THIS IS NO LONGER THE PROPERTY
OF THE SEATTLE PUBLIC LIBRARY

Toward Democracy

Other Works by James T. Kloppenberg

Uncertain Victory:
Social Democracy and Progressivism in European and American Thought, 1870–1920
Oxford University Press, 1986

A Companion to American Thought
Co-edited with Richard Wightman Fox
Wiley-Blackwell, 1995

The Virtues of Liberalism
Oxford University Press, 1998

Reading Obama:
Dreams, Hope, and the American Political Tradition
Princeton University Press, 2011

The Worlds of American Intellectual History
Co-edited with Joel Isaac, Michael O'Brien, and Jennifer Ratner-Rosenhagen
Oxford University Press, 2016

Toward Democracy

The Struggle for Self-Rule in European and American Thought

JAMES T. KLOPPENBERG

OXFORD
UNIVERSITY PRESS

Oxford University Press is a department of the University of Oxford. It furthers the University's objective of excellence in research, scholarship, and education by publishing worldwide. Oxford is a registered trade mark of Oxford University Press in the UK and certain other countries.

Published in the United States of America by Oxford University Press
198 Madison Avenue, New York, NY 10016, United States of America

© James T. Kloppenberg 2016

All rights reserved. No part of this publication may be reproduced, stored in a retrieval system, or transmitted, in any form or by any means, without the prior permission in writing of Oxford University Press, or as expressly permitted by law, by license, or under terms agreed with the appropriate reproduction rights organization. Inquiries concerning reproduction outside the scope of the above should be sent to the Rights Department, Oxford University Press, at the address above.

You must not circulate this work in any other form and you must impose this same condition on any acquirer.

Library of Congress Cataloging-in-Publication Data

Names: Kloppenberg, James T., author.
Title: Toward democracy : the struggle for self-rule in European and American thought / James T. Kloppenberg.
Description: Oxford ; New York : Oxford University Press, [2016] | Includes bibliographical references and index.
Identifiers: LCCN 2015033581 | ISBN 9780195054613 (acid-free paper)
Subjects: LCSH: Democracy—History. | Democracy—Europe. | Democracy—United States. | Autonomy.
Classification: LCC JC421 .K526 2016 | DDC 321.8—dc23
LC record available at http://lccn.loc.gov/2015033581

1 3 5 7 9 8 6 4 2

Printed by Sheridan Books, USA

For Mary
Forever

CONTENTS

PREFACE

THIS BOOK IS the result of a decision made twenty years ago. I had written a book about the intellectual revolution that lay behind the emergence of the liberal capitalist welfare states of our own day: *Uncertain Victory: Social Democracy and Progressivism in European and American Thought, 1870–1920* (Oxford, 1986). That book sought to explain why thinkers who rejected revolutionary socialism and laissez-faire liberalism turned toward more moderate approaches to political reform, which in turn fell out of favor in the wake of World War I. After the catastrophic interval of 1914–45, revised versions of social democracy and progressivism emerged to define North Atlantic politics for the half century following World War II. After the publication of *Uncertain Victory*, I spent a decade trying to decide whether to follow that story forward to the present or back toward the beginnings of democracy. I wrote articles on American thought in the late eighteenth century, on Tocqueville's visit to the United States in the 1830s, and on mid- to late-twentieth-century European and American politics and ideas, which came together in my book *The Virtues of Liberalism* (Oxford, 1998).

Still trying to understand why the liberal democratic welfare states of the present had taken such different shapes, and why they failed to address the persistent problems of inequality and injustice, I decided to plunge into the deeper past. Although I thought at first that this book would focus on the North Atlantic in the nineteenth century, I found myself drawn further back. The explanation for the different outcomes of eighteenth-century democratic revolutions, I came to believe, lay in the wars of religion ignited by the sixteenth-century Protestant Reformation, the dynamics and consequences of which could be understood only with reference to religious as well as political developments rooted in Athens, Jerusalem, and Rome. I became convinced that the effects of those earlier struggles were still reverberating in the twenty-first century. If the story told in this book begins earlier than I expected twenty years ago, its significance extends to our own day even more clearly than I imagined.

I have not changed my mind about the argument advanced in *Uncertain Victory* concerning the 1870–1920 period, nor do I think the struggles against dogma and for democratic inquiry and experimentation initiated during those years have been completed. It is certainly true that we have inherited the attempts of social democrats and progressives a century ago to extend the meaning of democracy from the political to the social and economic spheres. It is equally true, however, and less often acknowledged, that we have inherited the results of the unsuccessful attempts made in the nineteenth century to end regimes of economic, racial, and ethnic inequality, and the exclusion from power of women by men. Those forms of hierarchy, descended from ancient assumptions, hardened into distinct systems of white male supremacy on both sides of the Atlantic even as forms of self-rule were taking shape during the eighteenth and nineteenth centuries. Those assumptions and hierarchies continue to inflect European and American cultures today. This book is a study of the aspirations and achievements of thinkers who championed democracy through the end of the nineteenth century, the obstacles they faced, the conflicts they failed to resolve, and the unanticipated consequences of their struggle.

Completing a book of this magnitude takes a lot of time and a lot of help. I am happy to acknowledge the support of fellowships from the American Council of Learned Societies, the John Simon Guggenheim Foundation, and the National Endowment for the Humanities. I also want to thank the Nominating Committee for the Pitt Professorship, and the Fellows of Jesus College, University of Cambridge, for a memorable year in 2008–9; the Ecole des Hautes Etudes en Sciences Sociales, Paris, for an equally memorable spring in 2013; and, at Harvard, the assistance of the Cabot Fellowship, the Center for American Political Studies, the Center for European Studies, the Charles Warren Center for Studies in American History, the Mahindra Humanities Center, and the Radcliffe Institute for Advanced Study.

I am grateful to those who invited me to present my ideas about democracy, and those who discussed the topic with me, at the following colleges and universities: Brandeis, Cambridge, Catholic, Colby, Columbia, CUNY Graduate Center, Dartmouth, Denison, Dresden, Ecole des Hautes Etudes en Sciences Sociales, Free University of Berlin, Institut d'Etudes Politiques (Sciences Po) in Paris, London (University College), Northwestern, Notre

Dame, Nottingham, Ohio State, Oklahoma, Oxford, Rennes, Sheffield, Stanford, Sussex, Tokyo, Toronto, Turin, Vienna, Virginia, Washington University (St. Louis), and Yale; and also the Phillips Andover Academy, the Roxbury Latin School, St. Mark's School, the National Humanities Center in North Carolina, and the Woodrow Wilson Center in Washington, DC. Over the years I have relied on the splendid research staffs and extraordinary collections of libraries at Harvard, Cambridge, and Oxford, the American Antiquarian Society, the Boston Public Library, the British Library, the French National Archives, the French National Library, the Library of Congress, and the Massachusetts Historical Society.

Working with the staff of Oxford University Press has been a pleasure. The late Sheldon Meyer had confidence I could complete this book when it was still just an idea, and Susan Ferber waited patiently while I labored over a manuscript that kept getting longer. For helping transform that sprawling draft into this book, I am deeply grateful to Tim Bent. He shared my vision of what the book should be, and during the long months we worked on it he showed the intelligence, imagination, persistence, and generosity that all authors dream of finding in their editors. India Cooper, who lived up to her reputation for combining omniscience with meticulous attention to detail, proved that the art of copy editing, one of the most demanding aspects of scholarly production, remains alive. Alyssa O'Connell managed every stage of the intricate process with speed and grace, and Amy Whitmer skillfully guided me through the final stages of production. Niko Pfund reassured me, in moments of uneasiness, that everything was under control. At a time when many publishers are scaling back, urging authors to lower their sights and narrow their focus, it has been most satisfying to work with thoroughgoing professionals and a press committed to producing, according to the highest standards and without cutting any corners, a book of this scale and complexity.

Research and writing require isolation, but a scholar's life depends on communication and conversation. Without the affection and camaraderie of friends outside the study, the solitary days and nights of writing would be stifling rather than exhilarating. I would like to acknowledge first many of the current and former students who have helped with this project, over many years and in many ways, from sharing their ideas and their scholarship to checking notes and reading drafts: Tim Barker, Marco Basile, Mike Bernath, Kenzie Bok, Niko Bowie, Angus Burgin, Lucy Caplan, Tom Coens, Dana Comi, Yonatan Eyal, Jeanne Follansbee, John Gee, Scott Gelber, Katharine Gerbner, Glenda Goodman, Tina Groeger, Matt Hale, Dan Hamilton, Jared Hickman, Ben Irvin, Amy Kittelstrom, Mary Beth Klee, Sam Klug, Alison LaCroix, Ariane Liazos, Jason Maloy, Abbie Modaff, Elizabeth More, Darra Mulderry, Shaun

Nichols, Bill Novak, Arjun Ramamurti, Tim Roberts, Jennifer Ratner-Rosenhagen, Noah Rosenblum, Ganesh Sitaraman, Nico Slate, Tryg Throntveit, Darius Weil, Dan Wewers, Ben Wilcox, Tom Wolf, and Julian Zelizer. Working with these and many other superb students—many of whom have become, or are becoming, fellow scholars and teachers—has been a privilege.

The following people, who read parts of the manuscript (in some cases more than once) or discussed my ideas with me, helped either by sharing their own work, encouraging me to proceed, clarifying my thinking, or offering astringent criticism. The book is far better for their efforts. Since some of them remained unpersuaded, my expression of gratitude should not be taken to imply agreement with my arguments in the book, for which I alone am accountable. A partial list of those to whom I am indebted, for their generosity and their insight, includes Joyce Appleby, Nicolas Barreyre, David Bell, Duncan Bell, Tom Bender, Magalie Besson, Casey Blake, David Blight, Anouch Bourmayan, Holly Brewer, John Brooke, John Burt, Jon Butler, Leslie Butler, Charles Capper, Richard Carwadine, Catherine Colliot-Thélène, Stefan Collini, Saul Cornell, Paula Cossart, Andrew Delbanco, Suzanne Desan, E. J. Dionne, John Dunn, Michael Ermarth, Eric Foner, Richard Fox, Joanne Freeman, François Furstenberg, Jonathan Gienapp, Brad Gregory, Robert Griswold, Sandra Gustafson, Knud Haakonssen, Tom Haskell, David Hollinger, Axel Honneth, Daniel Walker Howe, Joel Isaac, Jonathan Israel, Hans Joas, Duncan Kelly, David M. Kennedy, Linda Kerber, Jim Livesey, Jim Livingston, John McGreevy, Françoise Mélonio, Sarah Mortimer, Mark Noll, Jim Oakes, Peter Onuf, Jason Opal, Tim Peltason, Janet Polasky, Jack Rakove, Andy Robertson, Dan Rodgers, Sophie Rosenfeld, Pierre Rosenvallon, Dorothy Ross, Alan Ryan, James Schleifer, Robbie Schneider, Bob Shalhope, Stephanie Shaw, Manisha Sinha, Steve Skowronek, Ruth Scurr, Rogers Smith, Steven Smith, Mitchell Snay, Mike Sonenscher, Gareth Stedman Jones, Jim Turner, Francesca Viano, David Waldstreicher, François Weil, Sean Wilentz, Caroline Winterer, Gordon Wood, Craig Yirush, Rosemarie Zagarri, and Olivier Zunz.

The Harvard Department of History and the programs in American Studies, History and Literature, and Social Studies have provided ideal conditions for sustaining the life of the mind. I am grateful to Janet Hatch, Ann Kaufman, Christine McFadden, Kimberly O'Hagan, Elena Palladino, and Arthur Patton-Hock for their kindness and efficiency; and to my faculty colleagues David Armitage, Bernard Bailyn, Anya Bassett, Eric Beerbohm, Sven Beckert, Ann Blair, Vince Brown, Larry Buell, Hannah Callaway, Dan Carpenter, Joyce Chaplin, Bob Darnton, Emma Dench, Drew Faust, Skip Gates, Peter Gordon, Annette Gordon Reed, David Hall, Jim Hankins, Jona Hansen,

Bryan Hehir, Patrice Higonnet, Maya Jasanoff, Andy Jewett, Walter Johnson, Jane Kamensky, Alex Keyssar, Mike Klarman, Jill Lepore, Charles Maier, Jane Mansbridge, Peter Marsden, Lisa McGirr, Sam Moyn, Eric Nelson, Bob Putnam, Sophus Reinert, Julie Reuben, Nancy Rosenblum, Emma Rothschild, Michael Sandel, Tommie Shelby, Theda Skocpol, John Stauffer, Brandon Terry, Richard Tuck, Laurel Ulrich, Cheryl Welch, and Daniel Ziblatt, who make Harvard such an invigorating place to exchange ideas. My friend and Harvard colleague Suzanne Smith, a tireless polymath who read, edited, and reread the entire manuscript with incisive intelligence, deserves special thanks for her heroic efforts. For any errors that remain, after all that help, I alone am responsible.

It is sobering to realize that this book has taken so long to complete that some of the scholars who guided my thinking about the history of democracy are no longer alive to see it come to fruition: Willi-Paul Adams, Carl Degler, Bill Gienapp, Stanley Hoffmann, Istvan Hont, Mark Kishlansky, Pauline Maier, Marvin Meyers, Michael O'Brien, and Jack Pole.

My deepest and most enduring debts are, as always, to my immediate family. My children, Annie Kloppenberg and Jay Kloppenberg, who grew up with this book, have become fearless creators, whose contributions to art and education have helped me see the many ways in which cultures of democracy can be built. As choreographer, dancer, scholar, and teacher, Annie has deepened the insights of the philosophers William James and John Dewey into the phenomenology of embodied aesthetic experience. Her explorations of collaboration and improvisation, beyond enriching the experiences of dancers and audiences on both sides of the Atlantic, show how the arts can foster democratic sensibilities. By establishing the African School for Excellence, now flourishing in townships near Johannesburg, Jay and his partner, Nonhlanhla Masina, are realizing their dream of expanding access to first-rate secondary education in sub-Saharan Africa. Imaginatively updating visions of democratic education from Dewey to Paulo Freire for the digital age, ASE is preparing students to pursue advanced studies in neighborhoods where few children have had that chance.

Besides reminding me often that Iceland, where her maternal grandparents were born, was the world's first democracy, my wife, Mary Kloppenberg, lived with this book from the beginning. She has devoted forty years of her life to young children and their families. For more than twenty-six years she has served as executive director of the extraordinarily successful early-childhood and after-school programs of the Wellesley Community Children's Center. Those of us lucky enough to work in higher education enjoy abundant respect and rewards for what we do. Those engaged in the far more challenging, and far more crucial, work of teaching our youngest children enjoy neither. The responsibilities and the urgency of Mary's work have made it impossible for her to weigh every word of this book, yet her unflagging commitment to the life of the mind, or, to be more precise, to the minds and hearts of young children during the years when scholars tell us the most learning occurs, has inspired my efforts as a teacher, scholar, and citizen. All the dimensions of democracy are encapsulated in the principle that has animated Mary's life and work: all children should have the care and nurturing necessary to enable them to reach their full potential. It is with deep gratitude for her life and her love, and with ever deeper admiration for her devotion to that principle, that I dedicate this book to her.

J. T. K.
Wellesley, Massachusetts
July 2015

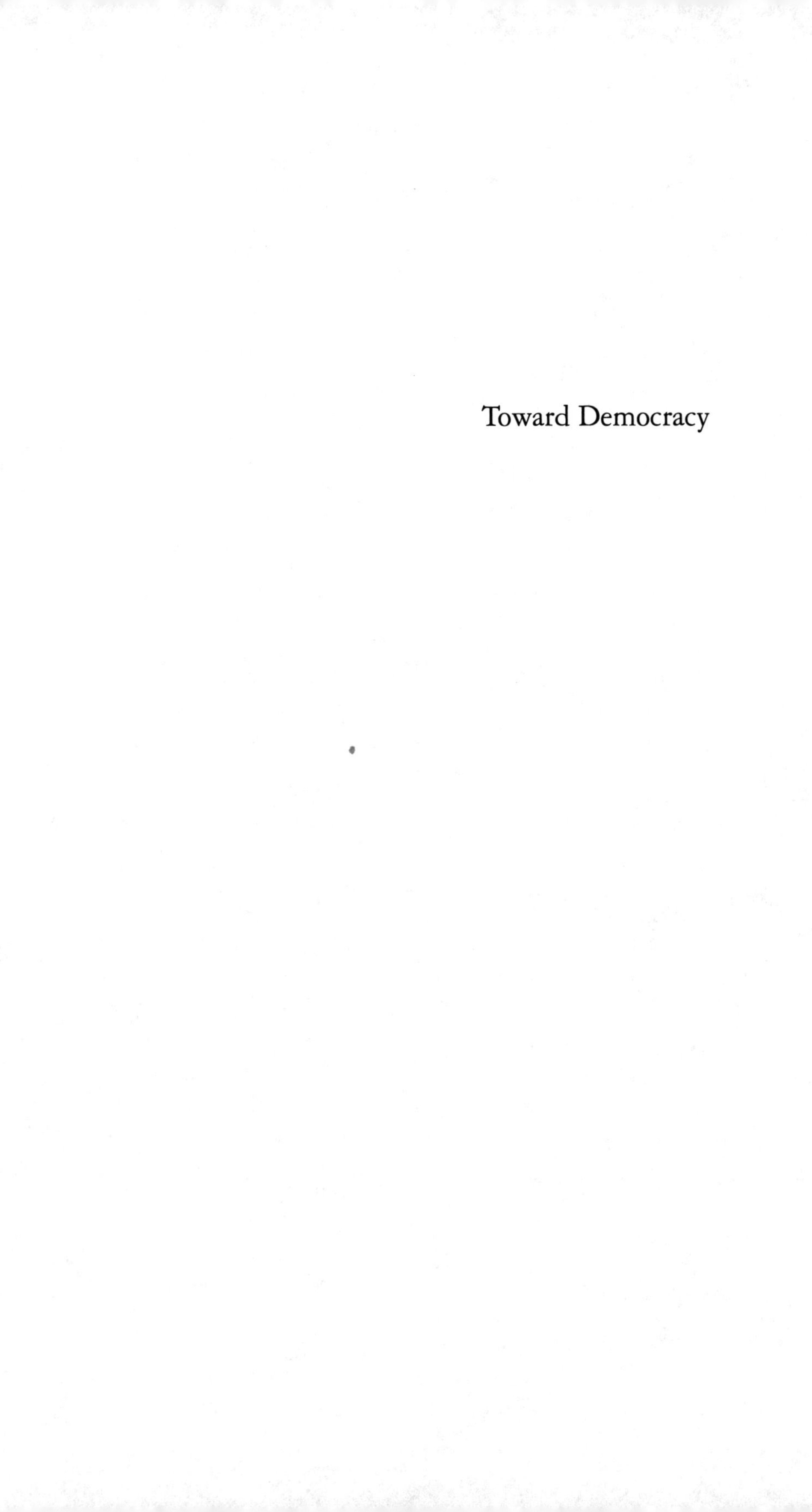

Toward Democracy

Introduction

The Paradoxes of Democracy

Swept forward by waves of popular passion, democracy has buried all alternatives to become the world's governing ideal. It was not always so. From the ancient world until the sixteenth-century Protestant Reformation, feelings about government by the people flowed in the opposite direction. "Democracy" was a term of abuse, usually yoked with labels such as "rabble," "herd," or "mob." By the end of the nineteenth century, however, things had changed. Over the course of four centuries, in many parts of the North Atlantic world the idea of self-government, scorned for nearly two millennia, emerged as a widely shared, albeit still controversial, model of government. This book, a history of democracy as it was imagined, understood, and practiced during those centuries, explores the reasons for that transformation and explains why the promise of democracy remains unfulfilled. If democracy gradually remade nations on both sides of the Atlantic, different preexisting cultural and institutional topographies, which lay hidden beneath the surface, helped determine the forms of popular government that emerged. From the early sixteenth through the late nineteenth century, conflicts over the people's proper role repeatedly exploded into war, and the long-term effects of those bloodlettings shaped the history of democracy everywhere.[1]

Democracy arose from violence and has never strayed far from it. Disputes over the form of governance appropriate for church and state, rooted in disagreements over theology and ecclesiology, spawned religious wars that convulsed sixteenth-century Europe. Struggles over questions of legitimate authority and the path to salvation drove many seventeenth-century English dissenters into exile, and those struggles ended in civil war and regicide. After self-government became the ideal of settlers in British North America, who declared their independence in 1776 and created the United States, the idea of democracy inspired successive revolutions in France that eventually spread across continental Europe. Changing attitudes toward popular government likewise fueled waves of reform that eventually transformed nineteenth-century Great Britain, though without fundamentally altering the nation's monarchical form of government. Democracy served as the founding ideal of the United States, yet in time rival understandings of what democracy means ignited a civil war that shapes the nation's history to this day.

In central Europe the slow tectonic shift toward self-government was more protracted. Although popular insurgencies, usually propelled by radical religious ideas, broke out as early as the sixteenth century, in the German states no governing political party outside Swiss-influenced Württemberg would dare designate itself "democratic" until 1918. The disputes that raged on both sides of the Atlantic from the early sixteenth century through the end of the nineteenth century, like struggles among competing groups within nations just emerging from long experience under autocracy in our own day, turned on questions as urgent now as they were then: What does democracy mean? How and why has it succeeded, and how and why has it failed?

This book traces the rise of democracy in European and American thought. Some of the thinkers examined here exerted influence only by the words they wrote; others played active parts in political and social life. Although people who did not write books, exercise political power, or possess cultural authority certainly contributed to the history of democracy, this book concentrates on those who wrote pivotal texts and framed arguments that helped change the terms of debate.[2] The history of democracy, in addition to being a story of social movements and political and economic developments, is also a story of ideas in history.[3]

The primary focus of this book is the shaping of democracy in what became the United States of America, but that does not make it an American history. All seventeenth- and almost all eighteenth-century North American thinkers wrote as members of European cultures, and Benjamin Franklin, Thomas Jefferson, and John Adams were almost as well known in France as they were in America. Nineteenth-century Americans likewise inherited European ideas and participated actively in transatlantic communities of discourse. Even self-taught Americans such as Frederick Douglass and Abraham Lincoln, whose educations were particularly hard-earned, frequently quoted sources ranging from the Bible and Shakespeare to contemporary European writers, and both were celebrated by reformers across the Atlantic. Most of those who contributed to democratic theory in America or Europe, from the sixteenth century through the nineteenth, thought of themselves as participants in a common cultural project. Europeans, from Michel de Montaigne through John Locke and Jean-Jacques Rousseau to Alexis de Tocqueville and John Stuart Mill, paid close attention to the New World. Most American thinkers were familiar with the ideas of John Milton and Algernon Sidney, Montesquieu and Adam Smith, Maximilien Robespierre and Mary Wollstonecraft. This book integrates European and American history to show how American ideas and practices descended from, and diverged from, earlier European, particularly English and French, models. It also shows that the influence of American thought and practice on European ideas about democracy—both negative and positive—was persistent and profound.[4]

Translating from one language or conceptual scheme to another is difficult. I have tried not to turn these thinkers into versions of each other or to find earlier versions of later ideas where they did not exist. Both the word "democracy" and the concept of self-government, however, were widely used from the ancient world onward. The word "democracy" derives from the ancient Greek word for "popular power." The Greeks distinguished the power (*kratos*) of the people (the *demos*) from government by the few (which came to be known as aristocracy) and government by one (monarchy). Just as they thought aristocracy could devolve into oligarchy and monarchy into tyranny, so they understood that rule by the people could dissolve into anarchy. Since its origins, democracy has been a protean idea that has attracted passionate advocates and equally passionate critics. The writers examined in this book read widely, across eras and across traditions. If comparing different cultures is as rewarding as it is challenging, so is studying ideas across a long time span.[5] This book does not trace a single concept of democracy from Periclean Athens to Gilded Age America, Victorian England, and the French Third Republic. Instead it examines the diverse meanings of terms used for multiple purposes, terms such as "democracy," "self-government," and "popular sovereignty," to designate a variety of ideas with contested meanings, not only across time but at every historical moment.

I offer this interpretation not as *the* history of democratic thought but as *a* history of democratic thought. The wide scope of this book means that it cannot be comprehensive. The number of people and events omitted inevitably dwarfs the number included. This book examines in some detail those thinkers who, in my judgment, made the most important contributions to the North Atlantic discourse of democracy through the end of the nineteenth century, many of whom shared an interest in the particular problems of representative democracy. Thinkers who dismissed all forms of democracy as undesirable, or who resisted the very idea of representation as antithetical to democracy, receive less attention here.

Most wide-ranging studies of democratic theory have been written by scholars of political philosophy who aim to offer a theory as well a history of democracy. While this book draws on that scholarship, it is a work of history that attempts to explain what happened and why. Ideas that are defeated often seem to disappear, but more often they persist, deep beneath the surface, slowly shifting the plates above. Although the discourse of democracy, over time and across cultures, has lacked the consistency or coherence of philosophical systems, a history focusing on ideas must address the flaws and inconsistencies of the arguments deployed by people trying to solve the problems of their day.[6]

This book does not seek to provide a theory of democracy. Nonetheless it emerged from and reflects a conviction that we need to change the way we think about democracy. Both the far left and the far right in Europe and the United States often view the institutions and practices of representative democracy as inadequate. For that reason, from the perspective of such critics, voting in elections and participating in mainstream public debate can be dismissed as a pale and shallow substitute for the more robust practices of direct democracy, which requires the active participation of citizens that is often held out as the defining feature of genuine self-government. That conviction, usually framed by romantic evocations of brief, evanescent moments of intense popular engagement such as those of 1789, 1848, or 1968, lacks historical foundation and rests on a misunderstanding of representative democracy.

Democracy has been—and remains—an ethical ideal rather than merely a set of institutions. It requires the willingness to allow differences to persist, a commitment to toleration that has long dissatisfied idealists. When you know the Truth, reasoning with your opponents or putting questions to a vote makes no sense. Democracy requires even those most sure of themselves to persuade a public often blind to what true believers find self-evident. For that reason democracy has always frustrated utopians. This book explains how and why champions of democracy in Europe and America, who understood that democracy is never merely a matter of institutional design, failed to achieve the results they sought. Though their ideals extended beyond voting to concerns with justice, they did not dismiss the casting of ballots or the reliance on representatives. To the contrary, almost all of them believed that representative democracy could help citizens develop the broadened sensibility of mutuality, or reciprocity, that democracy requires, and they believed that representatives, through deliberation, can identify the common good.

For the men and women examined in this book, voting was a necessary but not sufficient condition of democracy, just as self-government meant something more than a set of institutional arrangements. Of course they realized that such institutions, including constitutional government securing the integrity of the law, majority rule, and popular selection of those responsible for the work of government, are indispensable. The rise of democracy in the modern North Atlantic world, however, has had a broader cultural significance, one that can best be understood by examining the ideas of popular sovereignty, autonomy, and equality that lie at the center of this inquiry. Rather than thinking of democracy exclusively in terms of political—or even economic or social—arrangements, we should think of it as an ethical ideal. Modern democracy is rooted in the shared assumption that all citizens should have the capacity to shape their own lives within boundaries established by the standards and traditions of their communities, and that all citizens should be able to participate equally in shaping those standards and revising those traditions.

In the last century the meaning of democracy has gradually expanded, especially in Europe but also in the United States, from the political to the economic and social spheres. The category of citizenship has grown from a restricted group of white male property holders, usually of a certain religious affiliation, to include all adults regardless of race, gender, class, or religion. Along with those expansions of democracy and citizenship, however, and perhaps partly—and painfully—as a consequence of them, the ethical dimensions of democratic culture have become less and less evident in the last century. The thinkers who wrote most incisively about democracy as it took shape reveal why contemporary democracies fall so short of their promise. Nonetheless, despite widespread agreement about the desirability of democracy now, it would be antihistorical to assert the adequacy of a single understanding of what democracy has meant, not only across the time span of several centuries but also within individual nations. Disagreements about democracy constitute its history.

This book is not only a description of the experience of multiple nations with democracy; it is also an argument about the changing meanings of democracy, as well as the political, social, and economic conditions that have made it possible and necessary. Distinctive national traditions of popular government persist, and appreciating their roots and their continuity as well as signaling common processes of transformation is crucial. Rather than perpetuating debates about "American exceptionalism," this book seeks to contribute to the rise of a post-exceptionalist sensibility that acknowledges the uniqueness of each national history, not only American, British, and French but also Dutch, Swiss, and German, even though common threads justify placing these cultures in a single braided narrative. Especially searing events—notably the wars of religion, regicides in England and France, the European revolutions of 1848, and the United States Civil War—have shaped cultural understandings by imprinting particular experiences in collective memory. Such formative events impose frameworks through which cultures interpret what happened to themselves and to others, another reason why a general concept of democracy cannot be constructed independent of the particular historical experiences that filter popular memories, anxieties, and aspirations.[7]

At the heart of debates about democracy are three contested principles, popular sovereignty, autonomy, and equality; and three related, but less visible, underlying premises, deliberation, pluralism, and reciprocity. The persistent struggles over these principles and premises help explain the tangled history of democracy in practice as well as theory. This book also explores two underappreciated aspects of North Atlantic democracy, its religious origins and its ethical dimensions, which have profoundly influenced its development. Again, there is no single, essential, unchanging idea of democracy; its meanings have changed over time and been debated at every moment. These principles and premises are not meant to provide a transhistorical standard against which thinkers and institutions should be measured but only a conceptual framework for the historical analysis that follows.

To start with the first of the three principles, popular sovereignty holds that the will of the people is the sole source of legitimate authority. Although apparently unambiguous, its precise meaning has always been the central issue in debates about democracy. Champions of monarchical or aristocratic rather than strictly popular government have insisted that the people can legitimately choose to—and should—place themselves under the authority of a single person or a group of qualified individuals. Even partisans of democracy have expressed misgivings about the people's capacity to exercise judgment. Thomas Jefferson, by popular reckoning among the most passionately democratic of eighteenth-century thinkers, became increasingly ambivalent about those who considered him their champion. In a letter written in 1820, the seventy-seven-year-old Jefferson identified this perennial problem: "I know of no safe depository of the ultimate powers of the society but the people themselves," he wrote in an apparently unqualified endorsement of popular rule. "If we think them not enlightened enough to exercise their control with a wholesome discretion, the remedy is not to take it from them, but to enlighten their discretion."[8] Despite his genuine preference for democracy over monarchy or aristocracy, Jefferson did not identify the "we" charged with enlightening the people's discretion or explain what justification "we" have for presuming to instruct them. That problem has dogged even the most ardent champions of democracy, who have been forced by abundant evidence to admit, as Jefferson himself did in the wake of the French Revolution, that the people are capable of horrible excesses. Ever since Plato's Socrates likened statesmen to doctors and politicians to chefs—the former prescribe what is good for you even if it tastes terrible, the latter merely ask what tastes good—political thinkers have acknowledged the need to "enlighten" the people or to train (or restrain) their appetites. The principle of popular sovereignty itself, which assumes that the people are the source of authority and possess the potential to exercise good judgment, has been understood to be consistent with multiple forms of government.

Another perennial complication in the principle of popular sovereignty is the difference between representation and participation. Many ancient Greeks considered representation inimical to democracy; Athens relied on sortition, or lottery, to determine many positions of civic authority. But skeptics then and ever since have contended that chance as often empowers the reckless and foolish as the prudent and wise. In part to counter that concern, the practice of representative democracy, hardly unknown to the Greeks and further developed in the Roman republic, reemerged in late-medieval Europe. Elections appeared to offer a means of coping with the excesses of popular passion and the problem of scale, which made meetings of all citizens impractical in any political unit larger than a village. With the decline of hierarchy and the spread of literacy beginning in the sixteenth century, however, assumptions about citizens' different capacities, assumptions often invoked to justify representation rather than participation, again came under fire. That tension between direct and representative democracy, originating in the ancient world, has persisted into the present. As interest in democracy rose in the postmedieval world, its partisans as well as its critics argued that the principle of popular sovereignty must be balanced against other values such as individual rights, the common good, and stability, considerations that might serve as brakes on the people's sometimes unenlightened discretion. Although locating absolute, unquestionable authority in any single person or institution other than the people is anathema to democracy, examples of mob violence prompted uncomfortable realizations that some alternative source of legitimate authority, or some institutional check or legal constraint, must be available in practice to counter popular passions when they spin out of control.

Autonomy is the second principle of democracy. One of the principal arguments of this study is the centrality of the idea of autonomy in contrast to the impoverished conceptions of freedom that dominate contemporary scholarly and popular debate. The etymological roots of "autonomy" stretch back to the Greek words for "self" and "rule" or "law." "Autonomy" thus means self-rule. An autonomous individual exercises control over his or her own life by developing a self that is sufficiently mature to make decisions according to rules or laws chosen for good reasons. Autonomous individuals are in control of themselves, which means first that they are sovereign masters of their wills and second that they are not dependent on the wills (or whims) of others. Recent political theorists who have distinguished between "positive" and "negative" freedom, between the freedom to do something and the freedom from constraint, depart from the discourse of earlier democratic theorists, who understood that autonomy means self-rule in *both* the positive and negative senses: it requires a self both psychologically and ethically, as well as economically and socially, capable of deliberate action; and it requires the absence of control over individuals by other individuals and by the state. Autonomy has meaning only if individuals are understood as beings who act on the basis of consciously chosen goals developed in the framework of community standards and traditions. Thus in democratic discourse the idea of autonomy, like that of popular sovereignty, must be balanced against other ideas, in this case the dual awareness that constraints circumscribe individual choices and that the choices of the mature self must be weighed against the demands of the community.[9]

Equality is the third contested principle of democracy. The conflict arises not only from the familiar opposition between the values of equality and individual autonomy but also from the inescapable tensions within the concept of equality itself. The familiar distinction between equality of opportunity and equality of result again obscures the deeper problem, because equal opportunity is not possible in conditions of extreme inequality. There is nevertheless an inevitable contradiction between the principle of equality and the democratic commitment to majority rule. Imagine a simple community with three voters. Two of them decide that the third should become their slave, and they justify their decision by the principle of majority rule. When the third invokes the principles of autonomy and equality in self-defense—as oppressed minorities have often done, sometimes successfully—that strategy counterposes principles equally central to democracy to the principle of majority rule.

Although that example seems to suggest that an irreconcilable contradiction exists between different democratic ideals, it indicates only that the concepts of popular sovereignty, autonomy, and equality are mutually constitutive; they have no meaning except in relation to each other. The discourse of democracy, like the institutional frameworks of different democratic cultures, is complex and multilayered. It requires the careful weighing of different values rather than the passionate defense of one alone. As its emergence over the centuries shows, democracy is best understood as a way of life, not simply a set of political institutions. The internal tensions between the principle of popular sovereignty and the principles of autonomy and equality make the notion of a smooth-running, conflict-free democracy a contradiction in terms; history provides no examples of a placid democracy. Inherent in democracy, even when conceived of as an ethical ideal and a way of life, are the inevitable disagreements, and the victories, defeats, and compromises, that are inseparable from the commitment to allowing people to pursue their own ideals and refusing to specify in advance which of their different, and perhaps even incompatible, conceptions will triumph.

That commitment itself rests on three distinct premises that, as a result of the work done by the thinkers examined in this book, can now be seen to lie beneath modern democracy. Emerging from the wars of religion and contested for several centuries, these premises had become, by the end of the nineteenth century, the underlying pillars on which modern North Atlantic democracy stands. The first is necessity of deliberation. We cannot know, or impose on all persons, a fixed and unitary conception of the truth. In a democracy provisional truths emerge from the process of free inquiry, from the verification of truth claims in experience, and from democratic deliberation understood as the means of provisionally resolving remaining disputes. The English verb "deliberate" derives from the Latin *deliberare*, meaning to weigh well, to consider; that activity lies at the heart of democratic culture. Only when all citizens broaden their perspectives sufficiently to weigh well, or to consider seriously, the views of others who disagree with them is democratic deliberation possible. The mere tallying of individual desires, the elevation of unexamined and indefensible personal preferences to the level of privileged rights, although currently a common understanding of the meaning of democracy, is antithetical to this venerable conception of democracy as an ethical project necessarily concerned with the constitution of selfhood through dialogue with other persons engaged in the same process.

Democratic deliberation of this sort, despite its roots in classical, Christian, and Enlightenment thought, does not impose a certain form of reasoning or conversation to the exclusion of others. Instead the entire question of what is to constitute democratic deliberation must itself be subject to deliberation. That may seem to initiate an infinite regression but instead merely indicates that the procedures for interaction, as well as the outcome of that interaction, must themselves be considered provisional and subject to acceptance by the consent of those who participate in the conversation. The expansion of the relevant community is part of the democratic dynamic that has been developing since the revaluations of human capacity beginning with the Renaissance, maturing in the Reformation, and continuing into the present; challenging forms of argument preferred by those in power is a long-standing tradition that women and minorities have continued in recent decades by questioning established notions of reason, logic, and evidence. Those engaged in democratic discourse have long debated the role of rhetoric in shaping and enabling public debate. Does oratory—grand or simple—help citizens see the common good and embrace it, or does it distort their vision and obscure their understanding? In all conversations, eloquence, authority, shrewdness, and persuasiveness always intrude. A chasm falls between the ideal of deliberation—weighing well—and the reality of public debate.[10]

The second premise is that democracy does not specify once and for all, or impose on all persons, a fixed, unitary conception of the good life more specific or substantive than its commitments to popular sovereignty, autonomy, and equality. Achieving the shared understanding that democracy is necessarily both liberal and pluralistic was the work of the thinkers examined in this book, thinkers active in the era stretching from the sixteenth-century wars of religion to the end of the nineteenth century. That shared understanding was particularly difficult to establish because deeply held convictions about how life should be lived, usually but not exclusively grounded in religious belief, inspired so many of those who advanced the cause of democracy.

The third premise of modern democracy engaged by these figures, the ethic of reciprocity, provides the rationale for treating all persons with respect and weighing well their aspirations and their ways of looking at the world. This principle, which extends the category of those deserving consideration beyond the small body of citizens in ancient Greece and Rome or God's chosen people to embrace all humanity, originated in early Christianity. Absent commitments to deliberation, pluralism, and reciprocity, the call for popular rule can be a rationale for cruelty: as already noted, any group of three can yield a majority of two committed to enslaving the other one. Grounded on those premises, however, the democratic commitment to the principles of popular sovereignty, autonomy, and equality can translate into something more than a set of institutions and procedures, a way of life devoted to securing for all citizens autonomy and the equal chance to participate in shaping the institutions that affect their lives. This study traces the historical development of these interwoven threads in the emergence and transformation of democracy on both sides of the North Atlantic.

Those who contributed to the creation of modern European and American democratic regimes did not profess identical religious doctrines or ethical ideals, but the vast majority claimed to embrace the Judeo-Christian maxim of the sanctity of individual life. They also shared ethical assumptions about the superiority of some ways of life to others. We have inherited the myriad democratic procedures they put in place and their languages of popular sovereignty, autonomy, and equality—with their multiple layers of meaning. Perhaps because many people today have lost confidence in the universality of the religious ideas that originally infused democratic discourse, we tend to overlook the democratic ethic of reciprocity taken for granted by earlier generations, which leaves us with a flattened appreciation of the meaning and potential of democratic life. The significance for democracy of the transformation of North Atlantic cultures from a shared Judeo-Christian worldview to a more fragmented outlook is another principal question posed by this study.

It is clear that ideas about value judgments have changed dramatically. Greek and Roman philosophers generally conceived of reason as integral to ethical and political judgment. Early Christian thinkers insisted on unifying thought and action under the all-embracing command to love one another. By contrast, many social scientists in recent decades have tended to separate the category of rational thought, modeled now on supposedly neutral scientific and technical reasoning oriented toward maximizing individual utility, from the realms of faith, emotion, or taste, which are lumped together as "value questions" on which individuals need not, and cannot be expected to, agree. If greater tolerance for diversity has been gained in that translation, an idea of the good life as something shared by members of a community has been lost.

Looming ominously in the background of modern democratic discourse is the experience of religious warfare sparked by the Protestant Reformation, which destroyed the illusion of unity upheld in medieval Christendom. All sides were guilty of murderous excesses. In the St. Bartholomew's Day massacre of 1572, hundreds of French Protestants were rounded up and murdered. When Roman Catholic monasteries in England and northern Europe were sacked, thriving communities of devout persons were destroyed along with the corrupt hypocrites who were the original targets. In orgies of violence such as the sack of Magdeburg in 1630–31, rampaging soldiers robbed and butchered most of the townspeople who resisted them. Such abominations left a legacy of fear, suspicion, and hatred; not only were people willing to die for their beliefs, they were willing to kill for them. The early-modern fear of fanaticism was rooted not in irrational fantasies of what might happen if popular passions were unleashed but instead in the horrible reality of towns torched and innocents slaughtered. Apprehensions provoked by democratic revolutions in Europe and North America, both successful and unsuccessful, must be understood in the context of profound cultural anxieties concerning the balance between the desirability of empowering the people and the very real dangers of zealotry.

Historians and philosophers have often celebrated or pilloried early-modern advocates of popular rule by exaggerating particular dimensions of their thought and then interpreting their efforts through lenses provided by later developments that those historical figures could not have anticipated; a few notable examples include Roger Williams and John Milton, Jean-Jacques Rousseau and James Madison, and Mary Wollstonecraft and Frederick Douglass. This study seeks to present thinkers' ideas from their own perspectives. Many of the most influential contributors to democratic discourse from the sixteenth through the nineteenth centuries sought religious freedom not because they did not value faith but because they abhorred the consequences of religious warfare. They sought to enshrine reason not because they devalued emotion but because they recognized and abhorred the cruelty grounded in and justified by superstition and tradition. They sought economic freedom not because they did not value fairness and equality but because they recognized and abhorred the oppressiveness and stultifying effects of premarket economies and feudal arrangements confining individuals to particular social strata and worlds of work. They sought political rights for individuals not because they did not value community or solidarity but because they recognized and abhorred the consequences of absolutism. Finally, many of them preferred mixed government or representative democracy over direct democracy not because they did not value the ideals of popular sovereignty, autonomy, and equality but because they deplored the violent excesses displayed first in the wars of religion, then in the civil wars of the sixteenth and seventeenth centuries, later in the French Revolution and the nineteenth-century revolutions it inspired, and finally in and after the United States Civil War. They believed that if the crucial principle of popular sovereignty were established as the source of constitutional law, and if citizens learned from the experience of democratic political activity to embrace the principle of reciprocity, then the people could exercise responsible control of their culture and find the most effective means to achieve their goals in changing circumstances.

Those circumstances did indeed change in the aftermath of the democratic revolutions of the eighteenth century, but not in ways that the architects of those revolutions anticipated. As a result, the ideas and strategies of democratic thinkers and activists changed as well. The new freedoms secured for individuals unleashed forms of economic and political activity that dramatically transformed the world of restrictive feudal arrangements and aristocratic privileges. The new world of industrial capitalism and popular government, although the latter was even more severely restricted in Europe than in the United States until the end of the nineteenth century, gradually eroded inherited customs. In their place came more fluid social arrangements and rapidly changing forms of production and exchange. In the process a new set of problems developed, but these problems represented the unanticipated consequence of change, not the intended result. The social transformations set in motion by eighteenth-century revolutionaries' emphasis on individual freedom ended up making that freedom an end in itself rather than a means toward the end of an autonomous life of moral and civic virtue. A world dominated by instrumental reasoning and the scramble for economic success by any means was not the world that eighteenth-century champions of popular government sought.

Responding to the possibilities available thanks to the logic of democracy, nineteenth-century reformers aimed to address these new forms of dependency and inequality by widening the electorate and expanding the responsibilities of government. Their hope was to resolve the tension between the expressive individualism of liberated citizens and their yearnings for social solidarity and national community. Revolutions, wars of national unification, and the United States Civil War yielded different solutions to this problem. All of them reflected particular cultural and religious traditions. Because all of them built on the fissures of earlier wars that had shattered the ethic of reciprocity, all proved unstable. Toward the end of the nineteenth century new modes of democratic thinking and a new set of democratic reforms emerged, incorporating greater sensitivity to the problems of poverty, the domination of women by men, and the poisonous effects of racism, although those problems too persisted despite reformers' efforts. Many of these problems can be traced to the permanent scars left by the violence of earlier civil wars. In the case of the most recent of those cataclysms, the United States Civil War, those scars have not yet healed after a century and a half.

Framed by these events, the history of democratic theory and practice in modern Europe and America is a story of unforeseen and unintended consequences. Those who envisioned and helped implement democratic reforms did not succeed in securing the autonomy and equality they sought. Instead the tragic irony of democracy—for it is nothing less than that—has been the recurrent creation of social and political arrangements that, although often initially appearing to mirror popular desires, ended up either freeing previously repressed impulses that undermined democracy or generating other pressures that produced new and unanticipated forms of dependency and hierarchy. Eighteenth-century revolutions, the American and particularly the

French, ushered in new forms of oppression that resulted from what appeared to be democratic reformers' most successful achievements. The most conspicuous failures of modern democracy reflect neither villainy nor conspiracy, nor even shortsightedness or simple naiveté, but instead the tragic irony of democratic virtues.[11]

As this book attempts to show, we cannot understand the rise and consolidation of democratic institutions, or the successes and failures of democratic reformers, on either side of the Atlantic unless we look beyond our own contemporary categories of politics and economics, important as they are, and beyond the categories of conservative and radical, liberal and republican, capitalist and socialist, important as they have been, to see how such ideas have been changed and amalgamated in the historical discourse of democracy. From the early seventeenth century through the end of the nineteenth century, democracy was an ethical ideal as much as it was a political or economic ideal, and we cannot understand the historical development of American or European cultures without focusing on the moral and religious dimensions of the struggles that have given us the world we inhabit. This book shows how and why American and European champions of democracy understood the potentially democratic nature of state power, and how and why they conceived of autonomy within the context of equality and mutuality, in an effort to restore the contingency of outcomes to our historical imagination.[12]

Even if the history of democracy has not culminated in triumph, it does possess a certain directionality. Setbacks have been plentiful, yet it would be folly to deny that the political institutions in place in the North Atlantic West are more democratic in the twenty-first century than in the sixteenth. Illuminating the ways in which, and the reasons why, inherited ideas and existing structures gave way to new ways of thinking and new social practices, including the wider acceptance of the principles and premises of democracy, remains crucial. The history of democracy has never been unilinear, nor its outcome foreordained. Instead it has been a messy process with paradoxical gains and losses, unexpected advances and retreats, happening simultaneously in different places and often in different parts of a single nation.[13]

Ideas are weapons, instruments, tools used in argument, and they cannot be understood in the abstract, without reference to the particular purposes of those who employed them in any text, whether a philosophical treatise or a political tract. Meanings, particularly for those texts that have acquired a normative significance for cultures over time, are elusive and protean. To a certain degree, the meanings intended by historical writers and speakers, and those understood by historical readers and listeners, are lost to us, because we inherit knowledge and understandings through which we inevitably filter all the texts we encounter. Even though historians should acknowledge the obstacles that stand in our way, we can strive for understandings as close to the meanings intended by those whom we study as we can achieve. Comparative historical studies are complicated by the fact that meanings change over time and across languages, and as a result of later interpretations, yet meanings remain at least sufficiently stable to enable what we call communication.[14] This study resurrects the importance of ethical and religious ideas in democratic discourse because our contemporary scholarly and popular emphasis on economic efficiency and self-interested political behavior blinds us to the equally important role played by other considerations in the history of democracy.[15]

Recovering the ethical dimensions of earlier democratic discourse requires examining familiar figures in political theory as well as contributors of important ideas long marginalized in standard accounts. Eighteenth-century feminists, including Wollstonecraft in England, Judith Sargent Murray in America, and Olympe de Gouges in France, drew from their dissatisfaction with the constraints imposed by sexual stereotyping a critique of the often invisible oppression operating in male-dominated cultures. Feminists ever since have transformed democratic discourse, particularly with respect to the relations between logic and emotion in the exercise of reason, and between individuals and community in the exercise of rights. They have pointed out that even autonomous selves inevitably experience dependency at the beginning and end of their lives, an awkward and unsettling challenge to those who conceive of freedom simply as the absence of constraint. Such arguments can hardly be considered peripheral or supplementary to a supposed mainstream of cultural debate.

Likewise insights of racial minorities place mainstream Western ideas of selfhood and social responsibility in a different light. Those barred from power because of race or ethnicity illuminate the problematical nature of attempts to incorporate diversity within any culture premised on assumptions about fundamental commonality—most notably, the willingness to abide by the will of the majority—that must underlie democratic institutions. The scope of democratic citizenship expanded during the eighteenth and nineteenth centuries largely due to changing conceptions of the criteria appropriate for determining who should take part in the decision-making process. Few women and members of racial minorities were allowed to participate formally in the public debates that eventually enlarged the category of citizenship to include women and nonwhites. But the ideas of thinkers such as Douglass had explosive significance in shaping modern democratic thought and culture; like the ideas of feminists, such insights do not simply add another dimension to our thinking about democracy in conditions of ethnic diversity, they transform it.[16]

As noted, religious affiliation has been until recently one of the defining dimensions of personal identity for almost all members of North Atlantic cultures. Given the centrality of obedience to authority in such religious traditions, as well as the importance of concepts such as sin, evil, and repentance, and given the tendency of many secular scholars to associate religious faith with superstition, the contributions of religious communities to democratic theory and practice are often minimized. But understanding sixteenth-century Protestant challenges to the papacy, seventeenth-century Puritan challenges to royal authority, the mobilization of colonial American resentments against Britain, the violent spasms of the French Revolution, the nineteenth-century waves of social protest, and the fervor of both sides in the United States Civil War—to cite just a few of the more obvious examples—requires attending to popular religious ideals and to the writings of religious leaders, who often inspired democratic reform movements. Illuminating the vexed relation between traditional religious doctrines and democratic principles is among the main goals of this study. Many partisans of democracy, from unconventionally Christian thinkers such as John Locke and John Adams to champions of the rights of women such as Wollstonecraft and abolitionists such as Douglass, drew inspiration from their religious faith.[17]

There are multiple reasons for taking seriously the role of religion in modern democratic discourse. Historically it is undeniable that the source of the animating ideals of modern democratic movements in the Atlantic world has been the Christian principle of *agape*, selfless love for all humans because all are created in God's image, which lies beneath the democratic ethic of reciprocity. Astute critics from Erasmus through Friedrich Nietzsche to Jürgen Habermas have observed that the Christian ideas of humility, mercy, forgiveness, and equal respect for other persons form the backdrop against which modern concepts of autonomy and equality emerged, and they remain a crucial part of the cultural inheritance of North Atlantic democratic cultures.[18] Our own ideas and ideals, our own analytical tools and our most cherished values, have emerged through the historical process that we study. For that reason historians should treat the past we study with the respect that we ask our readers to show for the texts we produce. If we treat earlier texts with suspicion or cynicism, and refuse to take seriously the reasons that those we study offered for believing what they did, we invite the same suspicion and cynicism in our readers.[19]

Studying the history of modern democracy in the North Atlantic is urgent in the twenty-first century for two reasons. First, the disappearance of rival political systems has paradoxically made the internal inconsistencies and fuzziness of democracy even more apparent and nettlesome. Second, the flexibility and open-endedness of democracy make it particularly suitable for cultures increasingly attuned to a scientific sensibility, committed to testing multiple hypotheses through trial and error and examining the consequences through open inquiry. The culture of stable, unchallenged hierarchy faded as the culture of science emerged, because whereas authority dictates obedience, democracy should accommodate experimentation. That orientation toward open-endedness and innovation helps explain the steady rise of democracy toward its current status as a nearly universally acclaimed ideal, but it also disguises another dynamic.

Once possibilities are unbounded, both for individuals seeking autonomy and for cultures seeking solutions to all social problems, disappointment becomes inevitable. Whereas in predemocratic and prescientific cultures status was largely fixed and horizons limited, in democratic cultures everyone can aspire to the pinnacles achieved by the most honored, the most affluent, the most brilliant, or the most virtuous. The logic of equality that undergirds democracy encourages such ambitions. Yet frustration necessarily accompanies those hopes, because by their very nature pinnacles cannot accommodate everyone who aspires to them. Thus democracy as it expands breeds optimism and disappointment, euphoria and despair, in an ineluctable dialectic. Once the barriers erected by hierarchy are dismantled, the promise of satisfaction beckons all citizens. But the logic of democracy dictates that the horizons of exceptional achievement will inevitably continue to recede. If we can learn to understand that dynamic, perhaps we can appreciate the irony of democratic virtue and find in it not grounds for despair but reasons for continued resolution. The historical understanding of democracy might also help us get beyond our current tendency to frame disagreements as all-or-nothing struggles between good and evil, between freedom and oppression, and to see instead that democracy inevitably—necessarily—involves endless negotiation and compromise between competing values and worldviews. We can redeem the promise of democracy only if we realize that democracy, by always kindling hopes for change, forever feeds frustrations, in part because of the tensions between democratic principles and in part because our struggles to resolve certain problems inevitably create others.

Today's sophisticated diagnosticians of the social sciences know more about our condition than ever before, and not surprisingly many people infer that we should be able to cure what ails us. But the very bluntness of democracy, its inadequacy as a tool to slice through to the core of social problems with a single, penetrating stroke, might be what prevents fatal experiments of the sort that originated in quests for quick and sure solutions and ended with death and destruction. Democratic politics resembles ancient healing more than modern medicine: it promises no surgical miracles but usually keeps the patient alive. Studying several centuries of modern history shows how hard it has been to nurture democratic cultures. The frustrations of our imperfect democracies will continue to annoy us. The solutions we try will generate unexpected problems, and attempts to solve them will plunge us into new conflicts with unforeseeable and sometimes tragic consequences. The long and often bloody history of establishing self-government in the North Atlantic world, the story told in the chapters that follow, also shows why democracy, despite its difficulties, remains among our most precious cultural achievements.

The story told here may not inspire hope because it reveals how and why democracy, so inspiring as an idea, has proved so unsatisfying in practice. Democracy depends on cultural resources that the struggle to achieve democracy can erode, and the successful creation of self-government unleashes forces that can endanger the sensibilities it requires. War, particularly civil war, has an especially devastating effect, and for that reason the cultural consequences of civil war for democracy can last for generations, even centuries, as has been true of the European wars of religion, the English Civil War, the civil war that the French Revolution became, and the United States Civil War.

The consequences of establishing democratic institutions of government have been neither what the thinkers studied here intended nor what they anticipated. They thought that individuals, who come to consciousness in communities and traditions, both cultural and religious, would learn to form preferences not merely in response to their desires but in relation to ethical standards. This book explores the changing ideas of democratic theorists who probed and contested not only the operation of popular government but also the philosophical underpinnings on which democracy must rest, and it shows their nations' inability to construct cultures of democracy oriented toward the ideas of autonomy and reciprocity they prized.

These multiple discrepancies between intentions and results constitute the tragic irony of democracy. Awareness of the reasons why a shadow has fallen between democrats' aspirations and their achievements may temper—but need not extinguish—our hopes for democracy. Instead historical understanding should help us see how the legacies of past conflicts, particularly the still-smoldering embers from earlier civil wars, continue to obstruct efforts to fulfill the promise of democracy. Identifying those roots might enable us to see more clearly the nature and the depth of the challenges we face.

PART I | Roots and Branches

CHAPTER 1

Born in Bloodshed

The Origins of Democracy

FROM HIS CHÂTEAU situated between Bordeaux and Bergerac in southwestern France, Michel de Montaigne could see the ragged armies approach. Bands of soldiers, some Catholic, some Protestant, roamed the countryside of Périgord during the wars of religion that raged for decades in sixteenth-century France. In 1585, when the Catholic Montaigne returned to the writer's life he had abandoned to serve as mayor of Bordeaux, he found himself in trouble. One of his aristocratic neighbors, arriving on horseback, breathlessly begged him for refuge from the superior forces of a rival lord threatening to butcher his troops.

Montaigne knew the dangers of his age. He had been abducted, taken to a forest, and robbed earlier while traveling through a hostile region supposedly under a truce between Protestants and Catholics. As a result of "our civil wars," he had written, France was rich in examples of vicious cruelty. Catholic and Protestant soldiers alike showed a passion for inflicting pain. "I could hardly persuade myself, before I had actual evidence," Montaigne wrote, "that there exist any souls so unnatural as to commit murder for the mere pleasure of doing so." Alert to such threats, and already suspicious of the neighbor seeking his help, Montaigne could neither wholeheartedly believe his tale nor dismiss it. Everyone had enemies, and the story seemed plausible. When five more haggard-looking soldiers rode up, repeating their commander's story, Montaigne allowed them into his courtyard. Several more groups of armed horsemen followed them. Now, thanks to the trust he had extended, Montaigne found himself facing two dozen mounted soldiers who, he gradually realized, had come intending at least to rob and probably to kill him. As when he was kidnapped, he thought death was at hand.[1]

Montaigne escaped with his life on both occasions. The intruder to his château later told Montaigne that "my face and my open-heartedness had removed his treacherous intentions." In the forest, his captors' "miraculous repentance" extended even to returning all his stolen goods. The band's leader then removed his mask, identified himself, and told Montaigne that "I owed this deliverance to my face, to my freedom and firmness of speech." Montaigne's enemies expected him, as a distinguished member of the French nobility, to snarl with contemptuous defiance and demonstrate through heroic death the magnificence of his courage and his virtue. Instead, he conceded their advantage and met their threats with dumbfounding temperance and humility. His manner, Montaigne explained, sustained him not only in life-threatening moments but every day.[2]

Montaigne adhered to his ethic of reciprocity when powerful as well as powerless. While still serving as mayor of Bordeaux, he got word of a plot against his life hatched by dissident Catholic soldiers. Dissatisfied with his lack of zeal against the hated Huguenots (as French Protestants were called), they planned to murder him during a review of his troops. Again Montaigne understood the danger. An earlier mayor of the city had been killed by an unruly mob that he tried vainly to calm. Montaigne's aides urged him to disarm the troops; instead he called for "volleys loud and lusty" to demonstrate his confidence in them.

Montaigne's ethic was not utilitarian; its value did not depend on its results. In an unpredictable world, he reasoned, we can never know with certainty the consequences of our behavior. We can only act as we see fit. In place of the earlier aristocratic ethic of stoic hardness and haughtiness, which identified yielding with commoners, Montaigne cultivated an ethic of reciprocity in which the distinctions between the strong and the weak, the merciful and the forgiven, could be blurred through the mutual acknowledgment of autonomy and the extension of trust.[3] Whether submitting without fear or pardoning without fear, Montaigne believed that the willingness to yield might nurture respect that could otherwise never be achieved. Although the admission of vulnerability and the ethic of reciprocity might not bring an end to civil war or ensure one's safety, their absence assured the continuation of endless conflict. In 1576, Montaigne had a bronze medallion struck with two inscriptions. One side read "Je m'abstiens," or "I restrain myself," the principle that more than once saved his life. The other side asked a question equally out of favor in a time of religious fervor: "Que sçais-je?" or "What do I know?"[4] Whereas passion and certainty were watchwords during the wars of religion, the emergence of democracy would require an ethic of reciprocity grounded on restraint and doubt.

Like many other new ideas in sixteenth-century Europe, Montaigne's convictions originated in response to the new world of America. Reports from explorers and encounters with Indians brought to France jarred Montaigne's sensibility from the well-worn grooves of European culture. Some of his most provocative essays, especially "On Custom," "On Vehicles," and "On Cannibals," show how exposure to cultural diversity could unsettle conventional ideas. In the latter essay Montaigne contrasted the forms of torture preferred by Christians to the reported practices of some Indian tribes and warned his readers against reviling the natives' "horrible savagery" while remaining blind to their own. It seems no less savage, Montaigne observed, "to tear by rack and torture a body still full of feeling, to roast it by degrees," and then feed it to dogs and swine—a practice his French contemporaries had not only read about but also witnessed, and between their neighbors and fellow citizens, under the cover of religious fervor—"than to roast and eat a man after he is dead." Instead of finding in reports of cannibalism evidence of the superiority of Christian cultures, Montaigne challenged Europeans' tendency to "call barbarous anything that is contrary to our own habits."[5]

So devastatingly did Montaigne ridicule Europeans' pretension that their cultural standards conformed to reason and nature that he has often been characterized as a skeptic who doubted the very possibility of reliable knowledge. As he put it in "On Experience," which he placed at the end of his last volume of essays, "There is nothing inherently just; customs and laws make justice." Yet such judgments did not propel Montaigne toward skepticism. He did not doubt that we can acquire valuable knowledge from experience. He doubted only that we can achieve certainty.[6] Montaigne did not offer an early version of the thoroughgoing skepticism that later thinkers such as René Descartes and Francis Bacon felt compelled to confront and go beyond in order to begin what was later called the scientific revolution. Montaigne not only posed the crucial question "What do I know?"; he also insisted that we proclaim our answers not dogmatically but with chastened restraint. His sober commitment to continuing investigation derived from the experience of knowing how often we are proven not just wrong but inane: "One must learn that one is nothing but a fool."[7]

Against the warring zealots of his day, Montaigne counseled conversation. The give-and-take of discussion, when allowed to proceed freely, can pry open a mind sealed shut by dogmatism. Reading pales by comparison: "The most fruitful and natural exercise for our minds is, in my opinion, conversation." Because Montaigne so willingly conceded the limits of his own knowledge, he welcomed the challenge of different views. He conceded that since he frequently contradicted himself, as exasperated readers of his *Essays* have long noted, contradictory opinions "neither offend nor estrange me; they only arouse and exercise my mind." Only by exchanging ideas can we see our own errors or hope to persuade those who disagree with us. Conversation, by showing us how little we know and reminding us how little others think we know, helps us see our limits. It is a great school of restraint. Recalling Democritus, Montaigne contended that truth is not "hidden in the depths of the abyss" where we humans might uncover it. It is instead "situated rather at an infinite height in the divine understanding." His conclusion joins both sides of his medal: "The world is but a school of inquiry."[8]

France was plunged into civil war when Protestants and Catholics alike stopped arguing and starting fighting. Bloodshed would end only when they mastered their desire for dominance, conceded their ignorance, and extended to their enemies the mercy that both François, duc de Guise, and Montaigne, mayor of Bordeaux, had shown theirs. In a letter he wrote in 1590 to Henry of Navarre, a Protestant whom many moderate Catholics like Montaigne thought stood the best chance of bringing peace to France, Montaigne counseled Henry to demonstrate restraint and mercy. At the time Henry was still fighting to consolidate the control over his fractious realm that he would exercise after converting to Catholicism and reigning as Henry IV. "It has often been observed," Montaigne wrote, "that where conquests, because of their greatness and difficulty, could not be thoroughly completed by arms and by force, they have been completed by clemency and magnificence."[9] Montaigne practiced what he preached. He declined to fortify his château and declared himself ready to submit to royal authority. From his perspective, that submission was the sign of his autonomy, not its negation. The ethic of reciprocity requires mutuality, and that mutuality requires the autonomy of both parties. Trust cannot be secured until it is first extended.[10]

The central ideas Montaigne advanced in his essays correspond to those already identified in the introduction as central to democracy. Given his emphasis on mutual respect, his lampooning of convention, and his conception of truth as whatever is discovered through inquiry, Montaigne might seem a likely champion of democracy. But he was no democrat. Instead he decisively denounced democracy, for reasons that help explain why the idea of popular sovereignty found almost no adherents in Europe for another century. Montaigne's watchwords, restraint and doubt, required self-mastery of a sort he judged exceedingly difficult to achieve. As he wrote in his *Essays*, "The knowledge of his duty should not be left to each man's judgment; it should be prescribed to him, not left to the choice of his reason."[11] The mob, after all, had killed the mayor of Bordeaux. The people of Athens in their wisdom had condemned Socrates to death.

Montaigne returned repeatedly to the fate of that earlier proponent of doubt and paragon of freethinking virtue, whose trial and conviction showed how little faith ordinary people deserve. Montaigne admired Socrates for choosing death rather than renouncing his convictions, but he also likened his defiance before his accusers to that of the cannibals who refused ever to yield in battle and preferred death to surrender. From Montaigne's perspective, that courage expressed an ethic of stoic resistance quite distinct from the ethic of reciprocity he counseled. Even though he conceded that submission and mercy might be inadequate tools for forging justice, he distanced himself from the heroic ethic of Socrates—and that of the rumored cannibals—in order to advance an alternative that he thought only a few hardy souls could achieve. More demanding than the willingness to die is the willingness to forgive. The willingness to yield, when freely chosen, can be more heroic than courage. Before peace is possible, Montaigne suggested, we must be sufficiently in control of ourselves, sufficiently autonomous, to submit freely to authority. The alternative is endless war. Montaigne doubted that more than a very few could become members of a true aristocracy of spirit, capable of doubt, restraint, and the ethic of reciprocity. For that reason he urged obedience to monarchy and religious authority: "All deference and submission is due" to kings "except that of the understanding. My reason was not formed to bow and stoop—that is for my knee."[12]

In his essay "On Physiognomy," Montaigne proclaimed the two commitments that propelled him away from the principles of democracy. First, he asked plaintively, "Is there any political wrong so bad that it is worth fighting with so deadly a drug as civil war?" That haunting question has continued to echo into our own time. From Montaigne's perspective, only a powerful monarch could end the wars of religion, and for that reason establishing the legitimacy of authority and the obligation of obedience eclipsed every other consideration. Second, "True freedom is to have complete power over one's own activities."[13] Such autonomy, Montaigne believed, is compatible with monarchy because autonomy requires self-restraint, or self-mastery, rather than the absence of all constraint. Submission that is part of a deliberate exchange calculated to achieve the peace makes possible not only independence but life itself. Montaigne's experience of the masses' murderous credulity and his reading of Greek and Roman history convinced him that ordinary people could not achieve the autonomy that an ethic of reciprocity would require.

Most of his contemporaries rejected most of what Montaigne believed, especially the ideas that make him important to us and to the history of democratic cultures. But they agreed with him in dismissing the prospect of popular government. The evidence of two millennia proved to them the undesirability, and perhaps even the impossibility, of democracy. Montaigne nevertheless helped articulate the ideas on which democracy depends. Indeed, in the recurring pattern of unanticipated and unintended consequences that has marked the history of democracy in Europe and America, some of those most skeptical about popular government have advanced it. Conversely, its self-proclaimed stalwarts have at times obstructed its progress.

Democracy begins in bloodshed, in eras such as the one in which Montaigne lived. To survive, however, let alone thrive, it requires a culture of mutual respect. Popular government often emerges as a result of conflicts that turn violent, but it cannot be established or sustained unless people are willing to let their worst enemies exercise power if they win an election. That willingness requires the predisposition that I have characterized as the ethic of reciprocity. In its absence, democracy is impossible; even in its presence, democracy is fragile. Although issues in politics often seem too important to submit to a vote or a jury of randomly selected citizens, sustaining democracy depends on individuals' willingness to do just that. Either rejecting the outcome of established procedures such as elections or trials or responding to defeat with violence is fatal to democracy. Conceding legitimacy to opponents requires both Montaigne-like forbearance and humility, because it signals the realization that one might be wrong and one's foes might be right. That willingness has been uncommon in human history, which explains why democracies have been rare and why they have rarely lasted long.

All histories of democracy must begin by considering developments in the ancient Near East, the warring city-states of classical Greece, and the beginnings of Christianity during the mighty but brittle republic of Rome. As those early examples show, beneath the principles of popular sovereignty, autonomy, and equality lie commitments to deliberation, pluralism, and the ethic of reciprocity.

The admonition to treat your neighbor as you would like to be treated yourself, which we know as the golden rule, dates back at least to the tenth century BCE. Early versions of the golden rule appeared in the law codes of the ancient Near East, and the oldest books of the Hebrew Bible contain variants on the theme. "Thou shalt love thy neighbor as thyself," reads a verse in Leviticus. Elsewhere in the Torah the people of Israel are enjoined, as part of their covenant with the Lord, to treat each other with fairness, not to oppress strangers, and to care for widows, orphans, and the poor among them. The form of these Jewish laws follows the standard structure of covenant codes. Such treaties, in which subjects (or vassals) pledged to obey all-powerful rulers, were common in the ancient Near East. The distinctive feature of the Jewish scriptures had to do with God's commitment to treat with infinite mercy the people who had bound themselves to his law. By rendering even the King of Kings subject to the code of the covenant, the Torah itself established, over the seven centuries of its composition, the earliest irony of self-government: if their God bound himself to obey a self-imposed law, then his people were likewise bound to honor the covenant that their God had made with them.[14]

The logic of the covenant thus pointed in the direction of establishing the unlimited authority of the law and implied the limited authority of any particular king. Along with the Ten Commandments given to Moses, the covenant, as articulated in Exodus and Leviticus, elevated the principle of the golden rule. But the Torah did not provide clear guidelines indicating exactly how the people of God should arrange their own government. The authority of Saul, the first king of Israel, and his successors was said to descend directly, as did that of Moses, from the authority of Yahweh the lawgiver. Yet because a gap remained between the undeniable authority of the divine source of law and the necessity of interpreting the meaning of those laws, disagreements among people claiming to act according to God's will emerged almost immediately and never ceased. Claiming to interpret God's will more accurately, prophets repeatedly challenged the legitimacy of rulers. Centuries of rabbinical commentary offered layers of differing interpretation. Because none enjoyed unrivaled supremacy within the varieties of Jewish practice, over the course of generations disputing the law became the norm. By virtue of the Jewish commitment to deliberation, the meaning of humility as well as autonomy, and of equality as well as the ethic of reciprocity, both within Israel itself and in its relations with its neighbors, remained open to interpretation even though bound by law.[15]

In Greece, where no single god and no single idea of law reigned supreme, competing ideas about—and practices of—government likewise emerge from the earliest records of the archaic period (seventh and sixth centuries BCE). Although no direct line connects early Greek democracy to more recent forms of self-government, many of the controversies about democracy among contemporary historians and political theorists echo those among classical Greek writers—and among scholars who study the changing values and practices of Greek city-states from the fifth through the fourth century BCE. Ever since late-medieval and early-modern European thinkers, indebted to the work of Byzantine and Islamic scholars who kept these records alive, became acquainted with this Greek heritage, what happened in Greece has mattered profoundly to Europeans. Democracy in Greece originated in religious practice and matured as the best means to counter aristocratic rule. But Greek democracy differed strikingly from later versions, primarily because it depended centrally on the use of sortition, or lottery, to choose members of the assembly and other government officials. Although the earliest uses of sortition are disputed, it seems likely that reliance on a lottery was initially associated with fate or the will of the gods: decisions made by chance rather than by deliberate human choice could be interpreted as divinely sanctioned.

The reasons behind the initial appearance of democracy in Greek political life remain unknown. It is clear, however, that even in Homer and Hesiod individual choices were deemed important, and the people were thought to play a crucial role in public life by participating in the assembly and insuring that their leaders remained subject to the law. When the aristocratic rulers of archaic Greek city-states wanted to extend their power, they needed help. To secure the loyalty of the farmers whom they enlisted as soldiers in their military campaigns, they began experimenting with different forms of government. Herodotus, who wrote the first history of Greece, offered three criteria for popular rule: the use of lot to select officials, the accountability of those officials to the wider public, and the ultimate location of decision making in a popular assembly consisting of all citizens. Such forms of government emerged in some Greek city-states from the sixth through the fourth century BCE.[16]

In Athens democratic rule matured thanks to the innovations of Solon. Chosen as chief magistrate in 594 BCE, Solon challenged the oligarchic rule of a landed aristocracy by instituting debt relief and empowering a council of four hundred citizens. He changed the criterion for election to the council, which set the agenda for the assembly, from family to wealth, thereby at least opening the door to the more democratic forms of government that were to follow. In the words Aristotle used to summarize the assessment of later commentators, "Solon was an excellent lawgiver who broke the over-exclusive nature of the oligarchy, ended the slavery of the common people, and established the ancient democracy with a well-balanced constitution."[17] Solon sought to balance the power of the wealthy (the word *aristocratia* combined the Greek root for "the excellent" with the suffix for "power") against that of the community of citizens (*democratia*).[18] Although members of the council were elected, other officials were chosen by lot. Every citizen could participate in the assembly and enjoyed equal status before the law. After Solon's death, Athens slid quickly from democracy to tyranny, but given the already well-established traditions of popular engagement, even the ensuing "age of tyrants"—in Athens and elsewhere—could be seen as contributing to Greek democracy by galvanizing the people against autocratic rule.[19]

Athens emerged as a full-fledged, self-conscious democracy in the years following 508 BCE, when Cleisthenes was recalled to power by the people of Athens. He instituted reforms that weakened the power of the wealthy and consolidated popular government. Cleisthenes further broadened membership in the council to include five hundred citizens elected from those put forward by the *demoi* or demes, the villages in the vicinity of Athens or the districts of the city itself. Members of the council, who served for one year and no more than two nonconsecutive years, were responsible for administering the government, making decisions about foreign policy, and setting the agenda for the assembly. Roughly 25 percent of the 120,000 people of Athens were citizens, and as many as 6,000 of those 30,000 citizens gathered almost every week to speak, listen, and render judgment in the assembly. As important as rhetorical skills were for the minority of citizens who delivered speeches before the assembled citizens, members of the assembly did not deliberate. After hearing a series of formal orations, the assembly voted, by voice, simply yes or no. An even larger number of citizens, selected by lot as were those who served in the assembly, participated as members of juries in Athenian law courts.[20]

Sortition was thought to remove the dangers of faction and the possibility of rule by elites or experts. Only those who put their names forward could be chosen, yet sortition engaged more than half the citizens of Athens in public life, giving them both the opportunity and the responsibility to make laws and render judgments. A few crucial positions, notably those involving the administration of finance and military command, were always decided by election rather than lot, and those elected were subject to removal by the assembly. It was no empty threat. From time to time even the most celebrated, including Pericles (c. 495–420 BCE), were discharged from office. By breaking down the older kin-based networks and engaging more people in public life, sortition and the other reforms instituted under Cleisthenes not only invigorated public life but also turned Athens into a formidable military power. In time renewed jockeying for position among leading families prompted yet another round of democratic reforms, engineered by Ephialtes and consummated by his successor, Pericles, from 462 to 450 BCE. Once more aimed at the oligarchy that had again taken control of public life, this constitution, which also used sortition to secure citizens' participation, ushered in the golden age of classical Greek civilization.[21]

During the next century, as democracy matured in Athens, an unexpected rationale emerged thanks to the historian Thucydides. Although himself critical of popular government, Thucydides provided an enduring statement of classical democratic ideals. In his rendering of a funeral oration delivered in 431 BCE, after one of the early battles of the Peloponnesian War, Thucydides put these now-familiar words in the mouth of Pericles: "Our constitution is called a democracy because power is in the hands not of a minority but of the whole people." Since all women, children, and slaves, and all Athenians not born to citizens, were barred from participating, the claim was overblown. Yet the assumption that free, native-born, adult male property owners constituted the "whole people" governed Western democratic theory and practice until at least the late eighteenth century.

Whenever disputes emerged, Thucydides continued, "everyone"—i.e., every free male with property—was considered "equal before the law." Every time Athenians selected individuals for "positions of public responsibility," what mattered was not "membership in a particular class, but the actual ability which the man possesses. No one, so long as he has it in him to be of service to the state, is kept in political obscurity because of poverty." Although that claim expressed an Athenian ideal, it was another exaggeration: even after Cleisthenes introduced modest compensation for jury service, only citizens with a reliable flow of household labor from dependent women and slaves could afford the demands of extended public service. The ideals of equality and autonomy, however, as well as the institutions of sortition and rotation in office, did distinguish Athens from some of its rival Greek city-states.

Those differences extended from politics to culture, and the link between the two domains, although contested, has remained a crucial issue for democracies ever since. In the words Thucydides attributed to Pericles, "Just as our political life is free and open, so is our day-to-day life in our relations with each other." Athenian citizens did not mind if "a neighbor enjoys himself in his own way"; in their "private lives" they were "free and tolerant." Thucydides thus seemed to separate the private from the public sphere, a distinction later thinkers would inherit—and dispute.

The question of how we should understand the idea of individual rights in classical Athens remains hotly contested. Since all citizens considered themselves part of a civic community, the concept of rights to be exercised against that community seemed as incongruous as the idea of the wrist enjoying rights against the arm. If all Athenians shared but one common good, then the concepts of self-interest and an inviolable private sphere remained alien. No word expressing what we call "individual rights" existed in classical Greek. Although Pericles praised Athenians' open-mindedness toward each other, their toleration did not extend to open dissent or to the customs and ideals of other cultures. Whatever (limited) diversity Athenians might have accepted in private behavior, Pericles made clear that "in public affairs we keep to the law. This is because it commands our deep respect. We give our obedience to those whom we put in positions of authority, and we obey the laws themselves." Finally, although all citizens were thought equal before the law, Athenians understood that such equality was empty if it remained merely formal. It was necessary to pay particular attention, according to Pericles, to those laws concerned with "the protection of the oppressed." Athenian democracy was distinguished by an ethic of mutual respect among citizens and a particular concern with "the oppressed," two considerations that, although evidently not extending to women or slaves, did signal an awareness that democratic culture requires something more than the institutions of self-government.[22]

Periclean Athens was radically democratic compared with earlier and contemporary forms of government in the Greek city-states. Although Pericles thought that made "the school of Hellas" a model, some of the most influential philosophers of ancient Greece considered the democratic constitution of Athens its fatal flaw. When the works of Plato, Aristotle, and other writers such as Pseudo-Xenophon ("the Old Oligarch") were recovered in the hierarchical world of late-medieval Europe, the meanings of democracy were filtered through their criticism of popular government rather than the celebrations found in other classical texts. Orators such as Demosthenes, Aeschines, and Isocrates skewered wealthy individuals who dared put their own concerns above the public good. They extolled popular participation in public life because it provided freedom, equality, and justice for all citizens. Yet at times even these champions of the people lampooned sortition and praised elections as the best way to select qualified officials. Skilled rhetoricians speaking in the council, the assembly, or the law courts advanced conflicting ideas about the best way to secure the public good. At times criticizing democracy could prove dangerous.[23]

The best-known of these public trials concerned Socrates. According to his accusers, Socrates had characterized as "folly" the practice of "appointing public officials by lot." No one would choose "a pilot or builder or flautist by lot." That claim, his critics charged, had "led the young to despise the established constitution and made them violent."[24] Although Socrates denied the charge that his instruction corrupted Athenian youth, he rejected exile and accepted his sentence. He respected the legitimacy of the law, he explained, that had given him the freedom to think and teach and now condemned him to death. When Plato (428–347 BCE) immortalized his mentor in the *Apology*, however, he had Socrates dismiss democratic justice: "Please do not be offended if I tell you the truth," Plato's Socrates proclaimed. "No man on earth who conscientiously opposes either you or any other organized democracy, and flatly prevents a great many wrongs and illegalities from taking place in the state to which he belongs, can possibly escape with his life." From Plato's perspective, majority rule empowers the unenlightened many over the thoughtful few. For that reason "the true champion of justice, if he intends to survive even for a short time, must necessarily confine himself to private life" and leave politics—all forms of politics—alone.[25]

In the *Republic* Plato's Socrates described democracy as a travesty of justice in which all individuals, no matter how base their tastes or judgment, can do whatever they like. Authority, instead of being grounded on principles of truth and justice and exercised by those best suited to the task, is given to charlatans who promise to indulge the undisciplined passions and satisfy the insatiable appetites of the people. The "features of a democracy," in short, are "an agreeable form of anarchy with plenty of variety and an equality of a peculiar kind for equals and unequals alike." Thanks to interpreters of Plato, that unflattering image of democracy came to be as firmly associated with ancient Athens as its drama, art, or architecture.[26]

Of the many students in Plato's Academy, Aristotle (384–322 BCE) proved uniquely influential. In his *Nicomachean Ethics*, Aristotle argued that virtue should be understood as a mean between extremes, and in politics the best path lay in a "mean" between popular and aristocratic rule. Claiming to base his conclusion not on reflection but on careful study of the consequences of a wide variety of political arrangements, Aristotle wrote that man is by nature a "political animal" equipped with not only the capacity for speech but also the capacity to reason and discern good from evil. Only in his appropriate setting, as a citizen within the framework provided by social organization within the *polis* or city-state, could man develop his capacity for virtue.[27] Aristotle rejected any notion of a prepolitical or presocial individual who might then form a compact with others. "A social instinct is implanted in all men by nature," he insisted, and "when perfected," man is the "best of animals." But "when separated from law and justice," as occurs when political order dissolves into anarchy, "he is the worst of all."[28]

Although Aristotle's writings disappeared for centuries, when his works resurfaced in late-medieval Europe he was christened "the master of those who know," and his writings exerted an enduring influence on later thinkers. Aristotle observed, following convention, that most governments had been either monarchical, aristocratic, or popular. Whenever the purpose of government shifts from the public interest to the self-interest of those in power, these three forms devolve into tyranny, oligarchy, or democracy. Best of all would be a mixed constitution, which Aristotle called a polity (*politeia*), that would combine the strengths and control the weaknesses of all these forms in a hybrid variety of virtuous popular government, democracy tempered by aristocracy. Rather than depending too much on oligarchs' temptations to tyranny or the whims of an impoverished multitude, such a polity would rest most solidly on a dispersed agrarian or pastoral population of middling means.

Aristotle took for granted that all states contain poor, middling, and wealthy citizens. He linked the stability of his ideal mixed constitution with the virtuous moderation practiced by the rural middle class, those self-sufficient agrarians who do not covet the property of the rich but work too hard to be envied by the poor. Moreover, particularly if such a polity were large (yet not too large), it might escape the deadly tensions that derive from factions because "in small states it is easy for the whole body of citizens to become divided into two, which leaves no middle at all, and nearly everybody either rich or poor."[29] Aristotle agreed with Pericles that the principles of democracy are freedom and equality, but he insisted that in any real polity the passion for both must be constrained to prevent anarchy. In a democracy individuals want not to be ruled. They prefer to live as they choose, and precisely for that reason democracies spin out of control. When "whatever the majority decides is final and constitutes justice," people inevitably find that "freedom to do exactly what one likes cannot do anything to keep in check that element of badness which exists in each and all of us."[30] Aristotle thus identified one among the multiple unintended consequences of popular government: freeing individuals to follow their desires can erode the ethic of reciprocity on which democracy depends.

Collecting features from diverse historical and contemporary precedents, Aristotle listed those that characterize democracies. Public offices should be filled for short terms by different individuals, chosen by lot where appropriate or by election where necessary, because of either the need for expertise or the scale of the damage that could be done by the incompetent. In a democracy there should be few or limited property qualifications for citizenship. Citizens should be paid to serve on juries so all can participate in public life. Legislation should be decided by a sovereign assembly in which all citizens can speak. Finally, democracies tend to be dominated by those of "low birth, low incomes, and mechanical occupations," and it was Aristotle's obvious disdain for the judgment of such people that soured his admirers on democracy.[31] Aristotle's ideal mixed polity would adopt as many of those features as proved consistent with stability and exclude slaves, women, and foreigners, all of whom Aristotle deemed "irrational" because they lacked the deliberative faculty crucial for collective decision making. The capacity to see beyond narrow self-interest was the defining characteristic of the citizens of Aristotle's mixed polity. That commitment to the common good he considered both indispensable and fragile. Aristotle believed that sustaining an ethic of reciprocity when individuals enjoy the freedom to follow their narrower, less elevated desires would be the most difficult challenge facing citizens in a polity. Rotation in office, weighing alternative positions, and making judgments all engendered and required "considering the interest of others."[32]

Aristotle further claimed that "'ruling and being ruled in turn' is one element in liberty, and the democratic ideal of justice is in fact numerical equality, not equality based on merit."[33] In that simple sentence Aristotle collapsed three separable values that many later theorists of democracy struggled to keep distinct. First is the ethic of reciprocity, the awareness that all citizens rule and that no citizen is above the law. Second is the conception of liberty as self-rule, described later in the *Politics* as the ability to "live as you like," by which he meant freedom from domination; it was the opposite of being enslaved. Finally, democracy means that majorities rule whether their decisions are wise or foolish. Ideally, though, the majority rules according to "the idea of justice that is by common consent democratic," meaning that the poor "exercise no more influence in ruling than the rich, and do not have sole sovereign power, but all exercise it together on the basis of numerical equality." In sum, under a democratic constitution, based on an ethic of reciprocity, all citizens should enjoy both freedom and equality. But Aristotle distinguished between the arithmetical equality appropriate in many circumstances and the geometrical equality appropriate in public service. All citizens should be equal before the law, but political responsibilities and rewards should be proportionate to merit.[34]

Despite the appeal of a polity that would inculcate such a vibrant civic spirit, Aristotle worried that popular government can be unstable. The hybrid form he recommended would work best when citizens' interest in public affairs was tempered by a wholesome inclination to focus on productive labor rather than idle chatter. Aristotle's virtuous citizens thus "find more satisfaction in working on the land than in ruling and in engaging in public affairs." Busying themselves in their fields rather than scheming obsessively for individual gain or partisan political advantage, citizens should know the limits of their competency and trust the crucial issues of public life to the best qualified, most virtuous, and most politically adept of their neighbors.[35]

Such a polity would hardly suit all populations, Aristotle admitted, and his warnings echoed in the criticism expressed by later writers on democracy. Perhaps a city-state, lacking resources of its own, cannot be self-sufficient and must engage in extensive commerce. Perhaps, for various reasons, there must be more herdsmen than farmers, or, even worse, more mechanics, artisans, and merchants. Particularly in that case, in "the most extreme democracy," an urban population would insist that everyone should participate in politics. "Not every state can tolerate" that condition, "and it is not likely to last unless it is well held together by its laws and customs." If deeply rooted, those laws and customs might prevent two otherwise likely outcomes. First, the poor should avoid antagonizing the rich, which inevitably propels the emergence of a powerful oligarchic reaction. Second, the rich should understand that it is in their interest to use their surplus wealth for those "in need, if possible in lump sums large enough for the acquisition of a small piece of land, but if not, enough to start a business, or work in agriculture." Such moderation was the only way to escape the instability engendered by extreme inequality.

The middle road of virtue that Aristotle judged desirable for each individual citizen would become possible only in the context of *politeia*. Thus policies preventing poverty and facilitating the achievement of moderate prosperity would be necessary to preserve the mixed constitution Aristotle recommended. In his day exemplars of such moderation were scarce both in ethics and in politics. As Athens struggled for dominance with its rival city-states, its own "laws and customs" proved too weak to prevent a widening gap between rich and poor, its political culture too weak to stave off oligarchic rule, and its military too weak to resist the invading armies of Macedonia. When Athenian democracy was flourishing, however, the principle of *isonomia* (equality before the law) and the practices of sortition, rotation in office, and the widespread participation of citizens in collective decision making helped reinforce the ethic of reciprocity and inculcate the values of autonomy and reciprocity that later champions of democracy would seek to nurture.[36]

Commentators on classical Athenian democracy understood its fragility. They had seen how skillful orators could become demagogues and tyrants. They knew that the assembly could not always discern the difference between talented but unscrupulous speakers and truly virtuous leaders. Demosthenes warned that "he who shall prevail by his words will hold office" in a democracy. Although Thucydides admired Pericles, he conceded that Pericles was able, "by his rank, ability, and known integrity," to "exercise an independent control over the multitude." Thanks to his exceptional abilities, "what was nominally a democracy became in his hands government by the first citizen." Isocrates emphasized the importance of uniting the ability to speak well with moral excellence; the first quality without the second spelled trouble for democracy. Just as the misgivings expressed by Plato and Aristotle shaped later commentators' judgments of popular government, so the warnings of Demosthenes, Thucydides, and Isocrates shaped the ideal of a well-rounded citizen qualified for leadership in a democracy. A popular leader, one capable of moving the masses with his words, had to be educated in—and had to embody—both moral and civic virtues. Otherwise, from the perspective of those schooled in the lessons of classical Greece, skilled rhetoricians might subvert rather than inspire the people, and democracy could deteriorate from Aristotle's ideal of a balanced polity to his nightmare of passionate excess.[37]

Important as the ideas of Aristotle proved to be to later conceptions of democracy, the account provided by Thucydides is crucial for understanding the cultural predispositions and practices necessary for its development. Through historical analysis, Thucydides revealed that tensions between individuals and cultural ideals are inescapable. He showed the inevitable gaps between aspirations and behavior, and between individuals' intentions and the consequences of their actions, in particular the distance between the high ideals of Pericles's funeral oration and the austere realism of the equally familiar Melian Dialogue of 416 BCE. In that classic exchange, representatives of the Athenian military engaged the council of Melos, a small island that had sought to preserve its neutrality. Power, the Athenians announced grandly, generates the only "standard of justice" that matters: "The strong do what they have the power to do and the weak accept what they have to accept."[38]

Such cynicism boils down all human interaction to struggles of strength between self-interested parties. Thucydides showed that when that view prevailed within Athens itself, as well as in its relations with other states, it destroyed democracy. In short, whereas Aristotle suggested how a well-ordered state could avert conflict by suppressing unruly desire and cultivating virtue, Thucydides showed how and why Athenian democracy worked, and then why it failed not only to live up to its ideals but even to survive the city-state's efforts to dominate its neighbors. Whereas the intricate and unstable interactions of desire and reason, self-interest and responsibility, can be simplified or blurred by the abstractions of philosophy, they are less easily resolved in the messiness of human experience. The success of classical Athenian democracy, both in terms of citizens' internalizing its norms of self-rule and reciprocity and their ability to institutionalize them, fed its vanity. That inflated sense of its capacity drove Athens to assert its power, and that impulse collided with the equally ambitious aspirations of Sparta. As Thucydides made clear, even as Athenian leaders after Pericles failed to show his prudence or his judgment, so Athens itself proved unable to harness the qualities responsible for its ascension to prevent its defeat. When Pericles's successors abandoned his restraint, they found it impossible to satisfy either their own desire for military expansion or the rapidly expanding desires of their citizens. When the ethic of reciprocity faded in the later stages of classical Athenian democracy, so did the freedom and equality it made possible.

All the advantages Athens achieved by forging unity in the *polis* through a robust democracy—the fostering of participation, the suppression of individual ambition, and the prevention of factions—did not enable it to recognize its limits when it encountered equally powerful rivals. The institutions of classical Athenian democracy served one purpose: by checking and channeling desires that ran counter to the public interest, they prevented any individual or group of individuals from subverting the common good. As the cynicism Athens displayed in Melos made clear, however, such equilibrium proved too fragile when confronted with resistance. The unity achieved by democratic freedom facilitated the expansion of Athens. Through Pericles's final speech, much longer and more impassioned than his funeral oration, Thucydides showed him invoking the importance of sacrifice for the common good in an effort to inspire Athens to persevere.

None of the leaders who followed Pericles matched his ability to persuade Athenians to look beyond the desires of the moment to see the longer view or their shared interest. When the people of Athens and their leaders indulged their ambitions, particularly in the disastrous Sicilian expeditions of 427 and 413 BCE, without heeding the constraints imposed by their changed circumstances, their continued efforts to expand blinded them to the ethic of reciprocity integral to the success of their democracy.[39]

Roman experiments with forms of popular governance began in the fifth century BCE, but the eventual replacement of republican by imperial rule etched deeply into postmedieval European memory anxieties about the people's capacity to govern. Of the many achievements of the Roman Empire, its most lasting contribution to the long-term development of democracy might have been its failed suppression of Christianity. Rome's glory rested on manipulating, when possible, or suppressing violently, when necessary, the will of the people. Although at least formally acknowledged in the *concilium plebis* established in 471 BCE, which indirectly empowered the people to vote for magistrates, the people enjoyed little effectual involvement in public life beyond voting yea or nay in occasional plebiscites and public trials. Some Roman ideas about the people's limited role in government derived from earlier indigenous practices of absolute monarchy, some were borrowed from Greek and Greco-Roman Stoic philosophy, and others wove together strands from both sources. Even at the height of Rome's republic, the regime nominally devoted to *res publica populi Romani*, the public thing of the Roman people, it was run by and for a small number of its wealthiest citizens, who monopolized the positions of consul, senator, and magistrate. Although groups of plebes formed clubs or gangs, often associated with religious cults distinct from those favored by patricians, these plebeian groups existed outside the formal decision-making process. Like the Greek city-states, Rome was effectively an oligopoly rather than a democracy, and it was slave labor from conquests that enabled its citizens to play their part in *res publica*.

Whereas some Greek writers had identified the virtues of direct democracy and others its dangers, writers on the Roman form of republican government focused on its practices of elections, representation, and plebiscites. The most influential of these writers, Polybius and Cicero, lived during the second and first centuries BCE, when the republic was wracked by the threat of civil war and giving way to imperial rule. The Greek-born Polybius offered a standard typology of governments ruled by the one, the few, and the many. But unlike Aristotle and other Greek critics of popular government, for whom democracy untempered by aristocracy was malignant, Polybius argued that the legitimacy of all three forms depends on the consent of the governed. Absent popular approval, kingship degenerates into tyranny, aristocracy into oligarchy, and democracy into mob rule. But each form is capable of excellence, including a properly functioning democracy in which "the majority decision prevails, but which retains the traditional values of piety toward the gods, care of parents, respect for elders, and obedience to the laws." Polybius further proposed a cyclical progression through these forms of government. The impulse toward reciprocity, which Polybius traced to the natural interaction of family members, and which he thought underlay all stable governance, sooner or later gave way to the use of fear to maintain order.

From the perspective of Polybius, the ideal constitution, such as the one Lycurgus gave Sparta, combined the best features of all three forms. When a polity's constitution enables the one, the few, and the many to check each other's potential excesses, and when it reinforces the ethic of reciprocity that Polybius judged crucial, healthy relations between king, aristocracy, and people are possible. Unfortunately, history showed Polybius that such balance rarely lasts long. Eventually the cycle recurs. Although the writings of Polybius disappeared and were only rediscovered, in fragments, during the Italian Renaissance, the ideas presented in book 6 of his *Histories* would have a profound impact on later thinkers.[40]

The most influential Roman political thinker, Cicero (106–43 BCE), saw the potential of a less polarized society and a government that bridged the gap between the privileged and the people. His writings helped shape later ideas about the possibility of popular government, but as a political actor Cicero did little to improve its prospects. From a wealthy but non-noble background, Cicero was catapulted to the consulship in 63 BCE as a result of his brilliance as an orator and because he represented an alternative to his rival Catiline, whom members of the Roman elite perceived as a threat to their rule. When Cicero unearthed evidence of a conspiracy that seemed to confirm those suspicions, he ordered the plotters executed without trial. Cicero defended that extreme step as necessary to preserve the republic, but it led to his own brief exile after the First Triumvirate of Pompey, Crassus, and Julius Caesar took power in 60 BCE. Out of power, Cicero had time to write.

Because most of Cicero's writings take the form of dialogues between characters with distinctly different points of view, his own views cannot always be identified with confidence. Cicero presented skeptical and historicist arguments concerning the variability of cultures, the inevitable discrepancy between right and necessity, and the excellent reasons why we should embrace rather than deny uncertainty. He also disputed the cynical proposition that all notions of right and wrong are rooted in nothing more solid than the shifting sands of custom. He entertained the idea, gaining popularity among Roman jurists, of a universal natural law governing all people, although he doubted that individuals—or political leaders—could always know it or follow it. Coupled with the Stoic doctrine that all individuals possess a divine spark that makes them worthy of respect, Cicero's stern ethics required not only self-restraint but also, contrary to the practice of his time, reciprocity, which he considered a moral as well as political ideal. Against the savvy wisdom that counseled choosing the useful over the right course of action, Cicero insisted that the choice is false: in the long run only the good proves useful.

Cicero wrote many books but produced fewer new ideas. He proclaimed that public virtues such as generosity and patriotism "originate in our natural inclination to love our fellow men," which he deemed the "foundation of justice." Such inclinations, although natural, find expression only through the exercise of "right reason." Like Aristotle, Cicero was skeptical about popular government because he doubted the masses could master their inclinations in order to govern "as slaves to the public interest." Subordinating the self to advance the common good was the only path toward Cicero's goal of civic harmony, and he did not think ordinary people were up to that arduous task.[41] Cicero believed that the Roman republic, at its best, mixed elements of monarchy in its consuls, aristocracy in its senate, and democracy in the people's right to vote for those who would represent them.[42]

Cicero's admonitions to high-minded public service inspired many of his contemporaries and many later readers. They did not, however, save Cicero himself. In the wake of Julius Caesar's assassination, again fearing the end of republican rule and fatally abandoning his usual prudence, a tendency that many have interpreted as indecisiveness, Cicero delivered a series of orations attacking Marc Antony. Like many other Roman rulers denounced as tyrants,

Antony knew there are two ways to understand reciprocity. Cicero himself had written that "men are both the greatest benefit and the greatest harm to each other."[43] When Antony joined with Lepidus and Octavian (the future Caesar Augustus) to form the Second Triumvirate in 43 BCE, Cicero was declared an enemy of the state and executed.

Cicero's ideal of "mutual helpfulness" extended the individual's responsibility beyond family, clan, and republic to all humanity, at least in principle. But like Polybius and consistent with the hierarchical and patriarchal assumptions that governed Roman culture, Cicero did not doubt that duties could be ranked in order of importance from those to the gods, then to the fatherland, to one's parents, and so on down to the strangers whom one need only avoid harming. It was the connections dictated by the desire for honor and the realities of mastery and dependence that stabilized Roman society. Like every other Roman citizen, Cicero admired heroes who died with valor to enhance the glory of Rome and urged even the powerful to sacrifice their interests for the good of the whole. Yet the notion that the worthiest of all should allow himself to be humiliated and sacrificed for the sake of the least worthy never entered Cicero's mind. To most Romans of his day such sacrifice, motivated by selfless love, seemed absurd, contrary to all standards of honor.

Christian morality, by rejecting the Roman moral code and inserting in its place an ethic of love, implicitly threatened Rome's identification of honor with martial glory and the social and political structures that went along with it. Christians insisted on the spiritual potential of every soul and simultaneously emphasized human sinfulness and heavenly rewards, divine judgment rather than political justice. Early Christians stressed the importance of taking care of those in need, a theme prominent in books of the Hebrew Bible such as Isaiah and central to the Christian gospels. There were no Greek or Roman equivalents to the central theological virtues of Christianity: faith, hope, and especially charity. Nor did ancient philosophers see the value of humility or repentance, two other virtues that distinguished Christianity from classical thought and left a permanent imprint on the modern North Atlantic cultures in which modern democracy emerged centuries later. The first were to be last, the last first: "Whoever exalts himself shall be humbled, and whoever humbles himself shall be exalted." None—not even the shunned, such as tax collectors, or the most reviled, such as prostitutes—were to be excluded. Such admonitions were not unprecedented within Judaism. Hillel, a Babylon-born rabbi living in Jerusalem c. 30 BCE–10 CE, taught a moderate version of Jewish law that inspired a vibrant tradition centered on the ethic of reciprocity. According to Hillel, the core of Judaism, in addition to the love of the Lord, could be stated simply. In the familiar words of one of the central axioms attributed to him, "What is hateful to thee, do not unto thy fellow man; this is the whole law. The rest is commentary."[44]

Arising from the tradition of Judaism represented by Hillel and inspired by the life of Jesus Christ, Christianity originated in just such a series of commentaries, produced decades after Jesus died. Because Jesus, like Hillel, left no sacred texts proclaiming his teachings in his own words, differences of emphasis and interpretive disagreements among his followers marked the Christian community from the beginning. Such discursive proliferation might have inaugurated a diverse and pluralistic set of religious assemblies, relishing debate and encouraging dissent, faithful only to Christ's unambiguous central message that his followers should, above all, love one another. Just as Jews in Jesus's day disagreed over which interpretations of their tradition should prevail, those of the strict School of Shammai or those of Hillel, so Christians from the first century struggled to work out the implications of their faith, including its political consequences.

The most revolutionary aspect of the Christian message was the challenge to Roman assumptions concerning hierarchy and honor. Those Jews first drawn to the Christian message were themselves outsiders. Once Saul of Tarsus converted to Christianity, he carried that openness even further by suggesting that gentiles could become Christians without first becoming Jews. Although some Christians had and kept possessions, including the houses where the early Christians assembled, they departed from the Roman practice of using charity to demonstrate their own grandeur—and establish their dominance over those beneath them. Early Christian communities established instead the revolutionary practice of giving freely, anonymously, and on a regular basis to those in need, including foreigners who shared their faith but whom they had never met. If Hillel could encapsulate all of Jewish teaching into a single sentence, so the Gospel of Matthew could have Jesus compress his message into two equally brief admonitions: first love God, then love your neighbor as yourself.[45] Those two simple commandments, Jesus assured those who were trying to trip him up, contained all of Jewish law and all the wisdom of the prophets. Paul later underscored the point: "You, my brothers and sisters, were called to be free." But you should not use your freedom to indulge your desire for pleasure. Instead you should "serve one another humbly in love. For the entire law is fulfilled in keeping this one command: 'Love your neighbor as yourself.'"[46]

This ethic of brotherhood, grounded on the principle of universal benevolence that Jesus preached, did not entail a frontal challenge to the institution of slavery or the subordination of children and women to their fathers and husbands. Those relationships were not only taken for granted, by

Christians and Jews as well as Greeks and Romans, but also served as paradigms for every Christian's willingness to serve her or his divine master. Christian morality nevertheless did translate into a different attitude toward human relations that would prove profoundly important to later generations. In his letters to early Christian communities, Paul recommended the virtues of mercy, kindness, humility, meekness, and patience. He advised slaves to "obey your earthly masters in everything, not only while being watched and in order to please them, but wholeheartedly, fearing the Lord. Whatever your task, put yourselves into it, as done for the Lord and not for your masters, since you know that from the Lord you will receive the inheritance as your reward; you serve the Lord Christ." In principle at least, Christianity transformed the entire framework of domination as well as service. "Masters, treat your slaves justly and fairly, for you know that you also have a Master in heaven."[47] In another letter Paul counseled his friend Philemon to embrace his runaway slave Onesimus, now that both had become Christians, and treat him "no longer as a slave, but instead of a slave as a brother most dear, especially to me, and how much more to thee, both in the flesh and in the Lord!" In a culture saturated with slavery, Paul underscored the radicalism of his message: "If, therefore, thou dost count me as a partner, welcome him as thou wouldst me."[48]

Although there were, of course, significant precedents for the virtue of benevolence, in Christianity it became central. In the School of Hillel and in ancient Roman philosophy, notably in Stoicism and Cynicism, could be found scattered recommendations of a simple life of self-denial and generosity toward others. The Christian gospels carried the injunction further both by extending it to all people—not excluding women, slaves, and foreigners, all of whom were to be treated as equals—and by warning that even such praiseworthy behavior should not become a basis for pride, because pride was itself problematic. Such self-abnegation, patterned on Christ's crucifixion, served to remind humans to seek salvation rather than early success, and it carried ambiguous implications for the relation of Christians to the world around them. Unsettling to Greeks and Romans alike, early Christians forged communities practicing the virtues Jesus embodied and admonished others to do the same. In the first-century Acts of the Apostles, the earliest disciples were described as "holding all things in common" and distributing what they owned "according to each individual's needs."[49] The first Christians hoped thereby to influence others and draw them to the Christian faith, in the process widening and deepening the life of their assemblies.

As their numbers grew, differences inevitably emerged. Some welcomed the continuing proliferation of interpretations and practices, seeing in that diversity God's spirit at work. They agreed with Paul's advice in his letters about the fruitfulness of humility and forbearance—and the need to continue to experiment—as reflections of humans' limited understanding of God's will. In Paul's words to the Christian assembly of Thessalonians, "Do not extinguish the spirit. Do not despise prophecies. But test all things; hold fast that which is good."[50] Others disagreed with Paul's approach. Many, including those of Jesus's followers who produced the first gospels, feared diversity might end in anarchy. In that case Christ's example and his central message would be lost. Within several generations, a new authority, formalized in scriptures including Paul's letters and accounts of Jesus's life provided by the evangelists Mark, Matthew, Luke, and, later, John, had been established.[51]

The previously open-ended, egalitarian communities of Christians began to take a rather different shape, in part to stave off heresy and in part from fear of Roman authorities, who saw in Christians' renunciation of Roman gods a potential threat to Roman authority and law. The systematic persecution of Christians began during the catastrophic reign of Nero (54–68), gathered momentum under Domitian (81–96), and peaked in the second half of the third century. In response Christian communities turned inward. Christian writers, of whom Origen (??–251) was the most influential, began creating a theology to supplement Paul's admonitions and the narratives of Jesus's life. These writers worked to amalgamate traditions of Greco-Roman philosophy with the teachings of Jesus by replacing the centrality of the crucifixion and resurrection with a cosmic history that emanates from the divine Logos and culminates in the emergence of Israel and the eventual triumph of Christianity, now characterized as the world's first universal religion. Its rigorous ethic, its concern for the poor, and the devotion of its adherents, whose martyrdom testified powerfully to the depth of their commitment, helped Christianity gain support among the Roman elite. The identification of the church with the state in the fourth century, however, just when Rome was beginning to collapse, proved disastrous to the original ideas of unselfish love and humility. Christian writers had always been ambivalent about whether believers should be engaged in society or steer clear of its corruption. Now they began explicitly to deprecate public service of any sort, a dynamic that did not help Rome, now formally Christian, defend itself against invaders from the North.[52]

The long-term consequences for democracy of the most influential Christian writer of the fifth century, Augustine of Hippo (354–430), were profound and paradoxical. By his own admission, Augustine began his adult life as a libertine. He ended as the most influential theologian of the first millennium. From 395 until his death, with invaders at the gates of his city,

Augustine served as bishop of Hippo, in present-day Algeria. In his *Confessions*, the first spiritual autobiography ever written, he attributed his renunciation of a life devoted to pleasure to his reading of Cicero's *Hortensius*, a book based on Aristotle's *Protrepticus*. Both of these now-lost books invited readers to the satisfactions of a life lived in devotion to philosophy, and Augustine credited Cicero with setting him on the road that led eventually away from the paganism of Augustine's father and toward the Christianity embraced by his mother, Monica.[53]

Augustine wrote his other major work, the *City of God*, in the shadow of the barbarian invasions, and he challenged the prevailing identification of Rome as a Christian empire. Because the *City of God* distinguished the personal from the political and the sacred from the profane, it had an even more deflating effect on ideas of civic engagement and social reform. Some contemporaries were blaming the new state religion for the empire's failing condition. From Augustine's perspective, such critiques rested on a faulty understanding of the role Christianity could play in human history. Augustine shared with earlier Greek and Roman thinkers the conviction that man is a social being, but he disagreed that reason can guide men toward fulfillment through political life. Even at its best, when a polity finds justice of the sort that Cicero compared with the harmony achieved by musicians, a well-ordered republic cannot escape eventual corruption because of human imperfection.

The inheritance of original sin, Augustine claimed, prevents humans from escaping the propensity to evil. No earthly political order—no city of man, in his terminology—can offer more than a framework of peace and order within which individuals might orient their lives toward salvation. Augustine acknowledged the necessity and legitimacy of political and legal authority in the earthly city and did not recommend against participating in its affairs. He reminded Christians that no success or accomplishments in this life would last. The soul's destination, and thus the proper focus of every Christian, is eternal salvation. The two cities "have issued from two kinds of love. Worldly society has flowered from a selfish love which dared to despise even God, whereas the communion of saints is rooted in a love of God that is ready to trample on self." Whereas those in the city of man long for fame and material success, and "both the rulers themselves and the people they dominate are dominated by the lust for domination," in the City of God "all citizens serve one another in charity, whether they serve by the responsibilities of office or by the duties of obedience." Augustine judged the classical norm of honor merely the sin of pride; in its place he recommended the Christian virtue of humility.[54] Augustine's *City of God* was interpreted as a warning against placing too much hope in the possibilities of political activity and against the illusion that politics could ever be sanctified.

Augustine insisted that man could do nothing to merit a heavenly reward without divine grace. Against those Christian writers who had highlighted the role of individual free choice in earning salvation, an emphasis that could authorize active engagement in the world in order to bring into being Christ's ethic of love, Augustine stressed the grace of God. His dismissal of earthly things, and his emphasis on the relative insignificance of the physical world and human institutions compared with salvation, fed the later rise of the medieval monastic ideal of isolation from the corruptions of this life. Some early Christians considered political or social action the proper way to bring the kingdom of God and the earthly city closer together. Others judged such work a distraction from the proper focus on the soul's salvation. Augustine contended that the "wayfaring" community of Christians invited "citizens from all nations and all tongues" and united them "into a single band" rather than allowing them to continue to form themselves into diverse communities.[55] The church on earth should be one church, professing obedience to a single authoritative doctrine. Most Christians soon came to agree with Augustine that in the "earthly city" of politics perfection was impossible; no more could be achieved than "a kind of compromise between human wills about the things relevant to moral life."[56]

For the history of democracy, the effect of Augustine's writings is difficult to exaggerate. Combined with an authoritarian hierarchy that became sacralized and increasingly distinct from the laity, Augustine's writings helped blunt the revolutionary implications of Christianity. Although selfless love and the universal brotherhood of man remained its central ideals, theological and ecclesiastical developments obscured that democratic potential for nearly a thousand years.

Rome's disintegration left Europe in political chaos. Rulers great and small ruled as they saw fit, fending off challenges by other kingdoms or principalities, or from their own subjects, by consent if possible and by force if necessary. When their prerogatives were questioned, kings and princes conferred with the most powerful of their subjects; popes convened councils of cardinals. The German duchies elected a king in 911 and, in 962, designated him the Holy Roman Emperor. That emperor, however, managed to exert little authority over those ostensibly under his rule. In 1220 he conceded that he governed a confederation of effectively autonomous principalities, in which ecclesiastical princes ruled their own territories and secular princes established free cities, some of which combined to form the Hanseatic League.

The Golden Bull of 1356 not only sealed the authority of imperial electors to select the emperor but also secured their power in their own lands. In the duchies, assemblies of clergy, nobles, and townsmen constituted the Estates General, which could be convened only by the ecclesiastical or secular princes and met irregularly. Gradually this motley array coalesced into an assembly, the Imperial Diet, which brought together imperial electors, princes, and prominent townsmen, and an Imperial Governing Council, which existed briefly in the early sixteenth century. Neither diet nor council succeeded in bringing effectual authority, let alone order, to the crazy quilt of the German states. The French king Philip IV called an assembly of the three estates of his realm, clergy, nobility, and bourgeoisie, in 1302, but the Estates General did not become an effective force in the French monarchy as a result. It served primarily to ratify, not to challenge, the king's will, particularly concerning taxation. As was true in the Holy Roman Empire, only Philip's handpicked counselors, laws already in existence, and long-standing customs hemmed in the ruler's power. Authority was exercised from the top down.[57]

Such assemblies existed in England from the ninth century onward, and the legitimacy of the legislation passed—and of the judicial decisions reached—derived from the authority those assemblies shared with the monarch. Eadred succeeded his brother Edward as king in 946 "by the election of the nobles," including those from Wales and Scandinavia. Between that date and the return from exile of Edward the Confessor in 1041, the significance of the assembly's consent was sufficiently well established that Edward could become king only after he agreed to the terms laid down by the assembled nobles. The Norman rule of William interrupted that practice after 1066, but the crown's fiscal needs prompted renewed consultation with those whose compliance was required. Once King John signed the Magna Carta in 1215, the enduring institution of Parliament emerged from the models provided by the earlier assemblies and councils. The English aristocracy made increasing use of the bolstering phrase "vox populi" when asserting the rights of Englishmen in the fourteenth and fifteenth centuries. Parliament's approval was required for all taxes sought by the king, and it became an increasingly popular forum for focusing attention on grievances expressed in popular petitions. Even though the authority of Parliament remained constrained by royal prerogatives, the converse also held true. For ordinary Englishmen, as for the subjects of kings and princes elsewhere in Europe, popular sovereignty remained an abstraction. The very existence of the Imperial Diet and Council in the German states, the Estates General in France, and especially the rising authority of Parliament in England, however, did provide the common people with at least nominal representation in public affairs, and on that foundation far more ambitious claims would arise.[58]

The idea that citizens could play an active part in politics all but disappeared following the fall of Rome. When it returned during the twelfth and thirteenth centuries, it emerged alongside various civic and economic institutions that were habitually understood within an overarching religious cosmology. These included the first self-governing towns since the ancient world, medieval craft guilds, confraternities, and other voluntary associations that stressed the importance of subordinating the self to the whole. Whereas Medieval Latin was rich with terms concerning community, society, mutuality, and the common good, there was no word for "individual." The notion of a person existing outside the boundaries of multiple communities, rank-ordered from the universal church through various civic and economic groups, was unknown, even though ways of asserting legal claims against other individuals as well as associations were beginning to develop.[59]

Neither late-medieval political theory nor practice seemed likely to provide fertile soil for democracy. As papal authority expanded in the temporal realm ostensibly relegated to insignificance by *The City of God*, so did arguments justifying its power. From the time that Pope Leo IX (1049–54) proclaimed on rickety grounds the "imperial power and dignity" ostensibly ceded by Constantine to the pope, the papacy claimed increasingly comprehensive authority in the secular as well as the religious sphere.[60] From the very heart of that culture, however, the monastic communities most completely separated from public life and most completely devoted to the ideals of self-abnegation and obedience, emerged ideas that would eventually culminate in new ways of thinking about government.

The monks responsible for copying ancient Greek texts and translating them into Latin were venturing into dangerous territory. Gregory IX (1227–41) prohibited the study of the pagan Aristotle until his texts had been "examined and purified." That delicate task fell to the trustworthy Dominican Friars. William of Moerbeke, in Flanders, and Albert the Great and his student Thomas Aquinas, in Paris, undertook the translation of Aristotle's works and unwittingly began the process of transforming European thought. William of Moerbeke, responsible for translating Aristotle's *Politics*, is generally credited with having coined the Latin words *democratia* and *politizare* as a way of making sense of Greek ideas for which there were no Latin equivalents in use when he completed his translation in 1260. The latter verb meant "to take an active part in public affairs," or "to act as a citizen." From that point on, Western Europeans had at least the terminology for envisioning public life outside the framework of Church authority.[61]

Of course, not everyone greeted the new vocabulary of *democratia* and *politizare* with enthusiasm. After all, Aristotle had described democracy as a corrupt form of government. In the writings of Aquinas (1224–74), the division between the earthly and heavenly cities of Augustine vanished in the triumphant declaration of universal natural law governing all states and their ultimate subservience to the authority of God's church. Consistent with his aim of integrating Aristotle's philosophy with Christian theology, Aquinas praised the mixed constitution that incorporated monarch, aristocracy, and people. Aquinas made clear that an ideal citizen, rational and virtuous, must also strive to be an ideal Christian, obedient to divinely ordained natural law. Consequently Aquinas savaged the idea that the people themselves could constitute legitimate authority. In his book *On Princely Government* (1270), Aquinas declared that "a government is called a democracy when it is iniquitous, and when it is carried on by a large number of people." It is "a form of popular power in which the common people, by sheer force of numbers, oppress the rich, with the result that the whole populace becomes a kind of tyrant."[62] That argument clearly echoed the most pessimistic classical Greek and Roman writers' worries about the poor and vicious masses unjustly despoiling the wealthy and worthy few. Moreover, it nailed down the scholastic conception of authority descending from God to the "vicar of Christ," as popes had taken to calling themselves. There had once been an alternative model. Some early Church fathers conceived of authority as ascending from the scattered communities of early Christians to the bishops, and from them to the "servant of the servants of God," in the words of Pope Gregory the Great (590–604). After Gregory, however, that model of authority ascending from its foundation in the people all but vanished in Christian Europe.[63]

Challenges to the descending conception of authority began to emerge in the late thirteenth century. Writers such as Brunetto Latini, John of Paris, Bartolus of Sassoferrato, Ptolemy of Lucca, and especially Marsilius of Padua (1275–1342) rehabilitated the classical ideal of mixed government and began to envision legitimate forms of popular political engagement, albeit almost always within the frameworks of monarchical and papal power. Their writings offered early glimpses of a conception of popular sovereignty grounded on an ethic of reciprocity. All of them offered the Christian virtue of *caritas*, loving others above oneself, as the essential quality of social life. Without it, humans gravitated toward sinful self-centeredness. With it, according to Henry of Ghent, "men living together in civil society and community" might aspire to living as God intended: "bound together by supreme friendship, in which each considered the other as a second self, by supreme charity, by which each of them loved the other as himself, and by supreme benevolence, by which each of them wished for the other what he wished for himself."[64] Marsilius produced *Defender of the Peace*, the most influential of these writings, on behalf of the Northern Italian city-states, such as his native Padua, which were struggling to establish their independence from the papacy. Aquinas had claimed that the people, in principle originally sovereign, alienated that sovereignty when they delegated authority to a ruler. His critics countered that, in the words of Marsilius, "the elected kind of government is superior to the non-elected," and "the ultimate legislator in any well-ordered community must be the people or the whole body of citizens." Marsilius was launching a conceptual revolution.[65]

Challenges to the model of authority descending from God through the pope did not occur in a vacuum. Writers such as Marsilius deliberately invoked the early communities of Christians, governing themselves without central authority. They looked to the precedent of self-governing monastic communities such as the Cistercians. They also cited the practice of their own day, when various local organizations operating within communes, and the communes themselves, demonstrated the value of at least a measure of self-government de facto even though they might lack the formal authority de jure to legitimate that practice. Feudal relationships depended on mutual obligations. Almost all persons in England after 1066, in the northern parts of France, and to a lesser degree in the Italian city-states and the German territories, experienced such bonds in both directions, linking them to those to whom they owed fealty, and to others who owed them fealty. When those bonds were tight and responsibilities clear, the chain of obligations prevented the emergence of a clearly articulated theory of popular sovereignty. When the feudal order began to break down, however, and when newly emerging communities of various kinds began to employ the Aristotelian idea of a natural civic order independent of (even if consistent with) the spiritual order, as in the Padua of Marsilius and the Lucca of Ptolemy, then asserting the sovereign authority of the people became not only a plausible but also an attractive strategy to employ against the prevailing authority of monarch and pope.

In practice, democracy still had limited allure. Most of those who made the arguments for popular sovereignty in Italian city-states such as Padua, Lucca, and Florence had in mind empowering aristocrats against kings, or against the imperial papacy, rather than engaging the masses directly in politics. Although Marsilius elicited positive responses from critics of papal ambition, republican governments in Renaissance city-states remained oligarchic, and none enjoyed long-term stability. In the early years of the Italian communes, fear of factional strife led some communities in the eleventh and twelfth centuries to experiment with sortition or the use of indirect election. Fourteenth-century Florentine oligarchs appointed diplomats and military leaders, but Florence relied on a lottery to select magistrates. In his *History of the Florentine People* (1415–21), Leonardo Bruni challenged the logic of random selection by emphasizing that elections require candidates to put their "reputation on the line," an incentive missing when officials are chosen by lot. When the Medici seized power in 1434, Florence maintained the façade of republican rule beneath the reality of oligarchy, a disguise preferred by most of the Italian city-states that proudly declared themselves republics. After the revolution of 1494 ended Medici rule, the charismatic populist reformer Fra Girolamo Savonarola instituted a Great Council of nearly 3,400 citizens responsible for legislation and choosing magistrates. But Savonarola overplayed his hand, lost his popular support, and found himself arrested and executed as an enemy of the republic he sought to save from the threat posed by wealthy families.

Humanists such as Niccolò Machiavelli and Francesco Guicciardini split over the appropriate allocation of authority and the appropriate means of governing Florence, and their disagreements were echoed in other Italian city-states. Machiavelli was unusual among humanists not only because his *Prince* recommended the cynical manipulation of power but also because his (until recently) less well known *Discourses on Livy* and *Florentine Histories* presented stinging critiques of the oligarchies that controlled most so-called republics. Machiavelli applauded plebeian resistance in Roman and in Florentine politics and railed against ruling families' use of republican rhetoric to mask their abuses of power. Whereas Machiavelli championed lotteries and citizen juries to balance the power of wealth, Guicciardini, like Bruni, preferred to leave power in the hands of a smaller number of wise and virtuous public officials, whom they judged better able to discern the common good than were the people themselves.[66] Inventing Latin words for "democracy" and "political participation" was only a first step down a long road toward making that activity real for more than a few members of the most privileged segments of the population of Europe.

The Protestant Reformation fed democracy in two different ways. First, Protestants downplayed the role of the clergy and implicitly or explicitly challenged the prerogatives of hierarchies ostensibly authorized by divine authority. Second, Protestants emphasized the sacred dimension of ordinary life, the divine spark in every human that made possible, for God's elect, a life of sainthood in secular as well as religious callings. That vision of everyday life justified trusting the judgment of ordinary people as much as that of their supposed betters, whether in the clergy or, by extension, in the aristocracy. Within some religious communities, that confidence in the capacity of the people eventually manifested itself in a new commitment to the possibility of self-governing political bodies as well.

The tension between religious devotion turning into intolerant zealotry, as in the sixteenth- and seventeenth-century wars of religion, and religious devotion justifying popular government by providing the rationale for seeing the will of the people as the will of God has been a persistent feature of modern democracy. Accounts of democracy that treat it primarily as an economic struggle, a war between oppressed classes yearning for equality and elites trying to maintain their status, like accounts that focus exclusively on the struggle of individuals to attain and defend their rights to liberty and property against oppressive state power, overlook the independent significance of this crucial religious dynamic. Religious issues have persisted at the center of democratic discourse over the last four centuries.

Democracy emerged not only due to revulsion against religious fanaticism. It derived just as much from the revaluations of everyday life and of ordinary people's capacity to lead virtuous lives and exercise judgment responsibly. It is usually taken for granted that the Protestant Reformation advanced the cause of democracy, a truism that masks the more complicated dynamic at work in the sixteenth and seventeenth centuries. Challenges to the authority of Rome obviously eroded papal authority. Those challenges sparked religious wars that not only delayed the emergence of popular government by inadvertently ushering in royal absolutism but also left a poisonous deposit of hatred in the cultures of northern Europe. Establishing—or even reestablishing—an ethic of reciprocity in the aftermath of civil war has proven exceedingly difficult.

By the time *Defender of the Peace* was condemned as heretical in 1327, the papacy itself was widely considered a scandal. In the *Inferno* Dante included a number of popes and lesser clerics among those souls burning in hell. Some observers began to combine critiques of Church practices with critiques of the culture that both nourished such corruption and excused it.[67] Philology, which Renaissance humanists employed to pry open ancient texts and breathe life into medieval thought, provided unexpected leverage for that more radical project. The fifteenth-century Italian humanist Lorenzo Valla exposed the forgery behind the Donation of Constantine by demonstrating that, because it contained words unknown in classical Rome, it must have been written at least several centuries after Constantine's death. Taken as a whole, the inquiries of Renaissance philologists served to erode grander claims for a unity of truth and authority, and to suggest that all beliefs are specific to particular times and cultures. Although that historicist framework did not shatter the Christian faith of all humanists, combined with the recovery of ancient texts it provided a position from which to launch far-reaching social, political, and religious challenges to prevailing practices.

Two of the most influential of those critiques helped unsettle prevailing ideas about political authority. Written by two good friends, these books appeared in the same year, 1516, but in strikingly different rhetorical modes. The *Institutio principis christiani*, written by Desiderius Erasmus of Rotterdam, took the form of a sober advice book for the young Hapsburg monarch Charles V. Thomas More's *Utopia* used early reports from the New World as a pretext for a satirical attack on the England of his day and the pretensions of those who would advise princes. Both books manifested their authors' commitment to braiding political ideas drawn from the pagan classics with the moral precepts of Christianity. Neither Erasmus nor More shared the pessimism that some of their contemporaries derived from the writings of Augustine and others derived from the evidence of widespread corruption in the realms of church and state. Both invoked republican civic virtue and Christian brotherhood to advance an ideal of good government conceived as the pursuit of social justice rather than privilege.

More had the citizens of Utopia choose their magistrates democratically. All political decisions in Utopia emerge from careful deliberation because the Utopians "know that through a perverse and preposterous pride a man may prefer to sacrifice the common good to his own hasty opinions." More's Utopians pledge themselves to an ethical code that, although not explicitly Christian, bears an uncanny resemblance to More's and Erasmus's own efforts—and to the ethical ideas Montaigne would later advance in his *Essays*—to fuse sacred scripture with elements from Epicurean and Stoic moral philosophy. Utopians wisely "never discuss happiness without combining the rational principles of philosophy with principles taken from religion," an amalgam that produces something quite different from the medieval monastic ideal. "The Utopians do not believe that there is happiness in all pleasures, but only in good and honest pleasures. To such, they believe, our nature is drawn as to its highest good by virtue itself."

More's Utopians can choose their government officials wisely because they will what is good. Rather than distrusting all pleasure, as Christian ascetics did, or glorying only in the pitiless hauteur of classical or Renaissance nobles, the Utopians instead take delight in "those appetites to which nature leads us," that is, "only to the delights approved by right reason." They realize, more clearly than did More's own contemporaries, that if minimizing pain for others is a legitimate goal, then minimizing pain for oneself is equally legitimate. More's understanding of what constitutes "natural" virtue was, as Montaigne's was to be, as decisively shaped by reports of American Indian cultures as it was by his disaffection from the Italian civic humanist ideal of mastering fortune or the monastic ideal of self-abnegation. The most notorious dimensions of More's *Utopia*, its communal living arrangements and the absence of private property, manifested More's conviction regarding the desirability of equal access to—and the sensible use rather than immoderate accumulation of—the goods of the world, not their renunciation. Like his friend Erasmus, More used his learning to unsettle the assumptions of those comfortable with their own privileges. The Utopians deemed "basically unjust" any society in which those who did the most important work endured poverty to sustain the luxury of those who did not work. Such arrangements—typical of all European cultures of More's day—survived only because of what he called "a conspiracy of the rich."[68]

As explosive as More's social critique was his commitment to self-government. The citizens of Utopia not only elected their public officials, whom he called "phylarchs"; they also elected their priests. Every twenty households elected a representative to a one-year term, which ensured rotation of office and wide participation in public affairs. Those elected then chose a smaller group, one from every group of ten phylarchs, and this council chose a prince who ruled for life—unless he turned tyrant, in which case he could be deposed. By locating political power in the people of Utopia, More challenged the monarchical ideal that prevailed not only in England but in most of Europe. Even though *Utopia* concluded with the character called "More" dismissing its central ideas as a fantasy rendered impossible by human pride and the ubiquitous yearning for "nobility, magnificence, splendor, and majesty," the book nevertheless signaled the radical implications of ideas being entertained by humanists such as More and Erasmus.[69]

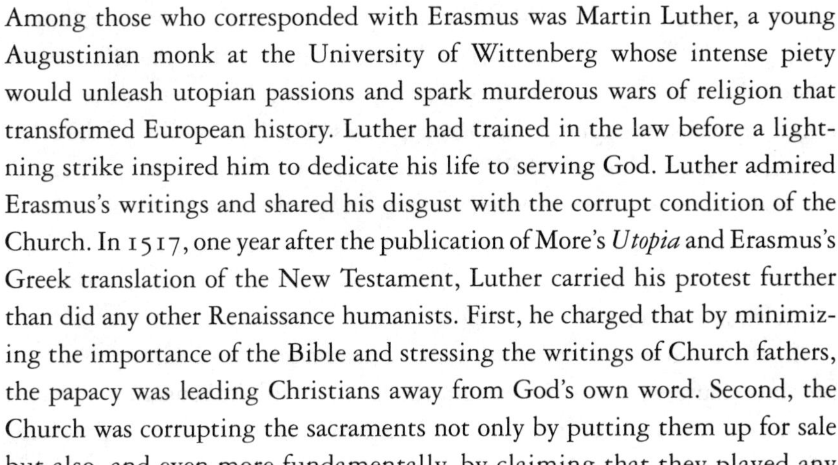

Among those who corresponded with Erasmus was Martin Luther, a young Augustinian monk at the University of Wittenberg whose intense piety would unleash utopian passions and spark murderous wars of religion that transformed European history. Luther had trained in the law before a lightning strike inspired him to dedicate his life to serving God. Luther admired Erasmus's writings and shared his disgust with the corrupt condition of the Church. In 1517, one year after the publication of More's *Utopia* and Erasmus's Greek translation of the New Testament, Luther carried his protest further than did any other Renaissance humanists. First, he charged that by minimizing the importance of the Bible and stressing the writings of Church fathers, the papacy was leading Christians away from God's own word. Second, the Church was corrupting the sacraments not only by putting them up for sale but also, and even more fundamentally, by claiming that they played any part in saving sinners from damnation. Third, Church authorities, losing sight of the central truths of revelation (and of Augustine's theology), were encouraging Catholics in the mistaken belief that their own righteousness, exhibited in good works, could earn their souls' salvation. Scripture, repentance, grace, and faith, Luther charged in the Ninety-Five Theses he posted in Wittenberg, not the forms of intercession provided by clergy, sacraments, indulgences, or works, lay at the heart of Christianity. By challenging the role of the Catholic hierarchy and endorsing "the priesthood of all believers," Luther seemed to undercut the legitimacy of all established authority and to suggest, at least implicitly, government by the people. Luther urged German princes to shrug off the papacy's illegitimate pretensions to power and assume responsibility for purifying religious practice in their own territories. Although he considered himself a loyal Catholic calling his church back to its animating ideals, Luther was excommunicated by the pope and declared an outlaw by the Hapsburg emperor Charles V.

Various complaints about the power of feudal lords and against the abuses of the clergy fueled radical criticism of social and political arrangements as well as religious orthodoxy.[70] The most systematic statement of these grievances, bearing the innocuous title *Twelve Articles*, circulated in southwestern Germany during the peasants' rebellion of 1524–25. Attempting to leverage support for Luther in his dispute against Rome, insurgent peasants clamored to appoint their own ministers and determine their pay.[71] In short, they were demanding autonomy and equality within the boundaries revealed in scripture as God's law. Champions of these revolts thought they saw in Luther an ally who could help mobilize support for ordinary people against the privileges and authority of the nobility. Luther disagreed. He clarified his own belief in an absolute distinction between the inner, spiritual life and the outer, temporal life. In his *Friendly Admonition to Peace concerning the Twelve Articles of the Swabian Peasants* (1525), Luther argued that the Bible commands obedience rather than liberation. By then hundreds of thousands were taking up arms throughout the German states. The most visible of the rebel leaders, Thomas Müntzer, challenged the feudal lords and Catholic clergy of Thuringia, at the heart of central Europe. In the decisive battle of May 15, 1525, his army of peasants, miners, textile workers, and religious enthusiasts was routed by the artillery of the dukes of Saxony and Brunswick. Müntzer himself was beheaded.

In the months that followed, tens of thousands who had rallied to the peasants' cause were put to death in the German states. Luther approved of the massacres as the only way to end rebellion and restore order, without which no Christian life is possible. Luther had warned the princes and lords facing rebellious peasants to "try kindness first" so as not to "strike a spark that will kindle all Germany and that no one can quench."[72] The savagery of the early sixteenth-century peasants' revolts—and the savagery of their suppression—fulfilled Luther's worst fears. They marked the beginning of a deadly age of warfare that not only infected German culture but also decisively transformed religion and politics all over Europe.

Unlike Luther, who denied that his challenge to religious authority implied a challenge to secular authority, many of the reformers inspired by his defiance of papal supremacy tried to work out the political implications of challenging Rome. Huldrych Zwingli, in Zurich, and Jean Calvin, in Geneva, thought the political consequences of the Copernican revolution meant rethinking the Christian responsibilities of civil authorities and the civic responsibilities of Christians. Zwingli contended that the division between magistrates and clergy could be healed if both followed the word of Christ: "The Christian is nothing else than the faithful and good citizen, and the Christian city is nothing other than the Christian Church."[73]

The contributions of Calvinism to democracy have long been acknowledged, but the irony of the outcome has attracted less attention. Calvin shared Luther's conviction that each Christian has unmediated access, through free inquiry in the Bible, to the word of God. He likewise embraced the idea that all humans are subject to the sovereign will of the almighty. Those principles might seem to translate without too much difficulty into the ideas of liberty and equality. The translation is complex, however, and not only because the doctrine of predestination—usually considered the central contribution of Calvin to Protestantism—seems inconsistent with any concept of self-determination, whether for individuals or the people as a whole. Calvin fled his native Paris for Basel after one of his friends was burned at the stake for heresy in 1535. The following year he completed the single most influential text of the Reformation, *Institutes of the Christian Religion*, which he continued to revise until four years before his death in 1564. In 1536 Calvin arrived in Geneva, which became a Protestant town that year by virtue of a vote by all the adult male citizens. So fervently did Calvin assert the independence of the reformed clergy that he was banished from the city two years later.

Calvin showed greater restraint when he returned to Geneva in 1541, and that strategy worked. In his writings and in later editions of his *Institutes*, Calvin proclaimed the supremacy of civil authority and invoked "Christian liberty" less frequently than "Godly discipline." In the final edition of the *Institutes*, Calvin elaborated on a divinely appointed "two-fold government," operating in the civic and ecclesiastical realms, with secular and church officials coordinating to provide moral and religious guidance and discipline while nevertheless remaining independent of each other. Following Luther's logic, Calvin counseled Christians not to rebel as individuals against unjust authority. He invoked the example of Spartan, Athenian, and Roman assemblies to show how the people could stand up to tyrants, and his followers were to cite those passages when they asserted the legitimacy of resistance.

Such arguments also emerged in sixteenth-century England, where a form of Protestantism became the official state religion in the 1530s as a result of royal initiative and parliamentary decree rather than popular agitation. Henry VIII, previously proclaimed "Defender of the Faith" by Pope Leo X for his denunciation of Luther, led England away from Rome in order to legitimate his divorce and the heir he expected from his second marriage in 1533. The king's lord chancellor, Thomas More, who had criticized the abuses of the Catholic Church and portrayed the happy consequences of religious toleration in his *Utopia*, in the 1520s had nevertheless proven himself a passionate foe of Lutheran heretics. After Henry's remarriage, the hunters became the hunted: More and dozens of other Catholic resisters died martyrs' deaths.

The tide turned again when Henry's oldest daughter, the Catholic Mary Tudor, took the throne after Henry's son (by his third wife) died. Mary restored Catholicism, executed several bishops who had done her father's will—along with almost three hundred ordinary people who had cheered them on—and sent hundreds more scurrying into exile. Among those were John Ponet, John Knox, and Christopher Goodman, radical Calvinists who adapted the arguments of sixteenth-century conciliarism to their own cause. Knox and Goodman escaped to Geneva, and Calvin urged the fiery Goodman to stay after Knox invited Goodman to join his Calvinist community in Edinburgh. Goodman's tract *How Superior Powers Ought to Be Obeyed by Their Subjects: And Wherein They May Be Lawfully Disobeyed and Resisted* (1558) made clear the potentially democratic implications of the idea of the covenant. Goodman reasoned that just as the early Christians had to redeem the covenant from the Jews, so now God's people must redeem it from papists. Goodman acknowledged the multiple admonitions to obedience in the Christian scriptures. He condemned the "Anabaptists and Libertines" who took the law into their own hands. As the Hebrew prophets counseled Israel to endure captivity and oppression, so Paul and Peter instructed the early Christians to follow Christ's own example. God's people now faced a different challenge. As God delivered Israel from bondage, and as redemption came through the death of Christ, now the covenant required the "Church of God" to resist the Antichrist in its papist form and restore God's rule.[74]

After only five years on the English throne, Queen Mary died in 1558, the same year Goodman's tract appeared, and the status enjoyed by the Church of

England was restored by Mary's half sister, Elizabeth. Although Mary's efforts to suppress Protestantism had been short-lived, she had sown seeds of bitterness. The rage that seethed through texts such as Goodman's would find different forms of expression in the violence of the English Civil War, in the death of Charles I, and in the busy little towns set up by Puritans in New England. Alive, Müntzer, More, and the Marian martyrs had little in common. Their executions transformed mistrust into hatred.

Bloody struggles between Catholics and Lutherans in the German states continued until 1555, when the Peace of Augsburg authorized nobles to determine the religious faith of their subjects. This arrangement, the end of a sequence originating with Luther's declaration of independence for the conscience of each individual believer, brought religious faith firmly under control of the nobility. The treaty nevertheless accomplished one of the principal aims of the *Twelve Articles*. To avoid massacres, Lutheran princes were instructed to allow their Catholic subjects to emigrate to territories where they could practice their faith; Catholic princes were to permit Lutherans to do the same. Such uprootings were painful, as were the conversions of convenience that enabled people to stay put and survive. The Peace of Augsburg, even as it tightened the control of princes over their people's religious practices, unexpectedly loosened some other bonds as the price of the peace it secured.

As the population shifts prompted by the Augsburg settlement slowed in the German states, tensions between Protestants and Catholics in France intensified. The conflict reached a crescendo in the days after August 25, 1572, when the violence originating in the St. Bartholomew's Day massacre of Huguenots in Paris culminated in the deaths of thousands of Protestants throughout France. From that moment on, murders, assassinations, and pitched battles between massed armies alternated with lawless raiding expeditions that terrorized populations caught in the crossfire, permanently defaced French abbeys and cathedrals, and—as we've seen—more than once nearly cost Montaigne his life. At the height of the violence in France, a series of books appeared extending the Calvinist argument for resistance and legitimating the formation of armies devoted to overthrowing a tyrannical monarch. These arguments took different forms. One proceeded on the basis of history: the early Frankish monarchy attained legitimacy only because all components of the culture authorized it. From this perspective, the Estates General was only the most recent in a long tradition of public assemblies. A second form of argument, revealing a clear debt to the 1560 edition of Calvin's *Institutes* and parallels with Goodman's incendiary tract, counterposed the authority of God to the authority of tyrants. The third, exemplified by

Philippe Duplessis-Mornay's *Vindiciae contra tyrannos* (1579), made even more radical claims.

Vindiciae contra tyrannos, which appeared in eleven Latin editions and was translated into French and English, surpassed the most controversial of Calvin's formulations to contend that all monarchy rests on popular consent. Because the greatest of kings remain but God's vassals, public officials not only may but also have a duty to challenge tyrants who flout divine law. The people unrestrained may be likened to "a raging beast," yet in extreme circumstances, when usurpers disregard the constitutive social traditions that undergird all authority, "even the least of the people" may legitimately resist tyranny.[75] In these successive contributions to public debate, the initial complaints of Luther and Calvin about the corrupt papacy all but vanished. In their place stood versions of the principle of popular sovereignty. By such circuitous routes did the initial proclamations of free inquiry and the challenges to clerical authority culminate in spirited assertions of popular government.

In France those arguments were drowned out by the din of war and demands that it should cease. Huguenot aristocrats, lawyers, and merchants consolidated control over walled towns in the more or less autonomous regions on the periphery of France. From those strongholds they fought fierce battles against Catholic forces. As in the German states, economic issues were a factor in these struggles, yet only religious convictions can explain the fury of these wars or the willingness of Catholics and Protestants to die for their faith.

Given the exhaustion and fears of anarchy elicited by such carnage, the idea of trusting the people to bring peace seemed a fantasy. More influential than the Calvinist tracts urging popular resistance was Jean Bodin's *The Six Books of the Republic* (1576), which likened a republic to a family. Just as a family is most stable when the patriarch exercises absolute authority, Bodin argued, so absolute rule by the monarch offers the best means to the universally desired end of tranquility. Bodin took direct aim at both the Aristotelian and Polybian arguments for mixed government. He drew a distinction, which was to prove widely influential, between states and governments. A state, he contended, could be monarchical, aristocratic, or democratic. Bodin classified the republics of ancient Rome and contemporary Geneva as democratic states because the ultimate authority resided with the body of the people. State sovereignty could not be divided, as government or administration could be—and indeed in most regimes had been. Rome, for example, combined quasi-monarchical forms of executive authority with an aristocratic senate and a plebeian assembly. For Bodin, sovereignty remained unitary regardless of the forms of government: "To institute the dominion of one, together with that of the few, and also with that of the many, simultaneously," is not only impossible but unimaginable: "sovereignty is by its nature indivisible."[76] Regardless of the administrative forms adopted, ultimate authority had to reside with the monarch, the nobility, or the people. The wars of religion showed why patriarchal states such as those of Europe relied on monarchical government: the alternative was chaos. When state sovereignty, Bodin concluded, resides in the king's will, the king is answerable only to God. Bodin helped inaugurate a tradition of arguments justifying royal absolutism that would dominate seventeenth-century political discourse throughout the Atlantic world. After a century of furious struggle, the idea of popular sovereignty seemed consigned to the margins of European thought.

By the early seventeenth century, democracy had few friends. Models of more or less popular or representative government were familiar from classical Greece, the Roman republic, and some late-medieval and Renaissance city-states. Arguments for liberty and against monarchy and hierarchy descended from those sources and from themes present in the writings of the Hebrew Bible, the Christian scriptures, and Protestant resistance theory. To understand why none of the roads leading toward democracy was taken before the seventeenth century, we must return to Montaigne's château.

Montaigne and other humanists had learned from classical thinkers—and from the example of American Indians—the appeal of autonomy and equality for all citizens. Montaigne had learned from his own experience, and the simple fact that he had lived to recount it, the appeal of an ethic of reciprocity. He placed those values within the framework of his watchwords uncertainty and restraint. The French wars of religion convinced him that because ordinary people had shown themselves incapable of doubting dogmas or restraining themselves, the values of deliberation, pluralism, and reciprocity could survive only if peace were restored by obedience to custom and established authority. The alternative was savagery worse than cannibalism. Attractive as civic and religious virtues were in the abstract, war rendered them irrelevant.[77]

The consequences of the Reformation and the wars of religion thus proved doubly ironic. In the short run they contributed to the rise of royal absolutism and deepened the distrust of the people whose revolts against authority took such destructive turns, a dynamic that delayed the emergence of democratic governments. In the longer run, the effect was as profoundly transformative as it was unanticipated. Because the violence of religious warfare showed the dangers of religious dogmatism, thinkers such as Montaigne and his successors began to contemplate a world in which uncertainty replaced certainty. Among earlier worldviews, however, were not only those that had undergirded the deeply hierarchical cultures of feudalism and sustained the royal absolutism of the seventeenth century. Equally important in the long run were those that had animated rabbis such as Hillel, the communities of early Christians, and the mendicant friars who cherished ideals of benevolence that challenged prevailing medieval patterns of thought and behavior. Montaigne's understandable revulsion against cruelty seeped into European culture as an aversion to all efforts to unify religious belief and political practice, which in time led skeptics to distrust faith and believers to distrust skeptics. The wars of religion ended with a truce, which seemed to silence calls for popular government yet eventually ushered in democratic cultures that displaced absolutism. When religious and political pluralists at last vanquished absolutists, however, among the casualties were the religious underpinnings of the golden rule, the ideal that had made possible the emergence of the ethic of reciprocity on which democracy depends.[78]

In the aftermath of the voyages of exploration and the wars of religion, violence cast a dark shadow over the idea of democracy. Despite lingering awareness of scattered experiments with popular government in the ancient world, and despite hints of alternatives to absolutism ranging from the practices of American Indian cultures to the ideas advanced by resistance theorists, very few Europeans in the early seventeenth century were thinking seriously about government by the people. Only when English settlers began arriving in the North American colonies were the first, albeit unintended, steps taken toward the emergence of democratic cultures in the modern North Atlantic world. Small and tentative as such steps were, they had lasting consequences.

CHAPTER 2

Voices in the Wilderness

Democracies in North America

When William Dyer gathered with other English settlers on an island in Narragansett Bay in the late winter of 1641, icy winds chilled his fingers. Meeting in Patuxit (now Portsmouth, Rhode Island), the group commissioned Dyer to record their judgments: "It is ordered and unanimously agreed upon, that the Government which this Bodie Politick doth attend unto this Island, and the Jurisdiction thereof, in favour of our Prince is a DEMOCRACIE, or Popular Government." How could these men in the same breath characterize their government as a democracy and acknowledge the authority of their "Prince," the English king Charles I?

This chapter explores that question by focusing on how and why English colonists transformed the abstract idea of popular sovereignty into practices of self-government. "It is in the Power of the Body of Freemen orderly assembled," Dyer and his associates continued, "or the major part of them, to make or constitute Just Lawes, by which they will be regulated, and to depute from among themselves such Ministers as shall see them faithfully executed between Man and Man." As their motto, the settlers chose "*Amor vincit omnia*," love conquers all. After reporting decisions concerning the bounty on foxes and the killing of deer, and the resolution of disputes over property and debts, the group ordered that the people, "being lawfully assembled at the place and hour appointed, shall have full Powrc to transact the business that shall be Presented" so long as the majority, "the Major part of the Body entire," participates. Finally, "such acts concluded and issued [shall] be of as full authority as if there were all present."[1] With those few words, the often-squabbling residents of fledgling towns of Newport and Portsmouth, situated at opposite ends of Aquidneck Island, constituted themselves a single representative democracy with laws to be made by the people. They did not renounce the English monarchy. They simply did not expect the king or Parliament to play a role in their civic affairs. They would govern themselves.

The formal declaration recorded by William Dyer made explicit the democratic thrust of compacts made in communities throughout New England after the colonies of Plymouth and Massachusetts Bay were established in 1620 and 1629. The sovereign people gathered together to make just laws, which they authorized their chosen officials to administer. As a result of their mutual love, and with God's help, they would survive the hardships they faced—if they didn't tear each other apart, or antagonize the Indians on whose forbearance their settlements depended. Compared with the world they left behind in England, a world of monarchy, dependency, and inherited status, the world these New Englanders made for themselves in America was marked by greater popular participation in government and relatively greater autonomy and equality.

That transition was anything but straightforward. Consider the gathering in Patuxit. William Dyer had abandoned his life as a prosperous London merchant and sailed with his wife, Mary, to join the Massachusetts Puritans in 1635. His family emigrated from Boston because Mary sympathized with her close friend Anne Hutchinson and their minister, John Wheelwright, both of whom had been banished by Massachusetts governor John Winthrop. After Mary Dyer walked out of church with Hutchinson, her stillborn child was exhumed and declared a "monstrous" example of the fruits of heresy. Two decades after her husband had helped establish the "DEMOCRACIE" of Patuxit, Mary Dyer was hanged when she returned to Puritan Massachusetts as an unrepentant and defiant Quaker.[2]

The less dramatic conflict between Mary Dyer's nemesis, John Winthrop, and another unorthodox Puritan, Roger Williams, brings into focus the challenge of reconciling popular sovereignty with autonomy. Williams left England with his wife and child in December of 1630, just six months after Winthrop's ship, the *Arbella*, had landed in New England. Williams was a precocious student and a brilliant linguist. He read law with the leading jurist of his day, Sir Edward Coke. As a boy he learned Dutch from neighbors in London and earned entry to Peterhouse College, Cambridge, by virtue of Coke's sponsorship and Williams's early mastery of Hebrew, Greek, and Latin. While training for the ministry in Cambridge, Williams gravitated toward the Puritan dissenters who feared that Catholic sympathizers led by Archbishop William Laud were conspiring to roll back the Reformation. Leaving behind his native England for North America, Williams later wrote, "was bitter as Death to me."[3]

Winthrop at first admired Williams as a talented and devoted minister, but soon the governor lost patience with the young firebrand. Williams spent two years in the colony of Plymouth, south of Boston, and while there he became acquainted with the Indians nearby. He learned enough about their language and their culture to question the legitimacy of English claims to their land. In 1633 he accepted an offer from the town of Salem to serve as its minister, an invitation that the magistrates of the Massachusetts Bay Colony, already aware of Williams's unconventional ideas, opposed. As Winthrop saw it, the uncompromising Williams then used his Salem pulpit to fan every spark of controversy in the colony, from the veiling of women in church and the presence of a cross on the English flag to the acceptability of using God's name in oaths. Williams went too far, as he had done in Plymouth, when he criticized the king for seizing Indian land. Twice he was called before the General Court and told to recant, which he did, reluctantly, behind closed doors.

Beneath all Williams's objections, however, lay a more fundamental challenge: he denied the state's authority to regulate religious belief. Because so many of the people who knew Williams were "much taken with the apprehension of his godliness," Winthrop wrote, the contagion of dissent might infect other Puritans. The General Court ruled that Williams must be banished.[4] Militia captain John Underhill was ordered to apprehend Williams and ship him across the Atlantic. When a storm prevented Underhill's men from leaving Boston, Winthrop, now no longer governor but still a member of the colony's Court of Assistants, secretly warned Williams that he had three days to escape.[5] Leaving behind his family in Salem—his wife had given birth to a second child, a daughter named Freeborne, only a few months earlier—Williams gathered what few things he could carry, bundled himself against the snow, and headed south.

Venturing into a New England blizzard in January requires courage and strength as well as faith. Alone and on foot, Williams wandered for fourteen weeks before arriving at the headwaters of Narragansett Bay, some sixty miles from Salem, in April of 1636. Seeing the hand of God in his exodus, Williams named the place of his deliverance Providence. Joined that summer by his family and others from Salem and Boston who shared his principles, or at least his uneasiness with Massachusetts, Williams and his neighbors deliberately established a community distinct both from Winthrop's Bay Colony and from the Pilgrims in Plymouth. Williams developed an explicitly religious argument for separating church and state. He reasoned that God inscribed the commandments he gave Moses on two separate tablets because the first four sins—sins against the deity—differed from the other six sins against humans. Civil authorities should enforce the latter to preserve order, but sins against God were His alone to judge and to punish. Whereas the magistrates of Massachusetts Bay presumed to regulate the beliefs as well as the behavior of the colony's residents, Williams denied all earthly powers the authority to discipline souls. Contemporaries familiar with the document establishing the government of Providence in 1637 knew that it stipulated the inhabitants would "subject ourselves in active and passive obedience to all such orders or agreements as shall be made for the public good of the body," orders relating only to "civil things," not religious beliefs. Unlike the oppressive theocrats of Massachusetts, Williams is revered as a precocious champion of individual liberty, a pioneer who pointed England's American colonies toward secular, popular government. As usual, such inspiring tales mask a more complicated truth.

The quarrels between Williams and Winthrop demonstrate the Janus face of early American Puritanism. Seventeenth-century New Englanders, who consciously yearned to recapture a world of ancient simplicity and berated themselves as failures, created institutions that irretrievably transformed their culture. The rise of democracy in America, like the creation of its most iconic and influential form, the New England town meeting, is a story of backing into uncharted territory, a story of surprising and unintended consequences rather than heroic trailblazing.

When Williams fled Salem, he placed himself not only in the hands of God but also at the mercy of the Narragansett Indians. Most English colonists took for granted that their Christian king authorized them, as God's designated agents, to occupy Indian lands and convert pagan Indians. Williams rejected that assumption on two grounds. First, he denied that the English king, or the English themselves, could be designated Christians. Only those willing to separate themselves from the corrupt Church of England—the small minority of Puritans called Separatists (like those in Plymouth) or Independents (those in the Bay Colony)—could even approach that lofty status. Second, Williams accepted the Indians' claim to their own lands and insisted that the English could assume dominion only by attaining the Indians' consent. If this double-barreled challenge to the authority of the English kings James and Charles elicited the earliest public censures of Williams, it was his rejection of civil authority in matters of faith that provoked his banishment.

On earth, Williams once wrote, humans are but "poor grasshoppers, hopping and skipping from branch to twig in this vale of tears."[6] When Williams found himself neither hopping nor skipping but slogging and sloshing through a "howling wilderness" covered by deep snow in that brutally cold winter of 1636, he stopped first in Plymouth.[7] Officials there, however, remembering the trouble he had caused them and fearful of antagonizing the Massachusetts magistrates who had banished him, warned Williams to keep moving south. When he arrived in Narragansett territory, Williams set out to practice what he had preached to so little effect in Salem and Plymouth, relying on the tool he had acquired earlier, a facility with Indian languages. While lodging with the Wampanoags, in what he called "their filthy, smoakie holes," he had indulged his "Constant Zealous desire to dive into their Native language." That investment now paid off.[8] Defenseless, hungry, and cold, Williams threw himself on the Narragansetts' generosity. He found "even amongst these wild *Americans*," he later wrote, "a savour of *civility* and *courtesie*," which they extended without making distinctions, "both amongst *themselves* and towards *strangers*."[9]

Williams did not romanticize American Indians. He judged them as susceptible to sin as the English and as likely to behave as "barbarous men of blood." When they did resort to violence, he later wrote in 1675, at the height of King Philip's War, they were "as justly repelled and subdued as wolves that assault the sheep," and he was remorseless about punishing those responsible for torching Providence.[10] Williams did not, however, imagine Indians occupying the lower rungs of a ladder reaching from degradation to civilization: "Nature knows no difference between *Europe* and *Americans* in blood, birth, bodies, &c. God having of one blood made all mankind *Acts* 17. and all by nature being children of wrath *Ephes*. 2." From Williams's perspective, unrepentant English Christians were no nearer to God than were unconverted Indians. Williams expressed that conviction in a brief verse addressed to English readers reluctant to reform:

> By nature, wrath's his portion, thine no more,
> Till grace, his soul and thine in Christ restore.
> Make sure thy second birth, else thou shalt see
> Heaven ope to Indians wild, but shut to thee.[11]

The unyielding rigor of Williams's own religious convictions prompted him to treat Indians with as much respect as shown by any English colonist of his generation. Since all people—Puritan as well as Wampanoag or Narragansett—are sinners, he urged the English to adopt an attitude of greater humility in their encounters with the native people of America. Williams confided that he himself had "been in danger of them," and, thanks to God, "delivered yet from them."[12]

Just how did Williams escape danger? First, his reputation as a friend of the Indians preceded him when he headed south. Second, he befriended the

Narragansett sachem Miantonomo. Finally, he agreed to purchase rather than simply claim the land on which Providence would stand. Overall, he treated the Narragansett with a degree of respect they did not enjoy in their dealings with Plymouth, with Massachusetts, or, later, with Connecticut. In a letter to the unruly settlers of Providence, Williams wrote, "It was not price nor money that could have purchased Rhode Island. Rhode Island was purchased by love."[13] Far-fetched as that claim might seem, in light of Williams's generally unsentimental attitude toward Indian culture it can be taken to show his unusual commitment to the principles of autonomy and reciprocity. That commitment helped make the colony he founded one of the first successful, if tumultuous, experiments in democratic government. Those principles emerge as well from the analysis Williams offered in *A Key into the Language of America; or, An help to the Language of the Natives in that part of America, called New-England*, published in London in 1643. Williams aimed to facilitate peaceful and fruitful interaction between Indians and English colonists, the "key," as he put it, to unlocking the puzzles of Indian culture. Williams translated not only words but also concepts and practices that the English found as incomprehensible as Indian languages. Although a Puritan minister, Williams focused less on converting Indians to Christianity than on trying to understand their ways and explain them. That broad-mindedness sprang from his understanding of Christian faith, not from a precocious cultural pluralism. Until Indians, like Anglicans in England and nonseparating Puritans in Massachusetts, felt of their own volition "true repentance and a true turning to God," attempts at baptism or coerced religious practice would mean less than nothing.[14]

Williams had learned Indian languages by living with Indians, gleaning the knowledge he needed to survive. As he explained in *A Key into the Language of America*, he depended on the Indians' hospitality and their food: "It is a strange truth that a man shall generally find more free entertainment and refreshing amongst these barbarians than amongst thousands that call themselves Christians."[15] From experience Williams came to respect the Indians' resourcefulness and their integrity; he "could never discern that excess of scandalous sins among them which Europe aboundeth with." These pagans committed fewer crimes of all sorts—"robberies, murders, adulteries, &c."—than did the English who claimed to practice Christian charity.[16] Williams found among the Narragansett hearts "sensible of kindnesses"; from them he had "reaped kindnesse" himself on too many occasions to recount. Whereas even "sinners will do good for good, kindnesse for kindnesse," Jesus had admonished his followers to do "good for evill."[17]

American Indians' own willingness to do good for evil, which would eventually prove fatal to them, enabled them to govern themselves in ways from which Williams thought the English might learn. The "wildest Indians in America," Williams wrote in 1644, chose their forms of government themselves. Some preferred a "civil compact" in towns; others dispersed more widely. Whatever they chose, he considered "their civil and earthly governments [to] be as lawful and true as any governments in the world." The diverse institutions the Indians established, Williams insisted, derived their legitimacy from the principle of popular sovereignty, which he stated succinctly: American Indians understood that the "sovereign, original, and foundation of civil power," Williams wrote, "lies in the people." For that reason "a people may erect and establish what form of government seems to them most meet for their civil condition." This principle of popular sovereignty, combined with the clear evidence of cultural variety Williams observed from living with the Wampanoags and Narragansetts, meant that no single form of government fits every situation. The divine right of kings, so often accorded quasi-sacred status among Europeans, he judged a particularly foul convention, which legitimated sinfulness at home, and covetousness in the New World, by allowing self-proclaimed Christians to pretend they were doing God's work. America's Indians "must judge according to their Indian or American consciences, for other consciences it cannot be supposed they should have."[18] English authorities who imposed their rule on American Indians were guilty of sinning against the God whose name they invoked.

Historians in the middle decades of the twentieth century took for granted that the story of America was, among other things, a story of democracy.[19] Scholars now often assume the opposite. The history of democracy in early America, however, is neither a triumphal procession nor a fiction.[20] Some English colonies embraced versions of the popular sovereignty that animated Roger Williams, and some of them, like William Dyer and his associates on Aquidneck Island, linked the "democracie" they proclaimed with their fealty to Charles I. Others were just as firmly committed to the principle of divine sovereignty, which officials such as John Winthrop invoked to discipline dissenters such as Williams. Most Puritans struggled to reconcile the two, and they adopted different positions depending on the circumstances and challenges of the moment. No one in New England emerged from these battles altogether satisfied with the outcome. By 1660, however, various forms of governance had emerged throughout England's North American colonies that rested more firmly and explicitly on the principle of popular sovereignty, and incorporated more elements of popular participation, than did any forms found in seventeenth-century Europe. No one set out deliberately to achieve that result. The irony of democracy in America thus begins with the first towns established in New England.

Debates among English settlers on the role of the people in government began before they landed in America. Preparing to embark for New England, Winthrop lamented the corruption and injustice prevailing in England. Papists threatened Puritans trying to practice their faith, the rapacious wealthy oppressed the defenseless poor, and the law offered no recourse. Trained in the law and serving as a justice of the peace at the court of his manor of Groton, in England Winthrop enjoyed gentry status and the relative affluence that went with it. The cruelties inflicted by the rich on the poor gnawed at his conscience and offended his Christian sense of obligation. A devout Puritan, Winthrop sold his lands and signed on with the Massachusetts Bay Company in exchange for the opportunity to live in a community devoted to the lofty ideals of his faith.

Winthrop laid out those ideals in the address he composed on the *Arbella*, "A Model of Christian Charity." This expression of an ancient Christian aspiration helps explain what happened when these otherworldly Puritans arrived in New England on June 12, 1630. Winthrop began by proclaiming that hierarchy, divinely ordained, is inevitable: "In all times some must be rich, some poor, some high and eminent in power and dignity, others mean and in subjection." The importance of that baseline assumption cannot be exaggerated: like almost all of his contemporaries, Winthrop took for granted that "all these differences" were God's will, no more the product of human volition than the weather. Adam's fall bequeathed to all humans a propensity to selfishness. Only divine grace enabled people to act with "Justice and Mercy" toward each other. Justice, the "Law of Nature," the moral law, stipulates that men should follow the golden rule. Mercy, the "Law of Grace," imposes a more stringent requirement on Christians: they must love not only their neighbors but also their enemies. The "rich and mighty should not eat up the poor," as English aristocrats were inclined to do, nor should "the poor and despised rise up against their superiors and shake off their yoke," as rampaging English peasants sometimes did. God's grace enabled, and Christian love required, all to sympathize with their neighbors. Those on the *Arbella* were to be "knit together by this bond of Love," so "the care of the public must oversway all private respects."

Winthrop assured his fellow sojourners that safe arrival at their refuge would ratify God's covenant with them, a covenant that made them, in the phrase from Matthew's Gospel, "a City upon a Hill." If they failed, if they put their "pleasures, and profits" before their love of God and of each other, their failure and their shame would be visible to all of England. Winthrop encapsulated their mission by invoking the counsel of Micah: "to do justly, to love mercy, to walk humbly with our God." Those embarking for America must "be willing to abridge ourselves of our superfluities" to provide for "others' necessities." The echoes of the Hebrew scriptures and the Christian Gospels, the lofty ethical ideals of ancient and simple communities of like-minded people, could not have been clearer in Winthrop's opening charge to his shipmates.[21]

Winthrop had been chosen governor by the stockholders of the Massachusetts Bay Company, who were empowered by the company's charter of March 4, 1629, to select the magistrates. These stockholders, designated "freemen," were to meet four times a year to elect a governor, deputy governor, and assistants. When Winthrop agreed to lead the migration of a thousand settlers in the spring of 1630, the company decided to meet henceforth in Massachusetts. Winthrop was permitted to take the company charter with him. Designated the leading figure in the expedition, he assumed he would continue to wield the unchallenged authority in America that he was accustomed to wielding at his manor in England. He was wrong.

Winthrop's problems originated in a tension apparent early in the Reformation. From the outset, Calvinists invoked the higher authority of God's law to legitimate their challenges to the pope. That strategy, as Luther saw immediately, threatened to dissolve all authority. For that reason he urged obedience to civil authorities. Calvinists on the continent and Puritans in England sought to evade the threat of anarchy by tying their challenge to divine law: disobedience to unlawful authorities such as the Catholic Church did not imply disobedience to God's own law as revealed in the Bible. When Puritans employed the language of the covenant, they envisioned a chain of command stretching all the way from God's word, as revealed first to Moses and then elaborated through the Christian scriptures, to the particular restraints imposed on his people by legitimate laws. Obedience to such laws involved no sacrifice of liberty; indeed, Christian freedom could be exercised only by following God's path. When rulers deviated from God's will, resistance was in order, and when civil authorities followed divine law, they must be obeyed. Who could be trusted to see the difference, the people or their magistrates?

The issue of authority became increasingly urgent for Puritans who migrated to New England. The issue had remained abstract in England, at least after the threat briefly embodied by the Catholic Mary Tudor (1553–58) disappeared when she was succeeded by the vigorously anti-Catholic monarchs Elizabeth and James I. When Puritans anxious about the creeping Catholicism of Charles I and Archbishop Laud undertook to reconstitute their communities across the Atlantic, however, they had to decide how to distinguish lawful authority from tyranny. Winthrop discovered right away that not all of those "knit together" in the Puritan covenant agreed that the governor's judgment accorded with God's wisdom. When these settlers first arrived in

New England, they formed themselves into churches and towns and drew up covenants that quite unself-consciously expressed the ambiguities of their attitude toward authority. They committed themselves to God's law, but those making the commitment took upon themselves the duty to decide its meaning. Those who established the First Church of Charlestown, which soon moved across the Charles River to Boston, signed the following covenant:

> Wee whose names are hereunder written, being by His most wise, and good Providence brought together in this part of America in the Bay of Massachusetts, and desirous to unite our selves into one Congregation, or Church, under the Lord Jesus Christ our Head, in such sort as becometh all whom He hath Redeemed, and Sanctifyed to Himselfe, doe hereby solemnly, and religiously (as in His most holy Proesence) Promisse, and bind ourselves, to walke in our wayes according to the Rule of the Gospell, and in all sincere Conformity to His holy Ordinaunces, and in mutuall love, and respect each to other, so neere as God shall give us grace.[22]

The men who signed the covenant pledged to unite under the Christian law of love. Although their commitment paralleled the high standards Winthrop erected in his "Model of Christian Charity," they acknowledged no authority but God's, and they explicitly pledged to bind themselves to no earthly authority except their own.

Compare the covenant of the First Church to the opening words of the covenant signed by the heads of the families who founded the town of Dedham, southwest of Boston, six years later: "We whose names are here unto subscribed do, in the fear and reverence of our Almighty God, mutually and severally promise amongst ourselves and each other to profess and practice one truth according to that most perfect rule, the foundation whereof is everlasting love." The Dedham Covenant further stipulated that only those who agreed to its terms would be welcome in the town. Others were free to settle elsewhere. If disagreements arose, "then such party or parties shall presently refer all such differences unto some one, two, or three others of our said society to be fully accorded and determined without any further delay." Conflicts would be resolved through mediation. Every individual who became a property holder "shall pay his share" of the charges "imposed on him" and "become freely subject unto all such orders and constitutions as shall be... made now or at any time hereafter from this day forward." That phrase "become freely subject" expresses an idea central to these early New England towns. Once individuals voiced their consent, they bound themselves to obey the authority of the community. That was the meaning of autonomy, the acceptance of self-imposed law.

Like the other founding covenants, the Dedham agreement was meant to cover not only the laws but also—and even more crucially—the spirit infusing the interactions of the townspeople "for loving and comfortable society in our said town."[23] As was true in the case of the Charlestown covenant, those who signed the Dedham covenant acknowledged only the authority of God beyond their own. They were constituting a church and a town in conformity to God's law but on their own terms. Their signatures gave the covenant all the legitimacy it needed.

These steps, grounded on an explicitly stated ethic of reciprocity, were fully consistent with the logic of the Puritans' Congregationalism. They denied the possibility of a single, united church. They insisted that each true church, gathered from among the elect of "visible saints," was independent of—but equal to—every other. Unlike Separatists such as the Pilgrims at Plymouth, however, Congregationalists refused to renounce the Church of England altogether because they cherished the hope that it could be reformed. Thus New England Puritans, although they declared the sovereignty of God and their subservience to his will, nevertheless took a significant step when they established their churches and their towns according to the principles of autonomy and popular sovereignty: their founding documents acknowledged only God's authority above them. The diversity in their interpretations of theology and their religious practice stemmed directly from their intense localism.[24]

The highly charged nature of the Puritan concept of the covenant itself became apparent in the first conflicts Winthrop faced in New England. The officials in charge of the colony convened as the Massachusetts General Court for the first time on October 19, 1630. The magistrates proposed that the stockholders—the freemen—should elect the assistants, who would then choose the governor and the deputy governor. Consistent with the deference typically accorded gentry such as Winthrop, the freemen accepted this proposal, not realizing that it actually curtailed the power given to them by the company charter. But then, and evidently without worrying much about the consequences of a decision that seems puzzling in retrospect, the magistrates decided to open the ranks of the freemen to all property holders who were church members. Perhaps even more significantly, a trading company became a commonwealth, evidently without anyone quite understanding or even noticing the change. Just as paradoxically, the second public meeting of the Massachusetts General Court administered the freeman's oath to 116 colonists—thereby further increasing their number—and determined that in the future only church members could become freemen—at least potentially diminishing their number. That pattern, complex, even contradictory, manifested the implicit logic of the Dedham covenant and provided a model for the confusion to come.[25]

The logic of the Puritan covenant required all members of the community to bind themselves together, as the Charlestown covenant put it, in "mutuall love, and respect." Unless everyone agreed to submit to the authority that emerged from their agreement to join together, no order, to say nothing of the Christian fellowship they envisioned, would be possible. The customarily firm distinctions between gentry and peasantry began to dissolve in the communities of saints that developed. By establishing church membership as the criterion of inclusion, the early settlers were rejecting another criterion with deeper roots in English tradition, socioeconomic status, for one available to all with whom God had made his covenant. No sooner had the colony's new government been empowered, however, than Winthrop's twelve assistants faced resistance. When they attempted to levy a tax, the people of Watertown, a settlement just up the Charles River from Charlestown and Boston, refused to pay. Watertown insisted that the government of the colony had no authority to "make laws or raise taxations without the people." That response signals the implicit logic of the Puritan covenant and distinguishes the pattern of popular government that emerged in New England from the English model.

In England Parliament had come into being because English kings had to raise revenues; members of the gentry were offered seats in Parliament in exchange for their financial as well as political support. Medieval English practice had involved constituencies choosing and instructing attorneys to represent their interests against the crown, given that Parliament had developed in a very different direction since the twelfth century. Members of Parliament were enjoined to consider the good of the entire realm, not the interests of a particular constituency. By the early seventeenth century, representation in Parliament usually expanded when monarchs assigned seats to boroughs controlled by country gentlemen friendly to the crown's designs. Such gentry often did not reside in such boroughs, and no one expected them to represent the interests of those who did live there.[26]

In response to protests such as that from the people of Watertown, the Massachusetts General Court established a system as early as 1634 whereby each town would choose, in Winthrop's words, "two men to be at the next court, to advise with the governour and assistants about the raising of a public stock, so as what they should agree upon should bind all."[27] Just as the covenant proclaimed by each church congregation emerged from the deliberations of the members—guided, to be sure, but not ruled by the minister they had chosen—so the people of Massachusetts would choose those who would make their laws. When they adopted covenants, the Congregationalists were unwittingly moving toward a position none of them envisioned, abandoning subservience to authority and assuming that authority themselves.

The elected representatives of the people of Massachusetts extended their authority further at the May 14, 1634, meeting of the General Court. The freemen chosen by the eight towns demanded to see the original charter of the Massachusetts Bay Company. They learned that not only were they empowered to choose the governor and his assistants annually but also that they, the freemen, and not these elected officials, were empowered to make the laws of the colony. Voting for the first time by secret ballot, the assembled freemen then dismissed Winthrop from office and elected as governor his deputy Thomas Dudley. Even more significantly, these delegates from the towns assumed the legislative power that Winthrop and his assistants had usurped. From that point on, the laws of Massachusetts would be those adopted by the representatives elected by the towns of the commonwealth. The General Court would include the governor and his deputy along with two or three delegates chosen by each of the towns of the Bay Colony.[28]

How had things slipped from Winthrop's hands in just four years? How had the Christian brotherhood of the *Arbella*, united under his leadership, become a self-governing assembly of small landowners? How did the people come to meet in separate towns and churches and delegate authority to their representatives, who then gathered to legislate for the colony as a whole? The answers to those questions explain the dynamic of democracy in seventeenth-century English North America: Once the colonists left home and spread out into the lands they settled, they stepped beyond the boundaries of existing government. They had to—and they were able to—make the rules by which they would govern themselves. Those who settled in New England had experience with the forms of town government operating in their native region of East Anglia. They also brought with them the assumptions of seventeenth-century Englishmen accustomed to hierarchal authority extending from God to his faithful king or queen, then from the monarch to the local justice of the peace. In the absence of traditional forms of monarchical and aristocratic dominance, their English experience proved inadequate, even irrelevant. They shared common-law assumptions about landownership and the legal rights and obligations of English subjects, but lacking manorial courts such as Winthrop's in England, they worked out the implications of those assumptions themselves.

The dispersal of the Massachusetts population into discrete settlements began almost immediately. Even though the original charter made no provision for town governments, they materialized anyway alongside the church covenants such as those of Charlestown and Dedham. The proliferation of colony-wide responsibilities prompted Winthrop and the assistants of the General Court from the outset to assign towns various responsibilities, including the provision of arms, the building of fences, and the setting of wage rates. Separate town governments sprang up as early as 1633 in Dorchester, 1634 in Boston, and 1636 in Dedham. If dispersing authority to these towns initially suited Winthrop's purposes, he learned quickly that they would be less tractable to his will than Parliament had been to the will of the monarch.[29]

Neither the townspeople nor the magistrates of the Bay Colony understood that these first town governments provided an enduringly influential template. By 1636 the General Court acknowledged the change: it gave to "the freemen of every town, or the major part of them," the authority to "dispose of their owne lands, and woods"; to "make such order as may concerne the well ordering of their owne townes, not repugnant to the lawes and orders here established by the General Court"; and "to chuse their owne particular officers."[30] These settlers did not intend to enact—nor realize they were enacting—a new form of self-rule. The power of local communities to dispose of their lands themselves and enforce their own laws shaped New England culture decisively. Again paradoxes abound. Although towns tended to distribute land to all heads of household, they did so in accordance with individuals' wealth and status. Although they policed behavior strictly, they made much less use of capital punishment for crimes such as theft than did English authorities. They aimed to follow the ethic of equity articulated by the Puritan theologian William Perkins, who urged his readers to avoid extremes, whether lusting after excessive wealth or enforcing the death penalty. Perkins preached moderation in everything except love, urging Christians "to practise this Christian *Equitie* of themselves" rather than being "compelled to it by authoritie." The ethic of equity translated into calls for fairness in the disposition of lands, the treatment of paupers, widows, and orphans, and the punishment of criminals. Conflicts, Perkins and his New England followers agreed, should be resolved through arbitration. Because mutuality and reciprocity were the ideals cherished by these Puritans, they sought to minimize friction.[31]

Widespread landownership meant that popular participation, at all levels of political organization, was from the beginning more widespread in New England than in England, or anywhere else in Europe up to that time. Since 1430, the right to vote in England had been limited to those few adult males who owned land sufficient to earn forty shillings in rent each year, typically around fifty acres. That effectively restricted the franchise to less than 10 percent of the population. The inflation of the seventeenth century changed that equation so that, in principle, perhaps as many as 20 percent of Englishmen could vote. Yet because the practice and significance of voting in England was governed as much by custom as by law, wide variations existed from borough to borough.[32] In New England, by contrast, the previously unimaginable availability of land that was unoccupied (at least as seen from the English perspective, if not from the Indians') meant that many more male heads of household met the standard of a forty-shilling freehold. In most towns, at least initially, church membership rather than property holding was prerequisite to voting. Because most male heads of household were church members, at least in the first years of settlement, as many as 60 to 80 percent of adult male New Englanders were eligible to vote in early colony-wide elections. As of 1647, when a law was passed extending the franchise to all "inhabitants," between 60 and 90 percent could vote in Massachusetts town elections. Those percentages diminished over the course of several decades. Fewer newcomers became church members as requirements for membership became more rigorous, and property restrictions became more common.

The practice of voting must be understood in the context of the prevailing Puritan commitments to comity and reciprocity. Freemen did not choose between contending candidates representing different positions or factions. New Englanders interacted in church congregations, town meetings, and courts of law. They submitted petitions to air grievances and brought suits when wronged. Even though most adult males *could* vote, participation rates varied wildly from town to town and decade to decade. Because the goal was reaching consensus about justice and equity, informed by an ethic of mutuality and reciprocity, voting was but one way to be involved in public life.[33]

These New Englanders did not set out to create a democracy, nor did most of them understand what they were doing as democratic. They respected authority and thought of themselves as entirely subject to God's will, the meaning of which they derived from the educated elite of ministers who spoke from the pulpits of their meeting houses. As Congregationalists they selected their own ministers, and as freeholders they elected their own selectmen at the local level and their own representatives to the General Court. Again and again they chose the same people—at first members of the English gentry such as Winthrop and Dudley, and later newly wealthy fellow New Englanders—to occupy town and colony offices. In Dedham, for example, ten prosperous men held most of the town's elected offices for five decades. Because such a small number of comparatively well-off individuals exercised power over such a long period of time, recent historians of New England have stressed the persistence of hierarchy, deference, and hegemony.

Most New Englanders did indeed denigrate democracy as a degenerate form of government, just as they denigrated "disordered" individuals who refused to obey just laws or accept the will of the community. They prized order, peace, and consensus, the very real cost of which became clear when individuals such as Anne Hutchinson, Mary Dyer, or Roger Williams challenged prevailing interpretations of scripture and law. The Puritans' greater interest in unity was consistent with a serious commitment to popular authority. They did not see how their reliance on the covenant, which they entered into voluntarily as individuals, would eventually erode the stability and hierarchy they wanted to preserve. They were more worried that toleration of fundamental disagreements might erode the fellowship necessary for the ethic of mutuality that makes people willing to accept defeat when they lose either a discussion or an election or a case in court. The Puritans tried to balance their ancient Christian law of love against the unprecedented freedom of movement available in a new land. They ventured beyond English custom and law equipped with a vision of harmony that the conditions of their settlements—unbounded, ever changing—shattered almost immediately. The world they created, a world of relative equality and unprecedented economic and social mobility, eventually upset the ideals of peaceful order, voluntary submission to authority, and Christian fellowship they brought with them to America.[34]

The Puritans' emphasis on unity persisted despite the conflicts that soon wracked Massachusetts Bay. When Winthrop, serving as deputy governor, was censured in 1636 for allowing Williams to escape, he recorded in his journal his acknowledgment that he should in the future "take a more strict course" in enforcing the law and discussed in detail the magistrates' determination to cope more effectively with disagreements that might erupt in the future by keeping alive the lingering dream of voluntary agreement: if individuals differed with each other in public meetings, they were expected "to express their difference in all modesty and due respect to the court and such as differ." Disagreements were to be expressed as questions rather than direct challenges, and once a consensual decision was reached, "none shall intimate his dislike privately, or if one dissent he shall sit down without showing any further distaste, publicly or privately." Early New Englanders frowned on dissent because they feared divisiveness.[35]

Although such proclamations surely indicate precisely what was not happening, they nevertheless confirm the overall impression left by records of the wrangling in political discussions at all levels of the commonwealth: the early settlers of Massachusetts sought to resolve conflicts by reaching consensus. The recourse to discipline, which could be exercised both by officials against outcasts and by the people or their representatives against figures in authority who fell from favor, meant that mediation and persuasion had failed. Sometimes there was no alternative, as when unruly tongues were silenced or when town meetings turned out their elected officials. Imposing order on the recalcitrant, whatever their place in the hierarchy of power, elicited regret, not congratulations.[36]

Any reference to the Puritans' stringent discipline conjures up an image of the stern John Winthrop. Having learned from his leniency toward Williams, Winthrop showed no such mercy to dissenters such as the Antinomians. When Anne Hutchinson and others claimed the authority to preach, arguing that the Holy Spirit dwelled within them, they were tried, excommunicated, and banished. In the midst of the controversy, Winthrop issued an order prohibiting the people of Massachusetts from allowing "strangers" to live with them for more than three weeks without the magistrates' permission. Winthrop's reasoning merits attention because it shows how he understood the complex relation between the origin of government, popular sovereignty, the ethic of mutuality, the covenant, and the legitimate exercise of authority.

A Puritan commonwealth such as Massachusetts originates in the "consent of a certaine companie of people," Winthrop began, to live together "under one government for their mutuall safety and welfare." It follows that "no common weale" and no privileges "can be founded but by free consent." All members must preserve "the wellfare of the bodye" of the whole community, which is not to be sacrificed for the wishes or "the advantage of any particular members." Just as towns and churches could legitimately expel those who refused to abide by their rules—as the Dedham Covenant, for example, explicitly stipulated—so a commonwealth may refuse to accept those "whose dispositions suite not with ours and whose society (we know) will be hurtfull to us." Winthrop concluded with an image frequently used by Puritan ministers: "A family is a little common wealth, and a common wealth is a greate family. Now as a family is not bound to entertaine all comers, no not every good man (otherwise than by hospitality) no more is a common wealth."[37]

To what extent does a commonwealth resemble a family? Is the authority of those empowered by the community similar to that exercised by the biblical patriarch? Having been censured by the magistrates and more than once voted out of office, Winthrop had personally experienced the difference: unlike voters, Puritan wives and children were not authorized to expel husbands and fathers. Yet Winthrop persisted in claiming privileges for those in positions of legal authority considerably grander than those he succeeded in exercising himself. In 1644 he wrote a "small treatise" claiming complete executive and judicial power for the magistrates of Massachusetts, a view the General Court rejected. Again in 1645, after he was impeached following a dispute with the town of Hingham concerning the election of its militia, he used the occasion of his vindication by the court to explain his views on authority. Winthrop immediately identified the central issue: the relation between the people's liberty and the magistrates' prerogative. Sustaining officials' authority did not diminish the people's power because "it is yourselves who have called us to this office" through election, "and being called by you we have our authority from God." By voting, the people of Massachusetts enacted God's will; the covenant between electors and elected "is to this purpose, that we shall govern you and judge your causes by the rules of God's laws and our own, according to our best skill."

If the official's authority descends from God through the people, what about the people's liberty? Winthrop distinguished, more fully than he did on the *Arbella*, between two kinds of liberty. "Natural" liberty is "common to man with beasts and other creatures." It is "a liberty to evil as well as to good." This liberty he judged "incompatible and inconsistent with authority"; it "cannot endure the least restraint of the most just authority." Exercising natural liberty makes men "grow more evil, and in time to be worse than brute beasts." Animals enjoy and sinners covet such liberty, which Winthrop branded "the great enemy of truth and peace." His enemies, Winthrop implied, were bewitched by the lure of natural liberty. The other kind of liberty he called "civil," "federal," or "moral." Only those who have entered voluntarily into covenants with God and with one another, covenants binding them to obey, enjoy such liberty. "This liberty is the proper end and object of authority and cannot subsist without it, and it is a liberty to that only which is good, just, and honest." The lesson was clear: Dissenters and rabble-rousers, those who "stand for your natural corrupt liberties," and prefer "to do what is good in your own eyes," refuse to "endure the least weight of authority." But those who are "satisfied to enjoy such civil and lawful liberties, such as Christ allows," will "quietly and cheerfully submit" to the authority exercised "for your good." When authorities err, Winthrop concluded, "we hope we shall be willing (by God's assistance) to hearken to good advice from any of you, or in any other way of God."[38]

Skeptical readers of Winthrop's speech, especially those who see invocations of God's will as veiled justifications of tyranny, dismiss it as a flimsy rationalization, as did some of his contemporaries who interpreted "all the magistrates' actions and speeches" as attempts to secure for themselves "an unlimited power to do what they pleased without control." From Winthrop's perspective, hatred and distrust heightened the "fears and jealousies" of the magistrates' critics to the extent that every step the officials took was perceived as a threat to "the people's liberty."[39] In only fifteen years, Winthrop's "Model of Christian Charity" had become a hornet's nest. Why?

Winthrop understood the challenges that New England Puritans had set themselves. He prophesied on the *Arbella*, and warned repeatedly afterward, that if the first settlers failed "to abridge ourselves of our superfluities for the supply of others' necessities"—if they failed to place the good of the whole above their individual desires—they would lose "the unity of the Spirit in the bond of peace." Whether or not such unity ever characterized the community, that is precisely what happened during their early decades in the New World. These Englishmen, hungry as most of them were for the moral liberty Winthrop contrasted to mere appetite, were also hungry for land. Without deliberately or consciously turning away from God's law, they found themselves also turning toward what Winthrop had called their "pleasures, and profits."[40] In the process they gradually transformed the underlying terms of their interactions from mutuality to competition. They established their religious and their political communities on the foundation of the covenant. The voluntarism implicit in that concept, however, enabled many of them to slip outside the ethic of love, the yearning for unity, and the voluntary acceptance of authority, and to begin exercising forms of freedom that Winthrop judged incompatible with authority and inconsistent with peace. Those who took that opportunity renounced an orderly covenant of Christian neighbors for a different model. Winthrop characterized that alternative disdainfully as a "mere democracy," in which all joined in "public agitation" and advanced their own private interests, instead of deliberating selflessly, under the wise guidance of the gentry, to find the common good.[41]

Democracy in Massachusetts emerged from the collisions of religion and politics. The ideals of Christian fellowship had from their origins in the Gospels challenged prevailing patterns of economic behavior. In Puritan New England that challenge assumed a new shape that mirrored the unprecedented opportunities available to these pious, driven people. It was the notorious case of the merchant Robert Keayne that prompted Winthrop's mournful observation that the Bay Colony had declined from a "mixte aristocratie" into a "mere democracy." Keayne, among the most successful merchants in Massachusetts, was fined by the General Court and censured by the First Church of Boston in 1639 for the offense of price gouging. Having charged more than the accepted profit of six pence on the shilling for goods ranging from bags of nails to golden buttons, Keayne was forced to pay eighty pounds to the commonwealth and "bewail his covetous and corrupt heart" before his congregation. In 1642, still a symbol of greed to many in the commonwealth, Keayne was accused of stealing a sow from Elizabeth Sherman. The General Court, finding itself deadlocked between wealthier pro- and more popular anti-Keayne factions, split into two houses, the assistants occupying the upper and the deputies, those representing the towns of Massachusetts, the lower.

Keayne has remained a symbol ever since; his significance is read in many ways. Having provided the occasion for the first emergence of bicameralism in America, he figures (albeit unwittingly) in the history of democracy. His case indicates, too, the conflict between an emergent market mentality and a lingering sensibility distrustful of market mechanisms to approximate what had been called for centuries a "just price." The Puritans have remained central players in the frequently retold drama of the rise of capitalism, and for good reason. They were among the first to glorify work, not for its own sake or because of the wealth unstinting work could win, but as a sign that one might be among God's chosen. Wealth did not guarantee membership in the elect—witness sinful Robert Keayne, censured for his calculating shrewdness—but the failure to prosper, if attributable to the failure to work hard, could be taken as a reliable indicator that one remained unregenerate. Thus the logic of Calvin's theology did indeed translate into a greater willingness to work, and a greater inclination toward asceticism, than was typical of ancient, medieval, or Renaissance aristocrats, who loved comfort but shunned work, or the laboring poor, for whom work was a cross to be borne, not a mark of distinction.

New England Puritans built themselves a trap that has fascinated scholars for a century: the harder they worked to demonstrate righteous mastery over sins such as imprudence or sloth, the more they prospered. The more they prospered, the harder they had to work to demonstrate their righteousness. And so on. Given those crosscutting pressures, there is nothing contradictory about the Puritans' simultaneous success and their self-abnegation.[42] From the beginning, feudal restraints on production and trade failed to take root in New England. Guilds fell away before the fluidity and mobility of the workforce. It was too easy for disgruntled workers, who could be detained or whipped in England, simply to relocate to another town. When the Puritans founded towns, they distributed the land without restricting the terms of resale or transmission through estates. They resisted the monopolies rampant in sixteenth- and early seventeenth-century England—monopolies that grated particularly on the industrious Puritan merchants and artisans central to the New England migration—unless a temporary monopoly was necessary to induce the building of a mill or a shop deemed necessary to the community.

Two Puritan peers, Lord Brooke and Lord Saye and Sele, discovered just how deep the desire for self-government was when they proposed transplanting heritable aristocratic privilege to New England. Winthrop instructed John Cotton, minister of the First Church of Boston, to explain, with all due deference, that Massachusetts would have no House of Lords. All offices in the Bay Colony were earned by "public election" rather than inherited rank. So indispensable were the principles of equity and reciprocity that only the "godly" were deemed capable of exercising proper judgment in civic affairs. Lord Saye and Sele complained to Winthrop that the spirit of New England's people ran so high that no wise man would choose to live where "every man is a master" and "fools determine" policy.[43]

Boisterous as the economy of Massachusetts was, it was the opposite of laissez-faire. Town or commonwealth authorities oversaw industry, commerce, and land tenure to ensure fair and honest dealing. Speculation in property was illegitimate: if land remained undeveloped, it reverted to the town, to be distributed to those who would put it to productive use. Ministers harangued with equal intensity against displays of wealth and displays of lassitude. They urged their congregations to balance hard work with hard virtues. Industrious striving was the rule, ease in wealth or poverty the exception. No one has expressed the heart of the Puritan sensibility better than the third governor of the Plymouth Colony, Edward Winslow, who observed as early as 1624 that in America "religion and profit jump together, which is rare."[44]

Imagining Puritan theology as a fixed, watertight worldview makes it difficult to square with the enterprising activities of seventeenth-century New Englanders, which can make the ministers seem irrelevant or the laymen hypocritical. If we focus instead on Puritanism as a lived religion, we see a series of negotiations, running from the sixteenth century into the eighteenth, between the demands of Calvin's theology and the challenges and opportunities faced by ordinary people living in extraordinary circumstances. New Englanders had a script, which Winthrop expressed clearly in his "Model of Christian Charity," but they found themselves in a situation in which the absence of traditional restraints, legal as well as physical, forced and enabled them to improvise. Although the culture that emerged had its roots deep in the traditions of English nonconformity, New Englanders developed religious, economic, and political practices unlike those prevailing elsewhere in the Atlantic world.[45]

A similar dynamic marked the emergence of democracy in the settlements ringing the Massachusetts Bay Colony, including the one that predated the Puritans' arrival and those established later. The earliest of the founding documents of New England was the Mayflower Compact, signed in 1620 by the original Pilgrims settling in the colony they established at Plymouth. These Separatists, who had given up hope for the Church of England, had first fled to the Netherlands in 1608. When a group of them decided to depart for the New World, their pastor, John Robinson, who chose to remain in Leyden, made clear the difficulty of establishing a government on the basis of equality. If these Pilgrims were to form their own body politic, they had to face the fact that, unlike their English brethren, they were not "furnished with any persons of special eminency above the rest, to be chosen by you into office of government." After Robinson urged them, in the absence of an aristocracy, to use their "wisdom and godliness" to select those who would govern in the interest of all, he emphasized that they must then yield to those chosen "all due honour and obedience in their lawful administrations, not beholding in them the ordinariness of their persons."[46]

The Pilgrims would have to remember their mutual dependence. "Wise men," Robinson observed, had endorsed as "good and lawful" three distinct forms of polity—monarchical, aristocratic, and "democratical"—and all had their place in Christ's church: "In respect of him the head, it is a monarchy; in respect of the eldership, an aristocracy; in respect of the body, a popular state." By joining together in independent congregations, the Pilgrims incorporated elements of all three forms, which Robinson thought should be balanced. The "external church government" he judged "plainly aristocratical, and to be administered by some choice men." But the elders' responsibilities do not exhaust all decision making. It remains "up to the people freely to vote in elections and judgments of the church."[47]

A decade later, Winthrop on the *Arbella* was echoing Robinson's words: "Let the elders publicly propound, and order all things in the church," and "let the people of faith give their assent to their elders' holy and lawful administration."[48] From the perspective shared by Robinson and Winthrop, only freedom consistent with the Gospel is true liberty; church elders had to refine untutored popular desire into genuine Christian volition. The Mayflower Compact committed its signers to terms strikingly similar to those Robinson had laid out for them: for God's glory they pledged to "covenant and combine ourselves together into a civil Body Politick, for our better Ordering and Preservation." To that end they came together to "enact, constitute, and frame, such just and equal Laws, Ordinances, Acts, Constitutions, and Officers" deemed necessary "for the general Good of the Colony; unto which we promise all due Submission and Obedience."[49] The forty-one names signed to the compact included individuals ranging from the wealthy merchant John Carver to ordinary sailors and servants.

Not all of those making the voyage shared the devout Calvinist faith of the Pilgrims. Indeed, the future governor of the colony William Bradford later explained that the Mayflower Compact was drawn up explicitly in response to "discontented and mutinous speeches" given on the ship by some non-Pilgrims—"strangers," as they were designated—who had let it be known "that when they came ashore they would use their own liberty, for none had the power to command them."[50] So even the apparently straightforward proclamation of popular sovereignty expressed in the Mayflower Compact reflects a deliberate and delicate balancing act between the longing to form a voluntary compact among equals and the need to secure order and avoid anarchy. Aboard the *Mayflower*, beyond the reach of English law—and especially among people committed to the equality of all believers—inherited assumptions about hierarchy withered. In their place emerged a framework of popular government erected at the intersection of the Pilgrims' hopes and fears.

In November of 1636 the Plymouth colonists laid down a new set of rules for their governance that resembled those established by their northern neighbors in the Massachusetts Bay Colony. Although Bradford would continue to serve as governor of Plymouth almost continuously from 1621 to 1657, the "whole body" determined that all freemen would meet once a year as a legislative body and formally limited the governor's privileges and responsibilities to administration. In 1638 the colonists reconsidered that framework and decided that instead of meeting annually as a body they would elect deputies who would serve in the General Court. The shift from direct to representative democracy occurred in New England less than two decades after the Pilgrims first landed at Plymouth, and the evidence indicates it was the freemen themselves who made that decision.[51]

The gears seldom meshed as smoothly in practice as the founding documents of New England Congregationalists—separating and nonseparating alike—indicated that they should. The similarity among the compacts and covenants signed in these years is nevertheless striking, whether one looks at documents written by the most well-educated divines or by colonists about whom little is known. When settlers headed north from the Massachusetts Bay Colony in 1639 to establish the town of Exeter, in what is now New Hampshire, their founding document invoked God's name, will, grace, sight, and law no fewer than eight times. They were as clear-sighted as the Pilgrims of Plymouth about the roles of the few who would rule and the many who would rule the rulers. According to the "Elders' or Rulers' Oath," those selected must "rule and govern His people according to the righteous will of God." The "Oath of the People" likewise empowers and restricts, limits and authorizes: "We will submit ourselves to be ruled and governed according to the will and word of God and such wholesome laws and ordinances as shall be derived therefrom by our honored rulers and the lawful assistants with the consent of the people." To this founding document twenty-four men signed their name; thirteen other men made their mark. All agreed to be bound by the government they created and the laws it would establish.[52] Those who wrote these compacts endorsed neither pure democracy nor aristocracy. Instead they placed rulers and ruled in conditions of mutual dependence, and above all they placed everyone under the dictates of God's law.[53]

Another group of emigrants from Massachusetts signed the "Fundamental Orders of 1639" to form the towns of Hartford, Windsor, and Wetherfield into a colony along the banks of the Connecticut River. Led by the eminent minister Thomas Hooker, who served the congregation in Newtown (later renamed Cambridge in honor of many early clergymen's alma mater) for four years after his arrival in 1632, these Connecticut settlers sought new farmland and a less restrictive polity.[54] Hooker argued in an election sermon of 1638 that public magistrates should be chosen by the people; such is God's will. The people should exercise that privilege not merely according to their whims but according to God's law. Those empowered to choose officials could circumscribe their authority. Citing a phrase from Proverbs, "in the multitude of counsellers there is safety," Hooker found scriptural warrant for the people's authority. The reason was simple: "The foundation of authority is laid," Hooker proclaimed, "in the free consent of the people."[55]

In *A Survey of the Summe of Church-Discipline* (1645), Hooker likened the role of the covenant in establishing order in congregations to that of charters in the civil sphere. In both cases, the whole body comprises members joined together by mutual dependence, the "sement that soders them all." That cement activates all the "parts and particular persons," and anyone entering such a congregation or polity willingly binds himself "to each member of that society to promote the good of the whole."[56] That choice entailed assent to prevailing laws. When a dispute prompted the town of Springfield to withdraw from the confederacy of Connecticut towns, Hooker objected. He complained that William Pynchon, the leader of the Springfield settlers, wanted to "devise ways to make his oath bind him when he will, and loosen him" when he saw fit. If Pynchon could explain how he could "engage himself in a civil covenant" when convenient, Hooker complained, "and yet can cast it away at his pleasure," he would have to write such a law himself, "for it is written in no law nor gospel that ever I read."[57]

The covenanting communities of Puritans that authorized the creation of congregations and town governments took themselves and their collective will too seriously to accept dispassionately either dissent or secession. They believed that disagreements, although inevitable, had to be resolved rather than allowed to fester. Such discord, they feared, would eventually break the bonds of sympathy that united them and enabled them to trust each other, thereby making possible their institutions of self-government.

A similar spirit animated the town of New Haven, founded in 1638 by followers of the London minister John Davenport, which joined with other towns established nearby to form a larger colony in 1643. Davenport's little band initially made church membership prerequisite to citizenship, and they experimented boldly—and, as it turned out, briefly—with direct democracy. The freemen chose twelve individuals suited for the magistracy, then selected seven of those by lot. When for unknown reasons those seven resigned, the freemen elected a magistrate and four deputies. From that point New Haven was unusual not for its use of sortition but instead because it required no rotation in office and had fewer rather than more individuals holding office. Davenport's New Haven colony tried to resolve the problem of dissent by foreclosing the possibility. If only the faithful could participate in civic affairs, the freemen of New Haven reasoned, squabbling was ruled out from the beginning. As Davenport made clear in the title of his *Discourse about Civil Religion in a New Plantation Whose Design Is Religion*, the purpose of a gathered church and town was "righteousness." If "unsuitable ones" were admitted, hell would break loose. Such ambitions, however, were short-lived in New Haven, as they proved to be in Massachusetts. When New Haven was swallowed up by the newly chartered colony of Connecticut in 1664, "godly rule" came to an end. Although New Haven began as an experiment in radical democracy as well as "righteousness," it developed into one of the less egalitarian Puritan settlements.[58]

Disagreements emerged everywhere in seventeenth-century New England. Winthrop believed that dissenters such as Williams and Hutchinson, and those such as Keayne who were censured for choosing to satisfy their own desires rather than living in accordance with the will of the community, could not be tolerated without sacrificing the unity demanded by the covenant. Notwithstanding the founders' commitment to consensus, conflicts proved to be pervasive in practice, and those in power invoked their authority to stifle the complaints of disgruntled minorities. It was their commitment to the covenant, constraining and intolerant as it often proved to be in practice, that made these communities willing to empower their congregations or popular assemblies to govern in the first place. Their power was no more fictional than a jail cell or an executioner's ax. As crucial as the ideas animating these founding documents was the experience of government that they made possible. In the crucible of conflict, more often resolved in the seventeenth century by imposing order from above than by accepting differences, English colonists struggled to cope with the disagreements that they knew sinfulness would breed, but that they hoped their commitments to equity and reciprocity would enable them to resolve.

Only a decade after the arrival of the *Arbella*, with twenty-six towns already established and others emerging, popular discontent in Massachusetts prompted the deputies to call for a fundamental, colony-wide code resembling that adopted by neighboring Connecticut. According to Winthrop's terse account, "The people had long desired a body of laws, and thought their condition very unsafe while so much power rested in the discretion of magistrates."[59] The General Court first directed John Cotton, distinguished minister of the Boston church, to draw up such a code, but the deputies were dissatisfied that Cotton's *Abstract for Laws and Government* still allowed the magistrates too much discretionary power. Nathaniel Ward of Ipswich, an experienced Puritan minister who fled England when he was suspended by Archbishop Laud, submitted another draft, *The Body of Liberties*. Unlike Cotton, Ward was trained in law as well as theology. He drew more heavily on the traditions of Greek, Roman, and English common law than did Cotton, who depended more explicitly on the Bible. Not surprisingly, Winthrop saw only "error" in Ward's approach, "for if religion and the word of God makes men wiser than their neighbors, we may better frame rules of government for ourselves than to receive others upon the bare authority of the wisdom, justice, etc. of those heathen commonwealths."[60] As happened often enough, however, the people's representatives disagreed with Winthrop. Although most of them preferred Ward's more careful delineation of the magistrates' prerogatives, they decided to submit both drafts to the people. After lively debates throughout the commonwealth, *The Body of Liberties* became law in 1641.

Ironies abound. The magistrates, jealous of their prerogatives, preferred Cotton's *Abstract for Laws and Government*. The people's representatives preferred *The Body of Liberties*, in part because they judged it friendlier to popular government and a sturdier bulwark against the magistrates' oligarchic tendencies. Ward himself, however, faithful to sixteenth-century English traditions of monarchy, and taking for granted the authority of church elders vis-à-vis their congregations, opposed submitting his draft for approval by the common people. He thought the decision was not theirs to make. The ratification of the code by Massachusetts freeholders inaugurated a tradition that persisted in England's North American colonies. *The Body of Liberties* codified legal practices already common in the commonwealth and clarified issues that had remained ambiguous. It protected freedom of assembly and movement; specified the legal rights of women, children, and servants; guaranteed due process and trial by jury; prohibited the legacies of feudal land tenure and transfer; and outlined the essential features of representative government. The General Court agreed to revisit the entire question in three years. As Winthrop summarized their decision, the rules specified in *The*

Body of Liberties were "revised and altered by the court, and sent forth into every town to be further considered of, and now again in this court they were revised, amended, and presented, and so established for three years, by that experience to have them fully amended and established to be perpetual."[61] Massachusetts thereby established another enduring tradition: the fundamental law should be reviewed, and altered if necessary, on the basis of experience.[62]

Vexing as religious intolerance proved to be, it was but one of the sources of conflict in seventeenth-century New England, as developments in Williams's Rhode Island made clear almost right away. The disposition of land ignited the fiercest squabbles. In 1640 thirty-nine heads of household in Providence agreed to choose five "disposers" who would resolve disputes that arose between the meetings of all the town's freemen. Confirming their commitment to "liberty of Conscience" was easy. So too was the decision to enforce payment of debts and fines by convening a posse, with the provision that "if any man raise a hubbub and there be no just cause," he that "raised the hubbub must satisfy men for their time lost in it."

Deciding how to divide land that had been claimed by more than one person proved more challenging, not only in Providence but everywhere. To that end the freemen resolved that each party in a dispute enter binding arbitration and select those who would resolve the conflict. Should those chosen fail to reach agreement, the five "disposers" would choose two more, and if that group deadlocked, the disposers would choose three more freemen whose decision would be final.[63] As that elaborate procedure suggests, conflict seems to have been endemic both within Providence and between its settlers and their neighbors. So was the longing for the peaceful and equitable resolution of disputes.

Six months later, the General Court met in Portsmouth to establish the government of the colony of Rhode Island. Although many provisions of this founding document concern specific points of disagreement, it was the unanimous affirmation of the colony as a "DEMOCRACIE" that remains its hallmark.[64] That first formal declaration of democratic government merely made explicit the democratic thrust of the provisions included in all the Puritans' compacts discussed so far. Government in the colony evidently continued to function after that meeting much as it had before, just as *The Body of Liberties*, enacted the same year, codified more than it modified existing practice in Massachusetts. The disputes dividing Rhode Islanders from each other likewise continued as before, but in the history of modern democracy, that document of March 19, 1641, is nevertheless a milestone.

Six years later the settlers who had established towns alongside Narragansett Bay and on the island of Newport formed themselves into a single government.

Following the lead of their Rhode Island predecessors in 1641, they designated that government a "democracy." In their words, "the due forme of government" was to be "democratical, that is to say, a government held by the free and voluntary consent of all, or the greater part of the free inhabitants." Laws were to be promulgated by a General Assembly, which was to be the sole source of authority acknowledged in the colony of Rhode Island. When these New Englanders hemmed in the authority of magistrates and empowered townspeople to elect public officials and make laws, they knew what they were doing. But they were equally self-conscious about the ethic of Christian love, mutuality, and equity—the ethic of reciprocity—on which they based the institutions of self-government they created as they attempted to put their religious principles into practice.[65]

The contrast between these boisterous but law-abiding New England towns and conditions in England, where such reformist efforts by dissenting Protestants ended in a crescendo of violence, is stark. In 1641, the same year that *The Body of Liberties* became law and Rhode Island formally declared itself a democracy, England began skidding toward revolution. Parliament's "Grand Remonstrance" signaled rising anger about legal practices still standard in England but now explicitly outlawed by the fundamental codes of Massachusetts, Connecticut, and Rhode Island. Within three years Roger Williams would be in England himself, fighting to preserve the principle of religious freedom—and to save his colony—from the specter of a greater New England. Before turning to the causes and consequences of the English Civil War, however, it is worth reflecting on the reasons why this study of democracy in early American settlements focuses on New England. The English had been in Virginia for more than a decade when the *Mayflower* landed, and the colony of Maryland was chartered before Williams was banished from Massachusetts. Why, and to what extent, did the institutions of popular government take a different form in those colonies?

The first English settlement in America did not last. In 1585 Sir Walter Raleigh sent a small band of men to Virginia. The colony they established on Roanoke Island survived only because the native Roanok Indians shared their supply of corn. This band of adventurers, as different from the devout Puritans of New England as Virginia's winters are from Boston's, evidently expected to flourish without work in the paradise described in early travelers' accounts. Instead they floundered, and soon they turned against the natives who had kept them alive. After a shipload of Englishmen returned home for provisions, the colony mysteriously vanished.

A second band of colonists, sent by a new investment company chartered by a new monarch, King James, arrived in Virginia in 1607. Hoping to avoid their predecessors' fate, they named both the river they sailed up and the settlement they founded after their king rather than the neighboring Indians. But they shared the earlier group's aversion to work and their desire to live off the fat of the land. These gentlemen-adventurers and unskilled vagrants failed to adjust to their conditions and refused to learn from the Indians how to keep themselves alive. Instead of planting corn, they prospected for gold. Instead of retreating from the summer heat, they stuck to the banks of the fetid river. Overmatched by Indian raiding parties, malaria-carrying mosquitoes, and the dysentery and typhus bred by their own carelessness, their numbers shrank.

Reinforcements and supplies were sent from England, but of the nearly two thousand who arrived in the colony's first decade, only a few hundred survived. Luring even men with little to lose proved increasingly difficult, so the members of the Virginia Company took a fateful step. They offered fifty acres to anyone who would fund his own passage, offered additional land for any servants or family members, and even promised land to servants who worked off their indenture. In 1619 the company authorized an assembly of representatives in Virginia and permitted them to review the decisions made in England. Within a few years, this first popularly elected lawmaking body in English North America had become indispensable: "Nothinge can more conduce to our satisfaction or the publique utilitie" than the General Assembly. The Jamestown settlement was still struggling, but the pattern of independent freeholders constituting themselves into a representative government, and meeting annually with the governor and his appointed council, was put in place.[66]

Then came tobacco. Although initially inhospitable to English ways of life, Virginia provided ideal conditions for raising a crop that would addict thousands of Europeans in the seventeenth century. Profits from 500 to 1,000 percent beckoned men willing to gamble their safety against the promise of unimagined wealth. Dreams of gold went up in smoke; energy replaced indolence. Looking back from 1624, Captain John Smith claimed that the prospect of prospering changed everything. In the words of Ralph Hamer, one of the first to venture to Virginia, "When our people were fedde out of the common store, and laboured jointly," anyone who could avoid working was happy to get away with it. Even "the most honest of them" did less work in a week than they now did in a day. Formerly, Hamer concluded, no one cared about increasing the harvest because the "generall store" provided for them, so they "reaped not so much corne from the labours of thirty men" as under the new rules "three men have done for themselves."[67]

Tobacco profits did not immediately improve Virginia's mortality rate or the colony's deteriorating relations with neighboring Indians. Finding enough

Englishmen willing to emigrate remained a problem. When the Virginia Company went bankrupt and King James assumed control of the colony in 1624, he sent governors to rule without interference from the meddlesome assembly. Those governors found themselves hamstrung without popular support, so they were forced back into cooperation with the assembly despite the King's wishes. In 1639, reluctantly—and, as it turned out, belatedly—conceding the need to consult his own Parliament at home, Charles acknowledged that his royal governors should cooperate with the colonial assembly in Virginia.[68] Limited disorder seemed preferable to inertia. By the 1640s the Virginia House of Burgesses enjoyed the consent of the crown. It had also assumed a judicial role, and it was meeting annually.

Then came slavery. West Africans had been trading slaves to Arabs for centuries and to Europeans since they began sailing the African coast in the 1450s. The Portuguese and Spanish depended on slaves in their Caribbean sugar plantations. Even though the condition of permanent, heritable enslavement had no precedent in England, English colonists began buying African slaves to work their land early in the seventeenth century. When the price of tobacco soared and the supply of indentured servants lagged, Virginia planters, desperate for labor and concerned only with profit, turned increasingly to slaves. Like other people enslaved by Europeans for centuries, Africans were foreign, they were already captives, and they were non-Christian. Hierarchy and dependence characterized every aspect of early seventeenth-century English society. Slaves and servants were subservient in varying degrees to the freemen who controlled their lives.

Initial patterns of black and white interaction in Virginia showed considerable variety. The lines between slaves and servants were fuzzy. Within just a few decades that distinction became rigid; the color line that separated blacks from whites became as sharply etched as that dividing slave from free. When the supply of indentured servants dried up, the two lines subtly merged into one. As the great planters of Virginia became exceedingly rich, they managed to convince their fellow English colonists that although they might be poor, they were at least free and white, which meant that they—unlike slaves—could participate in choosing which members of the planter elite might represent them in the colony's government.

As in New England, hierarchy persisted, but in Virginia the presence of an ever-growing slave population added a much sharper division to that separating wealthy landowners from ordinary people. Even many of the poorest whites, once they worked off their indentures, soon owned enough land to vote, whereas blacks—including the decreasing number of free blacks—were excluded from the franchise. There is no doubt that New England magistrates, ministers, and successful merchants constituted an elite. The distance separating them from their fellow townspeople, however, was tiny compared to the economic divide between great tobacco planters and small farmers in the Chesapeake by 1660. That gap, wide as it was, dwindled into insignificance compared with the gulf—social and legal as well as economic—between those poor white farmers and African slaves.[69]

The other southern colony founded in the early seventeenth century confirmed the Puritans' worst fears. In 1632 Charles authorized a Catholic, his friend Charles Calvert, the second Lord Baltimore, to establish on land north of Virginia the proprietary colony of Maryland, to be governed by Calvert's younger brother. When word reached New England that ships carrying Catholics as well as Protestants had embarked for the new settlement, an indignant Winthrop noted in his journal that "those which came over were many of them papists and did set up Mass openly."[70] Calvert did indeed want to establish a place where all Christians could worship freely; Charles hoped only that Maryland would show the viability of permitting Catholics to practice their faith alongside Protestants. As always in the New World, things took a series of unexpected turns.

English law prohibited official establishment of Catholicism in the colony, and few Catholics chose to emigrate at a moment when many hoped England itself would return to the fold. More numerous were dissenting Protestants harried north by Virginia's enforcement of Anglicanism. Calvert aimed to establish an orderly feudal society under his brother's firm governing hand, with aristocratic landlords ruling a colony of tenant farmers sprinkled with a few hardy yeomen. To entice emigrants he offered even more generous tracts of land than the Virginia Company, which meant that ambitious tobacco farmers, already experienced in the ways of Chesapeake cultivation, quickly moved to Maryland and established plantations of their own. The royal charter required Calvert to rule with the "Advice, Assent, and Approbation of the Free-Men" of Maryland, "or of the greater Part of them, or of their Delegates or Deputies, whom We will shall be called together for the framing of Laws, when, and as often as Need shall require." Such laws, of course, were to be made according to reason and were not to be inconsistent with those of England. When circumstances made it impossible to call together the freemen or their delegates, the governor was empowered to use his own discretion, but under no circumstances was he to restrict the liberty of English citizens.[71]

Those stipulations soon shook the Calverts from their neo-feudal dream. In 1635 Governor Leonard Calvert, perhaps envisioning himself as a latter-day King John assembling his liege men at Runnymede, gathered the settlers together to obtain their public assent. The records of the assembly of 1638, however, show that the colonists had already begun experimenting with their power in unanticipated ways. Some attended the assembly "as freemen" to register their own votes, others to cast votes as well for those who had sent them. Others attended specifically because they had *not* voted for the representative chosen by the majority of their neighbors. On February 16, 1638, Cuthbert Fenwick, one of the original settlers of Maryland, who later rose to the position of Speaker of the House of Burgesses, was said to have "claimed a Voice as not assenting to the election of St. Mary's burgesses and was admitted." Only gradually did the assembly assume the shape taken for granted today, in which each representative spoke for the entire population of his district—those who voted against as well as for him. Because some members of the Maryland assembly were sent by their towns or counties, and others, typically larger property holders, were summoned by the governor to advise him, a bicameral legislature emerged earlier, and more organically, in Maryland than it did in some of the other colonies.[72]

Similar forms of representative democracy soon became the norm throughout England's mainland colonies even though the processes of development differed. Legislatures were bicameral rather than unicameral. Whether those chosen for the assembly were called "burgesses," "deputies," or "delegates," they were tied to towns or counties where they resided, an older practice that had all but disappeared in England. Regulations required those serving in colonial assemblies everywhere to behave themselves. Inflammatory or defamatory speech was forbidden. Assemblymen who carried weapons, used tobacco, appeared intoxicated, or failed to show up for scheduled meetings were subject to fines. As such rules suggest, those selected for colony-wide office were not always genteel or prosperous. Over time, however, the membership of all the colonial assemblies showed increasing stability: a smaller and smaller group of people was elected more and more often throughout the colonies.

Despite some persistent local peculiarities, all these early English colonies north and south developed forms of representative democracy that emphasized the role of assemblies. Elections, less often contests than occasions for reaching agreement about delegates and linking them to the interests of their communities, became the standard method of choosing public officials. From diverse origins ranging from a commercial enterprise in Virginia, forms of religious pilgrimage into and around New England, and a medieval proprietary venture in Maryland, these colonies developed their own practices of popular government as they were crafting the theories or arguments to justify their existence. Gradually, increasing numbers of settlers dispersed from the

Atlantic seaboard, and the habit of electing representatives spread with them across all the English colonies in mainland North America.[73]

Of the European powers that succeeded in planting their own colonies across the Atlantic, only the English sought to occupy the land and brought people to settle it permanently. Like the Spanish and French, and the Portuguese and the Dutch, the English carried in their ships soldiers, traders, and missionaries. They differed in that they brought mostly farmers and artisans, and especially in New England they brought women of childbearing age, perhaps the most distinctive feature of the English migration. The English colonies—again, particularly the colonies in New England—developed as extensions of English culture rather than simply outposts on the frontier, as the Spanish missions and the French trading posts remained. The French at first hoped to build a version of their seigneurial system, with docile farmers tied to the land and obeying the lords of their manors. The Dutch exported their expertise as mariners and traders, building a worldwide commercial empire in which New Amsterdam, situated on Manhattan Island, lacked much significance despite its location at the site of a splendid harbor and at the mouth of the navigable Hudson River. With a booming economy and a polyglot population including Puritans and Jews as well as adherents to the official Dutch Reformed version of Calvinism, the Netherlands generated neither the roaming surplus population of England nor the missionary zeal of Counter-Reformation Spain and France.

In short, neither Spain nor France nor the Netherlands built in the New World the independent, self-sufficient, permanent colonies of settler families that came from England. Other Atlantic peoples sailed the oceans as avidly as the English did. For a variety of religious, economic, demographic, and cultural reasons, however, relatively few non-English Europeans wanted to make their homes in the western hemisphere. In none of those settlements did colonists establish forms of self-government like the assemblies that developed in the English colonies on the North American mainland. Compared with their continental rivals, the English monarchs were poor, weak, and distracted. For that reason the English who emigrated to America enjoyed remarkable autonomy in the first half of the seventeenth century. The English who stayed home, by contrast, endured civil war, revolution, and regicide, which delayed the further advance of popular government in England for more than two centuries.

CHAPTER 3

Democracy Deferred

The English Civil War

CHARLES I, THE only English monarch put to death in public by his subjects, understood the dangers of democracy decades before he was beheaded. When he mounted the scaffold in 1649, Charles remained defiant. "For the people," he announced, "truly I desire their liberty and freedom as much as anybody whatsoever." He insisted that their liberty and freedom consisted solely in "having of government those laws by which their life and goods may be most their own." To more than that, however, to a republic or a democracy, for example, they should never aspire. The people's liberty "is not having share in government, sirs; that is nothing pertaining to them."[1] The executioner's ax contradicted that claim. Yet by killing the king in the name of the people, the king's foes postponed further progress toward democracy in England for centuries.

To understand why dissatisfaction with monarchy led, after civil war, regicide, and republican rule, to the return of monarchy eleven years later, it is necessary to examine those whom the philosopher Thomas Hobbes later called "democratical gentlemen," or, simply, "the democraticals." After the return of royal authority, Hobbes could see that ideas of popular government lay at the root of England's midcentury convulsions.[2]

This chapter traces the rise, explosion, and final snuffing out of democracy in mid-seventeenth-century England. Challenges to monarchy emerged first, in moderate form, through the efforts of barrister Henry Parker and clergyman Philip Hunton in the early 1640s. Such ideas assumed a more radical cast in the fiery writings of figures grouped together by their enemies as "Levellers." As this unrest grew into war and revolution, democratic ideas found an unlikely home among members of the New Model Army, which seized power from moderates in Parliament who aimed to reform rather than end the monarchy. The waves of violence that swept across England from the outbreak of civil war in 1647 until the restoration of monarchy in 1660 were another expression of the same convulsive religious wars that raged in Europe throughout the preceding century. Contemporaries understood the connection. An anonymous pamphlet printed in London in 1648 lamented the chaos of "these late, bad, and worst of times," when "all the Christian world hath been imbroyl'd with Warre, and all the miseries of Sword, Fire, and Famine: when Nation did rise against Nation, and Realme against Realme." The pamphlet recited the familiar litany: Swedes fought Germans, Poles fought Russians, Spaniards fought Dutchmen, and worst of all, France fell into a "most bloody and cruell Civil War with itselfe." England watched while the continent was "drencht and neer drownd with blood and slaughter," but eventually it too caught the contagion. Not to be outdone in "killing and cutting throats, robbing, rifling, plundering," and "ruinating one another (under the fair pretences of Religion and Reformation)," the people of the British Isles set about their business with "barbarous inhumanity and cruelty" worthy of infidels and cannibals.[3] The king's execution merely underscored the savagery of the struggle.

Charles was raised by a father, James I, who longed to exercise absolute authority as God's chosen monarch. In 1623, when the headstrong Charles became interested in the daughter of the king of Spain, his reported willingness to convert to Catholicism to win her hand outraged mainstream Anglicans as well as already suspicious Puritans and Presbyterians. When Charles then married instead the teenaged sister of the king of France, with the understanding that she and her entourage could not only practice their religion openly but also raise their children—and thus the heir to the English throne—in her Catholic faith, English Protestants feared the worst. The marriage only cemented a diplomatic alliance to replenish the finances of the English crown and give England a formidable ally in Europe, just as the marriage to the Spanish infanta would have done. For the Protestant majority of the English population, however, Charles's marriage heralded a truly terrifying prospect, the triumph of the Catholic Counter-Reformation. The early successes enjoyed by Catholic armies in the Thirty Years War, which was to rage in central Europe from 1618 to 1648, convinced Protestants everywhere that a resurgent Catholicism threatened to roll back the Reformation. Changes within the Church of England restored the importance of ceremony, amplified the power of bishops, and threatened to enforce obedience to Anglican orthodoxy, all of which intensified dissenters' fears of popery.

Thus relations between king and Parliament, which had been deteriorating for years, were poisoned from the moment Charles ascended the throne after his father's death in 1625. Charles's father, James VI of Scotland, published his treatise *The Trew Law of Free Monarchies* in 1598, five years before he became James I of England on the death of Elizabeth, and two years before Jean Bodin's *Six Books of the Commonweale* appeared for the first time in English translation. James made a spirited case for royal absolutism, the doctrine that had gained favor among Catholic monarchs enthralled by Bodin's logic and its consequences for their legitimacy. Although the subtitle announced James's subject as "the Reciprock and Mutuall Dutie betwixt a Free King and His Naturall Subjects," the ethic of reciprocity could not have been further from James's mind. Rather than envisioning two autonomous parties with wills of their own, he imagined the king as father and the people as his adoring and obedient children. The monarch's authority, James declared, came from God, from traditional custom, and from the law of nature, all of which placed the king beyond the reach of any legal restrictions that his critics in Parliament could invoke. The people's only duty, as good subjects, was to "keep their hearts and hands free from such monstrous and unnaturall rebellions."[4] Half a century later, just such a rebellion, undertaken explicitly to protest royal absolutism on behalf of popular government, would take his son's life.

James and Charles sought harmony and order as sincerely as did the Puritans of New England, but on very different terms. They believed it should be proclaimed by royal decree rather than emerge from a process of public deliberation by God's people or their elected representatives. James and Charles operated on assumptions inherited from earlier English practice and apparently authorized by English common law. They encountered resistance, however, from the moment James took the throne.

Ever since King John granted Magna Carta to his subjects in 1215, the precise relation between king and Parliament had been contested. This conflict stemmed from the original ambiguity of the institution of Parliament itself, beginning in the thirteenth century, when county and borough representatives were summoned by the king to obtain their consent for laws and taxes. These representatives carried with them full powers of attorney, so that those back home could not challenge their decisions. When Parliament expanded from under 300 to 462 members in the early seventeenth century, the crown awarded most of the new seats to members of the gentry who controlled local elections but did not reside in the towns or counties they nominally represented in Parliament. Although from the beginning representation was thus imposed from above, by the king, rather than from below, Parliament nevertheless developed during the thirteenth and fourteenth centuries as a means of incorporating into English law the mutual agreements, typical of late-medieval practice, by which lords and vassals formally accepted their obligations to each other.

Such arrangements could hardly be characterized as egalitarian or interpreted as expressing the idea of popular sovereignty. Nevertheless they formed the basis on which developed the practice of Parliament's asserting its authority to defend the liberties of Englishmen against the crown, a tradition on which parliamentary critics of the Stuart monarchy drew. In principle the rights of Englishmen, secured by what was known as the ancient constitution and elaborated over centuries in the common law, were acknowledged by English kings and queens from the thirteenth century on, even though Parliament usually accepted limits to its ability to challenge the crown's authority.[5]

This tension was not confined to England. Conflicts over multiple issues, ranging from religion to taxation, pitted representative assemblies of various kinds against monarchs of varying strength. Kings triumphed in France and the Hapsburg states. After the Dutch republic secured its independence from Spain in 1581, the representatives sent to the States-General by ruling provincial oligarchs seldom agreed on any issue except the importance of encouraging commerce. Nonetheless they refused to acquiesce to the most powerful among them, William of Orange. Europeans everywhere wrestled with the question of whether the power of princes could or should be restrained by nobles or assemblies representing the people. The tradition of Calvinist resistance theory offered one alternative to Bodin's absolutism. Late-sixteenth- and early seventeenth-century French theorists of constitutionalism offered another. Guy Coquille claimed that it had been "the people who make the law" by forging agreements with their kings. They had retained the authority and the capacity to challenge royal authority through the institution of parlements, the provincial courts of law that had operated more or less independently of the French monarchy. Pierre Charron likewise stressed the customary practice of balancing different forms of authority, basing his ideas about politics on an insight as potentially unsettling as anything in the writings of his friend Montaigne: "There is no opinion held by all, or current in all places," that has not been "debated and disputed" by people holding "contrarie" points of view. Unlike the "dogmatists," the "wisest, greatest, and most noble Philosophers" admit their "ignorance" and rest content with "doubting, enquiring, searching."[6]

Another alternative to the doctrine of royal absolutism emerged in the writings of the German legal theorists Johannes Althusius and Christoph Besold, who offered different concepts of mixed government, grounded in the experience of divided power in the German principalities and towns, to challenge the idea of unitary royal authority.[7] The tradition of natural jurisprudence proved the most significant alternative. Arguments from natural law, originating with the jurist and legal theorist Hugo Grotius in early seventeenth-century Holland, helped shape democratic theory on both sides of the Atlantic.

Thus the struggles between Parliament and the Stuarts, played out within a distinctly English historical and religious framework, had parallels outside England. Until the seventeenth century such assemblies were called only occasionally, and their purpose was almost always to raise money for military campaigns. Such appeals were usually assumed to be urgent, even though precedents for resistance existed: beginning in 1367, English kings had been ousted five times. When Parliament began to challenge first James and then Charles—mainly over attempts to finance the royal army and navy—the compromise that had existed in the sixteenth century under Elizabeth began to unravel.[8]

Sustained partisan struggles between more or less stable groups emerged slowly in England. Crown as well as Parliament agreed that decisions should be made consensually whenever possible. At the local level the lingering legacy of feudal obligations—and the persistence of hierarchical relations—knitted together communities and provided the mechanisms for achieving such agreement. That was the system of bounded and balanced authority that scholastics such as Aquinas had recommended and that writers such as John Fortescue had described in the fourteenth century as "circumscribed monarchy." "The King of England is not able to change the laws of his kingdom at pleasure," Fortescue wrote, for he ruled his people with a government "not only regal but also political." Were the king's power purely regal, he could alter the laws at will, but he needed his subjects' assent, and the English people, "ruled by laws that they themselves desire," could thus "freely enjoy their properties" without interference.[9]

Parliament reflected the commitment to consensus that English colonists transported across the Atlantic. Those returned to the House of Commons were more often than not prominent citizens selected by local magistrates. In the fourteenth and fifteenth centuries, members of Parliament were seldom chosen by formal elections, in which qualified freemen cast ballots. Such contests signaled a failure to achieve the desired consensus. As Thomas Smith observed in *De Republica Angolorum* (1583), England was a "common wealth," which for Smith had a very particular meaning: "A common wealth is called a society or common doing of a multitude of free men collected together and united by common accord and covenauntes among themselves, for the conservation of themselves as well in peace as in warre."[10]

Religious passion was the solvent that made the system come unglued, and that passion was catalyzed by developments in Europe. In 1613 James married his daughter to Prince Frederick, the Protestant Elector of the Palatinate.

When Calvinists in Bohemia rose against their Catholic Hapsburg ruler, they named Frederick their prince and looked to James, Frederick's father-in-law and the Protestant king of England, for assistance in their struggle. They were disappointed when no such help arrived. Their armies were routed in the decisive Battle of White Mountain in 1620, in the aftermath of which Calvinists were slaughtered in Bohemia and Frederick's Palatinate fell to the Hapsburgs. From the perspective of Calvinists on the continent and many Puritans in England, James's failure to aid the Protestant cause against the Hapsburgs showed he was at best soft on Catholicism and at worst a pawn of the pope. When his son embarked on a campaign that failed pathetically to liberate the Palatinate from the Hapsburgs' grip, and then married a French Catholic princess, Puritans' fears became feverish. The Stuart kings were proving to be as incompetent as they were untrustworthy.

When Charles ascended the throne in 1625, he worried that the dissenters among his subjects were straying dangerously close to treason. They accused him of apostasy, and he regarded them as a threat to the Church of England because they challenged its rituals, its traditions, and the legitimate authority of its clergy. Parliament compounded his problems by resisting his call for funds sufficient to enable England to combat the principal forces of the Counter-Reformation, the Spanish and Austrian Hapsburgs. Thus Charles, like his father, found himself struggling against two almost equally hostile forces, resurgent Catholic empires and domestic critics who denied him the resources to do what they ridiculed him for failing to do.

The petitions issued throughout the 1620s demonstrate that from the final years of James's reign through the outbreak of civil war in 1641, dissenting Protestants and Parliamentarians alike accused the Stuart kings of conspiring with Catholics at home and on the continent. In 1621, a petition lamented the attempts of "swarms of Priests and Jesuits" in England conniving under the pope's direction to achieve "the subversion of the true Religion."[11] Another petition four years later warned Charles that papists in England were aiming "not only at the utter extirpation of our religion, but also at the possessinge of themselves of the whole power of the State." In two pamphlets of 1620 and 1624, entitled *Vox Populi* and *The Second Part of Vox Populi*, Thomas Scott added another dimension to such fears, distinguishing the rock-solid Protestantism of ordinary English people from the Spanish—and thus popish and anti-Christian—preferences of the great landowners allied with the crown.[12] Today such fears seem like paranoid rantings. At the time, however, they explained many of the otherwise perplexing innovations that Charles undertook during the early years of his reign. He proposed to shift the focus of Anglican worship from preaching to ritual, stamp out the endless theological squabbling of dissenters, restore not only the status of the clergy but also many of the lands turned over to the laity since the closing of the monasteries, and punish those who disobeyed. During the 1620s Catholics had been proscribed from government service; Charles reversed that trend and seemed to be directing his ire instead at antipopery.

The anxieties that propelled Puritans such as John Winthrop and Roger Williams across the Atlantic grew more pronounced in England during the 1630s, the decade when experiments among self-governing congregations were proliferating in New England. Tensions between king and Parliament might have continued to smolder had not religious animosities ignited them. For beyond the conflicts between Charles and Parliament over taxation and discretionary imprisonment lay mutual distrust between Anglicans and Puritans on the one hand and Anglicans and the resurgent Catholics of the Counter-Reformation on the other. The Church of England was pressed on both sides by critics who disputed its legitimacy and its authority. Scattered examples of dissent fueled Anglicans' anxieties. Members of the University of Cambridge, a hotbed of Puritan sentiment, openly debated whether election would be preferable to hereditary succession as a basis for kingship. Thousands of Puritans, seeking to practice their faith in peace, fled England for Holland or the New World. Archbishop Laud castigated Puritan preachers for encouraging sedition. As a result, Anglicans as well as Catholics thought they had ample reason to fear the loyalty of a dissenting sect widely deemed capable of treason. Anglicans as well as Puritans and Presbyterians suspected that Charles was preparing to return England to the papacy. It all seemed to add up: Laud became Archbishop of Canterbury and embarked on the series of reforms that further antagonized already-wary Puritans; the king's French wife practiced her Catholicism openly; the number of priests saying Mass in England mushroomed; and the Catholic population increased by as much as 50 percent between 1603 and 1640.

As rumors fanned the fears of both sides, the ingrained English inclination toward consensus faded. Moderates thought the only solution lay in excluding dissenting Puritans and Presbyterians as well as Catholics from public life. Yet the ranks of both groups, and the degree of danger they represented to their opponents, swelled during the 1630s. Charles's chartering of the proprietary colony of Maryland only inflamed fears of creeping papism. The king and Archbishop Laud may have wanted nothing more sinister than to solidify the Church of England against the threats they perceived in the agitation of Puritans and Presbyterians, but dissenters in the 1620s and 1630s thought royal policies signaled a conspiracy to make England Catholic. Dissenters who fled England were willing to gamble their lives on the seriousness of the threat they perceived. From their perspective Charles's program forced a choice between Rome and Geneva.[13]

Contemporaries understood that the tensions growing in England from the 1620s onward derived from the same source as those feeding the religious wars in Europe.[14] We cannot know whether the disagreements between the English Parliament and Charles I would have escalated to war without the apocalyptic dimension added by competing religious convictions. We do know that such convictions deepened the sense of crisis.[15] Scattered incidents indicated that the conflict was coming to a head. In 1627 a history lecturer in Cambridge was sacked for endorsing, in a study of Tacitus, the idea that monarchy derives its legitimacy from the free submission of the people. A year later Parliament's Petition of Right proclaimed the traditional liberties of Englishmen against what MPs perceived as the king's arbitrary exercise of his authority. The petition was drawn up by the patron and teacher of Roger Williams, Edward Coke, whose *Reports* (published between 1600 and 1615) established him as the preeminent champion of the authority of the common law. Coke's *Reports* also provided a sturdy historical foundation for the claim that English liberties were grounded in the consent of the king's subjects, and the Petition of Right invoked precedents stretching back to the thirteenth century.

Those who disputed royal power and hereditary right in the early seventeenth century were drawing on venerable traditions. According to English law and lore, an ancient constitution, unwritten but observed in practice from time beyond memory, limited the powers and prerogatives of monarchs and protected the liberties of the people. Allegedly established and enforced by Angles and Saxons and invoked to constrain even William the Conqueror after 1066, this ancient constitution was understood to lie behind Magna Carta (1215), behind the Statute of No Taxation without Consent (1297), and behind all later proclamations of the rights of the English people. As early as chapter 39 of Magna Carta, which invoked the "law of the land" against the presumptions of King John, the English nobility was drawing on earlier defenses of personal liberty. When Edward II ascended to the throne in 1308, he conceded that English law was the joint product of the king and the community.

Thus the concept of law as the product of a contract between monarchy and nobility emerged from late-medieval practice with more formal and explicit legitimacy in England than elsewhere. In the 1630s and especially the 1640s, holding office by hereditary right came under direct challenge. When critics substituted consent for birth as the basis of legitimacy, one of the casualties was the idea of lot as a means of selecting officeholders. In 1627 the Puritan cleric Thomas Gataker surveyed the widespread use of lot in ancient Israel, Greece, and Rome and in fifteenth- and sixteenth-century Italy. *Of the*

Nature and Use of Lots, however, was to be the last English book on the subject for three centuries. If the explicit consent of the governed was the standard of legitimacy, it followed that choosing political officers deliberately, by election, was superior to random selection. Thus a centuries-old technique fell into disuse. From the 1630s onward, champions of democracy emphasized the importance of explicit consent and preferred election to sortition.[16]

Those who invoked the ancient constitution stressed the consent of the governed as a limit on the power of the monarch. Speaking in the House of Commons on June 4, 1628, John Pym denounced the innovations of Charles I as a threat to cherished English liberties. The "government of the Saxons" provided laws that constrained all kings after the "Conqueror, whose victory gave him first hope." Although reckless rulers repeatedly challenged such ancient traditions, they were checked by acts of Parliament and by the petitions filed by subjects "demanding their ancient and due liberties." It was the king, not his critics, who proposed to undo centuries of careful work that had established consent as the basis of the English common law.[17]

Charles I dismissed such protests and the notion of the ancient constitution as powerless against his prerogative, which he grounded in the doctrine proclaimed by his father in *The Trew Law of Free Monarchies*. From the Stuarts' perspective, all the charters and rights supposedly secured by the ancient constitution, including Magna Carta, were granted by the English monarch to his subjects. Such claims of royal sovereignty now prompted resistance. In the words of John Selden, a moderate Parliamentarian who eventually turned against the king even though he dismissed the ancient constitution as nonsense, all legitimate English law was "either ascertained by custom or confirmed by act of parliament." From the perspective of Selden and others who shared his convictions, English monarchs after the imposition of what was commonly called the "Norman yoke" were consistently prohibited from disregarding Parliament by the need to secure the consent of the governed.[18]

The Petition of Right affirmed nothing more inflammatory than the traditional rights of Englishmen, yet it constituted nothing less than a direct challenge to the king, who had imposed loans to pay his debts and imprisoned five knights who refused. Charles was out of money and patience. He accepted the Petition of Right to secure the funds he needed, but he neither abandoned the policies that provoked it nor conceded the larger point. Fundamental disagreements on the relation between royal prerogative and parliamentary authority persisted. Parliament continued to defy the king. First it denied him the right to impose the traditional levies that had long funded the crown's military campaigns. Then, raising the stakes, it challenged Charles to enforce Protestant orthodoxy against those perceived to be sliding toward

Rome. Charles answered by refusing to call Parliament throughout the 1630s. The Elizabethan compromise was coming apart over the question of Parliament's authority and fears of popery.[19]

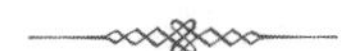

In Scotland the resistance of Presbyterians to the innovations introduced by Archbishop Laud and Charles became militant. When the king tried to impose the Anglican prayer book on the Scots, latent distrust turned to outrage: in 1639 Scottish troops invaded England. Now Charles needed money to defend his realm. He called Parliament, assuming loyalty to England would trump distrust of his reign. When he learned he was mistaken, he dissolved Parliament. Later that year, with his army in danger of being routed by Scottish Presbyterians, Charles again convened Parliament. Whereas the Short Parliament had met for only three weeks, this one would sit for thirteen years. Like its predecessor, though, the Long Parliament refused Charles the funds he needed. By then too few Parliamentarians wanted to see Charles's policies enforced in England or in rebellious Scotland. His chief political adviser, the Earl of Strafford, was executed; Archbishop Laud was imprisoned.

Challenges to the king's sovereign authority, previously veiled beneath the pretense that his advisers were to blame for arbitrary rule and papist tendencies, became increasingly provocative. In November 1640 Parliament passed the Triennial Act, which required the king to convene Parliament every three years. On December 1, 1640, Parliament issued the Great Remonstrance, which demanded the authority to approve the appointment of all royal counselors, an unambiguous sign that Parliament, not the king, would control government. In its Protestation of May 3, 1641, Parliament rendered the decisive verdict, in terms echoing those rattling around for two decades in the pamphlets of dissenters, against "endeavours to subvert the fundamental laws of England and Ireland, and to introduce the exercise of an arbitrary and tyrannical government by most pernicious and wicked counsels, practises, plots and conspiracies." Evidence of such tyranny included "many illegal taxations, whereby the subjects have been prosecuted and grieved," and many "divers innovations and superstitions" within the Church of England.[20]

At such charges Charles's rising impatience exploded into rage. In the summer of 1642 he left London, branded the Presbyterian and Puritan leaders of Parliament traitors, and declared war against them. Royalist loyalty centered in the North and West; parliamentary strength lay in the South and East. The armies of both the king and Parliament numbered over twenty thousand, and once the war began in October 1642, it set off a grim sequence of pitched battles, killings, and reprisals that continued sporadically, in Ireland even more murderously than in England, for nine years. Despite sharing most of the same convictions, the king's subjects were driven into rival camps by passionate disagreements over religious principles and royal versus parliamentary power—in short, over the ideas of monarchy and democracy.

In the polarization of opinion between 1628 and the outbreak of civil war in 1642, all sides said they wanted only to restore arrangements sanctified by a century of consensual practice. The Puritans and Presbyterians, however, were wrong. Both their demands for different purified forms of Protestantism and their demands for popular sovereignty, which were to take clearer shape during the Civil War, challenged enduring preferences. Whereas Puritans consistently embraced the idea of a self-governing covenanted community based on voluntary consent, forms of which had been adopted in many New England towns, and resisted attempts at either Anglican inclusiveness or Presbyterian hierarchy, the main current of English culture was flowing in the opposite direction. Puritans stressed the priesthood of all believers and relished discussion among those gathered into their churches. Charles, Laud, and most of their allies saw in such practices disorder, disobedience, and the eventual dissolution of the monarchy into the excesses of democracy and anarchy. Samuel Brooke, the master of Trinity College, Cambridge, spoke for many in 1630 when he identified Puritan dissent as "the roote of all rebellions and disobedient intractableness in parliaments etc. and all schisme and sausiness in the countrey."[21]

A glance back across the Atlantic illuminates the differences between England and the communities controlled by Puritans. Self-governing colonies had been established in the towns that became Connecticut and Rhode Island, a self-proclaimed "democracie." In 1641 the Massachusetts Bay Colony's *Body of Liberties* explicitly rejected the practices for which the Grand Remonstrance chastised Charles, including both neglect of habeas corpus and the combining of legislative, judicial, and executive power in Star Chamber. As the war between Parliament and Charles raged, the people of Massachusetts proclaimed that "ours is [a] *perfecta respublica*," a perfect republic or commonwealth, self-governing and subject to "no other power but among ourselves." Accused by Presbyterians of behaving as though they were not subjects of the king of England, the Massachusetts General Court announced defiantly that "our allegiance binds us not to the laws of England any longer than while we live in England, for the laws of [the] parliament of England reach no further [than the physical boundaries of England], nor do the king's writs under the great seal."

In the words of the Bay Colony's government, "The highest authoritie here is in the general court, both by our charter and by our owne positive laws." The "people are present" in the General Court by virtue of sending their representatives, so "nothing can passe" without the approval of "the democraticall part" of the government." Those simple observations, an early seventeenth-century declaration of legal independence, reflected and ratified the decade-long practice of autonomous decision making in New England. From the outset consent of the governed, not hereditary right to office, had determined who would exercise authority.[22]

Even as New Englanders applauded attempts to rein in the king, they were nevertheless wary when they learned that Scottish armies were advancing into England. Early skirmishes in the war of words that accompanied the military engagements suggested that compromise remained a possibility. Surprisingly, the king replied to another set of parliamentary demands, the Nineteen Propositions of 1642, by explicitly repudiating James's doctrine of royal absolutism. He acknowledged that the people, not the king, were the source of the unwritten constitution of the English realm and conceded that the king made the laws "jointly" with the Houses of Lords and Commons. Charles even endorsed the ancient formula of mixed government, admitting that monarchy could devolve into tyranny, aristocracy into oligarchy, and democracy into "tumults, violence, and licentiousnes." He went so far as to acknowledge that the "good of democracy is liberty, and the courage and industry that liberty begets." Having thus surrendered the claim of royal sovereignty, that most fundamental premise of divine right monarchy, *His Majesties Answer* then abruptly rejected the Nineteen Propositions on the grounds that they would upset the crucial balance among the three estates of king, lords, and commons.[23] Charles and his advisers were seeking a middle ground that would appeal to moderates torn between sympathy for Parliament and loyalty to the king. By admitting that sovereign power originated with the people, not the king, however, *His Majesties Answer* inadvertently invigorated those who would become his most radical critics.

The rumblings of unrest concerning royal authority had begun quietly enough. Henry Parker, a barrister who became secretary to the parliamentary army and a prolific pamphleteer, and Philip Hunton, a clergyman and later master of Durham College, both endorsed the king's argument, but they drew conclusions dramatically different from his. If the nation originated in the people's consent, and if the people then agreed to be governed by a monarch, then his legitimacy depended on their approval, which they could withdraw whenever arbitrary government overstepped the boundaries of the public good. *Salus populi suprema lex esto*, an ancient axiom equating legitimate law with the welfare of the people, began to appear in popular pamphlets endorsing Parliament and urging resistance to Charles.

In 1640 Parker had explored the logic of challenging the crown over the question of fees levied without the consent of Parliament. Only two years later, having been appointed the secretary of the parliamentary army commanded by the Earl of Essex, Parker argued that the people must rise to defend their threatened liberties. His *Observations upon some of his majesties late answers and expresses* (1642) provided the most frequently cited justification for Parliament's actions. Parker reasoned that hundreds of individuals deliberating in Parliament stood a better chance of coming to an understanding of the "common good" than did a single monarch. Thus the decisions reached by people's representatives should always take precedence over the will of any king. The representative nature of Parliament justified its speaking and acting on behalf of the people as a whole. Whereas Parker conceded that earlier rebellions typically manifested the will of an oligarchy seeking to establish itself in power, the English Parliament in its current form, "by vertue of election and representation," embodied the will of the people. Through its deliberations "the wise shall consent for the simple, the vertue of all shall redound to some, and the prudence of some shall redound to all."[24]

Parker extended his argument for the principle of popular sovereignty even further in *Jus populi*, a landmark pamphlet published in October 1644. "The truth is," Parker wrote, "both Monarchy and Aristocracy, are derivative formes, and owe a dependance upon Democracy, which though it be not the best, and most exact forme for all nations and Empires at all times, yet it is ever the most naturall, and primarily authenticall; and for some times, and places the most beneficiall." The Romans, for example, had never enjoyed a democracy, primarily because "the body of Plebeians" was nothing but "a vast, rude, confused, indigested heap of the vulgar," utterly unqualified to choose its representatives. So radically had warfare altered Parker's judgment about the appropriate roles of the king and the people of England that he characterized democracy—so long maligned as degraded and dangerous—as the most natural and authentic form of government. When proper elections, not lot, yielded a truly representative body, democracy was also the best form.[25]

Other writers went even further, although the circumlocutions and qualifications of many of the pamphlets of the early 1640s indicate how painful was the departure from the idea of the king's sovereign authority. Hunton, in his anonymous pamphlet *A Treatise of Monarchy* (1643), located the ultimate decision-making authority not in Parliament but—because neither king nor Parliament could claim absolute authority—in the conscience of individual citizens. Against the logic of divine right Hunton counterposed the argument that God remains indifferent to the forms of government chosen by his creatures. Such forms vary according to time and place, and it remains the prerogative and the responsibility of those who inherit particular traditions to judge their continued suitability.[26]

Although explicit endorsements of popular sovereignty remained scattered in the years immediately following the outbreak of war in 1642, arguments such as Hunton's and Parker's represented a direct challenge to monarchy. Promising as such attempts might have seemed in the abstract, they became increasingly unappealing as the war took its bloody course. Royalists shrieked that supporters of Parliament were leading the gullible people of England toward lawlessness and even regicide. Parliamentarians protested just as loudly that they intended no such abomination. Hunton insisted that "force ought not to be used against the person of the sovereign on any pretence whatever, by any or all of his subjects, even in limited and mixed monarchies" such as England.[27] In the early days of the war, reining in the monarch did not mean killing him.

The king hardly lacked loyal subjects willing to defend his authority with arguments as well as arms. Michael Hudson, a royal chaplain who became a soldier in the king's army, spoke for many Englishmen. His book *The Divine Right of Government* proclaimed absolute monarchy the only legitimate form. All others, which he lumped together as "*Polarchy*," or government by more than a single person, he characterized as the work of "that old grand Rebel," the "author of all mischief," the devil himself. The ground, however, was shifting. A year before Charles I met a similar fate, his champion and chaplain Hudson was put to death by soldiers of Parliament's army.[28]

Royalists were not the only ones fretting about the devil and his works. An anonymous pamphlet entitled *Regall Tyrannie discovered* charged that anyone claiming God's authority for himself stands in a direct line of descent from Satan.[29] Richard Overton and John Lilburne, among the most important Leveller agitators, were uneasy about the dominance of Presbyterians in Parliament in the early stages of the Civil War. Lilburne, after returning from exile in Holland, where like many other Puritans he had sought refuge because of his nonconformist views, joined the Parliamentary army. He resigned rather than accept the covenant imposed by Presbyterians, however, and in 1645 he was arrested by the House of Commons. Levellers such as Lilburne and Overton clamored for more dramatic changes, including a degree of religious toleration, than did Parker and Hunton. Their writings about popular sovereignty inspired a flurry of political pamphlets and wide-ranging debates advancing the principles of democracy.[30]

The year of Lilburne's first imprisonment, 1645, marked the beginning of his fertile association with Overton and William Walwyn. Like Lilburne (but unlike Overton), Walwyn lacked a university education, yet his pamphlets showed familiarity with writers ranging from Seneca to Montaigne. In pamphlets that appeared in June and July of 1646, Lilburne sketched out the ideas that would be central to the Levellers' view. *The Free-Mans Freedome Vindicated* established his radical premise: in the beginning, not only Adam and Eve, "the earthly, original fountain," but all men and women "were by nature all equall and alike in power, digni[t]y, authority, and majesty." Positions of authority emerged only after they came to "mutuall agreement or consent."[31]

These arguments coalesced in the most important and widely read of the Levellers' early pamphlets, *A Remonstrance of Many Thousand Citizens* (1646). There Overton, Walwyn, and Henry Marten challenged the legitimacy not only of Charles but also of kingship, not only of the Lords but also of Parliament, and not only the hierarchical excesses of Laud's Anglicanism but also the intolerance of Presbyterianism and the tyranny of an established church. They demanded that Lilburne, "that Famous and Worthy Sufferer for his Countrys Freedoms," be released from his "Illegal and Barborous Imprisonment." They chastised Parliamentarians for claiming economic and legal privileges as indefensible as those of the most corrupt lords who preceded them in power. By assuming "a Power to controule and force Religion, or a way to *Church Government*, upon the People," the Presbyterians controlling Parliament aimed to enslave the English people. In place of the corrupt monarchy descended from William's conquest, the authors of the *Remonstrance* proposed government by annual Parliaments, with members elected by residents of the boroughs they were to represent. Thus authority would spring from consent, its only legitimate source: "*the choice of the People, from whom the power that is just must be derived.*"[32]

In the months that followed, as Lilburne continued to write from behind bars, the Levellers broadened their attack. Overton proclaimed "all men are equally and alike borne to like propriety, liberty and freedom." Equal liberty, not hierarchy, is natural to humans. In other pamphlets Lilburne tied his imprisonment to the tyranny borne by his fellow Englishmen and called for universal manhood suffrage as the solution. Legitimate lawmaking authority, Lilburne argued, "*is originally inherent in the people, and derivatively in their Commissions chosen by themselves by common consent, and no other.*" In a phrase that was to echo for years, Lilburne declared that "the poorest that lives, hath so true a right to give a vote, as well as the richest and greatest."[33]

The Levellers bolstered their arguments with quotations from classical sources, but they were not seeking to reproduce an ancient model or merely to trade Anglican for Presbyterian hierarchy.[34] Instead they wanted a democracy, based on the consent of the governed, with unprecedented access to the vote and the freedom of conscience, just the features enshrined in the settlements that became Rhode Island. In Lilburne's words, "*the people in generall are the originall sole legislaters, and the true fountain, and earthly well-spring of all just power.*" The power of the House of Commons, by contrast, "*is merely derivative and bounded within this tacit Commission, to act only for the good of those that betrusted them.*"[35] Suspicious of their Presbyterian foes in the House of Lords and of many officers in Parliament's armies, the Levellers took their case directly to the Commons. They submitted a petition calling for a code of laws, written in plain English, and the end of mandatory tithes, the House of Lords, and the monarchy itself. The representatives of the people in the House of Commons were to be the supreme authority. They had badly miscalculated: the Commons responded to their invitation by jailing some of the petitioners and burning the petition itself.

If the Levellers had overestimated their persuasiveness, the Presbyterians who dominated Parliament then made an equally serious error of their own. Worried about grumbling in the army but disinclined to grant the soldiers' plea for guarantees of their back pay and future indemnity against impressment, Parliament threatened that any soldiers who persisted in pressing their case would be deemed enemies of the state. The army was to be disbanded; volunteers were to be sent to enforce peace in Ireland. Leveller agitators, seeing that such a direct challenge to its army undercut Parliament's standing, seized the opening. Overton put the point bluntly: having done the hard and dangerous work, the army deserved the nation's gratitude—and just compensation—rather than Parliament's threats. The time had come to resist the "false, traiterous, and deceitfull men" in Parliament who sought "to inthrall & inslave us." The army, having found to save England from Charles, now had to rescue the nation from Parliament, which was threatening to "raise up an Army of wicked men" to combat the authentic army of the people.[36]

The allegiance of at least part of the military was now shifting from the Presbyterians and toward the Levellers. Soldiers warned of a plot hatched by MPs who, having tasted power, now sought to become "tyrants."[37] Lilburne intensified such fears by charging that a conspiracy of "lawless, unlimited, and unbounded men" in Parliament kept him in prison and England in chains. Only the army could save the nation.[38] Ordered by an increasingly anxious Parliament to disband, the army refused. Throughout the summer of 1647 ever more fiery pamphlets and petitions circulated. Ideas that just a year before had attracted only the most radical of the London Levellers now generated enthusiasm among common soldiers, who began demanding not only their pay and support of widows and orphans but political reform as well. When some officers, sensing mutiny, gave grudging assent to their petitions, a conflict between the army and Parliament seemed imminent.

At that moment Oliver Cromwell, the yeoman MP from Cambridge who had risen swiftly to command one of Parliament's armies, drew back from supporting the Leveller-inspired program now embraced by increasingly prominent elements of the army. With army agitators clamoring for a march on London, Cromwell counseled restraint, and his words would resound as loudly as any of Lilburne's, both in the debates of the next few months and in the developments of the next two centuries. "Itt is the generall good," Cromwell advised, of "all the people in the Kingdome" that should determine England's course. "That's the question, what's for their good, nott what pleases them."[39] The notion that a shadow falls between the immediate wishes of the people and their deeper, more lasting interest, the intuition that the general good can be discerned more clearly by some individuals than by the people themselves, prevented Cromwell from taking his soldiers' demands as seriously as he took his own judgment of the nation's needs.

Overton disagreed. In *An Appeale*, a pamphlet printed on July 17, 1647, Overton consolidated arguments circulating among the Levellers for months.[40] In a culture marked by widespread literacy, and in which censorship could be evaded, such pamphlets became increasingly influential means of circulating ideas that previously had appeared in learned treatises accessible only to readers of Greek or Latin. Overton was writing from jail. Almost a year earlier, on the night of August 11, 1646, the Lords had sent an armed guard to Overton's house, without a warrant, and took him from his bed at pistol-point. Overton refused to remove his hat before the Lords or to answer the charges leveled against him, demanding instead to appear before his peers in the House of Commons. His behavior infuriated Parliament as much as Lilburne's did, and for the same reasons: he denied Parliament's authority to constrain his opinions. Overton was, in his words, "incivilly and inhumanely dragged" to Newgate prison, severely beaten, jailed with "Rogues and Fellons, and laid in double Irons." His house was ransacked, his wife and his brother imprisoned without cause, and his three helpless young children left "exposed to the mercy of the wide world."[41]

Overton was not powerless: his widely read *Appeale* helped widen the gulf opening between the more radical elements among the common soldiers and their more cautious officers. Overton grounded his argument in "*right Reason,*" which cannot be inconsistent with the law because it aligns with God's will. The principle of self-defense against tyranny, which initially justified Parliament's war against Charles, now justified Overton's appeal to the army. When the people's representatives in Parliament betrayed their trust, its authority reverted to its point of origin, "the *people*" whom Parliament had abandoned, whose authority alone "indureth for ever." Overton was appealing over the heads of Parliament to the "*Sovereign power*" of popular consent.[42] He argued that the principle of popular sovereignty depends on an ethic of reciprocity.

Challenging the king was merely an attempt to recover "our naturall human rights and freedomes" so that all Englishmen might do "*unto all men as we would be done unto.*" Failing to abide by the Golden Rule—as did those who insisted on the prerogatives of King and Lords to rule as they saw fit—was to reject God's will and natural law. Anyone violating the ethic of mutuality was "an *enemy to mankinde*" and "guilty of the highest kinde of Treason," treason against God himself.[43] Overton appealed to the ideal of reciprocity: the army's assistance to Parliament, and Parliament's service to the people, were "*dependent*" on each other.[44]

Overton appended to his *Appeale* a list of specific reforms, which indicate the necessary connection he saw between political democracy and the autonomy of all individuals. No titled lords or clerics should have automatic places in Parliament; all should hold seats only as a result of the "free choice and Election of the People." The law, too, should reflect the principle of equality rather than distinguishing between rich and poor. All congregations should voluntarily sustain their ministers instead of relying on compulsory tithes for a state church. The state should provide free schools and maintain public hospitals to care for the sick, the elderly, widows, and orphans. Finally, Overton resurrected a century-old protest: enclosed fields should be "laid open againe to the free and common use and benefit of the poore."[45] Such reforms would upset prevailing hierarchies and alter the distribution of wealth and power in England. "It must be the poore, the simple and meane things of this earth," Overton concluded, who "must confound the mighty and the strong."[46] Unless economic conditions improved and ordinary people had the chance to develop their God-given capacities, they would be indistinguishable from brutish beasts. By reducing the English people to an animal-like state, elites had created forms of degradation that served to justify their own monopoly on wealth and power. Overton believed, as did the other Leveller leaders, that the English people shared their commitment to popular sovereignty, autonomy, equality, and the ethic of reciprocity. For that reason they were confident that such ideas could be incorporated into a new kind of government by the consent of, and in the interest of, the people.[47]

The problem facing the imprisoned Leveller leaders was the problem facing any reformers intent on creating democracy where another form of government exists. Democracy can flourish only when its institutions and its ethos have the support of an overwhelming majority of the people. Until it is firmly in place, however, popular government often appears to threaten everything ordinary people cherish. In England reverence for the king, traditional deference to the clergy and to the gentry who maintained a hierarchical social order, and ingrained habits of respect for the centuries-old laws and customs all militated against support by more than a small minority for the Levellers' democratic ideas.[48]

As Parliament was cracking down on Lilburne and Overton in 1647, the divisions in the army between Presbyterians and Independents widened. Originally the Presbyterians enjoyed a decisive advantage because it was their alliance with the Scottish forces invading England that had enabled Parliament to wage war against the king. After the struggle had continued indecisively for three years, however, Parliament unified its three more or less separate armies in what was dubbed the New Model Army. Under the command of Thomas Fairfax, a religious and political moderate thought capable of unifying the fractious parliamentary forces, the New Model Army besieged the king's headquarters in Oxford in the spring of 1645. Multiple engagements culminated in the parliamentarians' victory at Naseby on June 14, after which royalist forces lost a series of costly battles until finally surrendering the formidable castle of Bristol in September, which brought to a close the first stage of the Civil War.

The triumph of parliamentary armies, however, did not bring peace, in part because of persistent quarrels within Parliament itself. Independents such as Cromwell and his son-in-law Henry Ireton, two of the cavalry officers responsible for the parliamentarians' success at Naseby, inspired other opponents of Presbyterianism to assert themselves. Independents in the New Model had much more in common with the Levellers than did the more hierarchically inclined Presbyterians, and the growing animosities within the parliamentary ranks deepened when Charles escaped from Oxford in May of 1646 and sought to ally with the Scottish army against Parliament.

Developments in the spring of 1647 cemented the bonds between Independents and Levellers. In April of that year each regiment of the New Model elected two delegates (called "agitators") to speak for the common soldiers, a step that signaled the emergence of a more democratic sensibility among at least some members of the army. In May similar organizing among the officers of several regiments prompted the resignations of some of those harboring more conservative religious or political convictions. Those promoted to fill the resulting vacancies gave the officer corps of the New Model a distinctly more popular quality than was typical of the English military. Originally the grievances of the army centered on issues of pay and benefits, but the process of organizing and debating proposals to advance their claims had an unexpected effect.

By the summer and fall of 1647, the army was debating issues of far broader significance. *The Heads of the Proposals* was written by a committee consisting of a dozen officers and a dozen of the soldiers' elected agitators. Many of the Levellers' democratic ideas surfaced in this document, perhaps because some of the officers, notably Colonel Thomas Rainsborough, son of a vice admiral and himself a member of Parliament, shared the ordinary soldiers' sympathy with Lilburne and Overton. *Proposals* called for biennial Parliaments, with seats redistributed according to population and chosen by free elections, the end of religious tests, tithes, and ecclesiastical courts, and most of the other judicial and economic reforms the Levellers had championed in their tracts. Notably the king's will, though constrained, remained the source of all governmental authority, and the House of Lords was not called into question. Those significant limitations indicated the very real differences separating the democratic radicalism of the Levellers from the more moderate approach of Cromwell, Ireton, and other Independents in the army. Other conflicts between the Levellers and the most powerful forces in the army, which came into focus during the next two years, proved decisive for the fate of popular government in England.[49]

In late October of 1647, as Cromwell was reconsidering an alliance with Charles, the Levellers consolidated their central arguments in the first *Agreement of the People*. They envisioned an England in which the sovereignty of the people would be manifested in a Parliament elected by manhood suffrage and constrained neither by king nor lords but only by the fundamental rights laid out in the *Agreement*, such as freedom of conscience, freedom from conscription, and equal protection—with no unequal privileges—before the law. Not only did the Levellers hope to convince senior officers, including Cromwell and Ireton; they intended to submit the *Agreement* to the people of England. Popular approval would provide the basis for a new constitution founded on the premise that all political power originates in a compact of "the people" themselves, whose "safety and well being" should be the sole objective of all laws.[50] Though this remarkable document has long been acknowledged as a landmark in Anglo-American political thought, the compacts of most New England communities founded in the preceding twenty-seven years already incorporated most of its principles. Those documents became law. In England, the *Agreement* remained a proposal for debate.

And debated it was. As the army, positioned on the outskirts of London in 1647, weighed its options, the abstract principles of democracy came vividly to life. Soldiers and officers deliberated over the *Agreement* in the village church of Putney. Thanks to the efforts of William Clarke, assistant secretary to the Army Council, a detailed record of their debates survived. Like the deliberations in early New England towns that yielded constitutions and charters, the Putney debates provide striking testimony of contemporary attitudes toward popular government. Many were appalled by the Levellers' straightforward challenge to monarchy and aristocracy. Cromwell, for example, opposed the *Agreement* because it called for "very great alterations of the very Government of the Kingedome."[51] Cromwell endorsed the principle of popular sovereignty: "The foundation and supremacy is in the people, radically in them." Acknowledging the principle was one thing, putting it in practice quite another.[52] Cromwell and Ireton, along with most of the senior officers and perhaps most of the soldiers as well, thought that no matter how deeply Englishmen loathed Charles, they were not prepared to do without a king.

On October 28 and 29, Levellers led by John Wildman, who appears to have been the principal author of both *The Case of the Army Truly Stated* and *An Agreement of the People*, were joined by several sympathizers among the officers, notably Colonel Rainsborough. Rainsborough understood how wide was the gulf between England's past and the future sketched in the *Agreement*, yet he faced it without misgivings: "When I leape I shall take soe much of God with mee, and so much of just and right with mee, as I shall jumpe sure."[53] With words that have been quoted ever since, Rainsborough stated with simple eloquence the logic of the Levellers' case for government by consent: "for really I think that the poorest he that is in England has a life to live as the greatest he." Because every individual ought to be autonomous, and government originates in the consent of all the people, everyone to be bound by the law should have an equal right to participate by voting. In Rainsborough's words, "I do think that the poorest man in England is not at all bound in a strict sense to that government that he has not had a voice to put himself under."[54]

The principal issues sparking disagreement at Putney were the army's covenant with Parliament, which Ireton contended it could not break, and the call of the *Agreement* for universal manhood suffrage, which Ireton predicted would lead to the abolition of private property and, ultimately, to anarchy. If every man enjoys a God-given, natural right to vote, Ireton argued, then likewise he will have an equal right "in any goods he sees: meat, drink, clothes, to take them and use them for his sustenance; he has a freedom to the land, the ground, to exercise it, till it."[55] Universal manhood suffrage, premised on equal natural rights, would end in chaos. Political rights are limited because they originate in history, Ireton insisted, not divine law. Cromwell agreed. No one accused the Levellers of intending the outcome foreseen by Ireton: "No man says you have a mind to anarchy," Cromwell acknowledged, "but the consequence of this rule tends to anarchy, must end in anarchy."[56] Colonel Nathaniel Rich estimated that since there were five propertyless Englishmen for every man who owned the forty-shilling freehold prerequisite to voting, universal manhood suffrage would lead to disaster by one of two routes. Either the electorate would choose representatives who would enact laws to establish "an equality of goods," or they would sell their votes, as he claimed the poor did in ancient Rome. In either case, by ending monarchy England would usher in the greater tyranny of military dictatorship.[57]

Wildman and Rainsborough addressed these objections as the debates progressed. No one can be held to an unjust covenant, Rainsborough reasoned, any more than a man can be justly forced to enslave himself. Nor is the fact of property its own justification. The privileges of the aristocracy, the excesses of property and poverty, may be protected by law, but members of the army would not know what they had fought for if property rights endured without challenge. No longer should the people of England "be bound by laws in which they have no voice at all."[58] Abandoned by Parliament, the people had to look to the army.

Wildman summarized the Levellers' case without the invective preferred by Lilburne and Overton. Invoking precedent was useless, Wildman began, because English laws had been made by their conquerors ever since the Norman invasion. It was time for the people to seek justice constrained neither by tradition nor fear. Wildman declared that "every person in England has as clear a right to elect his representative as the greatest person in England." That is "the undeniable maxim of government: that all government is in the free consent of the people." From Wildman's perspective, as from Rainsborough's, the Putney deliberations led irresistibly to a single question: "whether any person can justly be bound by law not by his own consent."[59] Looking back on the Putney debates during a lull in the Civil War several months later, Wildman judged the principle of popular sovereignty the central issue. The only authority with "an image of justice upon it" is that "derived from the People, either immediately by their personal consent, or agreement, or mediately by the mutuall consent of those, who are elected by the People to represent them."[60]

The Levellers' arguments at Putney proved less persuasive to their contemporaries than did their opponents' apocalyptic warnings. The enduring popular image of the Levellers emerged first in the widely read *Gangraena*, by the Presbyterian minister Thomas Edwards. The "gangrene" of the title were those who, "in divers Pamphletes and some sermons, have declared against Monarchie and Aristocracie, and for Democracy." They would make untutored people "the Creator and Destroyer of Kings, Parliaments and all Magistrates at there mere pleasure, without tying them to any rule, or bounding them by any lawes." According to Edwards, the goal of such democrats was "noe other than Anarchie."[61] The charge made in *Gangraena* was incoherent, as the Levellers never tired of pointing out. They challenged the privileges of the aristocracy so that more people could enjoy, along with their more prosperous neighbors, legal protection for the property they would be able to possess. The Levellers themselves hailed from the lower levels or the fringes of the English elite: roughly half were the sons of lesser gentry. Most were artisans, tradesmen, teachers, soldiers, or small businessmen who wanted to accumulate property, not abolish it.

Some among the few proponents of truly radical economic change in the seventeenth century, known as the Diggers, perceived the limits of the Levellers' ideas. Gerrard Winstanley, who later attracted the admiration of communists for his and his fellow Diggers' genuine commitment to communal property, understood that the Levellers sought only to alter the distribution of property. "A thing called *An Agreement of the People*," Winstanley observed derisively, "is too low and too shallow to free us at all: for it doth not throw down all the *Arbitrary Courts, Powers, and Patents*, as aforesaid: And what stock or way is provided for the *poor, fatherless, widows, and impoverished people*?"[62]

The Putney debates illuminated the attitudes of Levellers and Independents alike, but they proved inconclusive. Rainsborough proposed an extended meeting to continue the debate. The Levellers believed consensus would eventually emerge from deliberation and compromise and feared that a premature vote would harden positions and generate permanent factions. The chosen alternative, naming a committee to resolve the disagreements, proved equally unproductive. The General Council of the Army later agreed to extend the franchise to all native-born Englishmen except "servants or beggars," a standard lying somewhere between universal manhood suffrage and the forty-shilling freehold that remained vague.[63] Although calls for universal manhood suffrage faded soon after the Putney debates, the charges of anarchy stuck. A *Declaration by Congregationall Societies* accused the Levellers, in defiance of the Bible, of wanting not only communal property but also polygamy.[64] Thus the Levellers found themselves attacked from two directions. The more cautious of their contemporaries dismissed them as hopeless utopians blind to the harsh realities of power and to the legitimate concerns of property holders. Those even more radical maligned them as spineless moderates too timid to tackle the injustice of the institution of property itself.[65]

Events moved quickly after the Putney debates, and in the end they conspired to defeat the Levellers' hopes of bringing the *Agreement* to the people. At the first of the public meetings called to discuss the *Agreement*, a gathering at which Rainsborough and perhaps (on the fringes) a just-released Lilburne were present, Lilburne's regiment dismissed all but one of their officers and appeared on Corkbush Field on November 15, 1647, with copies of the *Agreement* fluttering from their hats. Their incipient revolt was put down decisively by

Cromwell. Three insurgents were court-martialed for insurrection, one was shot on the spot, and the soldiers' interest in the *Agreement* ended abruptly.[66]

Charles, returned by the Scots to England in the hope that a new Presbyterian form of church governance might be secured, now maneuvered against Parliament and tried to reestablish his authority among his discontented subjects. Cromwell renounced his earlier conciliatory stance toward the king and began mouthing the challenges to monarchy that he had previously dismissed. When he and Ireton sought to make peace with the Leveller sympathizers in the army whom they had opposed at Putney, it was the Levellers' turn to be suspicious. With Presbyterians in Parliament turning to the king, and royalism evidently resurgent among the populace, Cromwell and Ireton tried to rally the army only to find the Levellers now impugning their motives and warning the soldiers that the danger of military rule rivaled that of the Presbyterian majority in Parliament.

At this crucial moment, Lilburne and Wildman produced new arguments calculated to convince the army and the people to resist all the available options: Cromwell, Charles, and Parliament. Accused of treason, Lilburne was given a chance to address the Commons. He conceded that most Englishmen did not share his hatred of the king. Most preferred monarchy to popular government. Even so, Lilburne argued, it was necessary for reformers to come to the aid of the people. So dire was the condition of ordinary Englishmen that they could see neither the reason why they suffered nor any alternative. They required help, just as a righteous man would rescue a neighbor, even if against his will, from a burning house. The "great end wherefore God sent man into the world was, that he should do good in his generation, and thereby glorifie God." To that end, it was necessary to follow God's will, not man's.[67] Like Cromwell, Lilburne came to believe he could see the people's interest more clearly than could the people themselves. Unlike Cromwell, he lacked a political strategy to attract the most powerful forces in England to his side—or an army to enforce his will. Together with Wildman, Lilburne was again committed to the Tower of London.

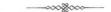

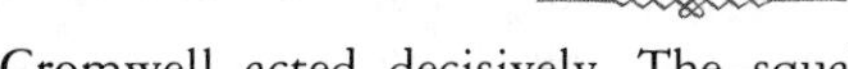

Now Cromwell acted decisively. The squabbles between the army and Parliament had emboldened Charles. Inciting his English followers to join with Scots who felt betrayed by what they saw as the army's obstruction of Presbyterianism's progress, he incited a Second Civil War. Cromwell rallied the New Model against the king and his Scottish allies, put down the last rumblings of dissent among his troops, and by the end of the summer of 1648 had triumphed over all his enemies. The Presbyterians in the Commons, fearful that Cromwell would overwhelm them, freed Lilburne in the hope that he might help them by turning his ire against Cromwell. To their dismay,

Cromwell's former adversaries in the army joined forces with him. Levellers and Independents prepared to ally behind a second *Agreement of the People*, a proposal much like the first version debated at Putney. Even though Ireton gave speeches indicating his greater willingness to entertain an end to monarchy and a broader suffrage than previously, his conversion struck many Levellers as more strategic than genuine. The amity between Levellers and Independents proved paper-thin; by the end of the fall it had been ripped apart.

The army had lost patience. After army units commanded by Colonel Thomas Pride purged the Presbyterians from Parliament on December 6, 1648, the army prepared to bring the king to trial immediately. The Levellers resisted this headlong rush to justice because they feared that ending the king's reign before establishing the terms of the new government would leave Cromwell too much latitude. When the Levellers insisted that a constitution, based on a revised form of the *Agreement of the People*, be debated and submitted to the people, Ireton advanced another version of the *reductio ad absurdum* he had employed at Putney. This time the issue was not popular sovereignty, which both Cromwell and Ireton were now prepared to embrace, but autonomy of the sort they considered most threatening. Both the first and second versions of the *Agreement* guaranteed freedom of conscience. Two weeks after Pride's purge had shifted the fulcrum of power in the Rump that remained in Parliament, Ireton addressed the question of religious toleration. If civil authorities lacked the power to regulate religion, then people would be free "to practice idolatry, to practice atheisme, and any thinge that is against the light of God."[68]

On the issue of state regulation of religion, though, the Levellers refused to compromise. They shared the conviction of Roger Williams: government could not be permitted to intervene on questions of conscience—at least among Protestant Christians. Even though Cromwell and Ireton were at pains to distinguish themselves from Presbyterians, and assured dissenting Protestant sects that their target was popery, the Levellers had built their entire constitutional theory on the foundation of free consent by autonomous and equal individuals, a premise derived from the model of voluntary assemblies of the faithful. In the words of the first *Agreement*, "We cannot remit or exceed a tittle of what our Consciences dictate to be the mind of God, without willfull sinne."[69]

The Levellers had not opposed Marian Catholicism, then the Anglican Archbishop Laud, then a Presbyterian settlement, only to embrace another version—any version—of a state church exercising the power to compel or exclude. The Christian law of love, Overton argued, should imply a policy of religious toleration: "The business is, not how great a sinner I am, but how faithfull and reall to the Common-wealth; that's the matter concerneth my neighbour," and all the state could properly police. As Overton echoed Williams on the implications of Christianity, so Walwyn echoed his mentor Montaigne. All of them agreed that the realm of politics should be considered independent from that of faith. In both spheres individuals should be able to choose freely the terms of the covenants by which they would be bound.[70]

After weeks of sustained and spirited debates stretching from mid-December to mid-January of 1649, the army finally agreed to present a revised version of the second *Agreement of the People* for consideration by the Rump. Several features distinguished this version from its predecessors. First, the officers now opposed presenting the *Agreement* to the Commons and insisted it go directly to the people. The officers' *Agreement* provided for the dissolution of the Commons so that new elections could be held. Many critics doubted that members of Parliament would agree to remove themselves from power. Perhaps for just that reason, the Rump never formally debated the officers' *Agreement*. The monarchy and the House of Lords were to be abolished and household suffrage established (again, with only paupers and servants excluded because their dependency rendered them incapable of autonomous judgment). There was to be no compulsion of religious belief among those professing "Faith in God by Jesus Christ," although that liberty did not "extend to Popery or Prelacy." This officers' *Agreement* stipulated that nothing was to be done to "levell mens Estates, destroy Propriety [property], or make all things common."[71]

In early 1649 printing presses released a torrent of pamphlets on all sides of all these issues. When the Levellers published critiques of the features of the officers' *Agreement* they disliked, they elicited the fury of assorted Anglicans, Presbyterians, royalists, and wealthier merchants and businessmen who accused them of secret alliances with everyone from Winstanley to the pope. The furor surrounding the Levellers subsided as attention shifted from their ideas to something much more radical: regicide. Charles had vowed that he would never renounce his claim to rule or accept parliamentary supremacy. Even from his isolation as a prisoner on the Isle of Wight, it was evident that Charles would continue to serve as a rallying point for disgruntled monarchists and that he would attempt to raise an army against Parliament. Despite protests from the Lords and to the astonishment of many of his subjects, Charles was put on trial by the Rump, found guilty of treason, and executed.[72]

As soon as Charles's headless body was carried from the scaffold, he was transformed from tyrant to martyr, his killers from patriots to traitors, and popular government from an idea under discussion to an instrument of murder. Sovereign power passed to the Rump, with its will presumably to be enforced by Cromwell and the army. When England was declared a republic eight days after the king was put to death, its birth through the shock of regicide identified the new regime with a horrible crime rather than a noble cause. To anxious royalists, Presbyterians, and Levellers alike, this arrangement seemed likelier to end in a new tyranny than to relieve England of arbitrary government.

The tide turned against the king when his critics charged him with placing his "personal interest" ahead of the "public good." The rationale for monarchy depended on the crown's ability to keep its distance from any particular faction. When the king himself was accused, from the summer of 1647 until his death, of turning his back on his people and maneuvering on behalf of his own "private interests," he metamorphosed in his critics' eyes from guardian of the common good to enemy of the people.[73] The prosecuting attorney at the king's trial, John Cook, later explained the rationale that had prompted so extreme a step. Monarchy, Cook insisted, had become its own faction, a threat to God's will. Because kings everywhere were secretly in league with the pope, Charles's death was necessary to end tyranny and "exalt Christ as Lord and King over mens Consciences, to magnifie and make the Law of God honourable and authentick every where and to give Justice and Mercy the upper hand."[74] That rationale, although consistent with the Levellers' and the officers' arguments against Charles, failed to convince many who remained unsure that dissenters from Anglicanism had as firm a grasp of God's will as they claimed.

A book purported to be Charles's final testament, *Eikon Basilike*, or *The Image of the King*, circulated widely. Thirty-five editions of the book were published, and over time it grew to include excerpts supposedly taken from Charles's speeches, prayers, and letters. *Eikon Basilike*, playing to the royalist sympathies of the gentry and many ordinary people, generated widespread sympathy for the dead king and intense hatred of those who killed him in the people's name. Monarchy never looked better than it did after Charles's death. Regicide could now be characterized as the inevitable fruit of democracy, and as Cromwell moved to consolidate his power, earlier predictions that republican rule always ends in tyranny began to seem warranted.

In pamphlets such as *The Hunting of the Foxes* and *The Second Part of Englands Newe Chaines*, Levellers charged that Cromwell and the Independents in the Rump had cynically maneuvered with, and then against, the king, the Lords, the Commons, and the army to achieve power for themselves. For people skeptical of parties and worried that something as apparently innocuous as a straw vote might cement animosities and prevent reconciliation, regicide constituted a disaster without equal. In reply to such criticism, the Rump had Lilburne, Overton, Walwyn, and their treasurer, Thomas Prince, sent to prison. A petition calling for their release, with ten thousand signatures, sparked a mutiny in some army units. One executed dissident's funeral inspired a wider revolt, which had attracted twelve hundred men by the time Cromwell's army surprised the insurgents, shot their leader, and finally halted the Levellers' organized resistance.[75]

The third and final *Agreement of the People*, which appeared just as that army revolt broke out, shows how Leveller ideas had crystallized during war and revolution. It also shows why they failed. Absent a monarch, the third *Agreement* placed even greater emphasis than the Levellers' earlier pamphlets and petitions on the mechanics of popular election. The "Supreme Authority of *England*" was to reside no longer in a king but in "a Representative of the people consisting of four hundred persons, but no more," to be elected annually by all men twenty-one and older "not being servants, or receiving alms." The new Parliament was to convene one day after the current Parliament disbanded; if Parliament refused to organize new elections, the people themselves were to do so. There was likewise to be strict separation of powers from the judiciary, with Parliament prohibited from convening any council of state or any courts of its own devising, excluding any citizen from public service because of his religious beliefs, or conscripting any citizen for army service against his conscience. All privileges or exemptions of any persons from the law were to end, as was the reliance on unwritten laws to punish individuals—such as, although they did not point it out, the laws enforced against the Levellers themselves: "Where there is no Law, there is no transgression." The economic reforms of the Levellers' early pamphlets returned to prominence in the third *Agreement*. It called for the end of excise or customs taxes to raise revenues and permitted no restrictions on trade or exemptions from property taxes. Parliament was instructed to "have speciall care to preserve, all sorts of people from wickedness misery and beggary," but again the goal was to expand rather than end property ownership. Parliament was specifically denied power to "level mens Estates, destroy Propriety, or make all things Common."

Central to the third *Agreement* was a call for democratic procedures. Suspicions about the tendency of power to corrupt individuals overshadowed any lingering concerns about the value of experience in government: there was to be strict rotation of office, with no member allowed to sit in two successive Parliaments. Officers were to be selected by vote, not lot. All ministers were to be chosen and supported on a voluntary basis by their parishes rather than appointed by the state and paid from compulsory tithes. As this shift from the customary practices of the Church of England to those of dissenting congregations makes clear, the Levellers remained, from first to last, committed to the principles animating the sects that founded communities in New England.

The similarity between this third *Agreement* and the compacts that established many New England towns was no accident. As in New England, the preference for local elections extended from the religious to the public sector. Whereas previously magistrates had been appointed, no longer was any authority to be empowered "to impose any publike officer upon any Counties, Hundreds, Cities, Towns, or Boroughs." Instead "the people" themselves should choose "all their publike Officers" for "one whole year, and no longer." As in New England, deliberations in the community were expected to yield consensus about who was best qualified to serve in positions of authority. The emphasis on consent translated into a preference for elections over random selection of officers.

Finally, since recent developments had shown that the military posed the greatest threat to stability, the third *Agreement* stipulated that "each particular County, City, Town, and Borrugh" be responsible for "raising, furnishing, and paying" its "due proportion" of the army and have "Free liberty, to nominate and appoint all Officers appertaining to Regiments, Troops, and Companies." Only the senior officers were to be appointed by Parliament; they were to be in charge of an army of citizen soldiers commanded by officers chosen by voters at the local level. The panoramic vision of popular control in the third *Agreement*, extending from politics to the law, from religion to the army, seems breathtaking until we realize that precisely such democratic forms of life were already functioning—with all the controversies, complications, and dissatisfactions inevitable in any democracy—in towns across the Atlantic, just as the Leveller leaders imagined they might do in England.[76]

The Levellers' third *Agreement* has been said to show their naïveté, their failure to grasp the realities of social life and political power. It does show that the world they envisioned would have required an ethical as well as an institutional transformation. Such a change would have required individuals to submit their individual wills to the collective will of the democratically constituted community. One of the most penetrating statements of the difference appeared in a pamphlet written by Walwyn, and signed by all four Leveller leaders, while they were imprisoned in the Tower of London in the spring of 1649. This *Manifestation* lays out, more clearly than the Levellers' other writings, the philosophical foundation beneath their democratic commitments.

"No man is born for himself only," Walwyn began. Everyone is obliged by the laws of God and nature to devote himself to "the advancement of a communitive Happiness, of equall concernment to others as our selves." In response to the Leveller leaders' efforts to end the sufferings of their day, Walwyn, Lilburne, Overton, and Prince had "reaped only Reproach." Even confined in the Tower, the Levellers believed the time was ripe for change. "When so much has been done for the recovery of our Liberties, and seeing God hath so blest that which has been done," the people of England had only to seize the moment to create "a *truly happy* and *wholly Free* Nation: We think our selves bound by the greatest obligations that may be, to prevent the neglect of this opportunity."

For the history of democracy, Walwyn's defense against charges that the Levellers were agents of the king, the pope, or the Jesuits, or champions of atheism or communism, mattered less than his arguments about the relation between self-interest and the requirements of a democratic culture. Despite the label stuck on them by their enemies, Walwyn insisted again that he and his allies opposed any compulsory "Levelling" of estates or confiscation of property. Even among the early Christians, Walwyn reminded his readers, such communal property holding was voluntary, experimental, and practiced only for a short time in a few scattered places. They wanted simply that every man, not merely the wealthiest, "may with as much security as may be enjoy his own propriety."[77] It was "unconscionable," Walwyn had observed in another pamphlet, "that one should have 10,000 pounds, and another more deserving and usefull to the Common-wealth, should not be worth two pence."[78]

Walwyn had learned that any criticism of inequality elicited shrieks of outrage. He insisted, though, that the traditional privileges of monarchy and aristocracy, the unequal rewards characteristic of a hierarchical society, "distinctions of orders and dignities," had been perverted from their purpose. Such honors "were never intended for the nourishment of Ambition, or subjugation of the People but only to preserve the due respect and obedience in the People which is necessary for the better execution of the laws." The Levellers believed that such respect and obedience was now likelier if the people ruled themselves than if they were ruled from above. Charges of anarchism and utopianism were off the mark. The Levellers' goal, to make government "as near as might be to perfection," meant what we now call representative democracy, government by the people through their elected officials. "Certainly we know very well the pravity [depravity] and corruption of mans heart is such that there could be no living without" government.[79] Bad as tyranny was, anarchy would be even worse. Democracy was the solution.

The fallen nature of humanity meant that unruly passions must be restrained. The Levellers were committed to popular instead of royal sovereignty, and to the ideas of autonomy, equality, and reciprocity rather than obedience to prevailing forms of authority, yet they remained committed above all to doing God's will. They wanted the people rather than a king or an aristocracy to exercise authority, and they wanted an end to enforced religious conformity. The purpose of such steps remained the creation of a culture in which the devout would voluntarily submit to divine authority. The Levellers presented popular sovereignty, autonomy, and reciprocity as norms consistent with God's law of love as revealed in sacred scripture, not as alternatives to it. Their efforts to change prevailing political, legal, and ethical norms must be understood within the framework of their religious sensibilities. Attaining liberty was important primarily because it would enable individuals to submit freely to God's commands. Freedom authorized men neither to act as they desired nor to find fulfillment in some path other than that laid out in scripture. Levellers sought neither ancient republican nor Renaissance humanist paths to virtue, neither "possessive individualist" paths to wealth or comfort nor any other form of self-fulfillment. They prized individual conscience only because it would enable them to practice their own faith freely, not because they valued pluralism. In *The Power of Love* (1643), Walwyn had characterized diversity of beliefs not as a goal to be reached but an evil to be endured.[80]

When Lilburne was given the chance to speak at his trial later in 1649, he underscored exactly that point. His life was not his own but God's; the purpose of all government was not to free men to make their own choices but to enable them to serve their omnipotent creator. We reason properly not when we follow our own inclinations but only when our reason conforms to God's will.[81] Popular government and freedom of conscience matter only because they make possible lives devoted to Christ. Walwyn concluded his *Manifestation* by explaining that the Leveller leaders wanted to submit the third *Agreement* to the "generality of the people" of England because establishing a democratic Constitution, which the third *Agreement* was designed to be, meant persuading a traditionally royalist nation to embrace popular government: "It is essentiall to the nature of such an Agreement to take its rise from the People."[82]

Because the Levellers denied the suffrage to paupers and servants and failed even to raise the question of women's rights, they do not qualify as democrats from a twenty-first-century perspective.[83] In the context of their time, however, the Levellers were radical democrats who aimed to expand popular control in political, economic, legal, military, and religious life. They failed not because they were insufficiently democratic, as some twentieth-century commentators intoxicated by the lure of communism claimed, but because their culture was insufficiently inclined toward democracy to embrace their ideas. The Levellers never had the power to enforce their will. Beyond lacking power, the Levellers lacked the leverage they needed to persuade the English people to exchange monarchy for democracy. Their ideas could take root only in a culture of democracy like that already established in some New England towns, a culture that existed in no more than a few scattered pockets of the England they were trying to transform.

The end of the monarchy in England brought not democracy but chaos. A High Court of Justice, which many of the king's subjects deemed illegitimate, had issued Charles I a death sentence that most of the people of England considered unwarranted. Four years after the king was beheaded, Cromwell tried to bring order to the warring factions in Parliament. In 1653 he accepted an Instrument of Government that proclaimed his authority as Lord Protector without giving him the legitimacy that only a parliamentary statute or a popular mandate might have provided. The Instrument of Government, which did incorporate some features of the Levellers' earlier *Agreements*, has been characterized as one of the first written constitutions of the modern era, a claim that overlooks the colonial charters already adopted and operating across the Atlantic. Moreover, the Instrument proved flimsy and short-lived. When Cromwell invoked it to justify ruling by ordinance and levying taxes by decree, at least until a new Parliament could be elected, he found himself challenged by an even wider array of foes than those who had opposed Charles. Levellers and ex-Levellers, royalists and republicans, and disordered bands of radical religious dissenters agreed on nothing except the inadequacy of the Protectorate and the Instrument. They were all dissatisfied for different reasons. Given the hubbub of dissent, the parliamentary elections of 1654 were remarkable for replacing the representation of rotten boroughs by a more general suffrage based on a more uniform standard of property holding. Those elected to the new Parliament represented—without being able to reconcile or even contain—all the factions and the passions unleashed during the preceding decade. Given an ever more urgent need of funds to pacify rebellious Ireland and stave off a perceived Dutch threat, Cromwell believed he had no choice but to disband the Parliament that refused him. When he took the same step two years later, this time to fight the Spanish, many thought his rule was becoming as arbitrary, and as brittle, as that of the monarch who preceded him. Proposals to make Cromwell king—proposals both he and his army found unpalatable—carried an odor of desperation.[84]

If the failure to establish a stable alternative to monarchy fueled mounting frustration, it also inspired a flurry of writing about the principles of government. Some of the greatest monuments of English political thought emerged during these chaotic years, including a book written by a member of the court of the dead king's exiled wife, Thomas Hobbes, and another by one of the dead king's friends, James Harrington. Harrington presented his scheme, *The Commonwealth of Oceana* (1656), in the form of a utopia in order to escape the strictures of censorship. The essential principles of Harrington's commonwealth, mixed government and rotation in office, were coupled with an agrarian law that prohibited primogeniture and guaranteed a rough equality of economic condition among all heads of households. Harrington's goal was a society in which all men owned sufficient property to keep them from being dependent on the will of another, and in which all held an arms-bearing status he thought necessary for a strong but unthreatening republican military force. Harrington envisioned a senate composed of members of a "natural aristocracy."

This elite of the wise and the good, selected not by birth but by merit, would deliberate and draft legislation. Their proposals would then be accepted or rejected—although not debated—by an assembly chosen by the people to protect the public interest. Unlike champions of democracy such as the Levellers, who believed that the consideration of competing ideas enabled ordinary people to refine their ideas and reach clearer understandings about issues of common concern, in *Oceana* Harrington envisioned a populace that, after initially discussing the constitution of the commonwealth, renounced public debate and placed its faith in the natural aristocrats serving in the senate.

Like his contemporaries Hobbes, Marchamont Nedham, and John Milton, Harrington had little faith in the ability of ordinary people. Unlike Hobbes, he believed that a Polybian mixed government, based on a careful balancing of the virtuous few and the self-interested many, might provide the lasting stability that had eluded previous monarchies, aristocracies, and democracies. Harrington adopted a self-consciously tough-minded approach to law, which he thought could shunt the interests of self-aggrandizing individuals into channels that would release their energies without ending in chaos. Harrington's now-familiar illustration of how to secure justice encapsulates his approach. If one of two self-interested girls is designated to slice a cake into two pieces and the other permitted to choose the larger slice, the procedure achieves rough equality without relying on the benevolence of either girl. Freedom of conscience was a crucial feature of the republic Harrington envisioned. The commonwealth described in *Oceana*, like the English Commonwealth, came into being when the existing government lost popular support and a visionary leader (Olphaus Megaletor, a thinly veiled version of Cromwell) embraced Harrington's ideals. His utopian vision proved an inspiration to many readers in later generations, ranging from monarchists to democrats. After the English monarchy was restored, Harrington was arrested for conspiracy.[85]

Harrington and Hobbes envisioned different forms of government independent of particular religious beliefs, an orientation not widely shared at the time. Despite the widespread realization that religious frictions sparked the Civil War, the vast majority of English people cherished some version of Christianity. The depth of their faith was among the principal obstacles preventing the establishment of order in the wake of the revolution. The fate of the radical Puritan vision, which had plunged England into civil war, can be seen in lives of Hugh Peter, Henry Vane Jr., and John Milton, and in the connections and contrasts between England and New England.

Hugh Peter, who trained at Trinity College, Cambridge, from an early age openly opposed Archbishop Laud and Arminianism. He became linked to the Winthrop family through marriage, and in 1628 he was involved in the formation of the Massachusetts Bay Company. He emigrated to Holland in 1631; there he became pastor of a church in Delft. Two years later he moved to Rotterdam, where he served alongside the dissenting theologian William Ames. Peter left for New England in 1635 to escape the pressure Laud was exerting on all nonconforming English churches, even those in Holland. In Massachusetts Peter served the Salem congregation after Williams left for Rhode Island, was appointed an overseer of Harvard College, and helped encourage the fledgling fishing and shipbuilding industries. Supporting Winthrop's authority and opposing the perceived threats of separatism and enthusiasm, Peter helped establish the New England Way.

Henry Vane the Younger also arrived in New England from Holland, where he had gone after his own conversion to Puritanism propelled him from Oxford to Leyden. The well-born Vane, described by John Winthrop as the "son and heir to a privy counsillor in England" and "a wise and godly gentleman," immediately rose to prominence in the Bay Colony. He chafed under Winthrop's strictures and supported Anne Hutchinson in the Antinomian controversy. Although only twenty-three years of age, the highly regarded Vane was elected governor and served briefly—and unhappily—between Winthrop's terms. Claiming to find the fissures opening up in the Bay Colony deeply disturbing, he returned to England in 1637. In England Vane again ascended quickly and ignited controversy. Knighted in 1640 and elected to Parliament from Hull, he criticized the king, Strafford, and Laud. He allied with the Independents against both Anglicans and Presbyterians and actively maneuvered on behalf of religious freedom and political reform. Even though he opposed the regicide, he became an influential figure in the Council of State established when the House of Lords was abolished after Charles's death. During the Commonwealth, perhaps only Cromwell held more power than Vane. His admirers extolled his intelligence as an administrator, first of the navy and then the army; his shrewdness as a negotiator during the twists and turns of civil war; and his virtue as a steadfast critic of tyranny, first of Charles and then of Cromwell. When Vane broke with Cromwell in 1653 over the reform of parliamentary elections, Cromwell's exasperated cry "Lord deliver me from Sir Henry Vane" punctuated his dissolution of Parliament and the beginning of the Protectorate. After his volatile political career ended, Vane wrote several murky books advancing his political and religious ideas, but none exerted the influence he enjoyed as a political operative.[86]

In 1641 Peter, too, returned to England. Sent by Massachusetts as one of the agents soliciting aid for the colony, and particularly for Harvard College, he likewise decided not to go back to the Bay Colony. Within five years Peter had become a chaplain in the New Model, which attracted the service of other fervent New Englanders, including Stephen Winthrop, one of John Winthrop's sons. During the Civil War, and in the debates at Putney, Peter sided with the Independents against the Presbyterians. Unlike Vane, Peter was among those who advocated executing the king in 1647, and he stood praying on the scaffold when Charles was beheaded. It is a measure of Peter's prominence in the following years that his Whitehall lodgings had been occupied by Archbishop Laud. As sentiment in England shifted back toward monarchy, the friends of Peter and Vane urged them both to return to the safety of New England. They refused. After the restoration of Charles II in 1660, both were arrested.

From first to last, Peter's and Vane's different challenges to established authority placed them outside the mainstream of Anglican theology and monarchism. They never doubted the legitimacy of authority per se, which they considered necessary to prevent the otherwise unruly impulses of wayward individuals from leading them astray. Their defenses of the Commonwealth, like that of Milton (who wrote a sonnet in praise of Vane), showed the distance separating many critics of monarchism from unqualified confidence in popular sentiment. Puritans abandoned established authority and set up their own communities. They inaugurated, permanently in New England and later—and, as it turned out, only briefly—in England, institutions of popular governance that they justified according to a particular version of the principle of popular sovereignty. They believed that their covenant with God legitimated the authority of the laws they created because they considered those laws consistent with, indeed authorized by their conformity with, God's will. When confronted with challenges to those laws, authorities in the Commonwealth of Massachusetts and in the English Commonwealth did not hesitate to enforce discipline, as Peter did in supporting Winthrop during the Antinomian controversy and the prosecution of Anne Hutchinson, and as Vane did during his short term as governor of the Bay Colony and as a member of the Council of State.[87]

The restoration of monarchy in England in 1660 reestablished the principle of divine right and all but obliterated the legacy of self-rule in England, while in many New England towns the institutions of self-government survived intact. Although forced to operate in a different environment after the restoration, to be sure, those institutions of democratic governance and the sensibility that inspired them nevertheless persisted beneath the reach of the ambitious new forms of authority that the crown tried to impose on the colonies.

Of all English writers active during the middle decades of the seventeenth century, the poet John Milton is no doubt the best known today. Champion of free speech, freedom of conscience, and divorce by consent, critic of monarchy and empire, Milton appeals to many twenty-first-century liberals and libertarians.[88] Milton's changing ideas demonstrate the appeal to Puritans of popular sovereignty and autonomy, but they also show the importance of contextualizing such ideas. Challenging the legitimacy of civil authorities to constrain belief or expression, Milton drew on the same Calvinist covenental tradition as continental resistance theorists. Milton's earliest writings questioned episcopacy and emphasized the inviolability of conscience, which God gave man to remind him of his status as a "servant," a "subordinate" free only when he submits to God's sovereignty.[89]

In *Aeropagitica* Milton rhapsodized about the power of the published word: "For books are not absolutely dead things, but do contain a potency of life in them to be as active as that soul was whose progeny they are." Books "do preserve as in a vial the purest efficacy and extraction of that living intellect that bred them," and are thus "as lively, and as vigorously productive, as those fabulous dragon's teeth; and being sown up and down, may chance to spring up armed men." Milton defended free expression as a Puritan, not as a civil libertarian; not from respect for the nobility of man, but because the divinity of God was at stake: "He who destroys a good book kills reason itself, kills the image of God."[90] The presence of the modifier "good" is crucial; Milton had no more sympathy for papists or nonbelievers than did most other Puritans. Milton advanced an argument that later had wide appeal—our inability to know the truth makes it necessary for us to consider a wide range of views—yet he never doubted either that God's will constitutes the truth or that man must submit to it.

Milton's vociferous justification of the regicide, *The Tenure of Kings and Magistrates*, published only two weeks after Charles's execution, established his republican credentials and laid out an argument of lasting persuasive power. No one, Milton began, "can be so stupid to deny that all men naturally were borne free, being the image and resemblance of God himself." Milton's pugnacious, even contemptuous tone masked the novelty of his argument. Earlier Protestant resistance theorists had distinguished between the legitimate challenges to royal authority by those designated "inferior magistrates," on the one hand, and the always illegitimate rebellions of individuals or groups of individuals against legitimate authority—no matter how unreasonable such authority was—unless the tyrant could be shown to be a usurper. Milton denied the distinction.

Milton argued that authority begins with, and remains in the hands of, God's people. Expelled from Eden, Milton contended, men fell to "wrong and violence," so as a solution "they agreed by common league to bind each other from mutual injury, and joyntly to defend themselves against any that gave disturbance or opposition to such agreement." Standard arguments for royal absolutism held that the authority of kings comes from God, and even Protestant resistance theorists had confined protest to lower-level officials. Milton reversed the sequence and reached a revolutionary conclusion. Governments originated when people saw the need for some authority to keep the peace, choosing either a single monarch or multiple magistrates to secure justice. Whenever power became absolute, however, it became arbitrary. In that case power reverted to the people.

Milton's conclusion has echoed for centuries. "The power of Kings and Magistrates" is "only derivative, transferr'd and committed to them in trust from the People, to the Common good of them all." Claims of absolute, God-given authority "are either arrogancies, or flatteries," rejected by classical authorities from Aristotle onward, by Isaiah and other writers in the Hebrew Bible, and by ancient Christians as inconsistent with the people's ultimate authority. Milton did not shrink from the radical implications of his argument: "since the King or Magistrate holds his authoritie of the people," they may "retaine him or depose him" in order "to be govern'd as seems to them best." Seldom had the principle of popular sovereignty been stated so directly: "The right of choosing, yea of changing their own Government is by the grant of God himself in the People." They may "reassume it to themselves" or "dispose of it by any alteration, as they shall judge most conducing to the public good."

To bolster his argument for democracy, Milton drew on every source available to him. He ranged from the "very principles of nature" to invocations of authorities and examples drawn from the Old and New Testaments and from ancient, medieval, and modern European, English, and especially—since Presbyterians in Parliament were among the most severe critics of the Commonwealth—Scottish history. From Milton's perspective, amassing evidence from nature and from Greek and Roman writers, from Renaissance humanists, from the Hebrew Bible and the Christian scriptures, from English common law, and from more recent republican experiments such as that of the United Provinces involved him in no contradictions. As he put it, all of "our ancestors" understood "that if any law or custom should conflict with the law of God or nature or, in short, reason, it should not be considered a valid law." Scholars now distinguish these traditions and choose among them. Milton drew on them all.[91]

The persuasive power of Milton's arguments in *The Tenure of Kings and Magistrates* might explain why he was chosen by Parliament to provide the official reply to *Eikon Basilike*, Charles's reputed self-defense. Milton insisted, in *Eikonoklastes* (1649), that kings remain bound by the rule of law to protect the good of the people. Legitimate monarchs deserve obedience; tyrants deserve death. Not just any people, though, but only the virtuous can discern the difference between authority and tyranny and reconstitute themselves after having deposed a tyrant. Milton concluded, "The happiness of a Nation consists in true Religion, Piety, Justice, Prudence, Temperance, Fortitude, and the contempt of Avarice and Ambition." Those in whom "these vertues dwell eminently" can do without kings because they "are the architects of their own happiness."[92] God gave his people the capacity to govern themselves.

Not surprisingly, the regicide prompted royalists in Europe as in England to reassert even more emphatically the doctrine of royal absolutism. The French Huguenot scholar Salmasius (Claude de Saumaise) was commissioned to indict those who murdered Charles. Salmasius reiterated the standard line: royal power comes from God, not from the people; therefore only God—and emphatically *not* the people—can judge a king. He condemned those responsible for Charles's death as licentious sinners and traitors to the true Protestant cause. Again designated to respond, Milton replied in his *Defense of the English People* (1651). There Milton moderated a few of the arguments advanced in *The Tenure of Kings and Magistrates*, a tendency already evident in the second edition of that work, but he refused to back down.[93]

From its understated opening line—"You empty windbag of a man, Salmasius"—to its closing invocation of God's wrath against a man he likened to Judas and Satan, Milton railed in his *Defense* against the claim that Puritans mistook license for freedom.[94] Nor had they renounced the rich tradition of legitimate resistance articulated by Calvin and Luther and developed by the Scots John Knox and George Buchanan. Freedom is but the opportunity God gives man to exercise his will; it can be used legitimately only in accordance with the laws God has inscribed in man's conscience. When men join together to place themselves under the authority of law, they entrust their original freedom to a king or magistrates only as long as their trustees act in accordance with justice. Freedom without the constraint of God's law, Milton insisted *pace* Salmasius, is not freedom, but obedience to a tyrant is a likewise a rebuke to God's will. God gave power to his people to determine how they would govern themselves. "Let God himself be heard," Milton thundered. Invoking the authority of Deuteronomy 17:14, Milton proclaimed that "God has decided then that the form of a commonwealth is more perfect than that of a monarchy as human conditions go, and of greater benefit to his own people: since he himself set up this form of government." God granted the Hebrews a monarchy only later, when they asked for it, "and then not willingly."[95]

Uncompromising as Milton's defense of popular sovereignty remained, he nevertheless conceded an important point to Salmasius, as the English champion of royal absolutism Robert Filmer later observed. Milton insisted that no people would choose to enslave themselves, yet he admitted that the judgment of "the lowest rabble" was as untrustworthy as Salmasius claimed.

The category of those actually qualified to exercise the sovereignty that God had ceded to the people, it turned out, did not include the people as a whole. Only the "most sensible and skillful in affairs" should exercise authority. "As for the rest, luxury and opulence on the one hand, poverty and need on the other, generally divert them from virtue and the study of statesmanship." Like republican theorists from Aristotle and Cicero to Ireton and Harrington, Milton wanted to empower the virtuous and restrain the rest. God might have preferred a commonwealth, but when he found out what kind of creatures he was dealing with, he agreed to give them a king. Milton gave no ground to Salmasius on the principle of popular sovereignty or the people's right to judge a king. Watching many of his fellow Englishmen slip back into royalism, though, he stipulated that only the virtuous should be permitted to rule. Vice infected the wealthy in the form of gluttony and pride, the poor in the form of covetousness and sloth. In principle democracy was God's will; putting God's will into practice required some adjustments.[96]

Milton's uneasiness about "the lowest rabble" intensified as popular support for the Commonwealth waned and royalist sentiment gathered momentum, not only in England but also on the continent. The Fronde, a prolonged uprising against the French monarchy spearheaded by French aristocrats and then fueled by uprisings of urban and rural mobs with agendas of their own, collapsed in 1652. The boy who would become the most powerful of all European monarchs, Louis XIV, ascended to the throne. Royal absolutism, in practice as well as theory, appeared to be reasserting itself. In February 1660 the army commanded by General George Monck, the same army that would reinstate the former members of the Long Parliament and facilitate the accession of Charles II to the throne, arrived in London.

Writing in the midst of this bleakness, with his failing sight giving way to total blindness, Milton gave voice to his fears as well as his fury. In his mordant *The Readie and Easie Way to Establish a Free Commonwealth*, Milton credited the regicide with exciting republicans everywhere, "stirring up" even Catholic France. It seemed at first as though the English revolution might be the contagion feared by Salmasius and his patrons, but that fervor faded fast. Milton was appalled that "a firm and free Commonwealth" would collapse as "a strange degenerate corruption" prompted the people to creep back so quickly to the "thralldom of kingship." Returning to monarchy dishonored those who died for the Good Old Cause, "making vain and viler than dirt the blood of some many thousand faithfull and valiant English men."[97]

By allowing monarchy to return, England squandered the rarest of achievements, "so dearly purchased, a free Commonwealth." Popular government, Milton observed, was "held by wisest men in all ages the noblest, the manliest, the equallest, the justest government, the most agreeable to all due liberties and proportioned equalitie, both human, civil and Christian." As in his earlier writings, Milton saw no need to distinguish between endorsements of republican rule originating in the humanist, common law, and religious traditions. A commonwealth is "enjoined by our Saviour himself, to all Christians"; in republics the ethic of reciprocity militates against either kings or lords claiming privileges over ordinary people. As Christ admonished his disciples: "*He that is greatest among you, let him be as the younger; and he that is chief, as he that serveth.*"[98]

Milton's *Readie and Easie Way* offered a passionate defense of the principles of popular sovereignty, reciprocity, autonomy, and equality against the threat of a king brought back less by force than by the servility of his former subjects. "I doubt not but that all ingenuous and knowing men will easily agree with me," Milton wrote, "that a free Commonwealth without a single person or house of lords, is by far the best government, if it can be had." Taking a step that signaled the depth of his disillusionment, he proposed a measure that might enable the wise and virtuous to stave off catastrophe. Milton's solution, though, has struck many observers as a cure worse than the ill.[99] Reasoning that the English people were dissatisfied with popular government because of "the frequent disturbances, interruptions and dissolutions" that Parliament had to face, he suggested an arrangement whereby "the ablest men" would serve for life in a Grand Council. After all, Milton reasoned, such men have experience in government, and the people trust them. Given lifetime tenure, they could better learn what must be done and do it. Frequent changes, as painful recent experience had taught, served only "to satisfie the ambition" of the wicked. Milton conceded that rotation in office might prevent unrest, but he judged it an inferior alternative because it would empower the less able and less experienced. History showed that a permanent council had succeeded best at suppressing the turmoil bred by ambition; illustrations included Greece, Rome, Venice, and, more recently, the United Provinces.[100]

In this final political intervention of his long career, unusual because of the doubts he expressed about the English people's capacity to maintain a popular form of government, Milton characteristically blended political with religious concerns. "The whole freedom of man consists either in spiritual or civil libertie. As for spiritual, who can be at rest, who can enjoy any thing in this world with contentment, who hath not liberties to serve God and to save his own soul, according to the best light which God hath planted in him to that purpose, by the reading of his revealed will and the guidance of his holy spirit?"[101] In Milton's writing, as in the writing of other prominent partisans of popular government in seventeenth-century England, it is impossible to disentangle the braided strands of Puritan theology, classical and civic humanist political theory, and traditional arguments about the rights of Englishmen from the tradition of English common law. If we view the champions of democracy in seventeenth-century England from their perspective rather than ours, we can see that they wove together arguments concerning God's will and the people's will to make a compelling case for popular sovereignty, reciprocity, equality, and autonomy.[102]

If so, then why did these "democratical gentlemen," as Hobbes scornfully characterized his foes, fail to consolidate their victories in the Civil War and the revolution that followed it? The dynamic that drove Hobbes from the position he took in *De cive* (1642), where he made democracy the original form of government, to the position he took in *Leviathan* (1651) is surely an important part of the answer. Reflecting on a century of unprecedentedly murderous warfare, whether on the continent or in England, Hobbes came to a conclusion similar to that reached by Montaigne: left to their own devices, ordinary people are incapable of self-government. Only an absolute authority—the more absolute the better—can end the slaughter sparked by the enthusiasms of "democraticals" everywhere.[103]

Champions of democracy have often celebrated the heroic, selfless struggles of those willing to fight and die for popular government. The English experience, however, like that of Europeans in the preceding century, illustrates that war, even when it is inescapable, makes democracy harder to attain and less likely to survive. Faced with chaos, ordinary people often choose order over the constant discord of democratic life. Political convictions, fortified by religious faith as profound as that of Milton, fuel partisan loyalties too fierce for moderation. The ethic of reciprocity requires a willingness to tolerate difference and disagreement. Autonomy is incompatible with enforced conformity. War fans the flames of passion and snuffs out the virtues of mercy and forgiveness. If democracy is a cultural project as much as a struggle over institutions, nothing represents a more serious obstacle than war, which breeds lasting resentments and destroys the trust on which democracy depends.

Milton stands among the most incisive observers of the role that trust must play in popular government. If the people are sovereign and entrust their authority to those who govern, the vitality of democracy depends on preserving that trust. In the wake of war, hatred takes its place. Estimates indicate that England lost almost 4 percent of its population in the wars between 1640 and 1660, Scotland perhaps 6 percent, and Ireland a stupefying 40 percent—death rates that exceed both of the twentieth century's notoriously bloody wars. Many deaths came in combat. Others occurred in massacres of noncombatants, public hangings, and even more grisly forms of execution, frequently, as on the continent, for the exalted cause of religious purity.[104] Such carnage did not advance the cause of democracy.

Overall, the long-term effects for England of civil war, revolution, and restoration were hardly what any of those involved would have expected. Every major faction—Anglicans and royalists, Presbyterians, and the various Independent or Puritan sects—sought unity, or at least harmony, rather than the permanent divisions of a stable party system. Each wanted that unity on its own terms, each vision was incompatible with the others, and all found compromise uncongenial. Without the degree of consensus enjoyed, and sometimes enforced, in the most democratic of New England towns, such discord could not translate into stable popular government. As a consequence none of the factions emerged triumphant after 1660. The monarchy of Charles II was a far cry from the egalitarian republic envisioned by those most inclined toward democracy, but neither did it approach the degree of absolute authority enjoyed by Louis XIV and other continental rulers.

We cannot know what "the people" thought, both because the people of England, Scotland, and Ireland were of several minds and because no reliable method existed to find out. There were no plebiscites, no opinion polls, and no elections that registered the thoughts of more than a tiny slice of the public. We know only that those who left written records disagreed on fundamental issues. We know, too, that each holder of power, initially Charles I, then the army that defeated him, then those who put him to death, then Cromwell, and finally Charles II, represented only a minority of Englishmen. At the end of those cycles, England brought back a monarch and a corrupt oligarchy whose successors shared power for centuries. If the size of the electorate had been slowly expanding prior to the 1640s, after 1660 it shrank dramatically and remained tiny and malapportioned for two centuries. The rigorous ethical standards and passionate religiosity of the Puritan sects, discredited as fanaticism and charged with responsibility for regicide, likewise all but vanished after the restoration, replaced by a lax, even cynical form of orthodox Anglicanism. Who was responsible? Traitors and villains abound. Heroes are harder to find.[105]

According to champions of popular government such as Milton, the ultimate advantage of a republic would have come from its commitment to educating all its citizens in the virtues conducive to autonomy and reciprocity. Such education, not just for literacy but "in all liberal arts and exercises," as Milton put it in *The Readie and Easie Way*, would in time spread civility as well as knowledge throughout England. Whereas monarchs preferred their subjects "well-fleeced for their own shearing," republics produced "flourishing, vertuous, noble, and high spirited" citizens.[106] Nothing in the remaining years of Milton's life altered that judgment. In his final years, writing in obscurity and isolation, Milton was a thoroughly disenchanted democrat. As he asked three years before he died, in *Paradise Regained* (1671), "And what the People but a herd confused, / A miscellaneous rabble . . . ?"

Ridding England of its monarchy was a monumental achievement. Were kings to return, Milton had warned in *The Readie and Easie Way*, their rule would be even more difficult to dislodge. They would, for good reasons, distrust their potentially rebellious people and thus check all the institutions—from local to national—in which they could exercise their liberties. The Commons would be weaker, a restored House of Lords stronger. Indeed, aristocrats would prove even more committed to doing the bidding of the king, who would in turn assiduously secure the Lords' loyalties by corruption of all sorts. In short, Milton predicted, bad as the English monarchy was before the regicide, a restored monarchy would be even worse. Milton's own experience confirmed his fears. Greeted with a mixture of joy, relief, and resignation by the common people on his return in 1660, Charles II quickly restored the House of Lords and the Anglican episcopacy. Copies of Milton's *Eikonoklastes* and *A Defense of the English People* were publicly burned. Milton himself was imprisoned.

What happened to Hugh Peter and Henry Vane? Puritans who had prospered in Holland and America, they had tried to bring their distinct understandings of the principles of self-government to England during the Civil War. Peter served in the New Model and, following Cromwell's death, delivered the funeral sermon. After Cromwell dissolved Parliament, Vane wrote a pamphlet entitled *The Healing Question*, which criticized the Protectorate. For his pains this strict adherent to the covenant of grace was accused of being a tool of the Jesuits or the Quakers. After the restoration, both Peter and Vane were tried for their part in the regicide, and both were convicted of treason. Peter was hanged, drawn, and quartered. As befitted a member of the gentry, Vane was beheaded.[107]

Meanwhile Roger Williams, another champion of popular sovereignty and freedom of conscience, spent 1652 in London seeking a new charter for his colony. While there, he lived with Vane and tutored Milton in Dutch as the poet descended into blindness and bitterness. Two years later Williams, unlike Peter and Vane, decided to return to New England, where he was elected president of a lively, thriving, ever-contentious colony of Rhode Island. He carried with him the new charter he had negotiated for the towns that proudly designated themselves "democratical."[108]

CHAPTER 4

Coup d'Etat

1688 in England and America

IN 1688 ENGLAND replaced one king with another. Usually described by contemporaries as "the happy revolution," that regime change has come to be known as the Glorious Revolution. Given its causes and consequences, however, it might better be described as a coup d'état. By sacking James II and bringing in the Dutch Protestant William of Orange, England's Anglican gentry rid themselves of a Catholic king they disliked and secured their own domination of English politics for nearly two centuries.

So widespread was anti-Catholicism in England that the coup generated little opposition. In the years preceding William's accession to the throne, a flurry of radical pamphlets and books advanced ideas about popular sovereignty and religious toleration with lasting significance for democratic theory. As became clear in its aftermath, not only did the counterrevolution of 1688 not advance democracy in England, it opened the door for oligarchy. Across the Atlantic, by contrast, English colonists applied many of the ideas advanced by dissidents during the Restoration—as the period after 1660 is called—as they continued to develop diverse cultures of self-government. After 1688 England became less concerned with religious uniformity and more committed to gentry rule, while England's North American colonies moved slowly toward greater religious toleration and wholeheartedly embraced political ideas that provided a rationale for their democratic political institutions. This chapter traces that process on both sides of the Atlantic, focusing first on England and then more briefly on the mainland colonies.[1]

John Locke and Algernon Sidney, the most enduringly influential English political writers of the 1680s, are now usually described as moderates. Their ideas are characterized as tepid challenges to the entrenched privileges of

England's ruling oligarchy. It is true that neither Locke nor Sidney disputed the legitimacy of constitutional monarchy. Neither denied the legitimacy of private property. Neither doubted the existence of God or the fundamental truth of Christianity. Neither would have extended to atheists or Catholics the degree of religious toleration they sought for dissenting Protestants.

Even so, Locke and Sidney were heretics and traitors. These two thinkers, widely read in England's colonies and later revered by the architects of the American Revolution, disputed central doctrines of Anglicanism and actively worked to unseat the king of England. They crafted arguments for the principles of popular sovereignty, autonomy, and equality that became touchstones among champions of democracy. They understood the indispensability of deliberation among people with diverse identities and interests, and they premised their democratic ideas on a shared commitment to the Christian ideal of mutuality. Their lives were tumultuous, their ideas explosive. Locke's friend and patron Anthony Ashley Cooper, the first Earl of Shaftesbury, was arrested in August of 1681 and charged with treason because of his political maneuvering against the crown. Shaftesbury was released and went into hiding, then sought refuge in Holland, where he died on January 21, 1683. Later that year Locke, himself under surveillance by the king's spies, fled to Holland to avoid imprisonment. Locke had reason to worry. Sidney, another critic of the restored monarchy, was arrested on June 26, 1683, for his alleged role in the failed Rye House plot to assassinate both Charles II and his Catholic brother—and heir to the throne—James Stuart, the Duke of York, later James II. On the basis of ideas expressed in manuscripts found in Sidney's home, he was accused of treason. Had Locke's own manuscripts, eventually published anonymously as *Two Treatises of Government*, been discovered, he too might have been arrested. In the 1680s, even entertaining the idea that sovereign power resided in the English people rather than the king-in-Parliament put dissidents' lives in danger.

Sidney and Locke's threatening radicalism consisted in their insistence that the original sovereign power legitimating the authority of government rests with the people rather than the king, their conviction that abuse of that delegated authority renders monarchs vulnerable to resistance, and their belief that enforcing conformity to Anglicanism unjustly constrained Protestant Christians' freedom of conscience. By sacking James and crowning William, England's threatened Protestant aristocracy secured control of England and the global expansion of British power until the late nineteenth century. The strategies and techniques employed by that oligarchy, which eighteenth-century critics came to call "corruption," led to the loss of Britain's most valuable North American colonies and the birth of the world's first democratic nation-state.

This chapter examines the ideas of 1688 and their consequences. Replacing James II with William of Orange accomplished more than was intended. Seventeenth- and early eighteenth-century Europe was dominated by entrenched authority and inherited privilege, and the concept of royal absolutism was almost perfectly embodied in the expansive monarchy of the Sun King, Louis XIV. Even so, admiration for post-1689 British culture, particularly its perceived religious toleration, its apparently vigorous institutions of government authorizing Parliament to rein in the power of monarchy, and its impressive economic growth, helped loosen the grip of absolutism on the imaginations of some European thinkers. The roots and the forms of the "century of light" varied widely across distinctive cultures ranging from Scotland to Italy, and up and down the Atlantic seaboard of North America. The most important political ideas, articulated most dramatically, and most influentially, by Jean-Jacques Rousseau and James Madison, descended from and extended the ideas advanced by those dangerous English moderates Sidney and Locke.

The restoration of the English monarchy in 1660 appeared to signal the end of the cultural ferment of the preceding several decades. Although regicide cast a shadow over the divine right of kings, the return to monarchy provoked surprisingly little protest. The Convention Parliament, which opened in April 1660, welcomed Charles II in the hope that he might restore peace, prosperity, and the security that not only aristocrats but also ordinary people sought. That yearning translated into harsh governance. Various measures passed in the early 1660s ended the physical mobility of the poor and outlawed both political and religious dissent.[2]

The doctrine of royal absolutism fed this passion for uniformity. Advanced in numerous pamphlets and books, including particularly those of Robert Filmer, absolutism drew ammunition from selective reading in the Bible and Jean Bodin, James I and Charles I, and especially from the lessons of the preceding two decades, which had demonstrated more conclusively than any text the horrors of popular unrest. Doctrines associated with the Levellers, the New Model Army, James Harrington, and John Milton were now anathema. Painful experience had taught the English that "Popery and Phanaticism, are equally dangerous to the Government by Law Established." Although "Papists" had plotted against England since the Reformation, "by God's Providence" they had not yet succeeded. But not for want of trying. "The Phanaticks" had "laid aside the Monarchy, Destroyed the Church," and wreaked havoc for two decades.[3]

Retrieving order from chaos required recovering the common-law maxims that no man can be a judge in his own case and that no inferior court can judge a superior court. Absolutists invoked those two rules to bolster claims for royal authority. Only a king was thought to enjoy sufficient distance from all disputes to exercise independent, disinterested judgment. Therefore only a king could discern the public good. No inferior power, whether vested in the law, the Lords, or the Commons, could challenge his authority. Defining all popular unrest as anarchy, champions of the restored monarchy substituted a comprehensive scheme for the more democratic ideas that had bubbled up in previous decades. In place of calls for popular sovereignty, royalists offered the unbending rule of absolute monarchy; for autonomy, the dependency of inferiors on their superiors; for equality, hierarchy; for toleration, enforced uniformity to an increasingly rigid Anglican doctrine; and for reciprocity, unquestioning obedience in both religious and civic spheres.

Absolutists faced a dilemma. If the king's power were unlimited, then on what basis had Parliament challenged English monarchs, as it had done dozens of times over the centuries? If the king were subject to Parliament according to custom as well as common law, then how could the blustery claims of royalists be sustained? This logical dilemma could not be evaded, as Sidney's good friend Henry Vane had made clear, albeit ineffectually, in the speech he delivered on the scaffold in 1662. From the perspective of Vane and many other critics of absolutism, the "Antient Foundations" of mixed government provided an insurmountable barrier to the claims of Filmer, Charles II, and their allies. Despite the king's pretensions and his power to execute dissenters such as Vane, he still had to answer to a potentially unruly Parliament.[4]

That parliamentary power reemerged soon enough, as Parliamentarians' twin fears of Puritans and papists sparked the first appearance of stable political parties in England. Fearing that Charles II might convert to the Catholicism of his brother, James Stuart, and that the Stuarts would eventually repeal the Test Act against James's coreligionists and bring the Counter-Reformation to England, wary Anglicans contemplated a preemptive strike. According to traders in conspiracy such as William Bedloe, England was the final "*Bull-work* of *Liberty*, *Protestantism*, and *Christian Faith* in General, throughout the world." England alone stood against the "tyranny and superstition" of Rome, so only a Protestant could occupy the throne.[5] Fewer than 2 percent of England's population remained Catholic by the late 1670s, yet Anglicans' anxiety was real and potent. The Exclusion Crisis inspired critics of the Stuarts to form the Whig Party, which venerated the ancient constitution empowering Parliament to defend the liberties of Englishmen. In response the king's supporters mobilized as the faction that became the Tories, and these two groups wrestled for supremacy during the next two centuries.

The Whigs' first ringleader was Locke's friend Shaftesbury, who initially welcomed the Restoration. In 1672 he assumed the post of lord chancellor in the cabinet of Charles II. He soon recoiled against the excesses of absolutist rule, however, and he was removed from the Privy Council in 1674. If divine right monarchy carried with it all the powers Charles claimed, Shaftesbury cautioned, then Magna Carta had been annulled, and "our Laws are but Rules amongst ourselves during the King's pleasure," because such a monarchy "cannot be bounded or limited by human Laws." The genius of the English system of government, according to Shaftesbury, derived from its mixture of king, Lords, and Commons. If the king overstepped his boundaries, the nobility provided a counterbalance. Mixed monarchy protected the English people: "Humane reason can hardly contrive a more excellent Government." Due to the equilibrium between king, Lords, and Commons, "the People are thus secure, no Laws can be made, nor Money given, but what themselves, though at home, fully consent and agree to." From the Whigs' perspective, English government derived its legitimacy from popular consent, which ideally manifested itself in the deliberations of both houses of Parliament. Absolutism and enforced Anglican uniformity rested on doctrines of infallibility repudiated by Protestants.[6]

The Whigs believed new elections would strengthen their leverage against the king, but Charles cited the insolence of speeches such as Shaftesbury's to justify suspending Parliament for fifteen months. When Parliament reconvened in 1677, Shaftesbury reiterated in the House of Lords—in even more intemperate language—challenges he had advanced in earlier sessions. The pattern of Whig charges and royal responses, parliamentary challenges and royal dismissals of Parliament, peaked with the publication in 1680 of Filmer's *Patriarcha*, an absolutist manifesto written fifty years earlier, and the appearance in 1681 of an equally fiery Whig reply. This pamphlet, entitled *Vox Populi*, rehearsed the centuries-old history of successful parliamentary challenges to royal prerogative and reminded Charles II how often his predecessors—and their lackeys—had been removed from power when they neglected the public good. Both Whig and royalist arguments had begun to echo those of the early 1640s. When Shaftesbury raised the stakes by charging that the act of proroguing Parliament was illegal, Charles confined him to the Tower of London. That step only briefly silenced the Whigs' champion and merely sidestepped the issue that had plagued the monarchy for decades, the question the Levellers raised and Vane addressed in his final speech. A king who refused to share power with Parliament had become a tyrant.[7]

That simmering controversy prompted the writing that led to Shaftesbury's and Locke's exile in Holland and to Sidney's death. The Stuarts were emboldened by their confidence that Louis XIV would redeem his promise to provide the funds they needed and that Parliament refused to authorize. The

Whigs maneuvered with equal confidence, believing that not only their countrymen but also the Dutch House of Orange and Protestants throughout Europe shared their commitment to preserving a Protestant England. A collision seemed inescapable.

Other dissidents were quick to pick up the Whigs' banner after Shaftesbury, having failed to engineer a rebellion, fled to Holland. The most fiery—and most lastingly influential—was Algernon Sidney. As a younger son facing life with limited prospects for advancement, he dutifully joined the army. He served under his father and brother in Ireland, then in 1644, at the age of twenty-one, was wounded in the Battle of Marston Moor. Elected to the House of Commons two years later, he agreed instead to a second stint in Ireland. He served as governor of Dublin before being recalled to England in 1647, when the government was reorganized by Presbyterians. Sidney opposed the regicide, but he remained a member of Parliament and became convinced that an English republic could thrive without a king. A prominent figure in the Rump who was forcibly removed by Cromwell on April 20, 1653, Sidney watched warily as Cromwell consolidated his power. When Parliament was restored in 1659, Sidney was elected to the Council of State and then sent on a diplomatic mission to conclude a peace between the kings of Denmark and Sweden. While there, he was said to have been given a book in which he inscribed the words that have been associated with him ever since. In 1775, these words became the motto of the Commonwealth of Massachusetts: "This hand, hostile to tyrants, seeks by the sword the tranquil peace of freedom."[8]

Like Shaftesbury, Sidney initially—albeit grudgingly—accepted the restoration, both because of his lasting enmity toward Cromwell and because it was effected by Parliament. He realized that his own republican predilections made him, as he put it, "a very unfit stone for such a building," so he decided to embrace "voluntary exile" in Rome.[9] The terms in which Charles II and his allies characterized the king's authority confirmed Sidney's deep-seated mistrust of monarchical power. While he stewed in Italy, his opposition to Charles deepened. The execution of his friend Henry Vane, whom Sidney described as unequaled in "vertue, prudence, courage, industry, reputation and godliness," prompted him to begin plotting revolution together with other radicals exiled in Switzerland. Visiting the Calvinist Academy in Geneva in 1663, he wrote in the visitors' book, "Let there be revenge for the blood of the just."[10]

Sidney's anti-Stuart scheming took him to Holland, where he met with other English dissidents, then to France, where he tried to interest the government of Louis XIV—implausibly enough—in the cause of English republicanism. Sidney's maneuverings drew the attention of an Englishman who reported back to Edward Hyde, Earl of Clarendon, that it was becoming necessary to keep an eye on the increasingly dangerous Sidney and his co-conspirator Edmund Ludlow, a leading figure among the English community on the shores of Lake Geneva. When Sidney returned from Paris to Rotterdam he became acquainted with the Quaker Benjamin Furly, a radical proponent of religious toleration who also befriended other English exiles including Shaftesbury, William Penn, and—later—Locke. During Sidney's time in Holland, according to another of Charles's informants, he was busy producing "a Treatise in defence of a Republique, & against Monarchy," a manuscript that he was reportedly seeking to place with a publisher.[11]

Charles's spies were right. Sidney's manuscript, *Court Maxims*, appears to have been written between 1664 and 1666. It remained largely unknown during his lifetime and did not surface until the late nineteenth century. Much about it remains dubious. Yet it is easy to see why its author was the object of persistent surveillance. Sidney described the Anglican hierarchy and the Stuart judiciary as a "goodly and sacred fellowship of tyrants," a "glorious army of thieves, murderers, and blasphemers" who "persecute and endeavour to destroy" God's holy people "throughout the world, adorning the gates and towers of the city with the mangled limbs of thy choicest servants, to gratify the lusts and uphold the interest of their two masters, the king and the devil." Turning from the bishops and judges to the English people, who had squandered the Commonwealth and willingly enslaved themselves again to monarchy, Sidney let loose his fury. "Burnt children dred the fire," he wrote, "but we, more childish than children, though often scorched and burnt, do again cast ourselves into the fire, like moths and gnats, delighting in the flame that consumes us."[12]

Beyond splendid invective, *Court Maxims* offered telescoped versions of the arguments that Sidney elaborated in his later *Discourses concerning Government*. He excoriated the restored monarchy for eradicating the ancient rights of Englishmen by insisting on unprecedentedly strict adherence to rigid codes of religious belief and practice. He was careful to specify that liberty must be distinguished from the simple freedom to follow any whim: "He is not happy that hath what he desires but desires what is good and enjoys it." Our passions tempt us from the eternal laws of God and nature, subjecting our potentially elevating "higher" selves to our base, contemptible, and brutish "lower" selves.[13] Sidney's conception of freedom as the exercise of virtue echoed Aristotelian, Augustinian, and English republican conventions as articulated by Levellers such as Overton and Wildman: "As there is no happiness without liberty, and no man more a slave than he that is overmastered by vicious passions, there is neither liberty nor happiness where there is no virtue."[14]

Sidney admitted no conflict between the dictates of reason and the prescriptions of revelation.[15] Not every individual merits freedom, and even those inclined toward virtue require both law and scripture to help them find the right path. The English people, liberated by the Reformation from bondage to Rome and by the republic from bondage to tyranny, had demonstrated that they were among that small number of nations capable of self-rule. "Full of men who excel in wisdom and experience," the people of England should "keep the power in their own hands of governing themselves or one another by turns," not allow themselves to be "perpetually governed by one man and his posterity."[16]

Sidney envisioned autonomous individuals following an ethic of reciprocity as they reasoned together in a self-governing polity. "Reason enjoins every man not to arrogate to himself more than he allows to others, not to retain that Liberty which will prove hurtful to him; or to expect that others will suffer themselves to be restrain'd, whilst he, to their prejudice, remains in the exercise of that freedom which Nature allows."[17] Sidney derived his understanding of autonomy, equality, toleration, and mutuality as the principles and premises of democracy from his religious faith, as did most other seventeenth-century English writers who disagreed with the doctrines of absolutism and religious uniformity. Whereas monarchists argued that a king's legitimate authority derives from God, republicans such as Sidney challenged that model without also denying that divine sanction undergirds law. He stated his own religious convictions less clearly than did many other republicans. It is clear, however, that his faith was not of the doctrinaire sort that prevented some of his contemporaries (such as Ludlow) from making strategically useful alliances. Indeed, Sidney and other critics of the Restoration monarchy helped transform English republican discourse by muting the more stridently religious tone of earlier champions of popular sovereignty, such as Vane and Milton, thereby creating the mistaken impression that late seventeenth-century political discourse had little to do with religious faith.[18]

Sidney believed the rumor about a popish plot to recapture England through Charles's conversion to Catholicism, a rumor swirling among English exiles in Europe, which was much later found to have been true. Sidney began inquiring about the possibility of returning to England not only because he was impoverished and politically marginalized on the continent but also because he thought he might better combat the Catholic threat closer to home. Through a French Huguenot named Marshal Turenne, Charles II learned in 1670 that Sidney now wanted to be of service to the crown. Sidney tried to persuade Charles that only by granting freedom of conscience to dissenting Protestants could the king effectively snuff out the embers of revolution. In that case the fractious English people might form a united front to oppose both of their rivals, Catholic France and Protestant Holland. Charles responded to Sidney's presumptuousness by exiling him to the far reaches of Languedoc. In 1673, however, for reasons that remain obscure, the king relented and invited Sidney to return home. He stayed in France another four years, then finally arrived in England in the fall of 1677.[19]

Alarmed by evidence of mounting political corruption and religious inflexibility and inflamed by new anxieties that the king, already widely known to sympathize with Catholicism, was intent on returning England to the pope, by January of 1679 the House of Commons had begun taking steps to prevent Charles's Catholic brother, James, from becoming king. Charles, himself fearful that republicans were plotting to rise against him—as they had against his father—succeeded in forging an ill-considered alliance with Louis XIV, then dissolved the Parliament that until then he had been content merely to suspend and recall. Sidney was but one among many radicals, inspired by fears of popery and royal tyranny, to stand for election to a new Parliament.

Sidney's campaign was managed by William Penn, a leading Quaker who had already been exiled and imprisoned for his unorthodox religious beliefs. Penn's wealth and connections—including his friendship with James, the Duke of York, which would prove less advantageous after 1689—had given prominence to his Quaker beliefs. Yet those connections did not protect him from the wrath of Anglicans scandalized by his denials of their authority and of the doctrine of the trinity. The Quakers were widely known as democrats committed to the principle of equality. Although Sidney was no Quaker, Penn admired him for defending the Quakers' central commitment to the freedom of conscience. Penn worked hard to secure Sidney's election from the borough of Guildford in Surrey, and the two also collaborated on Penn's "Frame of Government" for his new colony in North America.

Sidney was defeated in that campaign and in later attempts to win election to Parliament. He and Penn were convinced that the practice of buying votes had cost him a seat. As Penn put it, in most seventeenth-century elections English voters were invited to "make a *Swop* of our *Birthright* (and that of our Posterities too) for a Mess of Pottage, a *Feast* or a *Drinking-bout*."[20] Although Sidney was not returned to Parliament, he was deeply involved in the behind-the-scenes maneuvering that brought England to the brink of civil war by 1681.[21] As factions formed and dissolved, Sidney's alliances shifted rapidly. "We are heare in the strangest confusion that I ever remember to have seene in English businesse. There never was more intrigues, and lesse truth," Sidney wrote to the Quaker Benjamin Furly on October 13, 1680.[22]

As unrest reached a boil after 1680, Sidney became one of the targets of royalists, along with Shaftesbury and others such as John Wildman and Henry Neville. When Charles secured sufficient funds from Louis XIV to end the dependence on Parliament that had hamstrung his father, his government launched a sweeping campaign against its enemies. The first targets included Shaftesbury's circle, then radical republicans such as Sidney, who were suspected of plotting to murder both Charles and his brother, James.[23] Compelling evidence of criminal activity was thin when Sidney was arrested in June of 1683. When the prosecution found drafts of his writings, though, including the manuscript of *Discourses*, it had all the evidence it needed. Sidney's text contained "all the malice revenge and treason mankind can be guilty of," according to the Lord Chief Justice George Jeffreys. "There is not a line in the book scarce but what is treason." Unless such ideas were silenced, they would lead again to regicide. "The late unhappy rebellion," Jeffreys assured the jury, "was first begun by such kind of principles."[24] It was true that Sidney's manuscript indicted monarchy and called for popular government. Like his earlier—and unknown at the time—*Court Maxims*, Sidney's *Discourses* smoldered with the dangerous idea of democracy.

Like all examples of Protestant resistance theory since the mid-sixteenth century, Sidney's *Discourses* proclaimed freedom of conscience. Because Sidney shared the conviction of dissenters that religious belief is not a matter of will, he contended that coercion yields only hypocrisy. No regime can compel what it cannot control, including faith that is God-given and sincerely held. Like the Levellers who preceded him and contemporaries like Shaftesbury and Locke, Sidney held political principles that flowed from, and were inseparable from, his dissenting Protestantism.[25] As he had done in *Court Maxims*, Sidney began his *Discourses* by disputing the legitimacy of monarchy, then proceeded to establish the primacy of individual autonomy. Whether in terms of conscience, property, or political decision making, liberty meant an individual's freedom from "the dominion of another." Although such liberty was natural to man, it was to be exercised only in accord with reason, which Sidney described as "the law of man's nature," or "an emanation of the divine wisdom." Again as in *Court Maxims*, Sidney argued that as God's children, we are led by the dictates of reason in the direction of virtue. Our passions may mislead us, as Sidney's own notoriously unruly temper surely and frequently did, but reason can correct our impulses and redirect us toward God's will.[26]

Sidney's direct challenge to Filmer's denial of the right of revolution against monarchy was the central and most radical argument in his *Discourses*. Sidney reasoned that all communities, and all nations, originate in direct democracy, which is therefore the first and most natural form of government. Only when such communities grow, and the number of citizens and the size of the territory make gathering everyone together impossible or impractical, does representation emerge. Sidney discussed examples ranging from the tribes of the Hebrew Bible to Athens, Sparta, Rome, and the Germans and Saxons of northern Europe. In every case, he insisted, the people originally made decisions through deliberation that included all members of the community, then eventually decided to delegate authority to some of them. Invoking Tacitus to bolster his biblical citations, Sidney concluded that "the great matters" among the Germans and Saxons alike were transacted by "the whole people." Restating and incorporating the standard republican understanding of autonomy as freedom from dependence, Sidney explained that "the difference between *civis* and *servus* is irreconcilable; and no man, whilst he is a servant, can be a member of a commonwealth." Moreover, such arrangements constituted the norm; all the "northern nations had the like customs among them."[27]

Only at that late stage, after the earlier forms of direct democracy, representative democracy, and aristocracy were well established, did the people—remaining sovereign—occasionally opt to establish the institution of monarchy. Sidney insisted that it was up to them to choose among multiple options, including the pure forms of democracy, aristocracy, and monarchy, and the mixed forms most nations eventually adopted. Whatever form of government the people chose, they retained sovereign power and aimed for "the good of the publick."[28] Sidney readily conceded that no examples of direct democracy remained after the formative stages of human association. The transition to forms of mixed government occurred early in the process of development. Sidney thought Coke and the common lawyers had things backward: "The authority of a magistracy proceeds not from the number of years that it has continued, but the rectitude of the institution, and the authority of those that instituted it." That authority was, in every case, that of the people, the origin of all legitimate power. Sidney concluded that both time and right were on the side of the doctrine of popular sovereignty.[29] Royal proclamations derived their force not from a putative ancient constitution but from the people's grant of authority to their representatives, who had decided to constitute aristocracies and monarchies.

Sidney's crucial discussion of representation depended on his understanding of human fallibility and manifested his confidence in the productive power of deliberation. He conceded the truth of an ancient adage often invoked during the English Civil War: only the person wearing a shoe knows where it pinches. For that reason he acknowledged the importance of enabling citizens to express their own personal interests in politics; there was nothing illegitimate about wanting to ease the pinch.[30] Individuals did not always know why problems existed, however, or understand how to solve them. Their views, indispensable as they were, could best be refined through the institution of representative assemblies. Just as the realization that knowledge of religious truth was imperfect made necessary freedom of conscience, so the realization that individual citizens were not always capable of seeing beyond their own narrow interest meant that representative bodies could—not must, but could—find ways of aligning those interests with the general interest of the public. A national representative assembly has the capacity to transcend the perspectives of the individual communities that constitute it. Through the process of meeting with their constituents and deliberating with one another, representatives can help forge a public good from the inchoate and unconscious impulses of people initially incapable of seeing beyond their own narrow perspectives.

Sidney thus resurrected the parliamentary army's contention in 1647–48 and turned on its head the royalist claim that only a king can see more broadly than his own interest. To the contrary, Sidney reasoned, the king vis-à-vis the assembly has precisely his own interest in view, whereas the assembly brings together multiple perspectives and thus can determine—or, even more crucially, can create—through the back-and-forth of debate, the position that best approximates the interest of the public as a whole. This "publick good" might be visible from the standpoint of the national assembly but obscured from the sight of any of the individual constituencies, or their representatives. Instead of being fixed by royal proclamation, it would continue to develop through the processes of representative democracy.[31]

Sidney opposed the idea of binding instructions sent to representatives from those who had chosen them. Although he considered representatives the servants, or creatures, of those by whom they were sent, and therefore judged instructions to be appropriate and effective vehicles for communicating popular sentiment, on par with annual elections, he nevertheless cautioned that binding instructions undercut the chief benefit of deliberation. Neither representatives nor those who elect them can predict "what will be proposed when they are together; much less resolve how to vote till they hear the reasons on both sides." Binding representatives to their electors' prior wishes "would make the decision of the most important affairs to depend upon the judgment of those who know nothing of the matters in question, and by that means cast the nation into the utmost danger of the most inextricable confusion." Sidney understood that the process of forming public judgment is complex, dynamic, and multitiered. The people meet to find their own voice, which they then communicate imperfectly to their representative, who then meets with others in the assembly to weigh competing ideas. Only then can representatives return to those who sent them, explain what happened in the assembly, and seek their continuing support and reelection.[32] Messy, unpredictable, and necessarily indeterminate and unending, such was the nature of representative democracy.

The purpose of deliberation, as Sidney envisioned it, was not merely to balance competing interests. Instead it was to find, or rather to create over time, the elusive ideal that Sidney called "the publick good." Democracy for Sidney never involved choosing between the defense of individual liberty and the public interest, because in Sidney's mind no contradiction between the two was possible. Governments were created in the first place "for the good of the people, and for the defence of every private man's life, liberty, lands and goods." Protecting such rights was constitutive of the public good, not in conflict with it. "If the publick safety be provided, liberty and propriety secured, justice administered, virtue encouraged, vice suppressed, and the true interest of the nation advanced, the ends of government are accomplished."[33] Reaching that goal did not require individuals to renounce but instead only to reconsider their own personal interest in relation to the greater good. "Virtuous actions that are profitable to a commonwealth ought to be made, as far as it is possible, safe, easy, and advantageous."[34]

Sidney endorsed deliberation and representation because of human imperfection. It is "the condition of mankind," he wrote, "that nothing can be so perfectly framed as not to give some testimony of human imbecility, and frequently to stand in need of reparations and amendments." In the realm of public life, "no law made by man can be perfect," so ways must be found to correct "such defects as in time may arise or be discovered." The advantage of democratic decision making was its consistency with the flawed process of human reasoning; it provided, through the give-and-take of public argument among constituents, between constituents and their representatives, and among representatives gathered in a legislative assembly and then submitting to reelection, a way to "advance a good that at the first was not thought on."[35]

The humility required for democracy grows only on the apparently forbidding but potentially fertile ground of equality. Whereas hierarchical systems breed pride and resentment, insolence and subservience, democratic interactions are most likely and productive among equals. In the condition of equality into which men were originally born, Sidney wrote, "I cannot reasonably expect to be defended from wrong, unless I oblige my self to do none; or to suffer the punishment prescribed by the law, if I perform not my engagement." The ethic of reciprocity, which came naturally in the conditions of primitive equality, could be recovered by reining in the excessive leverage enjoyed by the monarchy, which resulted in widespread corruption of the public realm, and through the practices of deliberation required in a republic.[36]

Sidney's rationale for democracy rested on his Augustinian sensibility. Our human weaknesses render us unable to accomplish much on our own, particularly in the great projects of national politics. Left to their own impulses, the "fierce barbarity of a loose multitude, bound by no law, and regulated by no discipline," can produce only a "pestilent evil." The solution to this woeful condition is the formation of government, which creates a united force that renders men's talents no longer destructive but useful to everyone, a form of alchemy achieved only through discipline. Democratically elected officials, Sidney concluded, are "political architects," whose goal is to envision a republic that would, over time and always imperfectly, protect liberty and promote virtue.[37]

In time Sidney's *Discourses* became a classic statement of popular sovereignty and the right to revolution. Initially, however, it only sealed his fate.[38] Convicted of treason and condemned to death, Sidney mounted the scaffold on December 7, 1683, with an eloquent statement, which he handed to the executioner, defending the principles of self-government. The God-given power to establish governments originates with the people, not with the monarch: "God had left Nations unto the Liberty of setting up such Governments as best pleased themselves."[39] Sidney's final declaration was published by a government confident that all who read it would see its folly. Instead Whigs on both sides of the Atlantic embraced its message and flung it in the face of monarchy for the next century. Through Sidney's final testament and his *Discourses*, the identification of autonomy with self-government became a staple of Whig ideology: the only way to distinguish "between free nations and such as are not so" was that the free governed themselves.[40] Sidney's idea of self-government, enhanced by his martyrdom, proved a powerful resource for later agitators.

Influential as Algernon Sidney was, he was neither a systematic philosopher nor a shrewd political activist. John Locke was both. His writings on epistemology earned him a place among the most important figures in modern philosophy. His political acumen kept him alive. Having eluded arrest in 1683 and returned from Holland to London, when William of Orange secured the English throne in 1689, Locke arrived in England in the company of the new Queen Mary. He moved carefully, and skillfully, in the inner circles of England's most powerful families. The jagged edges of Sidney's prose were never honed through processes of revision, publication, and public debate. Locke's writings, although likewise prudently unpublished during the Stuart monarchy, went through elaborate revision before he made them available for public scrutiny, and even then the most important of his texts appeared anonymously.

As a philosopher Locke towers over Sidney. He was long misunderstood, by his admirers and his critics alike, as a founder of or precursor to versions of "liberalism" that did not exist in his day, and of which he thus could not even have been aware. Such once-common readings are now acknowledged as anachronistic and misleading.[41] A recent generation of scholars has retrieved the historical Locke by restoring his Calvinist religious faith to its proper place at the center of his thought.[42] Viewed as contributions to the late seventeenth- and early eighteenth-century discourse of democracy, Locke's well-modulated texts, crucial as they became in philosophy, political theory, religion, education, and economics, were no more influential than Sidney's impassioned diatribes. Locke's political writings, unpublished until after the Revolution of 1688, were drafted during the same period of crisis, 1681–83, in which Sidney produced the manuscripts for which he was executed. Locke's writings, less polemical but likewise devoted to demolishing arguments for absolute monarchy and establishing the case for popular sovereignty, manifest the precision of his mind and the prudence of his sensibility, both of which he refined during his long and valuable association with his patron the Earl of Shaftesbury.

Locke was born in a comfortable but hardly wealthy Puritan household in Somerset, in the southwest of England, grandson of a clothier and son of an attorney. His father, who served briefly as an officer in the parliamentary army during the Civil War, was clerk of the local magistrates. He also worked as personal attorney to Alexander Popham, who served in the House of Commons and who launched his son John down the path of patronage he was to follow throughout his life. Popham arranged a place for Locke at Westminster School, which prepared him for Christ Church College, Oxford, to which he was admitted, probably through Popham's intervention, in 1652. Both at Westminster and at Oxford Locke studied with teachers who opposed what they considered the extremism of both Roman Catholicism and Puritanism. During these formative years he developed the abiding commitment to a moderate form of dissenting Protestantism—and a wariness toward papists and High Church Anglicans, on the one hand, and religious enthusiasts of all kinds, on the other—visible in his mature writings.

Locke earned his master of arts degree in 1658 and was appointed a tutor at Christ Church in 1660. Two letters he wrote in the intervening year indicate the concerns that animated his first writings about politics, his *Two Tracts* of 1660–62. To his father Locke explained the reasons why, although he was tempted to follow his lead and take up arms when the restoration struggle broke out, he stuck to his studies in Oxford. He was not sure which side he favored, and he judged war the worst way to settle a political dispute:

"Wars have produced nothing but wars," the sword only more "work for the sword." To another correspondent he expressed his longing for "a Pilot that would steare the tossed ship of this state to the haven of happiness" and his faith that "God is the hand that governs all things, and manages our chaos." Those twin commitments, to the peaceful resolution of disputes and to God's benevolent will, remained with Locke throughout his life.[43]

After a comically brief career as a diplomat—he accompanied the royalist brother of the martyred republican Henry Vane to the court of the Elector of Brandenburg—Locke returned to Oxford to study medicine. There he met a friend of his patron Popham, Anthony Ashley Cooper, then Lord Ashley, who in 1667 invited Locke to live in his London home and serve as his personal physician. In that capacity Locke supervised a risky operation on Ashley's liver that saved his life and earned his lasting gratitude. Locke was invited to serve as secretary to the Lords Proprietors of Carolina, in which capacity he helped write the Fundamental Constitutions proposed for the colony. Deliberately designed to "avoid erecting a numerous democracy," this plan outlined a feudal Neverland in which great landowning lords would oversee—from the comfort of their homes in England—an army of serfs and slaves industriously doing their bidding in Carolina. Not surprisingly, given the way the American colonies were developing by the late seventeenth century, nothing came of this far-fetched and remarkably ill conceived scheme.[44]

Backward-looking as the Carolina Constitution was, it did guarantee freedom of conscience. Ashley was already committed to religious toleration, although more for economic than for philosophical reasons. Locke, having seen the consequence of Parliament's attempt to enforce religious uniformity through the so-called Clarendon Code that reestablished Anglicanism and outlawed other religions, had shifted his position from that of *Two Tracts*. As is evident from the first draft of his *Letter concerning Toleration*, written in 1673, Locke had embraced the idea of limited religious toleration. Charles II initially opposed the Anglican-gentry alliance that sought to impose religious conformity, not because he prized dissent but because, having already forged a secret pact with Louis XIV in which he pledged to convert to Catholicism, he wanted to pry open space for his future coreligionists. At this stage of his maneuvering, he named Ashley, by then the 1st Earl of Shaftesbury, lord high chancellor of England. In the face of rabid anti-Catholicism, however, Charles soon abandoned his doomed strategy of toleration. Thomas Osborne, Earl of Danby, supplanted Shaftesbury, and from Shaftesbury's mounting resentment arose the Whig Party, which coalesced around opposition to enforced religious conformity. With his patron out of power, and with Charles now apparently allied with the Anglican gentry and opposed to religious toleration, Locke embarked on a trip to France, where he remained until 1679. While he was away, Shaftesbury was imprisoned, released, and then, through a series of comic-opera intrigues and maneuvers, found himself lord president of the Council of State. As Shaftesbury's anxieties mounted, he summoned Locke to return from France. The Whigs needed his help.

If the Catholic brother of Charles II, James, the Duke of York, were to have a son, first James, then his heir, would presumably become Catholic kings of England, thereby ending the hope that James's older daughter, Mary, the Protestant wife of William of Orange, would assume the throne. Protestants throughout Europe feared that a wave of Catholicism, generated by the gravitational pull of the Sun King, was about to sweep across the continent and the English Channel. That was no fantasy: such a wave did drive Protestants out of Poland, Bohemia, and, after the Revocation of the Edict of Nantes in 1685, France. To prevent inundation by Catholics, Shaftesbury and his allies hatched a scheme to exclude James from the throne. What they needed was a compelling rationale to justify his exclusion. Locke was charged with the task of providing that rationale; his *Two Treatises of Government*, not published until after the Revolution of 1688 was complete, were written for that reason. The heightened tensions of the Exclusion Crisis not only cost Sidney his life and forced Shaftesbury into exile; they also led the already suspicious librarian at Christ Church College to investigate Locke's activities in Oxford. He wondered whether his fellow in medicine was more involved in political agitation than in medical research.

Locke was under suspicion for good reason: it now seems likely that much of the work on his *Two Treatises* was completed during the years before he followed Shaftesbury into exile in Holland in 1683. No sooner had he left England than inquiries were made in Oxford. Told that the king wanted Locke removed from his fellowship, the dean of Christ Church replied that no one in the college had "heard him speak a word either against or so much as concerning the government." The dean asked that Locke be afforded a chance to defend himself. That request was rejected, however, and Locke expelled. Informed that English authorities wanted him extradited from Holland, Locke went underground, assuming the pseudonyms "Dr. van den Linden" and "Dr. Lynne" and seeking refuge in Brandenburg.[45] At the end of 1684, with Shaftesbury dead, Locke wrote a letter to his friend and new patron the Earl of Pembroke, to whom he later dedicated his *Essay concerning Human Understanding*. Locke was eager to deny the charges that had prompted his expulsion from Christ Church: "I here solemnly protest in the presence of God, that I am not the author, not only of any libel, but not of any pamphlet or treatise whatsoever in print." Attempting to explain to Pembroke why he was not in France but in Holland, known for decades as the preferred refuge for English political as well as religious dissenters, the abstemious Locke offered a singularly unconvincing reason; he was there for the beer.[46] Having learned from Sidney's fate, Locke probably brought his explosive manuscripts with him to Holland, but he remained wary about the shifting tides of English politics. He did not acknowledge authorship of *Two Treatises* until the year of his death—fifteen years after their anonymous publication.

Within months after Locke arrived in Holland, Charles II was dead and his brother, James, had quelled a brief Whig uprising—engineered in part by refugees in Holland—and secured his succession to the throne. James II provoked a crisis when he decreed religious toleration for his fellow Catholics and for Protestant dissenters. Not only did the king imprison Anglican bishops who denied his right to suspend Parliament's laws; he began ignoring Parliament and invoking arguments descended from his grandfather's theory of royal absolutism. When his wife gave birth to a male heir on June 10, 1688, the Anglican gentry felt compelled to act. Leading Tories joined their Whig foes in opposition to James, and together they invited William of Orange to save England from Catholicism. William saw the opportunity to cement an alliance between the Protestant nations surrounding France, so for reasons of state more than reasons of conscience he decided to launch an invasion. When William's forces landed, James departed for Ireland to regroup, and Parliament declared the throne vacant.

Now what? It was assumed that William would accept the authority of Parliament, that he would oppose Catholicism, and that he might relax the strictures against other Protestant sects. After all, the Dutch were celebrated (or, among Anglicans, notorious) for tolerating nonconformist sects persecuted by Anglicans for a century, sects ranging from separating and nonseparating Puritans, many of whom ended up in New England, to Quakers, many of whom ended up in Pennsylvania, Delaware, and New Jersey. It was into that maelstrom of debate concerning religious and political authority that Locke launched his most influential political tracts, his *Letter concerning Toleration* and his *Two Treatises of Government*, both of which appeared in 1689. Although neither determined the outcome, their immediate and lasting notoriety derived from the neat fit between his arguments and the positions taken by the new regime. The Toleration Act of May 1689 did not declare complete religious freedom. At least compared with the alternatives being considered, however, it did end Anglican hegemony and cracked open the door to dissenters and even Catholics. In Locke's own words, "Toleration has now at last been established by law in our country. Not perhaps so wide in scope as might be wished for," but "it is something to have progressed so far."[47] The Declaration of Rights, declared law later in 1689, merely codified the fuzzy, centuries-old understanding that kings would rule with, and through, Parliament, rather than in defiance of it, as the Stuarts had tried to do. This arrangement only perpetuated the contradiction so often noted by dissidents in earlier decades. If William's accession depended on his formal acceptance of the Declaration of Rights, then England had become an elective monarchy. If instead he ruled independent of Parliament, then the king remained the sovereign power of the realm. In fact, ambiguity reigned, yet because it brought peace as well as Protestantism in its train, both monarch and Parliament were content.

If Locke's texts did not shape either the religious or political settlements of 1689, they did provide templates for understanding the outcome. Locke's religious writings reflect his own lifelong piety and his conscious internalizing of the religious faith he inherited. In the supercharged atmosphere of religious war, so many proclamations of faith were followed by rapid renunciations and conversions that all claims to sincere religious conviction deserve critical scrutiny. The evidence of Locke's steadfast religious convictions is so consistently manifested in his life and his writings that there seems no good reason to doubt it. Although Locke was clearly aware of alternatives, notably the materialism turned atheism of Hobbes and the skepticism turned fideism of Pascal, he chose instead, quite deliberately, an only slightly modified version of his father's strict Puritan faith. In his relations and his correspondence with his patrons, his family, and his friends, Locke hewed to the principles he found expressed in the Gospels and manifested in the life of Jesus. Locke dissented from orthodox Calvinists' emphasis on depravity to the extent that he emphasized the compatibility of Christian doctrine with the exercise of reason. Indeed, he did not contrast reason to revelation; instead he judged both necessary to finding the truth of the law of nature, which he judged consistent with the truth of Christianity.

Nor did Locke see the need to choose either a hedonistic or self-abnegating account of human motivation. We are drawn to pleasure and seek to avoid pain, inclinations that operate within the framework of God's law and the possibilities of eternal punishment or salvation. Locke counseled strenuous attention to the Puritan idea of a calling and our obligation, as part of God's creation, to develop the resources available in ourselves and the world we inhabit. Explaining his convictions to his friend Edward Clarke soon after finishing his *Letter concerning Toleration*, Locke wrote, "He that has not a mastery over his inclinations, he that knows not how to resist the importunity of present pleasure, or pain, for the sake of what, reason tells him, is fit to be donne, wants the true principle of Vertue, and industry; and is in danger never to be good for anything." The ability to see the standard of excellence as God's will rather than ancient or Renaissance heroic striving or simple material accumulation—older and newer measures of achievement that Locke explicitly rejected as unworthy—required God's grace, which individuals could receive but not command.[48]

Locke wrote *A Letter concerning Toleration* while exiled in Holland in 1685, soon after the attempt to unseat James II had failed in England and the Edict of Nantes, which had protected Protestants, had been revoked in France. Locke believed the wars of religion had demonstrated the folly of governments attempting to impose religious convictions on their people. Such efforts at best induced hypocrisy, at worst war. He began by stating with confidence a proposition rejected for centuries by most Christians: "The toleration of those that differ from others in matters of religion, is so agreeable to the Gospel of Jesus Christ, and to the genuine reason of mankind, that it seems monstrous for men" to reject it. Yet Locke was no cultural relativist. He proclaimed there is "but one truth, one way to heaven." The beliefs of a Roman Catholic, a Jew, and a "heathen" he judged "false and absurd." He drew a line, however, between the domains of government and religion. Magistrates could safeguard "civil interests" including "life, liberty, health," and "outward things, such as money, lands, houses, furniture, and the like," but their jurisdiction ought not extend beyond them to the "care of souls." God never gave man the power to compel religious belief, nor could "such power be vested in the magistrate by the consent of the people." Even if Protestant Christianity were true, as Locke believed, "no man can so far abandon the care of his own salvation as blindly to leave it to the choice of any other" to determine his religious convictions. Unless one's faith interferes with the faith of others, varieties of religious belief should be tolerated.[49]

Because faith is a matter of individual conscience, imposing religious observance has no effect on belief and only bolsters the power of the clerics who demand it.[50] *A Letter concerning Toleration* provides Locke's most ambitious argument concerning the need to separate the religious and civic spheres. Locke had witnessed the costs imposed by demands for religious uniformity, and his opposition to such intolerance was surpassed only by his anxiety concerning the even greater threat represented by "papists" and atheists.[51] On the one hand, Locke's argument that social cohesion did not require a common religious faith represented a dramatic departure from earlier assumptions about the relation between politics and religion. On the other hand, that argument hardly dented the profound and persistent anti-atheism, anti-Semitism, and anti-Catholicism of English culture. Compared with the more far-reaching toleration preached by Roger Williams in New England decades earlier, Locke's was a distinctly modest contribution to religious pluralism.

Locke's *Two Treatises of Government* undermined monarchists' demands for the king's absolute authority much as *A Letter concerning Toleration* undermined Anglican demands for religious uniformity. In the *First Treatise*, Locke attacked the claims for absolute monarchy and the divine right of kings in Filmer's *Patriarcha*, which Locke bought immediately after it was published in early 1680. Filmer's book quickly became a favorite of royalists, and Locke's detailed refutation reflects the importance he, like Sidney, attached to it.[52] Much as the critique advanced in the *First Treatise* mattered to Locke, Shaftesbury, and their fellow Whigs in the early 1680s, the arguments of the *Second Treatise* have had a much deeper and broader resonance.

The *Second Treatise* begins with a crisp summary of Locke's elaborate demolition of Filmer. These two pages culminate in the bold claim that "*Public Power*" consists in the right to make and enforce laws regulating property "for the sake of the 'Publick Good.'"[53] To explain what he meant by the public good, Locke proposed three interlocking ideas—the state of nature, the law of nature, and the will of God—on which his political theory rests. In Locke's state of nature, all individuals are free and equal. Both this freedom and this equality, "wherein all the Power and Jurisdiction is reciprocal," are immediately clear to all persons. There is "nothing more evident," Locke wrote, "than that Creatures of the same species and rank promiscuously born to all the same advantage of Nature, and the use of the same faculties, should also be equal one amongst another." From this perception of the essential sameness, their possession of "the same faculties," Locke contended that they come to certain conclusions concerning how they should treat one another.[54]

Locke's argument explicitly follows the lead of Richard Hooker, whose multivolume work *Of the Laws of Ecclesiastical Polity* was written between 1580 and 1600, during the last two decades of Hooker's life, and whom Locke quoted repeatedly in the *Second Treatise*. Hooker wrote to defend the Anglican episcopacy against challenges from Calvinists, and Locke might have thought he was defanging his own anti-Anglican arguments by invoking the authority of "the judicious Hooker." Hooker's argument was double-edged. He rested the authority of bishops on the prior authority of the people, to whom God had given the power to set over themselves any system of authority they chose.[55] Locke had two reasons for beginning his analysis of the state of nature with Hooker. First, he was invoking a respected Anglican writer on behalf of his own claims for the identification of natural law with God's will, and of human reason with the ability to discern God's will.

Second, he was laying the groundwork for his claim that legitimate government rests on the consent of the governed. The fundamental axiom governing social interaction is the golden rule. Men have learned, in Hooker's words, "that it is no less their Duty, to Love others than themselves," for they can expect to be treated as they treat others. "My desire therefore to be lov'd of my equals in nature, as much as possible may be, imposeth upon me a natural Duty of bearing to [all of them] fully the like affection."[56]

The ethic of mutuality prevails even before the creation of civil society. In the state of nature, according to Locke, the "*State of Liberty*" is "*not a State of Licence.*" Freedom means, as it did for the Levellers and for Sidney, freedom to act in accordance with God's will, freedom to live a virtuous life, not freedom to follow any desire, however base or unjustifiable. In a crucial passage that sets the terms of Locke's entire theory of government, he wrote, "The *State of Nature* has a Law of Nature to govern it, which obliges every one; And Reason, which is that Law, teaches all Mankind, who will but consult it, that being all equal and independent, no one ought to harm another in his Life, Health, Liberty, or Possessions." Not only did Locke identify natural law with reason; he also contended that reason teaches all people the principles of autonomy, equality, and reciprocity. The gulf separating Hobbes's egoism from Locke's conception of the mutuality entailed by reason is clear. Undergirding these principles, Locke continued, is God's will. Because all human beings are God's creatures, they deserve respectful treatment. "For Men being all the Workmanship of one Omnipotent, and infinitely wise Maker; All the Servants of one Sovereign Master, sent into the World by his order and about his business, they are his Property, whose Workmanship they are, made to last during his, not one anothers Pleasure." Interfering with the exercise of individual autonomy, denying the equality of all people, or ignoring the golden rule means challenging not merely human conventions but God's will.

Locke explicitly challenged the fixed hierarchical arrangements taken for granted almost everywhere seventeenth-century Europeans lived. "And being furnished with like Faculties," he continued, and "sharing all in one Community of Nature, there cannot be supposed any such *Subordination* among us, that may Authorize us to destroy one another, as if we were made for one anothers uses, as the inferior ranks of Creatures are for ours." As these passages indicate, Locke's *Second Treatise* bridged the earlier Christian law of love and the later Kantian categorical imperative. Humans naturally exist not for the sake of one another but to fulfill God's purpose for them. Thus no individual should be considered—or treated—as merely instrumental to the purposes of another. Instead each must be recognized as an autonomous being with a God-given will and a purpose, a being with capacities to be freely developed and exercised, albeit within the boundaries of virtue, rather than merely shunted onto a path prescribed by someone else. We are to engage in such behavior not because we benefit from it, not because we can calculate its rewards for ourselves, but because it conforms to God's will for us. Although Locke himself seems not to have protested the subordination in his own day of Africans in the slave trade, Indians in the Americas, day laborers in England, or women everywhere, it should be clear that the principles on which his theory of government rested provide ammunition for those who were to challenge—from his day to ours—the unjustifiable treatment of members of those groups.

A careful reading of these crucial sentences at the beginning of the *Second Treatise* also makes clear that Locke's conception of every human as a creature of God ruled out not only suicide, as Christians had always done, but also economic exploitation or simple neglect of the impoverished, treatment that was so common as to seem unproblematic to most of his contemporaries. Everyone is bound not only "*to preserve himself*" but also "ought he, as much as he can, *to preserve the rest of Mankind*." Earlier writers had denied that any individual has the right to take the life of another not guilty of a monstrous offense or representing a mortal threat. Extending that injunction from doing no harm to engaging actively in preserving the life, liberty, health, and property of everyone—"the rest of mankind"—was a dramatic step. As Locke himself restated his bold claim, "the Law of Nature . . . willeth the Peace and *Preservation of all Mankind*."[57]

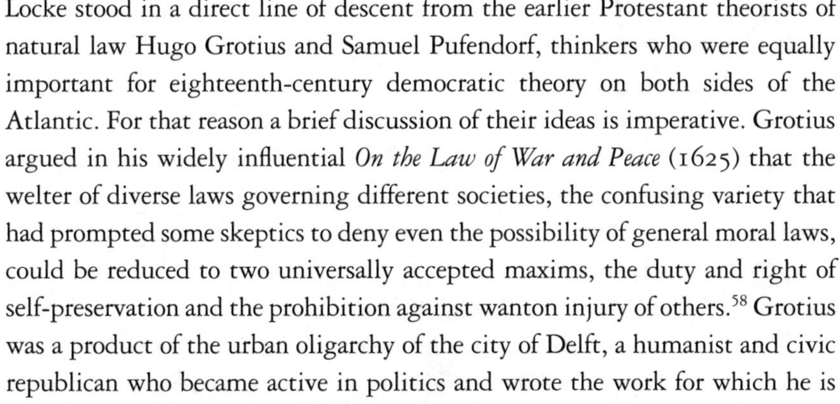

Locke stood in a direct line of descent from the earlier Protestant theorists of natural law Hugo Grotius and Samuel Pufendorf, thinkers who were equally important for eighteenth-century democratic theory on both sides of the Atlantic. For that reason a brief discussion of their ideas is imperative. Grotius argued in his widely influential *On the Law of War and Peace* (1625) that the welter of diverse laws governing different societies, the confusing variety that had prompted some skeptics to deny even the possibility of general moral laws, could be reduced to two universally accepted maxims, the duty and right of self-preservation and the prohibition against wanton injury of others.[58] Grotius was a product of the urban oligarchy of the city of Delft, a humanist and civic republican who became active in politics and wrote the work for which he is best known, *The Free Sea* (1609), to justify Dutch commercial activity.[59]

Grotius was also a champion of limited religious toleration. If his toleration, like Locke's, did not extend to Catholicism, it did extend at least to certain controversial varieties of Protestantism, particularly the views of the Dutch theologian Arminius, who argued that individuals have the choice of accepting God's grace and that predestination is less rigid than Calvin taught. The core beliefs of Christianity, Grotius argued, were shared by all Protestants, and most disagreements could be avoided if state authorities did not enforce uniformity. In the early seventeenth century, however, it was as dangerous to challenge orthodox Calvinism in the United Provinces as it was to challenge Anglicanism in England in the 1670s and 1680s. Whereas Locke managed to escape the fate of his patron Shaftesbury, Grotius's religious views led to his arrest in 1618, together with his patron Jan van Oldenbarnevelt, who was put to death for his unorthodox religious views. Spared execution, Grotius was imprisoned, and—appropriately enough for someone who had made his career as a writer—escaped by hiding in a basket of books that his wife had sent to him. He made his way to Antwerp, then to Paris.[60]

In his writings Grotius offered a minimalist account of the obligations individuals owe one another in the state of nature. When individuals join together to preserve peace and protect their property, they can choose among a variety of governments. Grotius was hardly a champion of popular government. He considered democracy so unworkable that he contended it had never even been tried. He believed that the sovereign people surrender their sovereignty once government forms; state authority can be resisted only if a tyrant attacks his people. Otherwise the desirability of order trumps the people's right to resist. Grotius learned from Europe's wars of religion that peace among citizens is the primary objective of government, and his principles of self-preservation and prevention of wanton injury were a bare-bones framework designed to achieve that end. He did postulate the natural autonomy of individuals. Reciprocity he also deemed valuable, if only because it provided a rule to prevent others from seizing one's possessions or infringing on the free exercise of one's will.

Pufendorf's major work, *On the Law of Nature and of Nations* (1672), differed from the writings of Grotius because Pufendorf denied the possibility that natural law could be grounded on reason alone rather than reason and revelation together. Through the possibilities of eternal damnation or salvation, God offered man unmatched incentives to develop his capacities not only for self-defense and self-preservation but also for "imperfect" rights to the resources necessary to sustain life. Pufendorf agreed with Grotius that human freedom is restrained by God-given reason and natural law. Challenging Hobbes's notorious portrayal of the state of nature as a state of war, Pufendorf insisted that humans never lived independently of each other. They learned from a very early stage that they must cooperate in order to survive, and obligations arose as a result of the need each person had for others.

The rights and obligations of individuals, though, had to be compounded somehow to form the sovereign authority of the state, and there the fragmented shape of the German city-states provided Pufendorf no easy answers. He reasoned that individuals achieve the standing of "moral persons" not merely as physical beings but as component parts of society through their jobs or callings, their stations, their communities, and their status as parts of the corporate body that makes up the category of "the governed." As such they not only enjoy rights but also have duties, all of which are transformed from the particular wills, rights, and duties of separate individuals into something else. A state, Pufendorf wrote, is a moral body with a single will. Since the distinct wills of many distinct persons cannot be compounded into a single will in "perpetual harmony," the unified will of the state is produced when "all the persons in the state submit their will to that of one man, or of a council, in whom the supreme sovereignty has been vested." Once that sovereign authority is constituted, Pufendorf claimed, it is absolute. It governs not according to the changing will or whims of the people, but is instead "guided by the rule: 'Let the safety of the people be the supreme law.'" It is up to the ruler, not the people, to decide the meaning of *salus populi*, public safety. Since the people rarely understand the reasons behind the ruler's decisions, "the supreme sovereign can rightfully force citizens to all things which he judges to be of any advantage to the public good." The people have no recourse except in the most extreme circumstances, when they have been attacked by a ruler turned tyrant.[61] In the normal course of things, rulers rule and the governed submit.

Pufendorf wrote history as well as theory, and he held the position of court historian to Frederick William of Prussia for much of his life. Three of his ideas helped shape later eighteenth-century thought. First, humans develop the quality of sociability over time. Whereas Grotius had claimed that the propensity to society is natural, Pufendorf argued instead that it arises through a process of historical development, in which the ethic of reciprocity or mutuality emerges at an intermediate stage.[62] Second, Pufendorf considered all rights adventitious, or artificial, rather than brute or fundamental. As they take shape over time they are naturally correlated with obligations, including the duty to take whatever steps the ruler deems necessary to ensure the survival of all members of the community. Third, as cultures develop historically, they pass through stages, from the most primitive condition to that marked by hunting and gathering, then to agriculture, and finally to the most advanced stage of commercial society, in which previously unimaginable luxury becomes possible. The lure of that luxury serves as both a spur to effort and a threat to moral and civic virtue.

Locke preferred Pufendorf's work to that of Grotius for several reasons, including its explicitly religious quality, its concern with the development and regulation of property, and its more extensive conception of duties as well as rights, and he relied on it more heavily in the *Second Treatise*. By making the preservation of all mankind the duty of every individual, however, Locke took the crucial step of broadening the tradition of natural law beyond the scope envisioned either by Grotius or by Pufendorf.[63] Locke shared the idea that sovereign authority originates with the people, but he disagreed with Grotius and Pufendorf that the people ever alienate it completely. Instead it is up to the people, when they form themselves into a body politic, to decide what form of government they want to have. They then entrust their sovereign authority to those in positions of power, whether in a democracy, an aristocracy, a monarchy, or some mixture of those forms, and they consent to be governed by those they have chosen. If rulers lose the trust of the people, Locke argued, it is not, as Pufendorf thought, a problem for the people but a problem for those in power, because the people retain a right to resist whenever their trust has been violated. An absolute ruler is particularly problematical, Locke reasoned, because he must be the judge in his own case, an obvious violation of the principle of reciprocity and the rule of law. For Locke, as for Grotius and Pufendorf, natural law, understood as God's will, remained the unbending framework within which legitimate political decisions could be made. Important as consent was for Locke, it could never legitimate deviations from God's law.

If popular consent is the principle undergirding political authority for Locke, once the people have constituted themselves as "*one Community* or Government," it then falls to the majority to make decisions. Gathering all individuals together is impossible, but logistical obstacles are not the only reason for majority rule. The "variety of Opinions, and contrariety of Interests, which unavoidably happen in all Collections of Men," would make forming a single, unitary judgment at any moment difficult and, over time, impossible. Unless the majority could make decisions for the entire people, the body politic would "be immediately dissolved again."[64] When people formed themselves into a body politic, they chose to concentrate authority in a single leader until they learned that their safety was best secured by locating power in "collective Bodies of Men." Only at that stage, when a representative assembly was constituted, did everyone from the monarch to "the Meanest Men" become subject to the same set of laws.[65]

Locke shared Shaftesbury's reservations concerning the haphazard and inexact system of representation that had gradually evolved in England. The selection of members of Parliament disfranchised not only women and propertyless men—a long-standing assumption rooted in republican ideas of dependency and autonomy[66]—but also certain towns and regions, some of which had sizable populations. The notorious "rotten boroughs" gave access to positions in the House of Commons independent of voters' preferences, and the House of Lords did not even pretend to be a representative body. That situation had emerged because of historical contingencies rather than good reasons, and the time had come to address such inequalities and reapportion electoral districts. "Things in this World are in so constant a Flux that nothing remains long in the same State," Locke observed. "People, Riches, Trade, Power, change their Stations." Cities rise and fall, vacant districts fill and flourish, so that "Customs and Privileges" no longer correspond to present conditions. So it often happens that when legislators are chosen to represent the people, "this *Representation* becomes very *unequal* and disproportionate," a process that had yielded "gross absurdities." Towns with nothing left but ruins, where only "a Shepherd is to be found," sent as many representatives to Parliament as "as a whole County numerous in People." Strangers were right to deride the English electoral system as a farce.[67]

What work should such assemblies do? Although Locke devoted considerable attention to the origin and justification of property rights, he never doubted that property rights are not only secured but also may legitimately be regulated by government. All customs—including those designed to preserve existing forms of inequality, such as primogeniture, which Locke had explicitly criticized in the *First Treatise*—were subject to critical scrutiny according to the same principles as the traditions shielding corrupt elections. Important as establishing principles to protect property holders from unjust incursions by other citizens was to Locke, so was protecting citizens from unjust taxation by a monarch seeking to finance projects inimical to the public good. The goal was to devise standing rules, "*promulgated, establish'd Laws*, not to be varied in particular Cases, but to have one Rule for Rich and Poor, for the Favourite at Court, and the Country Man at Plough." In short, the best means to achieve "the *Peace, Safety, and publick good* of the People" was to apply the same natural jurisprudential standard for regulating property, or voting, or anything else in public affairs.[68]

When the people constituted themselves as a body politic, Locke thought they could choose any form of government they wanted. Neither Christianity nor natural law dictated a particular arrangement. The majority "may imploy all that power in making Laws for the Community" and have those laws executed "by Officers of their own appointing," in which case "the *Form* of the Government is a perfect *Democracy*" of the sort set up by some English communities across the Atlantic. The majority might also choose oligarchy, or monarchy, either hereditary or elective. Finally, if the people wished to combine these pure types, "the Community may make compounded and mixed Forms of Government, as they think good."[69]

Locke was not the first English writer to claim that power, if abused, returns to the people's representatives.[70] In the *Second Treatise*, Locke proposed a practice that had not been tried in England but that was, as he knew from experience, already in place in some of the English colonies in North America. There the colonists had established, as a first step, through an original covenant, charter, or other founding document, the principles and form of their government. Only then did they choose, as a second step, the individuals who would fill those roles. The convention of differentiating between a constitutional assembly, representing the entire people and establishing the fundamentals of government, and a legislative assembly, which with executive and judicial officers would administer the government, did not originate with Locke. In his *Second Treatise*, though, that practice, already common in English colonies across the Atlantic, received an influential formulation.

Whereas Pufendorf held that such authority is constituted only in the form of the state, and can never return to the people once it has been alienated, the greatest long-term significance of Locke's argument for democratic theory was his contention that when rulers place themselves in a "state of war" with their people, sovereignty reverts to the people themselves, and it is up to them to decide how to reconstitute government once it has been dissolved. When James II abdicated, according to Locke and other Whigs, he brought the Stuart monarchy to an end. At that point the people reconstituted the government by welcoming William's army. For that reason Locke's *Second Treatise* seemed to provide a convincing rationale for the Revolution of 1688. Another set of questions, however, remained open. When a legitimate government is operating in accordance with the will of the people, how should a properly constituted representative assembly proceed? Locke's *Second Treatise* did not specify. Should members speak for their constituencies or in accord with their consciences? Were they to be delegates or agents? In either case, how could such an assembly follow natural law? How did the ideas of individual autonomy, equal standing, reciprocity, and popular sovereignty proclaimed in the *Second Treatise* translate into ordinary parliamentary politics? Those unanswered questions too were part of Locke's legacy.

We need not speculate about the implications of Locke's *Second Treatise* for the politics of his day. A document in Locke's handwriting, which dates from the spring of 1690, offers a justification of the rule of William of Orange. Not surprisingly, James's partisans remained unreconciled to William's reign. The former king was gathering a Catholic army in Ireland, where a contingent of English Protestant troops was starving for lack of supplies. The French were threatening to mount an invasion on James's behalf. Were James to return to the throne, the Counter-Reformation would gain momentum. Locke, a favorite of the new king who was invited to fill various prominent ambassadorial positions, would be forced back into exile. The stakes for England,

and for Locke himself, remained high.[71] In a letter to his friend William Clarke, Locke laid out arguments that Clarke could use in Parliament to show why those resisting William's rule should be forced to abjure the former king. As monarch, James had threatened English "laws, libertys, and Religion." Those still intent on his return would "betray England and expose it to popish rage and revenge, . . . a more violent inundation of all sorts of misery than that we were soe lately delivered from." Securing the alternative of peaceful and lawful government, Locke insisted, demanded a formal public declaration of consent, the foundation of all legitimate government. He urged Clarke to support the Abjuration Bill, which required all officials to condemn James's reign and acknowledge William as "the great Restorer."

Locke conceded that unanimity in Parliament on partisan issues was impossible: a "union of opinions" could be reached only through "compulsion," which would just make matters worse. So much did Locke want the legitimacy of William's reign acknowledged in public, however, that he recommended polemical language of the sort he usually eschewed. To skeptics reluctant to accept the Abjuration and Recognition Bills, Locke held out the prospect of conquest by the "potent and vigilant enemy" at our doorstep, Irish and French forces inimical to "our religion and nation." He urged Clarke to dangle before each Member of Parliament, Whig or Tory, the image of his "children stript and his wife ravished," because foreigners "with swords in their hands make no distinction" between parties, especially among those "of a contrary religion."[72] Preventing England from suffering that fate provided the only rationale necessary for William's Protestant forces to subject Catholics in Ireland to just such treatment. The hatreds spawned by that subjugation have persisted.

William himself, it should be noted, seems to have sought nothing so bold as Locke proposed. Instead he was content merely to be acknowledged as king in fact, if not necessarily king by right. Locke wanted more. Nothing loomed larger than a public declaration of consent authorizing William as the legitimate king of England. Only after such consent was formally granted, Locke argued, could politics proceed as usual. Different opinions concerning minor matters do not endanger the fundamentals. Whigs can be Whigs, Tories can be Tories: "Governments have always subsisted and often flourished with such factions as these." The people of England, through their representatives, must, however, acknowledge "the right of the prince they are to obey." Locke sought a public commitment to a polity dedicated to reaching a common understanding of natural law.[73] If his compatriots could embrace deliberative procedures premised on an ethic of reciprocity, they might eventually arrive at similar conclusions on substantive issues of politics.

To most commentators, then as now, such a goal has seemed either chimerical or ominous. Being of the same mind, according to such critics, would squelch the differences of opinion that are the lifeblood of public life. Like most seventeenth-century Puritans, Locke did not share that judgment. The reasons why he was willing to tolerate factions, even though he hoped for agreement, emerge more clearly in the book that made his fame, the only one of his books he acknowledged having written before William's reign was firmly established, his *Essay concerning Human Understanding*. Like the *Second Treatise*, that book was the product of a long period of gestation. Locke had worked on both books for more than a decade. When the two books appeared in 1689, the *Second Treatise* was published anonymously. The *Essay* bore Locke's name.

The supposed inconsistency between Locke's open reliance on natural law in the *Second Treatise* and the philosophical empiricism he inaugurated in the *Essay concerning Human Understanding* has long troubled his interpreters. In the *Essay* Locke denied the existence of innate ideas, a concept descended from scholasticism and given new life by the French rationalist philosopher and mathematician René Descartes. Locke counterposed experience to introspection as the source of human knowledge. He denied even that knowledge of God is innate and contended that "*if the idea of GOD be not innate, no other can be supposed innate.*"[74] Many philosophers have overlooked the common reliance of Locke's *Second Treatise* and his *Essay* on his religious faith. If one sees Locke as a somewhat more timid version of Hobbes or a somewhat less astute precursor of Hume, a would-be champion of atheism, skepticism, and individual interest who simply lacked the courage to carry his ideas to their logical conclusions, then his Protestantism is a distracting annoyance, an embarrassing quirk to be brushed aside as a remnant of an earlier, more credulous era. That attitude has blinded many commentators to the heart of Locke's philosophy, and as a result has distorted both his political ideas and his epistemology.[75]

It is only because we are God's creatures, Locke insisted as forcefully in his *Essay* as he did in the *Second Treatise*, that we have the capacity to reason. That conception of reason as God-given, with grace as the necessary precondition of its proper exercise, undergirds his most important epistemological arguments. In the *Essay* Locke defined man as a "corporeal rational being," by which he meant that humans have the capacity for abstract thought. That capacity is universal, which means that despite the varieties of culture and religious belief, all humans have the potential to reason to the existence of God and from there to their own duties. As creatures of God, all men have autonomous wills; the challenge is to develop the "power of abstracting" in order to reach the conclusion that all persons, as equal children of God, have that same capacity, and each thus has certain obligations to the others.[76] The capacity of abstraction must be developed and tested in experience. Since no ideas are innate, Locke argued, men must reason from certain knowledge of their own existence to the knowledge of an eternal, omnipotent, and all-knowing being. At the end of that process, Locke concluded, "we more certainly know that there is a GOD, than that there is any thing else" outside ourselves.[77] Our knowledge of God comes to us from divine revelation, rather than immediately, but in order to understand and judge the truth of revelation, and to distinguish God's word from that of false prophets, Locke argued, we must use reason.

Locke summarized his argument by asserting two propositions that may strike contemporary readers as contradictory: we must trust reason *and* trust revelation. On the one hand, "*nothing that is contrary to, and inconsistent with the clear and self-evident dictates of reason, has a right to be urged, or assented to, as matter of faith, wherein reason has nothing to do.*" But on the other, "Whatsoever is divine *revelation*, ought to over-rule all our opinions, prejudices, and interests, and hath a right to be received with a full assent."[78] Locke's simultaneous proclamation of both propositions helps explain why he ruled out toleration of atheists and Roman Catholics and worried about all forms of religious enthusiasm. Those who did not believe in God were guilty of failing to use reason and should not be allowed to participate in public life. Those who accepted doctrines such as transubstantiation likewise confused revelation with nonsense, thereby demonstrating their failure to develop their God-given capacity to reason. Fanatics who professed unshakable and unexamined faith, and who denied the possibility that reason might illuminate religion, threatened the moderate sensibility—the commitment to the project Locke called "inquiry"—on which public life as he envisioned it must rest.[79] The singular persuasiveness of Christianity,[80] as Locke understood it, lay in individuals' ability to confirm its truth through the proper exercise of reason.[81]

The older aristocratic ideal of well-bred hauteur, with its accompanying illusion of effortlessness, Locke dismissed. He associated it with the unthinking frame of mind he detested, the mental laziness that sustained absolutism and superstition and could neither understand nor embrace popular sovereignty. The deliberate exercise of reason would lead irresistibly to truth: "What upon full examination I find the most probable, I cannot deny my assent to." Only thoughtless, slavish conformity to prevailing opinion could short-circuit the process. We cannot "hinder our knowledge" nor withhold "our assent" once we perceive the truth, "yet *we can hinder both knowledge and assent, by stopping our enquiry*, and not employing our faculties in the search of any truth."[82]

A life of inquiry requires sustained commitment to critical thinking. Most people would prefer not to be bothered. A note in Locke's journal of 1681 suggests the link he saw between the exercise of reason and the understanding of duty: "Morality as well as mathematics," he wrote, is "capable of demonstration if men would employ their understanding to think about it and not give themselves up to the lazy traditional way of talking."[83] Although everyone has the faculty of reason, few use it. Locke was concerned that many of his contemporaries invoked the idea of natural law as a skyhook to legitimate their own prejudices. Instead he insisted that only through the careful and deliberate exercise of reason, a demanding and difficult process, could humans reach knowledge of truth. Harnessing appetite through will, the exercise that hedonists from his day to ours have contested, Locke affirmed as the path of inquiry.

Locke's lengthy and intricate analysis of liberty, desire, and will in the *Essay* turns on the "hinge," as he puts it, of man's capacity to subject his desires to critical scrutiny. This is "the great privilege of finite intellectual beings," Locke concluded, and "all the *liberty* men have, are capable of, or can be useful to them, and that whereon depends the turn of their actions," depends on their ability to "*suspend* their desires, and stop them from determining their *wills* to any action, till they have duly and fairly *examin'd* the good and evil of it." Our duty consists in holding "our *wills* undetermined" until we have reached a "judgment" concerning not what our passions may dictate but what God wills us to do. Exercising such judgment, using reason to command desire, was Locke's definition of liberty, and it was one of his principal contributions to democratic theory. Autonomy is freedom disciplined by reason and refined by judgment.[84]

Teaching children to develop their natural capacity to reason and "the art of stifling their desires" was the theme of Locke's treatise *Some Thoughts concerning Education*. Published in 1693, after the storms of the immediate post-revolutionary years had subsided and Locke was enjoying greater tranquility than in any earlier phase of his life, the book originated in letters Locke wrote from Holland in 1687 to Edward Clarke and his wife, Mary, Locke's cousin, on the subject of how they should raise their son. The childless Locke counseled avoiding the standard incentives and punishments, arguing that rewarding children with treats teaches them to prize "luxury, pride, or covetousness" instead of virtue. Frequent use of the rod breeds either aversion to the tutor or slavishness, neither of which conduces to the self-discipline that education should instill. The goal of education, to be reached by internalizing the ethics of the Bible more than by learning skills, was consistent with Locke's argument in the *Essay*. "As the Strength of the Body lies chiefly in being able to endure Hardships, so also does that of the Mind. And the great Principle and

Foundation of all Vertue and Worth, is placed in this. That a man is able to *deny himself* his own Desires, cross his own Inclinations, and purely follow what Reason directs as best, tho' the Appetite lean the other way."[85] The echo in Locke's *Education* of arguments in the *Essay* is hardly surprising. Indeed, some passages in his *Education* came directly from letters to Clarke written as Locke was completing the *Essay*, including the 1687 letter already quoted above: Anyone who lacks "a mastery over his inclinations," who cannot resist the lure of "present pleasure or pain" and follow the guidance of reason, does not understand "the true principle of virtue and industry" and will never amount to anything.[86]

Powerful as reason is in directing people toward virtue, the most profound ethical truths are disclosed only through revelation. In his tract *The Reasonableness of Christianity* (1695), Locke brought together his arguments on faith and reason in the *Letter concerning Toleration* and the *Essay concerning Human Understanding*. Locke published *The Reasonableness of Christianity* anonymously. Stepping into a prominent public role, first as one of the commissioners for trade and plantations, then on the Board of Trade, he had no desire to jeopardize his reputation, his position, or his salary. His prudence was warranted: his arguments undercut the authority of the privileged patrons who made Locke much more comfortable in his final years than he had been earlier in his life.

To illustrate his contention in the *Essay* that all humans could grasp the higher truths of Christianity, Locke pointed out that Jesus gathered "a company of poor, ignorant, illiterate men," simple but inspired fishermen.[87] Those original disciples, though, like Locke's own contemporaries, needed help. The supplement they required was not sophisticated philosophical training, however, but revelation, the model and teaching of Jesus, "one manifestly sent from God, and coming with visible authority from him."[88] If the models of Christian conversion were the untutored, ordinary people whom Jesus recruited, so the untutored, ordinary people of Locke's England might, by engaging in rational inquiry and accepting the gift of God's grace, come to understand the sublime ethical truth of Christian benevolence and the principles of natural law that should guide them in the public realm. Those central principles made Christianity "reasonable," as even members of other cultures might eventually come to see.

Locke's religiosity thus explains why he could hold out the hope—unlikely ever to be realized—that eventually all people would come to a shared understanding of the principles he derived from his Protestant faith and proclaimed in all his writings, the principles of natural law. That understanding, because it was not innate, would develop over time and through the exercise of reason in the process of critical inquiry. It was bound to result in differences of judgment concerning inevitably contentious issues. Representative government would not resolve disputes once and for all. The process of deliberation, however, might enable both representatives and those they represented to develop, gradually and fitfully, a clearer understanding of the principle Locke identified in the *Second Treatise*: "The Law of Nature stands as an Eternal Rule to all Men, *Legislators* as well as others. The *Rules* that they make," which must apply to everyone from the highest to the lowest, must "be conformable to the Law of Nature, i.e., to the Will of God, of which that is a Declaration, and the *fundamental Law of Nature* being *the preservation of Mankind*, no Humane Sanction can be good, or valid against it."[89]

The virtuous self that Locke envisioned would develop in multiple dimensions: first, by following the idea of a "calling" in the domain of productive labor; second, by seeking in the public sphere to make possible a polity devoted to the common good of all mankind; third, by aspiring to master unruly desires according to reason and the ethic of benevolence laid out in the Gospels; and finally, above all, by striving to do God's will and, through God's grace, gain eternal salvation. The lure of the virtuous self made some version of representative democracy possible, difficult, and necessary, even within the prevailing framework of constitutional monarchy. People devoted to the ideals of autonomy, equality, and reciprocity could make popular government work, but fallible humans, trying to operate within the boundaries of natural law, would necessarily come into conflict. Precisely the chafing felt by the virtuous self, when confronting ideas and activities that strayed from the strict guidelines of God's will, rendered essential the limitations that democratic decision making places on those who would presume to define the common good.[90]

If Locke's arguments for popular sovereignty were incendiary in the 1670s and even the late 1680s, after 1688 they were no longer anomalous, as the fierce pamphleteering of the immediate postrevolutionary era made clear. Prominent radical tracts from preceding decades, including works by Hunton, Lawson, Milton, and Sidney, were reprinted or adapted to the controversies of the day. As debates surrounding the work of the Convention Parliament and the Declaration of Rights in 1689 made clear, an understanding had emerged that the Convention, as a kind of constitution-drafting body, was "something greater, and of greater power, than a Parliament," an institution that "has more power than a Parliament, and is its creator."[91] Moreover, the Convention debates reflected the increasingly widespread idea that government rested on a prior agreement of the people, the concept of a social contract that had surfaced in Leveller tracts and received more detailed discussion in Hobbes, Sidney, and

Locke. Not only were these ideas articulated in the debates of the Convention; they found expression in the first draft of the Declaration of Rights.

Contemporaries understood that England was at a crossroads. "Remember that the Government being dissolved," urged a paper said to have been written by the Marquis of Halifax, "we are in such a state at present as a people are where no government is yet set up. In such a state, the people are to meet in their Representatives, and agree upon their constitution, before they choose their governour for the Administration." This preliminary step was momentous, the Convention was reminded: "Redeem us from slavery, what you omit now is lost for ever." Or in the words of another writer, the Convention enjoyed "an opportunity we are like never to have again in the World."[92]

The Convention adopted a watered-down version of the Declaration of Rights that reflected the anxieties shared by the Lords and by Tories in the Commons. Proclaiming a contract between the people and the king would limit the monarch's authority and enshrine the people's sovereignty, just as Sidney and Locke had suggested, and as indeed the first draft of the Declaration of Rights would have done. The Declaration as adopted nevertheless redefined relations between crown and Parliament, as William's resistance to the revised Declaration made clear. It established Parliament's role in a mixed monarchy rather than radicals' idea of parliamentary supremacy, and it lacked an explicit statement that the King's authority derived from the people. Yet the Declaration of Rights nevertheless marked an important shift in the relative authority of the monarch and the representative assembly. No longer would the king be allowed either to suspend or dispense with laws, nor to maintain a standing army, without the approval of Parliament. If William's acceptance of the crown did not depend (as was long thought) on his prior acceptance of the Declaration of Rights, which in fact he publicly ignored, Parliament did become, after 1689, both much more active and more influential in shaping English culture. The fact that many pamphleteers in the early eighteenth century took for granted the doctrines of social contract and popular sovereignty indicates how much the ideological ground shifted, even as the economic and political realities gradually moved in the opposite direction thanks to an increasingly hegemonic landowning elite.[93]

The other relevant achievement of the post-1688 settlement was the Toleration Act, a step toward democracy as small as that represented by the Declaration of Rights—but nevertheless equally significant. Left out were not only Jews and Catholics but also Quakers and Deists. Only those ministers who took the Oaths of Allegiance and Supremacy and embraced most of the Anglican Thirty-nine Articles were permitted to gather in their own places of worship. Such churches proliferated. By 1710 there were almost 10,000

Anglican parishes and more than 2,500 non-conforming congregations. England was on its way, slowly, toward at least limited religious pluralism. Not coincidentally, it was also moving simultaneously toward both somewhat greater toleration among Protestant sects and, at least within some parts of eighteenth-century English culture, a more relaxed attitude toward religion itself.

Throughout the following decades, religious anxieties and animosities became less pronounced, and public engagement with political issues likewise waned. Parliament stipulated in 1701 that all future kings must at least be Anglican, if not English, a step made necessary by the turn from the Stuarts to the German house of Hanover in 1701. Paradoxically, Parliament's increasing independence from the monarchy occurred at the same time that rival oligarchies were tightening their grip on public life in England. William's accession in 1689 set in motion a long-term transformation of English government. The consolidation of power in Parliament, the creation of the Bank of England and the financial revolution that followed, and the Union of 1707 that ended the legislative independence of Scotland all helped create the much more vigorous eighteenth-century state of Great Britain.[94]

All that stabilization and consolidation, however, came at the cost of diminishing even further the already limited significance of electoral politics. The unrepresentative nature of Parliament noted by Shaftesbury, Locke, and Wildman persisted, as each of the counties with much smaller populations, such as those in Wales and, after 1707, Scotland, sent two MPs to the House of Commons, just as much more populous counties did. Only males over twenty-one years of age, who owned freehold property worth forty shillings annually, could vote in elections for county seats in Parliament. The qualifications to vote in elections for borough seats, which were more numerous in the South and Southwest than in the North, followed local custom and sometimes permitted artisans or shopkeepers to vote.

Those were hardly the only practices limiting popular influence in politics. In many instances prominent local figures still decided among themselves who should stand for elective office, whether the two county seats should simply be divided between Tory and Whig candidates, and whether elections should even be held. Sometimes groups of voters gathered in advance to express their preferences, after which one or more candidates withdrew rather than face the humiliation of electoral defeat. At other times voters were offered no choice and simply told by local leaders who their "representatives" would be. Moreover, many borough MPs were simply selected, either directly or indirectly, by influential members of the House of Lords. Notwithstanding those limitations, the years between 1689 and 1714 were the high-water mark for the electorate's influence in English politics until the final decades of the nineteenth century. Perhaps as many as one-quarter of adult males were at least eligible to vote in some elections, a number higher than that reached in the mid-nineteenth century. As criteria shifted rapidly from election to election, an even higher percentage might have voted at least once during these years. There is evidence of lively public engagement with substantive issues in some electoral contests. From 1714 to 1721, as elections became less frequent and enclosures further diminished the number and independence of English farmers and craftsmen, this brief opening of heightened democratic engagement snapped shut.[95]

The House of Lords, of course, existed entirely outside the realm of popular politics, and as the eighteenth century unfolded, and kings needed more leverage to influence an increasingly independent Parliament, the creation of peerages and the awarding of pensions and places became ever more important in parliamentary politics. All of these strategies together earned the general name "influence" or, to use the term preferred by critics, "corruption." Kings used such techniques of patronage to stabilize but also further subvert the "popular" part of what the English revered as their "mixed" government, which ostensibly included democratic as well as aristocratic and monarchical elements but actually tended more and more toward rule by a closed elite. By the middle of the eighteenth century, fewer than 10 percent of elections for county seats in Parliament were being contested. Some counties went decades without voting, some boroughs over a century. Although Whigs and Tories originally divided according to their opposition to or approbation of the Stuart monarchs in the 1670s, by the time of George I that partisan divide gave way to ever more complex and shifting fissures, perhaps the most important being the divisions between the landed and the monied elites, and between the "Court" and "Country" factions who criticized the Whig oligarchy from different perspectives. During the middle decades of the eighteenth century, the earlier republican alternative to the English model of sovereignty, king-in-Parliament, faded from the position it had occupied from the 1640s onward.

From the writings of the Levellers and the New Model Army's debates to Sidney's *Discourses* and Locke's *Second Treatise*, the English people had at least entertained the possibility that the people should rule. During the eighteenth century that option slowly vanished from sight. Revulsion against the violence and anarchy of the midcentury was so intense that the change of monarchy effected by the coup of 1688 proceeded with little or no public opposition, as did the transition from the Stuart to the Hanover line of succession. The English people had experienced popular government, and they had turned against it decisively and, evidently, permanently. Although the scope and size of the electorate would again be debated in the nineteenth century, the more fundamental question about whether ordinary people could fill the roles played by the monarch and the aristocracy never again emerged as a live option in British politics.[96]

The historical significance of 1688 becomes clearer when its consequences in England are compared with those in England's North American colonies. After the restoration, England sought to tighten its grip on the colonies and profit from their products and their commercial potential. First, the Navigation Acts shunted European goods headed to North America through English port cities and channeled colonial products—especially the most profitable, sugar and tobacco—to England, on English ships, steps designed to increase the flow of commerce and the revenues from customs. Second, new proprietary colonies thought to be more likely to benefit the crown were established in New York, where the Dutch colony was conquered in 1664, in New Jersey, and in Pennsylvania. Royal charters issued for Rhode Island, Connecticut, and Massachusetts were likewise intended to reduce these colonies' notorious pretensions to self-government. The American colonies, according to the Duke of Portland, unfortunately thought of themselves as "little commonwealths" making their own laws "without having any regard as to their being repugnant to the laws of England."[97]

The Stuarts interpreted such impertinence as an intolerable affront to their authority. When representative assemblies in Virginia, Maryland, New Jersey, and New York protested against new taxes imposed without their approval, they were told brusquely that as a subordinate people they enjoyed only those rights the king deemed fit to grant them. James made clear, when the governor of New York requested permission to form an assembly, that such institutions of popular government threatened the principle of absolute monarchy: "I cannot but suspect they would be of dangerous consequence," he predicted, "nothing being more knowne than the aptness of such bodyes to assume in themselves many privileges which prove destructive to, or very oft disturbe, the peace of the govererment wherein they are allowed." The self-important assemblies of Virginia and Massachusetts had taught James a lesson. Against his better judgment, James reluctantly allowed the creation of an assembly to satisfy the governor of New York. When it produced a "Charter of Libertyes and Privileges" equating its power with that of Parliament, he dissolved it.[98]

The crown's bluntest challenge to the colonies' autonomy was the proclamation of the Dominion of New England in 1684. The Massachusetts assembly had greeted Charles's earlier attempt to issue a new charter in 1678 by claiming that "the lawes of England are bounded within the four seas and doe not reach America." The colonists' defiance echoed and extended the arguments advanced in the 1641 Massachusetts *Body of Liberties*. Only laws enacted by their own representatives could be enforced.[99] The Dominion not only revoked that charter but also ended the independent status of Massachusetts, which was henceforth to be submerged within a vast new colony stretching from Canada to the Delaware River. All the colonial assemblies in the Dominion were disbanded. Anglican military officer Sir Edmund Andros was given authority to rule the Dominion. Town meetings were severely restricted. Strictures against the Church of England were declared invalid. The validity of longstanding property claims was challenged. To enforce the rules of this new regime, English troops were to be quartered in America. To pay for this vastly expanded English presence, taxes were to be raised to unprecedented levels.

Not surprisingly, the Dominion infuriated almost everyone in New England. Sermons were preached and pamphlets printed, all expressing the colonists' outrage. In petitions submitted in 1683 and 1685, the people of Massachusetts advanced a proto-Lockean labor theory of property, rooting their claims to the land in their "sore labour and indefattigable industry" as well as their rights to be represented in their own assembly.[100] From the town of Ipswich, the Puritan minister John Wise inflamed his congregation to vote against the new tax. Their "Privilidges" as Englishmen, he insisted, meant that it was not "the townes Duties any wayes to Assist those ill Methods of Raising money without a General Assembly." Like critics of absolutism in England, Wise was arrested. At his trial, the judge, Joseph Dudley, flatly dismissed the colonists' case. In his words, "You have no more privilidges left you, than not to be sold for Slaves." Wise was convicted, jailed for three weeks, fined fifty pounds, and barred from preaching for a year.[101]

Dudley's claim, standard for absolutists everywhere, did not go down well in New England. Because not only the idea but also the practice of self-government through representative assembly were taken for granted, the Dominion represented a frontal assault on New Englanders' self-understanding. Andros and Dudley did not entirely lack allies. In Connecticut the onetime minister and onetime physician Gershom Bulkeley, serving under Andros as a justice of the peace in Hartford, savaged the sensibility of his fellow New Englanders as "a levelling, independent democratical principle and spirit," which he characterized as "a very churlish drug." This "frontier Filmer," as Bulkeley has been called, articulated the principles of divine right, hierarchy, and absolute monarchical authority that undergirded the reigns of Charles and James in England, Louis XIV in France, and countless rulers with equal ambition if less power scattered across Europe. Among political commentators in England's

North American colonies, however, Bulkeley stands out as an exception. Because absolute monarchy is divinely ordained, he reasoned, it "is the best form or kind of civil government," and the king is "the minister of God for our good, and the fountain of all lawful civil authority within all his dominions." So "rebellion against the king is a mediate rebellion against God, and is like the sin of witchcraft." Bulkeley's tract, published in Philadelphia because—significantly—no Boston printer would touch it, testifies to his unusual status as one of very few writers born in New England who disputed the legitimacy of the colonies' ideas and institutions of self-government. Indeed, when rumors of James's flight and William's accession to the English throne arrived in the New World, the colonists were quick to designate William their "deliverer" and proclaim their gratitude for having been spared the popish plot signaled by the Dominion. The Glorious Revolution set in motion a series of developments, some immediate, some taking several decades, that restored throughout the American colonies the extraordinary degree of political autonomy that Charles and James had sought to end.[102]

Not surprisingly, given their history of cantankerous resistance to the crown's authority, the most immediate changes came in New England. On April 18, 1689, dissident leaders in Boston gathered together a crowd two thousand strong and removed Andros from power before his English troops could be mustered to defend him. Andros's demise was greeted with as much enthusiasm and as little opposition in New England as was James's in England, and for some of the same reasons. Fears of popery were real on both sides of the Atlantic. New Englanders looked forward not only to restoring their political institutions and securing the title to their property but also to ending the imposed toleration of "rom-ish" Anglicans that Andros had inaugurated. Cotton Mather, then twenty-six years old, read a hastily written tract from the balcony of the Boston Town House. He denounced Andros and his "Crew of abject Persons" as "Tools of the Adversary," the instruments of Satan. Motivated by "their own insatiable Avarice and Beggary," these "Horse-leeches" imposed, on the basis of their own illegitimate authority, laws "as impossible for us to know" as they were "dangerous for us to break."[103]

The spring of 1689 found Cotton Mather's father, Increase Mather, already in London. The colony had sent Increase on a mission, while Andros was still in power, to restore its earlier charter. Although Increase welcomed William's accession as a sign of God's renewed favor toward the nonconformists whom Charles and James had persecuted, the Act of Toleration in 1690 came as a blow to him and to his fellow New England Puritans. Without abandoning his conviction that Anglicans, Presbyterians, Quakers, and others had no place among the saints striving to perform their divinely inspired errand, Increase had no choice but to accept the best deal he could get. The charter that he negotiated for Massachusetts represented a mixture of gains and losses. It restored an elected General Court and the autonomy of town government. It provided that members of the Governor's Council would be selected not by the governor but by the people's own representatives. The new charter repudiated the Puritans' principle that only church members should vote. Now property rather than the test of saving grace would be the criterion; a forty-shilling freehold became the standard in Massachusetts, as it did in neighboring Connecticut and Rhode Island. Toleration was extended to all Protestants. Neither papists nor persons deemed "vicious in life" would be permitted to vote anywhere in New England.

Masking his disappointment, Increase Mather characterized the new charter as "a MAGNA CHARTA" in which men's liberties and property were "confirmed and secured." Yet the result was hardly what he wanted. The charter of 1691, he conceded ruefully, was "more Monarchical and less Democratical than in former Times."[104] Even so, the combination of widespread church membership, widespread landownership, and the lax enforcement in the towns of restrictions mandated by the charter meant that as many as 75 percent of adult males in Massachusetts were eligible to vote in the early eighteenth century.[105] New Englanders continued to think of themselves, and to vote, as they had done for decades, not as atomistic individuals but as members of towns and congregations, as participants in local communities that had much greater significance for them than did the policies enacted in the provincial capital or the metropolis of London.[106]

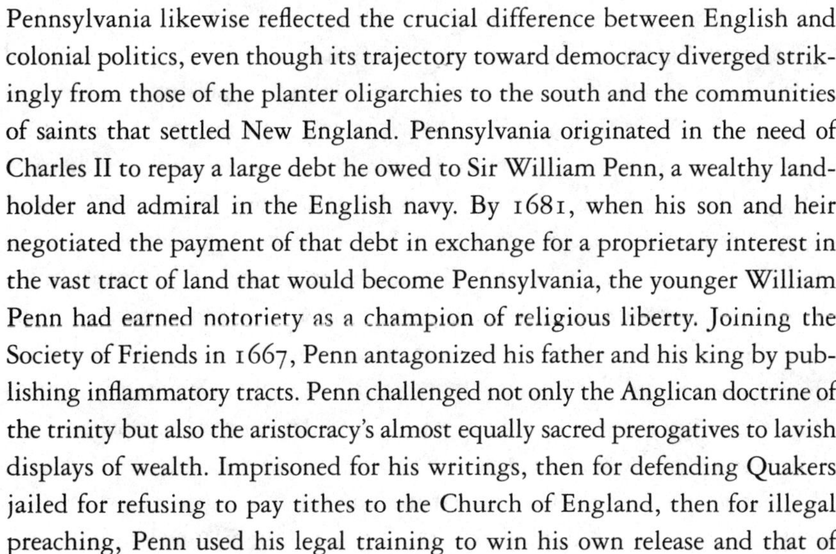

Pennsylvania likewise reflected the crucial difference between English and colonial politics, even though its trajectory toward democracy diverged strikingly from those of the planter oligarchies to the south and the communities of saints that settled New England. Pennsylvania originated in the need of Charles II to repay a large debt he owed to Sir William Penn, a wealthy landholder and admiral in the English navy. By 1681, when his son and heir negotiated the payment of that debt in exchange for a proprietary interest in the vast tract of land that would become Pennsylvania, the younger William Penn had earned notoriety as a champion of religious liberty. Joining the Society of Friends in 1667, Penn antagonized his father and his king by publishing inflammatory tracts. Penn challenged not only the Anglican doctrine of the trinity but also the aristocracy's almost equally sacred prerogatives to lavish displays of wealth. Imprisoned for his writings, then for defending Quakers jailed for refusing to pay tithes to the Church of England, then for illegal preaching, Penn used his legal training to win his own release and that of

Quaker leader George Fox, and to argue the cause of freedom of conscience. Not only were Quakers imprisoned for refusing to take oaths or remove their hats before earthly authorities; their refusal to conform to Anglican practices led to the confiscation of their property. Thus Penn and other dissenters began to link their crusade for religious liberty to the cause of inviolable property rights, not because the latter was real and the former a sham but because the persecution they suffered linked the two.

Freedom of conscience was a cause that made strange bedfellows in Restoration England. On the one hand, Penn had befriended the Catholic James, the Duke of York, while Penn was studying law, attending at court, and chafing at Anglican discipline in the 1660s. It was James who secured Penn's release from the Tower in 1668. On the other, while Penn was on a missionary trip through Holland in the early 1670s, he had been introduced by the Quaker Benjamin Furly to the dissident Algernon Sidney. In 1679, as previously noted, Penn managed Sidney's electoral campaign.[107] Penn had first attracted the attention of English radicals when the transcript of his 1670 trial was reprinted nine times in four months. In his trial he appealed over the heads of the court and Parliament to "the Law of *nature*," which he said protected the "liberty and property" of individuals against all intrusions of state authority. "Where Liberty and Property are destroyed, there must alwayes be a state of force and war," which "will be esteemed intolerable by the *Invaded*, who will no longer remain subject."[108] Penn's use of natural law echoed the arguments of Grotius and Pufendorf and uncannily resembled the argument Locke was to make in the *Second Treatise*. Penn's arguments for religious liberty in *England's Present Interest Considered* (1675) likewise paralleled Locke's later yoking of freedom of conscience with the right to property as among men's "natural and civil rights" under the will of God.[109]

Penn's conception of politics as the pursuit of the common good had surfaced earlier. His first contribution to shaping the politics of England's colonies, the West New Jersey Concessions and Agreements of 1676, provided far-reaching powers for the popularly elected assembly of the new colony.[110] In the process of trying to resolve a dispute between two Quakers engaged in establishing a colony west of the Delaware River, Penn acquired the land that became Pennsylvania.[111] The founding documents of Pennsylvania illustrate the extent to which Penn's convictions as a Quaker aligned with the principles of popular sovereignty, autonomy, equality, and mutuality. The Quakers were among the most democratic of sects; their commitment to human equality extended from pious proclamation to practice. Quakers were to be among the pioneers in opposing slavery and advancing women's rights, and that sensibility manifested itself in Penn's unusual approach to dealing with those already occupying the land on which he planned to build his colony. Penn stipulated in his original "Concessions to the Province of Pennsylvania" (1681) that the settlers must acknowledge the legitimate claims of those already there. Although Penn seems not to have focused on the gulf between English and Native American ideas concerning "improvement of their ground" and the meaning of law, his proposals for dealing with native peoples did inaugurate the relatively peaceful interactions with Indians that would characterize the colony that bore his name.[112]

The following year Penn submitted to the freemen of the new colony his ambitious "Charter of Liberties and Frame of Government of the Province of Pennsylvania in America," one of the most thoughtful and significant among the many reflections on government produced in the seventeenth century. Penn conceded that disagreements arise immediately whenever people contemplate the first principles of government. Indeed, there is "nothing the wits of men are more busy and divided upon. It is true, they seem to agree to the end, to wit, happiness; but in the means, they differ." Differences emerge primarily because "men side with their passions against their reason, and their sinister interests have so strong a bias upon their minds, that they lean to them gainst the good of the things they know." Penn contended that all frames of government are suited only to particular times, places, and people, so it was folly to imagine a universal model. Finally, he denied that choosing among the three standard forms of government, monarchy, aristocracy, and democracy, matters as much as the principle of popular sovereignty. Government is "*free to the people under it*," no matter what form it takes, whenever the rule of law prevails and "*the people are a party to those laws*." Wherever that animating principle is in place, government can flourish; wherever it is not, "tyranny, oligarchy, or confusion" reigns.

The mechanics of government matter less than the culture within which institutions and laws operate. "Let men be good," Penn insisted, "and the government cannot be bad; if it be ill, they will cure it." No airtight defense against corruption exists; bad men will "warp and spoil" even the best government. Therefore, educating citizens in "wisdom and virtue" is the most important responsibility of government, because men so instructed will "*secure the people from the abuse of power*, that they may be free by their just obedience." Quakers envisioned a world in which all citizens flourish by willing observance of the law: "Liberty without obedience is confusion," according to Penn, and "obedience without liberty is slavery." Achieving the proper balance requires citizens equal to and respectful of each other and a constitution rooted firmly in the commitment of the sovereign people to do the will of God.[113]

The specific form of government Penn offered to the freeman and pledged to honor, as proprietor and governor, proved as influential in the second half of the eighteenth century as it was controversial in his day. Penn proposed that all the freemen meet on December 20, 1682, and "chuse out of themselves seventy-two persons of most note for their wisdom, virtue, and ability," who would constitute the Provincial Council and meet once every month. One-third of the council would then be elected every year. No member of this body could serve more than a three-year term of office before cycling off for at least one year. Such rotation would ensure fresh blood in the upper house of the bicameral assembly, which had sole power to propose legislation and over which the governor or his deputy would preside. Besides erecting law courts and executing the laws of the province through the innovation of four standing committees, the council and governor were charged with laying out all towns and cities, markets and schools, and roads and highways, a provision still visible in the street grid distinguishing Philadelphia from other early cities established in England's colonies.

Beginning in 1683, Penn proposed that all the freemen of the colony gather, at the same time and place as the election of the Provincial Council, as the General Assembly to meet with, and discuss laws proposed by, the governor and the council. Although admittedly cumbersome, this review of all legislation would guarantee that all laws "have the more full concurrence of the freemen of the province." Because Penn hoped the population of the province would grow rapidly, as indeed it did, his plan specified that after the first year the membership in this assembly would be capped, initially at no more than two hundred representatives, which would then be permitted to grow ultimately to five hundred. Consistent with the concerns of dissenters such as Shaftesbury, Sidney, and Locke, Penn specified that representation be fairly apportioned as new towns and counties were formed to accommodate a growing number of families. All other government officials, including judges, sheriffs, and coroners, were to be selected by the Provincial Council from those proposed by the General Assembly.

So far this plan seems a dream vision, a utopia of representative government in which all decisions are made with the active participation of every property owner in the province. Penn was the sole proprietor of Pennsylvania as well as its first governor, however, and he intended to keep his office. Looking forward, the Frame also provided "that at all times when, and so often as it shall happen that the Governor shall or may be an infant, under the age of one and twenty years," the council should designate a committee of guardians until the governor reached adulthood. So amidst all the rotation of office, not only was the governor of Pennsylvania to rule for life, but also the position was to be hereditary. Even Penn, who made no provision for a landed aristocracy of the sort known for centuries in England and that Locke and Shaftesbury took for granted in Carolina, and who was as committed to the principles of popular sovereignty and equality as almost anyone of his generation, could envision representative government only if he served as the functional equivalent of the colony's monarch. Council membership would rotate, and the earliest General Assembly would include every property owner, but the executive enjoyed life tenure and could bequeath his position to his heir.

Freemen were to include every inhabitant who purchased one hundred acres of land, at a minimal price, and cultivated but ten acres of it; any former servant or bondsman who purchased half that amount and cultivated twenty acres of it; or anyone who paid property taxes. Moreover, "every such person shall, and may, be capable of electing, or being elected, representatives of the people, in provincial Council, or General Assembly." Penn's Quaker principles forbade any institutionalized inequality among members of the community. Nowhere in America was the principle of equality as rigorously proclaimed—or the goal of political, social, and economic equality as fully realized—as in Pennsylvania. Yet there were limits. Unlike Harrington, whose plan he otherwise followed in many respects, Penn provided no agrarian law, and very quickly the wealthiest merchants and landowners emerged to dominate the Provincial Council. Since suffrage was limited to men who paid a house tax, even elections for the General Assembly soon shut out not only slaves and servants but anyone—farm laborers, artisans, sailors, any adult sons still living with their parents—who did not live in his own home. The distance between the expansive, democratic language of Penn's Frame and the reality of Pennsylvania politics became apparent very fast.

The section of this founding document entitled "Laws Agreed Upon in England, etc." contains many of the provisions that distinguished Pennsylvania from many other English colonies. All voting was to be done by ballot, and no rewards were to be offered or received for votes. All trials "shall be by twelve men, and as near as may be, peers or equals, and of the neighborhood." All laws were to be published; all fees moderate, all prisons or workhouses local and free; all servants and the terms of their service registered and none kept beyond their time; and all children "taught some useful trade or skill, to the end none may be idle, but the poor may work to live, and the rich, if they become poor may not want." Not surprisingly, many of those provisions were consciously designed to address the features of English life that Penn found most problematic.

Finally, Penn specified that although all officers of the law "shall be such as possess faith in Jesus Christ," the religious tests standard in Restoration England and in most English colonies would be abandoned. In Pennsylvania, all persons "who acknowledge the one Almighty and eternal God, to be the

Creator, Upholder and Ruler of the world; and that hold themselves obliged in conscience to live peaceably and justly in civil society," were free to practice their own religion. Moreover, no taxes were to be assessed to support any sect. In short, everything having to do with religious establishment that Anglicans demanded in England—and Puritans demanded in Massachusetts—was outlawed in Pennsylvania.

Lest we forget the difference between the discipline expected by devout Quakers and the unrestrained personal freedom celebrated in our own day, note that Penn followed his ringing denunciation of religious persecution with his endorsement of the early Christians' practice of preserving Sundays for the worship of God, which settlers in the province would be expected to do in their own ways. Then came an equally passionate denunciation of prohibited "offences against God." These included not only "swearing, cursing, lying, prophane talking, drunkenness, drinking of healths, obscene words, incest, sodomy, rapes, whoredom, [and] fornication" but also a much longer list of other crimes, including treason, murder, felony, sedition, and activities such as staging plays, playing dice or cards, and other games such as "bull-baitings, cock-fightings, bear-baitings, and the like." Even Penn, no Puritan, a champion of religious freedom, an egalitarian, and one of the very few involved in European colonization projects willing to accept people of other faiths and from other nations, espoused—and expected to enforce—a strict code of personal behavior. That code extended from public life to what is now considered the private sphere, a distinction unfamiliar then. The banned forms of behavior and recreation, Penn wrote, "excite the people to rudeness, cruelty, looseness, and irreligion."

The culture of democracy requires an ethic of mutuality, which for Penn rested on what he called the ideal of "Christian love." When Penn deemed Pennsylvania "a holy experiment" and dubbed Philadelphia the "city of brotherly love," he meant it. Inasmuch as he judged certain activities or entertainments corrosive of the dispositions necessary for the flourishing of those public ideals, the cultivation of wisdom and virtue, Penn shared the view of many seventeenth-century English nonconformists that such practices were to be discouraged. Of course, the necessity of prohibiting everything on those lists confirms our smug assumption that such practices must have been widespread and commonly tolerated. Perhaps before we condescend to the priggishness of Penn and his contemporaries, we should reflect more carefully on the values implicit in those prohibitions, the reasons for our instinctive reactions to them, and the consequences for our democracy.[114] Penn was adamant about separating "Religion and Polity," which he considered "two distinct things" with "two separate ends." But that did not mean toleration should extend to behaviors inimical to the cultural foundations of democracy.[115]

Unlike the Levellers' pamphlets, or Sidney's *Discourses*, or Locke's *Two Treatises of Government*, the writings of the founders of American colonies turned into constitutions, spawned institutional forms, and ultimately yielded laws, all of which immediately collided with reality. Those collisions reveal the difference between political life in America and England after 1688. Penn fancied himself a friend of the people, but the people themselves were not so sure. He encountered resistance from the outset. Penn admitted that his motives were mixed. Although he intended to guarantee religious freedom, he expected to be compensated for his efforts.[116] Penn's fellow investors shared his desire to turn a profit from sales of real estate, and the rapid development of towns and roads reflected their desire to help colonists get their produce to market. Pennsylvania rapidly established itself as the "best poor man's country" because the land was fertile, the climate moderate, and the religious and political restrictions looser than anywhere else at the time. Penn and other promoters circulated tracts celebrating the province. In Penn's words, the "difference of labouring for themselves and for others" was never better understood than by those able to establish themselves as farmers west of the Delaware River.[117] Such promotional tracts had the desired effect: by 1686 the colony had attracted more than eight thousand setters. Many were Quakers from England, but Pennsylvania also attracted those who had already settled in New York or New Jersey, including Swedish Lutherans, German Pietists, and Dutch Calvinists, and immigrants fleeing other sorts of religious persecution or economic restrictions, including Catholics, Huguenots, and Jews.

During those first two years, Penn's spirits soared, but soon a combination of economic and political disappointments propelled him back to England in despair. Rents were not being paid, profits never materialized, and sharp disagreements divided the people who thronged to the colony. Early settlers, who had clustered on the lower banks of the Delaware before the Quakers' arrival, resented their presumptuousness. They clamored for an equal voice in public affairs and demanded better protection from pirates raiding their settlements. Among the Quakers themselves, disputes between rival groups exploded the dream of a peaceful community. Even the Philadelphia meetinghouse, dedicated to the peaceful resolution of disagreements, split in two, and Friends accustomed to waiting in silence for God's "inner light" found themselves instead shouting epithets at each other. As if those rivalries were not enough, competing factions emerged around Penn himself. Penn's supporters proclaimed themselves as deeply committed to the public good as Penn himself, but the anti-Penn camp saw in their policies only greed masked by pious hypocrisy. Disillusioned, demoralized, and losing money quickly, thanks in part to spending habits more in keeping with his English gentry status than with the plain clothes and humble manners preferred by most of his fellow Quakers, Penn pleaded in 1685 with the freemen whom he had welcomed just two years before: "For the love of god, me & the poor Country, be not so Governmentish, so Noisy & open in yr dissatisfactions."[118]

Penn returned to England hopeful that his friendship with James II might help him restore his wealth even if he could not regain his control over his colony. He continued to struggle, however, and politics in Pennsylvania grew ever more contentious as the colony's population became more diverse. Visiting the Quaker Benjamin Furly in Holland in 1686, Penn was introduced to Locke, who lived with Furly in Rotterdam for two years before returning to England after William's accession. Penn remained proud of his "holy experiment" and convinced that the problems he was facing in Pennsylvania resulted not from his Frame of Government but from the fecklessness of its contentious people. After reading the copy of the Frame that Penn gave him, Locke disagreed. He copied down in his journal some of the provisions of Penn's Frame, followed by his own commentary. The entries illuminate both men's ways of thinking.

Locke saw plenty of problems. He deemed "inconvenient" Penn's plan to have all the freemen of the colony meet in one place. He wondered what would happen if those selected for office proved not to be notable for their "wisdom, virtue, and ability." Locke judged "dangerous" Penn's plan to have the governor and the Provincial Council create the courts of law, and his plan to provide common schools "the surest check upon liberty of conscience, suppressing all displeasing opinions in the bud." Penn had stipulated that any person who "shall abuse or deride" others for their religion would be punished as a "disturber of the peace," which Locke predicted would lead to "perpetual persecution and animosity." Penn provided for fines or imprisonment for anyone speaking "loosely or prophanely" about God or the Bible; Locke wondered who would decide what constituted such speech.

In short, Penn's experience of persecution, his devotion to the Society of Friends, and his confidence in his own judgment had led him to worry more about the effects of establishment than about the costs of toleration, and more about lax observance than about the dangers of his own authority. Locke's experience of covert political activity followed by exile had alerted him to the possibility that yoking civil power to any religious authority threatened freedom of conscience. Penn's experience with Friends' meetings alerted him to the potential creativity of uncoerced deliberation. Locke's participation in the myriad schemes hatched during and after the Exclusion Crisis showed him that calculations of advantage tend to poison the discussions of even the most like-minded and engaged citizens. Locke believed the details of execution and enforcement were bound to bedevil Penn's bare bones outline. In Locke's words, "The whole is so far from a frame of government that it scarce contains a part of the materials."[119]

Unlike Harrington's utopian commonwealth or Locke and Shaftesbury's dream vision of a feudal Carolina, however, Penn's Frame did become law. To his dismay, problems of the sort Locke identified surfaced almost immediately. Maneuvering to improve his own situation in England, Penn fared no better than he did in his attempts to resolve the conflicts in his colony. In what would prove to be the final year of James's reign, Penn intervened to obtain a pardon for his fellow nonconformist John Locke, who was astutely reading the winds of change and did not want or, as it turned out, need that pardon.[120] When William III took the throne vacated by James II, it was Penn who found himself without a patron. Soon, through William's intervention, he also found himself without a colony.

Distrusting a longtime ally and associate of the Stuarts, the new King William replaced Penn as governor of Pennsylvania in 1692. The new royal governor, William Fletcher, less enamored of popular consent than Harrington, Sidney, Locke, and Penn, soon abandoned Penn's plan and began appointing members of the Provincial Council who would do his will. Only a minority of the twelve he named were Quakers, and some of those belonged to the anti-Penn faction led by William Keith. To mollify the outraged public, Fletcher permitted the General Assembly to initiate legislation, although he was careful to centralize as much executive and judicial authority as possible in his own hands and those of his handpicked council. It was becoming apparent that even in the absence of a hereditary aristocracy, the council was beginning to function as a de facto House of Lords.

Penn managed to regain control of Pennsylvania and to return as governor in 1699, but the intervening fifteen years had killed whatever slim chance of success his Frame might have had. Negotiations with the General Assembly yielded a new Charter of Liberties in 1701, a plan that eliminated the council and enabled the assembly to evade the veto often wielded by Penn, then Fletcher, to defeat popular initiatives. The new charter worked no better than the first in achieving the harmony Penn sought. Factions seemed to proliferate with every new disagreement. The relatively wealthy Quaker oligarchy found itself facing vigorous popular opposition no matter what it tried to do. Less legislation was passed in Pennsylvania, and the provincial government generally was much less active, than elsewhere in North America. Paradoxically, the colony exhibited lively local participation, on the one hand, because most officials were elected by towns or counties, and, on the other, relatively persistent domination of colony-wide politics by the shrinking minority of old Quakers opposed to the proprietary interests of the Penn family. Before Penn returned to England, where his fortune continued to unravel to the extent that this once-great proprietor died in debtor's prison, he pleaded one last time that the settlers of his colony should "be humbled and made more plyable; for what w[i]th the distance, & the Scarcity of mankinde [there], they opine too much."[121]

Thus the consolidation of democracy in Pennsylvania occurred both because of, and despite the opposition of, its architect. By authorizing widespread popular involvement at the outset, Penn helped set in motion the dynamic that ultimately secured a greater degree of power for the Pennsylvania General Assembly than he originally envisioned. By insisting repeatedly that his own interest was fundamentally the public interest, he engendered the active opposition, the lively fractiousness, and the recurrent and self-conscious invocations of a shared common good that became the hallmark of the colony's politics. Finally, by welcoming members of almost every European nation and tolerating the practice of almost every European religious denomination, Penn allowed the rise of an inadvertent pluralism that generated fierce loyalties and equally fierce animosities, and in time made possible—and necessary—a brand of coalition building, deal making, and compromise that prepared Pennsylvanians to govern themselves first without a council, then without a king-like governor, and, finally, without a king.

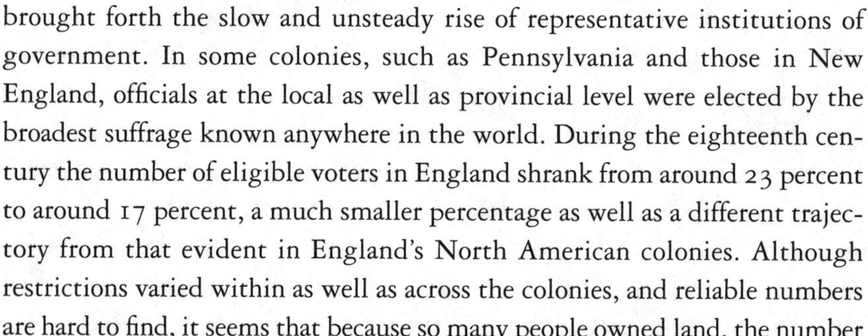

Throughout the American colonies, the aftermath of the Glorious Revolution brought forth the slow and unsteady rise of representative institutions of government. In some colonies, such as Pennsylvania and those in New England, officials at the local as well as provincial level were elected by the broadest suffrage known anywhere in the world. During the eighteenth century the number of eligible voters in England shrank from around 23 percent to around 17 percent, a much smaller percentage as well as a different trajectory from that evident in England's North American colonies. Although restrictions varied within as well as across the colonies, and reliable numbers are hard to find, it seems that because so many people owned land, the number of adult white males eligible to vote varied between a low of 50 percent in the areas most dominated by large landowners to a high of over 75 percent in parts of Virginia, Pennsylvania, and New England.[122]

For some people, reaching consensus through informal local meetings mattered more than the formal exercise of casting a ballot. For others, the danger of challenging the privileges of those in positions of power or authority militated against political participation. Whether the methods of enforcing discipline were as visible and violent as the whippings, maimings, burnings, and hangings on which authorities occasionally relied to enforce conformity or the subtler operations of respect and deference, early English settlers emphasized order and authority, which were assumed to be legitimate, necessary, and part of God's plan, rather than encouraging individual experimentation or celebrating difference. One consequence of that preference for order and authority was a clear yearning for homogeneity that persisted despite the overwhelming evidence of diversity and disagreement. Whether proclaimed from a pulpit, a town meeting, or a courthouse, or on the floor of an assembly, the idea of the common good reverberated throughout the colonies. Particular factions emerged, with particular interests. Yet partisans felt the need to declare their interest that of the whole, not just of their part, because only thereby could they establish its legitimacy in a world dominated by the ideal of organic communities.

Despite all the diversity of early colonial life, one conclusion is clear. Up and down the Atlantic seaboard, widespread landownership and institutions of representative governance appeared early and sent down roots that spread wide and deep. Those institutions gave white American males an experience of participation in political life at the local and provincial level quite different from those shaped by prevailing patterns of life in the more hierarchical and tradition-bound cultures from which they had come. The presence of slavery, especially but not exclusively in the South, meant that one man's freedom depended on another man's, or several other men's, unfreedom, and it depended on their coerced labor. Yet the presence of institutions of self-government, and the absence of a hereditary aristocracy to dominate those institutions, together made possible the vigorous, unruly cultures of the colonial assemblies. The people's representatives became accustomed to debating issues and returning to their constituencies, to instruct and be instructed, talk and listen, teach and learn, in a process that gradually familiarized the elected and the electorate with representative democracy—its requirements, its potential, and its limitations. As Roger Williams and the Levellers had seen, only where the habits of deference and hierarchy have eroded can a culture of democracy emerge.[123] Although no one among the North American colonists set out deliberately to challenge the assumptions about social order they carried with them from Europe, their first steps away from established authority nevertheless carried them in the direction of self-government. The experience of making their own decisions shifted the center of gravity away from a hereditary class of magistrates toward a set of officials selected by ordinary people to occupy positions in government.

Those steps did not require a dramatic or even conscious departure from inherited assumptions about hierarchy. As the Puritan minister John Davenport put it in an election sermon of 1669, the power exercised by magistrates belonged to God before it belonged to the electorate, and with every choice of an official the people were conferring God's authority by their vote. "In regular actings of the creature, God is the first Agent; there are not two several and distinct actings, one of God, another of the People: but in one and the same action, God, by the Peoples suffrages, makes such an one Governor, or Magistrate, and not another." This conferral of power, moreover, was granted by the people conditionally, because sinful men err, "so as, if the condition be violated, they may resume their power of chusing another."[124]

Davenport's listeners perceived no contradiction between the idea of divine sovereignty and the practice of popular sovereignty, no rejection of authority in the declaration that such authority was contractual rather than exercised by any individual on the basis of birthright. The aftermath of 1688 made clear that various forms of the contractual government that Sidney and Locke had sketched in theory were already being practiced in America. Not only in New England but also, to varying degrees, elsewhere, this pattern held. Even in the proprietary colonies, originally designed, for example, by Lord Baltimore in Maryland, or by Shaftesbury and Locke in Carolina, and to a certain extent by Penn in Pennsylvania, as more hierarchical fiefdoms controlled by—and yielding profits for—absentee landlords, sooner or later there emerged cultures of small landowners scattered across the landscape and electing representatives to their own assemblies.

Thus, after 1688, the contrast between English and American politics became increasingly clear. In England the landed gentry, threatened for a half century by a series of challenges from republicans as well as champions of absolute monarchy, recovered their equilibrium and reestablished their control over Parliament and over English life. The Revolution of 1688 facilitated the restoration of oligarchy in England. In America, the decades after 1688 saw the steady rise of representative democracy. As the quite different cases of Massachusetts and Pennsylvania illustrate, the early and feeble protests against royal authority that occurred episodically after the restoration of the Stuart monarchy in 1660 matured quickly into sustained challenges to the authority of the crown after the coup of 1688. The people of the colonies effectively expressed their power through their legislative assemblies. James Stuart was prescient when he warned that the creation of a representative assembly in his colony of New York would prove to be "of dangerous consequence," and Gershom Bulkeley was correct when he discerned in New England's opposition to the Dominion government of Edmund Andros "a levelling, independent democratical principle and spirit."[125] If asked, the colonists would have rejected the idea of democracy as an unbalanced and therefore unstable and undesirable form of government. Yet the absence of a hereditary gentry class and the diminishing power of the crown's appointed agents would gradually erase even the symbolic residue of aristocracy and monarchy, leaving a people who would stubbornly choose their own form of government and select those who would hold office in their name.[126]

PART II | Trial and Error

CHAPTER 5

Sympathy, Will, and Democracy in the Enlightenments of Europe

THE METAPHOR OF light has misled those who study the eighteenth century. If "Enlightenment" meant the emergence of greater faith in reason, sympathy, and progress, the process was gradual, intermittent, and transitory. The French referred to a "*siècle des lumières*," a century illuminated by rays of light. German thinkers coined the noun "*Aufklärung*" as a reference to the process of brightening or clearing, a term that was then translated into other languages. The nomenclature itself can obstruct understanding of a devilishly complex historical phenomenon. Across northern Europe and the English settlements in North America, the century of light brought neither brilliant nor blinding sun but only changing, and perhaps slightly brighter, skies. The clouds did not suddenly part.[1]

Most Europeans and Americans went about their lives as people always do, sometimes imperceptibly adjusting their ways of thinking and acting to make room, grudgingly or gratefully, for new ideas and changing social and economic circumstances, through a process more dialectical than linear.[2] Through an ascending spiral of rhetorical excess, however, the most vociferous champions of change provoked the most fiercely loyal traditionalists—and vice versa—in a process that by the end of the century culminated in violence that finally surpassed even the apocalyptic furor of the most overheated partisans on all sides.

Inasmuch as enlightened thinkers challenged tradition and hierarchy, they might also be expected to have championed the idea of democratic government. Yet the more radical partisans of the Enlightenment distrusted popular piety as much as they distrusted priestcraft. Because many radical philosophes or *lumières* tended to value reason over emotion, scientific truth over superstitious folklore, and freedom over obedience, they proved more inclined to trust sympathetic enlightened despots than to put their faith in the judgment of custom-bound ordinary people.[3] The complicated relation between democracy and Enlightenment varied over time and across cultures, but beneath those differences certain themes emerged, particularly in the work of the towering figures of the French Enlightenment, Montesquieu and Jean-Jacques Rousseau, and of the Scottish Enlightenment, David Hume and Adam Smith. This chapter concentrates on these protean and controversial thinkers, and situates them in a wider array of eighteenth-century contributors to debates about politics, because of the profound and paradoxical consequences of their ideas for democratic discourse on both sides of the Atlantic. By linking particular conceptions of autonomy and sympathy with the possibility of self-government, they helped inspire the democratic revolutions of the eighteenth century.[4]

The significance of England in the early Enlightenment shows the distance separating the complex historical record from the myths of an Age of Reason understood to be an age of science, skepticism, and secularism. In *Letters concerning the English Nation* (1733), one of the opening salvos of enlightened cultural criticism and a book first published, significantly, in English rather than French, Voltaire (born François-Marie Arouet) singled out Francis Bacon, John Locke, and Isaac Newton as thinkers who brought to life the new spirit of empiricism in science and philosophy. Bacon ranked as "the father of experimental philosophy." Newton, whom Voltaire elsewhere dubbed "the greatest man who ever lived," mattered not only for his discoveries in mathematics and physics but also because he destroyed "the Cartesian system," with its deductive procedures and reliance on innate ideas. Locke built on those foundations a radical philosophy based on observation and conceded, in the spirit of Montaigne, how much we cannot know.

The vitality of Voltaire's portrait of England derived from the comparisons he drew with his native France. Satirical verses written in 1717 had landed Voltaire in the Bastille for eleven months; an impetuous challenge to a well-connected aristocrat put him there again in 1726. Exiled from Paris and fed up with French autocracy and intolerance, Voltaire moved to England for two years and developed a lasting admiration for English institutions, moderation, balance, and tolerance of dissent. The power of English kings was limited, he observed, through centuries of effective resistance. English aristocrats, content to pay taxes and accept their status between their monarch and the common people, "are great without insolence." The English people "share in government without confusion."[5]

Voltaire's stay in London acquainted him with other features of English culture much admired by his fellow *lumières*, features put in relief by their contrast with conditions in early-eighteenth-century France. The Revocation of the Edict of Nantes in 1685 underscored the distinction between French Catholic intolerance and the less oppressive form of Anglicanism dominant after 1689. In England proliferating coffeehouses, periodicals, and clubs nourished a vibrant polite society in which drama, poetry, novels, and political tracts generated lively conversation; in France the combined authority of the Catholic Church and the Bourbon monarchy stood behind censors who stifled the flow of ideas and harried Huguenots into exile. Commercial activity buoyed the British economy, and in place of mid-seventeenth-century Puritan strictures emerged unprecedented luxury, as well as a class of merchants committed to the ever-wider distribution of an ever-expanding array of consumer goods. In England scientific advances, religious toleration, literary and artistic production, and constitutional monarchy seemed a formula for imperial expansion. By contrast French aristocrats successfully resisted being taxed and scorned commercial activity, the French parlements stubbornly clung to ancient and cumbersome feudal customs rather than uniform codes of law, and the once-proud regime of the Sun King, defeated in the War of Spanish Succession, was left staggering after the humiliating Peace of Utrecht in 1713.

The image of England conveyed by Voltaire's *Letters*, however, was as inaccurate as the image of the Enlightenment as a dramatic triumph of secular scientists over superstitious obscurantists. Bacon, after all, had emphasized the crucial significance of Christianity while advancing the cause of science. Not only his *Novum organum* but also his utopian fantasy *The New Atlantis* showed the complexity of his religious faith. Bacon could assume the benevolence of science because scientists operated not to augment their own power but to illuminate God's creation. Newton, despite his unrivaled contributions to scientific investigation and understanding, envisioned God as the source and sustainer of the natural world he investigated. Locke's epistemology depended as much as his moral philosophy and his political thought on a conception of God's will that derived from his devout Protestant faith.

Many of the early-eighteenth-century works most widely read in England sought only to soften the manners, regulate the morals, and temper the religiosity of their readers. That was equally true of the journalism and novels of Daniel Defoe; of Alexander Pope's "Essay on Man"; of the *Characteristics of Men, Manners, Opinions, Times* (1711) by Locke's former pupil Anthony Ashley Cooper, the 3rd Earl of Shaftesbury; of the *Tatler* (1709–11) of Richard Steele; and of the *Spectator* (1711–14) that Steele coedited with Joseph

Addison. In Addison's familiar words, "I shall be ambitious to have it said of me, that I have brought philosophy out of closets and libraries, schools and colleges, to dwell in clubs and assemblies, at tea-tables and in coffee-houses." Like many of his English contemporaries, Addison proclaimed a philosophy of moderation and embraced an ideal of clever, even playful conversation, not cultural revolution.[6]

Champions of Enlightenment in early-eighteenth-century England wrote for a rising middle class with unprecedented access to printed materials after the 1695 expiration of the Licensing Act. In the flood of print that followed, the principal message encouraged politeness and piety, temperance and conversation, and the deliberate balancing of self-interest and the common good. Writing to a Dutch colleague in 1706, Shaftesbury declared, "There is a mighty Light which spreads its self over the world especially in those two free Nations of England and Holland; on whom the Affairs of Europe now turn." Should heaven grant us peace, "a peace suitable to the great Successes we have had, it is impossible but that Letters and Knowledge must advance in greater Proportion than ever." That advance, Shaftesbury continued, need no more contradict religion than did the progress of science in the preceding century. "I am far from thinking that the Cause of Theisme will lose anything by fair Dispute." To the contrary, religion would only be strengthened by "the Establishment of an intire Philosophicall Liberty."[7]

Shaftesbury inaugurated the tradition of moral sense philosophy to resolve conflicts between self-interest and the common good that bedeviled classical, Christian, and modern moral philosophers and political theorists alike. He departed from Hobbes's egoism and from his teacher Locke, who emphasized the role of divine sanctions in motivating ethical decisions. Instead Shaftesbury argued that God has constituted humans such that properly cultivated individuals, trained to become virtuous much as they are trained to develop an appreciation of harmony in aesthetics, naturally approve of ethical acts—whether done by themselves or by others. The moral sense inclines toward benevolence; actions that benefit others bring happiness to oneself. Self-governing individuals, in tune with their moral feelings, act for the good of others without sacrificing their own self-interest. "Thus the wisdom of what rules, and is first and chief in nature, has made it to be according to the private interest and good of every one, to work toward the general good." If anyone "ceases to promote" that good, Shaftesbury wrote in the concluding words of his *Inquiry concerning Virtue, or Merit* (1699), he "ceases to promote his own happiness and welfare." So it is that virtue, "which of all excellencies and beauties is the chief, and most amiable," not only benefits all of society but also increases the "happiness and good" of every individual.

All humans possess the same moral sense, not merely privileged members of the gentry, those with a certain amount of property, or those engaged in certain elevated kinds of work. The challenge lay in bringing those moral feelings to maturity, which required no return to Spartan or Puritan simplicity but only the free circulation of ideas, the preservation of piety, and the participation in polite conversation so central to the English Enlightenment.[8]

Beneath all the talk of refinement and cultivation, and beneath the surface stability and prosperity of the British Empire, lay festering resentments, particularly in the provinces, but also among displaced English peasants and artisans and among those less than amused by the corruption of parliamentary politics. Those grievances eventually unsettled the apparently solid rule of king-in-Parliament. Voltaire correctly identified the features of political economy that distinguished England from France. In religion and philosophy, however, as in literature and art, he exaggerated the subversive and tolerant aspects of the English Enlightenment and minimized its more moderate and conventionally Protestant Christian framework for his own polemical purposes. As the English "became more enlightened" after 1688, in Voltaire's words, they further developed their distinctive "love of liberty" and "destroyed the fanaticism that shakes the most solid of states."[9] Voltaire envisioned for France a similar progression from religious fervor to moderate liberty via the path of Enlightenment. French authorities had a different vision. By order of the Paris parlement, his *Letters concerning the English Nation* was to be burned.

The other early champion of Enlightenment in France, Charles-Louis de Secondat, the Baron de Montesquieu, likewise lionized the constitutional monarchy of England. Appropriately enough, he was born in 1689. A member of the lesser aristocracy of Bordeaux, descended from both the older nobility of the sword and the newer, but often wealthier, nobility of the robe, Montesquieu inherited the position of magistrate in the parlement of Bordeaux, and he studied law diligently so that he might perform his duties responsibly.[10] Montesquieu was a noble of relatively modest means: his combined income from his office and his vineyards, although considerable, was but a fraction—perhaps around 10 percent—of Voltaire's. Yet he was no uncritical apologist of the Old Regime: the critical bite of his writings sometimes rivaled that of the other *lumières* at their most incisive.[11]

Montesquieu began his ascent to the pinnacle of French intellectual life with the publication of *The Persian Letters* in 1721. Although the book appeared anonymously, its popularity catapulted its author to prominence and prompted him to sell his office (a common practice in the Old Regime), travel extensively throughout Europe, then divide his time between the salons of Paris and his château La Brède, located south of Bordeaux. The novel recounts the adventures of two Persians, Usbek and Rica, who spend nine years in the West searching for wisdom. Trying to interpret the customs they encounter, they mistake the pope for a magician and the posturing audience at the theater for the performers. They judge fashions and parties absurd; colonies, universities, and the French Academy self-defeating; and religious warfare "a total eclipse of human reason." Meanwhile Usbek's seraglio back home is unraveling, as letters from his eunuchs and wives make clear, for reasons identical to those offered to explain the differences between despotism and popular government in Europe. Whereas royal absolutism breeds poverty, depopulation, and the surly servility of oppressed subjects, "gentle methods of government" are said to enable the Swiss and Dutch republics to prosper, grow, and enjoy freedom and equality.

The Persian Letters explores the psychology of degradation and its consequences in the microcosm of Usbek's harem and despotic cultures, East and West. By the end of the novel, Rica embraces Europe because he has internalized the culture of autonomy available to those who renounce oppression. He has learned to learn from experience as a good Lockean would do. Usbek, emotionally bound to the seraglio, feels compelled to return home, but too late: his favorite wife, Roxana, has renounced his authority, proclaimed her freedom, taken a lover, and committed suicide, the only option available for such an independent woman in a despotic world. In *The Persian Letters*, Montesquieu's views on history, political sociology, and constitutionalism, the principal subjects of his monumental *Spirit of the Laws* (1748), emerge only in scattered asides, notably in the fable of the Troglodytes that Usbek recounts to his friend Mirza because "moral truths" must be felt to be understood. If that allusion to the philosophy of Shaftesbury seems subtle, in the fable itself the references to him—and to Hobbes as well as Locke—are unmistakable.

The Troglodytes, according to Usbek, were a small nation in Arabia that suffered under a foreign tyrant whom they overthrew. The ministers elected to govern them became unendurable and were massacred. Each Troglodyte then became a Hobbesian egoist, looking out for himself and disregarding everyone else. Soon starvation, robbery, murder, and disease made life miserable for everyone, and the Troglodytes, in Usbek's words, "perished because of their wickedness, and fell victim to their own injustice."

The only two surviving Troglodyte families were headed by extraordinary men who loved virtue. Their example inspired their wives and their children, whom they taught "that the individual's self-interest is always to be found in the common interest." Virtue is not "a wearisome exercise" but accords with the deepest human impulses, and "justice to others is charity for ourselves." This small band of Troglodytes flourished, not because they feared God's wrath but because they acted according to their natural inclination toward benevolence. Not that they were impious: their religion softened "any roughness of manner left over from nature." In their festivals, "joy reigned equally with frugality." Because the Troglodytes considered themselves members of a single family, they proved fierce warriors who repulsed the attacks of envious neighbors.

This utopian reverie, however, could not last. The conclusion of the fable indicates Montesquieu's elusiveness as well as his characteristic historical sensibility. Elsewhere in *The Persian Letters* a correspondent explains to Rica that European republics originated in the "spirit of freedom" that first inspired Greeks, then Romans, and later northern tribes to establish governments, based on the sovereignty of the people, that restricted their rulers "in a thousand different ways." Just as these republics rose, prospered, and declined, so too did the Troglodytes fall victim to history. As their population grew, Usbek explained, the Troglodytes decided they should choose a king. They selected the most just among them, but rather than rejoice in the honor he greeted it with tears: "I shall die in grief," he lamented, because a formerly free people now wanted to subject itself to his rule. The reluctant king sensed they were willing to exchange self-government for monarchy because virtue had begun to be a burden. Now the people wanted merely to satisfy their ambitions, accumulate wealth, and live in idle degradation. Instead of continuing to act virtuously, they were ready to abandon autonomy and bow down to a king, whose laws would be less demanding than their own. The Troglodytes' tale, like the lessons to be learned elsewhere in *The Persian Letters* from the examples of Greece and Rome, suggested that the lure of luxury, which Shaftesbury linked with an enlightened culture facilitating lives of virtue, led toward either monarchy or despotism.[12]

In addition to drawing on the contrast between Shaftesbury and Hobbes, *The Persian Letters* indirectly addressed issues raised by two other writers, the Burgundian Archbishop François de Salignac de la Mothe Fénelon and the Dutch-born English provocateur Bernard Mandeville. Fénelon's influential novel *Télémaque* (1699) presented an ascetic utopia masking a critique of Louis XIV. He contrasted an innocent Platonic society, animated by simple communitarian virtues, to the more elaborate forms of self-discipline necessary for a complex monarchical regime depending not only on the virtue of the people but also on an aristocratic elite ruling according to the principles of hierarchy, order, and the pure love of God. Shaftesbury thought virtue remains possible with commerce and refinement so long as individuals are guided by the moral sense; Fénelon considered divine grace the only source sufficiently potent to redirect individuals' self-love toward the common good.[13]

Mandeville challenged both Fénelon and Shaftesbury in a little book that would be invoked—and reviled—throughout the eighteenth century. The lengthy subtitle of his 1714 book expressed its argument: *The Fable of the Bees: or, Private Vices, Publick Benefits. Containing Several Discourses to demonstrate, that Human Frailties, during the degeneracy of Mankind, may be turn'd to the Advantage of the Civil Society, and made to supply the Place of Moral Virtues.* Mandeville contended that self-interest provides a more reliable motive than Fénelon's love or Shaftesbury's moral sense. In place of antique simplicity, self-interest produces prosperity and greatness for modern commercial nations. Acknowledging the role of selfishness also eliminated the quaint notion (such as that found in Fénelon and Shaftesbury as well as Sidney and Locke) that humans are anything other than animals seeking pleasure and trying to avoid pain. *The Fable of the Bees* scandalized many readers; it also shaped later developments in political economy.[14]

Montesquieu charted a course different from those of Fénelon and Mandeville. In 1734 he published the book that would inspire Gibbon's history of Rome and Tocqueville's history of the French Revolution, *Considerations on the Causes of the Romans' Greatness and Decline*. Montesquieu's *Considerations* introduced the genre of "philosophical history" that has endured to our own day. He focused less on chronicle or military affairs than on the interaction between ideas, culture, politics, and socioeconomic conditions. Montesquieu claimed that the animating principle of the Roman republic, virtue, emerged from selfless love of the fatherland and disappeared when Romans lost interest in civic life. From the perspective of democratic theory, Montesquieu's emphasis on the role of conflict in republican government ranks among his most important insights. Valuable and reassuring as consensus might seem, Montesquieu argued that wrangling produces something more precious: "True union is a harmony in which all the parts, however opposed they may appear, concur in attaining the general good of the society, just as dissonances in music are necessary so that they may be resolved in an ultimate harmony. Union may exist in a state where apparently only trouble is found."[15] At its most republican, Rome showed that the capacity for self-correction was a distinctive feature of self-government. When republican austerity gave way to luxury, and empire distracted citizens from public affairs, despotism was not far behind.

Influential as Montesquieu's earlier books were, his most important contribution to political thinking was his chef d'oeuvre, *L'esprit des lois,* or *The Spirit of the Laws* (1748), a vast, sprawling survey of government now much more often cited than read. Ponderous proclamations about Man and Government clog the book's endless pages; typologies breed like rabbits. Formulas concerning the necessary relation between types of government and climate, geography, commerce, sex, etc., strike us as a comic parody of social science: Monty Python's quest for the ideal type. But impatience with Montesquieu as oracle can obscure the reasons for his book's landmark status. The persistent tension between his awareness of variety and dynamism and his longing for law-like generalizations makes the book seem divided against itself. Sufficiently controversial to earn censure from the faculty of theology at the Sorbonne and a spot on the Vatican's index of banned books, *The Spirit of the Laws* nevertheless ranked above all other eighteenth-century texts as a source of information and judgments concerning politics and society.[16]

In the most significant of his categorizations, Montesquieu divided governments into three types—republican, monarchical, and despotic—with three animating principles: virtue, honor, and fear. He emphasized the separation of powers among legislative, judicial, and executive branches and praised mixed and balanced government. He insisted that cultures and values vary, and that laws and customs are intimately connected with each other, and he condemned the despotic treatment of women and all forms of slavery.[17] The two forms of republican government, according to Montesquieu, are democracy and aristocracy. He took for granted that democracy is a legitimate form of government, well suited to particular cultures in particular circumstances. Direct democracy he considered dangerous. The history of the ancient world showed that the people as a mass tend toward impulsive and passionate decisions. Representative democracy had its own problems. Widespread corruption marred elections to the English Parliament, for example. Bribes were common currency among office seekers, and votes were sold to the highest bidder, which is why Montesquieu advised against a secret ballot.[18] Given Montesquieu's own noble status, we might assume he preferred aristocratic to democratic forms of republican rule, but his arguments are more nuanced.

Montesquieu's anxieties concerning the people, not only those governed by their passions but also those whose poverty induced them to sell their votes and those whose lack of education made them unable to follow political debates, led him to conclude that a republic is most secure when it rests on a balance between popular will and the judgment of an aristocracy—of birth or merit. Sometimes governments must act decisively. In such cases the endless deliberations of a large popular forum or the immediate emotional response of a mob can be fatal. Aristocracy without any popular participation, however, Montesquieu judged equally undesirable. Instead he recommended weighing the unmatched knowledge of the people, who know better than anyone else the conditions of life in their own communities, against the broader vision enjoyed by those either born into an aristocracy or elevated to its ranks by notable achievements. How wide a gap should divide an aristocracy from the people? The closer aristocracy comes to monarchy, Montesquieu wrote, "the more it is imperfect," whereas "the more an aristocracy borders on democracy, the nearer it approaches perfection." From Montesquieu's perspective, no pure form of government is flawless; various hybrids show intriguing potential.[19]

As Montesquieu understood, both space and time matter in democracy. Proximity generates intimate knowledge of problems and of people, and that intimacy not only breeds familiarity and sometimes contempt. It also produces the most precious quality of democratic life, commitment to the public interest, which requires sustained engagement with civic life and is the source of republican virtue. Unlike the honor that animates a monarchy, which depends on politeness and "greatness of soul"—precisely the values Montesquieu associated with the cultures prized by Anglophile partisans of Enlightenment such as Shaftesbury and Voltaire—popular governments instead require the "constant preference of public to private interest, and that can spring only from a love of the republic that can be neither manufactured nor feigned." If such public spirit cannot be created, how does it emerge? Montesquieu argued that only the *experience* of equality and frugality could generate the spontaneous love of those conditions on which popular government must rest. If these values are lived, they can be embodied in law through measures such as progressive taxation; if embodied both in law and in customs, or *moeurs*, these practices can be perpetuated from one generation to the next.[20] As Shaftesbury said of benevolence, civic virtue is, in Montesquieu's words, "a sensation, and not a consequence of acquired knowledge, a sensation that may be felt by the meanest as well as by the highest person in the state." Without it, democracy cannot survive. "A love of the republic in a democracy is a love of the democracy," which means that everyone must embrace equality. All individuals must share the same advantages, "taste the same pleasures and form the same hopes." Because "real equality is the very soul of a democracy," preserving it is as important as it is difficult.

If democracy is to survive, Montesquieu warned, only moderate degrees of wealth or poverty can be permitted. Otherwise "men of overgrown estates," who interpret as a personal affront everything that does not augment their own "power and honor," will no longer endure steps taken to level the playing field, such as graduated taxation. Instead, as some people prosper—for any reason, whether through talent, hard work, or simple luck—they will seek to separate themselves from everyone else, and they will seek ways to pass along those advantages to their children. Commercial expansion, from Montesquieu's perspective, is attractive because it fosters "frugality, economy, moderation, labor, prudence, tranquility, order, and rule." Unlike inherited wealth, commercial success requires effort and produces no ill effects. "Excessive wealth" of any sort ineluctably destroys democracy. He judged partible inheritance, like a progressive tax on income, a useful means to prevent the emergence of such cancerous extravagances.

In conditions of extreme inequality, as the examples of Athens and Sparta as well as Rome made clear, democracy gives way to despotism. Such had been the fate also of all extended republics that tried to preserve popular government over a vast expanse of land. In those circumstances some men of wealth—and equally inflated self-importance—come to prefer their own interests to those of the public, which are easy to see in the context of small states and easy to overlook in large empires. Although despotic regimes appeal to, and depend on, man's worst qualities and extinguish his best, they have existed more frequently because they require only passion, the least common denominator of all people. Democracy, by contrast, depends on the most difficult, most precious, and thus rarest of all qualities, virtue.[21]

Like all good historians of his day, Montesquieu knew that democracies had always failed. They had turned despotic not only because their populations had grown too large or too unequal; excessive equality generates problems of its own. The erosion of respect breeds license. When democracies mistake "the true spirit of equality for that of extreme equality," everyone commands and no one obeys. "The natural place of virtue is near to liberty; but it is not nearer to excessive liberty than to servitude." Montesquieu's conception of liberty shaped his judgment as clearly as did his conception of hierarchy. In democracies, because the people themselves authorize the laws, they act "as they please," but he cautioned that "political liberty does not consist in unlimited freedom." Instead "liberty can consist only in the power of doing what we ought to will," a formula that Montesquieu—like other notable eighteenth-century theorists, including both Rousseau and James Madison in rather different ways—considered consistent with, and even necessary for, popular government. For Montesquieu, democracy can survive only with equality and autonomy.[22]

From his observations on bounded liberty, Montesquieu launched into an elaborate discussion of England. He judged England the single contemporary example of a nation that "has for the direct end of its constitution political liberty." England proved the exception to most of Montesquieu's rules. He conveniently forgot what he had observed about shoddy contemporary English elections. He shoehorned English practices into his model of separated powers by misrepresenting its judicial system and whitewashing the relation between the king and Parliament, many of whose members the monarch manipulated at will despite the ostensible limits on royal prerogative achieved in 1689. In the "country of liberty" examined in *The Spirit of the Laws*, Montesquieu observed that "the legislative power should reside in the whole body of the people" (rather than in the tiny fraction of the population who could actually vote in eighteenth-century England). Since not everyone in large states can gather in one place, and even in small states such assemblies of the whole are "subject to many inconveniences, it is fit the people should transact by their representatives what they cannot transact by themselves." Because residents understand most clearly the wants and interests of the community, Montesquieu insisted that representatives should be elected by—and from among—the inhabitants themselves, a standard few English elections met.

Montesquieu developed a robust defense of representation. Originally designed as a device merely to make the best of a bad situation—as a way of compensating for the fact that people either lived too far away from each other, or were too numerous to fit into a single space, or would require weeks or months to reach a decision that must be made right away—the idea of a representative assembly had demonstrated its unique value: "The great advantage of representatives is their capacity of discussing public affairs. For this the people collectively are extremely unfit," which he judged among the "chief inconveniences" of direct democracy. Montesquieu was unconvinced that such representatives should carry instructions from their constituents. Such instructions enabled each deputy to control the entire assembly, and thus "the wheels of government might be stopped by the caprice of a single person." Montesquieu credited Algernon Sidney with having identified, in the Dutch republic, a better arrangement. When individual representatives are accountable to particular constituencies, as in Holland, representatives can deliberate freely; then voters can decide, at election time, whether they are content with their representative.[23]

Although Montesquieu denied that the people as a whole were qualified to make the laws, or that any large body could execute them, he believed the people should retain the power to accept or reject all legislation—a democratic variant on the power of the French parlements vis-à-vis the king. In a democracy sovereign power remains ultimately with the people, so they should wield the power to approve or disapprove both the persons who represent them and the laws those persons propose. Toward the end of *The Spirit of the Laws*, Montesquieu reflected on the likelihood that popular sentiment would divide into partisan attachments, whether around parties, as in

England's Whigs and Tories, or between the executive and legislative branches of the government. In either case such partisanship was unproblematic: as long as such passions are contained by the structures of government, with separations and balances maintaining a dynamic equilibrium, spirited disagreements represent something more than a necessary evil.

Controversies generate the public spirit democracies require. Debates about candidates, legislation, and executive decisions draw citizens into the public sphere and focus attention on public life. Representative governments have a great advantage over the direct democracies of the ancient world, in which skilled speechmakers prompted the people to make impulsive decisions. In a representative democracy, proximity of the electorate to the elected and the brief period between elections temper rash judgments by spurring debate, reflection, and reconsideration. Montesquieu argued that every inhabitant of a district ought to have a right to vote for a representative—except women, whom he judged dependent on their fathers or their husbands, and those "in so mean a situation as to be deemed to have no will of their own."[24] He differed from ancient and most sixteenth- and seventeenth-century republican theorists because he considered Greek and Roman ideals of civic virtue either too focused on martial qualities and imperial expansion or too all-encompassing. A republic that demanded all its citizens' attention all the time left no room for the joys of private life. That distinction catalyzed both those who agreed with him about circumscribing the demands of public life and those convinced that a domain separate from the civic sphere sapped vitality from politics and fed individuals' most selfish inclinations.[25] He extolled the advantages of England's mixed monarchy, with its distinctive (if in practice considerably less clear-cut) separation of legislative, executive, and judicial functions.[26]

In sum, Montesquieu's ideal form of republican government combined aspects of mixed monarchy with representative democracy. Despite his many departures from the *Persian Letters*—including his stated debts to Mandeville's hard-headed assessments of the potential rewards of self-interested behavior, and his borrowing from the English Tory Viscount Henry St. John Bolingbroke the notion that the different functions of government should be kept separate—Montesquieu remained drawn toward the Troglodytes' virtuous but fragile democracy, in which public-spirited individuals inspired others voluntarily to follow their lead. Much as that model appealed to Montesquieu's imagination, the evidence he adduced from his studies made him doubt its viability. The free choice of virtue made democracy possible. The lure of wealth made democracy vulnerable. The preference for luxury over self-government—the choice that reduced the Troglodytes' new king to tears—made despotism inevitable. In the second half of the eighteenth century, thinkers and activists on both sides of the Atlantic would work to break that cycle.[27]

In the *Preliminary Discourse* to the *Encyclopedia* (1751), the mathematician Jean le Ronde d'Alembert characterized Montesquieu as a "judicious figure," a "great philosopher" underappreciated in his native France but "honored by all Europe."[28] Articles in the *Encyclopedia* on law, custom, and politics incorporate concepts and information from *The Spirit of the Laws*. In a eulogy to Montesquieu included in volume 5, d'Alembert credited him with demonstrating that history is scripted neither by providence nor by chance, as Christian and classical scholars had argued, but instead unfolds according to the interaction of laws and customs, and of constitutional structures and socioeconomic pressures.[29] Because the *Encyclopedia* is usually considered the archetypal statement of the principles of the French Enlightenment, the explicit praise of Montesquieu and the integration of many of his insights into its articles illustrate either that the standard interpretation of Montesquieu as a conservative—or perhaps of the *Encylopedia* as radical—is mistaken, or, more properly, that the contrasts are misconceived. The tensions between Montesquieu's empiricism and his yearning for general laws, and between his insight into the attractiveness of a democratic republic and his anxiety about its workability, however, are real. They are echoed, albeit in a different key, by two related tensions present in the writings of other philosophes usually considered more iconoclastic than Montesquieu.

The first is the tension between diversity and uniformity, the second between democracy and despotism. Both tensions sprang from the difficulty many eighteenth-century thinkers had making the transition from a world of absolute truth and absolute authority to a world in which yearnings for stability persisted even though developments in science and politics were shaking their foundations. Many philosophes greeted with glee the discoveries of natural science that unsettled Christian cosmology by showing that traditional biblical understandings of the natural world were not merely false but absurd.[30] They relished the prospect that empirical investigations would yield useful—and unified—knowledge. In the *Preliminary Discourse*, d'Alembert singled out Bacon, Descartes, Newton, and Locke as "the principal geniuses" who had led the world from darkness. Bacon contributed the scientific method. Descartes began not with revelation but with radical doubt. Newton replaced conjecture with observation. Locke "reduced metaphysics to what it really ought to be: the experimental physics of the soul." Their efforts had reoriented humans away from revelation and Descartes's doctrine of innate ideas, which d'Alembert credited Locke with having demolished once and for all, and launched a wave of empirical inquiries.[31]

D'Alembert, whose expertise in mathematics had earned him a place in the scientific societies of France, England, and Prussia, preserved the hope that research would one day unite all the arts and sciences. That aspiration animated the *Encyclopedia*, which d'Alembert and his chief collaborator, Denis Diderot, envisioned as a reliable guide to knowledge of all kinds. "We can hope to know nature," d'Alembert wrote, only "by thoughtful study of phenomena, by the comparisons we make among them," and by reducing phenomena to the one "that can be regarded as their principle."[32] This quest for unity contrasts with an awareness of incommensurability or the acceptance of irreducible difference. In the words of Voltaire, history reveals that "whatever concerns human nature is the same from one end of the universe to the other, and that which is dependent upon custom differs." The variety of different forms of government did not shake the philosophes' confidence that beneath diversity lay a common denominator, human reason, and that is why democracy was a problem for many philosophes.[33] If reason can disclose truth, why should political judgment depend on or even allow the deliberation of uneducated or unreasonable people?

Civic life in France left little or no room for popular engagement—except as observers of spectacle. Public power was constituted and administered through arrangements descending from feudal practices and only imperfectly integrated into a national system of law. Even at the height of the powers of Louis XIV, royal absolutism operated only in times of crisis. Otherwise, and especially after the death of the Sun King, jockeying for position among the king's ministers, and between Versailles, the provincial parlements, and town officials was the order of the day, the messy reality beneath the grandiose theory. The conflicts between the rival aristocracies of the sword and the robe, Voltaire observed, meant that the effective privileges and prerogatives of these bodies floated in uncertainty. More generally, the history of France showed nothing uniform or stable. Chance, short-term thinking, and whims often dictated legislation.

When Louis XV emerged from his prolonged regency, he had to negotiate with distinct—and invigorated—constituted bodies. The crown's financial burdens increased as the century wore on, making it clear that new revenues were required if the monarchy were to exercise its authority within France and extend its war-making power in global affairs. Debates concerning the best way forward attracted the attention not only of traditional religious and aristocratic elites but also, by midcentury, those who envisioned themselves as independent of the church or the court. Partisans of the new program of

Enlightenment, devoted to the pursuit of knowledge modeled on the new national academies of science and pursued as avidly in their provincial imitators, emerged as influential challengers.[34] Detailed studies have revealed the multiple dimensions of the French Enlightenment and shown that many philosophes had little interest in democracy. Misguided popular subservience to the dogmas of religion showed why the common people were not to be trusted. Whereas "the Supreme Intelligence"—d'Alembert's phrase seems deliberately chosen to pique the pious—"seems to have tried to tantalize the human curiosity," only the enlightened could be expected to see "the flashes of light which should direct us along the way." Political power should be left in the hands of rulers whom those few might serve as ministers or counsel as men of letters.[35]

The most self-conscious champions of that approach to public service were those known as physiocrats, who left an imprint on French government that survived the disastrous consequences of some of their proposals in late-eighteenth-century France. François Quesnay, Pierre Paul Le Mercier de la Rivière, and Victor Riqueti, the marquis de Mirabeau, explicitly endorsed the concept of enlightened despotism—or, more precisely, "legal despotism"—as the best way to implement their new "science" of political economy. Quesnay, as personal physician to Louis XV, outlined his principles of free trade in the *Encyclopedia*. Mirabeau elaborated those principles in several books on population, taxation, and the grain trade. Mercier penned the physiocrats' political manifesto, *L'ordre naturel et essentiel des sociétés politiques* (1767). They considered government, the economy, and society subject to laws as unvarying and coercive as the laws of geometry. The challenge lay simply in applying those self-evident maxims, which included—for a nation such as France, at least—emphasis on agricultural production rather than commerce and, most importantly, free trade.[36]

The most dramatic—and disastrous—test of the physiocrats' ideas came under Anne-Robert-Jacques Turgot, a vigorous combatant on behalf of science and its cultural fruits.[37] Turgot's relation to the physiocrats was complicated. A member of the Paris parlement from 1753 to 1761 and a versatile civil servant, Turgot traveled to the famine-stricken Limousin region in 1770 and urged that steps inconsistent with physiocratic doctrine be taken in response to the widespread scarcity of corn. Despite his commitment to the idea of free trade, Turgot saw that its consequences, at least in the short term, occasionally required the government to intervene.[38] When the new king, Louis XVI, named Turgot controller-general of finance in 1774, Turgot immediately removed government restrictions on the grain trade. When harvests were again disappointing, and bread riots began to spread in April of

1775 from the provinces toward Paris (where the restriction had been preserved), Turgot again proposed modest steps to ameliorate the problem of widespread hunger. But public passions were aroused, and mobs had to be dispersed by force. Hundreds were arrested; some were executed. Enraged critics, ranging from religious and court conservatives to Turgot's rival Jacques Necker, charged that responsibility for the economic chaos lay with the physiocrats' commitment to free trade. The traditional idea of the just price was contrasted to the heartless rationality of enlightened science. Turgot was sacked, replaced by his archenemy Necker, and the reputation of physiocracy as disastrous for the poor was sealed.[39]

Turgot himself, however, and his protégé Jean-Antoine-Nicholas, marquis de Condorcet, learned from these disasters lessons about the relation between government policy and popular protest that would shape their responses, examined in later chapters, to both the American and French Revolutions. Given what they perceived as the irrationality of the public outcry against Turgot's policies, an outcry easily elicited and cynically exploited by their political opponents, Turgot and especially Condorcet saw that a science of government would depend on popular persuasion rather than simply the coercive force of scientific truth. Only if the obstacle of public unreason were uprooted, and only if power were even more effectively concentrated in a sovereign ruler, could science triumph and the public interest be advanced. Because the people had shown themselves blind to their own best interest, they would have to be either silenced, as Quesnay and other doctrinaire physiocrats advised, or enlightened.[40]

Diderot, like other prominent philosophes, was disenchanted with physiocracy and searching for an alternative approach to government. Attracted to rebellious spirits such as Voltaire, Diderot ended up behind bars because of his writing. In 1752, only a year after he and d'Alembert began publication, and though the multiauthored *Encyclopedia* adopted no clear stance on political issues and issued no explicit call for popular government, the *Encyclopedia* was banned until some of the philosophes' well-placed friends interceded with the authorities. Diderot's own contributions proposed that political authority originates in the sovereign will of the people, a subversive claim in a culture still officially dedicated to the principle that the king's authority embodies God's will. Government "is not private property," Diderot wrote, "but public property that consequently can never be taken from the people, to whom it belongs exclusively, fundamentally." All forms of "public *authority* are possessions, owned by the body of the nation, held as a usufruct by princes and as a trust by ministers."[41] According to Diderot's article "Citizen," the legitimacy of political decisions should be measured against not divine will but the "general will," a phrase coined by Diderot even though it is usually associated with Jean-Jacques Rousseau. Like Turgot, Diderot did not consider the people the best judge of the general will. Like Montesquieu, he recommended policies conducive to greater social and economic equality as the road to tranquility, yet he too warned that "complete equality" in any society is a chimera and judged a stable monarchy a safer alternative than a volatile and unpredictable democracy.[42]

In his article "Natural Right," Diderot offered the concept of the general will as a way for individuals to distinguish right from wrong. Diderot cut his teeth translating Shaftesbury's *Inquiry concerning Virtue* into French, and the influence persisted even though Diderot's belief in God did not. Apparently contrasting Shaftesbury to Hobbes (although no evidence indicates Diderot had read Hobbes when he wrote this article), Diderot offered as a maxim that "the unjust and passionate man feels inclined to do to others what he would not wish to have done to himself." That impulse can and must be constrained. "Particular wills are suspect; they can be good or evil, but the general will is always good: it is never wrong, it never will be wrong." Diderot proposed the general will as a guide for political reasoning and individual moral judgment, although the former, implicitly explosive, necessarily remained more vague. Inasmuch as he specified its meaning, it approximates the ethic of reciprocity on which democracy rests: what individuals consider "good, noble, exalted, and sublime" is "in the general and common interest."[43]

Between the conception of the *Encyclopedia* in 1747 and the appearance of the twenty-eighth and final volume in 1772, during which time some twenty-five thousand copies of the work were published,[44] Diderot's worldview changed. His initial moderation, sparked by Voltaire's early writings and confirmed by his immersion in Shaftesbury's philosophy, gave way to the materialism and atheism of the philosophes' small radical wing. This group included the physician Julien Offray de la Mettrie, whose book *L'homme machine* (usually translated *Man a Machine*) expressed its argument in its title; Helvétius, who characterized Shaftesbury's "theological philosophy" as "absurd" and dismissed the idea of a moral sense as equivalent to that of a moral castle or a moral elephant; and Paul Henri Thiry d'Holbach, a prolific writer who attributed vice and injustice to the ignorance instilled by religious authorities. The work of these writers elicited furious opposition. When Holbach's books were ordered burned, he was accurately described as belonging to a network of radicals equally opposed to the French monarchy and the Catholic Church, a group intent on toppling both the throne and the altar.[45]

Helvétius and Holbach believed that only self-interest motivates individuals. Maximizing utility for all individuals, without any billowing rhetoric about human dignity, was the simple purpose of government.[46] Holbach likewise concentrated on dismantling the claims of religious and state authorities to legitimate the illegitimate. Like La Mettrie and Helvétius, he proclaimed an uncompromising atheist materialism and reduced motivation to the quest for happiness, defined simply as pleasure. Government exists only to facilitate that pursuit; everything else is froth whipped up by zealots in order to distract people from the truth. The sole object of morality, according to Holbach's *Système social* (1773), "is to make men know that their greatest interest demands that they practice virtue; the end of government should be to make them practice it."[47]

Whatever appeal a republic might have in principle, most of Holbach's allies took for granted that in practice authority should be exercised by a sovereign ruler—ideally one whom they had enlightened. Yet Holbach's article "Representatives" in the *Encyclopedia* shows the ambivalence concerning democracy present in much enlightened discourse. In contrast to Asiatic despotism, Holbach argued, European nations understood the utility and necessity of developing forms of representation that enabled citizens to restrain their rulers in the name of the nation as a whole. Such forms of representation varied. When representatives are chosen, they become "depositories" of the people's authority, and "according to whether more or less power has been reserved by and for the people, the government becomes either an aristocracy or it remains a democracy." Holbach thus perpetuated the idea that only a direct assembly of all citizens constitutes a democracy and reflected the French preoccupation with unitary sovereignty, ideas that would prove consequential sooner than he could have imagined.[48]

Given the deterministic psychological egoism advanced by La Mettrie, Helvétius, and Holbach, and their denial that any independent faculty of judgment intervened between sense experience and decision, they saw no reason why individuals in public life should choose virtue rather than successfully feign it, or cooperate with their fellows rather than cynically manipulate them. If so, the critics of Helvétius and Holbach were quick to ask, then why should a king, or any of his enlightened ministers, be inclined to look beyond his own automatic calculation of immediate self-interest? The starkness of these egoists' ideas made even their fellow radicals such as Diderot squirm. Human passions, both the propensity to love and hate and the fondness for beauty and aversion to ugliness, seemed more mysterious, more variable, and less easily managed than materialists claimed. Perhaps, their critics charged, some philosophes' inclination to produce pornography as enthusiastically as they produced works of political criticism explained why the censors banned all works grouped under the rubric *livres philosophiques*.[49] Their contemporaries disagreed about whether the most radical philosophes were bravely facing facts or removing from human consciousness all the attributes that distinguish humans from other animals.

Even those philosophes who resisted atheism and materialism, however, shared the belief that contemporary French culture was corrupted by excesses of a different kind—those of the clergy and the nobility. From the performance of his first play, *Oedipe*, in 1718 until his death in 1778, no other individual epitomized the French Enlightenment as much as Voltaire. Yet his multiple critiques of Catholic doctrine and hatred of organized religion did not shake Voltaire's belief that God exists, and he believed that humans are constituted with a sentiment of benevolence as powerful as our instinct of self-preservation.

In Voltaire's one-man encyclopedia, his *Philosophical Dictionary* (1764), he wrote that "morality comes from God like light." He declared that "all the great moral philosophers," including Jesus, "taught us the same lesson," namely, "Morality is one, it comes from God." Jesus's admonition to love God and your neighbor as yourself was hard to improve on, Voltaire wrote, and he defined virtue himself simply as "doing good to one's neighbor." All the dogmas of theology, all the forms of self-denial practiced by ascetics, and all the superstitions that keep organized religions afloat Voltaire satirized mercilessly. He thus shared the critical posture of the materialists and atheists and devoted his life to his imperative—"*écrasez l'infâme*," crush the infamous thing—yet Voltaire never doubted the existence of God or a uniform moral code buried somewhere under the rubble caused by religious warfare. The only cure for religious and secular fanaticism was doubt and toleration: "the philosophical spirit."[50]

Voltaire's political ideas have stirred up nearly as much controversy as his anticlerical and antidoctrinal theism, in part because of his personal flirtations with monarchs. The admiration he and other philosophes shared for the so-called enlightened despots Frederick the Great of Prussia, Catherine II of Russia, and Joseph II of the Holy Roman Empire is impossible to disentangle from two complicating factors. First, the philosophes were under constant scrutiny in France and needed friends in high places. Second, such rulers possessed the power and seemed to show the inclination to effect change. Catherine II invited d'Alembert to Moscow, offered Diderot a pension, and quoted from *The Spirit of the Laws* and the *Encyclopedia* in her own writings. Joseph II extended religious toleration to Protestants, Eastern Orthodox Catholics, and Jews. His fact-finding missions through the empire seemed the very model of enlightened critical inquiry.

The most prominent and, at least initially, promising of these rulers was Frederick the Great. From his habit of signing his letters "Frederick the philosopher" and his offer to have Voltaire write the preface to Frederick's book *Anti-Machiavel* of 1740 (published anonymously but soon known to be the work of the Prussian ruler) to his invitations to Voltaire to join him in Potsdam and to Diderot to become head of the Prussian Academy of Science, Frederick seemed to show serious interest in the program of the philosophes. He declared religious toleration for Catholics, limited the use of torture, and offered asylum to persecuted writers. His open-mindedness had limits, though: he condemned Holbach's atheism and his naive belief in human perfectibility. Frederick proved a better general, brutally efficient and unflinching despite his early criticism of Machiavelli's *Prince*, than philosophe. He quarreled openly with Voltaire and even had him briefly imprisoned in 1753.[51]

When Voltaire settled in Geneva in 1755, he found himself drawn into the politics of the Calvinist city. Perhaps surprisingly, given how much time and effort he had expended ingratiating himself with the royal courts of France and Prussia, he sided with the citizens of Geneva against the ruling oligarchy. The citizens, less than 10 percent of a total population around twenty-five thousand, together constituted the General Assembly; they contested the role of elite families that had subverted Geneva's republican constitution by consolidating their control over the two-hundred-member Council. Voltaire wrote a tract entitled *Idées républicaines* (1765) that predictably called for freedom of expression, a uniform criminal code, and the removal of civil authority from religious authorities, but unexpectedly also embraced the idea of popular government: "The magistrates are not the masters of the people; the laws are," and the force of those laws derives from the people. Citizens enjoy the right, when assembled, to reject or endorse the magistrates and the laws proposed to them. Voltaire characterized civil government as "the will of all, carried out by a single person or by several, in accord with the laws that all have supported." As that final sentence indicates, Voltaire was willing to remain flexible concerning the appropriate form of administration, though at this stage he seemed to be moving toward the idea that sovereign power might reside in the people rather than necessarily being concentrated in a king.[52]

Yet Voltaire never entirely abandoned his royalism, at least where France or the states of central and eastern Europe were concerned. In his earliest poems and plays he celebrated the accomplishments of the heroic Henri IV. His history *Le siècle de Louis XIV* seasoned an admiring account of the glory the Sun King brought France with sharp criticism of his errors, most notably his revocation of the Edict of Nantes. Nevertheless, to Voltaire the mistakes of Henri IV were minor compared with the intransigence of the nobility and the parlements, who for centuries had resisted all efforts to reform French laws, revise the inequitable tax structure, or rein in the clergy. In 1766 Louis XV finally confronted the Parlement of Paris. He declared that sovereign power "resides in my person alone," that "legislative power belongs to me alone," and that "my courts derive their authority from me alone."

When Louis XV elevated to the position of chancellor René-Nicolat de Maupeou, who took further steps against the Paris Parlement, Voltaire published his *Histoire du Parlement de Paris*. This carefully documented but stridently partisan account can be reconciled with his *Idées républicaines* only by acknowledging that Voltaire judged different strategies appropriate in different contexts. His own allegiance depended on his judgment of the worst offenders against his principles of toleration and the rule of law. In Geneva he stood with the republicans, in France with the king. Voltaire's history demonstrated how the Parlement of Paris, although in principle responsible only for administering rather than making law, had for centuries obstructed all efforts to remove the remnants of feudalism that clogged French public life. As Voltaire wrote to d'Alembert just before the crisis of the Maupeou Parlement began, in France "the cause of the king is the cause of the philosophes."[53] Ultimately, none of the rulers initially embraced by the philosophes lived up to their hopes. In the 1770s Diderot wrote several critiques detailing the failures of these "enlightened despots." Voltaire ended up after 1759 far from any court, on the banks of Lake Geneva, near the austere city republic that gave birth to the most important—and most misunderstood—eighteenth-century European theorist of democracy, Jean-Jacques Rousseau.

Rousseau's life began in tragedy and ended in melancholy and isolation. Recurring quarrels with friends and confrontations with patrons punctuated a career marked by flashes of undeniable brilliance, outbursts of petulance and paranoia, and increasingly severe bouts with mental illness. His mother, who died days after giving birth to Jean-Jacques, hailed from a family of considerable wealth and some prestige. His father, a Geneva watchmaker who fled the city in 1722 after an altercation with a local notable not unlike the incident that landed Voltaire in prison, left his ten-year-old Jean-Jacques to be raised by the prosperous family of his wife's brother. As a child Rousseau himself thus experienced the bleakness of a motherless childhood, then a life of idyllic joy amidst the upper classes, before he was finally compelled to make his own way in the world. First Rousseau failed as an apprentice engraver, released by one master and beaten by another for various infractions. Demoralized by his treatment and his prospects, he was also haunted by memories of the "almost complete freedom" and "perfect equality"—as he later described that blissful interlude in his autobiographical *Confessions*—that he had enjoyed with his uncle's family.

One Sunday afternoon in the spring of 1728, returning from a stroll in the countryside with friends, the fifteen-year-old Rousseau found the gates of Geneva locked. It was not the first time; he was convinced a malicious gate-keeper had again raised the drawbridge early, this time when a sprinting Rousseau was only twenty strides away from it. Facing another certain beating, he made the fateful decision to leave Geneva. He knew he was exchanging the likelihood of "a calm and peaceful life in the security of my faith, in my own country, among my family and friends," for the wider horizons of an uncertain fate.[54] Rousseau's wanderings took him to the Counter-Reformation hotbed of Annecy, then to Turin, then back for an extended stay in the Savoyard town of Chambéry, at the foot of the majestic mountain known as the Grand Chartreuse. There he enjoyed a different sort of idyll in the company of a woman fourteen years older than he, Françoise-Louise de la Tour, baronne de Warens, successively his surrogate mother; his confidante, guide, and patron; and ultimately his lover. In his childhood Rousseau had read mostly tales and ancient history. He recalled that his earliest passion had been for the Roman heroes he found in Plutarch. While in Turin he converted to Catholicism. In Chambéry, during years when he and Madame de Warens enjoyed "the sweetest intimacy," he as her "little one," she as his "Mama," he discovered the Enlightenment. At this stage Rousseau reported reading Pascal, Descartes, Locke, Newton, Leibniz, the *Spectator*, Hobbes, and Pufendorf, among many others. Voltaire, in his estimation, towered over the rest.[55]

With the help of Madame de Warens, who supplied the books, the music, the house, and the company he needed, Rousseau educated himself. After toying with the idea of trying to reconcile the competing visions of the philosophers he read, he gave it up as a waste of time and decided to make his own mind a philosophical blank slate. For a while at least he would renounce "thinking independently" and follow the "thoughts of others unreflectively," so that he might build up "a great enough fund of learning to be self-sufficient and to think without the help of another."[56] According to his own account, Rousseau forged his intellectual independence through several trials. Serving as a tutor to the Mably family near Lyons tested his patience but earned him letters of introduction from the two brothers of his employer, the Abbé Gabriel de Mably and the Abbé Etienne Bonnot de Condillac. These two philosophes, later known respectively for a critique of private property and a

Lockean treatise on sensationalism, were years away from their mature work. They helped Rousseau develop his capacity for self-criticism, notably a painful appreciation of the inadequacy of his own first attempt at writing.[57]

Rousseau's next destination was Paris, where he soon met prominent philosophes—notably Diderot, who became for a time one of his closest friends—and many would-be philosophes and other hangers-on. His own interest in composing music had resulted in a novel scheme of musical notation that he hoped would make his fortune. He was mistaken. After scuffling around the edges of the worlds of the royal court and the salons that he longed to enter, Rousseau traveled to the Republic of Venice as secretary to the French ambassador. There he formed a fragile preference for its glittering world of music and spectacle over the still-too-sober and quasi-Calvinist culture of his native Geneva. He was beginning to wonder about the contrast. Did a successful republic require a Spartan simplicity? In what was to become a familiar pattern, he quarreled with the volatile French ambassador and abruptly returned from Venice to Paris. Soon indignation over the lack of sympathy he received from the Parisian *beau-monde* boiled over into rage: "The justice and fruitlessness of my complaints left a seed of indignation in my heart against our absurd civil institutions." From Rousseau's perspective, "the real welfare of the public and true justice" were always sacrificed to some false idol of order. Power, he seethed, "merely gives the sanction of public authority to the oppression of the weak and the iniquity of the strong."[58]

Not all Rousseau's Parisian friends abandoned him. For his efforts to turn one of Voltaire's minor works into an opera, he received the author's praise. The laundress at his hotel, Thérèse Levasseur, became his lover and bore his children while evidently asking little (and receiving less) in return. Diderot engaged him in the planning of a periodical patterned after Addison and Steele's *Spectator*. Diderot and d'Alembert invited him to write articles on music for the *Encyclopedia*. The parents of his friend Dupin de Francueil invited him to serve as an all-purpose researcher. In their employ he was asked to collaborate, at the Hôtel Lambert in Paris and at their estate in the Loire Valley, the exquisite Château de Chenonceau, on projects ranging from scientific experiments and a treatise on women's rights to various poems, plays, and pieces of music, all of which Rousseau did while continuing his own education in the Dupins' fine library.[59]

As Rousseau was beginning to think for himself, his friend Diderot was churning out texts, ranging from obscene novels to tracts on skepticism, that made him increasingly vulnerable to state censorship. On July 24, 1749, he was arrested and sent to the dungeon at the Château de Vincennes outside Paris. After a month there Diderot was moved to a fairly comfortable room in the château, where he lived with his wife and received visits from his friends, including Rousseau. It was on one of Rousseau's two-hour walks to visit Diderot in Vincennes that a life-changing revelation struck him. Reading the notice of an essay competition sponsored by the Academy of Dijon, Rousseau was stopped in his tracks by the question it posed: "Has the restoration of the sciences and arts tended to purify morals?"[60] Rousseau claimed that a single flash of insight en route to visit his friend inspired his entire oeuvre. "If I had ever been able to write a quarter of what I saw and felt under that tree, . . . I would have shown all the contradictions of the social system" and "exposed all the abuses of our institutions," demonstrating too "that man is naturally good, and that it is by these institutions that men become wicked."[61] Or, as Rousseau put it more briskly in his *Confessions*, "I beheld another universe and became another man."[62] The fruit of his transformation was his prizewinning *Discourse on the Sciences and Arts*, known now simply as the *First Discourse*, which surprised his friends and launched his writing career.

In the *First Discourse*, Rousseau rejected everything the Enlightenment embraced. He upheld an ideal of primitive simplicity antithetical to the values prized by learned societies in London or Paris (although evidently not that of Dijon), which celebrated science, technology, politeness, cultivation, and refinement as sure signs of progress. Rousseau argued instead that "advances" in the arts and sciences had, ever since the ancient world, always corrupted morals. Pleasure distracts citizens from their duties, luxuries lure them from the simple life, and pleasing appearances blind them to hardy virtue. The desire for fame leads individuals to conceive of themselves, and to construct their own ambitions, in relation to their hunger for esteem. Genuine concern for the common good thus gives way to a degraded form of reciprocity based not on authentic benevolence but on assumptions about the universality of self-interest. That culture of hypocrisy prizes a superficial self-regard, appraised only through the false perceptions of other equally shallow and egocentric individuals, and erodes even the possibility of deeper human bonds. A few truly brilliant minds—again Bacon, Newton, and Descartes serve as examples—can advance knowledge without being corrupted. The rest succumb to the temptations of sham profundity (such as shown by Berkeley, Spinoza, Mandeville, and Hobbes) or mere popularity. Recklessly, Rousseau cited Voltaire as an example of that danger, an impetuous step that earned him the chief philosophe's lasting enmity.[63]

Rousseau railed against the philosophes'—and his own—dependence on wealthy patrons. Against the decadence of his own day, he invoked the restraint of Socrates and Montaigne. Against the progress promised by Enlightenment, he offered the rustic virtue of American Indians, Spartan warriors, or Romans of the early republic. "What yoke," he asked in a phrase that points toward a principal theme of his later work, "could be imposed on men who need nothing?" Even more directly targeting the identification of Enlightenment with commerce and politeness, he defied the British and French philosophes' emphasis on economic growth: "What will become of virtue when one must get rich at any price? Ancient politicians incessantly talked about morals and virtue, those of our time talk only of business and money."[64]

Perhaps surprisingly, his friend Diderot was slow to react to the *First Discourse*, and Rousseau remained among the contributors to the *Encyclopedia*. In the conclusion to his "Preliminary Discourse," d'Alembert contended that despite Rousseau's complaints about the arts and sciences, his participation showed he accepted many of their ideas. Not only the notoriety of the *First Discourse* but also the successful performance of his opera *Le devin du village* made Rousseau a minor celebrity, welcome in the salons of the wealthy and fashionable. Even Louis XV wanted to meet him. Yet Rousseau was growing increasingly uneasy in polite society, increasingly wary of his dependence on the rich, and increasingly averse to the philosophes' growing materialism, in both the philosophical and the common-sense meanings of the term. His own religious faith, although unconventional in its pantheism, was deepening, as was his conviction that virtue requires simplicity. He abandoned the fairly lucrative position as a clerk that Francueil had secured for him, refused the pension that Louis XV offered him, and bravely—or foolishly, in Diderot's estimation—vowed to support himself and Thérèse on the modest income he could earn from honest work copying music.[65]

In 1754 lightning struck again. Rousseau wrote another essay for another competition, again sponsored by the Academy of Dijon, this time on the origins of inequality. Again he touched a nerve. Rousseau signed his *Discourse on the Origin and Foundations of Inequality among Men*, also known as the *Second Discourse*, as a "Citizen of Geneva." Since Rousseau did not meet the qualifications for citizenship in his native city-state, the claim was not strictly accurate. Yet the phrase signaled his admiration and aspirations for his homeland, the republic to which he had returned—after converting back to Protestantism—in 1754, and to which he dedicated the *Discourse on Inequality*. That dedication provides one of the most important (if least widely known or well understood) indications of the paradox at the heart of Rousseau's ideas about politics and culture. His more speculative statements of his political ideals pointed one way. His judgments concerning viable institutions and political practices in existing eighteenth-century polities—rather than ancient city-states or isolated mountain villages—pointed in quite another.[66]

According to Rousseau himself, the central contention of his life's work was that "everything is good when it springs from the hands of our Creator; everything degenerates when shaped by the hands of man."[67] Rousseau's *Discourse on Inequality* presents the first mature statement of that argument. Whereas savage man, "when he has eaten, is at peace with all nature, and the friend of all his fellow-man," modern man, even when well-fed, enjoyed neither peace nor freedom. "Luxury is a remedy far worse than the evil it claims to cure," because economic development eroded the original human instincts of self-preservation tempered by pity and yielded instead the unremitting cruelty and conflict of civilization.[68]

Rousseau's contemporaries, like his later interpreters, understood him to be urging a return to the simple life of primitive people. Voltaire, to cite just the best-known example, wrote playfully to Rousseau that reading the *Second Discourse*, "your new book against the human species," made "one long to go on all fours."[69] Rousseau denied such charges explicitly in the *Discourse on Inequality* itself. Although rare souls might find a simple life rewarding, the deeper tragedy of human development lay in its disfiguring men to the extent that they were no longer capable of such existence. "As for men like me, whose passions have forever destroyed their original simplicity," no such alternative was possible. The degradation occasioned by the human capacity of "perfectibility" could not be reversed. There was no going back to the state of nature. Rousseau insisted that man's original pity, which checked cruelties that had since become commonplace, had vanished with the emergence of inequality, a condition unknown in the state of nature. Only when property appeared did individuals need each other for any purpose other than reproduction. All that changed when "the first person who, having fenced off a plot of ground, took it into his head to say *this is mine*" managed to find "people simple enough to believe him." That individual, according to Rousseau's melodramatic formulation, "was the true founder of civil society."

Rather than treating property as natural or fundamental, Rousseau proclaimed it an artifice, a mere convention. Property perverted men from their original instinct of self-preservation, or healthy "love of self" (*amour de soi*), which was always softened by pity for others, and transmuted that quality into a corrupt "self-love" (*amour propre*). Social relations thus deteriorated into competition, dependency, or oppression, the conditions typical of all modern societies.[70] Pity had led individuals not to the golden rule but to a more instinctive version of Shaftesbury's benevolence. The natural exercise of pity "carries us without reflection to the aid of those whom we see suffer; in the state of nature, it takes the place of laws, morals, and virtue, with the advantage that no one is tempted to disobey its gentle voice." It leads to a "maxim of natural goodness" that is less perfect but more useful than the law of love: *"Do what is good for you with the least possible harm to others."* That more modest ethic prevented outright war, limited both the power of the stronger and the dependency of the weaker, and prevented the "instituted inequality" that developed only with the emergence of property and the laws of civil society. Champions of Enlightenment were wrong. Refinement did not bring a softening of morals; instead civilization destroyed natural benevolence and gave birth to the monstrous forms of manipulative hypocrisy and cringing dissimulation known as polite manners.[71]

On the other hand, as human cultures developed, the weakening impulses of self-preservation and pity gave way to the possibilities of virtue and vice, neither of which existed when humans merely followed their instincts. For a brief moment, Rousseau wrote wistfully, there must have been "a golden mean between the indolence of the primitive state and the petulant activity of our vanity." That era he portrayed rhapsodically as the "happiest and most durable epoch" of human history. Rousseau endorsed Locke's judgment: *"Where there is no property, there is no injury."* Yet that moment could not endure. With the advent of property, law became necessary. Individuals could then transform modest advantages in strength or intelligence—through the division of labor—into the more permanent, and more insidious, "contrived inequality" authorized by civil society. Property holders' clever usurpation became "an irrevocable right," and henceforth all of humanity was subjected to "work, servitude, and misery."[72] With the poor now dependent on the rich for survival, the rich thought themselves entitled not only to luxury but also to authority.

Rousseau's account of the institution of civil society both rested on the writings of earlier writers—he invoked Sidney, Locke, and Pufendorf, among others, to repudiate the claim that absolute authority in politics derives from a father's paternal authority[73]—and departed from them. He excoriated slavery, particularly heritable slavery, as an abomination without justification. Challenging Pufendorf's claim that one can alienate freedom as one can alienate one's property, Rousseau drew a distinction: the right of property is merely a human convention, so every man is free to do whatever he wishes with what he possesses. "The essential gifts of nature, such as life and freedom," by contrast, come from God, not man, and cannot be divested. Those who claimed that the child of a slave is born a slave pretended that "a man would not be born a man."[74]

Because the use of one's life and freedom comes to the individual from God, it follows that free individuals came together to institute government.

Absolute or arbitrary power should not be considered the origin of government but its "corruption and extreme limit." At this stage Rousseau envisioned the people making a contract with a ruler, as earlier theorists such as Sidney and Locke had held, a conception he later repudiated. Already in the *Second Discourse*, Rousseau adumbrated the concept of the general will that later became the centerpiece of his thought. "The people having, on the subject of social relations, united all their wills into a single one, all the articles on which this will is explicit become so many fundamental laws obligating all members of the State without exception." As that passage makes clear, Rousseau's general will is nothing more mysterious than the legitimate rule of law authorized by the people and grounded in popular sovereignty. He speculated that different degrees of inequality had spawned different forms of government. The most unequal conditions yielded monarchy. Moderate inequality bred aristocracy. Finally, "those whose fortune or talents were less disproportionate, and who were the least removed from the state of nature, kept the supreme administration in common and formed a democracy." Regardless of the form of government, however, "all magistrates were at first elective," with age, wealth, or merit providing the criteria of selection. If government officials abused their authority, power reverted to its source, the people.[75]

In the *Discourse on Inequality*, Rousseau said little about how government should operate beyond proclaiming that an egalitarian democracy most nearly resembled the happiest stage. Yet he made clear his conviction that people could not return to the state of nature. He advised readers wanting to address the problems he identified to "respect the sacred bonds of the societies of which they are members," meaning they should "love their fellow-men" and "serve them with all their power."[76] Through such obedience to law, obedience to the ethic of reciprocity, and obedience to legitimate authority, individuals might shake off the yoke of artificial norms and regain their freedom. That freedom would include freedom of the will, denied by the more materialistic and deterministic among the philosophes; freedom as persons no longer afraid to be honest or authentic, and no longer in competition with each other; freedom from the lures of luxury, prestige, and power; and freedom as citizens, exercising power over the magistrates who serve them rather than cowering before those officials' pretensions to unquestionable authority. Unfortunately, everything Rousseau said about the consequences and irreversibility of historical development militated against attaining those goals.

In the *Second Discourse*, Rousseau concentrated on diagnosing the disease of inequality. Only faintly did he sketch his own philosophical, social, and political ideals. His mature writings, particularly his treatise on education masked as a novel, *Emile*, and the *Social Contract*, filled in the details. Rousseau's paradoxical linking of freedom with obedience—his familiar maxim that citizens must at times be "forced to be free"—has generated a flood of critical commentary ever since these two books appeared in 1762. Both were condemned by officials in France and Geneva and severely criticized by many partisans of the Enlightenment. For the final sixteen years of his life, Rousseau found himself increasingly estranged from his former allies and harried from place to place by outraged authorities.

The anger and the acclaim that greeted *Emile* and the *Social Contract* in their first two decades have been drowned out by the furor generated by the use to which the books were put after Rousseau's death in 1778. Paradoxically, recovering these texts' historical significance means confronting the distorting influence of the French Revolution on our reading of Rousseau. He never imagined the Reign of Terror. Nor did he envision the guillotining of Louis XVI and his queen, Marie Antoinette, a headstrong young woman who was known, incidentally, to be an avid reader of Rousseau. Attempts to make Rousseau responsible for the violence of the Revolution or the fury of the civil war that followed show either a failure of historical imagination or at least an inclination toward anachronism. Later chapters examine the partisans of revolutionary violence who revered Rousseau. The responses to that violence, and the reflexive attribution of its horrors to Rousseau, show why radicals were drawn to him and their foes reviled him. Few understood what he meant by autonomy, equality, and the general will.[77]

Rousseau's *Emile* follows the education of the protagonist by a wise tutor who teaches him what he needs to know to live as a free and virtuous man, and as an ideal citizen, at least in a hypothetical republic. Rousseau's tutor places Emile in a series of situations in which he gradually learns, by being required to submit again and again to manifest necessity rather than to the masked will of the tutor, to follow the rules of self-sufficiency, on the one hand, and the ethical maxim to "let your duties come before your inclinations," on the other. Individuals who follow their appetites or their inclinations only appear to be free. They enjoy nothing but the empty freedom of slaves. Emile's education, by contrast, trains and enables him to "extend the law of necessity to moral things," as the tutor puts it, so that he can "reign over himself" and "sacrifice his interest to the common interest." Emile eventually comes to understand that his freedom lies in embracing the rules provided by his benevolent tutor. He becomes wise enough to see that those laws provide more reliable guidance than his own often wayward desires, always apt to be shunted by appetite toward vice. He implores his tutor to "make me free by protecting me against those of my passions which do violence to me. Prevent me from being their slave; force me to be my own master and to obey not my sense but my reason." Only when Emile has developed his own autonomy, only when he is capable of self-mastery in the tutor's absence, is he prepared for life as a husband, a father, and a citizen.[78]

Emile closes with the tutor assuring Emile and his new wife, Sophie, who agreed to postpone their marriage until Emile's education was complete, that they are now ready to live their lives independently. Emile has internalized the ethic of reciprocity, grounded in both conscience and sentiment rather than reason alone, and achieved the steely autonomy he needs. He has forged a fully developed conscience, which, in the words of the Savoyard vicar who contributes the philosophical reflections at the core of *Emile*, provides a "principle of justice and virtue" that enables us to judge our own actions as well as those of others.[79] Now the naturally beneficent Sophie will serve as the only guide Emile needs, not only aiding but also obeying her husband, "just as nature wanted it." (Eighteenth-century gender hierarchy was among the few conventions Rousseau left unchallenged.) The grateful young couple resists the tutor's invitation to independence. When they are to become parents, they ask the tutor to raise their children as he did Emile. "As long as I live," Emile confesses, "I shall need you." Does the virtuous Emile's humility reflect his awareness that his benevolent tutor sees his true interest better than he sees it himself, or, as critics suggest, does it reveal Rousseau's pathological need to perpetuate tyrannical control while calling such manipulation "freedom"?[80]

Rousseau began developing the ideas that would reach fruition in the *Social Contract* at least partly in response to the ideas of Diderot. In his article "Natural Law," Diderot had issued an implicit challenge to Rousseau's portrait of pity in the state of nature and its erosion over time. From the perspective of Diderot and other philosophes, understanding the requirements of the general will, or the common good, does not vary according to stages of historical development. It comes naturally to all humans as a function of reason. Rousseau disagreed. In his article "Political Economy," also appearing in the *Encyclopedia* (in volume 5, published in 1755), he credited Diderot with coining the term "general will." Rousseau then subtly transformed its meaning while drawing a crucial distinction between sovereignty and government that has too often been overlooked. Rousseau began by acknowledging that Sidney and Locke had refuted the arguments of Filmer and other apologists of absolutism. He concluded by arguing for a system of taxation directly opposite to that prevailing in France. Not only should the amount of tax paid be proportional to the amount of wealth individuals held, he contended; all taxes on property should be enacted "with the express consent of the people or its representatives."[81]

In addition to challenging the royal absolutism and laissez-faire economics preferred by many philosophes, Rousseau distinguished between the particular interests of individuals and of social groups, on the one hand, and the interest of the public on the other. In "Political Economy," Rousseau offered a clear, shorthand version of his central—and doubtless most influential and controversial—idea, the "general will." From Rousseau's perspective, the general will "always tends toward the preservation and welfare of the whole and of each part." It is "the source of the laws" and provides "the rule of what is just and unjust." The particular will of any individual, by contrast, and of any group within the society, may or may not correspond to the general will. Rousseau offered the general will as an abstract standard of judgment, an ideal of justice, a principle that provides the norm against which all considerations of individual or group interests must be measured.

In a democracy, in which the people are the source of law, individuals or groups might be expected to see that their deeper interests are identical to that of the public. Unfortunately, even in popular government "personal interest is always found in inverse ratio to duty." The people can be seduced by wily men to substitute private interests for the good of the whole. By definition "the general will is always in favor of the common good," yet the assembly's natural inclination is very often "bypassed for the sake of private views," which saps the strength of the general will. As society splits apart, members of specific groups make choices that benefit only one part rather than the whole from which they seceded. Just as an individual can become convinced that his own interest differs from the general will, so can members of a particular group reach that conclusion. Despite the shrewd justifications offered to defend those partial interests—"the most corrupt men always render some sort of homage to the public faith"—it is imperative, Rousseau insisted, to distinguish the general will from any and all particular wills.[82]

How is that to be done? Rousseau's answer was disarmingly simple. "These marvels are the work of the law. It is to law alone that men owe justice and freedom." Given the sublimity and indispensability of law, Rousseau not surprisingly recommended that the first duty of the legislator is to "make the laws conform to the general will."[83] How is the general will to be identified? "Must the whole nation be assembled at each unforeseen event?" Many of Rousseau's readers—both his champions and his critics—have concluded that he thought all citizens must assemble to make laws, but he considered such a step neither practical nor necessary. Moreover, Rousseau denied that even an assembly of all citizens would be dependable because its decisions would not necessarily conform to the general will. Of all Rousseau's paradoxes, this one seems at first the most nettlesome, but he had already explained how to resolve it. Given the inclination of individuals and groups to mistake their own particular interests for the general will, gathering such individuals together, or gathering members of such groups together, is as likely to generate conflict as resolution, as likely to provoke statements of unyielding loyalty to self or group as to illuminate what is truly in the general interest. Yet the problem is less vexing than it seems: "For the leaders know very well that the general will is always for the side most favorable to the public interest—that is, for the most equitable; so that it is only necessary to be just and one is assured of following the general will." Only the filters of particular interest, whether of individuals or of small groups, obscure the luminous truth of justice. Remove the filters, see the truth.

Viewed in that light, the lessons of autonomy and virtue learned by Emile seem not only pertinent but essential to public life. Since virtue consists in the "conformity of the private will to the general," the objective of government is simply to "make virtue reign." Achieving that goal is the purpose of law. "The most absolute authority is that which penetrates to the inner man and is exerted no less on his will than on his actions." Each individual "is virtuous when his private will conforms on all matters with the general will." Under the right conditions, no force is necessary, because "we willingly want what is wanted by the people we love." Just as Emile and Sophie trust the tutor because they know he has nothing but their best interests at heart, so citizens should have confidence that the laws embody the general will. "When citizens love their duty," Rousseau concluded, "all difficulties vanish."[84]

Neat trick, one might say. It is one thing for Rousseau to resolve such difficulties in the fictional tale of Emile, quite another to contend that they can be resolved in a world in which, by his own admission, particular interests obstruct the ability of all individuals and all groups to perceive the general will. What is to be done? Rousseau explicitly denied that coercion is the answer. If the doctrine of the general will "means that the government is allowed to sacrifice an innocent man for the safety of the multitude, I hold this maxim to be one of the most execrable that tyranny ever invented, the most false that might be proposed, the most dangerous that might be accepted, and the most directly opposed to the fundamental laws of society."[85] Although accused of endorsing just such steps, Rousseau insisted that individuals cannot be made means to the state's ends. If violence is ruled out, how can states inculcate virtue in their citizens? Rousseau's answer was visionary:

"Public education, under rules prescribed by the government and magistrates established by the sovereign, is therefore one of the fundamental maxims of popular or legitimate government."[86] In the 1750s such public education existed nowhere in the world. Its rise, first in New England and then elsewhere in North America and Europe, where it spread in the middle decades of the nineteenth century, both reflected and propelled the triumph of the idea that popular government must rest on the foundation of an educated citizenry. For Rousseau, as for some of his contemporaries (such as John Adams, Benjamin Rush, and Thomas Jefferson) and for many champions of the idea for the next century, the purpose of education had little to do with economic productivity and everything to do with virtue, both moral and civic.

Rousseau's economic ideas likewise turned standard assumptions on their heads. The "third essential duty of the government" is not "to fill the granaries of private individuals and dispense them from working," as landowning aristocracies throughout Europe had done for centuries. Governments should instead make abundance available to all people willing to work. Rousseau envisioned a gradual transformation through progressive taxation rather than confiscation and redistribution of property. Given the radical critique of property in the *Discourse on Inequality*, Rousseau's characterization of the right to property in "Political Economy" as "the basis of the social compact" is as surprising as his defense of inheritance and his critique of ceaseless changes in citizens' status.

Even so, Rousseau was convinced that inequality remained the deepest source of injustice. He concluded "Political Economy" by rejecting defenses of superfluous wealth and the tax systems designed to preserve and even widen those inequalities. "Someone who has only the bare necessities should pay nothing at all; taxation on someone who has superfluities can, if need be, approach the totality of what exceeds his necessities." Those with excessive wealth always defended such wealth as necessary for those of exalted rank, but Rousseau dismissed such claims as a lie. Even the richest noble has but one stomach and needs but one roof over his head. Rousseau criticized both mercantilist and physiocratic approaches to public finance and the expansionist impulses of all large states. Instead he praised the small-scale city-states of antiquity and systems of public granaries such as that maintained in Geneva, which was available to the public in times of need and was the principal, and most reliable, source of revenue for the state.[87]

Rousseau's argument in "Political Economy" rested on a distinction between the sovereign people and the government, or the people's representatives, whose job it is to identify the general will and ensure that its underlying principle of equity, premised on the ethic of reciprocity, informs all legislation. Challenging the philosophes' confidence in universality, Rousseau argued that both the form of such decision making and the decisions made would vary over time and across cultures. His convictions that laws must fit mores, that particular polities require particular political systems, and that founding moments are unique to individual cultures—and thus can be neither repeated nor generalized—stand among the most important (if least often acknowledged) of his insights.[88] In "Political Economy," Rousseau described individuals willingly adopting the principle of justice embodied in laws made by the people themselves, an economy oriented through progressive taxation toward the greatest degree of equity compatible with stable and secure property rights, and expressed his belief that every culture, and each historical moment, is unique. In his most influential work, the *Social Contract*, he presented the same ideas about popular sovereignty, autonomy, and equality, and he examined in detail the ethic of reciprocity underlying the idea of the general will.

We may never know when Rousseau began work on the *Social Contract*. Parts of his first version of the text, now known as the *Geneva Manuscript*, might have been written as early as 1752, before he wrote the *Second Discourse* or "Political Economy," or perhaps as late as 1761. Whenever it was written, the *Geneva Manuscript* illuminates certain features of his thought by bringing into sharper focus some of the arguments that appear in the version of the *Social Contract* published in 1762. Rousseau decided not to publish the chapter of the *Geneva Manuscript* in which he explicitly repudiated Diderot's idea of a universal general will of the entire human race. For that reason it is easy to overlook his strident objections to the ideas of natural law, premised on universal human reason and the right to self-preservation, and an unchanging human nature. Instead Rousseau claimed that "the soul's most delicious feeling, which is love of virtue," becomes possible only *after* humans leave the state of nature and enter civil society. Only then does individual interest stifle fellow feeling. What are called natural law and natural reason take shape only *after* "the prior development of the passions renders all its precepts impotent."

Those passages from the *Geneva Manuscript* illustrate more clearly than does the *Social Contract* itself the historicist irony that unlocks Rousseau's meaning. Rather than characterizing reason, natural rights, and natural law as inherent qualities of humans, as so many earlier theorists had done, Rousseau contended that such qualities emerged only after men had already joined together to form civil society. Only then was their initial and harmless love of self transmuted into a corrosive and egocentric self-love. Only then was their original instinct of pity transmuted, due to human perfectibility, into the capacity for virtue or vice. Likewise in the *Geneva Manuscript* Rousseau directly challenged the notion of a single, overarching social ideal. "It is only from the social order established among us that we derive ideas about the one we imagine. We conceive of the general society on the basis of our particular societies." Rousseau's emphases on historical time and cultural variability thus distinguished his ideas from those of many other philosophes—and from the ideas often attributed to him—a difference muted in the published version of the *Social Contract* but unmistakable in the *Geneva Manuscript*.[89]

The *Social Contract* appeared in at least thirteen French editions, three editions in English (all three of which John Adams bought), and one each in German and Russian, within two years of its publication.[90] Although the central arguments in the *Social Contract* did not surprise readers familiar with Rousseau's other work, bringing them all together made the ensemble even more explosive. Rousseau explicitly endorsed an ideal democracy as the regime most appropriate for angels, yet his explicit criticism of existing forms of popular government has caused readers for two centuries to contend that he opposed all forms of representation and favored only the direct participation of all citizens in all political decision making. Interpreters of the *Social Contract* have thus offered Rousseau as the founder of modern democratic theory while simultaneously offering as the only legitimate form of democracy a type of regime Rousseau himself never expected to see, not only because he understood that it would be impossible but also because he considered it undesirable.[91] Untangling that confusion is therefore critically important.

"Man is born free, and everywhere he is in chains." Controversies over the *Social Contract* begin with the first sentence of the book. Quite clearly, Rousseau deliberately chose words that carry the double meaning expressed in French. "*L'homme est né*" can mean either "man is born"—and thus remains free or should be free, or even more provocatively, should be freed—or "man was born"—and thus has evolved from an original condition of freedom to the current state of enslavement.[92] Almost equally controversial is Rousseau's claim that any individual who refuses to obey the general will "shall be constrained to do so by the entire body; which means only that he will be forced to be free." That provocative formulation echoes Rousseau's arguments in "Political Economy" and *Emile*; its meaning derives directly from that of the general will. In the *Social Contract*, Rousseau revised the understanding drawn from earlier contract theorists and contended that civil society is formed when individuals make a compact with each other—not, as Locke had it, with their rulers. *"Each of us puts his person and all his power in common under the supreme direction of the general will."* Each individual alienates all his rights to the whole community, which then constitutes the sovereign power and by its "act of association produces a moral and collective body, composed of as many members as there are voices in the assembly, which receives from this same act its unity, its common *self*, its life, and its will."[93]

Just as individuals cannot will themselves into slavery, so the people cannot alienate their sovereignty. Popular sovereignty remains the principle standing behind—and giving legitimacy to—the general will. Yet because individuals retain free will even after entering the social compact, they can make choices contrary to their own interest. To Rousseau's critics, being "forced to be free" conjures up images of the guillotine or the secret police. In the framework of Rousseau's conception of the general will as presented in "Political Economy" and *Emile* and elaborated in the *Social Contract*, it means nothing more ominous or sinister than the straightforward maxim that citizens must obey the law. Such obedience to law involves not renouncing one's will but fulfilling it. Wanting to have the advantages of citizenship without fulfilling its duties is a natural consequence of the disfigured self-love that causes everyone to see himself in competition with everyone else and causes everyone to want to take advantage of everyone else. The purpose of the general will is to prevent that from happening. Unlike other regimes, in which monarchs or aristocrats enjoy special privileges, a republic in which law conforms to the general will requires everyone to obey the law.[94]

In three brief paragraphs, Rousseau recapitulated the intricate argument for autonomy in *Emile* and laid out the rationale for the general will. When men become citizens, they substitute "justice for instinct" and "the voice of duty" for "physical impulse." In such circumstances, "right replaces appetite." Men lose their "natural freedom" but gain something of much greater value, "civil freedom, which is limited by the general will," and "moral freedom, which alone makes man truly the master of himself." In short, "the impulse to appetite alone is slavery, and obedience to the law one has prescribed for oneself is freedom."[95] Such arguments illuminate the distinction Rousseau drew between the "will of all" and the general will, a distinction crucial for subsequent democratic theorists on both sides of the Atlantic. As Rousseau pointed out in the *Second Discourse* and "Political Economy," the same dynamic that leads individuals to separate their own interests from the common interest leads them to form factions, or "partial associations at the expense of the whole." Such groups do not consider their interests distinct from the general will; instead they think their will is the general will. When such factions multiply, they form alliances, which are even more powerfully inclined to identify their interests with the common good, especially when a single association emerges to dominate all the others. Rousseau distinguished the "will of all," merely the sum of private wills, whether those are the wills of separate individuals or of small or even majority factions, from the general will, because individuals and factions can express only private interests rather than the general interest. "Take away from these same wills the pluses and minuses that cancel each other out, and the remaining sum of the differences is the general will." Inasmuch as the particular wills of individuals or factions correspond with the general will, they are unproblematical. When they differ from it—even if they constitute a numerical majority—they corrode the common good.[96]

Rousseau's distrust of individual interests and group interests contrary to the general will has generated fierce objections ever since the *Social Contract* appeared. When the general will is understood simply as the rule of law, however, such criticism seems misdirected. Immediately after his discussion of potentially divisive partial associations and the need to guard against the "will of all" masquerading as the general will, Rousseau qualified his earlier characterization of rights and noted that "each person alienates through the social compact only that part of his power, goods, and freedom whose use matters to the community." That is a considerable fraction, as Rousseau's discussion of taxation in "Political Economy" makes clear, yet it is hardly unlimited. Only mutual engagements are obligatory, and all such obligations must be general rather than directed toward any single individual. The only limits on rights are those on which all agree, and "every man can fully dispose of the part of his goods and freedom that has been left to him by these conventions."[97] Rights are not only preserved; they are solidified because they have the force of the general will behind them.

Rousseau, whose experience of politics was shaped by the contrast between the Calvinist theocratic republic of Geneva and the royal absolutism of Louis XV, was convinced that the selfishness of individuals was the problem of politics, not the solution. He sought an alternative that linked ideas about voluntarism stretching from Seneca and Augustine through Montaigne and Pascal to the hunger for universality that he saw in Christianity and absolutism.[98] That alternative, as he put it in a letter to Mirabeau, lay in "the most austere democracy," in which the rule of law depends on the will of the people but nevertheless places the law above every individual citizen. Such a solution, Rousseau conceded, seems "comparable to squaring the circle in geometry."[99] As that image makes clear, Rousseau understood that individual wills cannot be reconciled perfectly with the general will.

Rousseau himself admitted as much in a crucial passage in the *Geneva Manuscript* that might have clarified these issues had it appeared in the *Social Contract*. "The general will is rarely the will of all," he wrote, "and the public force is always less than the sum of the private forces, so that in the mechanism of the States there is an equivalent of friction in machines, which one must know how to reduce to the least possible amount."[100] Such friction can never be eliminated; the idea of two frictionless surfaces exists only as an abstraction. Even though the populace might always want the good, on its own it rarely sees it. "The general will is always right, but the judgment that guides it is not always enlightened," in large part due to "the seduction of private wills."

If the chafing between the particular wills of individuals and the general will cannot be avoided, the *Social Contract* offers several strategies for minimizing it, notably reliance on a wise lawgiver. The problem, of course, is that such omniscient and universally respected lawgivers are in short supply. Moreover, there can be no formula for dispensing such laws because every culture is unique, and a founding moment comes but once in the history of any people. Laws and political institutions must develop from the particular experiences and mores of particular peoples, and the appropriate circumstances for establishing a republic of laws based on the general will can never be recovered, not even, Rousseau proclaimed explicitly, by starting over: even revolutions cannot restore those conditions. The genius of Emile's tutor lay in knowing when Emile could take the next step in his education. So "one people is capable of discipline at birth, another is not after ten centuries."[101] Rousseau's stance in the *Social Contract* mirrors that of the *Second Discourse*, in which he showed why the conditions necessary to secure freedom in its philosophical, social, and political dimensions were becoming more unattainable every day.

Rousseau counseled careful attention to history and culture. Different peoples, in different geographical circumstances, at different historical stages, need different forms of government. As long as laws are just, the rule of law is supreme, and the sovereign people remain the source of its legitimacy, Rousseau contended, the state can take the shape of monarchy, aristocracy, or democracy. All of these forms of government admit of multiple variations and mixtures; no arithmetical calculations will yield the appropriate governments under all conditions. Those caveats notwithstanding, Rousseau did speculate on the appropriate situation for originating or founding legislation: when people are bound together by customs, but those customs are not too ingrained; when people are flourishing but not too numerous to know one another; when they are neither rich nor poor but self-sufficient; and when they are neither too simple nor too advanced but combine the "stability of an ancient people with the docility of a new people." As Rousseau noted, after ticking off these difficult and successively more delicate and elusive balances, such conditions are hard to find, which explains why one sees so few well-constituted states.[102]

Well-constituted democracies are even more rare.[103] The fundamental prerequisite of majority rule, which I have labeled the ethic of reciprocity, Rousseau deemed "contrary to the natural order" in that it empowers the majority to govern and the minority to be governed. Moreover, he dismissed the idea of full participation because the people cannot "remain constantly assembled to attend to public affairs." For that reason even democracies eventually deputize some citizens to administer the government. A few gradually acquire power, and thus democracy tends to degenerate into oligarchy or autocracy. Under modern conditions, Rousseau observed, it could hardly be otherwise. Whereas "a people who would always govern well would not need to be governed," the dynamics of self-love and particular wills make government inevitable and the decline of democracy predictable. The few historical experiments in democracy demonstrate that "there is no government so subject to civil wars and internal agitations as the democratic or popular one, because there is none that tends so strongly and constantly to change its form, nor that demands more vigilance and courage to be maintained in its own form." Rousseau's words convey the reasons behind his deep ambivalence about democracy, which he admired as an ideal for precisely the reasons he dismissed it as a viable option in most circumstances: "If there were a people of Gods, it would govern itself democratically. Such a perfect government is not suited to men."[104] Bleak as that judgment seems, Rousseau saw a way out: representative government.

Rousseau's discussion of "deputies or representatives" in the *Social Contract* has prompted many of his interpreters to disregard that possibility. Such readers conclude that only a direct democracy, in which all citizens assemble to participate in making all political decisions, meets Rousseau's standards. That mistake derives from neglecting Rousseau's crucial distinction between sovereignty and government, a distinction that he took from Bodin, and a distinction between "false" and "true" democracies that he took from the marquis d'Argenson, one of the few eighteenth-century French writers who endorsed democracy. D'Argenson considered monarchy indispensable for the unity all nations need. Pardoxically, though, he considered democracy, properly understood, more compatible with monarchy than France's existing aristocracy. Whereas aristocrats' love of luxury bred dissolution and dissent, and the common people lacked the capacity to govern directly without sliding into the chaos that befell ancient democracies, the principle of representation provided an alternative. "In a true democracy," d'Argenson wrote, "one acts through deputies, who are authorized by election; the mission of those elected by the people and the authority that such officials carry constitute the public power." Left to their own devices, individuals jealously seek their own advantage. When groups of citizens can assemble, "conciliate with one another, and act with a certain independence," they can discover a common interest otherwise hidden from view.[105]

Rousseau cited d'Argenson's *Considérations sur le gouvernement ancien et présent de la France* in the notes to the *Social Contract*, and he adopted several of its central ideas, notably d'Argenson's critique of luxury, his praise for the simple life, and his analysis of locally elected officials' capacity to discern the common good. Rousseau argued that the sovereign power of the people "cannot be represented for the same reason it cannot be alienated." Because it "consists essentially in the general will," and the will cannot be represented, only exercised, there is no way for individual deputies, no matter how legitimate their election, to "represent" the undivided will of the sovereign people. But government is something else entirely. Rousseau did not characterize the people's elected representatives as sovereign, as theorists customarily described the ruling power in a monarchy or an aristocracy. Instead he saw them only as the people's agents, the creatures of the people whose decisions the people themselves must then ratify before they can legitimately be considered consistent with the people's will. D'Argenson thought that was the king's job, but Rousseau believed it was up to the people.

Rousseau explicitly criticized the practice of elections in Britain, much praised by other philosophes. He contended that the English people were free only when they were electing members of Parliament. Once they were elected, the people were again slaves. Why? The notorious corruption of English politics—the buying and selling of votes, the rotten boroughs, the tiny fraction of the population entitled to vote—made a mockery of the idea that the House of Commons embodied the will of the people. English citizens had no other avenue of engagement in politics: most petitions were ignored, and there were no formal referenda, no chance to recall wayward representatives, no opportunities to instruct MPs, and no prospect of ratifying or rejecting any decisions of Parliament. Rather than sustained engagement, the system allowed only a few English citizens to vote, then dismissed them from civic life. Finally, neither the House of Lords nor the crown's appointed ministers nor the judiciary made the slightest pretense of representing anybody, and their combined power dwarfed that of the House of Commons.

Even the generous contemporary characterization of sovereign power resting with the king-in-Parliament reflected the extent to which the monarchy retained at the very least a substantial share of the sovereign power, which Rousseau contended could be neither divided nor relinquished by the people. Much as Rousseau's critical comments about British practice distinguished his stance from that of many French philosophes enamored of British traditions, they should not be taken as ruling out the viability of more robust forms of representative government. Rousseau acknowledged, as Montesquieu had done, that Athenian democracy relied on a combination of lot and election to fill offices. When citizens are asked to bear a burden, according to Rousseau, lot is the best mechanism because it distributes obligations without preference. Elections are called for when special skills are required, but for other positions, such as those involving judicial responsibilities, in which "good sense, justice, and integrity suffice," lot is preferable because all citizens, at least ideally, should possess such qualities.[106]

Despite the claims of many of his critics and admirers, Rousseau did not endorse direct democracy in all circumstances. In the constitutions he drafted for Poland and Corsica, and particularly in his dedication of the *Second Discourse* to Geneva, he stressed the role of representation even as he conceded that, in an ideal world—a world of gods, perhaps, or a world in which circles are squared and frictionless surfaces exist—such institutions would be unnecessary. The kingdom of Poland, a sprawling monarchy with an entrenched aristocracy and a mass of uneducated, dependent serfs, might seem among the least likely sites for a republic patterned on Rousseau's model in the *Social Contract*. Yet he complied with the request he received for a model constitution. The design Rousseau submitted for Poland, while taking into account the nation's cultural, social, and political traditions, emphasized the importance of moving gradually toward a republic by educating the serfs to prepare them for citizenship, eventually providing universal suffrage, and working to "perfect the form" of the existing representative assemblies.[107] Corsica, singled out in the *Social Contract* as ripe for a republican form of government, likewise invited Rousseau to envision a constitution. Again he turned to representative assemblies. Because Corsica's size prevented all citizens from assembling in a single place, Rousseau noted that a pure democracy, appropriate in "a small town rather than in a nation," was impossible. Instead Rousseau recommended a federal system similar to his scheme for Poland, with regional assemblies that would make laws and submit them to the people for approval.[108]

The clearest indication of the consistency between a particular species of representative democracy and Rousseau's political principles, however, comes from the dedication of the *Second Discourse*. There Rousseau lovingly described a country "where I would have wished to be born," a country that many readers have assumed to be Rousseau's native Geneva, the republic to which he had returned and to which he dedicated the *Second Discourse*. But mid-eighteenth-century Geneva was hardly a place where the "sweet habit of seeing and knowing one another turned love of the fatherland into love of the citizens rather than love of the soil." Geneva was instead racked by conflicts, not only between the people and the ruling oligarchy that controlled the government, but also among the factions operating within the popular party contesting oligarchic rule.[109]

Rousseau understood the tragic irony of democracy better than most later commentators. He knew that self-government had come to Geneva not through the efforts of Calvin or of ordinary people but through the calculating intervention of the pre-Reformation Catholic Bishop Adémar Fabri, who granted citizens the franchise in 1367 to secure their loyalty to the Holy Roman Empire against the Duke of Savoy. From Rousseau's perspective, the coming of Calvin's theocratic republic marked the beginning of a centuries-long decline of popular government in Geneva, not its apotheosis. His opposition to the unification of religious and civil authority in Geneva put him at odds with one of the popular factions challenging the Council of Twenty-Five. The other faction was calling for direct democracy, an option Rousseau opposed with equal fervor.

In his dedication, Rousseau endorsed the idea of a sovereign people, but he warned against precisely the sort of participatory democratic government he is often thought to have embraced. "Above all I would have fled, as necessarily ill-governed, a Republic where the people, believing it could do without its magistrates or only allow them a precarious authority, would imprudently have retained the administration of civil affairs and the execution of its own laws." Only immediately after people had emerged from the state of nature would they have chosen such a "rude constitution." Lest that criticism be misunderstood, Rousseau pointedly characterized such excessive democratic participation as "one of the vices that ruined the Republic of Athens." His goal, as the *Social Contract* made clear, was to find a way *beyond* the narrow interests of particular individuals or groups, and he worried that empowering an assembly of all citizens would muffle the voice of the general will, which would be drowned out by the clamor of competing particular wills.[110]

What was Rousseau's alternative? Immediately after having dismissed direct democracy as an unsatisfactory accommodation suitable only to primitive states, he extolled the virtues of representative democracy. "Rather I would have chosen that Republic" where citizens "elect from year to year the most capable and upright of their fellow citizens to administer justice and govern the State." Such officials should consider themselves representatives of all the people rather than narrow regions or factions. Whereas direct democracy throws states into chaos, according to Rousseau, democratic deliberation by the people's delegates would provide the means to resolve disagreements that might otherwise escalate. As he stressed in the *Second Discourse* itself and later elaborated in the *Social Contract*, in his dedication Rousseau emphasized "moderation, reciprocal esteem, and a common respect for the laws," precisely the qualities required for the smoothest possible meshing of particular wills with the general will. To ensure such veneration of the law, it is crucial to avoid the perpetual conflict excited by direct participation and work instead toward "a sincere and perpetual reconciliation" of differences. Many theorists of democracy assume that authentic politics requires the clash of competing interests, the supposedly realistic acknowledgment that because competition between self-interested individuals is fundamental to the human condition, all attempts to resolve or minimize such conflicts must be either evasions or elitist plots to silence the disempowered. Rousseau offered a different vision, an ethical ideal of autonomous selves voluntarily subordinating their own interests to the general interest. The best efforts of the people's delegates would yield proposals submitted for popular approval. Forging those proposals was to be the work of the people's delegates, not the people themselves.[111]

Rousseau confirmed his belief that in principle sovereign power remains with the people, who preserve in common the right to legislate, but he warned that their benevolence and sense of duty had been eroded by self-love. Their capacity to see the general will was clouded by an obsessive, shallow, and shortsighted self-interest. For those reasons, the people should exercise their authority not by proposing laws themselves—work better done by those suited to the task by training as well as virtue—but instead by electing qualified deputies, by making certain those elected act responsibly, and by voting to ratify or reject the rare changes in the laws proposed by the legislative assembly. The proper work of citizens, Rousseau proclaimed in words that would echo in *Emile* and in the *Social Contract*, is "to do wholeheartedly and with just confidence what you should always be obliged to do by a true self-interest, by duty, and for the sake of reason." To enjoy life in a state governed with the least possible conflict, then, Rousseau "would have wished to be born under a democratic government, wisely tempered," by which he meant a form of democracy in which sovereignty resides with the people, but the tasks of legislation and administration are performed by elected officials responsible to those on whom their authority depends.[112]

Of course Rousseau's ostensibly modest, statesmanlike effort to flatter the citizens of Geneva, both in his dedication to the *Second Discourse* and his later *Letters Written from the Mountain*, succeeded only in antagonizing almost everyone in his homeland and inflaming its smoldering conflicts. Church officials were appalled by Rousseau's challenges to Calvinist theology and his equally heretical call to separate church from state authority. The Council of Twenty-Five was incensed by his characterization of their power as oligarchic. The leaders of both principal factions of the popular parties were outraged by his failure to see the wisdom of either of their rival agendas. His books burned and banned, rejected by his erstwhile friends, and hunted by French and Swiss authorities, in the last fifteen years of his life Rousseau wandered through Europe in search of a haven. Rousseau's journey finally carried him to England, the birthplace of Enlightenment. There he sought out David Hume, a Scottish philosopher whom he had met in Paris, a potential ally who might, Rousseau hoped, provide refuge from his tormentors. Eighteenth-century Scotland produced a number of thinkers who proved significant throughout Europe—and even more influential in Britain's North American colonies. Not altogether surprisingly, given Rousseau's track record, Rousseau and Hume soon quarreled.[113]

Rousseau's falling-out with Hume was predictable. Rousseau believed fervently in a stripped-down version of Christianity and thought belief in God and an afterlife essential for any democratic culture. Hume was an atheist who mocked the credulity of religious believers. Rousseau shared Locke's empiricism and his confidence that the trustworthiness of sense data is underwritten by a beneficent deity. Hume was a skeptic who challenged conventional understandings of causality and of the relation between "is" and "ought." Rousseau distrusted polite society and saw greater virtue in simplicity. Hume lampooned the purposelessness of all "monkish virtues" such as humility and self-denial and celebrated commerce, luxury, and economic development as emblems of and avenues toward Enlightenment. Rousseau denied the persuasiveness of his contemporaries' claims concerning "natural man" and envisioned a dramatically different human condition in the state of nature. Hume proclaimed that human nature never changes and dismissed all visions of primitive peace as wishful thinking.[114]

Hume and Rousseau are usually thought to have held dramatically different views of democracy.[115] Rousseau prized democracy in principle, and he sought ways to approximate its ideals in practice by holding a government of elected delegates strictly accountable to the sovereign people. Hume, by contrast, rejected democracies because he judged them "turbulent." He distrusted "the lower people" and thought radical republicans' notions of popular government naive and dangerous. He believed that existing governments have "an infinite advantage" simply because they are established. If reformers were wise, as he put it, they would make only limited changes to the "ancient fabric" of existing institutions.[116]

Hume dismissed partisan squabbling as a shadow game. The hyperbolic rhetoric of both the Whigs' Court and Country factions in his day showed the folly and danger of inflaming political passions. History, although often and unfortunately put to partisan uses, provided the most profound and convincing evidence that politics follows a path of unpredictable and unintended consequences. From the ancient world through the Revolution of 1688, historical outcomes reflected contingent developments and the specific decisions of particular individuals. All sides in the seventeenth-century struggles over sovereignty failed to appreciate that the delicate institutional balance of English public life resulted from centuries of struggle. When Hume did refer to the "wisdom of the English constitution," he immediately caught himself and deflated it to "the concurrence of accidents." Zealots had destroyed more than they built.[117]

Whereas Rousseau saw history as a more or less steady decline into corruption, Hume saw slow and unsteady progress toward civility, or "politeness," which might continue only if reason could bridle passion through carefully manipulating law and institutions. Hume's essay "Of the Rise and Progress of the Arts and Sciences" (1742) preceded the publication of both of Rousseau's *Discourses*, and it tied political regimes to social relations in a way eerily similar to Rousseau's. But Hume reached a different conclusion. Politeness and civility flourish better in refined monarchies than in simple republics because the dependency ubiquitous in hierarchical societies necessitates deferential—and thus moderate—behavior. Equality breeds independence and thus discourages restraint. Hume acknowledged that "modern politeness, which is naturally so ornamental, runs often into affectation and foppery, disguise and insincerity"—precisely the dynamic that infuriated Rousseau. On the other hand, the "ancient simplicity" of republican cultures, to use Hume's phrase, "naturally so amiable and affecting, often degenerates into rusticity and abuse, scurrility and obscenity."[118] Better the "indissoluble chain" linking "industry, knowledge, and humanity" in "the more luxurious ages," Hume insisted, than the fierce honesty and unrestrained politics characteristic of simpler societies.[119] Hume's self-consciously tough-minded proclamations about politics have endeared him to generations of self-consciously tough-minded commentators. "It is therefore on opinion only that government is founded."[120] "It is, therefore, a just political maxim, that every man must be supposed a knave."[121] "Avarice, or the desire of gain, is an [*sic*] universal passion, which operates at all times, in all places, and upon all persons."[122]

Ancient experiments with democracy had failed. Even when the people were said to rule, as in classical Athens, which Hume considered "the most extensive democracy" in recorded history, only one-tenth of the adult males actually participated, and yet that severely limited democracy collapsed into anarchy. Hume contended that the Roman republic gave the people boundless legislative power, which they wielded directly rather than through representative government. The result was "a perpetual scene of tumult and sedition." When the government collapsed into anarchy, as democracies inevitably do, Rome turned to the despotism of the Caesars. One can almost hear Hume sigh: "Such are the effects of democracy without a representative." Far better to preserve a hereditary executive and a landed aristocracy beyond the temptations of corrupt electioneering than trust a naïve and fickle public.[123]

Might the excesses of democracy be cured and its benefits enjoyed? The ink was hardly dry on James Harrington's confident prediction that England would never see another king, Hume noted, when the monarchy was restored.[124] Democracy begets parties, and "factions subvert government, render laws impotent, and beget the fiercest animosities among men of the same nation, who ought to give mutual assistance and protection to each other." Once the weeds of faction have taken root, they persist for centuries, long after the original partisan differences cease to matter.[125] Even the most honest and intelligent individuals sacrifice "honour," normally a brake on excesses, to party loyalty and learn to despise their opponents.[126] On their own, individuals' self-interest is checked by the feelings of sympathy that Hume, like other eighteenth-century Scottish philosophers influenced by Shaftesbury, took to be a fundamental feature of human existence. Loyalties to party, however, inflame the passions; chaos reigns. Instead of speculating about reform, Britons should "improve our ancient government as much as possible, without encouraging a passion for such dangerous novelties." The rising power of the Commons, Hume cautioned, was already threatening the stability of Britain's fragile mixed monarchy. Only the crown's ingenious practice of dangling offices before ambitious MPs maintained a modicum of balance between the executive and the legislature. Although critics branded such manipulation of Parliament "*corruption* and *dependence*," Hume judged such practices indispensable to mixed government. With the Enlightenment weakening the religious and political enthusiasm that resulted in Cromwell's rule, further steps toward popular government were ill-advised.[127]

Democracy, Hume concluded, always ends in tyranny. The claim that government originates in the consent of the people "is not justified by history or experience, in any age or country in the world." Only time softens the sting of the "usurpation or conquest" with which governments originate and veils them with legitimacy. Democracies function only briefly before collapsing in fraud, violence, or both. People obey the law not because they have consented but because they would be worse off without government. The idea of a social contract "leads to paradoxes, repugnant to the common sentiments of mankind, and to the practice and opinion of all nations and all ages."[128] Hume's damning indictments of democracy in theory and practice notwithstanding, he merits attention for two reasons. First, for half a century Hume's political writings have been cited as a decisive influence on one of the principal architects and advocates of the United States Constitution, James Madison, and invoked to demonstrate the "conservative" or "aristocratic" dimensions of Madison's political thought.[129] Understanding Hume's thought is necessary in order to assess that claim. Second, Hume's writings about democracy are more complex, nuanced, and elusive than the familiar passages quoted above from his early essays suggest.

In his essay "Idea of a Perfect Commonwealth," Hume toyed with just the sort of speculation concerning democracy that he usually resisted, and the fruits of his playful imagination are tantalizing. Hume's wit, even more puckish here than in most of his other political essays, makes his meaning hard to pin down. Placed at the end of the collection published in 1752, the essay opens with Hume dismissing Plato's and More's utopias. Of Harrington's *Oceana*, "the only valuable model of a commonwealth," Hume offered a detailed and judicious critique.[130] Then Hume sprang a surprise, sketching a form of government "to which I cannot, in theory, discover any considerable objection." In other words, the anti-utopian Hume was offering his own ideal form of government. He proposed dividing a territory roughly the size of Great Britain and Ireland—for the sake of argument, evidently—into one hundred counties, each of which would then be subdivided into one hundred parishes. The qualified voters of each county meet annually, in each parish church, to elect a representative to an assembly. Those representatives in turn choose both ten local magistrates for the parishes and one member of a national senate. All legislative power resides in the one hundred county assemblies, which debate and vote on all laws proposed by the senate. Before they deliberate on legislation, the senators, shielded from public scrutiny like the College of Cardinals, choose a "protector," an elected executive who presides over the senate, and two secretaries of state concerned with foreign affairs.

The senate fills out the ambassadorial ranks and necessary councils of state, primarily from among its members.

Hume envisioned an elaborate "court of competitors" comprising those candidates who won more than one-third of the votes in every election, and he proposed multiple ways in which these bodies could expel wayward members and reconsider each other's decisions. He stipulated no strict rotation of office and no particular distribution of wealth. Turning Rousseau's formulation on its head, Hume meant to design a democracy for flawed humans instead of angels. Each county, "a kind of republic within itself," elects its own representatives, who make laws for their own county and submit them to the senate and other counties for approval. Clerical organization is Presbyterian, as in Hume's Scotland; the civil authority exercises power over the clerical. Electoral districts are reapportioned to take account of population changes every seven years. The mechanics of Hume's proposal thus echo many of the ideas resounding on the democratic fringe of British political debate, on both sides of the Atlantic, throughout the preceding century. Their presence in Hume's imagination suggests that such ideas, usually dismissed as appealing to no more than a few radical extremists, had migrated by the 1750s to the moderate center of British opinion. If Hume represents a voice of caution, his willingness to entertain the idea of a thoroughgoing, top-to-bottom representative democracy signals a shift in British political debate.

As Hume revised his scheme in later editions of his essays, he twice altered the qualifications of his voters to limit the franchise to wealthier citizens. Commentators have agreed that these revisions show just how limited was his conception of democracy. In light of Hume's familiar criticism of popular government, his willingness to imagine representative democracy—even limited to those with considerable property—did indicate that the appeal of these ideas was widening. Hume offered a set of "political aphorisms" to explain his proposal. First, "the lower sort of people and small proprietors are good judges enough of one not very distant from them in rank or habitation." For that reason they could be trusted to choose their own representatives. Yet Hume deemed such people "wholly unfit for county-meetings, and for electing into the higher offices of the republic" because their ignorance made it easy for clever grandees to deceive them. Without a senate, the people elected to county legislatures might lack sufficient wisdom to govern. But without the popular assembly scrutinizing its affairs, the senate could not be trusted. If all these officials, or even one-tenth of them, debated in a single assembly, Hume feared that chaos would ensue. Yet if the senate alone exercised effective power, the people would lose their voice, as Hume thought would happen in the commonwealth envisioned in Harrington's *Oceana*.

This apparently insoluble conundrum, Hume exclaimed, which had stymied the most imaginative statesmen, was surprisingly easy to remedy. The answer lay in decentralization: "If the people debate, all is confusion," but if they cannot debate, all power falls to the senate. So, Hume suggested, "divide the people into many separate bodies; and then they may debate with safety, and every inconvenience seems to be prevented." The secret lay in preventing those with great power or prestige from infecting the local assemblies, where the appeal of their authority might prove irresistible. Separate those members from the local assemblies, and the problem disappears. "Though every member be only of middling sense, it is not probable, that anything but reason can prevail over the whole." Absent the corrupting influence of an aristocracy, "good sense will always get the better of bad among a number of people." For such a cautious political thinker, that endorsement of representative democracy was a breathtaking step.

Representative democracy operating at multiple levels would also inoculate the government against faction. Because Hume's imagined senate consists of officials to be elected every year, and because its members can be challenged both by the court of competitors and by members of the county assemblies, power cannot become concentrated in the senate, the problem that ruined earlier republics. Because the senate was to remain relatively small, "factious members" would be removed by the senators themselves or by those who elected them, thereby ensuring that the good of the commonwealth remains the object—and the product—of their deliberations. The tone of Hume's conclusion is, by his standards, almost giddy: "A small commonwealth is the happiest government in the world," at least in its domestic politics, "because every thing lies under the eye of the rulers." This scheme, Hume declared with a flourish, "seems to have all the advantages both of a great and a little commonwealth." Hume rehearsed the standard observation that republics are better suited to small cities or states than to large nations (such as, say, Britain), but the federal structure solves that problem as well. "In a large government, which is modelled with masterly skill"—such as Hume himself had shown—"there is compass and room enough to refine the democracy from the lower people, who may be admitted into the first elections or first concoction of the commonwealth, to the higher magistrates, who direct all the movements." Hume offered one further safeguard in his revision of the prevailing wisdom (codified by Montesquieu) concerning states large and small. When "the parts are so distant and remote" as they are in a large republic, it would be "very difficult, either by intrigue, prejudice, or passion, to hurry them into any measures against the public interest." Although Hume conceded that his imagined republic—or representative democracy, for such it would be—would not last forever, "such a government would flourish for many ages."

Publishing his "Idea of a Perfect Commonwealth" did not turn the moderate Hume into a radical democrat, but it did suggest that he thought Britain might approach his ideal by taking just two small steps. First, reapportioning seats in the Commons would provide more equal representation and a more vigorous legislative body. Second, seats in the Lords should be made elective rather than hereditary, and some of the increased number of places he recommended should be made available to especially able members of the Commons. As a result, Hume predicted, "the house of Lords would consist entirely of the men of chief credit, ability, and interest in the nation," as the body emphatically did not in Hume's day. Reviving proposals a century old, yet all but dead by Hume's day, as but modest steps, embraced by the most moderate of men, was surprising in light of Hume's other writings.

Hume pointed to the success of the long-lived republic of the United Provinces to show that his plan of government was realistic. Addressing the few weaknesses he saw in the Netherlands, Hume suggested that the too-powerful aristocracy of the Dutch could be balanced by a "well-tempered democracy," which annual elections of county representatives would achieve. Second, if counties were less independent of each other, and less unequal, Holland and Amsterdam would not so easily dominate the other provinces. Hume considered the overall resemblance between his plan for an ideal state and such a refashioned government of the United Provinces decisive proof of its viability.[131]

The secret to political reform for Hume lay in recognizing that we must begin where we are, not where we might be if we were actually starting from scratch. Two of Hume's late essays balance his arguments in "Idea of a Perfect Commonwealth." "Of the Coalition of Parties" laid down "use and practice" as the chief maxim of government and advised against trusting the uncertain guide of reason. Abandoning existing forms of authority sunders the bonds of civil society, which leaves "every man at liberty to consult his private interest, by those expedients, which his appetite, disguised under the appearance of reason, shall dictate to him." Once the people proclaim themselves the sole sovereign, Hume predicted, they "become incapable of civil government." Lacking the restraint of any authority, they find themselves forced to accept "a succession of military and despotic tyrants." To pretend otherwise, Hume the meticulous historian insisted, was to ignore evidence stretching from Athens and Rome to the execution of Charles I and the intolerable rule of Cromwell.[132]

Hume's political caution, like Montaigne's, was the product of his skepticism. Both worried that profound convictions fueled not only heroic sacrifices but also pitiless slaughter. In an essay published after his death in 1776, "Of the Origins of Government," Hume speculated that the first governments originated during a state of war, when "the pernicious effects of disorder are most sensibly felt," and people had to submit or die. From that moment to his own time, there had been an unending struggle, either open or veiled, between liberty and authority. Even granting that "liberty is the perfection of civil society," as Hume believed, "still authority must be acknowledged essential to its very existence." Government officials must enforce the law, which means only, he concluded, that they must "oblige men, however reluctant, to consult their own real and permanent interests." The proper exercise of freedom, as Rousseau explained in *Emile* and the *Social Contract*, requires reason to suppress appetite.[133]

Hume was out of step with the other leading figures of the Scottish Enlightenment. The philosopher who most influenced Hume's moral philosophy, Francis Hutcheson, warned the University of Edinburgh not to hire Hume because of his atheism and skepticism.[134] On the issues central to Scottish thought, moral philosophy and political economy, Hume diverged less dramatically from his peers. As a province swallowed up by Great Britain in the Union of 1707, Scotland exchanged its own legislature for seats in the British Parliament. Absent an independent political life, the focus of Scottish thought shifted from questions of government to questions of culture and commerce. After the failed Jacobite rebellions of 1715 and 1745 ended the prospect of an independent state, Scottish writers resigned themselves to life in a province controlled by the metropolitan powers in London. If Scotland could not control its own political destiny, it could at least chart an independent course in culture by emphasizing the activity of autonomous individuals who pursued lives of virtue. Andrew Fletcher, a founding father of the Scottish Enlightenment, was among the first to see the civic value of Scotland's new place in a multitiered Great Britain. "So many different seats of government will highly encourage virtue," Fletcher wrote. If lesser government officials exercised authority over only a moderate number of people, opportunities and responsibilities will expand, and more people will have a chance "of doing good to their fellow citizens."[135]

In Edinburgh, Glasgow, Dundee, St. Andrews, Aberdeen, and elsewhere, ideas filtered through universities and coffeehouses into books, newspapers, and magazines that circulated throughout the British Atlantic. In place of the classical republican emphasis on the exercise of virtue in political or military activity, Scottish thinkers extended Shaftesbury's argument that virtue lies in cultivating the natural inclination toward sympathy, which enables individuals to realize their potential through moral behavior that advances the welfare of society. They also repudiated ancient condemnations of commercial activity and accepted trade as a potential avenue toward virtue.

The Irish-born Presbyterian Francis Hutcheson assumed the chair in moral philosophy at the University of Glasgow in 1729. He had already presented his philosophy of moral sense, which was to become widely influential on both sides of the Atlantic, in *An Inquiry into the Original of Our Ideas of Beauty and Virtue* (1725). Although Hutcheson grounded his arguments on the goodness of God, which he claimed never to doubt, he presented his philosophy as a species of induction. He began by characterizing Shaftesbury's idea of sympathy as a sense, not an intuition, similar in many respects to the other five senses, which gives us an immediate perception of moral goodness. Hutcheson wrote to combat Hobbes's egoism and Mandeville's emphasis on self-interest. "As soon as any action is represented to us as flowing from love, humanity, gratitude, compassion, a study of the good of others, and an ultimate desire of their happiness," regardless of where or when, humans spontaneously respond with a powerful feeling of sympathy. "We feel joy within us, admire the lovely action, and praise its author." Likewise at the other end of the spectrum: we respond to malevolent actions with "abhorrence and aversion." Those responses do not require the intervention of reason, nor are they merely intuitive, and they are certainly not motivated by selfishness. "The love of *benevolence*," in his words, "excludes self-interest."[136]

Hutcheson argued that all humans possess a moral sense that approves disinterested love, patterned on the Christian ideal. He was the first to use the formula later associated with utilitarianism: "*that action is best*, which procures the *greatest happiness* for the *greatest number*." Our greatest happiness, he believed, comes from the happiness of others, not from our own pleasure or personal benefit. The human disposition to approve actions done from benevolent motives shows God's infinite goodness to us and cannot be said to derive from the "prospect of any pleasure accompanying the affection itself." Jeremy Bentham developed his hedonic calculus as a direct challenge to Hutcheson's moral philosophy.[137]

Hutcheson gravitated toward republican rather than monarchical government. Popular government maximizes individuals' chances for benevolent action and thus provides the greatest overall happiness. The path to "*the most heroic virtue*," however, remains open under any form of government. Benevolence imposes an obligation to virtue that takes two forms. Perfect obligations, to be enforced by law, include respect for property, contracts, and promises, and the prohibition of slavery. Imperfect obligations, such as helping the poor and repaying generosity with gratitude, by contrast, cannot be enforced by law and require greater virtue. They are thus more highly prized by the moral sense.[138] When the moral sense is properly developed, Hutcheson wrote in his *System of Moral Philosophy*, "it makes the generous determination to public happiness the supreme one in the soul." Hutcheson was too circumspect to draw out the political implications of his philosophy beyond inserting Locke's right of resistance where Pufendorf, for example, had stipulated the people's irrevocable ceding of sovereignty to their rulers. Just as Calvinist conceptions of the divinely chosen elect could not survive Hutcheson's claims for a universal sense of benevolence, so institutional arrangements such as slavery, primogeniture, hereditary aristocracy, and monarchy seemed equally vulnerable. If sympathy guides the moral judgments of all persons, should it not also justify their exercise of political judgment?[139]

Hutcheson's successor at the University of Glasgow was his student Adam Smith, who elaborated his teacher's moral sense philosophy in his *Theory of Moral Sentiments*. First published in 1759, Smith's book appeared in six English editions before his death in 1790, and the book was also translated into French and German. Even though the renown of his later exploration of the principles of economics, *An Inquiry into the Nature and Causes of the Wealth of Nations* (1776), eventually eclipsed his work in moral philosophy, Smith's *Theory of Moral Sentiments* was far better known in his day. It was the most widely read exposition of the role played by sentiment in moral decisions throughout the late eighteenth and early nineteenth centuries on both sides of the Atlantic. Smith's *Theory of Moral Sentiments* opens with a memorable sentence that demonstrates his great debt to Hutcheson: "How selfish soever man may be supposed, there are evidently some principles in his nature which interest him in the fortunes of others, and render their happiness necessary to him, though he derives nothing from it except the pleasure of seeing it."[140]

Whereas Hume, who claimed to embrace Hutcheson's idea of sympathy, nevertheless qualified it by emphasizing the pressure exerted on benevolence by self-interest, Smith provided the most vivid elaboration of Hutcheson's moral sense in his image of the impartial spectator. Given that our passions are so often selfish, yet our inclinations to help others so strong, how can we account for the clear evidence that people are willing to "sacrifice their own interests to the greater interests of others?"

Smith did not consider Hutcheson's answer, the moral sense, altogether satisfactory. "It is not the soft power of humanity," he wrote, "not that feeble spark of benevolence which Nature has lighted up in the human heart," that does the trick. To counteract the "strongest impulses of self-love" we need a "stronger power, a more forcible motive," which Smith had trouble identifying with a single word. "It is reason, principle, conscience, the inhabitant of the breast, the man within, the great arbiter of our conscience," or, as he ultimately conjured it up with an enduring image, an "impartial spectator" whom we see before us whenever we wrestle with the proper course of action. This imaginary third party, dispassionately viewing our action from a distance, "shows us the propriety of resigning the greatest interests of our own, for the yet greater interests of others, and the deformity of doing the smallest injury to another, in order to obtain the greatest benefit to ourselves." The principles invoked by earlier moralists did not suffice to explain the dynamic at work in moral judgment. Neither the love of neighbor nor the love of mankind but a "stronger love, a more powerful affection," takes hold of us when we realize that we will be judged impartially according to the standard of benevolence even if our own sympathetic impulse does not exert adequate leverage always to determine our will.[141]

Whether the logic of Smith's moral philosophy was driven by, or was even consistent with, Christian religious faith is a question that has attracted spirited debate ever since Smith's death in 1790. His followers and allies worked to distinguish his views from those of his friend Hume. Later commentators have doubted that Smith's own religious faith survived and point to the steadily shrinking references to Christianity from the first to the last editions of *The Theory of Moral Sentiments*. In his own final (published) word on the subject, Smith contended that the idea of benevolence can provide "no solid happiness" to any humans not convinced that "all inhabitants of the universe" exist "under the immediate care and protection of that great, benevolent, and all-wise Being, who directs all the movements of nature." The idea that such a "divine Being" is constantly maximizing happiness "is certainly of all the objects of human contemplation by far the most sublime." Smith was willing to entertain Hume's suggestion that we are on our own in "a fatherless world," yet he resisted that "most melancholy of all reflections" because it implied that the universe was filled with "nothing but endless misery and wretchedness."[142]

Smith moved away from Hutcheson's strict reliance on the moral sense, arguing that reason also played a role, albeit subsidiary to that of sympathy, as we assess the judgment of the "impartial spectator." But Smith's greatest contribution to the tradition of Scottish moral philosophy came with his dual emphasis on sympathy and autonomy, which he called "self-mastery." The common belief that autonomy conflicts with benevolence, Smith insisted, was a mistake. "Our sensibility to the feelings of others, so far from being inconsistent with the manhood of self-command, is the very principle upon which that manhood is founded." Combining the two should be our goal. "The man of the most perfect virtue, the man whom we naturally love and revere the most, is he who joins, to the most perfect command of his own original and selfish feelings, the most exquisite sensibility both to the original and sympathetic feelings of others." So for Smith hardy independence and profound benevolence reinforce rather than undercut each other. To be autonomous is to obey the impartial spectator who demands benevolence over self-love. "The man who feels the most for the joys and sorrows of others, is best fitted for acquiring the most complete control of his own joys and sorrows."[143] For Smith, as for Harrington and Milton, Locke and Sidney, and Montesquieu and Rousseau, a commitment to individual independence was compatible with an equally deep commitment to responsibility. For Smith, self-command *meant* harnessing the will in service to a cause larger than one's own personal interest.

Smith's commitment to a union of benevolence and autonomy did not produce an equally pronounced commitment to republican or democratic reform. He shared too much of his friend Hume's doubts about "the man of system," the passionate reformer whom he derided near the end of the sixth edition of *The Theory of Moral Sentiments*, who imagines manipulating people as one would arrange pieces on a chessboard. Unfortunately for such reformers, humans possess their own motives and make their own decisions.[144] Smith shared the Scottish philosophers' approach to history: he envisioned a gradual process of development through four stages: first hunters and fishers, then shepherds, farmers, and finally merchants. Democracy figured only in the most primitive of these stages, then in Smith's account of the dynamics by which kings empowered ordinary people to help them control the landed gentry that threatened their rule. His system seemed to follow its own hydraulic mechanism independent of any principles of divine-right monarchy, natural aristocracy, or popular sovereignty. The dispassionate quality of Smith's analysis reflected his Humean aspiration to keep his distance from partisan politics in order to understand and explain how history works.[145] "No government is quite perfect," Smith wrote in his *Lectures on Jurisprudence*; "it is better to submit to some inconveniences than make attempts against it."[146]

The passionate call for sympathy evident intermittently in *The Theory of Moral Sentiments* always lay just beneath the surface of Smith's analysis. Throughout his writings about politics, he sought to balance deference for authority and respect for established forms of government against the widespread and "earnest desire to render the condition of our fellow-citizens as safe, respectable, and happy as we can." How could those competing inclinations be reconciled? In most cases, such as the squabbling factions of eighteenth-century British politics, Smith joined Hume in declaring a plague on both parties and guarding his independence. In moments of crisis, though, such as the one that began in America as he was working on *The Wealth of Nations* or the one that began later in France and soon convulsed all of Europe, it was necessary to take action. Deciding just what to do, however, required rare "political wisdom."[147]

In the case of American demands for independence, Smith recommended making seats in the British Parliament available to the colonists. Because American leaders were motivated principally by the fear that Parliament's efforts to annul their laws threatened the authority they enjoyed in American assemblies, he thought the prospect of places in Parliament would quiet their anxieties. Just as Union had brought an end to faction in Scotland, and just as a restored monarchy had brought peace to England in 1660 and again in 1688, so more thorough amalgamation in British politics might soothe the jangled sensibilities of American party leaders. More pertinent than the idle speculations of publicists, and more crucial than particular institutional arrangements, to Smith as to Hume, was the inevitable jostling occasioned by the universal human desire for approbation. "Men desire to have some share in the management of publick affairs chiefly on account of the importance which it gives them." The "natural aristocracy" of the colonies was no different. "The leading men of America, like those of other countries, desire to preserve their own importance." If American colonists could satisfy their ambitions in a greater British Parliament that extended across the Atlantic, peace would be restored.[148]

Yet the astringency of Smith's observations about politics must be balanced by the very different tenor of his moral philosophy. Indeed, when Smith sought to illustrate by example the combination of autonomy and sympathy that served as his moral ideal in *The Theory of Moral Sentiments*, he invoked the figure of the legislator, who combined the prudence Smith (and Hume) prized with "many greater and more splendid virtues," the most striking of which were "strong benevolence" and "self-command." In politics as in everyday life, that combination represented Smith's ideal. When he scanned history for an example of someone whose "public spirit is prompted altogether by humanity and benevolence," he settled on Solon, long considered the founder of the first democracy in Athens. When establishing the ideal regime—Smith's unspecified version of Hume's "perfect commonwealth," perhaps—is not possible, the legislator "will not disdain to ameliorate the wrong; but like Solon, when he cannot establish the best system of laws, he will endeavour to establish the best that people can bear." In the case of Athens, Smith understood that regime to be a combination of direct and representative democracy.[149] Unless or until the need or opportunity for a legislator arose, the best a reformer could hope to do with the chessboard of eighteenth-century British culture was to improve education and put an end to the state's mercantilist meddling in the marketplace. The advent of free trade, Smith predicted, might make possible further steady growth of the ranks of autonomous individuals. When the people had gained economic independence, they would have the opportunity to develop moral autonomy as well, autonomy balanced by benevolence rather than freed from responsibility for the common good.

When later commentators innocent of Smith's *Theory of Moral Sentiments* contended that he designed his free-market economics to liberate egocentric individuals to pursue their own narrow self-interest, unconstrained by government regulations or considerations of justice—the sensibility, long maligned as the vice of selfishness, recently designated by the singularly inappropriate term "rational choice"—it was difficult to see how such an economic program could be reconciled with Smith's moral philosophy. Now that *The Wealth of Nations* is properly understood as Smith's attempt to release people from the status of dependents so they could become autonomous and benevolent individuals, the problem has dissolved.[150] Smith offered his *Wealth of Nations* as a blueprint for a society in which autonomous individuals can follow the path of sympathy illuminated by the impartial spectator. Instead of being seen as ushering in a world of Dickensian workhouses and grinding industrial poverty, *The Wealth of Nations* can be restored to its appropriate significance as a critique of mercantilism.[151] That form of government intervention, perhaps well-intentioned but certainly counterproductive, had been responsible for famines. Smith's purpose in demonstrating the magic of the marketplace, the unintended consequence of individuals seeking to better their own lots in life, was not to make possible the emergence of unprecedented fortunes but to make available to everyone the opportunity to escape dependency and destitution.

Hume, Hutcheson, and Smith now stand as the towering figures of the Scottish Enlightenment, but in the eighteenth century others rivaled them in stature and influence. Thomas Reid, who held a professorship in Aberdeen before he was called to Glasgow, revised Scottish moral philosophy by insisting that both Hutcheson's sympathy and Hume's skepticism underestimated the capacity of reason. It is reason, according to Reid, not a moral sense, that enables us to make moral decisions. It is reason, furthermore, that enables us to distinguish our perceptions from the world outside ourselves. Reid and those who followed him, such as Dugald Stewart, Adam Ferguson, and Henry Home, Lord Kames, helped disseminate Scottish ideas about moral philosophy, historical stages, and the general benefits of commerce and luxury (especially for those not already rich). By the end of the eighteenth century, both Hutcheson's philosophy of the moral sense and Reid and Stewart's rival version, which emphasized the crucial role of reason and was designated common-sense philosophy, had become integral features of Anglo-American culture. As these ideas matured and spread, their radical thrust was blunted. Through a process examined in later chapters, they were gradually transformed from weapons directed against one form of privilege to props sustaining another.[152]

Hume was among the first British observers to see where the disgruntled provinces of North America were heading. As early as 1768 he was proposing and predicting their independence. Most Britons later designated "friends of America" continued to envision—as Smith did—some form of continuing affiliation between Mother England and her upstart progeny until the crushing defeat of British forces at Saratoga in 1777 began to change minds on both sides of the Atlantic. What explains Hume's prescience? In his *History of England*, Hume identified the unique trajectory of American development. The American colonies were "established on the noblest footing that has been known in any age or nation," by which Hume meant that the "spirit of independency" animating their founders "shone forth in its full lustre." Those who left Britain for America, dissatisfied with the established church and the monarchy, were seeking the freedom to govern themselves. Hume's glowing portrait of people establishing their own laws, and their own institutional frameworks, seems jarringly discordant with his familiar observations concerning the necessity of preserving whatever exists. As early as the 1730s, Hume made clear that he understood the distinctiveness of the colonial experiments: "The Charter Governments in America are almost entirely independent of England."

That "noblest footing," on which Hume thought the colonial governments were established, allowed them to experiment in ways not open to inhabitants of mature states. The American colonists did what Plato, More, Harrington, and Hume himself, the author of "Idea of a Perfect Commonwealth," never had the chance to do. They created their own institutions of government because, according to Hume, nothing was established when they arrived in America. Instead of conforming to existing models, they designed their governments to suit their "aspiring character." In New England, with ambitions nourished by the experience some had enjoyed beyond English authority in the republican atmosphere of Holland, they aspired to the Puritan ideal of gathered and self-governing congregations.[153] In light of that beginning and the colonists' subsequent experience with the self-governing assemblies of the middle and southern colonies, Hume found their claims against Parliament less startling than did almost all of his British contemporaries. No wonder Hume called himself, in a letter dated October 27, 1775, "an American in my Principles."[154]

This was Hume, though, so the starry-eyed vision suggested by the preceding paragraph must be tempered. As early as 1771 he had observed that "our Union with America," already fragile, "cannot long subsist."[155] In the fall of 1775 he urged withdrawing both the navy and army, leaving the colonists "entirely to themselves."[156] That counsel was informed by Hume's characteristic cynicism. In the letter in which he proclaimed himself "an American in my Principles," he also lamented the sorry condition of the "poor infatuated Americans" and explained why he thought Britain should "let them alone to govern or misgovern themselves as they think proper: The affair is of no Consequence, or of little Consequence to us." Hume's implication seems clear: the new government would probably go the way of all democracies and disintegrate soon enough.[157] By February of 1776 Hume was wondering how far "the frenzies of the people" for self-government would carry the Americans.[158] In another letter he observed that the colonists were falling into factions, and, as he had written so often, "Faction, next to Fanaticism, is, of all passions, the most destructive of Morality."[159]

Having begun with the "noblest footing" and the highest aspirations for their democracy, would the Americans succeed in building on their now-established traditions of self-government? Or, having chosen the least stable form of government, would they reap the whirlwind? Just those questions faced the principal figures in the American Enlightenment. Many of these thinkers emerged as leaders of the American Revolution, and some of them were then elected to wield power in the new nation they created. Although it would be up to Americans to respond to the questions Hume posed, some European philosophes thought they already knew the answer. Writing soon after the English colonies declared their independence, Diderot rapturously expostulated on the American achievement. Now that Americans offered "all the inhabitants of Europe an asylum against fanaticism and tyranny," he hoped the new nation would instruct rulers in the Old World "on the legitimate use of their authority!" Diderot was captivated by "these brave Americans," who "would rather see their wives raped, their children murdered, their dwellings destroyed, their fields ravaged, their villages burned, and rather shed their blood and die than lose the slightest portion of their freedom." As they struggled heroically to "prevent the enormous accumulation and unequal distribution of wealth, luxury, effeminacy, and corruption of manners," he concluded, "may they provide for the maintenance of their freedom and the survival of their government."[160] Except for the ever-ambivalent Hume, nearly all European partisans of Enlightenment, whether theists or atheists, monarchists or democrats, shared Diderot's enthusiasm for the American Revolution. If he was distinctive in using apocalyptic images reminiscent of the European wars of religion to describe the War for Independence, he was among the many eighteenth-century European thinkers who wondered whether a nation committed to self-government could survive when all earlier democracies had failed. Because the rebellious colonies seemed to embody enlightened ideas, most European champions of Enlightenment believed that the fate of their own ideals hinged on the future of the new nation.

CHAPTER 6

Faith, Enlightenment, and Resistance in America

MOST AMERICAN CONTRIBUTORS to the Enlightenment, unlike their European counterparts, played an active part in the political life of their colonial cultures. The American Revolution cannot be disentangled from the American Enlightenment. Neither can it be understood apart from the broader and deeper history of self-government in England's North American colonies, nor outside the framework of European ideas. The architects of the new American nation honed their political arguments on the work of Harrington, Milton, Sidney, and Locke, as well as Montesquieu, Rousseau, Hutcheson, and Hume. Their views of public life were shaped by their experience with political institutions and democratic cultures consistent with many of the ideas debated in the Enlightenments of Europe. Although this chapter concentrates on the particular relation between ideas and the emergence of commitments to independence and self-government, Enlightenment in America had multiple dimensions, of which politics was but one.[1] Consider the lives and thought of three prominent American philosophes, Benjamin Franklin, John Adams, and Thomas Jefferson, whose interests stretched from religion to the natural sciences.

Franklin established the first American political discussion group, reading club, and circulating library and one of the first American universities. He also negotiated the loans that financed the War for Independence from Great Britain and was three times elected president of the executive council (effectively, governor) of the fledgling state of Pennsylvania. Not only were Adams and Jefferson elected the second and third presidents of the United States, but they also served as the presidents of the leading American learned societies at the end of the eighteenth century, the American Academy of Arts and Sciences and the American Philosophical Society. Having established themselves as three of the most distinguished writers and most original thinkers among those engaged in colonial politics, in 1776 Franklin, Adams, and Jefferson were appointed by the Continental Congress as a committee charged with producing the Declaration of Independence, among the emblematic documents of the democratic Enlightenment. They were instrumental in the composition of a number of other foundational documents. Franklin's Albany Plan of 1754 provided the template for American federalism. Adams's *Thoughts on Government* in 1776 proved to be the most influential outline for the state constitutions then being framed throughout the colonies, and Adams wrote the 1780 Constitution of Massachusetts, which remains the fundamental law of the Commonwealth. Jefferson proposed a draft constitution for Virginia, the separation of church and state, the abolition of entail and primogeniture, a plan for the free public education of boys and girls, a university for Virginia, a library for the new nation, and the process whereby the western regions of North America would be organized and eventually incorporated into the United States. European thinkers stood apart from—or occasionally, briefly and usually to little effect, advised—the monarchs and landed gentry who exercised political power. As Britain's North American colonies defied a king and rejected hereditary aristocracy, American philosophers helped their fellow citizens lay out the plans for, and then were among those elected to office in, their new nation.

During the last several decades, historians have demonstrated the multiple ways in which the revolutionary upheavals of the 1760s and 1770s in America depended on the active engagement of ordinary colonists. Without spontaneous crowd actions, organized and sustained forms of social and economic protest, and political behavior ranging from attending local gatherings to voting for or against boycotts, candidates, and proposed constitutions, the American Revolution would not have occurred, or at least would not have taken the shape it took. For centuries, surging currents of popular protest in Europe either overflowed into anarchy or dissolved into abiding resentments against the rich. Together with more than a century of experience with self-government, Enlightenment ideas in America helped provide the frameworks that channeled popular protest into the particular forms that democratic government took in the new nation. Those forms themselves emerged from passionate, and unprecedented, popular debates over the writing and ratifying of new constitutions at the state and national level. We now know much more about the farmers, artisans, sailors, merchants, women, and slaves whose efforts gave force and shape to ideas that would otherwise have remained abstractions.[2] An intellectual history of democracy in eighteenth-century America concentrates on those who wrote the most widely read pamphlets, tracts, sermons, treatises, declarations, and constitutions. With few exceptions, though, the people who wrote those documents sprang from the same socioeconomic roots as those who read, discussed, and responded to their work. No clear-cut, stable divisions separated a single upper class from a single lower class, or leaders from followers. Social reality was always more fluid, inchoate, and blurred at the edges.[3]

This chapter and the three that follow it focus on particular individuals who helped shape the political ideas and institutions of late-eighteenth-century America, and whose thoughts reveal the complex interactions between concreteness and abstraction, religion and impiety, boldness and caution, cosmopolitanism and localism, shrewd calculation and unwavering principle. As the deliberate syncopation of those pairings is meant to suggest, the standard categories of the European Enlightenments were shaken into new forms in America. The result was explosive. The lives and work of Franklin, Adams, and Jefferson illustrate both the regional variations and the distinct phases through which enlightened ideas passed during the years leading up to the 1760s and 1770s, when unrest flared into revolution.

The most decisive and distinctive features of American democracy reflected simultaneously the colonists' experience with the unpredictability of self-government and their commitment to the principles of reasoned argument and testing hypotheses in practice. Rather than trying to freeze their institutions and laws in a particular form, a temptation given their serious commitments to the apparently fixed truths of Christianity and natural law, the creators of the new American state governments provided for open-ended experimentation. Their often conflicting religious, political, and ethical convictions heightened their awareness of their own fallibility—and of the very deep differences between their conceptions of democracy. Realizing their audacious project took courage and imagination, but a century of chastening experience with self-government had taught them that boldness must be tempered with humility and the willingness to tolerate inevitable disagreements.

The colonists had learned that differences of perspective and principle cannot always be resolved. The mechanisms of representative democracy that had emerged, however, could keep such differences from turning into cancers of the sort that had devoured or disfigured prior experiments with popular government. At least that was their hope. As loyal Britons became Americans, they renounced monarchy, at first reluctantly, and embraced the idea that sovereignty resides with the people, conceived now as autonomous citizens equal before the law and not differentiated into nobles and commoners. They did not altogether repudiate, let alone erase, the vestiges of hierarchy, inherited privilege, and racial and gender inequality that had marked European cultures for millennia.[4] Few people yet imagined ending slavery or enfranchising women. The principles articulated between the first stirring of revolutionary ferment and the ratification of the Constitution, however, provided ammunition for those who would later broaden the meaning of "the people." Almost no one in North America entered the 1760s entertaining the idea that the colonies should be independent of Great Britain and its king. By the 1790s, almost no one doubted that the United States of America was the world's first democratic nation. How did a cultural revolution of that magnitude occur?

The American Enlightenment varied by region and changed over time. Nowhere did it flower more luxuriantly than in Philadelphia, and no one embodied its early stages more fully than Benjamin Franklin. Like almost all other eighteenth-century inhabitants of the middle colonies, Franklin was born elsewhere and brought to the region skills, ambition, and a sincere but denominationally unmoored piety. Son of a Boston candlemaker who had left England in 1682 in order to avoid the penalties of nonconformity to the Church of England, Franklin was raised in a large Puritan family—his mother belonged to one of the first English families to settle in New England—and apprenticed as a printer to his brother. An avid reader who later reported in his celebrated *Autobiography* his encounters as a youth with Addison and Steele's *Spectator*, and the writings of Locke, Shaftesbury, and the English Deist Anthony Collins as well as John Bunyan and Cotton Mather, Franklin chafed under his brother's strict control and the equally rigid Calvinism of Boston's New South Church. At the age of seventeen, he decided to make his own way as a printer. Breaking his apprenticeship four years early meant he could not work in Boston, so he drifted to New York City and then to Philadelphia, where he found work as a printer and a patron in Pennsylvania's governor, Sir William Keith. Eighteen months in London then gave Franklin experience with English life and with his craft; he returned to manage the Philadelphia printing house where he had been employed. Already intrigued by the prospect of writing and intoxicated with the ideas of freethinkers such as Collins, Franklin moved quickly to establish Philadelphia as an American outpost of Enlightenment.[5]

Franklin joined with friends in 1727 to form "a Club for mutual Improvement," which they called the Junto (loosely derived from the Latin word for "join"), modeled on similar clubs in England. Members wrote essays and discussed issues of "Morals, Politics, or Natural Philosophy." Two years later Franklin established a newspaper, the *Pennsylvania Gazette*, which earned notoriety and subscribers due to his lively writing. He reported that the Massachusetts legislature, known as the General Court, was resisting a proposed tax to pay the governor's salary, a challenge showing that English colonists "still retain that ardent Spirit of Liberty" that "has in every Age so gloriously distinguished BRITONS and ENGLISHMEN from all the Rest of Mankind."[6] None of Franklin's readers imagined in 1729—any more than he did—the ultimate consequences of resisting the costs of empire.

Franklin never lost his belief in God or an afterlife and irregularly attended a Presbyterian church in Philadelphia, but he never embraced the doctrines of any denomination. The Pennsylvania Quakers' defense of free conscience suited Franklin's own latitudinarian inclinations. The ethical code he formulated owed less to revelation than to Shaftesbury and Hutcheson and to his conviction that the best we can do is to be useful to each other.[7] Franklin defended the unconventional Presbyterian minister Samuel Hemphill, threatened with dismissal by Franklin's own Philadelphia congregation for his refusal to subscribe to the Westminster Confession of Faith, by arguing that Jesus offered "an excellent Moral Discourse" rather than a theology. "Morality or Virtue is the End, Faith only a Means to obtain that End: And if the End be obtained, it is no matter by what Means."[8] Doctrinal squabbles reflected a parsimonious spirit alien to the spirit of Jesus.[9] Franklin's *Autobiography* surveyed a wide range of religions and expressed his conviction that "the most acceptable Service of God is doing Good to Man."[10] His ethics of benevolence unwittingly echoed Voltaire, who defined virtue as "doing good to one's neighbor." Against centuries of praise for asceticism and strictures against the sins of the flesh, Voltaire insisted that "there is no true good for us but what is good for society."[11] The most prominent figures in the Enlightenments of Britain and France sought to embody and encourage genteel refinement of the sort epitomized by Addison and Steele's *Spectator*. They aimed, as Hume put it, to serve as ambassadors "from the Dominions of Learning to those of Conversation."[12] Contrasting his emphasis to British wit and French *politesse* (the obsession with refinement that prompted Rousseau's break from the philosophes), Franklin focused more on solving his neighbors' problems than on entertaining them or elevating their taste.[13]

Franklin's contributions to Enlightenment in America, in addition to the Junto (and the five subsidiary reading and discussion groups it spawned) and the *Gazette*, included the first American subscription library, the Library Company of Philadelphia. The books acquired by the Library Company illustrate the mixture of classical, Enlightenment, and religious writers judged most important by Franklin and his associates. Greek and Roman history, natural history, poetry, philosophy, and political commentary, authors from China and the Arab world—all were available to the members of the Library Company, giving its self-governing subscribers access to an impressive array of ideas and information.[14] Franklin also advanced Enlightenment in America by helping to establish the American Philosophical Society, devoted at least as much to what would now be called the physical and biological sciences and the arts as to philosophical inquiry. Its distinguished members shared no particular religious outlook. Among those who participated in its activities were Calvinists, such as the physician and chemist Benjamin Rush; Presbyterians, such as the astronomer David Rittenhouse, who succeeded Franklin as president of the society; freethinking proto-Unitarians, such as John Vaughan, who served as treasurer; and Deists, such as the painter Charles Willson Peale.[15]

To continue the project of Enlightenment, Franklin urged the establishment of an academy in Philadelphia. In his *Proposals Relating to the Education of Youth in Pennsylvania*, Franklin outlined the subjects and the books that students should be required to master. His specific recommendations, like the lists of books ordered for the Library Company, demonstrate the persistence of his interest in classical and Christian texts alongside those of more recent writers such as Sidney, Locke, and Hutcheson. The most striking feature of Franklin's *Proposals* is his ringing declaration that the purpose of education is to inculcate virtue, which Franklin defined characteristically: "*Doing Good to Men* is the *Only Service of God* in our Power; and to *imitate his Beneficence* is to *glorify him*." To underscore the point, in his conclusion Franklin quoted both Hutcheson and Locke, who considered virtue the aim of education.[16]

A key to understanding why Franklin undertook all of these ambitious activities, and why he conceived of them as he did, lies in a set of reflections he wrote in 1731, the year in which the Library Company took shape, and later included in his *Autobiography* under the heading "Observations on my Reading History in Library." Franklin began by noting that "the great Affairs of the World, the Wars, Revolutions, &c. are carried on and effected by Parties." Different parties form to advance particular projects, and it is the differences among their views that "occasion all Confusion." While each party thus pursues its interest, each individual "has his particular private Interest in View." Once his party has succeeded, each person "becomes intent upon his particular Interest," which leads to ever more strident conflict. Franklin acknowledged that despite their pretensions, few men act from a genuine concern for the public interest. For that reason he called, perhaps wistfully, for raising a "united Party for Virtue, by forming the Virtuous and good Men of all Nations into a regular Body, to be govern'd by suitable good and wise Rules, which good and wise Men may probably be more unanimous in their Obedience to, than common People are to common Laws." All his activities, from the Junto to the Library Company to the American Philosophical Society to the academy he hoped to establish, were calculated to engage individuals in activities that carried them beyond their self-interest to the common good.[17]

Franklin's *Autobiography* is best known for the connections he drew between the virtues he consciously sought to cultivate in himself and the material success he considered the likely consequence. But that reading of Franklin misses the larger point, his conviction that a broader measure of cultural flourishing lay beyond individual success. He added humility to the list of virtues in the *Autobiography*, he later admitted, only when he learned he was thought proud. To Franklin humility meant trying to "follow Jesus and Socrates," but not toward sacrificial death. Instead he counseled using phrases such as "I imagine" or "it appears to me" in place of "certainly" and "undoubtedly." Franklin admitted achieving only the appearance of this virtue, yet his self-consciously adopted "modest way" won him forgiveness for many errors. Difficult as he found even counterfeiting humility, projecting it eventually became "so easy and so habitual to me, that perhaps for these Fifty Years past no one has ever heard a dogmatical Expression escape me." By his own admission a poor public speaker, Franklin succeeded precisely because he avoided inflammatory, dogmatic, or contentious forms of expression. Such passages do show Franklin's shrewdness. They also show what democratic discourse requires.[18]

Putting the endless search for truth in place of dogma, and substituting humility for arrogance, was the path toward a culture of self-government.[19] That aspiration seems oddly airy for the man who gave us the Franklin stove and the earthy aphorisms of *Poor Richard's Almanac*, yet it is the thread that connects Franklin's diverse civic projects, including the militia he helped organize to defend Pennsylvania from marauding pirates off its coast and French forces on its western border. The Quaker principles of the colony's founding families prevented them from taking up arms or establishing a force to defend themselves. Sharing his neighbors' anxieties, in the *Pennsylvania Gazette* Franklin reprinted Sidney's motto, usually translated as "this hand, hostile to tyrants, seeks with the sword a quiet peace under liberty." Franklin also published excerpts from Sidney's *Discourses* that he thought deserved attention. Cities should expand, Sidney wrote, for "that which does not grow better will grow worse." More pointedly, Sidney contended that the most valuable government, "in Point of Wisdom as well as Justice, is the Government given by GOD to the *Hebrews*, which *chiefly* fitted them for War, and to make Conquests." By invoking Sidney, the patriot most Pennsylvanians considered the cofounder of their colony, Franklin counterposed the martyr for English liberty to the Quaker pacifism of Penn's heirs.[20]

When Pennsylvanians responded to his appeal for action, Franklin proposed a militia charter consistent with his earlier initiatives. The self-governing body would constitute itself voluntarily, choose its officers democratically, and provide for its continuing governance. Ruling out hierarchies of rank or wealth would prevent people sorting themselves "according to their Ranks in Life, their Quality, or Station." The militia should "mix the Great and Small together" to achieve "Union and Encouragement." Because everyone would face the same danger, everyone had the same duty. More than ten thousand men responded to Franklin's call. Organized into more than one hundred companies, the militia did indeed elect its own officers and pay for its own artillery—through a lottery that Franklin organized for the purpose.[21]

Whether helping to organize the people of Philadelphia to defend themselves, clean their streets, or fight their fires, Franklin identified the principle at work. "The Good particular Men may do separately," he wrote in his call to establish a hospital, "is small, compared with what they may do collectively, or by a joint Endeavour and Interest."[22] Placing Franklin's contributions to civic life in the framework of his ethic of benevolence shows his rationale for self-government. His vision extended beyond elections and majority rule to the premises and predispositions on which democracy depends. No utopian, Franklin understood the hard fact of self-interest. But he also understood that transmuting self-interest into the common good is not only a matter of institutional design, completed when by-laws are adopted, but also an unending ethical project.

Pennsylvania suited Franklin. Founded as a haven for nonconformists, it had become the most diverse colony in North America. As early as 1681 Penn had observed that "No laws could be made, nor Money raised, but by the People[']s Consent," and he conceded that their jealous attention to circumscribing the power of government meant that not even "the highest in Authority" could "legally oppress the meanest." Penn's own later rejection by his colony's voters proved he was right. The popularly elected Assembly had achieved dominance over the governor and his council by 1701, but factions continued squabbling, and by midcentury these quarrels had intensified. Whereas Penn's son Thomas warned that the colony was in danger of falling into the chaos of "perfect democracy," Joseph Galloway, among the Quakers opposing the Penn family, criticized Penn's faction for threatening its proudly "democratical" Assembly.[23]

With its chaotic politics and its prosperous economy, Pennsylvania was a magnet for people longing for autonomy. The 1730s and 1740s saw a large influx of Scots-Irish Presbyterians, and in the 1750s so many immigrants arrived from central Europe that perhaps half the colony's population was German-speaking. The establishment of the militia in the mid-1750s reflected that growing diversity and marked the end of Quaker dominance in Pennsylvania politics. The multiplicity of religious sects and national communities, coupled with vast tracts of open and immensely fertile land that enabled most settlers to meet the modest property qualifications for voting, made Pennsylvania the least deferential, and least hierarchical, of England's colonies.[24]

That diversity, however, had another side. Weak churches, widespread landownership, and strong county assemblies meant no tithes, few rent payments, and extremely low taxes (by English or continental standards). While Franklin and other civic boosters built impressive institutions in Philadelphia with private funding, the public sector languished elsewhere in Pennsylvania. Freeholding farmers owned almost three-quarters of the land throughout the middle colonies, a far higher percentage than in England or continental Europe, and they vigorously resisted outside interference. Because none of the sects or national communities trusted the others, schools, hospitals, and other charitable institutions were built to serve particular groups rather than all citizens. One consequence, strikingly apparent when Pennsylvania is compared with the German states or the New England colonies, is the distrust of—and thus the relative weakness or even absence of—public authority and government institutions. The rise of new congregations sparked by the Great Awakening of the 1730s and 1740s only intensified the colony's intense localism.[25]

Even the usually upbeat Franklin reflected the darker side of that distrust. As early as 1751, he predicted that the continuing population explosion of the North American colonies would eventually, and inevitably, make them more prosperous and powerful than England itself. He was not predicting separation, merely the rise of the junior partners to equal status in the British Empire. In the first version of his *Observations concerning the Increase of Mankind*, Franklin expressed his fears that German immigrants flooding into Pennsylvania, whom he labeled "Palatine boors," would overwhelm its English-speaking population. These newcomers, refusing to learn English and insisting on their own schools, stores, newspapers, and other institutions, threatened "to Germanize us instead of our Anglifying them." Franklin understood that a democratic culture requires the humility to concede mistakes and an ethic of benevolence that tolerates difference, but he embodied those virtues as imperfectly as did his fellow colonists. At least he acknowledged the problem: "Perhaps I am partial to the Complexion of my Country, for such Kind of partiality is natural to Mankind." Moreover, he could admit an error. When he published his *Observations* in 1760, he omitted the offensive comments on German immigrants. The damage, however, had been done. News of the original passage circulated widely in 1764, and Franklin was defeated in his bid for the Pennsylvania Assembly.[26]

Slavery presented the most serious problem for colonial North America. Pennsylvania had fewer slaves than the southern colonies, but its merchants—like merchants up and down the eastern seaboard—participated avidly and profited handsomely from the slave trade. Franklin himself owned five household slaves; his *Pennsylvania Gazette* printed notices concerning slave sales and runaway slaves. Although slavery seems to us to contradict the ideals of the Enlightenment, most eighteenth-century writers, like Europeans since the ancient world, took its existence for granted. In the essay maligning German immigrants, Franklin lamented the presence of Africans in Pennsylvania and reflected on the consequences of slavery for slaves and nonslaves. Not only was slave labor in the Caribbean and North American colonies less efficient than wage labor in England, Franklin claimed, it was self-defeating. Because slaves were "work'd too hard, and ill fed," their mortality rate was higher than their birthrate, which made necessary a continual supply of newcomers. That lamentable situation, particularly acute in the brutal sugar islands, flowed from the nature of slavery and infected everyone: "The white Children become proud, disgusted with Labour, and being educated in idleness, are rendered unfit to get a Living by Industry." Many white Britons in North America shared Franklin's aversion to increasing the "Sons of Africa" and his desire to increase the number of European—especially English—settlers.[27]

Much white opposition to slavery for the next century sprang from such racism, but not all of it. Although Pennsylvania was home to slaves and slave traders, it was also home to some of the first organized antislavery activities in America. Scattered attempts to prohibit slavery had appeared in the seventeenth century—notably in Rhode Island in 1652—and a protest was lodged in Pennsylvania in 1688. Few whites, however, showed much interest. Then, in 1754, John Woolman and Anthony Benezet, Quakers from New Jersey and Pennsylvania, published tracts condemning slavery. The Yearly Meeting of Pennsylvania, New Jersey, and Delaware Friends issued a formal declaration calling for its abolition: keeping slaves "tends to harden the heart and render the soul less susceptible of that holy spirit of love, meekness, and charity, which is the peculiar character of a true Christian."[28] By the 1770s, organized opposition to slavery had emerged on both sides of the Atlantic, not coincidentally at just the same time that England's North American colonies began complaining about their own enslavement and demanding their independence. When the latent tension between the principles of autonomy, equality, and reciprocity on the one hand, and the virtues of toleration and humility on the other, came to a head, the racism shared by many white champions of democracy prompted them to sacrifice the former to the latter for the sake of colonial union.

When the colonies took their first, halting step toward formal unification in the same year that American Quakers formally condemned slavery, 1754, Franklin played a pivotal role. He had been impressed by the ability of the Iroquois to ally with other Indian nations while maintaining their own autonomy. His interest in science had put Franklin in touch with colonists elsewhere in North America, and he began wondering whether an alliance similar to the Iroquois Confederation might help English settlers defend themselves. Already alarmed by the threats from the French, from neighboring Indians, and from marauding pirates that gave rise to the colony's militia three years later, Franklin agreed to serve as one of Pennsylvania's emissaries to the six nations of the Iroquois confederation. What he learned came to fruition when he met with others in Albany, where the delegates adopted his "Plan for the Union of all the Colonies"—possibly because he so skillfully deployed his humility. Franklin's scheme, a general government regulating the colonies' trade with and defense from the Indians, required approval by Britain's Board of Trade as well as the colonies. Following his usual practice in Philadelphia, Franklin proposed that members of this Grand Council be chosen by the colonies' assemblies and that it be administered by a crown appointee.

The outcome of this initiative hinted at what was happening in the empire. The colonies distrusted the crown's appointed executive; the crown distrusted the colonies' elected representatives. As Franklin explained the result, "The Assemblies did not adopt it as they all thought there was too much *Prerogative* in it; and in England it was judg'd to have too much of the *Democratic*." Americans and Britons were developing distinct frameworks for interpreting the same phenomenon, divergent perceptions and mirrored fears. "The different and contrary Reasons of dislike to my Plan," Franklin reflected, "makes me suspect that it was really the true Medium."[29]

Franklin's mission to Albany, his first experience in intercolonial negotiations, inaugurated his career as a diplomat, a role he was to play the rest of his life. Quarrels between the Pennsylvania Assembly and the colony's proprietors, simmering for decades, boiled over when the people's representatives proposed taxing the proprietors' land. In 1757, the Assembly appointed Franklin to carry its case to the king. In London Franklin bolstered his ties with leading figures of the British Enlightenment. He met prominent figures in the natural sciences, who had already awarded him the Copley Medal for his work in electricity and elected him a member of the Royal Society of London. At the Club of Honest Whigs and in London's coffeehouses, he got to know dissenters such as Richard Price and Joseph Priestley, two radicals whose critique of English politics would become increasingly important. In Scotland, where the University of St. Andrews awarded him an honorary doctorate, he met the writers David Hume, Adam Ferguson, William Robertson, and Henry Home, Lord Kames, and developed a lasting respect for the Scottish Enlightenment.[30]

While Franklin was busy across the Atlantic, intellectual leadership in the middle colonies passed to a younger generation. Prominent among them was Benjamin Rush, whom Franklin advised to continue his medical studies in Scotland, where he would encounter "a Set of as truly great Men, Professors of the several Branches of Knowledge, as have ever appeared in any Age or Country." Rush took Franklin's advice and later wrote that his Edinburgh years were the most important of his life. Scotland profoundly affected Enlightenment in America, and not only through its writers and universities. Equally crucial were two immigrants to the middle colonies, James Wilson and John Witherspoon, the two Scots who signed the Declaration of Independence and exerted a shaping influence on the United States Constitution.[31]

Deep as Franklin's loyalty to England was, his growing confidence in America's future led to increasing friction with English officials in his role as the emissary of Pennsylvania's Assembly. Franklin later recounted his exchanges with John Carteret, Lord Granville, head of the king's Privy Council, who told Franklin that the king's instructions to his governors were "the Law of the Land" and "the King is the Legislator of the Colonies." Franklin saw things differently: "Our Laws were to be made by our Assemblies." Even though those laws were to be submitted to the king for approval, from the colonists' perspective the king lacked the power—and should not expect—to legislate for the colonies. The exchange between Granville and Franklin illustrates how even Americans loyal to the crown were coming to understand their practices of self-government and their place within the British Empire.[32]

Franklin's career as a diplomat kept him away from America almost continuously after 1757, and eventually he became nearly as comfortable with life at court as he was in the genteel conversations and intellectual exchanges of coffeehouses, salons, and scientific societies. For many Europeans, Franklin embodied the American Enlightenment. Voltaire's *Philosophical Letters* and articles in the *Encyclopedia* had identified Pennsylvania, and the culture of the American colonies in general, with the plain manners and morals of the Quakers. While in France in the 1770s, Franklin learned to play the part convincingly even though he was never a Quaker himself. When he and Voltaire were at last introduced to each other in Paris, those in attendance demanded a formal embrace to seal the alliance between the Enlightenments of France and America.

John Adams was among those who witnessed the embrace of Voltaire and Franklin, a gesture of showmanship that illustrated the gulf already separating the genial Franklin from the stolid Adams. With a mind more rigorous and a personality more irascible than Franklin's, Adams envied but did not always admire his older countryman's easy grace among Europe's courtiers and hostesses. Adams's letters back home to Massachusetts from European capitals are suffused with his sense of social exclusion, his confidence in his intellectual superiority, and his even greater certainty of his superior virtue. The feelings were mutual: Franklin once wrote that Adams "means well for his Country, is always an honest Man, often a Wise One, but sometimes and in some things, absolutely out of his Senses."[33]

Born in 1735, Adams was almost thirty years younger than Franklin, and the Boston experienced by his generation differed from the town where Franklin had been born. Bigger and more bustling, it was still vibrating with a religious intensity quite unlike that of the diverse sects jostling with each other in the middle colonies. The New England in which Adams was raised likewise shows the inadequacy of attempts to counterpose Enlightenment to religion. As in seventeenth- and eighteenth-century England, the ideas that attracted the most enthusiastic support in America were those that did not appear to contradict the revealed truths of Protestant Christianity. The emergence of Adams as a champion of resistance to royal authority is incomprehensible outside the context of the changes in New England Protestantism from 1715 to 1750.

Ideas and practices of self-government, present in New England from the first settlements, persisted as the monarchy worked to consolidate its control over its colonies after 1688. The Ipswich minister John Wise published *A Vindication of the Government of New England Churches* in 1717. Although the issue that immediately engaged Wise concerned ecclesiastical rather than civil authority, he linked the two explicitly. Wise insisted that the principles of self-government appropriate for Puritan churches were equally appropriate outside that domain, and his arguments influenced later developments in New England, including the ideas of Adams and his generation.[34] Wise pulled together strands from multiple traditions to justify self-government. *A Vindication* shows the compatibility between seventeenth-century Puritan ideas, such as those of Sidney, Locke, and Pufendorf on which Wise drew directly, and later arguments for popular sovereignty. "It is certain Civil Government in General," Wise wrote, "is a very Admirable Result of Providence, and an Incomparable Benefit to Mankind." Government is "the Effect of Humane [human] Free-Compacts and not of Divine Institution," a product of man's reason rather than God's wisdom. Governments must suit the "temper and inclination" of a particular people. Otherwise governments would be identical everywhere. Instead God gave humans reason and the freedom to use it, which enables them to understand the law of nature.[35]

In Wise's formulation, that law is simplicity itself. "A Principle of Self-Love" is accompanied by "a Sociable Disposition" and "an Affection or Love to Man-Kind in General," complementary inclinations that prevent man from being "so Wedded to his own Interest" that he is unable to "make the Common good the mark of his Aim." Echoing Winthrop as well as Sidney, Locke, and Pufendorf, Wise insisted that man's God-given "Liberty does not consist in a loose and ungovernable Freedom, or in an unbounded Licence." To the contrary, in a formulation Wise took from Plutarch, *"Those Persons only who live in Obedience to Reason, are worthy to be accounted free: They alone live as they Will, who have Learnt what they ought to Will."* All individuals have equal freedom to judge for themselves the path that leads to their own happiness and well-being. The only justifiable distinctions among individuals are those deemed "agreeable with the publick Good." Wise rejected out of hand the ancient assumption that some are fit to rule and others fit for slavery.[36] Man's "Inclinations to Society" impel him to "enter into a Civil Community," where he "puts himself under Government" and voluntarily agrees to "Sacrifice his Private, for the Publick Good." The original form of government is a democracy, in which each individual possesses the right to vote for the kind of government to be established, after which the majority rules. To achieve its aim, "*Salus Populi*, or the Happiness of the People," the government may "Use, and Apply the strength and riches of Private Persons towards maintaining the Common Peace, Security, and Well-being of all."[37]

Governments exist in three forms, monarchy, aristocracy, and the most ancient form of all, democracy. When "Free Persons, do Assemble together, in Order to enter into a Covenant for Uniting themselves in a Body," they constitute only an embryonic democracy. They must decide through a second covenant how their sovereign authority will be exercised. Only then can their compact be called a legitimate "Democratical Government." The people might continue to meet as an assembly of the whole, or they might choose to delegate their authority to some members. Because many people cannot administer a government, "it is most agreeable with the Law of Nature, that they Institute their Officers to act in their Name, and Stead." Wise distinguished between what came to be known as a constitutional convention and the ordinary processes of democratic government, and he reasoned that there is nothing undemocratic about the people choosing to select some members to execute their will.[38] Wise's central contention—that governments arise when naturally sociable individuals choose voluntarily to restrain their freedom within a democratic form of government constituted to secure the public good—consolidated arguments from a century of radical English political thinking and echoed through the writings of several generations of Americans.

The 1720s and 1730s saw two more strands woven into that braid of Protestant and republican arguments. With the frequency of parliamentary elections in Britain reduced to once every seven years after 1716, and with the ruling oligarchy tightening its hold on public life, Prime Minister Robert Walpole was able to manipulate Parliament through bribery, pensions, and the careful allocation of government positions. These strategies, which cynical observers such as Hume reckoned the price of peaceful government, outraged critics across the British political spectrum. The most prominent spokesmen for what was called the "Country" position, John Trenchard and Thomas Gordon, collaborated on articles in English periodicals from 1720 to 1723 that appeared in book form as *Cato's Letters*. The most prolific critic from the rival "Court" perspective, Henry St. John, Viscount Bolingbroke, assailed Walpole in almost five hundred issues of the *Craftsman*, published between 1726 and 1736.[39]

In the American colonies, the writings of Trenchard and Gordon and Bolingbroke were reprinted in papers from Benjamin Franklin's brother James Franklin's *New England Courant* to the *South Carolina Gazette*. Although suspect among conservative Puritans and Anglicans alike, these British critics appealed to American dissidents.[40] Concern with the corrupt practices and increasing power of Walpole's government merged with Americans' worries about the vitality of their own institutions of governance. Such anxieties, intensified by the crown's efforts to expand the authority of royal governors and diminish the power of the colonies' own assemblies, provided one of the contexts that framed Americans' political writings in the 1740s.

The threat of political corruption was only one of the frameworks that mattered. Equally important for many American colonists were their religious beliefs, including but not limited to a new and more emotional form of evangelical Protestantism later known as the Great Awakening. Itinerant ministers traveled throughout the colonies in the 1740s, delivering sermons that deviated from cool reason and elicited passionate responses that shattered the decorum and rattled the stability of many existing congregations. Figures such as Jonathan Edwards in western New England, Gilbert Tennent in New Jersey, Samuel Davies in Virginia, and the peripatetic George Whitefield sought to reawaken believers' zeal by stressing the need for God's intervention in their lives. Although such preachers emphasized spiritual conversion rather than political democracy, their message had the unintended effect of weakening their followers' acceptance of established authority—civil as well as ecclesiastical.[41]

As passionate as the popular response to these revivals was the reaction of orthodox ministers who sought to ban, and sometimes succeeded in outlawing, such forms of worship. After Connecticut passed such a law in 1742, Yale rector Elisha Williams, a great-grandson of the Puritan divine John Cotton, published (under the pseudonym "Philalethes") a widely circulated tract entitled *The Essential Rights and Liberties of Protestants*. Although Williams disapproved of the new forms of worship and worked to inoculate Yale from the contagion of enthusiasm, he resurrected arguments of earlier radical nonconformists such as Roger Williams, John Milton, and others concerning the sanctity of conscience. *Essential Rights* shows how the ideas of self-government, at least among some mainstream Congregationalists, were eroding the strict discipline against which dissidents had chafed a century earlier. "Every Christian," Williams thundered, "has *a Right of judging for himself* what he is to believe and practice in Religion" according to "the SACRED SCRIPTURES."[42]

Turning to civil society, Williams followed Locke. All individuals are born free and equal in the state of nature, equipped with reason to discern and the will to obey the laws of God and of nature. "*This natural Freedom* is not a Liberty for every one to do what he pleases without any Regard to any *Law*; for a *rational* Creature cannot but be made under a *Law* from its MAKER," that is, "the *Law of Nature*." God gave the earth to all of his children in common, but when an individual "removes any Thing out of the State that Nature has provided," then "he has *mixed his Labour* with it and joined something to it that is his own, and thereby makes it his Property." In the state of nature neither person nor property is secure, Williams reasoned, so individuals voluntarily form a social compact, in which property rights become subject to regulation according to "the Good and Safety of the society," as is "not only *necessary* but *just*." To underscore the prior claims of social justice over individual rights, Williams also invoked that standard to justify the exercise of free speech: "Every Member of a Community ought to be concerned for the *whole*, as well as for *his particular Part*."[43] Discussing the origins of civil society, Williams adopted, as did John Wise, Sidney's and Locke's view that democracy was the original form of government. To Williams, as to all colonists long accustomed to electing government officials, the shift from direct to representative government was straightforward. The people can either make the laws themselves or, "which comes to the same Thing, appoint those who shall make them, and who shall see them executed." Williams produced as democratic a tract as any written in the 1740s; like Wise, he considered representation unproblematic.

Anti-Catholicism remained powerful in these years. In the midst of Williams's plea for toleration of diverse Protestant sects, which had shown they could exist with "mutual Forbearance," he excluded "the *Papist*," whom he branded "an Enemy or Traytor to a *Protestant State*." "*Popery*" did not qualify as a religion but was instead a conspiracy against it, managed by none other than "the Vice-regent of the *Devil*." Under Henry VIII and Elizabeth, England had perpetuated the errors of the Roman Catholic Church by uniting religious and civil authority. Not until the Act of Toleration had freedom of conscience been secured. But within the Church of England—and even in New England, as the proposed Connecticut statute showed—there were latent seeds of authoritarianism that might still blossom any moment into popery.[44]

Fears of religious authoritarianism and fears of political corruption fused in the 1740s. A group of Bostonians, including the young brewer Samuel Adams, established the *Independent Advertiser* in early 1748 and immediately targeted the New England elite and the English gentry behind them. Whereas "all men are by nature on a level" and "born with an equal share of freedom," the conditions that had enabled the early settlers of New England to prosper were changing. "Liberty can never subsist without equality," so the rise of unprecedented wealth and unprecedented poverty likewise threatened even those who were holding their own. "When men's riches become immeasurably or surprisingly great," the people must ask how it happened. The *Independent Advertiser* offered the same explanation given by *Cato's Letters* and the *Craftsman*: luxury and corruption.[45]

If Boston's working people were growing uneasy about the wealthy, their uneasiness was beginning to alarm the well-to-do. Prosperous Bostonians thought the problem was democracy. The source of "the Mobbish turn in this Town," according to Governor William Shirley, was its constitution; "by which the management of it is devolv'd upon the populace assembled in their town meetings." In those raucous gatherings "the meanest inhabitants," with nothing more constructive to do, "generally are the majority and outvote the gentlemen" and merchants, few of whom choose to attend. From the ancient world to the present, critics of democracy had predicted it would end in anarchy. Shirley echoed their fear. The involvement in public life of too many "working artificers, seafaring men, and low sorts of people," as he put it, contributed to the rise of an ominous "mobbish spirit" that would lead to trouble if left unchecked. Shirley proved an excellent prophet.[46]

Practices of self-government spread throughout the colonies. Wherever Congregationalists or Presbyterians settled, and wherever the Great Awakening fired groups of the newly regenerate to establish churches, an intensely independent spirit emerged. Just as diverse denominations in the middle colonies withdrew into separate institutional frameworks, so in settlements far from the eastern seaboard self-rule took root. From political, economic, and religious sources, the experience of autonomous communities was undermining deference to authority by the mid-eighteenth century. After 1660 in England,

and for much longer elsewhere in Europe, the alliance of republicanism and Protestantism was less common than Luther's injunction to obey established authority. Only in England's North American colonies, where covenanted communities developed their own forms of government with a remarkable degree of independence, was Christianity yoked with democracy.[47]

Associating power with corruption became increasingly common in the 1740s. The Awakening spread throughout the colonies, challenging established sects. Then, in June of 1745, a band of New Englanders—with the former rector of Yale Elisha Williams as their chaplain—successfully launched an attack on the French stronghold of Louisbourg, on the eastern tip of Nova Scotia, in the North American theater of the War of the Austrian Succession. When colonial militias elsewhere managed to fend off French and Indian attacks, and when a French fleet sailing to retake Nova Scotia and Cape Breton went down in a storm at sea, Americans saw the hand of God at work. George Whitefield, preaching a thanksgiving sermon in Philadelphia in August of 1746, praised God's intervention and called on his listeners to repent lest the next challenge succeed: "If the Lord had not been on our side," Great Britain and its American colonies would have become "a field of blood." Without God's grace, a plague of "monks, Dominicans and friars, like so many locusts," would have overwhelmed the colonists. If not beset by papists, the colonists might have fallen victim to smallpox or yellow fever. In an atmosphere supercharged by religious fervor, corruption wore many guises. French monarchism, in league with the pope as Antichrist, was one; veiled popular yearnings for Catholicism, still festering within the Church of England, were another; the dissolute gentry, occupying the House of Lords and the colonial governors' mansions and exploiting public office for private gain, were yet one more. The links connecting those diverse fears hardened in the forge of a pervasive anti-Catholicism.[48]

As the Awakening gathered momentum, distrust of authority manifested itself even in more established churches. Boston's Charles Chauncy, an orthodox Congregationalist troubled by religious enthusiasm, delivered just such a message in 1747 before Governor William Shirley, his council, and the Massachusetts Assembly. Although Chauncy acknowledged the need for sinful men to obey the law and refrain from inciting unrest, he warned the Anglican governor that the people of Massachusetts had no intention of straying from "*that manner of worship and discipline*" that had led their ancestors to New England. Unusually in an election-day sermon, Chauncy identified a particular policy as consistent with God's mercy: more lenient terms of credit for the colony's struggling people. "As rulers would be just," he advised, "they must take all proper care to preserve entire the civil rights of a people." The thrust of Chauncy's sermon was clear: if Governor Shirley and his council did not take heed, popular protests would escalate.[49]

Shirley's worries extended well beyond the common people to prominent New England clergymen. Jonathan Mayhew ascended to the pulpit of Boston's West Church the same year that Shirley expressed his anxieties to the Board of Trade. Mayhew quickly earned a reputation for theological heterodoxy and radical politics. A 1750 sermon praising resistance to Charles I fed Shirley's anxiety: strident protests were now coming not only from artisans and seamen but also from Harvard-educated Congregationalist ministers. Whereas in England, at least since 1660, the nearly universal revulsion against regicide had moderated resistance to monarchy, Mayhew boldly defended Charles's execution as a just response to tyranny. Kings rule only "for the public welfare." When they turn despotic, "they may be *forcibly* resisted." No form of government tends so easily toward tyranny as monarchy; no one can better judge a king than ordinary people. In a crescendo of accusations, Mayhew declared despotism, not regicide, disloyalty: "'tis treason,—not against one *single* man, but the state—against the whole body politic;—'tis treason against mankind;—'tis treason against common sense;—'tis treason against God."[50] Linking individual reason with God's will and God's will with common sense, Mayhew was departing from Puritan emphases on human sinfulness and divine grace. In other national contexts, mixing together practices of self-government, republican critiques of corruption, revivalist ministers' calls for renewal outside the boundaries of established authority, and a shared, increasingly vitriolic anti-Catholicism had proved impossible. Would it work in the colonies?

Common-sense moral philosophy, by redefining human capacity, provided the ingredient that smoothed out the volatile mixture and made it palatable. As formulated first by Shaftesbury and refined by Hutcheson, and ultimately filtered into the colonies through the heterodox preaching of liberal ministers such as Chauncy and Mayhew as well as influential Scottish immigrants, Scottish common sense became Americans' philosophy of choice between the 1740s and the 1790s. Even thinkers who did not depart from orthodox Calvinism as dramatically as Franklin were seeking a form of Christianity that minimized miracles, widened the scope of free will and works, and made room for reason. Hutcheson's assurance that our moral sense provides guidance as reliable as our other senses enabled American readers persuaded by Locke to embrace empiricism without accepting the materialism of Spinoza or the skepticism of Hume.[51]

By the 1750s, Hutcheson's philosophy had become a central part of the curriculum at Harvard College and the College of Philadelphia. At William and Mary, it captivated Thomas Jefferson. When it became the centerpiece of instruction in Princeton, at the College of New Jersey, thanks to John Witherspoon, it shaped the sensibility of James Madison.[52] In sum, common sense not only was consistent with Locke's psychology and Newton's physics but also offered a way to resolve the squabbles among Protestant sects. Finally, and decisively, it jibed with the practices of self-government maturing throughout the colonies since the mid-seventeenth century. In Hutcheson's concept of a human inclination toward benevolence, a moral sense that naturalized as well as universalized the Christian law of love, Americans found their moral philosophy.[53]

Scottish common-sense philosophy did encounter resistance from some leading American theologians of the 1740s and 1750s, such as Jonathan Edwards and Samuel Johnson, but it offered an attractive alternative to the insistence of such figures—and their most influential followers, such as New Jersey's Gilbert Tennent, Virginia's Samuel Davies, and New England's Isaac Backus—on God's sovereignty and man's depravity. The Judeo-Christian idea of man's fall endured so long in part because it helped explain why humans so seldom measure up to the ideal of benevolence and so often show themselves to be selfish, even cruel. The notion that humans struggled between their capacity to love and their inclination to hate, between the love of God and the lure of the devil, corresponded so well to the experience of individuals wrestling with competing impulses that it survived centuries of criticism. Neatly as common-sense philosophy seemed to resolve many difficulties facing mid-eighteenth-century Americans, older ideas of human frailty persisted. The evidence of human sinfulness stood as a formidable barrier against claims of human benevolence.

John Adams illustrates the persistence of those conflicts and the process whereby changing religious and philosophical ideas bolstered ideas about self-government. He was born into an orthodox Puritan family in the town of Braintree, south of Boston. His father, John Adams Sr., descended from Puritans who had settled there in 1638 as part of the first great migration to New England, was a farmer and shoemaker of modest means. When his son showed a gift for reading, he took steps to prepare the boy for Harvard College and a life in the ministry.[54] In 1749, the year before the younger John entered Harvard, his father became embroiled in a controversy concerning the town's new minister, Lemuel Briant. Briant had preached a sermon taking aim at central doctrines of Calvinism. The meeting to decide the heretical Briant's fate convened in the Adams family home, a natural site because John Adams Sr., also a selectman, was a deacon in the First Church of Braintree.

Young John, bookish already at age fourteen, read all the pamphlets, attended the "Ecclesiastical Councils," and came away demoralized, even though Briant was exonerated, by what he called the "Spirit of Dogmatism and Bigotry" that prevailed. He decided "that the Study of Theology and the pursuit of it as a Profession would involve me in endless Altercations and make my life miserable, without any prospect of doing good to my fellow Men." Given that Adams was to spend his entire life embroiled in "endless Altercations"—albeit those of politics rather than religion—it seems unlikely that it was the contentiousness of the dispute that troubled him.[55]

Like Jonathan Mayhew, with whom Briant sometimes exchanged pulpits, Adams repudiated the Calvinist principles of total depravity—that the sins of Adam and Eve were sufficient "to damn the whole human Race, without any actual Crimes committed by any of them"—and of unconditional election, a "detestable" idea that characterized "eternal life as an unattainable Thing without the special favor of the Father." Such doctrines, Adams concluded, actually "discourage the practice of virtue." In a letter to a friend, the young Adams denied that the universe is governed by "such arbitrary Will or inflexible fatality."[56] Mayhew's preaching, with its confidence in reason and common sense, converted Adams from the strict Calvinism of his ancestors to the emerging liberal Protestantism of the English and Scottish Enlightenments. At Harvard, Adams encountered the natural sciences and came away a convinced Newtonian. After graduation, he accepted a job teaching school in Worcester. There he joined a provincial version of a typical Enlightenment reading club, encountered skeptics and Deists in person and in print, and solidified his liberal Protestant faith. Although exposure to Enlightenment thinkers helped Adams repudiate Calvinism, throughout his life he maintained a firm belief in God and an equally sturdy conviction that salvation must be earned by virtuous living rather than granted solely by God's grace. From teaching, which Adams found difficult and tedious, he learned that every social group possesses members with different talents and inclinations. He also learned that his aspiration to moral excellence would be complicated by his vanity and his ambition, flaws he acknowledged but never managed to suppress. His experience and his character pointed in the same direction: legal training leading toward a career in public life.[57]

During the time that Adams read law in Worcester and began his legal practice back in Braintree, he read voraciously, not only the law books he was required to study but also a remarkable syllabus the ambitious young man set for himself. From Virgil to Voltaire, from Milton to Montesquieu, from Leibniz to the English Latitudinarian theologians, he devoured books in his quest to form his own ideas about philosophy, law, and politics. Liberal Anglican theologians such as John Tillotson, Joseph Butler, and Samuel Clarke bolstered Adams's own religious convictions, cementing his confidence that reason fortified by will enables humans to lead the lives of virtue envisioned for them by God. Natural philosophers from Bacon to Newton showed Adams the "true sphere of Modern Genius." Towering above all these figures, though, stood Locke, whose *Essay concerning Human Understanding* had demolished Descartes's doctrine of innate ideas and explored "the unenlightened Regions of the human Mind," where Locke discovered "a new World," the world of experience and rational reflection.[58]

Locke's empiricism, linked with rather than divorced from religious faith, served as the armature of Adams's mature thought. As Adams wrote in 1756, "An intimate knowledge therefore of the intellectual and moral World is the sole foundation on which a stable structure of Knowledge can be erected."[59] In contrast to Puritans who distrusted depraved man's capacity to reason and choose, Adams declared, together with Locke, that God had given man reason to enable him to find "the Truth, and the real Design and true End of our Existence."[60] His reading caused Adams to question the adequacy of English common law; instead he looked to reason. "Law is human Reason," as he put it, and "the political and civil Laws of each Nation should be only the particular Cases, in which human Reason is applied."[61]

The same was true of the moral law. Reasoning roughly as Shaftesbury, Adam Smith, and Hutcheson did, and as John Wise, Elisha Williams, and Jonathan Mayhew did, Adams contended that God had provided humans with adequate means to discern and do his will. In his diary Adams observed that we associate vice with pain, and virtue with pleasure, and that a "Course of Impiety and Injustice, of Malevolence and Intemperance" appears "Shocking and deformed to our first Reflections."[62] Whether his conversion to something resembling the moral sense was the work of Mayhew or the Scottish philosophers, or, more likely, both, Adams appears to have embraced the idea. As he expressed it in a showy letter to one of his Harvard classmates, "Upon common theaters, indeed, the applause of the audience is of more importance to the actors than their own approbation. But upon the stage of life, while conscience claps, let the world hiss! On the contrary if conscience disapproves, the loudest applauses of the world are of little value."[63]

Our internal judge of vice and virtue—our conscience, our rational judgment, our moral sense, Smith's impartial spectator—is the only tribunal that matters. It registers our understanding of God's will and our knowledge that paradise or damnation awaits as our just reward.[64] The best use of reason, Adams mused, lay not in earning admiration or wealth but in doing God's will. To that end he filled his diary with admonitions not to stray from the path of virtue, and his correspondence makes clear that he showed an equally stern face to others. He also valued knowledge that might improve people's lives over mere speculation. Our "primary Endeavour" is to "distinguish between Useful and unuseful, to pursue the former with unwearied Industry, and to neglect with much Contempt all the Rest."[65]

To fasten his attention on such useful knowledge, Adams vowed to follow a strict regimen of study and virtuous activity; his diary reveals how seriously he took that pledge. After listing the virtues conventionally, dividing them between self-regarding ("Habits of Temperance, Recollection, and self Government") and other-regarding ("Habits of Love and Compassion to our fellow men"), Adams conceded that his most formidable challenge lay in controlling his unruly passions. As his diary reveals, mastering his will took more effort than following the golden rule.[66] His studies of history taught him that fame came in two varieties: benevolent when earned by those who saw and advanced the public good, malevolent when attained by corrupt means. He saw the same potential for virtue and vice in the great and the ordinary, a potential unchanged from the heroes and villains of the ancient agora to "our American Town Meeting." The learning Adams had gained, and the eloquence he hoped to develop, might "be employed wisely to persuade" or "employed wickedly to seduce."[67] Throughout his career Adams worked tirelessly, self-consciously, obsessively, to attain fame of the benevolent sort, and he proved quick to relegate to the other category anyone who dared disagree with him.

Adams realized from an early age that pride was his most serious flaw, which he neither mastered nor forgave in himself or anyone else.[68] Years later, after Adams had served as an undiplomatic diplomat in Paris with Jefferson and Franklin, Jefferson described him in a letter to James Madison as "vain, irritable, and a bad calculator of the force and probable effect of the motives which govern men." Even if, as Jefferson added immediately, "this is all the ill which can possibly be said of him," it was enough to cause Adams constant distress and embroil him in constant disputes.[69] As he continued teaching school in Worcester while preparing himself for the law, Adams berated himself repeatedly for his laziness and inattention to his own education.[70] Despite his vow to improve his mind, he found his interests shifting to politics. In a remarkable letter to his Harvard classmate Nathan Webb, Adams predicted—in terms strikingly similar to Franklin's—that England's North American colonies were destined to outstrip the mother country in population and power. In the aftermath of the Louisbourg expedition, when western New England was feeling quite full of itself, he speculated that England could preserve its superior position only by preventing the colonies from joining together. He closed the letter with a self-deprecating quip that became significant only later: "Be not surprised that I am turn'd Politician. This whole town is immers'd in Politicks."[71]

John Adams became a freeholder in 1761, when his father's death made him owner of the modest family farm in Braintree. He set aside one of the small rooms of the farmhouse as his law office. For the rest of his life Adams balanced his legal and political ambitions against the insistent demands of maintaining a farm in the challenging climate of New England. Again the contrast with European philosophes is striking: if Adams never attained the refined grace of the salon, perhaps it was because, even though he was often absent, he worked throughout his life not only in law courts and political meetings but also, with his own hands, in his own rocky fields and fragile orchards.

Adams's career, divided between farm and meetinghouse, was made possible by his marriage, in 1764, to a Congregationalist preacher's daughter from nearby Weymouth, Abigail Smith, who became the most important person in his life. Although as a girl she received none of the classical education reserved for boys, Abigail was as avid a reader as John and, as they both acknowledged, his intellectual equal. Her correspondence shows her early familiarity with writers from Shakespeare and Milton to Addison and Pope, writers later supplemented by Molière, Rousseau, historians ancient and modern—and even a few disreputable novelists. Abigail's sensibility, like John's, was shaped by Locke's philosophy. Her Christian faith was as unshakable as her husband's, even as both migrated from their parents' Puritanism toward a more liberal Christianity less attuned to depravity and election than to benevolence and duty.[72]

The intellectual capacity of women was hotly contested in eighteenth-century America. Although the legal subordination of wives to husbands was taken for granted—by many if not most women as well as men—as completely as the subordination of children to their parents, the proper role of wives and mothers remained open to debate. Because Bible reading was central to the Puritans' sense of themselves and their mission, teaching reading at home had been an important responsibility assigned to New England women for over a century. The achievements of independent thinkers and powerful writers, including Anne Bradstreet, Ann Hopkins, Anne Hutchinson, Sarah Whipple Goodhue, and Mary Rowlandson were well known. When Boston's Brattle Street Church was established at the end of the seventeenth century, female communicants were granted the right to participate in selecting the minister. Cotton Mather praised the intellectual vitality of Puritan women in his sermons and his writing. Though women were still expected to remain silent in church—and were still sometimes silenced outside it—more and more women began to think for themselves as the Great Awakening and the Enlightenment both shook the foundations of deference within and outside Congregational meetinghouses.

Women increasingly began to write as well as read. They were not, however, welcome to contribute to James Franklin's *New England Courant*, and his sister Jane presents a melancholy illustration of the limited opportunities for self-expression afforded most women. Her correspondence with her brother Ben showed that Jane had plenty of ideas. His letters were her principal source of information about the larger world, and writing to her celebrated brother enabled her to express what she was thinking.[73] The *New England Monthly Journal*, founded in 1727, encouraged women's education, but in terms that merely reinforced the prejudices women faced. In the issue of June 22, 1730, the editor, Reverend Mather Byles, placed women's intellectual capacity on a par with men's: "Is not their Reason as strong, their Memory as good, and is their Judgment less sound than ours?" His approbation of women's increasing interest in reading and writing indicated the sweeping changes occurring in New England culture more generally, as enlightened ideals of refinement, the allied phenomenon dubbed Anglicization, and the persistence of older Puritan ideals of modesty and virtue meshed somewhat awkwardly: "Thirst after Knowledge is a Sign of a virtuous Soul; and were the Ladies encourag'd in this glorious Pursuit of Wisdom, we shoul'd find the Face of Affairs change in the *Beau Monde*." Women needed only to shift their focus to their capacities, "and reflect what excellent Talents they suffer to be bury'd," in order to alter their condition. If women learned to "value themselves more for their Learning than their Dress, they wou'd have the Glory of reforming the Men, of introducing Modesty and good Sense, and of banishing Vice and Folly, the Twin Daughters of Ignorance."[74]

John and Abigail Adams seemed to share that perspective. In a letter to Abigail written after the death of her mother, John expressed his regret that her "Talents, and Virtues" were "too much confined, to private, social and domestic life." Crucial as that domain was, it need not exhaust women's contributions. If the "Benevolence, Charity, Capacity, and Industry" that were exerted by able women "in private life" could be "employed upon a larger Scale," to advance "the great Principles of Virtue and Freedom of political Regulations," the benefits would extend to "whole Nations and Generations." Byles and Adams were hardly alone in predicting the transformative effect of extending female virtue from the household to the public sphere, but as will become clear, there were limits to the role they and their contemporaries envisioned for women.[75]

New England women participated in a female version of the male reading clubs and coffeehouses of the French and British Enlightenments, even though signs of their Puritan heritage lingered. Abigail Adams belonged to a reading circle that also included Mercy Otis Warren, who lent her a copy of Molière that elicited a chiding reply: despite his charms, Abigail wrote, Molière would be of little lasting value because he "ridiculed Vice without engaging us to Virtue." She contrasted such trifles with the weightier stuff of *Cato's Letters*, then commended the exemplary civic virtue displayed in Warren's biting portrait of the wealthy merchant, British colonial official, and symbol of royal tyranny Thomas Hutchinson in her play *The Adulateur.* Warren's later writings, including *The Group*, another drama satirizing British oppression of the colonies, also earned the praise of Abigail's husband, who was sufficiently impressed by her work to solicit Warren's ideas about government. Spirited engagement in the republic of letters was preparing such women for roles in public life.[76]

Abigail and John alternately bolstered each other's faith in human capacity and reminded each other of the sober lessons drawn from history and their religious convictions. Abigail captured all three dimensions in a letter that showed she was turning into something of a "politician" herself: "I am more and more convinced that man is a dangerous creature, and that power whether vested in many or few is ever grasping." Her own misgivings concerning claims to republican virtue paralleled John's. "The great fish swallow up the small," she observed, "and he who is most strenuous for the rights of the people, when vested with power, is as eager after the prerogatives of government." Without disputing enlightened claims about human capacity, she advised caution. "You tell me of degrees of perfection to which humane nature is capable of arriving, and I believe it, but at the same time lament that our admiration should arise from the scarcity of the instances."[77] In her ability to turn a phrase as well as in her blending and balancing of ideas from multiple sources, and above all in her rock-solid reliability under conditions that would have tested not merely the patience of Penelope but the endurance of Ulysses, Abigail proved the ideal match for John. Both the patience and the endurance of English colonists were being tested by the time John and Abigail married in 1764. Conventionally, the events that led to the American Revolution are said to have begun in 1763, when the new government of Prime Minister George Grenville decided to enforce regulations on colonial trade in order to shift more of the rising cost of empire from England to North America. When the Treaty of Paris ended the Seven Years War, Grenville's ministry sought to bolster British authority over the colonies. The tensions that led to that decision, however, had already been rising.

Franklin and Adams were among many who noted the spectacular growth of population up and down the North American seaboard. The free population more than doubled between 1710 and 1740, then again between 1740 and 1770; the slave population grew at twice that rate. Rising colonial imports and exports were fueling the British economy, which brought both enthusiasm and anxiety. Like Franklin and Adams, many in Britain began to ponder the future of the colonial relationship in the face of that explosive growth. From the 1720s to the 1740s, moreover, colonial assemblies exercised ever greater authority, effectively constraining the royal governors' power and augmenting their own without directly addressing the shift or its implications. Revolts by tenants against landlords in New Jersey, New York, and North Carolina, which pitted small farmers against distant creditors, added another dimension to the spreading uneasiness: those who worked the land claimed ownership, either citing Locke explicitly or offering their own versions of his labor theory of property. Efforts to counter such squatters by asserting the ancient prerogatives of a landowning aristocracy made headway nowhere.[78]

When a new head of the Board of Trade attempted to tighten control of colonial politics and commerce after 1748, scattered protests signaled a new stage in the colonies' assertiveness. Attempts to rein in assemblies' issuing of paper money sparked resistance, and the colonists increasingly ignored directives issued by governors and by the Board of Trade. Britain's neglect of the colonies had enabled their institutions of self-governance to become established as the source of law. Mayhew's sermons were but one signal of that change. Efforts to annul—or even to review—colonial legislation foundered as Britain failed to enforce the instructions sent to governors. Throughout the Seven Years War, Britain tried vainly to control the colonies through piecemeal attempts to curtail the assemblies' power. Because the crown needed the colonies' assistance in the war against the French, however, those scattered efforts heightened the colonists' distrust without effectively challenging their self-rule.

Renewed efforts to police the colonies collided with enhanced colonial sensitivities in the writs-of-assistance case of 1761. The new governor of Massachusetts, Francis Bernard, had already ruffled feathers in 1760 by proposing to change Boston's town meeting to a "close corporation," patterned after a form of English city government in which officials named their own successors and the lord mayor exercised considerable power. "A Combination of Twelve Strangers," according to the *Boston Gazette* of May 5, 1760, wanted to "overthrow the ancient Constitution of our Town Meeting, as being popular and mobbish, and to form a Committee to transact the whole affairs of the town." This cabal, spearheaded by Bernard with assistance from local merchants led by Thomas Hutchinson, sought to prevent "those whom in contempt they usually term the low lived people" from participating in elections for the General Court. The term "strangers," still the preferred word for Anglicans in Puritan New England, signaled the lingering fear that the crown wanted not only to regulate colonial commerce but also to impose its corrupt forms of religion and politics.[79]

The writs of assistance empowered British customs officials to search Boston homes for illegal goods or evidence of smuggling. James Otis, the Harvard-educated brother of Abigail's friend Mercy Otis Warren, had been appointed the king's advocate general in the vice-admiralty court in Boston. He resigned that position to lead the dozens of Boston merchants protesting the writs. In the Superior Court of Judicature, Otis challenged Parliament's authorization of intrusions into the homes of English citizens, invoking ancient rights and warning against tyrannical excesses. John Adams, who witnessed Otis's speech, later testified to its impact. "Every man of a crowded audience appeared to me to go away, as I did, ready to take arms against the writs of assistance," Adams later wrote. "Then and there the child Independence was born." Even allowing for some retrospective hyperbole, Adams's own career took a sharp turn on that day.[80]

Among the many issues Otis broached in his address was slavery. Although 90 percent of slaves on the mainland lived in the southern colonies, and less than 5 percent of the New England population was enslaved, New Englanders certainly profited from the enormous Atlantic slave trade, either directly or indirectly. The number of slaves carried to the murderous islands of the Caribbean and to Latin America dwarfed the number brought to North America. The profits earned from slavery and the institution itself, however, elicited protests in New England from an early date. In a tract entitled *The Selling of Joseph* (1700), Samuel Sewall had written that "all men, as they are sons of Adam," possess what Sewall termed an "equal right unto liberty." Sewall condemned both slavery and the slave trade. "How horrible is the uncleanness, mortality, if not murder, that the ships are guilty of that bring great Crouds of these miserable men and women."[81] Otis picked up the themes of such early antislavery tracts. Opposition to slavery in New England did not begin in the 1760s, but after the writs-of-assistance case it became a recurrent theme in criticism of English policy, as indeed it was for both John and Abigail Adams, neither of whom ever owned slaves or saw any justification for the institution.

Otis extended his critique of slavery in *The Rights of the British Colonies Asserted and Proved* (1764). "The colonists are by the law of nature free born, as indeed all men are, white or black." Otis challenged centuries-old European assumptions about race used to justify enslaving Africans: "Will short curled hair like wool, instead of Christian hair, as tis called by those whose hearts are as hard as the nether millstone, help the argument?" It was impossible to draw any "logical inference in favor of slavery" from "a flat nose, a long or short face." Slavery not only visited unimaginable cruelty on slaves; it also made a tyrant of everyone involved in it. The climate of opinion was shifting. Massachusetts towns such as Worcester and Boston instructed their representatives in the General Court to oppose slavery. Debates on the issue were held at Harvard, where slaves were hardly unknown. Prominent writers joined the chorus.[82]

The focus of New Englanders' concern soon shifted from enslaved Africans to white colonists' fears of their own enslavement, to borrow the heightened rhetoric of the day. Otis made that move himself. Powerful as Otis's indictment of race-based slavery was, he began to focus his attention on an argument for democracy, descended from his Puritan ancestors, which never persuaded royalists or Anglicans. Popular government has "an everlasting foundation in the *unchangeable will of GOD*." As Puritans had claimed since the upheavals of the 1640s, Otis contended that sovereign power is "*originally* and *ultimately* in the people." Against the pretensions of monarchs, he proclaimed that only God's power can be called "supreme and absolute. In the order of nature immediately under him, comes the power of a simple *democracy*, or the power of the whole over the whole." Neither Otis nor those who joined him in succeeding years to protest British attempts to regulate the colonies shied away from the idea that they were counterposing democracy to monarchy and aristocracy. Neither did they differentiate between the traditions of civic republicanism, as articulated by a thinker such as Harrington, the tradition of liberalism now usually associated with Locke, and the doctrines of Christianity as it was understood in different parts of the colonies. Instead they drew on all three traditions, and on eighteenth-century ideas of reason and common sense, to forge a set of wide-ranging and supple arguments that they deployed against the threats of British authority.

The idea of popular sovereignty, as preceding chapters have shown, emerged before the English Civil War and developed afterward among British Whigs. The power of the king and the aristocracy, corruption in parliamentary politics, and revulsion at the memory of civil war, however, all militated against widespread acceptance in England of the proposition that authority resides in the common people. Power too obviously lay elsewhere. In Britain's North American colonies, by contrast, the majority of white adult males owned land or at least sufficient property to vote, and many of them did vote, usually every year. Those votes, moreover, translated directly into representation in local, county, or colony-wide assemblies. There people of ordinary means exercised effective power, determining the laws under which they lived. In such circumstances, popular sovereignty was a fact, not a fiction.[83] Despite its limitations, and from a twenty-first-century perspective they were considerable with respect to gender, race, and class, the self-government practiced by colonial societies went beyond anything practiced in Britain or anywhere on the continent of Europe, including the vaunted republics of the United Provinces and the Swiss Confederation, where oligarchies exercised effective control. When James Otis defended "the power of a simple *democracy*, or the power of the whole over the whole," and identified democracy with the will of God, he meant exactly what he said.[84]

The complicating dimension of Otis's argument derived not from his conception of democracy but from his identification of democracy with God's will, and of God's will with natural law. Whereas British legal theory was moving, with the publication of Blackstone's *Commentaries* from 1765 to 1769, in the direction of positive law, meaning that law is what the courts say it is and nothing more, Otis and many other Americans continued to adhere to an earlier conception that identified the foundation of law with the unchanging will of God. The challenge, in that framework, lay not with making law but rather with finding law. Thus the essence of law—the immutable will of God—never changes; only our understanding of it does. In that case it is difficult to see how the people, with their changing whims, can be the repository as well as the instrument of God's will. Otis invoked the example of ancient Greek city-states and New England towns to show the working of small-scale democracy, "a government of all over all." The question would become whether that model could apply—or should apply—for an entire colony, or for the colonies as a whole. Although that issue was not yet in the minds of many colonists in 1761, it would soon become more urgent.[85]

Franklin too had reason to worry about democracy. In the same year as Otis's impassioned defense of popular government, Franklin's impatience with the Penn family and its allies in the proprietary party in Pennsylvania came to a boil. He joined with other members of Philadelphia's elite to propose replacing the colony's proprietor with a royal governor. Invective and character assassination reached new lows in the ensuing struggle, which showed that electoral politics in the colonies was changing from a comparatively decorous contest between genteel candidates to a no-holds-barred slugfest. Both parties presented themselves as allies of "the people" of Pennsylvania. Both skewered their opponents as tools of unscrupulous elites out to swindle ordinary citizens. Many religious dissenters feared that a royal government would impose Anglicanism, a threat they judged more dangerous than the continuing control of the colony by Penn's heirs and their associates. When Franklin and his party lost, more dramatically and decisively than in any other contest in his public life, he learned a lesson in the new politics of democracy. He came away wary of the idea of "rights" and convinced that Hume was right: politics rests on nothing more solid than opinion, which flutters in the slightest breeze. Principles are but negotiating points; positions are to be defended when possible and abandoned when expedient. The goal is to win elections, not to find God's will or follow natural law. That perspective enabled Franklin to accomplish a great deal, but it put him at odds—again and again—with the very different sensibility of John Adams.[86]

Franklin's experience of defeat in 1764 helped make him the most skillful and successful American negotiator of the late eighteenth century. It was a lesson Adams never learned. In 1763 he outlined the strategy he would follow his entire career: "I would quarrel with both parties, and with every individual of each, before I would subjugate my understanding, or prostitute my tongue or pen to either."[87] If it takes two people to make an argument, Adams was always ready to be one of those two; wherever three were gathered, he usually disagreed with both of the others. In Adams's own mind, such disagreements were the price of principle. In the minds of those who had to deal with him, such as Franklin, they signaled instead a cantankerous temperament that disqualified him from all situations in which compromise was required—in other words, from politics itself.

Political life in the colonies was growing ever more rancorous. Britain's program to bring the colonies under tighter control began taking shape with Grenville's declaration, in early 1765, of the Stamp Act, despite protests lodged by delegations of colonists. More to enforce the principle of parliamentary authority than to generate revenue, Grenville stipulated that newspapers, ships' clearance documents, and most other legal documents must be printed on stamped paper. Taxes were also to be imposed on goods ranging from dice, playing cards, and liquor licenses to calendars, advertisements, and pamphlets. Grenville's program extended beyond merchants to ordinary colonists, and the Stamp Act thus created, from the disparate interests of farmers, artisans, and merchants, a shared sense of outrage. Like the earlier Molasses Act and the Quartering Act, the Stamp Act was intended merely to defray the costs of maintaining a British army in the colonies. The funds raised would remain in the colonies, and the troops would be housed in uninhabited buildings, but important principles were involved. Parliament wanted to show its authority to impose taxes independent of the colonial assemblies, and it wanted to remind the colonists that they should help pay for their defense. In the course of the debates, Treasury Secretary Thomas Whately promulgated the idea of "virtual representation," reasoning that the colonists were as effectively represented in Parliament as were those thousands of Englishmen who inhabited cities or regions that lacked an MP.[88]

Many colonists rejected the underlying principle as well as the particular measures. James Otis, in his *Vindication of the British Colonies*, insisted again that the colonists' rights were underwritten by "the laws of God and nature as well as by the common law and by the constitution of the country." Nothing Parliament did could "shake one of the essential, natural, civil, or religious rights of the colonists." Although it might be said that Otis's reasoning demonstrates the colonists' confusion over the relation between the law of nature, rooted in God's unchanging will, and laws made by assemblies such as their own, or Parliament, it also shows that they did not yet distinguish between the two.[89] One of Otis's most potent arguments concerned the claim of virtual representation. Using that logic, Otis pointed out, in a phrase that was frequently repeated in the coming years, one might "as well prove that the British House of Commons in fact represent[s] all the people of the globe as those in America," a notion both "futile" and "absurd." Moreover, if major cities such as Manchester, Birmingham, and Sheffield lacked representatives, Otis continued, that fact did not vindicate Parliament's claim but instead showed the illegitimacy of the entire corrupt patchwork of British political practices.[90] From our perspective, it appears that Otis was reasoning toward a categorical denial of Parliament's authority to impose laws on the colonies. From his own perspective, however, he was trying instead merely to show that Parliament's legitimacy could not extend beyond natural law, "uniform and inviolable," a very different argument indeed. Thus Otis's surprising conclusion, that the colonies could not deny parliamentary authority but must instead "submit"—even though they might remonstrate—might strike us as inconsistent. Instead it demonstrates just how difficult it was for the colonists to face directly the consequences for their relations with Britain of the premises concerning self-government many of them had begun to embrace.

Some of Otis's contemporaries grasped the problem. A few, outraged by his apparent surrender of the principles he had proclaimed so forcefully in the writs-of-assistance case and restated in the early sections of his *Vindication*, denounced him as a coward who must have been corrupted—and perhaps bought off—by the ministry he had challenged. Others, though, understood that a frontal assault on Parliament would effectively deny the colonies membership in the British Empire, a step too drastic for loyal subjects of the king to contemplate. The central issue for Otis, as for many colonists aggrieved by the principle underlying the Stamp Act, was the issue of legal authority.

Daniel Dulany contended that because the power to tax lay with the "order of Democracy," colonial legislatures were the only authorities that could legitimately establish internal taxes.[91] The colonists had established in fact the principle that they would make their own laws in their own courtrooms and legislatures. Because they were not represented in Parliament, Parliament had no authority to legislate for them. Their commitment to self-government might seem inconsistent with loyalty to a king, but to eighteenth-century Americans it seemed merely to perpetuate their tradition of effective self-government within the overarching framework of the British monarchy. The assumption undergirding their lawmaking from the outset had been that their laws would not be "repugnant" to the crown. Since the mid-seventeenth century, and particularly since 1688, British authorities had protested the colonies' presumption to legislate for themselves, and the colonies in turn had protested the crown's presumption to regulate their lawmaking power. Although the two sides had bargained, and accommodations had been reached, the principle had never been resolved. The realization that the two claims to sovereignty were fundamentally incompatible had not yet become clear to them—any more than it had been clear to Locke or Sidney, whose ideas Otis invoked in his *Vindication*.[92]

Caught in a similar set of contradictions was Jonathan Mayhew. Having established himself as a spirited critic of corruption fifteen years earlier, he now faced criticism for failing to address the latest crisis. The Stamp Act carried Mayhew to a precipice. Artisans calling themselves the Loyal Nine spawned a wider colonial network, the Sons of Liberty, which brought together people unhappy with Britain for reasons ranging from economic to social to religious. In the middle of August 1765, a mob organized by the Loyal Nine hanged an effigy of the stamp distributor Andrew Oliver, destroyed a building Oliver was having built in Boston, and gathered threateningly in front of Oliver's house. The crowd did only minor damage before dispersing, but they made their point: Oliver resigned his post.

Tensions continued to mount. Articles published in Benjamin Edes's *Boston Gazette* intensified the colonists' uneasiness, and Mayhew delivered a sermon in which he yoked together "civil and religious liberty" and denounced the Stamp Act, which "almost every person of understanding in the plantations" considered an unjustifiable attack on the colonists' liberties. The luxurious home of Oliver's brother-in-law Thomas Hutchinson, then lieutenant governor, chief justice, and to many Bostonians a symbol of British corruption and oppression, was torched by a mob the day after Mayhew's sermon.[93] That riot disturbed Mayhew even more than the revolutionary implications of his *Vindication* unsettled Otis. Had his sermon incited the mob? Writing to Hutchinson in "deep sympathy," Mayhew insisted he had "cautioned [his] hearers very particularly against the abuses of liberty."[94] In May of 1766, celebrating repeal of the Stamp Act, Mayhew delivered another sermon, *The Snare Broken*, in which he underscored his passion for liberty and explained why such liberty requires obedience to legitimate authority. The protests had gotten out of hand. "The general discontent" precipitated by the Stamp Act led some to legitimate protest and others to "abominable excesses and outrages."[95]

Mayhew aligned his love of liberty with the lessons of the Bible, which showed that an angry God gave the Israelites a king "only because they had not sense and virtue enough to like a free commonwealth." After detailing his debts to classical writers and to Milton, Sidney, and Locke, Mayhew reminded his congregation that America had been settled as a refuge for those escaping cultures "weakened by luxury, debauchery, venality, intestine quarrels, or other vices," and so the colonies should remain. He pleaded for union, urging his listeners to "abstain from all party names" and instead "promote the common good, 'by love serving one another.'" Strikingly, however, immediately after granting the legitimacy—indeed, the necessity—of lawful resistance in the face of oppression, Mayhew forcefully denounced illegal or violent activity. His encomium to the existing order must have surprised his congregation. "Let all therefore now join with heart and hand in supporting the lawful, constitutional government over us in its just dignity and vigor; in supporting his majesty's representative, the civil magistrates, and all persons in authority, in the lawful exercise of their several offices." Anyone objecting was "no true friend of liberty."[96]

Renouncing one set of identities and embracing another was wrenching. Generations of Britons and Europeans had engaged in forms of more or less harmless, ritualized gestures of protest that challenged or sometimes briefly unbalanced the social order. But such carnivalesque popular festivals never threatened the power of priesthood, monarchy, or aristocracy. The organized resistance that began in the wake of the Stamp Act, by contrast, did not follow scripts of Charivari, "rough music," Pope's Day events, or Guy Fawkes Day festivities.[97] Although no one in America in 1765 imagined that the colonies would be fighting for their independence only a decade later, these protests grew from a developing political sensibility rather than a fleeting wish for catharsis.

No one felt more immediately or acutely the tensions between liberty and democracy on the one hand, and legitimate authority and social order on the other, than did Adams. When he moved back to Boston he followed the pattern he had set in Worcester. He joined a reading and discussion club called the Sodality to improve his mind as he established his legal practice. During the early months of 1765, when unrest concerning the Stamp Act was gathering force, his reading included not only legal theorists but also Rousseau's *Social Contract*. Adams's relation to Rousseau is more complex than most interpreters have acknowledged, and his pivotal contributions to the escalating conflicts beginning in 1765 reflect the powerful impact of Rousseau's ideas. Adams purchased four versions of the *Social Contract* during his lifetime, and his assessment of its value changed dramatically over the three decades after he first read it in the fall of 1765. Initially Rousseau offered him a model for self-government, which Adams linked with the writings of Sidney and Locke. Only after the French Revolution turned violent, and the idea of the general will was pressed into service to justify that violence, did Adams repudiate Rousseau.

In light of the New England traditions of independent congregations and town meetings seeking to work through conflict to a shared consensus about God's will and the public good, the most beguiling feature of Rousseau's *Social Contract* was the general will. Just as New Englanders from the outset had expelled those unwilling to abide by their own strict discipline, so Rousseau's admission that sometimes people must be "forced to be free" showed his awareness that self-governing communities require discipline to preserve the common good. Whenever possible, consensus should emerge from instruction and discussion, but dissent and assertions of individual will could not be allowed to undermine comity. Not surprisingly, when Adams first read the *Social Contract* in 1765, he found Rousseau compelling.

The affinities between Adams and Rousseau, which Adams stridently repudiated when the Terror erupted, are first apparent in the articles that Adams wrote and rewrote in the summer and fall of 1765, at the time his first child was born and he first read the *Social Contract*. Originally published anonymously in the *Boston Gazette* and, when reprinted in London, attributed to Jeremiah Gridley, who had organized the Sodality, *A Dissertation on the Canon and Feudal Law* marked Adams's auspicious entry into public discourse. "Wherever a general knowledge and sensibility have prevailed among the people," Adams began, "arbitrary government and every kind of oppression have lessened and disappeared in proportion." When men's aspiration to power, unproblematic if "founded in benevolence, and cherished by knowledge," is accompanied by freedom, it stimulates an admirable aspiration to independence, and when harnessed by "equity and reason," it can bring out the best of man's "exalted soul." When exercised by malevolent monarchies and aristocracies in arbitrary government, by contrast, that love of power manifests itself in corruption and oppression.[98]

The Stamp Act, which Adams mentioned only in his final paragraph but which nevertheless hovered over his entire argument, endangered liberty because it threatened the free flow of information. As the "wicked confederacy" of priests and nobles embodied in "the Canon and Feudal law" enslaved the mediaeval mind, so Britain now aimed to restrict the publication of books, periodicals, and pamphlets in the colonies. Adams's first publication thus drew together his Puritan forbears' aversion to Catholic and Anglican hierarchy, his New England small farmer's hatred of a landed aristocracy, and his Protestant- and Enlightenment-inspired enthusiasm for an educated reading public and democratic citizenry that made up its own mind.[99] Adams quoted both Rousseau and the Scottish philosopher Henry Home, Lord Kames, to bolster his case. Rousseau called the union of episcopal and feudal law the "most iniquitous and absurd form of government by which human nature was so shamefully degraded"; Kames denounced it as "contradictory to all the principles which govern mankind." Adams conceded that his Puritan ancestors had embraced "a mild limited monarchy," but they abhorred the theory and practice of absolutism. They believed that "popular powers must be placed as a guard, a control, a balance, to the powers of the monarch and the priest, in every government." Otherwise power degenerates, as it had done under the Stuarts, into a regime "of sin, the whore of Babylon, the mystery of iniquity, a great and detestable system of fraud, violence, and usurpation."[100]

Education, Adams explained, provided the bulwark against absolutism. Ranging from the Bay Colony's early founding and its consistent support for higher education at Harvard to the requirement that every town should provide a grammar school, the Puritans had assured that "the education of all ranks of people was made the care and expense of the public, in a manner that I believe has been unknown to any other people ancient or modern." Visitors to New England, Adams boasted, agreed "that they have never seen so much knowledge and civility among the common people in any part of the world." Now those traditions were under siege. A party of royal agents and Anglicans, "missionaries of ignorance, foppery, servility, and slavery," criticized schools as an unnecessary expense imposed by the poor on the rich. Because New Englanders understood that "liberty cannot be preserved without a general knowledge among the people," the threat—nothing less than "a direct and formal design on foot, to enslave all America"—had been met by popular resistance.[101]

Adams offered a version of the argument for progressive taxation familiar from the work of Puritans in England and New England and from the writings of Harrington, Sidney, Locke, Montesquieu, and Rousseau. Adams reasoned that "the preservation of the means of knowledge among the lowest ranks, is of more importance to the public than all the property of all the rich men in the country." He argued that "the rich ought undoubtedly to contribute" to public education "in the same proportion as to all other public burdens, i.e. in proportion to their wealth." Since the security of property depends on government enforcing the law, those with the most property should contribute proportionately larger amounts to the institutions that sustain public order, the most fundamental of which are schools.[102]

Adams invoked the traditions of English liberty, from Magna Carta through regicide and the installation of William of Orange. Tyranny had always inspired resistance, even rebellion, among Englishmen. Now that a league of royal officials was conspiring to treat Americans "like servants, nay, more like slaves," the colonists had to defend themselves. Adams spoke in the languages of ancient republican virtue, Protestant resistance, and Enlightenment rationalism. Decades before Immanuel Kant declared the anthem of the Enlightenment, "*Sapere aude*," or "Dare to know," Adams wrote, with even greater audacity, "Let us dare to read, think, speak, and write." Kant distinguished between the freedom to think and the obligation to obey that charted the distinctive trajectory (and limits) of the German Enlightenment. Adams, by contrast, urged his compatriots not only to think for themselves but also to sustain a lively public sphere of democratic discourse, disseminating and openly discussing their ideas in town meetings, pamphlets, and periodicals. For a century and a half, he observed, that had been the New England way.[103]

Adams distinguished his preferred discursive mode from that prevailing in England. Whereas English writers marshaled "reason, imagination, wit, passion, senses, and all" in the "satire and invective" they hurled against the corruption of "vile and futile fellows who sometimes get into place and power," Americans could do better. The spirit of resistance, without a basis in understanding, would be no better than the useless and "brutal rage" apparent in much English protest. Instead New Englanders should cherish—and defend from attack—all "the means of knowledge" at their disposal, taking particular care to study the law of nature and "the grounds and principles of government, ecclesiastical and civil." Studying ancient and modern history would show that their British ancestors' defense of the "inherent rights of mankind" against "kings and cruel priests" was equal to the valor of Greek and Roman heroes.[104]

Not satisfied with the vulgar, often obscene critiques of English and French satirists and cartoonists, Adams expected from his compatriots protests more attuned to Enlightenment ideals of reason than to the Grub Street hacks or Parisian scandalmongers whom historians have made familiar in recent decades. "Let the public disputations become researches into the grounds and nature and ends of government." Resistance should spread by engaging ordinary people in political debate, not by ridiculing individual officials. Open public discourse should be the means "of impressing on the tender mind, and of spreading and distributing far and wide, the ideas of right and the sensations of freedom." If "every sluice of knowledge" were "opened and set a-flowing," then colonists facing tyranny would produce their own heroes in the great tradition of the "Vanes, Seldens, Miltons, Nedhams, Harringtons, Sidneys, Locks [*sic*]."[105]

The Stamp Act was an attack on ideas. The most insidious of its features, Adams concluded, lay hidden beneath the veil of Parliament's authority to tax the colonies. Designed "to strip us in great measure of the means of knowledge, by loading the press, the colleges, and even an Almanack and a newspaper, with restraints and duties," this measure represented only the thin edge of a broader and more dangerous campaign to come. England aimed to introduce nothing less than "the inequalities and dependencies of the feudal system, by taking from the poorer sort of people all their little subsistence, and conferring it on a set of stamp officers, distributors, and their deputies." England would replace the colonists' hardy culture of self-government with its own corrupted and corrupting politics and religion.[106]

The New Englander whom Adams credited with exposing aristocratic and Anglican subversion was the minister who shaped his own convictions, Jonathan Mayhew. Adams's *Dissertation* explains why he later wrote, in frequently quoted letters to Thomas Jefferson in 1815 and Hezekiah Niles in 1818, that the American Revolution "was in the minds of the people, and this was effected, from 1760 to 1775, in the course of fifteen years before a drop of blood was shed at Lexington." That "radical change" occurred because of changes in the colonists' "religious sentiments of their duties and obligations." In that process, which forced them to rethink their role in the British Empire, Mayhew figured prominently.[107] When Adams linked the activities of the Anglican Society for the Propagation of the Gospel to those of officials of the British army, navy, and customs houses, he showed the religious as well as the political and economic dimensions of the threat. Not all colonists judged those dangers equally significant. New Englanders' anxieties about creeping Anglicanism drew on wider and older fears of Catholicism, and the colonists' anxieties about customs officers and the proposed collectors of duties on stamps echoed English Whigs' persistent complaints about corruption. Adams's *Dissertation* illustrates clearly the colonists' inclination to blend together vocabularies and conceptual frameworks that might seem incongruous or inconsistent. Although unusual in his erudition, Adams was typical in his eclecticism.[108]

Later in 1765, which Adams was to describe as "the most remarkable Year of my Life," he was chosen by the people of Braintree as part of a committee to provide instructions for the town's representative to the Massachusetts General Court.[109] The instructions Adams drafted reflect the convictions underlying the colonists' resistance to the Stamp Act, their deliberate decision to blend high principles with hardheaded, practical considerations, and the reasons why they prized their representative institutions. The town of Braintree instructed its elected representative, Ebenezer Thayer, to oppose the Stamp Act and make clear to the king's agents the colonists' reasons for resisting. The first was economic. Money was scarce in the colonies, a problem that had already sparked considerable unrest and prompted British officials' efforts to clamp down on the assemblies' attempts to expand the money supply. In that context, additional taxes would "drain the country of its cash, strip multitudes of the poorer people of all their property, and reduce them to absolute beggary."[110]

A second reason loomed even larger. Speaking for all of Braintree's freemen, Adams deemed the tax "unconstitutional." The Stamp Act ran contrary to the long-standing principle, originating in Magna Carta and confirmed in common-law practice ever since, that no tax could be imposed, and no property seized, without popular consent. "No taxation without representation" was already a familiar phrase, common in subjugated Ireland for at least a generation. Adams pointed out the obvious: "We are not represented" in Parliament "in any sense, unless it be by a Fiction of Law." Implicit in that observation was a striking and revealing contrast: whereas Braintree had no voice in Parliament, its townspeople did indeed elect their own representative to the General Court of Massachusetts. They could—and often did—let him know what they thought he should do.

Finally, the Stamp Act outraged Braintree's people because it was to be enforced through courts of admiralty, in which judges ruled without juries. Even worse, these appointed officials would stand to profit from convictions because they would be rewarded with property seized from offenders. Both Magna Carta and common-law practice, Adams protested, prohibited the taking of an individual's property except "by lawful judgment of his peers." Expanding the reach of admiralty courts to enforce the unwise and unjust Stamp Act would expand the powers of appointed officials. Facing a "weak or wicked man for a judge," the "sordid and forlorn" colonists would become the "slaves of a slave of the servant of a minister of state." Combining the threat of impoverishment, the fact of unconstitutionality, and the likelihood of corruption, Adams the ambitious attorney believed he had constructed an irrefutable case against the crown.[111]

The most important feature of that case, however, is easy to overlook. The freemen of Braintree did not offer their objections primarily on the basis of calculating their individual self-interest. Instead they deliberated in town meeting, constituted a committee, selected its members, and then met again to discuss and approve its work. That multistep procedure reflected the shared assumptions of eighteenth-century Americans. To be sure, deliberations within assemblies such as the town meeting of Braintree reflected—indeed, took for granted—differences of age, gender, wealth, prestige, and other less obvious but decisive qualities such as wisdom and virtue as well as self-confidence and eloquence. Adams himself, however, was a young attorney who possessed neither wealth nor prestige. The son of a former deacon and selectman, he was hardly unknown, but it was the force of his personality and the persuasive power of his arguments, not the small farm he had inherited, that earned the young man the job of writing the first draft of the Braintree Instructions. Neither the wealthiest members of the town nor their minister nor their elected representative determined those instructions, which emerged from the procedures of democratic deliberation. Braintree understood that Ebenezer Thayer could no more decide how the General Court would vote than any single individual could decide how the town meeting would vote. Just as the Braintree Instructions moved from fears of economic ruin to invocations of the common good, so all the decisions of these years involved negotiating between particular interests and more abstract but nevertheless genuine—and constitutive—religious, political, and moral convictions.

The animating spirit of the American Revolution emerged from this dynamic, as formally elected representatives and informal, unelected participants in public discourse such as ministers, writers of pamphlets, and leaders of mobs all pushed and pulled public opinion toward an awareness that the American colonies had different interests and ideals from those who ruled Britain. One striking manifestation of this change came the next year, when construction began on the first public gallery for viewing the debates in the Massachusetts General Court, a process that had previously occurred behind closed doors. Pennsylvania followed in 1770, and the other colonies eventually fell in line. This symbolic change indicated the ways in which older patterns of deference and hierarchy were being put under new strains as the decisions of the king and Parliament came to be scrutinized more closely and their authority challenged more openly.

The colonists had grown accustomed to making their own laws through institutions they created and controlled. When threatened, they took steps to defend their democratic practices. The links connecting representatives to the electorate had always been tighter in the colonial assemblies than between members of Parliament, who were thought to represent the nation rather than a particular constituency, and the handful of voters who selected them. The colonies were shifting away from British practice and toward the idea that representatives should represent those who elected them. How to strike a balance between instructing delegates and respecting their independent judgment, however, remained unclear. Not only were representatives expected to look out for the interests of their constituents; they were also obliged to seek the common good.[112]

Repeal of the Stamp Act on March 18, 1766 gave the colonists a rich but fleeting sense of satisfaction. Almost immediately Parliament passed the Declaratory Act, reasserting its power to enact laws for the colonies "in all cases whatsoever." Declaring that authority proved easier than enforcing it. Writing anonymously as "the Earl of Clarendon," Adams observed that the people, "even to the lowest Ranks," had become notably "attentive to their liberties" and "determined to defend them." In response to British outrages, "the Presses have every where groaned; and the Pulpits have thundered." In consequence "Their Counties, Towns, and even private Clubs and Sodalities, have voted and determined; their Merchants have Resolved; the united Colonies have Remonstrated." As a result of such widespread activities, precisely what Adams had recommended in his *Dissertation* the preceding year, British officials "have every where trembled, and all their little Tools and Creatures have been afraid to speak, and ashamed to be seen."[113]

Writing in response to an English author who defended the Stamp Act and asserted Parliament's absolute authority over the colonies, Adams as "Clarendon" replied that the colonists' slumbering devotion to liberty had been awakened. The legitimate role of king and Parliament in colonial affairs had previously been taken for granted. The people of New England now understood the principle first articulated by the Levellers in the 1640s. The English Constitution was premised neither on the divine right of kings nor on the notion that "a few nobles or rich commonerss have the right to inherit the earth." It stood on the premise, Adams declared, "that the meanest and lowest of the people are by the unalterable, indefeasible laws of God and nature, as well entitled to the benefit of the air to breathe, light to see, food to eat, and clothes to wear, as the nobles or the king. All men are born equal." For that reason "popular power" was located in the legislature.

Adams explained how and why representation emerged, following closely not only the arguments of the Levellers but also those of John Wise in the 1710s, Elisha Williams in the 1740s, and Jonathan Mayhew in the 1760s. The power of legislation originally rested in "the universal and immediate suffrage of the people." Only when the population grew too large did the "expedient which we call a representation" come into being. Authority remains with ordinary citizens, who choose their representatives and reserve the power to instruct those representatives how to vote, just as Braintree had done, and reelect them or replace them with "wiser" and "better" representatives. The words of Adams's Puritan ancestors reverberated in his own.

Adams as "Clarendon" concluded by reflecting on the standard conception of the British monarchy as a "mixture of the three forms of government." It was thought to combine the best features of each, namely "the monarchical splendor, the aristocratical independency, and the democratical freedom." But recent developments had shown that the first two had been overvalued and the last underappreciated. "Popular power," manifesting itself in colonial assemblies and juries, provides "the heart and the lungs" of government. Without them "the body must die." Were the people to lose control of legislation or the courts, the consequence would be absolute monarchy or oligarchy. The purpose of the English Constitution was to secure the welfare of the people through representative assemblies and jury trials. Britons enjoyed no other defense against "being ridden like horses, fleeced like sheep, worked like cattle, and fed and clothed like swine and hounds." Resistance to the Stamp Act had reminded New Englanders that their colonies were founded by dissenters fleeing the tyranny of kings and priests. Now their heirs, possessing a "radical sense of liberty, and the highest reverence for virtue," were determined to protect their "whole system of popular power."[114]

If the crown's officers trembled when the colonial presses groaned, they also took steps to shore up their power. Recognizing Adams as the rabble-rouser he was becoming, and reverting to the only means at his disposal, Massachusetts governor Bernard offered Adams a position in the very admiralty courts he savaged in the Braintree Instructions. Adams knew corruption when he smelled it. Explaining his decision to refuse the offer, he wrote that he could not be "under any restraints, or Obligations of Gratitude to the Government for any of their favours." Nor would he participate in a "System, wholly inconsistent with all my Ideas of Right, Justice and Policy."[115] Such defiance was becoming contagious.

The Stamp Act transmuted squabbling colonies into a united body. Franklin's slogan from the time of the Albany Congress, "Join or die," which had persuaded few in 1754, now began appearing in newspapers from New Hampshire to Virginia. Patrick Henry's fiery speech in the Virginia House of Burgesses, denying Parliament's authority to counter the colonists' own representative bodies, was reprinted throughout the colonies. Even though the Virginia legislature had rejected it as too extreme, it was usually presented in the press, and received by readers, as if it had been adopted. Other colonies passed spirited declarations of democratic principles, challenging Parliament's authority to impose taxes not approved by the colonists' own elected representatives, meeting in their own legislative assemblies.

Still in England on his mission to replace Pennsylvania's proprietors with a royal governor, Franklin was caught in the furor over the Stamp Act. A friend of Hutchinson and an enemy of mobs, he was appalled by Boston's riots and fearful that his own new home in Philadelphia might be a target because he had urged the colonists to comply with the Stamp Act. The venom directed at Franklin and his newspapers in Philadelphia, New York, and Charleston came as a surprise. The new British ministry of Lord Rockingham wanted a solution. As Parliament weighed its options, Franklin was summoned to explain the colonists' perspective. In a four-hour examination, a cautious Franklin shrewdly balanced reassurances about the colonists' continuing loyalty to the king against warnings that Parliament's authority was growing precarious. Franklin asserted the distinction, soon popular in the colonies from John Dickinson's *Letters from a Farmer in Pennsylvania*, that regulation of colonial commerce (and thus "external" taxes on trade) remained acceptable. To "internal taxes," by contrast, the colonies would submit only if levied by their own legislatures. Franklin reported that his fellow Americans—and it is striking that these were the years in which English publications began referring to the colonists rather than American Indians as "Americans," and colonists such as Adams began self-consciously assuming that identity—had grown accustomed to ordering their own affairs through their own institutions of government.[116] Franklin was asked pointedly how the colonists could claim the authority to tax themselves when the Declaration of Rights explicitly stipulated that only Parliament possessed that right. His reply raised the stakes: "The Colonies are not supposed to be within the realm; they have assemblies of their own, which are their parliaments."[117] Franklin's remarks before Parliament, published in London and in American newspapers, restored his reputation in the colonies.

Like Adams's *Dissertation*, Franklin's defense of colonial self-government helped bring to consciousness an emerging democratic sensibility even as the colonists' loyalty to George III persisted. Both Adams and Franklin understood the deep roots of Americans' preoccupation with self-government and grasped its implications. As the measures known as the Townshend Acts were being formulated in England, Franklin explained to his Scottish friend Lord Kames why British-American relations were unraveling so rapidly. Although no one had planned or expected it, the reason was democracy. Parliament was operating with the mistaken assumption that because

England had founded the colonies, it retained authority over them. Many colonies, Franklin observed, were "planted at the Expense of private Adventurers" such as William Penn and others like him. Settlers, voluntarily remaining British subjects, established communities on lands they bought from the Indians. "Parliament had no hand in their Settlement, was never so much as consulted about their Constitution, and took no kind of Notice of them till many Years after they were established." Franklin claimed that Parliament never tried to "meddle with the Government" of the colonies until recently. Colonial laws were made "by their Assemblies or little Parliaments"; the assent of the king was assumed rather than sought. From their own perspective, then, the colonies were "separate little States," in principle subject to the king but in fact governing themselves. When Britons referred to the "*Sovereignty of Parliament*, and the *Sovereignty of this Nation* over the Colonies," the colonists contested the claim on the basis of long-standing, customary practice. Given the colonies' natural advantages and rapid growth, Franklin predicted they "must become a great Country, populous and mighty," fully able to "shake off any Shackles that may be impos'd." Britain's recklessness would only "sour their Tempers" and "hasten their final Revolt." Over a century of experience had given Americans an ineradicable sense of themselves as a people who made their own laws through their own representative institutions. No measures concocted by British ministers could shake that conviction or alter that fact.[118]

The Townshend Acts merely exacerbated these tensions. Scattered noncompliance with imperial regulations congealed into widespread protests against the quartering of British troops and the adoption of nonimportation agreements. Boycotts of British goods crippled trade. Dickinson's *Letters* were reprinted throughout the colonies in newspapers and as pamphlets. The Massachusetts General Court endorsed Samuel Adams's Circular Letter, denying the king the right to appoint colonial officials and Parliament the right to raise revenues in the colonies. While other colonies were deciding whether to follow suit, Wills Hill, the 1st Earl of Hillsborough, rashly ordered colonial governors to dissolve the assemblies.

The colonies exploded. The Massachusetts General Court denied that England had any authority whatsoever in the colonies. Members of Governor Bernard's administration had seen the confrontation coming months before. According to Thomas Hutchinson, Massachusetts town meetings had deteriorated into "an absolute democracy," an inevitable result of the promiscuous mingling of ordinary people with those Hutchinson considered their superiors.[119] A letter from General Thomas Gage to Hillsborough, written in Boston and dated October 31, 1768, was published in newspapers from

Boston and Providence to Georgia in the spring of 1769. Gage was furious that the unruly people of Massachusetts had thwarted all of Governor Bernard's reasonable attempts to find housing for British troops. He too identified the problem as democracy. Complaining that the governor lacked the leverage necessary to execute the law, Gage contended that "there is no government in Boston." The people simply did as they pleased because, in Gage's words, "the constitution of this province leans so much to the side of democracy, that the Governor has not the powers to remedy the disorders which happen in it."[120] From London, where Franklin observed the deteriorating relations between the colonies and England, and from Boston, where Hutchinson and Gage described the turmoil around them, the problem looked the same: Americans had grown accustomed to self-government, and Britain lacked the power to loosen their commitment.[121]

Resistance took multiple forms. Merchants complained about restraints on their trade. Landowners, both small and large, complained about illegitimate taxes not authorized by their elected representatives. In regions stretching from the frontiers that would become Vermont and upstate New York to the backwoods of North Carolina, tenants and squatters who worked the land, and wanted to own it, advanced claims against absentee landlords. From the richest to the poorest, from the biggest towns to the remotest regions, colonists of diverse backgrounds and aspirations found themselves coming together. Yet the gears did not always mesh. Some prosperous colonists resented the presumption of landless upstarts trumpeting their rights. Tenants and artisans bristled at efforts to rein in their political mobilization. Attempts to enforce nonimportation agreements, through crowd actions directed against suspected violators, threatened to transform peaceful boycotts into vigilante violence. Samuel Adams, one of the favorite writers and spokesmen of the Boston crowd, worried that such spontaneous upsurges of violence might prove counterproductive. Writing as "Populus" in the *Boston Gazette*, Adams urged caution: "NO MOBS—NO CONFUSIONS—NO TUMULTS."[122] Unless popular resentments were harnessed into a politically effective force, violence might prove as futile as most forms of resistance across the Atlantic. Symbolic gestures of protest, no matter how satisfying in the short run, would no longer suffice.

On the frontier, the same rebellious spirit manifested itself in tenant revolts that sometimes turned against native peoples. William Johnson, the English official in charge of Indian relations, wrote to London that settlers along the frontier "have a hatred for, ill treat, Rob and frequently murder the Indians." Such unruly behavior Johnson attributed to the backcountry colonists' overall attitude, not only toward Indians but toward all authority. They "are in general a lawless set of People, as fond of independency" as the Indians themselves, distrustful of government "owing to ignorance, prejudice, democratical principles, & their remote situation." More than a century before Frederick Jackson Turner linked the frontier with self-government, British officials likewise traced backwoods' colonists' unruliness to their "democratical principles."[123]

Two of the most violent crowd actions occurred in Boston early in 1770. Opposition to standing armies had long been a staple of Whig ideology. The troops sent to enforce customs regulations remained even after the Stamp Act had been repealed, and they were more than a symbolic irritant because they competed for part-time jobs with residents. Political and economic tensions fed each other. An insult sparked a fight, which led to a mob, which gathered in front of the Boston Customs House and began taunting and throwing sticks or snowballs at the soldiers. A frightened soldier slipped, fired his musket, and set off the Boston Massacre, in which five townspeople were killed and six wounded.

John Adams and Josiah Quincy accepted the job of defending the accused soldiers. Invoking the principle that every defendant deserves his day in court, Adams and Quincy could take the high ground and also satisfy their ambition to establish themselves as attorneys. Adams later claimed that defending the accused had cost him support in Boston, but even the Sons of Liberty agreed that showing respect for law bolstered their standing.[124] In his concluding remarks at the trial, Adams invoked Sidney's magisterial defense of the law in his *Discourses*, quoting the passage in which Sidney wrote that "no passion can disturb" the law, which "commands that which is good, and punishes evil in all whether rich or poor, high or low." The law, Adams concluded, remains equally unmoved by prisoners' "cries and lamentations" and "deaf as an adder to the clamours of the populace." Adams defended the rule of law while endorsing Sidney's resistance, distancing himself from this particular crowd action while embracing its larger program. From the perspective of the Sons of Liberty, devotion to law required them to defy Britain's illegal attempt to impose its will without the colonies' consent.[125]

The Boston Massacre became a treasured memory for New England. Sermons, speeches, and pamphlets commemorated the event and its martyrs, including Crispus Attucks, a runaway slave from nearby Framingham. Among those memorials was an address delivered by the Boston physician Joseph Warren; its themes indicate the multiple sources on which New Englanders drew as they moved unknowingly toward independence. "That Man is formed for *social life*," Warren observed, is the "wise and generous principle which actuated the first founders of civil government." Securing the "*strength and security* of all" is the purpose of government, and when well devised it is "one of the richest Blessings to mankind, and ought to be held in the highest veneration." But of course things did not always go well. Rome declined when autonomous citizens became "contented slaves" who forgot what Warren wanted his listeners always to remember: "HAPPINESS DEPENDS ON A VIRTUOUS AND UNSHAKEN ATTACHMENT TO A FREE CONSTITUTION." Just that attachment had driven the colony's founders across the Atlantic.

The English Constitution, Warren noted, was "a happy compound" of the three standard forms, monarchy, aristocracy, and democracy. Without the consent of all three, no legislation could be approved. Laws passed for raising taxes could be proposed only in the House of Commons in Britain or the House of Representatives in Massachusetts. Were the "*late acts of the British parliament for taxing America*" constitutional? Members of the House of Commons were neither "the people of this province" nor elected by them, so "nothing done by *them* can be said to be done by the democratic branch of our constitution." For that reason their will did not bind the colonists.[126] Like Adams and Mayhew before him, Warren drew on scripture, classical history, republican theory, and Sidney and Locke's social contract theory to establish the colonists' right of resistance. Without a native aristocracy, the colonies were governed by their own representative assemblies. The king's representatives, the governor and his council, lacked the legitimacy (and the power) to enforce Parliament's decrees.

In the two years after the Boston Massacre, despite his misgivings about having defended the accused soldiers, Adams found himself in ever greater demand. He prospered as an attorney and remained active politically. He published less, but he recorded his thoughts on democracy, on the eve of the American Revolution, in the notes for a speech in his diary in 1772. "There is no king or queen bee," Adams wrote, "distinguished from all others by size or figure or beauty and variety of colors, in the human hive," and no evidence, no "revelation from heaven," that anyone enjoys "any divine communication to govern his fellow men." Instead nature "throws us all into the world equal and alike." Given that equality, all should enjoy equal liberty, the preservation of which "depends upon the intellectual and moral character of the people. As long as knowledge and virtue are diffused generally among the body of a nation, it is impossible they should be enslaved."[127] Even champions of popular government, according to Adams, must acknowledge that no man can be trusted with power sufficient to endanger the people's liberty. Designing the institutional mechanics and sustaining the ethical commitment necessary to elevate "the united power of the multitude" from mob action to democratic deliberation would occupy Adams the rest of his life. His fears always clouded his hopes.[128]

A sign of the respect Adams had earned in Massachusetts came in 1772, when Governor Thomas Hutchinson declared that Parliament must retain complete authority over the colony and that the governor's salary henceforth would be paid by the crown, not by the colony itself. Although not yet elected a member of the General Court, Adams was selected to write the official reply to Hutchinson. In a brief that ranged from Magna Carta to 1689, Adams challenged the historical basis of the governor's claim.[129] To nail down his argument—and embarrass his adversary, whom he loathed as one of the worst of the "miniature infinitessimal deities" who sought to corrupt American politics[130]—Adams added evidence taken from Hutchinson's own history of Massachusetts. As Hutchinson himself put it, Massachusetts was established by a compact in which the founders agreed "*to be governed by Laws made by themselves*." Hutchinson further noted that the laws of England were "bounded within the four Seas, *and did not reach America*." There was general agreement that "Acts of Parliament had no other Force, than what they derived from Acts made by the General Court."[131] Over and over, quoting either Hutchinson or those on whom his history depended, Adams hammered home his argument. His coup de grace also deployed Hutchinson's own words. Hutchinson had acknowledged that he knew "no Line that can be drawn between the Supreme Authority of Parliament and the total Independence of the Colonies." Adams upended Hutchinson's conclusion: if forced to choose between independence and acceptance of Parliament's "absolute uncontrouled Supreme Power," Massachusetts knew its course.[132]

Adams's effort earned him widespread acclaim. In consequence he was chosen to reply to another of Hutchinson's charges, that the town of Boston was guilty of "unwarrantable" defiance to British authority. Hutchinson's claim would reduce the people's representative assembly, which had governed Massachusetts from the outset, to a "mere Phantom; limited, controuled, superceded and nullified at the Will of another."[133] The people of Massachusetts appreciated the logic of Adams's taunting replies to the governor; British authorities were outraged. Even after the repeal of the Townshend Acts—except the tax on tea—the colonial committees of correspondence redoubled their efforts to elicit popular resistance.

Perhaps just a straw in the wind, a decision reached at the oldest college in Britain's colonies illustrated the rising tide of popular sentiment. Only a tiny minority of Americans in the eighteenth century earned a college degree at one of the handful of colonial institutions of higher learning. Many graduates of Harvard College, including John Adams, Samuel Adams, and Joseph

Warren, hailed from families of distinctly modest means. Yet college graduates typically saw themselves—and were seen by others—as constituting an elite. So when Harvard decided, in 1773, to abandon its tradition of ranking each student according to his social standing, it registered the changing cultural climate. Such bows to European convention no longer suited a culture self-consciously committed to eradicating the remnants of feudal and aristocratic hierarchies. If forms of privilege were to survive, they would rest on a basis different from inheritance. Eventually, after the outbreak of the French Revolution, Adams would have reason to wonder whether his refutation of Hutchinson had carried him further than he should have gone.[134]

The democratic current was rising fast. Even Franklin, no friend of disorder and at this stage certainly no champion of independence, found himself carried along by it. In an article published in London in 1770, he pointed out that tyrants had typically begun abridging citizens' rights by beginning "with the more distant Parts." If such measures worked in America, England itself might become subject to the "Iron Rod." Like Adams defending British soldiers, Franklin concluded with words from Sidney's *Discourse on Government*: "Asiatic Slaves usually pay such Tributes as are imposed on them. We own none but what we freely give, none is or can be imposed on us, unless by ourselves." If the colonists renounced the principle of self-government, they would share the "shameful misery" endured by slaves. Unless England changed its course, precious liberties would soon be under siege at home as well.[135]

Yet Franklin harbored hope that not only George III but also his government sought the best for the colonies. The problem lay only with the corrupt officials they had placed in America, the continent-wide contingent of fools and knaves that Franklin conjured up in his imagination by extrapolating from his experiences with the proprietors in Pennsylvania. In 1772 Franklin came into possession of letters written by Adams's nemesis (then lieutenant governor) Hutchinson to Treasury Secretary Whately. The letters crackled with contempt for the colonists and called for decisive disciplinary action. To Franklin, the letters showed that officials such as Hutchinson were systematically misinforming British authorities. He sent them to Massachusetts for publication in the belief that the public would come to see things his way.

Franklin miscalculated. Instead of directing the anger of Massachusetts against Hutchinson, whom they already loathed, the letters turned New England against the crown itself. To the Boston Committee of Correspondence, the letters disclosed "the plot that has been laid for us by our malicious and invidious enemies." Again invective fed invective, and the growing rage found expression on December 16, 1773, when colonists masquerading as

Indians dumped a shipload of English tea into Boston harbor.[136] The English press tore into Franklin. Just as news of the Boston Tea Party was reaching England, Franklin was scheduled to address the Privy Council, in his capacity as agent of Massachusetts, to present a petition for redress of grievances. The timing could not have been worse. Franklin was forced to endure an hour-long tongue-lashing. Solicitor General Alexander Wedderburn called him "the first mover and prime conductor" of colonial unrest, a charlatan who had "forfeited all the respect of societies and of men." When Franklin finally exited the Whitehall room in which this ritual humiliation was enacted, a room known as the Cockpit, he had been transformed from England's best friend in the colonies to one of its worst enemies. By the end of that year, there would be few candidates for the former title south of Quebec and countless colonists contending for the latter.[137]

The swift and stern English reply to the Boston Tea Party startled the colonists. The Coercive Acts (also known as the Intolerable Acts) of 1774 closed Boston harbor, annulled the Massachusetts charter, and prohibited the calling of town meetings for any purpose other than the annual election of officials. The crown intended by this show of force to snuff out New England's impudence, but this time it was the king's advisers who miscalculated. Gouverneur Morris, a New Yorker of English aristocratic birth and inclinations, captured the change in a letter of May 20, 1774: "The mob begin to think and to reason. Poor reptiles! It is with them a vernal morning; they are struggling to cast off their winter's slough, they bask in the sunshine, and ere noon they will bite, depend upon it." Colonial rabble-rousers had failed to unite the colonies; the Coercive Acts just might do it. Unless the dispute was resolved, "we shall be under the domination of a riotous mob." Some of Morris's wealthy friends were beginning to see, in the spring and summer of 1774, that only by stepping forward to lead the rebellion could they avoid being submerged by it. Eventually Morris too sided with independence, and by the end of the struggle he had made his peace with a form of popular government.[138] Trying to isolate rebellious Massachusetts only provoked the other colonies to identify with aggrieved New England. When the royal governor dissolved the Massachusetts General Court in Boston, it defiantly reconstituted itself in Salem. The colonial response to the Intolerable Acts proved as decisive as the decrees themselves. From New England through New York and Pennsylvania to the southern colonies, previously squabbling factions put aside their differences.

Equally inflammatory was the Quebec Act, which established an English government in the colony recently acquired from France and infuriated England's other North American colonists. If the end of the Seven Years War had eased colonists' concern about France, the Quebec Act reawakened their slumbering paranoia about creeping Catholicism. A crown that countenanced popery and oligarchy, and renounced elections and jury trials, was careening toward absolutism. Concerns about an Anglican threat to dissenting Protestants returned. Serious as the Coercive Acts were, the danger latent in the Quebec Act loomed at least as large, and one source of anxiety fed another.[139]

On September 5, 1774, delegates gathered in Philadelphia from every colony but Georgia in the First Continental Congress. They established a Continental Association to coordinate their response and agreed to implement immediate nonimportation and eventual nonexportation if Parliament did not rescind the Intolerable Acts. Fearing that all colonial institutions of self-government might now be disbanded, as the Massachusetts legislature had been, the Congress authorized the creation of town and county Committees of Inspection to mobilize support for the embargo on British goods and engage more people in politics. In New England such committees flowed naturally from the practice of town meetings. In colonies such as New Jersey, New York, Maryland, and South Carolina, they helped loosen the increasingly firm grip that large landowners had held on power, and they expanded the number of people engaged in public life.

The significance of this reshuffling of American power, which might have led (and eventually did lead) to sharp conflicts within each of the colonies, was obscured by the focus on Britain. In the words of British observer Ambrose Serle, the dominance of the old families was diminishing everywhere, even in New York. Such families "have been long in a gradual Decay," Serle wrote in his journal, and "perhaps a new arrangement of political affairs may leave them wholly extinct." At the time, however, all such tensions, including "jealousies naturally arising from the variety of private interests in the Planter, the Merchant, and the Mechanic," were overshadowed by the colonists' obsessive concern with British authority.[140] With characteristic flair, the Virginian Patrick Henry announced the result of the Intolerable Acts and the colonists' response: "All government is dissolved," Henry proclaimed; the colonies were once again "in a state of nature." Starting with clean slates, they would build anew. "The distinctions between Virginians, Pennsylvanians, New Yorkers, and New Englanders are no more. I am not a Virginian but an American."[141] Even acknowledging Henry's hyperbole, the difference from the Albany gathering of 1754 was palpable: the First Continental Congress helped delegates begin the process of transforming their identities.

No one more eagerly or eloquently explained the consequences of these developments than Adams, who returned from the Continental Congress convinced that respect for the rule of law now required the colonies to oppose Parliament with even greater energy. In the late autumn and winter of 1774–75, replying as "Novanglus" to a series of articles written by Daniel Leonard as "Massachusettensis," Adams made a compelling case for active resistance by extending the logic of his earlier arguments. When the first colonists left England and established their own towns in North America, Adams argued, they made covenants and formed their own governments on their own authority. When they expanded throughout Massachusetts and spread into Rhode Island and Connecticut, they repeated the process. Although the first generation remained subservient to the authority of the king, those born later—and those who came from elsewhere—did not. English colonists in America remained loyal subjects by choice, not obligation, because they were "out of the legal jurisdiction of parliament." On their own, the colonists established their own institutions, customs, and laws.[142]

For a century and a half, Parliament had not presumed to impose its authority on the colonies. The original settlers enjoyed the right to establish "a British constitution, or a perfect democracy, or any other form of government they saw fit." Indeed, in different colonies they did experiment with different forms, all of which developed according to decisions made by the colonists themselves. Now Britain was trying to change the rules in the middle of the game. "The port bill, charter bill, murder bill, Quebec bill"—together they constituted "a frightful system." Yet the British gamble had failed. The colonists had learned that "nothing is so terrible to them as the loss of their liberties." Almost all American colonists, Adams proclaimed, were now determined to resist Parliament.[143] Nothing in international law or customary practice authorized Parliament to annul the work of colonial legislatures. From the beginning, American colonists "had precisely the same sense of the authority of parliament, *viz.* that it had none at all." If Parliament had been allowed to exercise any power, such as that it exercised over trade with the colonies, it did so "by the voluntary act of the colonies."[144] Critics of the Continental Congress such as Leonard had complained that the colonists wanted to enjoy the liberties secured by the ancient English Constitution without complying with English law. But Adams insisted that the blessings of that form of government lay in the colonies' own legislatures, not in the "complete oligarchy" of the British Parliament. Adams then raised the stakes, zeroing in on the constitutional issue that lay at the heart of the dispute: "America will never allow that parliament has any authority to alter their constitution at all." In that simple sentence Adams issued a categorical and incendiary challenge to the legitimacy of Parliament's power over the colonies.[145]

The ideas of Sidney, Locke, Grotius, and Pufendorf, all of whom Adams invoked in his "Novanglus" essays, remained central to his argument. The law of nations and the law of nature, grounded in God's will, authorized people to defend themselves against tyranny. Parliament, not the colonies, was upsetting established precedent by annulling laws enacted by colonial legislatures. Parliament had thrown the colonies, in Henry's phrase, back to a state of nature; thus they reflexively thought in terms of a compact. In the words from Locke's *Second Treatise* that Adams quoted, "This power in the people of providing for their safety anew by a legislative," when the previous government—in this case Parliament—had acted "contrary to their trust," is "the best fence against rebellion." So colonial resistance, deemed treason by Tories, should be seen as the lawful response to Parliament's unlawful and rebellious acts.[146]

Adams was being neither fanciful nor disingenuous. His rhetorical strategy in 1774–75 not only echoed his arguments in Braintree and against Hutchinson a decade earlier; they also reinforced his position in the Boston Massacre case. In the pivotal year of 1774, while Adams was composing the arguments that would establish popular sovereignty as the "revolution principle" that he counterposed to the "passive obedience" urged by Tories, Adams the attorney took another controversial case that puzzled many of his allies. He agreed to defend the Loyalist Richard King, whose home had been destroyed by a Boston mob. Writing to Abigail, Adams explained that "I do and will detest" all lawless attempts to settle private scores under the banner of principled political action. Adams consistently differentiated purposeful "Popular Commotions" (such as the Boston Tea Party, which he endorsed) from willful and self-indulgent exercises of revenge or mob violence. Although the chaos of events soon blurred that distinction, so clear to Adams, keeping it clear is crucial for understanding the promise and the problems of democracy.[147]

Adams's "Novanglus" essays illuminate the divergence of two strikingly different ways in which Americans were beginning to interpret the meaning and significance of the Glorious Revolution. For most English Whigs, 1689 had established the supremacy of king-in-Parliament, a conceptualization that allowed them to sidestep Sidney's and Locke's arguments for popular sovereignty and embrace mixed government. For Americans, 1689 had confirmed the principle that the Levellers had proclaimed and that English regicides had carried to its logical conclusion: all government rests on the consent of the governed, and all tyrants are to be forcibly resisted. Popular sovereignty was common practice in America long before it became, as Adams put it, a "revolution principle." If some New Englanders now feared that self-government was too unstable to contemplate, many others shared Adams's conviction that it was the best bulwark against tyranny.[148] "A democratical despotism," Adams wrote, "is a contradiction in terms."[149] Officials in democratic governments are accountable to voters; it was the absence of accountability that made Parliament dangerous.[150]

Colonists along the entire Atlantic seaboard were reluctantly coming to share Adams's views. Like Patrick Henry, they agreed that severing ties with England would return them to a state of nature. "The only distinction between slavery and freedom consists in this," New Yorker Alexander Hamilton wrote in 1774: man is governed either "by the will of another" or "by the laws to which he has given his consent." There could be no legitimate reason why man should govern others unless they had submitted "voluntarily."[151] James Iredell of North Carolina wrestled with the idea of divided sovereign authority before siding with Adams. In "the case of several *distinct* and *independent* legislatures" such as those of the colonies, Iredell reasoned, each with its own range of concerns, the old argument about *imperium in imperio* did not apply. Drawing on *Calvin's Case* of 1608 and arguments from Coke and Bacon, Iredell concluded that the colonists, although still loyal to the king, were not subject to the authority of Parliament.[152]

In Pennsylvania, James Wilson and Benjamin Franklin reached the same conclusion. The Scottish-born attorney Wilson had hoped to take a more moderate position on Parliament's authority vis-à-vis the colonial legislatures, but English law held "that there can be no medium between *acknowledging* and *denying* that power in all cases." Because the indivisibility of sovereignty was forced upon him by "principles of reason, of liberty, and of law," Wilson concluded that the colonies should admit only their voluntary loyalty to the crown and their independence from Parliament.[153] On this issue Franklin was ahead of most other colonists. As early as 1768 he had written to his son William that no intermediate position could be sustained. Either "Parliament has a right to make *all laws* for us" or "it has a power to make *no laws* for us."[154] By 1774, a growing chorus was choosing the latter option.

Of the Virginians who began to call for independence, the most influential proved to be among the youngest, Thomas Jefferson. Jefferson sprang from roots utterly different from those of Adams and Franklin. He was born into wealth, and from birth to death his life of comfort was made possible by the labor of slaves. Yet Jefferson took steps to end, in his native Virginia, the accumulation and perpetuation of landed wealth such as that he inherited and enjoyed. He wrote—and grudgingly published—a critique of race-based slavery so stinging that his fellow slaveholders condemned it and abolitionists invoked it. At the same time that he was working on that book, *Notes on the State of Virginia*, the evidence shows, Jefferson engaged in a long-term sexual relationship with one of his slaves, his wife's younger half-sister Sally Hemings. A bundle of inconsistencies so tightly tangled that no commentator has unsnarled it, Jefferson's life, like his ideas, shows both the promise and the pathos of the American Enlightenment and its paradoxical relation to democracy. Self-government in Virginia depended from the start on economic growth made possible by exploiting enslaved Africans and on political stability achieved by the shared racism that united rich and poor whites against the blacks among them. Those poisonous contradictions lay at the heart of Jefferson's life and thought.[155]

Only thirty-one years old in 1774, Jefferson was not among the delegates Virginia sent to the First Continental Congress. A rising lawyer, he had recently been elected a member of the Virginia House of Burgesses. Even more recently he had married a young widow, Martha Skelton, who, on the death of her prosperous father in 1773, brought to their marriage an inheritance equal to Jefferson's own, which, in his own words, "doubled the ease of our circumstances." Jefferson joined the insurgency against Britain almost as soon as he joined the House of Burgesses, which was dissolved by the governor soon after his election. He was among those who gathered at the Raleigh tavern in Williamsburg to establish a Committee of Correspondence in each colony to produce a "unity of action" in their "common cause" against Britain.[156]

In 1774, the little-known Jefferson established himself as a writer on a par with Adams and Franklin when he produced an anonymous pamphlet entitled *A Summary View of the Rights of British America, Set Forth in Some Resolutions Intended for the Inspection of the Present Delegates of the People of Virginia*. Immediately reprinted in Philadelphia and London, it circulated widely among critics of British colonial policy, including British Whigs such as Edmund Burke. Along with Adams's "Novanglus" essays, Jefferson's *Summary View* provided the most persuasive case against Parliament. Jefferson and Adams reasoned independently but reached the same conclusion: all persons possess "a right, which nature has given to all men, of departing from the country in which chance, not choice has placed them." Such emigrants, finding themselves in new lands without governments, can establish "new societies, under such laws and regulations as to them shall seem most likely to promote public happiness." Those who came to America did just that, and England did not interfere: "Nor was ever any claim of superiority or dependance asserted over them by that mother country from which they had migrated." The colonists, not the crown, paid for their new land in blood and treasure. Although under no obligation, they chose to submit to the king's authority. Britain had tried to tighten its grip on the colonies after 1660 and 1689, but to no effect, because the colonies were already accustomed to making their own decisions. "The true ground on which we declare these acts void is that the British parliament has no right to exercise authority over us."[157]

The colonies had always governed themselves through their own legislatures and their own courts, a practice they had no intention of surrendering. "Not only the principles of common sense, but the common feelings of human nature must be surrendered up, before his majesty's subjects here can be persuaded to believe that they hold their political existence at the will of a British parliament." Why should the "160,000 electors" who chose Parliament "give law to four millions in the states of America, every individual of whom is equal to every individual of them in virtue, in understanding, and in bodily strength?" Such a condition would render all Americans "slaves, not of one, but of 160,000 tyrants." British custom and the classical republican tradition distinguished between the people and the few aristocrats who exercised power in Britain, but Jefferson rejected that model.[158] When Parliament or the king's appointed officials disbanded colonial assemblies, power reverted to the sovereign people, who could choose their form of government. They might decide on direct democracy, "assembling together in person," or representative democracy, "sending deputies," or they might choose "any other way they may think proper." The power to constitute themselves remained with the people of the colonies, not with the untenable British notion of king-in-Parliament.[159]

Jefferson also challenged feudal traditions concerning the "fictitious principle that all lands belong originally to the king." He contrasted that fantasy, which he traced to William's Norman conquest in 1066, to the actual practices of landownership in America.[160] Jefferson disputed the prevailing practices of primogeniture and entail, the means by which great estates had been consolidated and handed down intact to firstborn sons across generations. Several years earlier he had written in his commonplace book this commentary on Montesquieu's *Spirit of the Laws*: "In a democracy equality & frugality should be promoted by the laws, as they nurse the amor patriae. To do this, a census is advisable, discriminating the people according to their possessions." With that information in hand, "particular laws may equalise them in some degree by laying burthens on the richer classes, & encouraging the poorer ones." From an early age Jefferson, himself a beneficiary of the practices of primogeniture and entail, saw that they worked against the equality on which popular government must rest. "In a commercial republic," he concluded, "where great wealth will be amassed by individuals, inheritances should be divided among all the children."[161]

In the *Autobiography* Jefferson wrote in 1821, he explained his crusade against landed estates of the sort he inherited and enjoyed. Grants of large parcels of land to some early Virginia settlers had set in motion a dynamic facilitated by feudal inheritance practices. By the second half of the eighteenth century, a fortunate few families enjoyed not only wealth and prestige but also political power, a situation inimical to the republican ideal of a virtuous citizenry focused on the public interest. Such families commanded deference and tried to establish a hierarchical polity. To achieve his goal of "a well-ordered republic," Jefferson deemed it necessary first to annul the privilege of handing down landed estates intact. Reckoning an "aristocracy of wealth" more harmful and dangerous than beneficial to society, he sought instead an "aristocracy of virtue and talent," qualities scattered equally throughout the population. Partible inheritance authorized each landowner to divide his property equally among his children, more nearly placing all of them "on the level of their fellow citizens." Given that eighteenth-century Virginia seems to have been moving toward ever greater degrees of hierarchy and deference as elites attempted to ape the power and lavish consumption of British aristocrats, Jefferson's successful campaign for partible inheritance put limits on what might otherwise have been an even more inegalitarian culture. The more hierarchical southern colonies surely differed from those of New England and the mid-Atlantic, but Virginia's gentry, accountable (albeit imperfectly) to voters, also differed from England's landed aristocracy, which ruled from the security of a political system in which no more than 3 percent of the electorate could vote.[162]

Considerable as was the economic gap separating wealthy planters from poor subsistence farmers, it was dwarfed by the distance separating all free men in Virginia from the vast number of slaves who worked the tobacco fields that spread rapidly during the eighteenth century. Here the gulf between Jefferson's words and his actions exposes the deepest tragedy of American history. In his *Autobiography*, Jefferson accurately noted that he advocated—without success—the emancipation of Virginia's slaves in his first term in the House of Burgesses. He introduced legislation to enable owners to free slaves without legislative approval—again without success. Also in 1769 he pleaded before the colony's highest court the case of Thomas Howell, a light-skinned indentured servant sentenced to thirty-one years of hard labor because his white mother and grandmother had been born out of wedlock. Howell was the victim of a statute usually applied to the children of unions between whites and black slaves. "Under the law of Nature," Jefferson argued, "all men are born free, every one comes into the world with a right to his own person, which includes the liberty of moving and using it at his own will." This "personal liberty" is the gift not of government but of "the author of nature." Again Jefferson—and Howell—lost.[163]

In *A Summary View* Jefferson contended that the "abolition of domestic slavery is the great object of desire in those colonies, where it was unhappily introduced in their infant state." He complained that the king had blocked all attempts to end the slave trade and lamented that the thirst for profit outweighed "the rights of human nature, deeply wounded by this infamous practice." If preserving the institution of slavery seemed to him "so shameful an abuse of a power," what justification might Jefferson have found for his own life as a slaveholder? He could have freed his own slaves every time he denounced "this infamous practice." He agreed to free the slaves of Tadeusz Kosciuszko, then failed to do so after his Polish friend died. Finally, he went to his grave without freeing even the slaves who were his own children. Critiques of slavery were a century old by the time of Jefferson's birth. Antislavery agitation gained momentum throughout his adult life. No amount of sympathetic imagination can veil the profound hypocrisy of Jefferson's lifelong dependence on a system of inhuman exploitation that he consistently described as indefensible.

Although Jefferson's condemnations of slavery in his drafts of *A Summary View* were rejected as decisively by southerners as was his earlier attempt to end slaveholding in Virginia, objections to slavery were mounting throughout the colonies. The Second Continental Congress followed the lead of Massachusetts, Connecticut, Rhode Island, Virginia, and North Carolina in outlawing the slave trade. More and more colonists were coming to share the judgment of Abigail Adams, who wrote to John in 1774 about her disgust with slavery and the awkward and "iniquitous scheme" of fighting "for what we are daily robbing and plundering from those who have as good a right to freedom as we have."[164]

Dependency remained the normal condition of laborers in the eighteenth century, in America as elsewhere. Slavery might have occupied only one point on a continuum of harsh and degrading forms of work, but the creation of heritable race slavery was the work of the seventeenth and eighteenth centuries, and placing it within a context of cruel and unforgiving labor relations does not mask the fact that it occupied the extreme end of that continuum. The population of slaves skyrocketed during precisely the period when Americans were becoming increasingly agitated about their own "enslavement" by Parliament. Their rhetoric should not blind us—as it did not blind contemporary critics—to the incongruity of the simultaneous blossoming of democratic sensibilities for many whites and an increasingly vicious form of slave labor for most blacks. If George Washington, who finally freed his slaves, and Jefferson, who did not, were generally thought to have treated their slaves better than did most planters, such praise today seems faint indeed.

Reconciling slavery with democracy might seem as challenging as reconciling slavery with Christianity. Yet defending slavery by quoting scripture was a venerable tradition rooted in at least some readings of the New Testament as well as the Hebrew Bible.[165] Just as the dissenting Protestant sects destabilized hierarchies outside as well as within the religious domain, however, so some of the denominations that dissented from established Protestant churches intensified criticism of slavery on religious grounds. First Quakers, then members of other evangelical sects that spread as part of the Great Awakening, increasingly invoked the ethics of Christianity as the rationale for ending slavery. When antislavery appeals were muted, however, as was the case with Baptists in Virginia, then dissenting or evangelical gentry could forge alliances between rich and poor whites against a common British target. Charles Woodmason, a southern Anglican minister, captured the dynamic when he charged that evangelical preachers in the Carolinas were "instilling democratical and common wealth principles" into the minds of otherwise sensible farmers, "embittering them" against established authority and "laying deep their fatal republican notions and principles, especially that they owe no subjection to Great Britain." Quakers, Baptists, and other independent ministers, he complained, were preaching to witless commoners the nonsense "that they are a free people."[166] Because Jefferson kept his religious beliefs largely to himself, we cannot say whether his Deism sprang from piety or was a mere convenience. He did not shy away from invoking God, however, or using the language of religious believers. The ringing conclusion of *A Summary View* harmonized the political, economic, and philosophical convictions he shared with almost all colonists: "The God who gave us life gave us liberty at the same time; the hand of force may destroy, but cannot disjoin them."[167]

A Summary View demonstrates that Jefferson, like Adams, Franklin, and the other most prominent figures in the debates leading up to the Revolution, drew promiscuously from a wide range of sources. In 1769 Jefferson purchased a number of books from London, including Locke's *Two Treatises of Government*, the complete works of Montesquieu, and the Swiss legal theorist Jean-Jacques Burlamaqui's *Principes du droit naturel*. Because the entries in Jefferson's commonplace book cannot be dated with precision, we cannot specify when he read which authors. A letter to Robert Skipwith, dated August 31, 1771, recommending a reading list on a wide range of topics as a basis for constructing a personal library, brings us back to the question of the Enlightenment in America.

Jefferson's list reflects the breadth of his intellectual interests. Consistent with his principle that "everything is useful which contributes to fix in the principles and practices of virtue," he recommended novels, plays, and poetry as well as nonfiction. His recommendations included classical Greek and Roman writers; Chaucer, Shakespeare, and Milton; Dryden, Pope, and Swift; the *Spectator* and the *Tatler*; Sidney and Locke; Blackstone, Bolingbroke, and Burke; Reid, Smith, Hume, Robertson, Kames, and Steuart; Montesquieu, Voltaire, and, finally, Rousseau. Jefferson recommended Rousseau's *La nouvelle Héloïse* and *Emile* rather than the *Discourses* or the *Social Contract*, two political texts that Adams evidently knew better than did Jefferson, but the concluding discussion of Emile's civic obligations conveyed the full force of Rousseau's explosive ideas.[168] Jefferson's list also provides a fair sampling of the diverse sources on which he drew in his early writings. He cited Roman philosophers such as Seneca and Cicero; English writers such as Milton, Sidney, Locke, and various dissenting Whigs of the Court and Country persuasions; and numerous figures from the Scottish and French Enlightenments. Scholars might separate those traditions; American thinkers did not.[169]

Already in *A Summary View* Jefferson showed the influences, principles, and perceptions that he shared with many of the most incisive writers of his time. First, his writings reflected his immersion in the traditions of republicanism ancient and modern. Second, he shared the belief, common among American partisans of Enlightenment regardless of their denominational affiliations, that principles of political, economic, and social equality derive from God's law and provide the foundation for the doctrine of popular sovereignty. Although exposure to ideas about politeness might have altered some colonists' tastes, for many Americans Enlightenment had less to do with refinement than with the relation between philosophy, religious faith, and public life. Finally, Jefferson's early references to the horrible consequences of slavery reflect his anguished realization that his indefensible life as a slaveholder contradicted his professed belief in human equality.[170]

Examining the early efforts of American writers and statesmen to explain the reasons for their growing discontent, illustrated in the work of Franklin, Adams, and Jefferson, reveals the complexity of the relation between enlightened ideas and the colonists' arguments for representative democracy. Rooted in their various forms of religious faith, their colonies' diverse histories and experiences with institutions of self-government, and their readings of continental European and British philosophers, historians, and political theorists from the ancient world through their own day, these thinkers' understanding of their own situation evolved in response to the changing pressures exerted by British officials and their increasingly dissatisfied fellow colonists. The legacies of classical, Christian, and republican traditions blended with newer ideas about science and reason to produce a rich and potent brew. In America, to an extent far greater than in France or even England, various forms of Christian theology and piety provided the framework within which, rather than against which, enlightened ideas emerged. Their political implications were clear.

In 1761 the faculty and students of Harvard College sent George III a volume of poetry, *Pietas et gratulatio*, welcoming the new king and expressing in verse their piety and respect. Yet that respect had an edge. Although predicting that "the increase of people and wealth will of course produce the improvement of arts and sciences" under George's reign, they also "presumed to express our thoughts upon the political relations of this Country." They noted that "Science is our business, but we find Science and Policy so intimately connected, that we cannot separate the ideas of the one from the other." They fully anticipated the advance of science but felt compelled to explain why they also expected improvement in the domain of politics. The admonitory tone of this ceremonial greeting from the college that produced Mayhew, Chauncy, Adams, Otis, and others soon to make trouble suggests the links between Enlightenment and self-government in America.[171]

If two-thirds of adult males throughout the colonies could read and write—a rate far exceeding those of England or the nations of continental Europe—and literacy in New England was almost universal by the early eighteenth century, the book more widely owned, read, and cited than any other throughout the colonies remained the Bible. In America enthusiasm for reason ran alongside, rather than against, the persistence of religious faith. Confidence in self-government was bolstered by belief in God's providence as well as increasing confidence in human capability. Few Americans professed a degree of faith in reason comparable to that of European philosophes such as the physiocrats, and few invoked the standard of reason to exclude ordinary people from political affairs. Given the number of people who owned land in the colonies, political participation had been widespread for over a century. A few eighteenth-century skeptics did dismiss the possibility—or the cogency—of simultaneously acknowledging human reason and maintaining belief in divine omnipotence. Most American Protestants, however, held both ideas simultaneously.[172]

Of course, not every American in these years shared the same ideas. Indeed, a sample as small as Franklin, Adams, and Jefferson shows three distinct forms of Enlightenment and three distinct intellectual trajectories. All three came to share a basic commitment with most of their contemporaries, up and down the Atlantic seaboard, a commitment to self-government that lay at the heart of some versions of American Enlightenment. Rooted in religious and political convictions and experience, that commitment manifested itself in the unexpected development of a new consciousness, expressed in different registers by Franklin at the Court of St. James's, by Adams in his "Novanglus" essays, by Jefferson in his *Summary View*, and by countless other colonists in countless different forms. During the spring of 1775, that emergent consciousness began to blossom into a spirit of revolution, which in turn gave birth, during the ensuing dozen years, to one of the greatest outpourings of democratic activism, writing, and institution-building in human history.

CHAPTER 7 | Democracy and American Independence

In the spring of 1775, when fighting broke out in Lexington and Concord, Massachusetts, just west of Boston, almost no one in the colonies was prepared for war. The First Continental Congress had wanted only to loosen the bonds tying the colonies to the mother country and strengthen the authority of colonial legislatures. Achieving those goals did not require independence. Many within Britain thought Parliament should abandon its punitive policies; most thought allowing the colonies to control their internal affairs would suffice. Within weeks of Lexington and Concord, however, the situation changed. Large numbers of colonists became determined to separate from Britain. Those who had led the protests now faced the challenge of justifying a war they had neither sought nor anticipated. As one of the first Americans to engage British soldiers at the Battle of Concord, former captain Levi Preston, later explained to an interlocutor, "Young man, what we meant in going for those redcoats was this: we had always governed ourselves, and we always meant to. They didn't mean we should."[1]

Americans struggling for independence from Britain knew they were fighting for self-government. In June of 1776, the New Hampshire *Freeman's Journal* described a "Proper Democracy" as a government "where the people have all the power in themselves" and choose their own representatives. That is what "Spartanus" wanted when he wrote that New York should now become "a proper Democracy." In August the *Maryland Gazette* endorsed "a well regulated democracy," and a few months later Mecklenburg County, North Carolina, recommended "a simple democracy," or as near to it as possible, and instructed its delegates to oppose anything leaning toward aristocracy. According to the *Providence Gazette*, "By a *democracy* is meant that form of government where the highest power of making laws is lodged in the common people, or persons chosen out of them." Some people, the *Gazette* continued, call such a government a democracy; others prefer "a republic, a commonwealth, or a free state." By whatever name, however, it was "the most agreeable to *natural right and liberty*," and it was the aim of the war for independence.[2] During the decisive years of the war against Britain, Americans increasingly used the words "democracy," "republic," and "commonwealth" as synonyms to describe the nonmonarchical, nonaristocratic government they wanted. Initially the word "republic" was more common than "democracy," but systematic differentiation between the meanings of the two is a product of later debates.[3] More importantly, besides using different words, Americans had different ideas about the framework and purpose of popular government, differences that came into sharper relief during the years of the Revolution.

Democracy provides channels for resolving conflict. It also engenders conflict, in times of war as well as peace. Of the many wealthy Americans who remained loyal to Britain, most left during or after the war. Others among the well-to-do, like Gouverneur Morris and his friends, maneuvered to protect the privileges they had enjoyed as Britons. Many other prominent figures, including John Hancock, the wealthiest merchant in Boston, and big planters like Thomas Jefferson, entered the struggle for independence vowing to expunge all vestiges of monarchy and inherited aristocratic privilege. Many middling men like John Adams, who was later skewered as a champion of hierarchy, in the 1760s aligned themselves with the "meanest and lowest of the people." Adams had bristled at the "sneers and snubbs" of those who, presuming "Airs of Wisdom and Superiority," radiated contempt for the people with whom this shoemaker's son identified: "the multitude, the million, the populace, the vulgar, the mob, the herd and the rabble, as the great always delight to call them." George Hewes, himself a shoemaker, remembered considering his fellow patriot John Hancock his equal as they took part, shoulder to shoulder, in extralegal crowd actions during the 1770s. Yet the appearance of a united front is misleading.[4]

During the War for Independence, the people fighting to establish a new nation also struggled with each other. The wealthy not only distanced themselves from middling men like Adams but also worked to secure political, economic, and legal arrangements that many farmers, mechanics, and artisans—members of "the herd and the rabble"—deemed as unfair as those they were fighting to escape. In 1775, in an account of his lengthy visit to North America more than a decade earlier, the Englishman Andrew Burnaby reported that the colonies' internal divisions were too severe to be bridged. Masters and slaves, rich and poor, northerners and southerners, were united only by their shared fear of Indian attacks. Their "mutual jealousy" meant that a "voluntary coalition, at least a permanent one," was as hard to imagine as a union of fire and water. When Adams was traveling to Philadelphia for the Continental Congress, the New York merchant Philip Livingston sputtered against the "levelling spirit" of Adams's New England and predicted that without Britain to unite them, the colonies "should instantly go to civil wars among ourselves."[5]

Burnaby and Livingston were right that the war revealed new fissures as well as old ones: between rich, middling, and poor; between conservative Protestants, members of evangelical sects, and those of other faiths or no faith; between artisans, merchants, and farmers; between red, black, and white; between women and men; and between the daring and the cautious. A wide range of regional differences appeared, not only between the southern, middle, and New England colonies but also between the settled countryside, the western frontier, and the eastern seaboard, and within as well as between villages, towns, cities, and the colonies' peripheries. Equally significant were the tensions between those who trusted and those who feared the people, between those who embraced and those who abhorred diversity, and between those willing to compromise and those who saw in every disagreement a struggle between Life and Death, Good and Evil, God and Satan.

Few in Britain were eager for war. Benjamin Franklin had met throughout the fall of 1774 with former prime minister William Pitt, now the Earl of Chatham, in the hope that the crisis might still be resolved. Chatham proposed withdrawing British troops and recognizing the authority of colonial legislatures to determine internal taxation, two of the central issues in the dispute. The House of Lords immediately rejected the measure, with particular opprobrium directed at Franklin, who was in the gallery and was assumed to have been the source of Chatham's plan. Franklin now abandoned hope of reconciliation; the Lords' insults severed the last strands of his loyalty to Britain. "To hear so many of these *Hereditary* Legislators declaiming so vehemently against, not the Adopting merely, but even the *Consideration*" of Chatham's proposal, Franklin wrote, "gave me an exceeding mean Opinion of their Abilities, and made their Claim of Sovereignty over three Millions of virtuous sensible People in America, seem the greatest of Absurdities." The haughty Lords were unfit even "to govern a Herd of Swine." It would make more sense, Franklin fumed, to have "Hereditary Professors of Mathematics" than to have "Hereditary Legislators." The House of Commons was no better, and it would remain corrupt as long as votes could be sold to the highest bidder. Having witnessed precisely the corruption decried by British and American Whigs, Franklin sailed from London for Philadelphia to preside over the Second Continental Congress.[6]

When that Congress convened in May of 1775, many prominent delegates worried that the colonies had overreacted and must back down. A number of prosperous southerners doubted the wisdom of pushing Britain further. Quakers were only among the most prominent of those colonists who hated and feared the violence and destruction of war. Even John Dickinson, who had helped ignite colonial resistance to British taxes and provided the official rationale for establishing the Continental Army under General George Washington, now urged caution. He believed that colonial resistance should aim toward a reformed British Empire, not its dissolution. Of course, these divisions were hardly new. When the Continental Congress first convened eight months earlier, Adams recalled, Benjamin Rush had greeted the New England delegation on the outskirts of Philadelphia to warn them that many of those representing other regions were leaning toward reconciliation. Now delegates from the middle as well as southern colonies worried that the battles of Lexington and Concord had put all the colonies in jeopardy. Adams estimated that roughly one-third of the delegates shared his New England colleagues' preference for independence. Another third, including many of those sent by the six colonies that had instructed their delegates to vote against independence, argued fervently for conciliation with Britain. The final third were unsure.

Adams knew what was at stake. He wrote to Abigail's uncle that "this American contest will light up a general war" that might last a decade or more. He proved a poor prophet: the conflicts exposed during the war never did end completely. In July a divided Congress voted to extend an "Olive Branch Petition" to the crown, protesting the policies adopted by Parliament and pleading with George III, as his loyal subjects, to intervene on their behalf. The petition, opposed by many colonists, was rejected.[7] Early in 1776, the Congress learned that Britain had prohibited all trade with the colonies and declared them outside the crown's protection, effectively branding the colonists traitors and threatening punishment by death. Both the furious naval bombardment of Norfolk, Virginia, and the decision to send ships carrying supplies and twenty thousand German mercenaries across the Atlantic illustrated Britain's hardening resolve to discipline its upstart colonies. The lingering hope of those colonists who believed that British critics of colonial policy such as Edmund Burke might sway the crown began to fade.

With war came talk of the need for new colonial constitutions, the moment for which Adams had been waiting and preparing. As early as June of 1774, after Britain had dissolved the Massachusetts legislature, Adams wrote to his friend James Warren, imagining himself and his fellow colonists playing the role of lawgiver enacted by Solon, Lycurgus, and Cicero. The chance intoxicated Adams even though he saw the risk: "Brutus and Cassius were conquered and slain. Hampden died in the Field, Sydney [*sic*] on the Scaffold, Harrington in jail."[8] A year later, Adams advocated authorizing the colonies to begin forming new governments. In the spring of 1776, he saw his opportunity. He presented a resolution urging Congress to instruct all the colonies that lacked permanent constitutions based on the principle of popular sovereignty to produce such statements of fundamental law. It was time to act on the "Theories of the Wisest Writers" and make explicit the principle that lay beneath political practice in the colonies. Proclaiming the people "the Source of all Authority and Original of all Power," Adams advised Congress to "invite the People, to erect the whole Building with their own hands upon the broadest foundation."[9]

When Congress voted to adopt that resolution on May 15, 1776, the history of democracy in America entered a new stage. As Adams wrote, it was "a decisive Event," because "no Colony, which shall assume a Government under the People, will give it up."[10] Having already shown the persuasive power of his arguments for popular sovereignty, Adams immediately found his ideas in demand. Delegates from other colonies, charged with drafting constitutions, asked Adams for help. In response to a request for a sketch of his ideas from William Hooper of North Carolina, Adams wrote his *Thoughts on Government*. It was the most decisive proposal advanced at this crucial moment and among the most influential documents in modern history.[11] Word of the document traveled fast. Soon Adams was sending copies to John Penn, another delegate from North Carolina involved in drafting that colony's new constitution; Jonathan Sergeant of New Jersey; and two delegates from Virginia, Richard Henry Lee and George Wythe. When a Philadelphia printer agreed to publish *Thoughts on Government* as a pamphlet, Adams's vision of representative democracy quickly circulated throughout the colonies.

As the celebrated final paragraph of his *Thoughts* made clear, Adams appreciated the magnitude of the moment. "You and I, my dear friend," he wrote to George Wythe, "have been sent into life at a time when the greatest lawgivers of antiquity would have wished to live." The lawgiver envisioned by Rousseau, and the Greek and Roman lawgivers Adams had studied, would have envied the American colonists: "How few of the human race have ever enjoyed an opportunity of making an election of government, more than of air, soil, or climate, for themselves or their children!" Whereas the theorists of social compacts had only imagined people coming together from a state of nature to frame governments of their own choosing, the colonists now found themselves in such circumstances. Britain had thrust Americans into a situation unlike the hypothetical condition envisioned by earlier theorists.

Significantly, Adams listed Sidney first in the litany of republican theorists he invoked in *Thoughts*. Whereas Locke had justified giving the people responsibility for accepting or rejecting a king, Sidney had envisioned a more active and continuing role, which the colonists had been playing for over a century. Adams aimed to make Americans conscious of the ethos animating their institutions. "When, before the present epocha," Adams asked, "had three millions of people full power and a fair opportunity to form and establish the wisest and happiest government that human wisdom can contrive?"[12]

The seas of public opinion had already turned turbulent by the time Adams's *Thoughts* appeared, without the acknowledgment of authorship, in the spring of 1776. Earlier that year, another anonymous pamphlet had stirred up intense debate. Written by a recently arrived Englishman soon known to be Thomas Paine, the pamphlet helped transform American opinion by launching a frontal assault on the idea of monarchy, which most American colonists still took for granted despite their dissatisfaction with British policy. Like Adams, Paine saw how extraordinary the moment was. "We have it in our power," he wrote, "to begin the world over again. A situation, similar to the present, hath not happened since the days of Noah until now. The birthday of a new world is at hand."[13]

Paine had arrived in Philadelphia from England in 1774. Having been dismissed from his position as a collector of excise taxes, he decided to divorce his young wife and seek a new life in the New World. Equipped with a letter of introduction from Benjamin Franklin, whom Paine met in London, he soon found work editing the *Pennsylvania Magazine*. In England he had written a political pamphlet urging Parliament to improve the conditions of excise collectors, work he found more engaging than any of his earlier jobs as corset maker, sailor, tobacconist, schoolteacher, or tax collector. Quickly Paine got to know Philadelphia artisans and dissenters, including David Rittenhouse, Thomas Young, Timothy Matlack, James Cannon, and Christopher Marshall, and also John Adams, Samuel Adams, and Benjamin Rush. It was Rush who urged Paine to write *Common Sense*, a pamphlet so inflammatory that at first no printer would agree to publish it, and who suggested its title.

Using an increasingly familiar form of popular appeal, Paine presented a straightforward defense of self-government. Without citing any learned philosophers or quoting adages on the rights of Englishmen, Paine outlined Locke's argument about free individuals coming together under laws they gave themselves. Using the idea of an original contract to challenge monarchy itself, Paine treated the Bible, on which earlier royalists had based claims for the divine right of kings, as a lever for republican government. Paine contended, as Milton and Sidney had done, that the people of Israel lived a thousand years under a republic. Only when gripped by "a national delusion" did the Hebrews opt for a king, which proved a fatal error. When there were no kings, there were no wars. From "Heathens" the Hebrews borrowed monarchy, "the most prosperous invention the Devil ever set on foot for the promotion of idolatry."[14] Paine also lampooned English kings. The tradition began dishonorably, when "a French bastard" crowned himself king "against the consent of the natives." Neither history nor logic could redeem the corrupt system of hereditary monarchy, which rested on nothing but tyrannical usurpation.[15]

For Paine, as for Adams, the solution was self-government. Against England's rotten monarchy Paine contrasted the virtue of republican government as practiced in North America. Like his friend Rush, Paine characterized the colonies as an "asylum for the persecuted lovers of civil and religious liberty," not just from England but from all over Europe.[16] The mongrel quality of Pennsylvania's population stirred Paine's hopes for a new form of popular rule. Americans' desire to separate from England sprang neither from selfishness nor disloyalty but from "unextinguishable feelings" of justice that "the Almighty hath implanted in us." America had nothing to gain from associating with England and a destiny to fulfill on its own. In a world filled with oppression, freedom had been "hunted round the globe. Asia, and Africa, have long expelled her.—Europe regards her like a stranger, and England hath given her warning to depart." Only Americans could offer "the fugitive" liberty a home. Upholding religious orthodoxy was the rule elsewhere, but in America "it is the will of the Almighty" that religious diversity should prevail.[17] Echoing almost precisely Adams's arguments as "Clarendon" in 1766, Paine reasoned from a hypothetical state of nature. In that original condition society predated government, which was "rendered necessary by the inability of moral virtue to govern the world." At that stage "every man, by natural right," had a seat in the parliament in which laws were made. But population increased; people spread out over the land. Simple or direct democracy was no longer an option. It became "too inconvenient for all of them to meet on every occasion as at first, when their number was small, their habitations near, and the public concerns few."

The problem was easy to solve. The key for Paine, as for Adams, was representation. The people decided "to leave the legislative part to be managed by the select number chosen from the whole body." Elected representatives, possessing "the same concerns" as those who elected them, were empowered to act "in the same manner as the whole body would act were they present." As the society continued to grow larger and more complex, it became "necessary to augment the number of the representatives" so that "the interest of every part" of society could be considered. Thus it was "found best to divide the whole into convenient parts, each part sending its proper number." Frequent elections were Paine's preferred means to prevent the representatives from forming "an interest separate from the *electors*." Such a procedure had two advantages. First, "the *elected* might by that means return and mix again with the general body of the *electors*," thereby ensuring by "prudent reflexion" their "fidelity to the public." Second, "this frequent interchange will establish a common interest with every part of the community," so that the people and their elected representatives "will mutually and naturally support each other."[18] Annual elections would secure trust and accountability.

Common Sense has been acknowledged since 1776 as the most influential text spreading the revolutionary sensibility in America. At a time when political pamphlets were thought successful with a circulation of one or two thousand copies, between seventy-five thousand and one hundred thousand copies of *Common Sense* were sold throughout the colonies. Because of his no-holds-barred invective and the popularity of the pamphlet among America's working people, Paine has been lionized as the founder of many forms of American radicalism, from left- and right-wing populism to libertarianism. Strikingly, Paine rejected direct democracy in favor of representative government and argued that elected representatives could and would "establish a common interest with every part of the community." Paine was a passionate egalitarian who rejected the idea of separate classes with stable, conflicting interests and embraced representative democracy in principle because he thought it capable of resolving all kinds of differences. Not only did representation keep legislators informed through frequent communication between electors and elected; it enabled representatives to see the sources of conflict and address them. By confronting and understanding differences, representatives could forge a shared sensibility, based on an ethic of reciprocity, and through that process individuals might learn to "mutually and naturally support each other."[19]

That logic also underlay Paine's proposed "Continental Conference" to establish the new nation's institutional framework. After it completed its work, it would disband and the business of government commence. For the same reasons that he recommended electing representatives for legislative assemblies, Paine proposed selecting two delegates from each colony to "frame a *Continental Charter*, or Charter of the United Colonies," a procedure that would unite "*knowledge* and *power*." Those selected would have had wider experience in national affairs and thus be capable of good judgment. The convention itself, empowered by the people themselves, would enjoy "a truly legal authority."[20] Paine's rationale for a constitutional convention proved nearly as influential as his case for independence.

In *Common Sense* Paine tried to answer the question that gnawed at many of his contemporaries, even those who embraced the idea of independence: Who would be king? Paine suggested randomly choosing the name of one colony, then letting all the delegates to the Congress select one of that colony's representatives to serve as executive officer, or "president," for a year, then repeating the process until a member of each colony had served in turn. Paine devalued the executive because "in America," he wrote, "THE LAW IS KING." In absolute governments, by contrast, "the King is law," so "in free countries the law *ought* to be King; and there ought to be no other."[21] Paine paid little attention to the execution of the law and its application. He focused on legislation, the most important work to be done by the people's representatives, and the processes whereby those people would be elected. Representative democracy, he presumed, was plain common sense.

Paine's ideas had a long lineage, but he gave them a distinctive twist. In England he had associated with the dissenting groups, either affiliated with his father's Quaker community or with other bands of dissident artisans whose ideas descended from seventeenth-century radicalism. Although it is hard to know just what the self-educated Paine had read, he had clearly encountered various currents of English political writing before he arrived in Philadelphia. Many critics aimed to restore the proper balance (as they saw it from their quite different perspectives) between the church, the king, the Lords, and the Commons. They did not seek to topple the monarchy altogether, the aim of Paine and the most enthusiastic of his American readers and allies.[22]

Paine's critics registered his impact. Maryland Loyalist James Chalmers warned that repudiating monarchy meant "our Constitution would immediately degenerate into Democracy," a condition much more turbulent than the mixed government Britain had enjoyed for centuries—except for the unfortunate years of the Commonwealth. From the ancient Greek and Roman republics to more recent examples such as those of Holland and Switzerland, democracies inevitably ended in chaos. America's republics too would fall victim to an oppressive government "imposed on us by some Cromwell of our armies."[23] Another of Paine's critics described him as "a crack-brained zealot for democracy" and "an avowed, violent republican" who, like the Commonwealthmen before him, would lead the colonists toward the dead end of tyranny. Only a fool would trust "every silly clown and illiterate mechanic" to choose representatives, let alone elect those who would write a constitution. Another Loyalist, writing as "Cato," denied that the Bible endorsed popular government and ridiculed Paine's ostensible preference for "a pure Republick," even though Paine had explicitly endorsed representative government rather than direct democracy.[24]

Other critics savaged Paine's savage tone. American pamphleteers aiming to mimic the acid wit of British satirists had usually missed the mark, coming across instead as tin-eared provincials. Paine was different. He dispensed with aphorisms recycled from learned authorities. In a screed characteristic of the denunciations *Common Sense* provoked, Loyalist Charles Inglis accused Paine of aiming for "the passions of his readers, especially their pity and resentment." Paine "seems to be every where transported with rage—a rage that knows no limits, and hurries him along like an impetuous torrent." Surely such "fire and fury" signaled that either a terrible disappointment or dangerous ambition drove the author of *Common Sense*. The status-conscious Gouverneur Morris dismissed Paine as "a mere adventurer" who lacked fortune, family, and "connexions."[25] On the last count, however, Morris was mistaken.

Paine's many allies ranged from urban artisans and sailors to Franklin and other prominent members of the Continental Congress, who agreed that he had made a convincing case. George Washington wrote of Paine's "sound doctrine and unanswerable reasoning" and expressed a widespread belief that the arguments in *Common Sense* would inspire the converted and persuade the ambivalent. Tens of thousands bought or borrowed the pamphlet; countless others heard parts of it read aloud in all kinds of settings. One colonist likened Paine's work to a flood that swept all before it. Others claimed *Common Sense* had brought sight to the blind and had awakened wealthy and prominent public officials to the convictions shared by "tens of thousands of farmers and tradesmen."[26]

Paine also attracted criticism from among those who shared his taste for independence. Some colonists struggling to enjoy the prosperity that Paine identified with America disagreed with his economic analysis: whereas he traced poverty to personal shortcomings, others blamed the wealthy who oppressed the poor. Other critics faulted his discussion of religion. John Witherspoon, the Presbyterian cleric who as president of the College of New Jersey taught several prominent leaders of the American Revolution, excoriated Paine for treating the doctrine of original sin as an object of "contempt or abhorrence." By dismissing ideas still held by a majority of different Protestant denominations, the author of *Common Sense* showed that he was either "astonishingly ignorant" or, as Witherspoon was among the few to suspect, "an enemy to the Christian faith."[27] When Adams complained to Paine about his use of the Bible, he reported that Paine "expressed a contempt of the Old Testament and indeed the Bible at large" and vowed to write a book exposing the folly of all religion.[28] Paine had tried to cloak his doubt by feigning reverence, but Witherspoon, Adams, and others already discerned the skepticism Paine expressed decades later in *The Age of Reason* (1794), a book that would earn him the opprobrium of the increasingly religious people of the new United States.[29]

Even those who disagreed with Paine, however, had to acknowledge the powerful influence of *Common Sense*. John Adams wrote to Abigail that Paine's pamphlet contained "a great deal of good sense" in a "clear, simple, concise" style that many people found compelling. Adams complained, characteristically and (in this case) justifiably, that Paine had offered nothing more than "a tolerable summary" of his own arguments. Adams thought that criticizing Britain was useful but inadequate: "This Writer has a better Hand at pulling down than building."[30] Although Adams shared Paine's desire for independence and his preference for representative rather than direct democracy, their differences were many.

Paine acknowledged at the beginning of *Common Sense* that government originates in the need to control human weaknesses. At best, "government, like dress, is a badge of our lost innocence."[31] Adams feared that Paine forgot those sensible warnings when he proposed a form of government requiring an impossible degree of virtue. Paine's preference for a single legislative body seemed to Adams overly optimistic. Once the institutions of representative democracy were in place, Paine envisioned no lasting disagreements among the people or between the people and their representatives. Paine was ignoring what Adams considered the most dangerous and the likeliest of all prospects, the outcome that had sunk ancient and more recent experiments with popular government. That was the tendency of the legislature, evident in republics ever since the ancient world, to declare itself an interest separate from that of the people and devolve into an oligarchy. To prevent that from happening in America, Adams set to work to counter the influence of Paine's *Common Sense*. In the process he identified one of the most divisive issues of the coming years.

Adams differed from many enthusiasts of Enlightenment ideas by virtue of his interest in history and culture rather than unchanging reason or natural law. In 1772 he outlined the prerequisites to becoming a lawgiver: "Human Nature" and "human Life," he wrote, "must be carefully observed and studied." Only by considering the entire range of human experience, surveying societies operating in different climates, with "different Religions and Customs," and in different stages of historical development, would it be possible to assess the options and choose institutions wisely.[32] Consequently, Adams tailored each of the three versions of the text that became his *Thoughts on Government* to the features of the colony whose representatives had asked his assistance. Unlike his native New England, where "ideas of equality" were from the outset "so agreeable" that practices of self-government had been entrenched for generations, the colonies of North Carolina, Virginia, and New Jersey contained great landowners whose power and preferences Adams felt obliged to acknowledge. Thus his recommendations reflected the "Inclinations of the Barons of the south, and Proprietary Interests in the Middle Colonies." For them he proposed a senate selected by the house of representatives, rather than by the people themselves, and a governor chosen by both houses of the legislature. Adams himself preferred annual elections, and as his later plan for the Massachusetts Constitution made clear, he wanted lawmakers in both the upper and lower houses of the legislature and the governor to be elected directly by the people. He also recommended a wider franchise than existed anywhere in America at the time. He knew very well that the relatively egalitarian convictions and practices of New England were not shared throughout the colonies. Writing to Horatio Gates, a former British general now joining the Continental Army, Adams complained that "all our misfortunes" derived from southerners' resistance to genuinely popular government as it was understood in the northern colonies. Unless that problem could be overcome, the colonists' plans to unite against Britain would fail. Even so, Adams suggested to Patrick Henry that the people of Virginia might alter his scheme if they found the idea of annual elections "too popular"—i.e., too democratic—or if any other features of his plan seemed unsuitable.[33]

Adams understood that the matter of representation, which Paine considered a straightforward solution to the problem of government, would prove to be one of the thorniest issues facing the new nation. Like everyone else who had attended the First Continental Congress in 1774, Adams witnessed the debate between representatives from large and small states. Virginia's Patrick Henry proposed that each colony be represented according to its (nonslave) population, which Thomas Lynch, from the wealthy but sparsely populated colony of South Carolina, suggested amending to include both property and population. Samuel Ward of Rhode Island, the smallest and least populous of the colonies, protested. Ward grounded his call for the equal representation of each colony on the practice in Henry's own Virginia, where every county, from the most to the least populous, sent two representatives to the House of Burgesses. That practice reflected long-standing assumptions brought from Europe, assumptions that were only beginning to be questioned.

American colonists in the seventeenth and eighteenth centuries took for granted that every individual exists within a collectivity. Whether that community was conceived as a family, a congregation, a town, or a county, or, now, in the Continental Congress, an entire colony, every individual was understood to be part of an entity larger than the self. Thus each representative at the Congress spoke for a collectivity, not for particular individuals within it. In the face of Ward's compelling argument, which rested on practices accepted in all the colonies, and faced with the even more compelling need to reach unanimity, the more populous colonies grudgingly accepted the proposal that every delegation should have one vote.[34] Two distinct conceptions of representation, the first, proportional or equal, and the second, by population or "property" (the euphemism for slaves), surfaced in the very first meeting of the Continental Congress. The colonies' distinct patterns of representation were rooted in their different experiences, and the discrepancy between any single concept of representation and the colonies' diverse practices meant that this difficulty would remain nettlesome.[35]

When Adams addressed the issue of representation in his *Thoughts*, that unresolved controversy shaped his argument. A chorus of complaints concerning the inadequacy of their representation in Parliament had unsettled the colonists' inherited assumptions about government. The challenge of any republican government, Adams observed, lay in deciding how "to depute power from the many to a few of the most wise and good." The representative assembly, he continued, "should be in miniature an exact portrait of the people at large. It should think, feel, reason, and act like them." To achieve that goal, the assembly should offer equal representation to all the people with an interest in it. How would that determination be made, and by whom, even under the best of circumstances? Given the chaos of war in the spring of 1776, and given the urgent need of the colonies to form governments, Adams advised each colony to follow its own established modes of selecting representatives.[36]

Adams's preference for practices shown by experience to be viable shaped his judgment that Paine was "very ignorant of the Science of Government."[37] Paine's proposal for a unicameral legislature disturbed Adams more than any other feature of *Common Sense*, and he offered multiple reasons to reject it. A single assembly "is liable to all the vices, follies, and frailties of an individual," including dangerous "starts of passion" and "flights of enthusiasm" that can and often do lead to "hasty results and absurd judgments." Adams had not only learned of such tragedies from reading histories classical and modern but also had witnessed them—indeed, he had been guilty of them—himself. Because a single assembly "is apt to be avaricious," its members might exempt themselves from the burdens laid on their constituents. Because it is "apt to grow ambitious," in time it is likely "to vote itself perpetual." Adams singled out a range of examples from the ancient world to Britain's Long Parliament. He then focused on Holland, where those in the assembly first moved from annual to septennial elections, then declared themselves members for life, and eventually decided to fill vacancies caused by death without submitting their decisions to the people. Beyond these dangers lay the legislature's inability to perform executive or judicial functions. It would be far wiser, Adams reasoned, to take Montesquieu's advice and separate the judiciary and the executive from the legislature, and wiser still to constitute a second, distinct assembly, which could mediate between the representatives of the people and the power of the executive and enjoy "a free and independent exercise of its judgment."

Adams was not warning against representative democracy. Instead he urged caution because he considered the success of these new republics crucial for the future of popular government. Nowhere in his *Thoughts* did Adams suggest that those selected to serve in the second house, to be called the council or the senate, should be categorically different from those in the assembly itself. As the War for Independence raged, Adams expressed no interest in creating an American aristocracy, the absence of which seemed to him a distinctive virtue of American colonial society and law. Government simply needed institutional brakes—such as a second legislative body and an independent judiciary—to prevent each individual legislator from being empowered (or forced) to serve, effectively, as a judge in his own case.[38]

Although Adams opposed Paine's plan to concentrate power in a single legislative body, he cherished the principle of popular sovereignty far more than he feared unicameralism. The constitution proposed in Pennsylvania during the spring of 1776 was unusual in calling for a single assembly. Adams rebuked critics of the Pennsylvania plan who invoked his *Thoughts* to support their position. Those opposed to the new Pennsylvania Constitution, he wrote to Abigail, "are making a factious use of my Name," and they do so "much against my Will." Despite his reservations about a unicameral legislature, "yet I think it is agreable to the Body of the People, and if they please themselves they will please me."[39] Adams's early writings, particularly his *Thoughts on Government*, complicate the now-familiar charge that he always distrusted democracy. Indeed, Adams's correspondence during the spring of 1776 makes apparent the depth of his commitment to democracy—and his contemporaries' awareness of it. Virginia and New Jersey both quickly adopted new constitutions patterned on Adams's *Thoughts*. Some prominent Virginians, including Washington and Jefferson, were away when a committee of the Virginia legislature produced a Declaration of Rights and a new constitution, but those present knew the heart of the issue was democracy. Patrick Henry, whose commitment to popular government was widely known,[40] identified himself as "a Democrat on the plan of our admired friend, J. Adams, whose pamphlet I read with great pleasure." Richard Henry Lee described the new Virginia Constitution as "very much of the democratic kind." Virginia and New Jersey, the first two colonies to adopt new constitutions in June of 1776, decided to create bicameral legislatures, with all members of both houses popularly elected, and an independent executive and judiciary, just as Adams had recommended.[41]

Critics of these proposed schemes of government saw them in the same light as their champions. Virginia's Carter Braxton, for example, undertook to answer Adams's *Thoughts* with a defense of traditional mixed government patterned on the British model. Braxton considered the plans for popular government being adopted in the colonies defective precisely because "the principle of democratical Governments" put too much trust in the people. As democracies and republics had always done, they would collapse in anarchy or end in despotism. In a blunt letter to Landon Carter, his uncle and one of the colony's wealthiest planters, Braxton lamented the "purely democratical" ethos of New England and predicted those colonies would use the crisis to "embrace their darling Democracy."

The words of Henry, Lee, and Braxton underscore the more or less interchangeable use of the words "democratical" and "republican" by friends and foes of popular government during these crucial years of colonial constitution writing.[42] The connotations of both words, as we have seen, had long been negative in England, particularly since the Restoration. Most British writers took for granted that the Commonwealth had been a disaster. Most agreed that Holland had quickly devolved from its republican promise into a simple oligarchy. Britain's dissenting Whigs, notwithstanding their desire to reform the corrupt British political system, remained monarchists. Beginning in the spring of 1775 and gathering momentum during the years that followed, a growing number of Americans for and against independence saw clearly that the colonists' plans for government, like those advanced by both Paine and Adams, were blueprints for democracy.[43]

The New England colonies, with the longest and most deeply rooted traditions of democratic rule, were quick to confirm that their governments rested squarely on the principle of popular sovereignty. Even before Congress authorized the colonies to begin creating constitutions, Rhode Island affirmed its democratic Charter of 1663, which followed closely the Acts and Orders of 1647. Connecticut likewise adopted its Charter of 1662, which differed little from the earlier Charter of 1639.[44] In both colonies, bicameral legislatures and governors had long been elected by the people, practices they voted to perpetuate. When the *Providence Gazette* addressed the topic of different forms of government in the summer of 1777, it registered the shared and uncontroversial commitment of New Englanders to the idea that "democracy" and "republic" both meant popular sovereignty, government by the people through their elected representatives.[45]

Loyalists, to their dismay, saw the same dynamic at work. An exasperated Jonathan Sewall, the last British attorney general in Massachusetts and a good friend of Adams until the outbreak of hostilities, wrote in 1775 that the first settlers of New England carried with them the seeds of sedition. The current crisis developed from "that ancient republican independent spirit, which the first Emigrants to America brought out with them; and which the Forms of Government, unhappily given to the New England Colonies, instead of checking, have served to cherish and keep alive." Ambrose Serle, a British official stationed in New York, agreed with Sewall. America's Congregationalists exhibited "a pretty strong Inclination to every sort of Democracy." From Serle's perspective, the struggle between England and her colonies was "at the Bottom very much a religious War" echoing the one fought in the seventeenth century between Anglicans and dissenters.[46]

Within months of the battles of Lexington and Concord, the Massachusetts Bay Colony likewise committed itself to democratic government. In June of 1775 Massachusetts replaced its office of royally appointed governor, which had been the focus of so much agitation since the 1760s, with an executive council. Otherwise it adopted the 1691 Charter as its first constitution. New Hampshire, without a similar charter to affirm, became the first state to adopt a freshly written constitution in January of 1776. As in Massachusetts, replacing the governor with an executive council chosen by the popularly elected legislature was the principal change from existing practice. As Adams noted, the "ideas of equality" so familiar in the New England colonies enabled them to embrace forms of representative democracy with great speed and little dissent.[47]

New controversies emerged soon enough. Questions of who should participate in civic life, and how, and why, bled into questions about the culture and institutions necessary for democracy to survive, let alone thrive. Although the data are fragmentary, it is clear that voting in colony-wide elections hardly conformed to the image of widespread engagement conjured by activists' rhetoric in the 1770s. In the eighteenth century, nearly two-thirds of white men could vote in the colonies, but fewer than half of those eligible in the colonies actually voted. Voter turnout in the middle decades of the century ranged from a high of 40–50 percent in Virginia, where elite planters were routinely returned to office, to a low of only 15–30 percent in New England and the backcountry, with the middle colonies falling somewhere in between. Although voting could spike in particularly contentious elections, it usually settled back to those levels. Elections in the South were boisterous affairs, with the wealthy often resorting to bribes or liquid inducements to lure voters to the polls. Even then, less than 10 percent of the electorate typically turned out in areas such as rural South Carolina. Voting in New England was more decorous and less corrupt than elsewhere, yet—or perhaps for that reason—fewer people voted.

For most colonists, politics had been a distraction rather than a passion. Colonial farmers, who constituted 95 percent of the population, had limited contact with the world outside their villages. In all the cultures these settlers had left behind them when they crossed the Atlantic, between 5 percent and 20 percent of adult males enjoyed the franchise, and few of them exercised it. Political decisions affecting ordinary people were made by monarchs, princes, and a tiny circle of aristocrats untethered to the consent of the people. Although protests, rebellions, or food riots gave outlets to discontent, voting served primarily to endorse decisions already made by the sovereign and his ministers. In the 1760s and 1770s, however, the level of engagement began to change in North America. The number of petitions submitted to colonial legislatures jumped, and periodicals featured politics more prominently. When the colonists began to mobilize against Britain, popular government began to matter more. Conflicts that had seemed minor loomed larger. Political attitudes and behaviors that had been inherited now had to be evaluated and reconstituted.[48]

The strident invective of Paine's *Common Sense* was less novel than the idea that representatives chosen by the people should meet in constitutional conventions to frame the laws by which they would be governed. Adams had made the case for self-government in his "Novanglus" essays, Jefferson in his *Summary View*, and countless others in the flurry of pamphlets provoked by the imperial crisis. To translate that principle into practice, ordinary Americans now had to authorize forming new governments. In 1775 and 1776 a chorus of voices began making the case that special, extralegislative conventions, constituted by popular election or appointed by the people's representatives in the legislature, should meet and establish forms of self-government to be ratified by the people. Once Britain had disbanded the colonial legislatures, the colonists were forced—and enabled—to begin again. In the words of Scottish-born James Wilson in Philadelphia, calling extraordinary conventions was "authorized by that which weighs much more in the scale of reason" than opponents' objections: "the spirit of our constitutions," which dated back to the seventeenth century. Once Britain shut down the colonial assemblies by "lopping off one or more of their branches," according to Jefferson, "the power reverts to the people, who may use it to unlimited extent, either assembling together in person, sending deputies, or in any other way they may think proper." Similar proclamations emerged everywhere.[49]

Most colonies took Adams's advice that the new constitutions should conform to existing practices rather than to an abstract model. Almost all adopted bicameral legislatures, weakened executives, and independent judiciaries. The close relation between those plans and Adams's *Thoughts* indicated either his influence or his understanding of existing practices and his fellow colonists' fears and aspirations. Debates in Virginia illustrate some of the reasons why the writers of almost all the new constitutions opted for bicameral rather than unicameral legislatures.[50] Signing himself—significantly—"Democritus," a writer in the *Virginia Gazette* endorsed Adams's ideas because of the difference he saw between America's natural aristocracy and Britain's hereditary aristocracy. Democritus saw in the institution of the senate a way for "the ablest men in the nation," distinguished by experience, education, and wisdom rather than their families' wealth, to emerge as powerful political figures. Whereas the House of Lords merely perpetuated inherited privileges, the additional legislative body proposed for Virginia would provide nothing more than a check on the deliberations of the popularly elected assembly, a second perspective to supplement that of the people's representatives. Just as bringing together the representatives of various towns, counties, and interests enabled a democratic assembly to come to an understanding different from those of any of the voters whose choices brought it into being, so a senate, a second legislative assembly selected from the members elected to the first, might further reflect on, and refine, the judgment of their associates. In the absence of an aristocracy, Democritus insisted, lingering fears about an "upper house" made no sense. When Americans abolished all hierarchies of rank, they replaced birth with ability as the sole criterion of excellence.[51]

Jefferson, who submitted a draft constitution for Virginia in June of 1776, shared the perspective of Democritus and Adams. He proposed that "every person of full age"—meaning every white, male adult—"neither owning nor having owned 50 acres of land, shall be entitled to an appropriation of 50 acres or to so much as shall make up what he owns or has owned 50 acres in full and absolute dominion." Since Jefferson's draft constitution specified that all taxpayers who owned twenty-five acres of farmland, or a quarter of an acre in town, would be able to vote, his plan would have expanded the franchise to include all white men who were not indentured servants. Moreover, Jefferson proposed that everyone who could vote could also be elected to the assembly. Notwithstanding his explicit exclusion of Indians, blacks, and women, the egalitarianism of Jefferson's draft was consistent with his insistence that the abolition of entail and primogeniture in Virginia marked the end of "the aristocracy of wealth" and the beginning of an "aristocracy of virtue and talent."[52]

Yet even the self-consciously egalitarian Jefferson also envisioned a senate, to be appointed by members of the assembly. To prevent the senate from naming itself perpetual, as other such assemblies had done, he stipulated that no senators could be reappointed after serving a single nine-year term. Nothing in Jefferson's draft constitution suggests that he envisioned the senate as a refuge for the wealthy. Instead, like Adams and Democritus, he argued that the senate would simply refine the judgment of the legislature. Jefferson's goal was simple: "to get the wisest men chosen, & to make them perfectly independent when chosen." Elaborating on his reasoning, Jefferson aligned his position even more closely with that of Adams: "In general I believe the decisions of the people, in a body, will be more honest and more disinterested than those of wealthy men." It was explicitly because he sought the filtration or refinement of judgment, not the representation of wealth, that Jefferson opposed the popular election of senators. He confessed that he would be almost equally content with his fellow Virginian Edward Pendleton's idea "that the people of each county should chuse twelve electors, who should meet those of the other counties in the same district & chuse a senator." Why? Jefferson wanted the senate as well as the assembly to "have an opportunity of superintending & judging of the situation of the whole state & be not all of one neighborhood as our upper house used to be."[53]

Jefferson aimed to broaden the sensibilities of all the people's representatives, and he conceded that there might be multiple paths to that goal. George Mason, principally responsible for both the draft of the Virginia Constitution and the Virginia Declaration of Rights, shared Pendleton's preference for a senate chosen by special electors. The convention rejected such plans, as did almost all the state constitutions written at this stage, in favor of popularly elected upper houses. The decision made by many of the state conventions to create new and distinct districts for senatorial elections, as the Virginia Convention did, reflected an awareness that the principle of representation for the upper house should be different, and the horizons of those elected widened, relative to those of representatives elected to legislative assemblies. Many champions of bicameralism among the writers of these new state constitutions shared Rousseau's goal in the *Social Contract*. They sought to find a way for legislators to move beyond the representation of particular interests to considerations of the public good, or what Rousseau termed the general will. Their aim, as Adams put it in *Thoughts*, was everywhere the same: the upper house should serve as a "mediator," and it should enjoy "a free and independent exercise of its judgment."[54]

Finally, although Jefferson proposed a nine-year term, he emphasized the importance of limiting senators to a single term so that they would "return into the mass of the people & become the governed instead of the governor." Knowing that condition to be their future would ensure the concern with "the public good" that senators might otherwise "perhaps be induced by their independence to forget." Jefferson proposed a lengthy term for the same reason: to insulate senators from the evanescent passions and narrower perspectives of the particular constituencies selecting representatives for the assembly. Jefferson, Pendleton, Mason, Democritus, and Adams were all trying to differentiate those in the upper house from those in the lower without resorting to aristocracy, the same challenge being confronted everywhere in the colonies.[55]

Of course, not everyone shared their view. Pennsylvania took a strikingly different course, and the architects of its 1776 constitution offered their variant as a more democratic alternative.[56] Although delegates were chosen for the colony's constitutional convention by an unprecedentedly broad electorate, those who opposed independence were prevented from voting. This procedure produced a separate Loyalist assembly, which included many members of the popularly elected legislature ousted by the constitutional convention. Incongruously enough, the Loyalists gathered across the street from the Continental Congress in Philadelphia, even though the members of the Loyalist assembly inhabited a different conceptual universe from them and from those who wrote the 1776 Pennsylvania Constitution.

Those elected to that constitutional convention deliberately rejected Adams's counsel to follow the colony's existing practice. According to one delegate, the convention "determined not to pay the least regard to the former Constitutions" but chose to "clear away every part of the old rubbish" and "begin upon a clean foundation."[57] The convention was filled with critics of Pennsylvania's cautious elite and enthusiasts for Paine's ideas, including not only his friend Benjamin Rush but also shopkeeper Timothy Matlack, physician Thomas Young, painter Charles Willson Peale, watchmaker and astronomer David Rittenhouse, and Scottish-born teacher of mathematics James Cannon, who spoke for the colony's militia.

Almost as influential among these delegates as Paine's *Common Sense* was an anonymous pamphlet printed in Philadelphia in the spring of 1776, *The Genuine Principles of the Ancient Saxon, or English Constitution*. Written under the telling pseudonym "Demophilus," *Genuine Principles* drew on the most radical ideas of the dissenting Whig tradition and emphasized local institutions of government. The ancient Saxons' experience in public life had bred republican virtue, and when such active engagement gave way to mere voting, "men fell into a political stupor, and have never, to this day, thoroughly awakened, to a sense of the necessity there is, to watch over both legislative and executive departments in the state." Adams valued traditional colonial forms and practices; Demophilus saw in them only paralysis. "Fixed establishments" and "rooted habits and prejudices" had to be overcome if popular government were to flourish.[58] Those who wrote the 1776 Pennsylvania Constitution endorsed local participation and resented "the Aristocratic party" that had controlled Pennsylvania since its founding. Just as *Genuine Principles* emphasized annual elections to bind legislators to the will of the people, so the convention emphasized the importance of preventing another group of "*great men*" from seizing power through an upper house of the legislature.

The centerpiece of the radicals' model was a unicameral legislature, a less dramatic departure than the rhetoric mustered for and against it might suggest. Pennsylvania had, after all, been governed by a unicameral legislature (albeit together with an executive council and a governor who had to approve all legislation) since Penn's 1701 Charter of Privileges. The Continental Congress, meeting in Philadelphia as the nearest thing America had yet seen to a national government, was itself a unicameral assembly. Unicameralism was not without precedent, and it attracted some surprising supporters. Writing to Gouverneur Morris, Alexander Hamilton rejected the common charge that instability is inevitable in popular governments. Hamilton contended that history reveals a different source of trouble. Mixed governments failed because they "introduce distinct interests; and these interests will clash, throw the state into convulsions and produce a change or dissolution." Hamilton did not endorse, any more than Paine did, direct government by the people, which would end in "error, confusion and instability." A representative democracy with a single legislature, however, might avoid this danger without risking the more dangerous prospect of a senate becoming "purely aristocratical." Hamilton was only one among many whose judgment changed during the following decade.[59]

The language used by Pennsylvanians in support of unicameralism underscored the interchangeability of "republican" and "democratic" as clearly as did Virginia's Henry, Lee, or Braxton, New York's Hamilton, or the *Providence Gazette*. Writing in the *Pennsylvania Gazette*, "Salus Populi" contended that "popular Government—sometimes termed Democracy, Republick, or Commonwealth—is the plan of civil society wherein the community at large takes the care of its own welfare." In such circumstances, establishing an upper chamber, which "Salus Populi" considered a fake House of Lords, was admitting defeat, "creating *separate*, and *jarring interests*" where there should properly be only "one *common interest*." In the absence of a monarch or "hereditary nobility, different from the general body of the people," there was no need for an upper house that might nurture hierarchy.[60]

In an anonymous pamphlet published in the summer of 1776, James Cannon extended the widespread critique of an aristocracy by birth to include a denunciation of education and expertise, precisely the qualities prized by Adams, Jefferson, and many other champions of independence. America is fortunate, Cannon contended, "that there is no rank above that of Freeman," and "much of our future Welfare and Tranquility will depend on it remaining so for-ever." Convention delegates had to be chosen with care because "great and over-great rich Men" are "too apt to be framing Distinctions in Society." Those with "great learning" are likewise apt to "indulge their Disposition to refinement," so Pennsylvania should take care to avoid having too many educated delegates in its convention. Fortunately, an antidote to the perils of excessive learning was available. "Honesty, common Sense, and a plain understanding, when unbiased, by sinister Motives, are fully equal to the Task" of government. By linking wealth with education as disqualifying characteristics for the people's lawmakers, Cannon was drawing a distinction quite unlike that envisioned by most constitution writers in the other colonies, themselves well educated as well as well-to-do.[61]

Even Pennsylvania, however, placed limits on the suffrage. The writers of the Pennsylvania Constitution proclaimed "that every member of society hath a right to be protected in the enjoyment of life, liberty and property, and therefore is bound to contribute his proportion toward the expense of that protection, and to yield his personal service when necessary, or an equivalent thereto." Those who contributed by paying taxes earned protection of their property—and owed a debt proportional to the protection they received.[62] Although the 1776 constitution broadened the franchise by eliminating property as a criterion, the taxpaying qualification did exclude paupers, indentured servants, slaves, and women and children thought to be already represented in the collectivity of the household. Others, too, were ruled out. Those unwilling to take an oath of loyalty to the constitution were excluded from the franchise, and those who doubted the existence of a single God (such as Tom Paine, as became clear later), or denied the divine inspiration of the Old and New Testaments, could not be elected to the legislature. As "popular" as defenders of the 1776 constitution claimed it was, it still limited participation to a minority of the white, male, God-fearing taxpayers, whose elected representatives were to make, judge, and administer the law.

Understandings of representation were in flux during these crucial years. The uncertain and problematical nature of representation—who and what was to be represented, and according to what principle—was clear in the discrepancy between the procedures followed in determining membership in the Pennsylvania Constitutional Convention in 1776 and in the resulting constitution's provision for reapportionment every seven years. Consistent with the belief that communities rather than individuals deserved a voice in any assembly, each county elected one member in 1776. The constitution promulgated by that convention, however, offered a different rationale: "Representation in proportion to the number of taxable inhabitants is the only principle which can at all times secure liberty, and make the voice of the majority of the people the law of the land."[63]

Unfortunately for the partisans of the 1776 Pennsylvania Constitution, the provision for reapportionment according to population rather than representation by county meant that in the future an increasingly large number of representatives would be chosen from the populous and diverse regions of eastern Pennsylvania and Philadelphia. There unicameralism commanded less support, more people bristled at the oaths required by the constitution, and rival ideas such as the separation of powers appealed to a large number—eventually, the majority—of voters. Two competing ideals, one of local communities in which a common interest should prevail against all others, the other of individuals speaking their minds freely and clamoring for policies in line with their own personal interests, would collide in the coming decades. Both groups thought of themselves as speaking for "the people," and both branded their rivals antidemocratic. The results of their clash would come as an unpleasant surprise to many Pennsylvanians, both rural and urban, and transform the understandings of representation shared for centuries in Britain and by most Americans as late as 1776.

As the spring of 1776 turned to summer, debates heated up among the other group of colonists gathered in Philadelphia, the elected members of the Second Continental Congress. Now that the colonies had been instructed to frame new constitutions, declaring independence from Britain was the next step. The Congress was meeting in the same State House where the soon-to-be-disbanded Pennsylvania Assembly of Loyalists was digging in its heels against independence. Several colonial legislatures, including those of Pennsylvania and Virginia, had issued instructions binding their delegates to the Continental Congress to oppose independence. News that British warships and Hessian mercenaries were descending on Philadelphia, however, alarmed even the most cautious delegates, and Adams seized the moment to introduce a resolution branding continued allegiance to Britain contrary to Americans' "preservation of internal peace, virtue, and good order" and "absolutely irreconcilable to reason and good conscience."[64] Some legislatures formally rescinded their opposition to independence; events mooted any lingering hesitancy. Although the delegates had not yet been able to agree even to vote on whether they should act as a single nation, the Congress appointed Franklin, Adams, and Jefferson to draft a Declaration of Independence.

Jefferson is known to have written the first and final drafts of the Declaration of Independence submitted to the Continental Congress. Adams and Franklin are known to have read early drafts and to have made suggestions. Beyond that we have little more than competing and inconsistent accounts from Adams and Jefferson and speculation concerning their accuracy.[65] It is known, however, that more than ninety declarations of independence had tumbled forth from town, county, and colony-wide assemblies in the spring of 1776. Jefferson never disputed their significance, and he later claimed only to have offered an "expression of the American mind" and to have placed "before mankind the common sense of the subject, in terms so plain and firm as to command their assent."[66] Jefferson's Declaration did bring together many of the colonists' indictments of Britain and justifications of their cause. Speaking before the Massachusetts legislature, the Reverend Samuel West eerily foreshadowed Jefferson's words. After proclaiming that "all men" are "by nature equal," West contended that "if magistrates have no authority but what they derive from the people; if they are properly of human creation; if the whole end and design of their institution is to promote the general good, and to secure to men their just rights," then it follows that the people who gave them their authority can take it away from them if they act against the public interest.[67] Since it seems unlikely that Jefferson could have seen the text of West's sermon, the parallels suggest merely how conventional such arguments had become by May of 1776.

The dozens of other declarations produced in these months likewise drew on a set of shared, interlocking principles. They invoked the concept of self-preservation central to Christian doctrine, natural-law theory, and the English common law. They made use of Locke's and Rousseau's arguments about a state of nature and a social contract that individuals enter to establish laws and protect their rights. Finally, they deployed the idea that republican citizens must demonstrate their virtue through devotion to the common good. Reviewing these declarations shows how central the themes of community and responsibility—or an ideal of autonomy and an ethic of reciprocity—were to Americans' thinking.

In the words of the revolutionary law of Rhode Island, "in all states existing by compact, protection and allegiance are reciprocal; the latter being only due in consequence of the former." Because the king had shown no interest in protecting the colony's people, it became their "highest duty" to oppose his power and defend their "invaluable rights and privileges."[68] Because the king had "violated his compact," Maryland declared, they owed him no allegiance. Confident of the "justice of our cause," Maryland urged "every virtuous citizen to join cordially in defence of our common rights."[69]

Pennsylvania's Conference of Committees declared that the "despotism" of George III had dissolved "the obligations of allegiance (being reciprocal between a King and his subjects)."[70]

Communities from South Carolina to Massachusetts issued similar calls to create institutions of self-government authorized by the people. Now "the poorest man" of "virtue and merit" could be elevated to public office, then again be "blended in the common mass."[71] The benefits of self-government, the community of Charleston, South Carolina, predicted, would be felt "generally, equally, and indiscriminately" by all, "from the richest to the poorest." At the opposite end of the colony, the Cheraws grand jury declared that the "rights and happiness of the whole, the poor and the rich, are equally secured" in the new government of South Carolina. "The virtuous fruits" of the new constitution would be enjoyed forever because it established a government of the people.[72]

One of the principal themes uniting these declarations was confidence in, and deference to, the Second Continental Congress. Even as ordinary people were gathering on village greens, in meetinghouses, or in courtrooms to express their commitment to independence, and formally declaring it themselves, they took pains to specify that the ultimate decision would be made by their representatives in Philadelphia. A Congress of "wise and good men," in the words of the town of Topsfield, Massachusetts, in the northeast corner of the colony, was appropriately standing "at the helm of affairs, consulting measures which will be most for the safety and prosperity of the whole." In western Massachusetts, the townspeople of Palmer agreed to "submit the whole affair" to the "wise consideration and determination" of the Congress, and southwest of Boston, Wrentham expressed its "highest confidence under God" in "the honourable *American* Congress."[73] Just as it is impossible to separate the strands of religious, ethical, and political language running through these documents, so it is impossible—even at the moment of formally declaring war for independence—to separate the colonists' deference from their defiance. To eighteenth-century Americans, the shift of loyalty from king to Congress was jarring, but it happened fast. A new, shared sensibility emerged as English subjects began to think of themselves as members of a new American nation in the process of being born. From the shared sense of having been wronged sprang a shared sense of how to make things right. The answer was democracy.

Jefferson later claimed that he did not consult the books of learned philosophers as he composed his draft of the Declaration of Independence. It was unnecessary. He had already internalized the arguments of writers from Aristotle and Cicero through Grotius and Pufendorf, Harrington and Milton, Locke and Sidney, to Hutcheson, Reid, and the English dissenting Whigs.

He had read the Declaration of Rights in which his fellow Virginian George Mason had written, just weeks before, that "all men are born equally free and independent, and have certain inherent natural rights" including "the enjoyment of life and liberty." Like the other members of the Congress, he had read in a pamphlet by James Wilson, like Adams an avid reader of Rousseau, that "all men are, by nature, equal and free; no one has a right to any authority over another without his consent; all lawful government is founded on the consent of those who are subject to it." Of course, Jefferson was also aware of Adams's *Thoughts*. Moreover, he had already written his own *Summary View* and had just completed his own draft constitution for Virginia.[74]

Four particular features of Jefferson's Declaration had a lasting impact on democracy in America. First, Jefferson invoked the "laws of nature and nature's God" to justify independence to other nations. The "self-evident truths" included both "that all men are created equal" and that "they are endowed by their creator with inalienable rights." Jefferson did not invoke the words of Jesus,[75] yet his explicit reference to God the creator signals the religious sensibility he shared with those who would read the Declaration and embrace it.

Second, Jefferson altered Locke's triad of "life, liberty, and property." His reasons have generated considerable speculation. Property had been considered an adventitious—i.e., alienable—right ever since Aristotle. The colonists' complaints about taxes were real, yet Jefferson did not claim that property rights have the same sacred status as the rights to life and liberty. He understood, as did all the other members of the Continental Congress required to fund the war, that all governments depend on the power to tax citizens in order to provide—and enforce—the laws on which other rights depend.[76]

Third, Jefferson wrote that governments derive "their just powers from the consent of the governed," a proclamation of popular sovereignty expressing the colonists' shared understanding of their own experience and aspirations. Governments are instituted to secure the rights to "life, liberty and the pursuit of happiness" for all, and Jefferson balanced the people's legitimate desire to "secure their safety and happiness" against the prudent desire not to change "governments long established" for "light & transient causes." In place of their traditional allegiance to monarchy, the colonists were substituting a new commitment to self-government.

Finally, Jefferson's references to the unchanging "laws of nature" could be reconciled with popular sovereignty only because he assumed that each individual's judgment was directed by an internal gyroscope, the moral sense. Many of Jefferson's writings show his commitment to the ideas of Scottish common-sense philosophy. For those who ratified the Declaration of Independence, that moral code was consistent with the code of the Christian gospels, which insisted on the brotherhood of men and each individual's obligation to love his neighbor as himself. That brotherhood, of course, did not extend to the five hundred thousand slaves, roughly one-eighth of the American population, whose independence the Declaration did not address.[77] If there was tension between natural law and popular sovereignty, for Jefferson—as for Locke and Sidney—that tension was to be resolved in accordance not with man's whims but with God's will.[78]

Ambitious as these plans for independent institutions of government were, they were not the only changes Americans had in mind. Many were equally intent on launching a campaign for cultural reform. Countless writers identified the need for republican virtue that had been associated with forms of popular government since the ancient world. Two features were said to distinguish the American colonies from other republics that had failed to endure. First, those not enslaved enjoyed much greater social and economic equality. Celebrations of the unprecedentedly wide ownership of property went along with challenges to the last vestiges of feudal traditions such as primogeniture and entail, and unprecedentedly broad electorates were the natural consequence. Second, countless sermons up and down the colonies reminded Americans that they enjoyed the chance to achieve self-government thanks to God's grace, and ministers warned that they would be able to preserve their republics only by living up to the ethic laid down in the gospels.[79]

Older dreams of a city upon a hill, the dreams of John Winthrop, Roger Williams, and Thomas Hooker, continued to reverberate. Adams's *Thoughts on Government* proclaimed, conventionally enough, that a republic's "principle and foundation is virtue." If a republican constitution of the sort he was recommending helped to improve the level of education among the people of Massachusetts and inspired in them the "conscious dignity becoming freemen," from that spirit might spread "good humor, sociability, good manners, and good morals." Adams explicitly distinguished his vision of republican virtue from the genteel Addisonian refinement that appealed to many of his European contemporaries. Self-government inspires "sober, industrial, and frugal habits" and "makes the common people brave and enterprising." Observers might find among Americans "some elegance, perhaps, but more solidity," and "some politeness, but more civility." Adams might have moved from Puritan to liberal Protestant theology, but he remained wedded to his ancestors' stern civic and cultural ideals.[80]

As the new state constitutions were being debated, and shortly before the Continental Congress took the precipitous step of declaring independence, Adams wrote to Abigail that the new governments taking shape throughout the colonies "will require a Purification from our Vices, and an Augmentation of our Virtues or they will be no Blessings."[81] Many shared the view of Benjamin Rush, who predicted that the rigors imposed by the War for Independence would "purge away the monarchical impurity we contracted by laying so long upon the lap of Great Britain." Because "liberty without virtue would be no blessing to us," Rush continued, "peace at this time would be the greatest curse that could befall us."[82] Rush had in mind, along with both John and Abigail Adams, the ideal that Samuel Adams captured with a memorable phrase. Americans were building a "Christian Sparta," and they shared his fear as well as his hope: "I am infinitely more apprehensive of the Contagion of Vice than the Power of all other Enemies," Samuel Adams wrote in the summer of 1777. "We shall succeed if we are virtuous."[83]

Sentiments such as Rush's were as widespread in the middle colonies as in New England. The New Jersey Presbyterian minister John Witherspoon, the only minister to sign the Declaration of Independence, was crucial in forging an alliance between Congregationalists in New England and Presbyterians and Anglicans in colonies farther south. Having battled with Francis Hutcheson before leaving Scotland in 1768 to become president of the College of New Jersey, Witherspoon helped cement Scottish common-sense philosophy in America. He trained many of the ministers who took over pulpits throughout the middle colonies, and he taught several of the most influential delegates to the Constitutional Convention in 1787, including James Madison.[84] Witherspoon thus exerted a powerful influence on American civic as well as religious life, and his 1776 sermon *The Dominion of Providence over the Passions of Men* shows how religious language was woven together with political arguments.

Witherspoon took issue with Paine's dismissive treatment of religion and insisted that the spirit animating the drive toward independence began with the Protestant Reformation. It was religious persecution that led to the settling of New England, where many practiced their faith "in as great a degree of purity" as could be found "in any protestant church now in the world." That purity now fed the revolution.[85] The colonies united not from "pride, resentment, or sedition," Witherspoon continued, but from "a deep and general conviction, that our civil and religious liberties" and our "temporal and eternal happiness" were at stake. Respecting God's will meant shielding citizens' freedom. History contained no examples of nations preserving religious liberty and losing civil liberty. Succumbing to Britain's demands would "deliver the conscience into bondage." Britain was too distant and too corrupt to control the colonies, which were now ready to govern themselves.

Witherspoon conceded that some "selfish persons" were trying to profit from the conflict—to be expected given original sin—but he was more surprised that "so great a degree of public spirit" marked the colonists' efforts. Now they must avoid the temptation of "provincial pride," prevent themselves from separating into "different classes," and find the common cause that would unite them in their struggle to achieve self-government. The ethic of reciprocity, from Witherspoon's perspective, was the ethic of Christians as well as members of a self-governing polity. Learning to internalize the self-denial, restraint, and moderation enjoined by the gospels was appropriate for Christians and necessary for independent citizens aiming to meet their civic obligations. Remember, Witherspoon urged in conclusion, "that your duty to God, to your country, to your families, and to yourselves is the same."[86]

Beyond the regeneration of souls urged by Witherspoon and his fellow preachers, how would Americans secure the virtue required for their democratic or republican forms of government?[87] Beneath the ubiquitous encomia to virtue lay submerged tensions and resentments. The extraordinary Abigail Adams, although hardly a typical American in these or any other years, expressed and questioned the multistranded and dynamic discourse of virtue. The letters she wrote to her son and future president John Quincy display the sensibility historians associate with the ideal of republican motherhood; her letters to her husband and her friend Mercy Otis Warren show her chafing under the constraints of that role.

The precocious twelve-year-old John Quincy Adams accompanied his father when he was sent to Europe, in the midst of the Revolution, to secure loans from France and Holland. "These are times in which a Genious would wish to live," Abigail wrote to her son, striking the same chord as her husband and likewise piling up numerous ancient examples. Abigail urged her son to reflect on God's grace in preserving him and his father through the perils of their voyage, which included a frightening attack by a British vessel and a dangerous storm that blew them off course to Spain. "Every new Mercy you receive is a New Debt upon you, a new *obligation* to a diligent discharge of the various relations in which you stand connected; in the first place to your Great Preserver, in the next to Society in General, in particular to your Country, to your parents and to yourself." Abigail reiterated the advice that her son, like almost everyone else in the colonies, would have heard for years from preachers such as Witherspoon: "The only sure and permanent foundation of virtue is Religion."

John Quincy's mother counseled him to discharge his debts through the "performance of certain duties which tend to the happiness and welfare of Society," encapsulated in the command to "Love thy Neighbor as thyself." In the midst of a revolution being fought to establish a republic, however, there was more to be said on the subject of responsibility. "Justice, humanities and

Benevolence are the duties you owe to society in general," Abigail continued, and "to your Country the same duties are incumbent upon you with the additional obligation of sacrificeing ease, pleasure, wealth and life itself for its defence and security." She brought home her message with a single phrase. Whatever our fate after death might be, "Virtue alone is happiness below."[88]

The Adams family shared that conviction with countless other colonists. It extended beyond the clergy and the devout to learned scientists. Abigail and John's physician friends John Warren, martyred at Bunker Hill, and Benjamin Rush expressed similar sentiments in their writings. Rush wrote to Abigail that religion is "the only foundation for a useful education in a republic." Without faith there can be "no virtue, and without virtue there can be no liberty, and liberty is the object and life of all republican government."[89] Rush's formulation captures the standard American identification of republican virtue with religion and education, two aspects of colonial life reflected in many of the new state constitutions.[90] As Adams wrote in *Thoughts*, "Laws for the liberal education of youth, especially of the lower class of people, are so extremely wise and useful, that, to a humane and generous mind, no expense for this purpose would be thought extravagant."[91] If our reflex now is to focus on Adams's reference to "the lower class of people," the point of the passage is that no expense should be spared to help the less prosperous alter their condition.

Adams made clear his commitment to equality in a letter to Massachusetts Superior Court judge James Sullivan on May 26, 1776, in which Adams invoked Harrington's agrarian: "the balance of power in a society" follows the ownership of land. The only way to preserve that balance "on the side of equal liberty and public virtue"—his principal aim in *Thoughts*—"is to make the acquisition of land easy to every member of society; to make a division of the land into small quantities, so that the multitude may be possessed of landed estates." Like Jefferson in his draft constitution for Virginia, Adams wanted to extend the tradition of widespread landholding in the New England countryside. Self-government required no less. If most people own property, power will be widely dispersed, and in that case "the multitude will take care of the liberty, virtue, and interest of the multitude, in all acts of government."[92]

If that was the advantage of equality, Adams also knew from personal experience the drawbacks of inequality. As "Humphrey Ploughjogger" he had expressed his loathing of Boston's gentry, and in the years of the Revolution he condemned "that exuberance of pride" that produced "an insolent domination" by a very few "opulent, monopolizing families." He vowed that such grandees would have to be brought down, in a republic, to a degree of reasonable moderation. Unequal as property distribution had been in much of New

England, Adams understood that slavery made conditions more poisonous in the southern colonies. There the far wider gulf between rich and poor gave "an aristocratical turn" to social life and politics, which accounted for the "strong aversion" many wealthy southern planters expressed for Adams's *Thoughts* and Paine's *Common Sense*. No matter, Adams concluded. In the independent republics that the colonies were about to become, "the spirit of these barons" would be broken.[93]

Yet Adams's passion for equality had limits, as Abigail knew. "In the Code of Laws which I suppose it will be necessary for you to make," Abigail wrote to John in March of 1776, when the departure of the British fleet from Boston and the expectation that independence would soon be declared had lightened her heart, "I desire that you would Remember the Ladies, and be more generous and favourable to them than your ancestors. Do not put such unlimited power into the hands of the Husbands." After Abigail quoted Daniel Defoe's familiar adage, "Remember all men would be tyrants if they could," she put its wisdom to her own uses. "If particular care and attention is not paid to the ladies," Abigail warned, "we are determined to foment a rebellion, and will not hold ourselves bound by any laws in which we have no voice or representation." Not only the men but also the women of America were tired of having others make decisions for them.

Abigail's tone changed as she continued. "That your sex are naturally tyrannical is a truth so thoroughly established as to admit of no dispute, but such of you as wish to be happy willingly give up the harsh title of master for the more tender and endearing one of friend," as indeed John had done with her. "Why then not put it out of the power of the vicious and the lawless to use us with cruelty?" Why allow men to subject their wives to endless indignities "with impunity"? Surely, Abigail reasoned, those proclaiming the glory of self-government should abide neither race slavery nor the subjection of women. "Men of Sense in all Ages abhor those customs which treat us only as vassals of your Sex. Regard us then as Beings placed by providence under your protection and in imitation of the Supreem Being make use of that power only for our happiness."[94]

Abigail Adams spoke for many, and other women went further than chiding their husbands. Some raised the question of woman suffrage, which she herself was not ready to entertain. In January of 1776, the New Jersey Provincial Congress decided to grant the suffrage to "all freeholders, and householders" who possessed "fifty pounds clear estate." The absence of any pronouns specifying gender appears to have been deliberate. The issue was debated again in 1790, and the pronouns "he or she" removed any ambiguity from the earlier language. Until 1807, all single adult women, whether unmarried or widowed, enjoyed the right to vote in New Jersey. Although that landmark provision sparked other discussions of the issue, it remained an achievement puzzling in its singularity.[95]

Replying to his wife Abigail's call for a new and "extraordinary Code of Laws," John struck the light tone he correctly perceived in the opening sentences of her letter. "I cannot but laugh," he wrote, in a sarcasm-laden reply that has been read as an earnest statement of patriarchal, even misogynist principles. "We have been told that our Struggle has loosened the bands of Government every where. That Children and Apprentices were disobedient—that schools and Colledges were grown turbulent—that Indians slighted their Guardians and Negroes grew insolent to their Masters. But your Letter was the first Intimation that another Tribe more numerous and powerfull than all the rest were grown discontented." After trying out what he clearly considered the stock rhetorical strategy *reductio ad absurdum*, Adams essayed another already familiar trope: "In Practice you know We are the subjects. We have only the Name of Masters, and rather than give up this, which would compleatly subject Us to the Despotism of the Peticoat, I hope General Washington, and all our brave Heroes would fight."[96]

There the matter appears to have been left. At least it was not the subject of any further surviving correspondence from husband to wife. Writing to her close friend Mercy Otis Warren, Abigail observed that in his reply John had simply called her "sausy" and shrugged off her complaint. But her tone with her friend was more serious, and more annoyed. She had asked John to frame a code of laws "upon just and Liberal principles" that would control the currently limitless power of a husband "to use his wife ill." Abigail would rechannel her resentment, she confided, by telling John she had "only been making trial of the Disinterestedness of his Virtue, and when weigh'd in the balance have found it wanting." Abigail saw already the quality that John's critics would see demonstrated two decades later: his interpretation of civic virtue could be as narrow as it was deep.[97]

Abigail had reason to suspect that Mercy Otis Warren would be sympathetic with her protests. Her brother James Otis had asked as early as 1764, in *The Rights of the British Colonies Asserted and Proved*, "Are not women born as free as men?" Since they are, Otis insisted, every woman as well as man possesses a "right to be consulted" in forming any compact or government.[98] Abigail's knowledge that some of her friends shared her views strengthened her resolve. After writing to Mercy Otis Warren, she wrote another letter to John. It was inappropriate, she observed, for the Continental Congress to proclaim peace and goodwill toward all men and nations while still "retaining an absolute power over Wives." To deliver her coup de grace she selected a weapon from Adams's own arsenal: "Arbitrary power is like most other things which are very hard, very liable to be broken." No matter how wise your laws, she concluded, we women enjoy the power "not only to free ourselves but to subdue our Masters."[99]

If John Adams never again directly addressed the issue of women's rights in his letters to Abigail, he did not forget his run-in with her on the subject. He respected her judgment too much to dismiss her suggestions out of hand.[100] In the letter to James Sullivan quoted above, in addition to his comments on the widespread nature of property-holding in New England, Adams addressed existing limits on suffrage. If "the only moral foundation of government is consent," as all Americans except a few Loyalists now agreed, then on what basis could any limits be placed on the franchise? Should not children, the destitute, and women vote? For the last, Adams suggested that Sullivan would advance the most common answer: "their delicacy" rendered them unfit for "the great businesses of life," including war and politics. Besides, he imagined Sullivan continuing, nature fitted them for "domestic cares." John worried that even raising the question of changing existing qualifications would open the floodgates. As Abigail had shown, out would come women, children, slaves, and the "penniless and shiftless." No, Adams reassured himself and Sullivan, better to limit the franchise to those men deemed independent by virtue of the property they owned. Otherwise all dependents would grow restless, "and there will be no end to it."

Adams's rambling letter suggests he knew he was stuck. He endorsed a wider distribution of property in New England. He understood that continuing such practices would mean that ever more adult males would vote. Yet he clung to restrictions because the alternative would "confound and destroy all distinctions, and prostrate all ranks to one common level," an outcome leading to anarchy and thus fatal for a democracy. Removing one set of rulers might set in motion a process that would cause authority itself—even that authorized by the people—to lose its force. The result would be mob rule, the persistent fear of democracy's critics since the ancient world. In that case, Adams concluded, Tories would watch gleefully as the fragile new republics collapsed. Abigail yoked women's rights with the injustice of slavery, just as James Otis had done when he proclaimed that all Massachusetts colonists "are by the law of nature free born, as indeed all men are white and black." Otis denied that race justified slavery, a view that attracted a growing number of adherents in the ensuing decades. Abigail asked whether the "passion for Liberty" could persist among those "accustomed to deprive their fellow Creatures of theirs." Her husband, who deplored slavery as a "foul contagion in the human character," agreed with her."[101]

Adams waxed vitriolic about delegates to the Continental Convention who urged moderation when he was passionately calling for independence, yet his respect for New England traditions—including widespread landownership and public participation in public life, and also the tradition of patriarchy, coupled with his anxieties about radical egalitarianism—made him resist Abigail's call for equal treatment. Having just urged the colonies to act rashly in severing their ties with Britain and setting up democratic governments of their own, Adams now counseled caution when dealing with the rights of women and the propertyless. His clumsy attempts to reconcile his democratic radicalism with his cultural conservatism would end up transforming him from the prophetic champion of popular government into the most visible target of self-proclaimed democrats.[102]

The colonists had come a long way during the year leading up to the fateful decision to declare independence. They had settled on the need for constitutional conventions. They had forged from the precedents and practices of their diverse modes of governance a group of strikingly democratic polities. They had decided that an unprecedentedly large electorate, but an electorate still limited to white males who owned property, would be able to participate in their postmonarchical experiment in representative government. Finally, they had committed themselves, or at least they had been urged again and again to commit themselves, to building the culture of virtue—ethical, civic, and religious virtue—that would be necessary to sustain their democracy.

The Declaration launched Americans into the sea of independence without providing any clear sense of what lay on the horizon. The brave proclamations of unity among the new United States of America and the confidence expressed in the citizen soldiers who would volunteer to serve, and who would then defeat the combined military force of Britain and its Hessian mercenaries, could not long conceal the unsteady grip of the new nation's central government or its meager resources. With some of the former colonies failing to provide enough money or men to fight the war, the states seemed able to agree only that the others were not doing their fair share. Sturdy yeomen farmers proved less eager to enlist than the Congress had anticipated; typically only the very poor proved willing to fight.[103]

The War for Independence was a nightmare for most Americans and a near-catastrophe for American democracy. During eight long years of warfare, it deepened existing divisions and opened new ones, and many of those social, cultural, geographical, regional, and economic rifts did not heal. Some places, such as Westchester County, New York, and parts of Pennsylvania, New Jersey, and North Carolina, experienced protracted warfare, and the pitched battles between armies constituted only part of the carnage. Armed bands of Patriots and Loyalists, poorly equipped, disorganized, and pitiless, raided, torched, looted, and commandeered farms, livestock, and food throughout the colonies. Women found themselves impoverished and endangered, forced to endure not only the absence of their husbands, sons, and brothers but also the presence of ragged partisans lacking supplies and discipline.

The American economy was slumping even before the war began. The imperial crisis meant that all trade was disrupted. Money was even scarcer than before; per capita income plummeted. Eight years of warfare left almost all Americans poorer, but shortages of food, money, and credit had the deepest impact on those who had the least. The livelihoods of sailors, dockhands, and other maritime laborers vanished with colonial boycotts and did not return while the war raged. Artisans and craftsmen lacked supplies and markets for their work. Unable to trade, people in the countryside returned to subsistence farming. Women planted cotton or sheared sheep to compensate for the absence of imported textiles. They carded fibers, spun thread, and wove cloth, but they could not meet demand at home or on the battlefield. A shrinking number of women and girls had to do the work of missing, wounded, or dead menfolk. Lord Dunmore promised freedom to any slaves willing to fight for Britain, and tens of thousands of African Americans fled to the crown only to be shipped to Canada or the Caribbean with their Loyalist owners. In the backcountry, clashes with Indians, some allied with Britain and others striking back at the settlers who had occupied land and resources they considered their own, compounded the violence.

With almost everyone suffering, resentments and scapegoats multiplied. Merchants, bankers, and lawyers became targets for rowdy mobs, not only in the coastal cities but also in towns scattered through the countryside. Preexisting tensions turned violent, as artisans and mechanics in Philadelphia turned against merchants and shopkeepers. Established families from New England through New York to Georgia found their positions challenged by upstarts emboldened by talk of equality. Some patriots enforced boycotts, engineered rent strikes, and threatened the lives and property of fence-sitters. Given the depth of many colonists' loyalty to Britain, the shaky prospects of the ill-trained and under-funded Continental Army, and the uncertain future facing a nation ringed by European powers, many Americans—perhaps even a majority—wavered between the warring nations. By some estimates, 20 percent actively supported the Loyalist cause, another 40 to 60 percent favored independence, and perhaps nearly half remained neutral or disengaged throughout the conflict. The soaring rhetoric of Jefferson's Declaration, widely printed and read aloud throughout the colonies, persuaded some who heard or read it. But many people with little interest in politics before the crisis kept as much distance as possible from the struggle against Britain, and from the myriad internal conflicts the war intensified.[104]

The new nation was fortunate that France, seeing an opportunity to weaken its principal imperial rival, agreed to help it survive. Without the soldiers and ships sent by Louis XVI, and without financial support from the Dutch as well as the French, the British might have preserved their North American empire. Although the troops Washington commanded did manage to become an effective army, which performed well in the decisive battles of Saratoga and Yorktown, on their own they would have had trouble persevering over eight and a half years, a longer time span than that of the Civil War or World War II. Casualties numbered upwards of thirty-five thousand, a percentage of the American population higher than in any conflict except the Civil War. As the struggle dragged on, public support grew as ragged as the winter uniforms of the Continental Army, whose chief engineer, Louis Duportail, was among the French imports who provided needed expertise. The Americans' lack of devotion to the cause disappointed him. He reported home to his government, with only slight exaggeration, that "there is a hundred times more enthusiasm for this Revolution in any Paris café than in all the colonies together."[105] That enthusiasm cost less in Paris than it did where the battles were being fought, but it would prove consequential soon enough.

As war raged in March of 1778, Massachusetts decided to write a new constitution, which the specially elected body then submitted to a popular referendum. A growing consensus held that constitutions, the formal expression of popular sovereignty, required the people's approval. By a margin of almost five to one, 9,972 to 2,083, the constitution was rejected by an electorate that included all adult males. Explanations ranged from discontent about property qualifications for voters and officeholders, on the one hand, to fears that ordinary people were unqualified to exercise such authority, on the other. A particularly pointed critique of popular grumbling emerged from twelve of the twenty-one towns in Essex County in northeastern Massachusetts. The *Essex Result*, read to the constitutional convention by Theophilus Parsons, the Newburyport lawyer who wrote it, acknowledged that concern with the common good can "result from a democracy" but contended that Massachusetts now also needed qualities such as "wisdom, learning, and firmness and consistency of character," qualities found only "amongst gentlemen of education, fortune, and leisure." Others traced the problem to their wealthy neighbors. They argued that representatives to the legislature should advance the interests of the ordinary people they represented, not chase some amorphous, chimerical "common good," which appeared very different to struggling farmers and artisans than to those whose pretensions to "greater wisdom" veiled efforts to shield their wealth. Could these contrasting arguments, which would echo through the next century, be reconciled?[106]

John Adams, already skeptical about the prospect of unity as a result of his experience at the Continental Congress, was sent to Europe as an American envoy in 1777. There his anxieties deepened. Traveling to Paris from Bordeaux, Adams observed lush fields of grain and vast vineyards. "The delights of France are innumerable," he wrote to Abigail. "The politeness, the elegance, the softness, the delicacy is extreme." But France was hardly paradise: "Every place swarms with beggars." The contrast between the aristocracy's wealth and the poverty of the masses shocked him, "stern and haughty republican that I am." He found himself ill-suited to the *beau-monde* that delighted Franklin. Adams returned from European court life convinced that Americans must maintain their equality and their "stern" virtue, and that the latter could not survive without the former. Exposure to luxury confirmed his fears about the lure of self-indulgence, which Parsons and others had reported was markedly on the rise. It was during this trip, when he saw the gulf dividing the dissolute French aristocracy from the simple life that Adams linked with republican virtue, that he first wrote to Abigail advising her to read Rousseau. The author of the *Social Contract* was "too virtuous for the Age, and for Europe," although perhaps not for "another country," by which he meant the American republic of John and Abigail's dreams. Adams's first experience with grandeur only deepened his affinity with its most notorious critic.[107]

Massachusetts decided to try again. This time Adams was elected to the convention, and when he was named "principal engineer" of the new constitution, as he put it, he could barely contain his delight. Now he could bring to life the commonwealth Rousseau had only imagined. Adams was hardly alone. Massachusetts was alive with ideas, and debates about the earlier constitution of 1778 spawned many new proposals, several of which brought together ideas from the Puritans, the Levellers, Sidney, and Locke as well as those articulated in the decade leading to independence. The delegate from the town of Stoughton, north of Boston, came to the constitutional convention equipped with propositions that expressed convictions widely shared throughout the Commonwealth. Starting from a bedrock assumption that "a republican form of government is the most agreeable to the Genius of the people," Stoughton laid out the ambitious theory of government that would prevail in the new nation. People join together to obtain the advantages of common life, yet they preserve all the rights necessary to limit the state's power. Even so, individuals must subordinate their personal desires "where the good of the whole Requirest it." Turning to institutions, Stoughton stipulated that the powers of government should be kept separate and balanced, and all those powers must be understood to flow from the people, "the Grand fountain of Supreme Power." Only if the citizens of Massachusetts remained careful sluice keepers could they avoid drowning in a "flood of Tyranny."[108]

The constitution Adams drafted for Massachusetts incorporated both Stoughton's spirit and most of its details. Adams had been selected to draft the constitution because he had proven to be a leading champion of self-government. The congruence between the Stoughton proposals and other, similar proclamations and the writings of Adams and other Patriot leaders indicates the tight connection between popular discussions of government and the documents crafted by the most prominent political figures in the new nation. Significant disagreements existed, and those differences would be magnified in the coming decades. Yet few Americans would have quarreled with the principles drawn up by the Stoughton town meeting, and very few Britons would have endorsed them.

Adams's preamble, which emphasizes the will of the community rather than the choices of individuals, and underscores the continuing authority of the people as a whole, deliberately echoed Rousseau's ideas even more clearly than Locke's: "It is a social compact by which the whole people covenants with each citizen and each citizen with the whole people, that all shall be governed by certain laws for the common good." Rather than forming a compact with their government, the people were contracting with each other. They—not their government once it was formed—remained sovereign, just as Rousseau had argued in the *Social Contract*. Reflecting the conviction that such founding documents must be submitted for popular approval rather than merely declared in force (as had been done, for example, in Pennsylvania in 1776), the convention amended Adams's phrase "the delegates of the people" so the preamble opened with the words that would ring throughout the states thereafter, "We the people."[109] After his draft was adopted with only minor revisions, Adams reflected on its significance: "There never was an example of such precautions as are taken by this wise and jealous people in the formation of their government. None was ever made so perfectly upon the principle of the people's rights and equality. It is Locke, Sidney, and Rousseau and de Mably reduced to practice." Although Adams later denounced Rousseau, until the mid-1790s he remained a resolute defender of "the people's rights and equality" as understood by the author of the *Social Contract*.[110]

Adams emphasized the implications of popular sovereignty for the Massachusetts Constitution. This was the unifying theme of his thought from the 1760s onward, and the close resemblance between his formulation and the Stoughton principles indicates the widely shared understanding of this fundamental idea. "The people of this commonwealth have the sole and exclusive right of governing themselves, as a free, sovereign, and independent state." They will maintain "every power, jurisdiction, and right" not expressly delegated to the national government. Because all power resides in the people and derives from them, all officers of government—appointed as well as elected—"are at all times accountable to them." No laws, and no taxes, could be imposed without popular consent, as expressed by the judgment of "the representative body of the people." Any attempt to subvert the common good, Adams declared categorically, was inconsistent with republican government. As in Jefferson's Declaration and in Rousseau's *Social Contract*, Adams made the rights of individuals subservient to the welfare of the community. That understanding of self-government, so widely shared as to be conventional at the time, shows why Adams described his blueprint as Rousseau "reduced to practice."

Invocations of the common good in these early state constitutions justified the hardheaded insistence that because all government officials held in trust the public interest, they could be removed from office for breach of that trust. If public servants in Massachusetts were thought to have placed their personal interests, or the interests of a particular group of citizens, above the interest of the Commonwealth, they could be removed from office. Because Adams considered the virtues of "piety, justice, moderation, temperance, industry, and frugality" crucial in popular government, he urged the people to remain vigilant about public servants' observance of those ideals. Adams believed all elected officials should be held to a high standard and kept on a short leash. He wanted all members of the assembly and the senate, as well as the governor, chosen directly by the people in annual elections. That feature of his plan, emphasizing popular control of both houses of the legislature, distinguished it from many other state constitutions written during the late 1770s.

Massachusetts never had to wrestle with the question of a bill of rights. Perhaps because of the intolerance of the early Puritans or because of the tradition inaugurated by the work of Nathaniel Ward a century earlier and incorporated into the colony's practices, by 1780 protecting rights was taken for granted in the commonwealth. Adams included in his original draft many provisions of the first ten amendments to the United States Constitution. To ensure the responsible exercise of these rights, Adams proposed that Massachusetts support education from the primary grades through college. Here the legislature did him one better, further stipulating support of Harvard College, and insulating it from any intrusions on its financial or intellectual independence, because a Christian republic could survive only with an educated citizenry. Adams underscored the importance of funding expensive elementary and secondary schools and various "private societies and public institutions" devoted to diffusing "wisdom and knowledge, as well as virtue" among the populace, underscoring once again the links between the American Enlightenment, Christianity, and self-government. Universal education was necessary "to inculcate the principles of humanity and general benevolence, public and private charity, industry and frugality, honesty, punctuality in their dealings, sincerity, good humor, and all social affections and generous sentiments among the people." Without virtue, which was understood within the three overlapping frameworks of Christianity, moral philosophy, and politics, Massachusetts would fall victim to the ancient dangers of anarchy; tyranny would inevitably follow.

The question of whether representatives are free to use their own judgment or bound by instructions from those who elected them is perennial in democracy, and it generated lively debate during the American Revolution. Adams and many others worried about the assertiveness of local gatherings—particularly in the increasingly boisterous western part of Massachusetts—yet he included in his draft constitution a provision for the people to "consult upon the common good, give instructions to their representatives," and petition for "redress of the wrongs done them, and the grievances they suffer." Given the direct annual election of all legislators and the governor by the people of the state, some thought further encumbering their deliberations unnecessary. But such encumbering was precisely the aim of those Americans who viewed all attempts to concentrate power as a threat to the republic.[111]

The issue of instructions was among the most vexed and complex debated during these years. It brought into focus the discrepancy between two views. According to the older conception, the general good existed apart from particular interests and was likeliest achieved by the deliberations of wise legislators who represented everyone and sought the general interest. According to the newer view, which had emerged before and during the American Revolution, the interests of different parts of the society required representatives to speak on behalf of the particular constituencies that elected them. When that difference centered on the gulf dividing the colonies from Mother England, colonists could agree. When the interests were those of, say, rural versus urban, or agrarian versus commercial regions of a state, or between states—divisions becoming increasingly bitter in the 1770s and 1780s—the "republican" or "democratic" solution to the problem was murkier. From the Levellers and Sidney to Rousseau, Paine, and Jefferson, theorists sympathetic with self-governing nations had envisioned representative assemblies sifting, or refining, the preferences of individuals and groups through a process of deliberation that generated new perspectives and a broadened understanding of the common good. Now that ideal was under fire. Because the controversy with Britain had centered on the difference between "virtual" and "actual" representation, many colonists had become suspicious of allowing elected officials any leeway at all. Compounding the problem, some towns and counties had traditionally issued binding instructions to their representatives, as Braintree had given Adams in 1765, so it made sense, to Adams and to many others, to continue that practice.

Some saw a problem. As the Massachusetts Constitution was being debated, a writer for Boston's *Independent Chronicle* feared that townspeople now saw "the common interest" only in terms of "private or particular advantages to their own towns or persons, the prejudice of other towns." The president of Yale College, Ezra Stiles, complained that legislators were weighing only "particular local interests." This tension, intrinsic to representative government, was intensifying everywhere. In South Carolina, brewer William Hornby insisted that abandoning instructions would "at a stroke transform us into *legal* SLAVES to our *lordly* SERVANTS" in the legislature, whereas a critic of the practice predicted that "fettering" representatives would disable them from attending to "the *general combined* interest of *all* the state *put together*."[112]

The intense localism of the western regions of most American states derived from their increasingly sharp perception that their interests differed from those of the more urban and commercial centers on the Atlantic seaboard, and it manifested itself in various demands. Some western writers insisted that each town or county, no matter how small, ought to have its own representative in the state legislature because each corporate body differed from every other. Inhabitants of rural New Hampshire complained that joining together separate towns and giving them a single representative was akin to taking "the souls of a number of different persons to say they make one, while yet they remain separate and different."[113] Many of those clustered in cities along the Atlantic coast, by contrast, believed that acknowledging and encouraging such parochialism would paralyze legislatures and prevent the forging of coherent republican governments. Reflecting on this problem in 1778, Massachusetts resident William Whiting predicted that following the lead of Berkshire County would transform the fledgling United States of America into "the *infinite number of jarring, disunited factions of America*." Such blinkered, cranky provincials, "now erecting little democracies" in every village, would not only destroy the nation but also prevent the creation of a genuinely democratic Commonwealth of Massachusetts, in which the good of the whole, not the interests of particular parts, remained the objective.[114]

Adams aimed to solve that problem. If the people assembled peacefully in their communities "to consult upon the common good," then gave their representatives instructions derived from that broadened understanding rather than reflecting their particular, narrow interests, then their instructions would initiate rather than obstruct the deliberative process on which representative democracy depends. Both of these conceptual advances, it is worth emphasizing, depended on Rousseau's reformulation of English theorists' version of the social contract. Sidney had argued in his *Discourses* that the public good emerges from the give-and-take of debate. Rousseau had recommended to Geneva the value of deliberation by representatives for the same reason: it was the best way for men (although of course not for angels) to come to a rough understanding of the general will. That understanding of the purpose and potential of democratic deliberation, confirmed by Adams's personal experience in town meetings, state legislative assemblies, and the Continental Congress, manifested itself in all of his writings about government from his Braintree Instructions through his draft of the Massachusetts Constitution. No wonder Adams wanted Abigail to read Rousseau.[115]

Adams envisioned a notably broad suffrage by the standards of the day. Voters would include all men over twenty-one with a modest stake in the state, a freehold estate yielding a mere three pounds or "other real or personal estate of the value of sixty pounds." Almost all adult males in Massachusetts not living at home would pass that bar, as low as any in the new United States.[116] Adams also stipulated that voters must have resided for a full year in the community in which they were to vote, a requirement more stringent than had been in place to that point. Residency requirements were becoming a standard feature of American politics as a result of the colonists' protests against "virtual representation" in Parliament. Revealingly, in 1774 England abolished even the fig leaf of formal residency requirements in parliamentary elections, thereby underscoring the gulf dividing American from British ideas and practices. Two years later, Pennsylvania decided formally to require residency for candidates running for office in any electoral district. When Montesquieu had envisioned the proper functioning of representation in his *Spirit of the Laws*, he specified requirements of the sort being put in place in America, and his American admirers, including Adams, Jefferson, and many others, echoed his rationale. Unless representatives resided in the same place as those they represented, they could neither understand nor be perceived by their constituents to understand the conditions under which citizens lived.[117]

Adams was proposing a constitution that provided more explicit local control than he did in his *Thoughts on Government*. He tried to balance the desire for fair apportionment of legislative districts against the concerns of small towns.[118] When he specified the characteristics of those eligible for elective office, he deviated from his earlier pattern. His first two criteria, Christian faith and residency in the district, were uncontroversial, although the second remained somewhat innovative at a time when practices patterned on England's rotten boroughs remained common in some parts of America. Adams proposed much higher property requirements for officeholders, particularly for senators and the governor, which the Massachusetts convention did not adopt. Instead it used the proportion of tax revenue contributed by different districts to determine representation in the senate.[119]

Without a hereditary aristocracy that all Americans opposed, the states were wrestling with the question of how to justify the existence of a senate—and how to distinguish it from the lower house. Adams had savaged the upper house of colonial Massachusetts, the Governor's Council, in his "Novanglus" essays. He resisted the ideas, floated elsewhere, that senators should hold life tenure or, as George Mason proposed for Virginia and as Maryland enacted, that they should be selected indirectly by the legislature or by special electors. With few (and brief) exceptions, Americans agreed about the need for a second chamber, but they were not sure how it should be constituted. Jefferson too was fretting about the branches of the new state governments. In his *Notes on the State of Virginia*, a rambling reply to queries about Virginia sent by François de Margolis in 1781, Jefferson addressed this issue. He first traced the development of democratic government from the initial meetings of the assembly in the early seventeenth century and showed how that practice of self-government had laid the groundwork for the Revolution. He then observed that Virginia's assembly and its senate too nearly resembled each other. "The purpose of establishing different houses of legislation is to introduce the influence of different interests or different principles." Perhaps thinking of the recent innovations in Massachusetts, he wrote, "In some of the American states the delegates and senators are so chosen, as that the first represent the persons, and the second the property of the state. But with us, wealth and wisdom have equal chance for admission into both houses." In Virginia these legislative bodies controlled the judiciary and the executive, a situation that Jefferson described as "the definition of despotic government."

Having just completed a disastrously ineffective term as governor of Virginia himself, Jefferson knew that legislatures could turn dangerous. "An *elective despotism* was not the government we fought for." Instead Americans wanted the powers of government "divided and balanced among several bodies of magistracy, as that no one could transcend their legal limits, without being effectually checked and restrained by the others." Although Virginia's legislators acted "with no ill intention," their obsession with control and distrust of the judiciary and executive might precipitate a broader shift from virtue to corruption.[120] Finding the common good would require balancing popular enthusiasm with the judgment that only temperate deliberation could produce.

Others shared the anxieties of Adams and Jefferson concerning the new state legislatures. James Madison wrote in 1785 that state senates lacked the necessary "*wisdom* and *steadfastness*," and executives were unable to constrain the ambitious assemblies. Because Americans also remembered the dangers posed by councils and governors appointed by the crown, Madison wrote, weak executive officers were the worst features of these faulty constitutions. Madison pointed to Maryland, with its indirect election of senators, as a good model.[121] Samuel Chase, who had feared that exceptional individuals would be submerged into the mass and in 1776 approvingly characterized the Maryland senate as "the aristocratical part of the government," now downplayed the differences between the two houses. Popular sovereignty did the trick. "Both branches of our legislature," in his words, "derive *all* their power from the people, and *equally* hold their *commission* to legislate, or make laws, from the *grant* of the people." The vaunted difference between the senate and the house had been exaggerated: "There is no difference between them but *only* in the *duration of their commission*. Their authority proceeds from the same source, and is co-equal and co-extensive." The senate as well as the house "must be equally the *representatives, trustees*, and *servants* of the people, and the people are equally the *constituents* of both."[122] Among the more hierarchical of the colonies, Maryland was now clearly moving toward the new understanding of popular sovereignty that was beginning to come into focus as the War for Independence came to an end.

Attitudes were shifting rapidly during these tumultuous years; even Pennsylvania was reconsidering its unicameral legislature. When Benjamin Rush first argued for instituting a senate in 1776, he contended that increasing inequality made it necessary. Wealth had "introduced natural distinctions of rank in Pennsylvania, as certain and general as the artificial distinctions of men in Europe." Concentrating such men in a senate would let the people's representatives in the assembly counter their influence. Rush's argument did not die; in fact, John Adams would make a version of it only a decade later. During the 1780s, however, a different rationale emerged to justify the existence of another legislative house. James Wilson and others agitating for constitutional reform now argued that the senate would simply provide a second deliberative body. "It is because I abhor every species of aristocracy," declared Arthur St. Clair, "that I object to a single branch in a legislature." A senate without a landed aristocracy would be, like the house, "your representatives, the breath of your nostrils." Advocates called for an upper house "without distinction either in the electors or elected."[123] In more egalitarian

Pennsylvania, as in more stratified Maryland, talk of different social orders had vanished. Despite the claims of those who wrote the Pennsylvania Constitution of 1776 that they spoke for "the people," it had been simply declared law by the convention that wrote it. Within a decade its architects found themselves besieged by a new set of reformers who demanded a new constitution. These challengers, who called their party "Republican," observed that Pennsylvania had departed from the model chosen by other states and echoed Adams's warning: unicameral governments had always ended in tyranny.[124]

The Pennsylvania model of unicameralism proved fragile, either because it was undermined by a cabal of antidemocratic elitists or because it was the flawed product of a deck stacked from the outset. Yet it exerted a degree of influence incommensurate with its brief history. In the 1780s it became—at least to many French writers and especially to critics of the French monarchy—the prototype of democracy. According to the French philosophes Mirabeau, Turgot, and Condorcet, the Pennsylvania Constitution of 1776 stood alone, among the new state constitutions, as an appropriate framework for a popular government. From their perspective the very idea of bicameralism, just as Paine and his Pennsylvania allies James Cannon and Thomas Young had argued, betrayed the fundamental object of republican rule, the identification of a unitary public interest. That conviction not only animated thoughtful philosophes surveying the American scene but also inflamed the passions of Maximilien Robespierre and the Jacobins he inspired, and it helps explain why the democratic revolution in France differed so dramatically from the democratic revolution in Britain's American colonies.[125]

Benjamin Rush, who had prompted Paine to write *Common Sense*, emerged as one of the most prominent figures to call for the reform of the 1776 Pennsylvania Constitution. The fact that Pennsylvania lacked a landed aristocracy did not mean all citizens could exercise equal power. History showed Rush that "the rich have always been an over-match for the poor in all contests for power." Unequal leverage meant that everyone but the richest few should ally to protect themselves. Only by cordoning off such would-be aristocrats in their own chamber could ordinary people preserve the assembly as their own.[126] Adams had struggled with just this issue as he witnessed deplorable poverty in stark contrast to French aristocrats' spectacles of decadence; others in Massachusetts were also wrestling with it. Writing in Boston's *Continental Journal* in April of 1778, Roxbury minister William Gordon contended that the absence of an aristocracy changed everything, yet the people had become convinced that two legislatures were better suited to preserving liberty than a single assembly.[127] If all citizens were now freeborn, as Adams emphasized, and all officials elected, it made no sense to claim that senators differed categorically from other public servants.

Most states adopted that logic. They limited the number of senators, elected them from districts larger than those choosing representatives to the lower house, and usually raised the property qualifications. Novel as that strategy was, most commentators emphasized its continuity with older ideas. The pastor of Boston's Brattle Street Church, Samuel Cooper, in a sermon devoted to the glories of the new Massachusetts Constitution, began with a passage from Jeremiah indicating that God's chosen people chose their own government. According to Cooper, the pact between God and Israel was "not imposed" but instead "freely adopted." The Bible thus called it a "covenant" or "compact," which "depended entirely on the consent of the people." Cooper invoked Sidney to nail down his point: "'As it was democratically sent,' says a great author, who wrote conclusively, who fought bravely, and died gloriously in the cause of liberty, 'it was democratically received.'" Until Israel declined into monarchy, it had enjoyed a republic founded on the principle of popular sovereignty.[128] The new bicameral frame of government established in Massachusetts, Cooper concluded, reflected the "sacred oracles" of God's revelation, the dictates of "reason and common sense," and the principles articulated in "the immortal writings of Sidney and Locke."[129] Yet not everyone embraced the proposed constitution. Adams himself, sent to Europe again to negotiate a loan from the Dutch, was unable to participate in the debates, and the assembled delegates raised numerous objections. After the Massachusetts convention deliberated, revised, and finally approved the constitution, it was submitted to a deeply divided citizenry for ratification. Although many towns voted to accept it, others voted for diverse modifications, and others rejected it outright. Negotiations dragged on until the convention followed the precedent of other states, including Pennsylvania, and finally just declared the constitution law on October 25, 1780.[130]

One of the most distinctive and crucial features of the Massachusetts Constitution, and one of those that would later distinguish the United States Constitution as well, was the power "expressly reserved to the people" of amending the constitution "after a fair experiment of fifteen years." It is difficult to exaggerate the significance of that provision for amendment or disentangle it from the self-consciously religious sensibilities of those who wrote and voted on the document. Lacking the Promethean confidence of earlier (and later) constitution writers, these Americans conceded that their experiment would succeed only if sinful men maintained, as Cooper put it, their focus on "the public interest in all its extended branches."[131] Cooper's hopes and fears reverberated throughout the new nation during the decade that followed.

Other writers, including those who expressed themselves in newspapers or pamphlets rather than from pulpits, shared his emphasis on the necessity of virtue, the importance of piety to sustain public spirit, the need for harmony between the demands of Christianity and the dictates of reason, and his wariness about the possibility of preserving those qualities.

As the war dragged on, signs of a new sensibility began to emerge among the American colonists. A spirit of equality quickly filled the vacuum left by the displacement of monarchy and aristocracy, and it expressed itself in a new confidence that the state constitutions would enable the people to maintain direct control over all the officers of their governments.[132] As it rose, that spirit of equality remained yoked to the idea of autonomy, the older conception of liberty restrained by God's will and man's laws. In a sermon commemorating the sixth anniversary of the Battle of Lexington, Henry Cumings, the pastor of the First Congregational Church of Billerica, Massachusetts, reminded his congregation that beyond the precious sphere of civil liberty lay another, even more precious kind of freedom, "freedom from the dominion of sin." Echoing Adams and a chorus of preachers ranging from Winthrop through Ward to Mayhew and Cooper, Cumings spoke for many Americans when he cautioned against confusing the individual freedom to pursue one's own interests with the more urgent obligation to pursue God's will even if it meant subordinating one's own.[133]

Such language was also deployed in Massachusetts by African Americans with their own reasons to invoke God's will against the willfulness of sinful individuals. Encouraged by the *Somerset* decision rendered in 1772 by Lord Mansfield, England's chief justice, slaves began filing petitions against slavery in Massachusetts. Only after the Massachusetts Constitution of 1780 declared all people "free and equal," however, was one of the slaves, Elizabeth Freeman, able to challenge the institution successfully in *Brom and Bett* v. *John Ashley*, the case that marked the beginning of the end of slavery in New England.[134] Although many of the slaves who fled during the war ended up without freedom, others managed to forge new lives in the northern states. Connecticut-born Lemuel Haynes, son of an African father and a white mother, worked off an indenture and fought at Bunker Hill and Fort Ticonderoga. He wrote an antislavery pamphlet, entitled *Liberty Further Extended; or, Free Thoughts on the Illegality of Slave-keeping*, which marshaled Biblical and secular arguments to establish that every African possesses "an undeniable right to his liberty" equal to that of any European. Haynes later became the first black minister to serve in white Congregational churches in Massachusetts, Vermont, and New York, delivering thousands of sermons widely praised for articulating the inconsistency between slavery and democracy.[135]

For years American writers had emphasized the link between democracy and equality. Now increasing inequality showed the challenges American democracy would face. Small farmers were finding it increasingly difficult to maintain ownership of their land. Residents of western regions continued to worry that their concerns were drowned out by the demands of urban merchants and artisans. Residents of seaboard towns feared that a majority of farmers would outvote them. By the summer of 1783, the war had ended and the army had been disbanded, yet enraged and unpaid former members of the Continental Army descended on Philadelphia demanding justice. With the war's end came new fears of conflict.

A former general in the Continental Army, Benjamin Lincoln, addressed those anxieties in a series of articles in Boston's *Independent Chronicle* in the fall of 1785 and the winter of 1786. Lincoln observed matter-of-factly that the vaunted equality of American society was slipping away. If not addressed, the different interests that already exist when governments are instituted become "seeds of destruction" that ripen into dissolution. In republics, Lincoln wrote, such divergent interests "may all of them be easily and directly traced to the rights of persons and of property."[136] Because inequality was far more pronounced in 1783 than it had been twenty years earlier, many struggling families wondered if democracy offered a solution to their problems or merely compounded them. A dawning awareness of clashing social and economic interests complicated earlier expectations that virtuous Americans would find a way to resolve their differences.

Among the most obvious of those divisions was that separating Patriots from Loyalists. More than a hundred thousand Loyalists left England's former colonies during and immediately after the war. Loyalists who cherished antidemocratic and monarchical principles found comfort by returning to England or its colonial outposts in Canada or the Caribbean. Many lost everything: their families were forever divided, their property confiscated without compensation, their plans for the future shattered. As Benjamin Franklin wrote in justification of the taking of Loyalists' lands, private property "is a creature of society, and is subject to the calls of that society whenever its necessities shall require it, even to its last farthing."[137]

Loyalists were hardly the only wealthy people in America, however; nor were they alone in their suffering during the war. Indeed, some of the richest planters and merchants threw their energies into the cause of independence, and many of them emerged less prosperous than they had been before the war. The least wealthy, though, paid the highest price. Small landholders were prominent among those who fought and died in combat, and many who survived the war found that the shift back from subsistence to commercial farming rendered them vulnerable to the tightening of credit provoked by eastern bankers' and merchants' desire to stabilize the new nation's financial situation with European financiers. The religious, social, and economic rifts dividing Americans in every state came into sharp focus by war's end.[138] Not only were many hierarchies leveled or inverted during the war for independence; new rivalries as well as new solidarities emerged.

Some things did not change so fast, including the prominence of religion in public debate. Almost no one in the new democracy separated religious principles from political or economic principles. There was no secular public sphere in eighteenth-century America.[139] Americans inherited multiple traditions that they did not consider incompatible. They drew religious principles from the different strands of the Reformation and from those in the moderate wing of the Enlightenment who saw faith as compatible with reason. They adapted political principles from the diverse dissenting traditions of English writers ranging from the radical Levellers and republicans such as Milton through Sidney and Locke to eighteenth-century Whig and Tory critics of corruption, and they borrowed ideas from Montesquieu and Rousseau. Finally, they took principles of moral philosophy from those texts and from the French, the English, and especially the Scottish Enlightenments. All those diverse sources furnished inspiration for republican government and reasons to harbor misgivings about its durability.

Franklin had identified as early as 1731 the challenge that would continue to bedevil and beguile champions of democracy on both sides of the Atlantic for a century and a half. It was a problem inextricably linked to, but not resolved by, the prominent role played by religion in American culture. How could the citizens of the new nation identify and inculcate Franklin's "principle of benevolence," a democratic ethic that would either convince individuals to subordinate their particular interests to the general interest or create a process whereby individuals could learn from each other how to resolve their differences? By 1785 even the enterprising Franklin was identifying as a threat to American democracy the emergence of new wealth and the growing gap between rich and poor, and other commentators from New England to the South voiced similar concerns.[140] Writing in 1780, with the war's outcome still in doubt, Adams claimed that Americans had already separated themselves from Britain because their "democratical sentiments and principles were not confined to one Colony, but they run through it." Carried forward by a "popular torrent," every state had already "instituted a democracy," and, he noted, "the people are universally fond of their new government."[141] As soon as the War for Independence ended, however, the new nation was shown to be a rickety raft. Those trying to establish its equilibrium, having hurriedly lashed together its rough logs, now had to construct a sturdier vessel even as they struggled to keep it afloat in choppy waters.

Britain's departure left Americans on their own. They were now free to show either that their individual, regional, denominational, or economic interests would obscure the common good, or that that they could, in the phrase Condorcet applied to Franklin, commit themselves to "the power of reason and the reality of virtue."[142] When the war finally came to an end in 1783, Americans began creating new wealth as quickly as they had begun creating new constitutions in 1776. As they did, they began arguing over what sacrifices, if any, they should be prepared to make for the sake of their new democracy.

CHAPTER 8 | Constituting American Democracy

DEEP DISAGREEMENTS SURFACED as soon as the United States secured their independence from Britain. For some Americans peace brought an economic upturn fueled by renewed commercial activity. For many others the end of the war brought years of continuing hardship. Because of either greedy merchants and bankers or the "uncurbed enthusiasm and licentiousness" of those protesting debt collection, or perhaps simply due to "a want of authority in our executive power," according to Philadelphia's *Pennsylvania Packet*, something had gone awry. "Was it with these expectations" that Americans "waded through oceans of blood" and "experienced all the horrors of a cruel and destructive war"?[1]

Food riots and crowd actions triggered by reports of suspected hoarders had broken out intermittently during the War for Independence. Rural insurgents had been active since the North Carolina uprising of the Paxton boys in 1763. Once independence was secured and the presumed sources of corruption and injustice had sailed back to Britain, the rise of those who took privileged and remunerative government places vacated by departed Loyalists fed other Americans' growing resentment. A 1780 proposal to change the name of Massachusetts to "Oceana" failed, but the conviction that inspired it—the belief that all should have more equal access to land ownership, as in Harrington's utopia—spread. In a nation now formally committed to the principle of equality, the fact of inequality became harder to endure. Well-established merchants, ship captains, and some artisans prospered while most farmers and many traders, seamen, and mechanics floundered. The nation had piled up enormous debts during the war, and the end of hostilities brought demands for payment from domestic and foreign creditors.[2]

Personal indebtedness soared. The gulf between rich and poor grew. The prices for agricultural products plummeted as the cost of provisions rose. The paper money used to finance the war lost almost all of its value, and much of what little circulating specie remained was sent to England for cheap imported goods. With interest rates soaring from 6 percent annually to 6 percent a month, indebted farmers everywhere found themselves facing foreclosures. William Findley, born in Ulster and trained as a weaver, became a small landowner in western Pennsylvania, where many farms were "subject to be sold for debts." Findley had volunteered in the War for Independence and rose to the rank of captain; after the war he moved farther west and was elected to the state legislature. He told the General Assembly that his constituents were being forced to sell "the last cow and sheep to procure a little money."

Farmers and the traders who did business with them faced dire conditions throughout the former colonies. In the absence of bankruptcy laws, a legal vise tightened on those who failed to meet their obligations, and the threat of debtors' prison loomed for those unable to pay tax collectors or creditors. The complaints of unpaid soldiers merged with those of debt-strapped farmers who could not market their crops and urban artisans unable to afford the materials they required or find buyers for the goods they produced. All of them believed the war had been fought to improve their lot, and they grumbled that only the rich had gotten richer. Rumors about soldiers who refused to surrender their weapons until they were paid, and rumors about legislatures threatening to authorize paying those soldiers with worthless paper money, combined with rumblings from wealthy citizens about the unworthy rabble and the inevitable return of monarchy, fed fears that another revolution might follow the first.[3]

Outlying regions languished as wealth grew increasingly concentrated in the coastal cities. In Massachusetts, fisheries were devastated by the war, and small-scale merchants left medium-sized towns for Boston. Many bankrupt farmers abandoned their land for western or northern frontiers, where all expected to find opportunity and some hoped to escape creditors. Those who stayed on their farms found themselves responsible for higher taxes assessed on collapsing land values. The nominal property valuation of all land in Massachusetts was estimated at $11 million; the tax bill was over $4 million. When the commonwealth began in earnest to collect those taxes to pay down the war debt, one contemporary estimated that taxes swallowed a third of the state's income.[4] To creditors, many of whom had purchased government securities at a deep discount, debtors appeared to be evading obligations incurred through self-indulgence. Farmers who had fought the Revolution to win economic as well as political independence insisted that corrupt bankers, merchants, speculators, and officers of the law were responsible for their predicament. Government officials, particularly the courts and sheriffs charged with administering and enforcing most statutes, simply wanted citizens to obey the laws enacted by their representatives.[5]

Having expelled the Loyalists and British officials who had oppressed them, newly empowered white, male property holders expected to control their own destiny (as well as that of the women, African Americans, and Indians whose inferior status they took for granted). Their experience did not match their expectations. Newspaper editors pleaded for "benevolence, and a regard for your fellow creatures, your fellow citizens," who had "bravely struggled in the cause of liberty." In the Loyalists' absence, bitter squabbling replaced the "harmony and concord" the nation needed.[6] The struggle to solve these problems eventually yielded a constitution designed to bring order and to secure the common good by channeling popular sentiments into productive political engagement.

Creating that constitution would be a challenge. Political differences among Americans in the 1780s were as deep as their social, economic, and cultural divisions. They shared anxieties about the new nation's standing in the international order, the security of its borders, and its prospects for economic growth. They also shared convictions about limiting government authority, circumscribing officials' discretion, and trusting their elected representatives to protect their rights. Nonetheless, they disagreed about the implications of those anxieties and those convictions for the loose union of independent states created by the Articles of Confederation. Under the Articles, the obligations of regulating the economy and ensuring citizens' welfare fell to the governments of the states. The national government, charged with conducting foreign affairs and resolving disputes between the states, lacked the authority to exercise its powers or enforce its decisions.

Different states and regions inherited different political cultures. These ranged from traditions of republican self-government by more-or-less stable elites in New England and Virginia, and those run by increasingly unsteady oligarchies in New York and South Carolina, to the noisy diversity of Pennsylvania and New Jersey and the cantankerous resistance to all authority in the rough backcountry of almost every state. In all parts of the nation, conflict between rich and poor, debtors and creditors, and farmers and merchants, as well as struggles based on geography, religion, ethnicity, or language was the rule. Partisan loyalties to particular leaders, groups, or causes developed from disputes at the local, county, or state level.[7]

When ordinary people mobilized to express their grievances in the 1780s, all of these rifts came into focus. The proportion of ordinary farmers serving in state legislatures doubled from the mid-1770s to the mid-1780s, jumping from one-eighth to one-quarter in the South and from one-quarter to over one-half in states such as New Hampshire, New Jersey, and New York. Quite different challenges faced urban artisans and merchants, who also found new outlets for their grievances after the war. Larger numbers of people voted throughout the nation, and turnover in all elected offices increased, in part because of the exodus of prominent Loyalists who had long held important administrative positions.[8]

Some Americans had an entirely different frame of reference. Nationalists such as New York's Alexander Hamilton, an immigrant from St. Croix who had risen to become one of George Washington's closest aides by the end of the war, and Pennsylvania's Robert Morris, who served as superintendent of finance during the War for Independence and secured the crucial loan from France, saw the fledgling nation in an international perspective. Unlike most of their countrymen, whose loyalties and interests focused on their local communities, Hamilton and Morris believed the nation's future depended on establishing sound credit, facilitating national and international commerce, and developing sufficient military capacity to fend off threats from indigenous peoples and European powers.[9]

Political ideals also varied, especially concerning the tension between the pursuit of private interest and the general welfare. Some thought autonomous individuals could flourish in the new nation if they respected each other and placed the public interest above personal desires. For others, wealthy and impoverished alike, deference either to persons or to some notion of the common good seemed antithetical to individuals' freedom to pursue their own aims without interference. "Prejudice and private interest," a disillusioned Hamilton wrote in 1779, "will be antagonists too powerful for public spirit and the public good." Those urging selfless pursuit of the common interest were wasting their words: "We may preach till we are tired of the theme, the necessity of disinterestedness in republics, without making a single proselyte." Partisans as well as critics of the Articles of Confederation included those who valued what they considered civic virtue and others who stressed personal freedom. Despite profound differences within as well as between these groups, almost all of them claimed to be speaking for "the people."[10]

Long-standing disagreements about the appropriate procedures for self-government outlived the British surrender at Yorktown in 1781. Given that the states of the new nation had the widest franchise anywhere and aristocracy was outlawed, election was preferred to lottery as the appropriate way to select government officials. But unanimity ended there. Sharp disagreements emerged about who owed what to whom, how the states should govern themselves, and how much authority the Articles of Confederation conferred on the national government. Diplomats negotiating with Britain, France, Holland, and Spain felt powerless given the states' failures to make payments to the nation. Debtors negotiating the depression of the mid-1780s felt equally powerless and even more bitterly aggrieved.

The most widespread demands focused on the need for currency and tax relief. Many legislatures printed paper money in response. In 1785 alone, Pennsylvania, South Carolina, North Carolina, New York, New Jersey, Georgia, and Rhode Island expanded the money supply. Wherever legislatures resisted, there was trouble. In Virginia courthouses were burned. In New Hampshire farmers surrounded the Assembly. From South Carolina through Maryland to New England, popular agitators for debt relief and tax relief blocked auctions of seized property and shuttered courthouses. Such actions shattered officials' confidence in their capacity to enforce the law. Angry bands of citizens subjected tax collectors, judges, and sheriffs to humiliating and sometimes violent ritual assaults. Taxpayer resistance was a "cause of alarm to all," according to Pennsylvania merchant and banker Thomas FitzSimons, and officials reported that the "infection" of unrest had reached "epidemic" proportions there. Former North Carolina congressman Thomas Hawkins wrote that "disorderly behaviour" by South Carolina citizens in 1785 interrupted tax collections and threatened chaos. In the judgment of Connecticut attorney David Daggett, fury over taxes and "the alarming state of our finances" had sparked "civil discord in almost every state in the union." Because Americans were accustomed to having local juries render decisions that respected local customs, attempts to impose statewide norms in local courthouses brought tensions that could erupt into armed clashes.[11]

The best-known and most consequential of these revolts broke out in August 1786 in Berkshire County, Massachusetts, where former army officer Daniel Shays organized neighboring farmers to protect their property and protest the legislature's refusal to provide relief from debt and taxes.[12] Shays's Rebellion elicited diverse reactions. Massachusetts governor James Bowdoin did not wait to see whether the rebels would make good their threats. He mustered the militia, supplemented by volunteers keen to suppress what they considered simple lawlessness, and crushed the insurgency, leaving four dead, dozens wounded, and two who were later hanged. In the first *History of the Insurrections*, published in Worcester just two years after Shays's Rebellion, George Richards Minot traced the conflict to a timeless "distinction of interests" between "men of property" and the "debtors, speculators, and persons otherwise interested against them." Minot concluded that only dispassionate enforcement of law could keep the peace; violence just made matters worse.

Massachusetts voters, however, had a different response. The many critics of the governor's overreaction contended that the Shaysites were merely continuing a decades-long tradition of legitimate protest. They voted Bowdoin and his allies out of office and elected a government that pardoned Shays and worked to address the sources of the unrest. In the words of a Massachusetts farmer looking back on that outcome, "Everything appeared like the clear and pleasant suncchin after a most tremendous storm." According to Minot, the result, overall, had proved "a striking demonstration of the advantages of a free elective government."[13] From another vantage point, however, there was a decisive difference between pre- and postrevolutionary acts of violence. The ordinances now in force were, after all, the work of the people's elected representatives. In the words of Boston's Thomas Dawes, "If our constitution is the perfect law of liberty, whence those mighty animosities which have so latterly distracted the bosom of peace, and stained the first pages of our history with civil blood?" The problem was bigger than Berkshire County: "Our sufferings have arisen from a *deeper fountain*," the absence of a "proper *federal authority*."[14]

Plenty of commentators outside Massachusetts shared Dawes's judgment. Pennsylvania's James Wilson, the Scottish immigrant who was to emerge as a pivotal figure in the debates of these years, agreed that unless the United States replaced the Articles of Confederation with a stronger national government, it would see the return of "insurrections and tumults."[15] At the height of the anxiety occasioned by the Shaysites, a correspondent wrote to Virginian James Madison that Shays had attracted tens of thousands of supporters; the usually calm George Washington warned Madison that farmers throughout New England were rumored to be joining an armed insurrection. When he was told that British troops along the nation's northwestern border were poised to give the rebels encouragement and supplies, the already worried Madison turned frantic.[16] Up and down the continent and up and down the social and economic ladder, anxieties were rising.[17]

James Madison and James Wilson were two of the most ingenious, influential, and controversial figures of the years of the Critical Period. Both believed the United States faced two dangers—unrest at home and threats from abroad—which only a stronger national government could check. Yet they were as determined to preserve self-government as they were to restore domestic order and secure the nation's international standing. The consistency of those three commitments, to popular sovereignty, economic and political stability, and a solid financial and military stance vis-à-vis other nation-states, was not always apparent to their contemporaries, and critics ever since have echoed that skepticism. Madison and Wilson believed that the complexity of the problems dictated a multifaceted solution, and they came to think that the new United States Constitution, forged in Philadelphia and submitted to the states for ratification in 1787, offered the best available option.

Wilson and Madison had much in common. Both were shaped intellectually by versions of Scottish common-sense moral philosophy. They considered individuals' passions inferior to, and subject to control by, the rational faculty of the moral sense. Both judged the Confederation government too feeble to defend the nation from its enemies and too weak to prevent individual states from ignoring their responsibilities. When delegates gathered in Philadelphia for the Constitutional Convention in May of 1787, Wilson's influence in the deliberations was second only to Madison's. Afterward both wrote influential articles and delivered dramatic speeches, Madison in Virginia and Wilson in Pennsylvania, in favor of ratification. Both then enjoyed spectacularly successful careers as public servants, Madison as Jefferson's secretary of state and ultimately as the fourth president of the United States, Wilson as one of the nation's first Supreme Court justices. Both also endured assaults on their homes, albeit in strikingly dissimilar circumstances: Wilson's was attacked by an angry crowd in central Philadelphia in 1779, Madison's when the British torched the White House during the War of 1812. Despite the stark differences in their standing today, Madison acclaimed or reviled and Wilson forgotten, in the 1780s these allies were pivotal figures in creating the United States Constitution. From the moment that document was ratified, democracy in America has been a glass at once more than half empty and more than half full, an unstable potion of largely unrealized yet unlimited potential. The reasons American democracy has simultaneously inspired the fury and the hopes of people everywhere drawn to the idea of popular government can be traced to its origins, specifically to the ideas of James Wilson and James Madison.

At James Wilson's birth in Scotland in 1742, his devout Presbyterian parents dedicated their son to the ministry. He had all but completed his postgraduate studies in divinity at the University of St. Andrews when his father's death forced him to return home. He took over the struggling family farm and worked as a tutor to supplement his income. When his youngest siblings grew old enough to assume responsibility for their mother and for the farm, Wilson left for America. He arrived in Pennsylvania in the fall of 1765 and found work teaching ancient languages and Scottish moral philosophy in the College of Philadelphia. Wilson's ambitions, however, extended beyond a tutor's world. He read law with the prominent John Dickinson, expanding his studies from Greek and Roman philosophy to include Pufendorf and

Grotius, Locke and Sidney, Coke and Blackstone, Montesquieu and Rousseau. Wilson also continued reading eighteenth-century Scottish philosophy, supplementing studies of Hutcheson and Reid with Ferguson and Hume, broadening his intellectual horizons without unsettling his Presbyterian faith. His earliest forays into journalism, articles coauthored in 1768 with William White, later an Episcopal bishop, reflected Wilson's immersion in Enlightenment ideas and his staunch Christian faith.

After Wilson moved to Pennsylvania, he began to dabble in politics. He drafted an article on the limits of Parliament's authority in the colonies. He married the wealthy Ruth Bird and moved west, to Carlisle, where he established a law practice. Elected a delegate to the provincial convention, Wilson published a pamphlet, *Considerations on the Nature and Extent of the Legislative Authority of the British Parliament*, which propelled him to prominence. His claim that "all power is derived from the people" established him as a leading advocate of democracy.[18] Known as a spokesman for popular sovereignty, Wilson surprised his fellow radicals by opposing the unicameral legislature proposed for the 1776 Pennsylvania Constitution. His historical studies had convinced him that such legislatures had a bad track record. Unbridled power in the hands of popular assemblies, not only in the ancient world but as recently as the period after the English Civil War, transmuted righteous anger into murderous rage that ended in tyranny.

Elected a delegate to the Continental Congress in the spring of 1776, Wilson arrived in Philadelphia with instructions to oppose independence, which he did until the British navy's arrival nearby altered the perspective of Pennsylvania legislators. Wilson's reversal shifted the balance of the Pennsylvania delegation, and he signed the Declaration of Independence without second thoughts. Some observers misinterpreted Wilson's early reluctance as hesitancy about the Revolution itself, however, and his criticism of the Pennsylvania Constitution was said to reveal aristocratic leanings. His defense of several Quaker Tories accused of treason prompted even more venomous accusations and, despite his flamboyantly democratic *Considerations*, questions about his loyalties persisted. In Philadelphia Wilson found that criticizing unicameralism put him in league with some of Philadelphia's wealthiest citizens, people who shared his wariness about the new Pennsylvania regime but none of his democratic principles. As the War for Independence continued, Wilson became increasingly involved with successful businessmen, including the financier Robert Morris, who already enjoyed the wealth that Wilson sought.[19]

Pennsylvania's economy was sagging as the war dragged on. Food was scarce. Prices were rising. Many Philadelphians, unable to find work or afford the imported goods they enjoyed before the war, accused merchants and bankers of price gouging. Soldiers in the Continental Army were not being paid, as colonial legislatures refused to remit the funds demanded by the Continental Congress to support the military. Pennsylvania militiamen, impatient that Congress offered them only excuses, gathered on May 12, 1779, demanding back pay and urging the legislature to control the prices of the goods their families had to buy. Their efforts failed, in part because many humble tradesmen and artisans, who also had families to feed, opposed their demand for price controls. By autumn economic conditions had deteriorated further. On October 4 a crowd of two hundred militiamen and sympathizers formed in Philadelphia and marched through the city calling for justice.

Outside a tavern the crowd encountered several dozen men who did not share their sympathies, including several prominent bankers and merchants. The businessmen "retreated" to the substantial home of their friend Wilson, midway between the Delaware River and the State House, and from there they watched the parade pass by Wilson's house. When a Captain Campbell shouted at the crowd from one of Wilson's windows, the reply from a musket in the street ignited a gunfight. Shots flew in all directions, killing six men: Campbell, four militiamen, and an African American who had joined the march. Eventually the city's cavalry and a troop of dragoons arrived, commanded by Joseph Reed, then serving as president (as the state's chief executive officer was called) of Pennsylvania. Twenty-seven of the militiamen were arrested. Order was restored.

The "Fort Wilson Riot," as the skirmish came to be known, can be interpreted as an American version of the food riots that broke out periodically in early-modern Europe, or an example of ordinary people banding together (as in other, later revolutions) to take the law into their own hands. But the event's other dimensions show the deeper roots of the conflict and the differences between popular and autocratic government. First, "the people" of Philadelphia were divided over the causes and the proper response to wartime inflation. Many artisans and traders as well as bankers blamed the Pennsylvania Assembly for mismanagement and denounced the proposed price controls. The parties for and against the 1776 constitution had divided along social and political rather than class lines, and those alignments persisted. Second, President Reed dismissed the charges against the jailed militiamen, released them the next day, and ordered the distribution of one hundred barrels of flour, with explicit instructions that preference be given to the families of militiamen.[20]

The battle waged outside James Wilson's home did not turn him against popular government. He understood and sympathized with the demands of those in the street. Only a national government stronger than that created by the Continental Congress, and a more stable flow of money from an adequate set of financial institutions, would secure paychecks for the Continental Army and economic stability to people struggling to make ends meet. Wilson was among many members of the Continental Congress who tried repeatedly, and fruitlessly, to pressure state governments to fund the Continental Army. In 1780 Wilson helped Robert Morris to create the Bank of Pennsylvania, a short-lived institution that provided the model for the later Bank of North America. Not only did Wilson serve as legal adviser to the Bank of Pennsylvania; he was also a client. He borrowed money to fund his speculation in western real estate, as did Morris and other wealthy Pennsylvanians who dreamed big and, like Wilson, ended up losing their shirts. Loans had enabled Wilson to read law, establish his law practice, buy land in the West, and set up a company to manufacture nails. Though nobody wanted a free flow of money more than Wilson did, and few stood to benefit more from inflation than those with big debts, he considered the rising tide of state-issued paper money a poor substitute for a stable currency. The teetering tower of loans that funded Wilson's risky land deals should not obscure, and might even help to explain, the powerful and persuasive arguments he made for popular government before, during, and after the War for Independence.[21]

James Madison's life unfolded in a fashion very different from Wilson's. He was born on March 16, 1751, on a sprawling, 2,850-acre tobacco plantation, the firstborn child of a leading family of Orange County, Virginia, that owned perhaps a hundred slaves. His tutor Donald Robertson had graduated from the University of Edinburgh, and from Madison's first educational experiences until the end of his life, Scottish common-sense philosophy shaped his sensibility. Although Madison's family, like almost all of Virginia's leading planters, belonged to the local Anglican congregation, his father sent him north, to the Presbyterian College of New Jersey, to continue his education. Under the leadership of John Witherspoon, who arrived from Scotland in 1768, one year before Madison began his studies, the college in Princeton was one of the centers of common-sense philosophy in North America. During Madison's time there, it emerged as one of the centers of resistance to British policy.

In Princeton Madison read widely. He studied the classics of Greek and Latin literature, and he encountered in Aristotle's *Politics* the argument that large states are "freer from faction" than small states because "their middle element," the independent citizenry capable of virtuous behavior, plays a larger role.[22] He also read the work of those who shaped the continental tradition of natural law as well as the principal contributors to seventeenth-century English political theory, including Hobbes, Harrington, Selden, Sidney, and

Locke. Of eighteenth-century authors he read Ferguson's *History of Civil Society* and Hume's *Essays*, and he was particularly enamored of Montesquieu. Twenty years later Madison could still quote from memory lengthy passages from *The Spirit of the Laws*. By far the deepest influence on Madison, though, was Scottish common-sense philosophy. The sensibility of his teacher Witherspoon was shaped by Francis Hutcheson, whom Witherspoon prized for reconciling Enlightenment science with Presbyterian theology. Like Locke, Hutcheson saw no conflict between serious engagement with science and devotion to God. Witherspoon taught his students to balance empiricism and revelation under the calm control of reason. Individuals could develop their potential sociability only if they learned, with God's grace of course, to combat their natural egoism. Although communal associations could help individuals bridle their selfish propensities, they could also, if unchecked, become factions undermining the common good.

The temperate Madison left Princeton equipped with an arsenal to be deployed against challenges coming from Hume's philosophical skepticism and from the religious enthusiasm of the Great Awakening. Throughout his life Madison adhered to what he learned from Witherspoon, including his ideas about the risks posed by aristocracy to self-governing cultures. Having dressed in homespun clothing and taken part in protests against the Townshend Acts at the College of New Jersey, Madison became convinced that democracy and duty are as compatible as rationality and religiosity. He completed his three-year course in two years, but the pace that suited his eager mind did his body no good. Too weak to travel, he remained in Princeton as Witherspoon's assistant, working closely with the future signer of the Declaration of Independence and architect of New Jersey's constitution.[23]

After Madison returned home to Montpelier, he read law and government as he recovered his strength. Compared with the rich diet of ideas that sustained him in Princeton, reading law left him feeling stranded in "a barren desert." An attorney's life appealed to him less than the ministry, though Virginia Anglicanism seemed overly hierarchical and less satisfying than the moral uplift he had breathed in Princeton's bracing atmosphere. Having imbibed Witherspoon's commitment to religious toleration along with his rigorous Presbyterian ethics, Madison pondered the cultures bred by particular forms of religiosity. Inspired by New England's protests, Madison grew preoccupied with politics, and traveling to Pennsylvania and New York only heightened his interest. Back home in Virginia, the diminutive Jemmy—as his family called him—joined the Orange County Committee of Safety and wrote stinging essays and letters praising American radicals. "If the Church of England had been the established and general Religion in all the Northern colonies as it has been among us here," Madison mused about his Virginia homeland, resistance to Britain would have withered into "slavery and subjection."

The problem stemmed from the religious uniformity of the Anglican South. "Union of religious sentiments begets a surprizing confidence" in the authority of rulers, Madison observed, "and Ecclesiastical Establishments tend to great ignorance and Corruption." Inhabitants of New Jersey and Pennsylvania showed a "liberal catholic and equitable way of thinking as to the rights of Conscience," a sensibility that fueled a lively and productive culture. In Virginia, by contrast, "religious bondage shackles and debilitates the mind and unfits it for every noble enterprise, every expanded project." Not only did an established religion breed "Pride ignorance and Knavery among the Priesthood and Vice and Wickedness among the Laity"; it also perpetuated "Poverty and Luxury" rather than the general prosperity of the middle colonies. What "vexes me the most of any thing whatever," Madison wrote, was the problem of religious intolerance. Not only did a "diabolical Hell-conceived principle of persecution" rage among some Virginians; the Anglican clergy, "to their eternal Infamy," fanned the flames of hatred. Not far from Madison's home, Baptist religious dissenters had been jailed merely for publishing their religious writings. That fact violated the principle of toleration Madison had learned from Locke, internalized thanks to Witherspoon, and pursued in the writings of Joseph Priestley and Josiah Tucker. Motivating Madison's critique was the seriousness of his faith and his respect for others' religious convictions. The earnest young Madison contrasted the moral and political lethargy of Virginia planters, whose comfortable lives depended on the abominable institution of slavery, to the self-disciplined productivity and vibrant self-government of New England and the middle colonies.[24]

Intensifying resistance to Britain buoyed Madison's spirits and softened his assessment of his neighbors' mettle. Commitment to the slogan "Liberty or Death" was transforming the "vice and wickedness" of Virginia's citizens. If all power were to rest on "the favor of the people," political and religious authorities would have to measure up to higher standards. Almost all of Orange County's eleven hundred white males owned enough property to vote, and they typically elected as their representatives people such as Madison's father, prosperous and prominent men who served as justices of the peace, vestrymen in their congregations, and, with the intensifying of sentiment against Britain, leaders of the militia.[25]

The young James Madison formally entered politics when elected to represent Orange County at the Virginia Constitutional Convention.[26] Despite his youth, Madison drafted an amendment to the Declaration of Rights, proposed by George Mason, which extended Locke's principle of religious freedom beyond the liberty of conscience and challenged the very institution of an established church: "No man or class of men ought, on account of religion," be "invested with peculiar emoluments or privileges; nor subjected to any penalties or disabilities unless, under color of religion, any man disturb the peace, the happiness, or safety of society." Sensing correctly that the amendment would disestablish Anglicanism, the delegates rejected Madison's attempt to secure toleration of all religious beliefs and guarantee that their expression remained "unpunished and unrestrained." Instead they endorsed "the free exercise of religion unless the preservation of equal liberty and the existence of the state are manifestly endangered," a less far-reaching provision that did circumscribe the state's authority.[27] Madison's foray into representative democracy whetted his appetite. When he stood for election to the General Assembly in 1777, he adopted a posture consistent with what he called "the purity of moral and of republican principles." Rejecting the "corrupting" practice of wooing voters with alcohol, he was defeated by a tavern-keeper who deferred to popular expectations. Madison recounted the story often later in life, making sport of his youthful abstemiousness. But he learned his lesson. From then on he played by the rules, observed local customs, and never lost another election. In 1779, the Assembly chose him as a delegate to the Continental Congress.

In Philadelphia Madison's horizons broadened and his commitment to national unity deepened. He began to worry that without a reliable flow of revenue, the new nation would starve its army and navy before it could establish its independence. After adopting the Articles of Confederation in 1781, the states failed to meet their financial obligations to the nation. Increasingly doubtful that the feeble union could survive under its existing government, Madison supported the efforts of Wilson's friend Robert Morris, named superintendent of finance in 1781, to stabilize the economy of the United States, a confederation consisting of effectively independent states united in name only. Pressure from unpaid soldiers in the Continental Army—the pressure that eventually boiled over in the riot at "Fort Wilson"—continued to intensify. New Jersey was threatening to pay its soldiers, and Pennsylvania its civilian creditors, with funds the states owed Congress. Morris threatened to resign if Congress failed to act. Madison was coming to agree with Morris, Wilson, and Hamilton that the new nation required a better financial system to survive. "Justice" to creditors, "gratitude" to our soldiers, the nation's "reputation abroad, and our tranquillity at home," Madison wrote to Edmund Randolph, "require provision for a debt of not less than fifty millions."

Madison knew state governments distrusted Morris's plans: he was under explicit instructions from Virginia to oppose them. Yet he persisted. "If there are not revenue laws which operate at the same time through all the States, and are exempt from the control of each—the mutual jealousies which begin already to appear among them will assuredly defraud both our foreign and domestic creditors."[28]

Within weeks, however, Madison became aware that Morris and Hamilton had a very different vision of the purpose of funding and perpetuating the national debt. Madison and Wilson aimed to repay the soldiers, along with domestic and foreign creditors who contributed to winning independence, through a funding scheme consistent with their democratic convictions. Morris and Hamilton envisioned a national government directed by interlocking political, financial, and commercial elites leveraging their financial heft to establish an American equivalent of the British court party. Wilson and Madison, like Adams and Jefferson, wanted instead a democratic empire of liberty.[29] After Madison returned from the Continental Congress to Montpelier at the end of 1783, he was elected to the Virginia House of Delegates and plunged into a debate that altered his view of his neighbors' capacity for responsible self-government as he understood it. Presbyterians had joined Anglicans in favoring the assessment of a tax to support Christian ministers, which meant that a majority of delegates seemed likely to approve the measure. Instead of bolstering the Christian sensibility that the bill's sponsors claimed was flagging, Madison argued, assessment would not only impede the continuing "progress of religious liberty," it would "dishonor Christianity." After Madison managed to persuade enough delegates to vote to postpone consideration of the bill, he set to work writing a petition, to be circulated throughout Virginia, explaining his objections. The resulting *Memorial and Remonstrance against Religious Assessments* evidently expressed the sentiments of many Virginians. When the General Assembly reconvened in 1785, only eleven of the over one hundred petitions submitted favored the assessment bill. Many of those opposed presented versions of Madison's arguments, and thirteen simply copied the text of his *Memorial*.[30]

Offering a barrage of reasons to oppose the bill, Madison drew not only on Locke but on multiple sources to attract adherents from different denominations and to appeal to those with little interest in religion. Like his mentor Witherspoon and his friend Jefferson, Madison saw no contradiction between reason and religion. "It is the duty of every man to render to the Creator such homage and such homage only as he believes to be acceptable to him," he wrote in his *Memorial*. "This duty is precedent, both in order of time and in degree of obligation, to the claims of Civil Society. Before any man can be considered as a member of Civil Society, he must be considered as a subject of the Governour of the Universe." For that reason religious beliefs are "wholly exempt" from restrictions instituted by government. These words reflect the seriousness of Madison's own religiosity as well as his misgivings about the assessment bill. Madison's earlier attempt to disestablish Anglicanism had failed. In the version of the Virginia Declaration of Rights that was adopted, however, he found a phrase he could use: "Because we hold it for a fundamental and undeniable truth, 'that Religion or the duty which we owe to our Creator and the manner of discharging it, can be directed only by reason and conviction, not by force or violence.'" Civil authority had no place in regulating religion.[31]

For fifteen centuries, Madison wrote, established religions had been on trial. The result had been only "indolence in the Clergy, ignorance and servility in the laity," and "superstition, bigotry, and persecution" in the broader society. Religious assessment would "destroy that moderation and harmony" among rival sects made possible by Virginia's reluctance to "intermeddle with religion." Madison echoed Montaigne in judging the European example decisive: "Torrents of blood have been spilt in the old world, by vain attempts of the secular arm, to extinguish Religious discord, by proscribing all difference in Religious opinion." Americans—or at least those who lived in some parts of America—had learned that the "true remedy" for the disease of religious hatred was to limit the power of government in matters of faith. Even the appearance of the assessment bill on the horizon, Madison observed, had transformed "Christian forbearance, love, and charity" into "animosities and jealousies" that threatened to persist. Virginians should have learned from Europe's convulsive wars of religion and from the relative peacefulness of those American states that permitted the free exercise of religion. Established as well as proscribed denominations suffer, and the culture itself is poisoned, by attempts to force faith into particular channels.[32]

Madison added other, less abstract arguments that show how his ideas about popular government were evolving. If the legislature possessed the authority to establish some forms of Christianity, it could equally easily establish or prohibit others, and it could force its citizens to support other causes too. If the legislature could abolish this fundamental right, what rights were safe? If all citizens were declared equal by the Virginia Declaration of Rights, then the legislature could not give advantages to some sects and discriminate against others: "We cannot deny an equal freedom to those whose minds have not yet yielded to the evidence which has convinced us." Established religions, Madison argued, inevitably pervert religious faith.

Substituting artificial for pure motives not only weakens believers' confidence in the truth of their beliefs but also fosters in skeptics the unhealthy suspicion that "its friends are too conscious of its fallacies to trust it to its own merits." Moreover, the proposed assessment stood in contradiction to Christianity itself: Christians before Constantine actively disavowed "dependence on powers of this world." Thus tacking back and forth between efforts to persuade Anglicans and Presbyterians that assessment would weaken their standing, on the one hand, and appeals to Baptists, Methodists, and other dissenters, on the other, Madison's *Memorial* had something for everyone. Beyond its significance in establishing the separation of church and state, it provided Madison the occasion for developing arguments about the value of deliberation, pluralism, and reciprocity that he would soon deploy for a different purpose.[33]

Although Madison and his allies defeated religious assessments, his experience as a legislator overall left him demoralized about his neighbors' parochialism and attentiveness to public affairs. As a result he began searching for more comprehensive solutions to a variety of problems. Issues ranging from funding the national debt to the question of navigation rights on the Mississippi River pitted southerners against northerners and those who thought locally against those who thought more broadly. On the regional issues Madison was every bit a Virginian. Spain had banned American traffic on the Mississippi River in 1784, and Madison disagreed vehemently with northerners who supported a proposal by Secretary of Foreign Affairs John Jay to relinquish American claims to the river in exchange for better commercial relations with Spain. Like all southerners who expected the nation to spread westward quickly, Madison considered access to the Mississippi indispensable.

On national issues Madison sided with those who were losing confidence in the Articles of Confederation. He eagerly attended a conference in Annapolis, Maryland, in September 1786 at which twelve delegates from five of the eight invited states gathered to address the issue of regulating commerce. While he was there, Madison wrote an exasperated letter to his fellow Virginian James Monroe, in which his anxieties about the danger to the South of the nation's abandoning its claims to the Mississippi merged with his larger concerns about the increasingly acrimonious relations among the fractious thirteen states comprising the nation. In that letter, Madison's hope that the flickering idea of a national common good might survive the storm of regional scheming led him to reflect on the relation between democracy and justice. Jay's plan to negotiate with Spain over the Mississippi, although couched in terms of the value of free trade, seemed to Madison designed to benefit northerners at the expense of southerners moving westward. Even if the proposal won support, "I shall never be convinced that it is expedient," Madison wrote to Monroe, "because I cannot conceive it to be just. There is no maxim in my opinion which is more liable to be misapplied and which therefore more needs elucidation than the current one that the interest of the majority is the political standard of right and wrong." If one were to take "the word 'interest' as synonymous with 'Ultimate happiness,' in which sense it is qualified with every necessary moral ingredient," then of course the proposition is true. But taken as it usually is to mean the "immediate augmentation of property and wealth," as would be the case for the northern merchants, nothing could be more false, because in that sense "it would be the interest of every majority" to do everything possible "to despoil & enslave the minority."

As in the assessment battle in the Virginia legislature, Madison argued that a majority does not possess the right to impose its will on the minority simply by force of numbers. Instead Madison envisioned a process whereby majorities would be forced to consider the arguments of minorities. In that way, different perspectives could be weighed against minority rights and against an emergent standard of justice. Confrontations between competing points of view might spawn more attractive alternatives better attuned to "every necessary moral ingredient" and driven less by avarice.[34] Witherspoon's lessons in Scottish common-sense philosophy, emphasizing the capacity of reason to master the passions in accord with the virtue of sympathy, echo through such formulations. Minority rights was but one dimension of Madison's developing conception of how deliberation and reciprocity might enable republican government to approach his ideal of justice.

Other Americans, in circumstances very different from Madison's, were also thinking about the relation between property and justice in democratic cultures. Neither Jefferson nor Adams—the former growing more comfortable in Europe while the latter grew increasingly restless away from home—shared Madison's deepening anxieties about democratic unrest. Two months before Madison wrote his nearly hysterical warning about the global conflagration that would spring from the ashes of Shays's Rebellion, Jefferson had sent him an equally remarkable letter expressing a dramatically different view. Jefferson blithely observed that the apparent "evil" of democratic "turbulence" would prove "productive of good" because "it prevents the degeneracy of government and nourishes a general attention to the public affairs." Jefferson continued with one of the celebrated observations that have made him the hero of revolutionaries ever since: "I hold it that a little rebellion now and then is a good thing & necessary in the political world as storms in the physical." Governors in republics should take care to be "mild in their punishment of rebellions, as not to discourage them too much. It is a medecine necessary for the sound health of government."[35] In case Madison had missed the point, Jefferson later wrote that "the late rebellion in Massachusetts has given more alarm than I think it should have done." From Jefferson's perspective, in the comfort of Parisian salons, the protests of a few Berkshire farmers represented at worst but a trivial nuisance and more likely a sign of vitality.

More surprisingly, Adams, in London, seemed equally calm. "Don't be allarmed at the late Turbulence in New England," Adams reassured Jefferson. The unrest was prompted by the zeal of the Massachusetts General Court, which in its eagerness to retire its debt had imposed a tax too heavy for the people to bear. The paradoxical result, Adams concluded, would be stability through "additional Strength to the Government" because it had shown its responsiveness to popular protest. The unruffled Jefferson chided Madison that even authoritarian France had seen three insurrections in the three years he had been there. Each time more people were involved than in Massachusetts and "a great deal more blood was spilt."[36] Within a few years Americans would be debating whether such blood, no matter if it is the blood of patriots or tyrants, refreshes or poisons the tree of liberty.

Jefferson's experience in Europe confirmed his conviction that democracy in America rested on a different social foundation than in France. Although he admired the smooth surfaces of European polite society, he contrasted the "tranquil, permanent felicity" of companionate marriage that he had enjoyed before his wife's death in 1782 with the sexual "intrigues" made necessary by the absence of "conjugal love" among French aristocrats.[37] He warned that European travel and education would breed in American youths "a fondness for European luxury and dissipation" and a weakness for aristocracy and monarchy, temptations made even more irresistible by the contempt they would feel for Americans' "simplicity" and for the "lovely equality"—relative to Europe—"which the poor enjoy with the rich" citizens of the United States.[38]

The most significant of Jefferson's Paris letters to his friend Madison were those in which the Virginia slaveholder reflected on the extreme inequality of French society. The nation's property was concentrated in the hands of a tiny minority, with "the flower of the country" serving as domestic servants and countless other people working on the estates of the nobility as artisans, tradesmen, and farmers. The most numerous of all, though, were "the poor who cannot find work," a fact Jefferson found incomprehensible in a land blessed with such extraordinary resources. Far too much land remained uncultivated merely for the sake of game preserves kept wild to satisfy aristocrats' whims.

At the root of the problem lay France's colossally wrongheaded attachment to primogeniture, which perpetuated the grandeur of privileged firstborn sons and their families at the expense of everyone else. American strictures preventing such concentrations of wealth Jefferson judged both "politic" and "practicable."

Jefferson also recommended another strategy to Madison. This proposal, which stood in equally stark contrast to the French tradition of exempting the nobility from taxation, was "to exempt all from taxation below a certain point, and to tax the higher portions of property in geometrical progression as they rise." The approach that Jefferson endorsed, which has come to be known as graduated or progressive taxation, seemed to him a natural corollary to democratic governance. Whenever there are "uncultivated lands and unemployed poor, it is clear that the laws of property have been so far extended as to violate natural right. The earth is given as a common stock for man to labor and live on." In situations in which there is no land available to those who want it, "we must take care that other employment be provided to those excluded from the appropriation. If we do not, the fundamental right to labor the earth returns to the unemployed." The United States still enjoyed plenty of empty land, from Jefferson's perspective if not from those of the American Indians who occupied it, and thus the nation should "provide by every possible means that as few as possible shall be without a little portion of land. The small landowners are the most precious part of a state," he concluded, the part most conspicuously absent in France and most essential for a democracy to succeed.[39]

Adams had arrived in Paris in 1778, and his encounters with Jefferson and his friends among the French intelligentsia sharpened Adams's convictions concerning the cultural and economic underpinnings of a republic. Adams shared Jefferson's aversion to the inherited privileges of the French nobility, many of whom struck the earnest Adams as frivolous fops. Having negotiated loans, alliances, and finally the treaty of peace that ended the War for Independence, Adams had reluctantly become familiar with the capitals of France, Holland, and Britain. Having seen the *hauteur* of aristocrats and the poverty endured by ordinary people, he was trying to see how the American experiment with popular government could avoid degenerating into a similar morass. Before Adams left Paris to serve as the first American ambassador to the Court of St. James's, conversations with members of the French nobility, especially Lafayette, fixed in his mind the need to clarify his conception of democracy.

In London Adams chafed under the preferences expressed by French writers, notably Turgot and Condorcet, for the idea of a unicameral legislature, which he had opposed for a decade. Adams remained adamant that his own draft of the 1780 Massachusetts Constitution was a better blueprint for republican government. His convictions were hardened, and his pride wounded, when Turgot's criticism of plans such as his became a controversial subject of debate in London as well as Paris. The English radical Richard Price, in an appendix to his *Observations on the Importance of the American Revolution*, printed a letter from Turgot denigrating Americans' bicameral legislatures and multiple layers of government as inconsistent with republican principles. If the sovereign people had become the source of all authority, then separating the legislative, executive, and judicial branches of government had become an incoherent anachronism. The people's representatives, meeting in a single legislative assembly, should exercise power directly. By offering only awkward imitations of British government, the writers of America's constitutions showed their lingering attachment to aristocracy.

Adams was livid that his republican convictions had been questioned yet again. More troubled than ever that Paine's wrongheaded unicameralism was making progress in France and Britain, Adams rushed into print a book written in three frenzied months in the fall of 1786, his *Defence of the Constitutions of Government of the United States of America*. Adams also feared that political and social unrest in America, a broader phenomenon of which Shays's Rebellion was merely one manifestation, might rekindle efforts to bring America's governments into line with Pennsylvania's misguided experiment, to which Turgot's endorsement gave added cachet. When the French Assembly of Notables convened in 1786–87, Adams fretted that forms of centralized and, from his perspective, unbalanced government might now be adopted in France as well as America.[40] Adams criticized Turgot and Condorcet, whom he knew and respected, for presuming to think about politics a priori, to proceed from reason rather than history. Adams surveyed constitutions from the ancient world to the present. He wanted to follow Machiavelli, Bacon, Newton, and Locke in explaining empirically the causes of change over time rather than deducing from abstract principles ostensibly universal truths, as did Descartes and "some celebrated Academicians," to use Adams's phrase for the physiocrats. Even the revered Montesquieu, Adams argued, failed to understand that history, not typology, provides the experimental evidence on which political science must rest. The success of the best American constitutions, Adams insisted, with characteristic immodesty, derived from simple truths of nature disclosed in history.[41]

Adams grounded his *Defence* on "the real constitution of human nature, not upon any wild Visions of its perfectibility."[42] If Turgot and Condorcet wanted to dispute the need to balance a bicameral legislature against an elected unitary executive and an independent judiciary, they would have to reckon with history. Adams narrated the fall of over fifty republics, from Athens, Carthage, Sparta, Corinth, and Rome through the medieval Italian city-states to the short-lived little duchies embroiled in the sixteenth-century wars of religion. Simple governments, Adams showed, always deteriorated into despotism. Those states in the modern world often described as democratic republics, including San Marino, the Swiss cantons, and the United Provinces, in fact combined features of monarchy and aristocracy with those of democracy.[43] In short, the existence of so-called simple democracies was "a speculative phantom" that history shows "never can exist." Even the American example proved his point. Adams contended that only the exigencies of war made possible the colonies' self-discipline as they struggled to establish themselves. Now that they were at peace, Americans had become "addicted to luxury" and reduced to squabbling among themselves. Duty kept the frustrated Adams in England during the Constitutional Convention and the debates over ratification. His strident critique of the unicameral Articles of Confederation, however, together with his praise of balanced government resting on popular sovereignty that many Americans mistakenly associated with Britain rather than Massachusetts, caused many Americans to infer that he now preferred aristocracy to democracy. As both Jefferson and Madison knew, that charge was untrue.[44]

Adams wrote the *Defence* in part to convince European statesmen that the United States was a good credit risk, so he emphasized the century of gradual development that lay behind the nation's balanced political institutions. Americans, particularly the vast majority who did not tackle the massive, rambling, and eventually multivolume *Defence* but depended on reports from others who claimed (often without foundation) that they had read it, misinterpreted Adams as recommending that they renounce self-government. Adams intended nothing of the kind. "Our people are undoubtedly sovereign," he wrote. He applauded the fact that "all the landed and other property is in the hands of the citizens," that the people's representatives, senators, and governors were all chosen in annual elections, that there were no hereditary offices or privileges of any kind, and that the powers of the legislature, the executive, and the judiciary were strictly separated.

Americans understood the adage, known since the ancient world, that it is the people who know best "'where the shoe wrings, what grievances are most heavy,' and, therefore, they should always hold an independent and essential part in the legislature and be always able to prevent the shoe from wringing more and the grievances from being made more heavy." The pretensions of superiority taken for granted by Europe's nobility would be ridiculed in America, Adams wrote, where the egalitarian sensibility insured that "the vainest of all must be of the people or be nothing." Because every office was open to every citizen, and the people chose every government official—again, governors and senators as well as representatives—"no such airs" as those assumed by European aristocrats "would ever be endured." Adams was proud that no legal inequality by reason of birth (with the exception of slavery, which he abhorred) was allowed to exist anywhere in America, yet he pointed to the paradoxical pattern of deference that puzzled European observers. In the elections of any New England town, from the beginning more open than anywhere else, people from the same three or four families usually held positions of authority from one generation to the next. From Adams's perspective, the end of aristocracy did not mean the end of respect for those whom voters judged best able to serve the public.[45]

Notwithstanding his encomia to popular government, the hardheaded realism that marked Adams's political writings surfaced in his *Defence*. "The passions and appetites are parts of human nature," the self-aware Adams observed, "as well as reason and the moral sense." Adams had been studying Smith's *Theory of Moral Sentiments*, and Smith's ideas about the relation between self-love and the desire for approbation were reshaping Adams's sensibility in ways that became even more apparent in his later *Discourses on Davila*. "Although reason ought always to govern individuals, it certainly never did since the Fall, and never will till the Millennium."[46] Notwithstanding such warnings about human perfidy, punctuated with endless examples of failed republics, Adams's commitment to popular sovereignty remained as steadfast as his awareness of human fallibility, even though many critics failed to see it. In the ratification debates, both Federalists and Antifederalists would draw heavily on the arguments that Adams advanced in his *Defence*.[47]

In the spring of 1786, months before Adams wrote his *Defence* and Shays organized his regulators, and state delegates gathered in Annapolis, Maryland, to assess the adequacy of the Articles of Confederation, Madison was immersing himself in the history of confederacies ancient and modern. He was troubled by the central government's inability to establish a viable nation capable of maintaining order and paying its debts to its army and its American and European creditors. Nowhere did Madison find an enduring model for the United States. Just as Adams found nothing resembling the physiocrats' utopia in republics from ancient to modern days, Madison concluded that all confederations had either lacked sufficient central authority to remain viable or vanished when a powerful center eclipsed their component parts.[48] The United States, beset by domestic unrest and threatened by European powers eyeing its borders, seemed to Madison on the brink of following one form of failure or the other.

The twelve delegates who gathered in Annapolis later that year reached no conclusions, but they agreed to propose a more general convention to discuss the problems of the Confederation government. Since amending the Articles required a unanimous vote that no proposal had yet received, the alternatives appeared to be stalemate, with the danger of possible dissolution along regional lines, or a bold initiative to scrap the Articles and start over. Almost all the state legislatures agreed that something had to be done, but they had different complaints, and it was far from certain a constitutional convention would be called. To Madison's surprise, all the states but Rhode Island chose delegates to meet in Philadelphia in the spring of 1787. Given that those state assemblies included an unprecedented number of new members from relatively modest backgrounds, the almost-unanimous decision to send delegates indicates widespread support for reconsidering the Articles of Confederation.[49]

No one knew what would happen in Philadelphia. Some delegates expected they would tinker with the Articles, refine them at the margins or make cosmetic changes, then return home. It was not clear what authority the gathering of delegates had, and no plans for an alternative had circulated. Few delegates anticipated the creation of a new constitution. Among those few, however, was Madison. Although Madison initially resisted the idea of revising the Articles because he feared the entire structure might be too fragile to withstand such a quick alteration, the urgency of the problems changed his mind.[50] In the weeks before the Constitutional Convention opened on May 29, 1787, Madison prepared a detailed memorandum entitled "Vices of the Political System of the United States." He drew on this document, never published during his lifetime, not only for his crucial speeches at the convention in Philadelphia and the letters he wrote about the Constitution to Washington, Jefferson, and others but also for his later arguments in support of ratification. Writing for himself alone, Madison laid down the principles that would guide him in the decisive fifteen months ahead.

Madison's "Vices" began with the three interlocking issues he had raised often in the Continental Congress and in Virginia: the states' failure to meet their obligations to retire the national debt; their encroachments on each other's rights; and the printing of paper money, which he considered unwise. He applied the same logic to economic relations among individuals, states, and nations. The citizens of every state stand in relation to the citizens of other states either as creditors or debtors. When a debtor state acted in favor of debtors, it affected the creditor states just as it would affect "its own citizens who are relatively creditors towards other citizens." Madison extended the same logic to foreign nations. He believed that all citizens have a shared interest in preserving a stable money supply and preventing frauds on citizens of other states or other nations. All stood to gain more from stability than from fluctuations in the value of money. Consistent with the logic of Adam Smith in particular and Scottish common sense in general, and with the emerging consensus on the general benefits of stimulating trade, Madison emphasized predictability and trust as conditions of economic—as of political—relations. Although obscured by the unequal situations of debtors and creditors, the logic underlying his argument was the ethic of reciprocity. To Madison the payment of debts was a simple matter of justice.[51]

Madison's principal concern was the "want of concert in matters where common interest requires it." The United States would continue to lag behind other nations because it lacked the means to undertake essential national projects (such as a national university). Even during the War for Independence, Madison wrote, when danger made cooperation urgent, most of the states failed to fulfill their obligations to the nation. The burdens of government would always fall unevenly on different states. If each state could choose whether to comply, "distrust of the voluntary compliance of each other may prevent the compliance of any." Madison understood that the problem of collective action is perennial. If things continued to get worse, "dissolving the Union altogether" loomed as a real possibility. The history of earlier confederations illustrated how easily and how often such unions came unglued.

A deeper problem lay beneath the troubled relations between and within the states. As a Protestant Christian and a student of Scottish common-sense philosophy, Madison understood the friction between individual desires and conscience, between self-interest and benevolence, which raised a stark question about "the fundamental principle of republican Government." Is it true, he asked, "that the majority who rule in such Governments, are the safest Guardians both of public good and of private rights"? The chaos of the postwar period made the answer anything but obvious. In a veiled reference to Shays's Rebellion and other instances of armed violence, Madison noted that "a minority may in an appeal to force, be an overmatch for the majority." Should that minority possess "the skill and habits of military life," the possibility became ominous. History showed countless examples of military forces overwhelming civil authorities.

Insurrection by the propertyless presented another obvious danger: if their conditions deteriorated further, the poor would surely side with the forces of sedition rather than order. Curiously for a man who owned more than one hundred slaves himself, Madison added, almost as an afterthought, "Where slavery exists the republican Theory becomes still more fallacious." As Jefferson observed in his *Notes on the State of Virginia*, slaves could hardly be expected to support the laws that kept them enslaved. Madison seems never to have focused directly on the relation between impoverished white men and African American slaves. Like so many other southerners from the seventeenth century on, he internalized a categorical division between white and black that blinded him to the very real constraints operating on debtors of any color during the 1780s.[52]

A contemporary reader working through Madison's list of "Vices" now cannot help wondering how—or even whether—he thought popular government could be saved. Although the people could always "displace the offenders" and elect public-spirited officials, it was possible that even the most "base and selfish measures" could be disguised, and "honest but unenlightened" representatives were often duped by a leader "veiling his selfish views under the professions of public good." Madison had seen talented but unscrupulous orators work their magic in assemblies. Overall, the legislatures of the states were too strong, the government of the nation too weak, and a practicable solution to both of those problems was hard to envision.[53]

The answer lay elsewhere. Only if the ethic of reciprocity could be inculcated might popular government be redeemed from its vices. Sketching in outline the arguments he would make in the Constitutional Convention and in the most celebrated and influential—and most often misinterpreted—of his contributions to the *Federalist*, Madison offered a shrewd analysis of social conflict. "All civilized societies are divided into different interests and factions." These multiple interests and factions include divisions between "(1) creditors or debtors; (2) rich or poor; (3) husbandmen, merchants, or manufacturers; (4) members of religious sects; (5) followers of different political leaders; (6) inhabitants of different districts; [and] (7) owners of different kinds of property."

Madison's seven distinct divisions correspond uncannily to the conflicts of the 1780s. Experience and his reading of history convinced him that societies rupture along multiple fault lines; the resulting groupings are messy and unpredictable. The divisions between agrarians, traders, and artisans in his day made clear that struggling farmers did not have the same interests as struggling merchants or struggling craftsmen. James Wilson and Robert Morris, high-flying land speculators who ended up penniless, showed that rich debtors did not have the same interests as rich creditors, nor did wealthy holders of securities necessarily have the same interests as wealthy holders of real property. Adherents to rival religious sects had always persecuted each other irrespective of their wealth or any other characteristic, and Madison had seen evidence of the crazy quilts of religious alliances and antagonisms in the middle colonies as well as in his home county. Successful political leaders, such as Virginia rivals Patrick Henry and Edmund Randolph, often won support independent of their economic programs—sometimes even in spite of their economic programs—on the basis of clan, creed, or what was later called charisma. Finally, Madison the Virginian knew that loyalties to race and region—and animosities toward other races and regions—follow a merciless illogic all their own, especially when hierarchies rest on race-based slavery.

Madison's understanding of human motivation and human association cannot be captured by a simple division between rich and poor, or "elites" versus "the people." He had seen successful and prominent planters disgraced and rejected, as he was in 1777 and again in 1785, and as Jefferson was at the end of his term as governor of Virginia. He had seen immigrants such as James Wilson rise during the space of fourteen years from poverty and anonymity to become wealthy and powerful—and targets of public abuse as enemies of the "common people" from whose ranks they sprang. Madison's world had all the complications of any human community, and he understood that no single rift captured those complications.

Madison's solution to the "Vices of the Political System" required harnessing all these crosscutting divisions and, through the use of explicitly political institutions, creating institutions of government and nourishing a culture of democracy oriented toward the pursuit of justice understood as the common good. How would it work? Madison suggested three reasons why members from such diverse "interests and factions" might join together. First, they might seek "the general and permanent good of the Community." Despite the "decisive weight" of that objective, however, he had learned from experience that it rarely sufficed. Like individuals, nations tended to forget that "honesty is the best policy." Relying on a few farsighted and virtuous citizens to provide the necessary leadership might seem attractive, but Madison considered it chimerical: the multitude would never follow the example of such paragons. Might religion do the trick? Given that Christianity had failed to prevent vice despite Christ's message, and given the clear evidence of religious motives for some of history's cruelest acts, Madison dismissed the possibility: religion was as likely to become a "motive to oppression" as a barrier against injustice.

No thoughtful Christian from Jesus through Witherspoon would have objected to these observations, which Madison followed with a sobering assessment of majority rule: "Place three individuals in a situation wherein the interests of each depends on the voice of the others, and give to two of them an interest opposed to the rights of the third." In such circumstances, Madison asked, "will the latter be secure? The prudence of every man would shun the danger." Madison knew these objections were ancient and that regimes had coped with them in myriad ways. Monarchies trusted the king's neutrality; small republics circumscribed the power that governments could deploy against their people. Such measures, history showed, rarely proved adequate.

Madison did a have solution in mind: representative democracy, understood as a process of deliberative and experimental truth-testing. Drawing from the arguments of Aristotle, Hume, and Adam Smith concerning the moderation of conditions in large states and the value of crosscutting interests, and leveraging their ideas against Montesquieu's familiar warnings about the impossibility of a large republic, Madison proposed "such a process of elections as will most certainly extract from the mass of the Society the purest and noblest characters which it contains; such as will feel most strongly the proper motives to pursue the end of their appointment." Madison had already stipulated that the goal of government is not merely to manage conflict or preserve order. Instead the "great desideratum in Government is such a modification of the Sovereignty as will render it sufficiently neutral between the different interests and factions." Or, in the words Madison used nine months later in *Federalist* 51, "justice is the end of government. It is the end of civil society. It ever has been, and ever will be pursued, until it is obtained, or until liberty be lost in the pursuit."[54] The advantage of a large over a small republic, Madison argued in "Vices" and in the *Federalist*, depends precisely on the crosscutting nature of the different interests he had identified. Given the myriad complexities of those conflicts, he judged it all but impossible in a large nation that any single constellation of interests could form, or mobilize a majority, around any interest other than the "public interest."

In "Vices" Madison expressed this crucial point somewhat obliquely. The aim of the electoral process is to prevent "one part of the Society from invading the rights of another," and at the same time to keep each part "from setting up an interest adverse to that of the whole Society." By the time he wrote *Federalist* 51, he had found a more felicitous formulation: "In the extended republic of the United States, and among the great variety of interests, parties and sects which it embraces, a coalition of a majority of the whole society could seldom take place upon any other principles than those of justice and the general good." Madison sought a system that would do more than merely balance competing groups, play off factions against each other, or allow for the stark contests of naked self-interest, which he considered the problem rather than the solution. Instead Madison remained committed to the ideal shared by Witherspoon and Hutcheson, and by Rousseau and Paine: through the institutions of representative democracy, individuals might learn to internalize the ethic of reciprocity and find a way to treat each other with benevolence.[55]

Is there a difference between the interests of individuals and the general interest? That question lay at the heart of the controversies that raged in late eighteenth-century America. The gulf separating Madison from other champions of a vigorous national government such as Robert Morris and Hamilton began to be clear as early as the debates over the Bank of Pennsylvania in 1786. The Pennsylvania legislature was debating whether or not to renew the charter of Morris's bank. The small landowner and assemblyman William Findley of Carlisle spoke for the same rural elements that gravitated toward Daniel Shays, and he spoke directly about the economic conflicts that Minot saw at work in the Shaysites' struggle with the merchants and bankers of eastern Massachusetts. Findley and his western allies contended that Pennsylvania had no business chartering a bank from which only certain people, particularly Robert Morris, stood to benefit. "The government of Pennsylvania being a democracy," Findley proclaimed, "the bank is . . . inconsistent with our general laws, customs, and circumstances, and even with the nature of our government." We "divide our estates, both real and personal, more equally among our heirs" than do any other nations. For that reason we are so equal in wealth and power that we lack the leverage necessary to "check or control an institution of such vast influence and magnitude" as the Bank of Pennsylvania. It had long been common practice in rural areas to accept the slow repayment of debts, and paper money had shown its "amazing usefulness, before the revolution," in helping most Pennsylvanians prosper.

Now the concentration of wealth was threatening the independence made possible by such practices. Whereas "wealth in many hands operates as many checks," Findley continued, "one wealthy man has a control over another." Such dependency is inimical to democracy. An autonomous individual can "act upon his own principles. His virtue, his honour, his sympathy, and generosity" determine his behavior: "He is in a state of personal responsibility." But the bank run by Morris and his cronies had "no principle but that of avarice, which dries up and shrivels up all the manly—all the generous feelings of the human soul." Findley argued that while those backing the bank had a "right to advocate their own cause, on the floor of this house," he challenged them to admit that they were doing only that. Findley charged Morris with departing from the republican values to which Americans had declared allegiance throughout the revolutionary era. If the power and "special temper" of the bank continued to grow, Findley concluded, "like a snow ball perpetually rolled," increasing "its dimensions and influence," it would end by "overturning our government. Democracy must fall before it."[56]

Although Madison and Wilson shared Morris's desire to put the nation's finances on a sounder basis, they resisted his departure from republican ideals. True to their intellectual formation in Protestant Christianity and Scottish common-sense philosophy, they believed, together with Findley, that pursuit of self-interest could and should be governed by the moral sense. They also believed that social interaction, both outside and inside forums of political debate, provides the occasion for cultivating the autonomy and reciprocity on which democratic culture and institutions depend. A chasm separated their sensibility from that of Morris and other like-minded figures such as Hamilton. Both Wilson and Madison had learned the difference between a hereditary aristocracy, which exercises political power by right and without question, and democratic leadership, which possesses only revocable authority by virtue of voters' ballots.

They had also learned that nothing in democracy is final. Contingent developments alter perceptions and options. With extralegal actions by impoverished citizens unable to pay their debts or their taxes obstructing the operation of government, many shared Findley's fears for the future of democracy. Many farmers vilified Wilson because of his ties to Robert Morris. Yet after the "Fort Wilson" incident, most urban artisans, sailors, and small merchants, perhaps surprisingly, threw their support behind Wilson and his allies in their battle against the 1776 constitution. They opposed that framework not because they were antidemocratic but because—in the absence of an independent judiciary and effective executive to balance the all-powerful legislature—they judged it potentially despotic. The volatility of the states convinced Madison, too, that popularly elected legislatures could threaten the survival of self-government as much as tyrants. The delegates to the Constitutional Convention in 1787 were about to find out whether apparently solid convictions, grounded in interest, affiliation, and aspiration, could become more malleable preferences under the pressure of debate.

Madison left little to chance in the months leading up to the convention. He wanted to replace the Articles of Confederation with something altogether new, and we have an idea what he was thinking from the plan of government he had sketched for a friend two years earlier. If the Kentucky region of Virginia were to become a state, his college friend Caleb Wallace asked him in 1785, how should it organize its government? Madison had been studying an edition of the new state constitutions, and his letter to Wallace shows how deeply indebted he was to Adams's Massachusetts Constitution in particular. He proposed for Kentucky a bicameral legislature, with members of the upper house serving four- or five-year terms, to provide stability, and periodic reapportionment to secure fair representation. He considered an executive officer crucial, but he declared himself agnostic about whether he should be elected by popular ballot or chosen by the legislature. He also recommended as "very practicable" a declaration of rights, which he considered indispensable to restrain the legislature. He offered a familiar classical republican argument for a wide electorate of autonomous rather than dependent individuals. He advised against limiting the electorate to landowners, which would exclude too many citizens from the franchise, and also against giving too much power to those who would "either abuse it themselves or sell it to the rich who will abuse it." Determining the appropriate qualifications for voting, in short, would be a delicate matter contingent on economic as well as political circumstances. Finally, referring to the independent judiciary he proposed, Madison concluded that it would be unwise to rule out amendments made necessary by experience. The people of Kentucky would have to decide how their constitution was working and adjust it accordingly.[57]

The two years between his 1785 letter to Wallace and his memorandum on "Vices" convinced Madison that the confederation government had to be scrapped. He sent Washington a detailed report on the Annapolis meeting, and the two Virginians exchanged letters on the reasons why Americans should rethink their national government. Madison also sent Washington copies of his thoughts on confederacies and his "Vices" essay; Washington read and took detailed notes on both documents. Eager to begin work, Madison arrived in Philadelphia early. In the eleven days before the convention was scheduled to open, he forged a crucial alliance between himself, Randolph, Washington, and the members of the Pennsylvania delegation.[58] Not only were all the Virginians but Mason and all the Pennsylvanians committed to a stronger national government; Madison discovered that Wilson in particular shared his ideas about establishing the new nation on a popular foundation. Some of the wealthiest delegates, including Robert Morris, Gouverneur Morris, and Hamilton, surely did distrust the judgment of ordinary people. Madison and Wilson, by contrast, believed that a stable national government must rest on the principle and the practice of popular sovereignty. Wilson and Madison preferred direct popular election of members of the lower house and argued that representation in an indirectly elected upper house, like that of the lower, should be proportional to population. Among the first members of the convention to settle on the idea of an individual executive officer, Wilson thought the president (a modest-sounding term to camouflage the role of an executive who would "preside" rather than "govern") likewise should be elected directly by the people. Given Americans' persistent fears of monarchy, most members of the convention were wary of a single executive. Few besides Wilson trusted ordinary voters to choose such a potentially powerful official no matter what he was called.

Although Madison probably met Franklin for the first time in the spring of 1787, he had worked with the other Pennsylvanians before. Wilson, Robert Morris, and Gouverneur Morris had served with Madison in the Continental Congress, as had forty-two of the fifty-five delegates to the Constitutional Convention. Robert Morris, hated as he was by many other Americans striving to become equally prosperous themselves, was a self-made man, as were Wilson, Franklin, and Hamilton. Gouverneur Morris, by contrast, descended from one of New York's wealthiest and most prominent families. He wrote undergraduate and MA theses at King's College (later Columbia) on the topics of wit, beauty, and love, and he demonstrated a lifelong commitment to all three. Clever, self-confident, and physically imposing, Gouverneur Morris moved among the highest social circles of New York and, eventually, his adopted city of Philadelphia, where he established himself after a carriage accident in 1780 left him with an artificial leg. After settling in Pennsylvania, he developed a desire to succeed in politics as well as finance.

Neither the well-to-do Robert Morris nor the well-born Gouverneur Morris was naturally prone, as Madison observed, to "incline toward the democratic side." Yet both had their own reasons to share Madison's and Wilson's desire for a new national government. During informal sessions in Philadelphia taverns before a quorum finally allowed the convention to begin meeting on May 25, Madison and Wilson reached an understanding with each other. They also helped shape the thinking of the more voluble Randolph and Gouverneur Morris, skilled orators who introduced and ably defended many of Madison's and Wilson's ideas in the convention. Although their many differences would later become apparent, at the convention these moderate nationalists managed to present a more or less united front. Their alliance caused contemporary and later commentators to misunderstand Madison's and Wilson's dual objectives, a strong and stable national government and a sturdy foundation of continuing popular engagement.[59]

Debates concerning the meaning and significance of the Constitutional Convention began even before it opened.[60] Locating the debates in the context of contemporaries' concerns illuminates the range of objectives sought by various delegates and shows why the resulting compromise, which satisfied almost no one completely, satisfied almost everyone just enough to ensure that it would be sent to the states for ratification. The Constitution emerged from hardheaded deal-making by shrewd politicians with diverse religious and political ideas and varied experience as lawmakers in their own states. Delegates balanced their desire to satisfy the legislative assemblies that sent them against their willingness to change their minds in the face of other delegates' arguments, convictions, preferences, and prejudices. Their deliberations reflected all the divisions Madison had identified in "Vices," and the convention's outcome likewise reflected the unpredictable developments inevitable in the course of any unscripted gathering of individuals. When the historian Jared Sparks later edited Madison's detailed notes on the convention, he wrote that "opinions were so various and at first so crude that it was necessary they should be long debated before any uniform system of opinion could be formed. Meantime the minds of the members were changing, and much was to be gained by a yielding and accommodating spirit." Inasmuch as such a sensibility, a prerequisite to democratic deliberation, surfaced at all, it emerged slowly and imperfectly in the debates as they unfolded.

Since the only detailed record of the convention that exists comes from the notes Madison kept, historians have had to trust the accuracy of his transcriptions. Sparks reported that no delegate, including Madison, appeared to feel "obliged to retain his opinions any longer than he was satisfied of their propriety and truth." All were "open to the force of argument." Even if not always persuaded by the logic of each other's reasoning, delegates did make concessions that facilitated the final outcome. Had they been bound by their constituents' instructions and lacked sufficient independence to change their positions, had their deliberations been held in public or leaked to the press, no progress would have been possible, and no constitution would have been created.[61]

Those procedures, however, sparked controversy from the start. Jefferson wrote to Adams from Paris denouncing the secrecy imposed in Philadelphia. "Tying up the tongues" of the delegates established an "abominable precedent." Although critics of the convention have echoed that judgment, the next attempt to forge a national constitution in a public setting, in Paris a few years later, did not work quite as well as Jefferson predicted. Despite his misgivings, Jefferson had faith in those gathering behind closed doors to frame a new government. "Nothing can justify this example," he wrote, "but the innocence of their intentions, and ignorance of the value of public discussions. I have no doubt that all their other measures will be good and wise. It really is an assembly of demigods." Demigods or not, delegates understood that free-flowing discussion would be impossible if they took formal rather than straw votes on every proposal and if their every comment and query were made public. George Mason, a Virginia planter who owned three hundred slaves and ranked among the wealthiest men in the nation, characterized the controversial rule of secrecy as "a necessary precaution to prevent misrepresentations or mistakes, there being a material difference between the appearance of a subject in its first crude and undigested shape, and after it shall have been properly matured and arranged." In his letter to Adams, Jefferson himself noted that he felt obliged to present "every truth of any consequence" about developments in France because accounts published in the newspapers were so unreliable: "Floating in the mass of lies which constitute the atmospheres of London and Paris, you may not have been sure of their truth."

Apprehensive about such a "mass of lies" poisoning debates in the sometimes stifling Pennsylvania State House, the delegates agreed to keep the windows closed and to keep their discussions to themselves. Madison later wrote that "no Constitution would ever have been adopted by the convention if the debates had been public." Only under strictly regulated conditions, with the stipulations that every speaker was to be treated with respect, that informal votes would not be recorded, and that secrecy would be respected, were the delegates able to deliberate.[62] Many delegates were so frustrated by the wrangling, or so upset by the prospect of the stronger national authority they feared, that they went home. Others, including Madison, were ready to abandon the convention at several moments. The veiled threat that other delegates, particularly those from Georgia and South Carolina, might leave surely constrained debate.[63]

The decisive breakthrough, locating the authority of the Constitution in the people at large instead of the states, occurred right away. The Articles of Confederation provided for a Congress chosen by the state assemblies. Perhaps citizens and their legislative representatives did not trust the central government with much power because the people at large had not voted for those who sat in the Confederation Congress. Almost as soon as the Constitutional Convention opened on May 29, after preliminary rule-setting discussions, Virginia governor Edmund Randolph presented a proposal, drafted primarily by Madison and Wilson in the days before the convention opened, that came to be known as the Virginia Plan. Besides Madison and Randolph, the Virginia delegation included George Washington, unanimously elected to preside over the proceedings, and Mason, one of twenty-five slave owners of the fifty-five delegates at the convention. Not coincidentally, Randolph's speech echoed almost perfectly the concerns articulated in the first part of Madison's "Vices."

The Virginia Plan included a popularly elected bicameral national assembly, which its architects hoped would solve several problems at once. It legitimated the national government by locating authority in the people themselves, thereby making concrete the abstract principle of popular sovereignty. Americans had been electing representatives to local, colonial, and now state assemblies for over a century; under the Virginia Plan they would choose members of the national legislature. Because we take for granted a popularly elected House of Representatives, it is difficult to recapture how stunning the Virginia proposal seemed. Randolph also proposed an upper house, a "national executive" to be chosen by the national assembly, and a set of federal courts. The plan featured two of Madison's obsessions. A national veto of any state legislation deemed inconsistent with the Constitution reflected his concern that majorities might not respect creditors' or property holders' rights. A provision to use "the force of the Union against any member of the Union failing to fulfill its duty" would compel states to pay their debts.

Another novel feature of the Virginia Plan was that "provision ought to be made for amending the Constitution not by Congress but by the people, who would retain the power to alter their framework of government." Those who hammered out the Constitution did not imagine themselves demigods standing outside history. Just as crucially, the Constitution was to be ratified not by currently sitting state legislatures but by special assemblies elected by the people for that purpose. That step, previously taken only in Massachusetts (and imperfectly executed there), further signaled the location of sovereignty, though critics later charged that the legislative assemblies would have been more responsive to popular sentiment than were these specially chosen ratifying conventions. Finally, although the delegates assumed the states would impose qualifications for voters and officeholders, the Virginia Plan stipulated neither age nor sex nor race. The words "We the People," which stand at the head of the Constitution as ultimately adopted, express a commitment to popular government visible from the first proposal to the final document submitted for ratification.[64]

Alignments concerning the ideal distance between the people and the national government began to emerge as soon as debate on the Virginia Plan began. Roger Sherman of Connecticut, who later introduced a decisive compromise, began by objecting to the direct election of representatives. "The people," he said in an unconscious echo of Cromwell in the Putney debates of 1647, "immediately should have as little to do as may be about the Government." Because they lack information, they are "constantly liable to be misled." Elbridge Gerry of Massachusetts agreed: "The evils we experience flow from the excess of democracy." It seems to be "a maxim of democracy," he joked, "to starve the public servants" by refusing government the funds necessary to operate. Randolph too, perhaps to Madison's surprise, expressed concern about popularly elected legislatures: the problems besetting state governments flowed from "the turbulence and follies of democracy."[65]

The prosperous planter George Mason responded by endorsing a popularly elected legislature as "the grand depository of the democratic principle of the Government." If the states had sometimes been "too democratic" under the Articles of Confederation, his anxious colleagues should not "incautiously run into the opposite extreme" and forget their duty to "every class of the people." Whereas the first two delegates to question the people's capacity were themselves of humble birth, the wellborn and now even wealthier Mason spoke passionately about trusting the people's judgment. Delegates did not always play to type.

In his opening remarks, Wilson introduced an image he would use repeatedly in the coming years. He envisioned a pyramid of government resting on the most solid foundation imaginable; the entire people. That image eventually became part of the nation's great seal, designed by Wilson's friend Francis Hopkinson. Because Wilson wished to raise "the federal pyramid to a considerable altitude, and for that reason wished to give it as broad a basis as possible," he urged direct popular election of all national officials. "No government could long subsist without the confidence of the people," he argued, which explains Wilson's conviction that not only both houses of Congress but also the executive should be elected directly by the people. Madison echoed the sentiments expressed by Mason and Wilson. If all the officers of the national government were chosen indirectly, "the people would be lost sight of altogether; and the necessary sympathy between them" and the national government would fail to grow. Madison did admit some misgivings. He favored "the policy of refining the popular appointments by successive filtrations" but warned that such filtering might go too far. Following Wilson's lead, Madison argued "that the great fabric to be raised would be more stable and durable, if it should rest on the solid foundation of the people themselves, than if it should stand merely on the pillars of the Legislatures."[66]

On June 6 Wilson and Madison delivered major speeches laying out the logic of their case for direct popular engagement. Wilson advanced an argument concerning popular sovereignty that became a central lever for those who favored the Constitution and a target of those who opposed it. Wilson wanted the "vigor" in the national government "to flow immediately from the legitimate source of all authority," the people. The nation's government "ought to possess not only firstly the force but secondly the *mind or sense* of the people at large," which was accomplished through representation only because "it is impossible for the people to act collectively." The public would accept increasing the power of the central government if they understood that its power originated in their will. Wilson seconded Madison's point: "There is no danger of improper elections if made by *large* districts. Bad elections proceed from the smallness of the districts which give an opportunity to bad men to intrigue themselves into office." Such shenanigans were less likely in districts with more people. Mason agreed that representatives should "sympathize" with their constituents, should "think as they think, & feel as they feel." He contended that candidates in larger districts would have to appeal to a wider range of voters and that the filtration process would improve the electoral process more generally.

Even among these unusually well-educated delegates, twenty-nine of whom were among the tiny minority of Americans who had earned college degrees, Wilson stood out because of the breadth of his learning. William Pierce, a Georgia delegate who penned word portraits of those at the convention, deftly captured him: "Wilson ranks among the foremost in legal and political knowledge. He has joined to a fine genius all that can set him off and show him to advantage." No armchair scholar, Wilson was "well acquainted with Man, and understands all the passions that influence him." With Adams stuck in Europe, Wilson's erudition distinguished him from everyone at the convention except Madison: "Government seems to have been his peculiar Study," according to Pierce. Wilson knew "in detail" all the world's political institutions, and he could "trace the causes and effects of every revolution" from ancient Greece to the present. Unfortunately, Wilson liked to display his encyclopedic knowledge every time he spoke. With daily sessions beginning around 10:00 a.m. and wrapping up five or six hours later, Wilson's long-winded remarks sometimes ran from one day to the next. Yet only Madison's speeches rivaled Wilson's for sheer density of ideas. From the opening of the convention through ratification sixteen month later, Wilson validated Pierce's judgment: though he was "no great Orator," no one was "more clear, copious, and comprehensive than Mr. Wilson," who commanded "attention not by the charm of his eloquence, but by the force of his reasoning."[67]

That same day, June 6, Madison delivered the first of many speeches and essays drawn directly from ideas outlined in "Vices." To the question of what the filters of popular election and democratic deliberation would do, Madison answered that they would provide "the security of private rights and the steady dispensation of justice." Enlarging the sphere would split the nation into so many interests and parties that a majority could only form around the public good. By empowering the people to choose representatives to the national legislature, the new system would be self-correcting. Such procedures would not enable the new government to escape historical time, as commentators more familiar with Machiavelli than Madison have contended, but would instead yoke the new republic to a process that could unfold only in time, through the back-and-forth of debate. Whether delegates changed their minds or simply realized they would be outvoted, as Madison eventually did with his pet national veto, deliberation required everyone either to yield to the force of the better argument or just face facts. When ideas do not mesh, grinding their edges can mangle them, bring them into alignment, or make their edges even sharper. In any case, the process takes time.[68]

Madison did want merely to manage conflict. Finding a way for those conflicts to generate a "common interest," he declared from the outset, was "the only defence against the inconveniences of democracy consistent with the democratic form of government." In his first extended speech in the convention, Madison did not refer to the inconveniences of a "*republic*" or the value of a "*republican* form of government," as he later did in the celebrated *Federalist* 10. Speaking to the colleagues he had to convince, he spoke about solving the problems of a *democracy* by taking steps consistent with *democratic* government. Adopting Wilson's bold formulation, Madison deployed the word "democracy," a word often used to denounce popular government and used for that purpose by Sherman of Connecticut, Gerry of Massachusetts, and others in Philadelphia, and defiantly turned it back on them. Far from repudiating the idea of democracy, at the convention Madison embraced it openly. He wanted a democratic national government.[69]

In the early stages of debate, many of Madison's and Wilson's arguments seemed persuasive. Hamilton grudgingly conceded that there was much truth in Madison's arguments for the democratic thrust of the Virginia Plan, even though he complained that they "do not conclude so strongly as he supposes." The proposal for popular election of one branch of the national legislature passed with only two dissenting votes. Although Madison fought with terrier-like tenacity for a national veto on state laws, it went down to defeat, as did more than half of Madison's specific policy proposals. He was the most influential figure in the convention and, as Georgia's Pierce noted, along with Wilson the "best informed man at any point in debate"—at least in part because he was the one keeping a detailed record—but in Philadelphia Madison lost as many battles as he won.[70]

Wilson gradually enlisted support for his idea of locating executive authority in a single person, whom the Committee on Detail eventually decided to call the president, but reaching agreement on the procedure for selecting that person seemed impossible. Wilson's own preference, popular election by the people whom the national executive would represent, elicited shrieks of outrage from Mason and Gerry. Mason likened the idea to asking a blind man to choose among colors, and Gerry warned that "the ignorance of the people" would make them susceptible to easy manipulation. The delegates debated whether the president should be chosen by the state legislatures, by the national legislature, or by another body altogether. At one stage, perhaps from desperation born of deadlock, Wilson proposed the fanciful idea of selecting a group of congressmen by lottery and letting them choose the executive. It is an indication of the extent to which the ancient Greek institution of sortition, which has recently attracted the enthusiasm of so many contemporary political theorists, had vanished from sight that Wilson's suggestion attracted no support from anyone; even Wilson conceded that the notion was half-baked and "liable to strong objections." Wilson's own preference for direct election of the president was defeated nine to one; he stood almost alone in his conviction that the people themselves should elect the most important officer in the federal government.[71]

In the comforting presence of Washington, the great Cincinnatus who presided over the convention, delegates eventually accepted a single rather than multiple executive. Fears that such a national leader was bound to become, as South Carolina's Pierce Butler put it, "a Cataline [sic] or a Cromwell," were exacerbated by Hamilton's unsuccessful proposal that both the executive and those in the upper house of the legislature should serve for life, after the model of Britain's kings and lords. To quell such fears, the convention initially endorsed a single seven-year term for an executive to be chosen indirectly rather than through the popular vote that Wilson explicitly endorsed. Had it not been assumed that Washington, renowned throughout the nation and esteemed as being above personal ambition, would be the nation's first chief executive, the convention might have deadlocked on the issue of the presidency. It was an office thought fit, in an age of monarchy, for tyrants-in-waiting.[72]

But the deepest rifts, which threatened to rupture the convention from the outset, divided the delegations from small states from those representing large states and the North from the South. Delaware, the least populous of the thirteen states, was prepared to scuttle the entire project of revision if the principle of representation proportional to population were adopted for the national legislature. Corporate entities such as towns and parishes had always been the basis of representation in the colonial legislatures, and that practice remained unquestioned until the 1760s.[73] Individuals' membership in communities mattered everywhere; identity was still largely determined by a person's town or state. Bolstered by custom, delegates from smaller states resisted proportional representation with growing fervor. William Paterson declared flatly that New Jersey, like Delaware, would never accept representation proportional to population and proposed an alternative plan featuring a single national legislature with equal representation for all states, a plan augmenting the power of Congress to levy taxes and regulate commerce but in other respects replicating the Articles of Confederation.

Wilson and Madison likewise dug in their heels. Wilson responded to Paterson that Pennsylvania would accept no basis for representation other than population. Madison's reply was more temperate and more elaborate.

Madison explained ad nauseam why revising the Articles of Confederation would not suffice. He cataloged all of history's failed confederations, showing how the analogs of the American states had usurped authority and brought "confusion & ruin on the whole." Madison concluded by insisting that the larger states, with all their differences, would never ally on the basis of size anyway, and he observed that the New Jersey plan for equal representation of the states violated the principle of majority rule fundamental to democracy. Enabling the minority of the nation's population to legislate for the majority, Madison declared, Americans should never accept.[74]

Even after the delegates killed the New Jersey plan, disagreements persisted. Obvious conflicts over the fate of slavery, which was already in the process of being outlawed in many northern states, put the North at odds with the South over another issue that might have deadlocked the convention. Slavery might be endangered even if, as the convention ultimately decided, slaves were to be counted as three-fifths persons for the purpose of apportioning representation.[75] The idea of two houses, one popularly elected according to the principle of proportionality, the other with two representatives from each state, earlier suggested by Connecticut and rejected, now emerged as a solution to both the large-small and the North-South divisions. Yet for two long, hot weeks, Madison, Wilson, and a few allies held out against the Connecticut compromise. Wilson reverted to his metaphor of the pyramid: "If the Government be not laid on this foundation" of fair representation in both branches of the national legislature, "it can be neither solid nor lasting."[76] The convention disposed of subsidiary issues, including the size of the lower house, which Madison wanted to be twice as large as the sixty-five members the convention endorsed. But the conflict over the composition of the Senate, as many upper houses had been called since the time of the Roman republic, remained unresolved.

The venerable Franklin, frail and suffering from kidney stones, finally decided it was time for him to speak. In an address read by his colleague Wilson because Franklin was too weak to deliver it, Franklin pleaded for compromise. The convention had begun with delegates agreeing to exchange ideas freely, but since they had turned to the issue of representation, "declarations of a fixed opinion and of determined resolution" had obstructed further progress. To break the logjam, Franklin urged each delegate to "consider himself rather as a representative of the whole, than as an Agent for the interests of a particular state." From that perspective, delegates should be able to see that the number of representatives should be proportional to the number of people represented, and that decisions should be made by "the majority of members, not the majority of States." Perhaps because his conclusion (as well as his premises) aligned too closely with the ideas of Madison and Wilson, and perhaps because Franklin proposed implementing his plan by having the richer states contribute more in taxes than the poorer states, his impassioned plea elicited no response from anyone. The delegates appeared stymied.[77]

The convention finally broke the deadlock by voting, on July 16, by the narrowest of margins, in favor of Connecticut's proposal, a "great blow" to which Madison and Wilson could not manage to reconcile themselves immediately.[78] Accepting the Connecticut compromise, however, ensured that the delegates would reach a conclusion and submit a constitution to the states for ratification. The final weeks of the convention were devoted to debates over suffrage. After lengthy discussion, the delegates decided against specifying any limits on the right to vote and left that issue to the states.[79]

During the convention some delegates simply took a position and held it unflinchingly. Yet only a few delegates, in the words of Madison that Sparks later echoed, "did not change in the progress of the discussions the opinions on important points which they carried into the convention." Almost no one denied that their ideas changed because of "the enlightening effect of the discussions."[80] Although the debates altered Madison's thinking on some issues, and he ended up defending provisions of the Constitution he had initially opposed, his judgment never wavered on three issues: the need for a national veto; the undesirable, antidemocratic form of representation in the Senate; and, perhaps above all, his enduring conviction that slavery constituted "the most oppressive dominion ever exercised by man over man."[81]

Understanding how men who spoke eloquently about freedom and equality could own slaves challenges our historical imagination. No one is more unfathomable than Jefferson, who inadvertently brought to the attention of Europeans and well as Americans his profound inconsistencies on the issue of race. In a letter to his law teacher George Wythe sent from Paris in the summer of 1786, Jefferson wrote that a "bad French translation" of his *Notes on the State of Virginia* was being circulated in France. As a result he felt compelled to prepare and make available an improved English edition. Having been persuaded by Madison that the book "will not do the harm I had apprehended but on the contrary may do some good," Jefferson was readying it for publication. The "harm" had to do with his discussion of slavery, and he had reason to worry. Musing in response to queries about the laws and manners of Virginia, Jefferson had expressed ideas that would not only indict him as the worst of hypocrites but also become powerful ammunition for critics of slavery.

Jefferson pointed out that he had called for the emancipation of slaves in the proposals he submitted to the Virginia legislature in 1776, and he explained that, although no action was taken then, he remained committed to ending slavery. After emancipation, though, he favored colonizing former slaves "to such place as the circumstances of the time should render most proper." Jefferson offered a remarkable list of reasons for colonization: "deep rooted prejudices entertained by the whites; ten thousand recollections, by the blacks, of the injuries they have sustained; new provocations; the real distinctions which nature has made; and many other circumstances, will divide us into parties, and produce convulsions, which will probably never end but in the extermination of one or the other race." Implicit in the list were not only Jefferson's awareness of the injustice and cruelty of slavery but his own deep-seated racism. When he wrote about the differences between American Indians and European settlers elsewhere in *Notes*, he did not hesitate, as a good Lockean, to attribute the differences to circumstances and to predict rapid development of Indians' capacities due to their increasing interaction with Europeans. In the case of the blacks on whose abilities his own prosperous life depended, however, he invoked only supposedly natural "real distinctions."[82]

Despite his racism, Jefferson realized that slavery was indefensible. That knowledge nagged at him, and later in *Notes* he returned to the subject in a searing passage on "customs and manners" that deserves to be as well known as the Declaration of Independence. "There must doubtless be an unhappy influence on the manners of our people produced by the existence of slavery among us," Jefferson began. "The whole commerce between master and slave is a perpetual exercise of the most boisterous passions, the most unremitting despotism on the one part, and degrading submissions on the other." When white children witness such behavior, they "learn to imitate it; for man is an imitative animal. This quality is the germ of all education in him. From his cradle to his grave he is learning to do what he sees others do." Even if a parent could find no other reason for "restraining the intemperance of passion towards his slave, it should always be a sufficient one that his child is present." Jefferson himself had been raised by a slave owner, and he knew from his father's example that his own presence had proved no impediment to a master's rage. "The parent storms, the child looks on, catches the lineaments of wrath, puts on the same airs in the circle of smaller slaves," and sets free his worst passions. Children "nursed, educated, and daily exercised in tyranny, cannot but be stamped by it with odious peculiarities. That man must be a prodigy who can retain his manners and morals undepraved by such circumstances." Although Jefferson's reckoning of slavery's costs is heavily weighted toward masters rather than slaves, he was hardly blind to the fact that slavery was a "perpetual" nightmare of "degrading submissions" for slaves.

Jefferson did not flinch at drawing the obvious, if excruciating, conclusion: "And with what execration should the statesman be loaded, who permitting one half the citizens thus to trample on the rights of the other, transforms those into despots, and these into enemies, destroys the morals of the one part, and the amor patriae of the other?" Former slaves could hardly be expected to live amicably with former masters. "For if a slave can have a country in this world, it must be any other in preference to that in which he is born to live and labour for another." When Jefferson focused on the consequences of slavery for the slave, he underscored its endless horror. Given that admission, how could he answer the haunting question posed by his sentence about the "execration" due to statesmen, such as Jefferson himself, who perpetuated slavery?

The disastrous effects of slavery, odious as they were for the enslaved, extended to the owners who lived off their labor. Jefferson noted yet another dimension of the damage slavery did to slaveholders and the world they made. Along "with the morals of the people" dependent on slaves, "their industry also is destroyed." In warm climates, "no man will labour for himself who can make another labour for him," so few slave owners ever do any work themselves. Having rhapsodized about the accord between autonomous small farmers and self-government, Jefferson understood the pathetic folly of resting democratic government on citizens made ever lazier by, and ever more dependent on, the labor of those who worked so they might rest. Jefferson recognized that slavery threatened the survival of American democracy: "Can the liberties of a nation be thought secure when we have removed their only firm basis, a conviction in the minds of the people that these liberties are of the gift of God? That they are not to be violated but with his wrath?" Then came the terrible crescendo that would echo into our own day. "Indeed I tremble for my country when I reflect that God is just: that his justice cannot sleep for ever: that considering numbers, nature and natural means only a revolution of the wheel of fortune, an exchange of situation, is among possible events: that it may become possible by supernatural interference?" Jefferson's verdict could not have been more severe. "The Almighty has no attribute which can take side with us in such a contest.— But it is impossible to be temperate and to pursue this subject through the various considerations of policy, of morals, of history natural and civil." Jefferson's dash after imagining slavery ending by God's wrath, like the succession of colons that arrest the progression of the words before it, signals the barely buried dread of cataclysm he shared with all slaveholders.

After Jefferson recovered his equilibrium, he continued in a more characteristically forward-looking tone: "I think a change already perceptible, since the origin of the present revolution. The spirit of the master is abating, that of the slave rising from the dust." The condition of slaves was "mollifying, the way I hope preparing, under the auspices of heaven, for a total emancipation." With luck, Jefferson concluded, that end would arrive with the masters' consent instead of their "extirpation."[83] This final, extraordinary sentence, which concludes Jefferson's discussion of slavery in *Notes*, seems to have a momentum of its own. It begins calmly enough, with both the slave owner and the slave learning moderation. As it progresses toward emancipation, the reader sees the energy and enthusiasm of Jefferson's hope for a peaceful resolution. But that hope inevitably collides with the violence on which slavery depends, violence that might at any moment unleash the righteous fury of the oppressed and culminate in slaves' self-emancipation and their owners' annihilation. One wonders how the author of those sentences faced any of his own slaves, let alone the one who was the mother of his children.

Jefferson knew that oppression and inequality were inimical to democracy. He worked hard to help institute laws, create a political framework, and inculcate cultural practices that would enable the United States to preserve its democracy by avoiding the traps of luxury and privilege that poisoned France. Slavery mocked all those efforts. When Adams left France for good in May of 1785, Jefferson presented him with a copy of *Notes on the State of Virginia*, which Adams read—perhaps aloud to Abigail and their daughter Nabby—as they traveled toward the English Channel. Many of the ideas in the book, in particular those on the value of mixed government and the horror of slavery, resonated with Adams's own convictions. He sent Jefferson a letter praising the book. The passages on slavery in particular, Adams wrote, were "worth diamonds."[84] Their value evidently diminished, however, when they reached the United States.

The delegates at the Constitutional Convention perpetuated the American tradition of talking about slavery but doing little about it. Madison's internal conflict was as deep as Jefferson's. When one of his slaves escaped to join the British army during the Revolution, Madison understood he was seeking only "that liberty for which we have paid the price of so much blood," the goal Americans proclaimed the "worthy pursuit of every human being." Madison released that slave from bondage, a fact complicated by Madison's apprehension that returning an escaped slave to Montpelier might "corrupt" his other slaves. Madison knew that slavery and democracy were incompatible, but like the man in Jefferson's image who held a wolf by the ears, and like most other late eighteenth-century Americans, he had no solution.[85]

Few delegates even mentioned this most obvious issue underlying many disagreements at the convention.[86] Madison was an exception, as was Wilson's teacher John Dickinson. In his speech of June 6, Madison described slavery as an injustice justified according to the flimsiest of pretexts, "the mere distinction of color."[87] Dickinson wrote in his notebook that the record's omission even of "the WORD" slavery "will be regarded as an Endeavour to conceal a principle of which we are ashamed." If more delegates had confronted the reasons for that shame, they might have written a different constitution, but it is likelier that the effort would have failed completely.[88]

Delegates from Georgia and South Carolina, the only states to keep importing slaves from Africa legal after the Revolution, threatened to bolt if the issue so much as came to the floor of the convention. When Gouverneur Morris delivered a thunderous attack on "a nefarious institution" that he called "the curse of heaven on the states where it prevailed," he was only restating a characterization made with increasing frequency in the North since the 1770s. Slavery had been condemned in the new constitutions of Vermont, Pennsylvania, and Massachusetts, and some states were adopting plans of gradual abolition. Gouverneur Morris had already demanded abolishing slavery in his native New York, reasoning that every human being should enjoy the same privileges as every other. Slavery was under attack in many northern states by the late 1780s, for economic reasons as well as the ethical reasons Morris offered. The Society of Friends made opposing slavery a condition of membership, and many Methodist congregations followed suit, but such religious fervor only antagonized many fence-sitters.[89]

The status of slavery in the Upper South was changing. As Virginia farmers diversified from relying solely on tobacco cultivation, many indebted planters sold slaves to eager buyers in the Deep South and the growing Mississippi region. The only other delegate besides Madison and Morris who denounced slavery in the convention was George Mason, who owned as many slaves as anyone but had criticized the institution in 1773 for its disastrous effect on whites. In an essay similar in tone to Jefferson's indictment and equally hypocritical, Mason had called slavery a "slow Poison" responsible for "contaminating the Minds and Morals of our People." Like many planters in the Upper South, however, Mason realized that ending the slave trade would increase the value of his slaves; he had no interest in ending slavery itself.[90]

After his opening speech, Madison never returned to the issue of slavery at the convention. Dickinson kept his reservations to himself. Gouverneur Morris found no allies willing to denounce slavery or call for its abolition. Even the date proposed for ending the slave trade was moved forward from 1800 to 1808 in response to pressure from Georgia and South Carolina. From the perspective of many contemporaries and later abolitionists, the founders' moral cowardice in countenancing slavery poisoned the Constitution. Although the assumptions undergirding slavery were being questioned as debates about liberty and equality churned sentiments during the 1770s and 1780s, those challenges failed to dislodge a practice centuries old. The convention's failure to address the evil of slavery directly gave legitimacy to the institution, which had exactly the consequences that Jefferson, Madison, and Mason among southerners, and Adams, Wilson, Dickinson, and many others in the North, predicted: it naturalized oppression and inequality, fixing in place a regime of white supremacy that encouraged white males to see all nonwhites, including not only slaves but also free blacks and Indians, as their inferiors. From that assumption unfolded the tragic irony of United States democracy: white men expanded their own rights and privileges at the expense of everyone else, women and children as well as nonwhites. If the deliberations in Philadelphia provided a chance for Americans to imagine how ideals of reciprocity, autonomy, and equality might be nourished in a federal system of representative democracy, the convention instead produced a document that made possible the emergence of something very different, a culture of domination, dependency, and inequality.[91]

CHAPTER 9 | Ratification and Reciprocity

When the constitutional Convention adjourned on September 17, 1787, Madison was exhausted. For almost four months he had spent his days debating and his nights transcribing the debate. In the last stage of rewriting the Constitution for presentation to the public and the state ratifying conventions, he and several associates were working nonstop. They knew that the challenge of rallying supporters and persuading skeptics still lay ahead.[1] One of the more moderate proponents of a stronger national government among the pro-ratification forces, Madison began his campaign of persuasion with Jefferson, a champion of decentralization who had expressed doubts about important features of the Constitution. Their exchange foreshadowed much of the ensuing debate.

Madison wrote his fellow Virginian, still in Paris, a long and detailed letter explaining the intricacy of the compromises struck in Philadelphia and his own surprise at the outcome. Given the breadth of controversies and the depth of disagreements, he wrote, and "adding to these considerations the natural diversity of human opinions on all new and complicated subjects, it is impossible to consider the degree of concord which ultimately prevailed as less than a miracle." Madison had not only decided the Constitution was the best that could be expected, given the delegates' differences, but he was also beginning to see value in a federal as opposed to a strictly national framework because it combined two different forms of deliberation in two legislative branches chosen by different means. Although Madison was still disappointed with his failure to achieve the popular election of senators (as well as his hobbyhorse, the national veto over state legislation), his long letter to Jefferson shows evidence of a crucial shift with lasting if unexpected consequences.

Madison gave Jefferson yet another version of his argument from "Vices" to explain why a national government made possible a degree of harmony otherwise unattainable. His vocabulary, though, was changing. Whereas in the convention he had spoken of a remedy to the problems of a *democracy* consistent with a *democratic* form of government, he described to Jefferson his search for a solution to be found so that "no common interest or passion will be likely to unite a majority of the whole number in an unjust pursuit." The key was inverting Montesquieu: "The true principles of Republican Government," he continued, "prove in contradiction to the concurrent opinions of theoretical writers, that this form of Government, in order to effect its purposes, must operate not within a small but an extensive sphere."

Earlier writers could no longer help, Madison explained, because the world had changed. "Those who contend for a simple Democracy, or a pure republic," which would operate "within narrow limits," have to assume a "fictitious" situation in which all individuals have "precisely the same interests, and the same feelings in every respect." Madison distinguished his alternative from the two identical forms of "simple Democracy" and "pure republic" because it relied on representatives not merely presenting constituents' unitary, fixed preferences but creating from the people's diverse and fluid sentiments a new sense of the common good. Whereas Alexander Hamilton and other champions of a strong national government, on the one hand, and implacably localist critics such as William Findley, on the other, still envisioned a world of fixed interests, a world in which "elites" wrestled with "the people," Madison disassembled those categories. In their place he substituted complicated citizens whose nuanced, shifting, and internally inconsistent preferences and aspirations were irreducible to their current economic positions.[2]

In the debates over ratification, which continued from September of 1787 until the Congress declared the Constitution ratified on September 13, 1788, Madison adjusted his vocabulary to position the Constitution between two undesirable alternatives. That rhetorical sleight of hand, effective at the time, was so subtle that it confounded his later interpreters, who have savaged or lionized him for something he did not do. In the convention Madison spoke of a "democratic form of government." The Constitution explicitly outlawed all titles of nobility and established the people as the sole source of the national government's authority. After equating a "pure republic" with a "simple democracy" in his letter to Jefferson, Madison contrasted Americans' universal use of representation and deliberation to that classical model, which commentators since Aristotle had criticized for its instability. Madison was inching toward an argument he would advance in print less than a month later, which helped persuade his contemporaries but has misled generations of commentators who have read his words but missed his point: the United States Constitution created a "democratic form of government."[3]

As the convention had drawn to a close, one more complication had emerged, and Madison had to address it in order to convince Jefferson and others who shared his misgivings. Several state constitutions, including notably Virginia's, included bills of rights that strictly limited the powers of government. The United States Constitution itself secured some rights against government intrusion, including the right of habeas corpus. Some delegates in Philadelphia, including Mason, who had drafted the Virginia Declaration of Rights in 1776, objected to the absence of a more robust proclamation of rights in the Constitution. Those who shared that concern were not persuaded by Madison's and Wilson's arguments about the transformation that had occurred since independence was declared. They were still thinking as Britons did at the start of the Revolution. "The origin of all civil government," Alexander Hamilton had written in 1775, "must be a voluntary compact, between the rulers and the ruled." All the bills of rights in English history, from Magna Carta onward, had been granted grudgingly by the king to his subjects in response to popular demands. Now, for the first time, the people themselves had established a government. If sovereign power originated with them and flowed from them, Madison asked Jefferson, why should they require a bill of rights to protect them against themselves? In Wilson's hyperbolic formulation, the need for a bill of rights "never struck the mind of any member" at the Convention, so thoroughly had the conceptual transformation swept the gathering. If "we the people" authorized and directly or indirectly chose all government officials, why would—and how could—that government threaten their rights?[4]

Jefferson, however, still shared the conviction expressed in Philadelphia by George Mason and others. Writing to Madison, Jefferson first listed features of the Constitution that he liked, including the separation of powers and the location of the power to tax in the branch of the legislature directly elected by the people. Although he was "captivated" by "the compromise of the opposite claims of the great & little states," he did not equivocate about what he disliked: "the omission of a bill of rights providing clearly & without the aid of sophisms for freedom of religion, freedom of the press"; guaranteed trial by jury; and explicit protections against monopolies and standing armies. Jefferson was hardly unaware of Madison and Wilson's arguments concerning popular sovereignty. He was simply unpersuaded.[5]

Jefferson was not alone. Despite Wilson's claim that none of the delegates worried about a declaration of rights, Mason refused to sign the Constitution for just that reason. So did his fellow Virginian Governor Edmund Randolph and Elbridge Gerry from Massachusetts. Their reservations, although rooted as much in their anxieties about regional differences between the agrarian South and the more commercial North as in concerns about rights, proved contagious. As soon as the Constitution was sent to the states, where it was to be debated by popularly elected ratifying conventions, opposition began to form. Even before the Constitutional Convention began, Noah Webster from Massachusetts had identified the opposing groups that would emerge: those seeking to replace the Articles of Confederation with a stronger national government he dubbed "foederal," their foes "antifoederal."[6] To the chagrin of those Webster dubbed Antifederalists, who believed their loyalty to the existing Confederation government made them the authentic champions of a federal rather than national scheme, the terms stuck.

All the arguments that had played out in Philadelphia during the summer of 1787 were revisited in the yearlong battle over ratification, only this time the debate involved not dozens but thousands of participants.[7] When Congress finally declared the Constitution ratified in September of 1788, it established a novel federal scheme of representative democracy with provision for self-correction by amendment.[8] The divisions that opened up during the debates of 1787–88, however, inaugurated new ways of thinking about self-government, and about the future of the United States, which created new complications for the ethic of reciprocity on which democracy depends.

The long-standing tradition of counterposing the haughtiest and wealthiest advocates of the Constitution to its most plebeian backwoods critics, inaugurated by Charles Beard's *Economic Study of the Constitution* in 1913 and continuing to the present, obscures more than it clarifies.[9] Most Americans instead agreed with George Turner of the Society of the Cincinnati, who thought there was "a middle walk to be trodden, as the directest Road to Truth." Like Turner they endorsed the general framework proposed in Philadelphia, yet they found themselves, with John Breckinridge, "at a loss to decide absolutely" on the Constitution. "I am for it," he mused, "and against it."[10] Yet the choice was stark: up or down, yes or no. Writers in newspapers and speakers in the state ratifying conventions ranged themselves across a wide spectrum of opinion, but more people clustered toward positions in the middle—even overlapping on central issues such as securing rights and separating powers—than occupied the poles. They understood that the new nation required a stronger central government, which would empower ordinary people through institutions of representative democracy operating at the local, state, and national levels. They wanted a government with limited powers divided among separate branches, a form of government suitable for a nation with no monarch, no aristocracy, and deep commitments to equal rights. Whether the people decided to adopt the new constitution or merely to amend the Articles of Confederation, they would remain sovereign. No alternative source of authority was conceivable. Speaking for many, a Pennsylvania Antifederalist writing as "William Penn" declared that neither monarchy nor aristocracy had any place in the United States. "Liberty can be attained or preserved," Americans agreed, in a single form of government, "*democracy*, or *government of the people*." Although all Americans could agree to oppose European forms of government, they differed on the shape their democracy should take.[11]

Opponents to ratification first mobilized in New York. The Confederation Congress, although inactive, remained in session, and members of Madison's own Virginia delegation, including not only Mason but also Richard Henry Lee and William Henry Grayson, attempted to kill the document before it could be considered for ratification. Madison, for months far from home, was cash-poor as well as energy-depleted, but he knew he could not return to Montpelier to regain his strength and replenish his wallet. He was needed in New York, so he borrowed one hundred dollars from fellow Virginia delegate John Blair and hurried north. In the Confederation Congress Mason, Lee, and Grayson found like-minded foes of the Constitution ranging from the often inebriated Luther Martin of Maryland to the still-angry New Yorkers Robert Yates and John Lansing, whose unwavering opposition to any strengthened national government had prompted them to leave the Constitutional Convention long before it concluded. This coalition of wealthy southern planters and northerners fearful of consolidated government power failed to persuade their associates, however, and the Confederation Congress empowered the states to elect ratifying conventions that would decide the fate of the Constitution. The ensuing war of words, the most consequential debate ever conducted on the principles of democracy in the United States, exposed fault lines that have continued to divide Americans.

If the Antifederalists attracted a wide range of supporters in their time, they have continued to appeal to Americans whose loyalties range from far right to far left. Antifederalists presented themselves as the true friends of "the people" against their many enemies. They shared a conviction that the Articles of Confederation were preferable to the proposed Constitution. All Antifederalists feared the federal government would end up too big for the people to control, too distant for the close contact between representatives and constituents required for democracy, and too prone to develop a standing army that would be sustained by ever-rising taxes. They differed from one another, however, in economic status, occupation, religion, section, region, age, and outlook.[12]

Antifederalists' attitudes toward democracy were strikingly diverse. Most proclaimed their confidence in the judgment of ordinary citizens and their anxiety that the institutions of the federal government would be manipulated by the wealthy and well connected, who would exclude "middling" people from any meaningful participation. Yet others disagreed. Mason and Elbridge Gerry, two of the earliest and most prominent Antifederalists, had expressed their deep mistrust about popular involvement prior to and during the Constitutional Convention. They and other Antifederalists opposed the scheme precisely because it would undercut the prominence of local or state elites and compromise their own authority.

The contradictory nature of the Antifederalists' positions posed a problem. Southerners worried that because the Constitution authorized Congress to end the foreign slave trade in 1808, it established the federal government's power to abolish slavery altogether. Russell Lowndes of South Carolina declared that northerners "don't like our slaves, because they have none themselves, and therefore want to exclude us from this great advantage."[13] Virginia's Patrick Henry asked "why it was omitted to secure us that property in slaves," and answered that the federal government would "lay such heavy taxes on slaves, as would amount to emancipation."[14] In Philadelphia George Mason had condemned the slave trade, but now he complained that there was nothing in the Constitution to prevent the northern and eastern states from "meddling with our whole property of that kind." Mason conceded that slavery was "far from desirable" yet observed that the South would face "great difficulties and infelicity" were it abolished.[15] Antislavery Antifederalists, by contrast, vehemently denounced the institution of slavery. According to "Brutus" (possibly New York's Robert Yates or Abraham Yates Jr.), slavery denied "every idea of benevolence, justice, and religion" and mocked "all the principles of liberty." By this logic, permitting the slave trade to continue and including the three-fifths clause rewarded the South by increasing its representatives in the House of Representatives with "every cargo of these unhappy people" and proportionally decreasing the share of taxes owed by slave states.[16]

The self-conscious emphasis on localities in most Antifederalist articles and speeches undercut their effort to mount a united front, as Federalists never tired of pointing out. From the Antifederalist perspective, however, it was that diversity of the United States that called into question the desirability of a stronger national government, which they denounced as a "heterogeneous phantom" or a "thirteen-horned monster." Federalists treated the differences between northern and southern, urban and rural, and religious and nonreligious Antifederalist objections either as a mark of their incoherence or, occasionally at least, as a sign of the Constitution's fairness to all Americans, since it evidently distributed its dangers across so many cultural and regional divisions.[17] Everyone involved in these debates understood immediately that winning popular support would be the key to ratifying or rejecting the Constitution, so the most popular or persuasive articles were reprinted many times throughout the nation.

Antifederalists included the full range of Americans, from self-consciously plebeian spokesmen for backcountry interests such as Pennsylvania's William Petrikin to wealthy, well-educated New Englanders such as Mercy Otis Warren and prosperous southerners such as Mason, Grantham, Richard Henry Lee, and Arthur Lee. Others were middling sorts, often from the middle states, including notably New York's Melancton Smith and Pennsylvania's William Findley. Many opted to use pseudonyms to mask their identities and enable them to speak in the guise of still-familiar classical republican figures such as Brutus, Centinel, or Agrippa. Others preferred homegrown monikers such as "Federal Farmer" (possibly New Yorker Melancton Smith or, as contemporaries thought more likely, Virginian Richard Henry Lee). Not only contrasting and incompatible versions of localism but also different religious and economic convictions divided even those Antifederalists who enjoyed similar standing at the top, middle, or bottom of the scale.[18]

The tone of their essays showed similar diversity, ranging from the learned and scholarly to the deliberately down-to-earth. Among the first Antifederalist texts to appear was that of "Centinel," written by Samuel Bryan, the son of Pennsylvania Supreme Court justice George Bryan. Centinel failed to show the respect commonly accorded venerable figures such as Washington, Franklin, and John Adams. "Wealthy and ambitious men," Bryan charged, had used the occasion of the postrevolutionary period to hatch a plot against popular government. Concealing their plan behind innocuous elder statesmen and national heroes, "these characters flatter themselves that they have lulled all distrust and jealousy" from the general population. The Constitution bore the face of democracy, but its heart was despotic.[19]

Despite the Antifederalists' variety, certain themes ran through many of their most widely circulated essays. Whether they were themselves wealthy and prominent, and thus anticipated remaining in control of local politics under the Confederation government, or poor and powerless, and eager to challenge the continuing domination of elites, Antifederalists warned that the consolidation of power in the federal government would sap all authority from town and state institutions. Antifederalists clamored for more democracy, citing the absence of rotation in office, the departure from annual elections, and the sheer size of electoral districts as evidence that "the few and the great" would seize control from the people.[20] Old World habits of lordly domination would take root in the presidency, the Senate, and the federal judiciary, and from them would sprout the distinct social orders Americans had destroyed by separating from Britain. Americans would now see "a monstrous aristocracy" emerge to "swallow up the democratic rights of the union, and sacrifice the liberties of the people to the power and domination of the few."[21] Almost all Antifederalists feared that the federal power to tax would fund a standing army, always a potential tool of autocracy, which the swift and brutal suppression of Shays's Rebellion had shown to be more than a paranoid fantasy.[22] By contrast, few Antifederalists criticized representative democracy or called for direct democracy. They argued only that such representation worked better when constituents knew the candidates for office personally. They offered different explanations for that preference. For example, "Agrippa" (James Winthrop of Massachusetts) contended that the old republican emphasis on civic virtue was outdated. Power must remain local to protect and advance local interests. "No man when he enters into society does it from a view to promote the good of others, but he does it for his own good."[23]

Such blunt endorsements of the legitimacy of self-interest, however, were less common among Antifederalists than were versions of the argument for popular sovereignty offered by Wilson and Madison at the convention. According to Antifederalist "William Penn," writing in the Philadelphia *Independent Gazetteer*, "it is universally agreed upon, in this enlightened country, that all power residing originally in the people, and being derived from them, they ought to be governed by themselves only, or by their immediate representatives." Because the purpose of democracy, according to most Antifederalists, is to secure citizens' autonomy, the power of government must be limited. "What is liberty?" Penn asked. Far from the simple absence of restraint, it is "*the unlimited power of doing good*," which individuals identify by attending to the "internal voice" of Christian ethics and Scottish moral philosophy. Choosing representatives from their own communities, Antifederalists argued, gave them a chance to select virtuous citizens who could identify and advance the common good.[24] An Old Whig echoed that conception of liberty constrained by the public interest. "If the good of his country should require it," the Pennsylvania Antifederalist wrote, "every individual in the community ought to strip himself of some convenience for the sake of the public good." Such "cheerful obedience" did not infringe on citizens' rights but instead made possible liberty under law. Complete self-sacrifice on the Spartan model was unrealistic and, in a democracy, not required. Were citizens to contribute too little, the government would be too feeble to protect them. The goal was to "yield up" just so much of their liberty "as is necessary for the purposes of government" and retain the rest. Middling Antifederalists sought to secure autonomy in self-government.[25]

Antifederalists and Federalists alike believed that self-rule had been the ethos of colonial and state assemblies, and almost all called for its continuation. Moderate Antifederalists wanted power located at the local and state levels, moderate Federalists at the national level. Selecting representatives made sense in neighborhoods and counties, but once the scale of government encompassed the entire nation, representatives inevitably became too remote and government too dangerous. This conviction, standard among republicans for centuries and canonized by Montesquieu, had tradition on its side. The Federalists proposed to extend a democratic revolution by means the Antifederalists thought likely to extinguish the popular government all Americans claimed to cherish.[26]

Despite the depth of their disagreements with each other, many Antifederalists paradoxically prized homogeneity to a degree that distinguished their arguments from those of Federalists such as Madison and Wilson, who saw value in diversity. When Mason began writing in opposition to ratification, he turned his argument concerning the need for a tight connection between representatives and their constituents, which he used in Philadelphia in favor of the direct election of representatives to Congress, against the Constitution. Not only the Senate, he and other Antifederalists insisted, but also members of the House, the president, and the judiciary were bound to be detached from the concerns of most Americans. In the words of Brutus, "In a republic, the manners, sentiments, and interests of the people should be similar. If this be not the case, there will be a constant clashing of opinions; and the representatives of one part will be continually striving against those of the other."[27]

Other writers elaborated on this theme. Federal Farmer warned that the "different laws, customs, and opinions" of the different states would inevitably impede the national unity touted by supporters of the Constitution. Melancton Smith echoed that anxiety: representatives should "resemble those they represent; they should be a true picture of the people; possess the knowledge of their circumstances and their wants; sympathies in all their distresses, and be disposed to seek their true interests."[28] But that was the rub: Who would be better placed to see their "true interests," those who most nearly resembled ordinary people or those who took a wider view, as both Federal Farmer and Smith thought middling men could do? "Cincinnatus" took Wilson to task for locating sovereignty in the people, and he quoted Locke and Pufendorf to establish that sovereign power must reside instead in the government.[29] Madison and Wilson's conception of a public good emerging from clashing opinions seemed incomprehensible to some Antifederalists and incoherent to others. Disagreements stemming from regional, religious, economic, or social differences, from the perspective of many Antifederalists wedded to the idea of fixed social orders and distinct local cultures, would never be resolved through deliberation. The only solution was to locate authority at the level at which a shared viewpoint and common values could be expected to yield unanimity. From the perspective of Madison and Wilson, of course, that level was left behind as soon as any three people gathered in a room. Madison thought the Antifederalists' confidence that local or state communities nurtured consensus was misplaced: spirited disagreements were likely to break out anytime a handful of people got together in any church, any town hall, or any tavern anywhere in America. Smith and Federal Farmer both admitted the problem, but they thought citizens neither too rich nor too poor to sympathize with others could solve it on their own.

Among the most cogent of Antifederalist interventions on this pivotal question were the letters from Federal Farmer, published as a pamphlet in New York in the first weeks of debate, on November 8, 1787. Federal Farmer framed the issue as a struggle among three contending forces. First came the "aristocrats," those "dangerous men" with "servile dependents" who "avariciously grasp at power and property." Second were the "little insurgents, men in debt, who want no law, and who want a share of the property of others." If the first group included those enthralled by New York's Hamilton and Pennsylvania's Robert Morris and Gouverneur Morris, whom Antifederalists dubbed "morrisites," the second group consisted of "levellers" and "Shaysites." Between these groups lay "the weight of the community," the middling men who were not in debt and keen to preserve popular government. It was such men, those "not aiming at immense fortunes, offices, and power" but representing "the solid, free, and independent part of the community," that Federal Farmer identified with and set out to persuade.[30]

The first letter signaled most Antifederalists' anxieties about the ambitions and abilities of the new nation's most prominent citizens. Variants on the word "aristocracy" appeared no fewer than five times in two early paragraphs. Whereas those who had gathered with Madison in Annapolis in 1786 merely discussed amending the Articles of Confederation, the "aristocratical" delegates sent to Philadelphia concocted their own scheme. If we "recollect how disproportionably the democratic and aristocratic parts of the community were represented" at the Constitutional Convention, we will realize that their plan, although spiced with "democratic phrases," effectively consolidated the power of a wealthy cabal. Given the centrifugal forces of the nation's diversity, the only possible consequences were anarchy, if the central government remained weak and the states strong, or despotism, the outcome Antifederalists judged most likely. Holding the powers to tax, raise a standing army, and determine the law through the Supreme Court, the federal government would inevitably manifest "a strong tendency to aristocracy, or the government of the few." Unless the people were vigilant, the "transfer of power from the many to the few" would be complete.

According to Federal Farmer, Americans currently enjoyed equal power and equal representation in their state governments. Even granting that a few "levellers" did not respect law or property and "abused democracy," the proposed cure was worse than the ill. "I am not among those men who think a democratic branch a nuisance." Instead that branch should be "sufficiently numerous, to admit some of the best informed men of each order in the community into the administration of government." Federal Farmer's conception of representation, like that of other middling Antifederalists, mirrored Madison's. He agreed that voters should select the best-qualified citizens to serve in government, but he feared the size and diversity of the United States made centralization inevitable. Although the Constitution "uses the democratic language of several of the state constitutions, particularly that of Massachusetts," Federal Farmer feared that the consolidation of power would eviscerate the authority of state governments.[31]

Melancton Smith, who had risen from running a store in Poughkeepsie to become a substantial landowner, lawyer, and merchant in New York City, addressed Hamilton directly on this subject in the New York Ratifying Convention. Although "it is our singular felicity that we have no legal or hereditary distinctions," Smith observed, "there are real differences: Every society naturally divides itself into classes." Even in the United States, national elections would inevitably cause a "natural aristocracy" to emerge, and the Constitution failed to counteract that danger. Smith had no objection to representative democracy, which he valued for reasons that paralleled Madison's. The problem was scale. Modest farmers, artisans, or traders would not be elected over those possessing education, talent, and wealth. Smith contended that the best shield against that danger of elite domination was "a strong democratic branch in the legislature," with members chosen annually and featuring "a number of the substantial, sensible yeomanry of the country." Such people could secure election to state legislatures and state ratifying conventions, as Smith did from his native Dutchess County, but Antifederalists doubted such men would ascend to the United States Congress.

Smith proposed a solution. Because "the same passions and prejudices govern all men," care for the public good should be entrusted to those in middling circumstances. Compared with the wealthy, who share the same attitudes and motives as members of a "hereditary nobility," middling men are inclined "to set bounds to their passions and appetites" and thus offer an antidote to the poison of Hamilton and his ilk. They are "more temperate, of better morals and less ambition than the great," who lack sympathy for the poor and "consider themselves above the common people." Representative assemblies filled with such middling men provide the strongest protection of liberty, because when their interests are pursued, "the public good is pursued."

Extending one's vision beyond one's own interest disclosed the interlocking and interdependent nature of American society. Smith thought that the deliberation, pluralism, and reciprocity he prized could be nurtured only at the local or, at best, the state level. Because Madison, by contrast, thought individuals' interests formed and changed for reasons besides their "middling" economic status, he reasoned that the distillation process would function at all levels of the federal system.[32] Whereas Federalists like Hamilton and Antifederalists like Winthrop considered self-interest the sole engine of politics, Smith explained the working of representative democracy, in terms similar to those used by Federal Farmer, William Penn, Brutus, and other moderate Antifederalists, as the process whereby people learned to see beyond self-interest.[33]

If the strikingly diverse Antifederalists were united principally by their shared opposition to the Constitution, differences among the Federalists were only slightly less sharp. They agreed that the Constitution should be ratified; their reasons and their expectations varied widely. The Federalists enjoyed strategic advantages. Newspapers were clustered in cities that leaned toward the new constitution, and many of the nation's most venerated figures had participated in the convention and endorsed its work. Most of the ratifying conventions were held in Federalist strongholds. On the question of democracy, Hamilton, Robert Morris, and Gouverneur Morris stood at one end of the Federalist spectrum as skeptics and critics, Wilson and Madison at the other. Those who supported the Constitution, like those who opposed it, ranged from the top to the bottom of the socioeconomic scale. Urban artisans and sailors expected a revival of shipping and a tax on imports to enliven domestic consumption. Farmers imagined new markets for their produce. Small-town merchants and lawyers expected the national framework would bring them new business. The Philadelphia artisans and tradesmen who attacked the boardinghouse where prominent Antifederalists Findley and John Smilie were lodging showed that supporters of the Constitution were not all wealthy bankers and merchants.

Federalists agreed with Antifederalists that popular persuasion was crucial, and they were quick to pick up the challenge posed by their opponents. Indeed, if denouncing the aristocratic Constitution united many Antifederalist tracts, so most Federalist essays and speeches answered critics' charges by insisting that the Constitution would empower the people.[34] The first public statement of the Federalist position to be widely reprinted, cited—and attacked by Antifederalists—was James Wilson's speech at a lively Saturday night political rally in Philadelphia on October 6, 1787. Wilson's arguments on behalf of the Constitution in that State House Yard speech show his deep debts to "the eloquent Rousseau," whose *Social Contract* he later cited on page two of the *Lectures on Law* that he delivered in Philadelphia in 1790–91.[35] During the debates over ratification, Wilson echoed Rousseau's insistence that citizens can never alienate sovereignty and that they should strive to internalize the general will.

The argument for popular sovereignty that Wilson and Madison had advanced in the convention depended on their transferring the ultimate legitimating authority of government from the rulers to the ruled, who then authorized the division of that power however they saw fit among the different authorities of their local, state, and national government. The sovereign people did not need to restrain themselves against themselves.[36] The only restraint necessary, identified by Rousseau in the *Social Contract*, was the requirement to will the common good, manifested in laws created by the people's representatives. That similarity is no accident. Wilson wrote his speeches with an English translation of Rousseau's *Social Contract* at his side, the same edition of Rousseau that John Adams used when writing the Massachusetts Constitution of 1780. Wilson conceded that he would have preferred a constitution different in certain respects from the version the delegates adopted. He had argued for direct election of senators and the president as well as representatives. Yet he was content because "the seeds of reformation are sown in the work itself." The provision for amendment made the plan for history's first national democracy "the best form of government which has ever been offered to the world."[37]

Wilson's Rousseauvian ideas became even more apparent in his speeches at the Pennsylvania Ratifying Convention in November of 1787, where he provided exhaustive answers to all the objections raised by Antifederalists. In the state of nature, he argued, an individual can act to further his personal pleasure or self-interest, and people leave that condition only when animosities generated by their incommensurable interests drive them to form a social compact. Although each individual surrenders the liberty he previously enjoyed, he gains more than he loses by the limits placed on others. Again echoing Rousseau, Wilson declared that "the aggregate of liberty is more in society, than it is in a state of nature," precisely because in society individuals are governed by law. Europeans still did not understand representation because they still thought distinct social orders must correspond to the distinct parts of mixed government. In the United States, by contrast, the people as a whole authorized the creation of the Constitution. For that reason "the welfare of the whole," Wilson's phrase for Rousseau's general will, "shall be pursued and not a part, and the measures necessary to the good of the community, must consequently be binding upon the individuals that compose it." When the fundamental law emanates from the people rather than the monarch or aristocracy, is framed by the people's chosen representatives, and embodies the people's understanding of the common good, individuals must obey—even if, Wilson might have added, they must be forced to be free.

Rousseau's ideas reverberate clearly in the conclusion of Wilson's opening speech at the convention, on November 24, 1787, where his explicit use of Madison's arguments in Philadelphia indicates the unacknowledged parallels between Rousseau's and Madison's central ideas. "In its principles," Wilson proclaimed, the new government "is purely democratical; varying indeed, in its form, in order to admit all the advantages, and to exclude all the disadvantages" of that form. When we reflect on "the streams of power that appear through this great and comprehensive plan, when we contemplate the variety of their directions, the force and dignity of their currents," we can "trace them all to one great and noble source, THE PEOPLE." The framework served the same purpose as Rousseau's general will. By drawing on the talents and abilities of all citizens, "without regard to birth or fortune," representative government made possible the creation of laws bringing order along with maximum enjoyment of individual liberty consistent with equal liberty for all. Achieving that goal, "the welfare of the whole," was the explicit aim of the Constitution and what made it "purely democratical."[38] Like Rousseau, Wilson cherished a concept of law distinct from the common law Americans inherited from England, but it was hardly a static concept derived from an unchanging ideal of abstract reason. Wilson's models were those of Rousseau and of the Scottish Enlightenment, models in which the individual struggles constantly to internalize the general will, as Rousseau's Emile did, and to cultivate the ideal of benevolence against the steady tug of selfishness. That too was the purpose of law as Wilson saw it: not to protect self-interested behavior from government but to prevent self-interest from blotting out the "welfare of the whole."[39] The means to that end was democracy.

Near the end of the Pennsylvania Ratifying Convention, on December 11, 1787, the indefatigable Wilson delivered an address that went on for an exhausting four and a half hours. He explained why the Constitution should be seen as an "experiment" that would have to change as the nation adapted to new circumstances and challenges. Wilson insisted, as Rousseau and Adams had done, that the people were entering into an agreement with no one but themselves. He underscored the democratic character of representation. "If it could be effected," he declared, "all the people of the same society ought to meet in one place, and communicate freely with each other on the great business of representation." Although distance renders such meetings impossible, they provide the principle undergirding representative democracy, which Wilson articulated in terms similar not only to those of Rousseau and Madison but also to those of Federal Farmer and Melancton Smith: "Every member is the representative of the whole community, and not of a particular part." The object of legislation is the general will, the welfare of the whole, and individuals obey because they learn to internalize that public good, aligned with the dictates of the moral sense, and to will it themselves.

Wilson's mechanism for institutionalizing that broadened perspective was the same as Madison's: the larger the district, the likelier "wise and virtuous characters" will be selected. Far from securing titles or positions for individuals or their heirs, all the offices of government were open to all candidates. At the end of an oration that began before 10:30 a.m. and concluded—when the delegates returned from a much needed break in the middle of the day—after 6:00 p.m., Wilson reverted again to the pyramid as the image best suited to a plan "purely democratical." The Constitution "is laid on the broad basis of the people; its powers gradually rise, while they are confined, in proportion as they ascend, until they end in that most permanent of all forms." But every stage preserves "the essential mark of free governments—a chain of connection with the people." That pyramid would in time serve as a beacon, not only attracting freedom-loving immigrants from Europe but also transforming the Old World by its example.[40]

The purpose of the ratification debates was to persuade the public. Despite the shrieking denunciations that peppered many contributions, defenders and critics nevertheless engaged in sustained and mostly civil debates about the merits of the Constitution itself and about the proper procedures for deciding its fate. Delegates on both sides claimed God was with them. Particularly vociferous debaters sometimes elicited applause, at other times abuse, and occasionally warnings from the chair to moderate their tone. Some people thought headstrong delegates should be issued binding instructions from their constituents; others claimed instructions undercut the purpose of representative government. When Connecticut towns gathered to discuss ratifying the Constitution, for example, many of them voted explicitly to empower their representatives to make the decision on their own. Of the ninety-eight towns in Connecticut that sent delegates to the ratifying convention, only fourteen are known to have instructed their representatives one way or the other, and those towns split down the middle.[41] Associating instructions with democracy only misled the people, according to Connecticut Federalist Roger Sherman, because it suggested "they have a right to control the debates," which would defeat the purpose of meeting. Once the people had voted and chosen their representative, he was obliged to consult with other delegates from throughout the state before reaching a decision "for the general benefit of the whole community." If representatives were bound by instructions, Sherman concluded, "there would be no use in deliberation."[42] Many Federalists were experienced debaters, mostly attorneys accustomed to arguing cases in courts of law. Since they relished the prospect of showing their skills, it is no surprise that they wanted delegates to enjoy sufficient independence to think, reflect, and adjust their positions.[43]

Federalists were likelier to rhapsodize about the productive value of debate than their opponents. James Innes told the Virginia convention that he arrived inclined toward ratification but "with a mind open to conviction, and a predetermination to recede from my opinion, if I should find it to be erroneous." Edmund Randolph had opposed the Constitution, but he said he changed his mind after "further consideration of the subject" and paying "attention to the lights which were thrown on it by others." John Jay expressed a similar conviction in New York. "If the gentlemen will convince me I am wrong, I will submit." Jay intended to give his views "frankly upon the subject. If my reasoning is not good, let them show me the folly of it. It is from this reciprocal interchange of ideas that the truth must come out."[44] In that way alone could new understandings form, and the fruits of such understandings would be much more valuable than any of the ideas available at the outset. The forging of the Constitution itself was their prime example.

Many Antifederalists distrusted the eloquence of their better-educated and often wealthier opponents; for them the Constitution demonstrated the dangers of free-flowing debate. If only the delegates had been held to the people's preferences, they complained, debate would have remained focused on amending the Articles of Confederation rather than replacing them. In North Carolina opponents of ratification called for an immediate vote, reasoning that their job was simply to register the opposition of the voters who sent them. But other delegates protested and proceeded to debate the Constitution, presenting objections and answering them one provision at a time, while their Antifederalist foes fumed in silence. Archibald Maclaine insisted that instructions defeated the purpose of the convention, to gather "the united wisdom of the state" and "*deliberate* and *determine*" what was to be done. His colleague James Iredell agreed. "Shall it be said," he asked, "of the representatives of North Carolina, that near three hundred of them assembled for the express purpose of deliberating upon the most important question that ever came before a people, refused to discuss it, and discarded all reasoning as useless?" Iredell and Maclaine persisted even though they knew some delegates had made up their minds. Iredell volunteered that he came to the convention to learn, to judge, and then to decide the question on its merits. He was scornful of those who refused to do the same. Others may "believe that they are never in the wrong, may arrogate infallibility to themselves, and conclude deliberation to be useless." But Iredell rejected that stance. "I have often known myself to be in the wrong, and have ever wished to be corrected. There is nothing dishonorable in changing an opinion. Nothing is more fallible than human judgment."[45]

Not all Federalists, of course, shared Iredell's humility or his belief that debate is the lifeblood of democracy. Fisher Ames of Massachusetts, to cite one prominent example, was among those later driven by the French Revolution to repudiate popular government as inherently unstable. Others, such as Hamilton, conceived of the Constitution less as a vehicle by which the people could exercise sovereignty than as a means to consolidate and extend their own power as well as that of the nation. Their misgivings mattered little, however, because the fate of the Constitution would turn on the decisions made by popularly elected state ratifying conventions. For that reason even the least democratically inclined Federalists had to participate in the struggle to persuade the people. Everyone knew the battles in New York and Virginia would be decisive, which is why Madison accepted the invitation of Hamilton and Jay to join them in writing a series of articles defending the Constitution in New York.

The three authors of the *Federalist* adopted a classical pseudonym, "Publius," because they had in mind Plutarch's observation that Publicola had not left Rome after giving the laws but had remained to participate in the hard but crucial work of government.[46] The eighty-five essays of the *Federalist* appeared in multiple publications from October 27, 1787, through May 28, 1788, during the most crucial stage of the debate on the Constitution. The *Federalist* was the work of three men with different political principles who wrote to counter arguments advanced by New York Antifederalists, and the essays were produced very fast—roughly a thousand words a day for several months.[47] The anonymity provided by their shared pseudonym masked the real tensions between Hamilton, Madison, and Jay.[48] Hamilton, as noted, thought government originated not from the people but from a compact between the people and their rulers. He envisioned an expansive republic, which he often and revealingly termed an "empire," securely controlled by a national financial elite. At the Constitutional Convention, he proposed life terms not only for the judiciary but also for the executive and members of the Senate. Even if he was merely staking out ground from which the Federalists could retreat to the four- and six-year terms eventually adopted, which departed dramatically from the annual elections still common in the United States, his proposals struck his fellow delegates as characteristic of his disdain for principles almost all Americans embraced. Though Madison also sought to insulate the federal government from volatile popular passions, he disagreed with Hamilton on central questions. Thus it was decisive for the shaping of the *Federalist* that Hamilton and Jay wrote the first nine essays, which established Publius's stance on crucial issues and the framework within which Madison had to work, before Madison contributed a single word.

Hamilton began by raising doubts about the Antifederalists' doubts. They were simply wary about losing their perches of power and privilege in state governments, he assured his readers, so they were spinning tales to mislead the public and keep things as they stood. Hamilton then retreated, denying he meant to impugn his foes' motives, but he had made his point. He also sketched out Publius's rhetorical strategy. Throughout history, the greatest threat to popular government had come from those masquerading as the people's champions. Americans should be suspicious of those paying "obsequious court to the people," who were the real enemies of "the true principles of republican government" embodied in the Constitution.[49]

For three weeks Hamilton and Jay pounded home two arguments. First, partisans of self-government endorsed the Constitution. Its enemies preferred the Articles of Confederation, which protected their own standing but endangered the nation. Second, disunion was the greatest threat facing the United States, a point that deserves more attention than it has received. Hamilton and Jay considered union their strongest retort to the Antifederalists. Americans' reverence for a united nation did not take decades to develop, as has sometimes been alleged; it was present in 1787 and persisted.[50]

In *Federalist* 9, Hamilton introduced the terminology that would define Publius's approach. The institutional architecture of the Constitution provides the means by which "the excellencies of republican government may be retained and its imperfections lessened or avoided." Thus Hamilton distanced Publius from the demagogic false friends of direct democracy and aligned the Constitution with "the excellencies of republican government," otherwise known as representative democracy. Hamilton remained committed to Madison's logic concerning "the ENLARGEMENT of the ORBIT" of national government: Virginia, Massachusetts, Pennsylvania, and New York were already far larger than Montesquieu envisioned as appropriate for republican government, yet not even the angriest Antifederalists quarreled with those states' governments. Hamilton positioned himself as Federal Farmer did, between "levellers" and "morrisites." His rhetoric, however, convinced later commentators that the Constitution had metamorphosed from the "democracy" Madison proposed in the Convention to a "republic."[51]

When Madison sat down to write *Federalist* 10, the first essay he contributed to the project, he inherited a problematic rhetorical strategy. Hamilton had diverged from the terminology Madison used in his "Vices" essay and proclaimed straightforwardly in his opening speech in Philadelphia. Publius had already designated the Constitution "republican" and distinguished it from the democratic regimes of antiquity that had proved susceptible to homegrown demagogues and foreign conquerors. Madison had no choice but to adopt that distinction between ancient and modern republics, which he had already hinted at in his letter to Jefferson.

Madison's case for the Constitution in *Federalist* 10 has remained among the most significant pieces of American political writing.[52] His first intervention as Publius extended his campaign to achieve ratification of the Constitution, which he now considered the best hope for securing stable self-government for the United States. As his writings and speeches before the fall of 1787 made clear, Madison conceived of the Constitution as a democratic solution to the problems of democracy. Despite his misgivings when the convention adjourned, no alternative seemed better. The conflicts that had surfaced in Philadelphia convinced him that a second convention stood no chance of succeeding, and he believed the nation would disintegrate if the Confederation government were not replaced.[53] When Madison reproduced a version of his argument from "Vices" in *Federalist* 10, for strategic reasons he framed it differently. "The latent causes of faction are sown in the nature of man; and we see them brought into different degrees of activity, according to the different circumstances of civil society." The cause of factions could be removed only by extinguishing liberty, a solution worse than the problem. Because Madison believed that factions originate in "the diversity of faculties of men from which the rights of property originate," and he declared that "the protection of these faculties is the first object of Government," many readers have taken him to mean that defending property rights, not protecting "the diversity of faculties," is the principal goal of government.

In *Federalist* 10 Madison did indeed contend, as he did in "Vices" and elsewhere, that the causes of faction are ineradicable. Ranging from religious beliefs to political ideas, from the magnetism of particular leaders to "the most frivolous and fanciful of distinctions," he outlined a few of the many diverse sources of conflict explored in his earlier musings. The human tendency of men to fall into "mutual animosities" is universal. Although the "most violent conflicts" can be rooted in the least rational obsessions, the most familiar and stubborn source of factions has been the "unequal distribution of property." Yet as Madison noted in "Vices," economic conflicts—even if they could be isolated as the sole source of division, an idea he dismissed as simple-minded—cannot be reduced merely to the division between rich and poor. At a minimum, a "landed interest, a manufacturing interest, a mercantile interest," and "a monied interest" have formed explosive coalitions across divisions of class. Late-eighteenth-century alliances between urban artisans and wealthy merchants in seaboard cities such as New York and Philadelphia, and between poor farmers and wealthy landowners throughout the South, illustrate his point. Drawing a simple distinction between rich and poor, then asserting that the rich favored the Constitution and the poor opposed it, distorts the multidimensional reality that Madison knew from his own experience and that modern history has confirmed.[54]

Since the causes of faction cannot be removed, the challenge is to counter its undesirable effects. Legislators must be prevented from serving as "advocates and parties to the causes they determine." Whether the issue is debt, taxes, or domestic manufactures, government needs to be impartial, yet legislators are always tempted to choose their own or their constituents' narrow interests over "justice and the public good." Adams was among those who saw through Madison's strategic distinction between a republic and a democracy and understood that Madison was now embracing the logic of his own case for bicameralism.[55] For Madison as for Adams, faction was not a healthy sign of a vibrant culture, as mid-twentieth-century American pluralists claimed, but a troubling indicator of malignant growths to be controlled if they could not be excised. As anyone familiar with the Scottish philosophers of common sense might expect, the causes lay in the human propensity to sin; the solution required cultivating the human capacity for virtue.

Madison thought the objective was not merely to find a way to pit interest against interest, or faction against faction, so they might cancel each other out. Madison has been glorified (and demonized) as the champion of America's unique liberal pluralism, particularly since self-consciously tough-minded political scientists of the early years of the Cold War, scholars such as Martin Diamond and Daniel Boorstin, distinguished the "genius" of American moderation from communist and socialist "extremism." Madison was aiming higher than a stable conflict between rival interest groups. His goals were liberty, equality, and justice, to be achieved through democratic government: "To secure the public good, and private rights, against the danger" of faction, even a majority faction intent on pursuing its own goals against the common good, and simultaneously preserving "the spirit and the form of popular government, is then the great object"—or what he called "the great desideratum"—of popular government. Madison's goal remained "the public good," an ideal that lay beyond the interests of any particular group.

Federalist 10 elaborated the ideas Madison had been sketching for a year. His ideas did not change, but thanks to the rhetorical strategy he inherited from Hamilton, his mode of presentation did. Writing now as Publius, he argued for the first time that in a "pure Democracy," in which a "small number of citizens" assemble to make decisions, faction is given free rein, as are passion and interest, with the result that there is no check against the temptation to "sacrifice the weaker party" for the stronger. The historical consequences, as Hamilton observed earlier in the *Federalist*, were "spectacles of turbulence and contention" culminating in the violent death of popular government. To that nightmare vision of life in democracy—as solitary, poor, nasty, brutish, and short-lived as many feared the United States might be—Madison contrasted another image. "A Republic," he wrote, "by which I mean a government in which the scheme of representation takes place, opens a different prospect, and promises the cure for which we are seeking." Representation makes a republic more temperate because deliberation enables legislators to see a wider horizon previously hidden from view. Deliberation serves "to refine and enlarge the public views, by passing them through the medium of a chosen body of citizens, whose wisdom may best discern the true interest of their country, and whose patriotism and love of justice, will be least likely to sacrifice it to temporary or partial considerations." The turn to representation was no mere expedient. It was likelier to generate policies "consonant to the public good" than were "the people themselves convened for the purpose." Representatives engaging in debate have a better chance of seeing what Rousseau had designated the general will, the common good beyond the limited horizon of self-interest. The larger the number of citizens voting, and the more extended the sphere, the more likely that people with broader, more "enlightened views and virtuous sentiments" will be elected.[56]

The challenge lay in identifying threats to the common good and checking them, not in order to preserve unjust hierarchies but to protect a precious experiment in popular government. Like his mentor Witherspoon, Madison considered passion and self-interest ubiquitous. Just as Scottish common-sense philosophers emphasized individuals' capacity to harness their unruly selves by cultivating a disciplined conscience, or by consulting Adam Smith's impartial spectator, so Madison thought representative democracy might nourish the public good. The Constitution, Madison concluded, offered "a republican remedy for the diseases most incident to republican government." With a stroke of his pen, Madison turned the "democracy" he proposed and defended in Philadelphia into a "republic." Although he banished the specter of "pure Democracy," a straw man that no one in 1780s America preferred to representative democracy, Madison's commitments to autonomy and the common good remained intact.[57]

New Yorkers who read Madison's first contribution to the *Federalist* could not know it would become the most influential essay in the history of American political thought.[58] The Federalists' focus shifted away from the issues Madison raised because their success in showing that the Constitution would preserve the union inadvertently fueled Antifederalists' fears of centralization. Any national government powerful enough to hold the nation together might prove dangerous to the states. Whereas Hamilton in *Federalist* 9 made a virtue of the Senate because there the states would continue to be represented as collective entities, by numbers 14–18 Publius was quelling anxieties that the Senate would become a breeding ground for a new aristocracy. The power to tax, defended because it would enable the nation to defend itself, now sparked concerns about the continuing viability of state authority vis-à-vis the federal government. Publius had many fires to extinguish,[59] which Madison tried to do in his later contributions to the *Federalist*.[60] Publius's strategic maneuvering required him to situate defenders of the Constitution between two exaggerated threats. The Antifederalists were cast as "pure democrats," radical anarchists opposed even to the principle of representation; similarly imaginary aristocratic foes longed for positions of hereditary privilege. In some essays, though, Madison stopped shadowboxing and flexed his mind.

In *Federalist* 37, Madison highlighted the tentativeness of the American Enlightenment, a quality that reflected not only the Christian doctrines of human sinfulness and humility but also Americans' appreciation of just how imperfect both reason and deliberation are. He admitted that the Constitution had emerged from a process of contestation; delegates representing competing interest groups, different factions, had forged a compromise. The precise operation of the new framework of government, though, could not be settled in the abstract but would be worked out, over time, in practice. In short, Madison emphasized—instead of denying—the unpredictability of the outcome of ratifying the Constitution. Precisely because it instituted an open-ended democracy, designed to reflect the shifting judgments and aspirations of the people, the United States government would change. Unlike classical or Renaissance republicans, who equated change with decline, Madison embraced the idea of progress through stages of development advanced by writers in the Scottish Enlightenment. The future had to remain a mystery; further changes were unavoidable.[61] Both Benjamin Franklin in his impassioned closing speech at the Constitutional Convention and Madison in *Federalist* 37 marshaled the distinctive humility that characterized the American Enlightenment. They urged individuals to put aside their own parochial concerns for the sake of the greater good of the new nation. Designating it either a strategic move or an expression of Franklin's and Madison's deepest convictions is misleading. It was both.[62]

Both Federalists and Antifederalists deployed an idea that originated during these debates: the concept of responsibility. Although we assume the idea is timeless, the word has a history, as all words do. Mercy Otis Warren introduced "responsibility" in a stinging critique of the Constitution in general, and of Wilson in particular, published in February 1788. The Federalists described their scheme of representative government as democratic, and John Stevens of New Jersey had asserted confidently that "recurrence of elections" meant that "representatives cannot fail of proving the faithful and effectual guardians of the people." Ancient democracies collapsed because they lacked the stability and moderation that representation ensures.[63] Warren countered that only "annual election is the basis of responsibility." Only the knowledge that elected officials have to face the electorate every year would them induce to act responsibly. Otherwise they would be free to behave as they wished; the consequence would be corruption.

Whether or not Madison had read the *Observations on the Constitution* that Warren published under the pseudonym "A Columbian Patriot," he addressed the point directly in *Federalist* 63. Although ancient republics had made some use of the mechanism of representation, which the Federalists considered among the strongest features of American government, the Greek city-states were too small for the filtering process to work. The refinement of views would be particularly pronounced in the Senate. Although misconstrued by Antifederalists as an aristocratic body, it was simply another deliberative assembly, representing the states as communities rather than their citizens as individuals. Senators would have a broader, statewide perspective while retaining "a due responsibility" in the government of the people. "Responsibility," Madison argued, "in order to be reasonable, must be limited to objects within the power of the responsible party." Even though senators would be elected for six-year terms, they still had to answer to the representative assemblies that chose them. That was the purpose of elections.[64]

In essays published between February 6 and February 20, 1788, Madison presented arguments said to indicate his hostility to democracy and his tough-minded acceptance of perpetual conflict as the normal condition of politics. "In all very numerous assemblies," Madison began, "passion never fails to wrest the scepter from reason." Even the most rational individuals surrender to emotion when swept away by the crowd: "Had every Athenian citizen been a Socrates, every Athenian assembly would still have been a mob." By contrast, both the popularly elected House of Representatives and the Senate would be, unlike the assemblies of Athens and Sparta, large enough to represent the diverse interests and views of the American people, yet small enough to prevent rule by a passion-crazed mob. Again the nation's size, and the winnowing accomplished by elections, promised an escape from chaos. Madison's conclusion sounded a note of realism while reflecting his belief that his hopes had a solid foundation. "As there is a degree of depravity in mankind which requires a certain degree of circumspection and distrust," that depravity is balanced by a saving capacity: "So there are other qualities in human nature, which justify a certain portion of esteem and confidence." Admittedly, popular governments require more of the latter qualities to survive than do other forms. If the Antifederalists' portraits of human perfidy were accurate, then one might conclude that humans lack sufficient virtue for self-government. Indeed, one might conclude that "nothing less than the chains of despotism can restrain them from destroying and devouring one another." The Antifederalists' concerns about the Constitution revealed a distrust so deep, Madison suggested, that it would also rule out popularly elected state governments, a conclusion the Federalists at their most tough-minded refused to draw.[65]

In the *Federalist* Madison went out of his way to display his realism. Those who opposed the Constitution were warning New Yorkers that the Federalists' fine talk about the common good masked aristocratic schemes beneath their republican language. Madison sought to show they were wrong. No single group could control the nation's government. Not only was power divided between the federal, state, and local governments, and at each level divided between legislative, executive, and judicial branches. American society was "broken into so many parts, interests and classes of citizens, that the rights of individuals or of the minority, will be in little danger from interested combinations of the majority." To illustrate the point, he returned to the issue of religious diversity that had attracted his attention—and Jefferson's—in their quest to disestablish Anglicanism in Virginia. "The security for civil rights must be the same as that for religious rights. It consists in the one case in the multiplicity of interests, and in the other, in the multiplicity of sects."

In both domains—religious and secular—the more diversity the better. Up to that point, Madison seemed to posit conflict itself as the alternative to tyranny, pitting power against power, interest against interest, in eternal agonistic conflict. But he did not stop there. "Justice is the end of government," he declared. "It is the end of civil society. It ever has been, and ever will be pursued, until it be obtained, or until liberty be lost in the pursuit." From the confrontation between competing interests, perspectives, or ideals would emerge the closest, albeit provisional, approximation of justice. The "great variety of interests, parties and sects" masked an important benefit: "A coalition of a majority of the whole society could seldom take place upon any other principles than those of justice and the general good."[66]

Antifederalists worried that ordinary people were bound to lose control of the federal government; only unworthy members of "the better sort" would be chosen. Lofty phrases such as "justice and the general good" did not assuage their fears, because many, including Federal Farmer and Pennsylvania congressman William Findley, believed that politics usually boils down to a clash of interests, and only those close enough to ordinary citizens could understand their world and represent their interests responsibly. The Federalists' impatient insistence on immediate ratification showed they were less committed to deliberation than they claimed. They were up to something.

Madison replied to such charges in *Federalist* 57. The objection that members of the House of Representatives would lose "sympathy with the mass of the people" and seek their own "aggrandizement," Madison wrote, "strikes at the very root of republican government." The integrity of the American electoral system, top to bottom, depended on tying representatives to those who elect them. All forms of popular government aimed to secure positions of authority for those possessing the "most virtue to pursue the common good of the society." Antifederalists were challenging the fundamental principle of representative government. "Who are to be the electors?" Madison asked. "Not the rich more than the poor; not the learned more than the ignorant; not the haughty heirs of distinguished names, more than the humble sons of obscure and unpropitious fortune. The electors are to be the great body of the people of the United States," precisely those who already elected all the members of every state assembly. If the Antifederalists were content with state legislators, many Federalists asked, why did they doubt the people's ability to choose their representatives to the federal government? "No qualification of wealth, of birth, or religious faith, or of civil profession," Madison concluded, "is permitted to fetter the judgment or disappoint the inclination of the people." The framework of the Constitution would make available the resources necessary for the people to undertake egalitarian as well as hierarchical initiatives. Power lay with the people.[67]

The full documentary record of the state ratifying conventions, held between December 1787 and early 1788, demonstrates both the intense public engagement with ideas about instituting representative democracy and the depth of Americans' disagreements.[68] More than 1,700 people participated formally in the deliberations of these conventions, and more than 1,700 points of view emerged, so summarizing the debates even in individual states is enormously challenging.[69] Two of the first three states to ratify, Delaware on December 7 and New Jersey on December 18, 1787, did so unanimously and almost immediately. But in the other ratifying conventions, lively disputes reflected preexisting social, economic, political, and cultural divisions. The party splits that developed less than a decade later make it irresistible to read those divisions back into the debates in the ratifying conventions, but that brings a misleading clarity to a much more amorphous process. In New York, prominent Federalists such as Hamilton, Jay, Robert R. Livingston Jr., and Philip J. Schuyler barely concealed their desire to perpetuate the dominance of wealth, including that of families descended from the earliest Dutch settlers. The gulf dividing more moderate Federalists from prominent Antifederalists such as George Clinton and Melancton Smith, however, is easy to exaggerate. All of the participants in the New York debates, wealthy merchants and middling farmers alike, sought to secure property rights, stabilize the money supply, protect the state's frontiers against attack, use government to build roads and waterways that would facilitate commerce, and establish a wide franchise.

In Pennsylvania, Wilson led the Federalist contingent throughout the debates. He had kicked things off in his State House Yard address on October 6, 1787. Beyond being received with great enthusiasm in Philadelphia, that speech was reprinted ten times in the next month and widely hailed as one of the most convincing arguments for the Constitution. Wilson was the only member of the Pennsylvania Ratifying Convention who had served in the Constitutional Convention, and throughout the proceedings he responded energetically, and usually effectively, to all the objections Antifederalist delegates raised. In his final address, another marathon lasting over four and a half hours, Wilson reiterated his and Madison's arguments and characterized the national government as "purely democratical." No individuals would enjoy special privileges; "no peculiar rights have been reserved to any class of men." No males were excluded from any office, an openness Wilson claimed was unprecedented in history. At each step of the great pyramid of institutions, a "chain of connection" linked elected officials with those to whom they remained responsible. If the states ratified this new and democratic Constitution, its example would be followed "in every part of the earth."[70]

Unlike the closed Constitutional Convention earlier in 1787, the debates in the Pennsylvania Ratifying Convention were reported in the partisan press, and there was little evidence that twenty-two days of deliberation changed any minds. The delegates, whether under instructions from their constituents or merely acting as though they were, seldom deviated from the positions they staked out at the start. Antifederalist delegates Findley, John Smilie (of Lancaster County), and Robert Whitehill (from the region near Harrisburg) countered every claim made by Wilson and his allies; no one gave ground. The tone also differed dramatically from the relative decorum of the Constitutional Convention. Speakers interrupted each other. Speeches elicited angry cries of dissent and loud shouts of acclaim. Each side admitted distrusting the other. Each side accused the other of attempting to thwart the will of the people or the will of God. For some commentators, then and now, the no-holds-barred free-for-all embodied the spirit of democracy. Others found the spectacle demoralizing. On December 12, 1787, by a vote that mirrored almost exactly the earliest soundings of the delegates' leanings, the convention voted to ratify by 46 to 23, a substantial majority but far from the unanimous approvals registered in Delaware and New Jersey.

Federalists applauded the outcome in Pennsylvania, but it only intensified the struggle. The victors organized a procession in Philadelphia to celebrate ratification. The *Pennsylvania Packet* described it as "a great gathering," but critics in the *Independent Gazetteer* and the *Freeman's Journal* scoffed at the low turnout and lamented the "astonishing indifference" ordinary people had shown. Antifederalist Thomas Shippen dismissed "the mob in the streets," mindlessly "huzzaing triumphantly on the great event" although they were "perfectly ignorant whether it will make them free or slaves." All but two who voted against ratification signed a widely circulated petition not only criticizing the Constitution also but condemning the tactics of Pennsylvania Federalists. Outside Philadelphia these simmering emotions boiled over. In Carlisle, long a hotbed of opposition to Philadelphia merchants and bankers, Antifederalist anger exploded. On the day after Christmas in 1787, Federalists who had gathered there to celebrate ratification were attacked by a crowd of bitter Antifederalists. In an ill-advised move, the triumphant Federalists rolled out cannons, which they intended to fire in celebration at the end of the festivities. When the enraged crowd seized the cannons, scuffles escalated into fisticuffs. The next day an effigy of Wilson, the figure who had spoken most effusively about the "purely democratical" Constitution, was burned by another Antifederalist crowd.

As in the earlier riot at "Fort Wilson," Wilson had become the symbol for some Antifederalists of the infuriating use of democratic rhetoric to describe a project they deemed antidemocratic, and the Federalists' critics have echoed their judgment ever since. From that perspective, the Carlisle riots reveal the sophistry of Wilson's claim to speak on behalf of the interests of the people. But not all contemporaries agreed. If the Federalists overreached by asserting that Pennsylvania's vote ensured ratification, the Carlisle radicals' agitation also backfired. Prominent Antifederalist leaders, including many previously opposed to ratification in Pennsylvania, now lined up behind the Constitution, condemning the mob's violence as a dangerous sign that those opposed to the Constitution were now opposed to the rule of law. After Carlisle, moderate Antifederalists increasingly distanced themselves from their erstwhile plebeian allies, a division that sealed ratification but contributed to the deepening alienation of struggling farmers in western Pennsylvania from the increasingly moderate sensibility of the rest of the state.[71]

The struggle for ratification in other states continued into the summer of 1788 and, for Rhode Island, into 1790, and a torrent of arguments continued to flow. The early votes in favor of ratification were followed by similar outcomes in states ranging from those of New England to Maryland and Georgia, though such victories came only after protracted and sometimes violent conflicts that reflected deeply divergent views of the extent to which the Constitution embodied or betrayed the principles of democracy.

The Massachusetts contest was nearly as rancorous as that in Pennsylvania. Massachusetts had already debated first principles from 1778 through 1780, when the first draft of its state constitution was rejected and Adams's draft was examined critically before it was declared ratified. Memories of these debates were fresh, and everyone knew that Shays's Rebellion had sparked interest in replacing the Articles of Confederation. Voters in Massachusetts, accustomed to making their own decisions by long experience with town meetings, bristled at the idea that they could vote only up or down on the Constitution.

Almost three hundred Massachusetts towns elected 370 delegates to the ratifying convention that opened in Boston on January 9, 1788. Although in principle the towns were authorized to send to the ratifying convention only the same number of delegates that they sent to the legislature, a hundred towns, reasoning that their populations had grown, sent more. Very few of those delegates carried explicit instructions from the towns they represented. As in Connecticut, Massachusetts voters understood, from over a century of experience, that representatives should possess sufficient autonomy to deliberate freely. In a widely circulated and influential address prepared by a committee chosen by the voters in Northampton and Easthampton, a group of Massachusetts citizens expressed their understanding of representative democracy: The voters decided "not to give you positive instructions relative to your voting for or against the reported constitution." Instead they trusted their elected delegates to debate, form the "judicious opinion" warranted by the deliberations, and then vote in accord with the "collective wisdom of the state." The townspeople of Massachusetts wanted to empower their delegates, who had listened to their misgivings about the Senate, the power to tax, and the absence of a statement of rights, to come up with the appropriate collective response.[72]

Spirited debates occurred in the Massachusetts press in the run-up to the ratifying convention. Two writers from Cambridge assailed the Constitution tirelessly. Agrippa (James Winthrop) repeatedly denounced the Constitution as a plot to end popular government. Elbridge Gerry wrote a letter on October 18 explaining to the Massachusetts legislature why he had refused to sign the Constitution. At the Constitutional Convention Gerry had made, and Connecticut's Sherman had seconded, a motion to add a declaration of rights, but not one state had voted for it. Now demands for a bill of rights were gathering momentum, and Gerry reiterated that concern along with his worries about the powers given to Congress and the judiciary. Even though Gerry chose not to restate, back home in Massachusetts, the objections he voiced in Philadelphia concerning the excessively democratic quality of the proposed government, Cambridge voters elected neither Winthrop nor Gerry as delegates to the convention. Those whom the champions of ratification had begun lumping together as "Antifederalists" thus lacked a prominent, persuasive voice. Massachusetts Federalists adopted a strategy to mollify and marginalize the implacable Gerry, whose letter to the legislature was reprinted in almost all the state's newspapers in late October and helped galvanize the opposition. As the only elected delegate to the Constitutional Convention not elected to the state's ratifying convention, he was seated at the convention but authorized only to reply to written questions, not to speak. Samuel Adams, another potential leader of the opposition, had also expressed doubts about ratification. After almost four hundred Boston artisans and craftsmen met and "UNANIMOUSLY" endorsed the Constitution, however, Adams decided to wait and see.

John Hancock, recently elected governor by an electorate unhappy with the way his predecessor had handled the Shaysites, was a consensus choice to chair the ratifying convention. No one knew where Hancock stood. His sphinx-like silence became only more enigmatic when poor health prevented him from presiding in person. Another prominent public official was ailing in the winter of 1787–88: Charles Dana, an associate justice of the Massachusetts Supreme Judicial Court, had been elected to the Constitutional Convention, but frail health had prevented him from attending. Although Hancock and Dana were hardly alone among the experienced political figures elected as delegates, there were also many young first-timers whose towns had not given instructions and whose leanings were unknown. The ratifying convention in Boston was open to the public, and the crowd swelled to almost eight hundred people when the proceedings moved from the statehouse to a larger church that could accommodate the passionately curious public. In this highly charged atmosphere, the outcome was unpredictable.

The proceedings got off to a rocky start. Gerry was furious with his restrictions, and when he insisted that he be allowed to speak, an "altercation" between him and Dana was on the brink of devolving into a fistfight before the two old combatants were separated. The incident left both of them aggrieved and their supporters on edge. Those who opposed the Constitution articulated the anticipated objections. Annual elections had been the rule in New England. Surely those officials elected for two-year or, even worse, six-year terms would become autocrats. Not only was the abomination of slavery allowed to continue; even the slave trade could not be touched for twenty years. Disputes in Boston over the taxing power had set off the American Revolution; granting that authority to the central government might spark another rebellion. Finally, New Englanders had guarded their rights ever since John Wise had written his *Vindication of the Government of New England Churches* six decades earlier. No federal charter could be legitimate without a bill securing citizens' rights.

To all of these complaints the Federalists had ready answers.[73] Debate raged, with crowds of six to eight hundred filling the galleries of Reverend Jeremy Belknap's Congregational Church, until the recovering Dana and his ally Fisher Ames finally brokered a deal with Hancock. They proposed that Massachusetts ratify the Constitution on the condition that Congress agreed to adopt a declaration of rights. In that case they would support Hancock, either in his bid for reelection as governor or as the new nation's first president (if Virginia were to reject the Constitution, thereby making Washington, the odds-on favorite, ineligible to serve). Once Massachusetts Federalists conceded the tactical necessity of guaranteeing rights, the tenor of debate changed.[74]

Farmers such as Jonathan Smith, a self-styled "plain man," had already registered the uneasiness that he and other farmers had felt with the Shaysites and embraced the order promised by the Constitution. Other favorites of the common people, including the Baptist minister Isaac Backus, also came out for ratification. Backus pointed out that all government officials would hold office "by the consent of the people," and he judged the Constitution, with its explicit denial of any inherited privileges, more democratic than any other ever offered to "any people on earth." More Antifederalists announced their support because debates at the ratifying convention—and the provision for amendments securing rights—had persuaded them that the Constitution they had resisted had now become irresistible. At first the Federalists' education and eloquence had only hardened many rural farmers' and tradesmen's distrust of the Constitution. Over time, however, the Federalists' arguments softened their apprehension, and the declaration-of-rights deal proved decisive: enough delegates changed their minds for the Constitution to squeak through by a vote of 187 to 168.[75]

Even after ratification was secured in Massachusetts, Virginia and New York remained crucial. A nation without those two states was hardly viable. During these crucial months, though, Jefferson and Adams remained in Europe as emissaries of the new nation. Because Jefferson was known to approve many features of the Constitution and to be uneasy about others, both Federalists and Antifederalists in Virginia claimed him as an ally. Jefferson insisted to Madison that "a bill of rights is what the people are entitled to against every government on earth, general or particular, & what no just government should refuse."[76] Madison was hearing choruses of similar protests at home. He wanted the Constitution ratified, and the prospect of adding a declaration of rights troubled him less than the possibility that its absence might scuttle the entire effort. Again Madison had learned the difference between what he wanted and what the democratic process made it possible to achieve.[77]

In the early days of the Virginia convention, the opponents of ratification seemed in control, but slowly the Federalists gained the upper hand. However much the delegates might want a bill of rights, Madison pleaded that it would be better to ratify the Constitution first, and then amend it, as he was at last willing to concede was necessary, than to squander the chance to achieve a stronger national union. Finally, and this time decisively, he once again challenged the persistent claim that the Constitution handed the reins of government to an elite of merchants and bankers. In a crucial speech on June 20, 1788, speaking to his friends rather than writing anonymously as Publius, Madison made a final impassioned plea for the Constitution. He disputed both the charge that members of the federal legislature were likely to do "every mischief they possibly can," on the one hand, and the claim "that we are to place unlimited confidence" in elected officials "of exalted integrity and sublime virtue," on the other. Instead Madison reiterated his confidence in "this great republican principle, that the people will have virtue and intelligence to select men of virtue and wisdom." The people would choose as they saw fit. "Is there no virtue among us?" he asked plaintively. "If there be not, we are in a wretched situation," and "no form of government can render us secure." Imagining that institutions might secure liberty or happiness without popular virtue he dismissed as "chimerical." No legal or structural solution alone, but only a culture of democracy, would suffice. It was up to "the people who are to choose" the officers of government to exercise their "virtue and intelligence" in selecting them. Madison continued to situate the Constitution between the extremes of anarchic lawlessness and centralized control by elites and to hold out against those dangers the safeguard of representative democracy. The people would hold all the power. If they exercised it wisely, the nation would prosper. If they squandered it by choosing demagogues or reinstituting hierarchies, they would have themselves to blame.[78]

Virginia was the crucial state. Though New Hampshire had brought the number to the required nine, Virginia's decision meant the United States Constitution would now take effect. At that point New York, where the conflicts were as deep as they were in Pennsylvania and Virginia, quickly fell in line, because the disadvantages of remaining separate from the new nation became clear even to die-hard opponents.[79] Had Madison and his allies not persuaded their fellow Virginians to ratify, the entire project might have failed. Had Madison not acceded to demands for a declaration of rights, however, the project certainly would have failed. Madison agreed in part because he was understandably wary of a second constitutional convention, which some contemporaries considered the best way to secure a guarantee of rights. He feared that delegates this time would arrive with binding instructions, which would prevent them from reaching compromises. With the Constitution ratified, adding a declaration of rights would no longer threaten its prospects and might instead bolster the popular support on which its long-term success would depend. Although Madison acceded to amendments because he had no choice, he played the hand he was dealt with considerable skill. As he did when it became clear in Philadelphia that the Constitution would not contain his preferred national veto or proportional representation in the Senate, once he realized the inevitability of amendments he made the best of it. Once ratification was secured, Madison shifted his ground on a bill of rights, just as he promised the Virginia Ratifying Convention he would do. In meetings with groups of voters during his campaign for election to the House of Representatives, he learned that support for such a declaration of rights was even more widespread than he realized.

Madison's letter to Jefferson on October 17, 1788, shows him rethinking these issues, particularly because he now saw another opportunity to disestablish religion. His opening claim that "my own opinion has always been in favor of a bill of rights" was clearly exaggerated, but the record sustains his explanation: "At the same time I have never thought the omission a material defect, nor been anxious to supply it even by *subsequent* amendment, for any reason other than that it is anxiously desired by others." He aligned himself with Wilson's contention, which Jefferson had found unpersuasive, that "the people retain all the rights not specifically granted to the government."

Madison then reminded Jefferson that the "rights of Conscience," which both of them had worked to secure, were likely to remain threatened by intolerant popular majorities in most states, and an amendment to the United States Constitution might help establish the principle that would be codified in the Bill of Rights as "the free exercise of religion." Whereas earlier proponents of toleration such as Locke had recommended that established religions should deign to permit the existence of other faiths, that approach left in the hands of government the power to regulate religion.

Madison and Jefferson wanted to remove state authority from the domain of religion altogether. Although Madison remained skeptical that what he called "parchment barriers" could restrain popular passions, particularly in the case of religion, he nevertheless had begun to think that solemnly declaring such maxims might help them "acquire by degrees the character of fundamental maxims of free Government" and perhaps even, over time, "counteract the impulses of interest and passion." Second, if a threat were to emerge from the government rather than a popular majority, a statement of rights might stiffen popular resistance.[80]

Soon after the first United States Congress convened in the spring of 1789, Madison made good that promise, submitting nineteen propositions from which were carved the ten amendments that came to be known as the Bill of Rights. Madison explained in Congress that adopting these amendments would show Antifederalists that those who had supported the Constitution "were as sincerely devoted to liberty and a republican government" as were those who feared the new government would "lay the foundations of an aristocracy or despotism." The willing acceptance of the Constitution by Americans who wanted their rights guaranteed, in Madison's words, "calls upon us for a like return of moderation." Improving the Constitution "in the opinion of those who are opposed to it" allowed Congress to resolve rather than exacerbate tensions and "act the part of wise and liberal men."[81] Madison's about-face on a bill of rights reflected both his shrewd political instincts and his understanding that nurturing an ethic of reciprocity was the best chance the nation had to inoculate itself against the poison of permanent partisan struggle.

In the first Congress, as in the debates over ratification, Madison once again found himself facing opposition from two sides. Obstructionist Antifederalists thought the proposed amendments did not go far enough; some of his erstwhile allies thought they went too far. As in Philadelphia, Madison did not get everything he wanted from Congress. He proposed opening the revised Constitution with a ringing declaration of popular sovereignty, "All power is originally vested in and consequently derived from the people," and an equally unequivocal statement of the power to amend: "The people have an indubitable, unalienable, and indefeasible right to reform and change their government whenever it be found adverse or inadequate to the purposes of its institution."[82] Madison also wanted to extend these rights to all the states: "No *state* shall violate the equal rights of conscience, or the freedom of the press, or the trial by jury in criminal cases." Yet this principle, which Madison judged the most valuable of all, was defeated in the Senate, not established in law until the Fourteenth Amendment was ratified after the Civil War, and not secured in practice until a century later. The rights Madison proposed were more sweeping than the amendments adopted by Congress and approved by the states.

The decisive steps that Madison took in the direction of those who had opposed the Constitution demonstrate how self-consciously he sought to build a broad basis of support for the new national government. Unlike those who fought the English Civil War, killed the king, and earned the undying enmity of a royalist majority, Madison after the ratification debates worked to reconcile Federalists and Antifederalists around a set of shared principles. Instead of preserving a patrician distance from the electorate, he and his allies learned to learn from voters, and many of them came to believe that all elected officials should do the same. Unquestionably a shrewd coalition builder, Madison aimed for something more ambitious than a coalition. He sought a broad cultural commitment to democratic deliberation, the best way to strike provisional balances between liberty and equality and the only available approximation of "justice and the general good" attainable by fallible humans.[83]

In the aftermath of the acrimonious state debates, and especially after the final ratification of the Constitution in the fall of 1788, many voices throughout the new United States called for reconciliation instead of recriminations. In Massachusetts even the staunchest opponents conceded that they had been outvoted. Some were magnanimous. Because "a majority of wise and understanding men" had prevailed, as William Widgery put it, the time had come to "sow the seeds of union and peace among the people." Or in the words of Dr. John Taylor, perhaps the least temperate of the Constitution's New England critics, he and his allies were "fairly beaten." When he returned to his home in Worcester County, not far from the center of Shaysite unrest, he vowed to "infuse a spirit of harmony and love" among those who had feared the Constitution and fought hard against it. Conflict did not cease, particularly in western regions where discontent persisted. Occasionally it flared into violence, as in a 1794 insurgency in western Pennsylvania. But many former opponents of the proposed government, including the former Antifederalist—and now United States congressman—William Findley, were ready to see regulators suppressed and the law of the land upheld.

Whether support from former opponents was grudging or genuine, most agreed to support the Constitution.[84]

The Federalists' campaign to generate enthusiasm for the Constitution began with celebrations held immediately after the state ratifying conventions. Dissatisfied with the first Philadelphia parade and the chaos in Carlisle, organizers elsewhere took great pains to orchestrate unity. The Boston procession on February 7, 1788, included four thousand people and took five hours to complete. Leading the way were ax-wielding lumberjacks, hacking their way into the nation's uncharted but glorious future. Behind them, setting a festive tone, was a marching band. Then, perhaps surprisingly given the Antifederalist inclinations of the state's rural precincts, came farmers from Roxbury, complete with horses and oxen. In their wake walked the artisans and tradesmen of Boston, a contingent fifteen hundred strong that included federal butchers, bakers, candlestick makers, and assorted tailors, stonemasons, shoemakers, shipbuilders, printers, plumbers, painters, glaziers, coopers, cartwrights, carpenters, and cabinet makers. Two floats dominated the procession: a whaling ship transformed into a warship, the *Federal Constitution*, pulled by thirteen horses and manned by thirteen sailors; and, bringing up the rear, a dilapidated vessel dubbed the *Old Confederation*, which at the conclusion of the parade was set alight in a great bonfire that established a precedent followed elsewhere.[85]

Not content with its earlier festival, Philadelphia undertook to top other cities' efforts on July 4, 1788, when more than five thousand participants paraded through the city. Again farmers and their animals featured prominently, along with eighty-eight separate categories of workers and bands, ministers arm in arm with rabbis, and three especially impressive floats. One carried an elaborate structure designed by the painter Charles Willson Peale, the Grand Federal Edifice, whose domed roof stood on thirteen pillars; on another sailed a ship christened *Union*; and the third featured the Constitution itself, held aloft by the chief justice of the Pennsylvania Supreme Court. After James Wilson delivered the inevitable lengthy oration celebrating America's democracy and its citizens' public spirit, seventeen thousand people—half the city's population—gorged on four thousand pounds of roast Pennsylvania beef, twenty-five hundred pounds of smoked Pennsylvania ham, and enough locally brewed beer to float the good ship *Union*.[86]

As such festivals continued throughout the nation, organizers took care to accentuate harmony and avoid antagonizing erstwhile Antifederalists. The sentiment expressed in a toast by Boston artisans, "May a just sense of their mutual interest and dependence on each other forever unite the husbandman, the merchant and mechanick," captured a widespread aspiration. If the unity itself proved elusive, a modest postratification economic upsurge contributed more to closing the rifts than civic festivals and the renaming of federal hats, salutes, ships, and streets.[87]

Americans knew that such rituals of reconciliation had been orchestrated since the ancient world, which helps explain the profusion of classical motifs and allusions in so much early American design and architecture. Organizers deliberately brought together rural and urban, eastern and western, and low, high, and middling folks to generate a sense of shared pride and patriotism. Benjamin Rush explained how the festivals cemented the "connection between religion and good government." By deliberately placing ministers of different faiths together, organizers aimed to show that a free government could promote Christian charity. A Jewish rabbi, marching alongside two Protestant ministers, was a "most delightful sight" testifying to the commitment to religious freedom in the new nation, which "opens all its power and offices alike, not only to every sect of christians, but to worthy men of *every* religion." The presence of clergymen in these civic festivals was intended to sanctify the Constitution, soften old animosities, and renew Americans' sense of themselves as united in a common cause.[88]

The amendability of the Constitution manifested the most important insight of American democratic theorists, and it was the subject of much commentary in these years, particularly after the Bill of Rights was ratified in December of 1791. Shaped by a blend of Protestant Christianity, Enlightenment principles, and Scottish common-sense philosophy, the sensibilities of Madison, Wilson, Adams, Jefferson, and other members of their generation combined confidence in the human capacities of reason and benevolence with a sober assessment of the dangers of passion and self-interest. Never imagining they could construct a perfect set of political institutions, they made provision for improvements, and many contemporaries understood the magnitude of that step. The government of the United States, according to John Stevens of New Jersey, was "formed" by the people, and it could be "new modelled" whenever the people chose. James Iredell of North Carolina noted that "a constitutional mode of altering the Constitution itself, is perhaps, what has never been known among mankind before." The people's "power of altering and amending" their constitution, and improving it based on experience, impressed David Ramsay. Thomas Pownall praised the "*healing principle*" and Nathaniel Chipman the "plan of reformation" built into the constitutions.[89]

Though Thomas Paine, now living in France, remained dissatisfied with certain aspects of the Constitution, he wrote that he would have voted for it had he been in America—or for a constitution "even worse rather than have none." Not only did the Constitution provide the stronger central government that Paine considered necessary. The provision for amendment provided a way of "remedying its defects by the same appeal to the people" by which it was established. As Paine wrote in *The Rights of Man* (1791), "One of the greatest improvements that has been made for the perpetual security and progress of constitutional liberty, is the provision which the new constitutions make for occasionally revising, altering, and amending them."[90] John Adams, who almost never agreed with Paine, shared that sentiment: the Constitution "appears to be admirably calculated to cement all America in affection and interest, as one great nation." The result of necessary "accommodation and compromise," it would match no one's ideal of perfection, but that quality was hardly fatal because "provision is made for corrections and amendments, as they may be found necessary."[91]

Soon after the United States Constitution was ratified, a convention was called in 1790 in Pennsylvania to debate the state's contentious 1776 constitution, which had established a unicameral legislature and a controversial religious test. Defended vigorously by many agrarians, such as the Irish-born Presbyterians William Findley and John Smilie, that state constitution was opposed by many urban artisans and merchants, and by many Quakers and Congregationalists excluded from civic life since 1776. The foes of the 1776 framework, fresh off their success in winning ratification of the United States Constitution, outmaneuvered and outnumbered its champions. To the surprise of many, then and now, some prominent former Antifederalists, including Findley, who chaired the drafting committee, voted to enact a constitution more closely resembling those of the other states. Wilson made the case for a second legislative body by stressing the creative quality of debate in terms that reminded one of his colleagues of Rousseau, and again the comparison rang true. Like Rousseau, Wilson had no interest in perpetuating social orders or creating a new hereditary aristocracy. He preferred bicameralism only because he wanted more opportunities to discern the common good.[92] Like Madison, Wilson embraced a vision of popular government not committed to a static ideal of unchanging perfection but to development through time. He described that ideal in the *Lectures on Law* he delivered in Philadelphia in 1790–91: "This revolution principle—that, the sovereign power residing in the people, they may change their constitution and government whenever they please—is not a principle of discord, rancour, or war: it is a principle of melioration, contentment, and peace."[93]

Given the rancor that democracy both allows and engenders, and given the bitter conflicts that began almost as soon as the Constitution and the Bill of Rights took effect, Wilson's judgment may seem peculiar. But he understood that as long as no-holds-barred contests occur in the context of shared commitments to autonomy and reciprocity, debate enriches democracy. Instead of allowing discontent to fester and develop into civil war, deliberation by democratically chosen representatives can—not must, but can—enable them to reach shared understandings. Government, Wilson contended, "is only the creature of a constitution," and the United States Constitution was the creature of the American people: "In their hands it is as clay in the hands of the potter; they have the right to mould, to preserve, to improve, to refine, and to furnish it as they please."[94] Grounded on the people's will, the structure might have the stability of a pyramid, but it would remain forever unfinished, always subject to revision.

The delicate hydraulics of the nation's new constitutional system depended on balancing self-interest and the restraints imposed by conscience. It also required moderation. Rapid economic development and equally rapid cultural changes, however, were making that equilibrium increasingly precarious by the mid-1790s. Once the new federal government assumed the states' debts, farmers' tax burdens declined. A stable money supply eased credit for individuals and the nation, and commercial expansion fueled a booming economy.[95] Many Antifederalists had spoken frankly about the gap they perceived between their interests and those of their foes, a perception shared from the very different perspective of Hamilton and Robert Morris. It quickly became apparent that a large number of Americans, economically ambitious farmers and traders as well as already wealthy bankers and merchants, were quickly moving away from the Spartan simplicity of classical republicanism. Where they were headed, and what it meant for the culture and politics of American democracy, remained unclear.[96]

Many late-eighteenth-century thinkers on both sides of the Atlantic hoped the softening effects of commercial activity might provide an unexpected compass. According to the doctrine of "*doux commerce*," economic and social intercourse required and promoted promise-keeping and reliability, just as representative government did. As we've seen, Scottish Enlightenment thinkers, particularly Adam Smith, had conceived of the restraints of the earlier ideal of a moral economy and republicans' idealized agrarian small producers as obstacles to the development of a free society. Whereas individuals under feudal arrangements had been encumbered by various legal obligations, individuals in Smith's *Wealth of Nations* were free to pursue their own interests. The only constraints were those imposed on the one hand by the dictates of law, which enforced contracts, and on the other by the moral sense of benevolence, instructed by the "impartial spectator" imagined in Smith's *Theory of Moral Sentiments*.

The *doux commerce* thesis operated at numerous levels in American society. Benjamin Rush presented a clear version of it in his "Plan for the Establishment of Public Schools" in 1786. Commerce, Rush pointed out, had been thought of primarily in relation to "the wealth of the state," the view we now call mercantilism. But Rush argued instead that commerce should be seen "in a much higher light," in part because it was "the surest protection against aristocracy." Its effects were "next to those of religion in humanizing mankind," and it offered the prospect of uniting the world's nations "by ties of mutual wants and obligations." Just as commercial links could replace war between nations, so a commercial society could soften manners and improve morals by replacing earlier forms of subordination by smooth, albeit impersonal market relations.[97]

The result of this social and economic as well as political transformation would be either an expanding agrarian nation, the "empire of liberty" that Jefferson, Madison, and others projected on the basis of Scottish ideas, or the commercial power that Hamilton and his allies had in mind. Hamilton was forthright in his preference for an unequal society. From the different perspectives of both Rush and Hamilton, freeing people to engage in economic activity—or rather embracing that increasingly unconstrained activity that had been happening at an ever more frantic pace in the colonies for a century or more—would enable the United States to continue moving forward with the trajectory of history. The question was whether it would develop toward the benevolence and equality Rush predicted or toward the acquisitiveness and hierarchy Hamilton had in mind.[98]

The Scots' other enduring contribution was the idea of the moral sense. Not only Wilson and Madison, and Jefferson and Adams, but also former Antifederalist Mercy Otis Warren showed the impact of that idea in their writing, whether they understood it as a rational or intuitive faculty. During the summer of 1787, when Jefferson was in Paris and his daughter Mary arrived with her companion and maid Sally Hemings, he produced an especially rich series of letters. He wrote to his English friend Maria Cosway about the conflict between his head and his heart, to Abigail Adams about the salutary effects of "a little rebellion," to his friend Lafayette about the injustice of French landownership patterns, to Adams about diplomacy, and to Madison about a declaration of rights. He also sent a long meditation to Peter Carr, a young Virginian who was just beginning to read law with Jefferson's teacher and friend George Wythe, that provides a window into Jefferson's ideas of moral philosophy.

Given how many topics Carr had to study, Jefferson recommended against attending lectures on ethics because he judged them unnecessary: "He who made us would have been a pitiful bungler if he had made the rules of our moral conduct a matter of science." Although only some people have the chance for advanced study, all are obliged to behave morally. "Man was destined for society. His morality therefore was to be formed to this object. He was endowed with a sense of right & wrong," and "this sense is as much a part of his nature as the sense of hearing, seeing, feeling." In Jefferson's words, "The moral sense, or conscience, is as much a part of man as his leg or arm. It is given to all human beings in a stronger or weaker degree." This moral sense is "the true foundation of morality," yet it varies among individuals, as does physical strength, and it too could be strengthened by its exercise. Although our moral sense is "submitted indeed in some degree to the guidance of reason," only a "small stock" is required, a point Jefferson illustrated by suggesting that a "ploughman" is as likely to reason well about an ethical dilemma as a "professor." Jefferson never wrote a treatise on moral philosophy, but his correspondence reflects his conviction that the idea of a moral sense explains the operations of conscience.[99]

Because Adams started out with a different intellectual formation in New England Congregationalism, his convergence with Jefferson, Madison, and Wilson on moral philosophy is especially striking. Having abandoned his ancestors' Calvinist convictions concerning human depravity, Adams preserved a certain skepticism concerning the capacity of reason: "The passions and appetites are parts of human nature," he wrote, "as well as reason and the moral sense." Adams had read Adam Smith's *Theory of Moral Sentiments* by the time he wrote those words, and Smith's influence shows clearly in the emphasis Adams placed on the motivational force exerted by "the *esteem* and *admiration* of others," a force he knew all too well. Nature had given men "reason, conscience, and benevolence," which made them responsible for their actions and capable of virtue, the source of their "highest felicity." We all possess this "passion for the notice and regard" of others, and we will be tortured from cradle to grave if we neglect our duties. Like many other eighteenth-century Americans, Adams felt no need to choose among Hutcheson, Reid, and Smith concerning the source of the moral sense or its mode of operation. It was enough to note that earning the admiration of others requires "constant exertions of benevolence." This dynamic Adams deemed universal: "Old or young, rich or poor, high or low, wise or foolish, ignorant or learned," all people want others' respect.[100] Perhaps the vanity of which Adams was accused so often—and so fairly—sprang from his particularly acute awareness of the power of approbation, which proved more elusive the harder he tried to win it.

Adams's friend Mercy Otis Warren thought republican virtue and individual interest could be reconciled by benevolence. Conceiving history as the Scottish historians did, as a series of stages moving from barbarism to civilization, Warren argued that "manners" provide the necessary lubricant smoothing the strains as individuals learn to soften their selfishness, cultivate sympathy, and act responsibly. Warren perceived the difference between freedom conceived as the absence of all restraint and autonomy conceived as the willing acceptance of ethical laws. She believed the nation could fulfill its promise only if Americans learned, through manners, to internalize norms that would enable them to make the most of the democracy they had struggled to create: "What is generally called politeness is but the imitation of what we ought to be: civil, kind & attentive, but never servilely complaisant."[101] These thinkers' unanimous judgment concerning the presence in all people of the moral sense, and its indispensable role in reining in the excesses of individuals' appetites, gave them hope that Americans could keep alive sufficient virtue, or benevolence, as Madison, Wilson, Jefferson, Adams, and Warren all put it, to sustain the nation's new democratic government.

Many Americans continued to emphasize the role of religion in stabilizing republican government. The organizers and participants in the grand civic festivals of these years self-consciously highlighted the links they saw between Americans' religious and civic faith. Ezra Stiles of Yale had led the way, claiming in an election sermon in 1783 that adherence to Christian principles would enable the new nation to complete "our system of dominion and civic polity" and bring to fruition the promise of Harrington's *Oceana*.[102] The aged Charles Chauncy of Boston's First Church elaborated on this theme in *The Benevolence of the Deity*, an influential text that helped shape the emerging liberal Protestant sensibility around the ideas of liberality and benevolence: "the GREAT WHOLE" of the world was "a universal, gloriously connected system" in which political, economic, and ethical activity meshed smoothly.[103] Vermont's Asa Burton, preaching to his congregation in 1785, said that "political virtue may serve as a support for a while, but it is not a lasting principle." Only piety could bring it to fruition.[104] According to Charles Backus, addressing the citizens of Longmeadow in western Massachusetts, reason is "to be reckoned among the choicest gifts of the beneficent Creator," but it is not enough to sustain "the principles of the late Revolution." Only if Americans remained faithful to Christian ethics as well as reason would the republic flourish.[105]

During the final years of the eighteenth century, a number of New England Congregationalist ministers began to stray from the binaries of Calvinism and embrace the idea of "liberality" and "universal benevolence," an ethic of "piety and virtue," in the words of Aaron Bancroft, consistent with a wide-ranging acceptance of all of God's creation. David Barnes preferred a formulation similar to Jefferson's: because our "benevolent" creator "has wisely planted within us, an affection for this world and the things of it," we can best fulfill his plan by seeking "universal benevolence among men" based on the Christian ethic of love. Whether blending Scottish common-sense philosophy with the broader stream of early national Protestantism widened the appeal of Christianity or, by making it indistinguishable from a secular ethics of benevolence, weakened its hold on Americans remains an open question.[106]

All these economic, ethical, and religious ideas came together in a sermon preached by Enos Hitchcock, a western Massachusetts minister. When stopped on the road by armed rebels under the command of Daniel Shays, Hitchcock explained, he responded with a degree of calm that impressed the Shaysites and inspired them to reflect on loving one's enemies. The United States had proclaimed itself a nation of laws, not men, but the most important of those laws by far was Christ's law of universal benevolence. From Hitchcock's perspective, that law encompassed and should inform both political and economic activity. Commerce not only generates wealth, he told his flock, but also "unfetters and expands the human mind" and "enlarges the benevolent affections." Taken in the largest possible sense, commercial activity freed citizens of other nations as well as Americans; coupled with "a mild and benevolent religion" it might eradicate "bigotry, superstition, and persecution." Hitchcock published a children's catechism in 1788 that focused attention on Jesus's Sermon on the Mount and expanded the scope of the golden rule from the family, neighborhood, or nation to encompass all of God's creation. Just as the Almighty had shown "indiscriminate liberality" and "promiscuous benevolence" toward all his creatures, so they should develop "the generous feelings of a benevolent mind." Hitchcock saw a link between Christian love and the democratic ethic of reciprocity: "Virtue is the only sure basis on which the great social Fabrick can rise."[107]

Benjamin Rush, too, stressed the mutually reinforcing ethics of Christianity and self-government. "The precepts of the Gospel and the maxims of republics," he wrote to Adams, "in many instances agree with each other," a point he made later to Baptist minister Elhanan Winchester: "Republican forms of government are the best repositories of the Gospel." Finally, writing to Jefferson, Rush explained that the Christian gospel is "the *strong ground* of republicanism." The ethos of Christianity is opposed to the splendor of monarchy and encourages "republican liberty and equality as well as simplicity, integrity, and economy in government." Rush concluded that the powerful bond between Christianity and republicanism would "overturn all the corrupted political and religious institutions in the world."[108]

Both Adams and Jefferson shared that conviction. Adams wrote to his son Charles that the animating principles of American democracy originated in the Christian scriptures. "How the present age can boast of this Principle [of equality] as a Discove[r]y, as new Light and modern Knowledge I know not," because it descended directly from the admonition of Christ to love one's neighbor as oneself. When Adams declared all men equal in the Massachusetts Declaration of Rights, he meant a "moral Equality," because people are "not all equally tall, Strong wise handsome, active: but equally Men," in other words, all the handiwork of the same creator and entitled to the same justice. The principle of equality was grounded in the Christian principle that all people are equally the children of God.[109] Jefferson, although as previously noted a most unconventional believer, nevertheless found in the Christian gospels a uniquely admirable ethical code. He replied to Rush that his own views of Christianity would "displease neither the rational Christian nor Deists"; claims he was hostile to religion were "absolute falsehoods." His animosity was directed not against religion but against intolerance: "I have sworn upon the altar of god, eternal hostility against every form of tyranny over the mind of man."[110] To Moses Robinson, Jefferson described Christianity, at least when rid of its excrescences and returned to the "original purity and simplicity of its benevolent institutor," as the religion "most friendly to liberty, science, and the freest expansion of the human mind."[111] The members of this generation expressed, over and over, an extraordinary degree of confidence concerning the mutually reinforcing dynamics of commerce, Christianity, and democracy.[112]

All of them were startled by how rapidly the virtue they trusted, and which they thought consistent with commercial development, came under pressure. The source of that pressure, which would come to be considered one of the defining characteristics of the United States, was the unprecedented and unanticipated dismantling of hierarchies—and the deference that had sustained them—through ambitious individuals' frantic pursuit of self-interest. Before the ink dried on the Bill of Rights, older critiques of egoism evaporated. Whether bankers, merchants, or urban artisans, planters, commercial farmers, or pioneers on the edge of settlement, Americans sloughed off earlier constraints and spread out across the new nation. In defiance of the delicate balance envisioned by the framers, they constructed a dizzying array of new forms of enterprise and association, creating and discarding ways of life at a previously unknown pace. Although most Americans continued to employ the rhetoric of republican simplicity, they scrambled to acquire wealth and material goods in the democratic framework secured by the Constitution. It enabled individuals such as Hiram Harwood, a lonely farmer in rural Vermont committed to a vision of austere civic virtue, to participate in the civic life of his town and the growing economy of his region. Lured into an emerging market economy he neither sought nor understood, he was gradually ensnared in a web of commerce and eventually driven to suicide. For those living the new lives made possible by the new laws of the new nation, the risks could be as great as the opportunities.[113]

In *The Spirit of the Laws*, Montesquieu had asked, "When the whole world, impelled by the force of corruption, is immersed in voluptuousness, what must then become of virtue?"[114] Many Americans had carried that question with them into the era of the American Revolution, and it explains their anxiety about popular unrest and their hopes for the Constitution that seemed to promise stability at last. But the nation's rapid transformation strained those hopes; by the end of the eighteenth century some observers worried that the Americans' much-admired republican sensibility had vanished. François Alexandre Frédéric, duc de la Rochefoucauld-Liancourt, wrote a book about the United States after visiting for thirty-six months from 1795 through 1797. The new nation, he reported to readers eager to know about the nation France had helped to create, was in a state of constant change. Viewed in the context of Montesquieu's warnings and the disputes between Americans concerning personal interest and the public good, those changes showed just how prosperity threatened virtue. Rochefoucauld-Liancourt had produced one of the first French translations of the new nation's founding documents and state constitutions as early as 1783, and his abiding interest in the United States extended from his initial focus on its laws and its penitentiaries to the customs and manners of its people. In his two-volume account *Travels through North America*, he provided one of the earliest detailed portraits of its emerging culture. "The manners of the people display great simplicity," he reported, which some Europeans took as rudeness but which was better understood as a consequence of Americans' equality.

Rochefoucauld-Liancourt paid particular attention to the cultural consequences of democracy. He identified the absence of a hereditary aristocracy, the shared heritage of all the cultures of Europe, as the crucial difference. Rotation in office meant that elected positions in the United States were held for only a short time. As a result public service was generally undervalued; those holding office earned no particular distinction. Perhaps for that reason, Americans were turning away from the civic sphere and focusing their energies primarily on "the universal desire of amassing property." Such industriousness produced prosperity that merited praise, yet "an immoderate love of money hardens the heart, and renders it callous to humanity, to civility, nay to justice itself." Although such materialism did not necessarily rule out all "good and noble action," Rochefoucauld-Liancourt found Americans intent on a very particular sort of advantage that accrued from a "universal interest, which unites and supports society," namely, that "no member can enrich himself, without promoting at the same time the prosperity of others."[115] This peculiar American propensity, which several decades later Alexis de Tocqueville would call *"l'intérêt bien entendu"*—enlightened self-interest, or self-interest properly understood—was already apparent to Rochefoucauld-Liancourt, less than a decade after the Constitution was ratified, as the progeny of commerce and democracy.

The United States changed dramatically during the first decades of its existence. The Articles of Confederation gave way to a new constitution, which sparked a prolonged and productive debate about the meaning and possibility of democracy. In the debates over the Constitution, a particular sort of democratic sensibility emerged. Reflecting the creative power of debates conducted by popularly elected representatives, and pointing toward shared understandings that might emerge from such deliberations, it was a democratic sensibility sturdy enough to survive prolonged battles. But the issues that had inspired feverish debate over ratification quickly faded into the background, replaced by new and enticing prospects. The interlocking social, economic, cultural, religious, and political underpinnings on which Americans' democratic sensibility rested were changing even as the Constitution was becoming law, and those foundations were immediately put under stress. Perhaps the American culture of democracy could have survived, and achieved over time the stability that seemed possible or even likely to commentators in the late 1780s and early 1790s, had it not been for the tragedy that changed not only the life of the duc de la Rochefoucauld-Liancourt but everything on both sides of the Atlantic, the French Revolution.

PART III | Failure in Success

CHAPTER 10

Delusions of Unity and Collisions with Tradition in the French Revolution

THE SUCCESS OF America's democratic revolution caused the French Revolution. The failure of the French Revolution postponed for nearly a century the further development of democracy in Europe. Americans' replacement of monarchy by self-government inspired French critics disenchanted with the ancien régime, and the economic costs of helping America win its independence from Britain stretched the French monarchy beyond its breaking point. When Louis XVI convened an Assembly of Notables in January of 1787, he and his ministers anticipated finding a solution to their fiscal crisis. Instead the king initiated a process that immediately spun out of his control, quickly became a challenge to his rule, and eventually spurred the monarchies in the countries ringing France to ally against the Revolution.

Many observers on both sides of the Atlantic thought the failure of the French Revolution discredited democracy. The most ardent self-proclaimed champions of democracy in France, Maximilien Robespierre and his radical faction of the Jacobin party, misunderstood the meaning and mechanics of self-government. By identifying democracy with unanimity and enforcing it through violence, they tarnished the meaning of popular government not only in France but throughout Europe and even in America. Political debate in Europe and the United States was transformed by the Terror, by Robespierre's fatal confusion of his personal will with the will of the people, and by the wars, both foreign and civil, declared by the Jacobins against their enemies outside and within France. By repudiating the institutions of representative democracy in favor of tyranny, then abandoning the pretense of self-government for the glories promised by Napoleon Bonaparte's expansionist empire, the French Revolution confirmed for observers throughout the Atlantic world the suspicions expressed for centuries by critics of democracy: when the people exercise power, chaos inevitably results. But that irony is compounded by tragedy: unlike the Americans who inspired them, the Jacobins had no choice. Threatened by armies at their borders and by equally determined foes at home, champions of popular government in France turned to war, and ultimately to terror, as they tried to consolidate their new republic.

The French Revolution suffered from two delusions and failed because of two collisions. French observers imagined that the American Revolution brought unity and harmony to an Arcadian paradise. Interpreting the institutions of representative government in the new nation as the triumph of Enlightenment rationalism rather than as the maturation of already existing practices rooted in the experience of autonomy and an ethic of reciprocity grounded in Christianity, commentators in France rapturously characterized the United States as the land where reason had banished tradition and enthroned an uncomplicated system of popular rule. The second delusion was economic. The vast expenditures of the French monarchy, the most extravagant of which was the decisive aid provided for the American Revolution, left the nation's finances a shambles. Yet successive ministries deceived the French people, from the nobility to the peasantry, by pretending that solutions required only minor tinkering. Thus either miscalculation or personal corruption was blamed for problems that stemmed from the untenable practices of an anachronistic regime that starved the poor to protect the ancient privileges of the rich.

The collisions were religious and cultural. Misreading widespread misgivings about the French Catholic Church as evidence of the loss of religious faith, and seeking to curb the independent authority of the Catholic hierarchy, revolutionaries made a tragic and fatal error. The Civil Constitution of the Clergy, proclaimed on July 12, 1790, made the institutions and personnel of the Catholic Church subordinate to the state. That step changed the attitudes of many who had previously embraced the Revolution and confirmed the doubts of others. Most significantly, it transformed many of those already opposed to the Revolution into implacable enemies ready to die for their beliefs. The cultural collision involved the contradiction between new and old. The ideas of individual initiative, personal autonomy, economic change, and the perfectibility of man, at least when governed by reason and employing the tools of science—in short, the ideals of the French Enlightenment generally—collided with the still-strong pull of tradition. The embedded cultural forms of corporatism, whether of clan, guild, parish, or social order, did not persist only because of the strength of inertia; they persisted as well because of deep, constitutive loyalties felt by millions of French people, of all classes and regions, who proved unwilling to surrender the commitments that for centuries had defined their lives.

The force of those collisions in France would have been sufficient to cause serious damage in any case, but international rivalries compounded the problems exponentially, transforming civil strife into a much wider war between new and old, and between the Revolution and its opponents, that eventually spread throughout Europe and across the Atlantic. By the end of the eighteenth century, the French Revolution had metamorphosed from a struggle over the shape of French politics and society to a broader clash over fundamental cultural values, which gave rise to previously unknown and self-conscious forms of conservatism and radicalism throughout the Atlantic world. The consequences remain with us two centuries later. Although the substantive issues on both sides of the Atlantic have changed dramatically in recent decades, the symbolic structure remains that created by the French Revolution, whose tragic legacy has continued to poison democratic politics.

Whether or not France was suffering from a crisis of confidence in the mid-eighteenth century in the wake of its defeat at the hands of Britain in the Seven Years War, the role played by France in America's triumph precipitated a wave of self-congratulation in France and unbridled enthusiasm about the United States. Abbé Raynal's *Histoire philosophique et politique des établissements et du commerce des européens dans les Deux Indes*, a work of multiple volumes produced by multiple authors, had already raised the stakes concerning the future of the New World. Originally published in French in 1770, and translated into every major European language and reprinted more than fifty times in the late eighteenth century, Raynal's book highlighted the novel features of Europe's colonial outposts and predicted that they—like the slaves they contained—might one day turn the tables: "Europe may someday find its masters in its children."[1] The books of Thomas Paine and Richard Price extolling the American Revolution were immediately translated into French in 1776.[2] When Abbé Raynal invited Europeans in 1783 to answer the question whether the discovery of America "had been useful or harmful to the human race," most respondents answered in the affirmative. Abbé Louis Genty proclaimed, with restraint characteristic of many who replied to Raynal, that the "independence of the Anglo-Americans is exactly the right event to accelerate the revolution that must spread happiness on earth. In the bosom of this nascent republic lie the true treasures that will enrich the world."[3] Or as Raynal himself put it, referring to the outbreak of the American Revolution, "One day has given birth to a revolution. One day has transported us into a new century."[4]

The testimony that carried the most weight in France was that of a French migrant to the New World, St. Jean de Crèvecoeur, who wrote in his *Letters of an American Farmer* (1782) about a culture of independent-minded egalitarians who thought for themselves and were making a world of their own, free from the obstacles of inherited and outdated traditions. The marquis de Lafayette agreed with Crèvecoeur. In a letter to his wife, Lafayette too identified the feature of American culture that struck French observers as the most remarkable: "The richest and the poorest are on the same level here; and although some people are immensely rich, I defy anyone to find any difference in the way the rich and the poor behave toward each other."[5]

When Jacques-Pierre Brissot, a writer who would play a decisive role in the French Revolution after visiting the United States in 1788, first read Crèvecoeur, he thought he could see in America just what the French had been longing for: "a country, a government, where the desires of their hearts have been realized, a land which speaks to them in their own language. The happiness for which they have sighed finally does in truth exist."[6] With his collaborator the Swiss émigré and failed Genevan revolutionary Etienne Clavière, Brissot offered the American model as an alternative to the oligarchic regime France had put in power in Geneva.[7] Intoxicated by the American example, Brissot joined with Clavière, Crèvecoeur, and Nicolas Bergasse to establish in 1787 the short-lived and inefficacious Gallo-American Society.[8] Brissot returned from his trip across the Atlantic the following year inspired to write a plan to guide his French compatriots as they prepared to think about the fundamental principles of government. In the United States Brissot grasped the principle of popular sovereignty that animated the American system. He contended that all legitimate power must derive from the people themselves, which the new United States Constitution accomplished as a result of the process of popular ratification. This new and profound understanding of how to write and authorize a constitution, Brissot wrote, we owe to "the free Americans, and the convention which has just formed the plan for a federal system has infinitely perfected it." Fatefully, Brissot predicted that this "device or method" could be "very easily adapted to the circumstances in which France now finds itself."[9] That confidence, widely shared and badly misplaced, was the problem.

Despite the rapturous claims of French enthusiasts for the American Revolution, the political institutions and social structure of France in the 1770s and 1780s stood in stark contrast to those of the United States. The population of France was divided into three categories known as estates: the clergy, the nobility, and everyone else. Of a population rising from 26 million to 28 million from the 1750s through the 1780s, the first estate numbered roughly 130,000 clergymen and nuns. Including a wide range of institutions, the Catholic Church owned perhaps 10 percent of the land in France.

The nobility included somewhere between 100,000 and 300,000 people. That estimate testifies to the ambiguous and changing status of the second estate, which expanded rapidly during the eighteenth century through the monarchy's sale of offices, an acceleration of a long-standing practice that ennobled perhaps as many as 50,000 people during these years. This hereditary aristocracy, divided between an older nobility of the sword and a newer, but often wealthier, nobility of the robe, owned between a quarter and a third of the land. Neither clergy nor nobility paid taxes on land; nor were they liable for other obligations such as militia service or the unpaid compulsory labor, usually on public works such as roads, known as the *corvée*. The nobility monopolized positions of prestige and honor in church and state alike. Bishops were typically the younger sons of greater nobles. Positions in the provincial parlements, which combined legislative and judicial functions, were held by members of the nobility.

The weight of paying for the privileges of the monarchy, and of the first and second estates, fell on the remainder of the French nation, and primarily on the peasantry. Their tithes paid the living expenses of the clergy and the upkeep of church lands and buildings. Their taxes to the crown and the remaining feudal dues they paid to the nobility provided the funds that kept the system running. Roughly 80 percent of the population lived in villages of fewer than two thousand inhabitants, and most of them survived on what was raised on meager landholdings farmed according to traditional methods. This pattern of subsistence farming had changed little, and the standard of living—after generations of dividing and subdividing already small plots of land—was as meager for the vast majority as it was grand for those at the top of the pyramid. Guilds regulated the lives of artisans in French towns and cities, and those thrown off the land and into urban life had few opportunities to enter such lines of work.

The only non-nobles prospering from this system were the bourgeoisie, especially those in the cloth trades or the industrial enterprises springing up in the northeastern region of France, and the several hundred financiers who handled the taxes and skimmed off a healthy portion for themselves. Otherwise life in France was precarious for the majority of the population. Bad harvests or price increases, or both, could drive people either to the edge of starvation or over into vagrancy, begging, or crime. After the middle decades of the eighteenth century saw a brief and modest rise in living standards for most French people in towns and the countryside, a series of bad harvests running from the late 1760s through the 1790s brought that boomlet to a halt. Prices rose much faster than wages, and rents and taxes kept escalating to pay the rising expenses of the nobility and the court at Versailles.

No quick sketch of eighteenth-century French socioeconomic conditions can capture the wide disparities among regions, because not only variations of climate and soil but also deep-rooted cultural differences divided the parts of the nation from each other. The political system mirrored that diversity. Thirteen parlements, thirty-nine different provincial governorships, and 136 Catholic dioceses presided over a crazy quilt of administrative districts, and the customs and rules prevailing in one often differed from those prevailing in the neighboring district. Some territories on the western, southwestern, or southern margins of the nation, such as the Vendée or the Basque region, jealously guarded distinctive practices centuries old. Other eastern and southeastern regions recently incorporated into France, such as Brittany, Burgundy, and Provence, preserved considerable autonomy as a legacy from their earlier status as independent states. Although the proud claims of an absolute monarchy unified under the king of France had been expanding steadily for centuries, the reality of multiple language groups, customs duties that impeded the flow of commerce, and long-standing local as well as regional animosities marked the nation far more deeply than did the grandeur and pretensions of the royal court at Versailles.[10]

Religious practices and identities were likewise far more variegated than uniform. Eighteen different Catholic archbishops presided over flocks nominally Gallican, as the French Catholic Church was called after 1682, that strayed into forms of syncretic folk religious practices on the one hand and coexisted with varieties of Protestantism, Judaism, and Jansenism on the other. Although most Protestants in western and southern regions had been driven underground by the Revocation of the Edict of Nantes in 1685, the German speakers of Alsace continued to practice openly several varieties of Protestantism. Even more problematic were the Jansenists, who promulgated an Augustinian brand of Catholicism that counterposed an austere asceticism to the pomp and majesty preferred by the French hierarchy. Often characterized as the Puritans of France, the Jansenists considered themselves not only more authentically Catholic than the pope but also much closer to the teachings of Jesus than were the officially sanctioned forms of Gallican Catholicism.

Efforts to rein in Jansenist ideas and practices had been advanced, including an order from the Archbishop of Paris that prevented Jansenists from receiving the sacraments during the 1750s, but such efforts, like most attempts to enforce conformity since the outbreak of the Reformation, more often hardened resistance than eroded it. The powerful Parlement of Paris in particular remained a hotbed of Jansenism and a powerful counterweight to the Gallican hierarchy. Jansenist writers such as François Richer carried the fight to their foes, locating the authority of the Church in the lay faithful rather than the clergy and denying that the Church could legitimately own any property.

Nor were the Jansenists the only problem facing the hierarchy of the French Catholic Church. The Jesuit order was as cantankerous and independent-minded in France as elsewhere. Having been accused of taking orders from the head of the Society of Jesus in Rome and of complicity in a plot on the life of Louis XV, the Jesuits were suppressed in 1764. Thus from the struggles over the meaning of Catholicism in France, its relation to Rome, and its close connections with the king and the nobility, emerged lively discourses concerning the proper relation between popular authority and religious hierarchy and the propriety of preaching the gospel of poverty and humility from perches of wealth and privilege. Although the Church exercised almost sole authority over educational institutions, hospitals, and care of the poor, its central role in the provision of social services hardly mollified its many critics.[11]

It was in the realm of politics, however, that the fuse was lit. A gap was growing between the theory of royal absolutism and the prerogatives exercised by the parlements. Since the glory days of Louis XIV, when Bishop Bossuet had declared, without eliciting much dissent, that "all of the state resides within the person of the prince,"[12] the effective power of the monarch had eroded considerably. The consequences of that erosion became increasingly serious after Louis XV's chancellor René-Nicolas-Charles de Maupeou challenged the considerable authority of the Parlement of Paris in 1771. Although in principle the king retained final authority in the public realm, in practice the parlements could limit the effectiveness of his initiatives by resisting or failing to register his edicts. In the wake of the disastrous Seven Years War and catastrophic crop failures in the late 1760s, Maupeou announced a drastic reorganization of the parlements to prevent them from opposing Louis XV's financial reforms. Formerly venal offices were to be turned into administrative appointments, ostensibly a move toward rewarding ability and increasing effectiveness. But given the almost simultaneous transformation of thousands of local offices from elected to venal, a change ordered to raise funds for the monarchy, Maupeou's real purpose in transforming the parlements became clear. When the Parlement of Paris resisted, it was dissolved.

The resulting pamphlet war pitted the king's champions, including those (such as Voltaire) who preferred a reform-minded monarch to the tradition-loving *parlementaires*, against the Jansenist-led opposition. The king's critics drew a contrast between treasured and venerable liberties, sustained by the rule of law, and the rising threat of despotism. During the course of these debates, arguments concerning efficiency, justice, and the general will began crowding out older arguments concerning the monarch's divine right, on the one hand, and divinely sanctioned popular resistance, on the other, even though the public played a negligible role in this squabble between the king's advisers and the nobility. A heightened degree of contentiousness, hardened by scurrilous attacks on the monarch from the underground press, further corroded the glitter of royal authority. Shortly after Louis XV succumbed to smallpox, his *avocat-général* Antoine-Louis Séguier observed the costs involved in the falling of "the veil with which the prudence of our fathers had enveloped all that which pertains to government and administration."[13] The advisers chosen by the new king, Louis XVI, abandoned Maupeou's campaign against the parlements and restored them to their former condition.

The furor provoked by the Maupeou coup, however, had done lasting damage. Now every step taken by the king or his ministers was met with suspicion; every sign of resistance by the parlements was interpreted as insubordination. If the powers claimed by the British king's royal governors over his North American colonies had swollen beyond the limits of their effectiveness, the situation in France was doubly incendiary. Both the king's ministry and the parlements now jealously interpreted each other's every move as a potentially dangerous challenge to their own authority, yet neither possessed sufficient power to control the other. Although French political reality was drifting ever further from absolutism, the pretense of royal omnipotence persisted. In Alexis de Tocqueville's autopsy for prerevolutionary France, *The Old Regime and the French Revolution*, he identified the heart of the problem: "This is the old regime in a nutshell: a rigid rule, lax implementation; this is its character." That formula bred contempt for the law, and for those in positions of authority, with consequences far different from those of the American Revolution.[14]

By 1787 Louis XVI finally understood the scale of the fiscal crisis he faced, yet his government's ambitious scheme to raise taxes, float loans, and fundamentally reform the finances of the realm was nevertheless resisted by the parlements. When the king himself decided to join his ministers in making the case at a session of the reconstituted Parlement of Paris, he was stunned by the duc d'Orléans, who protested that the crown's plan to proceed despite the opposition of parlements was unconstitutional. The king's notorious reply, "It is legal because I will it," underscored the imperiousness of royal absolutism as decisively as the continuing intransigence of the entrenched nobility demonstrated the monarch's inability to impose his ostensible authority and make his will law. Despite scattered riots and popular protests, sustained opposition stemmed principally from the body of nobles ensconced in the parlements, who cloaked their stubborn refusal to surrender their privileges beneath silken invocations of the rule of law and the public good. If the king needed more money, that was his problem. The nobility had no intention of helping him solve it by paying the taxes he sought to impose, and France lacked political institutions (such as Britain's House of Commons or America's town meetings or state assemblies) capable of rallying the people to the side of the crown or the aristocracy.[15]

The distribution of wealth in France was so dramatically skewed that the king had no alternative to raising taxes on the nation's richest citizens. By the late 1780s the peasantry and townspeople were already facing higher rents, higher taxes, higher prices on bread, and a lower standard of living. The extravagance of court life in Versailles was stretching the resources of the crown, and even the grandest nobles were living beyond their means. The nation was unable to pay its debts or meet its obligations on the international front, where one of its allies, the neighboring Dutch republic, was overrun by Prussian troops while France looked on helplessly. The temporary euphoria brought on by the part France played in helping the United States defeat Britain had given way to the stark reality of economic catastrophe. Something had to give.

Thomas Jefferson, residing in France during these crucial years as a representative of the United States government, understood the problem. As the fiscal crisis in France worsened, Jefferson sharpened the point of his earlier letter to Madison concerning the disastrous consequences of France's dramatically unequal distribution of property and its exclusion of the people from political activity.[16] Writing to his law teacher George Wythe from Paris in the summer of 1786, Jefferson applauded the liberty enjoyed by Americans in speech, religion, and political activity. "If anybody thinks that kings, nobles, or priests are good conservators of the public happiness," he advised, "send them here. It is the best school in the universe to cure them of that folly." Distinct social orders "are an abandoned confederacy against the happiness of the mass of the people." Although France possessed the "finest soil" and best climate on earth, and a populace Jefferson judged "benevolent" and "amiable," the people of France were "loaded with misery by kings, nobles, and priests, and by them alone." Only by continuing to educate its citizens to resist all forms of aristocracy could America escape that fate. In a letter written January 16, 1787, Jefferson adopted a different image. European governments "have divided their nations into two classes, wolves & sheep. I do not exaggerate. This is a true picture of Europe." Whereas Americans had learned over decades the importance of remaining engaged in the public sphere, the wolves had denied Europe's sheep the benefits of such invigorating political activity.[17]

Jefferson watched the events leading up to the outbreak of the French Revolution with keen attention. The king's minister Charles-Alexandre de Calonne had attempted to marshal support for fiscal reforms by calling an Assembly of Notables, which disappointed him by declaring that only the Estates General possessed the authority to approve tax increases. A gathering of representatives of the three orders of the realm created in 1302, the Estates General had functioned in the next two centuries much as the English Parliament did, enabling the king to raise needed revenues and legitimating his reign. As squabbling between the estates made reaching agreement harder, and as the French monarchy consolidated its power under Louis XIV, however, the Estates General had faded into a distant memory. It had last been convened in 1614, when the young Louis XIII was not yet prepared to exercise power, and it had disbanded then without accomplishing anything. By the 1780s, nobody was quite sure about its purpose or its powers. In August of 1788, Jefferson wrote to Crèvecoeur that the struggle appeared to be shaping up as "a contest between the monarchical and aristocratical parts of the government," both of which sought to establish "a monopoly of despotism over the people." The nobility was dividing into reformist and uncompromising wings, the latter of which Jefferson predicted would drive the king to make great concessions to the people rather than giving any ground to his nemesis, the aristocracy that dominated the increasingly obdurate parlements. The urgent need to reconvene the nation's law courts and the king's reasonable fears of bankruptcy had driven him to agree, reluctantly, to convene the Estates General, and now the only questions concerned the timing of that event and its consequences. Compounding these political, legal, and financial difficulties was another disastrous harvest and a devastating hailstorm that had already ruined the crop of the next year, that of 1789. Whatever short-term remedies France might envision, Jefferson concluded, the only lasting solutions would require a dramatic economic, political, and cultural transformation. A way must be found to "bring the people to such a state of ease, as not to be ruined by the loss of a single crop." As Jefferson wrote to another friend, France needed a constitution sufficiently enlightened to secure fundamental rights and sufficiently moderate not to provoke "an appeal to arms" by an alarmed and fearful king.[18] Neither proved possible.

Even before the French Revolution began, Jefferson understood the reasons why it would take a course different from the American Revolution. The two revolutions diverged because of their different histories: Americans enjoyed two centuries of experience with self-government, theorized by Jefferson himself, Adams, Madison, Wilson, and many others in terms of representation and the search for the common good to be created through the process of deliberation. France lacked such experience. It was thus not possible for the

French to build on traditional and familiar democratic practices, as did those who wrote new constitutions for the new American states and those who framed the United States Constitution. Instead, as Tocqueville later argued, it was necessary in France to destroy all that remained of the old regime, both the absolute monarchy and the obstinate and isolated intermediate bodies of the clergy and the nobility.[19]

The differences between America and France derived from the dramatically different cultural, religious, political, and economic contexts within which the ideas of the common good and the general will came to prominence, not from different attitudes toward those ideas. In the United States the idea of the common good posed no threat because it was understood to be whatever would emerge from the multiple processes of democratic deliberation by the elected representatives of the people. In France, by contrast, the general will had to be seen as unitary, in the same way that the national will expressed by the monarchy had been unitary, at first because of the expectations of the French nation and later because of the very real threats to the Revolution. The monarchy, the refractory clergy that resisted challenges to its status, the stubborn nobility, the ordinary people who preferred their traditions to radical changes, and other European nations working in league with members of those groups meant that disagreements had a very different significance in France than in America, where the Loyalists departed and did not return.

Another major difference was the prominence in France of the physiocrats, those self-proclaimed champions of Enlightenment who thought reason could yield a science of society. Thinkers such as the economist François Quesnay, his follower Anne-Robert-Jacques Turgot, and the mathematician the marquis de Condorcet believed that rational administration by the central government should replace the long-standing privileges enjoyed by the clergy and the nobility, and they believed their own judgment should trump that of the people and their representatives. The continuing appeal in France of traditional affiliations and communities such as guilds, parishes, and parlements stood in stark contrast to the physiocrats' emphasis on individuals making rational choices.[20] No equivalent group existed in America, where the ideas of the Enlightenment were filtered through Protestant Christianity and Scottish common-sense philosophy rather than enthusiasm for the capacity of reason to generate timeless laws of politics, society, and economics.

During the years following the American Revolution, competing political ideas swirled through French culture. The writings of Montesquieu and Archbishop Fénelon remained influential—the latter's *Télémaque* served as a model for the young Louis XVI—and the ideas of Rousseau and the philosophes continued to attract lively commentary. Turgot had conceded, following the logic of the *Social Contract*, that sovereignty resides in the people, but like the other physiocrats he did not think that entitled the people to participate in the complex decision-making processes of government. The outrage over grain prices that sank Turgot's own ministry had demonstrated conclusively to the physiocrats the irrationality of ordinary people, and thus a chasm yawned between the abstract idea of popular sovereignty in the ideal republic and the real need to govern without paying attention to the people's mistaken judgment. As Condorcet put it in his *Vie de M. Turgot*, in theory "all property owners" should have an equal right to "participate in legislation, regulate the assemblies that draw up and promulgate the laws, give them sanction by their suffrage, and change the form of all public institutions by a formal decision."

In practice, however, Turgot had a different plan. Given the unenlightened state of public opinion, the right of political participation had to be shelved: "If the laws are regarded not as the expression of the arbitrary will of the greatest number, but as truths deduced by reason from the principles of natural law and adopted as such by the majority," then that majority should be content to allow those with the necessary training and expertise to rule in their place. Rather than worrying about "being subjected to the arbitrary will of another," the people of France should agree to submit "only to an enlightened reason," which would impose laws conducive to general happiness. Given the greater concentration of authority in an absolute monarchy, such a form of government seemed to Turgot better suited to the people's interests than the decentralization of power in provincial assemblies charged with legislative responsibilities. Although Turgot advocated establishing assemblies of that sort, he envisioned them only as sources of more accurate and reliable information on which the officials of the central government would base their decisions. Such assemblies, he cautioned, must not be able to oppose the steps required to effect necessary reforms. "They would have all of the advantages of assemblies of Estates with none of the inconveniences: neither the confusion, nor the intrigues, nor the esprit de corps, nor the animosities and prejudices of one order against another." As that characterization makes clear, Turgot longed for centralized administrative authority as a way to sidestep the inevitable opposition of the clergy, the nobility, and the peasantry to his plans to streamline the economic affairs of France.[21]

Turgot's own practice in the chaos that followed the famine of 1770 was more flexible than his principles seemed to allow. The public outcry in 1775, however, after he instituted free trade in grain, cost him his position and hardened his opposition to popular participation in politics. He wrote a critique of Louis XVI, which was made public only in 1787, in which he contrasted the particularity of the king's decrees with the generality that should characterize the rule of law.[22] Turgot aspired to a science of political administration that permitted no meddling by the emotional and uninformed masses. In his words, "The truths of moral and political science are capable of the same certainty as those that form the system of physical science, even in those branches like astronomy that seem to approximate mathematical certainty."[23]

After Turgot read Richard Price's account of the new American state constitutions in March of 1778, he wrote to Price complaining that the Americans had foolishly mimicked the British notion of mixed government rather than adopting a more centralized, and thus more rational and efficient, model. "Instead of bringing all the authorities into one, that of the nation," Turgot wrote, "they have established different bodies, a house of representatives, a council, a governor, because England has a house of commons, a house of lords, and a king." From Turgot's perspective, such intermediate institutions merely perpetuated antiquated forms of local authority and the "bodies" of nobles and clergy that exercised power and jealously guarded their autonomy. Although ostensibly looking after the public interest, such groups actually concerned themselves only with obstructing the efforts of the central government to bring order to chaos and prosperity to people mired in counterproductive traditions. This letter, which was published in 1784, three years after Turgot's death, sparked a lively debate between Price and John Adams, who had already bristled at the criticism of American governments lodged by another prolific and controversial French writer, Abbé Mably.[24]

Mably's stature has shrunk since the eighteenth century, but his contemporaries considered him a giant.[25] Mably's collected works ran to fifteen volumes; only Rousseau was cited and invoked more often during the French Revolution. During the 1740s Mably served as secretary to the French minister of state, Cardinal de Tencin, and in that capacity he drafted reports and prepared for negotiations with various heads of state. Mably preferred the life of the mind, however, to the intrigues of court. After leaving the cardinal's side he retired from public life to write, which he did incessantly until his death in 1785. One of his early books, *Des droits et des devoirs du citoyen*, was written in 1758 but published only in early 1789, when the uncanny echoes of the issues Mably addressed made readers wonder if the book had been revised with the current crisis in mind.

The book takes the form of a dialogue between Lord Stanhope, an English Commonwealthman enamored of the ancient republics and wary of the flagging virtue of his own nation, and the French author he is visiting. The characters lament the fading of their nations' earlier republican character and the emergence of royal absolutism. The problem, according to the English visitor, was popular disengagement from politics: Although the people are the sovereign power, at least originally, they have ceased to play that part. Whereas Turgot lamented the obstructionism of the parlements and other intermediate bodies in France, Mably's characters in *Des droits* looked to the people, awakened from their lethargy by political education and rising to seize the reins of government, to restore republican rule. Such dramatic action, however, was bound to rouse the monarchy to violent repression, so the best strategy was to convene the Estates General, avoid the temptation to divide into separate social orders, and maintain pressure on the king to authorize permanent institutions of popular government. None of Mably's characters in *Des droits* recommended doing away with the monarch. Reasoning from the experience of republics ancient and modern, they agreed that only a king—properly hemmed in by the institutions of representative government—could prevent the otherwise inevitable descent into despotism. But Mably seemed convinced that such revolutionary action would never occur in France. The nation's experience of the chaos and violence of the wars of religion had made it unwilling to risk tampering with the stability achieved by royal absolutism, even if that stability was purchased at the cost of corruption. As Mably put it, "Civil war is an even worse evil than slavery."[26]

Events in France seemed to confirm the anxieties expressed by Mably's characters in *Des droits*. The Maupeou coup showed that the French were not capable of making common cause against royal despotism. Instead the rivalries between the nobility and the ordinary people, made manifest in the parlements' resistance to the crown, seemed destined to block any successful challenge to the king's authority. In his *Observations sur l'histoire de France* (1772), Mably again pointed to the legacy of the wars of religion. In the absence of a mature populace with a sustained engagement in politics, the dangers posed by the threat of civil war would keep France from ever again challenging absolute monarchy. Whereas Turgot had dismissed American federalism as a foolish experiment because "all public authority should be one," by which he meant "that of the nation," Mably disagreed. He had met John Adams in Paris in 1782, and their spirited conversations gave Mably the impression that Adams wanted him to produce a book on the subject of American government. Although Adams reported being impressed by the "very agreeable" and "polite, good humoured, and sensible" Mably, he denied that he deserved credit for inspiring Mably's *Observations sur le gouvernement et les lois des Etats-Unis d'Amérique* (1784), a book published in the form of letters to Adams. Mably dismissed Turgot's call for unicameralism and endorsed the idea of two legislative chambers, a judgment that caused him, as it did

Adams, to be characterized as an aristocrat. The charge was as incoherent in the case of Mably as it had been in the case of Adams in the years leading up to the French Revolution. Both of them directed their fire against heritable privilege and pondered the ways in which the wealthy could be prevented from taking power in republican governments.[27]

Mably shared Adams's dislike of inequality, which both of them considered a threat to self-rule. The remedy Mably proposed in *De la législation*, however, the common ownership of property, seemed to Adams "stark mad," a cure considerably worse than the ill.[28] Also like Adams, Mably savaged atheism as incompatible with popular government. He endorsed the adoption of sumptuary laws against extravagant displays of wealth, such as those Adams built into the 1780 Massachusetts Constitution, to prevent the lure of luxury from draining republics of their virtue. Mably saw, as did Adams and Jefferson, that the greatest difference between France and the United States lay in the relative social and economic equality of American citizens and the absence of separate, stratified ranks legally separating the clergy and nobility from everyone else. Mably also perceived the difficulties those differences would present were France ever to attempt a republican revolution. Given his pointed warnings about the legacy of the wars of religion and his identification of popular government with virtue and social equality, Mably provided the revolutionary generation with an exceptionally rich vein of ideas to ponder and plunder for purposes ranging from the dangers of civil war to the promise of radical egalitarianism, and from the need for monarchical rule to the desirability of popular sovereignty.[29]

Unlike Mably's many texts, which permit and even encourage multiple interpretations, the writings of the marquis de Condorcet have seemed to many readers all too definite in their calculations of the probability of truth and the possibility of error in decision making. Condorcet has been held up by critics and admirers alike as the prime exemplar of Enlightenment rationalism, the founder of what is now called social choice theory, and an illustration of the appeal, as well as the perils, of using mathematical reasoning to make sense of human behavior. From the time of his early veneration of Turgot until Condorcet's death in 1794, probably by suicide, Condorcet's life either proved that irrational mobs cannot abide champions of reason or showed the folly of overreaching scientism. Or both. Placed in the context of late-eighteenth-century arguments concerning democracy, Condorcet emerges as a more complex, elusive figure, although his unshakable confidence in the capacity of reason still distinguishes him from many of his contemporaries.[30]

Condorcet's father, following a long family tradition of military service, was killed in combat only a month after the birth of his son, who was then raised by his mother in an atmosphere of intense Catholic piety and educated by Jesuits in Reims. Condorcet's exceptional aptitude for the natural sciences emerged only in the final year of his university training in Paris, where he concentrated on mathematics and physics. He earned membership in the Academy of Sciences on the strength of his first book, *Calcul intégral* (1765), and by 1776 he was serving as the academy's official spokesman. During the years of his ascent in the Parisian world of letters, Condorcet gravitated toward the salon of Julie de Lespinasse, where he became acquainted with *lumières* such as Jean le Rond d'Alembert, Denis Diderot, the abbé de Condillac, and Turgot. He also became involved in their plans to remake France by applying the leverage of reason to uproot obscurantist traditions in philosophy, literature, and politics.[31] Condorcet sharpened his wit and his pen in the controversies of the 1760s and 1770s. Siding with Turgot in the debates over the price of grain, he insisted that the liberalization of trade was a cause of science, a matter of simple logic, and that resistance to this application of reason to economics showed the dangers of popular adherence to tradition.[32]

Condorcet was working as a mathematician as well as an adviser to Turgot. In 1785 he published his *Essai sur l'application de l'analyse à la probabilité des décisions rendues à la pluralité des voix*, a landmark work applying mathematics to public affairs. Condorcet had already asserted the proposition that would drive all of his mature writing. Because the moral sciences are based on the observation of facts, they must follow the scientific method, develop "an equally exact and precise language," and culminate in "the same degree of certainty."[33] Condorcet never wavered in his confidence that the natural sciences should serve as the template for the human sciences. Unlike Turgot, whose experience in public life made him doubt the applicability of science to politics, Condorcet intended to demonstrate that the use of probability renders decisions about politics as definite as decisions in the sciences.[34] He agreed with Turgot that unless the people were enlightened by education, involving them in decision making was perilous—as Turgot learned the hard way. If the people could be made cognizant of scientific method, however, it would be possible to determine the probability that any popular assembly would arrive at the truth. Condorcet believed that replacing custom with science would make possible a system of representative government, based on the principles of equality and popular sovereignty, from which would emerge decisions both rational and freely chosen, decisions reached by an elite but to which the masses would freely consent.

Condorcet shared the widespread French enthusiasm for the American Revolution, and he wrote *L'influence de la Révolution d'Amérique* in 1786 to explain why he considered Americans the only people without the least bit of

Machiavellian maneuvering, "whose leaders do not profess the impossibility of perfecting the social order or reconciling public prosperity and justice."[35] Five years after Raynal had asked about the consequences of America's discovery, Condorcet replied that the Revolution had established the rights of man. Those rights, he wrote, included the right to personal liberty and security; the right to property; the right to equal standing before the law, which he insisted must be understood as unchanging in contradistinction to Montesquieu's pernicious historicist relativism; and the right to participate—even if only indirectly—in making laws. These principles Condorcet proclaimed true always and everywhere: "They are in effect the necessary result of the properties of sensitive beings capable of reasoning," laws that derive from the nature of man. "It is sufficient to suppose the existence of these beings for the propositions founded on these notions to be true; just as it is sufficient to suppose the existence of a circle to establish the truth of the propositions which develop its different characteristics." The fourth principle, however, the principle of participation, although highly prized by "zealous republicans," was not only less important than the others but was also contingent on the education of the people. Its advantages would be lost if "ignorance or prejudice" diverted those making decisions from "the immutable laws of justice." Judging in terms of public happiness, a republic instituting tyrannical laws would be far less desirable than a rationally governed monarchy.[36] Perhaps because the French lacked experience with self-government, Condorcet was but one of many French thinkers uneasy about the idea of popular participation.

Among the most striking features of the French response to the American Revolution was the almost universal French preference for the unicameral legislature of Pennsylvania over the bicameral legislatures adopted in all the other states. The French misapprehension of the virtues of unicameralism, as John Adams saw it, provoked not only Adams's own spirited *Defence of the Constitutions* but also a four-volume work by the Italian-born physician and merchant Philip Mazzei. Mazzei had worked with Jefferson to establish olive and grape growing while living near Monticello in the 1770s, then tried to secure arms and money in Europe to support the War for Independence. Like Adams, Mazzei sought to demonstrate and explain, in great detail, why Americans opted for the separation of legislative power.[37] By the time Adams's and Mazzei's books were published, their arguments were beginning to seem less abstract—and considerably more urgent—in France. In 1787, after the Assembly of Notables refused to authorize Calonne's proposal to increase taxes and called for convening the Estates General, French commentators were buzzing about the next step in the increasingly tense confrontation between the monarchy and the parlements. Calonne's successor Brienne tried in 1788 to persuade the provincial assemblies to accept new fiscal arrangements and disempower the parlements. Condorcet endorsed this initiative, which came to be known as the Brienne Coup. Condorcet worried that convening the Estates General would only exacerbate the problem of separate orders with separate interests, a situation inimical to finding and implementing policies calculated to advance the good of the nation as a whole. At this crucial juncture Condorcet wrote two pamphlets, *Lettres d'un citoyen des Etats-Unis à un français sur les affaires présentes* and *Sentiments d'un républicain sur les assemblées provinciales et les états généraux*, and a book, *Essai sur la constitution et les fonctions des assemblées provinciales*, all of which appeared in 1788.

Condorcet saw in the provincial assemblies the potential for developing, in time, the public's capacity for rational decision making in the public interest. He followed Turgot in preferring a suffrage limited to those with sufficient property to guarantee their subsistence. Only such men and women—Condorcet was an early advocate of limited woman suffrage—could resist corruption, an argument descending from familiar assumptions about self-sufficiency as a prerequisite to republican citizenship. Condorcet opposed the Estates General because he denied that the clergy and the nobility had special claims to rationality, the only relevant criterion for politics. Dividing the people into aristocrats, clerics, and everyone else would inevitably accentuate their differences, especially their inherited prejudices and distinctive perspectives. Those were precisely the differences that Condorcet hoped education would eventually eradicate.

As an alternative to the Estates General, Condorcet envisioned an elaborate system of assemblies ascending from the local to the district and the provincial and, finally, the national.[38] To prevent the emergence of particular interests, a special danger in a culture as divided into separate corporate bodies as France was, he specified that deliberation and administration must be kept separate from each other. Condorcet also proposed elaborate systems of voting designed to minimize the risk of irrationality and maximize the likelihood that reason would triumph. He outlined a scheme requiring increasing proportions of votes depending on the significance of the issue at stake or of the position for which a candidate was being chosen. The goal of these elaborate procedures, Condorcet emphasized, was not to conjure up Rousseau's general will, which he dismissed as a quasi-mystical something beyond the wills of particular individuals, but to achieve results consistent with "public reason." Mathematical calculations of probability took the place of deliberation as the best means to that end. What "should one be looking for?" Condorcet asked. Is the aim "the expression of the will of an assembly? No, without doubt; it is one that can be regarded as conforming with the truth, because it is that of the plurality of voters, who are assumed to pronounce in favor of truth rather than error."[39]

Ideally, Condorcet argued, assemblies need not even meet, since in such circumstances reason often yields to passion. If the choices—ideally simply "yes" or "no"—were properly framed, and offered to representatives in the correct sequence, rational decisions could be reached without assemblies needing to deliberate. If assemblies were to convene, Condorcet envisioned brief gatherings lasting no more than a single day, the better to prevent the emergence of factions or the dominance by charismatic individuals more intent on exercising power than on finding and following the dictates of public reason. Discussion could "create divisions" where none existed.[40] For precisely that reason Condorcet preferred indirect to direct democracy. He endorsed property qualifications as a precondition to voting, but even more important, from his perspective, was ensuring the greatest probability of outcomes he deemed "rational." When the Estates General were convened in 1789, the question of what form popular government would take in France diverged from Condorcet's probabilities toward multiple, less elegant, alternatives. His prerevolutionary writings, however, introduced into the political debates of the late 1780s a consideration carried over from many philosophes, a preoccupation with preventing irrational popular passions from swamping the exercise of dispassionate reason.[41]

Appeals to reason echoed in the political debates of 1788. Joining Condorcet, the darling of many self-styled forward-thinking aristocrats, was Abbé Emmanuel Joseph Sieyès, another champion of representation who was challenging the privileges of the nobility and the Church. Himself a cleric from Fréjus, in the South of France, and the son of a minor government official, Sieyès was educated in the rigorous seminary of St. Sulpice in Paris. Though he chose not to complete his training for ordination in the priesthood, Sieyès rose through the ranks of the Catholic Church to the position of vicar general in Chartres. Having immersed himself in the texts of the eighteenth-century French Enlightenment, particularly those of Montesquieu, Rousseau, Condillac, Quesnay, and the writings of Adam Smith, Sieyès in 1788 was bursting with ideas and indignation.

In three anonymous but widely discussed pamphlets—"Essay on Privileges," "Views of the Executive Means, Which Are at the Disposal of the Representatives of France in 1789," and "What Is the Third Estate?"—Sieyès challenged the central assumptions undergirding the Estates General. He also laid out an ambitious alternative framework for establishing legitimate state power. Rather than descending from divine mandate to the king, sovereign authority as Sieyès conceived of it came into being through the decisions made, and laws enacted, by representatives chosen by a greatly expanded electorate. Like Condorcet, Sieyès aimed to replace tradition with reason, but his concept of representation rested on an ambitious rethinking of the fundamental relation between representatives and those they represented.[42]

First circulating in manuscript and then published between November 1788 and May 1789, Sieyès's writings established him as the most widely read theorist of the first stage of the French Revolution. Sieyès offered a novel idea of representation. In all but the most primitive of human social relations, he argued, humans trade with one another, first through barter, then through some medium of exchange that ultimately evolves into money. Those trades enable individuals to meet their needs without having to provide everything they want by themselves. Neither the nation as a whole nor each citizen individually produces everything everyone needs, so "all the work undertaken in society is *representative*." Thus, Sieyès reasoned, representation is fundamental to the division of labor and to social life itself.[43] In the political domain, Sieyès argued that representation is equally valuable—and equally unproblematic. Representative government, rather than being second-best compared with direct democracy, instead simply transfers the elementary division of labor from the domains of social and economic life into the domain of public life. Just as individuals could acquire food or clothing by trading some goods for others, so they agreed to acquire peace and law by trading their consent for the service provided by their representatives. Representative government emerged as part of the natural transactions among individuals. As societies progressed, it became increasingly apparent that public service, like other kinds of work, should be carried out by professionals.[44]

The government empowered by that choice did not derive from individual decisions; nor did it result from a contract between the people and their government. Instead it embodied the fundamental, elemental will of the nation. Just as individuals developed particular skills in every other domain, so in mature nations the people selected the best-qualified individuals to perform the "public functions" of government. The notion of a purely democratic system of direct government, according to Sieyès, rested on "obscure and false" assumptions and led to a "chaos of contradictions."[45] Thus Sieyès substituted for older forms of social contract theory, and for the versions of resistance theory from which they descended, a conception of government that made the role of political representation central to human life but distinct from the representation characteristic of other forms of human interaction. Both forms involved a division of labor and an exchange, but whereas the exchange of goods and services satisfied the needs and desires of individuals, the exchange of consent for public order satisfied the needs and desires of the people as a whole. Only in the most primitive epoch did Sieyès envision individuals existing prior to society. As soon as they joined together, they wanted to accomplish a common purpose, and henceforth "power resides solely in the whole. A community has to have a common will. Without this *unity* of will, it would not be able to make itself a willing and acting whole." It was by conferring with each other that members of societies in this second epoch came to understand that common, united will. Finally, in the third epoch, as their numbers grew and they spread across the land, they agreed that government should be performed "by proxy," by representatives selected for that purpose. In that mature form, "the common will is exercised as a delegation or trust" rather than through direct participation.[46]

Sieyès conceived of two different kinds of decisions, those made in the socioeconomic sphere, in which material considerations predominate, and those made in the public sphere, in which the considerations are moral.[47] In the sphere of socioeconomic exchange, instrumental reasoning is appropriate. Individual relationships are functional; people strike bargains simply in order to acquire goods or services they want. The political sphere is different. There individuals should not serve as means to an end: the aim of all decision making, from the individual's vote to the legislative acts of the representatives meeting as a national assembly, is the common good.[48]

Sieyès began his "Views of the Executive Means," an essay written in 1788 and published as a pamphlet in 1789, with a formulation that echoed the celebrated opening of Rousseau's *Social Contract*: "We take it for a maxim that there are no slaves in France." Yet if all twenty-five million individuals are free, "how can it be conceivable that the nation is not?" If a citizen is "deprived of the right to consult his own interests, to deliberate, and to impose laws upon himself," then he is not free. The only legitimate source of legal obligation is will, and only free individuals, individuals not subject to domination, can "come to be united by a social engagement." Like Rousseau in the constitutions he wrote for Poland and Corsica, Sieyès embraced majority rule. He denied even the possibility of unanimity and explicitly rejected Rousseau's concept of the general will as Sieyès understood it from the *Social Contract*: "The common will cannot consist of anything other than the citizens' individual wills. It is this and this alone that entitles it to establish a genuinely binding obligation for all—and to make law for the whole community." If individuals disagree with the majority, they are free to leave. Otherwise they must obey.[49]

Sieyès acknowledged the misgivings that many people expressed about representatives. Some argued that all citizens must assemble to make laws.

The size of the French nation, Sieyès replied, made that impossible. Others argued that delegates must be bound by instructions. Sieyès rejected that option for the same reason the United States Congress rejected a proposed constitutional amendment authorizing constituents to issue binding instructions to congressmen: it would guarantee stalemate. The only solution, Sieyès insisted, lay in coming to a proper understanding of the meaning and purpose of representation. Although all individuals should be able to participate in electing their representatives—and Sieyès, like Condorcet, was among the few who favored woman suffrage—citizens must understand the obligation of their representatives: "What has to be kept as a maxim is the principle that each deputy represents the whole association," not just some part of it.[50] The task of writing a constitution should fall to a particular group of well-qualified representatives, but Sieyès, perhaps impressed by the model of the United States Constitutional Convention, considered it imperative that the individuals charged with producing that document must disband afterward.[51] That would be the challenge facing the Estates General, which would have to construct new institutional frameworks for legislation, administration, and the judiciary—and then dismiss itself.

Although his ideas about the role of an executive changed over time, Sieyès never ruled out the possibility that a monarch might also appoint members of the government, thereby further multiplying the officials charged with finding and acting on the will of the nation. Alongside all these, who were charged with deliberating and deciding on legislation and who might sit in two or even three different assemblies, Sieyès envisioned a body of administrators responsible for implementing the assemblies' decisions while remaining independent of them. He denied calling for the abolition of the clergy and the nobility; he wanted only to empower those excluded from power and privileges, the third estate.[52] When the Estates General had done its work and established a national assembly, Sieyès at this stage thought the parlements could return to their proper "judicial functions," operating "independent of all other authority." Such law courts would then be free "to adopt the principle of *judgment by one's peers*" and eventually to provide a new civil and criminal code. In place of the incoherent tangle of traditions constituting French law, Sieyès imagined a law code consistent with the dictates of reason rather than the whims of individual judges.[53]

To accomplish the ordinary work of governing, Sieyès had in mind an elaborate system of upward and downward elections. Local voters would elect representatives, from that body another tier of representatives would be selected, and finally a third set of representatives would constitute the national assembly. Those elected to the national assembly could serve only three years at a time because "every legislature has a continuous need to be refreshed by the democratic spirit." Legislators could not be reelected until three years had passed, then, after any subsequent term of service, only after six years. Sieyès was adamant that government service should be performed by the best-qualified individuals, not by ordinary citizens with only passing interest in affairs of state, because "it is up to the legislature to watch over the common needs of the society." Yet he insisted that as many people as possible should be involved in public affairs and warned against domination by a few families. Otherwise the general will might be "lost in harmful aristocratism."[54]

Writing in 1788, Sieyès was hardly sanguine about the challenges such a constitutional convention would face. "In France," he acknowledged, "faith in absolute authority is still the prevailing social belief." To ensure that the meetings of the national legislature would become as predictable as those of the English Parliament, Sieyès urged the Estates General to make the collection of taxes both the work of the various representative assemblies rather than the king's agents and contingent on the crown's continuing commitment to convening the assembly, thereby "riveting taxation to the constitution and the constitution to taxation." The French people were clamoring for a constitution to replace the prevailing "disorder" of French public life and finances. In place of the existing system, Sieyès concluded, France had to accept "the simple, natural, effective principle that the public treasury should be in the hands of those who pay and not at the disposal of those who spend." "Simple" and "natural" as that maxim seemed to Sieyès and other reformers, it represented nothing less than a revolution.[55]

In his "Essay on Privileges," written in 1788 and reprinted in 1789, Sieyès explained and excoriated extralegal and indefensible exceptions to "the law of the land" in France. With vitriol reminiscent of Rousseau's *Second Discourse*, Sieyès recounted the deformations of individual character and social interaction bred by privilege, "unjust, odious, and contrary to the supreme end of every political society." Inasmuch as individuals are awarded special favors, their minds are poisoned by the "true antisocial malady" that turns them against the common good and prompts them to focus exclusively on preserving their own status. Not only do the privileged consider themselves a different, more elevated order of human; they believe society *needs* them.

To the contrary, Sieyès thundered, all citizens should be equal before the law. The leeches who enjoy opulence while contributing nothing to the common weal suck the civic and economic blood from the nation. The lure of luxury and the charms of court life deformed individual sensibilities and distorted public and private spending without slaking aristocrats' insatiable thirst for distinction. Sieyès judged legitimate only the forms of inequality commensurate with wielding necessary public authority; all the others—military, religious, and civic—rested on an indefensible prejudice that he termed "the most pernicious that ever affected the earth."[56] Although there is no evidence that Sieyès either produced or consumed the scandalous underground literature that circulated in late-eighteenth-century France, his critique of the obscene excesses made possible by privilege drew fuel from, and contributed to, the growing sense of injustice that precipitated the impending explosion of French society.

The most familiar and influential of Sieyès's contributions to that explosion was the third of his early pamphlets, "What Is the Third Estate?" His revolutionary argument could not have been simpler: whereas the third estate had traditionally been excluded from all honors and deemed "nothing" in French public life, in fact it was "everything." Its members did all the productive work while receiving only the puniest of rewards. The clergy and the nobility, who savored drawing the finest of distinctions within their ranks, dismissed all members of the third estate as equally contemptible. Their monopoly on power excluded everyone else from decision making. "Until now, the third estate has never had genuine representatives in the Estates General. Thus its political rights are null." In the months leading up to the convening of the Estates General, reform-minded members of the nobility of the robe argued that because the older nobility of the sword dismissed them as parvenus, they should instead represent the third estate themselves. Sieyès replied that their appetites for hierarchy prevented them from speaking for those from whom they were eager to distance themselves. Only members of the third estate should represent the nation.

Because the third estate vastly outnumbered the first and second estates by twenty-five million to two hundred thousand—at least by Sieyès's estimate in "What Is the Third Estate?"—it would be a travesty if votes from each estate were counted equally. Only if the number of representatives of the third estate equaled those of the other two estates added together, only if the third estate met independently, and only if voting were done by head count rather than by estate would the results be legitimate.[57] Against the charge that members of the third estate lacked the requisite ability to participate in public life, Sieyès replied that, unlike the clergy and the nobility, "these classes have no other interest than that of the rest of the people." Within their ranks were plenty of "educated and honorable citizens"—such as Sieyès himself, perhaps—"all eminently well-qualified to be good representatives of the Nation."[58] Finally, Sieyès demanded that the tax burden be shifted away from those who lacked resources toward those who enjoyed, as a result of their illegitimate privileges, all the benefits of France's vast productivity and thus had the ability to pay the expenses necessary for public life.

Despite the strident tone of his attacks, Sieyès denied that he sought to abolish the French monarchy or the nation's distinct social orders. He understood that venerable and widely accepted traditions undergirded such distinctions. He merely wanted to see the legal, political, and economic privileges attached to such roles severely curtailed. He was not opposed to inequality or hierarchy per se. He denied wanting to limit individuals' ability to enrich themselves, whether their wealth resulted from their talents, their efforts, or simple good luck. Nor did he characterize his scheme of representative government as "democracy," a term he associated, as did most other mainstream eighteenth-century French political writers, with chaotic direct rule rather than sensible, indirect, representative government by those best qualified to exercise power. Only if individuals were prepared to submit their interests as individuals and members of factions to the considered judgments reached by such officials could popular government succeed. "Democracy," as he put it, "is the complete sacrifice of the individual to the common good, that is, the submission of the tangible person to the abstract person." Earlier efforts had foundered on the failure of just that submission, and the problem facing France was to find a way around it.[59]

Sieyès offered an account of self-interest in relation to the common good that paralleled some of Madison's central arguments.[60] There are three kinds of interest, Sieyès contended: the common interest, the interest of some individuals forming themselves into a divisive faction, and the self-interest of particular individuals. The latter is "not to be feared," Sieyès wrote, because it is "isolated" and particular to each person. "Its very variety is its own solution." Factions, however, generate "projects that are a danger to the community." For that reason, as history shows, factions must be prevented from forming or eradicated if found to exist. Given that self-interest makes the formation of factions likely, it would be dangerous—"a grave misjudgment of human nature"—to trust the fate of society, as classical republicans had done, to civic virtue alone. Success lay instead in a properly ordered state, in which "individual interests remain isolated and the will of the majority cleaves consistently to the public good even during those long periods when public manners are in a state of decadence and egoism seems to be the universal rule." The similarity to Madison's formulation is uncanny. The national assembly must consist of representatives of all the people, not of distinct social orders: "The right to be *represented* belongs to citizens only in respect to what they have in common and not to what serves to differentiate them."[61] In a widely quoted passage, Sieyès asked, "Who then would dare to say that the third estate does not, within itself, contain everything needed to form a complete nation?" The third estate "resembles a strong, robust man with one arm in chains," and without the privileged orders, this "everything" would be "free and flourishing."[62] Sieyès shared the interest of Condorcet and other philosophes in diminishing the role of tradition in French government and accentuating the role of reason. His idea of organizing France into departments, among the most enduring ideas articulated in his early writings, signals that aim.[63] Fundamentally, he envisioned rational organization supplanting outdated traditions and aimed to replace the other staple of the *ancien régime*, inherited privilege, with merit.

A third feature of his writing aligned Sieyès with another figure, prominent in the early phase of the Revolution, who later dominated its most tumultuous phase, Maximilien Robespierre. Sieyès and Robespierre shared a quality that many of their contemporaries admired, a quality often held up as praiseworthy by those interested in politics: intransigence. Although Sieyès spoke glowingly about the value of deliberation and over time showed far greater flexibility than did Robespierre, he frequently spewed venom when referring to his opponents. He had provided, he wrote, "sufficient proof of the fact that any privilege is by nature unjust, odious, and contrary to the social pact." Although he conceded that some readers might find his arguments unpersuasive, he was confident the French people would come around: "Public opinion will take shape and principles that were at first taken to be wildly illusory will finally come to be felt entirely practicable." It was not his job, as "a philosopher whose ardor is excited yet further at the sight of every difficulty," to moderate his message. The privileged class, he concluded, was "a pestilence" upon any nation forced to endure it, "a frightful disease devouring the living flesh of the body of its unhappy victim."[64] One does not compromise with such a disease. One expunges it or dies from it.

That stark choice, the choice between life and death, became the signature challenge posed by Robespierre, the most iconic figure of the French Revolution. Known from boyhood for his determination and his exemplary character, Robespierre arrived in Versailles in 1789 as an ambitious, fastidious, and only modestly successful attorney. Elected to the Estates General from his hometown of Arras after giving speeches and writing pamphlets and compiling lists of grievances sizzling with indignation, Robespierre from the start of his public career presented himself as the scourge of the dissolute rich and the champion of the virtuous poor. In a pamphlet entitled "Enemies of the People Unmasked," he announced his signature themes in typically florid language. He called on God to "inspire in all citizens the spirit of righteousness, truth, courage, and disinterestedness, the celestial love of humanity, and that healthy passion for the public good on which depend the happiness of the people."[65] Within a year Robespierre was receiving fan mail from admirers, including one letter that characterized him with the sobriquet "the incorruptible," a term that captured not only his self-image but also the reputation he cultivated.

Like Sieyès, Robespierre emerged from a conventional provincial background when the chaos of 1789 opened the door to previously obscure individuals with a flair for political debate. Contemporaries unanimously agreed that Robespierre was unique: his perfectly powdered wig and perfectly tailored waistcoat masked a passionate conviction about the injustice of privilege and the need to destroy it. Like Madison, Robespierre stood just over five feet tall and spoke with a reedy, shrill voice. It was not his physical presence but the intensity of his convictions that explained his forcefulness. Later interpreters of the French Revolution, from Thomas Carlyle and Jules Michelet to Max Weber, and from Jean Jaurès and Albert Mathiez to François Furet, have seen Robespierre as his contemporaries saw him in the early years of the Revolution—as the embodiment of revolutionary virtue. No one is neutral about Robespierre: he represents either the indomitable, uncompromising spirit of democratic revolution or the fatal betrayal of democracy by a despot who mistook his own willfulness for the will of the people. Educated to admire the Roman republican ideal of self-sacrifice and frustrated by the constricted opportunities open to him at home, in Versailles Robespierre seized the chance to adapt that classical ethos to the needs of eighteenth-century France as he perceived them. His selflessness and charisma were so apparent, to friends and foes alike, that for five years Robespierre managed to exert an influence far beyond his official power.

Robespierre rose rapidly. By March of 1790 he had parlayed his participation in the debates of the Constituent Assembly into the presidency of the Society of Jacobins, a political organization formed in late 1789 and nicknamed for the former Dominican monks' residence in the rue St. Jacques where the Jacobins met. From that perch Robespierre enjoyed a degree of authority—perhaps even more powerful because its source remained so mysterious—over the tone, volume, and tempo of revolutionary public opinion. Although he held only one official post, when he was elected to the Committee on Public Safety in July of 1793, he was nevertheless acknowledged as the personification of the revolutionary spirit, the one person who would never confuse his individual interest with the fate of the Revolution.[66]

When the Estates General opened on May 5, 1789, representatives elected by the three orders had very different agendas and expectations. In towns ranging from Aix-en-Provence and Marseilles in the south to Rennes in the north, the war of words was already becoming an armed struggle. Some mobs protested food prices and taxes, others forced notables to fight their way from their meeting rooms. Most of the clerics elected from the first estate were parish priests who shared the poverty and the worldview of the French peasants in their congregations; fewer than one-fifth were bishops seeking to protect the privileges and wealth of the church hierarchy. Plenty of reform-minded clerics instead sided with Sieyès, who stood for election by the third rather than the first estate. When the decisive moment came, many of these clerics would abandon their separate sphere, join with the third estate, and spark the Revolution. The second estate was equally divided. Some wealthy scions of France's oldest families resented even having to consort with commoners. Others had been aware of, or meeting with, philosophes such as Condorcet, himself of noble birth, in Parisian and provincial salons to discuss the prospects for rational reform. Others saw a chance to rein in the king without knowing how to do it. A few, including the comte de Mirabeau, knew from experience the exclusion and resentment fueling the anger of ordinary people, although none of them expressed it as effectively as Mirabeau did.[67]

Previously unknown figures from the provinces, such as Robespierre, dominated the third estate. Most of them were either attorneys or magistrates, and they stitched together political arguments drawing on sources that ranged from Polybius and Cicero to Montesquieu and Rousseau. Most critics in early 1789, including Sieyès, Condorcet, Mirabeau, and Robespierre, envisioned a reformed monarchy. Although many imagined a regime in which the public would participate by electing representatives, only a few republicans, such as the refugees from Geneva, Brissot and Clavière, dared to think about a France in which popular sovereignty would be more than merely a slogan. Delegates of the three estates had little in common, but they all shared one quality that proved decisive: a lack of experience in political deliberations.[68]

When the Estates General opened in the spring of 1789, no one imagined that France stood teetering on revolution. The decision to reproduce the pomp and the ceremonies of the last meeting in 1614 enabled the king, the wealthiest members of the nobility, and the church hierarchy to flaunt their grandeur. The protocols for opening the Estates General either deliberately or inadvertently provided multiple occasions for the king and the nobility to demonstrate the gulf separating them from the representatives of the third estate, thereby intensifying both the elite's feelings of superiority and the resentments of those "beneath" them.[69]

The complexity of the process whereby delegates were chosen for the Estates General mirrors the complexity of French society and the variety of local and regional traditions. France lacked a uniform political structure. In some provinces assemblies had been established in 1778, and election of delegates by property holders rather than selection by estates had been tried. In other regions the parlements vied for control with elected bodies meeting in three different chambers, according to estate. In each of the 234 constituencies of France, at least in principle, all clergy outside monasteries and all nobles could vote. All adult male taxpayers could attend a local assembly to choose those who would elect the representatives of the third estate. Such procedures perpetuated the customary exclusion of wage laborers and the effective overrepresentation of the bourgeoisie over peasants and artisans. They also reflected and registered the traditional assumption that choices were to be made by consensus rather than by individual ballot. Those recording the votes often indicated not who voted for whom but merely how many people were present and which delegates were chosen. Voters did not elect "candidates" who were "running for office" on a "platform." Instead the results reflected the status of individuals, families, and groups, existing patterns of affiliation, and long-standing rivalries.[70]

In all the elections from 1789 through the advent of Napoleon, turnout varied wildly, ranging from less than 5 percent to well over 50 percent. In 1789 villages, guilds, and corporations were permitted to submit *cahiers de doléances*, or lists of grievances, as they did customarily. Representatives elected that year, however, unlike earlier delegates who had been bound by the mandates of those who elected them, were not restricted by such directives. Instead they were declared free to deliberate, at least in principle, in order to determine the general will on their own, just as Sieyès had insisted they must be. Given the great diversity of procedures as well as the diversity of the French people who chose their representatives, the consequences of the meeting of the Estates General in 1789 were impossible to predict.[71]

Early in June the third estate rejected the customary division into separate estates and declared itself the Commons. Although that step outraged many clerics and aristocrats, few thought the monarchy was at risk. Sieyès had placed a "grand elector" at the pinnacle of his scheme of elected officials; it was hard to imagine doing without the functional equivalent of a king. But a dramatically new way of thinking was about to emerge. Drawing on the arguments he had advanced in his earlier pamphlets, Sieyès announced in a speech on June 10 that the time had come for representatives "to begin finally to concern themselves with the national interest, which alone, and to the exclusion of particular interests, appears as the great goal toward which all deputies must strive through common effort."[72]

The days of identifying with separate estates, regions, or interests were over. Now the representatives had a new duty: on June 15, Sieyès made explicit his debt to Rousseau. Forming themselves into a "national voice," those gathering in Versailles now faced the challenge of "interpreting and presenting the general will of the nation."[73] According to Sieyès, the Americans had erred by continuing to think in terms of a contract between the people and their government. It was Sieyès, though, who was in error. Although some Americans still thought in those terms, Adams and many state constitution writers, followed by Madison, Wilson, and many of their Federalist allies, had quite explicitly rejected that earlier conception and embraced Rousseau's idea of a people contracting with themselves to form a government. That was the conceptual revolution beneath the phrase "we the people." According to Sieyès, France would need to acknowledge that "there is only *one* power, only *one* authority," that of the sovereign people, which was precisely the idea embodied in the United States Constitution. The mesmerizing force of the idea of the general will grew throughout the years from 1789 through 1800, when multiple editions of Rousseau's *Social Contract* mushroomed in France and throughout Europe and the United States.[74]

The first crisis, sparked by the third estate's defiance, appeared to be resolved on June 27 when Louis XVI finally invited the first and second estates to join what had been proclaimed ten days earlier the National Assembly. Yet the concessions offered by the king were abruptly dismissed as inadequate. A new dynamic was emerging. Because the meetings of the National Assembly in Versailles were held in public, unlike the closed Constitutional Convention that met in Philadelphia, speakers such as Mirabeau, who could entertain and satisfy a popular audience, possessed a distinct advantage. The more compelling the speaker and the more strident his tone, the likelier he was to earn the crowd's approval.

In Paris, too, tensions were rising. Crowds in the thousands met daily in the Palais Royal. Rumors flew about bread prices increasing and profits soaring. Inflammatory speeches heightened emotions. Jacques Necker, a Swiss banking wizard charged by Louis XVI with the task of healing the crown's financial miseries, had become a favorite of the Parisian crowd. Necker preferred borrowing to taxing, for one thing, and the procedures he established for electing representatives from Paris to the third estate widened the suffrage dramatically. By late June, Parisians were growing increasingly wary. The king was rumored to be gathering an army of mercenaries to quell any unrest in the capital, and when the crowd learned that he had sacked their favorite, Necker, their anxieties boiled over. A crowd of around nine hundred, seeking gunpowder for a new militia established to defend Paris from an anticipated attack by the king's army, approached the Bastille, a notorious prison now all but evacuated and only lightly defended. They stormed the fortress, suffering nearly one hundred casualties, and released the handful of prisoners they found. After marching the soldiers to the city hall, the crowd killed two of the officers in charge, mounted their severed heads on pikes, and paraded through Paris for a day before dumping their bloody prizes in the Seine. Nine days later, the crowd carried the mutilated bodies of two more government officials in a similar triumphal procession.[75]

Robespierre described the events dispassionately. Necker's replacement, Joseph-François Foulon, whom many blamed for the famine in France, "was hanged yesterday by the people's decree." Not the mob but the king's decision to muster the army, from Robespierre's perspective, had sparked the violence. "The terror inspired by this national army, ready to present itself in Versailles, determined the Revolution." Events were unfolding rapidly; justice was being done. "The present revolution," Robespierre wrote with typical understatement, "has produced greater events in a few days than the whole previous history of mankind." Within days the taking of the Bastille had been sanctified as the first act of a now sovereign people. Louis XVI announced on July 15 that he was withdrawing the army. The king's brother, the comte d'Artois, decided that it was time to leave France.[76]

Artois's worries were widely shared. The wealthy American Gouverneur Morris, principal author of the Preamble to the United States Constitution, had arrived in Paris from Philadelphia in the winter of 1789 and taken up residence in a hotel near the Palais Royal. Aided by Jefferson, the American minister plenipotentiary, Morris quickly made his way into the upper reaches of French society.[77] Despite having participated actively and prominently in the United States Constitutional Convention, the wealthy Morris confidently advised his French friends that they should preserve their separate social orders and create an institutional home for the nobility, a chamber roughly akin to the British House of Lords or—at least as Morris now envisioned it—the United States Senate. By carefully moderating their positions and compromising with the increasingly radical rabble, Morris reassured his new friends, the French nobility could survive the crisis. Events in the middle of July, however, changed Morris's mind. Walking in the Palais Royal, he saw the body of Foulon being dragged toward the home of his son-in-law Bertier de Sauvigny, who was likewise, in Morris's words, "put to Death and cut to Pieces, the Populace carrying about the mangled Fragments with a Savage Joy." From that moment, Morris reported, he was eager to return home to Philadelphia. He conveyed his shock to Jefferson, who never personally witnessed such violence and who persisted in thinking, as he had explained to Madison during Shays's Rebellion, that such upheavals signaled a healthy democratic spirit.[78]

Jefferson, of course, was better acquainted with Parisian high society than was Morris. Although Jefferson (like every other American) lacked Franklin's wit and easy sociability, his authorship of the Declaration of Independence and *Notes on the State of Virginia* and his admiration for the *lumières* established his stature in France. Initially he counseled his French friends, including Condorcet and Lafayette, to moderate their reformist schemes. By March of 1789, however, he was more optimistic: a "complete revolution in this government," a revolution accomplished by a change in "public opinion," had made possible a much more dramatic transformation. In a detailed letter to John Jay dated May 9, 1789, he narrated the early stages of the Revolution.[79]

A month later Jefferson outlined an ambitious plan for a Charter of Rights. He claimed, in a letter to Jean-Paul Rabaut Saint-Etienne, to have concocted the scheme in a late-night conversation with Lafayette and Jefferson's aide William Short. After a ritual denial—"I know too little of the subject, & you know too much of it to justify me in offering anything but a hint"—he laid out a detailed ten-point charter to be submitted to the king for his signature. Proposing the plan was audacious; the ideas themselves seem sensible given where things stood at the time. Jefferson (and Lafayette, if Jefferson is to be believed) recommended that the Estates General should meet annually in November, should regulate their own elections and procedures, and should be responsible for levying taxes and making laws—with the king's consent, of course. The rule of law should govern all arrests and imprisonments. All prisoners should have the right to appeal to an impartial judge. The military should be subordinate to civil authority. The press should be free of all restraints except the publication of falsehoods. All persons should be subject to taxation, all debts contracted by the king should be paid by the nation, and the king should be loaned enough money to tide him over until the new tax system was put in place. Finally, the Estates General should now disband and reconvene when scheduled in November.[80]

If the violence of mid-July did not dampen Jefferson's enthusiasm, developments in the following weeks left him enthralled. On August 3 he rhapsodized in a letter that the French "nation has made a total resumption of rights, which they had certainly never before ventured even to think of. The National Assembly now have as clean a canvas to work on here as we had in America." That judgment, which at first seems misguided, appears less naive if one sees that in neither nation was the canvas clean. Instead layers of experience prepared the surface for what was to come. It was not yet clear, Jefferson admitted, whether there would be one legislative assembly or two, or what sort of veto the king would hold, but his faith overcame his doubts. "I have so much confidence in the good sense of man, and his qualifications for self-government, that I am never afraid of the issue where reason is left free to exert her force." As if that forecast were not bold enough, Jefferson continued,

"I will agree to be stoned as a false prophet if all does not end well in this country." From the failure of the Dutch Revolution of 1787 Jefferson had drawn the lesson that even a disgruntled nobility might ally with the monarch if reformers pushed too hard. Yet he believed that the National Assembly would heed that warning and successfully carry things to completion. In his words, the ongoing French Revolution was "but the first chapter of the history of European liberty."[81]

Not everyone shared Jefferson's confidence. Alliances formed and dissolved; issues came into focus and vanished without trace or resolution. As the representatives wrangled through July and into August, conditions in France deteriorated. Incidents of looting, pillage, and general lawlessness multiplied, feeding worries of even greater violence to come. These heightened anxieties culminated in *La Grande Peur,* the Great Fear. Interpreted as originating (at the time and since) either as an urban panic sparked by suspicions of the provincial aristocracy, or a rural panic that gripped peasants and their lords anxious about shadowy brigands said to threaten the harvest, the Great Fear raced across France as uncertainties mounted. Even so, no one anticipated the next step.[82]

On the night of August 4, the Assembly dismantled the feudal traditions that had governed France for centuries. In a lightly attended session from which many prominent delegates, including both Mirabeau and Sieyès, were absent, two nobles introduced measures intended to abolish serfdom that elicited unexpected enthusiasm. A frenzy of denunciation and dispossession followed. By morning the entire elaborate network of laws and informal practices enjoyed by the privileged few and resented by almost everyone else in France had collapsed. No more buying or selling or inheriting of offices. No more exemptions from taxation, or from the law, which would now apply to every citizen of France without exception. Subsequently, and after much debate, properties owned by the nobility and the Church were confiscated and sold. Hunting rights, manorial income, dues, tolls, tithes, and special standing for some cities or regions came to an end.

The nobility and the clergy had long clung to all those privileges and had denounced attempts to modify them even slightly. Now, in an apparent orgy of selflessness, nobles, priests, and commoners voluntarily surrendered their inheritance. Although it took a week to sort out the details, the decrees of August 4–11 stand among the few enduring achievements of the French Revolution. In place of the traditional corporate structures that had ordered life in France, the National Assembly instituted a new regime consisting of individual citizens, equal before the law, unprecedentedly free to compete in the marketplace and in public life.

Only a day after Jefferson had expressed his confidence that things in France would "end well," the National Assembly had taken a step even more dramatic than he had imagined possible. After August 4, France was working on a canvas not just as clean as but instead far cleaner than those on which Americans sketched the frameworks for their governments. Whereas the former British colonies could and did make use of a century and a half of experience at the local and colony-wide level, and quite consciously and deliberately drew on that experience when designing the United States Constitution, the French attempted to erase their traditions so they could start from scratch. The work of August 4–11 represents the most dramatic departure in French history.[83] Two of Mirabeau's quips captured the significance of August 4: after three months of "disputing over syllables," Mirabeau observed, the Assembly "in a single night overturned the whole venerable edifice of the monarchy." To the complaint later registered by Sieyès, who, like most churchmen and (at least as indicated by the *cahiers de doléances*) most ordinary Frenchmen, had sought more income for parish priests rather than the end of tithing, Mirabeau replied, "My dear Abbé, you have let loose the bull, and now you complain that he gores you."[84]

During these heady weeks, Jefferson was invited to share his ideas with the committee charged with writing a new constitution for France. Although he declined official involvement, he nevertheless collaborated with Lafayette on a draft, and just before he left for Virginia in September, Jefferson hosted a dinner with some of those involved. Included were the moderate Jean-Joseph Mounier, who favored an absolute royal veto, and Antoine-Pierre Barnave, who preferred giving the monarch only the power to delay legislation, which was called a suspensive veto. The discussions over dinner convinced Jefferson that reason was indeed emerging triumphant. He came away impressed by his guests' "coolness and candor of argument unusual in the conflicts of political opinion." They displayed a commitment to "logical reasoning, and chaste eloquence, disfigured by no gaudy tinsel of rhetoric or declamation, and truly worthy of being placed in parallel with the finest dialogue of antiquity." He neglected to note that Mounier and Barnave left the dinner as they arrived, in unyielding disagreement, and that the National Assembly continued to quarrel over issues ranging from the nature of the royal veto to the future of monarchical government in France. The refusal to compromise on issues large and small, in many instances petty stubbornness dressed up as a commitment to lofty principles, was hardly limited to Robespierre.[85]

The Declaration of the Rights of Man and of the Citizen, a document intended as a prologue to a constitution and adopted on August 26, 1789, signaled the victory of the principle of popular sovereignty that Sieyès and others had advanced in the preceding year. It indicated just as clearly the depth of the problems that had not yet been resolved. The National Assembly had renamed itself the Constituent Assembly precisely because its members understood that producing a constitution was their principal responsibility. They failed to achieve that goal precisely because the vaunted unanimity of purpose and shared understanding, which partisans of the Revolution later claimed to have been present in its early stages, was never complete. Profound differences—or at least ambiguities—remained concerning the source, the exercise, and the limits of the nation's power.

Various proposals for a declaration of rights surfaced throughout July. Prominent among those submitting and debating these ideas were several figures popularly associated with the United States, including not only Lafayette but also another veteran of the American War for Independence, Comte Mathieu de Montmorency; Condorcet, the author of *De l'influence de la révolution de l'Amérique sur l'opinion et la législation de l'Europe*; and the duc de La Rochefoucauld d'Enville, who had translated the thirteen state constitutions into French. The version of the Declaration of the Rights of Man and of the Citizen adopted on August 26 was the work of many hands. It mirrored many of the ideas endorsed by the Assembly between August 4 and August 11 and some that Jefferson had proposed to Rabaut Saint-Etienne. It also reflected many of the ideas articulated in the declarations of rights that had preceded the American state constitutions, and some of those that Americans were appending to the recently ratified United States Constitution.

The prologue of the Declaration immediately exposed one striking difference of emphasis from the Anglo-American tradition: in addition to proclaiming "the natural, inalienable, and sacred rights" of "all members of the social body," the Declaration also reminded "all members of the social body of their rights and duties."[86] Whereas the idea of an obligation to the common good was implied in most of the American state constitutions, with particular clarity in that of Massachusetts drafted by John Adams, and was understood by most Americans as implied in the phrase "promote the general welfare" in the United States Constitution, the yoking of rights and duties was made more explicit in the French Declaration than it was in Britain or America. Although some members of the Assembly argued for incorporating an even more robust conception of duty to balance the bold assertions of individual rights, the reference provided an opening wedge for the more vigorous assertion of duties that was to come.

The first articles of the Declaration addressed the question of rights explicitly, proclaiming that all men are "born and remain free and equal in rights. Social distinctions," heretofore rooted in traditional privileges, "can be based only on public utility." Political associations exist to preserve "the natural and imprescriptible rights of man," namely "liberty, property, security, and resistance to oppression." Liberty means "being able to do anything that does not injure another," and no one can be "accused, arrested, or detained"—or punished—except in accordance with law. Nailing down the end of feudal privileges, article 6 of the Declaration specified that all citizens "are equally admissible to all public dignities, places, and employments, according to their ability, and on the basis of no other distinction than that of their virtues and talents." The Declaration secured both freedom of expression in speech, writing, and print, and freedom of opinion "even in religious matters, provided their expression does not trouble the public order established by law," a provision that soon enough proved open to multiple interpretations. Taxation, to be determined by "all citizens" or "their representatives," was to be "shared equally among all the citizens," no longer according to their privileges, as in the *ancien régime*, but "according to their means," a phrase originating in *La code de la nature* (1755), attributed to the utopian writer Etienne-Gabriel Morelly, and echoed by many later socialists, including Charles Fourier and Karl Marx. This dramatic reversal of French practice cemented the decree of August 11 and specified at least one of the duties proclaimed in the prologue.

Numerous delegates raised the question of embedding the individual's rights in a web of social bonds. Sieyès urged the adoption of more robust language concerning the state's obligations, not only for "a good system of education" but also for economic aid: "One knows that those citizens whom misfortune has rendered unable to meet their own needs have a just right to assistance from their fellow citizens."[87] Such calls for a commitment to social assistance failed to survive in the final document. Instead, the Declaration proclaimed only that public officials held power "for the benefit of all and not for the personal advantage of those to whom it is entrusted." All public officials were to be accountable for upholding the law. In its final article, the Declaration addressed the issue on everyone's mind, in light of the demolition of feudalism and mounting uncertainties concerning the disposal of property formerly owned by members of the first and second estates: "Property being an inviolable and sacred right, no one can be deprived of it, unless legally established public necessity obviously demands it, and upon condition of a just and prior indemnity." Given how much was at stake, the guarantee of compensation was a matter of profound significance for clerics, nobles, and commoners alike, but a gap had already begun to open between that promise of indemnification and the reality of confiscation.

The central problem in the Declaration, however, did not have to do with rights, which certainly received adequate attention, or the duties of citizens or officials. Instead it had to do with resolving an apparent contradiction—or was it merely a paradox?—between articles 3, 6, and 16. According to article 3, "The source of all sovereignty resides essentially in the nation. No body, no individual can exercise authority that does not explicitly proceed from it." That straightforward proclamation of popular sovereignty appears to have descended to the Assembly from Rousseau via Sieyès. Taken by itself, its meaning seems unproblematic. The final version, though, masks the debate that preceded its adoption and the misgivings that persisted afterward. Locating the *source* of sovereignty in the nation left open the possibility that the *exercise* of sovereignty should be located elsewhere: in the monarch and his officials, perhaps, or in the representatives elected to the National Assembly. This vague language was preferred by moderates such as Mounier and resisted by the more radical delegates.

Article 6 called to mind Rousseau: "Law is the expression of the general will. All citizens have the right to take part personally, or through their representatives, in its formation." Here was the rub. The reference to the "general will" unambiguously echoed Rousseau's *Social Contract*. But what about Rousseau's critique of representation in that work, in which he characterized it as an inadequate method of identifying the general will, and what about Sieyès's critique of Rousseau? All citizens were declared eligible to compete for public offices "according to their capacities, and without any other distinction than that of their virtues and talents." That formulation left an urgent question unanswered: Were such virtuous and talented representatives obliged to do the will of their constituencies, or were representatives expected instead, as Sieyès urged and the Constituent Assembly itself explicitly endorsed, to be bound only by their understanding of the requirements of the general will? In that case, representatives were empowered to determine, through reasoned deliberation, the course of action that best conformed to the public good whether or not it conformed to the stated preferences of the electorate.

Sieyès offered the Constituent Assembly a spirited version of the argument he had earlier laid out in his pamphlets: "When a meeting is held, it is for the purpose of deliberation, of finding out other people's opinions, of taking advantage of their complementary enlightenment, of contrasting particular wills, of modifying them, of reconciling them, and finally of obtaining a decision supported by a plurality." It was clear, he continued, that deputies in the National Assembly were not merely to announce the "already formed will of their direct constituents" but instead to "deliberate and vote freely" in accordance with the positions they reached "by such enlightenment as the Assembly may bring to each of its members." The striking resemblance between Sieyès's reasoning and that of Madison for the creative role of deliberation in assemblies suggests that the contrast scholars usually draw between those who framed the United States Constitution and those who made the French Revolution is, in the case of Sieyès and Madison at least, overstated. Members of the Assembly were indeed freed from the obligation to vote in accordance with the mandates submitted by their constituents.[88] By charging the Assembly with identifying the general will, the Declaration raised but did not answer the questions Rousseau himself had posed: If there is a difference between the general will and the will of all, who can discern the difference? How can that problem be solved? Here the disagreement between Condorcet and Sieyès became crucial. Whereas Condorcet trusted reason and feared the distortions of rhetoric and emotion inevitable in debate, Sieyès denied the possibility, even in principle, of a general will existing independent of the wills of the actual individuals engaged in just such debates. Condorcet believed that reason yields truth. Sieyès thought provisional agreements would have to be hammered out through deliberation.

Finally, according to article 16, "A society in which the guarantee of rights is not secured, or the separation of powers not clearly established, has no constitution."[89] The Declaration had stipulated repeatedly the rights to be guaranteed, but the questions of how these rights were to be secured, and by what institutions, remained unclear. Even more ominously, the precise nature of the separation of powers, the issue to which the framers of the United States Constitution had devoted so much attention, was not resolved; in fact, it was not even addressed. Sieyès had warned against following the Americans' example and focusing obsessively on the separation of powers because he, like almost all of his contemporaries in France, continued to be haunted by the idea of unitary authority.

The challenges facing France differed from those of the United States because France first had to destroy before it could create. In striking contrast to debates in America, where the words "republic" and "democracy" had both been used for well over a century to designate nonmonarchical government, in France "democracy" continued to be used as an epithet. Brissot complained in 1789 that "the word 'democracy' is a scarecrow that the mischievous are using to fool the ignorant."[90] Americans from Roger Williams and Thomas Hooker to John Adams and James Madison had described American practices of government as "democratic." In France, by contrast, the word "democracy" was so closely linked with anarchy, violence, and civil war—the inevitable consequences of direct popular involvement from the ancient world through the sixteenth-century wars of religion—that it did not even appear in debates about suffrage throughout the era of the French Revolution.

Whatever changes lay in store for France, even those calling for popular sovereignty and representative government tended to distinguish their ideas from the divisiveness associated with democracy. In a democracy, according to Sieyès, "the citizens themselves make the laws," whereas he envisioned citizens electing "deputies to the legislative assembly." Thus "lawmaking ceases to be democratic, and becomes representative." In France, Sieyès insisted, there must be "only *one* power, only *one* authority," and for that reason rule by the multitude, or democracy as the Greeks and Romans knew it, was out of the question.[91] Given the need to begin anew, specifying the precise relation between the monarch and the legislature, to say nothing of the relation between the existing parlements and a new judiciary, threatened a return to the rancor of ancient democracy.

Debates over these issues continued in September, after the Declaration of the Rights of Man and of the Citizen was adopted. At that point the contending theories of sovereignty and governance descended from the realm of abstraction and came into focus over the royal veto. The king's authority remained unquestioned, but the ground was beginning to shift. Sieyès and Robespierre were both prominent among those who challenged the idea, which Mounier had defended at Jefferson's dinner, that the king should retain an absolute veto over the decisions of the National Assembly. Moderates worried that limiting the king's prerogatives would make him the servant of the legislative assembly, thereby transforming France from a monarchy into a republic, a step neither in their power nor consistent with the will of the French people as they perceived it. At the opposite end of the spectrum were those such as Abbé Grégoire and Rabaut Saint-Etienne, radical critics of monarchy passionately committed to just such a dramatic departure from tradition. From their perspective, not only were the people the source of sovereignty; they should exercise sovereignty in a unitary assembly expressing the unitary general will.

Sieyès, who remained consistent in opposing both of these views and arguing for the autonomy of the deliberations of the elected legislature, nevertheless opposed even a suspensive veto. Although he believed the king could retain his position, his will should not be allowed, even for a limited time, to trump that of the people, forged in the debates of the legislative assembly. Whereas the monarch is "hereditary [and] permanent," and constitutes "a separate interest," Sieyès contended, the "legislative body is elected, numerous," and "interested in the good." From his perspective sovereign authority, assumed at least since Bossuet and Louis XIV to reside solely in the king, was to be relocated in the French people and exercised by the National Assembly.[92] As late as September of 1789, Robespierre still distanced himself from radical republican ideas and aligned himself with Sieyès, whose reasoning he endorsed in a speech before the National Assembly that was immediately printed as a pamphlet. Since a large nation cannot govern directly, Robespierre pointed out, echoing Sieyès and challenging Grégoire and the radicals, it elects representatives, and the "will of these representatives must be regarded and respected as the will of the nation." This collective will possesses "sacred authority, superior to any particular will." For that reason, Robespierre characterized the idea of an absolute royal veto as an ominous threat that had to be rejected in order for the sovereign authority of the National Assembly to be affirmed.[93]

Thus, only months after the fall of the Bastille, both Sieyès and Robespierre were already thinking of a united national will, something akin to their understandings of Rousseau's general will. Neither of them, however, was ready to challenge the idea of the monarchy. Whereas some historians have claimed that references to a fictive "people" or "nation" were imaginary creations of the Revolution, the evidence indicates that the idea of the people as a sovereign body possessing a single will was not produced by the Revolution but existed before it began and persisted throughout its course. Commentators who deny the possibility of a general will often take for granted the priority of individual interest and hence the artificiality of the concept of the common good. Sieyès, Robespierre, and many other partisans of the French Revolution—like Rousseau, Adams, Madison, and Wilson before them—challenged precisely that claim.

By the time the Estates General was transformed into the National Assembly, and then the Constituent Assembly, some champions of popular sovereignty such as Sieyès and Robespierre were making arguments very similar to those made by Madison in the *Federalist* concerning the goal of popular government and the means by which it could be achieved. Instead of representing the particular privileges, preferences, or aspirations of their own narrow constituencies, which the Estates General had been thought able to do only in the presence of the monarch, representatives elected to the Assembly were now obliged to identify policies in the general interest of the entire French nation, which was as badly divided as were the delegates to the Estates General. Initially Sieyès and Robespierre agreed that a representative assembly could meet that objective. When critics insisted that only direct democracy would do, both of them, although in different ways, abandoned their early enthusiasm for representative government.[94]

While Louis XVI and his ministers sent muddled signals to the Constituent Assembly about what the king would and would not accept, Paris exploded. Persistent shortages of bread eventually led the women of Paris to riot on October 4. The next day they marched in the rain, seven thousand strong, to

Versailles. When a delegation of twelve was admitted to the Constituent Assembly, Robespierre welcomed them and identified himself with their cause. He ordered an immediate inquiry into the greed and corruption that he blamed for the food shortages, thereby winning the crowd's support and redirecting their anger away from the Assembly.[95] Trying to prevent a riot at the royal palace and forestall a full-scale mutiny, Lafayette, commander of the national guard in Paris, marched a force of fifteen thousand to Versailles. During the night, however, some of the women protestors managed to penetrate the royal apartments. Shots were fired, and in the chaos two members of the royal guard and one of the women were killed. The next day it was learned that Louis XVI had agreed to accept the Declaration of Rights, release a supply of flour, and accompany the crowd back to Paris. By then he had little choice. Along the way, riding in a ragged procession including perhaps sixty thousand soldiers and a crowd growing ever larger, the king and queen were mocked as the baker and the baker's wife. Whatever grandeur the monarchy enjoyed during the heady reign of the Sun King, the combination of scandal-mongering, economic crisis, and political unrest had transformed Louis XVI and Marie Antoinette into objects of the crowd's contempt.[96]

If the people had effectively captured the royal family and brought them to Paris, the challenge facing the Constituent Assembly remained the same: it had not yet produced a constitution, and it was not clear how, and with what authority, it should announce whatever decision it reached. Robespierre's attempt to find the appropriate language shows the persistence of his moderate and monarchist sensibility: "Louis, by the will of the nation, king of the French, to all citizens of our empire: People, here is the law that your representatives have made." Although Robespierre opposed a royal veto as late as October, neither he nor almost anyone else in the Constituent Assembly was opposed to monarchy itself. Not "We the People," as in the Preamble to the United States Constitution, but only "Louis, King of the French" could legitimate the constitution of France.[97]

That traditional reverence for the monarch, however, was fast eroding. When the Assembly moved from Versailles to Paris in mid-October, positions began to harden. Condorcet, elected by Saint-Germain to the new municipal government organized in Paris after the fall of the Bastille, tried to strike the right balance between the popular sovereignty he applauded and the anarchy he feared. When royal power was challenged in Britain or crumbled in America, traditions of representative government sustained the legitimacy of law and popular confidence in legislative decision making. "But in France," Condorcet observed in a perceptive essay written toward the end of 1789, "where all kinds of authority were hereditary, venal, or conferred by the will of the prince," the situation was explosive. The French people did not know the representatives they elected, and half of those had been chosen by members of the first and second estates whom the people considered their enemies. Peasants distrusted their lords, and urban dwellers their officials and judges. Most Frenchmen knew nothing about "the small number of enlightened men," such as Condorcet himself, who spoke on their behalf; nor had they understood the books that had been written for their benefit. Not surprisingly, the people distrusted everybody and wanted to judge everything by themselves. The pendulum of popular sentiment, Condorcet warned, could swing swiftly from forced impotence to delusions of omnipotence. Excluded so long and so completely from any engagement in political decision making, the crowd was beginning to toy with the false idea that "the tumultuous will of the inhabitants of a city, a town, a village and even a quarter" had the same authority as law. A specter of democracy, understood as unbounded and unmediated popular passion, was now haunting France.[98]

It was a concern with lawlessness rather than opposition to representative government that prompted Condorcet, along with Lafayette, Sieyès, and other moderates, to form the Society of 1789, an organization committed to bringing the Revolution to fruition and staving off chaos. Both Condorcet and Sieyès wrote pamphlets articulating the group's commitment to educating the French public by using the members' preferred methods: careful research and rational discussion. As Condorcet put it, "This is neither a sect nor a party, but a *company* of the friends of humanity and, one might even say, of those who deal in social truths."[99] By social truths, the Society of 1789 meant the truths that would be ascertained by nonpartisan inquiry into social life. "We regarded the social art as a true science," in Condorcet's words, "founded like all the others on facts, experiment, reasoning and calculation," and "susceptible, like all the others, of indefinite progress and development." The findings of the society would become "progressively more useful as its true principles are spread."[100]

As the Society of 1789 expanded to over four hundred members by the spring of 1790, its reputation grew. By June one friendly newspaper observed that its ranks were "becoming daily more numerous and more brilliant. It counts among its members many deputies to the national assembly, many distinguished men of letters, many persons who have given proof in the revolution of patriotism and zeal." The Society of 1789 attracted progressive aristocrats, philosophes active in the learned academies of the eighteenth century, and a substantial number of bankers. As they saw it, these were the friends the Revolution needed, serious men of ideas with independent minds and substantial means.[101] It was just those qualities, however, that attracted the suspicion of another group of partisans who fancied themselves the true friends of the Revolution, the members of the Jacobin Society.

Because the Jacobins have been associated for more than two centuries with the worst excesses of the Terror, it is hard but important to remember the group's innocuous origins. First called the Breton Club (because its founders hailed from Brittany) and then, after the Assembly moved to Paris, the Society of Friends of the Constitution, its purpose was to coordinate proposals from regional organizations concerning the constitution. Most of the Jacobins were members of the National Assembly who were committed to the principle of popular sovereignty and wary of royalist schemes to defuse the Revolution. Delegates did not arrive at the National Assembly with fully formed programs or ideologies. For that reason the meetings of organizations such as the Breton Club, the Society of 1789, and later the Society of Friends of the Constitution were valuable sites for presenting and wrangling over ideas. Even at the pinnacle of its influence, the Jacobin Society never attracted more than perhaps 4 or 5 percent of the French populace. There was always at least some variation in the positions taken by different Jacobin clubs in different regions of France, and Jacobin politics played out in distinct ways in different places. Initially the Jacobin Society in Paris attracted a range of people with different ideas: Mirabeau, Robespierre, and Lafayette were all members. Only gradually, as different groups of moderates seceded or were thrown out, did it become more radical, and only briefly, from early 1792 until late 1793, did the Jacobin Society harden into a band of ruthless killers.

Even as the Jacobins became a more organized party, the internal tension between their commitment to individual rights and their equally firm commitment to community gave their ideas both their vitality and their instability. From the perspective of later Marxists, the Jacobins were, from first to last, bourgeois individualists. Nineteenth-century French liberals thought it was the Jacobins' fervent commitment to selflessness that overwhelmed their concern with rights and tempted them toward terror. From yet another perspective, the Jacobins' sustained attempt to combine freedom with fraternity, in increasingly perilous circumstances, makes their successes fascinating and their failures tragic.[102]

The Jacobins' fascination with community and authority is customarily attributed to the influence of Rousseau, but another source deserves equal attention: the Roman Catholic Church. Catholic theologians insisted on locating each individual believer within the universal church, conceived as the mystical body of Christ. Each parish was nested within an organizational hierarchy stretching beyond bishops and the pope to God. Given the injunctions to obey religious as well as royal authority, the notion of inviolable individual rights never harmonized fully with French Catholic tradition, at least in principle. In practice, however, challenges to Catholicism and disputes about the relation between church and state were nothing new. Disagreements about the authority of the Roman Catholic Church in its own domain and the authority of secular officials in the domain of politics had simmered at least since Augustine's *City of God.* Dissenters from papal authority had long quoted Marsiglio of Padua, William of Ockham, and John of Paris. In France the tradition of resistance to royal authority, the tradition known as monarchomach dissent, had never been extinguished. Lively controversies over the independence of the French Catholic Church had raged ever since the Declaration of the Liberties of the Gallican Church in 1682 established the independence of the French king and his church from papal authority. By 1713, Louis XIV had reason to reconsider and renounce that bold proclamation. Fearing that dissident ideas from the Jansenist tradition were threatening his own as well as his bishops' authority, he urged Pope Clement XI to issue the bull *Unigenitus* that reaffirmed the pope's authority over the entire Church.

Yet Jansenism refused to die. Instead it served as a constant irritant to crown and episcopacy alike. Priests who resisted abandoning Gallicanism formed an awkward alliance with Jansenists to resist the renewed fusion of royal and papal authority and insist on the legitimacy of the Estates General. Although no human assembly, whether of churchmen or secular authorities, could "make an aristocracy or democracy out of the monarchical government established by Jesus Christ himself," it was nevertheless true that representatives of the nation possessed "the right to change the form of its government when it has good reasons for doing so." That passage, from the *Maximes du droit public françois* (or Maxims of French Public Law) published by Gabriel Maultrot and Abbé Claude Mey in 1775, suggests how at least some religious dissenters tied their program to a vision of French history. Maultrot and Mey drew from an eclectic array of sources ranging from the late-medieval School of Paris to more recent writers including Grotius, Pufendorf, Locke, and Sidney. According to an influential strand of eighteenth-century French writers, then, representatives of the medieval French nation, meeting in the Estates General, had established long before 1789 that the king's authority was contingent on their approval.[103]

In response to such self-consciously Christian challenges to royal absolutism on behalf of popular sovereignty, other French Catholics advanced a pugnacious argument in defense of the king and the pope. As early as the 1750s, such writers introduced an early form of an argument that would come to fruition in the conservatism of the nineteenth century, a form dubbed "ultramontane" because it was associated with the supreme authority exercised by popes on the other side of the Alps. Those challenging the king, according to this line of reasoning, were drawing on English Protestant traditions rather than an authentically French inheritance, and they were flirting with the chaos that enveloped England during its civil war. By contrast, in "pure monarchies" such as France, in the words of Abbé Capmartin de Chaupy, "the king is the state." No pretense of popular sovereignty should be allowed to distract the French people from the maxim appropriate for their nation: "the will of the king is the will of the state."[104] Writing in 1769 an unwitting prediction of what was to come, Jean-Georges Lefranc de Pompignan, bishop of Le Puy, testified that if forced to choose between the pope on the one hand and the people on the other, he and his fellow "ultramontane theologians" would choose unhesitatingly a "mixture of aristocracy with monarchy" over the "tumults and discords" of "popular tribunals."[105]

Older depictions of the French Revolution as a melodrama pitting progressive secular rationalists against reactionary religious obscurantists are thus doubly mistaken. Lively debates abounded on all sides. As already noted, most Jansenists, although often characterized as French Calvinists, considered themselves more faithful Catholics than their critics. In addition to their noisy controversies with Jansenists, practicing French Catholics split along several fault lines, political as well as theological and ecclesiological. Different religious radicals challenged the *ancien régime* from various angles of attack. Prominent revolutionaries had studied theology at the Sorbonne, and Sieyès was hardly the only cleric to call for popular government.[106] In the earliest stages of the Revolution, devout Catholics of various stripes could and did rally behind the National Assembly without thereby repudiating their religious faith. The *cahiers* submitted before the opening of the Estates General called for ambitious changes, including the institution of representative government and a constitutional monarchy, but they did not call for the Catholic Church to become subservient to the state. Most French peasants and artisans remained tied to the Catholic traditions that gave shape to the rhythms of the year and meaning to their lives.[107] Many clergymen favored reform in the Church and the state alike. Inspired by Sieyès and led by Abbés Jacques Jallet and Henri Grégoire, a majority of priests had chosen to abandon the first estate to sit with the third even before Louis XVI finally instructed the clergy and nobility to do so. The idea of a reform-minded Catholic priest was hardly an oxymoron in eighteenth-century France.[108]

Those reformist clergy, however, were unprepared for the dramatic steps the Assembly began to take in the early stages of the Revolution. Not only was the tithe abolished and church lands taken on August 4, 1789. Those decisions were followed in rapid succession by the measures collectively known as the Civil Constitution of the Clergy. Religious freedom had been proclaimed in the Declaration of the Rights of Man. Dissolving most religious orders, insisting on residency requirements for priests, limiting the luxuries enjoyed by the French hierarchy, and paying church officials a standard salary did not trouble most French Catholics, including most parish priests. Many Catholics—even many priests—had called for such reforms themselves. Yet when the Assembly ignored the reservations of its own ecclesiastical members and declared, on August 24, 1790, that all church officials were servants of the nation to be elected by the laity, many priests as well as bishops balked.[109]

New battle lines began to form in the fall of 1790. Coalitions sprang up, both among those who now opposed the Civil Constitution of the Clergy as a threat to life as they knew it and among those who denounced such emerging opposition as counterrevolutionary. More than two hundred delegates to the National Assembly were now members of the Jacobin Society in Paris. Jacobin clubs began appearing throughout France, countered by newly energized groups of Catholics who protested the Assembly's unwanted and unwarranted intrusion into French religious life. As more clerics resisted, claiming that they must meet in council to decide whether they could adopt the changes, popular dissent became more widespread. By November the Assembly felt compelled to take a dramatic step to enforce its decree. Henceforth all clerics would be required to take an oath "to be faithful to the nation, the king, and the law, and to uphold with all their power the constitution declared by the National Assembly and accepted by the king."[110]

The oath enforcing the Civil Constitution was a disaster, the worst mistake the National Assembly made. Although many of the oath's component parts had emerged from Jansenism or from other reform efforts within the Gallican Church itself, requiring clerics to swear their fidelity to the nation antagonized too many of the rural peasants and urban artisans who might have endorsed significant religious as well as political reform. The Civil Constitution galvanized a disorganized opposition and alienated many French citizens who previously had either been ambivalent about the Revolution or supported it actively. It forced everyone in France, for the first time, to take sides, thereby transforming a series of fragmentary, poorly coordinated, poorly understood measures into what many devout believers now interpreted as an unambiguous assault on French Catholicism. Millions who had been unsure or puzzled about the scope of the Revolution now found themselves joining an increasingly vocal and well organized resistance rallying to the standard of French traditions symbolized as much by the Church as by the king. Wounds dating back to the wars of religion reopened. In Nîmes, violence that claimed the lives of three hundred Catholics and twenty Protestants ended with Protestants in control of the municipal government and Catholics furious. In Avignon, long a papal possession and now annexed by France, conflicts were predictable. A Catholic mob, already angry over the takeover of church property and inspired by rumors that a statue of the Virgin Mary was weeping as a sign of God's anger, stabbed to death an official who had melted down church bells. In response, members of the new regime killed a number of their opponents, including six officials in the Avignon municipal government whom they had replaced.[111]

The French clergy split into two principal factions. The constitutional clergy, comprising less than half, accepted the new framework; the majority, the refractory clergy, rejected it. As previously squabbling individuals coalesced into those two groups, increasingly vociferous speakers in the National Assembly, particularly Robespierre, began denouncing the persistence of all independent corps or intermediary bodies within the nation. The loyalties to the nation felt by members of such groups, Robespierre argued, were compromised by their allegiance to a foreign prince, either the pope or perhaps one of the monarchies ringing France and warily watching developments within its borders.[112]

Robespierre had first garnered the attention of the third estate with a ringing denunciation of the opulence enjoyed by French bishops. He had urged the Church's aristocracy to "forego that luxury which surrounds them and that splendor which makes indigence blush."[113] On the eve of the Revolution many fervent Catholics would have embraced Robespierre's critique. After the Civil Constitution, as bishops began actively encouraging French Catholics to resist the Revolution, widespread and deeply rooted resentment of the bishops' wealth transmogrified into broader distrust of the Church itself, on the one hand, and an equally volatile antagonism toward the Revolution on the other.

Just a week after the promulgation of the Civil Constitution, one of Jefferson's friends among the French aristocracy, Madame de Houdetot, wrote to him that the new United States could build without regret because it had nothing to destroy. The American Revolution was the fruit of civic virtue; chaos was unfolding in France because of the nation's faults and its crimes.[114] With the emergence of the conviction that a unitary national authority was vested in the National Assembly and distinct from that of the Church, the king, or any other traditional sources of authority in France, references to counterrevolutionary groups and plots began to proliferate throughout France. By proclaiming the Civil Constitution, the Assembly froze a previously fluid situation, thereby creating precisely the fierce, implacable, and united opposition that had previously been only a fantasy shimmering in the imaginations of the king's brother Artois and a few scattered nobles.

If democracy depends on an ethic of reciprocity, the Civil Constitution of the Clergy marked the beginning of its repudiation and the emergence of an ethic of mutual animosity, even hatred, that recalled the worst features of the wars of religion and doomed democracy in France for almost a century. Once the Revolution became resolutely anticlerical, most devout Catholics became antirevolutionary, and reciprocal antagonism spiraled downward toward violence. Although both the Jacobin Society and the Catholic Church claimed to stand for an ethic of brotherhood and community, in practice partisans of both proved willing to resort to violence. Some revolutionaries assumed that religious faith always fuels subservience to authority and fanatical opposition to political change. Had they paid closer attention to English and American history, they would have seen that faith can also infuse reformist political action with the fervor of religious zeal. In the eighteenth century the assumption that kings embody divine authority lost its solidity. That shift might have led France—as it did England for a brief moment in the 1640s and as it did more enduringly England's North American colonies in the century before 1776—toward belief that the voice of God is embodied instead in the will of the people. By foreclosing the possibility of a France that was both Catholic and democratic, the Civil Constitution of the Clergy sent the French Revolution careening toward civil war.

CHAPTER 11

Virtue and Violence in the French Revolution

NOT ONLY DID the French Revolution, and in particular the Civil Constitution of the Clergy, split France into two separate camps less than two years after the fall of the Bastille; it had an almost equally swift and profound effect across the English Channel. British Whigs who had sympathized with the American Revolution hoped for even more dramatic consequences in France. British romantics such as William Wordsworth and Samuel Taylor Coleridge felt blissful to be alive for the dawning days of the Revolution, and the various bands of British Jacobins allied with the London Correspondence Society shared their initial enthusiasm.[1]

No one exceeded the enthusiasm of Richard Price, who had characterized the American Revolution as the most significant event since the Incarnation and saw similar promise in what was unfolding in France. In "A Discourse on the Love of our Country," an address originally delivered on November 4, 1789, to commemorate the Glorious Revolution of 1688, Price placed the French Revolution in a direct line of descent from the English champions of liberty Milton, Locke, and Sidney and like-minded French thinkers such as Montesquieu, Fénelon, and Turgot. Price argued that genuine patriotism, a true "love of our country," would lead his fellow Britons to address the most important defect of their political system, "the inequality of our representation." Price was a prime example of a devout clergyman who believed not only that Christianity is compatible with democracy but also that the free exercise of religion, coupled with robust representative government, would do more to stimulate renewed commitment to Christian principles than any attempts to enforce religious conformity or impose authoritarian rule. Whereas "vice and venality" brought "God's displeasure" on Britain, America and now France showed the promise of an alternative path. "Tremble all ye oppressors of the world!" Defenders of "slavish governments and slavish hierarchies" now had only one option: "Restore to mankind their rights and consent to the correction of abuses, before they and you are destroyed together."[2]

Of course, many Britons disagreed with Price. Edmund Burke, like many other critics of George III, believed that Britain incited the American Revolution through a series of miscalculations; he considered the French Revolution categorically different. Burke replied to Price with his *Reflections on the Revolution in France* (1790), a fiery diatribe that surprised even some of his friends. Tom Paine, for example, expected Burke to applaud developments in France just as both of them had embraced the American Revolution. Paine had Burke wrong.[3] Burke had already expressed doubts about natural rights and popular government. He could see the logic of the Americans' claims, grounded in centuries of English political tradition and "the ancient, manly, homebred sense of this country."[4] Burke was no friend of popular government, though, and he dismissed Price's claim that 1688 established a precedent for the people choosing their own rulers. Born in Ireland, Burke had shown some sympathy for extending toleration to Catholics and dissenters, but 1789 changed his mind. He found repellent the airy and indefensible notions of natural rights so fervently invoked by Price and his chief ally, Joseph Priestley. Burke made good his vow to "expose" Price and Priestley "to the hatred, ridicule, and contempt of the whole world." When Priestley dared reply in his *Letters to Burke: A Political Dialogue on the General Principles of Government* (1791), Priestley became the target of a mob that destroyed his home, laboratory, and church on the second anniversary of Bastille Day.[5]

Reflections on the Revolution in France went through eleven editions, sold over thirty thousand copies in its first year, and became the foundational text of Anglo-American conservatism. Burke portrayed popular government as a dangerous illusion based on dreams of benevolence; in his view, hierarchical authority alone could check human depravity. The French Revolution not only disregarded all of French history and tradition but also repudiated the fundamental building block of all societies, the family. Although some High Church bishops and conservative laymen had prepared the ground for Burke's offensive, his critique captured the public imagination.[6] Repeatedly asserting the licentiousness of revolutionaries and their desire "to uncover our nakedness by throwing off that Christian religion" that reined in man's sinfulness, Burke indulged in near-pornographic fantasies of sexual violation. Claiming inside knowledge of the October Days, Burke painted a vivid portrait of violence spiced by innuendo. The Jacobins' faulty social philosophy conceived of individuals "stripped of every relation in all the nakedness and solitude of metaphysical abstraction."[7] Whereas the philosophes made the French eager to "cast away the coat of prejudice" to expose pure reason, the English knew "that man is by his constitution a religious animal; that atheism is against, not only our reason, but our instincts; and that it cannot prevail long." Unfortunately, according to Burke, France had already lured some otherwise sensible Britons into degradation.[8] The claims of enlightenment and reason masked a more ominous unveiling: "All the decent drapery of life is to be rudely torn off." All the constraints of custom, "which the heart owns and the understanding ratifies as necessary to cover the defects of our naked, shivering nature," are to be "exploded," thus exposing man's animality. "On this scheme of things, a king is but a man, a queen is but a woman; a woman is but an animal, and an animal not of the highest order." The revolutionaries would legitimate bastards, legalize divorce at a moment's notice, and erase the natural differences between men and women.[9]

Burke's *Reflections* was but one of the breathless accounts of the Revolution's early days that circulated throughout Europe and intensified widespread fears of anarchy. The book was quickly translated into French—by Louis XVI himself, it was claimed—and into German by Friedrich von Gentz, generously paid for his efforts by the British government. Gentz repeated Price's prediction that the French example would prove contagious, but what had enraptured Price and Priestley appalled Gentz. With the advent of self-government, Priestley had claimed, the world would move from darkness, servitude, and conflict into light, freedom, and harmony, all because in the new age "the many will rule as they see fit." In a democracy, minorities and majorities learn to accommodate themselves to each other, and "reason will be the umpire in all disputes and extinguish civil wars as well as foreign ones." Gentz instead warned of "other revolutions into infinity" leading to "never-ending civil war."[10]

The exchanges between Price, Burke, Gentz, and Priestley set off a pamphlet war that began at the level of their already inflated rhetoric and escalated from there. By far the most widely read of these texts was Thomas Paine's *Rights of Man*, a book that maintains its status on the left just as firmly as Burke's does on the right. Within several years of its publication in 1791, more than two hundred thousand copies of *Rights of Man* were circulating not only in Britain and America but throughout Europe. In Paine's account, the French Revolution proceeded with almost serenedecorum. The women of Paris marched calmly to Versailles, and on the night of October 6 the king and queen voluntarily appeared on the palace balcony instead of hiding for their lives. The next day everyone—three hundred thousand strong, royalty, soldiers, and ordinary people—returned to Paris together, with "tranquility restored" and "all suspicions extinguished." If Burke exaggerated the violence of the Revolution's early stages, Paine underestimated the turmoil in almost equal measure.[11] On March 16, 1790, a year before the publication of *Rights of Man*, Paine had written to Benjamin Rush explaining his enthusiasm for the French Revolution. "Little inconveniences" were inevitable—"the necessary consequences of pulling down and building up"—but overall progress was steady. Because the French considered the United States "the Country from whence all reformations must originally spring," Paine had been asked to carry the American flag in the festivities marking the expected completion of a new constitution, and Lafayette was sending to George Washington, as a gesture of France's indebtedness to its American friends, the key to the Bastille.[12]

Paine's optimism proved unwarranted. In April of 1791, Louis XVI declared his intention to travel with his family to the recently renovated château of St. Cloud, one of Marie Antoinette's pet projects, to celebrate Easter in the countryside just west of Paris. When a mob prevented the royal carriage from leaving the city, the king realized he had become a prisoner of the Revolution and began making plans to escape. April also saw the death of Mirabeau, who was buried in the former Church of St. Geneviève, newly rededicated as the Panthéon. Mirabeau's soaring rhetoric, which had dominated early debates, led to his election as president of the National Assembly. His death left a vacuum among revolutionary leaders, which expanded when the Assembly voted to send all sitting delegates home once they finished work on the new constitution.

The principal champion of that measure was Robespierre. In an impassioned speech the Incorruptible challenged his fellow delegates to show their devotion to the Revolution by renouncing their positions. By shaming his rivals into retirement, he emptied Paris of many of those who had spent two years gaining valuable political experience. Although he had established himself as an influential figure within the Jacobin Society, Robespierre's own role in the negotiations leading up to the constitution had been minimal. His particular projects (strange in light of later events), outlawing the death penalty and ensuring freedom for the press, had gone nowhere.[13] Now Robespierre's speeches grew ever more ambitious. He invoked Rousseau's paeans to the general will and praised the "good, patient, and generous" people of France, who sought "nothing but peace, justice, and the right to live." He also began warning of vague dangers hiding in the shadows, unnamed political operatives driven by personal ambition to oppose the general interest.[14] As a legislator and constitutional architect Robespierre enjoyed little success. As an orator trafficking in conspiracies (and as a shrewd operator maneuvering behind the scenes), however, he was hitting his stride, confirming the worst fears of Burke, Gentz, and other critics of the Revolution throughout Europe.

Louis XVI, now convinced the Revolution threatened the monarchy, fled Paris with his family on the night of June 20, 1791. Through a string of misadventures worthy of comic opera, they were apprehended in Varennes and returned by a mob to Paris two days later. Compounding his predicament, the king had left a manifesto in which he denounced the Revolution and complained of his family's incarceration in Paris. Except for the Civil Constitution of the Clergy, the flight to Varennes did as much as any single event to transform the Revolution. Until then almost no one doubted that France would remain a monarchy; afterward people began to talk of putting the king on trial for treason. Moderates in the Assembly, including some prominent Jacobins, concocted an implausible explanation: the king had been kidnapped and forced to sign the message condemning the Revolution. Robespierre and the radicals scoffed at that transparent fiction. In a melodramatic but effective speech, Robespierre railed against the Revolution's enemies, who not only ringed its borders but also lurked within France itself. The royal family now stood on the wrong side of an increasingly wide gulf that separated the people from their foes. More than sixty Jacobin clubs demanded that the king be put on trial; the Paris Jacobins split over the question of the king's fate. The moderates, including Lafayette, formed a new club at the former home of another religious order, the Feuillants. Robespierre found himself left with a rump of no more than a hundred like-minded radicals.

When it was time to commemorate the fall of the Bastille, anger toward the king and impatience with the Assembly had replaced the festive mood of the preceding summer. Fifty thousand people gathered on the Champ de Mars to show their dedication to the Revolution and their fury with the king. Two men found hiding beneath the altar to the fatherland, assumed to be enemies of the people but likely just in the wrong place at the wrong time, were lynched. The ensuing tumult prompted Lafayette, still commander in chief of the National Guard, to call out his militia, and the citizen soldiers killed perhaps fifty demonstrators before the frenzy ended. Martial law was declared. The most radical figures of the Revolution—Georges-Jacques Danton, Jean-Paul Marat, and Camille Desmoulins—went underground.

As smoldering doubts about the king clouded the Paris air, the newly elected Assembly convened in August, submitted its plan, and proclaimed a new constitution. The king, lacking any viable alternative, accepted it. A Feuillant newspaper in Lyon captured the ambivalence of many observers and the ambiguity of the Assembly's achievement: "The people are sovereign, but it would injurious for it to exercise that sovereignty."[15] The Constituent Assembly, having completed its task, dissolved. As the delegates returned home, however, anxieties about the future muffled their sense of accomplishment. The pervasive uneasiness in France during the summer of 1791 came into focus in an exchange between Paine and Sieyès published in both Paris and London. Paine dismissed the "whole Hell of Monarchy," which the Americans had wisely abandoned, and praised the republican system of "Government by Representation." From Paine's perspective, the French and American Declarations of Rights were "one and the same thing in principles"; the only difference lay in the execution. In his reply, Sieyès carefully distinguished "republicanism," which he defined vaguely as government in "the public interest," from any particular institutions of government. Monarchies, whether hereditary or elective, aristocracies, and even "polyarchies," with power widely dispersed, might all serve the public interest. Because a single person incorporates the entire national interest in a monarchy, whereas all other individuals, whether elected or appointed, inevitably have particular interests, Sieyès still expressed a preference for monarchy over purely popular government. Notwithstanding his influential critiques, Sieyès's longing for a unitary voice to express the public interest prevented him from abandoning monarchy.[16]

Paine explained his alternative solution in *Le Républicain*, a newspaper he founded along with four French associates, Brissot, Condorcet, Clavière, and Achille François de Lascaris d'Urfé, Marquis du Chastellet, none of whom would survive the Revolution. Whereas critics of popular sovereignty always claimed that democracy is impossible in a large country, Paine insisted that representation is the solution: "The true *republican* system, by election and representation," provides the only way to distribute "the wisdom and the information of a government" regardless of the size of a country. Those nations often characterized as republics, including the Netherlands and Switzerland, Paine observed accurately, were governed by aristocratic oligarchies rather than by the people. Popular election of legislators distinguished the United States—and, potentially, France—from all others. "The system of *representation* is the strongest and most powerful center that can be devised for a nation. Its attraction acts so powerfully," Paine continued, that whenever it is instituted, its legitimacy is immediately taken for granted. Thanks to the Constituent Assembly, that would now become true even in Europe's largest nation: representation would make France "whole." In the Assembly citizens' rights would be protected, and soldiers would feel themselves no longer slaves of a despot but citizens committed to defending their nation.[17]

Deliberating representatives, Paine insisted, form from the individuals in far-flung regions a united nation with a shared interest, a general will. That logic, which had taken hold in the United States by 1789, Paine considered self-evident and irrefutable, but he and his allies misread conditions in France. The Constituent Assembly had proposed a mixed regime, a constitutional monarchy with a representative assembly, that satisfied neither the nobility nor at least a substantial fraction of the increasingly uneasy populace. The king had already declared—and demonstrated in attempting to flee Paris—that he shared neither Paine's faith in representation nor Sieyès's faith in a republican monarchy. In the aftermath of the Civil Constitution and the flight to Varennes, the new constitution was only a bandage applied to a severed artery.

Paine, Sieyès, and Condorcet offered three different diagnoses and three different remedies, and were haunted by three different nightmares. Paine trusted a representative assembly to conjure up a shared public interest, Sieyès a monarch assisted by an assembly. Condorcet, by contrast, insisted that reason alone was adequate to the task regardless of the form of government. In his *Mémoires sur l'instruction publique*, likewise written in 1791 as the Constituent Assembly did its work, Condorcet warned that royal despotism would give way to popular despotism if dramatic change were to precede widespread education. The more the law respects the independence and equality of individuals, the likelier that ruse would rule the ignorant and folly trump reason: an alliance of "accomplices and dupes" would empower "a troop of audacious hypocrites." Although the people might unmask charlatans, truth "is all-powerful only over minds accustomed to recognize and cherish it."[18] Condorcet feared that emotion would dominate democratic decision making; he trusted reason, disseminated through an ambitious scheme of education instilling the principles of mathematics, to discipline passion. In an ideal world, rational people would choose rational representatives, but Condorcet felt the ground shifting beneath his feet. He was growing increasingly anxious about the radicals clustering around Robespierre in the Jacobin Society—and around Danton in the Cordeliers Club, which took its name from the former Franciscan monastery in which it met. As revolutionary rhetoric grew ever more incendiary, Condorcet abandoned Lafayette and his former allies among the enlightened nobility. Making arguments for the connection between reason and representative government, Condorcet threw in his lot with moderates who promised a sensible path forward toward representative democracy, including Paine and Brissot.

Once the new Legislative Assembly began meeting, it seemed for a few months that the center might hold. But events beyond France's borders brought renewed conflict. Although different people had different reasons, many partisans of the Revolution welcomed the prospect of war against the monarchies encircling France. Brissot, Clavière, and Condorcet hoped war might unify a badly divided nation. Comparisons with the American war against George III multiplied. Louis XVI imagined that appearing to favor war would solidify his standing at home, even though many in France believed (correctly) that he was secretly negotiating with the rulers of other nations to roll back the Revolution. Popular disturbances spread from the north to the Midi, as bands of peasants and artisans and some units of the National Guard sacked châteaux and attacked refractory priests. Rumors of food hoarding, price-fixing, and counterrevolutionary plots fed popular dissatisfaction with continuing economic stagnation. If the Revolution seemed stuck, perhaps war against despots would jolt it forward.

Robespierre, having been elected president of the Paris Jacobins, denounced war as counterrevolutionary, as did Danton, his counterpart at the Cordeliers. Robespierre reasoned that only a people's army could simultaneously advance the Revolution and defend the nation. Lafayette might have fought against George III in America, but in France he had commanded the militia against the people. Robespierre mocked the enthusiasm for war and warned of "a gaping chasm filled with victims."[19] At the Jacobin Club he began explicitly invoking Rousseau more often, insisting that "only the people are good, just and generous," and "corruption and tyranny are the monopoly of those who hold them in disdain." He made a fateful distinction: "The people want what is good, but they do not always see it." Although that might evoke Jefferson's concern about enlightening the people's discretion, Robespierre had confidence he knew how to give sight to the blind.[20] Again claiming the mantle of the people and advertising his selflessness, Robespierre resigned his position as public prosecutor in Paris. He accused his rivals of abandoning the Revolution to embrace personal power. From Robespierre's vantage point, declaring war would bolster Clavière's financial interests, Brissot's political standing, and Lafayette's power as commander of the National Guard, all of which intensified the danger of civil war. In April of 1792, when the Holy Roman Emperor Leopold II, Marie Antoinette's brother, declined Louis's ultimatum to disavow all anti-French activities and instead mustered troops in Alsace, France declared war. Brissot and his allies were delighted. The consequences were disastrous.

In the months leading to that declaration of war on April 20, 1792, news arrived in France from the French colony of Saint-Domingue, where more than half a million slaves labored in conditions even more miserable and murderous than those in North America. A slave rebellion had been under way since August of 1791. Opinion on race and slavery among French revolutionaries was as divided as it was in the United States. Fewer than five thousand free blacks lived in France, without the chance to become citizens. Belief in racial equality was as rare among European whites as it was among whites in North America. Like Paine and Benjamin Rush in the United States, however, some prominent leaders of the French Revolution, including Brissot, Condorcet, and Robespierre, had followed the lead of Montesquieu, Raynal, and the *Encyclopedia* in denouncing slavery. In *Réflexions sur l'esclavage des nègres*, Condorcet simultaneously condemned slavery and warned against immediate emancipation, just as Raynal had done. Brissot had established the Societé des Amis des Noirs in 1788; Sieyès, Condorcet, Clavière, Lafayette, and Grégoire were among its members. The Sociéte des Colons Américains, established in Paris in 1789 by free blacks from Saint-Domingue, likewise helped alert France to the horrible condition of nonwhites in its Caribbean colonies.[21] When the word "slavery" appeared in French publications in the 1780s, it typically referred to feudalism or despotism and ignored enslaved blacks, just as American revolutionaries in the South hurled the word at George III without worrying about their own slaves. As was true in the United States, no one successfully mobilized French public opinion against the arrangements that brought cheap and plentiful sugar and coffee to France, enriching not only Caribbean planters but also shipping interests in Bordeaux, Le Havre, and Nantes.[22]

Forty-nine *cahiers* in 1789 called for ending either slavery or the slave trade. Most delegates to the National Assembly, however, like their American counterparts, considered slavery too important to the French economy to challenge it, and delegates sympathetic to colonial planters or merchants drowned out efforts to criticize slavery or the slave trade. Arguments made popular by the prominent philosophe Georges-Louis Leclerc, Comte de Buffon, demonized blacks and mulattos and lionized white Europeans for elevating and invigorating the otherwise degenerate tropical islands of the Caribbean. Only one delegate mentioned slavery on the night of August 4, 1789, when feudalism was dismantled. The Constituent Assembly failed to address the issue.[23]

Responding to the pleas of prosperous free blacks in Haiti, in 1784–85 Louis XVI had begun the process of reforming the *Code Noir* of Louis XIV. He decreed that those killing slaves were to be treated as murderers and that slaves could cultivate their own gardens. The wealthy white planters and merchants in Saint-Domingue resisted such efforts at reform. They insisted instead that they, like those in Britain's former North American colonies, should be governed by laws made in their own assembly. Their merchant allies in France shared an interest in maintaining hegemony over the slaves and free blacks of the island.[24] In a letter to Benjamin Rush in 1790, Paine had written that the abomination of slavery would persist until blacks were "enabled to take their own part" in abolishing the system.[25] Beginning as early as the mid-1780s, precisely that process began to gather momentum in Saint-Domingue. Louis's reforms sparked hopes of emancipation. Free blacks, notably Julien Raimond and Vincent Ogé, petitioned the king, then the Constituent Assembly, for further reform. When their efforts failed, the wealthy Ogé raised a military force and sailed to Saint-Domingue. There he, most of his soldiers, and many native rebels were captured and executed.

The National Assembly did not ignore the question entirely. On September 28, 1791, it voted to outlaw slavery in France, where there were few slaves to free, and began inching toward granting rights to free blacks in the Caribbean. Legal disputes and decrees from colonial governments throughout the French Caribbean made clear that officials and planters were increasingly nervous as word of the French Revolution spread. They censored publications or letters mentioning "liberty" and worried obsessively that news of unrest would inspire slave revolts. Once such uprisings broke out in 1791, the Colonial Assembly of Saint-Domingue immediately enacted a decree prohibiting the "sale, printing, or distribution of any pieces relative to the politics and revolution of France," which testifies as clearly as planters' memoirs to the presence in the Caribbean of antislavery literature. Félix Carteau wrote that "all it took among the slaves of a plantation was one who could read to the others, as the plots were being formed, to give them proof of how much they were pitied in France, and how much people wanted them to free themselves of the terrible yoke of their pitiless masters."[26] Because of the king's initiative in 1784–85 and because of African traditions of kingship, slaves often invoked royal authority in their resistance to planters. Once word of the French Revolution finally reached the Caribbean, references to the "rights of man" began to rival appeals to Louis XVI. Slaves in Saint-Domingue, like those in North America, looked for allies wherever they could be found, and in the coming decades different groups forged alliances with France, with Spain, and with Britain as they struggled for freedom.[27]

The slave revolts that began in 1791 and culminated in Haitian independence in 1804 were emphatically the work of the slaves and free blacks themselves, not the fruit of European political ideas. Multiple languages of liberty, from African, Afro-Caribbean, American, and French sources, reverberated in the French Caribbean throughout these decades. When Brissot replied in the Assembly to those who criticized the first, tentative extension of voting rights to free black property owners—a step that would affect probably no more than 25 percent of the roughly twenty-eight thousand free blacks in

Saint-Domingue—he mocked the claim that such steps endangered slavery. By the time he delivered that speech, on September 12, 1791, just such a slave revolt had already begun, even though news of it did not reach Paris until weeks later.[28] French officials failed to contain the revolt, which spread quickly throughout Saint-Domingue and brought to a halt the export of most commodities. Aiming to regain control, the Assembly in Paris awarded full civil rights to all free blacks in Saint-Domingue on April 4, 1792. Commissioners sent from France failed to quell the revolt, and on August 29, 1793, to save their lives as well as a semblance of French authority, they declared the end of slavery in Saint-Domingue. It was not until February of 1794 that the National Convention in Paris finally got around to ratifying the abolition of slavery that the slaves themselves had already accomplished.

In Saint-Domingue itself, war continued after slavery ended. The Spanish, then the British, became involved, and free blacks and former slaves in different parts of the island allied with French, Spanish, and British forces as they tried to consolidate political and economic control. Only when Toussaint Louverture and two other military leaders, former slave Jean-Jacques Dessalines and free black Henri Christophe, ended their alliance with Spain and sided with France did the French reestablish a shaky degree of control. The power of the *grands blancs*, the wealthy French whites who had ruled Saint-Domingue, was broken, and ten years after the revolt began in 1791, Toussaint emerged in complete control of the former colony.[29] The government put in place by the Haitian Constitution of 1801, although it reflected some ideas about self-government, can scarcely be characterized as a democracy. Toussaint Louverture, named Governor for Life, exercised far more power than the elected Assembly. He enjoyed sole authority to propose legislation, police public morality, censor all publications, and name his own successor. Following Napoleon's reassertion of French military power in 1802, Toussaint was captured and sent to France, where he was imprisoned and died a year later.

Napoleon later aimed to reestablish French control throughout Haiti and return slavery to the formerly Spanish part of the island, a project that provoked widespread resistance and escalated into civil war. Eventually the French forces, at their peak over a hundred thousand strong, were forced off the island, and Toussaint's former comrade Dessalines took control. The French had killed tens of thousands of blacks; now the tables were turned. Rejecting a draft proclaiming Haitian independence written by an admirer of Jefferson's Declaration of Independence, Louis Boisrond-Tonnerre wrote that Haitians had no desire to reconcile peacefully with France. "To draw up the act of independence," he wrote, "we need the skin of a white man for the parchment, his skull for an inkwell, his blood for ink, and a bayonet for a pen." The Declaration itself, which Dessalines proclaimed on January 1, 1804, renounced any future amity with the bloody-minded French, who had turned the people of Haiti into "the *prey of vultures*." Haitians would respond by killing any Frenchman who dared to soil by his presence this new land of liberty.[30] In the grim assessment of Dessalines, "We have repaid these cannibals, war for war, crime for crime, outrage for outrage."[31]

The triumphant Dessalines declared himself emperor of Haiti and permitted no opposition to his rule. Within two years he was killed by his own soldiers, who left his mutilated body to rot in an open field. His successor, Henri Christophe, turned down the chance to become president in the only nondictatorial constitution Haiti produced. Instead he chose to become king of a secessionist state to the north. Although a few references to terms and phrases familiar from the Enlightenment and the French Revolution popped up occasionally in the Haitian Revolution, from beginning to end it was a struggle for control among white French planters, free blacks, and slaves intent on securing their freedom. Because its leading figures never renounced monarchy or embraced the principle of popular sovereignty, what happened in Haiti should be understood as a war to end slavery rather than a failed effort to establish democracy.[32]

The Haitian Revolution culminated in a series of murderous autocracies ruled by merciless dictators. Its violence, understandable in light of the inhuman conditions that prevailed on Caribbean sugar plantations, evoked a range of responses among whites in the Atlantic world. The barbarity of the conflict struck observers with short memories as unprecedented; others recalled the sixteenth-century wars of religion, when Catholics and Protestants throughout Europe hacked each other to pieces with similar ferocity. In the United States, some slaveholders invoked the Haitian rebels' excesses to justify their own ruthlessness whenever they suspected slave revolts. Others smugly contrasted the supposedly benign conditions slaves enjoyed in the United States against the brutal conditions slaves endured in the Caribbean sugar islands and viewed the "contagion" of Saint-Domingue with equanimity. Whether one blamed those who kept slaves, as did abolitionists, or those who encouraged them to rebel, as did slaveholders, the example of Haiti lingered in the minds of everyone thinking about slavery in the nineteenth century.[33]

Critics and partisans of the French Revolution, like critics and partisans of the American Revolution, never tired of pointing out that the existence of slavery mocked the sentiments expressed in documents such as the Declaration of Independence and the Declaration of the Rights of Man and of the Citizen.

Glaring as that contradiction was, the treatment of women by self-styled champions of liberty on both sides of the Atlantic struck some contemporaries as equally jarring. Abigail Adams had chided her husband for neglecting to address the question of women's rights. The coming of the French Revolution provoked women on both sides of the Atlantic to articulate more insistent demands.

In the months leading to the outbreak of the French Revolution, women were not invited to participate in submitting *cahiers de doléances*. Yet thirty-three *cahiers* called for reforms to improve women's education, and some women did not wait for an invitation to submit their grievances. One entitled *Doléances des femmes françaises*, dated March 5, 1789, challenged the legitimacy of the Estates General, which pretended to "represent the entire nation, while more than half the Nation is excluded." As the writer concluded, "That, gentlemen, is a problem, and a problem injurious to our sex." Another of the *cahiers* asked "whether men could continue to make women the victims of their pride and injustice at a time when the common people were entering into their political rights and when even blacks were to be free." No longer could a man be said to "represent" any woman; it was time for women to participate in politics.[34]

Such claims to equality were rare; most of the *cahiers* took for granted the separate, domestic sphere to which French women were confined by custom as much as law. Most philosophes did not challenge gender roles. Diderot criticized the subordination of women but stressed their biological constraints. Rousseau's *Emile* and *La nouvelle Héloïse* reinscribed earlier ideals within an emerging romantic framework and elevated the quality of chaste simplicity, long judged defective among the nobility, into the most charming of women's characteristics. These admirable qualities still did not equip women for political action; only in the domestic sphere, where they could serve their husbands and their children, could Rousseau's ideal women flourish.

Notable exceptions included Condorcet and Olympe de Gouges. The discourse of equal rights for women had to overcome an all but unbroken legacy of assumed inequality dating from classical antiquity. Virtue in the ancient world was gendered male, and the supposed weaknesses of women disqualified them from participation in public life.[35] Condorcet dismissed such sexual stereotypes as remnants of an irrational world. Married in 1786 to the brilliant Sophie de Grouchy, who helped establish a women's rights organization, le Cercle Social and later translated both Paine and Adam Smith, Condorcet challenged gender stereotypes and called for women's education.[36] Equality in work and public life, far from making women less feminine, would immeasurably enrich men's as well as women's lives. Both in his writings about America and in his 1790 *Mémoires sur l'instruction publique* (usually translated as "The Nature and Purpose of Public Instruction"), Condorcet urged equal education for women and men. The Constitution of 1791, however, excluded women from public life and envisioned educating women for lives as wives and mothers.[37]

De Gouges seems to have been the first writer to use the phrase "rights of woman," when she submitted to Marie Antoinette in 1791 her *Declaration of the Rights of Woman and of the Citizen*, the text for which she remains best known. The illegitimate daughter of a nobleman who never acknowledged his paternity, she was raised by a butcher's family in southwestern France. Widowed in her early twenties, she traveled with her son to Paris, where she maneuvered into the salons of prominent writers, including the Condorcets, and began to write herself. Her antislavery play *Zamore et Mirza* (1785) was accepted by the Comédie Française but not performed. A two-volume collection of her plays appeared in 1788, when she also published the first of several dozen political pamphlets. During the next five years the prolific de Gouges challenged, with increasing boldness, the customary exclusion of women from political debate. She addressed topics ranging from finance and politics to legal and social reform, including inequalities in the tax system and marriage laws, the injustice of slavery and illegitimacy, and the desirability of divorce and women's education. She continued writing plays, including *Les aristocrates et les démocrates* and a revised version of *Samore et Mizra* that was closed down by proslavery forces after only three performances.[38]

Echoing as well as challenging the exclusions and ambiguities of the Declaration of the Rights of Man, de Gouges yoked rights with duties and grounded both in natural law. She repeated the echo of Rousseau—"The law must be the expression of the general will"—and expanded the formula to include "All female and male citizens must contribute either personally or through their representatives to its formation." The implications of adding "and women" to the articles of the Declaration of Rights were unmistakably radical: women as well as men, de Gouges proclaimed, should be equal before the law and eligible for "all honors, positions, and public employment according to their capacity." Only individuals' "virtues and talents," not their gender (or race, as she argued in her antislavery pamphlets), should determine their roles. In their contributions as well as their benefits, de Gouges deemed women equal to men, so women deserved their share of jobs and honors. De Gouges closed her *Declaration* as she closed many of her tracts, urging women to wake up and demand their rights. "The powerful empire of nature is no longer surrounded by prejudice, fanaticism, superstition, and lies." Men had invoked reason to justify revolution. Now it was up to women to extend that argument to the injustice of male hegemony. "It is in your power," she told women, "to free yourselves. You only have to will it."

De Gouges was hardly blind to the constraints facing women. The most fundamental, however, was their complicity in their subservience. Constrained to obey, they learned to dissimulate and deploy their charms instead of demanding their rights. In the decadent *ancien régime*, only those women whom men bought like African slaves could achieve wealth and ease. Under such conditions women abandoned all aspirations except marriage to a wealthy man. Conceived as the only bargain women could strike in a culture that closed off every other avenue, marriage was "the tomb of trust and love," as she knew from experience. To reform such corrupt arrangements, de Gouges turned Rousseau's phrase against him and framed a new social contract between men and women. She proposed to make all wealth within a marriage communal and to replace primogeniture with partible inheritance.

For de Gouges, as for most eighteenth-century Europeans and Americans, the family was the fundamental building block of society. Following Rousseau, whose work she valued despite the stark difference between his vision of women and hers, in *Le bonheur primitif* she sketched a model of primitive culture in which families, not Rousseau's individuals, are at the heart of social organization. That equilibrium, in which equal men and women shared work and were content with what they had, was upset when ambitious individuals severed the marriage bond and sought satisfaction elsewhere. They returned with technology, wealth, and learning, and their new lives bred dissatisfaction among their previously happy neighbors. De Gouges, like Rousseau, seemed ambivalent about progress. Her *Declaration* ended by challenging France to take seriously its claim to embrace reason. First, she offered "a foolproof way to elevate the soul of women; it is to join them to all the activities of man." The consequence of extending the rule of nature, she predicted, would be dramatic: the end of prejudice and the purification of morals. Second, France must recognize that abolishing slavery was the logical corollary of declaring equal rights. Continuing to assert despotic authority based on "the scantiest tint" of blood was indefensible: "A divine hand seems to spread liberty abroad through the realms of man."

Yet de Gouges was no republican. She wanted a stronger Legislative Assembly, which would represent women as well as men, and she also wanted a less corrupt priesthood, which she thought might be accomplished by allowing priests to marry. Above all she wanted a more stable monarchy. She linked her call for women's rights with her preference for constitutional monarchy: "I think that these two powers," the reformed executive and the reformed legislative, "like man and woman, should be united but equal in force and virtue to make a good household." A radical critic of the old regime, she nevertheless thought care of the poor, women's rights, and the end of slavery likelier in a reformed French monarchy.[39]

Mary Wollstonecraft, although not the first to employ the term "women's rights," proved more influential than de Gouges in the Anglo-American world. Wollstonecraft's *Vindication of the Rights of Woman* (1792) became the galvanizing text for generations of women's rights advocates on both sides of the Atlantic. Neglected as a child and unsatisfied by the conventional forms of work available to her as a lady's companion, schoolteacher, and governess, Wollstonecraft began working as an assistant for the London publisher Joseph Johnson. Expanding her already solid knowledge of the Bible, Milton, and Shakespeare, she reviewed and translated books by authors ranging from Leibniz, Kames, and Adam Smith to Rousseau, Kant, Swedenborg, and Necker, thereby acquiring a first-rate education, sharpening her critical sensibility, and cementing her own convictions.

Wollstonecraft became acquainted with Richard Price, and although she never renounced her Anglican faith, she became sympathetic with his unconventional form of Protestantism. Her first book, *Thoughts on the Education of Daughters* (1787), amalgamated Lockean and dissenting ideas about reason, habits of virtue, and the desirability of providing girls as well as boys a solid foundation in morality as well as academic subjects. Wollstonecraft's Christianity was the source of her twin pole stars of duty and universal benevolence. She warned that women, learning from romantic novels to relish refined sensibilities over ethics and reason, became enmeshed in the culture of artifice, making them accomplices of the manipulative males who lusted after their bodies and refused even to acknowledge their minds. To avoid the temptations of vanity and self-love, girls as well as boys required rigorous schooling. To inculcate reason and hone the moral sense, she compiled an anthology of writings grounded on the Bible but including selections from Shakespeare and various eighteenth-century moralists.[40]

Wollstonecraft was among the first of the several dozen British writers who replied to Burke's critique of Price. She had written a detailed and enthusiastic review of Price's celebration of the French Revolution, the target of Burke's diatribe. Her defense of Price, *A Vindication of the Rights of Men, in a Letter to the Right Honourable Edmund Burke*, was published—anonymously—only a month after Burke's book on France appeared. Drawing on Locke as well as Price, Wollstonecraft defended religious toleration, natural rights, and the duties individuals owe mankind, all of which Burke derided. She counterposed a commitment to social progress to Burke's emphasis on history.

Taking aim at Burke's celebrated *Philosophical Enquiry into the Origin of Our Ideas of the Sublime and Beautiful*, in which he identified sublimity with man and mere beauty with woman, she mocked his contentions that "*littleness and weakness* are the very essence of beauty" and that only men aspire to "truth, fortitude, and humanity." Burke's gendering of virtue, Wollstonecraft wrote, itself exemplified the shallow romanticism he linked with women, whereas her analysis proved her capable of the cold-eyed reason his caricature denied them. Challenging stable social orders, Burke predicted, would lead to anarchy. "Inequality of rank," Wollstonecraft countered, "must ever impede the growth of virtue," and she included among the disadvantaged not only non-noble men but also all women.[41] Wollstonecraft charged Burke with inconsistency, as did many of his other critics. Burke had defended Americans claiming their rights as Britons; now he denigrated French efforts to do the same. Whereas Burke had ridiculed Price for celebrating the progress of Britain's enemy, France, Wollstonecraft considered such generous sentiments consistent with Christianity: "In my eye all feelings are false and spurious, that do not rest on justice as their foundation, and are not concentrated by universal love." The sublime for Wollstonecraft was neither male nor female; it was the universal benevolence shown by God toward all his creation.[42]

A second edition of *A Vindication of the Rights of Men*, this one bearing Wollstonecraft's name, soon appeared; within a year she was working on a more systematic critique of the culture of tradition, hierarchy, and politeness that Burke defended. Her *Vindication of the Rights of Woman*, the best known of the eight books she published during her lifetime, reflects her deep commitment to the form of Christianity that she, like Price and Priestley, characterized as "rational religion." Most of the critical commentary on Wollstonecraft has centered on her proto-feminist critique of patriarchy and her declaration of women's equality. The religious framework within which she wrote has received less attention. Wollstonecraft aimed not merely to empower women but to show that all humans, women as well as men, require God's grace to find fulfillment—and earn salvation—through virtuous living. Like the Scottish common-sense philosophers, she argued that following the path of virtue requires autonomy, without which no human can live according to God's plan. Women, as much as men, must be independent, not to enjoy the unbridled exercise of their "rights" but so they can choose to do God's will. Duty and universal benevolence, not freedom to follow any whims proposed by desire, provide the armature of Wollstonecraft's *Vindication*. The human soul is unsexed. All humans possess the capacity to lead virtuous lives, and all should aim for salvation rather than successful marriages or careers.

Wollstonecraft deserves her reputation as a pioneer. There is no evidence that she was familiar with de Gouges's *Declaration of the Rights of Woman*. Earlier champions of women's education such as Mary Astell, whose work Wollstonecraft did know, had not advanced arguments as bold as those contained in her *Vindication*. Wollstonecraft embedded women's rights in the broader reformist campaigns of her day, including those led in America by Adams, Jefferson, Madison, and Wilson, and in Britain by Price and Priestley: human progress through reason, the end of oppressive regimes, and the principles of natural rights and social equality. Her contribution was to extend those principles to women, which ranked among the most radical ideas of the eighteenth-century age of democratic revolutions.

Wollstonecraft's *Vindication* opens with arguments for independence, equality, and benevolence and a stinging critique of the polite culture of lust and duplicity, which together chased sincerity out of society. If women are not educated to become men's companions, she argued, the continuing progress of knowledge as well as virtue will come to a halt. Truth can triumph only if it is shared by all. A woman can become virtuous only if she is free to "strengthen her reason till she comprehend her duty." Virtues, which spring from a love of others, can be produced only if mothers raise their girls as well as their boys to prize the moral and civic interests of all people.[43] Wollstonecraft challenged prevailing ideas of domesticity. Why should we assign a sex to virtue or morality when all humans are created to "unfold their faculties"? Only if all avenues are open to women—in all worlds of work and in civic life—can they develop their God-given capacities.[44]

Wollstonecraft aligned herself with Rousseau's conception of the social contract as an agreement of the people with each other, not with their rulers. She also shared his conviction that sovereignty rests in the people. Like de Gouges, however, she used her embrace of his political ideas to challenge his portrait of Sophie in *Emile*. Conceding the brilliance of Rousseau's strategy for teaching Emile to learn autonomy, she insisted that Sophie needed precisely the same instruction. Only by learning to think for herself and act on her own could Sophie become more than the simple-minded, weak-willed, fashion-obsessed, pleasure-addled, superficial, domestic adornment that Rousseau—and most other eighteenth-century male writers—idealized as the standard of female perfection. Wollstonecraft's conviction sprang from her belief that God created all humans with "an immortal soul" and a capacity for virtue to be developed. She credited Adam Smith with tracing to the court of Louis XIV the mania for frivolous beauty and "false refinement" that supplanted respect for "knowledge, industry, valour, and beneficence," the values Wollstonecraft herself prized.[45]

Some critics have accused Wollstonecraft of misogyny for denouncing women's "stupid acquiescence" in the "imbecility" and "listless inactivity" scripted for them. Others have criticized her treatment of passionate, romantic infatuation, which she dismissed as a sham compared with the enduring friendship she portrayed as the ideal of marriage. Such judgments nicely capture the distance between Wollstonecraft's austere Christian worldview and our own culture's obsession with liberating individuals from all constraints on behavior.[46] Wollstonecraft's sensibility took shape within the traditions of astringent Protestantism and Scottish moral philosophy, and she invoked her faith to explain the convictions about women's autonomy that her contemporaries found shocking: It was God who had impressed these "utopian dreams" of sexual equality on her soul, "and gave me sufficient strength of mind to dare to exert my own reason, till, becoming dependent only on him for the support of my virtue, I view, with indignation, the mistaken notions that enslave my sex." She acknowledged only one reliable basis for morality, the God who instilled in all humans, as an "emanation of divinity, the tie that connects the creature with the Creator," the power to reason for themselves. Wollstonecraft concluded her chapter criticizing Rousseau and other writers equally content to encourage women to limit themselves to the domestic sphere with an arresting sentence. "For it is the right use of reason alone which makes us independent of every thing—excepting the unclouded Reason—'Whose service is perfect freedom.'" Given Wollstonecraft's invocation of the familiar Christian adage about subjecting oneself voluntarily to God, her reference to "Reason" with a capital *R* should be understood as an unclouded reference to the divine master whom the faithful serve. Interpreters who take "Reason" itself to be Wollstonecraft's God only indicate the gulf that separates her world from ours. From her perspective, only through the ancient Christian practice of self-emptying, or kenosis, could humans find themselves capable of serving God by loving all of his creation.[47]

Instead of devoting all their love to a single man, as women in search of husbands—or wives trying to keep them—were urged to do, Wollstonecraft counseled women that they should "let love to man be only part of that glowing flame and universal love, which, after encircling humanity, mounts in grateful incense to God." In contrast to Burke, who had insisted Britons should limit their loyalty to their own nation, Wollstonecraft argued that "the tie which draws man to the Deity" leads the faithful to feel "drawn by some cord of love to all his fellow creatures." The love God commands extends beyond the boundaries of family. Thus women as well as men must tend to the public as well as the private sphere. "Public spirit must be nurtured by private virtue, or it will resemble the factitious sentiment which makes women careful to preserve their reputation and men their honour."[48]

By lifting the tightly drawn mask of sentimental love, Wollstonecraft exposed the self-loathing of men consumed by lust and women confined to coquetry. Such deformations were inherited along with hierarchy and wealth; health could be restored only through radical reform. "There must be more equality established in society, or morality will never gain ground. Moreover, this virtuous equality will not rest firmly even when founded on a rock, if one half of mankind be chained to its bottom by fate, for they will be continually undermining it through ignorance or pride."[49] Beyond the shiny but brittle surface of politeness prized by Burke, her vision extended from the autonomous self to civic engagement, an alternative model of egalitarian social interaction for both sexes grounded in and aspiring to the universal benevolence of God.[50]

Wollstonecraft's model of womanhood, like that of de Gouges, included citizenship. She called for women to escape the few "menial" occupations open to them, study politics and history instead of reading only romantic fiction, and find work wherever their talents took them, as physicians, farmers, shopkeepers, or artisans. Having become independent, women should select representatives in Parliament, thereby redeeming a corrupt institution that functioned only as a "convenient handle for despotism." Instead of serving as ornaments, women could then raise the economic, political, and moral standard of civilization. "Would men but generously snap our chains," Wollstonecraft concluded, "and be content with rational fellowship instead of slavish obedience," they would gain from the bargain. They "would find us more observant daughters, more affectionate sisters, more faithful wives, more reasonable mothers—in a word, better citizens. We should then love them with true affection, because we should learn to respect ourselves."[51] Wollstonecraft's *Vindication of the Rights of Woman*, as critics correctly observe, is repetitive, rhetorically overblown, and innocent of the stubbornly murky depths of both identity and sexuality, yet it was the first critique of gender roles to elaborate an alternative model for autonomous women and men. It also stands as the first sketch, at least in outline, of a democratic world that women and men might make together.[52]

Wollstonecraft's book became a sensation. She earned the gratitude of Price and the admiration of his circle of radicals, including William Godwin, Tom Paine, and the Americans Joel Barlow and Thomas Cooper, in part because she also assailed economic inequality. She called Burke's defense of the existing distribution of wealth "hard-hearted sophistry" and, also like de Gouges, Paine, Barlow, and Cooper—as well as Adams, Jefferson, and

Madison—she advocated dividing the large estates of the aristocracy into small farms on which the indolence of the rich would be replaced by the industry of the poor. Civic virtue, she concluded, "can only flourish among equals."[53]

Such arguments for economic equality were hardly unprecedented. They had surfaced in England in the 1630s and 1640s, and they had reverberated in America from that time through the end of the eighteenth century.[54] Wollstonecraft was the first writer to embed those proposals within an analysis of the inequality of men and women; such egalitarian ideas remained scandalous in the refined circles to which Burke appealed. When Paine published the second part of his *Rights of Man*, in February of 1792, he described the moral sense as "a system of social affections" implanted in every human. His arguments for progressive taxation and social insurance programs, premised on that principle of universal obligation, provoked predictable outrage. Paine elaborated on the ideas he had first broached four years earlier, in the letter he wrote to Jefferson from Paris in February 1788. He distinguished natural rights, by which he meant the right to think and speak freely, from civil rights, particularly the right to acquire and preserve property, which derive not from nature but from society, and which exist only as a result of society's guarantee to enforce its rules.[55] Paine argued that property came into existence only because of the implicit social power that provides each individual with security against the threat of everyone else. His calls for unemployment relief, old-age pensions, and assistance to the poor for their children's education flowed directly from that premise.[56]

Burke had focused his attack on the intellectual underpinnings and cultural consequences of the French Revolution, but he also criticized the radicals' proposed political institutions. From Burke's perspective, the Revolution began by proclaiming an obvious falsehood, the equality of men, then compounded the problem by using wealth to distinguish among those qualified to vote at different stages of the electoral process. Robespierre and others who opposed that measure had emphasized the same point. Burke did not have to choose between the principle of equality and its application in practice: he condemned both. He also differentiated between ancient republics, in which different classes and interests were balanced, and the Assembly's "tyranny and usurpation" in arrogating all power to itself.[57] Though Burke disdained the very idea of a republic, he chided the French for disregarding Montesquieu's advice to balance democracy, aristocracy, and monarchy. Paine took direct aim at that argument in *Rights of Man*. Burke knows so little about the principles of government, Paine began, "that he confounds democracy and representation together." Paine contended that "representation was a thing unknown in the ancient democracies." Instead, citizens of the small Greek city-states met together in a forum. When populations increased and territories expanded, however, that "simple democratical form became unwieldy and impracticable." Since the small-scale polities of the ancient world were unfamiliar with "the system of representation," they degenerated into tyranny or were conquered by the monarchies surrounding them.

Paine offered his own taxonomy: "The only forms of government are, the democratical, the aristocratical, the monarchical, and what is now called the representative." It has since become conventional wisdom that the United States was to be categorized as a republic rather than a democracy. Paine disagreed. "What is called a *republic*," he insisted, "is not any *particular form* of government." The word indicates instead only the purpose for which government should be instituted, "RES-PUBLICA, the public affairs, or the public good; or, literally translated, the *public thing*." A republic stands in sharp contrast to monarchy, which means instead "arbitrary power in an individual person," government focused on the interest of the king, not the good of the people. Although multiple forms of government might thus be described as republican, Paine contended that "it most naturally associates with the representative form, as being best calculated to secure" the public good. Paine had embraced the characterization of a republic that Sieyès offered in their exchange in the summer of 1791. Now he rejected Sieyès's claim that a monarchy could be a republic.

Although other states had called themselves republics, the United States, resting "wholly on the system of representation, is the only real republic in character and practice, that now exists." Paine was adamant in his response to the already common claim, popular among some Antifederalists in the United States, that the Constitution had diverged from its proper form by instituting government by representatives rather than by the people themselves. The American government aimed at nothing but the public good, and "therefore it is properly a republic." The United States rejected all hereditary honors and offices, "establishing government on the system of representation only." The problem of extending the size of the territory governed by the people could be solved only by representation: "Retaining, then, democracy as the ground, and rejecting the corrupt systems of monarchy and aristocracy, the representative system naturally presents itself; remedying at once the defects of the simple democracy as to form, and the incapacity of the other two" to attain the public good.

By "ingrafting representation upon democracy," Paine argued, "we arrive at a system of government capable of embracing and confederating all the various interests and every extent of territory and population." Through the deliberation of representatives chosen by people of different kinds, with different interests, an interest distinct from all of their personal interests—the *common* interest—could emerge. Echoing Adams, Jefferson, Madison, and Wilson, Paine designated America as much "the admiration and model of the present" as Athens was, "in miniature," the "wonder" of its day. Even "Athens, by representation, would have outrivalled her own democracy" because it could have identified thereby the public good that eluded it. Uniquely "conducive to the various interests of the community," representative democracy "concentrates the knowledge necessary to the interest of the parts, and of the whole," and avoids both the "nonage" and "dotage" of monarchies: power remains with the people, "never in the cradle, nor on crutches." It is refreshed by the constant infusion of new blood, and new ideas, in the form of newly elected public servants. Whereas monarchy is "all a bubble, a mere court artifice to procure money" that allows the royal family to live in splendor, democratic government performs only necessary functions. In the United States, a much wider range of citizens paid taxes than in aristocratic and monarchical France and England. More Americans were self-sufficient and fewer impoverished, and Paine considered his legislative proposals for addressing poverty in European nations irrelevant to the United States. Because extremes of wealth and poverty were unknown in America and, he predicted, representative democracy would surely prevent their emergence in the future, such measures would remain unnecessary.

Compared with monarchy and aristocracy, Paine argued that fewer people are uninformed in a democracy because "the representative system diffuses such a body of knowledge throughout a nation on the subject of government, as to explode ignorance." In monarchies all decisions are made in secret councils; in a representative system, because every citizen has a personal stake in government, all decisions are made in public. Because those decisions reflect the will of the majority, those who lose must accept the outcome. *Rights of Man* showed how Paine's experience in America had shaped his understanding of government. He first explained how the people empowered their representatives to write state constitutions, then traced the developments leading to the Constitutional Convention in Philadelphia. The ratification debates showed representative democracy at work. Although most state constitutions were ratified by large majorities, bitter disputes marked others, particularly in Massachusetts and Pennsylvania. Yet after the acrimonious debates in Massachusetts ended, Paine wrote, and the vote was taken, the minority opposition made a crucial decision. They declared, in Paine's words, "*that though they had argued and voted against it, because certain parts appeared to them in a different light to what they appeared to other members; yet, as the vote had decided in favour of the constitution as proposed, they should give it the same practical support as if they had voted for it.*" Of course, Paine was exaggerating. Struggles over issues ranging from taxation and the militia to the structure and functions of government continued. Even so, Paine's assertion reflects his judgment that a shared commitment to reciprocity enabled Massachusetts to endure the persistence of deep conflicts.

Paine knew from experience that equally deep conflicts marked Pennsylvania politics. After the United States Constitution was ratified and Pennsylvanians decided to revise their 1776 state constitution, the citizens elected delegates to a convention called for that purpose. Critics grumbled, and some observers predicted the worst, but the crisis passed: The proposals were published, the people accepted them, and they became law. The fact that such alterations could be made in nations ruled by constitutions, Paine argued, obviated the need for revolution. Whereas monarchists in Britain and France cherished traditions instead of political engineering, Paine pointed out that because all the constitutions in the United States were "established on the authority of the people," the people retained the power to revise their fundamental laws without resorting to violence.[58]

Paine became acquainted with Wollstonecraft while he was writing the second part of *Rights of Man*. They had a lot in common: an aversion to Burke, enthusiasm for the French Revolution, and confidence that representative democracy was the wave of the future. In December 1792, Wollstonecraft traveled to France to witness the changes endorsed in her *Vindication of the Rights of Men*. Several months later, accused by British authorities of seditious libel for his *Rights of Man*, Paine began thinking about leaving England for France himself. By the time he and Wollstonecraft arrived in Paris, the Revolution had entered its second phase.

Beginning in the summer of 1792, armed radicals in Paris seized control of the Revolution. Known as *sans-culottes* for their aversion to the breeches worn in polite society, they became the battering ram of the Paris Jacobin Society.[59] Paris had been divided into forty-eight *sections*, each with its own assembly. Some members of the assemblies, impatient with economic conditions and wary of the threat of counterrevolution, had begun to embrace a conception of democracy very different from that of Paine and Wollstonecraft. They considered themselves "the people," and they believed that they should be making the decisions about the pace and direction of the Revolution themselves. Some *sectionnaires*, as the members of these municipal assemblies were known, affiliated with the Paris Jacobins, others with the more radical Cordeliers Club, which had been calling for the king to step down or be deposed. A few demanded that he should be tried for treason. Bad news from the war's front lines bolstered rumors that the royal family was plotting with the queen's brother the Holy Roman Emperor to roll back the Revolution. Uprisings against the remnants of the old regime were on the rise in the provinces, and simmering anger between champions of the Revolution and those loyal to the king and refractory clergy was bubbling into violence.

The Assembly, never unified, voted to require the refractory clergy to swear another loyalty oath and established in Paris a new military force of twenty-thousand soldiers. These *fédérés*, faithful to the Revolution, would replace the king's loyal (and therefore untrustworthy) Swiss Guard. When the king vetoed both measures, as the constitution empowered him to do, his critics, including members of the ministry, exploded with rage. The dissenting ministers were sacked; unrest mounted. On June 20 a crowd estimated at more than ten thousand gathered at the Tuileries Palace to cheer speeches denouncing the king, the queen, France's enemies, and the ineffective army led by the increasingly unpopular Lafayette. Louis XVI sat expressionless at a window, wearing a red liberty hat as an unconvincing sop to the crowd, which eventually dispersed without satisfaction. Gouverneur Morris wrote in his diary, "The constitution has this day I think given its last groan."[60] Lafayette, fearing a more violent replay of the Bastille, returned to Paris. Speaking at the Assembly, he denounced everyone responsible for the events of June 20 and ordered the National Guard to disband the Jacobin Society. Ominously, the militia ignored his order.

In the next few weeks the positions of both the king and Lafayette became increasingly precarious. Forty-seven of the forty-eight Paris *sections* voted for the king to be deposed. Robespierre, speaking before the Jacobins on July 29, announced that "serious ills call for drastic remedies" and implied that the time had come for an insurrection to defend France from a king who had shown that he "wants to destroy the state." Rather than signaling that the law and the constitution were being abandoned, in the present circumstances insurrection had become a "necessary measure for health."[61] The Cordeliers, the now-armed *sections*, a momentarily unified Assembly, and *fédérés* from all over France—including those from Marseille with their bloodthirsty battle song—were joining together in opposition to the monarchy. When the Assembly refused a call for Lafayette to be indicted, the *sections* demanded action.

A group calling itself the Insurrectionary Commune, which included Robespierre, seized control of the Paris government on August 10, 1792. Declaring that its authority derived from the general will of the *sections*, the Commune ordered the National Guard to march on the Tuileries. Aware that his Swiss Guard of nine hundred would be no match for the twenty thousand soldiers and armed *sans-culottes* massing against him, the king sought refuge in the Assembly. The crowd advanced, the Swiss Guards fired, and the Marseille *fédérés* responded with devastating force. By the end of the massacre, six hundred of the Swiss Guards were dead and the royal family were prisoners. Robespierre interpreted the events as the fulfillment of the people's will. Writing on August 11 an account that appeared only ten days later in *La defenseur de la constitution*, he gave a detailed narrative of the events. Seizing the king was made necessary by the discovery of a counterrevolutionary plot to slaughter the people of Paris in "a new St. Bartholomew's Day massacre." The Commune had acted in self-defense. "The French people," Robespierre proclaimed, long "dishonored" and "oppressed," had chosen at last to fulfill "the sacred duty imposed by nature on all living beings, and with even more reason on all nations, of being able to take care of their own preservation by a generous resistance to oppression."

Robespierre contended that the August uprising was consistent with—indeed fulfilled the promise of—the principles of 1789: the people had exercised their sovereignty and deployed their power to secure their safety and happiness. Those who rebelled in Paris acted on behalf of the entire nation and inspired others to follow their example. In Robespierre's judgment, the storming of the Tuileries and the Assembly marked a new stage of "the most glorious revolution that has ever honored humanity," the first ever devoted to the principles of equality, justice, and reason.[62] Sieyès, Condorcet, and Paine had invoked those principles with a fervor equal to Robespierre's. The distance separating his understanding from theirs would become clear in the months following the insurrection of August 10.[63]

France was at a crossroads. When documents found in the Tuileries confirmed the king's complicity in treasonous plots, the Legislative Assembly took up the question of a new constitution. On August 11 it proclaimed that a two-stage election would be held without the former distinction between active and passive citizens. The result, however, was hardly the wide suffrage long celebrated by enthusiasts of this "second revolution." Only those males above twenty-one years old, "resident in a canton for a year, living upon an income or from the proceeds of employment, and not working as a domestic servant," were permitted to vote. Not only were women and servants excluded. The residency requirement ruled out many peasants and casual laborers who moved often in search of work. Long-standing assumptions about dependency persisted even at the height of the French Revolution, as did the filtering device of a two-stage electoral process. Traditional limits on suffrage remained in place even after direct action had brought down the monarchy.[64]

Still more significant, however, were other constraints imposed in the chaotic days following the August uprising. Before the Assembly disbanded, it decreed that nonjuring priests were to be banished. Local authorities throughout France imposed new rules of their own, sometimes extending sanctions to include even those priests who had taken the oath. The Paris Commune, which together with the *sections* had taken effective control of the capital, established tribunals to judge everyone suspected of disloyalty. Danton and Marat, among the most ruthless members of the Commune, ordered homes to be searched and suspects apprehended. Those found guilty—or, in many cases, merely accused—of treason were tried and killed by the newly devised instrument of humane execution, the guillotine.

Thousands died during the emergency of August and September. Those executed included not only nobles, members and friends of the royal court, refractory priests, and the Swiss Guards who survived the battle of the Tuileries, but also ordinary people who had the misfortune of falling under the suspicion of newly empowered *sectionnaires*. Gangs of vengeance-seeking *sans-culottes* passed through the prisons and the remaining monasteries, rectories, and convents of Paris, in some cases indiscriminately murdering those unfortunate enough to be in their way. Between September 2 and September 7, between 1,100 and 1,400 people were killed, some of them self-proclaimed friends of the Revolution and others ordinary criminals. Violence was hardly confined to Paris. The second revolution generated intense resistance in many regions; loyalists and republicans attacked and counterattacked in an increasingly murderous spiral.

The war too took a more dangerous turn. Lafayette escaped Paris, tried and failed to turn the army against the capital, and made his way to Belgium, where Austrian forces rewarded the disillusioned champion of liberty, the "hero of two revolutions," with immediate imprisonment as a dangerous insurgent. The Prussian army passed the fortifications at Verdun and appeared ready to attack Paris. As panic spread, elections for the new National Convention were held, and the second round occurred just as the September massacres began. Not surprisingly, despite the fact that the potential electorate had grown by perhaps 50 percent, only about 15 percent of those eligible turned out to vote. Turnout was not much higher for municipal elections at the end of the year. Although ordinary Frenchmen were now citizens entitled to vote, lacking traditions of participation and experience with mobilization, they were not immediately prepared to exercise the franchise; popular turnout for elections remained haphazard. The most prominent citizens, including absent members of the nobility and clergy who remained under suspicion, were still often returned to office. More insidiously, several years of increasingly bitter criticism of the Assembly had bred pervasive distrust of representative government, particularly in Paris. Many newspapers as well as speakers in the clubs and *sections* disparaged elected officials and rhapsodized about the direct action of "the people" in the streets.[65] Anxious legislators in the National Assembly, fearing enraged Parisians would target them next, commissioned Condorcet to defend them. "Any nation in which the title *representative* is not sacred," he wrote, "is necessarily a nation without government and without law." Unless representatives remained free to express their ideas without apprehension, their decisions would be determined not by their judgment or the dictates of conscience but by fear and expediency. In that case the Assembly could no longer express the general will of the nation. It would reflect instead merely the passions of individuals exercising power for their own purposes.[66] For a time at least, elected officials were spared.

The undeniable effectiveness of mass social action was made clear not only in the capital but also on the battlefield. In response to Danton's call to arms, more than twenty thousand citizens mustered to fight the Prussian army. At the decisive Battle of Valmy on September 20, the "people's army," as it came to be called, defeated the better-organized and -equipped but less spirited invading force. On that day France was declared a republic.

The newly formed National Assembly contained many men with impressive political experience and deep convictions. More than 85 percent had served either in the Legislative or Constituent Assembly or held local elective office. It soon divided into three principal factions. The moderate Brissontins, many of whom hailed from the Bordeaux region, were dubbed Girondins after the Gironde estuary north of the city of Bordeaux. The more radical members, mostly from Paris, who sat in the upper part of the Assembly and to the left of the speaker, came to be known as the Montagnards, or the Mountain. Between them lay the other delegates, sometimes called either the Plain or the Swamp, aligned with neither of the principal camps. The Assembly contained most of the celebrated writers, orators, and activists of the Revolution, including not only Brissot, Sieyès, and Condorcet but also Robespierre, Danton, and Marat. Reflecting the sense of international solidarity that had animated the deliberations of the Assembly since 1789, Paine and Price had also been elected. Paine was delighted by the honor, and he decided to sail for France as the date of his London trial for libel approached. Greeted with enthusiasm as a friend of the Revolution, he voted to proclaim the republic and was named, along with Sieyès and Condorcet, to the eleven-member committee responsible for drafting another new constitution. Having written extensively about how representative democracy should work, the three of them seemed well suited to the task. Paris in 1792, however, was hardly Philadelphia in 1787. Americans contended with activists opposed to their efforts, but they did not face members of the clergy whose followers were instigating a civil war. Nor were they threatened by a coalition of neighboring nations, whose armies were massed at their borders and bolstered by prominent members of their own centuries-old nobility. Above all, they did not have to decide what to do with a captured king.

Those elected to the Constitutional Convention in Philadelphia in 1787 disagreed with each other, but they were not at each other's throats. Compared with the tone of debate in Paris, disagreements in Philadelphia were decorous. In France poisonous rivalries were visible to everyone watching, listening to, and reading about the debates. Strategic disagreements and personal animosities were quickly inflated into matters of principle. Rhetoric calculated to inflame public sentiments usually crowded out efforts at calm deliberation. In a new journal launched to air his views, Robespierre ostentatiously invoked the general will of the nation and the virtue that "resolves all private interests into the general interest." He derided those unidentified enemies who doubted the wisdom of the people and cloaked himself in the gauzy robes of Rousseau's demigod lawgiver.[67] Brissot's allies replied to such charges with accusations that Robespierre wanted to end the Revolution by installing himself as tyrant. In response Danton denounced the Girondins. The never-subtle Marat also took up the challenge, defending Robespierre from Brissot yet insisting that only a dictatorship would end the "fifty years of anarchy" that would be France's fate otherwise. Robespierre called for Brissot's expulsion from the Jacobins, then in turn found himself accused, at the Convention, of responsibility for the September massacres.[68]

Robespierre was a lightning rod throughout these tumultuous debates. Even moderates split. On the one hand, Condorcet wrote scornfully of Robespierre that "he is a priest and will never be other than a priest." On the other, Olympe de Gouges wrote to Robespierre proposing that the two of them demonstrate their selfless patriotism by drowning themselves together in the Seine. His reply has not survived. Robespierre himself did not deny his role in helping arouse the people on August 10 to the glorious cause of the Revolution. Nor did he deny that innocent people had died. Yet France, while mourning such injustice committed on behalf of justice, should "keep back some tears for more touching calamities" and "weep instead for the hundred thousand victims of tyranny." Weighing centuries of oppression against a relatively few years of bloody vengeance, and aligning that violence with the general will, became a standard trope for Robespierre in the coming months. The cord tying his conception of popular sovereignty to elections, representative institutions, and law was fraying.[69]

At that pivotal moment, with radical sentiment in Paris and royalist sentiment in the west and south intensifying, the Convention voted to put the king on trial. The case against Louis XVI was made most forcefully by radicals such as Robespierre and Louis-Antoine de Saint-Just. Robespierre's conclusion was blunt: "Louis cannot be judged; he has already been condemned, else the republic is not cleared of guilt." Even suggesting a trial for the already dishonored king was "counter-revolutionary because it would bring the Revolution itself before the court." The people's will does not render its judgments in a court of law; rather it "hurls down thunderbolts." Robespierre's final judgment left no room for equivocation: "Louis must die because the nation must live."[70]

Yet wrangling persisted. Taking the life of Louis XVI remained a wrenching decision even for many French people who relished the end of monarchy in the abstract. After the king was declared guilty of treason on January 14, 1793, heated debates about his fate continued. Only the barest majority in the Convention voted for his execution. Robespierre denied that a vote could have any bearing on the king's guilt. Neither truth nor virtue is determined by majority rule: "The minority retains an inalienable right to make heard the voice of truth, or what it regards as such. Virtue is always in the minority on earth." When polled one final time for his vote on the king's execution, Robespierre announced, "I am inflexible in relation to oppressors because I am compassionate toward the oppressed. I do not recognize the humanity that butchers the people and pardons despots."[71] The conviction that the truth could be known by the virtuous and compassionate, regardless of evidence, undergirded a conception of government in which elections, assemblies, and juries were superfluous.

Moderates divided on the king's fate. Sieyès voted, reluctantly, in favor of execution; that vote probably saved his own life. De Gouges and Paine were opposed. De Gouges had written that since women had the right to mount the scaffold, they should have the right to mount the rostrum in public debate. Consistent with her conception of woman's role, she volunteered to defend the king at his trial. That was a step considerably more audacious than her advocacy of women's rights, a dangerous-enough stance after the Jacobins had shuttered the Paris women's clubs for challenging the Jacobins' official doctrine of separate spheres. Paine invoked Robespierre's earlier critique of capital punishment and expressed his fear that killing the king would intensify the hatred of other nations. Paine's opposition to regicide soured him on the Revolution, and the revolutionaries on him.[72] The judicious Condorcet, upset by the increasingly heated rhetoric of erstwhile moderates now calling for the king's head, replied to Saint-Just and Robespierre that the king as a public official deserved a trial. Condorcet's mediating argument, lodged between the claims of loyalists, who insisted that Louis XVI stood above the government and was thus not subject to its authority, and those of Saint-Just and Robespierre, who countered that he already stood condemned, carried the day. At the end of the proceedings, however, there appeared to be no moderate position between life and death.

For centuries France had aspired to unity. Saint-Just and Robespierre insisted that the Revolution establish its legitimacy by removing the person as well as the symbol of the united authority that had preceded 1789. Yet as Paine understood, and as the contrast with the United States made clear, the radicals were demanding unity on the principle of popular sovereignty even as they denied the legitimacy—and as they destroyed the possibility—of the institutional as well as cultural resources necessary for democracy to survive.[73]

Anguish about the consequences of voting on regicide was justified. The final tally in the Convention reflected public sentiment in France. A plurality of 361 voted to execute the former Louis XVI, now known as Louis Capet, 288 voted against putting him to death, and 72 voted—for various reasons, including Paine's judgment that it should be up to the next national assembly—to delay the decision. That margin, a single vote, signaled the division prevailing in 1793 more clearly than did the later roll-call votes that yielded a margin of seventy in favor of execution. When Louis Capet went to the guillotine on January 21, 1793, his death cemented the already deep rift that transformed the meaning of the Revolution for its friends and its foes alike. As Brissot had quipped during the debates, "The blood of Charles I gave new life to royalty." So it proved again. After the death of Louis Capet, France was not only at war against the monarchies of Europe, which intensified their efforts in the wake of the king's execution. France was at war against itself.[74]

As the Revolution was metamorphosing into civil war, those charged with constituting the new French republic were doing their best to create a framework that might keep the nation from disintegrating. Although Paine and Condorcet were in conversation during the fall of 1792, the draft of the constitution produced by Condorcet's committee contained few of the social democratic features characteristic of Wollstonecraft's *Vindication* and Paine's *Rights of Man*.[75] Instead it concentrated on decentralizing the institutional structures of government in order to give reason—and the common good—a chance to triumph. "The great art of governing," Condorcet wrote, "consists therefore in ceaselessly countering the one-sided restlessness of factions of people with the confidence of the mass of the people, and contrasting to the opinions of parties and factions the shared opinion of the whole." Consistent with his earlier writings, Condorcet intended the elaborate system of elections, with its multiple layers of assemblies voting on multiple officials and issues, to align democracy with reason. Condorcet's Girondin constitution, in certain respects patterned on the Pennsylvania Constitution of 1776, was presented to the Convention on February 15, 1793, and debated until the middle of May. It sought not only to empower local assemblies throughout France but also to limit the possibility that violent mass insurrections could preempt representative democracy. The constitution provided citizens with avenues to protest "in a legal and peaceful form" by giving each local assembly the power to initiate meetings to address any issue, then take their grievances to the intermediate levels of government, and eventually to the national assembly. The plan required revising the constitution every twenty years and allowed more frequent amendments if necessary.[76]

Condorcet's committee had issued an undeniably democratic plan. It provided nearly universal manhood suffrage—though not woman suffrage, which remained beyond imagining for almost all the men in the Convention. It stipulated that the selection of officials, not only legislative representatives but also national and departmental administrators, lay in the hands of voters. The constitution's emphasis on local engagement and its provision for multiple stages of deliberation—or, more precisely, for multiple stages of decision making, since Condorcet still wanted voters to choose between "yes" and "no" as often as possible—prompted the Jacobins immediately to brand it "federalist" and thus an affront to the unity of the nation. Condorcet deliberately tried to channel volatile popular sentiment into the institutions of representative democracy.[77] Identifying the will of the people with the triumphant violence of the Paris Commune, the Jacobins denounced Condorcet's committee as counterrevolutionary. Addressing the Convention on April 15, 1793, Robespierre focused his attention on the urgent need to address the economic problems plaguing France. He called for progressive taxation, government intervention to stabilize prices, and strategies to provide sustenance to those in need, and he excoriated unnamed villains guilty of making personal profit at the public's expense. Robespierre's hyperbolic characterizations of good and evil, punctuated with sharp contrasts between the virtuous poor and greedy merchants, brought the language of the streets, and the older vocabulary of republican moral economy, into the postmonarchist republic. It aligned the Jacobins with popular resentments against all members of all elites, real and imagined.[78]

Condorcet's constitution, by contrast, with its emphasis on reason and distrust of emotion, came from the austere world of the philosophes and the physiocrats. The success of the constitution Condorcet envisioned was contingent on an equally ambitious plan for education designed to ensure that the most discerning individuals would rise to positions of leadership. Its five levels, as he imagined them, would culminate in a National Society of Arts and Sciences to guide the entire system. Critics denounced Condorcet's plan as an insult to untutored republican citizens. The people had shown that the ability to discern—and especially the strength to act on behalf of—the general interest depends on virtue, not education. In the overheated atmosphere of the Convention, Condorcet's contention that better-educated individuals would make better judgments as citizens did not appeal to those deciding France's future.[79]

The Convention wrangled over the Girondin proposals for five months. In late May 1793, renewed unrest in Paris shifted the locus of power from the moderates to the radicals. The Girondins were expelled from the Convention on June 2, and the remaining representatives voted to adopt the Jacobin alternative to Condorcet's plan. Conventional ideas of representation now seemed suspect. From Robespierre's perspective, decisions made by elected representatives could never express the general will. Only the people themselves, either through active insurrection or passive acceptance of the Convention's decisions, possessed that capacity. "There exists for all men but one morality, one single conscience." Any deviation, of the sort demonstrated not only by royalists but also by moderates openly disagreeing with each other in the Convention, reflected a dangerous lack of virtue. Ordinary people, "leaving the hands of nature," were naturally trustworthy. Only the presence of conspirators threatened their ability to discern the public good. For that reason true patriots had to be vigilant in defending the people from their enemies, including those who disguised themselves beneath masks of moderation (the Girondins) or zeal (the ultraradical *enragés*).

Robespierre's attempt to justify enforced unanimity became more desperate during the coming months. On Christmas Day it reached a crescendo of grandeur or obfuscation. "The goal of constitutional government," he explained, "is to preserve the Republic; that of revolutionary government is to found it." From Robespierre's perspective, France was still in the midst of its revolution, so conspirators' venom could smother republican virtue in its cradle. "The revolution is the war of liberty against its enemies; the constitution is the regime of liberty victorious and peaceful. Revolutionary government requires extraordinary activity, precisely because it is at war." Until the Revolution had consolidated its control against it enemies, both internal and external, no ordinary constitutional government, with power vested in elected representatives, would suffice.[80] The Jacobins' constitutional proposals fed such appetites for national unity—at least as it was understood by Robespierre and the

Committee of Public Safety, a new executive council established by the Convention in the spring of 1792. Although the Jacobins' scheme provided for popular election of legislators, real authority was vested in an executive council of twenty-four to be chosen by the Convention. Condorcet, Sieyès, and Paine were appalled by this concentration of power in the hands of an appointed body and the abandonment of the multiple sites of deliberation proposed in the Girondin constitution. The center of gravity in the Convention, however, had moved from the moderates to the most extreme faction of Montagnards. The plan was adopted and submitted to the people for ratification.

Opposition to the Revolution was also intensifying, particularly in the west and south of France, throughout the spring and summer of 1793. Even so, the Jacobin Constitution was quickly declared ratified. The popular vote in favor of the new constitution, held on August 20, 1793, was reported to be 1,784,377 in favor and 11,531 opposed. Turnout was higher in Paris and in the east, where the war continued and enthusiasm for the Revolution ran high, than in the south and the west, where resistance was concentrated and where many disgruntled cantons did not even organize a vote. The results of the referendum on the Jacobin Constitution indicated that the concept of individual voting had not yet become firmly established. Many local authorities throughout France still registered a collective vote or sent emissaries to report their decision: Jaussier, a village in the Alps, sent delegates who declared, in good Rousseauean fashion, that the three of them represented "the general will of their community." In several neighborhoods in Paris, the vote in favor of the constitution was said to be unanimous. Such signs of consensus, however, masked underlying discord that was not dissipating but intensifying.[81]

The extent of that resistance became increasingly apparent in the winter and spring of 1793, after the Convention had decided the fate of Louis Capet and tried to raise a mass army against the monarchies threatening France. Those opposed to the Revolution began forming into more durable bands of armed counterrevolutionaries, who were already beginning to flex their muscles from Brittany to Provence and in other cities including Bourges and Lyon. By far the most significant resistance took shape in the west, along the Loire River in the region known as the Vendée, where a core of around ten thousand rebels ballooned into a ragged force of perhaps sixty thousand in the spring and summer of 1793. The Vendée had previously been just one among many regions uneasy with aspects of the Revolution, particularly the Civil Constitution of the Clergy. The conscription of soldiers to fight in the revolutionary army now prompted a full-scale rebellion in the name of God and (the now-dead) king. After armed peasants seized control of several towns and defeated troops sent to put down the uprising, scattered raids blossomed into an insurrection that stretched from Caen in the north to Bordeaux in the southwest. Charlotte Corday's murder of Marat on July 13, although unconnected with any organized movement, convinced those inclined toward conspiracy—an ever-increasing number—that the Revolution was besieged.

As evidence of counterrevolution within France mounted, military threats loomed at France's borders. From Flanders to the Mediterranean port of Toulon, French defenses were crumbling. The radicalism of the Parisian *sans-culottes* rose with food prices, and demands for more drastic action accelerated through the summer. As the now-discredited Girondins, with whom Corday had been identified, attracted increasing suspicion as agents of counterrevolution, the most incendiary of the Montagnards took the initiative. On September 5, 1793, the Convention responded to perils internal and external by declaring terror "the order of the day." The Revolutionary Tribunal, established six months earlier to address threats in the Vendée, was reorganized to streamline the progress from accusation to execution. Paine had written to Danton and Marat in the spring, complaining of the rising "spirit of denunciation" that enabled every individual to "indulge his private malignancy" by denouncing enemies "at random and without any kind of proof." Before the end of the year, Paine himself was accused of counterrevolutionary activity and imprisoned in the former Luxembourg Palace.[82]

On September 17 the infamous Law of Suspects was proclaimed. This measure, prompted (or justified) the arrest of more than eight hundred thousand people and set off the notorious butchery of 1794. The Place de la Révolution in central Paris (formerly the Place Louis XV, later renamed the Place de la Concorde) was home to the guillotine, which yielded the most vivid, grisly, and durable images of the Terror. It claimed not only Marie Antoinette but also Girondins such as Brissot and de Gouges, and radicals such as Danton, condemned by the Revolutionary Tribunal he had created. De Gouges, denounced as an enemy of the people for voting against the execution of Louis XVI and writing tracts condemning Robespierre, continued to proclaim her "truly republican soul" and her loyalty to the Revolution as well as the king. "Your blood alone," she wrote to Robespierre in the final text smuggled from her prison cell, "can wash away the stains that you have imprinted on the French nation."[83]

Visible and grisly as such beheadings were, fewer than two thousand people were guillotined by order of the Revolutionary Tribunal, and their deaths shrink to insignificance compared with the quarter of a million people slaughtered throughout France in executions, massacres, and pitched battles between pro- and counterrevolutionary forces. Horrific as contemporaneous violence was—whether in Saint-Domingue, Ireland, or Poland, where similar outrages occurred—the tales of devout Catholics drowned by the thousands in the Loire, or of other atrocities no less horrific, endure as testimony of the hideous violence perpetrated by revolutionaries and their foes. As in the wars of religion, entire towns and stretches of countryside were put to the torch. In parts of France, as in Ireland during the mid-seventeenth century, the population was cut in half, leaving a legacy of bitterness that contaminated French politics for more than two centuries.[84]

Condorcet too was charged with conspiracy against the Revolution in the fall of 1793. He was accused of having abandoned the people, just as he thought the Convention had abandoned his constitution. Instead of plotting, however, he was sequestered in a hideaway in Paris, working intently to complete a book bearing the cruelly ironic title *Esquisse d'un tableau historique des progrès de l'esprit humain*. There he wrote rhapsodically about human progress. "How welcome to the philosopher is this picture of the human race, freed from all its chains, released from the domination of chance and from that of the enemies of its progress, advancing with a firm and sure step in the path of truth, virtue, and happiness!" How welcome indeed, particularly for the philosopher forced into hiding to escape execution. How such progress consoles a philosopher when he contemplates all the "errors, crimes, and injustices that still defile the earth," Condorcet wrote, with uncanny predictive accuracy, "of which he is often the victim!" Only in contemplating this panorama of human progress, he concluded, does the philosopher find a reward for his work on behalf of reason and liberty.[85]

Condorcet's confidence in science, if not his confidence in the French Revolution, never flagged. When a decree outlawed him in March of 1794, he became worried about the safety of those who were shielding him and abandoned his Parisian refuge. Turned away by other friends he expected would take him in, he was captured on March 27, in a country inn located on the outskirts of Paris, imprisoned, and found dead, perhaps by his own hand, two days later. Given the circumstances of his death, Condorcet's undying faith that science would yield continuing progress seems either heroic or mad. The Revolution to which he had devoted so much energy had rejected his constitution and his plan for universal education, which he considered the cultural precondition for any successful democracy. Condorcet's was not the only constitution that failed. Soon after the Jacobins' alternative, the Constitution of 1793, was ratified, the Convention suspended it until after the end of the war. It never took effect.

The most elaborate rationale for suspending the Constitution of 1793 and governing instead by terror came from Robespierre, particularly in a rambling, fascinating speech delivered in the Convention on February 5, 1794. Speaking on behalf of the Committee of Public Safety, he first listed the sins of the *ancien régime*, then declared the "principles of political morality that should guide the National Convention." Only in his closing remarks did he turn to the enemies against whom he believed the full fury of that morality should be unleashed. Robespierre's statement of the Revolution's aims seems almost innocuous, a paraphrase of the language of Adams or Madison. "What goal are we aiming for? Peaceful enjoyment of liberty and equality; the reign of eternal justice whose laws are engraved, not in marble and stone, but in the hearts of all men, including the slave, who forgets them, and the tyrant who denies them."

Robespierre's desiderata—and the contrasts he drew between the *ancien régime* and France reborn by revolution—could have come from Wollstonecraft or Paine, de Gouges or Brissot. Robespierre wanted the Revolution to substitute "probity for honour, duties for proprieties, the rule of reason for the tyranny of fashion," and "a magnanimous, powerful, happy people for an amiable, frivolous, and miserable people." In sum, he sought to exchange "all the virtues and miracles of the Republic for all the vices and absurdities of monarchy." Here was the Enlightenment's critique of the *ancien régime* amalgamated with Rousseau's critique of the Enlightenment. Robespierre indicted the entire elaborate structure of French culture, the ideals of nobility, glory, and polite sensibility, as a sham masking putrid corruption. Only after the entire *ancien régime* had been swept away could the regeneration of France begin.

Perhaps more surprisingly, the familiar tones of Madison and Paine still echoed in Robespierre's discussion of representative democracy. What sort of government did the Revolution seek? "Only democratic or republican government: these two words are synonymous, despite the abuses of vulgar language; for aristocracy is no more republican than monarchy." In light of standard characterizations of the Jacobins' ideal as direct democracy in the form recommended by Rousseau in the *Social Contract* rather than in his plans for representative democracy in Poland and Corsica, Robespierre's words are jarring. "A democracy is not a state in which the people, continually assembled, manages all public business for itself." Instead, Robespierre claimed, his model was a form of representative democracy, a state "in which the sovereign people, guided by laws which are its own work, does for itself all that it can do properly, and through delegates does all that it cannot do for itself." Would Robespierre have felt at home in Philadelphia?

The decisive difference between Robespierre's vision and Madison's soon became apparent: a democratic government, in Robespierre's view, cannot allow "a hundred thousand fractions of the people, through isolated, precipitate and contradictory measures," to decide "the fate of the whole society." No such government, he declared, had ever existed, and if it did it would surely end in despotic rule. The pluralism that Madison considered inevitable, according to Robespierre, leads straight to tyranny. Instead authority must be unified and a single public interest identified by the central government. Replacing the French monarchy required an equally concentrated power, only this time operating in the interest of the public rather than the interests of the king, the nobility, and the clergy.

Robespierre's legitimating principle was popular sovereignty rather than monarchy, but the form of government he envisioned would remain centralized, unified, and intolerant of difference or dissent. The people had to remain vigilant in overseeing their representatives—Robespierre's verb is *surveiller*—because corruption was as likely among them as among the courtiers at Versailles. "If there is a representative body, a primary authority constituted by the people, it has the continuous task of supervising and repressing all public officials." But, Robespierre asks, "who will repress the body itself, if not its own virtue?" In other words, who will *surveiller* the *surveillants*? "The more elevated that source of public order is, the purer it should be; so the representative body needs to start with itself, by subjecting all its private passions to the general passion for public good. Happy are the representatives when their glory and their very interests, as well as their duty, attach them to the cause of liberty!" Implicit in Robespierre's final ejaculation, of course, was the contrary condition, the unhappiness of representatives, and of a people, when the interests of those serving in government diverged from the public good. That, Robespierre lamented, was the problem facing revolutionary France. "If you only had to steer the vessel of the Republic in calm waters," he sighed, then liberty, equality, and fraternity might flourish in a sea of civic virtue. "But the tempest howls; and the stage of revolution" in which France found itself "imposes another task."

France's greatest virtue, Robespierre claimed, was also its greatest weakness. On the one hand, virtue leads republican citizens to trust each other. On the other, though, Robespierre breathlessly listed all the demons tormenting such people. Their virtue only tempts the vicious, who imagine plundering the innocent and escaping unpunished, who reject liberty and eye the republic as prey. Such perfidy explained why so many ambitious or greedy men abandoned the Revolution; they had veered away from virtue from the start. Among self-proclaimed revolutionaries lurked traitors, people doubly dangerous because of their duplicity. Against such people the Revolution had to arm itself. It could survive only by showing no mercy.

In the melodramatic conclusion of his speech, Robespierre painted in chiaroscuro the perils facing France and the measures necessary to defend the people, virtuous but naïve, from their enemies. "Two opposed spirits that have been represented as disputing the dominion of nature are fighting during this great epoch of human history to decide the destinies of the world once and for all." France, Robespierre warned ominously, "is the theatre of that formidable struggle." Against the tyrants' armies surrounding France, the French people were engaged in a war to the death. Likewise, within France itself, conspirators never slept. The republic had no choice: it must strangle its enemies or die. The emergencies of war required extreme measures. "If the mainspring of popular government in peacetime is virtue, the mainspring of popular government in revolution is virtue and terror both: virtue, without which terror is disastrous; terror, without which virtue is powerless." Frightening as terror seemed to those blind to its necessity, it should be recognized as nothing more ominous than swift and unyielding justice, "an emanation of virtue" and the consequence of the principle of democracy directed against threats to the homeland. In the hands of a democratic people, the sword of terror might resemble that wielded by tyrants, but its purpose elevated and redeemed its use. "Who does not hate crime," Robespierre declared, "cannot love virtue."

Robespierre claimed that France now had its external enemies on the defensive. The people's army had shown its mettle. But complacency was a trap: the army's victories had not vanquished the republic's foes. Because "veiled malevolence" threatened democracy everywhere, vigilance remained necessary. That phrase, "veiled malevolence," captured the threatening tone of Robespierre's closing paragraphs. Mentioning no names, the Incorruptible charged everybody from moderates to ultrarevolutionaries with a long list of crimes. They had revived the poisonous spirit of party against the unity of the people. They had sown division by slandering the Committee of Public Safety, officials who had selflessly shielded France from its enemies. By meting out "inflexible justice for culprits," the revolutionary government prevented individual interests from interfering with the "general will and the indestructible power of reason." Conspiracies involving even prominent and honored revolutionaries had to be exposed and those guilty executed.[86]

Because Robespierre was spearheading the worst excesses of the Terror when he delivered that speech, commentators have focused attention on its hypocrisy or highlighted how self-serving was his denunciation of the moderate Girondins and the ultrarevolutionary Hébertists, as the followers of the journalist Jacques Hébert were known. With critics to his right and left swept away, Robespierre alone would be seen to embody the unsullied virtue of the republic. Such criticism, however, mutes the unambiguous critique of direct democracy and Robespierre's equally straightforward endorsement of representative democracy in the first part of his February 4 speech. Even Robespierre accepted the principle of representation. He had come to understand, as had Sieyès, Condorcet, Paine, and Wollstonecraft, as well as Adams, Jefferson, Madison, and Wilson, that a nation the size of France had to rely on representation. Whereas Montesquieu associated ancient democracy with sortition and direct rule by the people and tied elections to aristocracy, Robespierre acknowledged that all the citizens of the nation cannot meet continuously and administer their government directly. They must depend on their representatives.

What distinguished Robespierre was his insistence on unanimity. Unlike other champions of representative democracy, who saw deliberation as the means to hammer out provisional compromises from their inevitable disagreements, Robespierre had learned too well from the tradition of French monarchy the lesson that a single authority must declare and enforce the national interest. Thus when Brissot or de Gouges, or Paine or Condorcet, or, eventually, even Danton and Hébert disagreed with Robespierre, he interpreted their dissent as evidence of conspiracy. Robespierre agreed with Madison that factions exist. Whereas Madison thought representatives should manage disagreements and find, through deliberation and compromise, the closest approximation of the general will, Robespierre thought the aim was to end disagreement and enforce consensus.[87]

Robespierre's zeal to ferret out enemies and consolidate power in his own virtuous self led, predictably, to his demise. When even his childhood friend Desmoulins and the charismatic Danton were declared dangerous counterrevolutionaries in the spring of 1794, their crimes were hard to discern. Desmoulins had written euphorically that the Revolution forged the French into "a great family, a great body," a nation no longer divided by social orders and separate provincial traditions but at last united, "all French and all brothers." When the disillusioned Danton was delivered to the Luxembourg Prison where Paine was held, he remarked, "Mr. Paine, you have had the happiness of pleading in your country a cause which I shall no longer plead in mine."[88] From their perspectives, Desmoulins, Danton, and Paine were guilty only of having disagreed with Robespierre. By then, however, dissent itself was treason. By achieving unanimity, the Revolution had shown, according to Robespierre, that "the French are the first people in the world to have established true democracy."[89]

The circle was closing around Robespierre. He had criticized the Hébertists' relentless campaign of dechristianization, arguing that the attempt to rein in the power of the Catholic Church did not entail the atheism that Hébert and others proclaimed. Now Robespierre called for a new revolutionary religion, the cult of the Supreme Being, in service to which Notre Dame was to be rededicated. Robespierre announced a festival to inaugurate the rites of the new faith; he would officiate as president of the Convention. His critics scoffed that he now envisioned himself not as redeemer but as Supreme Being, a godlike figure to be revered—and feared. Two attempts on his life intensified Robespierre's paranoia, and his charges of conspiracy expanded to encompass almost everyone still left in the Convention. The pace of the guillotine picked up, reaching sixty heads a day, as did the fury of Robespierre's denunciations of the enemies of the Revolution.

On July 26 Robespierre delivered an impassioned defense of his own virtue and of the Revolution. He knew the recent wave of executions had intensified suspicions. He was being described as a dictator, a despot, a tyrant. He denied he had been too severe. Not Robespierre but conspirators plotting against the Revolution had committed crimes against the nation. Three times he proclaimed his innocence and leveled a countercharge against "the monsters who have accused us." They were the guilty ones. Hébert deserved to die because his writings made the revolutionary government look "ridiculous and intolerable." Desmoulins and Danton deserved to die because they defended Hébert. At times during his directionless, almost incoherent attempt to exonerate himself, Robespierre seemed to acknowledge that he had reached the end. "Who am I, who stand here accused? . . . Others are forgiven their offenses; my zeal is labeled a crime. Take my consciousness away," he cried. "I am the most unhappy of men." Yet he went down swinging, shouting charges of a conspiracy against liberty and denouncing a shadowy coalition of criminals plotting from within the Convention itself. The only solution now was a general purge of the Convention, the Committee of Public Safety, and the Committee of General Security in order to "crush all the factions with the weight of national authority, to raise on their ruins the power of justice and liberty." By then no one remained, even within the tiny revolutionary vanguard Robespierre trusted to redirect the wayward "true democracy" of France, to stand alongside the Incorruptible and effect that final purge. After Robespierre was denounced by the Convention on July 27, he was shot in the jaw—either by soldiers sent to arrest him or by his own hand—and went to the guillotine two days later, his sky-blue waistcoat stained with blood.[90]

The same fervor that fed the Terror also fueled the military campaigns that put France's enemies on the defensive. So successful were the people's armies raised in 1793, less dependent on professional soldiers and more savage in their treatment of the enemy, that they inaugurated a new style of warfare, which paved the way toward later "total wars" involving not only soldiers but unarmed noncombatants as well.[91] The intensity of the Terror within France rose with each military success, which undercuts the effort to explain away undercuts the effort to explain away its excesses by emphasizing France's peril. Victories against its external and internal enemies not only inflamed the paranoia of the Committee of Public Safety. They also solidified the fear outside France that the ruthlessness of the Terror would eventually be unleashed on all of Europe.

CHAPTER 12 | Democracy in the Wake of Terror

AFTER THE TERROR, no one in Europe or the United States could remain neutral about the French Revolution. Critics, already skeptical from the accounts of Edmund Burke and Friedrich von Gentz, were appalled; others were enraptured. The death of the king, followed by the spectacle of an all-conquering revolutionary army bent on, and apparently capable of, projecting indefinitely the principles of liberty, equality, and fraternity throughout Europe, thrilled many observers. Genevan and Dutch political exiles believed the transformation of France might lead to republican rule at home; Italian and Russian critics of absolutism shared their enthusiasm. In the German-speaking states, the Mainz Jacobins were inspired, and writers such as Immanuel Kant, Johann Gottfried von Herder, and later Johann Fichte, Goethe, Friedrich Schiller, and Wilhelm von Humboldt were fascinated. The success of the American Revolution had excited reform-minded Europeans everywhere; with the advent of revolution in France, the Atlantic no longer separated them from the promise of popular government.

The enthusiasm of those Europeans who sympathized with the French Revolution, however, had limited immediate impact. Social movements aiming toward democracy, suffocated by repressive regimes and stymied by the revulsion of ordinary people against the horror that many now associated with revolution, were stalled for decades. Although dissatisfaction with political as well as economic conditions persisted—and despite the fears of those who wanted those conditions to persist—that dissatisfaction generated few broadly popular, sustained, and successful democratic reform movements during the decades after the French Revolution.[1]

Surprisingly, the convulsions in France had the deepest and perhaps most lasting impact on the course of democracy in the United States. The responses varied, but it is possible to identify three stages: first curiosity, then alarm, and finally jingoism. Americans' initial responses to the French Revolution ranged from positive to ecstatic. Attitudes did not begin to change until news of the Terror prompted a lasting transformation of American partisan politics. Then, with the dawn of the nineteenth century and Napoleon's consolidation of his control in France, came the third stage, the emergence of a self-consciously democratic American nationalism, the consequences of which persist into the twenty-first century.[2]

Early reports from France filtered in slowly, mostly from British newspapers. In the late 1780s and early 1790s, they did little to capture the imaginations of Americans who were much more intent on establishing their own republic than worrying about what was happening in France. Their anxieties centered on the role of Britain and unresolved tensions left over from the debates over ratification of the Constitution. More than half a million Loyalists had left during the War for Independence—perhaps as high a percentage of the population as left France during the Revolution. Many Loyalists who remained in the United States felt a persistent tug of affection to their native Britain.[3] Worries about falling under the magnetic pull of monarchical culture outweighed interest in a few reforms to the French monarchy being discussed by clergymen, nobles, and some disgruntled commoners in the dusty halls of Versailles and Paris in 1789–91. Deciphering the meaning of events in the early stages of the French Revolution was no easy feat. The Reverend Elijah Parish, a Congregationalist minister in Massachusetts who later became a fiery critic of the Revolution, initially welcomed it as France's redemption from popery. Robespierre's call for freedom of the press was reprinted in nine American newspapers in 1789, and a year later the *Gazette of the United States* welcomed the Jacobin Club as a healthy sign of vitality in French civil society.[4]

It was not events in France but a fracas surrounding Thomas Paine's *Rights of Man* and involving Adams and Jefferson that kicked off the earliest controversies over the Revolution in America. Adams's *Defence of the Constitutions of Government* earned Jefferson's approval, which was not surprising because of the similarity between Adams's arguments and Jefferson's in his *Notes on the State of Virginia*. Doubts about Washington's presidency, and especially about Vice President Adams, however, began to surface very quickly after both took office in April 1789. Adams committed two major blunders early in his term. First, he suggested that the use of an elevated title—"His most benign Highness," perhaps—would impart to the president of the United States the majesty appropriate for a head of state equal to the kings of Europe. Second, Adams's anxiety about the vanishing of civic virtue led him to propose adorning public servants with visible signs indicating the honor attached to their selfless service. In the absence of virtue, he argued, only "ambition" could inspire people to devote themselves to the common good; that is when "Ribbons and Garters become necessary."[5]

Critics instantly lampooned both ideas as inappropriate for a democracy and labeled Adams an unreconstructed monarchist. Congress deemed the title "Mr. President" sufficiently grand for Washington. A writer who called himself "Mirabeau" warned against the "folly of idolatry." Benjamin Franklin Bache, editor of the *Philadelphia Aurora* and grandson of Benjamin Franklin, warned against draping "pontifical robes" around a figure others called "a political pope."[6] Adams's idea of decorations was met with almost universal derision, and the vice president was made the butt of jokes for proposing it. The ever-prickly Adams quickly came unglued in the face of such criticism, which almost overnight became standard in American politics but which he took as irrefutable evidence that the public spirit necessary for self-government was vanishing. Alarmed by the emergence of partisan spirit, he warned in the spring of 1790 of a rapid rise in "the tendency to civil war."[7]

Claiming that Adams's almost comical suggestions concerning titles and ribbons revealed his inclination toward creating a monarchy or a hereditary aristocracy was ludicrous. Adams had defended equality and popular sovereignty as energetically in his *Defence* as he had done in his earlier *Thoughts on Government*. As long as "sense and virtue remain in a Nation in sufficient Quantities to enable them to choose their Legislatures and Magistrates," he wrote to Benjamin Rush, "elective Governments are the best in the world."[8] Adams was hardly alone, though, in recognizing that the sense of common purpose driving Americans' efforts to establish their independence from Britain was being replaced by a different sensibility, a grasping individualism that seemed—not only to Adams but also to many other observers, including the duc de la Rochefoucauld-Liancourt—incompatible with, or corrosive of, the ethic of reciprocity. Adams observed in his "Reply to the Massachusetts Militia" on October 11, 1789, "Our constitution was made only for a moral and religious people. It is wholly inadequate to the government of any other."[9]

The distinctive features of the American state and federal constitutions stood out in even bolder relief to Adams when he learned of the plans being discussed in France with the convening of the Estates General. The French preference for a unicameral national legislature, articulated clearly in Condorcet's writings of 1788, indicated to Adams a dangerous blindness to the need for balance. Writing to Richard Price on April 19, 1790, to thank him for sending his "Discourse on the Love of our Country," Adams expressed his enthusiasm for Price's defense of the French Revolution as the culmination of the struggle for popular government. "From the year 1760 to this hour," Adams wrote, "the whole scope of my life has been to support such principles and propagate such sentiments." Underscoring his devotion, Adams continued, "No sacrifices of myself or my family, no dangers, no labors, have been too much for me in this great cause." Yet Adams had learned to "to rejoice with trembling" about France. He worried that "encyclopedists and economists" had shaped the revolutionaries' sensibilities "more than Sidney, Locke, and Hoadley, perhaps more than the American Revolution." Knowing that Price, despite his unorthodox religious convictions, remained a Christian minister, Adams confided that "I know not what to make of a republic of thirty million atheists." Creeping unbelief now competed with popery and excessive egalitarianism in his roster of anxieties.[10]

Adams's letter to Price offered just a hint of what was to come from his pen on the subject of France. In 1790 Adams published an anonymous series of articles that have come to be known as his *Discourses on Davila*, one of the first critiques of the French Revolution to appear in the United States. Adams took as his inspiration an obscure Italian writer, Enrico Caterino Davila, whose *Historia delle guerre civili di Francia* probed the causes and consequences of the French civil wars of the sixteenth century.[11] When Adams's articles first appeared in the *United States Gazette*, puzzled readers wondered why the scattered musings of Juvenal, Alexander Pope, Samuel Johnson, and Voltaire, preceding lengthy passages and commentaries taken from Davila's history and Adam Smith's *Theory of Moral Sentiments*, had any bearing on the United States.

Adams wanted to establish two truths. First, as Smith had shown, individuals' longing for esteem must be checked by instilling the internalized judgment of Smith's impartial spectator. Second, the most valuable lesson of history for politics is that faction, rooted in human ambition, will defeat every effort to eradicate it. Attempts to establish unitary authority in government, which the French had failed to accomplish during the wars of religion and were now trying again to do with their National Assembly, were doomed. Instead institutions of government must be designed to control faction, just as Madison had argued in Philadelphia and in the debates over ratification. Although Adams approved the balance between Britain's two houses of Parliament, he drew a categorical distinction between election to the United States Senate and the heritable privileges of British lords, which he considered an abomination. He neglected the advice of his wife, Abigail, at home while Adams was in Europe, who understood that it was foolhardy to say anything positive about "aristocracy"—natural or otherwise—while Antifederalists were hurling the word as a weapon.[12]

In *Davila*, Adams undertook to use his own theory of government—established by countless historical examples in his *Defence*—as a crowbar to dislodge the ideas of Turgot and Condorcet. Employing a faulty deductive rather than a fruitful inductive method, the philosophes had failed to reckon with history. Adams worried that their ideas would undergird a fatally flawed new regime that would concentrate power in France and end in despotic rule. In his *Defence* Adams had written that sovereignty is "unalienable and indivisible" and rests "in the whole body of the people."[13] He proclaimed repeatedly that "the people are the fountain and original of the power" of all branches of government, including "governors and senates" as well as the "assembly of representatives." His critics' charge that the *Defence* revealed Adams's penchant for aristocracy cannot survive a reading of the book, as Jefferson acknowledged. The "body of the people"—the whole people, not some fraction—never surrenders its authority: the people reserve the right "to interpose, and to depose for maladministration—to appoint anew." Such changes, however, Adams counseled, should come gradually, through elections, and should build on practice rather than theory, precisely as the institutions of popular government had grown over more than a century in Britain's North American colonies.[14]

The sovereign people neither could nor should exercise their sovereign authority directly. Adams considered representation the great advance in modern political theory and practice. He judged the American experience, particularly that of his home state of Massachusetts, which he believed had the broadest franchise in the world, an irrefutable demonstration of its value. Adams had in mind two audiences for *Davila*. He was instructing the French—and Anglo-American enthusiasts for the French Revolution, such as Price—about the wisdom of representative democracy and the separation and balance of power. He was instructing Americans that people seeking to establish their superiority are bound to emerge in any society, regardless of efforts to prevent that from happening, because of the differences among individuals. He did not applaud that development. He contended only—as he had done in the *Defence*—that history demonstrates it is ineluctable, and that steps must be taken to prevent such people from kidnapping popular government. In the 1770s that observation was commonplace; by the 1790s it had become anathema due to the emergence of partisanship in America, a development inextricably tied to the French Revolution.

The initial readers of *Davila* were not members of the French National Assembly but Americans, who interpreted Adams's meaning in light of a divide that opened almost as soon as Washington and Adams took office in 1789. Jefferson, who feared that the clique of High Federalists around

Secretary of the Treasury Alexander Hamilton wanted to turn the presidency into an imitation of the British monarchy, thought Adams intended to wield his critique of faction to silence critics of Washington's administration. At that pivotal moment, in the spring of 1791, Paine's *Rights of Man* snapped the already weakened bond connecting Adams and Jefferson.[15] Madison loaned Jefferson a copy of the English edition of *Rights of Man*, with its ringing endorsement of the French Revolution and Price's defense of it. Jefferson then sent the book to Paine's American publisher, along with a brief note recommending it as a counterweight to unspecified "political heresies" circulating in the United States. "I have no doubt our citizens will rally a second time," Jefferson wrote, "to the standard of Common Sense." When the American edition of *Rights of Man* appeared, with Jefferson's words as a preface, it generated riotous enthusiasm among Jefferson's and Paine's friends and fury in the Washington administration.[16]

Jefferson should not have been surprised by *Davila*. When he and Adams had exchanged letters about the United States Constitution while they were still in Europe, Jefferson had criticized the office of the president as a "bad edition of a Polish king," and Adams replied by noting that Jefferson was "afraid of the one, I, the few." Adams worried that an aristocracy (of merit, or ambition, to be sure, not inherited status), unless cordoned off in its own chamber and balanced by a popularly elected legislature, would inevitably dominate the federal government. To that extent Adams shared the anxiety of those Antifederalists who worried about an aristocratic Senate. But he and Jefferson concurred on the structure of the government: "We agree perfectly that the many should have full, fair, and perfect representation" in the House of Representatives. "You are apprehensive of monarchy; I, of aristocracy. I would therefore have given more power to the President and less to the Senate."[17] Concerning France, Adams had written a letter to Jefferson as early as December 10, 1787, expressing similar fears. In any unitary assembly, Adams predicted, a "simple aristocracy or oligarchy in effect" would eventually seize power. Such had been the fate of every regime lacking the separation and balance of powers built into the American political structure, every "simple democracy," contained in the historical record. In none of Adams's exchanges with Jefferson did he ever express any doubt about the superiority of representative democracy to monarchy.[18]

When Paine's *Rights of Man* appeared with Jefferson's reference to "political heresies" prominently noted in its foreword, Adams was apoplectic. Jefferson claimed that he had not intended the note for publication. He wrote to Adams, explaining that he did not hold the vice president himself responsible for such apostasy, but neither Adams nor Jefferson's jubilant allies believed a word of it. From June 8 to July 27, 1791, the Boston *Columbian Centinel* published a series of articles by "Publicola" lashing out at Jefferson. If those aligning American democracy with English traditions of liberty were now branded heretical, Publicola asked, was there now an American orthodoxy tying the United States with France? If so, the nation had slipped quickly from its original commitments to freedom of thought and belief. Instead Publicola advised Americans to "remain immovably fixed at the banners of our constitutional freedom," safe from visionaries' delusions within "the impregnable fortress of our liberties."[19]

Most readers assumed that the widely reprinted Publicola essays were the work of John Adams, but Madison quickly discerned a difference and correctly attributed them to the vice president's son John Quincy Adams. Working behind the scenes as the leader of those gravitating toward Jefferson because of their opposition to Hamilton, Madison quietly helped spread the emerging narrative, which persists to our own day, that Adams had abandoned democracy and become a monarchist.[20] Given the sharp critiques that had only recently characterized Madison himself as an elitist because of his defense of the Constitution in the *Federalist*, his rapid transformation into the scourge of Federalists is curious. Madison's own arguments in support of the Constitution owed a clear debt to Adams's early writings. Yet Madison's tale about Adams converting to royalism served the purposes of those now gravitating toward Jefferson—and beginning to coalesce as a party opposed to Washington's presidency—so well that it eventually took on a life of its own.[21]

Sitting in Congress as the French Revolution unfolded, Madison found his attention being drawn away from pressing issues such as slavery and the National Bank, both of which he opposed,[22] to the broader and deeper questions of political theory to which he had devoted such effort in the preceding years. Madison contributed a series of articles to Philip Freneau's *National Gazette*, in which he launched critiques of Adams and the Hamiltonian tendencies of Washington's administration. If the people effectively expressed their will, Madison argued, they could prevent usurpations of power by those who favored using government on behalf of private interests. The nation had already experienced three different party systems, Madison wrote. The first emerged during the Revolution, the second during the battle over the Constitution, and now there was a third, the divide between the new Federalist party of rank, money, and military power, on the one hand, and "the party of the people," that of Jefferson and his followers, on the other. Only by minimizing the distance separating rich from poor could the passions feeding partisanship be contained. The most effective means to that end was encouraging the "reciprocity of dependence" that knitted independent small farmers to each other and to the nation as a whole.

Madison claimed that Americans had "invented" republican governments, and that they would continue to make improvements as experience guided theory. In contrast to an unnamed "anti-republican" (presumably Adams or another member of the Washington administration, such as Alexander Hamilton) who considered citizens incapable of self-government and urged them to obey their betters, the "republican" (a loyal ally of Jefferson) insisted that ordinary people, enlightened and united, were the best guardians of their liberty. If such friends of the people were allowed the power to decide on war, for example, and if the present generation had to pay the bill for any wars the government declared, then, Madison contended, Rousseau's and Kant's dream of perpetual peace among republics might become a reality. As Madison's persistent discussions of war suggest, hovering over all of these essays was the threat of being drawn into the conflict between republican France and the monarchies united against it.[23]

By May of 1793, Freneau's *National Gazette* was warning its readers that if the monarchies were able to defeat revolutionary France, the United States would be next in line. In the ominous formulation of the *Providence Gazette*, "If liberty is extinguished in France, America falls next." According to the *Newport Mercury*, "With France we survive, with France we perish."[24] The cause of the French Revolution, according to some who were beginning to think of themselves as Jeffersonians, or Jeffersonian Republicans, or Democratic Republicans, had become the cause of democracy everywhere. Liberty caps assumed iconic status from New Hampshire to South Carolina. "Exalt the CAP of LIBERTY," urged the *National Gazette*. Jeffersonians defended their public display with the fervor of true believers against equally passionate Anglophiles intent on desecrating such symbols of Francophilia.[25]

Many Americans applauded when revolutions purporting to be inspired by the American and French examples broke out in Poland, Genoa, and Holland. In the *New York Diary*, a writer who called himself "Civis Mundi" called for a cosmopolitan conception of American nationality. Americans should embrace and learn from the best that all nations have to offer. Since "mankind are the Children of education," according to Civis Mundi, every nation ought to work "to improve upon the experience of others" and "observe an open, manly conduct with all nations." Because "true republicans consider all men as their brothers," they "wish to cultivate an acquaintance with their manners, their virtues and vices, and to improve upon their knowledge." The United States could spearhead a new coalition of broad-minded republics.[26]

American enthusiasm for the French Revolution, however, was far from universal. British sympathizers among the Federalists of the northern states, people drawn more toward Washington and Adams than toward Jefferson and Madison, accused Francophiles not only of promoting airy cosmopolitanism rather than hardy patriotism but also of fomenting division among Americans by slavishly aping French follies. According to a writer in the *Gazette of the United States*, those purporting to champion broad-mindedness were actually encouraging Americans "to hate every man, every measure and every principle that is British. To be any thing British is enough to damn truth and hang innocence." Such hatred "is a very pretty specimen of the liberal philosophy that pretends to fraternise the globe and to banish prejudice and government craft out of the world." The accelerating pace of change in France encouraged party formation by altering Americans' sense of time and their awareness of conflict, a development few people welcomed. After ratifying the United States Constitution and electing George Washington, Americans thought they could see before them a placid and glorious future. The storms of the French Revolution, initially exhilarating as a sign of triumphant democratic principles, also suggested that the fortunes of popular sovereignty might rise and fall with the military success and political stability of France, which the Terror clearly called into question.[27]

Although Anglophiles were horrified when snippets of information about the Terror reached the United States, some champions of the French Revolution rejoiced that royalist conspirators were finally being chased from their holes and exposed as the traitors they were. In Philadelphia, the caps worn by the "Sans Culottes Light Infantry Company" sported tricolored feathers. A Jeffersonian who had visited France and witnessed the revolutionary "people's army" at work reported with admiration that they "possessed the same spirit as the Protestants in the beginning of the reformation," who expunged "every vestige of Popery in painting and sculpture, that could be found."[28] Joel Barlow, who had arranged for the American publication of Paine's *Rights of Man*, was elected with Paine to the French National Assembly. Barlow, best known for his epic poem *The Columbiad*, composed a little ditty to be sung to the tune of "God Save the King." It began with the cheery words:

> God save the guillotine
> 'Till England's King and Queen
> Her power shall prove;
> 'Till each annointed knob
> Affords a clipping job,
> Let no vile halter rob
> The guillotine.[29]

Of course, such bloodthirsty delight sparked angry rebukes. Francophobes accused their opponents of inciting not only anti-British sentiment but also quasi-traitorous denials of the legitimacy of the Washington administration. By aligning the United States with France, according to such critics, Barlow and other champions of the French Revolution were encouraging Britain to view its former colonies as an enemy. Partisan divisions between the emerging parties of Federalists and Jeffersonian Republicans deepened as the enmity between Francophiles and Francophobes gathered momentum. Although Paine himself was imprisoned in France, his American partisans in the growing Democratic Societies enthusiastically celebrated his *Rights of Man*, the cause of the government that had jailed him, and the partisans of Jefferson who embraced the same ideals. Only gradually, as word of its excesses trickled in, did Americans begin to reconsider the meaning of the Terror and its implications for democracy.[30]

After the fall of Robespierre on July 27, 1793, the French Revolution quickly declined into a form of government by clique that endured for fifteen months, conventionally designated the "Thermidorian Reaction."[31] The group that assumed control was repelled less by the concentration of authority in the hands of the Committee of Public Safety than by the way Robespierre and his allies used that power. They replaced the slogan "Terror is the order of the day" with the apparently unobjectionable "Justice is the order of the day." But what would such "justice" mean for those imprisoned during the Terror—and for its victims' kin? Thousands of prisoners were released. In Paris almost five hundred were freed in just five days. Instantly new demands—for revenge—replaced those of Robespierre for enforcing the virtue of "true democracy" through terror. Girondins came back from exile. Cathartic trials revealed the extent of the barbarity unleashed against those who resisted the Revolution, particularly in Nantes, along the Loire, and in Marseille. Now hundreds, perhaps thousands, were killed for following the dictates of the Revolutionary Tribunal and executing those condemned to death. Butchers formerly celebrated as virtuous revolutionaries were rebranded *buveurs de sang* (drinkers of blood). The Jacobin Club in Paris was closed down.

Such reactions to the Terror, understandable as they were, inevitably provoked a counterreaction on the part of those who had not abandoned Jacobin aspirations even when Robespierre was discredited. They began to organize on behalf of the never-implemented Jacobin Constitution of 1793, which had been shelved as soon as it was ratified. If the replacement of "terror" with "justice" had ushered in a flurry of revenge killings, the end of price controls ushered in food shortages that threatened starvation. Again popular anger about the price and availability of bread in Paris, exacerbated now by the mutual mistrust of those incensed by the Terror and those incensed by the reaction against it, ignited a riot reminiscent of those that had effectively ended the monarchy and then toppled the revolutionary government. This time, however, it was difficult to discern the mob's aims or the purpose of its violent assault on the Convention. "Bread and the Constitution of 1793," the slogan of the revolt of May 15, 1795, known as the Prairial Uprising because it occurred during the time bearing that designation in the secular calendar imposed by the revolutionary government, reflected both the urgency and the vagueness of the crowd's demands. The Terror had been unleashed under the implicit authority of the Constitution of 1793; two years later the Convention still had no solution to the food shortages. The Prairial rampage brought a return to repressive policies and a decisive repudiation of the Constitution of 1793. Former Jacobins and anyone associated with the Terror were rounded up and imprisoned, or confined to their homes, even as the "official" policy of ending such violence was proclaimed with solemnity.[32]

That difference proved important. The violence of Prairial lacked the legal sanction Robespierre had given the Terror, and the Convention that produced a new Constitution in 1795 explicitly renounced popular uprisings of the sort celebrated in the Jacobin Constitution and in the Law of Suspects that followed. Democracy was now identified with the worst excesses of the Terror. With the insurgencies that had tarnished earlier ideals of "the people" through spontaneous crowd actions repudiated, the Constitution of 1795 drew a bright line between representative democracy and popular agitation. Yet even those who shared this chastened sensibility and denied that mobs embodied the nation's general will still sought the mirage of political unanimity. The Constitution of 1795 put in place safeguards designed to protect the French people from themselves, or at least from the perceived threat of excess democracy, now discredited by the murderous Prairial riots. François-Antoine Boissy d'Anglas, speaking for the committee that drafted the constitution, dismissed the Jacobin Constitution of 1793 as "the organization of anarchy." Instead, he proclaimed, France must renounce the "chimera" of "absolute equality" and agree to be "governed by the best; the best are those who are best educated and most interested in the maintenance of the laws."

Thomas Paine was all but alone in continuing to call for universal suffrage. He was spared execution by a fluke, when the inside rather than the outside of his prison door received the fatal chalk mark only because the door happened to be open when the officers passed his cell. Ill but still full of fight, Paine was freed from prison thanks to the intercession of the new United States envoy James Monroe, whose predecessor Gouverneur Morris had made little effort on Paine's behalf. When he was released on November 4, 1794,

Paine's enthusiasm for democracy remained undimmed. The Convention, however, was less sanguine. Erstwhile democrat Jean-Denis Lanjuinais spoke for many when he chided Paine: "The time for toadying to the people is past." France could no longer tolerate "the spectacle of political assemblies given over to crass ignorance, to contemptible greed or vile drunkenness." Merlin de Douai was even more blunt: "I cannot believe that you would wish to entrust the direction of the state to men who own nothing and produce nothing, to those men who are nothing but a burden upon society." Things had changed while Paine was in prison.[33]

The Constitution of 1795 enumerated specific duties as well as rights. Utterly repudiating the Jacobins' encomia to the *sans-culottes*, it instead identified those fit to govern with those who owned property. Although all adult male taxpayers were declared citizens, only about 310,000 men, or roughly 20 percent of the population holding considerable assets, were empowered to vote for deputies. Eligibility for the second-tier electoral colleges was even more restrictive; only 10 percent qualified. The constitution also outlawed instructing delegates, a common practice from 1790 to 1793, and prohibited all political gatherings other than the electoral assemblies, which were restricted to ten days' duration. The nation's legislature, strikingly, was now to be bicameral, with a much larger Council of Five Hundred proposing laws and an upper chamber, the Conseil des Anciens (Council of Elders) responsible for voting measures up or down. Disenchanted with monarchy and with Robespierre's tyranny, the constitution empowered a Directory of five, chosen by the Council of Elders from a list nominated by the lower chamber, to perform the executive functions of government. Sieyès, who had kept his head down during the Terror and chosen not to participate in the shaping of the Thermidorian Constitution, was among those selected, yet he declined to serve. Unnerved by the shattering experience of the Terror, he remained anxious about individual liberty in light of the ideal of national unity invoked by the new regime.[34]

The Constitution of 1795 and the Directory that governed under its aegis still made no room for legitimate political disagreement. Having been whipsawed by radical changes, France now steered toward a new goal, stability. Amending the constitution was made all but impossible: any change would require nine years to take effect. The constitution stipulated that two-thirds of the members of the new councils must come from the body that drew up the constitution, a dramatic reversal from Robespierre's "self-denying" ordinance of May 1791, which had elicited grumbling because it exiled experienced leaders from office. The constitution and the two-thirds law were submitted to a vote, and the returns suggested both the assent of the majority and the depth of the division that still marked French culture. Many royalists and Catholics, still hoping for a miraculous return of the *ancien régime* in some guise, were forced to concede defeat after the constitution was ratified. Although no reliable numbers have ever been compiled, the vote recorded—1,057,390 in favor and 49,978 against—seemed decisive enough to persuade even skeptics that ratification was achieved.

About the two-thirds law there was much less agreement. Many towns and departments expressed sharp disapproval, and the announced vote affirming the controversial arrangement seemed to many observers to strain credulity. Riots broke out across France protesting the result. Paris, where resistance was most pronounced, exploded. On October 4 an insurrection was declared, and the next day a crowd twenty-five thousand strong converged on the Convention. Sustained efforts to disarm the populace in the wake of the Prairial Uprising, however, made a difference. Although the pitched battle between the army—under the command of General Napoleon Bonaparte—and the rioters lasted six hours, it was a mismatch. With vastly superior firepower, Napoleon's troops decisively defeated the insurgents. It would not be the last uprising in Paris, but never again would the crowd manage to upend the army.

The Directory was off to a bad start. With unrest still smoldering, dissent again prompted accusations of treason. Demoralized *sans-culottes* and former Jacobins began to organize, and to their left an even more radical challenge to the very idea of private property coalesced around the journalist Gracchus Babeuf. Self-proclaimed democrats again organized to overthrow the government, to restore the more egalitarian Constitution of 1793, and to distribute free bread and lands seized from the church and the nobility. In response, the government rounded up the usual suspects, shuttered clubs and newspapers, and executed those found guilty of conspiracy. Only a few years after Robespierre had tried to sanctify it—and primarily because it had been Robespierre and it was now Babeuf who endorsed it—"democracy" was becoming a dangerous word in France. Once again it appeared synonymous, as it had been before July of 1789, with anarchic violence rather than representation, deliberation, and majority rule. Emboldened by the crackdown on radicals, royalists and Catholics decided the moment had come to restore some version of the *ancien régime*. Their attempt to mobilize support from within the ranks of the army, however, failed as miserably as had the left's efforts to gather support the preceding year. Having unleashed the army to pacify the left, the Directory now set out to discipline the disordered ranks of the right. Conservatives and Catholics were arrested as threats to the state, which meant that parallel trials were conducted simultaneously to suppress challenges from radicals and royalists alike. Suspected royalists were dismissed from both councils; two new directors were installed.

The peaceful coup d'état of September 1797, which ended the First Directory and inaugurated the Second, merely delayed its ultimate disappearance a year and a half later. Just as Robespierre eventually found himself isolated from those to his left as well as his right, so the Directory found itself more and more vulnerable in the ever-shrinking center. By February of 1798, when the Directory proscribed both white cockades, the symbols of royalist and Catholic counterrevolution, and red bonnets, symbols of the now-discredited popular insurgencies, it was clear that it was fighting a losing battle. With conspiracies and insurrections cascading in endless succession, the stability that was the Directory's primary objective became increasingly elusive.

In the only one of these regime changes engineered by the elected councils against the appointed directors, Sieyès took power on June 18, 1799. With Jacobins again fomenting rebellion in Paris, royalists threatening unrest in the usual hotbeds of counterrevolution, and Toulouse careening toward civil war, Sieyès gave up on the institutions of representative democracy that he had worked to establish. And no wonder: the results of elections were now routinely contested, either by those who lost or by those in Paris who were displeased by the results. The separation of powers between the two chambers of the legislature and the executive was hopelessly muddled. The rule of law had given way to chaos. The ethic of reciprocity, the willingness to accept the victory of one's enemies and the legitimacy of the democratic process, fragile from the outset in France, had crumbled under the pressure of unending conflict. Both sides saw their enemies as fundamental opponents of the regime. Both sides were right.

Finally, a coup engineered by General Napoleon Bonaparte—with the help of Sieyès—ended the farce that the Directory had become less than five months after Sieyès had taken control. Sieyès proposed a new constitution, with a Great Elector at the apex and a version of his original scheme of indirect elections to the assembly. Still aiming for stability, he was offering a scheme almost indistinguishable from the constitutional monarchy he had envisioned a decade earlier.[35] Sieyès's plan reduced the people to "a fiction," as Jacques Necker observed, because they no longer had any direct connection to the process of choosing representatives. "The prime utility of participation by the people in the nomination of its magistrates and its legislators," in Necker's words, "is to form a continuous, more or less tight link between the leaders of a state and the whole mass of its citizens." If one severs that relationship, either by robbing the people of the right to vote or reducing it to "a simulacrum, a simple fiction," as Sieyès did, then, Necker concluded, "there will no longer be a republic or it will exist only in name." When Napoleon seized control of the machinery of government on November 9, 1799, he effectively ended the Revolution. Under the Directory, however, the government of France had already ceased to be representative. In the wake of the Terror, the Directory, and Napoleon's manipulation of Sieyès's scheme to proclaim himself First Consul, all remaining prospects of democracy in France vanished.[36]

Many of the proposals advanced during the Directory's four-year life paralleled proposals adopted in the United States. The differences between their acceptance in America and their rejection in France make clear why democracy flourished in one culture and withered in the other. Conjuring up the spirit of "*le bon* Condorcet," the Directory did make a concerted effort to institute a new system of education, reasoning that a literate citizenry would be a rational citizenry, a people more inclined to trust its elected representatives and less likely to take matters into its own hands.[37] Those who proposed these reforms and the teachers who would implement them, however, had dramatically different conceptions of what was to be taught. The government officials envisioned a curriculum that would reflect their own relentlessly rationalist, secular, and materialist philosophy. Many teachers, by contrast, were drawn toward the Moderate Enlightenment and wanted students to read Locke, Rousseau, and the philosophers of Scottish common sense. Like Roger Martin of Toulouse, they believed that unless French children learned "to develop in the heart honest, generous sentiments, and to learn to feel the ills of others," they would never internalize the ethic of reciprocity, the moral sentiments on which civic life must rest. Without such instruction, these educational reformers insisted, children would never escape their families' inherited prejudices and learn both to reason and to exercise their moral sense.[38]

Unfortunately these reformers' plans, which recall the ideas of prominent Americans such as John Adams, Rush, Jefferson, and Madison, fell on deaf ears. Not only did the ideologues of the Directory resist their emphasis on ethical instruction; the peasants and artisans in France's provinces wanted no part of their scheme. Generations of devout Catholics had survived with the meager education provided by their priests in church, and neither the priests nor many of their parishioners saw any reason why those venerable truths would no longer serve them well. If forced to choose between the teacher equipped to offer instruction in Locke and Smith or the priest teaching the Gospels, most French families knew which option they preferred. Particularly in the northern and middle regions of the United States but also for many whites in the South, universal literacy and Bible study, conducted by preachers from multiple Protestant denominations, went hand in hand. By contrast, events since 1789 had only intensified the cultural polarization of France.

The idea that commercial farming contributes to the civic life of the republic by fostering autonomy and mutual regard, an idea with ancient roots that also lay at the heart of Jefferson's, Madison's, and Adams's social ideal (although emphatically not Hamilton's), likewise fell on rocky soil in France. The Directory's minister of the interior, François de Neufchâteau, believed deeply in the political and moral as well as economic advantages of a system of independent farmers in control of their own holdings. "Agriculture is either a pleasant or a useful occupation for everyone," he wrote. "It alone unites all the interests of the different classes of citizen." Many writers and rural reformers shared this ideal, and they believed it likelier to emerge were France to establish vigorous commercial relations with the United States, another nation of citizen farmers. The Washington administration, however, particularly after Jay's Treaty in 1794 resolved disagreements and facilitated trade with Britain, had other ideas. The dream of a Franco-American alliance of free-trading farmers collapsed in partisan divisions on both sides of the Atlantic.[39]

The Directory likewise aimed to establish a new set of civic traditions to inculcate a spirit of loyalty to the new regime. To that end it sponsored festivals and tried to establish new rituals to replace those of the Catholic Church, which were deemed hopelessly superstitious and irredeemably imbricated with the symbols of the *ancien régime*. The revolutionary calendar, with its twelve thirty-day months (such as Prairial) each of which had three ten-day weeks, was among the most ambitious of these attempts. Adopted on October 5, 1793 (and abolished on January 1, 1806), it took direct aim at the tradition of celebrating Mass on Sundays and Christian feast days throughout the year. Partisans of the Revolution from the inception of the revolutionary calendar until the present have claimed that it was designed primarily to rationalize an irrational and capricious system of time and dates.

Contemporaries knew better. They understood that the principal aim of the calendar was to decouple French culture from Christianity and reorient the French people toward a new, civic, secular rationalism. Unfortunately for the Revolution, the new calendar never caught on. Not only peasants but even the families of government officials responsible for implementing it—and increasingly vigorous efforts were made to enforce it almost until it was abolished—continued to follow the Gregorian calendar and to observe traditional Christian holidays. Other reforms instigated with the same purpose in mind, including the designation of regions as departments and the adoption of the metric system, took hold and flourished, some not only in France but elsewhere.

The Revolution's most fundamental attack on French culture, though, its assault on the by then conventional measurements of time and dates, failed miserably.

At that most basic level of how lived experience was to be understood, Enlightenment rationalism never entirely supplanted the older traditions of Christianity. The costs—both human and political—of the Civil Constitution of the Clergy were no doubt greater than those exacted by the revolutionary calendar, which since its disappearance has been easy to mock. While it was in force, however, the calendar served as a daily reminder, like a wound that would not heal, of the assault against cherished traditions that the Revolution represented to a very large fraction of the French population. The Revolution consciously sought to replace sacred time with secular time, and to shift the focus of daily life from the festivals of the church to the things of this world. Judgments on the wisdom and desirability of that attempt remain almost as divided in the twenty-first century as they were in the eighteenth.[40]

Unlike the culture that developed in England's North American colonies during the second half of the eighteenth century, France was fractured between Enlightenment rationalism and French Catholicism. Most French Catholics professed a very traditional form of Christianity deeply imbued with a reverential deference toward hierarchy. As revolutionaries understood, that sensibility made monarchy attractive and democratic ideas and institutions suspect. From the moment the Civil Constitution of the Clergy was declared, every person in France was obliged to choose, at least once a week, whether to profess loyalty to church or nation. In the United States, thanks to the fact of religious pluralism and the separation of church and state that Madison and Jefferson had engineered to prevent state authority from corrupting religious belief, no one had to face that wrenching choice.[41]

Moreover, compared with the local and colonial assemblies that Americans had elected and dealt with, often contentiously, for generations, the French people by the time of the Directory still had enjoyed only fleeting (and often unsatisfactory) experiences with representative democracy. In Necker's formulation, there was no substitute for "the free, direct elections that form the essence of a republic," yet Sieyès felt obliged to abandon elections in his constitution for the Directory.[42] The lingering lure of unitary authority, whether embodied in a monarch, a unicameral legislative assembly, or a single man of incorruptible virtue, continued to bewitch those who wrote the Constitution of 1795 and those who tried to make it work. The continuous squabbling that constitutes political life in a democracy, in which the electorate and its representatives engage in unending arguments about policies and people as the next election looms on the horizon, requires a degree of trust that the French Revolution made less rather than more likely. When disagreements multiplied and mushroomed into rebellions from right and left, the only recourse was a coup that would reestablish a single source of national power, now in the person of the Corsican general who built an empire that transformed modern Europe.

The twists and turns—and the ultimate failure—of the French Revolution not only had a profound effect on the prospects of popular government in France but also transformed American democracy. The almost universal enthusiasm Americans expressed at the beginning of the Revolution did not survive news of the September Days in the fall of 1792. Traditional anti-Catholicism had combined with pride in exporting American democratic institutions to overshadow lingering gratitude to the French monarchy for its help in securing America's independence from Britain. When reports of mob violence were followed in quick succession by news of the regicide, and then by increasingly grisly accounts of the Reign of Terror, however, many Americans were shocked.

But not everyone. In late December 1792, just before Louis XVI was put to death, Secretary of State Thomas Jefferson wrote to the United States minister to France, Gouverneur Morris, instructing him to resume payment of American debts now that "a Convention ha[d] been assembled" and "invested with full powers" as the "lawful representatives of the Nation." Indeed, the decision to remove the king, according to Jefferson, meant that the United States should quickly establish "the closest union" with France since the two nations were committed to "similar principles of government."[43] Four days later Jefferson wrote to his former secretary William Short, now serving as the American chargé d'affaires in France, chastising him for his harsh criticism of the Jacobins. The Jacobins, Jefferson insisted, were no different from the Feuillants or any other party of patriots. Once the king had demonstrated his disloyalty, they were right to demand his removal. "In the struggle which was necessary" to establish the republic, "many guilty persons fell without the forms of trial, and with some of them innocent. These," Jefferson wrote, "I deplore as much as any body, & shall deplore some of them to the day of my death. But I deplore them as I should have done had they fallen in battle." Ending the monarchy required using "the arm of the people, a machine not quite so blind as balls and bombs, but blind to a certain degree." Yet proclaiming the republic was worth the violence: "The liberty of the whole earth" depended on the struggle, "and was ever such a prize won with so little innocent blood?" Jefferson then offered a judgment as chilling as his blithe endorsement of

Shays's Rebellion. Wounded as he professed to be by the deaths of "the martyrs to this cause," he would rather have "half the earth desolated" than see the Revolution fail. "Were there but an Adam & Eve left in every country, & left free, it would be better than as it now is."

The vast majority of the American people, including President Washington, Jefferson assured Short, shared such sentiments. Only a minority, notably wealthy and inveterate Anglophiles who hoped the United States Constitution would somehow lead the nation back to monarchy, disagreed. Everyone else cheered the French Revolution because it had given the "coup de grace" to royalism. "This country is entirely republican, friends to the constitution, anxious to preserve it and to have it administered according to it's [*sic*] own republican principles." The adoption of the Bill of Rights helped Jefferson get over his initial misgivings about the Constitution. He now acknowledged that those who secured its ratification—including his friend Madison—had established a representative democracy controlled by the American people.[44]

Although support for the French Revolution was stronger, and endured longer, in the South than in the North—in part because so many planters were in debt to British merchants—some New Englanders backed the Jacobins with enthusiasm rivaling Jefferson's. James Sullivan of Massachusetts published a pamphlet, under the pseudonym "Citoyen de Novion," defending French radicals by explaining that they were doing only what was necessary to establish democracy in difficult circumstances. Joseph Eckley looked forward to the arrival of a "reign of virtue" made possible by the Terror. Most southern whites turned against the French Revolution only around 1800, when fears mounted that the Haitian Revolution might spark slave rebellions in the United States, and even then not all planters read the event the same way.[45]

In the northern states, criticism of the violence of the French Revolution began to appear late in 1792 and escalated through the next several decades. Calvinist preachers who emphasized human depravity saw in murderous mobs and in the state-sponsored killings of the Terror evidence both of man's sinfulness and of the long-standing French (and Catholic) propensity toward violence. For more than a century New Englanders had been blaming the French for all manner of crimes. Antipopery waxed and waned but never disappeared; whenever neighboring Indian tribes attacked colonists, allegations of French involvement—at times justified—were predictable.[46]

As divisions between partisans of Washington's administration and his critics heightened during the 1790s, Americans' responses to the French Revolution assumed a different and more ominous quality. Within just a few years, Federalists were claiming that their critics, coming to be known as Jeffersonian Republicans, had magically metamorphosed into Jacobins intent on bringing the Terror to America. New England Federalists claimed that their own political ideas descended from the ideology of the American Revolution, were encapsulated both in the state constitutions and the United States Constitution, and received their most eloquent expression in the writings of Vice President Adams. From their perspective, liberty exists only in law, and freedom requires order. "All rights are social," proclaimed Noah Webster. "Civil liberty, therefore, instead of being derived from *natural freedom* and *independence*, is the creature of society and government." Such formulations owed a clear debt not only to Adams but also to Wilson and Madison, now Jefferson's chief lieutenant, who had made similar arguments, as we have seen, in defense of the United States Constitution. When government and law were products of arbitrary monarchical authority, resistance was necessary and appropriate, but popular sovereignty changed everything. When government and law embodied the will of the people, as articulated by their elected representatives, following the law became a civic duty as well as a moral imperative.[47]

As Federalists distanced themselves from the French Revolution, they began warning that its American enthusiasts among the newly formed Democratic Societies and the emerging Democratic Republican Party would import its excesses to America if given the chance. Many of Jefferson's followers did embrace the Jacobin cause with enthusiasm. Toasts and festivals celebrating French victories and French democracy popped up throughout the United States. Bache translated and printed in the *Philadelphia Aurora* a pamphlet version of Robespierre's "Report upon the Principles of Political Morality," with its unsettling identification of virtue and justice with terror.[48] Partisans of the Whiskey Rebellion in western Pennsylvania aligned themselves with the Jacobins. When news of Jay's Treaty with Great Britain reached them in 1795, they expressed their dismay by toasting to "The Guillotine: May it Maintain its empire till all crowned heads are laid in the dust."[49]

Such enthusiastic celebrations of violence elicited horror from Federalists and dramatic conversion narratives from some erstwhile Francophiles. The 1796 ratification of Jay's Treaty elicited French fears of a new Anglo-American alliance. The following year, American commissioners were sent to soothe French nerves and conclude a new commercial treaty. Elijah Parish, who had earlier seen promise in the Revolution, now lamented the turn to violence. "We have seen a great kingdom of old possessed with a political enthusiasm rushing into unheard of cruelties & their soil deluged with blood." Even worse, American critics feared the violence might be exported. Parish saw "clouds of war" heading toward America, and "a shower of blood seems just ready to crimson our fields."[50] When Americans learned that French foreign minister Charles Maurice de Talleyrand had dispatched three envoys (after whose sobriquets the incident came to be known as the XYZ Affair) to meet the Americans and demand both a loan and a bribe from the United States, animosity toward the new French regime intensified. Earlier references to the interdependence of the new sister republics and the yoking of liberty and equality vanished. In Philadelphia, the Sans Culottes Light Infantry Company removed the tricolored feathers from their caps and shortened their name to the Light Infantry Company.[51] Offending logic but illustrating the dynamic shifting of categories, an epithet printed in the *Massachusetts Minerva* on Bastille Day 1798 erased the lines between American Loyalists and French radicals in an all-purpose denunciation: "Democratic Jacobin French tory foes are sinking down as low as their nothingness and the public scorn can sink them."[52]

The rapid reversals of American opinion did elicit some criticism. One writer in western Pennsylvania expressed the weariness shared by many: "First, we decomposed with Britain, and united with France; then we qualified with Britain, and renounced the French. Now we are temporising with France, and exciting England! What the devil next shall we get to?" He was exasperated with his fellow Americans for incessantly doing just what scholars of nationalism insist all nationalists inevitably do: "Is there an Englishman, a Frenchman, an Irishman, or any foreigner whatsoever, who does not endeavor to preserve his national character, and even put the Americans to blush for not preserving theirs?"[53]

After the Terror had been extinguished and the Directory spiraled into its desultory failures, Americans took a look at the consequences of the French Revolution and began to acknowledge its impact on their own democracy. In an anonymous contribution to the *Aurora* published on February 23, 1799, Madison identified the most important and most unfortunate effect of the controversies: "The French Revolution has produced such a ferment and agitation in the world, and has divided it, according to the different turns given to men's minds by temper, by interest, and by political principles, into such violent parties, that nothing depending on opinion, nor much even on facts, is received without a strong tincture from the channel through which it passes." In other words, the French Revolution had so exacerbated partisan positions that either pro- or anti-French filters colored all the news that arrived in America.

Federalists now claimed that the government of France had "entirely separated itself from the people, and erected itself into a Tyranny." Madison based his challenge to that contention on the logic of representative democracy. "The French Republic, like ours, is founded on the principles of representation and responsibility. The members of the legislature are chosen by the people." Although the Directory's repeated repudiations of electoral results had invalidated that claim, Madison's contention remains instructive: In principle at least, representatives were held accountable to their constituents by frequent elections, and the creation of two legislative branches provided "further security" against chaos. In short, inasmuch as the 1795 French Constitution resembled the United States Constitution, it provided popular participation through the people's continuing communication with their elected representatives. Inasmuch as the Directory and the bicameral legislature were insulated from the French people—as experience would show they were, just as Necker pointed out in his critique of the Constitution of 1795—that insulation showed why the people must remain vigilant if democracy is to survive.

"The true lesson" of the French Revolution, Madison continued, was that "in no case ought the eyes of people" be "shut on the conduct of those entrusted with power." Citizens should be encouraged both to criticize and commend their representatives. If elected officials were tempted to betray the trust of their constituents, it was better to "add new bits to the bridle" than to remove it altogether. That simple formulation expressed Madison's theory of representative democracy. Although the intensity of their rhetorical assaults on each other masked their common allegiance, not only all the Democratic Republicans coalescing around Jefferson but almost all Federalists—including especially President John Adams, the target of Madison's attack—shared that conviction.[54]

At a time when Adams was wrestling with the Quasi-War against France that he inherited from Washington, Madison warned against the dangers of war, a standing army, and the consolidation of power in the national government, all threats that most Americans had feared since the 1770s.[55] Madison and his fellow Democratic Republicans worried that the Adams administration was secretly hatching a plot to align with Britain, defeat France, and undo American democracy by enforcing the Alien and Sedition Acts. To their surprise, however, and to the consternation of Hamilton and his cronies (often grouped together as "High Federalists"), Adams defused tensions with France and refused to enforce the Alien Act. Federalists were equally anxious about their foes. Based on some Jeffersonians' expressions of enthusiasm for violence in France and their sometimes violent denunciations of the Washington and Adams administrations, paranoid Federalists fretted that their critics were anarchists at heart. Nevertheless, as a moment's reflection on the gulf separating pro- from antirevolutionary forces in France throws into relief, all but a few outliers in both American parties shared a commitment to the same principles of representative democracy.[56]

That commitment was tested and confirmed in 1800, when former friends and now bitter rivals Adams and Jefferson, two learned men who had served as president of the American Academy of Arts and Sciences, vied for the presidency of the United States. During the latter half of the 1790s, elections assumed a new significance throughout the nation. Aggressively mobilizing constituencies resulted in higher voter turnout, particularly but not exclusively in elections at the state level, and recently mined data suggest that turnout varied depending on the perceived salience of the issues emphasized by rival candidates. Even though no stable party organizations existed yet, affiliations established as early as the 1760s showed surprising persistence. Given the already strong anti-British sentiments of many Americans, particularly those in the South and sections of Pennsylvania and New Jersey that had seen the most intense fighting during the War for Independence, pro-French attitudes became intertwined with pro-Jeffersonian loyalties. The Federalists' aversion to France—and to the Jeffersonians, who began calling themselves "democrats" and their party Democratic Republican, and who tarred their foes as "aristocrats"—grew stronger at the same time. It was precisely during these years that uses of the words "democracy" and "democrat" spiked, appearing three times as often in 1793 as in 1792, and twice again as often the following year, as Federalists abandoned the word's association with the United States and began using it solely as an epithet for their Jeffersonian Francophile foes—at just the same time that the emerging party of Democratic Republicans was embracing the term.[57]

In light of that crescendo of political passions, the results of the fiercely contested election of 1800 demonstrated with particular clarity the distance separating the practice of popular government in the United States from the sorry state of the French Directory. As the election approached, Americans gradually came to realize that all of them could abide by the result. Even a passionate supporter of Adams, writing as "Candor" in the *Independent Chronicle*, admitted that he could accept Jefferson's election, if necessary, because the candidate was a "true friend to his country, and his character has ever been free from impeachment since he has been in public office." Although Jefferson erred in supporting the Jacobins, he "would neither be biassed by French politics, or be duped by British intrigues; but like a true American, would bid defiance to any nation who would dare insult our flag."[58]

Strikingly, a writer in the *Centinel of Freedom* voiced the ethic of reciprocity that Jefferson would himself express in his celebrated inaugural address, the sensibility that enabled the American republic to survive the Revolution of 1800: "One party cries jacobin, disorganizer! the other aristocrat, tyrant." Such overheated rhetoric masked the deeper truth that the writer, who called himself by the apt pseudonym "Moderate," saw beneath it. "Are we not all federalists and republicans, according to the true and literal meaning of these terms? Are we not all for supporting the constitution, which has confederated these colonies, into one federal republic?"[59]

A moderate stance finally did emerge from the supercharged debates of the 1790s, though the United States first had to endure yet another spirited debate between rival groups contesting the meaning of democracy in the election of 1800. Adams put his finger on this central feature of American culture, the triumph of what is often called the Moderate Enlightenment, in diary entries written before and after the French Revolution. Musing on the cultures of Europe while in Paris in 1783, Adams observed that "the human Mind contracts habits of thinking from the Example" set by government. In aristocracies people grow "accustomed to look up to a few"; they "imitate the same practice in private Life, and in common Things." In monarchies they admire "one Man in great Affairs" and display "a similar disposition in little ones." In the democratic colonies still fighting to extricate themselves from British rule, things were different. "In Democracies We contract the habit of deciding every Thing by a Majority of Votes. We put it to a vote whether the Company sing a Song or tell a Story." Whereas in aristocracies people "ask 2 or 3 of the better Sort," and in monarchies "the Lady or the Gentleman, in whose honour the feast was made," in democracies—such as the nation struggling to be born—people learn to trust each other's judgment rather than deferring to one king or a few members of the nobility. In matters great and small, the majority rules.[60]

Reflecting on the French Revolution thirteen years later, after the Terror, Adams drew an equally sharp distinction between religious and antireligious sensibilities. "One great advantage of the Christian Religion," Adams observed in 1796, at a time when Americans were obsessed with reports from France concerning the Jacobins' plans for dechristianization and the slaughters of Catholics in the Vendée, "is that it brings the great principle of the Law of Nature and Nations, Love your Neighbor as yourself, and do to others as you would that others should do to you, to the Knowledge, Belief and Verification of the whole People." The civic value of that ethic, against which the French Revolution represented a sustained attack, was incalculable. In a nation oriented toward rather than away from Christianity, Adams wrote, "The Duties and Rights of The Man and the Citizen are thus taught, from early Infancy to every Creature. The Sanctions of a future Life are thus added to the Observance of civil and political as well as domestic and private Duties." Having as little fondness for Catholicism as any other New Englander, Adams understood why the French Revolution had to challenge the authority of the pope and his bishops. He distanced himself, as did most partisans of the Moderate Enlightenment, from papists and atheists, and embraced a form of Protestantism that amalgamated the Bible with Locke's writings and Scottish common-sense philosophy. That blend permeated much of American culture through the words of countless ministers, schoolteachers, college professors, and newspaper editors.[61]

Adams's contemporary critics, as we have seen, accused him of favoring aristocracy, but that charge confuses Adams's fetish for mixed or balanced government with an aversion to representative democracy. Adams shared Madison's conviction that the lines of conflict in every culture run all the way down and in many directions. Individuals will always emerge from the ranks of the ambitious and talented to contend against each other and attempt to establish their dominance. But they will never form a united class interest. Instead the landed gentry face off against merchants and bankers; the well-educated set themselves against both of those groups (as Adams himself did). Adams believed that the people are equally likely to be divided against themselves, and even more likely to be irrationally exuberant, particularly on the question of property, yet he remained convinced that "there can be no free government without a democratic branch in the constitution."

Adams still preferred a government like the one he had designed for Massachusetts, the plan that had served as a model for other state constitutions and for the United States Constitution. He conceded that representation, by introducing an aristocracy of merit into government, constitutes a "departure" from direct democracy, but he continued to insist that such a scheme differed categorically from an aristocracy of birth. "Democrats, Rebells and Jacobins," he wrote to Jefferson, "when they possessed a momentary Power, have shewn a disposition, both to destroy and to forge Records, as vandalical, as Priests and Despots." Not worse than priests or despots, to be sure, but equally execrable.[62] Representation Adams deemed valuable because it acknowledges and harnesses exceptional individuals' talents without allowing them to become a permanent separate interest. Rivalries are bound to emerge from social and economic differences such as those between rich and poor, industrious and idle, learned and uneducated. From those differences parties will inevitably coalesce, but no group "should ever be suffered to be the masters" of all the others. The French erred fatally by trying to eliminate such conflicts in their quest for unitary authority.

Adams's admirers saw him as a realist. All people, according to Noah Webster, including "the most noisy democrat," want their children to find a dependable livelihood and a spouse from a well-connected and respectable family. Although perhaps "wrong and vicious," Webster continued, "the propensity exists—these things are true—they cannot be contradicted. And Mr. Adams, instead of advocating aristocracy and its exclusive privileges," wanted merely to explain that tendency and guard against "its pernicious effects in government." The term "aristocracy," Webster argued, should be reserved for the "hereditary titles" used in Europe to give certain individuals legal "claims and rights against others." Nothing of the sort existed in the United States, in large part thanks to the good work of constitution writers such as Adams. Rather than branding him with the misleading epithet "aristocrat," which was emerging into prominence along with the word "democrat" as partisan battles heated up in the 1790s, Webster contended that Adams deserved to be known as "a firm intelligent republican."[63]

As Madison had explained in the *Federalist*, so Adams insisted in *Davila*—the book that Madison excoriated as aristocratic—that the poor and the rich "should have equal power to defend themselves" against each other, just as the legislature and the executive must be balanced against each other. The alternative is despotism.[64] Because party formation springs from the human propensity for emulation, which creates rivalries within and between families, towns, and every other social grouping, conflict itself can never be extinguished. The only viable option for controlling conflict is a well-balanced government. These arguments, which Adams presented energetically, albeit less than diplomatically, in his *Defence* and *Davila*, might well be recognized as standing alongside the writings of Jefferson and Madison as classic defenses of representative democracy—had Jefferson, Madison, and their followers not savaged Adams's familiar arguments as aristocratic.

As president, Adams certainly gave the Jeffersonians plenty of material to work with as they tried to cast him as a curmudgeonly and antidemocratic Francophobe, and some of his Federalist supporters made things worse. Adams hankered neither for monarchy nor aristocracy, but he never doubted the legitimacy or inevitability of hierarchies based on merit, and he detested both the ideology of the Jacobins and the Democratic Republicans' perceived admiration for it. When President Adams formally recognized the new nation of Haiti, many Federalists cheered as many southern slaveholders fumed. Democratic Republicans' effort to extend the franchise to all white men, a campaign already under way in the second half of the 1790s, was accompanied by the formal exclusion of free blacks and women, many of whom had either enjoyed the franchise or had at least not formally been excluded from its exercise prior to 1800. Federalists, more intent on preserving social and cultural hierarchies, were less intent on gender and racial exclusions than were their Republican opponents.[65]

By the time Adams had been out of office and back on his farm in Quincy for a few years, he was playing the part of Democratic Republican scourge with such gusto that the author of the radical manifesto *Thoughts on Government* and the uniquely influential Massachusetts Constitution convinced not only his contemporaries but also posterity that he was the creature conjured up by his most venomous critics. By 1806, in the middle of Jefferson's second term as president, for example, Adams had so soured on his successor's party that his gloom blotted out the substantial similarities between his own political ideas and Jefferson's. "I once thought our Constitution was quasi or mixed government," Adams complained to Benjamin Rush. The Jeffersonian Republicans, however, "have now made it, to all intents and purposes, in virtue, in spirit, & effect, a democracy. We are left without resources but in our prayers and tears, and having nothing that we can do or say, but the Lord have mercy on us."[66] His son John Quincy Adams reinforced Republicans' suspicions when he translated and arranged an American edition of Gentz's analysis differentiating the French Revolution from the American.[67]

The differences between Federalists and Republicans were real and important. The hyperbolic rhetoric deployed by both sides from the 1790s through the War of 1812, however, makes it as difficult to discern their underlying agreement on representative democracy as it is to place them all within the Moderate Enlightenment, though that is certainly where they belong. Unlike the followers of Spinoza, Voltaire, or Hume, they shared respect for the value of religious faith and had little sympathy with materialist philosophy. Unlike Jeremy Bentham, James Mill, and the founders of the utilitarian tradition in Britain, the American partisans of Moderate Enlightenment never abandoned older traditions of moral philosophy grounded in Christianity and revised by Scottish common-sense philosophers. Unlike those in the French Revolution who hated Catholic Christianity with as much fervor as they hated monarchy, these American thinkers, despite the differences between Jefferson's and Madison's versions of Deism and Adams's Scottish-philosophy-inflected liberal Protestantism, considered religious faith an essential dimension of American culture (even though Jefferson and Madison worked more assiduously than Adams to separate church and state). These Americans wanted to divide and balance government, not only in its branches but also in its levels, keeping distinct local, state, and national government in a federal system without parallel elsewhere in the eighteenth century. They valued reason, order, balance, and compromise.[68]

Their respect for religious faith helped moderate their enthusiasm for some forms of democracy and helped determine the kind of democracy they endorsed. Whereas some French champions of democracy considered all religion obscurantist and all tradition reactionary, Adams, Jefferson, and Madison understood that a thoroughgoing democracy acknowledges the force of popular piety. If individuals think of themselves as capable of making decisions in every realm, they are inclined to elevate their potential and resist any criticism of their abilities. Those with humility doubt their own judgment and defer to sources of judgment other than their own. Those for whom democracy is the only norm possess Promethean confidence in human capacity. Those more skeptical about human capacity—or more alert to human frailties and foibles—might be described as chastened about the people even though only the people would exercise power. Neither the skeptical nor the revolutionary Enlightenment attracted as many Americans as the moderate strand, which balanced reason with faith, liberty with law, and democracy with institutions designed to constrain human passions.

Moderation in defense of Enlightenment certainly had its costs. Critics of slavery in the North and the South compromised with those who defended that indefensible institution. Without the willingness to compromise, which allowed slavery to persist while pointing vaguely toward ending the slave trade in 1808, there would have been no United States of America. Defenders of the Constitution such as Wilson and Madison contended that ratification would set in motion processes leading to eventual abolition of slavery in the United States, a step not possible under the Articles of Confederation. Defenders of slavery such as Charles Pinckney of South Carolina, on the other hand, contended with equal conviction that ratifying the Constitution would enable the South to preserve slavery forever. The Constitution itself did not address slavery, thus implicitly authorizing the perpetuation of one of the least enlightened modes of human interaction known to mankind.

The Congregationalist minister Samuel Hopkins, who had relocated from western Massachusetts to Newport, Rhode Island, spoke with uncanny prescience, and for many others in the North, as he agonized over the question of slavery. How must it "appear in the light of Heaven" that the United States, the nation that declared itself champion of liberty and flattered itself as "the highest and most noble example of zeal for it," could not end this abomination? Without the Constitution the nation would have fallen into "a state of anarchy, and probably civil war; therefore, I wish to have it adopted; but still, as I said, I fear. And perhaps civil war will not be avoided" in any case. Such torturous reasoning lay beneath many northerners' acquiescence in the survival of slavery after the Constitution took effect. With the complete breakdown of law in France and the reports of horrific violence in Haiti, fear in the United States mounted. More and more Americans realized that self-government by slaveholders was a contradiction in terms, yet widespread anxieties about the prospect of disunion or the prospect of slave revolts helped most of them avoid facing the contradiction.

Whereas in France Robespierre had silenced individual wills as counter-revolutionary when they differed from the general will as he understood it, in the United States after the 1790s the legitimation of the individual wills of slaveholders silenced the general will. The escalation of rhetoric in partisan debates had very little contact with reality, since the stakes were hardly life and death—except in relation to one issue, slavery, which eventually grew to resemble the conflict at the heart of the French Revolution. Critics of slavery such as Hopkins were right: slavery was a perpetual reign of terror that unleashed violent passions, a system with consequences every year more deadly than the worst excesses of the most bloodthirsty Jacobins at the height of the Terror. Moreover, it was beginning to appear to many Americans that slavery could be abolished only through the equally ferocious violence of war. The tragedy is doubled because there was no alternative, yet the consequences reproduced those of earlier civil wars: the ethic of reciprocity was buried along with slavery, stalling further development of democracy in America.[69]

The question of women's rights was the other glaring omission in most late eighteenth-century discussions of democracy. The United States, like Britain and France, produced plenty of women writers during the era of the French and Haitian Revolutions, but like Britain and France, it produced only one prominent figure who focused explicitly on issues of social and political theory rather than history, fiction, or poetry.[70] Judith Sargent Murray, like Wollstonecraft and de Gouges, championed women's intellectual capacity, challenged prevailing gender norms, and called for expanding women's access to education. Although Murray, also like Wollstonecraft and de Gouges, did not succeed in altering gender roles and relations during her lifetime, comparing her political views with theirs illustrates the different conditions prevailing in the democratic United States, monarchical Britain, and revolutionary France during the 1790s, and it also shows how partisanship and nationalism in America developed out of competing ideas about democracy. For Murray, as for many Americans trying to make sense of the contrast between the American and French Revolutions, it was the self-discipline and mutuality extolled by figures in the Moderate Enlightenment that accounted for the success of the United States and their absence that doomed France to chaos.

Murray was born Judith Sargent in Gloucester, Massachusetts, to the family of a successful merchant, but after she married John Stevens she never again enjoyed her parents' prosperity. Her merchant husband fell into debt after the American Revolution, evaded prison by leaving the United States, and died without ever returning home. His widow then married John Murray, an unorthodox minister who had abandoned his natal Presbyterianism, worked briefly under the revivalist George Whitefield, and embraced the heterodox form of Christianity known as Universalism. Hounded by creditors in Britain, John Murray emigrated to New England. There he attracted followers and met Judith, whom he married in 1788. John Murray was pastor of the Gloucester Universalist congregation until 1793, when he was called to the Boston Universalist church, where he served until a stroke in 1809 left him paralyzed and unable to continue preaching. Having experienced a sharp decline in status during her life, Judith Sargent Murray wrote in part to keep her family on the lower fringe of the middle class.

Murray began writing when she felt the need for a catechism to help her instruct the children of her extended family in her Universalist faith. Although committed to the divinity of Christ as the savior of mankind and the impossibility of earning salvation except through God's grace, Universalists renounced the doctrine of depravity and Calvinists' belief that the vast majority of humans were damned. Universalists were part of the vanguard that eventually shifted many American Christian denominations toward the more inclusive orientation that would eventually become liberal Protestantism, though at the time they were vilified for their waywardness. Murray's catechism was well received, and it emboldened her to begin writing on other subjects and in other genres.[71] She wrote articles for magazines both anonymously and under her own name, and she wrote everything that appeared in a one-woman magazine, the *Gleaner*, which she marketed aggressively and which attracted enough subscribers—including both George Washington and John Adams—to earn $2,375 in 1798, its single year of publication. After Murray had established herself as a significant commentator on a wide range of issues, at the peak of her productivity she stopped writing.

Other obligations intervened. Her young daughter, born in 1791, when Murray was forty years old, needed her attention. After her husband's stroke, so did he. Two years later her daughter, like the heroine in a romantic novel, fell for a Mississippi-born Harvard student who was living in the Murrays' home, became pregnant, and in 1812 gave birth to a daughter while she was living alone with her mother. During the five years the women waited "in a state of corroding suspense" for him to come back for his wife and child, Murray confessed to becoming a "confirmed maniac." Her son-in-law finally did return, then left with her daughter and her grandchild for Mississippi, where Murray joined them on their Natchez plantation in 1818 for the last two years of her life.[72]

The triumph of domesticity and the emerging ideology of separate spheres confined women to a set of duties that Murray had criticized in her writing as unjustified and unjustifiable. She was among the many women who read Wollstonecraft's *Vindication of the Rights of Woman*, available after 1794 in one of its four American editions. She found in Wollstonecraft's arguments confirmation of many of the ideas she had advanced in essays she began writing in the 1770s. Murray challenged the idea of women's natural subservience to men. She drew on Locke's environmentalism to suggest that only the differential upbringing and education of boys and girls accounted for their differences as adults. The physical differences between the sexes were not unimportant, and Murray never abandoned her belief that women, as mothers, were uniquely suited to nurturing and more attuned to "sensibility," "sympathies," and "affections." Those differences, however, invoked to rationalize the superior status of men and the necessity of women's obedience, seemed to Murray irrelevant in most domains of life. She granted that men were physically stronger than women. Jungle cats were stronger than both, but that did not entitle them to rule the earth. The most important criteria, Murray argued, were spiritual and intellectual, and in both she argued women are men's equals.

Murray first ventured to challenge women's role in two early essays. "Desultory Thoughts upon the Utility of Encouraging a Degree of Self-Complacency Especially in Female Bosoms," which appeared in 1784, announced its argument in its title. She established her notoriety as a social critic with "The Equality of the Sexes," published in March and April 1790, in the *Massachusetts Magazine* under the pseudonym "Constantia." She had written the bulk of the essay in 1779, when she was seething with resentment. Her parents insisted that her brothers, as sons of a prosperous merchant, were to receive a classical education whether they liked it or not. Denied that opportunity, Judith educated herself and became a champion of women's rights. Murray identified the intellectual powers as imagination, reason, memory, and judgment. She insisted, by turns lightheartedly and earnestly, that women had proven themselves equal to men in imagination and memory. Just think of their flair for fancy, fashion, and scandal, she suggested, or their ability to recall even the tiniest details of the entertaining stories they tell. If women fall short in the exercise of reason and judgment, the explanation lies in their inability to stretch their minds by pursuing the same level and kind of education as men. The resulting difference in intellectual ability gives women "a mortifying consciousness of inferiority," but if they were merely allowed the same instruction as their brothers, they could develop their minds to their full potential. Educated women would "have little room for the trifles with which our sex are, with too much justice, accused of amusing themselves, and they would thus be rendered fit companions" for men. Equal education would enable women to demonstrate their equal abilities in reason and judgment. As Wollstonecraft later did in her *Vindication*, Murray challenged the notion that men's and women's souls differed: "Yes, ye lordly, ye haughty sex, our souls are by nature *equal* to yours, the same breath of God animates, enlivens, and invigorates us." If women were given the chance to engage in "serious studies," Murray predicted, "we will bid our souls arise to equal strength." Murray concluded by turning Eve's alleged perfidy to women's advantage: What was Eve seeking from the serpent, after all, but knowledge?[73]

Few women dared venture into the public sphere in the eighteenth or early nineteenth centuries. Such behavior was judged, by men and by many women, as unladylike, unseemly, and perhaps even dangerous. Wollstonecraft herself became the most notorious example. In 1798, one year after her death, William Godwin published *Memoirs of the Author of "A Vindication of the Rights of Woman."* Although Godwin intended the book as a tribute to the woman who had become his wife, it disgraced her. Godwin revealed that while Wollstonecraft was in Paris, where she had gone to observe the French Revolution, she had fallen in love with an American, Gilbert Imlay, with whom she conceived a child. Like Murray's daughter, Wollstonecraft soon found herself abandoned, and she returned to London with her infant daughter. When Imlay rejected her for another woman, her desperation led to two unsuccessful suicide attempts. She gradually returned to her English friends, including Godwin, with whom she conceived another child. Complications from the birth of that child led to Wollstonecraft's death.

Godwin's *Memoirs* provoked a scandal. Even those who had applauded Wollstonecraft's writings rebuked her life. Two illegitimate children, two failed marriages, and two suicide attempts were too much for respectable people on both sides of the Atlantic. For much of the last two centuries, it has been assumed that Wollstonecraft's ideas about women's rights died with her. Recent research, however, indicates that her *Vindication* continued to be read, and many of the women's rights advocates who began agitating in the 1840s traced their militancy to her work. Just as the savagery of Dessalines's revenge in Saint-Domingue provided defenders of slavery with the pretext they needed to justify preserving an institution that served their interests, so Wollstonecraft's behavior served to illustrate, for cultural conservatives, the inevitable and shocking consequences of the very idea of gender equality. Although many Anglo-American women as well as men felt justified in treating Wollstonecraft's life as an unanswerable rebuttal of her ideas, others throughout the North Atlantic world mobilized for women's rights during the century that followed, albeit with limited success.[74]

Murray was among those who refused to renounce Wollstonecraft or abandon her ideas. In a letter to an unknown correspondent, Murray challenged the common contention that Wollstonecraft's radical ideas led directly toward her unconventional life and her scandalous death. "Her real *crime*," Murray wrote, was not her life but "*her able defence of the sex*." The blame lay with Imlay, not Wollstonecraft, whose marriage to Godwin, even if belated, showed that she was willing to uphold the sacred institution that Murray herself revered despite her criticism of women's subjection.[75] Murray's ideas strikingly illustrate the differences between American and British political culture. Murray criticized gender roles, the customs limiting women's education and their participation in civic life, and assumptions concerning their ability to contribute to the life of the mind. Like most Federalists, though, she did not criticize social or economic hierarchy. From her perspective, women's subjugation was unjustifiable because it denied equal opportunity to individuals of exceptional intelligence, talent, and ambition—women like herself. Murray believed in what is now called meritocracy, and her parents' refusal to educate her grated on her throughout her life because it prevented her from competing fairly with the men she most admired.

Murray's writings demonstrate the compatibility of the ideals of Christianity, classical republicanism, and the liberalism of natural rights philosophy. Murray argued that women excelled at the selflessness preached by Jesus. In the political sphere, women had demonstrated ever since the ancient world that they are "as capable of supporting with honour the toils of government" as men are. She characterized the ideal of political engagement in terms familiar to republicans aiming for civic virtue: "a capability of distinguishing that which will probably advance the real interest of a Community." Women, she concluded, are as concerned with the common good as the most public-spirited men.[76] Like those urging autonomous citizens to carry their independence into entrepreneurship and profitable participation in the marketplace, Murray envisioned a world including not only men but women, farmers and "farmeresses," merchants and "she-merchants." "With proper attention to their education, and subsequent habits," in short, women "might easily attain that independence, for which a Wollstonecraft has so energetically contended."[77] Murray's vision did not conform to the emerging ideology of separate spheres, and yet her vision of woman's role continued to include devotion to husband and children in a traditional monogamous relationship. From her perspective, as from that of most New England Federalists with whom she aligned herself, the American Revolution had accomplished its aim of establishing popular sovereignty and representative democracy. Americans should not now undermine the order without which liberty would be impossible; they should instead uphold the laws created by the people's representatives. She savaged "anarchy" with as much fervor as any other Federalist.

In *Gleaner* 26, an essay written in April of 1794, Murray celebrated the progress of the new American nation and lamented the chaos in France and the war raging in Europe. How could Americans decide between the combatants? Our former ally is in turmoil; our own benefactors have been imprisoned. Moreover, Murray observed, factions have arisen at home in response to the conflict abroad, and some critics dared even to assail the federal system itself. Although without naming the Jeffersonian Republicans, she accused them in the very terms they applied to the Federalists: "What is your object? . . . Why are you ambitious of forming an *aristocracy* in the midst of your brethren?" She pleaded for unity. "Ought not the nation at large to constitute one vast society of people, bound by common ties, common wishes, and common hopes?" That unity, Murray argued, had been made possible by the Constitution, which established a system of democratic government beyond reproach. If any government ever deserved to be characterized, "in a rationally republican sense, *the government of the people*," the United States "is indubitably that government." Delegates to the Constitutional Convention were chosen "*by the people*, invested with authority to weigh, ponder, and reflect; they assembled, they deliberated, examined, compared, and finally arranged." The next step was equally consistent with democratic principles. The ratifying conventions rigorously scrutinized the text, and only after they had deliberated did they decide that it embodied the "interests of *the people* at large." Murray considered her case complete: "A government thus originating, thus sanctioned, and thus established, may be unequivocally pronounced, in every *proper sense, the government of the people*." Like most Federalists, Murray thought the process as well as the product embodied the idea of popular sovereignty.

Lest her readers confuse her with Jeffersonian Republicans, though, Murray immediately signaled the move made reflexively by most Federalists in the 1790s. "This new world is the heritage of liberty; but it is of that liberty which decidedly avoweth her *systems*, her *regulations*, her *laws*, her *subordination*; to all of which she exacteth the most scrupulous obedience." Summarizing the principles of Moderate Enlightenment, the *Gleaner* compared liberty with "an informed, elevated, and well regulated mind," whose "mildly beneficent" operations are "authorized by reason." When such liberty rules, "tranquility" and "contentment" result. Murray closed by contrasting that charming, pastoral scene, a Federalist utopia, with a sketch of the world of "licentiousness" their Jeffersonian opponents would make: "Intoxicated by the inebriating draught, and having renounced his understanding," a Jeffersonian Republican would upend nature's order, leveling all virtues and annihilating all distinctions, leading the nation through riot and confusion to its ultimate destruction. Her foes were deluded: the alternative to Adams was not Jefferson but Robespierre.[78]

Without authority, Murray contended in the following essay, "anarchy" and "desolation" reign supreme. A state without any recognized authority would prove calamitous. Were each individual allowed to exercise "an absolute and uncontrollable right to consult his own feelings, submitting himself to no other empire than that of his wayward passions," the result would be a nightmare. Murray asked her readers to envision people in a state of nature who came to realize that they must form a social compact or endure anarchy. Anxious to frame laws for their fledgling state, they mused over governments ranging from the ancient republics to modern monarchies. When history and theory yielded no clear answer, Murray concluded, they would have to follow common sense. The resulting government, complete with two elected legislative bodies, an independent judiciary, trial by jury, and an executive officer elected by the people, uncannily resembled that of the United States. Such, Murray explained, are "the *lineaments of nature*" and the necessary consequences of self-discipline, "without which, GENUINE LIBERTY would no longer irradiate our hemisphere."[79]

Given the opprobrium heaped on Adams by his critics in the 1790s and ever since, it is easy to forget that he was elected president in 1796. Like many other New Englanders, Murray revered both John and Abigail Adams, and she opened the *Gleaner* with a fawning preface addressed to the president. "The homage we yield to eminent abilities" is fully appropriate in a representative system of government. "Genius, elevated by virtue and unimpeached integrity," always commands "the esteem and veneration of mankind." Although Jeffersonians sneered at such sentiments, Federalists considered respect for ability consistent with their veneration of American institutions of self-government, which they distinguished sharply from the lawlessness they associated with the French Revolution.[80] The same John Adams who had excoriated Wollstonecraft for her defense of the French Revolution warmly praised Murray's vindication of Federalism as well as her plans for female education. Other women and men shared Murray's convictions, and the early years of the nineteenth century saw a dramatic increase in the number of academies devoted to the education of women. Abigail Adams had observed in her letter to John in 1782 that female republican virtue was "the most disinterested of all virtues" because women stood to gain nothing as a result of their selflessness. Eventually the impulses that led to the creation of women's academies and reading societies would spark a women's rights movement. At the turn of the nineteenth century, however, the false dawn of increasing opportunities for women in American democracy proved a harbinger of nothing but the reassertion of male prerogatives. According to the American critics of Wollstonecraft and of the French Revolution, a lack of discipline and deference led inevitably to violence and tragedy.[81]

European critics of the French Revolution said much the same thing, and on both sides of the Atlantic commentators tried to explain why only the United States had successfully consolidated its democratic revolution. Revulsion against the violence of the Terror—and against the nation at war with the monarchies of Europe until Napoleon's final defeat in 1815—prompted almost universal recoil from radical reform. Across the continent, brief revolutionary explosions flared up and vanished. In Britain an especially harsh, unremitting system of laissez-faire liberalism emerged, softened only by the English upper classes' gauzy expressions of affection for crown and country. In France the bourgeoisie and landowners, who emerged from the turmoil of the Revolution energized, scrambled to occupy the spaces left open for economic and cultural occupation by the former nobility and the Catholic Church. In France as in England, the losers included the poor in cities and in the countryside, people who had depended on the nobility for jobs and patronage. In France, the poor had also depended on the Catholic Church for what little education and health care they received. In the early nineteenth century, France, like England, entered a period of retrenchment, both from social services and from political radicalism, a period in which the newly rich took for granted the legitimacy of their wealth and their power.[82]

The dramatic, souring effect of the French Revolution was apparent not only in the rise of the British and French bourgeoisie and the decline of the fortunes of the rural and urban poor. It was equally apparent in the eclipse of movements for economic reform championed by figures such as Paine, Condorcet, and Wollstonecraft. Paine inadvertently identified the gulf that would separate democracy in the early-nineteenth-century United States from the polarized and reactionary cultures of France and Britain in a letter he wrote to Danton in the spring of 1793. In addition to protesting the "spirit of denunciation" that landed Paine himself in prison, he also warned that if such "private malignancies" continued to be indulged, "all confidence will be undermined and all authority be destroyed."

The sharp contrast between the depth of the hatred in France—and its murderous consequences—can be seen in Paine's own response to the dramatically different situation he had experienced in Pennsylvania during the American Revolution. The skirmish between Pennsylvania radicals and Wilson's Federalist friends known as the "Fort Wilson Riot" was treated by some American commentators as evidence of the deep enmity between rich and poor in the United States during the 1770s and 1780s. Paine, however, characterized the fracas in Philadelphia as an "unfortunate blunder of friends" and minimized the extent and significance of the conflict. Compared with what he considered the legal and lawless violence prevailing in England and in prerevolutionary France, the aftermath of the incident outside Wilson's home indicated to Paine Americans' shared commitment to resolving differences through politics rather than arms. Although Wilson was hardly "a favourite" of many people in Pennsylvania, a fact that Wilson himself knew Paine pointed out that "the difference is exceedingly great, between not being in favor and being considered as an enemy." Once the shots were fired and "the parties in and out of the house were known, and became known to each other, the animosity began to subside," Paine explained to Danton, "and the whole, exclusive of the imprudence, explained itself into a tragedy of errors." No one was imprisoned as result of the "Fort Wilson" incident, even though six people died, and nothing similar happened afterward in Philadelphia. Real as the disagreements in American politics were, Paine assured Danton, Philadelphians agreed to settle their differences at the polls rather than turning to armed insurrection or violent repression. Democracy, neither contained nor rolled back from Paine's perspective, instead provided the means to repair rather than exacerbate divisions.[83]

After Paine's release from the Luxembourg Prison in late 1794, he had reason to reconsider his upbeat judgment of American democracy. While in Paris, he wrote the first part of *The Age of Reason*, which was published in two parts in 1794 and 1795. The book made Paine a hero to agnostics and atheists and elicited furious criticism from Christians. Neither his supporters nor his critics grasped what Paine was trying to do, even though he explained his aim in the book's opening paragraphs. Paine was troubled by the Jacobin mania for dechristianization, and he worried that "the people of France were running headlong into atheism." It was one thing to demolish "superstition" and expose "false systems of government and false theology," but now the Revolution threatened "morality," "humanity," and, strikingly, what Paine called "the theology that is true." Paine offered an apparently clear statement of his own Deist creed: "I believe in one God, and no more; and I hope for happiness beyond this life. I believe in the equality of man, and I believe that religious duties consist of doing justice, loving mercy, and endeavouring to make our fellow creatures happy." So far, one might suppose, so uncontroversial, at least among many freethinking eighteenth-century champions of Enlightenment.

The trouble began, at least from the point of view of Paine's Anglo-American readers, when Paine made clear that he wanted to disassociate himself not only from Judaism, Catholicism, and Islam but also from all denominations of Protestant Christianity. "My own mind is my own church." He declared that "all national institutions of churches, whether Jewish, Christian, or Turkish, appear to me no other than human inventions set up to terrify and enslave mankind, and monopolize power and profit." With that bold claim, Paine antagonized many of those who might have accepted his spare opening statement of belief in one God. All religions pretended to have been established by someone whom the creator had singled out. "The Jews have their Moses; the Christians their Jesus Christ, their apostles and saints; and the Turks their Mahomet; as if the way to God was not open to every man alike." Christianity, Paine explained, far from being a special revelation, had "sprung out of the tail" of "heathen mythology." The gods of the ancients became the saints of Christianity. The ritual practices of modern churches likewise descended from earlier pagan traditions. Paine claimed to admire the person of Jesus Christ, "a virtuous and amiable man" who had preached and practiced a benevolent morality and bequeathed to his followers a "most excellent" but hardly unique code of ethics. Paine contended that similar moral systems had been formulated by Confucius, by some early Greek philosophers, more recently by Quakers, and by "many good men in all ages." Paine saw no reason to accept preposterous claims concerning the birth, miracles, resurrection, or ascension of Jesus, and he chided Christians for accepting a "fable, which for absurdity and extravagance is not exceeded by any thing that is to be found in the mythology of the ancients."

When *The Age of Reason* appeared in the United States, a shadow fell over Paine. Christians of all stripes rushed to distance themselves from the darling of the Democratic Societies, a man so many had lionized. Although Paine continued to attract defenders, few Americans could accept his description of "the obscene stories, the voluptuous debaucheries, the cruel and torturous executions, the unrelenting vindictiveness" that filled the Bible. Fewer still could contemplate dispassionately his judgment that the Bible was likelier the "word of a demon" than the word of God. The rest of *The Age of Reason*, which only a few eighteenth-century Americans apparently had the stomach to read, consisted of unrelenting ridicule of the beliefs, practices, and implications of Christianity. American reviewers of *The Age of Reason* competed to find words adequate to express their disdain. Paine replied by appending a second part in the edition of 1795, pouring oil on the fire and transforming the cultural significance of Deism in America. Prior to *The Age of Reason*, Deists such as Franklin, Jefferson, and Madison could express their reservations about organized religion without declaring themselves irreligious or antagonizing all believing Christians. Paine's diatribe foreclosed that option. Much as the Civil Constitution of the Clergy forced French Catholics to take sides in a suddenly stark battle between orthodoxy and anticlericalism—a choice that few had previously felt forced to face—so *The Age of Reason* raised the stakes for dissenters in America. Now even serious doubters felt compelled to dissociate themselves from Paine's pugnacious attacks, and a much deeper gap opened between skeptics and believers—a diverse group that included freethinkers and Universalists such as Murray as well as more orthodox Christians.

A reverent, albeit somewhat bemused attitude toward Christian belief and Christian ethics, accompanied by a willingness to treat the Bible as poetry and its stories as metaphors, joined together many of the educated Americans who were attracted to the ideas of the Moderate Enlightenment. Paine's *Age of Reason* threw down a gauntlet. Unbelievers found Paine's argument compelling; never again would they take seriously either the Bible or the people who read it. Believers found Paine's argument repellent; never again would they take seriously either his ideas or those of people who admired him. Paine himself, like other moderates affiliated with the Girondins, had been targeted by Robespierre because his support of the Revolution had been judged insufficiently fervent. Now the fervor of his critique of Christianity made him a lightning rod in the Anglo-American world.[84]

Paine was harried out of England by his prosecution for the second part of *The Age of Reason*. When he returned to the United States, he anticipated a greeting as warm as the enthusiastic embrace he had enjoyed as the author of *Common Sense*. Much had changed, however, not only as a result of the publication of *The Age of Reason* but also, and even more profoundly, as a result of the French Revolution, on the one hand, and the election of Jefferson in 1800, on the other. Paine himself had written about the consequences of a mirror image of that dynamic when he described what had happened to the Revolution in France. "Had a Constitution been established" in France, Paine wrote, "the nation would then have had a bond of union, and every individual would have known the line of conduct he was to follow." That was why Paine had joined Condorcet and Sieyès to write the Girondin Constitution. They intended to stabilize French government and allow for representative democracy to take root. Instead, Paine pointed out, the Jacobins substituted their own constitution, which they then immediately suspended until the end of the war—an end that never came: "Instead of this, a revolutionary government, a thing without either principle or authority, was substituted in its place."[85]

Paine failed to draw the obvious inference from that astute observation. The United States did ratify its Constitution. As a result, as he predicted, a "bond of union" had emerged, and Americans knew the "line of conduct" they had to follow. Once the Jeffersonians elected their candidate to the presidency in 1800, those who continued to call for radical change now found themselves no longer described as Democratic Republicans. Overnight they had become, in the eyes of their opponents, Jacobins, anti-Americans, people who refused to accept as legitimate the "line of conduct" established by the Constitution. As soon as Jefferson was elected president, though, he wanted to heal partisan wounds and end party conflict. Democracy became a shared standard, the ideal of Federalists as well as Jeffersonians. Now those who stood on the outside, the radical Paineite critics of Jefferson, could be doubly demonized as atheists as well as Jacobins.[86]

By 1803 Paine was writing to his old friend Samuel Adams to clear up what Paine considered two common misconceptions. First, he did indeed believe in God. Second, he believed that the Federalists were trying to "overturn the Federal constitution established on the representative system, and place government in the new world on the corrupt system of the old."[87] Although doubtless an exaggeration as extreme as Adams's complaint to Rush that the United States was no longer a "mixed government," Paine's anxiety illustrates—as clearly as the equally faulty judgment of Adams that it mirrored almost perfectly—the ways in which heightened rhetoric masked from both of these champions of representative democracy what was actually happening in the United States. Within the system they had both helped put in place, the system of representative democracy, two dynamics operated simultaneously. On the one hand, it made conflict appear more pronounced. Partisan newspapers mushroomed, and citizens vilified each other as they positioned themselves and their candidates for elections. Yet the political system nevertheless channeled those conflicts into provisional resolutions, through the institution of elections and the legislative debates that followed, at which point the entire cycle began again.

Jefferson provided a clear description of that democratic process in his justly celebrated First Inaugural Address. His speech displays the best overview of the cultural resources of the Moderate Enlightenment, which made possible a peaceful transition that contemporaries dubbed, with good reason, the Revolution of 1800. Federalists had subjected Jefferson to attacks at least as savage as those his supporters had hurled at Adams. Jefferson and other Democratic Republicans had been accused of participating in the global conspiracy whereby the Illuminati had plunged France into chaos as the opening act in a campaign that would target the United States next. Seldom in American history have partisan accusations flared as spectacularly, or with as flimsy a foundation in fact, as in the election of 1800.

Jefferson began his inaugural by addressing the depth of the invective. "During the contest of opinion through which we have passed," what he delicately called "the animation of discussion and of exertions" would have prompted strangers to think that Americans were at each other's throats and ready for civil war. But the election "being now decided by the voice of the nation," Jefferson observed, "according to the rules of the Constitution, all will, of course, arrange themselves under the will of law, and unite in common efforts for the common good." His followers had done so after Adams was elected four years earlier; he predicted the Federalists would do so now. Jefferson renounced the temptation to declare that the election had rendered him omnipotent. "All too will bear in mind this sacred principle, that though the will of the majority is in all cases to prevail, that will to be rightful must be reasonable; that the minority possess their equal rights, which equal law must protect, and to violate would be oppression." Rarely has the ethic of reciprocity, that fundamental cultural precondition of democracy, been stated with equal clarity. In the aftermath of an election, no matter how fiercely contested, the obligation to heal the wounds opened by partisanship is paramount. "Let us, then, fellow-citizens, unite with one heart and one mind. Let us restore to social intercourse that harmony and affection without which liberty and even life itself are but dreary things." Given the hateful words that had passed between Jefferson and his followers and the administrations of Washington and Adams, Jefferson knew he was asking a lot of both sides.

Jefferson's call for unity did not blind him to the reality or legitimacy of differences nor to the inevitability of continuing conflict. "Let us, then, with courage and confidence pursue our own Federal and Republican principles," distinct as they are even though we share a common "attachment to union and representative government." The distinctiveness of that form of government, Jefferson explained in terms that he knew would resonate with any Federalist, lay in the confidence it assumed in the people's ability to discern. The "honor and confidence" of the people in their elected officials, in Jefferson's words, resulted "not from birth but from our actions and their sense of them." As Jefferson, Adams, and Madison all knew from experience, no individual, no matter how highly regarded, was immune from rejection by the electorate. Unlike the unassailable power exercised by so many officials in European governments, the authority of every American official depended on the will of the people rather than privileges inherited from birth.

Finally, when Jefferson provided a litany of the "essential principles of our Government," his formulation distinguished the United States from France—and was indistinguishable from those offered by Adams loyalist Judith Sargent Murray. At the heart of American democracy lay "the right of election by the people—a mild and safe corrective of abuses which are lopped by the sword of revolution where peaceable remedies are unprovided." Jefferson urged his listeners to understand that toleration is crucial for democracy. After putting an end to the "religious intolerance under which mankind so long bled and suffered," the United States would have achieved little "if we countenance a political intolerance as despotic, as wicked, and as capable of as bitter and bloody persecutions." It is tempting, Jefferson acknowledged, to take ourselves and our rhetoric seriously, and to believe that our invective accurately reflects reality. "But every difference of opinion is not a difference of principle." Our fancied political differences lie mostly on the surface. What binds us together, "the principle" of democracy, is deeper than what divides us. It is possible, of course, to discern just beneath the surface of that call for unity something akin to Robespierre's conception of "true democracy," a conviction that all Americans, at heart, were Democratic Republicans. Given the eventual triumph of Jefferson's party and the extinction of the Federalists, some commentators have contended that Jefferson had that outcome in mind. In the absence of clear evidence suggesting that he sought to snuff out any flickers of opposition to his government, however, his familiar words can also be read as his acknowledgment of Americans' commitment to the institutions of self-government and the ethic of reciprocity: "We are all Republicans, we are all Federalists."[88]

Democracy requires, as Jefferson understood, the willingness to endure division. Revolutionaries in France, by contrast, tried repeatedly to achieve unity and unanimity by force. The bloody struggles in France had resulted from different judgments about when to declare the Revolution over and let the republic begin. The Feuillants, the Girondins, the Jacobins, and the Directory all had different answers to that crucial question. Their refusal to bargain with each other plunged France into a civil war as gruesome as the sixteenth-century wars of religion or the English Civil War. Such wars eliminated any chance that a culture of reciprocity would take hold. In the United States, as the election of 1800 demonstrated, even profound disagreements would be settled peacefully. At least for another sixty years.

CHAPTER 13

Diagnosing Democratic Cultures in America and Europe

UNLIKE COMBATANTS ON all sides of the French Revolution, Thomas Jefferson understood that an ethic of reciprocity must undergird democracy. So did his successor as president, James Madison, whose variations on that theme had helped secure ratification of the Constitution. In part because the Jefferson and Madison administrations adopted the moderate nationalism of Washington and Adams, the fortunes of the Federalist Party declined so dramatically after Jefferson's inauguration that when Virginian James Monroe was elected president in 1816, even the *Columbian Centinel* in staunchly Federalist Boston declared the nation united. Now that the partisan rancor of a half century had been washed away, an "era of good feelings" had begun. Yet in the United States, as across the Atlantic, obstacles impeding the further progress of democracy remained so formidable that those "good feelings" were soon exposed as a veneer laid over hatreds as murderous as those that had plunged France, then all of Europe, into war.

Arguments for the central components of democracy were hardly new in the nineteenth century. The United States, formally committed to the principles of popular sovereignty, autonomy, and equality, had put in place institutional structures prerequisite to a robust democratic government. After the French Revolution, however, democracy stalled. Recovering from cultural, political, and socioeconomic trauma in the laboratories of democratic experimentation took time. Choruses of self-congratulation marked the exploits of Napoleon's armies and the expanding "empire of liberty" made possible by Jefferson's purchase of Louisiana and the nation's survival of the War of 1812 against Britain, but deep rifts remained. This chapter traces arguments to advance self-government from the early nineteenth century until 1848, when the Mexican-American War touched off new debates in the United States over the meaning of popular sovereignty as well as the future of slavery, and the failed European revolutions of 1848 enshrined moderation by rekindling fears of violence.

The enmities exposed by the French Revolution, and by the wars and domestic battles it provoked on both sides of the Atlantic, fed fears and fueled partisan struggles sufficiently bitter to stifle further development of an ethic of reciprocity. When the allied monarchies that ringed France finally defeated Napoleon, cultural and political conservatives cemented their grip on power. The mature regimes of market capitalism that emerged during these years throughout the Atlantic world, coupled with the poisonous persistence of chattel slavery in the United States, increased inequality and closed off the prospect of expanding and deepening democratic experiments. Noisy advocates of white male supremacy in the United States, including the followers of slave owner and Indian fighter Andrew Jackson, proclaimed themselves champions of democracy, as did some partisans of competing forms of utopian and revolutionary socialism in Europe such as Louis Blanc and Etienne Cabet. Yet such self-styled democrats did little to advance the practice of deliberation, the toleration of difference, or the ethic of reciprocity. Despite their grand rhetoric, reformers' paltry achievements paled beside the continuing denial of political and legal rights to women everywhere and the subjugation of African Americans, American Indians, and a growing industrial working class in Europe and America.

The shortcomings of early-nineteenth-century democracy first came into focus in the work of writers who explained why the dynamics of economic, social, and political development simultaneously fed interest in and stymied democracy. Prior to the nineteenth century, appeals to freedom were almost always balanced by reminders, usually although not always religious in inspiration, of the necessity of order and self-discipline. As self-interest came to be considered socially useful rather than shameful, which is the central dynamic examined in this chapter, earlier constraints of tradition and propriety that had also propped up hierarchy and paternalism gave way to the unrestrained exploitation of resources and people. The ethical framework within which Adam Smith had defended free markets collapsed under the ostensibly scientific political economy of David Ricardo and Thomas Malthus and the powerful people who embraced their ideas. Their understanding of social life placed competition at the center and consigned benevolence to the margins of human interaction, leaving the poor—now without the last remnants of the earlier "moral economy" that authorized charity—even more vulnerable.[1]

The internal contradictions that bedeviled nineteenth-century liberal democracy were the central focus of influential individuals on both sides of the

Atlantic, including Alexis de Tocqueville, John Stuart Mill, and Abraham Lincoln. Tocqueville's writings offered vivid accounts of both the American and French experiences with democratic revolution and identified the ironic consequences of freedom for democracy. He understood that liberating individuals from the bonds of feudal traditions enabled many individuals to escape poverty or at least become self-sufficient, but he also saw what such free-flowing, frenzied economic development masked: the deleterious consequences for community life of the unbounded grasping by individuals that he associated with such freedom. The word "individualism" first entered the English language when Henry Reeve translated Tocqueville's *Democracy in America* from French into English in 1835.

Mill, perhaps the most wide-ranging and influential English intellectual of the age, likewise probed the idea of individual liberty within the new framework of utilitarian calculations and located that analysis alongside searching inquiries into the continuing subjugation of women and the pervasive corruption of English politics. He identified the social and economic as well as political obstacles that impeded laying the cultural foundations necessary for robust self-government. Many of Mill's contemporaries misunderstood his analysis of those obstacles, including the denial of rights to women and the lack of education among potential voters, as a species of elitism and a denial of the possibility or desirability of democracy. Instead Mill, like John Quincy Adams, Jared Sparks, and other like-minded Americans who helped shape Tocqueville's analysis of democracy, advanced a cultural ideal that would require more of citizens than the simple pursuit of self-interest.

Lincoln agonized over the problems of justice and national unity under conditions of popular sovereignty. He rose to prominence by counterposing an ethic of reciprocity to majority rule, which he deemed an inadequate guide when the majority preferred injustice to justice. He inspired many Americans who were indifferent to the sufferings of slaves to commit themselves to fighting a war to preserve the Union, then fell victim to the hatred engendered by his challenge to the overwhelmingly popular doctrine of white supremacy. Like Tocqueville, Mill, and those whom they engaged in debate, Lincoln contrasted an ethical ideal of democracy to an increasingly popular but shallow conception of popular government as nothing more than the summing of choices made by self-interested individuals.

The nineteenth century witnessed a steady escalation of rhetoric against as well as for democracy. The reigns of George III and Victoria in Britain, and of Louis XVIII and Charles X in France, bolstered by an upsurge of evangelical

Protestant and conservative Catholic religiosity and romantic nationalism, channeled much popular enthusiasm away from self-government. So too did widespread revulsion against the perceived excesses of the French Revolution. Only in the United States did the language of democracy emerge unambiguously triumphant. After Jefferson's defeat of John Adams in the presidential election of 1800, very few Americans spoke openly on behalf of aristocracy or inequality. A few backward-looking critics such as the Federalist Fisher Ames decried "the mire of a democracy," which he claimed "pollutes the morals of citizens before it swallows up their liberties." Another conservative penned a satirical poem, *Democracy*, lampooning as "greasy caps" the workers who styled themselves the common people. Such sentiments were becoming increasingly uncommon, though, and Adams by then had deliberately disassociated himself from Federalists growing ever more reactionary.[2]

Ames's fellow conservative George Cabot explained why antidemocratic rhetoric was on its way out. He denied that a sharp distinction could be drawn between the radical French Revolution and the supposedly more moderate American republic because both, despite the Jacobins' excesses, originated "*in the political theories of our country*" and its embrace of popular sovereignty. As the Baptist preacher Elias Smith observed in a July 4, 1809, sermon, "The government adopted here is a DEMOCRACY," and though a handful of Americans like Ames ridiculed the term and insisted on designating the United States a republic, the distinction was nonsense. "All the power in the great and strong body, the people, is used for the benefit of the whole. My friends, never let us be ashamed of *DEMOCRACY*!" By 1820 not only was the Federalist Party dead. Americans had embraced the ideal, if not yet universally the label, of democracy.[3]

On all sides of almost all issues that roiled the early national period—the question of an active national government, slavery, education, Indian removal, and the reform of prisons, asylums, and alcohol use—public figures in the United States sought to align themselves with "the people," even though they attached different meanings to the word "democracy." When a new party division opened up in the 1820s, the majority of northerners agreed that a successful democracy requires thoroughgoing moral as well as economic uplift, autonomy in the sense of self-rule for individuals and an ethic of reciprocity. An increasing number of northerners committed themselves not only to commercial development but also to addressing the unjust treatment of African Americans, Indians, and, in some cases at least, women. Harvard professor Edward Tyrrel Channing, for example, decried the "dangers of false excitement" being whipped up by the "corrupt eloquence" of demagogues who claimed to speak on behalf of "the people" and insisted that he and his ilk were democracy's genuine friends. From the founding of the *North American Review* in 1815 through the Civil War, those who clustered first in the National Republican Party (which split from the Jeffersonian Democratic Republicans after the election of John Quincy Adams in 1824), then flocked to their successors the Whigs a decade later, and finally joined Lincoln's Republican Party in the 1850s, insisted on "self-culture" or moral elevation as a prerequisite for responsible deliberation.[4]

Americans held two rival conceptions of the democracy they all claimed to embrace. If Federalism had all but expired by the end of Madison's presidency in 1817, so too had the fervor that had fueled the Democratic Republican societies of the 1790s. During Jefferson's presidency it became clear that American politics would be contested within a shared framework. John Quincy Adams himself bolted from the Federalists over their opposition to Jefferson's embargo against Britain, and most of Jefferson's supporters applauded when the president augmented national power by purchasing Louisiana from France. Although Jefferson's 1800 inaugural hardly put an end to partisan squabbling, his presidency and Madison's did bring the first party system to an end. The seeds of the second party system were planted almost as soon as the first one ended, making the vaunted "era of good feelings" only a brief hiatus between eras of strident partisanship.

Among the most striking developments of the early nineteenth century were the rapid expansion of the franchise and the explosion of voter participation. The Northwest Territory was settled so fast, and so chaotically, that the old fifty-acre freehold requirement for suffrage made little sense. The new states carved from it abandoned such restrictions, and most northern states soon followed suit. Boston's J. T. Austin anticipated Tocqueville when he argued in 1820 that concern for the public good did not depend on "property, but upon institutions, laws, habits, and associations." The time had come for Massachusetts to enfranchise voters without regard to wealth. A year later, retired New York senator Nathan Sanford accurately attributed ideas about the fifty-acre freehold to lingering European notions of "three estates" and pointed out that "here there is but one estate—the people." Commencement speakers at William and Mary, long a bastion of southern privilege, endorsed universal manhood suffrage as early as 1808 and 1812, and another Virginian joshed that property requirements made no sense "unless there be something in the ownership of land, that by enchantment or magic converts frail, erring man, into an infallible and impeccable being."[5]

Along with the expanded suffrage of white men, however, came the systematic disfranchisement of women and free blacks. Women's subordinate condition had been so generally assumed that their status was seldom addressed in voting laws, yet some women, usually unmarried women and widows, had voted in the early years of the new nation, particularly in New Jersey. Likewise African American property owners, a growing number of whom resided in northern states, routinely exercised the franchise. With the elimination of property qualifications, however, came formal restrictions on the legal rights of women and African Americans. To deepen the paradox, one northern state after another abolished slavery during the same years when they were establishing all-but-universal suffrage for white men. Yet the end of slavery failed to dislodge whites' racism, which not only persisted but deepened throughout the United States during the early nineteenth century. As wealth ceased to differentiate members of the expanded white male electorate, gender and race took its place.[6]

The apotheosis of this *herrenvolk* democracy came with the rise of Andrew Jackson and his followers. Although they came to call themselves "the Democracy," they first became aware of their distinctiveness after the hotly contested election of 1824. With their hero denied the presidency by what they (inaccurately) charged was a "corrupt bargain" between Henry Clay of Tennessee and the new president, John Quincy Adams, the Jacksonians projected an image of themselves as the authentic champions of the common man in contrast to their "elitist" enemies. Jacksonians saw in the emerging commercial power of the Northeast precisely the aristocracy that John Adams, John Quincy Adams, and their allies claimed the United States had repudiated. In the words of the pro-Jackson *Washington Globe*, it was Nicholas Biddle, the president of the Bank of the United States, who was "the MONARCH whom the monied aristocracy have chosen to manage, with undivided effect, the instrument of their power."[7] Such rhetoric cut both ways. After Jackson won the presidency in 1828, his use of executive power prompted his critics to signal their opposition to his bloated authority by calling themselves Whigs and christening the executive "King Andrew I." Almost all African Americans who could still vote condemned Jackson as the head of a party of white supremacy and gravitated toward his enemies. By the 1820s, both parties deployed the rhetoric of aristocracy to tar their opponents and dubbed themselves friends of the people.[8]

Nineteenth-century uses of the term "democracy" across the Atlantic were equally hyperbolic but usually pejorative. Invigorated monarchies and religious movements burnished hierarchy and tradition to a gloss they had not enjoyed since the death of Louis XIV. In France a "white terror" followed the restoration of the Bourbon monarchy in 1814. It differed from the absolutism of the *ancien régime* because it was founded on a constitution that acknowledged the legitimacy of an elected lower chamber of the legislature and provided basic liberties, but its ultraroyalist spirit energized conservatives and enraged those with lingering republican or even moderate sympathies.

A less venomous form of conservatism also reigned in Britain, where it fed on centuries of tradition rather than decades of resentment and a passionate desire to settle scores. Voting in Britain had long meant little more than ratifying the decisions made by the crown's appointed ministers. Ordinary people, perhaps because they had so little influence on public life, showed more interest in royal pageantry than in politics. In Britain less than 20 percent of adult males were enfranchised even after the Reform Act of 1832. By contrast, the overwhelming majority of white males could vote in the United States by the 1830s, and more than 80 percent of those eligible participated in the presidential election of 1840. In France voting was even more restricted than in Britain: during the 1840s fewer than 3 percent of adult males enjoyed the franchise, with only 10 percent of that tiny group meeting the qualifications for election to the Chamber of Deputies.[9]

The accession to the French throne of Charles X in 1824 made obvious the contrast with both Britain and the United States. As the comte d'Artois, notorious since the outbreak of the Revolution as the most vehemently antirepublican member of the exiled French nobility, the new king, crowned at Reims with all the symbols of the old monarchy, embodied the worst excesses of the Restoration. With his blessing, the Jesuits returned and the Catholic Church reasserted its control over French education. Faint rumblings of dissent prompted government crackdowns. When Charles demanded that ministers answer to him, not to the legislature, the few left-leaning independent members of the very moderate (and very wealthy) Chamber of Deputies engineered a vote of no confidence in the government. Charles promptly disbanded the Chamber and called for new elections. When voters returned an equally unfriendly Chamber, the infuriated king dissolved it again and proposed new voting rules that slashed the already limited electorate by another 75 percent, reduced the clout of the ascendant bourgeoisie, and empowered the old, fading aristocracy. That move provoked the July Revolution of 1830, in the face of which Charles unceremoniously abdicated. The *ancien régime*, at last, appeared dead.

Monarchy of a different sort persisted in Britain. Looking back from midcentury, the social critic Matthew Arnold proclaimed that "the growing power in Europe is democracy," even though it would have been hard to identify a thoroughgoing democratic state when he made that claim. Between 1825 and 1829 Tory governments in Britain, strategically conceding the right of trade unions to organize and the right of Dissenters and Catholics to civil rights, defused some of the tensions. Moderate Whigs such as John

Cartwright and radicals such as William Cobbett pushed for modest expansion of the suffrage, but Whigs typically allied with Conservatives to preserve the rule of the propertied against the claims of the "unworthy" masses, whom both parties deemed unqualified to participate in public life. British debates over popular political involvement began in the 1820s and heated up in the following decades. Even the smallest gestures toward democracy were judged certain either to redeem or destroy civilization. Three reform bills generated bitter controversy, became law only after protracted struggles, and accomplished little. Merely expanding the electorate in England and Wales from 17 percent to 18 percent of adult males required heroic efforts against fierce opposition.[10]

From the perspective of democracy's critics on both sides of the English Channel, popular government promised dangerous and despotic mob rule, a return to the nightmare of the Terror. In Britain after 1815, high tariffs assured high prices for food; low wages assured poverty for industrial workers. Protestors demanded an expanded suffrage, higher wages, and lower prices, to be achieved through repeal of the Corn Laws that kept landowners happy. As the traditions of paternalism and charity that had made poverty endurable weakened and calls for representation of the new industrial cities in Parliament mounted, conflict became inevitable. In the Peterloo Massacre of 1819, soldiers attacked a peaceful crowd of demonstrators, leaving hundreds injured, eleven dead, and a legacy of mutual hatred and mistrust between workers and the wealthy. Yet not even radical agitators such as William Cobbett and Henry Hunt embraced the dangerous cause of—or the word—democracy. The appearance in 1819 of the *Democratic Recorder*, a periodical that proudly proclaimed its allegiance in its title and whose writers enjoyed thumbing their noses at Britain's ruling class, stood out among more moderate voices of popular protest.[11]

Although small-scale uprisings were a persistent feature of early-nineteenth-century French culture, even the most significant upheavals had limited consequences. The Revolution of 1830, which ousted the restored monarchy, was followed by a new monarchy shielded by a new oligarchy. The venerable Lafayette, having fled the Terror in 1792 only to be imprisoned for five years by the Austrians and Prussians, had remained a staunch critic of the Directory, Napoleon, and the restored monarchy ever since he returned to France in 1800—especially since his election to the Chamber of Deputies in 1827. Offered the chance to head a new government after Charles abdicated, the seventy-two-year-old hero of two revolutions declined. When he appeared in public with the man who would be king, the modest and apparently unthreatening duc d'Orléans, the two wrapped themselves in the tricolored flag of the Revolution rather than the fleur-de-lis proudly flown by the Bourbons. Lafayette, celebrated on both sides of the Atlantic as a foe of autocracy, thus helped legitimate the new monarchy. Although the king was declared subservient to the constitution, the changes, to Lafayette's chagrin, proved more symbolic than substantive. The violence of the French Revolution left a lasting suspicion of direct popular rule and a willingness to accept government by elites, either by a restored monarchy or, after 1830, by a bourgeois autocracy. The Revolution of 1830, like the Reform Bill of 1832, reflected the central role in the French and British constitutional monarchies of an emerging middle class. Neither was a triumph of democracy. Elites in France and Britain, insulated from popular pressures, instituted few measures to address rising poverty, declining health, and limited education.[12]

Resurgent popular religiosity played a part in this conservative turn. Assessing the role of religious faith, however, is among the most challenging puzzles of early-nineteenth-century Atlantic history. When Napoleon signed the Concordat with the Vatican in 1801, he appeared to end the religious war set off by the French Revolution. Yet the enforced subservience of the Church to the new Napoleonic order generated not only resentment but also, after Napoleon's defeat, French Catholics' passionate commitment to preventing secular authorities from dictating terms to religious believers. Throughout early-nineteenth-century Europe, those in charge of new and increasingly elaborate forms of government administration maintained control only by allying with church hierarchies and masses of believers who were, in many cases at least, becoming increasingly inclined toward more paternalistic—and authoritarian—regimes in church and state alike.

When monarchical rule was restored to France and to the other regions conquered by Napoleon, it usually returned in league with religious authorities and unencumbered by the aristocracies and traditions that had limited its power. Because these new alliances of church and state rested on shallower foundations, and because European cultures were undergoing rapid socioeconomic changes, these regimes proved to be less stable than those toppled by the French Revolution and the wars that followed in its wake. Various forms of romantic nationalism, fueled by nostalgia for an imagined world, encouraged aspirations of grandeur and provided alternative sources of popular adhesion from the Italian and the German states to England and Ireland. Because these new varieties of nationalism rested on sentimental attachment to the idea of the people themselves rather than to divine-right monarchy, the gaudy regimes of Restoration Europe stood on shaky ground. Tensions between Catholics and Protestants intensified to a level at times reminiscent of the sixteenth century.[13]

In England and the United States, new and newly energized evangelical Protestant denominations, marked by more emotional brands of religiosity, deprecated strictly secular versions of Enlightenment rationality and used the fervor of the faithful to campaign against evils ranging from alcohol abuse to inhumane prisons. By the 1840s, the Second Great Awakening had transformed American culture. Between 50 and 80 percent of Americans now belonged to religious congregations, a dramatic rise from the 1770s. Popular piety, paradoxically, seemed to inspire democratic reform in Britain and the United States and to block it in much of continental Europe. Groups of believers clustered on all sides of every issue, convinced that their own version of Christian faith undergirded their ideas about society and politics, which means it is impossible to generalize about—or to exaggerate the significance of—religion when examining nineteenth-century democracy on both sides of the North Atlantic.[14]

Nowhere is the significance of religion to democracy more apparent than in the work of Alexis de Tocqueville. Tocqueville was a child of the *ancien régime* who grew into the anatomist of democratic culture, the individual who most incisively probed the tension between popular involvement and "competence"—who should be allowed to participate and who should not—that defined much of the debate over democracy in the nineteenth century.[15] He was a great-grandson of Guillaume-Chrétien de Lamoignon de Malesherbes, who had helped conduct the defense of Louis XVI at the king's trial in 1792, and grandson of Louis Le Peletier de Rosanbo, head of the Parlement of Paris. He was a son of the Comte Hervé de Tocqueville, a substantial landowner who believed he was improving his prospects when he married into the Malesherbes family. Hervé sympathized with the Revolution in its early stages, but his hopes evaporated when terror became the order of the day. Malesherbes and Le Peletier de Rosanbo were arrested in December of 1793 and guillotined four months later. Hervé himself was imprisoned, along with his wife and her mother and grandmother, and released only after Robespierre's fall. It took decades for him to recover his land and his title.[16]

France during the Restoration was uneasy about both monarchy and democracy. If the Revolution had shown the dangers of popular passion, the extremists who returned to power with Charles X made the *ancien régime* look good. Benjamin Constant, the leading early-nineteenth-century French political commentator and a crucial figure for Alexis de Tocqueville, captured the ambivalence of many in his influential reflections on liberty and democracy.[17] Successful regimes outside France had shown that the ancients' civic virtue, which required selfless sacrifice for the public good, was no longer appropriate in the modern world. Because ordinary people were now free to enjoy the pleasures of everyday life, and because the complexity of modern nations ruled out the direct engagement in politics still possible in ancient city-states, moderns were disinclined to surrender their private satisfactions and embrace the austere virtue extolled by republicans like Mably and enforced by Robespierre. Instead they preferred what Constant called "modern liberty," with ample space reserved for private and family life, to the liberty of the ancients.[18]

Despotism, Constant argued, whether monarchical or democratic, poisons all facets of culture. Autonomy is required not only in the domains of politics and the arts but even in the military, where unthinking obedience issues in lust and pillage; in commerce, which requires more than self-interest to flourish; and in religion, which must elicit voluntary professions of faith rather than blind subservience. "Independence of thought is as necessary," Constant wrote, "as air is to physical life." In despotic regimes "everything degenerates." Despite the "vain brilliance" once relished by the court of Louis XIV and Napoleon's entourage, despotism divides thinking people into revolutionaries and those who "plunge into selfishness" and corruption.[19] Turning from liberty to government, Constant emphasized limiting the power of the state. He called for preserving a domain beyond government intrusion, within which individuals could think freely about religion and politics and enjoy their property without threats of confiscation. Constant came to believe that the Jacobins' obsession with now-obsolescent civic virtue blinded them to such limits. "It is in the name of liberty," he wrote, "that we were given prisons, scaffolds, countless persecutions."[20]

The Directory and the Empire convinced Constant that authoritarian rule always threatens freedom. "Variety is life," he wrote, "uniformity, death."[21] The Bourbon Restoration of 1815 and the onset of Louis-Philippe's monarchy in July of 1830 intensified his anxieties about oligarchic government in France. First to last, Constant emphasized the importance of historical development and the desirability of nurturing productive rather than destabilizing forms of civic engagement. The excesses of the Revolution had permanently discredited direct democracy, but Constant worried that France might swing too far in the other direction. He recommended steps taken by postrevolutionary American governments: annual elections to keep elected officials accountable; federalism to divide power; and a bicameral legislature with deputies elected by the people.[22] Balancing public participation against the danger of popular enthusiasm, and balancing liberty against the danger of inwardness, Constant attracted critics from both left and right.[23]

Yet Constant hardly stood alone. The emergence of a moderate alternative to radical republicanism and royalism was the (always unfinished) story of nineteenth-century French politics. Like-minded if hardly identical thinkers, including François Guizot, Pierre-Paul Royer-Collard, and Tocqueville, variously designated liberals, independents, doctrinaires, or champions of the *juste milieu* (middle course), took positions between what they considered the no longer viable revolutionary left and the equally unpalatable ultraroyalist right. They disagreed about the value of reason versus sentiment, freedom of conscience versus religious education, and decentralized versus centralized political power.[24]

Guizot was raised in Switzerland, where his Calvinist mother relocated after his father went to the guillotine in Nimes. When the young Guizot moved to Paris, he proved himself a precocious scholar and politician: he earned a professorship at the Sorbonne in 1812 and a post in the Interior Ministry in 1814. For the next four decades he churned out collections of historical documents, histories of Europe, England, and France, and influential political commentaries, all premised on his dual convictions about safeguarding rights and securing a limited but significant popular role in public life. Against the wishes of many royalists, the Restoration monarchy allowed a tiny percentage of wealthy citizens to vote, and that toehold prompted efforts to expand the suffrage.[25] Guizot and his fellow doctrinaires contended that a "right to vote" is nonsensical. All citizens are equal before the law, but only those with the "capacity"—the competence—to act responsibly should be able to exercise the franchise. Instead of popular sovereignty, Guizot enshrined the "sovereignty of reason," which *Le Globe* declared the "philosophy of the century" in an editorial of 1826.[26] It was despotism that was new, Guizot's histories showed, not representative democracy. The experiment with nearly universal manhood suffrage could be tried in the United States, a mere "*société enfant*," a child society, but the sophisticated societies of modern Europe were another matter.[27] The French Revolution had shown conclusively the danger of direct popular participation in developed nations.[28] Guizot was not hankering for a return to earlier eras or longing to see the Revolution completed. France enjoyed a government resting on civic equality, the rule of law, and the sanctity of representative institutions, the existence of which made universal suffrage—and "political democracy"—unnecessary and undesirable.[29]

The most important legacy of Guizot and Constant was their belief that public-spiritedness is the most crucial ingredient in modern political life. When the Revolution of 1830 ended by empowering the July Monarchy of Louis-Philippe, Guizot played an active role in broadening access to public schools in his term as minister of education (1832–37), even though he did not envision the process culminating in universal suffrage. Guizot's cooperation with the July monarchy has clouded his reputation. His notorious advice to those who complained that only a few wealthy individuals controlled national elections in France—"get rich"—has been frequently lampooned. His role propping up the Orléanist regime, which he served as prime minister in the months immediately preceding the outbreak of the Revolution of 1848, has likewise cast a shadow over his legacy.[30] The writings of Constant and Guizot highlighted the inevitable tensions in postrevolutionary France. First the Jacobins, then Napoleon, and finally the restored monarchy tried to resolve those tensions by establishing or reestablishing absolute authority. A republican left countered by keeping alive the flame of revolution. For that reason both radicals and conservatives assailed Constant and Guizot. Although their *juste milieu* now strikes critics as a flimsy excuse for rule by an emerging *haute bourgeoisie* that was neither moderate nor just, their juggling act set the stage for the more incisive ideas of Alexis de Tocqueville.

More clearly than any other nineteenth-century French thinker, Tocqueville discerned that both the twin forms of autocracy in France, that of the Jacobins and their heirs, on the one hand, and that of the liberals who provided the rationale for the July Monarchy, on the other, descended from the absence in postrevolutionary France of the intermediate, voluntary associations that marked democracy in America. Inasmuch as those organizations, often originating in religious congregations, had undergirded the earliest forms of political association in England's North American colonies, they had set in motion the developments that made possible vibrant popular government in America. Their absence was equally decisive in France. In the contrast between Tocqueville's account of democracy in America and his account of the Revolution in France lies the explanation for the distinct challenges that democracy has faced in the two nations since the 1830s.[31]

Given Tocqueville's family background at the heart of the French aristocracy, his own trajectory remains surprising. During his lifetime Tocqueville traveled not only to the United States and Canada but also throughout Europe and to Algeria. In his native France he witnessed two republics, two monarchies, and two empires. In none of them did he feel at home. Whereas his brothers both entered the military, married women from wealthy families, and made themselves rich, Alexis married an Englishwoman without fortune and, having studied law, embarked on an unpromising career at the bottom rung of the French judiciary. Tocqueville's formal education came from an ultraconservative priest who refused to acknowledge the Revolution, from mediocre schools in Metz, where his father was posted in his late adolescence, and above all from immersing himself in his father's library. There he encountered writings by all the philosophes, but it was Montesquieu, Voltaire, and Rousseau who made the most lasting impression. Tocqueville later recalled that he suffered from a debilitating personal crisis, probably brought on by a crisis of faith, at age sixteen. "Doubt entered, or rather hurtled in with an incredible violence, not only doubt about one thing or another in particular, but an all-embracing doubt." The tremors of this earthquake, to use his metaphor, left him "seized by the blackest melancholy, then by an extreme disgust with life."[32] Recurring fits of doubt periodically plunged him into despair in the succeeding decades. His friendships and his marriage, although hardly blissful, were the anchors that kept him from drifting into prolonged bouts of depression. He found few challenges and no satisfaction in his work. He was restless.

When the Revolution of 1830 ended the reign of Charles X and inaugurated the July Monarchy, Tocqueville did not share the anxiety of his friends or his father. His own letters and writings indicate his prior dissatisfaction with the restored Bourbon monarchy and his awareness that the world of aristocracy was giving way to a newly emerging, although as yet unshaped, culture. In the months leading up to the revolution, Tocqueville hinted that Charles would not survive the crisis. The new Orléanist regime of Louis-Philippe, aware of the opposition from right and left, required all civil servants to sign an oath of loyalty. After careful reflection, the twenty-five-year-old Tocqueville agreed to pledge himself to a regime that repelled most of the Bourbon aristocracy, including his father and others in his family. Looking back regretfully decades later, Tocqueville observed that Louis-Philippe epitomized the contrast between the old monarchy and the new: "He was enlightened, subtle, and tenacious, but all his thoughts turned to the useful, and he was filled with such a deep contempt for truth and such a profound disbelief in virtue that they clouded his vision." It was no surprise that the king removed the Catholic Church from the position of privilege to which the Bourbons had restored it.[33] Louis-Philippe ruled on behalf of a new class, the bourgeoisie, intent not on preserving tradition but making money. If that France offered little to offend Tocqueville, it offered even less to attract him.

Tocqueville and his best friend, Gustave de Beaumont, proposed to the new government of Louis-Philippe that they embark on a research project. The French penal system, by almost any measure a scandal, was ripe for reform. Tocqueville and Beaumont suggested that the most advanced experiments were emerging not in Britain, France's rival, but in the United States, the home of the world's most advanced democracy. Like the duc de la Rochefoucauld-Liancourt before them, Tocqueville and Beaumont would survey the topography of American penal reform. The two friends shared the belief that the July Monarchy was a paper bag over a ticking time bomb. Tocqueville and Beaumont wanted to visit the future. Their stated purpose, studying American penitentiaries, was only an excuse. Even before the 1830 Revolution, Tocqueville later wrote, he had become convinced that "we are irresistibly drawn by our laws and our mores toward an almost complete equality of social conditions." Once conditions became equal, "I no longer see any intermediary stage between a democratic government," on the one hand, and "the unchecked rule of one man," on the other. By the word "democratic" Tocqueville meant "not a republic but a state of society in which everyone, to a greater or lesser degree, takes part in the political process." In time, he predicted, all nations would "arrive at one or the other."[34] Beaumont shared Tocqueville's sense of what was at stake.[35]

Tocqueville and Beaumont were hardly alone in writing about the United States. Such travelers' accounts were a growth industry in the nineteenth century.[36] Like Chateaubriand and de la Rochefoucauld-Liancourt before them, the French visitors' aspirations soared beyond description to cultural analysis. Tocqueville's *Democracy* reflects his commitment to what he later called "philosophical history."[37] He was less interested in recounting the details of his experiences in America than in assessing the significance of the emerging democratic culture that he and Beaumont encountered. The result was Tocqueville's *Democracy in America*.[38]

Before embarking for America, Tocqueville had learned from Montesquieu about institutions and regimes, from Rousseau about states of nature and the general will, and from Guizot about the history of local life and government in France. Tocqueville attended Guizot's lectures at the Sorbonne in the late 1820s and took extensive notes. Guizot argued that medieval French *communes* had been more or less self-governing before the absolute monarchies of the sixteenth and seventeenth centuries systematically subjected them to royal authority. But Tocqueville was hardly an uncritical auditor. Guizot had praised the monarchy for quelling local upheavals, achieving national unification, and facilitating the orderly government of France, a process that also made possible the rise of a productive and apolitical bourgeoisie. Tocqueville's notes indicate that he was not persuaded by Guizot's characterizations of the self-governing *communes* as "ferocious" or by his rosy characterizations of the monarchy and the bourgeoisie. The young Tocqueville was already wondering whether the "excessively timid" French people had exchanged the vitality of self-government for the "calm of servitude" and "equality under a master."[39]

By the time Tocqueville arrived in America in 1831, then, he was already attuned by contemporary French political discourse to the problems of self-government, centralized authority, and the relation between social and economic development and political institutions.[40] What he learned in America, though, changed his ideas about democracy. His thinking developed, both during the time he spent in the New World and after he returned home to write the first volume of *Democracy in America*, which was published to immediate acclaim in 1835. Tocqueville's understanding of American democracy went through multiple stages. First, he was powerfully influenced by his New England informants, including Jared Sparks, John Quincy Adams, Josiah Quincy, and Francis Calley Gray. Second, by studying Joseph Story's *Commentaries on the Constitution*, Jefferson's *Notes on the State of Virginia*, and the *Federalist* he learned about American politics and government, which he supplemented by reading about English and Swiss local government. Finally, his view of America was colored by his anxieties about the continuing centralization of French government under the July Monarchy and its consequences for public life in France. In the United States Tocqueville learned to appreciate how crucial was the interaction between the social and the political, but he never lost sight of the essential role of government in associational life or democratic culture.[41]

The nation Tocqueville encountered in 1831 reflected the ambivalence about representative and direct democracy common on both sides of the Atlantic, which no one expressed or symbolized better than Thomas Jefferson. In several letters written in the spring and summer of 1816, Jefferson offered three variations on the question of a "pure republic." To his French-born friend Pierre du Pont de Nemours, who had sent Jefferson a plan for a new French government after the fall of Napoleon, Jefferson wrote "that action by the citizens in person, in affairs within their reach and competence, and in all others by representatives, chosen immediately, and removable by themselves, constitutes the essence of a republic." Unlike those Antifederalists who judged Madison an enemy of the people for endorsing a national government, Jefferson considered representative democracy ideal for the United States because "a government by representation is capable of extension over a greater surface of country than one of any other form."[42] To John Taylor, Jefferson wrote that a republic is a "government by its citizens in mass, acting directly and personally," but he noted that "such a government is evidently restrained to very narrow limits of space and population." Indeed, he doubted whether "it would be practicable beyond the extent of a New England township." In larger settings power must be exercised by representatives, elected for short terms to ensure their responsiveness to their constituents.[43] Jefferson prized local government, the "townships" of New England and the "wards"

he recommended for Virginia. These he deemed "the wisest invention ever devised by the wit of man for the perfect exercise of self-government, and for its preservation."[44] Inasmuch as Jefferson both praised direct involvement of ordinary people in local government and explicitly acknowledged that national affairs must be managed by the people's representatives, those with the "competence" to perform the tasks of government, he stood on both sides of the controversial debate about democracy that rocked America and France and defined party politics in the United States.

In the years immediately after Jefferson wrote those letters, his ideal of a vibrant American politics, which would extend from vigorous local participation in town government through a national politics oriented toward the common good, was replaced by a new ethos. Although labeled "Jeffersonian," "republican," or "democratic republican" at the time and since, this new conception of politics envisioned individual citizens voting their economic self-interest, a transformation that its partisans celebrated as democratic and its critics, including Jefferson himself and his loyal lieutenant Madison, denigrated as selfishness. In these years northern and northwestern states widened the franchise, abolished slavery, and outlawed black suffrage, and southern states established an unbreakable alliance of rich and poor white men dedicated to protecting white supremacy at all costs.[45] Beneath Americans' shared racism, which animated restrictions on the voting rights of the more than two hundred thousand free blacks in all but four American states and the scattered efforts to interest them in emigrating to Africa, however, a deep division was opening between North and South. The question of whether slavery would be permitted to expand westward with southern slaveholders was only papered over by the Missouri Compromise of 1820, which Jefferson likened to a "fire bell in the night" and John Quincy Adams called, somewhat cryptically, "the terrible sublime." The day of reckoning with slavery could not be deferred forever.[46]

The message presented to Congress by the newly elected John Quincy Adams on December 6, 1825, contained ideas that many northerners, including his aged father, could endorse. He proposed expanding support for education and internal improvements and establishing a national university, a national observatory, and a naval academy. He also took the occasion to reflect on the broader purposes of democratic government. If government exists for "the progressive improvement of the conditions of the governed," then Congress shouldering its responsibilities was "a duty as sacred and indispensable as the usurpation of powers not granted is criminal and odious." Adams expected Congress, after due deliberation, to take up "your obligations to your country" and "the common good." By that Adams meant more than building schools, roads, and canals to facilitate communication and commerce. "*Moral, political, intellectual improvement*," he continued, "are duties assigned by the Author of Our Existence to social no less than to individual man." Knowing his program would face opposition from those who distrusted all government initiatives, regulation, and the implicit assertion of the legitimacy of the authority of the federal government to act, he chided Congress not to "slumber in indolence or fold up our arms and proclaim to the world that we are palsied by the will of our constituents."[47]

Those were fighting words. Adams's message to Congress antagonized the many southerners—and northerners—already suspicious of this former Harvard professor, the son of a disgraced Federalist president, who was thought to have "stolen" the presidency from Andrew Jackson in 1824 and brazenly named Jackson's rival Henry Clay his secretary of state. Although the sentiments Adams expressed in his message to Congress caused his presidency to be stymied from the start, his ideas grew organically from convictions about democracy he had held since childhood. Duty, stoic endurance, and civic virtue had been drummed into him by his parents and reinforced in his adolescence by his reading of Cicero, Locke, Montesquieu, Adam Smith, and especially Rousseau, whom he admired as much as his father and mother did (at least before the Terror), and whose *Confessions* he called "the most extraordinary work I ever read in my life." While his father was serving as emissary of the fledgling United States government, the adolescent Adams spent five and a half years in Europe, becoming fluent in French and learning German while studying in Paris and Amsterdam, serving as Francis Dana's secretary on a mission to St. Petersburg, and finally forging a lasting friendship with Jefferson in Paris before returning home. Adams's political ideas, however, although familiar to the generation of the nation's first four presidents, had now become anathema to many self-designated "American democrats."[48]

Adams understood that popular government generated popular passions, and he knew that the animosity of many Jeffersonians toward his father's administration had been rooted both in partisanship and in a genuinely different conception of democracy. From the 1770s until the 1820s, many Americans believed the point of self-government was to wrest power from people who talked endlessly about education, self-control, and moral uplift, and put it in the hands of the common man. The younger Adams had written in 1802 that Jefferson's administration "rests upon the support of a much stronger majority of the people throughout the Union" than the Federalists (including his father) had ever enjoyed. He had abandoned the party himself, and resigned his seat in the Senate in 1808, because he thought Federalists' strident opposition to Jefferson's embargo, and particularly Massachusetts senator Charles Pickering's threat of disunion, showed they valued their own interests above those of the nation. Initially welcomed by the Jeffersonian Republicans as a uniquely valuable convert, the cosmopolitan Adams spent the decade before his election to the presidency immersed in foreign affairs, first in various European capitals he already knew well, then as James Monroe's secretary of state. Those experiences only deepened his commitment to the measures he brought before Congress in 1825, but he knew that any proposals to strengthen the federal government were bound to antagonize the South.

Adams advanced arguments already familiar to Americans, not only from the writings of his father, Jefferson, Madison, Wilson, and others but also, more recently, from speeches given by Daniel Webster. In his Plymouth address on December 22, 1820, the former New Hampshire congressman (and future Massachusetts senator) Webster contrasted New England democracy, epitomized by town meetings and animated by virtues resting on the cultural foundation of education, religious faith, and widespread property holding, with the failed democracies of Greece and Rome. Not only did those earlier democracies depend on slave labor; they also fueled conflict through reliance on direct democracy in the case of Greece and class conflict between plebeians and patricians in the case of Rome. New England democracy, in Webster's words, "originates entirely with the people and rests on no other foundation than their assent." In New England, ordinary citizens deliberated, then elected representatives to the assemblies of the commonwealth and the nation. The South that boasted about its democracy nurtured a planter aristocracy, exploited its slaves, and cherished states' rights, all of which Webster contrasted sharply with the legacy and current practices of New England. The difference was apparent to all who had gathered to celebrate the bicentennial of the Pilgrims' landing, including former president John Adams.[49]

Webster struck many of the same chords in his replies to Jacksonians' embrace of states' rights a decade later. Champions of the Jackson Party designated themselves the Democracy, but the people's will, according to Webster, was located not in the states alone but in the people of the entire nation. It was the people of the United States who had ratified the Constitution and authorized legitimate democratic government at the national as well as the local and state levels. American democracy had never been a mere patchwork of "fragments," Webster insisted, and for that reason he proclaimed "Liberty and Union, now and forever, one and inseparable!" The Jacksonians' celebration of individuals' interests, and the interests of individual slave states, over the unity and general good of the nation repudiated rather than fulfilled the promise of American democracy. Democratically elected representative bodies, according to Webster, were designed to "insure deliberation and caution" in their proceedings. He prized that commitment above the uncompromising defiance spewing from the mouths of southern fire-eaters, intent on defending slavery at all costs, who invoked self-government as their justification even as their slave societies undermined the ethic of reciprocity.[50]

Although increasing numbers of white men did indeed vote in antebellum American elections as a result of the second round of constitution writing, historians have demonstrated just how thin and episodic formal political engagement was. The Jacksonians' disregard for the rights of women, Indians, and African Americans showed the limits of their egalitarianism just as surely as their foes' misgivings about the "common man" or "the multitude" revealed lingering inclinations toward preserving hierarchy and deference. Neither party deserves to be characterized, without qualification, as democratic or antidemocratic. Instead, as Adams and Webster agreed, "the people" were capable of becoming either a nation devoted to autonomy and equality or a mob bent on lawless destruction. Evidence of both capacities could be found in nineteenth-century England, France, and the United States.[51]

Among the most articulate spokesmen for the Jacksonians was the prolific New York writer William Leggett, who championed a particular conception of democracy tirelessly in the late 1820 and 1830s. Although neither Leggett nor anyone else could represent the entire spectrum of Jacksonian opinion, his opposition to the phrases "general welfare" and "public good" captured the skepticism about do-gooders' use of government voiced by those who saw in such notions only the attempt to perpetuate rule by elites over ordinary people.[52] Government, Leggett insisted, must be confined "within the narrowest limits" to facilitate free competition. Laissez-faire was the essence of democracy and Leggett's answer to all of society's problems: the "fundamental maxim of democracy and of political economy is the same. They both acknowledge the equal rights of mankind" and seek to achieve it through the simplest possible means. Against these democratic principles, Leggett contended, Jackson's foes stood for rule by the rich, the heirs of aristocrats, whom Americans had expelled in the War for Independence and now had to reject again.[53]

Others framed these partisan battles in equally stark but very different terms. *A Voice from America to England*, written in 1839 by Whig publicist Calvin Colton, claimed that the Jackson Party aimed not toward Americans' highest ideals but toward "the lowest level of democracy," whereas the reformist agenda of the Whigs aimed toward "a spiritual supremacy." According to Colton, those who wrote the Constitution "purposely constructed this instrument to arrest the downward progress" they feared. The founders had in mind, and the Whigs now sought, "a return of the people in the good sense," the people who sought something beyond narrow partisan self-interest. Jackson's party had corrupted the noble term "democracy" by identifying it with people who threatened "a dissolution and overthrow" of the United States government. Because the vocabulary of politics had changed, neither party could do without the word "democracy," a word of "deep meaning and great potency in America," but Colton insisted it must be used accurately.[54]

Jacksonians and Whigs alike drew distinctions from the founding generation, which both parties claimed to revere and accused their opponents of dishonoring. What did the remaining founders themselves think? Whereas Jackson's supporters trumpeted the age of the common man as the apotheosis of democracy, both Jefferson and Madison were ambivalent about the party that claimed descent from their leadership. "A popular government, without popular information, or the means of acquiring it," Madison wrote, "is but a Prologue to a Farce or a Tragedy; or, perhaps, both."[55] Although the former presidents did not despair, they worried that their generation's commitment to pursuit of the common good was being trampled as individuals scrambled for wealth. If politics, as Leggett and other Jacksonian publicists conceived of it, was no more than a means to that end, what would happen to the public interest?[56]

Inasmuch as the National Republicans of John Quincy Adams, and their successors the Whigs, stood for cultural homogeneity, evangelical Protestant morality, an interventionist state, and an integrated nation, they were vulnerable to Democrats' criticism. The Jacksonians claimed that their own commitments to personal liberty, toleration of diversity, limited government, and localism more closely aligned with the desires of newly empowered individuals, people who shook hands rather than bowing, in the rapidly changing United States. Because the governing ethos of American law, *salus populi*, the people's welfare, originated in the idea of popular sovereignty conceived as the quest for the common good, not the interests of particular individuals, states, or sections, the tension between the Whigs' reformist agenda and the Jackson Party's commitment to laissez-faire could never be resolved by simple appeals to democracy. From the nation's origins, the idea of democracy contained within it both the Whigs' aspiration to a shared purpose and the Jacksonians' defense of local traditions and individual rights.[57]

The question raised by Jefferson (and later by Tocqueville, Mill, and especially Lincoln), turned on the question of competency and the purpose of popular government. Democracy rests on commitments to autonomy, or freedom bounded by moral constraints, and an ethic of reciprocity, which Jefferson in his letter to Kercheval called "the common reason of the society."

In the South at least, what has been called the "lodge democracy" of the Jacksonians resembled the *herrenvolk* democracy of other nominally popular but substantively antidemocratic regimes in Europe more than it did a thoroughgoing culture of democracy.[58] Although the new state constitutions adopted from the 1820s through the 1850s generally did expand the electorate to include almost all white males, they excluded—with bipartisan support, to be sure—free blacks, women, and the propertyless. Whigs fell back on assessments of capacity or competency, Jacksonians on white male supremacy. Both parties abandoned the eighteenth-century notion of natural rights as the criterion for voting, because that concept would have made it difficult to exclude everyone but white males. Instead they conceived of voting as a privilege, one for which only whites and only men qualified. Forms of biological essentialism were invoked with greater frequency to provide ostensibly scientific justification for maintaining traditions of racial and gender hierarchy.[59]

Slavery shaped American politics from the 1820s through the Civil War, but it was wrapped up with religious, ethnocultural, and economic issues as well. The division between those who became Jacksonians and those who, in the 1830s, became Whigs was apparent in the animosities that developed during the Adams and Jackson presidencies. The close elections of these decades indicate that the American voting public was equally divided between the two parties. Challenges to slavery and its expansion emanated from the North; defenses of slavery as a positive good, for slaves as well as slave owners, developed in the South. Evangelicals out to Christianize the nation allied with well-to-do reformers who targeted multiple forms of cruelty, ranging from abuses committed by alcoholics and slave owners to those committed against prisoners and the insane. The Jacksonians targeted by such reformers, on the other hand, considered the moral absolutism, paternalism, and meddling of self-righteous do-gooders alien to the nation's ethos of individual freedom. From the legacy of Jefferson and Madison, in short, had emerged two distinct democratic cultures.[60]

The symbol and leader of the Jacksonians had captured the nation's imagination when his valor fighting Indians on the frontier and the British in New Orleans established him as a rough-hewn American hero. Given four years to mobilize against John Quincy Adams, his supporters successfully contrasted his backwoods manner and physical courage to the secret scheming of political and economic elites. To his friends and foes alike, Jackson's 1828 electoral victory marked the end of hierarchy and deference. The ideal that John Quincy Adams embodied and extolled—his critics called it the "gentry ideal"—had long been under attack; it died with Jackson's election. Once

Jackson was inside the White House, his war against the Bank of the United States, a symbol of insiders' unfair advantages, and his removal of southern Indian tribes from their homelands, proof that he would defend the prerogatives of white settlers against self-styled humanitarians, thrilled his supporters as much as they antagonized his critics. Jackson rode a wave of white supremacy; by 1830, all the southern states had outlawed manumission. The rise of the Jackson Party showed the extent to which many Americans had moved away from the earlier pursuit of a shared public interest, the ideal Adams still espoused, to the unapologetic scramble of individuals seeking "the main chance" without government intrusion.[61] Adams was as committed to popular government as Jackson, but their deep differences manifested divergent understandings of democracy. That United States, divided between Adams and Jackson, North and South, slave and free, regulation and laissez-faire, was the nation Tocqueville sought to understand.[62]

A brief outline of what Tocqueville learned in America demonstrates how substantially his previous ideas were transformed by his travels and his reflections on them. The relative equality of conditions—at least among whites—extended from property holding (achieved in part as a result of the decision to abolish entail and primogeniture) and political rights to the relative absence of social hierarchies, deferential behavior, and, less happily, diversity of thought. Tocqueville distinguished sharply between the social and political conditions of the North, where equality was pervasive both as a fact and an ethos, and the South, where the pretense of equality between rich planters and poor whites was sustained by their shared commitment to enslaving blacks. In the North there were "no great lords, no common people, and, one may almost say, no rich or poor." Almost everyone in the North was better educated than almost anyone in the South. The "austere principles" of northern Protestant sects, especially Puritanism, combined devotion to work with "wonderful elements of order and morality." Those who emigrated to New England, Tocqueville wrote, "tore themselves away from home comforts in obedience to a purely intellectual craving." They endured exile for one reason only: "They hoped for the triumph of *an idea*." The Puritans who settled New England shared not only a religious doctrine but also a common devotion to "the most absolute democratic and republican theories." John Quincy Adams, Tocqueville would later learn, had made almost exactly the same point thirty years earlier in Plymouth.[63]

Change was more rapid and incessant than Tocqueville anticipated. New Englanders prized both innovation and geographic mobility, and by 1830 they were spreading westward across the northern tier of the nation. Quoting

John Winthrop on liberty and authority, Tocqueville argued that Americans combined two elements elsewhere kept apart, "the *spirit of religion* and the *spirit of freedom.*" Unlike European champions of liberty, Americans valued equality too. Americans' embrace of Christian moral principles enabled them to espouse democracy, in which "everything is in turmoil, contested, and uncertain." Their "jealousy of all authority" rested on their religious commitments, which allowed these "two apparently opposed tendencies" toward chaos and order to "work in harmony."[64] Because the American Enlightenment filtered democratic ideas through religious faith, challenges to authority were channeled into healthy political activity rather than spawning the destructive cynicism of the French philosophes, which bred skepticism without offering constructive outlets for the criticism they unleashed.

Tocqueville contrasted Americans' commitment to the "sovereignty of the people" with the prevailing French concept of the sovereignty of reason. Whereas the principle of popular sovereignty was "buried" in most regimes beneath the hard facts of intrigue and despotism, it was from the outset "the creative principle of most of the English colonies in America." Although cloaked by proclamations of fealty to the monarchy, democracy in England's North American colonies operated beneath that rhetorical cover in the provincial assemblies and especially in the townships. Once the Revolution began, "the dogma of the sovereignty of the people came out from the township and took possession of the government." At that stage "every class enlisted in its cause," and "the war was fought and victory obtained in its name." When independence was secured, popular sovereignty "became the law of laws." That achievement might have remained as illusory as invocations of the principle had been in European history. In America, however, "a change almost as rapid took place within society. The law of inheritance succeeded in breaking down local influences." Tocqueville understood that the end of primogeniture and the availability of land gave the abstract doctrine of popular sovereignty a force in American life that it had not enjoyed elsewhere. Widespread landownership meant that voting was equally widespread, and the practice of participation in local or colonial government, already well established by the time of the Revolution, was solidified in its aftermath.

Tocqueville confronted the question that had plagued his own class in the aftermath of the French Revolution: What would happen to inherited privileges in a democratic government? Wealthier Americans understood that it was futile to resist, so they "submitted without complaint or resistance" to the principle of democracy, equality, which "had by then become inevitable." Tocqueville understood that it was prosperous planters such as Jefferson and Madison, ambitious land speculators such as Richard Morris and James

Wilson, and successful attorneys such as John Adams who had helped to lead the Revolution and produced the state and federal constitutions: "The most democratic laws were voted by the very men whose interests they impaired." For that reason the wealthy "aroused no popular passions" and instead "themselves hastened the triumph of the new order."

The result of this extraordinary cross-class alliance, Tocqueville wrote, was clear by 1830. "The people take part in the making of the laws" by choosing both the lawgivers and those who execute the laws. Comparing the obvious control exercised by American voters at the ballot box with government officials' puny prerogatives, and contrasting that situation with what had prevailed for centuries in Europe, Tocqueville observed that Americans "govern themselves." The authority of government was "so feeble and restricted," and the administrators were "so obedient" to "the fount of power" in the electorate, Tocqueville concluded succinctly, that "the people reign over the American political world." Their power "is the cause and end of all things; everything rises out of it and is absorbed back into it."[65] In the absence of a king, a hereditary aristocracy, and a state church, and relative to governments everywhere else in the nineteenth century, popular sovereignty was not an abstract idea or a fiction. It was a fact.

Much of what Tocqueville saw surprised him. The harsh treatment of those kept in the prisons that he and Beaumont had expected to admire, the stupefying cruelty of slavery, and the mistreatment of America's "noble savages" all disgusted him. The contrast between the North and South, on the other hand, intrigued him. The American Revolution shattered the foundation of the southern planter aristocracy by removing the institutions of primogeniture and entail that had propped it up—just as Jefferson and Madison had intended. Yet the effect of that change was limited because of race-based slavery. Tocqueville understood that white racism was intensifying everywhere: "The prejudice rejecting the Negroes seems to increase in proportion to their emancipation, and inequality cuts deep into mores as it is effaced from the laws." Tocqueville's experience confirmed Jefferson's contention in *Notes on the State of Virginia*. Obviously and undeniably cruel for the slave, slavery was also "fatal" to the humanity of the master, so much so that it threatened the long-term survival of democracy in the United States. Tocqueville worried that the widening cultural, economic, and political gap between the free (albeit racist) North and the slave (and even more viciously racist) South would eventually rip the nation apart.[66] He also predicted that all of America's Indians were "doomed to perish." Even the cultures that had embraced European ways, such as the Creeks and the Choctaws, were destined to vanish as the United States expanded, either with violence, through war, or quietly, through treaties. After recounting the process of removing the Five Civilized Tribes from the South, he commented acidly, "It is impossible to destroy men with more respect for the laws of humanity."[67]

Finally, Tocqueville worried that the "mediocrity" encouraged by the celebration of equality would snuff out greatness and individuality. Absent the grandeur of the French nobility, American democracy faced the ominous threat of conformity, the oppressive weight of accepted opinion that Tocqueville dubbed "the tyranny of the majority."[68] Yet he was impressed by the widespread literacy among Americans and the proliferation of newspapers, which together generated what we know as a vital public sphere or civil society. It was during the years surrounding his visit that variations on the words "democracy" and "democratic" replaced "republic" and "republican" as the most common terms in newspapers' titles, indicating the relative change in place between the two words that Americans often used as synonyms.[69]

Bred in the French tradition of centralization, Tocqueville wrote at length about the novelty of American federalism, particularly the role of judicial review, the balance of powers, and the decentralization of authority. He paid special attention, of course, to Americans' habit of associating with each other in groups devoted to diverse political, social, religious, and moral causes. These voluntary associations inculcated the "habits of the heart," the *moeurs* or mores, that Tocqueville judged the indispensable feature of democratic culture, and in that judgment he was confirming the wisdom of Franklin's many civic projects and Jefferson's emphasis on the community institutions undergirding New England town government.[70] The institutions of civil society worked alongside formal political participation, particularly service on juries, to foster the sensibilities necessary for self-government.

Juries "teach men equity in practice. Each man, when judging his neighbor, thinks that he may be judged himself." The ethic of reciprocity, so pivotal for democracy, emerged from and was cemented in such experiences. In addition to teaching citizens to accept responsibility for their actions, a characteristic prerequisite to civic virtue, juries "make all men feel that they have duties toward society and that they take a share in its government." The experience of judging others, and the experience of having to deliberate with other jurors, help forge the sense of civic responsibility that democracy requires. "By making men pay attention to things other than their own affairs," Tocqueville wrote, juries "combat that individual selfishness which is like rust in society."

Equally important in moderating American passions was the "religious atmosphere" that, according to Tocqueville, was the first thing that struck him on arrival. In Europe religious fervor engendered conflicts that erupted into violence, but in America multiple religious traditions and the prevalence of Protestantism produced religiosity of a very different sort, intense but not exclusive. A function of the peculiar history of American colonial settlement, many thriving sects enabled Americans to be simultaneously devout and tolerant, a quality absent among atheists as well as believers in Europe. Tocqueville's account of the distinctive, unintended cultural mechanisms whereby autonomous individuals internalized an ethic of reciprocity was central to volume 1 of *Democracy in America*.[71]

Tocqueville concluded by reflecting on the lessons Europeans might learn from the United States. Despite the many positive features of his account, he did not recommend democracy for the Old World. The historical contingencies that made possible the experience of democracy in England's North American colonies and the emergence of the United States Constitution could not be replicated in European nations, where traditions of monarchy, aristocracy, and religious warfare rendered impossible the political, social, economic, and cultural transformation that would be necessary for democracy to take root. "It is hard to make the people take a share in government," he wrote. "It is even harder to provide them with the experience and to inspire them with the feelings they need to govern well."[72] Whereas Europeans viewed government as an ominous, alien power beyond their reach, Americans identified with the local institutions under their control. The distinctive decentralization of government meant that Americans viewed local officials as their servants rather than their masters. By contrast, in France all sides, during and after the Revolution, thought only in terms of freedom and despotism, regardless of whether they considered themselves republicans or monarchists. Whereas changes in public sentiment registered themselves in electoral change in the United States, in France the sole outlet was revolution. The American citizen, from Tocqueville's perspective, reveres the law as his own creation; the European, forever excluded from participating in public life, "oscillates between servility and license." America's democratic sensibility could not be exported to subjects who detested the power of the law, whether they flouted it or were forced to obey it.[73]

Tocqueville made two trips to Britain, in 1833 and 1835, after he had returned from America; those journeys altered his perspective. Whereas the United States alerted him to the contrast between France, with its centralized authority and legacy of hierarchy, and American democracy, in England he encountered a world strikingly different from the other two. There decentralized representative government operated alongside an entrenched landed aristocracy.

Tocqueville worried that the consequences of the Reform Act of 1832 threatened greater centralization that would jeopardize local control. Emerging industrialization and a commercial spirit were making money the measure of all things, a prospect that Tocqueville found unsettling. Little England presented more intricate puzzles than the vast United States. It was, he wrote his father, a tangled web with "lines that cross one another in every direction, a labyrinth" in which he felt "utterly lost."[74]

The paradoxical effects of the 1832 Reform Bill help explain Tocqueville's confusion. By widening the suffrage slightly, Parliament simultaneously succumbed to and fended off increasing pressure for greater democratic reform. The language employed by the champions of the Reform Bill indicates that they understood their dual aims. On the one hand, they wanted to respond to the widespread unrest concerning the overrepresentation of older agrarian interests and the underrepresentation of rising cities. They wanted to acknowledge that Britain was changing, even though they downplayed fears that the changes pointed toward a revolution of the sort endured by France. The best way to prevent such a dramatic transformation was to include only those voters who could be trusted to exercise good judgment. By that they meant the judgment of the most intelligent, best-educated, most rational people in Britain, who just happened also to be the wealthiest. Thus those living on land or in houses worth ten pounds a year qualified to vote, as did those who already exercised the franchise. The champions of suffrage reform included not only members of the rising middle classes, some of whom stood to benefit, but also anxious members of the gentry who wanted to assuage rising popular discontent.[75]

Lord John Russell, who represented London in the House of Commons, was named a junior minister in the new Whig government of Earl Grey in 1830 and led the fight for the Reform Bill. In that year Russell argued that the right to vote is unlike the right to property in that it exists as a "public trust" and serves a public purpose. For that reason it should be altered rarely, only if its reform is clearly in "the public interest." The architects of the Reform Bill envisioned it not as a way to undermine hierarchy or deference, as a wider suffrage was thought likely to do in revolutionary France or the United States (and as Tocqueville found that it did), but instead to solidify the control of those who should be in charge. In Russell's words, the goal was to "bring into the constituency those who are best qualified to exercise the important privilege, from their education, from their general intelligence, and from the stake which they have in the country."[76] Conservatives took for granted that such voters would ratify the legitimacy of those already directing public affairs in Britain. "Our principle," Earl Grey proclaimed in the House of Lords, is "to give to the nation contentment, and to all future governments the support of the respectability, the wealth, and the intelligence of the country." That was "the surest ground of stability" and the strongest bulwark "against all wild and unreasonable attempts at innovation."[77] No wonder Tocqueville was confused. During the debate, Russell conceded that those granted the suffrage should be "intelligent, incorrupt and independent," by which he meant they should have "the capacity to make a choice, the wish to make a good choice, and the power to carry that wish into effect." In the words of John Campbell and other like-minded members of Parliament, the suffrage was "a sacred trust," a trust conferred "for the public good."[78]

The language of capacity, or competency, in Britain echoed that of Constant and Guizot. In Britain, however, it was used to justify expanding the franchise slightly, not restricting it further. In politics as in economics, Britain scrambled Tocqueville's analysis. The Reform Bill worked just as its champions anticipated. Those who designed the first serious attempt to expand the franchise in England for three centuries denied that it would open the floodgates to an ever wider suffrage. So endlessly did Russell, its principal author, hammer home that point that he earned the nickname "Finality Jack." The Reform Bill was framed not in terms of empowering the previously powerless or giving voice to the voiceless. It was presented instead as a means of discovering the common good: "public opinion," according to Henry Bunbury, should not be confused with "a mere popular cry." Public opinion manifested in the votes of those now to be trusted with the franchise was "an abstract of the sentiments which prevailed through the intelligent, educated, observant, reflecting classes of the community." The decisions rendered by the expanded electorate would transcend mere personal or group interests to express the will of the public more generally—at least that part of the public qualified to register its judgment.[79]

Not everyone shared the enthusiasm of Russell and the other liberals who maneuvered the Reform Bill through Parliament. Many conservatives denounced the idea as "democratic," by which they meant to associate it with France and the United States, two enemy nations whose tendencies toward popular government they deemed self-evidently unwise. Occasionally another bogeyman, Irish Catholic immigrants, surfaced in warnings against "the Demon of Democracy and Papal Tyranny." Tories alternated between hinting that working men and shopkeepers might lower the tone of public discourse and shrieking about revolution. For much the same reason, Whigs carefully avoided adopting the term "democrats" for themselves, even though they happily branded their adversaries "aristocrats." These spirited debates over the franchise widened the focus of British public life in the 1830s and 1840s.[80]

Indeed, the limited effect of the 1832 Reform Act fed the most dramatic upsurge of democratic sentiment in Britain, the People's Charter. This six-part program, drafted by cabinetmaker William Lovett and tailor Francis Place, was published with a preamble written by radical MP John Arthur Roebuck. A close friend of John Stuart Mill, Roebuck had written, in his *Pamphlets for the People* (1835), that "the people, if they be wise and moral, can govern themselves well." He contended that "if good government is to be hoped for on earth, it must be the off-spring of democracy," and he insisted that it was the inadequacies of "aristocratic rule" that impelled Britain toward the "experiment" of democracy. The Charter eventually attracted millions of Britons to sign petitions submitted to Parliament in 1839, 1842, and 1848, the last time amid controversy over allegedly inflated claims and forged signatures. The sources and focus of Chartism varied widely. Although its ultimate objective was national, its organization was local. For that reason its central ideas varied considerably from place to place, and it sparked unprecedented popular participation in various associations of the sort Tocqueville considered crucial for American democracy.[81] Like most other political movements, Chartism divided between more and less moderate elements. The moderates, led by Lovett, Place, and others, found themselves dismissed by the more radical factions, which careened wildly under the passionate leadership of orators such as Feargus O'Connor and Bronterre O'Brien. One fiery partisan who had cheered the French *sans-culottes*, George Julian Harney, established the East London Democratic Association and aligned with the periodicals *London Democrat* (1839) and the *Democratic Review of British and Foreign Politics, History, and Literature* (1849). The best-selling and most visible organ of Chartist sentiment was O'Connor's *Northern Star*, which peppered its pages with references to "democracy" and "democratic."[82]

In *Chartism: A New Organisation of the People* (1840), Lovett and fellow Chartist John Collins conceded that ancient democracies had spun out of control. "*Popular representation*," however, which they termed the "peculiar feature of modern democracy," had solved the problem. "While every man can exercise influence over his representative, to effect his political desires, the passions and the prejudices of the multitude are kept back from the deliberations of legislation." John Adams, Madison, and Wilson had advanced similar arguments for representative democracy in American constitutional conventions, which Tocqueville emphasized in the first volume of his *Democracy*, but there was one difference: Lovett and Collins were writing from Warwick Jail.[83]

Chartists called for a comprehensive array of democratic reforms: universal male suffrage, the redrawing of electoral districts, annual elections, the secret ballot, and ending property qualifications and providing salaries for MPs. Dividing between more and less radical wings, Chartism drew its sustenance from an unstable alliance of working-class radicals, evangelical Christians, and socialists of various stripes. Although once thought to be primarily economic in focus and inspiration, Chartism has more recently been shown to be a movement driven as much by a desire for political inclusion as by class resentment, a challenge to corruption on behalf of virtue as much as a challenge to the wealthy on behalf of the poor.[84]

Parliament voted overwhelmingly against the Charter: by 235 to 46 votes in 1839, then by 287 to 49 votes in 1842. In 1848 it was simply dismissed. All three rejections sparked outbreaks of labor unrest, which the Chartists interpreted as popular support for the cause. The evidence, however, suggests that these disturbances resulted more from particular economic grievances, usually concerning unemployment and wages, than from workers' desire for the vote itself. Chartist moderates focused on politics; radicals proposed a variety of measures ranging from land reform to armed insurrection. At its peak, Chartism was the largest popular political movement in Britain. When the 1848 uprisings on the continent turned violent, however, British sympathy for the Charter seemed to evaporate. Many Chartist organs, including the *Northern Star*, had remained monarchist, and the movement splintered in 1848 as the more radical wing abandoned reform to embrace revolution. In the short term Chartism inflamed sensibilities against as well as for democracy. In the longer term, however, it eroded the almost universal support for parliamentary sovereignty after the French Revolution and planted the seeds that eventually—a century later—flowered into universal suffrage in Britain.[85]

When the first volume of Tocqueville's *Democracy in America* appeared in English translation in 1835, it was greeted with much enthusiastic praise from writers trying to make sense of the Reform Act, Chartism, and other forms of popular agitation. The most discerning and detailed analysis, from Tocqueville's perspective and from those of later commentators, came from John Stuart Mill, who reviewed the book in his recently founded journal the *London Review*. The rich correspondence between Mill and Tocqueville that developed after Mill's review turned into a friendship that lasted into the 1840s, when it withered over disputes about British and French imperialism. Mill invited Tocqueville to become a contributor to the *London Review* in 1835, and Tocqueville's reply expressed some of the central commitments that linked the two thinkers' views on democracy.

"I love liberty by taste," Tocqueville wrote to Mill, "equality by instinct and reason." His travels made the challenge of uniting those competing "passions" even more difficult. England enabled Tocqueville to triangulate between France and the United States, which yielded a different and more complex account in volume 2 of *Democracy in America*. Tocqueville expressed his tortured, ambivalent thinking about democracy at this pivotal moment in his June 1835 letter to Mill. One of the greatest miseries of France, Tocqueville wrote, was to watch democratic ideas, which alone had a future in modern society, advanced by people "whose efforts only serve to remove from the cause of Democracy many good minds who of themselves would tend toward it." That problem, which had plagued France since the Revolution, persisted. "A French democrat," Tocqueville continued, would "place the exclusive direction of society not in the hands of all the people, but in the hands of a certain portion of the people and who, to arrive at this result, understand only the use of material force." At a time when fewer than 3 percent of French males could vote, and only 10 percent of that tiny fraction could hold office, France remained a long way from democracy.

By contrast English democrats, Tocqueville continued, "do not seek to force the people to be happy in the fashion they consider the most appropriate." Instead they want to enable the people "to find that out for themselves, and, having found it out, to act accordingly. I myself am a democrat in that sense." Like Constant and unlike the Jacobins, Tocqueville denied that self-designated democrats could determine the public will on their own. Unlike Constant and like Mill, however, he affirmed the need to nurture public-spiritedness, a greater concern with the common good than with the pleasures of the private life. Achieving that goal in England and France would require a cultural transformation of the sort already occurring across the Atlantic. Unfortunately, the ultimate meaning of that change remained unclear.[86] Tocqueville did not specify what the English people would "find out," and his vagueness suggests the elusiveness of his own democratic commitments. Yet that passage from his letter to Mill signals recurring themes in their work. First, the future would belong to democracy, though England and France were far from ending the culture of ingrained and institutionalized deference that sustained aristocratic rule. Second, cynical politicians often subverted democracy into plebiscites that authorized their power at the people's expense rather than in their interest. Third, the people had to become, through better education, capable of self-government. That idea linked Tocqueville and Mill with John Quincy Adams and other like-minded Americans, which has led some commentators to deny that they should be considered democrats at all. Jefferson too, however, had referred to the need to enlighten the people's discretion, a judgment shared by many nineteenth-century advocates of democracy.[87]

The son of the philosopher James Mill, the young John Stuart Mill began life as a lab rat. James Mill and his friend Jeremy Bentham, founder of the philosophy of utilitarianism and an avid champion of democracy, decided to illustrate the wastefulness of most education by conducting an experiment. In his article "Education" in the 1825 supplement to the *Encyclopedia Britannica*, James Mill wrote that the "primary habits" formed in childhood are pivotal for shaping "the fundamental character of the man." "Education, then, or the care of forming the habits, ought to commence, as much as possible, with the period of sensation itself; and at no period, is the utmost vigilance of greater importance, than the first."[88] Upon the blank slate of John Stuart Mill, his father and Bentham worked to imprint their philosophical principles. The boy began studying ancient Greek at three, was reading Plato by four, and at five moved on to history and novels. At age eight he was ready for step two, learning Latin and then tutoring his reluctant younger sister, a chore he disliked as much as she did. Relief came from geometry, algebra, chemistry, and an expanded reading list of Greek authors culminating in Aristotle. At twelve Mill entered the final stage, working again through ancient texts with his father, honing his own critical sensibility, and at last turning his attention to contemporary affairs. By age fourteen, his formal training complete, Mill's tutors judged him ready for anything. Mill himself had doubts.[89]

Not surprisingly, given the boy's immersion in the thought world of his father and Bentham, he threw himself into their projects. Bentham's formula, the greatest good of the greatest number, became the omega point of Mill's tireless reformist efforts. He formed a discussion group, with his friend Roebuck and others, devoted to utilitarianism. He read, debated, and wrote his own pamphlets on issues of the day. He edited Bentham's unpublished manuscripts. The study of child development was undeveloped in the early nineteenth century, so his family was astonished, even if we are not surprised, that in 1826, the year Mill turned twenty, a gear in the finely tuned mechanism snapped.

Mill slipped into a prolonged depression. He realized that even achieving all of his father's and Bentham's schemes would give him no great joy. With that awareness, "my heart sank within me: the whole foundation on which my life was constructed fell down. All my happiness was to have been found in the continual pursuit of this end." In short, he felt, he had no reason to go on living. Mill sought relief from his favorite books, to no avail. He could hardly turn to his father or Bentham for sympathy or understanding. Not surprisingly, he had few friends. Gradually he came to realize, as he put it, that British empiricists' prized "associations" left something out. "The habit of analysis," Mill observed, "has a tendency to wear away the feelings." Mill knew that happiness comes from making "the good of others" the object of all one's efforts, and yet he was "left stranded at the commencement of my voyage, with a well equipped ship and a rudder, but no sail." He lacked any desire for the goals toward which he had been aimed, "no delight in virtue, or the general good, but also just as little in anything else." Becalmed when he thought himself ready to embark, Mill learned during what he called the "melancholy" winter of 1826–27 the same lesson Tocqueville learned from his own similar crisis. Only passion, in Tocqueville's estimation, rescued him from despair, and only by consciously cultivating his "feelings," not continuing to develop his rational faculty, did Mill begin his ascent. Reading the French writer Jean-François Marmontel and the English poets William Wordsworth and Lord Byron, together with a newfound appreciation of the English countryside and eventually an affinity for the romantic philosophy of Thomas Carlyle, restored to Mill the emotional life that his father's and Bentham's austere tutelage had suppressed.

Important as the Romantics were for Mill, his recovery depended just as much on his discovery of free will. Mill complained that "the doctrine of what is called Philosophical Necessity weighed on my existence like an incubus." If he was struggling pointlessly against the scientific proof that he was only "the helpless slave of antecedent circumstances," then his efforts were wasted. But he reached a different—and liberating—conclusion. "I saw that though our character is formed by circumstances, our own desires can do much to shape those circumstances." We are hardly pawns of "Necessity." The aspect of the "doctrine of free will" that Mill found "really inspiriting and ennobling" was "the conviction that we have real power over the formation of our own character; that our will, by influencing some of our circumstances, can modify our future habits or capabilities of willing." The realization of his own autonomy restored to Mill his energy and his engagement with political life. He understood that "representative democracy" should not be judged "an absolute principle" but instead a question of the proper cultural circumstances, not simply a matter of determining the single correct system but instead "a moral and educational question." Together with Roebuck he remained "a radical and democrat, for Europe, and especially for England." That conviction, which animated his political activities and his writing for the rest of his life, led him to embrace an idiosyncratic ideal of liberal democratic socialism quite distant from the laissez-faire political economy of his father and Bentham.[90]

In 1830 Mill met Harriet Taylor, who became his best friend for the twenty years before her husband died, after which she and Mill married. She was without question the most important person in his adult life. Even granting that Mill's extravagant praise of her influence manifested his intense devotion as well as her talent and insight, their love clearly exerted a shaping effect on his ideas, particularly his attitudes toward women's rights and equality between men and women. Mill's discovery of the indispensable importance of emotion had profound consequences for his life and for his philosophy. "The maintenance of a due balance among the faculties," especially the faculty of sensibility that he had previously dismissed as a frivolous distraction, "now seemed to me of primary importance. The cultivation of the feelings became one of the cardinal points in my ethical and philosophical creed." Bentham had held any pleasure to be as good as any other. "Quantity of pleasures being equal," his formula ran, the pleasures derived from a simple game ("pushpin" was his example) are as valuable as those derived from appreciating poetry. Departing from that way of thinking, Mill embarked on a quest to develop his own ethics, a qualitative utilitarianism with its own handy axiom: better Socrates dissatisfied than a fool satisfied. Mill's romanticism had given his father's stoic creed a new twist, and it cost him his friendship with, although not his admiration for, Roebuck. Although he continued to revere his father's self-discipline and commitment to social reform, the younger Mill now distinguished between those activities and forms of life that elevate human sensibilities and those that merely satisfy cravings for pleasure.[91]

Mill's aim shifted from politics toward "improvement in life and culture," particularly educational reform, to nudge England's people away from the thoughtless pursuit of "riches" toward goals with more substantial rewards. The problem was not the capacities of ordinary people but the misplaced values of British culture. Despite the best efforts of reformers such as Roebuck, a tireless champion of the cause of national education, public opinion after the Reform Act settled back into contentment with the status quo. As Mill wrote to his friend John Sterling in 1833, "The cause of the evil is one which I foresaw and predicted long before—the anomaly of a democratic constitution in a plutocratically constituted society."[92] Mill's altered view of democracy, he reported in the *Autobiography*, began when he read and reviewed the first volume of Tocqueville's *Democracy in America*.

Tocqueville too began to reassess the meaning of democracy after 1835. The effects of his British experience and the effects of the July Monarchy's policies of censorship combined to give the second volume of *Democracy in America*, published in 1840, a tone very different from the first. In the first volume Tocqueville worried that the majority might stifle dissent; in the second that there would be no dissent to stifle. The first raised the specter of uncontrolled masses careening toward tyranny; the second the specter of passionless drones incapable of acting. The first registered no concern with industrialization; the second Tocqueville's anxiety about a dangerous new aristocracy of industrialists. Tocqueville himself emphasized the continuities between the volumes, which surely do exist, but he acknowledged that readers could discern a change.[93] Tocqueville's second trip to Britain, in 1837, heightened his awareness of industrial poverty and the danger of a new plutocracy. In a speech about England delivered in 1835 he lamented that poor relief rendered its recipients indolent and condemned them to a life of dependence, but two years later his analysis shifted. He became far more critical of British industrialists and more optimistic about the future of the working class. He predicted that labor conflicts might lead to the education of workers, the formation of unions, and the promising readjustment of workers' status in industrial economies.

Between the completion of volume 1 and the writing of volume 2, Tocqueville's visits to England served to deepen his anxieties. He became increasingly worried that a combination of industrialization and centralization of the sort he witnessed in both Great Britain and France might extinguish the spirit of participation that he identified in America. In volume 2, he offered a complex and subtle account of that process. The democratic inclination to concentrate on material gain, a tendency he associated with the equality and mobility that he saw in America, might end in either of two outcomes. The economic opportunities available to Americans made entrepreneurial activity more attractive than art, scholarship, or martial honor and contributed to an ever-expanding middle class. If Americans lost interest in politics, gave up on the intermediate associations that engaged them in public affairs, and concerned themselves only with material goods, they might end up suffering from haunting isolation or as passive citizen-clients, lulled into relying on government to do for them everything that needs to be done. Only public spiritedness, the quality that Tocqueville called "*l'intérêt bien entendu*," best translated as "self-interest properly understood," prevented Americans' *moeurs* from deteriorating either into simple egoism or dependency and demoralization.[94]

Mill noted the double-sided quality of Tocqueville's *Democracy* in his review of volume 2. The "impartiality" of Tocqueville's analysis Mill judged exemplary. Though Tocqueville himself clearly leaned toward Radicalism, Mill observed, some of his observations were "susceptible of a Tory application." Indeed, British conservatives applauded Tocqueville's warnings about the potential tyranny of the majority, which suited their purposes perfectly, and these "country gentlemen" mistakenly portrayed him as "one of the pillars of Conservatism."[95] Even if Tocqueville's double-sidedness is acknowledged, it is necessary to take into account both his changing perceptions over time and the extent to which his different writings reflected particular observations and varying purposes.

Examining what remains more or less constant in both volumes of *Democracy in America* helps illuminate Tocqueville's central concerns. Despite the differences, there are at least two threads connecting the two volumes, reciprocity and religion. First, the characteristic of American democracy that has impressed commentators on Tocqueville from the earliest to the most recent is the importance he attributed to voluntary associations. Participation in such associations prepared Americans for civic life by prompting them to focus on solving concrete problems as members of community groups of all kinds, from the most benevolent and/or ambitious to the most self-serving and/or trivial. All of these experiences produced "self-interest properly understood"—the crucial concept that Tocqueville introduced to characterize the sensibility he associated with healthy democratic culture—and prevented that quality from degenerating into either the old-fashioned egoism that earlier moralists abhorred or the equally unattractive, newfangled individualism that Tocqueville considered a threat.

Tocqueville described egoism as a vice as old as humanity, "a passionate and exaggerated love of self which leads a man to think of all things in terms of himself and to prefer himself to all." Individualism, by contrast, was unprecedented, "a calm and considered feeling which disposes each citizen to isolate himself from the mass of his fellows and withdraw into the circle of family and friends." In the comfort of that nest, he happily leaves society to take care of itself. Egoism, which originates in "blind instinct" and "sterilizes the seeds of every virtue," is an ancient failing, the sin of selfishness. Individualism, by contrast, derives more from faulty understanding than from "perversity of heart." Although at first individualism "only dams the spring of public virtues," over time it chokes the other virtues too. If individualism were to merge into egoism, it would leave the public sphere desolate. Without the vibrant associational life central to democracy in the United States, the American individual would be "shut up in the solitude of his own heart."[96]

Tocqueville believed that voluntary associations, service on juries, and all kinds of participation in public affairs sustained democracy. Yet he certainly did not consider Americans uniquely virtuous. In fact, he refused even to associate "self-interest properly understood" with virtue, either in its republican or Christian form. He did, however, identify it closely with the practice of deliberation and the ethic of reciprocity, which he believed associational life fosters and which makes democracy work. The *experience* of associational life inclines Americans toward benevolence, or sympathy, whether they are virtuous or not. Even at the end of volume 2, where Tocqueville stressed the threat of government centralization in nations such as France, which lacked experience with the practice of deliberation and the ethic of reciprocity that undergirds it, he emphasized this feature of American democracy. By participating in such associations, "Americans of every station, outlook, and age day by day acquire a general taste" for working together. From that experience citizens "see, speak, listen, and stimulate each other to carry out all sorts of undertakings in common," which they then extend into civic life.[97] There was nothing analogous in France.

In America, Tocqueville wrote in his concluding pages, "interest as well as sympathy prompts a code of lending each other mutual assistance at need." As people's conditions become increasingly similar, they become increasingly alert to the "reciprocal obligation" they owe each other.[98] This ideal of reciprocity, which underlay the exercise of deliberation in voluntary associations and in public life that was central to what Tocqueville meant by democracy, provides the first thread of continuity between the two volumes of *Democracy in America*. Reciprocity prevents a tyrannical majority from stifling dissent through the decentralization of authority in volume 1 and prevents the decline of "self-interest properly understood" into egoism or selfish inwardness in volume 2. Equality, Tocqueville wrote, was crucial to the ethic of reciprocity. "The Americans have this advantage, that they attained democracy without the sufferings of a democratic revolution." Unlike those who sought to create equality in late eighteenth-century France, Americans "were born equal instead of becoming so."[99]

Tocqueville valued associational life for reasons similar to Madison's. Indeed, Madison's contributions to the *Federalist* were among the most important sources of Tocqueville's arguments. He understood Madison to argue that by participating in common projects, Americans learned how to see beyond the simple clash of competing interests. Through the process of confronting and filtering different ideas, clashing interests, and divergent ideals, people in associations can learn to see things from other points of view. By encountering the other, people learn how to appreciate the instabilities and complexities of judgment and think dialogically. That hope underlay Madison's commitments to representation and federalism, just as it underlay Tocqueville's belief that American democracy might survive despite the dangers it faced. In Tocqueville's words, through democratic participation "feelings and ideas are renewed, the heart enlarged, and the understanding developed only by the reciprocal action of men one upon the other."[100]

Tocqueville's commitment to taking seriously other ways of thinking and allowing those differences to alter one's own ideas was among the signal features of his own thought.

Mill singled out the importance of reciprocity in his review of volume 2. It was not just elections or voting that made America democratic. It was instead "the administration of nearly all the business of society by the people themselves." That experience gradually fostered a different attitude toward other people. Whereas an individual might otherwise "fasten his attention and interest exclusively upon himself, and upon his family," a focus "making him indifferent to the public, to the more generous objects and the nobler interests," if you "give him something to do for the public, whether as a vestryman, a juryman, or an elector," his perspective shifts. His horizon widens to encompass a wider range of concerns. As a result he comes "to feel"—the verb is important in light of Mill's own shifting sensibility—that "besides the interests which separate him from his fellow-citizens, he has interests which connect him with them; that not only the common weal is his weal, but that it partly depends upon his exertions." This altered perspective, which Mill characterized as "public spirit," must be engendered by "an extensive participation of the people in the business of government in detail," an experience that leaves a permanent deposit.

Mill identified the laudable goal of diffusing education from top to bottom of English society—and also its limitations. Inculcating the desired "public spirit" can be achieved not merely by providing better schooling or eliciting discussion of civic affairs at the local level, valuable as those are, but only "by a corresponding dissemination of public functions, and a voice in public affairs." Whereas in England the "public interest" had traditionally been identified with that of the monarch and the landed gentry, Mill wrote, in America only those arguments survive that address themselves "to the interest of the many." The challenge for democratic cultures lay in preserving aspirations toward the common good rather than allowing it to be reduced to the concerns of a majority narrowly focused on its material interests.[101]

The other common thread connecting both of Tocqueville's volumes is the importance of religion. Having experienced a crisis of religious faith himself at the age of sixteen, and acutely aware of the havoc caused in France by the wars of religion fought during the Reformation and after 1789, Tocqueville was puzzled that Americans' heated religious passions did not lead to religious conflict. By separating church and state, Americans had removed a potential source of tension and provided anchors tethering a culture otherwise at risk of drifting toward chaos.[102] From Tocqueville's perspective, the principal historical contribution of Christianity had been its revolutionary commitment to "the equality, the unity, the fraternity of all men," a commitment distinct from the prior acceptance of human inequality as inevitable. Moreover, the most influential form of religiosity in America, Puritanism, provided a template for the all-important institution of self-government, the New England town, and valorized the forms of behavior that Tocqueville designated "self-interest properly understood." His education and experience had acquainted him only with Christian or classical civic virtue, understood either as self-abnegation or self-sacrifice, and with the sin of egoism or the vice of unremitting self-centeredness. In America he encountered something new, a disposition that he thought rooted in Puritanism but manifested now in various forms of religiosity, including American Catholicism, and especially in the multiple forms of association that reinforced an ethic of reciprocity. Such experiences of communal life inclined Americans toward benevolent activity, which prevented ambitions from becoming vicious and softened the edges of competition whether individuals were motivated by Christian or civic virtue or not.

Tocqueville detested slavery. He insisted that even though some slaveholders and their apologists professed a belief in Christianity, such ideas disgusted Christians who took seriously the brotherhood of all races. Hypocrisy, however common, should not blind us to the ideals being mocked: "My heart rebels daily at seeing the little gentlemen who pass their time in clubs and wicked places, or great knaves who are capable of any base action as well as of any act of violence, speak devoutly of *their holy religion*. I am always tempted to cry out to them: 'Be pagans with pure conduct, proud souls, and clean hands rather than Christians in this fashion.'"[103] Tocqueville emphasized the importance of acknowledging the difference between the commitment of those who lived according to Christian principles and the hypocrisy of those who called themselves Christians without embracing Christ's stern ethic of love.

In a democratic age, according to Tocqueville, religion alone could draw people away from the materialism that might otherwise obsess them, thereby keeping alive the precious sense of mutual obligation that animated community life. "Despotism may be able to do without faith," Tocqueville reasoned, "but freedom cannot. Religion is much more needed" in a republic than in a monarchy, "and in democratic republics most of all. And what is to be done," he asked, "with a people master of itself if it is not subject to God?"[104] Historians in recent decades have misunderstood the significance of Tocqueville's argument for the importance of religious faith, which he advanced with explicit reference to Pascal's wager: if you believe in God, live a righteous life, and are proven wrong when you die, you lose nothing; if you are right, you win eternal life.

Some scholars have faulted Tocqueville for underestimating the importance of revivalism and for paying too much attention to the exceptional views of a few New England Unitarians.[105] Those informants, however, were important not because their own Unitarianism gave Tocqueville a skewed perception of American Protestantism but because their insights made a crucial difference in Tocqueville's understanding of democracy in America. Religious faith was inextricably intertwined with associational life in the structure of Tocqueville's argument. As his emphasis on the Puritan concept of the covenant at the beginning of volume 1 makes clear, he believed that Americans' practice of association embodied the ethic of reciprocity that derived from their common Christian heritage. Although such an ethic elevates benevolence in principle, in practice it could and did serve to justify activities driven by hatred instead of sympathy, including slavery, lynching, and assassination.[106] The value of community activities should be judged, then, by the precise nature of the activities ostensibly inspired by religious faith.

Both Tocqueville and Mill not only emphasized the habits of the heart but also advanced hardheaded assessments of the calculations of self-interest that such habits must struggle to restrain and redirect. Only within relatively equal social and economic conditions, such as those prevailing among white men in antebellum America, could the practice of deliberation and the ideal of reciprocity flourish. As people became accustomed to the freedom they enjoyed in a democratic culture, though, their exercise of that freedom endangered the commitment to mutuality that prevented self-rule from degenerating into a war of all against all.[107]

Tocqueville's sources for his crucial ideas concerning reciprocity and religion were the French thinkers who had shaped his ideas about politics and society, thinkers ranging from Pascal through Montesquieu, Rousseau, and Voltaire to Guizot.[108] It was his reading of Madison, though, that convinced him American democracy was something new under the sun, a culture that made possible the survival of self-government without the small scale or the reliance on classical civic virtue that earlier writers such as Montesquieu and Rousseau had considered indispensable. Just as important as Madison's reworking of republican political theory in the *Federalist*, however, were the insights of some of the people Tocqueville met in the United States. Tocqueville and Beaumont spent almost a month in Boston, where they felt more at home than anywhere else in America. Tocqueville himself never witnessed a town meeting. That might explain why he could be convinced that this often fractious, sometimes maddening institution, which could be traced back to the first settlers' practice of gathering in Puritan meetinghouses and deliberating over issues of shared concern, held the key to American self-government.

Tocqueville talked with many New Englanders, including not only prominent merchants, preachers, and writers but also a former president of the United States who was intimately acquainted with France, John Quincy Adams, the current president of Harvard College, Josiah Quincy, and a future president of Harvard, the historian Jared Sparks, equally passionate and ambivalent democrats whose animating principle was "ordered liberty."[109]

Tocqueville admired Adams and considered Sparks a man of rare knowledge and judgment, an assessment Sparks seems to have shared. He told Tocqueville that "New England is the cradle of American democracy." In addition to spending a good deal of time talking with Sparks, Tocqueville studied a lengthy essay Sparks sent him just before Tocqueville embarked for Washington, DC. The earliest English settlers had come to New England as "republicans and religious enthusiasts," according to Tocqueville's notes from their conversations. In contrast to most societies in human history, in which authority was concentrated and legitimated by tradition and law, these early settlers were "abandoned to our own devices, forgotten in this corner of the world." In that isolation, they existed in what Sparks called "a state of nature." Each settlement they established, beginning in Plymouth and then spreading through Massachusetts to Rhode Island, Connecticut, and the rest of New England, was self-governing.

In the essay Sparks sent to Tocqueville, "On the Government of Towns in New England," he wrote that "each person" had a voice in their discussions, and "all rules and decisions were established by a majority of voices. As circumstances required it, they adopted new regulations, or laws, but always upon the same principles, that is, the equal rights of each individual, and the power of a majority to control the whole." All new towns operated, in other words, as "independent republics." When they needed to unite, either to fight Indians or resist the crown, they constituted a self-governing commonwealth, but their citizens retained in their church congregations and town meetings the sovereignty they exercised before joining together for particular purposes.[110]

Sparks's insistence that sovereignty in America derived from individual Puritan congregations in New England towns provoked many features of Tocqueville's analysis, including the importance of voluntarism, association, and majority rule as well as religion. The New England *practice* of democratic governance differed dramatically from the opposite extremes of royal sovereignty and royal centralization that he identified with his native France. Sparks belonged to the generation of Americans who first began retrieving, cataloging, and making use of the early records of colonial America. These were the antiquarians and historians who began to compile the records of early American settlement as part of a broader cultural project of telling the story of the rise of the United States. In documents stretching from descriptions of debates over the state and federal constitutions all the way back to the earliest records of the charters establishing towns and colonies, they found evidence of contentious disputes over their institutions of governance. Throughout the colonies, ordinary citizens, often with an unsure grip on English grammar and spelling, nevertheless revealed a grasp of the principles—if not necessarily the texts of Locke and Rousseau—underlying the ideas of covenant and social compact, expressed in just the language that Sparks relayed to Tocqueville. In short, from the 1620s until the 1820s, the self-understanding of New Englanders remained pretty much the same: many of them saw themselves as Sparks saw them, as the "cradle of democracy."[111]

What about the South? As in New England, Tocqueville relied on a combination of texts, interviews, and his own impressions. Perhaps the most important written source was Jefferson's *Notes on the State of Virginia*, his reply to an earlier Frenchman's queries about America. There Tocqueville learned about Jefferson's awareness of the undeniable cruelties of slavery and the importance to democracy of social equality—at least among white men. As previously noted, one of Jefferson's first acts after he returned home from Philadelphia in 1776 was to file legislation abolishing primogeniture and entail, steps he considered essential for Virginia. If prosperous planters were unable to consolidate their wealth and power across generations, the way would be clear for ordinary white male farmers to live autonomous lives of the sort Jefferson thought desirable for a self-governing people.[112]

Tocqueville had learned about the southern states from various northerners even before arriving in Baltimore and beginning his journey through the South. After his dinner with John Quincy Adams in Boston, at which the former president had confirmed Sparks's judgment concerning the centrality of "the religious and political doctrines of the first founders of New England," Adams gave Tocqueville an account of slavery that left a deep impression. "Slavery has modified the whole state of society in the South," Tocqueville wrote in his notes after talking with Adams. "The whites form a class which has all the ideas, all the passions, all the prejudices of an aristocracy." The appearance, however, was misleading. Nowhere did equality among white men appear "greater than in the South," where "equality before the law" prevailed, "but it ceases absolutely in the habits of life. There are upper classes and working classes. Every white man in the South is a being equally privileged, whose destiny is to make the negroes work without working himself." Northerners did not understand that white southerners considered work "dishonourable," and the absence of a work ethic, the "laziness in which the southern whites live," resulted in "great differences of character." Southern whites, Adams concluded, focused their energies on hunting, racing, and other quasi-aristocratic forms of physical exertion, and they were so obsessed with "honour" that, more than anywhere else in the United States, duels were frequent.[113]

If Tocqueville's American informants powerfully shaped his perceptions and judgments of American democracy, his own arguments just as powerfully shaped Mill's. Just as his earlier personal crisis prompted Mill to repudiate the philosophy of his father and Bentham, so he testified that the second most important intellectual transformation of his life commenced with his careful study of Tocqueville, which prompted Mill to renounce Bentham's faith in "pure democracy."[114] Mill's encounter with Tocqueville awakened him to the historical sources of American democracy, alerted him to the potential dangers of democratic excess, and inspired him to rethink the relation between cultural particularity and political institutions. Mill never mentioned Jared Sparks, whose name appears nowhere in the voluminous literature on Mill. Yet the ideas Mill derived from Tocqueville strongly resembled the ideas Tocqueville derived from Sparks.[115]

Mill's review of the 1840 *Democracy* called attention to the darker premonitions that shaded Tocqueville's second volume.[116] Democracy would be possible, Mill came to believe, only under conditions of relative economic and social equality, conditions of the sort that Sparks singled out as enabling both the civic spirit and the lively give-and-take of town government in early New England. "Interest in the common good is at present so weak a motive" in Britain, Mill concluded, because individuals concentrate from dawn to dusk on their own "personal advantage." This was precisely the problem Tocqueville had identified. "The deep rooted selfishness which forms the general character of the existing state of society," Mill continued, "is *so* deeply rooted" because everything in contemporary life "tends to foster it." Compared with civic life in Athens or Rome, both under renewed scrutiny in Mill's day, contemporary Britons were far less often called upon do anything for the public than had been citizens of ancient republics—or, as Sparks and Tocqueville observed, townspeople in seventeenth-century New England.[117]

When the first American edition of *Democracy in America* appeared in 1838, with a preface by New York state assemblyman John C. Spencer, whom Tocqueville had met during his American travels, American reviewers immediately applauded Tocqueville's apparent enthusiasm for his subject. Not surprisingly, they downplayed the darker tone of volume 2. The more troubling dimensions of democracy, which Tocqueville himself identified and even emphasized, had caught the eye of Mill, whose review singled out the burning of an Ursuline convent in Boston and of abolitionists' homes in New York City and Philadelphia. By the late 1830s, as fears of conspiracy and disunion mounted, such acts of violence were increasing in frequency and intensity. Southern writers, unnerved by the growing boldness of antislavery agitators, began to develop new strategies for defending the legitimacy and expanding the geographic scope of slavery, attempting to transform what earlier generations had characterized as an unfortunate but necessary evil into a positive good.

Into that highly charged atmosphere of growing antagonism and mutual mistrust stepped the lanky young Abraham Lincoln, an Illinois state legislator invited to address the Young Men's Lyceum in Springfield, Illinois, on January 27, 1838. There is no reason to think that Lincoln had read Tocqueville, yet the thrust of his first major public address dovetailed with themes central to *Democracy in America*. Addressing "the perpetuation of our political institutions," Lincoln told his Springfield audience that democracy depends fundamentally on "the *attachment* of the People" to their government and its laws. Blessed with safe borders and thus invulnerable to foreign powers, the United States would face only those dangers that spring up from among the people themselves, dangers growing more serious due to an increasingly pervasive disregard for the law and the inclination to substitute for reliance on the legal system "the wild and furious passions" of "worse than savage mobs." To illustrate, Lincoln recounted a particularly horrifying incident in St. Louis, where an innocent free black man had been dragged through the streets, chained to a tree, and burned to death.

The lesson Lincoln drew from mob violence inverted Tocqueville's ethic of reciprocity: when gangs mistakenly execute the innocent today, "the mob of tomorrow may, and probably will, hang or burn some of them, by the very same mistake." Mob rule denies the adequacy of government to enforce justice. The "lawless in spirit" are unleashed. Having always disliked government, "they make a jubilee of the suspension of its operations" and become judge, jury, and executioners. Should that "mobocratic spirit" erode public confidence in the reliability of the law, "the feelings of the best citizens will become more or less alienated from it; and thus it will be left without friends, or with too few, and those few too weak, to make their friendship effectual." That sullen distrust of law and government characterized the attitudes of most Europeans, according to Tocqueville. Now Lincoln saw it creeping into America.

The American experiment with democracy depended fundamentally on the people's commitment to the rule of law, the "*political religion*" that Lincoln thought should be inculcated in homes, schools, churches, and legislatures. Even "bad laws," which should be changed, must nevertheless "be religiously observed" because the alternatives were anarchy or dictatorship. The world's first democratic nation represented a grand and "undecided experiment." The founding generation undertook "to display before an admiring world, a practical demonstration of the truth of a proposition, which had hitherto been considered, at best no better, than problematical; namely, *the capability of a people to govern themselves*." Throughout the nation, impatience with laws was translating into lawlessness that could destroy the American experiment. The Revolution succeeded only because it temporarily "smothered" the inclinations toward "jealousy, envy, and avarice" natural to human beings. Shared animosity toward the crown turned passions such as hatred and revenge, normally destructive of comity, against Britain alone. As a consequence, "the basest principles of our nature" either went dormant or were directed toward the best of causes, establishing and preserving "civil and religious liberty."

Memories of the Revolution, however, had grown fuzzy as those who fought its battles had died. Their shared devotion to democracy, once so fresh among Americans, had likewise begun to fade. Those memories and that history, "a fortress of strength," had been leveled by "the silent artillery of time." The American "temple of liberty" stood on pillars of memory that had crumbled, so a rising generation must provide another foundation "hewn from the solid quarry of sovereign reason." It was time to exchange fervor for moderation. The heated emotions fueling mob violence had become an enemy that only "reason, cold, calculating, unimpassioned reason," could defeat. Important as the example of leaders such as Washington had been, individual embodiments of virtue would no longer suffice. Instead the sensibilities of the people must be "moulded into *general intelligence, sound morality* and, in particular, *a reverence for the constitution and laws*." In short, precisely the qualities that Tocqueville had identified as prerequisite to the success of the American experiment, public-spiritedness and adherence to the laws generated by the people themselves, Lincoln identified as the barriers protecting democracy against mob rule.[118]

Like Mill and Tocqueville, Lincoln was convinced that democracy must rest on education. Lincoln himself, of course, was largely self-taught, and what education he had came through his own extraordinary efforts, under circumstances that could scarcely have been further from those of Tocqueville and Mill. Whereas the former roamed freely in the well-stocked library of his family's château and the latter was tutored by two of Britain's liveliest minds, Lincoln scrambled to find anything to read in the hardscrabble frontier towns of Kentucky, Indiana, and Illinois where his family scraped out a living.

Lincoln focused on schools in one of his first public addresses, delivered to the residents of Sangamo County, Illinois, in 1832, as a candidate for the state legislature. He closed with a paean to "the most important subject which we as a people can be engaged in," public education. Only if all individuals had access to an education adequate to enable them to read the histories of their own and other nations would free institutions be appreciated and secure. Only people who could read for themselves works of religion and ethics were prepared to participate in and elevate democratic culture.

Lincoln offered himself as a modest example of the fruits—as well as an advocate—of education. His characterization captures the distrust of dogmatic certainty that persisted throughout his journey from dirt-floor frontier cabins to the White House. He admitted that he could be wrong about any of the subjects he had addressed, then explained his personal outlook on politics: "Holding it a sound maxim that it is better to be only sometimes right, than at all times wrong, so soon as I discover my opinions to be erroneous, I shall be ready to renounce them."[119] Even if such self-deprecating jabs elicited a few smiles, Lincoln did not elicit enough votes. Not until two years later, after sustained study of law and oratory, did he win a seat in the Illinois legislature. His early self-awareness, along with an abiding distrust of claims to absolute truth in religion, ethics, and politics that resembled Montaigne's, stayed with him.

Lincoln placed as much emphasis on the importance of feelings, on "sensibility," as he did on rational thought and argument. Throughout his life Lincoln read and memorized poetry. He also wrote simple verses that conjure up, in theme if not in quality, the work of the romantic writers so important to Tocqueville and Mill. Something akin to the "circuitous journey" of Wordsworth's *Prelude*, to cite one example, was on Lincoln's mind in 1844, when he revisited for the first time in fifteen years the region in southern Indiana where he had grown up. "My childhood's home I see again, / And sadden with the view; / And still, as memory crowds my brain, / There's pleasure in it too." Lincoln doubted whether, as he put it, "my expression of those feelings is poetry," yet he grasped that the sentiments he was struggling to express were as powerful as the words were ungainly.

Death was omnipresent in Lincoln's life. It was in Indiana that his mother had died when he was nine. A sister died when he was nineteen. The woman who was probably his first love died when he was twenty-six. His brother died in infancy, his sister in childbirth, and two of his four children were also dead before the corpses of the Civil War began piling up in 1861. Memories came flooding back when Lincoln returned to his childhood home, "Where things decayed, and loved ones lost / In dreamy shadows rise." Now that he was, in his words, "freed from all that's earthly vile," he had to put away such sorrows, yet the earlier days intruded, as he put it, "Like scenes in some enchanted isle, / All bathed in liquid light." If Goethe was right that the "dark side" or "night side" of the romantic sensibility rendered it "fundamentally unhealthy," the Romantics' poetry nevertheless provided Lincoln with a set of tools for thinking about loss and the possibility of recovery. Although deeply worried about the passions inspiring rising mob violence, as his 1838 Springfield speech made clear, Lincoln himself can be described as a Romantic—moody, death-obsessed, and struggling with recurring bouts of melancholy.[120] Lincoln's deep commitment to the American national project may be read as another aspect of his romanticism. From his earliest speeches to his last, he harbored hopes for his homeland as ambitious as those of any nineteenth-century romantic nationalist. For Lincoln those hopes were rooted not in blood, soil, or other *volkish* notions but in his commitments to individual autonomy and human equality, principles only democracy could safeguard.

Lincoln entered electoral politics as a member of the Illinois Whig Party and served four terms in the state legislature in the 1830s and 1840s. He adopted most of the standard Whig Party positions, including government support for education, internal improvements such as roads, bridges, and canals, and economic development. From the Whigs' perspective, supporters of Jefferson and Madison, and then of Andrew Jackson—those who proudly called their party the Democracy—had simply "filched" the label. According to the Whig *American Review*, they had no right to the designation. Whereas self-proclaimed Democrats saw in their opponents' nation-building projects and reformist moralism the manipulation of authentic American freedom and popular government by scheming elites, Whigs designated themselves by the name proudly adopted by the patriots of the Revolution and called their foes not Democrats but the Jackson Party, in thrall to the autocratic King Andrew I. An editorial in the *American Review* called the United States a species of "representative government" located midway between "pure democracy" and "pure monarchy." Americans had repudiated all forms of inherited authority, whether of aristocracy or monarchy. All power lay with all the people, but the Constitution empowered the people to exercise their sovereignty by electing, for short terms only, those who would manage government for the common good, in the interest of "the *whole* people," not for a particular group of them such as those to whom Jackson distributed spoils. Legislators were not chosen as "business agents" to represent the "pecuniary interest" of particular persons or factions. Instead they were expected not only to attend to the legitimate concerns of their own constituents but also to see beyond them to the needs of the nation.[121]

By the time that Lincoln became politically active, Whigs were as adamant as Jacksonians that they embodied the spirit of democracy. The Washington *National Intelligencer* crowed in 1834 that unlike Jacksonians such as New York's scheming Martin Van Buren, who merited the label "Tories" for their steadfast opposition to change and their blind fealty to a single man, the Whigs were "the true Democracy of the Country." When the Whigs found their own war hero, William Henry Harrison, they won the 1840 election by mounting the first recognizably modern presidential campaign. After emerging victorious in a contest that attracted the votes of 80 percent of the eligible electorate, Whigs even more lustily trumpeted their own democratic credentials.[122]

One of the most prominent of the Whig statements of principle was a short pamphlet with a long title, *The Social Compact Exemplified in the Constitution of the Commonwealth of Massachusetts, with Remarks on the Theories of Divine Right of Hobbes and Filmer, and the Counter Theories of Sidney, Locke, Montesquieu, and Rousseau* (1842), written by John Quincy Adams. In this widely read text, Adams ventured an argument even more ambitious than his title suggests. He traced the origins of democracy back to ancient Greece, then noted the more proximate sources for American constitution writers in the work of Sidney, Locke, Montesquieu, and Rousseau.[123] Adams considered the use of the term "democratic" to describe the Jackson Party a category error. Neither party was more democratic, or more aristocratic, than the other. Even though the multitude could never govern directly, identifying democracy with the American form of representative government, distinct from monarchy or aristocracy, made perfect sense: "Democracy is the oxygen or vital air, too pure in itself for human respiration," which together with other elements, themselves less pure but equally destructive on their own, formed the "moral and political atmosphere" of the United States. The curse of party spirit should be banished; in its place should be the cause of the entire nation.[124]

Nowhere did the contest between rival parties claiming to embody democracy come into sharper focus than in tiny Rhode Island. Originally among the most self-consciously "democratical" governments in British North America, Rhode Island by the 1840s had among the most severely restricted electorates in the nation. Only around 50 percent of white males owned enough property to qualify to vote. Thomas Dorr bristled under the Rhode Island Whigs' dismissal of ordinary people's ability to exercise political judgment, and he emerged as the leader of a movement challenging the state legislature's continuing refusal to reconsider the outdated restrictions on suffrage. The product of a prominent Providence family and a graduate of Phillips Exeter Academy and Harvard College, Dorr broke with the Whigs and established a radical movement that championed free public education as a constitutional right, envisioned an independent judiciary, and sought to remove restrictions on suffrage. Frustrated by rural conservatives' and entrenched elites' vise-like grip on political power, Dorr's party wrote their own People's Constitution, which established universal white manhood suffrage. A majority of that much-enlarged electorate, including many foreign-born workers in urban centers, then ratified the proposed constitution in an extralegal referendum and elected Dorr governor—unanimously, they claimed.

The sitting legislature, unsurprisingly, denied the legitimacy of the new government and pursued Dorr and his lieutenants as lawless insurgents. Dorr enlisted the aid of radical Democrats from New York and twice tried to seize control of the state government through military action. But his supporters lacked the will to make a revolution, and they were turned back both times by superior numbers and firepower. When Dorr's movement excluded free blacks from voting under the People's Constitution, Frederick Douglass and other blacks disowned Dorr. When the sitting legislature countered the People's Constitution with a Law and Order Constitution that offered male free black taxpayers the vote, antislavery northerners thought it exposed the white supremacist strategy implicit in the Democrats' courtship of immigrants' votes. When Dorr's opponents asked John Quincy Adams if they could reprint his pamphlet *The Social Compact* to bolster their arguments against the dangers of mob rule, he complied willingly. To their critics, Jacksonian Democrats were lawless thugs. Jacksonians in turn skewered the Whigs' aversion to popular government—at least as they understood it—as a sign of their paternalism.[125] Although both parties wrapped themselves in the rhetoric of democracy, their understandings of its meaning were diverging in ways that would eventually endanger the ethic of reciprocity and the long-term prospects of democracy in America.

In 1844 Calvin Colton accurately recounted the origin, etymology, and history of "democracy" in his pamphlet of the same name, then observed that "the whole world" is striving "for *democracy* as opposed to *monarchy*." In the United States, because the powers of government spring from the people and return to them at every election, the American people are sovereign and the nation is therefore a democracy. The confusion of the 1830s and 1840s, according to Colton, originated in the false accusations of aristocracy and monarchy that killed the Federalist Party. Jefferson's Republican Party came to power because it did indeed embody "the power of the PEOPLE." Jackson's "Democracy," by contrast, Colton likened to Napoleonic rule, nothing but "the ascendant star of one man." No single party could presume to call itself "the Democracy" in a political system that was itself a democracy. The sacred name "*democrats* was *stolen*" by the Jackson men, oligarchs and monarchists who had no claim to the title because "it is an *American*, not a party name." Colton urged his fellow Whigs to use the older term "Locofocos" for their Jacksonian opponents and designate themselves "Democratic Whigs." Having thus cleared the air, they could continue to show, as they had by winning the presidency in 1840, that "the Whigs are the *only true* Democrats." The stakes were great. "The word, *Democracy*, is a *universal symbol*, of *uniform* import, and no power can arrest or limit its influence. It will prevail over everything, and carry all before it." Lincoln identified with the Whigs for all the reasons John Quincy Adams and Colton offered, and above all because, like those who would come to be known as "Conscience Whigs," he was passionately opposed to the expansion of slavery.[126]

Orestes Brownson, an idiosyncratic writer whose personal evolution tracked many of the possibilities running from populist Jacksonian to skeptical Whig, and whose writings for that reason appealed to different readers at different times, expressed his own ambivalence in his later judgments on the Jackson Party and Jackson's legacy. Brownson admitted he had agreed with most of Old Hickory's policies during his presidency. Indeed, his 1840 essay "The Laboring Classes" on Chartism was one of the most influential statements of working-class radicalism written by an American. Brownson advocated abolishing not only inheritance but also the entire wage system in order to replace what Karl Marx and Friedrich Engels later called the "cash nexus," the bond between individuals established by money alone, with what Jesus called an ethic of love. But enthusiastic as Jacksonians were about Brownson's critique of the Whigs' reformism, which he thought skirted the economic issue at the root of the political ills they identified, he refused to stay within any party boundaries.[127]

The problem with the Democratic Party became evident to Brownson only in the late 1830s, and it did not surface in "The Laboring Classes." Writing in the inaugural issue of the journal he founded, the *Boston Review*, in January of 1838, Brownson reflected on the multiple meanings of democracy. He noted first that all Americans had become democrats in the sense that they rejected monarchy and aristocracy. That much could be taken for granted. Brownson identified several distinct meanings of the word "democracy," and his description clarifies much of what differentiated many northern partisans of democracy from the Jackson Party. Democracy is "a form of government under which the people, either as a body or by their representatives, make and administer their own laws." Since democrats are simply those who embrace a popular form of government, almost all Americans are democrats in that sense. Occasionally, however, people associate with the word "democracy" something quite different, "the great body of the people, the unprivileged many, in opposition to the privileged few." Understood in this way, democrats are those in sympathy with the masses, those who contend that "all political and governmental action should have for its end and aim the protection of the rights and the promotion of the interests of the poorest and most numerous class." In this sense too, Brownson insisted, "the whole, or nearly the whole American people are democrats." No preferences for aristocracy had survived the transformation of American politics in the 1820s and 1830s.

Brownson rejected the Jackson Party's claim that its appeal to "the people" entitled it to adopt the term as its own. Like most Americans, Brownson disliked "party tyranny," which kept individuals from expressing their convictions freely. "In politics, as in morals, theology, and philosophy, we are eclectics, and hold ourselves free to seek, accept, and support truth and justice wherever we can find them." Blind partisanship, Brownson warned, was obscuring the real meaning of democracy, which was both "a great social and political doctrine" and a mass movement for better socioeconomic conditions. It was in this broader sense, Brownson wrote, that "the word is used in England and on the continent of Europe, though not often in this country," where the Jacksonians tried to monopolize it. Properly understood, a democrat was one who understood the word not in a partisan sense but as "philosophical democracy, or democracy as it should be." Modern democrats saw that the power of the state, expressing the will of the democratic majority, must be bounded by a robust commitment to individual autonomy. Circumscribing both the power of the majority and the exercise of individual rights must be the dictates of justice.

When Brownson undertook to explain how justice was to be identified, he took a step common among Whigs, and by the late 1850s among Republicans, who professed allegiance to democracy. The answer lay in education, in "enlightenment," because individuals' judgment is untrustworthy only when darkened by prejudice. The principle of popular sovereignty was a powerful and necessary weapon when the people were challenging kings, but the time had come for Americans to embrace autonomy, "the highest conception of liberty," which "leaves every man free to do whatever it is just to do, and not free to do only what it is unjust to do." Otherwise liberty is nothing but license, and people are slaves to their impulses. Only when people live "under the 'perfect law of liberty,'" the "immutable law of justice," are they free to seek "the full and harmonious development of all their faculties." Brownson explicitly eschewed violence, arguing that the end of all remaining privileges could come only slowly, by educating the electorate. Like most Whigs, Brownson judged democracy the best form of government only when the majority is restrained by respect for individual autonomy and by the ultimate standard, God's will, the "sovereignty of justice."[128]

Looking back from 1849, Brownson identified the mistake that Jackson had made by identifying his will with the will of the people, a mistake that his followers continued to make after his presidency. "The evil was done," in Brownson's words, "by the principles on which he acted and defended himself and his measures from the attacks of his enemies." Jackson was the first president to confuse the will of the people, as expressed in party meetings and partisan newspapers, with the will of the people as embodied in laws. Jackson thereby did irreparable harm to the nation, because he unchained the "spirit of wild and lawless democracy which the constitution was avowedly intended to repress." Neither Adams, Jefferson, Madison, nor Wilson had put the point better than Brownson did. When channeled through the institutions of representative democracy, the people could express their preferences rationally. When they operated outside the framework of law and political debate, the people spoke in the voice of "corrupt nature, of faction, of demagogues, disorderly passion, and selfish interests to which it is always fatal to listen."[129] Those mob-like tendencies, dependent less on deliberation than on blind fury, were displayed in the violence that attracted not only Brownson's attention but also Mill's in his review of Tocqueville and Lincoln's in his 1838 speech at Springfield.

Brownson's restless intellectual independence, which led him through multiple religious and political affiliations, renders him unclassifiable. A radical who championed the "laboring classes" against the rich, Brownson came to believe that majoritarian democracy would never unseat the wealthy manipulators who easily duped the poor into voting for their projects. His attempts to forge a link between northern and southern working people led him to each of the major parties and then, in the early 1840s, to a brief alliance with the strangest of bedfellows, South Carolina's John C. Calhoun. Calhoun, for whom the defense of slavery was the beginning and end of politics, had earlier dreamed up an ingenious conception of democracy. He claimed that his "concurrent majority" was designed to stave off despotic majoritarianism, but its sole purpose was to protect slavery. Calhoun contended that only if every "interest" in society could exercise an effective veto over every other interest could democracy avoid slipping into tyranny. The fact that Brownson, among the most strident partisans of social and economic egalitarianism in antebellum America, could briefly make common cause with Calhoun, among the most ingenious reactionaries in American history, shows how jumbled political affiliations were in the 1830s and 1840s.[130]

During these years, when Tocqueville and Mill were trying to make sense of democracy and Lincoln was embarking on his political career, the abstractions used by both American political parties to demonize each other became concrete over the issue of slavery. Nothing else in nineteenth-century American public life fed passions as did slavery, the antithesis of reciprocity. In the first half of the century, multiple streams converged into a rising current of antislavery sentiment. Early abolitionists such as John Woolman, Anthony Benezet, and John Wesley had reconceptualized slavery as the sinful infliction of pain, and others began arguing that those who tolerated slavery and enjoyed comfortable lives as a result were complicit in sin.[131] Grassroots mobilization by African Americans manifested itself in slave revolts that amplified the power of published testimony from free blacks.

Many Protestant ministers, such as Elijah Lovejoy, who vociferously criticized the use of alcohol, the faith of Roman Catholics, and the "amalgamation" of the races as degrading sins nevertheless castigated slavery and denounced those who found warrant for it in the Bible. When Lovejoy was murdered by a mob in Alton, Illinois, on November 7, 1837, he became the first white martyr to the antislavery cause. Lovejoy had lost three earlier printing presses to mob violence because he dared challenge the prevailing sentiments of whites in the vicinity of St. Louis. He had relocated across the Mississippi to the free state of Illinois to escape such attacks. But the hatred that followed him knew no bounds and respected no law. Writing in the newspaper he edited, the *Alton Observer*, shortly before his murder, Lovejoy articulated the arguments that would turn an increasing number of northern whites against slavery. Drawing on sources ranging from the Bible to the Declaration of Independence, Lovejoy summarized his case in these words: "Abolitionists, therefore, hold American slavery to be a *wrong*, a legalized system of inconceivable injustice, and a SIN." Slaveholders transgressed not only against slaves but against God himself. Whatever is "morally wrong," Lovejoy concluded, "can never be politically right." Abolitionists also believed that "slavery is a political evil of unspeakable magnitude, and one which, if not removed, will speedily work the downfall of our free institutions, both civil and religious."[132]

Fueled by shifting conventions concerning individual responsibility, changing cultural views of pain, and an emerging ethic of sympathy, antislavery sentiment spread throughout northern society. It also transformed southern defenses of slavery. Whereas earlier apologists of slavery had agonized over an indefensible but indispensable form of labor, beginning in the 1840s southerners harnessed new ideas about inflicting pain and sympathetic identification in service to a new rationale for slavery. Justifying it as a species of paternalism supposedly made necessary by blacks' inability to compete in the dog-eat-dog world of market society, southern ideologues presented slavery as a peculiar form of kindness to slaves.[133]

If slavery was evil and sinful, and threatened church and state alike, however, as its critics insisted, then it had to be eradicated. Lincoln began moving toward that conclusion in the speech he delivered in Springfield just months after Lovejoy's murder. Like Lovejoy himself and most other antislavery northerners, Lincoln believed that slave owners had to end slavery voluntarily, through manumission. Also like Lovejoy, he worried about the consequences of ending slavery in a nation as racist, and as obsessed with the supposed dangers of "amalgamation" of whites and blacks, as the United States. Events in the 1840s and 1850s gradually changed his mind.

Slavery emerged as the inescapable issue in American politics during the 1840s. Between the time of Tocqueville's visit to the United States and Lincoln's election to Congress, efforts to postpone its resolution or silence debate about it had failed. The Missouri Compromise, which had permitted slavery in Missouri but banned it elsewhere north of the Mason-Dixon line, had kept the issue from boiling over through the 1820s and 1830s. But anxieties kept mounting. Many Protestants worried about the influx of Catholics from Ireland and central Europe, and others fretted about an alleged conspiracy of Freemasons. All these fears congealed around two great threats. Northerners believed that a "slave power conspiracy" was committed to extending slavery across the continent, not only below but above the Mason-Dixon line. Southerners believed that Britain was trying to encircle the United States, challenging the nation's southern and western frontiers with the ultimate aim of ending slavery around the world. These fears were not without foundation. Antislavery firebrands, losing patience and gaining momentum, had a prominent new recruit in former president John Quincy Adams, who served in the House of Representatives from 1830 until his death in 1848. England did appear bent on occupying both the Oregon Territory and the land that would become California, a vast territory, containing fewer than ten thousand white inhabitants, that appeared ripe for plucking by the world's premier naval power. Ostensibly to prevent that incursion, and using the pretext of Britain's unpaid debts to America, President James Polk sent the United States Army into Mexico to seize much of what later became Texas, California, and the rest of the Southwest.

The Mexican War enraged northern Whigs, heightened sectional tensions, and raised new questions about the meaning of democracy. Opposition to slavery had begun to gather adherents in the late eighteenth century, but it became a powerful force only in the 1830s. David Walker's *Appeal to the Coloured Citizens of the World* (1829), a bitter indictment of slavery, racism, the United States Constitution, and all whites who considered blacks inferior, signaled a new stage in the struggle. Walker not only condemned the hypocrisy of Christians who managed to justify the oppression of fellow humans; he took the far more radical step of urging slaves to revolt against their masters and end slavery by force. Denying citizenship to African Americans, Walker declared, made a mockery of claims that the United States was a democracy, and he demanded that Americans return to the principle that all men are created equal.

Walker's *Appeal* fueled the efforts of the dozens of antislavery societies that African Americans had established in the years since slavery was outlawed in most northern states. Massachusetts, which had abolished slavery in 1783 and where Walker lived in the Boston community of free blacks from 1820 until his suspicious but still unexplained death in 1830, was an especially lively site of such agitation. Walker's *Appeal* went through three editions within a year. It circulated widely among free blacks throughout the nation and among escaped slaves in the maroon communities of the Upper South and the lower northern states. Southern journalists condemned the book for presuming to declare blacks equal to whites. Southern legislatures declared possession of Walker's *Appeal* illegal and put a bounty on his head. Walker grounded his arguments against slavery and for black equality on the principles of the American republic and on the evangelical Christianity he shared with many African Americans as well as whites. Although Walker's *Appeal* attracted much more vocal criticism than support from northern as well as southern whites, it nevertheless helped inspire the antislavery agitation that grew steadily after his death.

Most northern whites condemned calls to end slavery. As Tocqueville correctly observed, northern whites' racism was as deep as that of many southern slave owners. Some foes of slavery, still as fearful as Jefferson that whites and blacks could not live together peacefully in the aftermath of slavery, formed the American Colonization Society to ship free blacks back to Africa. The very conception of a multiracial democracy still appalled most white Americans, including Lincoln's hero, Henry Clay, who advocated colonization as much because of his racism as because of his opposition to slavery, and John Quincy Adams, who hated slavery but expressed "disgust" at the "unnatural" mingling of whites and blacks in marriage.[134]

In 1831 William Lloyd Garrison established his newspaper the *Liberator* and called for the immediate abolition of slavery. Garrison had earlier urged its gradual termination, but Walker and other free blacks convinced him that all slaves should be freed and all black citizens enfranchised. In the 1820s Garrison had worked with the Baltimore abolitionist editor Benjamin Lundy on the *Genius of Universal Emancipation*, and he was converted to the cause by his conviction that slavery was ruining America's reputation in Europe and thus impeding the global progress of democracy. Like others in the international abolitionist community, Garrison saw in France's 1830 Revolution and Britain's Reform Act clear evidence that the world was moving toward democracy. It was time for America to resume its leadership: "Ours is a representative Government, subject to the will of the people," he wrote in 1833. "Public opinion is the lever of national reform," and he envisioned the *Liberator* as a means of pressing that lever. "I will be as harsh as truth," Garrison wrote in the first issue of his paper, "and as uncompromising as justice." Let others moderate their message; "on this subject I do not wish to think, or speak, or write with moderation." Garrison, who in 1854 would denounce the United States Constitution as a pact with Satan, accused the nation, as Walker did, of denying its democratic birthright.[135]

Wendell Phillips, too, grew more radical as time passed and antislavery agitation seemed powerless to effect change. Phillips was powerfully influenced by Tocqueville and Mill, and he frequently cited the argument of *Democracy in America* concerning the power of public opinion in democracy. The problem, as Phillips learned from encounters with the abolitionists' sometimes vicious and violent opponents, was that opinions on slavery were not susceptible to persuasion by rational argument. As the 1840s unfolded, Phillips's outlook shifted from confidence in the power of voluntary associations to engender empathy, broaden citizens' horizons, and counter the tyranny of majority opinion, the argument of Tocqueville's volume 1, to a darker assessment of the public's willingness to think at all, the conclusion of Tocqueville's volume 2. At his most upbeat Phillips described America as his alma mater, Harvard College, writ large: "an educated community, where ideas govern;—ideas stamped into laws by the majority, and submitted to by the minority."[136] Mired in self-interest, however, Americans either failed to see or shrugged off the pain slavery inflicted. Although Phillips agreed that the ethic of reciprocity identified by Tocqueville was necessary to provide a counterweight to "the selfishness of men" undergirding slavery, he came to doubt that education in "the ideas of justice and humanity" could dislodge "the organized selfishness of human nature."[137]

Other Americans, less averse to moderation than Garrison and Phillips, also began to challenge slavery in other settings. As more prominent publicists and politicians rallied behind the antislavery banner, the movement, transatlantic from the outset, slowly spread throughout the northern states. Reformers such as Lydia Maria Child, William Ellery Channing, Theodore Dwight Weld, and eventually Ralph Waldo Emerson, Theodore Parker, Henry David Thoreau, and Margaret Fuller, all of whom devoted their energies primarily to other causes, gravitated to antislavery and helped in various ways to mobilize further support. Extending the Christian ethic of benevolence across all denominations, expanding the rights of women to include access to citizenship and suffrage, and ending the institution of slavery all seemed to a growing number of northerners consistent with the demands of democracy. When Frederick Douglass published the first version of his autobiography in 1845, armored by two prefaces written by Garrison and Phillips to vouch for Douglass's authorship, his *Narrative of the Life* galvanized northern sentiment much as David Walker's *Appeal* had done. Douglass demonstrated once more not only the undeniable cruelty of slavery but also the equally undeniable character, resiliency, and intelligence of this former slave.

The Mexican War brought abolitionist agitation to a head. Many northerners thought it was a war fought only to expand the reach of slavery. When Congress debated an apparently innocuous resolution commending the army for its heroism, George Ashmun from Massachusetts succeeded in having the following words placed at the beginning: "in a war unnecessarily and unconstitutionally begun by the President of the United States." Every Whig but one voted in favor of the amendment; every Democrat opposed it. Some abolitionists thought that paying taxes to fund the war made them accomplices in the crime of slavery. After Henry David Thoreau refused to pay his poll tax and spent a night in jail, he denigrated democracy in his essay "Resistance to Civil Government" (1849) as "a sort of gaming" because it left issues of good and evil to the caprice of majority opinion.[138]

In the South—and, to be fair, in many parts of the North as well, because the Mexican War was popular with much of the public—the war represented simply one more step toward fulfilling America's "manifest destiny."[139] When David Wilmot, a Democratic congressman from Pennsylvania, proposed to prohibit slavery in any land acquired from Mexico, he attracted considerable support. Most Whigs, including Lincoln, and some northern Democrats signed on for reasons that Lincoln later elaborated in the landmark speech he delivered in Peoria, Illinois, in 1854. Although the Wilmot Proviso was defeated by Democrats in the Senate, and voted down again when it resurfaced at the end of the Mexican War, it had a lasting effect. Debate over the measure intensified southern fears that the North was now prepared to vote slavery out of existence, and its defeat confirmed antislavery northerners' suspicions that the slave power conspiracy had consolidated its control of the nation. The "*attachment* of the people" to their government, to use Lincoln's phrase, was coming unstuck.

As Tocqueville anticipated, France too was moving toward a crisis, but of a very different sort. In the United States, ethnic, racial, and religious differences, visible geographic and economic mobility and, perhaps even more important, the widespread belief in such mobility, all combined with white male suffrage to discourage the emergence of a revolutionary working class.[140] France and Britain, however, lacked the "safety valves" built into American society. The confidence of propertied elites, who believed that governing the nation was up to them, was bolstered by centuries of privilege and decades of Terror-driven fear. As a result, unrest was mounting. Whereas Americans left, right, and center embraced democracy and griped only that their opponents misunderstood and misappropriated the term, in Britain and France democracy continued to spark sharp conflict precisely because both the left and the right associated universal suffrage with radical, even revolutionary transformation. The rumblings of Chartism suggested that widespread popular unrest lay beneath the apparently placid surface of parliamentary politics, in which both Tories and Whigs squabbled incessantly but refused to yield to the demand for a wider suffrage. In France, Tocqueville joined liberal critics of the restricted suffrage to argue that education was as important a marker of civic capacity as wealth. In the first of these debates, in 1842, one deputy proclaimed that the superior judgment of the educated made it dangerous as well as foolish to exclude them from participating in politics. The aristocracy of wealth currently recognized by the French electoral system "pales before the aristocracy of intelligence and genius," and education should "constitute in the eyes of the legislator a moral wealth at least equivalent to landed riches."[141]

Debates in 1842 and 1847 over these proposals, however, went nowhere. Guizot, who was serving as minister of foreign affairs when the issue again surfaced in 1847, squelched it. "I think today what I thought and what I said in 1842" on electoral reform, he declared. "The principle of universal suffrage is in itself so absurd that none of even its partisans dare accept it or support it completely. None." When a voice cried out, "Its day will come," Guizot replied, "There will never be a day for universal suffrage. There will never be a time when all human beings, whatever they are, can be called to exercise political rights." Whereas Guizot previously had held out hope that the capacity of French citizens could be enhanced through education, by 1847 he had dug in his heels. His intransigence mirrored that of the government of Louis-Philippe, and it helped set off the wildfire that became the revolutions of 1848.[142]

The cataclysmic year of 1848 marked the end of an era on the European continent. Starting with a string of uprisings that expanded across the Italian peninsula, then spread to France and eastward through much of central Europe, these revolutions recalled the contagion—and the hopes and fears—set off in 1789. The Italian revolts led quickly to the proclamation of new forms of constitutional monarchy, some patterned on the French settlement of 1830. But in France that option was obviously unavailable. After the failed legislative challenge of 1847, French champions of electoral reform concocted a new strategy. With political meetings outlawed, they upped the ante. They began to stage ever-larger gatherings, called "banquets" to evade the prohibition on political rallies, to convince Guizot and his allies of the need for political change. The government's anxiety grew with the size of the banquets. Tocqueville later observed in his *Recollections* that neither side was interested in a showdown, but when both raised the stakes, the result was something neither side anticipated or sought: radical leaders considered a revolution premature, and conservatives were prepared to make major concessions. The ensuing tragedy taught Tocqueville a lesson about politics that would inform his later writing about the Revolution of 1789. "One has to have spent long years in the whirlwind of party politics to realize how far men drive each other from their intended courses." Experience showed "how the world's fate is moved" by such inadvertent escalation, "but often in opposite directions from the wishes of those who produced the current, like a kite which flies by the opposing action of the wind and the string."[143]

When the government canceled a banquet scheduled to be held in Paris, the response was immediate and decisive. Crowds surged through the streets on February 22. As Tocqueville watched workers calmly erecting one of the barricades that clotted the streets of Paris, he remarked to his companion, "Believe me, this time it is not another riot, but a revolution." Reflecting later on what had happened, he mused, "In France a government is always wrong to base its support on the exclusive interests and selfish passions of a single class." The aristocracy of the *ancien régime* had already shown, and the bourgeoisie was showing now, that every group, when in power, finds "it clever to criticize its own prerogatives and thunder against the abuses on which it lived." Instead, he warned (too late to be of use), "the best way for a government of ours to keep itself in power is to rule well and, especially, to govern in the interest of everybody." But even then, he sighed, "it is still none too certain that it will last long."[144] Ordered to control the unrest, units of the National Guard and the army seemed instead to melt away, and the crowds grew. Calls to oust Guizot mingled with calls for a republic. The next day Guizot resigned. When an unruly crowd of several hundred people gathered outside his former office in the Ministry of Foreign Affairs, a soldier disobeyed the order not to fire. In the ensuing chaos more than fifty people were shot. Knowing that crowds were descending on the royal palace, Louis-Philippe decided against martyrdom, unceremoniously abdicated, and escaped to England.

The provisional government that met in the Hôtel de Ville declared a republic and announced, only two days after the revolution began, that elections would be held in April for a new Constituent Assembly. Disagreements and mutual distrust among members of the new government mirrored the divisions in France itself: rural versus urban; Catholic versus secular; south versus north; Bourbons versus Orléanists; and, perhaps most important, the small shopkeepers of the towns and the small landowners of rural France versus the urban masses and radical republicans.

Competing forms of radicalism had been proliferating in France since 1830, and radicals' inability to make common cause plagued the Second Republic during its brief existence. A partial list of the diverse groups on the left would include the followers of Charles Fourier and Henri de Saint-Simon, who had little interest in democracy because, like Turgot and Condorcet, they trusted an educated elite; Louis Blanc, who in his organ *La Réforme* called for universal suffrage as the means toward the end of cooperative workshops; Etienne Cabet, who championed Christian socialism and direct democracy in *Populaire*; Philippe Buchez and Anthime Corbon, whose journal *L'Atelier* advocated producers' cooperatives animated by a romantic, less hierarchical Catholicism; Auguste Blanqui, a longtime revolutionary whose prison term had only hardened his hatred of the wealthy; and the anarchist Pierre-Joseph Proudhon, who distrusted democracy because he was sure elites could manipulate the electorate to do their bidding. The elections held in May 1848 proved Proudhon the best prophet. The Assembly of nine hundred, chosen by universal manhood suffrage, included only one hundred radicals or socialists. Conservative candidates throughout rural France had actively courted the dramatically enlarged electorate, which swelled from two hundred thousand to over nine million. Some 84 percent of those eligible turned out to vote. These new voters, enfranchised thanks to the constant pressure on the new government exerted by its most radically democratic members, responded by siding with those who opposed their enfranchisement.

Tocqueville had served in the French Chamber of Deputies since 1839. Despite his family's aristocratic background, he chose to sit on the left. He thought of himself as a reformer who opposed Louis-Philippe's "hard right" repressive regime. As he explained to Pierre Royer-Collard in 1841, however, he was a man without a movement: "The liberal but not revolutionary party, which alone suits me, does not exist, and certainly it is not given to me to create it." He described himself as "a wheel that goes around very quickly, but which, having missed its gear, does nothing and is useful for nothing." Initially that dissatisfaction was balanced by his conviction that he could better serve the nation by preserving his "moral force" as a critic than by playing a more active role in the government, but his desire to contribute to a cause rather than remaining a "sterile" outsider propelled him to become involved with the new republic in 1848.[145]

Tocqueville ran for a seat in the spring elections, and in his *Recollections* he provided a vivid account of the new political dynamic of 1848. He did not campaign for a seat in the Assembly to represent his neighbors in rural Normandy; he merely published an address declaring his loyalty to the newly proclaimed republic. He announced his own moderation and renounced the desire of some republicans to declare "a dictatorship in the name of freedom" and immediately "reshape society itself." So popular did the address make Tocqueville that even his conservative opponents pledged their loyalty to him. Tocqueville then gave equally successful speeches to the citizens of Valognes and the workingmen of Cherbourg. He had not joined the revolution because he opposed violence. He supported the republic, though, for the same reasons he had worked for nine years "to steer the government that has just fallen into more liberal and honest paths." On the day of the election, he walked to the polls with the 170 voters from the little village of Tocqueville. According to his account, the townspeople asked him to lead their procession, and they asked him to address them when they stopped along the way. In the end, he was confident that almost all of them voted for him. Tocqueville understood from his visit to America and his experience in France that patterns of deference, if sufficiently well entrenched, could survive revolution and persist even under conditions of democracy. The men "formed themselves into a double column in alphabetical order; I preferred to take the place my name warranted, for I knew that in democratic times and countries one must allow oneself to be put at the head of the people, but must not put oneself there."[146] Tocqueville had learned from his visit to America and his studies of New England towns that respect for traditional authority need not be antithetical to democracy.

Not all of those involved in establishing the Second Republic had learned that lesson. The provisional government included a range of republicans, including moderates who clustered around the journal *Le National* and radicals such as the socialist Blanc and his ally Alexandre-Auguste Ledru-Rollin of *La Réforme*. Committed to Blanc's principle of a "right to work," the provisional government had adopted his plan for National Workshops, which did put the poor of Paris to work on various public projects funded by increasing taxes on rural landowners—large and small. Predictably, the specter of Jacobinism haunted the imaginations of those who preferred either the Bourbon *ancien régime* or the Orléanist monarchy. Those who feared another assault on the privileged position of Catholicism in France were equally worried. Because conservatives harboring such anxieties constituted a majority in the new Assembly, the executive council named by that Assembly reflected its rightward tilt. Excluded from the government they had fought to establish, Blanqui and other radicals launched another revolution to rescue the republic from its enemies. Using the government's decision to shut the National Workshops to rally the people, they mounted a desperate challenge to the regime. From Tocqueville's perspective at least, most of the people of Paris supported the insurrection. Only fear that the radicals' success would set off endless cycles of violence, as in 1793, stiffened the army's backbone. The National Guard, which had been reluctant to suppress the revolt by force, was now under different leadership and demonstrated pitiless resolve. Guard reinforcements poured in from outside Paris, and after three June days of combat, the army put down the Blanquists' uprising, imprisoned its leaders, and restored order.[147]

In addition to the hundreds killed in the June Days, the republic itself and the cause of democracy in France were seriously wounded. For a second time, most observers believed, France had demonstrated to all of Europe that popular government ends in lawlessness and bloodshed. Tocqueville judged himself unusual in yoking his preference for moderation with an equally strong commitment to democracy. He felt himself moving alongside the majority "in the only direction that my tastes, reason and conscience could approve," which was a novel experience for him, and he came to understand that "this majority would rebuff the socialists and the Montagnards but sincerely desired to support and organize the Republic." Tocqueville agreed with the republicans in opposing the monarchy. "I had no cause to defend except freedom and human dignity." He sought only to "make the clear will of the people of France triumph over the passions and desires of the Paris working men, and in this way to conquer demagogy by democracy, such was my only design. Never has an aim seemed to me higher or clearer."[148]

The new constitution, adopted in November, provided for direct election of a president. The enlarged electorate again disappointed the radicals. Voters resoundingly preferred the candidate least likely to lean leftward, an obscure nephew of Napoleon Bonaparte, Louis Napoleon. The electorate chose him, Tocqueville wrote, because "the whole nation was like a flock of frightened sheep running hither and thither, following no path." Everyone thought they saw in Louis Napoleon the answer to their prayers—whatever they happened to be.[149] A year later he extended the length of his term; a year after that he proclaimed himself emperor. Although Marx had it right in *The Eighteenth Brumaire* when he quipped that history had repeated itself, first as tragedy and then as farce, the consequences of the Second Empire for democracy in France were hardly comic.

Tocqueville's account of the Revolution of 1848—and of his role in it—has prompted fierce debate ever since his *Recollections* appeared in French in 1893 and in English three years later. Tocqueville's candid memoir, although he claimed it was not intended for publication, constitutes a fascinating meditation on the revolution. It illuminates his part in the ambitious effort to write a constitution for a new republic that would endure, and it provides his explanation of the reasons why the revolution collapsed into the regime of Louis Napoleon. By turns incisive and infuriating, arrogant and self-deprecating, the *Recollections* contains something to offend readers of all political persuasions. Tocqueville reprinted the perspicacious speech he delivered in the Chamber of Deputies on January 29, 1848, in which he proclaimed, "Gentlemen, my profound conviction is that we are lulling ourselves to sleep over a volcano." He pointed out why the logic of democracy might lead France inexorably to a revolution of the propertyless against the propertied, and he portrayed the chaos leading up to the lava flow of the June Days with a rare dramatic immediacy. Perhaps most cruelly of all, he compared the Constituent Assembly of 1848 unflatteringly to the Philadelphia Constitutional Convention of 1787, and he claimed he knew then that the republic would fail: "Whichever way I looked, I could see nothing either solid or durable amid the general malaise affecting the nation; everybody wanted to get rid of the Constitution, some through socialism, others by monarchy." As for Louis Napoleon, the most ordinary man who was elected president and then made himself emperor, Tocqueville wrote that his fellow members of the government, who "wanted to make the republic live," offered him "no more than ministers when he needed accomplices." Ultimately, the republic vanished and the empire appeared because "we had lost our taste for monarchy but had preserved the spirit of it."[150]

For well over a century critics have disputed Tocqueville's claim that moderates like him, elected by the broadest suffrage in French history, spoke for the people in rejecting the socialists who made the Revolution. Tocqueville confessed that his election in 1848 gave him "a sense of happiness I have never known before." Of course that happiness did not last. Tocqueville was part of a Constituent Assembly that he denigrated. He was troubled by the powers vested in the president, by the fact that the executive was to be elected directly by the people, and by the possibility that the president could be reelected, which Tocqueville judged especially dangerous in France. Above all, Tocqueville was troubled by the centralization of authority in the republic, the characteristic weakness of the French, and by the fact that amending the new constitution was rendered impossible. "I have long thought that, instead of trying to make our forms of government eternal, we should pay attention to making methodical change an easy matter."[151] By 1851, after Louis Napoleon's coup landed Tocqueville briefly in jail, he was again isolated politically, as he remained for the rest of his life.[152]

The convulsions that began in 1848 ended with more conservative regimes in place everywhere in Europe—except Switzerland, where a civil war ended quickly and a stable federal republican government emerged. The events in France had a particularly chilling effect on popular government because it was self-proclaimed democrats like Blanqui who engineered a coup against the elected government of the republic, and that coup set off the chain of events that culminated in the Second Empire. In Britain, too, the momentum behind Chartism died with the revolutions of 1848. In Mill's wistful words, it was "wretched to see the cause of legitimate Socialism thrown so far back by the spirit of reaction against that most happy outbreak at Paris in June." He feared that the explosion of violence set back the larger cause of democracy everywhere. As some radicals' interest veered toward revolution, Chartists dyed their green flags red. G. J. Harney shifted his emphasis from Chartism to Marxism, publishing the *Communist Manifesto* in his *Red Republican* and announcing his new conviction: "Henceforth Chartism is *Démocratique et Sociale*."[153]

Marx argued that 1848 should be seen as a death struggle between the bourgeoisie and the proletariat. To his chagrin, he was proven right. The bourgeois order not only survived; its increasing stability ended the shaky alliance between liberals and democrats for nearly half a century. Marx's own brand of revolutionary socialism, grounded in a philosophy of dialectical materialism and scornful not only of democracy but also of the religious or romantic radicalism that had fed earlier versions of socialism, emerged as the principal challenger to the increasingly conservative regimes in place after 1848. The militant atheism of communist revolutionaries transformed French Catholics, many of whom—like those in the circle around *L'Atelier*—had opposed hierarchical traditions and worked for democratic reform, into bitter foes not only of Jacobinism but also of those elements of the working class that espoused Marxism. As Madison had predicted and Tocqueville explained, multiple rifts opened in the politics of all

European nations, thwarting all attempts to establish enduring alliances of the powerless against the powerful.

By erecting a wall of mistrust and misunderstanding between liberals interested in democracy and an increasingly militant revolutionary movement, the rise of Marxism after 1848 split the left for at least a century and a half. That rupture weakened the forces of reform by driving many moderate democrats, throughout the Atlantic world, into what would prove a fateful embrace with political, cultural, and economic conservatives, and leading many members of the working class to dismiss democracy as a delusion. Like the French Revolution, the revolutions of 1848 had a chilling effect everywhere even though they failed. In their aftermath popular reform movements sputtered for decades, as fears of violence extinguished the flickering hope that champions of democracy harbored for its eventual success.

CHAPTER 14 | The Tragic Irony of Democracy

SHORTLY AFTER THE autocrats who ruled the German states had turned back the latest wave of failed democratic revolutions in 1848, King Maximilian II of Bavaria invited Leopold von Ranke, the most celebrated historian of the age, to help him understand his subjects' puzzling discontent. In a series of private lectures for the new king, Ranke explained that "ideas spread most rapidly when they have found adequate concrete expression." When the American colonies rebelled against Great Britain, Ranke observed, they "introduced a new force in the world," the revolutionary idea that "the nation should govern itself" and "power should come from below." Only when the government of the United States had actually taken shape "did the full significance of this idea become clear. All later revolutionary movements had this same goal." Whereas all Europeans had previously agreed that "a king who ruled by the grace of God had been the center around which everything turned," after 1787 that idea was contested by those rallying to the idea of democracy. The conflict between those two principles, Ranke continued, would now determine "the course of the modern world."[1]

Ranke was right. The central conflict since the late eighteenth century has pitted partisans of inherited authority against partisans of self-government. In the immediate aftermath of the revolutions of 1848, champions of democracy made only limited progress. Given that France established an enduring republic during these years, that Britain twice expanded the franchise (albeit modestly), and that the United States abolished slavery forever, that claim might seem puzzling. Yet the forms of democracy established in the 1870s left many European and American farmers and urban workers impoverished, women excluded from civic life, and African Americans subjugated, and those limitations prompted the next generation of democratic reformers to broaden their focus and rethink their objectives as well as their strategy. As democracy moved from the margins to the center of political discourse in the second half of the nineteenth century, it failed to redeem its promise because necessary commitments to deliberation, pluralism, and reciprocity remained unfulfilled. Rethinking the meaning of democracy in light of that failure was the work of a later generation. Between 1870 and 1920, democratic reformers on both sides of the Atlantic shifted their focus from the political to the social and economic spheres.[2]

In the wake of 1848, many Americans saw ominous harbingers in the return of conservative governments in Europe. Increasingly strident critiques of slavery from the North, and of abolitionism from the South, threatened disunion, and newspaper editors across the United States were quick to identify such talk on both sides as treasonous fodder feeding the "morbid delusions" of "fanatics." Claiming to speak for the "immense majority" of northerners and southerners alike, the *Philadelphia Public Ledger* gasped that splitting the sections would "*Europeanise* this continent." If Americans began to contemplate division, they would soon find springing up, in the place of their solid union, "national subdivision, war, standing armies, aristocracy, dynasties, poverty, ignorance, degradation," and a protracted struggle between upper classes seeking to preserve their privileges and "occasional bloody struggles of lower classes for rights which they would not know how to recover, enjoy or maintain." Frightening as that prospect was, political rhetoric continued to escalate.[3]

Though everyone in the United States claimed to embrace the principles of democracy, both Jacksonians and their opponents continued to accuse each other of treason to Americans' shared ideals. A contributor to the Whiggish *Christian Inquirer* accurately observed that all Americans were so comfortable with democracy that "one would as soon think of defending the solar system" as feel obliged to defend its legitimacy. Calvin Colton's phrase "Democratic Whig Party" found a home in Horace Greeley's *New York Tribune*, which responded to the 1848 revolutions by contending that "*true* Democrats" embraced the social democratic ideas of the French republic. Americans could prevent the European extremes of revolution and reaction only if, unlike the Jacksonians, they acknowledged the need to use government to address social and economic problems.[4]

Conservatives and Whigs in Britain thought their nation had demonstrated just such flexibility, thereby enabling Britain to escape the contagion of chaos that swept the continent. As he had shown in reversing his position to support the Reform Act of 1832, Conservative Robert Peel committed his party, and as prime minister his government, to measures such as the Factory Act of 1844 and the repeal of the Corn Laws in 1846, both of which antagonized large landowners and industrialists but won the Tories much working-class support. Peel said he took such steps "to fortify the established institutions of this country" and "discourage the desire for democratic change," yet his ministry contributed to the long-term decline of Britain's landed gentry. If aristocratic control of the boroughs began to slip after 1832, repealing the Corn Laws marked the beginning of the end of their domination of elections in the counties.[5]

As Britain became the world's workshop, both middle-class and working-class Britons found themselves disenchanted with the Liberals' laissez-faire doctrines. A Manchester businessman described himself to William Gladstone as just one of many long-time Liberals becoming increasingly "conservative in all that relates to the further infusion of the democratic elements into our constitution." Due to the Whigs' stubborn adherence to free trade and the Conservatives' flexibility, party affiliations were scrambled from the 1840s through the ministries of renegade Conservative Benjamin Disraeli. Britain's old aristocracy, its new working classes, and its rising middle class all found their status at risk as the nation became the world's leading urban industrial power. For that reason the relation between democracy and the Victorian ideal of "respectability" remained more vexed than in the United States, even though British policies addressing social problems relieved some of the pressure that continued to build in France between 1848 and the turbulence of 1870–71.[6]

The principle of universal manhood suffrage was firmly established in France in 1852. Though it was the gift of Louis Napoleon rather than accomplished by the Second Republic, and though the appointed rather than elected Senate continued to embody the spirit of the *ancien régime* in its personnel and its resistance to democratization, once universal suffrage was expanded it proved impossible to constrict. Yet the emperor, as Louis Napoleon styled himself after taking the name Napoleon III, shrewdly controlled the electoral process, which meant that universal manhood suffrage in the Second Empire only masked the emptiness behind the facade of French democracy. Napoleon III, master of display and (with his planner Baron Haussmann) creator of modern Paris, tried to resolve the tension Ranke identified by proclaiming himself the embodiment of popular sovereignty while prohibiting anything (free speech, party politics, citizens' associations) that might have enabled the people of France to express their voice.

Democracy in America, for reasons Tocqueville had explained to his compatriots, was not only livelier; during the 1850s it was becoming explosive.

The Compromise of 1850 and the Kansas-Nebraska Act, although intended to ease sectional conflict in the United States, only intensified it. The former, a complicated legislative package, stipulated that voters in all the territories would determine the status of slavery. Thanks to the designer of this scheme, Senator Stephen A. Douglas of Illinois, it came to be known as "popular sovereignty." Although resting on the evidently unproblematic principle of majority rule, Douglas's proposal satisfied almost no one. Northerners considered it a challenge to the sacred Missouri Compromise because it cracked open the door to slavery anywhere. To southerners it meant that voters might repudiate slavery even south of the 36°60' line. The most problematic provision was the fugitive slave law, which required all citizens to hand over runaway slaves to legal authorities so they could be returned their masters. In the eyes of many northerners, even those not active in the antislavery crusade, the fugitive slave law made them accomplices in the crime of slavery. Tensions rose further in 1854. In the United States Senate, Douglas introduced legislation to carve two new territories, Kansas and Nebraska, from the vast expanse of the Louisiana Purchase that lay north of the Indian Territory—and north of the Mason-Dixon line. The Kansas-Nebraska Act outraged many northerners because it made the question of slavery in these territories too a matter of "popular sovereignty." Now slavery could be introduced anywhere a majority of whites endorsed it. Abolitionists burned effigies of Douglas.

A new party, calling itself "Republican," began to take shape as several groups coalesced. Refugees from the crumbling Whig Party joined with Nativists (or "Know Nothings") who were opposed to immigration in general and the influx of Catholics in particular, and "Free Soilers" who opposed the further expansion of slavery as a threat to free labor. In the Kansas Territory, proslavery agitators arrived from neighboring Missouri, bringing with them tactics used against Elijah Lovejoy and other abolitionists. They tangled with Free Soilers who traveled from New England to establish communities opposed to slavery.[7] The rival groups' struggle to control Kansas sparked an increasingly bitter political debate in the neighboring states and in Congress. Abraham Lincoln, who had settled into a successful private legal practice in Springfield, Illinois, was among those inspired to address the issue. The speech he delivered in Peoria, Illinois, on October 16, 1854, a reply to Douglas's defense of the Kansas-Nebraska Act, catapulted Lincoln to prominence in the emerging Republican Party. It also established the terms on which he and

Douglas—and an increasingly large number of Americans in the North and the South—would wrangle over the meanings of democracy.

Lincoln's Peoria address, one of the most searching explorations of democracy offered in nineteenth-century America, began with a history lesson. He carefully traced the steps leading away from the nation's early ambivalence about slavery, starting with Jefferson's support of the Northwest Ordinance, which banned slavery north of the Ohio River and west of New York and Pennsylvania. He recounted the terms of the Missouri Compromise of 1820, the Wilmot Proviso, and the Compromise of 1850. Earlier generations, including the founding generation more broadly and slaveholders like Jefferson specifically, had agreed to limit the expansion of slavery. Now Douglas and the Democratic Party contended that settlers in the territories should decide for themselves, a decision Douglas characterized as "democratic" because it would reflect voters' preferences. Lincoln saw things differently.

"This *declared* indifference, but as I must think, covert *real* zeal for the spread of slavery," Lincoln began, "I can not but hate." Lincoln offered three different reasons. First, "I hate it because of the monstrous injustice of slavery itself." This conviction, which Lincoln had reached earlier, was now leading him toward new conclusions. Second, "I hate it because it deprives our republican example of its just influence in the world." Slavery gave the enemies of self-government good reasons to dismiss Americans as hypocrites. Those who favored the expansion of slavery were forced to repudiate the principle of equal rights proclaimed in the Declaration of Independence, instead "insisting that there is no right principle of action but *self-interest*." In that stark contrast, between his own characterization of the "fundamental principles" of American democracy and Douglas's principle of "self-interest," Lincoln echoed the distinction at the heart of American political debate since the seventeenth century and established the terms on which he would fight against slavery for the rest of his life.[8]

By framing the issues as he did in Peoria, Lincoln was issuing a fundamental challenge to Douglas and his proslavery allies. It was a challenge as old as the Christian scriptures, the Puritans' ideal of ordered liberty and their conception of the public good, the Scottish philosophers' idea of sympathy, and the insistence of John Adams, Madison, and Wilson that, as Rousseau saw, the purpose of democracy is to identify and advance the common interest. It was as contemporary as the antislavery arguments of Walker, Douglass, Garrison, Phillips, Lovejoy, and John Quincy Adams. Lincoln's argument in Peoria also paralleled central insights of Tocqueville and Mill. Tocqueville had already examined the problem of egoism and argued a healthy democracy depends on citizens' benevolence. Mill was formulating arguments about balancing individual liberty against the "permanent interests of man as a progressive being" that he would advance in his landmark books *Utilitarianism*, *The Subjection of Women*, and *On Liberty*. The contrast between Lincoln and Douglas was the contrast that has distinguished those champions of democracy who embrace the values of autonomy, equality, toleration, and mutuality from those who do not—and who nonetheless still consider themselves democrats.[9]

Later in his Peoria address Lincoln elaborated on the crucial distinction between self-interest and justice. "Slavery is founded on the selfishness of man's nature," he said bluntly, whereas opposition to the institution is grounded in "his love of justice. These principles are an eternal antagonism."[10] Americans would have to choose between them. Lincoln denied that he was calling for social equality between blacks and whites. He shared with many other nineteenth-century white antislavery writers assumptions about the superiority of the white race that remind us of the distance separating his day from ours. Although some whites and most blacks challenged the racism undergirding white supremacy, few whites, even those active in the antislavery crusade, envisioned social equality as the consequence or purpose of bringing slavery to an end. Lincoln's Peoria address illustrates the persistent racism that was an unmistakable feature of his sensibility at this stage in his development. Should blacks become equal with whites? "My own feelings will not admit of this," Lincoln confessed, and even "if mine would, we well know that those of the great mass of white people will not."

The next step in Lincoln's argument, which strikes contemporary readers as a non sequitur, is arresting today precisely because it seemed self-evident to Lincoln and his audience: "Whether this feeling accords with justice and sound judgment, is not the sole question, if indeed, it is any part of it." Why was it not the sole question, since that is how it seems to us? "A universal feeling, whether well or ill-founded, can not be safely disregarded." Perhaps, we are inclined to protest, but is that not the reason why addressing the question of justice and the soundness of popular judgment was the most urgent challenge of the day? Not from Lincoln's perspective. He concluded, "We can not, then, make them equals."[11] In 1854, Lincoln was no partisan of racial equality; that observation is as important as it is inescapable. So too is the central point in the final sections of Lincoln's speech, in which he made clear the trajectory of his thinking and signaled the direction in which he would move in the remaining years of his life. It is the reason Lincoln's Peoria address matters to the history of democracy.[12]

If Lincoln conceded that the prejudices of "the great mass of white people" could not be ignored, neither did he think those prejudices sufficient to justify slavery. To the contrary, he pointed to the shared sensibility of Americans concerning the universality of sympathy as the taproot of ethical reasoning, and he stressed the implications of that conviction. "The great majority, south as well as north, have human sympathies, of which they can no more divest themselves than they can of their sensibility to physical pain." Such sympathies, even among slaveholders, revealed "their sense of the wrong of slavery, and their consciousness that, after all, there is humanity in the Negro." If not, Lincoln asked pointedly, why did southerners agree to end the slave trade? Why did southerners, even those who owned slaves, "despise" slave dealers and slave catchers? Why had so many slave owners freed their slaves? The answer to those awkward questions, Lincoln asserted, lay in "SOMETHING which has operated on . . . white owners, inducing them, at vast pecuniary sacrifices, to liberate" their slaves. "In all these cases it is your sense of justice, and human sympathy, continually telling you, that the poor Negro has some natural right to himself—and those who deny it, and make mere merchandise of him, deserve kickings, contempt and death."[13] As clear as Lincoln's reluctance to embrace racial equality was his willingness to brand slavery an injustice inconsistent with human sympathy. People throughout the world, he proclaimed toward the end of the speech, had decided that slavery was evil, and their feelings about it, he insisted, were "not evanescent, but eternal." The judgment to condemn slavery "lies at the very foundation of their sense of justice."[14] Although few white Americans in the 1850s could envision social equality between themselves and African Americans, Lincoln declared that most people everywhere had learned to recognize slavery as "a great moral wrong." Lincoln's opposition to slavery was as deep as his ambivalence about race.[15]

Lincoln then addressed the premises underlying Douglas's doctrine of so-called popular sovereignty. On the face of it, Douglas appeared to be taking his stand on a principle congruent with American democracy. For Lincoln, though, the ethic of reciprocity trumped Douglas's reliance on the idea of majority rule. "The doctrine of self-government is right—absolutely and eternally right," Lincoln proclaimed, "but it has no just application" in the case of extending slavery, a question that could not be answered merely by asking whites to vote on it. Like Adams, Jefferson, and Madison before him, Lincoln declared that there are moral principles that must take precedence over the will of the majority and constrain its decisions. The justification of slavery, Lincoln insisted, instead "depends upon whether a Negro is *not* or *is* a man. If he is *not* a man, why in that case, he who *is* a man may, as a matter of self-government, do just as he pleases with him." In that case, Douglas's notion of "popular sovereignty" provided the solution. "But if the Negro *is* a man, is it not to that extent, a total destruction of self-government, to say that he too shall not govern *himself*?" This was the crux of the matter. "When the white man governs himself that is self-government." Fair enough. "But when he governs himself, and also governs *another* man, that is *more* than self-government—that is despotism." In other words, the principle of democracy, instead of justifying slavery, ruled it out. "If the Negro is a *man*, why then my ancient faith teaches me that 'all men are created equal'; and that there can be no moral right in connection with one man's making a slave of another." The demands of sympathy and autonomy in ethical and political judgment foreclosed enslaving another human being.

Douglas and his allies had extracted one aspect of the American creed of democracy, the will of the majority, without understanding that it rests on other principles. When placed in the framework of sympathy toward all humans and the value of autonomy for all humans, those values taken together yielded the dictum "that no man is good enough to govern another man, *without that other's consent*. I say this is the leading principle—the sheet anchor of American republicanism." Slavery, Lincoln concluded, constitutes a "total violation of the American conviction" that "the just powers of government are derived from the consent of the governed." When masters give themselves a different set of rules from those applied to their slaves, they violate democratic justice. "Allow ALL the governed an equal voice in the government, and that, and that only is self-government."[16]

Lincoln explicitly invoked the ideas of sympathy and autonomy in his Peoria address; the ethic of reciprocity, implicit there, shone through clearly in an unpublished fragment that dates from roughly the same time. There he reasoned that if those with light skin can enslave those with darker skin, they are in danger of enslavement themselves the first time they encounter people with skin lighter than their own. If the criterion is intellect, "you are to be a slave to the first man you meet, with an intellect superior to your own." Finally, he suggested, it could come down to a question of self-interest. In that case, if anyone else can make your enslavement "his interest, he has the right to enslave you." As Lincoln understood, anyone taking seriously the ethic of reciprocity would see through all the arguments offered in defense of slavery. As early as the end of 1854, Lincoln had arrived at the position that southerners accurately saw as a direct threat to slavery. If the institution was inconsistent with the core principle of American democracy, as Lincoln declared in Peoria, why should it—how could it—be allowed to survive?[17]

The violence raging in Kansas, where pro- and antislavery forces engaged in skirmishes of escalating violence, both real and rhetorical, was mirrored in

Washington. Debates in Congress became increasingly vitriolic, although they hardly rivaled the burning and looting of the antislavery hotbed of Lawrence, Kansas, where the Free State Hotel was torched. Senator Charles Sumner of Massachusetts, who had risen to prominence as a critic of slavery, racial segregation, and the abysmal conditions in schools and prisons, delivered an impassioned speech on May 19 and 20, 1856, that inspired abolitionists and infuriated southerners. Sumner denounced the "crime against Kansas" and insulted proslavery senator Andrew Butler of South Carolina by accusing him of taking up with a mistress, that "harlot, slavery." In response South Carolina congressman Preston Brooks, defending the honor of his cousin and his state, attacked Sumner with a cane and left him seriously injured. Sumner's grandiloquent speech and Brooks's response deepened the sense of outrage in North and South alike. As a million copies of Sumner's speech circulated in the North, Brooks received canes from admirers hoping he would have more occasions to put abolitionists in their place.[18]

Then came the *Dred Scott* decision of 1857. The Supreme Court declared that Scott remained a slave, even after his owner's death, despite Scott's having lived in free states. The complicated ruling, in which all nine justices wrote opinions, was understood by many northerners to vindicate the most extreme versions of proslavery ideology.[19] Lincoln's apprehensions deepened. Worried that the slave power conspiracy now included Douglas, Chief Justice Roger Taney, and both Presidents James Buchanan and Franklin Pierce, Lincoln and many others feared that slavery was free to expand throughout the United States. *Dred Scott* troubled even Douglas, who acknowledged that the decision denied the primacy of the principle of popular sovereignty as he understood it. Proslavery firebrands agreed on the significance of the decision, but instead of sharing Douglas's misgivings they exulted that the Supreme Court was on their side. When Missourians crossed into Kansas and elected a legislature that outlawed even questioning the legality of slavery, antislavery voters vehemently denied its legitimacy. With their opponents boycotting the entire process, proslavery Kansans representing less than 10 percent of the electorate in the territory authorized a convention that enacted the proslavery Lecompton Constitution. Again even Douglas was exasperated by the brazenness of the act and outraged when Buchanan and the Democratic Party endorsed it. Before Kansas could be admitted to the Union as a slave state, however, Kansas voters rejected the Lecompton Constitution by a margin of more than ten to one, an outcome that frustrated southerners as much as Lecompton had outraged northerners. From the perspective of Lincoln and many others, *Dred Scott* and Lecompton confirmed their fears: the "slave power conspiracy" was determined to extinguish American democracy.

The legendary debates on democracy between Lincoln and Douglas in 1858 unfolded against that backdrop. Douglas, in many respects a typical Jacksonian Democrat, believed in individual freedom and the sanctity of popular choice. Introducing moral issues into politics he considered a category error sure to end in disaster. Lincoln disagreed. He hated slavery and, as a good Whig, cherished the ideals of free labor and autonomous citizens acting according to their moral responsibilities. Although Lincoln remained skeptical about whether the Constitution would permit the abolition of slavery in the South against the wishes of southerners, his opposition to the expansion of slavery into the territories had grown more passionate as a result of Kansas-Nebraska and *Dred Scott*. Lincoln also cherished the ideal of Union, which had an almost mystical significance for him that cannot be understood outside the context of the democratic nationalism that developed along with romanticism in European and American culture during the first half of the nineteenth century.[20]

Lincoln's emotional attachment to the American Union is easier to understand when placed alongside the nationalism of Benjamin Constant and François Guizot in France, William Wordsworth, Thomas Carlyle, and Thomas Babington Macaulay in England, Johann Gottfried Herder in Germany, and Giuseppe Mazzini in Italy, as well as that of historians George Bancroft and Francis Parkman in the United States. Lincoln's passionate, quasi-religious nationalism, apparent in his Lyceum address of 1838 and in his Peoria address, came into sharper focus in his debates with Douglas in their 1858 contest for election to the United States Senate. Although not conventionally religious himself, Lincoln used religious imagery with increasing frequency in the last decade of his life, at first in response to the deaths in his own family, later because the deaths of hundreds of thousands of his countrymen deepened his sense of tragedy and his belief in providence.

Lincoln and Douglas established their positions in preliminary speeches given before the debates began. Lincoln's convictions concerning national unity surfaced powerfully in one of the most familiar of his addresses: "'A house divided against itself cannot stand,'" he declared. "I believe this government cannot endure, permanently half *slave* and half *free*." Sooner or later, "it will become *all* one thing, or *all* the other."[21] As soon as Douglas learned of Lincoln's formulation, he pounced on it. If Lincoln was warning that slavery would die if it could not expand, then it seemed clear that eradicating slavery was Lincoln's ultimate goal. Douglas hammered on that issue throughout the campaign. Knowing that Illinois voters' racism ran deep, he did not hesitate to accuse Lincoln of wanting to end slavery in order to give blacks the same status as whites. Trying to establish himself as a moderate distinct from the veiled abolitionist Lincoln and from those who would expand slavery everywhere, Douglas reiterated his opposition to the "fraud" of the Lecompton Constitution and his embrace of the apparently unobjectionable principle of popular sovereignty. Douglas pointed out bluntly that he and Lincoln held competing and incompatible conceptions of democracy. Whatever the people choose, Douglas insisted, should be law. "The great principle is the right of every community to judge and decide for itself, whether a thing is right or wrong, whether it would be good or evil for them to adopt it." Elaborating a principle held by many Americans before and since, Douglas continued, "The right of free action, the right of free thought, the right of free judgment" on every question, including slavery, "is dearer to every true American than any other under free government." Individual freedom, in short, is the ultimate American value.

Douglas then quoted Lincoln's "house divided" speech and challenged it, as he did throughout the campaign. Accusing Lincoln of demanding "uniformity in all things," including racial equality, Douglas aligned himself with the venerable American traditions of local self-government and white supremacy: "I am free to say to you that in my opinion this government of ours is founded on the white basis. It was made by the white man, for the benefit of the white man, to be administered by white men, in such manner as they should determine." As for blacks, Indians, and others, it should be left to the states to determine their status. Just as the northern opponents of Jackson's Indian removal policy lacked authority to dictate what southern states had to do with people under their jurisdiction, so northerners should not determine the fate of slavery.[22] Douglas knew how much the hardy people of Illinois hated being told what to do. Just as Democrats bristled at the other items on the Whigs' reformist agenda, so they resented being told how they should think about slavery. Douglas explicitly linked antislavery sentiment to reformers' ideas about liquor, schools, banks, and families. In every domain, Douglas concluded, Lincoln and his ilk wanted to tell the people of Illinois what they must do. The "black republicans," as Douglas and others dubbed adherents to the Republican Party emerging from the reshuffled partisan loyalties of the decade, stood outside the American mainstream. As a Democrat who believed in the principle of majority rule and a loyal member of the Jackson Party, Douglas believed it was up to the people to make such decisions for themselves. Some states allowed slavery; others did not. Some allowed free blacks to vote; others did not. That was the essence of American federalism, which Douglas charged Lincoln with repudiating because he wanted every state squeezed into a rigid antislavery mold.

The themes introduced in those two preliminary speeches echoed throughout the seven debates that followed. The contrast in the two candidates' appearance and rhetorical style was as sharp as that contrast between their understandings of democracy. Douglas, smooth, unruffled, and self-confident, traveled in style, dressed in style, and was accompanied by his stylish twenty-two-year-old wife. Lincoln relished the role of hayseed, playing up his ungainly, awkward appearance, his rumpled attire, and his plain-speaking manner.[23] Lincoln understood exactly what was at stake. To accomplish his goal, dislodging Jacksonian Democrats' understanding of democracy as the simple assertion of individual self-interest, Lincoln could not afford—even had he been able—to present himself as the embodiment of everything that well-educated, proper people thought America should be. Instead he had to beat Jackson's heirs at their own game. He had to establish his vision of democracy, with its respect for every human's right to determine his own fate and its insistence that duties accompany those rights, as the authentic American doctrine. Moreover, he had to demonstrate that Douglas's notion of popular sovereignty betrayed the core principles of American democracy properly understood. Even for a rail splitter who shared his fellow Whig David Crockett's fondness for making points by spinning yarns, it was a tall order.

In their first and second joint appearances, on August 21 and August 27, 1858, Douglas thundered about the inferiority of blacks, the superiority of popular sovereignty, and black republicans' abhorrent abolitionism. After Douglas had finished his hour-long address, according to the standard rules of the debates Lincoln had an hour and a half to reply before both then gave thirty-minute rebuttals. Lincoln distanced himself from other Republicans who embraced abolition. He denied he was calling for social equality and insisted that whites would remain in a "superior position" throughout the nation even if slavery were confined to the South. How much that argument reflected a conscious strategy designed to win over skeptical white listeners and how much it expressed Lincoln's own beliefs by 1858, perhaps not even Lincoln himself knew. As he continued, he dismantled the familiar white supremacist position he had sketched. Although an individual black man, Lincoln continued, might not be his equal in the lightness of his skin or perhaps even in "moral or intellectual endowment," those facts had no consequences for his rights as a human being. On that central issue Lincoln laid down a challenge to Douglas and to his audience. "In the right to eat the bread, without leave of anybody else, which his own hand earns, *he is my equal and the equal of Judge Douglas, and the equal of every living man*."[24] That was the crux of the matter.

Lincoln's moral critique of slavery, which aligned with the fundamental commitments of American democracy as he understood it, unwittingly followed the lead of another of the nation's most persuasive orators, Frederick Douglass. Before he diverged toward a more radical brand of abolitionism, Douglass's evolving ideas for a time paralleled Lincoln's. Unlike Garrison and some others who denounced the Constitution as a proslavery document, Douglass argued that the premises underlying American democracy categorically ruled out slavery. Beginning with *The Narrative of the Life of Frederick Douglass* and continuing through the newspapers he edited from 1847 through 1863 and his countless speeches, Douglass pounded home the injustice of slavery. He refused to rule out any strategy that might advance the cause of abolition, including everything from moderate antislavery agitation to violent slave insurrections.

In his lecture "What to the Slave Is the Fourth of July?" Douglass lashed out at the hypocrisy of Americans who could simultaneously congratulate themselves on their commitments to freedom and equality and accept an institution committed to the denial of those values. "Fellow-citizens!" Douglass thundered, "the existence of slavery in this country brands your republicanism as a sham, your humanity as a base pretence, and your Christianity as a lie." As Lincoln did in Peoria, Douglass charged that slavery "destroys your moral power abroad; it corrupts your politicians at home. It saps the foundations of religion." The problem could not be traced to the Declaration of Independence or the Constitution, both of which extolled freedom and equality. Douglass defied anyone to find "a single pro-slavery clause" in the Constitution. Instead it proclaimed principles "entirely hostile to the existence of slavery." Like Lincoln, Douglass was drawn to a species of romantic nationalism that linked the United States with what he considered a global movement toward equality and self-government. "The doom of slavery is certain," in his words, because slavery was inconsistent with the "obvious tendencies of the age."[25] Americans now had only to embrace the challenge implicit in their founding documents and live up to their democratic ideals.

Although Douglass would later become an enthusiastic supporter of Lincoln's election to the presidency, he remained a staunch critic of all who temporized on the question of bringing slavery to an end, including Lincoln, whom he continued to characterize as the "stepfather" of African Americans. Although on occasion generous in his praise of Lincoln, Douglass remained of two minds. As he later put it in the appendix to his *Life and Times*, Lincoln seemed "tardy, cold, dull, and indifferent" when viewed from the perspective of genuine abolitionism. But "measuring him by the sentiment of his country," by which Douglass meant the racism pervasive among whites, Lincoln instead appeared "swift, zealous, radical, and determined." In his "heart of hearts," Douglass wrote, Lincoln "loathed and hated slavery" despite his stated misgivings about racial equality. Lincoln tried to walk just that line in his debates with Stephen Douglas, and different people in their Illinois audiences praised or condemned him depending on their own points of view—just as Americans have done ever since.[26]

Most decisively, in his debates with Douglas, Lincoln explicitly reiterated the pivotal arguments from his earlier speeches in Springfield and Peoria: the expansion of slavery weakens the nation because it exposes the hypocrisy of American invocations of liberty. Champions of slavery ignore every fundamental principle of American government, as Frederick Douglass argued, and instead elevate only the principle of "*self-interest*." Unlike the founders, who saw the evil of slavery, sought ways to contain it, and hoped eventually to end it, the slave power conspiracy had become bolder. *Dred Scott* implied that even free states could not outlaw the practice of slavery. These audacious steps, Lincoln concluded, threatened the American tradition of free labor and American ideals of autonomy and justice. To cheers from his sympathizers, Lincoln's rhetoric rose with his invocation of the Declaration of Independence. Stephen Douglas liked to invoke "the era of our Revolution," yet he was committed to "muzzling the cannon which thunders its annual joyous return" in the Fourth of July speeches that were reverberating around the North in the 1850s condemning slavery. When he "invites any people willing to have slavery, to establish it, he is blowing out the moral lights around us." That familiar image, used by Henry Clay to condemn slavery when he addressed the American Colonization Society three decades before, predictably elicited a noisy mix of cheers and jeers from the crowd in 1858. Only after the clamor died down could Lincoln continue. When Douglas said he did not care whether slavery was voted up or down, because it was up to white voters to decide for themselves, Douglas was "in my judgment penetrating the human soul and eradicating the light of reason and the love of liberty in this American people." The contrast could hardly have been more stark.[27]

Although the following five debates (ending in Alton, Illinois on Oct. 15th) occasionally introduced variations on these themes, overall Lincoln and Douglas echoed the arguments from their preliminary speeches and initial exchanges. Douglas worked hard to identify Lincoln with "Fred Douglass," whom he characterized as Lincoln's radical abolitionist friend, and with other "black republicans" he was sure Illinois voters would reject. Lincoln resisted the affiliation with Frederick Douglass and tied Stephen Douglas himself to Democrats who had opposed the expansion of slavery. Douglas claimed Lincoln criticized slavery more stridently in northern than in southern Illinois. Lincoln denied it. Douglas held out the prospect of continuing American expansion, to Cuba perhaps, or Mexico, or Canada, and suggested that slavery might prove ideally suited to such new territories. Who are we to say, Douglas asked, whether the future should be slave or free? Lincoln replied to Douglas's continuing defenses of slavery, which Douglas treated as a feature of American history sanctified by law as well as practice, by reaffirming his conviction that the principles laid out in the Declaration of Independence did indeed include blacks. No one before the 1850s, he argued, had ever doubted that claim. Lincoln quoted the passage from Jefferson's *Notes on the State of Virginia* that had become a staple among abolitionists. Jefferson "used the strong language that 'he trembled for his country when he remembered that God was just.'" Douglas, Lincoln observed correctly, had never said anything of the sort. Those who now claimed Jefferson's mantle did not share his tortured convictions concerning the injustice of slavery.[28]

By the end of the debates, that ethical dimension of the issue had emerged as decisive. "The real issue in this controversy," as Lincoln put it, was the morality of slavery. The debates turned on "the eternal struggle between these two principles—right and wrong—throughout the world. They are the two principles that have stood face to face from the beginning of time; and will ever continue to struggle." Lincoln framed their disagreement in terms of their different understandings of legitimate authority: "The one is the common right of humanity and the other the divine right of kings." Or, as he had put the point earlier, slavery repudiated the principles that lay beneath Douglas's slogan of popular sovereignty. Slavery was "a moral, social and political evil,"[29] an excrescence deforming American democracy.

From beginning to end, Douglas exploited the racism of his audience more effectively than Lincoln did, and that success earned Douglas election to the Senate. Although Lincoln repeatedly denied calling for abolition and for black equality, he did challenge the morality of slavery directly, repeatedly, and unflinchingly. That strategy cost him the votes he needed. Douglas invoked popular sovereignty as the essence of democracy. Lincoln denied that voting for slavery erased its injustice. Like Frederick Douglass, he judged slavery inconsistent with the principles of autonomy, equality, and reciprocity on which democracy as he understood it must stand. Voices from deep in American history echoed in the Lincoln-Douglas debates, and their competing conceptions of democracy have continued to reverberate through American political life. Are individuals free to do whatever they choose, or should moral limits constrain their choices?

Democracy faced different challenges on the other side of the Atlantic. The battle against race-based heritable slavery and the battle to expand the electorate were both won, but not the larger war for democracy, which Ranke characterized as the idea that "power should come from below." Edouard Laboulaye, liberal partisan, prolific legal scholar, and after Tocqueville's death in 1859 the most prominent writer on the United States in France, argued in his book *Le parti libéral, son programme et son avenir* that the future now lay with democracy. The restraints on free expression in France reduced Laboulaye's writings in the 1850s and 1860s to an elaborate form of Kabuki theater, yet he pressed on nevertheless, ingeniously marshaling veiled calls for effective popular government outside the hard shell of imperial rule. Although nostalgia for the *ancien régime* would lure some French citizens to declare allegiance to the more repressive and authoritarian dimensions of the Second Empire, Laboulaye admitted, others would look forward, and for those the model of the United States beckoned.

Appropriately enough for the man responsible for the idea that eventually became the Statue of Liberty, Laboulaye passionately defended the Union during the Civil War and the cause of representative democracy in France throughout the 1860s. Though France was now governed by a peculiar hybrid form of (effective) hereditary and (nominal) democratic rule, Laboulaye consoled his readers by contending that the momentum of history was carrying the world toward popular government. Perhaps the alliance between Louis Napoleon's government and representative democracy actually corresponded best to the nation's character and temperament. On the one hand, "universal suffrage satisfies the passion for equality that is dear to us, and which is legitimate when it respects liberty." Voting by those formerly excluded from the franchise expressed a forward-looking spirit now widespread, particularly in French cities. On the other hand, those who perhaps "live too much in the past" remained a vital part of France, and their constitutive commitments to tradition should not be ignored. Laboulaye concluded that "the liberal party sincerely embraces the principle of universal suffrage as a guarantee of liberty, as a means of government, and as an instrument of political education." Universal suffrage, Laboulaye continued, can "sustain a government or overthrow it." From Laboulaye's perspective, attempting to limit the suffrage now would be futile. But before democracy could become effective, it was necessary to "instruct" and to "elevate to a higher moral level" the sensibilities of the electorate, which was precisely the challenge facing the political parties in Britain.[30]

In the aftermath of the revolutions of 1848, British critics of democracy thought they saw in popular government the dawn of chaos. Macaulay wrote to one of Jefferson's biographers in 1857 that the United States Constitution was "all sail and no anchor." Macaulay spoke for many of his countrymen when he predicted that "institutions purely democratic must, sooner or later, destroy liberty, or civilization, or both."[31] Few of Victoria's subjects questioned the institutions of monarchy or aristocracy, which most Englishmen revered as defining features of their nation. When Liberal William Gladstone announced his support for widening the suffrage in 1864, he stipulated that voters must show evidence of "self-command, self-control, respect for order, patience under suffering, confidence in the law," and, perhaps most important, "regard for superiors." He conceded that a mass electorate could be dangerous and acknowledged that in calling for its modest expansion, he was speaking "only of a limited portion of the working class." By aligning himself with those in favor of expanding the suffrage beyond the scope of the Reform Act of 1832, Gladstone was moving no further than Disraeli had done five years earlier.[32]

Gladstone, Disraeli, and Macaulay were hardly out of step with the population. The Second Reform Act of 1867, engineered by a Conservative government, doubled the number of voters and ushered in a flurry of moderate political changes. The slow growth of democracy in England—the percentage of the population entitled to vote increased only slightly between 1833 and 1866—reflected, at least in part, the tepid support shown by the people themselves for the idea of universal suffrage. Matthew Arnold observed that English democracy developed slowly because the English "aristocracy has been more in sympathy with the common people than perhaps any other aristocracy," and the people responded with the respect the gentry considered appropriate. Moreover, he contended that "the feeling of admiring deference to such a class" was more deeply rooted and persistent among the English people than it was anywhere on the continent. Were that situation to change, Arnold warned, England was bound to be "Americanised," by which he meant that the Hyde Park ruffians who demonstrated for electoral reform in 1866 (and trampled some flower beds) gave a taste of the anarchy that would follow. Even so, Arnold conceded that the French Revolution and Napoleon's empire had given common people everywhere a degree of self-respect that had "raised them in the scale of humanity." For that reason Arnold concluded with a rare, even majestic ambivalence rivaling—indeed inspired by—that of Tocqueville's *Democracy in America*. Meriting neither its champions' extravagant praise nor its critics' scorn, the progress of democracy was merely "natural and inevitable."[33] In 1867–68, after yet another monumental struggle, the British electorate grew to 30 percent of adult males. Disraeli's Conservative government was able to take credit even though some Tory back benchers urged restrictions because "we *must* make a stand against 'Democracy.'" By only slightly easing taxpaying requirements and judiciously redistributing seats to protect Conservative strongholds, the Second Reform Act did just that.[34]

The Representation of the People (often called the Third Reform) Act of 1884 extended the vote to as much as 60 percent of Britain's male population, prompting Scottish Labour Party leader Keir Hardie to declare that "the battle of the franchise" had been won. Yet Britain remained a monarchy controlled by a small oligarchy. The widening of the suffrage seemed only to consolidate the power of the most antidemocratic forces in British life, just as it did in France. At Queen Victoria's death in 1901, MPs were still drawn from the wealthiest segments of British society, and only the most radical English democrats envisioned a franchise as broad as that already operating in the American colonies in the late eighteenth century.[35]

Alongside the battle against slavery, the struggle to establish women's rights was one of the great reform causes of the late nineteenth century. The campaign for woman suffrage, which faced implacable resistance on both sides of the Atlantic, showed the depth of the problem confronting reformers seeking to establish thoroughgoing cultures of democracy. The problem of slavery was at least being addressed. As Lincoln pointed out, American political debate in the 1850s pivoted on the morality of slavery. Britain had abolished slavery almost everywhere in the empire in 1833. France had followed suit, after several false starts, in the aftermath of the 1848 revolutions. When English abolitionists, who influenced and supported American antislavery efforts from the 1830s through the Civil War, could declare their own battle against slavery won, they directed their efforts toward eradicating it elsewhere. From the perspective of many women and eventually some men, including John Stuart Mill, woman suffrage was the next step in the struggle for democracy. Now that slavery had been outlawed in Britain, democratic reformers should address the condition of women, another group systematically excluded from civic life.

The early struggle for women's rights stalled after William Godwin's biography of Mary Wollstonecraft had tarnished her reputation. On both sides of the Atlantic polite opinion came to associate criticism of gender roles with immorality, much as the excesses of the French Revolution were used to justify limiting popular participation in both France and Britain. As the concept of virtue gradually shed its associations with the earlier republican ideal and assumed new meanings linked to female chastity, women found themselves confined to an increasingly narrow sphere of action, which was considered appropriate in light of the purportedly God-given differences of biology and the distinct duties of the two sexes.[36]

Tocqueville's account of American women and family life in volume 2 of *Democracy in America* shows the centrality to his broader analysis of this understanding of women's roles. On the one hand, American girls "are less restricted than they are anywhere else"; on the other, "wives submit to stricter obligations." As both a "puritanical nation and a commercial people," Americans "require of women a degree of self-denial and constant sacrifice" not demanded in France or elsewhere in Europe. In his portrait of family life, Tocqueville captured the separate sphere of domesticity and the ideal of companionate marriage, both of which he contrasted sharply with the situation of aristocratic and nonaristocratic families in France.[37] He sought to identify a capacity he associated not only with American women but with also democratic men, the capacity to control one's inclinations and marshal one's energies for purposes other than self-promotion. By contrast, just as male aristocrats in France prized their lordly disdain of others, so their elite female counterparts in the old regime cynically engaged in intrigues to manipulate power indirectly.

Tocqueville offered the ethic of reciprocity, gendered male in his analysis, and the female embrace of domestic obligations as democratic alternatives to such corrupt forms of self-aggrandizement. Just as Tocqueville was using his reflections on American democracy to suggest ways in which moribund public life in France might be awakened by invigorating public debate, local government, and the intermediate associations long distrusted in France as corrosive of national unity, so his portrait of democratic wives implicitly celebrated the newly religious, newly domestic elite women seeking a place for themselves in the July Monarchy. Like most other males of his generation on both sides of the Atlantic, Tocqueville cordoned off family life from public life and confined women to their own domain.[38]

Within the home women might reign supreme, and florid celebrations of women's achievements as mothers and homemakers flowed from the pens of nineteenth-century writers on both sides of the Atlantic. Yet the topic of women's rights remained strangely taboo in the England of Queen Victoria. Unlike the powerful women who ruled eighteenth-century monarchies, including Maria Theresa of Austria and Catherine the Great of Russia, Victoria defended and paradoxically even seemed to embody the ideal of female domesticity. Calls for woman suffrage in the United States ran afoul of the similar domestic ideal captured in Tocqueville's *Democracy*. In addition, Anglo-American reformers' rising commitments to eradicating slavery made achieving equal rights for women seem less urgent in the 1830s and 1840s. At least to men.

A growing number of women disagreed. Over the decades from the 1830s through the 1850s, their voices increased in volume as well as number. One of the first to emerge was Frances Wright, a wealthy Scottish-born woman who first visited the United States in 1818–20. She returned after spending three years in France as Lafayette's "adopted daughter," and during her second

American visit he arranged for her to meet both Jefferson and Madison. Initially thrilled by the evident success of American democracy, the Benthamite radical Wright had written *Views of Society and Manners in America* (1821) extolling the nation's virtues. Her return visit showed her the pervasiveness of slavery, "in the free winds of America odious beyond all that the imagination can conceive." Intrigued by Jefferson's plans for colonization, she used part of her inheritance to buy land in western Tennessee, where slaves might earn the money to purchase their freedom, then depart for Haiti or Africa. The experiment, called Nashoba, failed miserably, after which she tried to reorganize it as a utopian community. Despite its undeserved reputation as a haven of interracial harmony and "free love" between equal women and men liberated from marriage laws, Nashoba was soon abandoned.[39]

Two sisters, Sarah Grimké and Angelina Grimké, made less sensational but more lasting contributions to reform. They renounced the proslavery stance of their South Carolina family and embarked on a scandalous speaking tour in New England. For publicly challenging the biblical warrant on which many defenses of slavery rested, the Grimké sisters elicited outrage. Not only were they challenging God's authorization of slavery in the Bible; women had no business discussing politics in the male arena. Sarah Grimké issued a spirited reply to such criticism in her *Letters on the Equality of the Sexes and the Condition of Women, Addressed to Mary S. Parker, President of the Boston Female Anti-Slavery Society* (1838). Renewing arguments rooted in the Reformation and deploying them on behalf of women's rights, she declared it "the solemn duty of every individual to search the Scriptures for themselves, with the aid of the Holy Spirit, and not be governed by the views of any man, or set of men." From just such independent reading, Grimké wrote, she derived her conclusion that men and women "were both made in the image of God; dominion was given to both over every other creature, but not over each other."

By 1838 Grimké was already deploying the logic Lincoln later used against race slavery. Instead of men being destined to control women, the two sexes were "created in perfect equality." Their shared sin banished them from Eden "and consequently from happiness, *but not from equality*." To the contrary, their sinfulness produced no distinction between them as "moral, intellectual and responsible beings." Men had long exercised authority over women, who had succumbed to the temptation to consider marriage "the one thing needful." But a woman's obedience was destructive to her status as a moral being, and the doctrine that women should be dependent on men was "monstrous" and "anti-christian." Defying the assignment of rights to men and duties to women, Grimké insisted that "WHATSOEVER IT IS MORALLY RIGHT FOR A MAN TO DO, IT IS MORALLY RIGHT FOR

A WOMAN TO DO; and that confusion must exist in the moral world, until woman takes her stand on the same platform with man, and feels that she is clothed by her Maker with the *same rights*, and, of course, that upon her devolve the *same duties*." Achieving autonomy, or "self-rule," in Grimké's formulation, was a human goal, not a male goal. Women were not meant to be uncontrolled, or controlled by men, but to control themselves.

Self-government was God's plan for women as well as men. Grimké envisioned mutual obligations grounded on an ungendered ethic of reciprocity. The conventional means of cultivating that spirit, treating a woman "like a spoiled child" and encouraging "her selfishness and vanity" through ostentatious deference, demeaned rather than elevated her. Such ostensibly benevolent and courteous attention only reinforced women's inferior status. Instead, Grimké wrote, "I want my sex to claim nothing from their brethren but what their brethren may justly claim from them, in their intercourse as Christians. I am persuaded that woman can do much in this way to elevate her own character." Grimké electrified her readers by using language far more direct than American women—even those who had dared challenge male supremacy—had customarily directed against men. She asked no favors for women and refused to surrender their claims to equality. She wanted men only to "take their feet from off our necks, and permit us to stand upright on that ground which God designed us to occupy." Think of it, Grimké suggested, as an experiment: if God did not intend women to exercise their capacities and give them "the rights which have, as I conceive been wrested from us, we shall soon give evidence of our inferiority, and shrink back into that obscurity, which the high souled magnanimity of man has assigned us as our appropriate sphere."[40] As Olympe de Gouges, Mary Wollstonecraft, and Judith Sargent Murray had suggested in the 1790s, women should be able to test assumptions about their weakness, and democracy should provide the forum for that experiment.

Because expressing such views exposed women to ridicule as "manly," few of the women who might have embraced such ideas in private chose to go public. One who did was Margaret Fuller, whose life became in time a scandal almost as notorious as Wollstonecraft's. Fuller edited the Transcendentalist journal the *Dial*, wrote for Horace Greeley's *New York Tribune*, and spent her final years in Europe before she died in a shipwreck while returning to America in 1850. Fuller's ideas about politics are as difficult to characterize as those of her close friend Ralph Waldo Emerson. She resisted the enthusiasm some of her Transcendentalist friends expressed for the turn taken by the Massachusetts Democratic Party toward the Locofocos' economic radicalism in the aftermath of the 1837 depression. Orestes Brownson's articles in the *Boston Review* expressed the reasons for that enthusiasm, which came to be shared not only by other radicals such as Theodore Parker but eventually by Emerson himself. Given the Transcendentalists' deep commitment to individual self-culture and their romantic longing for transcendence of humdrum existence, however, everyday political activity struck them as intolerably constraining, the insistent demands of organizing and mobilizing a distraction from the deeper and richer life of the spirit. Even when they did embrace political action, it was often in the self-consciously hyperindividualist vein of Thoreau's "Resistance to Civil Government" or his later essay in praise of John Brown, in both of which Thoreau expressed at least as deep concern with his ability to keep his conscience clear as with effecting social change.

In *Woman in the Nineteenth Century*, Fuller articulated, more fully than she did elsewhere in her voluminous writings, her hopes for the ultimate consequences of women's rights. If every woman could cultivate her own mind and then—most likely through teaching, as Fuller herself did—help cultivate the minds of others, American women, and eventually American men, might reorient their lives away from the mindless busyness that consumed their energies. They might then concentrate on emancipating themselves to become the "God-centered" creatures they had the capacity to be. Although Fuller emphasized more than some of her contemporaries the "radical dualism" that divided women from men, she believed men as well as women could better fulfill their potential by escaping conventionally scripted gender roles. "Man can never be perfectly happy or virtuous, till all men are so," she wrote, and she meant by that dictum that "the growth of man is two-fold, masculine and feminine." Only when women were permitted to think, act, and choose for themselves, as men were able to do, would they really know what they need. They would be able to stretch toward that goal, deliberately left indefinite because at present not fully imaginable, only when they had achieved "self-reliance and self-impulse."[41]

Fuller did not join women's rights advocates who subordinated their cause to that of abolition. Instead she argued that women should educate themselves in order to participate in all aspects of public life. To that end she established and coordinated a series of "Conversations" among women in the Boston area, which met weekly from 1839 to 1844 and gave roughly thirty women a chance every Saturday to exercise their minds by discussing issues ranging from the ancient world to their own day. She conceived of her work on the *Dial*, then her work as a scholar of as well as traveler to the lands of several Indian peoples of the Midwest, and then her work as a foreign correspondent for the *Tribune*, in the same way: she was demonstrating concretely women's capacity to do precisely what most men doubted they could do. Because her book *Women in the Nineteenth Century* had been reprinted (without her approval) by an English publisher, Fuller was already well known in Europe by the time she crossed the Atlantic in 1846. Fuller encountered many notable writers and activists during her European travels, and her horizons widened with her accomplishments. When she arrived in Italy in 1848 she fell in love with the cause of Mazzini and Italian nationalism and also with Count Giovanni Angelo Ossoli, who embodied the multiple dimensions of the romantic ethos. Fuller had earlier characterized the highest form of love as "intellectual communion." By all accounts the rapturous love she shared with Ossoli ascended to that level as well as producing a baby boy, who died with them on the ship that ran aground sixty miles from New York and less than a hundred yards off the shore of Fire Island.

Like the other individuals often grouped together as Transcendentalists, Fuller expressed ambivalence about democracy. Her aspirations for humanity centered more on the untapped potential of the individual spirit. She worried, as did Emerson and Thoreau, that immersing oneself in a cause might lead to submerging rather than elevating the self. Inasmuch as the Transcendentalists envisioned individuals unshackled from tradition and hierarchy, their writings helped loosen the bonds of social constraint and contributed to the further development of an egalitarian sensibility. Inasmuch as many of them scorned conventional political action, however, they focused little of their attention on the public sphere. They believed that a culture could become fully democratic only after individuals had become fully self-reliant. For that reason emancipating individual sensibilities had to precede empowering citizens. Merely asking people as they were what they desired was pointless. Instead of following their impulses unreflectively, individuals had to learn to interrogate their desires critically.

Emerson himself was notoriously wary of politics, including in his disdain the political party that called itself the Democracy, because he believed that most people in politics never scratch beneath the surface of their lives. In "Man the Reformer," Emerson minimized the significance of institutions because only the individual matters. In the emerging world of market capitalism, the Transcendentalists saw at work only self-interested and shallow deal makers, not the ethic of reciprocity they thought might guide individuals aware of their deeper selves and attuned to their richer capacities. The Transcendentalists' analysis implicitly acknowledged what Tocqueville identified as the irony of Jacksonian America: by freeing individuals and empowering them to prosper economically, American champions of democracy inadvertently undermined both the ideal of autonomy, or "self-reliance," and the ethic of reciprocity. Emerson contended that by returning to a simpler life, by renouncing wealth and the obsessive materialism it encouraged, individuals might free themselves from the mundane. Only if the individual could transform himself or herself to become the "transparent eyeball" that Emerson envisioned in "Nature," thereby coming to understand the self's independence from the constraints of traditions and institutions, would it be possible for anyone to approach oneness with the world spirit.

Whereas Fuller herself developed into a radical enthusiast for the 1848 revolutions in Europe, some women reformers who opposed her revolutionary radicalism advanced women's rights by devoting themselves to other causes such as temperance, antiprostitution, and antislavery agitation. Many women, like men, who advocated moral reform thought that self-government meant not only democracy but also the government of self, the discipline of the self. That was the point of Horace Mann's Tenth Annual Report of the Secretary of the Massachusetts Board of Education (1846); of novels such as Catharine Sedgwick's *Home* (1841); and of advice manuals such as Lydia Maria Child's *The Mother's Book* (1831), Henry Ward Beecher's *Lectures to Young Men* (1833), and William Ellery Channing's *Self-Culture* (1844).[42]

Many of the early champions of women's rights clustered around the antislavery movement, but others focused explicitly on changing women's status before the law. Slowly, the demand for women's rights began to make itself heard. Women at Sarah Pierce's school in Litchfield, Connecticut, celebrating the Fourth of July in 1839, challenged Jefferson's Declaration. The differences between the Litchfield "Ladies Declaration of Independence" and the original aligned it more closely with de Gouges and Wollstonecraft than with Murray. The premise underlying the Litchfield Declaration, that men have "undervalued our talents, and disparaged our attainments," was not widely shared, however, by women or men outside the circles of radical reform, where abolitionists and advocates of women's rights clustered.[43]

If the women in the vanguard of the battle for woman suffrage were also abolitionists, the converse was hardly true. When women gathered in the first all-female public meeting in American history, the Anti-Slavery Convention of American Women of 1837, the speakers condemned not only slavery but also the "unnatural prejudice against our colored population" that undergirded it.[44] Lucretia Mott, an especially well-educated woman active in the antislavery movement, provided the spark that woman suffrage needed. In 1840 Mott, who had presided at the 1837 Anti-Slavery Convention, traveled to London with Elizabeth Cady Stanton, a young woman recently married to an abolitionist, to attend the World Anti-Slavery Conference. Mott, Stanton, and five other American women, all elected delegates, were refused entrance to the conference hall by the leaders of the British and Foreign Anti-Slavery Society. Consigned to nonvoting status as spectators, the women were made acutely aware of their unequal status—even among male reformers devoted to abolishing race-based slavery—by their exclusion from the London conference. Stanton and Mott met other women's rights advocates, notably Anne Knight, while in England, and they returned to the United States determined to forge a link between antislavery and the cause of women's rights. But cultural obstacles seemed insurmountable and family obligations intervened, so they were able to do little organizing until news of the European revolutions of 1848 fired their imaginations.[45]

Inspired by the model of 1848, Mott and Stanton, together with Martha C. Wright, Mary Ann McClintock, and Jane C. Hunt, organized a meeting in Seneca Falls, New York, on July 19–20, 1848, and drew up a "Declaration of Sentiments and Resolutions." Like the Litchfield Ladies Declaration of Independence and a similar manifesto drawn up by women in Jefferson County, New York, in 1846, the Seneca Falls Declaration began by proclaiming the "self-evident" truth that "all men and women are created equal," then detailed the "long train of abuses" by men against women. In the authors' words, "The history of mankind is a history of repeated injuries and usurpations on the part of man toward woman, having in direct object the establishment of an absolute tyranny over her." Although the litany of abuses was long, aspirations for a broader democracy held a central place in the Declaration. Despite Americans' professed devotion to the principle of popular sovereignty, only half the people legislated for the whole body. "He has made her, if married, in the eye of the law, civilly dead" and denied her the right to own property. Married women, like slaves, were not only disfranchised but also lacked equal standing before the law.

The women of Seneca Falls, like Grimké and Fuller, demanded a wider range of options from men who had "monopolized nearly all the profitable employments." They observed accurately that the work women were permitted to do earned them only "a scanty remuneration," which, if they were married, their husbands controlled. The Declaration of Sentiments complained that women were shut out from higher education, which was effectively true even though a few small colleges were already following the lead of Oberlin in embracing coeducation. The Seneca Falls Declaration concluded by addressing the question of autonomy: "He has endeavored, in every way that he could, to destroy her confidence in her own powers, to lessen her self-respect, and to make her willing to lead a dependent and abject life." As Grimké, Fuller, and the authors of the Connecticut and upstate New York manifestos had done, the Declaration of Sentiments zeroed in on the exclusion of women from public life and the enforced dependency that prevented women from achieving self-rule as individuals.

Perhaps for the first time at Seneca Falls, and certainly numerous times afterward, Stanton delivered a speech in which she yoked arguments from Wollstonecraft, de Gouges, and Judith Sargent Murray together with a ringing endorsement of the 1848 revolutions. She noted that women in the Christian countries of England, France, and the United States were degraded no less than in those cultures ranging from the Arab world to the German states. She scoffed at men's universal presumption that woman is an inferior being whom he has the right to control. Men flattered themselves as rational while demeaning women as "mere creatures of the affections," and she boldly disputed the common claim of men's superior physical strength. Given the opportunity to develop their capacities for thinking and acting, Stanton argued, women might show previously unexpected powers and abilities of all sorts.

Stanton's frequently delivered speech also made clear a dimension of her worldview that would later assume much greater significance, her nativism, and another that would vanish, her enthusiasm for revolution. Even if women failed to show the eloquence of a Webster, she insisted, they deserved the same right to vote as "the most ignorant Irishman in the ditch." It was past time to remedy these injustices, and the women on the barricades in France had shown the way earlier in 1848. Men would keep calling women "angels" to persuade them they were not suited for the tumult of public life, but women were now ready to reply. They did not need men's "care and protection—such as the wolf gives the lamb—such as the eagle the hare he carries to his eyrie." The rights men denied women, "rights which are dearer to him than life itself," and which, thanks to the 1848 revolutions, "have been baptized in blood," were worth the struggle women were now beginning to wage. Just as the popular insurgencies engulfing Europe were "rocking to their foundations the kingdoms of the Old World," so now American women were ready to fight for inclusion in American democracy.[46]

The most radical message of these declarations concerned women's confidence in their own abilities and their determination to establish their independence from men. The most contentious resolution debated at Seneca Falls, the call for woman suffrage, passed by only a narrow margin. All the other resolutions, like the Declaration itself, were adopted unanimously by the sixty-eight women and thirty-two men in attendance. Suffrage was controversial for three reasons. Some of those present judged it less significant than the other issues under consideration. Others judged it unnecessarily inflammatory and thus counterproductive. Still others judged it merely a means toward upending men's domination of women, simply a signal of their deeper aspirations to the autonomous status that went along with full citizenship.[47] These early American calls for women's rights had in common both confidence in women's capacity and an urgency about the role women could play in redeeming the promise of popular government. Although the Grimké sisters were born in the South, most of the early women's rights advocates in the United States were northern women who shared the conception of democracy identified with the "Conscience Whigs" who favored the expansion of education and opposed slavery and Indian removal, then with the "Free Soilers," and eventually with the Republicans who picked up the antislavery banner. Some upper-class women's rights advocates were distressed by the popular tone of the Jackson Party's appeal, others by its evident lack of concern with anything but the freedom of white men to do whatever they wanted with anyone or anything in their way. The early champions of women's rights, and especially of woman suffrage, were convinced that once women could vote, the quality of American public life would veer from simply facilitating the economic success of white males toward moral uplift of universal benefit.

Much as Lincoln challenged Douglas's claim that popular sovereignty was consistent with white supremacy, and advocates of women's rights challenged the justice of male supremacy, John Stuart Mill questioned an array of inherited privileges. One of his many books, *The Subjection of Women* (1861), which he sketched out with Harriet Taylor Mill before her death in 1858, elaborated the case for women's rights. Mill's earlier writings had established him as a moderate liberal reformer, a champion of education and a modest expansion of the franchise for those members of the working class qualified to vote responsibly. *The Subjection of Women* altered Mill's profile on both sides of the Atlantic. The *North American Review* lampooned the book's "air of hot vehemence" and chided its author for abandoning his characteristic "fairness," the secret of his persuasive power. Men were bound to reject Mill's call for women's independence, the reviewer wrote, because they wanted their wives to remain subservient.[48] Harriet Taylor Mill had already predicted that response in an essay of 1851, in which she wrote that the only reason "why each woman should be a mere appendage to a man" was that men like it that way.[49] Yet the detailed discussion in the *North American Review* ended on a surprising note. The book should be read "by every one who cares in the least degree for social questions"; it might even convert skeptics. Although tempted to dismiss Mill's commitment to "absolute equality, 'justice,' and personal independence" as merely a personal quirk, the reviewer concluded instead that the arguments of the "far-seeing" Mill for women's equality pointed toward the future "path of progress." Most males were sure to dismiss Mill and Taylor as wild-eyed radicals, yet he conceded that they might be recognized one day as pioneers.[50]

Mill had come a long way. One early women's rights tract, published in 1825, quoted a passage from an article his father, James Mill, had contributed to the 1824 edition of the *Encyclopedia Britannica*: "One thing is pretty clear, that all those individuals whose interests are indisputably included in those of other individuals," may be disregarded when considering who should enjoy political rights. Thus, like children whose interests their parents can be assumed to look after, the interests of women were safely covered by either their fathers or their husbands. The greatest good of the greatest number of humans, in short, could be attained by consulting considerably less than half of them.[51]

Harriet Taylor Mill and John Stuart Mill adopted a position distinct from his father's, but a half century after Wollstonecraft's *Vindication*, it was hardly new. Bentham had expressed sympathy with the cause of women's rights, and he was not alone. Harriet Taylor Mill had first articulated her arguments about women's rights in response to the Seneca Falls Convention, and her connections with the women's rights movements in the United States and France were part of a much wider Atlantic network that predated by decades the publication of *The Subjection of Women*. Growing from roots in abolitionism, religious reform, and socialism, the international women's rights movement worked to expand male reformers' conceptions of democracy. When the English Chartists, for example, congratulated themselves on their demand for "universal suffrage," Taylor scoffed that "half the race are excluded" from their conception of "universal."[52] Because none of these male-dominated reform movements, which fancied themselves progressive, even radical, paid serious attention to the women who did much of the work required to advance the causes they championed, by the late 1830s women reformers were losing patience with their male associates.[53]

Things were changing on both sides of the Atlantic. When Harriet Taylor's son traveled to the United States in the summer of 1851, he delivered a copy of her essay "The Enfranchisement of Women," originally published in the *Westminster Review* in July of 1851, to Lucretia Mott. The essay featured prominently in the second National Women's Rights Convention, held in Worcester, Massachusetts, in October of that year. Those in Worcester also heard a translated letter written in solidarity by two French radicals, Jeanne Deroin and Pauline Roland, who had been imprisoned in Paris for participating in the 1848 Revolution. The attention paid in Worcester to "The Enfranchisement of Women" and the letter from Deroin and Roland was appropriate. Both Harriet Taylor Mill and her husband, along with other socialists interested in women's rights such as Deroin and Roland, had been inspired by the women of Seneca Falls. In a letter to his future wife, Mill had applauded the American Declaration for its boldness: it contained "not the least iota of compromise." He compared its tone to their own: "It is almost like ourselves speaking—outspoken like America, not frightened & servile like England." The American women had proclaimed the principle of women's equality and embraced its consequences, by which Mill meant the opprobrium they faced at the high tide of Victorian domesticity.[54]

A not untypical response to demands for women's rights, printed in the *New York Herald* after the Third National Women's Rights Convention in Syracuse in 1852, characterized the proceedings as a "farce." Dominated by shrill "old maids" and others slighted by men, the gathering showed that such vain and "mannish" women, who pathetically considered themselves superior to men in intellectual capacity, threatened the stability of society. Just as earlier generations had condemned the writings of Wollstonecraft and de Gouges because of their association with the discredited radicalism of the French Revolution, so at the height of Victorian domesticity it was easy to dismiss the clamor for women's rights as a species of revolutionary fervor that had to be resisted lest anarchy follow.[55]

Early women's rights advocates expressed their democratic sensibilities in various keys. Many renounced the paternalism and hierarchy of mainstream religious denominations, which had tended to become increasingly conservative in the decades after 1815. Some champions of women's rights adopted versions of socialism associated with Robert Owen, Charles Fourier, or Henri de Saint-Simon. By renouncing religious orthodoxy or embracing utopian socialism, many of those affiliated with the women's rights movement in its early years invited almost automatic accusations of harboring revolutionary sentiments. Nor were such charges altogether inaccurate. When the revolutions of 1848 broke out across Europe, women's rights advocates participated actively and visibly. In Paris Jeanne Deroin wrote for the feminist newspapers *La Voix des Femmes* and *L'Opinion des Femmes*, then ran for the legislature in the spring of 1849. Even some of the most radical voices in the revolutionary movement were aghast. Deroin's riposte to the comment of Pierre-Joseph Proudhon, who had objected that women cannot be legislators for the same reason men cannot be wet nurses, deserves its classic status: "Now we know what organ is needed to be a legislator."[56]

The revolutions of 1848 sparked publication of various radical newspapers throughout Europe and in the United States, including several explicitly focused on women's rights. The euphoria prompted by the revolutions faded as quickly as they did; the repression that followed them was more enduring. After the restoration of conservative regimes in France and the Italian and German states, socialist parties were outlawed and women were forbidden to attend political meetings. Some, including Deroin, spent time in jail; others, including Roland, died there. Still others emigrated. Deroin went to London, others to the United States. With the fledgling organizations and newspapers that sustained their activity extinguished in the postrevolutionary wave of reaction that swept across Europe, women's rights advocates went underground. Although they continued to correspond and worked to keep the cause alive, they experienced little visible success for the half century between 1860 and World War I.[57]

Their arguments, though, like those of Wollstonecraft and de Gouges before them, had established the terms on which later feminists would continue to struggle for equal rights and inclusion in political life. Mill's *The Subjection of Women*, which stated the case for expanding the framework of democracy to include women, amplified arguments advanced in Taylor's earlier "The Enfranchisement of Women." In her widely reprinted article, among the texts most frequently discussed by reformers on both sides of the Atlantic, Taylor portrayed the women's movement as a natural extension of the democracy she associated with the United States. She concluded her essay by forecasting that "the example of America will be followed on this side of the Atlantic." From its origins, the women's rights movement was an international phenomenon.[58]

Because there is no reason to doubt Mill's claim to his wife's effective coauthorship, *The Subjection of Women* should be considered Taylor and Mill's book. The book opens with Taylor and Mill challenging, in terms familiar from the late-eighteenth-century writings of women's rights advocates, the common opinion concerning women's unequal capacity. That judgment Taylor and Mill described as a mere emotion, an "instinct" located in the realm of irrational prejudice, deep beneath the level of rational argument. For that reason it was hard to defend but difficult to dislodge. Although reading the Romantics had enabled Mill to recover from his own psychic collapse, *The Subjection of Women* identified the nineteenth century's trust in nonrational "instinct" as one of the worst features of contemporaries' reaction against Enlightenment rationalism. Disentangling judgments of the progressive, productive potential of the emotions from critiques of the destructive power of irrationality is as challenging in the historical analysis of romanticism as separating Enlightenment thinkers' celebration of reason from their irrational distrust of rational religion.[59]

Women's inequality, according to Mill and Taylor, rested on a single foundation: force. "From the very earliest twilight of human society," men had used physical power to enslave women. All other forms of slavery in Europe had been abolished. It was past time to abolish the slavery of women. The law of force had endured through most of human history. Only the Stoics in the ancient world, then the early Christians, had dared to challenge it. Only in recent centuries had the law begun to protect the weak against the strong. Taylor and Mill admitted that all forms of domination, like all customs, appear natural when in place and taken for granted. Their barbarity becomes apparent only when they have been challenged and dislodged. Slavery they identified as a case in point: Europe rejected it, but in the American South it remained customary and thus seemed natural. Likewise women's subjection, Taylor and Mill reasoned, might seem a natural condition, but in time its barbarity too was bound to become equally apparent.[60]

Women had expressed objections to their condition for at least as long as they had been able to write, Taylor and Mill observed, and women's rights organizations were developing in the United States, France, Italy, Switzerland, and Russia to amplify those objections. Everywhere and forever men tried to get women not only to obey but also to submit willingly to men's authority. That, Taylor and Mill insisted, was precisely what women were now refusing to do. The distinctive feature of modernity, they argued, was the end of ascribed status at birth; only women, slaves, and royalty still could not determine their own course of life. Taylor and Mill contended that the environmentalism of the eighteenth century was on target. What was called the "nature of women" was "an eminently artificial thing." Although subjugation remained the rule, it should not be elevated into a norm or naturalized as inevitable.[61]

Despite women's ostensibly privileged position within the family, Taylor and Mill courted controversy by arguing that women were caught in an even worse predicament than slaves. Whereas slaves had their own quarters and controlled at least some of their own time, women could not legally resist their masters in "the last familiarity" of sexual intercourse. Most marriages might escape such cruelty; otherwise life for women would be hellish. Yet Taylor and Mill contended, offering a variant of Jefferson's argument about the effects of slavery, that the structure of relations between husband and wife defiles the love that should flourish in marriage. Power was "the nursery of these vices of character." Neither men nor women were well served by the sensibilities of autocracy on the one hand and self-abnegation on the other. "Command and obedience are but unfortunate necessities of human life," Taylor and Mill declared. "Society in equality is its normal state." Given the authors' categorical denial that woman's nature could be identified based on experience with women in their current condition, this equally categorical assertion of equality between the sexes as "normal" is jarring.[62]

Instead of backing down, Taylor and Mill extended their claim. It was past time for "the morality of justice," by which they meant equality between women and men, to be established. All of modern history consisted of the slow and steady "wearing away" of distinctions separating citizens by rank or by birth. After the distinctions taken for granted in the ancient world, which prevented anyone but free male citizens from being considered equal to each other, were challenged by early Christian communities, it had become possible to imagine a fuller equality among human beings. Although nineteenth-century critics of Christianity typically blamed religion for women's subjugation, Taylor and Mill offered the Christian ethic as the solution rather than the source of the problem. The ethic of love and mutual respect, if internalized by men and women, would heal the afflicted relation between the sexes. The future, they predicted, held out the promise of democracy because it would provide equal autonomy for all persons in a society governed by an ethic of reciprocity. All women and men would regard command of any sort as a temporary expedient and prefer "the society of those with whom leading and following can be alternate and reciprocal."[63]

Taylor and Mill addressed—and dismissed—the standard objections to women's equality. "The law of servitude in marriage" contradicted all modern principles of law and society and was the only legal form of bondage left in Britain. "There remain no legal slaves, except the mistress of every house." Equality in marriage would enable a deeper intimacy, a union built on the foundation of shared responsibilities rather than command and obedience.[64] The emancipation of women would culminate in the full development of human capacity, under the conditions of individual self-command and collective self-government, when women were able to join men as citizens in a democracy. Writers since Herodotus had praised the "ennobling influence of free government." With the inclusion of women, that influence would finally extend beyond the minority of free male citizens to include every adult. Participation in civic life, Taylor and Mill argued, echoing Tocqueville's treatment of the ethic of reciprocity that he saw operating in New England local government, "elevates the individual as a moral, spiritual, and social being." Mill and Taylor envisioned sexual equality as the means enabling individuals to attain happiness under conditions of social justice.[65] Mill is often lionized as a liberal who considered individual freedom the highest value and criticized as an elitist who opposed popular government. He was neither.

Mill participated much more actively in public debates, and consequently his work was much more widely read, after Harriet died in 1858. Having retired from his position with the East India Company and having lost his closest companion, he threw himself into controversies on behalf of the principles that he and Taylor cared most about, equality and democracy. In *The Subjection of Women* they addressed the domination of women by men, and despite hyperbolic criticism the first two editions sold out within months. The two other topics that animated Mill's major writings in the last fifteen years before his death in 1873 were the tyranny of the majority and class domination, which he considered the two deepest dangers to democracy.

First came the analysis of autonomy in his classic meditation *On Liberty* (1859). Against the threat of conformity that Tocqueville had identified, Mill urged individuals to safeguard personal freedom and counseled resisting government intrusion and regulation of thought and behavior except in extreme cases. In his *Considerations on Representative Government* (1861), a book that shows even more fully his concern with democratic despotism, Mill advocated universal suffrage, proportional representation, and plural voting to amplify the voices of the educated segments of British society. He called for open voting, rather than the secret ballot, for a reason that seems incomprehensible to many twenty-first-century commentators. His argument indicates the distance between the view of democracy that Mill shared with Tocqueville and Lincoln and the view that has become common in our own day. Like Montesquieu in *The Spirit of the Laws*, Mill wanted public voting so individuals might be ashamed to vote their own self-interest instead of choosing the common good. His belief in the luminous clarity of the public interest and his lack of concern with the potential intimidation of voters, both of which seem surprising, illustrate Mill's faith in the capacity as well as the self-confidence of an educated electorate. Given proper cultivation and the internalizing of the appropriate norms of self-government, Mill believed, voters could rise to the level of public-spiritedness that Tocqueville associated with the New England town, a quality threatened by the tyranny of the majority. In his *Autobiography*, Mill explained that he aimed in *Representative Government* to solve the problem set by Bentham's work: "the combination of complete popular control over public affairs with the greatest attainable perfection of skilled agency."[66]

These qualifications of Mill's earlier commitment to "pure democracy" reflected his Tocqueville-inspired concern that the "commercial society" of his day was driving individuals further away from the vaunted civic virtue of ancient republics and headlong toward a dog-eat-dog competition from which only education could redeem them. From Mill's perspective, as from Sparks's and Tocqueville's, voting was but a piece of the democratic puzzle. Of much greater significance were the social and cultural practices that either predisposed people to concern themselves with public life or encouraged them to narrow their conception of "interest" from "self-interest properly understood" to a shallower obsession with their short-term economic well-being. Creating a more vibrant civic life mattered because only religion mattered more than the form of government in making people what they are and enabling them to fulfill their potential.[67] That conviction was shared by Sparks, John Quincy Adams, Tocqueville, and other like-minded reformers troubled by the rise and legitimation of unvarnished egoism.

Despite these significant qualifications, Mill nevertheless vigorously defended democracy as the best form of government. His reasons are striking, particularly in the context of Tocqueville's writings. In the "ordinary life" of most people, Mill observed, there is little "to give any largeness either to their conceptions or to their sentiments." Their jobs are merely routine exercises in self-interest, in which neither what is done nor the process of doing it provides any escape from selfish concerns. Only participation in the civic sphere frees individuals from such confinement. There citizens must weigh competing claims by other standards than their own "private partialities" and apply instead the maxim of the common good. Without such experiences the individual, isolated from the rest of society, "never thinks of any collective interest."

Mill aimed toward the fullest possible development of the moral potential of all individuals, characterized in *On Liberty* as the "permanent interests of man as a progressive being," which he considered possible only in democracy. "The only government which can fully satisfy all the exigencies of the social state," he wrote, "is one in which the whole people participate." Any limitations on suffrage or other participation should be temporary, persisting only until education becomes universal. From that point on, citizens should participate not only by voting and serving on juries but also in "the details of judicial and administrative business." The goal, in Mill's words, should be the most free and transparent discussion possible, so that not only elected officials but the entire public shares in the instruction to be derived from active engagement with civic life.[68]

By the mid-1860s Mill had repudiated the mechanisms for limiting participation to the educated and become an advocate of democratic reforms. Even though he refused to campaign for office, he was elected to Parliament, as Leslie Stephen put it, strictly on his reputation. As an MP from 1866 to 1868, he spoke in favor of the Reform Bill and introduced a woman suffrage amendment, which failed but, to his surprise, attracted more than seventy votes. He was involved with a variety of other causes as well as women's rights, including the abolition of slavery in the United States and what came to be called economic democracy or democratic socialism. In the last years of his life, Mill championed a national system of education such as that advocated by

Sparks and Tocqueville, who identified it as the foundation of republican institutions. Mill also "looked forward to a time when society will no longer be divided into the idle and the industrious; when the rule that they who do not work shall not eat, will be applied not to paupers only, but impartially to all." That formula expressed for Mill the ethic of reciprocity underlying democracy. Or as Mill put it, he looked forward to the day when wealth would be distributed according to considerations of justice rather than accidents of birth.[69] Extending the principles of autonomy and mutuality from politics to society, however, like extending them from men to women, would require an ethical and cultural adjustment as much as legal or institutional reforms.

Mill elaborated on that transformation in *Utilitarianism* (1863), which shows the distance he had traveled from the philosophy of his father and Bentham and how much he had learned to value sympathy. He discarded their premise of hedonism and contended that the highest human happiness comes from cultivating moral excellence, by which he meant internalizing duty and contributing to the common good by "regard to the pleasures and pains of others." Champions of laissez-faire had prevented the state from fulfilling its moral obligations, which could be addressed by taking on land reform, taxing unearned income, securing women's rights, and attacking many other social ills.[70] An adequate social ethics, neither sacrificing the individual to the whole nor vice versa, would derive its force from "sympathy and benevolence and the passion for ideal excellence." For those not up to that exalted standard, a version of Adam Smith's impartial spectator, "the approbation" of those "whom we admire and venerate," should suffice to generate the sympathy Mill thought necessary to address evil and injustice.[71]

Mill agreed with Lincoln that the most egregious injustice of his day was American slavery, but Tocqueville was more ambivalent. In 1843 Tocqueville wrote a series of articles on abolition. He pointed out that slavery contradicted the universalist claims of the French Revolution concerning the Rights of Man. He also expressed anxiety that the pattern of the Haitian Revolution might repeat itself: former slaves from Britain's colonies might forcibly emancipate French slaves before they could be set free without violence. Debates over slavery continued ineffectually in France until 1848, when governments in the French Caribbean islands, faced with the imminent threat of slave revolts precipitated by the uprising of February 22–24, unilaterally freed their slaves. As he did in the reports he filed on Algeria when the situation had already spiraled downward, Tocqueville penned a powerful critique of slavery—after emancipation was accomplished. In 1855, in a letter published only after Tocqueville's death by the American Anti-Slavery Society in

Letters on American Slavery, he complained that slavery "pained and astonished" him and expressed his hope that it would end in America too one day. But his anguish, like Jefferson's in *Notes on the State of Virginia*, rings hollow in comparison with many of Tocqueville's contemporaries, who were calling not just for someone, somewhere, someday, to do something to end slavery but demanding its immediate abolition.[72]

The contrast with Mill is striking. Although Mill shared Tocqueville's sense that values change over time and his awareness that dogmas are vulnerable to change once their foundations are exposed to scrutiny, Mill felt no hesitancy concerning slavery.[73] He was aghast that the government of Britain toyed with recognizing the Confederacy when the onset of war threatened the cotton supplied by the American South for British mills. In his *Autobiography*, Mill noted that only the working classes and a few "literary and scientific men" resisted the "general frenzy" of "pro-Southern partisanship." He found the spectacle demoralizing: it showed how little "the minds of our influential classes" had changed. Mill considered the war "a turning point, for good or evil, of the course of human affairs." He had decided, as had Lincoln and many others, that the developments of the 1840s and 1850s should be understood as slaveholders' deliberate campaign to extend their domain, an ambition Mill traced to their "pecuniary interest, domineering temper, and the fanaticism of a class for its class privileges."

Mill wrote two articles about the United States Civil War, the first protesting the tendency among the British middle and upper classes to portray the war as a squabble over tariffs or, even worse, as a noble struggle for southern independence, rather than seeing it for what it was: a war over the survival of slavery. Were the South to succeed, Mill wrote, that "victory of the powers of evil" would discourage the friends of democracy and fortify "the enemies of progress" everywhere, especially among the aristocracies of Europe. Mill hoped that the shock of southern secession would inspire the Union to end slavery. He praised the radicals whom most English commentators loathed, including Garrison, the "courageous and single-minded apostle" of abolition, and Wendell Phillips, himself an admirer of Mill's *Representative Government*. Mill wanted his countrymen to continue the struggle that abolished slavery in the British Empire and regretted that his own generation did not feel as strongly as their fathers "the enormities of slavery."[74]

Lincoln's criticism of those "enormities," although it cost him the Senate election in 1858, aroused sufficient support in the North to earn him the Republican Party nomination and election to the presidency in 1860. His views also aroused the hatred of southerners, who discounted Lincoln's promises not to touch slavery in the southern states and voted to secede after his election. Lincoln's debates with Douglas had received national attention, but his speeches during the 1860 campaign made even clearer his opposition to slavery and his determination to prevent its expansion. He insisted that the founding generation had agreed only to tolerate slavery where it was already established; attempts to expand it were unwarranted. Yet Lincoln explicitly rejected the call for immediate abolition: "Wrong as we think slavery is," he declared in his Cooper Union address of February 27, 1860, "we can yet afford to let it alone where it is, because that much is due to the necessity arising from its actual presence in the nation."[75]

Lincoln was quick to repudiate John Brown's raid, which was, except for slave revolts, the most radical and dramatic assault on slavery before the Civil War. Other responses were less moderate. Mill compared "the voluntary martyr" Brown to Sir Thomas More, a "true hero" of an earlier day. Henry David Thoreau called Brown "a superior man," an "angel of light" who refused to be bound by unjust laws. The future governor of Massachusetts John Andrew declared emphatically that whether the attack was right or wrong, "John Brown himself is right." Frederick Douglass, a friend of Brown's, quoted Andrew's judgment approvingly. Brown's raid, which according to Douglass touched off the war, had to be seen in historical context: "The bloody harvest of Harper's Ferry was ripened by the heat and moisture of merciless bondage of more than two hundred years." Wendell Phillips, who delivered the eulogy at Brown's funeral, claimed that Democrats as well as Republicans in Massachusetts were sorry Brown did not succeed and expressed "sympathy with the attempt." Whether or not Brown started the war, southerners saw in such responses a harbinger of the inevitable.[76]

Measuring his words carefully, Lincoln explained that even moderate Republicans could not allow slavery to expand because it threatened the doctrines of individual autonomy and free labor on which the nation was built. His vision resembled Jefferson's and Madison's as well as that of Whigs such as Henry Clay: most men in the United States, Lincoln contended, start out working for someone else, then gradually save enough money to buy their own tools and work for themselves. Eventually they end up possessing their own tools, their own land, and their own home. A nation founded on those expectations could not allow slavery to expand, because it would undermine the nobility of free labor and transform a nation of self-directed farmers, artisans, and shopkeepers who worked for a living into a nation of listless dependents and the lazy drones who owned them. Although impatient abolitionists and Brown's admirers rebuked Lincoln for refusing to tackle slavery in the South, southerners saw in the logic of his arguments only the promise of slavery's eventual extinction.[77]

Lincoln tried hard to allay southerners' anxieties. In his First Inaugural Address, he quoted one of his campaign speeches and reinforced its message: "I declare that 'I have no purpose, directly or indirectly, to interfere with the institution of slavery in the states where it exists. I believe I have no lawful right to do so, and I have no inclination to do so.'" So the South had nothing to fear. The Republican Party platform, Lincoln noted, reiterated that pledge. But Lincoln resolutely rejected the right of secession. "I hold, that in contemplation of universal law, and of the Constitution, the Union of these States is perpetual." The Union, he argued, was even older than the Constitution, and he denied that any state could choose to leave it. Any "acts of violence, within any State or States, against the authority of the United States, are insurrectionary or revolutionary." Lincoln vowed to take the steps necessary to preserve the Union and tackled the question of majority rule and minority rights. If a minority, when it loses a dispute or an election, "will secede rather than acquiesce, they make a precedent which, in turn, will divide and ruin them; for a minority of their own will secede from them, whenever a majority refuses to be controlled by such minority." A democratic majority, restrained by law and subject to change with every election, is "the only true sovereign of a free people." Because unanimity is impossible in politics, those who reject majority rule "fly to anarchy or to despotism."[78]

Lincoln wanted the nation to continue debating slavery. As the laws had developed in response to changing beliefs, so those laws had been enforced, including the suppression of the slave trade, on the one hand, and the fugitive slave law, on the other. A year earlier, Lincoln had distilled the essence of the ethic of reciprocity: "The inclination to exchange thoughts with one another is probably an original impulse of our nature. If I be in pain I wish to let you know it, and to ask your sympathy and assistance; and my pleasurable emotions also, I wish to communicate to, and share with you." Such communication, God's gift to mankind, enables individuals to exchange ideas. By combining their "powers of observation and reflection," they advanced knowledge and reached a result that "neither *alone* would have arrived at."[79] Lincoln never relinquished the belief that a common good lay beyond the contending arguments even on issues as contentious as slavery. Whereas many Americans in his day considered, as they do in ours, partisan struggles for power the only way in which people with different interests can advance their cause, Lincoln embraced the view of thinkers ranging from the founders of New England towns and the Levellers through Rousseau and Madison to Tocqueville and Mill. He believed that debates in a democracy help individuals learn how to see what lies beyond their narrow self-interest.[80]

Lincoln's conception of communication as the fundamental fact of democracy informed his approach to slavery in his First Inaugural. He implored the South not to give up on the national conversation and turn to war. Some southerners had proposed amending the Constitution to stipulate that the federal government could never interfere with the institutions of individual states. Lincoln promised that he would abide by that amendment if it were adopted. Why, he asked, did the South now want to abandon the proper means of securing the changes it desired? "Why should there not be a patient confidence in the ultimate justice of the people? Is there any better, or equal hope, in the world? In our present differences, is either party without faith of being in the right?"

Lincoln, unlike Douglas, did not think any majority ruling on any issue was necessarily the voice of God, but he expressed confidence that the wisdom of the nation as a whole would, in time, guide it to a just resolution of the slavery question. The same principle that enabled voters to choose different representatives, Lincoln reminded the South, would give voters a chance to render a verdict on Lincoln himself. "While the people retain their virtue, and vigilance," no presidential administration could do much damage in just four years. Southerners who felt threatened by Lincoln's election should resist the temptation to act rashly. "Intelligence, patriotism, Christianity, and a firm reliance on Him, who has never yet forsaken this favored land, are still competent to adjust, in the best way, all our present difficulty." Lincoln's own religious faith was unconventional. He expressed misgivings about mainstream Protestantism and the evangelical denominations springing up during his lifetime. The trust he expressed in divine providence, however, is unmistakable.[81]

Lincoln admitted that he was reluctant to end his inaugural address. He was apprehensive about what would happen next. His unforgettable concluding words expressed his conviction—and his hope—that the continuing battle to persuade would not give way to warfare. "We are not enemies, but friends. We must not be enemies. Though passion may have strained, it must not break our bonds of affection. The mystic chords of memory, stretching from every battle-field, and patriot grave, to every living heart and hearthstone, all over this broad land, will yet swell the chorus of the Union, when again touched, as surely they will be, by the better angels of our nature."[82] Lincoln knew he was restating the plea of Jefferson's First Inaugural, and he prayed southerners would take heed as northerners had done in 1800.

Of course, the South did not agree. Southerners knew that Lincoln had inherited a tradition of active government from John Quincy Adams, Henry Clay, and Daniel Webster, which authorized using the power of the federal government to regulate state laws concerning political, economic, and social practices. Ending slavery, they feared, was merely the next step. Whereas many southerners in the 1840s and 1850s, and many Americans in later decades, pretended that the authentic American tradition is localist and that authentic Americans always resist federal authority, the historical record shows that active use of federal as well as state and local government was a persistent feature of United States history from the late 1780s, and through the presidencies of Jefferson and Jackson, to Lincoln and the Civil War.[83]

The firing on Fort Sumter ignited a war that began very badly for the Union, and grumbling about the wisdom and viability of fighting the Confederacy started right away. Should not the Union merely let the straying states go? If slavery had soiled the nation, would not secession purify American democracy rather than undermine it? On July 4, 1861, Lincoln delivered a message to Congress, meeting in special session, to explain why the war must be fought. Not merely the fate of the nation but a much deeper question, the viability of democracy, was at stake. The secession crisis "presents to the whole family of man, the question, whether a constitutional republic, or a democracy—a government of the people, by the same people—can, or cannot, maintain its territorial integrity, against its own domestic foes." The question was whether a minority, too small to win an election, could legitimately dissolve the government by withdrawing from it. If so, that would "practically put an end to free government upon the earth." The South's decision forced Americans to ask themselves whether any republic must necessarily "be too *strong* for the liberties of its own people, or too *weak* to maintain its own existence?"

Could Lincoln maintain control against those who wanted to see the Union fail, and who were willing to risk violence to attain their ends? He acknowledged that suspending the writ of habeas corpus inflamed northern critics and signaled desperation to the Confederacy. He admitted that raising an army constituting 10 percent of the northern male population, and shouldering a massive debt to pay for it, raised objections among those who elected him. But he saw no alternative. As commander in chief he aimed to defend democracy, to maintain "in the world, that form, and substance of government, whose leading object is, to elevate the condition of man—to lift artificial weights from all shoulders—to clear the paths of laudable pursuit for all—to afford all, an unfettered start, and a fair chance, in the race of life." Keeping that government alive meant to Lincoln, as it had meant to Robespierre when he faced the combined threat of counterrevolution within France and the massed armies of monarchies at its borders, prosecuting the war with all the resources his government could muster. Union victory, Lincoln concluded, would vindicate one of democracy's central premises:

what cannot be won by elections cannot be taken by arms. To that end, Lincoln asked Congress to authorize waging war against the insurrection. "And having thus chosen our course, without guile, and with pure purpose, let us renew our trust in God, and go forward without fear."[84]

For Union forces, the war went from bad to worse. Lincoln found himself besieged on all sides. As southern armies threatened to encircle the nation's capital, abolitionists assailed Lincoln for refusing to free the slaves in the border states and liberate all who joined the Union army. His advisers urged caution, warning him that such steps would weaken the cause by antagonizing slave-owning Union sympathizers in the border states. Lincoln agonized over emancipation. He counseled a delegation of free blacks to pursue colonization in Central America rather than expect equality in the United States.[85] He admitted in a letter to Horace Greeley that his goal was to save the Union; he would end slavery or let it survive if either course would effect that end. To Lincoln's critics, then and now, such calculations reveal the contemptible absence of any genuine commitment to abolition.[86]

Lincoln's options narrowed as Union armies continued to struggle. Now that the tide was turning against the Union, some of his advisers urged desperate measures. Robespierre had turned to terror and all-out war; Lincoln had an alternative. After the Union army finally won a decisive, and deadly, battle at Antietam, Lincoln at last issued the Emancipation Proclamation, on September 22, 1862, at a stroke freeing the slaves and altering the war's significance. Many abolitionists and other antislavery activists, ambivalent about fighting to save the Union, could now wholeheartedly support the war.[87] Britain decided not to recognize the Confederacy. And black troops, although they would face immediate execution if captured, formed regiments (including the Massachusetts 54th authorized by Governor John Andrew) to fight for the Union. The *levée en masse* had fueled the resurgence of the armies of the French Republic; the Terror had momentarily stilled the voices of many vocal foes of the Revolution. By issuing the Emancipation Proclamation, Lincoln sought to redefine the struggle against the South and bolster the resources of the army. He risked antagonizing northerners whose racism made them indifferent to the fate of slavery, but he enlisted the enthusiastic support of those for whom the military struggle now assumed sacred status.[88]

Battlefield victories transformed the mood of the northern states as decisively as did the Emancipation Proclamation. Early projections of defeat in 1864, both of Lincoln in his campaign for reelection and of Union armies against those of the Confederacy, began to look less certain after Union triumphs—albeit at immense cost—in the battles of Vicksburg, Gettysburg, and Lookout Mountain. At Gettysburg, in contrast to Edward Everett, who preceded him on the podium and delivered a ringing denunciation of the Confederacy that lasted over two hours, Lincoln refused to condemn the enemy. Instead he introduced the themes that decisively differentiated his strategy during the war from that of Robespierre. Still facing an uncertain outcome, Lincoln at Gettysburg did not malign the Confederacy but spoke of sacrifice, dedication, humility, and the possibility of transcendence. His Gettysburg Address has been interpreted as transforming America by making equality a value in a nation previously committed to the ideals of freedom and individualism. Its significance lay instead in Lincoln's decision to frame the Union's sacrifices in relation to its citizens' commitment to democracy. One need not read beyond the writings of John Adams, Jefferson, Madison, or Tocqueville to know that equality had long enjoyed equal status with freedom as an American ideal. It was not up to Lincoln to remind his listeners that the Declaration of Independence declared all men born equal. The "unfinished work" of restoring the Union, Lincoln resolved, would continue so that "this nation, under God, shall have a new birth of freedom—and that government of the people, by the people, for the people, shall not perish from the earth." The Civil War, at least as Lincoln saw it, was fought above all to fulfill the promise of American democracy. That meant, among many other things, that the South would not be treated as a vanquished enemy but welcomed back to the Union when peace was restored.[89]

Lincoln understood the emptiness of rights talk in the absence of equality. The thrust of his free-labor ideology centered on securing equal opportunities for all individuals. It was the denial of that principle for slaves that gnawed at him even though he persisted in thinking blacks inferior to whites. In the spring of 1864, he addressed a crowd in Baltimore and ruminated on the meaning of freedom. "We all declare for liberty, but in using the same *word* we do not all mean the same *thing*. With some the word liberty may mean for each man to do as he pleases with himself, and the product of his labor; while with others the same word may mean for some men to do as they please with other men, and the product of other men's labor." These meanings, Lincoln noted wryly, are "not only different, but incompatible," and their champions call them by "two different and incompatible names—liberty and tyranny."

Lincoln spun a yarn to make his point. "The shepherd drives the wolf from the sheep's throat, for which the sheep thanks the shepherd as a *liberator*, while the wolf denounces him for the same act as the destroyer of liberty, especially as the sheep was a black one." Just as the sheep and the wolf saw things differently, "precisely the same difference prevails to-day among us human creatures, even in the North, and all professing to love liberty."

Former slave states such as Maryland, Lincoln said, were undergoing dramatic transformation: thousands were being freed from bondage, a transformation some welcomed as the triumph of liberty and others mourned as its destruction. The metamorphosis was cultural as well as legal. The people of Maryland were repudiating "the wolf's dictionary." By precisely locating the distinct meanings of freedom within or outside conditions of equality, Lincoln was restating the premises of American democracy, applying to slave owners the same logic that eighteenth-century Americans applied to the landed aristocracy.[90]

Lincoln's reelection in 1864 and the Union's shifting fortunes on the battlefield vindicated his strategy. As the months wore on and the bodies piled up, Lincoln resisted any temptation he might have felt to gloat—or to wield the sword of righteousness against his enemies. Instead his mood darkened. He turned increasingly somber. Instead of taking credit for having made wise decisions, he invoked God's will. More than once he conceded that the war's outcome was out of his hands. "I claim not to have controlled events, but confess plainly that events have controlled me." In contrast to Robespierre, whose sense of his own significance and identification of his fate with that of the French Revolution only increased over time, Lincoln grew increasingly humble as the pain of war grew worse.[91]

Lincoln delivered his Second Inaugural Address, surely the most eloquent statement of democratic principles in the American record, in the spring of 1865, as Union armies tightened the noose around Confederate forces and the war rolled toward its climax. Lincoln's second inaugural demonstrates the gulf between his chastened sensibility and Robespierre's. Whereas the public expected a lengthy address celebrating the Union triumph and laying out Lincoln's plans to restore the authority of the national government in the South during the postwar period, he offered instead a brief meditation on the causes and consequences of the war.

The words of Lincoln sing. He began by conceding that his First Inaugural came as Americans were anxiously awaiting war. "All dreaded it—all sought to avert it." But while most worked to prevent it, some maneuvered to make it happen. "Both parties deprecated war; but one of them would *make* war rather than let the nation survive; and the other would *accept* war rather than let it perish. And the war came." That simple sentence, with its absent subject and its flat affect, achieves its power by evacuating blame for the tragedies that ensued. Instead of conjuring up villains or scapegoats, Lincoln was looking toward reconciliation. He acknowledged directly the fundamental fact that generations of Americans have tried unsuccessfully to dispute or deny. The Civil War was fought over the issue of slavery. "One eighth of the whole population were colored slaves, not distributed generally over the Union, but localised in the Southern part of it. The slaves constituted a peculiar and powerful interest. All knew that this interest was, somehow, the cause of the war." Despite all the ingenuity and obfuscation that have been devoted to pretending otherwise, Lincoln had it right. Slavery caused the Civil War, and Americans at the time knew it did. Yet Lincoln resisted the urge to bask in the knowledge that he had unleashed the forces of light to defeat the forces of darkness.

The Confederacy had proved willing to destroy the nation to preserve slavery. The federal government, Lincoln's government, claimed only the right to prevent its territorial expansion. No one on either side, Lincoln recalled with chilling accuracy, "expected for the war, the magnitude, or the duration, which it has already attained." Moreover, Lincoln himself was as surprised as anyone else by what the war had accomplished. Neither side expected that "the *cause* of the conflict," slavery, "might cease with, or even before" the end of the war itself. Each side "looked for an easier triumph, and a result less fundamental and astounding." It is worth remembering that almost 2 percent of the nation's population died in the Civil War.[92]

Not surprisingly, many of Lincoln's contemporaries, north and south, expressed hatred toward their foes akin to that voiced in 1793 by the proponents of the Terror. Northerners blamed the South for the death and destruction of war; they wanted blood. Lincoln adopted a tone of forbearance. He stressed the common heritage and shared cultural commitments that united Americans who had fought so passionately and killed so mercilessly. Both sides "read the same bible, and pray to the same God; and each invokes His aid against the other." Lincoln warned his allies, who had struggled to keep slavery from spreading and now wavered between satisfaction and surprise at its abolition, against triumphalism by invoking the words of the Bible that both sides cherished: "It may seem strange," he admitted, "that any men should dare to ask a just God's assistance in wringing their bread from the sweat of other men's faces; but let us judge not that we be not judged." A just God could not answer the prayer of both parties, and in the event "that of neither has been answered fully." No one on either side could have asked for destruction on the scale of Antietam or Gettysburg.

Above all, the Union should avoid seeing God's will in its armies' victories: "The Almighty has His own purposes. 'Woe unto the world because of offences! for it must needs be that offences come; but woe to that man by whom the offence cometh.'" The Confederacy alone was not to blame for the war. North and South shared responsibility for the "offense" of slavery, and Lincoln believed that slavery came to an end only through "this terrible war" for just that reason. As Frederick Douglass said, the war's destructive toll reflected the centuries of cruelty that northern as well as southern whites countenanced. "Fondly do we hope—fervently do we pray," Lincoln intoned, "that this mighty scourge of war may speedily pass away." Yet of course it might go on. And on. And "if God wills that it continue, until all the wealth piled by the bond-man's two hundred and fifty years of unrequited toil shall be sunk, and until every drop of blood drawn with the lash, shall be paid by another drawn with the sword," then all Americans should remember that divine justice is incomprehensible to man. They should recall, Lincoln reminded them, the words of Psalm 19, "so still it must be said 'the judgments of the Lord, are true and righteous altogether.'"

Lincoln restated, in the closing words of his Second Inaugural, the ethic of reciprocity that undergirded his critiques of slavery. "With malice toward none; with charity for all; with firmness in the right, as God gives us to see the right, let us strive on to finish the work we are in." For Lincoln, finishing that work did not mean continued violence, vengeance, and retribution. Once the war ended, northerners and southerners should close ranks, "bind up the nation's wounds," and care for the wounded veterans, widows, and orphans the war had made. Only then, only when the nation had found a way to "achieve and cherish a just, and a lasting peace, among ourselves, and with all nations," would the work of preserving American democracy be complete.[93]

Reports of Lincoln's speech in Europe expressed admiration for its rhetorical grandeur and its remarkable equanimity. Responses in the United States were more muted. Northerners had expected Lincoln to declare victory and condemn the enemy. If he was unwilling to gloat and reluctant to blame those guilty of causing four long years of chaos, most northerners, bursting with self-righteousness, were eager to do just that. Lincoln understood their unhappiness. As he wrote to his friend Thurlow Weed, "Men are not flattered by being shown that there has been a difference of purpose between the Almighty and them." In this case, though, denying that difference would have been "to deny that there is a God governing the world. It is a truth which I thought needed to be told." Lincoln knew he had deflated the swelling chests of northerners keen to celebrate the imminent Union victory. Yet he was unrepentant. "I expect," he wrote to Weed, that in time the Second Inaugural "will wear as well as—perhaps better than—any thing I have produced."[94]

The spirit of reconciliation that Lincoln recommended for the United States did not survive his assassination. Whether he could have succeeded in managing the firebrands in his own party, who demanded the demolition of antebellum southern political culture and its replacement by a dramatically different form of democracy, will never be known. We do know that, in his absence, the imperfectly implemented plans for Radical Reconstruction antagonized the South without successfully establishing a stable foundation for postwar government. That government would have had to incorporate the freedmen in a viable project constructing social, political, and economic bridges that would stretch from the past of slavery into the future of a racially mixed culture. Instead the early postwar forays into equality were greeted with a violent counterrevolution engineered by southern whites who refused to accept the verdict of Appomattox. The quick emergence of the Ku Klux Klan, night riders who used terror and lynching, and the Black Codes that reestablished the power of white supremacy against the attempts of newly freed blacks and their northern allies combined to prevent a smooth transition from slavery to freedom. Efforts to combat that counterrevolution and enforce the Fourteenth and Fifteenth Amendments ended abruptly when the North abandoned the military occupation of the former Confederacy in the Compromise of 1877.[95]

In exchange for awarding the presidency to the Republican nominee, Rutherford B. Hayes, who had lost the popular vote, Republicans in Congress agreed to remove the army from the southern states, thereby clearing a path for the consolidation of white power and the eventual triumph of Jim Crow legislation in the 1890s. Though the attempt to uproot white supremacy during the short-lived era of Radical Reconstruction had almost nothing in common with the Reign of Terror, it elicited an equally vituperative, and equally long-lasting, reaction that erased any prospect of racial justice or democratic government in the former Confederacy from the 1870s through the 1960s. The moral fervor that sustained the Union throughout the Civil War, a fervor dramatically intensified by Lincoln's assassination, proved indispensable for inspiring the sacrifices that enabled the North to win the Civil War. It also rendered unlikely the forgiveness that Lincoln prayed would come with the war's end.

Perhaps that outcome was inevitable. Perhaps the "sons of master and man," to use the formulation of W. E. B. Du Bois in *The Souls of Black Folk*, could never have realized Lincoln's hopeful vision of reconciliation. As it happened, whatever loose knitting bound the sections together in the aftermath of the Civil War occurred through a process of repressing memories of slavery's cruelty, forgetting visions of racial equality, and imposing a new regime premised on old white supremacist assumptions almost as widely shared after the 1880s, by whites throughout the United States, as they had been in the South in the 1850s.[96] That result forestalled the further progress of democracy in America for almost a century. Although formal efforts to roll back the tide of universal suffrage failed throughout the North, in the post–Civil War South the rights won by former slaves were effectively eliminated, first by violence, then by law.

During the Civil War, events compelled Lincoln, as they did Robespierre in the tumultuous days of 1793, to deny the legitimacy of dissent. Lincoln suspended habeas corpus; Robespierre relied on the guillotine. Although their methods differed, their determination won them similar degrees of veneration and hatred. Both were hailed as saviors and denounced as Caesars. The contrast between them became clear toward the end of Lincoln's life, when he admitted his errors, assigned blame for the war to North as well as South, and committed the North to reconciling with the South. The legacy of Robespierre was murder and unreconciled hatreds—on both sides. Lincoln's successors failed to steer the nation toward the goal he had set in his Second Inaugural. They failed because white southerners refused to accept defeat, and at least in part because Lincoln's assassination provoked a wrathful zeal to avenge his death along with the deaths of hundreds of thousands of Union soldiers. Lincoln's example would prove useful after a century passed, when later generations restored the postponed struggle for equality to American public life, at least briefly. Lincoln's assassination and its aftermath, coming as they did at the end of the most devastating war in American history, silenced his calls for justice and reconciliation and left a wound that permanently scarred American democracy.

Mill had written, in the early stages of the war, that the North had no choice but to respond to secession by fighting to save the Union. The southern states had committed themselves to the principle of expanding slavery throughout the nation, Mill wrote in "The Contest in America." Terrible as the prospect of war was, even worse was "the decayed and degraded state of moral and patriotic feeling which thinks nothing is *worth* a war." By rallying the North to the cause of union and challenging the Confederacy on the twin issues of secession and slavery, Lincoln had demonstrated that democracy was a better form of government than most Englishmen had been willing to admit. Popular support for the war effort in the North had shown that "the aberrations even of a ruling multitude are only fatal when the better instructed have not the virtue or the courage to front them boldly." Like Jefferson before him, Mill had not abandoned his wariness about the "multitude" or his confidence in the "better instructed," but the American Civil War had demonstrated convincingly the potential of democracy.[97]

Lincoln earned admiration from a wide range of European radicals. Marx praised this "single-minded son of the working class" for the same reason that British Chartists revered him: he worked on behalf of all people, however humble their backgrounds. Mill admired Lincoln as a "very favourable specimen of an American public man" who seized the chance to abolish slavery even though he had not set out to do it. Mill's admiration was complicated by Lincoln's failure to see from the beginning that ending slavery had to be the objective of the war, but Lincoln did come to that conclusion at last. After Lincoln was assassinated, Mill termed Lincoln "a glorious martyr if ever there was one." Lincoln lived to see slavery ended and the war won, and Mill mused that his death might put "the seal of universal remembrance" on Lincoln himself and the principles for which he died. His martyrdom consecrated his name for all time and enshrined antislavery as the noblest of crusades.[98]

It was perhaps fitting that Lincoln died as the world that produced him, the world of self-made, self-governing men who had internalized a stern moral code, was fading away. In its place came a world in which the *moeurs* identified by Tocqueville as the armature of American democracy gave way to the ethos of dog-eat-dog competition and winner-take-all capitalism. The achievement of individual rights had been among the aims of the eighteenth-century revolutions, but those rights had been conceived within a framework of moral obligations. By the 1880s the obligations had fallen away, leaving only self-interested individuals to pursue prosperity unrestrained by the older conception of responsibility to the public good. The achievement of freedom, as Tocqueville had seen, made possible a world in which ambitious individuals could treat each other with diminished respect as they became more free and less equal.

Tocqueville addressed this nightmare vision in the bleak preface to his final book, *The Old Regime and the French Revolution*. Written in response to an inquiry from Mill and addressing the challenges of his own day, Tocqueville's history explained why the French Revolution took its tragic course and why France failed to establish a viable democracy afterward.[99] Four themes stand out: the consequences of the centuries-old French experience of, and yearning for, centralized authority; the related absence of public experience or engagement with local political institutions; the war waged by the philosophes against Catholicism and their preference (the only thing they shared with the Catholic hierarchy) for rule by experts instead of ordinary people; and finally the stubborn adherence of the French people to a cluster of cultural traditions losing ground elsewhere.

Every dimension of Tocqueville's analysis sharpened the contrast between France and the United States. The differences deepened the gloom settling over Tocqueville as his health faded in the final years of his life. The French aristocracy and the French Catholic clergy still cherished a conception of freedom tied to their privileged status, whereas the revolutionary vanguard of the French people nurtured a vision of solidarity that prized national glory over civic participation. Neither was conducive to democracy, and together they explained why the revolutions of 1830 and 1848 followed the same trajectory as that of 1789: neither religious nor secular elites nor the French people could abide resolving conflicts through negotiation and compromise. Midcentury France was the worst of both worlds: the loosening of older "ties of caste, class, guild, or family" left individuals "preoccupied with their own private interests," obsessed with "looking out for themselves alone and withdrawing into a narrow individualism where all public virtues are smothered." The despotic rule of Napoleon III, like that of the old regime and the governments that followed, robbed citizens of "all common feeling" and "all occasion for common action." Without Americans' sustained and sustaining involvement in public life, the French shared only the desire to make money, an obsession that succeeded "in demoralizing and degrading the entire nation." The only antidote, Tocqueville sighed, was the liberty enjoyed by citizens in a democracy, who have countless occasions "to mingle, to join together through the need to communicate with one another, persuade each other, and satisfy each other in the conduct of their common affairs."[100]

The balance between simply responding to the electorate's increasing individualism and working to inculcate civic responsibility was the challenge facing democrats in the United States and Britain as well as France. Laboulaye, reflecting in 1866 on the arguments advanced in his widely read *Histoire des Etats-Unis*, emphasized the difference between the United States Constitution, which constrained the authority of government by the separation of powers and the Bill of Rights, and the unlimited authority of the people when "set loose" by Robespierre in the Terror. Although Americans shared the French commitment to finding "the general will as applied to the common good," they channeled that quest in constructive ways through representative government and respect for individual rights, which explained the different outcomes of the American and French Revolutions. Laboulaye, editor of Constant's writings, implicitly located in the mid-nineteenth-century United States Constant's "liberty of the moderns," a form of individual liberty cordoned off in a private sphere, where individuals pursued their goals independent of government intrusion or concern with the public interest. If "self-interest properly understood" devolved into simple self-interest, Tocqueville had warned, the promise of democracy would be squandered. Of course, as was true in the United States, not everyone accepted that diagnosis. In the 1864 "Manifesto of the Sixty," French workers clamored for working-class candidates who would advance their particular interests rather than those of the public as a whole, but little came of their effort. In the rigged game of midcentury French politics, the minority holding power kept it; the majority lacking power had no means to acquire it. By the 1860s, operating under the heavy fog that was public life in the Second Empire, Tocqueville's nightmare had become a beacon of hope for French liberals such as Laboulaye. Those who held out an alternative were no more committed to a politics of negotiation and compromise than was anyone else in France.[101]

France finally established a durable republic only after military defeat discredited the empire and the violent repression of another revolution again alarmed the resolutely conservative French countryside. The Third Republic, erected on the embers of the Commune, proved paradoxical: universal manhood suffrage again only secured the power of elites, who continued to rule on behalf of wary rural voters and members of an urban bourgeoisie content to pursue their economic interests. After the Franco-Prussian War, when Laboulaye helped frame the constitution of the Third Republic, he and his fellow liberals tried to infuse precisely the spirit of an educative culture of democracy that Tocqueville had admired in the United States. Absent popular engagement in public life, the effort proved futile.[102]

In his plan for a new form of government, *La république constitutionelle*, which Laboulaye published on the eve of the establishment of the Third Republic, he articulated the central ideas of moderate French liberals. He drew heavily on the United States Constitution, which he had studied as carefully as anyone else in France. He emphasized the importance of a bicameral legislature with indirect election of senators and the head of state, separation of church and state, and an educational system free of control by the Catholic Church. It was almost identical to the model advanced by Mill in *Representative Government* and by the first American political scientist, the German-born Francis Lieber, in *On Civil Liberty and Self-Government* (1853). Like Laboulaye and Mill, Lieber endorsed the idea of balancing public engagement in electoral politics against preserving order and providing expert administration. The American model, grounded on the principle of popular sovereignty, with universal manhood suffrage and defenses of individual liberties built in, loomed large on both sides of the Atlantic.[103]

Between the first appearance of such proposals in France and the final consolidation of authority under the Third Republic in 1875, France had to pass through another ordeal. Three different dissident groups jockeyed for position: the liberals, led by Adolphe Thiers; the republicans, led by Léon Gambetta; and the socialists, who followed the lead of Louis-Auguste Blanqui. Humiliated by the Franco-Prussian War, France proclaimed a republic in September 1870. The ensuing elections revealed a nation divided between the still-royalist countryside, which elected a monarchist National

Assembly, and the increasingly radical urban population inclined, as Laboulaye had accurately gauged, toward direct rather than representative democracy. When radicals seized the initiative in Paris and other large cities and defied the National Assembly, the battle lines shifted from Alsace and Lorraine to Paris itself.

The suppression of the Commune that controlled Paris in the spring of 1871 rekindled memories—and hatreds—from the worst years of the 1790s. Buildings were torched. The archbishop of Paris was captured, then killed when he could not be exchanged for the imprisoned Blanqui. Both monarchy and capitalism were declared dead. Hopes and fears spiraled upward toward a brutal denouement that cost ten thousand lives. Before the Third Republic was secured in 1875, popularly elected loyalists of both the Bourbon and Orléanist regimes had battled each other to a standstill, and the rifts between monarchists and republicans deepened. Liberal democrats such as Laboulaye withdrew into bitterness: once again violence rather than deliberation, military authority rather than a peaceful constitutional convention, had been necessary to establish the simulacrum that passed for democratic government in the early Third Republic.[104]

The sort of democracy that was emerging in the mid-nineteenth century made the generation of Mill, Tocqueville, and Lincoln—and many of those who admired them—increasingly uneasy. It was a culture of scrambling individualists that left little room for older ideals of the common good. Those who continued to evoke the earlier democratic creed after the death of Tocqueville and Lincoln, such as Mill in Britain and his friend Charles Eliot Norton in the United States, struck many of their critics as increasingly out of touch. They still thought of democracy as an ethical ideal, a way of life, an idea a rising generation seemed eager to discard.

Mill enthusiastically praised Norton's essay "American Political Ideals," which was published in the *North American Review* in 1865. Norton, son of a noted philologist and one of the most prominent writers in post–Civil War America, traced the history of American democracy from its origins in early New England. From the start, he noted, the colonies "had a moral rather than a political foundation." Early New Englanders understood that politics is "a branch of ethics," and together with other English colonists in North America they embarked on the unprecedented project of empowering "the *people*" to govern themselves. Their circumstances, Norton pointed out, echoing Sparks and Tocqueville, combined to promote not only individualism but also "the habit of combined action in the community." The American Revolution advanced that project, knitting together the citizens of the colonies "in a common cause." Unlike governments in Europe, which stood apart from their populations, Norton argued, state power in the United States was, for the first time, "authorized by the consent of the governed." Against those of his contemporaries who were trumpeting individual freedom as Americans' ultimate ideal, Norton countered that "the community requires, and must always require, an external government to control those wills, and to regulate the pursuit of those interests in such a manner as to preserve the moral order, to secure the general welfare."

Individual wills, Norton conceded, inevitably chafe against other wills. That tension, however, could be minimized by realizing the promise of democracy, which Norton called the "most promising ideal of modern Christian civilization,—the true brotherhood of man." In self-governing communities, individuals no longer felt themselves isolated but instead found their happiness and fulfillment in the "relations of mutual dependence" existing between self and community. Rights freed from obligations can render individuals self-centered. Community norms without an ethical anchor can authorize the barbarous behavior of "vigilance committees and lynch mobs." Although Norton considered moral ideals eternal, their application altered as conditions changed. The vista opening up with the end of slavery presented a fresh opportunity for the "uncivilized" South to adopt a new and more inclusive set of values. But that outcome was hardly inevitable. Although "the South has sullenly laid down its arms, beaten and dispirited, it has not laid down its hate."

The former Confederacy still clung to the idea that animated secession and inspired its armies. Norton shared Tocqueville's insight into the mutual dependence of government and extragovernmental organizations that embody the spirit of the community. Unless civil society in the South changed to align with the democratic ethos embodied in the nation's founding documents, the end of slavery would merely facilitate a new form of domination under the rule of selfishness. The North had a duty to impose justice on the South, conditions of liberty rather than tyranny—in other words, not Lincoln's liberty of the wolf but liberation from servitude and freedom of thought, conscience, and speech. The North had to enforce justice, develop "controlled and regular processes of moral and legal organizations," and harness the still-dangerous passions of individuals accustomed to a culture of white supremacy that persisted despite the Confederacy's military defeat.

It was a tall order. Norton's concluding litany of the nation's duties echoed the central themes articulated by Tocqueville, Lincoln, and Mill on the cultural prerequisites of democracy. As Lincoln had insisted, the United States must compel the rebellious South to acknowledge "the right of every man to be equal to any other man."[105] Unfortunately for Norton, Mill, and others on both sides of the Atlantic who shared their sensibility, the emphasis on balancing effective rights and civic duties in democracy would be lost, not only by the North's decision to leave former slaves at the mercy of their former masters but also in the laissez-faire ideology revived by interpreters of Charles Darwin, who insisted in the closing decades of the nineteenth century that life is nothing but a struggle for survival in which the strong inevitably dominate the weak.[106]

The letter Mill wrote to Norton in praise of "American Political Ideals" captures the affinities between Mill and the Americans who shared his commitment to a culture of democracy extending beyond suffrage to autonomy and reciprocity. Mill was alert to the immediate challenges facing the nation after the Civil War. Americans were more attached to their Constitution than were other people, such as the British, because the United States Constitution actually "*has* principles." Whereas Britain could boast only of the "unpremeditated and unplanned" outcomes of contingent conflicts, the United States was committed from the outset to freedom and equality. The triumph of the Union, although deeply satisfying, was not enough. Extending those principles from white to black, then from men to women, remained to be done. First, though, the United States had to clear the hurdle of Reconstruction. Unless southern society were "democratized in law and in fact," Mill warned, "the sufferings and sacrifices of these glorious years will be more than half lost." The North had the power, both military and economic, to enforce its rule. It needed only the will. When it became clear that the North lacked just that, the result was even worse than Mill predicted. Both parties pandered to the electorate's worst impulses, and Jackson's heirs in particular debased the name of their party by excluding the freedmen in the South and ever more brazenly trading favors for votes in the urban machines of the North. Whereas Norton identified American democracy with the radical Christian ideal of brotherhood, in the aftermath of Reconstruction it came down to exclusion and patronage.[107]

Disillusionment was widespread. The indomitable Walt Whitman hoped the arts might enable Americans to transcend the corrupt politics and obsessive money chasing that followed the heroic sacrifices of the Civil War. Whitman urged his countrymen to look beyond the superficial mechanism of voting, the stuff of mere political democracy, to the "moral conscience" required for real self-government. In his essay "Democratic Vistas," inspired by Mill's *On Liberty* and aimed at Thomas Carlyle's denunciation of democracy in his vitriolic essay "Shooting Niagara," Whitman lamented the triumph of an unbridled individualism and extolled its completion in the "adhesiveness or love, that fuses, ties, and aggregates, making the races comrades, and fraternizing all." For Whitman, finally, "the breath of life" animating American culture must be a benevolent religious spirit, the pulsating heart of democracy.[108]

Like Tocqueville, Mill, and Lincoln, both Norton and Whitman feared that their world was becoming so thoroughly infected by instrumental rationality that all discussions of values and norms were deemed illegitimate intrusions into individuals' freedom. Tocqueville warned that democracy, under such conditions, would deteriorate into a vicious and destructive egoism, a war of all against all in which the subtle power of the majority to produce uniformity might prove unstoppable. The wills of unreflective and self-centered people, unwilling to make arguments on behalf of their preferences, were likelier to veer into destructive antagonism than to forge the multiple solidarities on which these thinkers thought democracy must stand. From their perspective, democracy requires humility, restraint, benevolence, and brotherhood, and it is threatened by the idea that all personal preferences are sacred and all constraints tyrannical.

These late-nineteenth-century democrats, like many who preceded them, emphasized education because they thought that only people willing to subject their impulses to critical scrutiny and submit them to interrogation by other members of their communities—Socrates dissatisfied, in Mill's formulation—develop preferences that deserve respect. Such examination invites criticism. Democracy thrives, however, when individuals must articulate the reasons for their commitments; it withers when individuals retreat to unexamined willfulness. Champions of Constant's "modern" liberty see oppression and invasion in such invitations to discourse, whereas inheritors of the Judeo-Christian tradition or Mill's ethics of benevolence see the call to love others for their own sake, and interaction with others premised on that principle, as occasions for self-reflection and self-transcendence. Such communities can become dangerous when they confine individuals within visible or invisible forms of domination, or when they look to a disembodied, unchanging, universal "reason" to provide answers that emerge only from the give-and-take of argument and are thus always provisional.[109] That is why Lincoln, Mill, and Tocqueville insisted so vehemently that democracy works best when majorities are constrained by respect for individual liberty, when liberties are exercised in the context of rough equality, and when preferences are measured against a developing standard of justice. Maintaining that balance is the perpetual challenge of democracy, as daunting and inspiring now as it has always been.

Empowering the community, as Robespierre did by invoking the nation's general will to silence everyone he declared counterrevolutionary and tied to aristocratic plots, can justify terror. Empowering individual wills, however, or rather the wills of some individuals, which has been among the principal goals of politics since the late nineteenth century, can mute appeals to the animating principle of democracy, the idea of the common good. Both the outcome of the French Revolution and the American retreat from Reconstruction were tragic, although in opposite ways. The Terror inspired revolutions in 1830, 1848, and 1871, the reactions against which long suppressed popular engagement in French politics. The sense of injustice felt by white southerners at the end of the Civil War was deepened by the brief entry into southern politics of northerners and African Americans from 1865 to 1877. Together with the hardening of racism in American culture more generally, the urge to reconcile North and South rationalized the reinstatement of white supremacy. Animosity toward African Americans intensified throughout the United States in the wake of the Civil War, just as conservative opposition to radical calls for toleration and equality intensified in France throughout the nineteenth century. The aftertaste of that bitterness is perceptible in the politics of both nations today.[110]

The Hebrew Bible and the Christian scriptures offer an alternative to such animosity that still beckons those drawn toward the vision of democracy traced in this book. Hillel and Jesus both condensed the law to two simple duties: love God and love your neighbor as yourself.[111] Or as St. Paul wrote to the Christian community in Philippi, if you wish to live consistent with the ideals of Jesus, you should learn to see through one another's eyes, to think with one another's minds, and to treat each other with charity. Resist contentiousness and pride, Paul counseled, and act from humility, letting each one look "not to his own interests but to those of others."[112]

Democracy has proven malleable over the four centuries in which it has been debated and attempted in the modern world. Its meanings will always be contested. Democracy will always be unfinished precisely because it is an ethical ideal as well as a set of institutions and practices. Tocqueville captured the tragic irony of democracy in his conclusion to the second volume of *Democracy in America*. Although he was writing about the United States, he was thinking, as always, about France. "In the heat of the democratic revolution, men busy destroying the old aristocratic powers which opposed it displayed a strong spirit of independence." With the coming of equality, however, its French champions succumbed to "the instincts natural to that condition, strengthening and centralizing the power of society." Those who gave the world democratic government "had sought to be free in order to make themselves equal. But in proportion as equality was established by the era of freedom, freedom itself was thereby rendered more difficult to attain." Achieving a balance between freedom and equality has remained a challenge everywhere.[113]

Fulfilling the promise of democracy depends on individuals' internalizing limits on the freedom that democracy gives them. That is the meaning of autonomy. It depends on citizens' willingly interrogating their own preferences rather than taking for granted their legitimacy. That requires restraint. It also depends on their willingness to weigh their own preferences against the preferences of others, and it depends on their ability to understand that their own interests might not always align with the public interest. From the funeral oration of Pericles through Montaigne's reflections on the wars of religion to the consequences of the English Civil War, the French Revolution, and the American Civil War, it has been clear that civil war impairs the operation of that ethic of reciprocity.

Restoring trust in the aftermath of civil war takes time and deliberate cultural effort. It requires identifying the legacies and confronting the dormant sources of hate that lie just beneath the surface of contemporary political debate. Necessary as those steps are, history provides ample evidence that they might not be sufficient. If the obstacles to a culture of democracy are perennial, because self-interest never meshes smoothly with the ideal of reciprocity, then the consequences of civil wars have deepened, and made even more urgent, the need to confront the persistence of struggles thought buried in the past.

NOTES

Introduction

In general, these notes identify only the sources for passages quoted in the text. Many of the notes are followed by an asterisk, which indicates that fuller documentation, and in many cases extended critical discussion of the secondary literature, can be found in the five hundred pages of endnotes available in the electronic version of this book, which is accessible at www.scholar.harvard.edu/jameskloppenberg/home.

1. See the UNESCO report edited by Richard McKeon, *Democracy in a World of Tensions* (Chicago, 1951), 522; Amartya Sen, "Democracy as a Universal Value," *Journal of Democracy* 10 (1999): 3–17; and the widely circulated report by Freedom House, *Democracy's Century: A Survey of Political Change in the Twentieth Century* (New York, 1999), which reported that the number of democratic nations had mushroomed from a mere handful in 1900 to over 60 percent by the end of the century.*
2. See Ellen Fitzpatrick, *History's Memory: Writing America's Past, 1880–1980* (Cambridge, MA, 2002); Eric Foner and Lisa McGirr, eds., *American History Now* (Philadelphia, 2011); and William H. Sewell Jr., *Logics of History: Social Theory and Social Transformation* (Chicago, 2005).*
3. Whenever possible I have cited widely available editions of these thinkers' writings. For American writers, I have usually cited volumes in the series published by the Library of America. When those editions are unavailable, I have usually cited standard scholarly editions of writers' complete works. When I quote from texts with multiple English translations, such as the writings of Montaigne, Rousseau, and Tocqueville, the notes indicate the rendering that I prefer. Readers should note that I have sometimes slightly altered translations when I think different word choices more accurately convey the author's meaning.
4. See Joel Isaac, James T. Kloppenberg, Michael O'Brien, and Jennifer Ratner-Rosenhagen, eds., *The Worlds of American Intellectual History* (New York, 2016).

5. The same features of contemporary scholarship that make this book necessary have made it difficult to write. There is simply too much to know. See Daniel Lord Smail, "History and the Telescoping of Time: A Disciplinary Forum," *French Historical Studies* 34, no. 1 (2011): 1–5; Jo Guldi and David Armitage, *The History Manifesto* (Cambridge, 2014); and, on how scholars coped with earlier versions of this problem, Ann Blair, *Too Much to Know: Managing Scholarly Information before the Modern Age* (New Haven, 2010).*
6. See Bernard Manin, *The Principles of Representative Government* (Cambridge, 1997); Pierre Rosanvallon, *La démocratie inachevée* (Paris, 2000); Nadia Urbinati, *Representative Democracy: Principles and Genealogy* (Chicago, 2006); Pierre Rosanvallon, *Democratic Legitimacy: Impartiality, Reflexivity, Proximity*, trans. Arthur Goldhammer (Princeton, 2011); and Alan Ryan, *On Politics: A History of Political Thought from Herodotus to the Present* (New York, 2012). On genre differences, see James T. Kloppenberg, "A Well-Tempered Liberalism: Modern Intellectual History and Political Theory," *Modern Intellectual History* 10 (2013): 655–82; and for the method of historical analysis practiced in this book, James T. Kloppenberg, "Thinking Historically: A Manifesto of Pragmatic Hermeneutics," *Modern Intellectual History* 9 (2012): 201–16.*
7. See George Reid Andrews and Herrick Chapman, eds., *The Social Construction of Democracy, 1870–1990* (New York, 1995), 1–30; John Dunn, *Democracy: A History* (New York, 2005); Charles Tilly, *Democracy* (Cambridge, 2007); and John Keane, *The Life and Death of Democracy* (New York, 2009).*
8. Thomas Jefferson to Charles Jarvis, September 28, 1820 in *The Works of Thomas Jefferson*, ed. Paul L. Ford, 12 vols. (New York, 1905), 12:161–64.
9. Isaiah Berlin, "Two Concepts of Liberty," in Berlin, *Four Essays on Liberty* (Oxford, 1969), 118–72; Charles Taylor, *Sources of the Self: The Making of the Modern Identity* (Cambridge, MA, 1989); Joseph Raz, *The Morality of Freedom* (Oxford, 1986); and Stein Ringen, *What Democracy Is For: On Freedom and Moral Government* (Princeton, 2007).*
10. See Jane Mansbridge et al., "The Place of Self-Interest and the Role of Power in Deliberative Democracy," *Journal of Political Philosophy* 18, no. 1 (March 2010): 64–100; and Charles Girard, "La démocratie doit-elle étre délibérative?" *Archives de Philosophie* 74 (2011–12): 223–40.*
11. Historians need to recover the richness and complexity of eras incomprehensible in terms of our own flattened cultural lexicon, a world in which individuals took seriously not only their own personal aspirations but also the obligations that bound them to other people and, perhaps most importantly, to their God. The vocabularies of contemporary Anglo-American philosophy, behaviorist social science, and evolutionary psychology have made it difficult for us to understand the meanings that our ancestors imputed to words such as "autonomy" and "equality," or "liberty" and "justice," because many scholars now see such words as smokescreens obscuring the self-interest that is said to motivate all humans. See Carles Boix, *Democracy and Redistribution* (Cambridge,

2003); Daron Acemoglu and James A. Robinson, *Economic Origins of Dictatorship and Democracy* (Cambridge, 2006); and Daniel Ziblatt, "How Did Europe Democratize?" *World Politics* 58 (January 2006): 311–38.*

12. Standard analytical categories, such as the traditions of American liberalism and European statism, are too flat and too static. See James T. Kloppenberg, "*Requiescat in Pacem*: The Liberal Tradition of Louis Hartz," in *The American Liberal Tradition Reconsidered: The Contested Legacy of Louis Hartz*, ed. Mark Hulliung (Lawrence, 2010), 90–124.*
13. This analysis rejects the assumptions beneath the Whig and the anti-Whig views common in much contemporary historical writing. Whereas the Whig interpretation of history treats change as a progressive process culminating in our current success, I see the history of democracy less as a story of triumph or progress toward a definite telos than as a story of struggles with persistent obstacles, a story of some successes along with repeated failures. Although the principle of popular sovereignty and practices of democratic government were formally established in the United States and much of Western Europe by the end of the nineteenth century, the struggle to realize the ideals of autonomy and equality continues today.*
14. One of the merits of recent poststructuralist criticism is the emphasis placed on the unstable meanings and the strategic significance of language and the often surprising twists texts take as they are disseminated to readers in multiple forms. But those insights can be carried too far: the awareness of instability need not make historical interpretation impossible, nor must it culminate in the cynical belief that ulterior motives render all statements of principle suspect and make "unmasking" our paramount objective. See James T. Kloppenberg, "Objectivity and Historicism: A Century of American Historical Writing," *American Historical Review* 94 (1989): 1011–30.*
15. Historians should be increasingly self-conscious about our own unexamined assumptions and subject them to critical scrutiny, and we should be cautious about imputing our own values to the historical process itself. See James T. Kloppenberg, "The Canvas and the Color: Tocqueville's 'Philosophical History' and Why It Matters Now," *Modern Intellectual History* 3 (2006): 495–521; and Giovanni Capoccia and Daniel Ziblatt, "The Historical Turn in Democratization Studies," *Comparative Political Studies* 43 (2010): 931–68.*
16. W. E. B. Du Bois, *The Souls of Black Folk* (1903), in *Writings*, ed. Nathan Huggins (New York, 1986).*
17. It is both ahistorical and inaccurate to assume that the power of religion has always been arrayed against or with the power of the people. In the eighteenth century, perhaps only the Anglo-American radical Thomas Paine and the French revolutionary Maximilien Robespierre spoke with as much enthusiasm for democracy as did the future Pope Pius VII, who preached in 1797 that democratic government is consistent with the message of the Christian Gospel. R. R. Palmer, *The Age of the Democratic Revolution: A Political History of Europe and America*, vol. 1, *The Challenge* (Princeton, 1959), 13–20.*

18. See Charles Taylor, *A Secular Age* (Cambridge, MA, 2007); Jürgen Habermas et al., *An Awareness of What Is Missing: Faith and Reason in a Post-secular Age* (Cambridge, 2010); and Peter Gordon, "Religion within the Bounds of Democracy Alone: Habermas, Rawls, and the Trans-Atlantic Debate over Public Reason," in Isaac, Kloppenberg, O'Brien, and Ratner-Rosenhagen, *The Worlds of American Intellectual History*.*
19. The traditions of democratic discourse examined in this book are among the most complex and important parts of our cultural inheritance. The premises of pluralism, deliberation, and reciprocity on which North Atlantic democracy stands are products of those contested traditions. In the natural sciences as in the human sciences, everything we know is perspectival, provisional, and subject to revision in light of new evidence. On the thinkers who pioneered this approach, such as Wilhelm Dilthey, Max Weber, William James, and John Dewey, see James T. Kloppenberg, *Uncertain Victory: Social Democracy and Progressivism in European and American Thought, 1870–1920* (New York, 1986); and James T. Kloppenberg, "Democracy and Disenchantment: From Weber and Dewey to Habermas and Rorty," in Kloppenberg, *The Virtues of Liberalism* (New York, 1998), 82–99.*

Chapter 1

1. It was not uncommon, Montaigne observed, to see soldiers "hack and cut off other men's limbs" and "sharpen their wits to invent unusual tortures and new forms of death" without any particular hatred or hope of gain. Instead innocent victims were slaughtered "for the sole purpose of enjoying the pleasing spectacle afforded by the pitiful gestures and motions, the lamentable groans and cries, of a man dying in anguish." Surely, Montaigne concluded, such behavior represented "the extreme limit to which cruelty can attain." Michel de Montaigne, "On Cruelty," in *Essays*, trans. J. M. Cohen (London, 1958), 186; and Montaigne, *The Complete Works*, ed. and trans. Donald M. Frame (New York, 1943), 383; hereafter cited as *CW*.*
2. Montaigne, "On Physiognomy," in *Essays*, 339–43; *CW*, 988–92.
3. Montaigne, "By Diverse Means We Arrive at the Same End," in *CW*, 3–6.
4. Because of Montaigne's scandalous judgments, his books were confiscated by a papal censor on a trip to Rome in 1581. A century after his medal was struck, the Catholic Church finally placed his *Essays* on the index of banned books. David Lewis Schaefer, *The Political Philosophy of Montaigne* (Ithaca, 1990), 13n28.
5. Montaigne, "Of Custom," in *CW*, 93–108; Montaigne, "Of Cannibals," in *CW*, 182–93.*
6. In Montaigne's words, "Assertion and dogmatism are positive signs of stupidity." Montaigne, "On Experience," in *Essays*, 352; *CW*, 999.
7. Montaigne, *Essays*, 355; *CW*, 1002.*
8. Montaigne, "On the Art of Conversation," in *Essays*, 285–93; *CW*, 854–60.

9. See David Quint, *Montaigne and the Quality of Mercy* (Princeton, 1998), 102–44; for Montaigne's letter to Henry, see *CW*, 1332–34.*
10. "To submit and entrust oneself to others is an excellent way to win their heart and will," Montaigne wrote, but the submission must be done "freely and without the constraints of any necessity," and the situation must "be such that we bring to it a pure and clean trust," the outward sign of which would be "a countenance free of any misgiving." Montaigne, "By Diverse Means We Arrive at the Same End," in *CW*, 3–6.*
11. Montaigne, "Apology for Raymond Sebond," in *CW*, 436.*
12. Montaigne, "On the Art of Conversation," in *Essays*, 301; *CW*, 867.
13. Montaigne, "On Physiognomy," in *Essays*, 318, 322; *CW*, 971, 974.
14. Leviticus 19:18; see also Exodus 22:21.*
15. Paul R. Mendes-Flor, *Love, Accusative and Dative: Reflections on Leviticus 19:18*, B. G. Rudolph Lectures in Judaic Studies (Syracuse, 2007).
16. Herodotus, *Histories*, trans. Robin Waterfield (Oxford, 1998), 5.62–78.*
17. Aristotle, *Politics* 1273b.*
18. Josh Ober, "The Original Meaning of 'Democracy': Capacity to Do Things, Not Majority Rule," *Constellations* 15 (2008): 3–9.
19. All scholars of Greek democracy rely on the pathbreaking work of J. W. Headlam, *Election by Lot at Athens*, 2nd ed., rev. D. C. Macgregor (1891; Cambridge, 1933); and Mogens H. Hansen, *The Athenian Democracy in the Age of Demosthenes* (Cambridge, 1991). See also Eric W. Robinson, ed., *Ancient Greek Democracy* (Oxford: Blackwell, 2004); and Kurt A. Raaflaub, Josiah Ober, and Robert W. Wallace, *Origins of Democracy in Ancient Greece* (Berkeley, 2007).*
20. As was true of self-designated democracies from the ancient world through the end of the nineteenth century, the exclusion of women and the presence of slaves seemed to male Athenians so unproblematic as to be unremarkable. See Moses Finley, *Ancient Slavery and Modern Ideology* (London, 1980).*
21. On the role played by institutions or by the people of Athens in the time of Cleisthenes, see Hansen, *The Athenian Democracy in the Age of Demosthenes*; and Josiah Ober, *Mass and Elite in Democratic Athens: Rhetoric, Ideology, and the Power of the People* (Princeton, 1989).*
22. Thucydides, *The Peloponnesian War* 2.37.*
23. See Josiah Ober, *The Athenian Revolution: Essays on Ancient Greek Democracy and Political Theory* (Princeton, 1996).*
24. Xenophon, *Memorabilia* 1.2.9.
25. Plato, *The Apology* 31e–32a.*
26. Plato, *The Republic* 558c.*
27. See Jonathan Barnes, "Aristotle and Political Liberty," in *Aristotle's Politics: Critical Essays*, ed. Richard Kraut and Steven Skultety (Lanham, MD, 2005), 185–202.
28. Aristotle, *Politics* 1253a25.*

29. Aristotle, *Politics* 1296a7.* Unfortunately, Aristotle concluded glumly, his ideal "middle constitution has never occurred anywhere, or only seldom and sporadically," precisely because the conditions had never been right for it, and he gave no guidance about how it could be instituted. Aristotle, *Politics* 1296a7; see also Aristotle, *Nicomachean Ethics* 10.8–9.
30. Aristotle, *Politics* 1317a40, 1318b6.
31. Aristotle, *Politics* 1317a40, 1317b17.
32. Aristotle, *Politics* 1725b, 1279a.
33. Aristotle, *Politics* 1317a40.
34. Aristotle, *Politics* 1317b17.
35. In short, "the inevitable result is this most valuable of principles in a constitution: ruling by respectable men of blameless conduct, and without detriment to the populace at large." Aristotle, *Politics* 1318b6.
36. Aristotle rejected most of Plato's ideas, just as his own student Alexander the Great seems to have ignored most of Aristotle's teachings about moderation, yet Aristotle did agree with Socrates and Plato that philosophers should aim to discern universal norms from the particularities of experience. Although a wide range of political systems exists, Aristotle observed in the *Nicomachean Ethics*, and customs vary even more widely, "only one system is by nature the best everywhere." That ideal combination of aristocracy and democracy, the mixed polity, appealed to Aristotle because it filtered out of public life the narrow ambitions, petty jealousies, and self-interest that cause people to place their own advantage ahead of the public interest. Aristotle, *Nicomachean Ethics* 5.6, 1135a.*
37. Aristotle's aspiration toward moderation, however, stood in dynamic tension with the spirit of open-ended inquiry and public argumentation that emerged in Greek democracy, the spirit apparent in the historical writing of Thucydides. From that dynamic relation emerged the pathbreaking achievements of Greek culture in mathematics, science, logic, and literature, all of which manifested a commitment to public discourse, critical analysis, and reasoned debate rather than the blind observance of inherited traditions or customs. Demosthenes, *Against Boeotus* 1.39.10–11; Thucydides, *History of the Peloponnesian War* 2.65.1–11; and on Isocrates, *Antidosis*, see Yun Lee Too and David C. Mirhady, trans., *Isocrates I* (Austin: University of Texas Press, 2000); and Darius W. Weil, "Cultured Nobility and the Ideal of the Stately Elm: The Debate on Classical Education in 19th-Century America" (unpublished senior thesis, Harvard University, Fall 2009).
38. Thucydides, *The Peloponnesian War* 5.89.
39. On these issues see Cynthia Farrar, *The Origins of Democratic Thinking: The Invention of Politics in Classical Athens* (Cambridge, 1988), 126–91; and G. E. R. Lloyd, *Demystifying Mentalities* (Cambridge, 1990).*
40. Polybius, *The Histories* 6.3.5–8, 6.6.1–5, 6.10.1–14. See Arthur M. Eckstein, *Moral Vision in the Histories of Polybius* (Berkeley, 1995).

41. By his own reckoning, Cicero aimed primarily to translate classical Greek ideas into Latin. He addressed a range of issues in his many speeches and in his writings on political and philosophical subjects, notably in *De re publica* (*On the Republic*); *De legibus* (*On the Laws*), which he left unfinished; and the ethical treatise he addressed to his son, *De officis* (*On Duties*).
42. Whereas agrarian reformers following the lead of the Gracchi persuaded many in Cicero's day of the need for economic redistribution, Cicero advocated limiting the people's role to electing public-spirited citizens to the assembly. Cicero, *On Laws* 1.15.43; *On Duties* 1.10.31; *On the Republic* 1.53–54.*
43. Cicero, *On Duties* 2.17.*
44. A recent introduction to the life and writings of Hillel is Joseph Telushkin, *Hillel: If Not Now, When?* (New York, 2010).
45. Matthew 22:34–40.
46. Galatians 5:13–15.
47. Colossians 3:18–4:1.
48. Philemon 1:15–20.*
49. Acts of the Apostles 4:32–35.
50. Thessalonians 5:19–21.
51. See Wayne Meeks, *The Origins of Christian Morality* (New Haven, 1993); and Hans Küng, *The Catholic Church: A Short History* (New York, 2001).*
52. When Christianity became an accessory to the authority of the emperor, wealthy Romans began to share their wealth through a newly ambitious Catholic hierarchy and its institutions. Some of it helped the needy; much of it enriched and empowered the church. See Peter Brown, *Through the Eye of a Needle: Wealth, the Fall of Rome, and the Making of Christianity in the West* (Princeton, 2012).*
53. Cicero's vision of the good life, Augustine wrote, lifted his eyes from "evil without purpose" to a lifetime devoted to the study, clarification, and preaching of God's word. Augustine, *Confessions*, trans. John K. Ryan (Garden City, NY, 1960), 70, 81. Still standard is Peter Brown, *Augustine of Hippo: A Biography* (London, 1967).*
54. Augustine, *City of God*, trans. Gerald G. Walsh et al. (Garden City, NY, 1958), 72–75, 321.
55. Augustine, *City of God*, 425.
56. Acts of the Apostles 4:32–35; Augustine, *City of God*, 463–466.
57. Joachim Whaley, *Germany and the Holy Roman Empire*, vol. 1, *Maximilian I to the Peace of Westphalia, 1493–1648* (Oxford, 2012).
58. See J. R. Maddicott, *The Origins of the English Parliament, 924–1327* (Oxford, 2010).*
59. See Richard Tuck, *Natural Rights Theories: Their Origin and Development* (Cambridge, 1979).*
60. Leo IX quoted in I. S. Robinson, "Church and Papacy," in *The Cambridge History of Medieval Political Thought, c. 350–c. 1450* (hereafter *CHMT*), ed.

J. H. Burns (Cambridge, 1988), 281; and see Janet Nelson, "Kingship and Empire," in *CHMT*, 230–31.*

61. David Knowles, *The Evolution of Medieval Thought* (New York, 1962), 191–92; Jeannine Quillet, "Community, Counsel and Representation," in *CHMT*, 526–27; and Walter Ullmann, *A History of Political Thought: The Middle Ages* (Baltimore, 1965), 171.
62. Aquinas, *De regimine principum*, in *Aquinas: Selected Political Writings*, ed. A. P. D'Entrèves, trans. J. G. Dawson (Oxford, 1959), 6.
63. Gregory the Great quoted in Küng, *The Catholic Church,* 65.*
64. Henry of Ghent quoted in Anthony Black, "The Individual and Society," in *CHMT*, 597.*
65. Marsilius challenged the authority of the pope and argued that the apostles of Jesus had reached decisions through the "method of common deliberation." Marsilius of Padua, *The Defender of Peace*, ed. and trans. Alan Gewirth (New York, 1956), 32–33, 45.*
66. Bruni quoted in Bernard Manin, *The Principles of Representative Government* (Cambridge, 1997), 43; see also 51–67; John Najemy, *A History of Florence, 1200–1575* (Oxford, 2008); John P. McCormick, *Machiavellian Democracy* (Cambridge, 2011); and James Hankins, "Exclusivist Republicanism and the Non-Monarchical Republic," *Political Theory* 38 (2010): 452–82.*
67. Dante, *The Divine Comedy*, vol. 1, *Hell*, canto 19, trans. Dorothy Sayers (Harmondsworth, 1949), 188–91.*
68. Thomas More, *Utopia*, ed. and trans. H. V. S. Ogden (Arlington Heights, IL, 1949), 33, 47–49, 83.*
69. More, *Utopia*, 32–33, 75, 82.
70. Ulinka Rublack, *Reformation Europe* (Cambridge, 2007).
71. The peasants called for wider access to game and fish, wood and water, and meadows and fields, the use of which, often denied by feudal law, was being further restricted by the movement to enclose open lands that was spreading across Europe. *Twelve Articles*, in *The Protestant Reformation*, ed. Hans Hillerbrand (New York, 1968), 63–66.*
72. "The fact that the rulers are wicked and unjust," Luther wrote, "does not excuse tumult and rebellion, for to punish wickedness does not belong to everybody, but to the worldly rulers who bear the sword." Luther, *Friendly Admonition to Peace concerning the Twelve Articles of the Swabian Peasants*, in Hillerbrand, *The Protestant Reformation*, 67–87; quotations from 73, 80, 83, 70.*
73. Zwingli, *Jeremiah-Erklärungen* (1905–59), 14:424, quoted in Francis Oakley, "Christian Obedience and Authority," in *The Cambridge History of Political Thought, 1450–1700* (hereafter *CHPT, 1450–1700*), ed. J. H. Burns with Mark Goldie (Cambridge, 1988), 184.
74. Christopher Goodman, *How Superiors Ought to Be Obeyed by Their Subjects: And Wherein They May Be Lawfully Disobeyed and Resisted*, ed. Charles H. McIlwain (1558; New York, 1931), chap. 9.*

75. The most recent English edition of the most notorious of these monarchomach tracts is available as *Vindiciae, contra tyrannos: Or, Concerning the Legitimate Power of a Prince over the People, and of the People over a Prince*, ed. and trans. George Garnett (Cambridge, 1994). See also François Hotman, *Francogallia*, ed. R. E. Giesey, trans. J. H. M. Salmon (1573; Cambridge, 1972); Theodore Beza, *Du droit des magistrats*, ed. R. M. Kingdon (Geneva, 1971); and Philippe Duplessis-Mornay, *Vindiciae, contra tyrannos*, ed. H. Weber et al. (Geneva, 1979), 210, quoted in Robert N. Kingdon, "Calvinism and Resistance Theory," in *CHPT, 1450–1700*, 213.*
76. Jean Bodin, *De republica libri sex* (Paris, 1586), 2.1.176, trans. Julian H. Franklin, in *CHPT, 1450–1700*, 303.
77. See Mack Holt, *The French Wars of Religion, 1562–1629*, 2nd ed. (Cambridge, 2005); Denis Crouzet, *Les guerriers de Dieu: La violence au temps des troubles de religion* (Paris, 1990); and Brad S. Gregory, *Salvation at Stake: Christian Martyrdom in Early Modern Europe* (Cambridge, MA, 1999).*
78. See Charles Taylor, *A Secular Age* (Cambridge, MA, 2007); Jerome Schneewind, *The Invention of Autonomy: A History of Modern Moral Philosophy* (Cambridge, 1998), 15–57; Brad S. Gregory, *The Unintended Reformation: How a Religious Revolution Secularized Society* (Cambridge, MA, 2012); Alister Chapman, John Coffey, and Brad S. Gregory, eds., *Seeing Things Their Way: Intellectual History and the Return of Religion* (Notre Dame, 2009); and Benjamin Kaplan, *Divided by Faith: Religious Conflict and the Practice of Toleration in Early Modern Europe* (Cambridge, MA, 2007).*

Chapter 2

1. The document establishing the government of Rhode Island, March 16–19, 1641, is in *Records of the Colony of Rhode Island and Providence Plantations in New England, 1636 to 1792*, 10 vols., ed. J. R. Bartlett (Providence, 1856–65), 1:111–13.
2. *The Journal of John Winthrop, 1630–1649*, ed. Richard S. Dunn and Laetitia Yeandle (Cambridge, MA, 1996), 142–43.*
3. Roger Williams to Anne Sadleir, ca. April 1652, in *The Complete Writings of Roger Williams* (hereafter *CWRW*), 7 vols. (New York, 1963), 239.
4. Winthrop's complicated relations with Williams are evident in Winthrop, *Journal*. The quotation from January 1636 is on 87.
5. Although the tone of Winthrop's discussion of Williams in his journal entries in January of 1636 suggests he shared other officials' contempt for Williams, Williams later claimed, in a letter written to John Mason on June 22, 1670, that Winthrop tipped him off. See Winthrop, *Journal*, 82–89; and cf. Williams's letter in Perry Miller, *Roger Williams: His Contribution to the American Tradition* (1953; New York, 1974), 227–35.*
6. Roger Williams to John Winthrop, November 7, 1648, in *CWRW* 6:158–59.

7. Roger Williams, *Mr. Cottons Letter Lately Printed, Examined and Answered*, in *CWRW* 1:313.
8. *The Correspondence of Roger Williams*, ed. Glenn W. Lafantasie, 2 vols. (Providence, 1988), 1:750.
9. Roger Williams, *A Key into the Language of America*, ed. Howard M. Chapin, 5th ed. (1643; Providence, 1936), 9–10.
10. Roger Williams to John Winthrop Jr., December 18, 1675, in *CWRW* 6:377–78.
11. Williams, *A Key into the Language of America*, 53.
12. Williams counseled the following policy, which guided his own interactions with the Narragansett: first, "kiss truth where you evidently, upon your soul, see it"; second, "advance justice"; third, "seek and make peace, if possible, with all men"; finally, "secure your own life from a revengeful, malicious arrow or hatchet." Roger Williams to John Winthrop, May 28, 1647, in *CWRW* 6:146–47.
13. *Testimony of Roger Williams relative to the deed of Rhode Island, dated Providence 25, 6 (August 25), 1658,* in *CWRW* 6:305.
14. Williams, *A Key into the Language of America*, 138.
15. Williams, *A Key into the Language of America*, 16.
16. Williams, *A Key into the Language of America*, 143.
17. Williams, *A Key into the Language of America*, 7–8.
18. Williams, *The Bloudy Tenent of Persecution for Cause of Conscience Discussed and Mr. Cotton's Letter Examined and Answered*, ed. Edward Bean Underhill (1644; London, 1848), 215.*
19. This common assumption has its roots in Tocqueville's *Democracy in America*. See James T. Kloppenberg, "Life Everlasting: Tocqueville in America," in Kloppenberg, *The Virtues of Liberalism* (New York, 1998), chap. 5.*
20. See Jon Butler, *Becoming America: The Revolution before 1776* (Cambridge, MA, 2000), 90; and Alan Taylor, *American Colonies* (New York, 2001), 294–97.*
21. Winthrop, "A Model of Christian Charity," written in the spring of 1630, is reprinted in *Journal*, 1–11. On this backward-looking sensibility, see Theodore Dwight Bozeman, *To Live Ancient Lives: The Primitivist Dimension in Puritanism* (Chapel Hill, 1988). On covenants, see David A. Weir, *Early New England: A Covenanted Society* (Grand Rapids, 2005); and Patrick Collinson, *The Religion of Protestants: The Church in English Society, 1559–1625* (Oxford, 1982).*
22. *The Publications of the Colonial Society of Massachusetts*, vol. 40 (Boston, 1961), 12.*
23. The Dedham Covenant is reprinted in *The Early Records of Dedham, Massachusetts*, ed. Don Gleason Hill, 7 vols. (Dedham, 1892), 3:2–3. For detailed analysis, see Kenneth A. Lockridge, *A New England Town: The First Hundred Years* (New York, 1970), 4–22.*
24. On the Puritans' critique of Anglicanism, see Stephen Foster, *The Long Argument: English Puritanism and the Shaping of New England Culture, 1570–1700* (Chapel Hill, 1991).*
25. On the first and second meetings of the General Court, see Winthrop's *Journal*, 31–39, and the editors' note 73 on 31.*

26. On these issues, which have vexed generations of medieval English historians, see J. R. Maddicott, *The Origins of the English Parliament, 924–1327* (Oxford, 2010), 41–56, 139–47, 440–53.*
27. John Winthrop, *The History of New England from 1630 to 1649*, ed. James Savage, 2 vols. (Boston, 1853), 1:91.
28. For Winthrop's account of this challenge, see Winthrop, *Journal*, 64–67. On popular authority in early Massachusetts, see Jason S. Maloy, *The Colonial American Origins of Modern Democratic Thought* (Cambridge, 2008); and David D. Hall, *A Reforming People: Puritanism and the Transformation of Public Life in New England* (New York, 2011).*
29. See Hall, *A Reforming People*, 53–95; and David Hackett Fischer, *Albion's Seed: Four British Folkways in America* (Oxford, 1989), 181–205.*
30. "Att the Genrall Court, holden att Newe Towne, March 3, 1635," in *Records of the Governor and Company of Massachusetts Bay*, ed. Nathaniel B. Shurtleff, 5 vols. (Boston, 1853), 1:172.*
31. William Perkins, *Epieikeia, or a Treatise on Christian Equity*, in *The Work of William Perkins*, ed. Ian Breward (Abingdon, 1970). A selection from Perkins's *Treatise* is in *Puritan Political Ideas, 1558–1794*, ed. Edmund S. Morgan (Indianapolis, 1965), 59–73; the quoted passage appears on 71. On arbitration, mutuality, and equity, see also Hall, *A Reforming People*; and Mark Fortier, *The Culture of Equity in Early Modern England* (Aldershot, 2005).*
32. Edmund S. Morgan, *Inventing the People: The Rise of Popular Sovereignty in England and America* (New York, 1988), 42; Derek Hirst, *The Representative of the People? Voters and Voting in England under the Early Stuarts* (Cambridge, 1975).*
33. Robert J. Dinkin, *Voting in Provincial America: A Study of Elections in the Thirteen Colonies, 1689–1776* (Westport, 1977); Alexander Keyssar, *The Right to Vote: The Contested History of Democracy in the United States* (New York, 2000).*
34. John Demos, *A Little Commonwealth: Family Life in Plymouth Colony* (New York, 1970); John Demos, *Circles and Lines: The Shape of Life in Early America* (Cambridge, MA, 2004).
35. Winthrop, *Journal*, 90.*
36. Jane Kamensky, *Governing the Tongue: The Politics of Speech in Early New England* (New York, 1997).*
37. Winthrop, "A Declaration in Defense of an Order of Court Made in May, 1637," in Morgan, *Puritan Political Ideas*, 144–49.
38. Winthrop, *Journal*, 268–69, 280–84.
39. Winthrop, *Journal*, 284.
40. Winthrop, "Model of Christian Charity," in *Journal*, 1–11.
41. Winthrop, *Journal*, 278.
42. Winthrop, *Journal*, 165; Bernard Bailyn, "The 'Apologia' of Robert Keayne," *William and Mary Quarterly*, 3rd ser., 7 (1950): 568–87; and Stephen J. Innes, *Creating the Commonwealth: The Economic Culture of Puritan New England* (New York, 1995).*

43. Lord Saye and Sele and Lord Brooke abandoned their lands in America; Winthrop affirmed that the Bay Colony would have no hereditary aristocracy. See "Certain Proposals Made by Lord Say, Lord Brooke, and Other Persons of Quality, as Conditions of Their Removing to New-England, with the Answers Thereto," in *The History of the Province and Colony of Massachusetts-Bay*, ed. Lawrence S. Mayo, 3 vols. (Cambridge, MA, 1936), 1:410–13; *The Correspondence of John Cotton*, ed. Sargent Bush Jr. (Chapel Hill, 2001), 245; and Winthrop, *Journal*, 192.*
44. Edward Winslow, *Good Newes from New England* (1624; Bedford, MA, 1996), 70; Innes, *Creating the Commonwealth*.*
45. These compacts sought to balance obedience to authority, popular decision making, and the sovereign will of God. David D. Hall, "Narrating Puritanism," in *New Directions in American Religious History*, ed. Harry S. Stout and D. G. Hart (New York, 1997), 51–83.*
46. John Robinson's letter is in William Bradford, *Of Plymouth Plantation*, ed. Francis Murphy (New York, 1981), 57.*
47. John Robinson, *Mr. Bernard's Counsels of Peace Debated*, in *The Works of John Robinson*, ed. Robert Ashton, 3 vols. (Boston, 1851), 2:140–41.
48. John Robinson, *A Just and Necessary Apology of Certain Christians*, in *Works* 3:42–43.*
49. "The Mayflower Compact," in *The Federal and State Constitutions, Colonial Charters, and Other Organic Laws of the States, Territories, and Colonies Now or Heretofore Forming the United States of America*, ed. Francis Thorpe (Washington, DC, 1909), 1841. On its Christian and Roman origins, see Maloy, *The Colonial American Origins of Modern Democratic Theory*, 100.*
50. Bradford, *Of Plymouth Plantation*, 83.
51. *Records of the Colony of New Plymouth in New England*, ed. Nathaniel B. Shurtleff and David Pulsifer, 11 vols. (Boston, 1855–61), vol. 2, *Laws, 1623–1686*, 6, 7, 3; John D. Cushing, ed., *The Laws of the Pilgrims* (Wilmington, 1977), 21.
52. "Agreement among the Settlers," in *Remarkable Providences*, ed. John Demos, rev. ed. (1972; Boston, 1991), 230–31.
53. The distinctiveness of these compacts is clear when they are compared with others that explicitly recognized the continuing sovereignty of the English monarch. See, for example, "The Combinations of the Inhabitants upon the Piscataqua River for Government, 1641," in Thorpe, *The Federal and State Constitutions*, 2445. On the relation between English and colonial law, see Mary Sarah Bilder, *The Transatlantic Constitution: Colonial Legal Culture and the Empire* (Cambridge, MA, 2004).*
54. "The Fundamental Orders of 1639" and "The Fundamental Agreement, or Original Constitution of the Colony of New Haven, June 4, 1639," both in Thorpe, *The Federal and State Constitutions*, 531, 523–4, respectively .*
55. Proverbs 11:14, a passage also favored by the Pilgrims' pastor John Robinson. For Hooker's election sermon of 1638, see *Collections of the Connecticut Historical Society* 1 (1860): 20.*

56. Commentators who associate democracy with toleration of dissent and diversity have a conception of order, authority, membership, will, and liberty different from that of Winthrop and Hooker, who thought the town, like the covenant establishing the congregation, could survive only if the cement of mutual dependence remained the spirit soldering together individuals' disparate inclinations. Self-government required such unity. Thomas Hooker, *A Survey of the Summe of Church-Discipline* (London, 1648), pt. 1, 50; and see the discussion in Perry Miller, *Errand into the Wilderness* (1956; New York, 1964), 44–47.*
57. Thomas Hooker to John Winthrop, n.d. [fall 1638], *Collections of the Connecticut Historical Society* 1 (1860): 14.*
58. John Davenport, *A Discourse about Civil Government in a New Plantation Whose Design Is Religion* (Cambridge, 1663), 14–16.*
59. Winthrop, *Journal*, 168.
60. Winthrop, *Journal*, 189. On the similarities and differences between Winthrop's and Ward's conceptions of magistrates' authority, see David D. Hall, *Ways of Writing: The Practice and Politics of Text-Making in Seventeenth-Century New England* (Philadelphia, 2008), chap. 5.*
61. Winthrop, *Journal*, 198–99.
62. That commitment derived not from skepticism similar to Montaigne's but from the tradition of English common law and Paul's counsel to the Thessalonians that they should "test everything" and "hold on to what is good." 1 Thessalonians 5:21.*
63. "The Plantation Agreement at Providence, August 17–September 6, 1640," in Thorpe, *The Federal and State Constitutions*, 3205–7.
64. "The Document Establishing the Government of Rhode Island, March 16–19, 1641," in Thorpe, *The Federal and State Constitutions*, 3207–9.
65. John D. Cushing, ed., *The Earliest Acts and Laws of the Colony of Rhode Island and Providence Plantations, 1647–1719* (Wilmington, 1977), 12. See Hall, *A Reforming People*, 125–56, on New England towns' self-conscious practices of a Christian ethic of love, mutuality, and equity in making and enforcing law and distributing land to residents and newcomers.*
66. See Warren Billings, *A Little Parliament: The Virginia General Assembly in the Seventeenth Century* (Richmond, 2004); Peverill Squire, *The Evolution of American Legislatures: Colonies, Territories, and States, 1619–2009* (Ann Arbor, 2012); and Jack P. Greene, *The Constitutional Origins of the American Revolution* (Cambridge, 2011).*
67. Ralph Hamer, *A true discourse of the present estate of Virginia and the successe of the affaires there till the 18 of June, 1614* (London, 1615); see also Edmund S. Morgan, *American Slavery, American Freedom: The Ordeal of Colonial Virginia* (New York, 1975), 83.*
68. Morgan, *Inventing the People*, 124.
69. On the recourse to slavery in the Puritan colony of Providence, founded on an island off the coast of Nicaragua, see Karen Kupperman, *Providence Island, 1630–1641: The Other Puritan Colony* (New York, 1993).*

70. Winthrop, *Journal*, 67.
71. "The Charter of Maryland, 1632," in Thorpe, *The Federal and State Constitutions*, 1677–86; the passage quoted appears on 1679.*
72. *Proceedings and Acts of the General Assembly*, January 1637–38 to September 1644, *Archives of Maryland*, vol. 1 (Baltimore, 1883), 1–39; the quotation concerning Fenwick's appearance is on 32.*
73. Michael Kammen, *Deputyes and Libertyes: The Origins of Representative Government in Colonial America* (New York, 1969); Squire, *The Evolution of American Legislatures.**

Chapter 3

1. Charles I quoted in David Wootton, ed., *Divine Right and Democracy: An Anthology of Political Writing in Stuart England* (Harmondsworth, 1986), 337.
2. On Hobbes and ancient ideas of popular government, see Quentin Skinner, "Classical Liberty, Renaissance Translation and the English Civil War," in Skinner, *Visions of Politics*, vol. 2, *Renaissance Virtues* (Cambridge, 2002), 308–43; for the reasons why we should accept Hobbes's judgment about the "democraticals," see David Wootton, "Leveller Democracy and the Puritan Revolution," in *The Cambridge History of Political Thought, 1450–1700* (hereafter *CHPT, 1450–1700*), ed. J. H. Burns with Mark Goldie (Cambridge, 1991), 412–42.*
3. *Wee have brought our hogges to a faire market; with some remembrances of the estates and conditions of Church, King, kingdome, Parliament, Armie, and citie of London. And the one, and onely way to cure all our miseries described* (London, 1648), 1–2.
4. James I, *The Trew Law of Free Monarchies; or, The Reciprock and Mutuall Dutie betwixt a Free King and His Naturall Subjects*, in *The Political Works of James I*, ed. Charles Howard McIlwain (Cambridge, MA, 1918), 53–70.
5. See J. G. Edwards, *The Second Century of the English Parliament* (Oxford, 1979); and J. C. Holt, "The Prehistory of Parliament," in *The English Parliament in the Middle Ages*, ed. R. G. Davies and J. H. Denton (Manchester, 1981), 1–28.
6. Guy Coquille, *Les oeuvres de Maistre Guy Coquille*, 2 vols. (Bordeaux, 1703), vol. 2, pt. 2, 124–25. Pierre Charron, *De la sagesse*. . . , in *Of Wisdome Three Bookes*, trans. Samson Lennard (London, 1615), 247–48. See Nannerl O. Keohane, *Philosophy and the State in France: The Renaissance to the Enlightenment* (Princeton, 1980), 135–44; and Richard Tuck, *Philosophy and Government, 1572–1651* (Cambridge, 1993), 82–94.*
7. See Otto Gierke, *The Development of Political Theory*, trans. B. Freyd (1929; New York, 1966); and Julian Franklin, "Sovereignty and the Mixed Constitution: Bodin and His Critics," in *CHPT, 1450–1700*, 298–328.
8. See Mark Kishlansky, *A Monarchy Transformed: Britain, 1603–1714* (New York, 1996); and Jonathan Scott, *England's Troubles: Seventeenth-Century English Political Instability in European Context* (Cambridge, 2000).*
9. John Fortescue, *De laudibus legum Anglie*, ed. and trans. S. B. Chrimes, 2nd ed. (1942; Cambridge, 2011), 25.
10. Thomas Smith, *De Republica Angolorum*, ed. Mary Dewar (Cambridge, 1982), 57. On Parliamentary selection, see Derek Hirst, *The Representative of the People?*

Voters and Voting in England under the Early Stuarts (Cambridge, 1975); and Mark Kishlansky, *Parliamentary Selection: Social and Political Choice in Early Modern England* (Cambridge, 1986).*

11. John Rushworth, *Historical collections of private passages of state, weighty matters in law, remarkable proceedings in five Parliaments. Beginning the sixteenth year of King James, anno 1618. And ending the fifth year of King Charles, anno 1629...*, vol. 1 (London, 1721), 40–43.
12. *Debates in the House of Commons in 1625*, ed. Samuel Rawson Gardiner (Westminster, 1873), 18–19.* On Thomas Scott, see Christopher Hill, *The World Turned Upside Down: Radical Ideas during the English Revolution* (1972; New York, 1984), 34–35.
13. On the dangers of dissent, see Richard Hooker, *Of the Lawes of Ecclesiasticall Politie*, ed. W. Speed Hill, 4 vols. (1553 or 1554; Cambridge, 1977–82).*
14. A widely read contemporary account of the "warre, plagues, fires, inundations, massacres, meteors," and other calamaties, "of townes taken, cities besieged, and "so many men slain" was Robert Burton, *The Anatomy of Melancholy* (Oxford, 1621), 15, 3.*
15. For a warning that Charles I threatened the "original rightes and constitutions" of England, see Robert Phelips, in Gardiner, *Debates in the House of Commons in 1625*, 110.*
16. Thomas Gataker, *Of the Nature and Use of Lots*, 2nd ed. (London, 1627), 36–45.*
17. John Pym's speech at Manwaring's impeachment, June 4, 1628, is reprinted in *The Stuart Constitution, 1603–1688: Documents and Commentary*, ed. John Phillips Kenyon (Cambridge, 1986), 14–16. See also Robert Ashton, "Tradition and Innovation and the Great Rebellion," in *Three British Revolutions: 1641, 1688, 1776*, ed. J. G. A. Pocock (Princeton, 1980), 212; and J. G. A. Pocock, *The Ancient Constitution and the Feudal Law*, 2nd ed. (Cambridge, 1987).*
18. John Selden in *Commons Debates 1628*, vol. 3, *21 April–27 May 1628*, ed. Robert C. Johnson, Mary Frear Keeler, Maija Jansson Cole, and William B. Bidwell (New Haven, 1977), 33. On the religious basis of Selden's ideas and why he allied with Parliament against the king in 1642, see Richard Tuck, "'The Ancient Law of Freedom': John Selden and the Civil War," in *Reactions to the English Civil War, 1642–1649*, ed. John Morrill (London, 1982), 137–61.*
19. The Petition of Right is reprinted in Wootton, *Divine Right and Democracy*, 168–71.*
20. The Protestation is reprinted in *The Constitutional Documents of the Puritan Revolution, 1625–1660*, ed. Samuel Rawson Gardiner (Oxford, 1889), 84–85.
21. Samuel Brooke quoted in Nicholas Tyacke, *Anti-Calvinists: The Rise of English Arminianism, c. 1590–1640* (Oxford, 1987), 57.*
22. *Winthrop's Journal: History of New England, 1630–1649*, ed. James K. Hosmer, 2 vols. (New York, 1908), 2:186, 301; and "Fundamentalls of the Massachusetts

[*sic*]," in *The Hutchinson Papers*, ed. William H. Whitmore and William S. Appleton, 2 vols. (Albany, 1865), 1:231.

23. Charles I, *His Majesties Answer to the Nineteen Propositions of Both Houses of Parliament* (1642), in Wootton, *Divine Right and Democracy*, 171–74.
24. Henry Parker, *Observations upon some of His Majesties late answers and expresses* (London, 1642), 8, 15.* See also Michael Mendle, *Henry Parker and the English Civil War: The Political Thought of the Public's "Privado"* (Cambridge, 1995).*
25. Henry Parker, *Jus Populi; or, A discourse wherein clear satisfaction is given as well concerning the right of subjects as the right of princes shewing how both are consistent and where they border one upon the other: as also, what there is divine and what there is humane in both and whether is of more value and extent* (London, 1644), 61.*
26. Philip Hunton, *A Treatise of Monarchy*... (1643), in Wootton, *Divine Right and Democracy*, 175–211.*
27. Hunton, *A Treatise of Monarchy*, 195, 203, 204.
28. Michael Hudson, *The Divine Right of Government: 1. Naturall, and 2. Politique*... (London, 1647), 89–99.
29. John Lilburne, *Regall Tyrannie discovered* (London, 1647), is discussed in *Leveller Manifestoes of the Puritan Revolution*, ed. Don M. Wolfe (New York, 1944), 7–18, 154. A fine recent collection is *The English Levellers*, ed. Andrew Sharp (Cambridge, 1998).*
30. Parker ridiculed Lilburne in *A Letter of Due Censure*..., dated June 21, 1650, quoted in Wolfe, *Leveller Manifestoes*, 5 n. 6. The most recent comprehensive study of the Levellers is Rachel Foxley, *The Levellers: Radical Political Thought in the English Revolution* (Manchester, 2013).*
31. Lilburne urged a fresh start for England, based not on history but on reason, in *The Free-mans Freedome Vindicated* (London, 1646), 11.*
32. *A Remonstrance of Many Thousand Citizens*, July 7, 1646, is reprinted in Wolfe, *Leveller Manifestoes*, 112–30; and see Overton, *A Pearle in a Dounghill*, quoted in Wolfe, *Leveller Manifestoes*, 8–9.
33. Richard Overton, *An Arrow against All Tyrants and Tryany* [*sic*] (London, 1646), 3–4; John Lilburne, *Londons Liberty in Chains*... (London, 1646), 4; Lilburne, *The Charters of London* (London, 1646); and see Wolfe, *Leveller Manifestoes*, 11–14.
34. S. D. Glover, "The Putney Debates: Popular versus Elitist Republicanism," *Past and Present* 164 (August 1999): 47–80, shows that Leveller leaders such as Lilburne, Overton, Waldwyn, and Wildman sought to empower the poor, not only the propertied.*
35. Lilburne, *Regall Tyrannie discovered*..., 99.
36. Anonymous (Overton?), *A New Found Strategem*... (London?, 1647), 9.
37. *A Declaration of the Engagements, Remonstrances, Representations*... *from Fairfax, and the Generall Councel of the Army* (London, 1647), 8.
38. John Lilburne, *Rash Oaths unwarrantable*, May 31, 1647, in *The Clarke Papers: Selections from the Papers of William Clarke*, ed. C. H. Firth, 2 vols. (London, 1992), 1:6–7, 38. See also Wolfe, *Leveller Manifestoes*, 28–29, 133–34.

39. Cromwell in Firth, *The Clarke Papers* 1:209.
40. Overton, *An Appeale, From the degenerate Representative Body the Commons of England assembled at Westminster: To the Body Representing The free people in general of the several Counties, Cities, Townes, Burroughs, and places within this Kingdome of England, and Dominion of Wales* (London, 1647), in Wolfe, *Leveller Manifestoes*, 156–88.*
41. Overton, *An Appeale,* 163–65.
42. Overton, *An Appeale*, 158–63, 176–83, for Overton's denials that he and Lilburne were disloyal and his accusation that Parliament was guilty of "High Treason."*
43. Overton, *An Appeale*, 182.
44. Overton, *An Appeale*, 173.
45. Overton, *An Appeale*, 189–90, 194, for Overton's arguments for electing magistrates and guaranteeing freedom of conscience.*
46. Overton, *An Appeale*, 188.
47. On Overton's place in the wider battle of ideas, see Nicholas McDowell, *The English Radical Imagination: Culture, Religion, and Revolution, 1630–1669* (Oxford, 2003).*
48. The innovations of the Stuart monarchy led the people of England to civil war, revolution, and republic. The Restoration showed that the vast majority never abandoned their loyalties to the monarchy and the Church of England. See Robert Ashton, "Tradition and Innovation and the Great Rebellion," 208–23; Conrad Russell, *The Causes of the English Civil War* (Oxford, 1992); and Austin Woolrych, *Britain in Revolution* (Oxford, 2003).*
49. Convinced that only a small fraction of soldiers shared the Levellers' views, Cromwell considered a Presbyterian-dominated Parliament a greater threat to his fellow Independents than the king, with whom he recommended beginning negotiations. *The Case of the Army*, October 15, 1647, in Wolfe, *Leveller Manifestoes*, 198–224.*
50. *An Agreement of the People*, November 3, 1647, is in Wolfe, *Leveller Manifestoes*, 225–34; the quotations are from 228.
51. Cromwell in Firth, *The Clarke Papers* 1:236–37.
52. Cromwell in Firth, *The Clarke Papers* 1:277–78.
53. Thomas Rainsborough in Firth, *The Clarke Papers* 1:271. It is worth noting that the Putney debates were unknown until they were published in this collection in 1891. To place the Putney debates in context, see Mark Kishlansky, "Consensus Politics and the Structure of Debate at Putney," and David Underdown, "Commentary," in *The Origins of Anglo-American Radicalism*, ed. Margaret Jacob and James Jacob (Boston, 1984), 70–85, 127–129, respectively; and Mark Kishlansky, "Ideology and Politics in the Parliamentary Armies," in Morrill, *Reactions to the English Civil War*, 163–83.*
54. The Putney debates of October 29, 1647, are reprinted in Wootton, *Divine Right and Democracy*, 285–317. Rainsborough's celebrated opening speech is on 285.*
55. Wootton, *Divine Right and Democracy,* 291–92.

56. Wootton, *Divine Right and Democracy*, 292–93.
57. Wootton, *Divine Right and Democracy*, 296–97.
58. Wootton, *Divine Right and Democracy*, 294.
59. Wootton, *Divine Right and Democracy*, 198–99.
60. John Lawmind (the pseudonym chosen by John Wildman), *Putney Projects*, December 30, 1647, 44, British Library, E. 421 (19).
61. Thomas Edwards, *Gangraena* (London, 1646), pt. 3, preface.*
62. Anonymous (attributed to Winstanley), *More Light Shining in Buckingham-shire* (London, 1649), 16.
63. See the preface to Firth, *The Clarke Papers*, li, where these phrases appear in "a letter from the Agents to the regiments which they represented, dated November 11."*
64. On the *Declaration by Congregationall Societies*, November 22, 1647, see Wolfe, *Leveller Manifestoes*, 58n11.
65. On the Levellers' awkward situation and the tendency of recent scholars to reproduce the judgments rendered by their contemporaries, see the discussion of these issues in Wootton, "Leveller Democracy and the Puritan Revolution," in *CHPT, 1450–1700*, 430–34.*
66. On Corkbush, see G. E. Aylmer, *Rebellion or Revolution: England from Civil War to Restoration* (Oxford, 1986), 86–90.
67. John Lilburne, *An impeachment of high treason against Oliver Cromwell...* (London, 1649), 23.
68. Ireton in Firth, *The Clarke Papers* 2: 98.
69. *Agreement of the People* (1647), in Wolfe, *Leveller Manifestoes*, 227.
70. Richard Overton in *The Leveller Tracts, 1647–1653*, ed. William Haller and Godfrey Davies (Gloucester, MA, 1964), 231.*
71. *An Agreement of the People* (January 15, 1649), in Wolfe, *Leveller Manifestoes*, 333–50.
72. Jason Peacey, ed., *The Regicides and the Execution of Charles I* (New York, 2001).
73. On private interest and the common good in the *Declaration* of June 14, 1647; the *Remonstrance* of June 23, 1647; the *Declaration* of August 2, 1647; the *Remonstrance* of November 1648; and the *Declaration* of December 6, 1648, see Mark Kishlansky, "Ideology and Politics in the Parliamentary Armies," in Morrill, *Reactions to the English Civil War*, 163–83.*
74. John Cook, *A compleate collection of the lives speeches private passages, letters and prayers of those persons lately executed...* (London, 1661), quoted in J. C. Davis, "Religion and the Struggle for Freedom in the English Revolution," *Historical Journal* 35, no. 3 (1992): 507–30. The quotation appears on 521.
75. The Leveller leaders proposed an arbitration process that mirrored the proposal enacted in Rhode Island in 1640. In England, the idea came to nothing.*
76. The third *Agreement of the People*, April 14, 1649, in Wolfe, *Leveller Manifestoes*, 400–10.
77. William Walwyn, *Manifestation*, April 14, 1649, in Wolfe, *Leveller Manifestoes*, 388–96.

78. William Walwyn, *Walwins Wiles* (1649), in Haller and Davies, *The Leveller Tracts, 1647–1653*, 302.
79. Walwyn, *Manifestation.*
80. William Walwyn, *The Power of Love* (London, 1643), 43. The other Leveller leaders shared Walwyn's Puritan convictions. Reflecting on his career from his cell in the Tower in June 1649, Lilburne wrote that he had sought only to be "entirely and solely the servant of God." John Lilburne, *The Legall Fundamentall Liberties of the People of England* (1649), in Haller and Davies, *The Leveller Tracts*, 403.*
81. John Lilburne, *Strength out of Weaknesse...* (London, 1649), in Haller and Davies, *The Leveller Tracts*, 21–22. On the role of religion in the English Civil War, see John S. Morrill, "The Religious Context of the English Civil War," in Morrill, *The Nature of the English Revolution* (London, 1993); and Glen Burgess, "Was the English Civil War a War of Religion? The Evidence of Political Propaganda," *Huntington Library Quarterly* 61 (1998): 173–201.*
82. Walwyn, *Manifestation.*
83. On Katherine Chidley, who championed women's rights but insisted women remain subservient to God's will, see Ian Gentles, "London Levellers in the English Revolution: The Chidleys and their Circle," *Journal of Ecclesiastical History* 29 (1978): 281–309.*
84. See J. S. Morrill, ed., *Oliver Cromwell and the English Revolution* (London, 1990).*
85. Harrington's writings are available in many editions, including *The Political Works of James Harrington*, ed. J. G. A. Pocock (Cambridge, 1977); see 332–33 on liberty of conscience in *Oceana*.*
86. *The Journal of John Winthrop, 1630–1649*, ed. Richard s. Dunn and Laetitia Yeandle (Cambridge, MA, 1996), 84–85, 94, 109–13, 118–22. On Vane's ideas, see Michael P. Winship, *Making Heretics: Militant Protestantism and Free Grace in Massachusetts, 1636–1641* (Princeton, 2002); and Violet A. Rowe, *Sir Henry Vane the Younger: A Study in Political and Administrative History* (London, 1970), which includes, as Appendix F, "The Character of Sir Henry Vane by Algernon Sidney," 275–83.*
87. On Hugh Peter, the standard biography remains Raymond P. Stearns, *The Strenuous Puritan: Hugh Peter, 1598–1660* (Cambridge, MA, 1954).*
88. For Milton's writings on these subjects, see *The Complete Prose Works of John Milton*, ed. Don M. Wolfe et al., 8 vols. (New Haven, 1953–82). Two of Milton's texts, *The Tenure of Kings and Magistrates*, published two weeks after Charles I was put to death in 1649, and *A Defense of the People of England* (1651), are available in Milton, *Political Writings*, ed. Martin Dzelzainis (Cambridge, 1991); a third, *The Readie and Easie Way to Establish a Free Commonwealth* (1660), is reprinted in *The Struggle for Sovereignty: Seventeenth-Century English Political Tracts*, ed. Joyce Lee Malcolm, 2 vols. (Indianapolis, 1999) 1: 505–25.*
89. Milton, *An Apology against a Pamphlet...* (London, 1642).*
90. Milton, *Aeropagitica*, in *Prose Writings*, ed. K. M. Burton (New York, 1958), 149–50.

91. Milton, *The Tenure of Kings and Magistrates*, in Dzelzainis, *Political Writings*, 3–48.*
92. Milton, *Eikonoklastes*, in Wolfe et al., *Complete Prose Works* 3:542.
93. On the subtle changes in Milton's arguments, see the introduction by Martin Dzelzainis to Milton, *Political Writings*, especially x–xxv.*
94. Milton, *A Defense of the English People*, in Dzelzainis, *Political Writings*, 67, 251, 252.
95. Milton, *A Defense of the English People*, 80; see also 156–57, 184–91.
96. Milton, *A Defense of the English People*, 194; see also Dzelzainis's introduction, xxiv–xxv.
97. Milton, *The Readie and Easie Way*, 509–10.*
98. "The happiness of a nation must needs be firmest and certainest in a full and free Councel of their own electing, where no single person but reason only swayes." Milton, *The Readie and Easie Way*, 510–12.*
99. For the judgment that "patrician social prejudices" tarnished Milton's "radical intellectual convictions," see Hill, *The World Turned Upside Down*, 401.*
100. Milton, *The Readie and Easie Way*, 514–17.
101. In Milton's judgment, "liberty of conscience" and "the civil rights and advancements of every person according to his merit" would be best "obtained, if every county in the land were made a little commonwealth." Milton, *The Readie and Easie Way*, 520–23.*
102. See Charles W. A. Prior, *A Confusion of Tongues: Britain's Wars of Reformation, 1625–1642* (New York, 2012); Steven Pincus, "Neither Machiavellian Moment nor Possessive Individualism: Commercial Society and the Defenders of the English Commonwealth," *American Historical Review* 103 (1998): 705–36; and Scott, *England's Troubles*.*
103. See Tuck, *Philosophy and Government, 1572–1651*, 279–348; and Quentin Skinner, *Visions of Politics*, vol. 3, *Hobbes and Civil Science* (Cambridge, 2002).*
104. See Scott, *England's Troubles*, 46–48; and Charles Carlton, *Going to the Wars: The Experience of the British Civil Wars, 1638–1651* (London, 1992). Things could have been even worse, as they were in Europe's wars of religion: see Barbara Donagan, "Atrocity, War Crime, and Treason in the English Civil War," *American Historical Review* 99 (1994): 1137–66; and Benjamin Kaplan, *Divided by Faith: Conflict and the Practice of Toleration in Early Modern Europe* (Cambridge, MA, 2007).
105. On the consequences of the Civil War, see Hill, *The World Turned Upside Down*; Lawrence Stone, "The Results of the English Revolutions of the Seventeenth Century," in Pocock, *Three British Revolutions*, 23–108; Kishlansky, *A Monarchy Transformed*; and Aylmer, *Rebellion or Revolution*.*
106. Milton, *The Readie and Easie Way*, 523.
107. For Vane's speech and the record of his trial, see Malcolm, *The Struggle for Sovereignty*, 531–62.*
108. Edwin S. Gaustad, *Liberty of Conscience: Roger Williams in America* (Grand Rapids, 1991), 137–40; John M. Barry, *Roger Williams and the Creation of the*

American Soul: Church, State, and the Birth of Liberty (New York, 2012), 341–57. David Hall, *A Reforming People: Puritanism and the Transformation of Public Life in New England* (New York, 2012), 49–50, observes that English reformers "fell significantly short of what the colonists had accomplished."*

Chapter 4

1. See Scott Sowerby, *Making Toleration: The Repealers and the Glorious Revolution* (Cambridge, MA, 2013); Julian Hoppit, *A Land of Liberty? England, 1689–1727* (Oxford, 2000), 25; and Jonathan Israel, ed., *The Anglo-Dutch Moment: Essays on the Glorious Revolution* (Cambridge, 1991).
2. See Paul Seaward, *The Cavalier Parliament and the Reconstruction of the Old Regime, 1661–1667* (Cambridge, 1989); and Jonathan Scott, *England's Troubles: Seventeenth-Century English Political Instability in European Context* (Cambridge, 2000).*
3. On Filmer, see Peter Laslett's introduction to Robert Filmer, *Patriarcha*, ed. Peter Laslett (Oxford, 1949); and for the *Presentment of the Grand Jury of Ossulston* (1662), see Tim Harris, *London Crowds in the Reign of Charles II* (Cambridge, 1987), 144.*
4. Vane's speech, delivered June 6, 1662, and the account of his trial are reprinted in Joyce Lee Malcolm, ed., *The Struggle for Sovereignty: Seventeenth-Century English Political Tracts*, 2 vols. (Indianapolis, 1999), 2:531–62.*
5. William Bedloe, *A Narrative and Impartial Discovery of the Horrid Popish Plot...* (London, 1679), 2. On anti-Catholicism, see Jonathan C. D. Clark, *The Language of Liberty, 1660–1832: Political Discourse and Social Dynamics in the Anglo-American World* (Cambridge, 1994).
6. Anthony Ashley Cooper, Earl of Shaftesbury, "Two Seasonable Discourses concerning this Present Parliament" and "A Letter from a Person of Quality, to His Friend in the Country," both from 1675, are reprinted in Malcolm, *The Struggle for Sovereignty* 2:592–602, 606–49.
7. *Vox Populi; or, The Peoples Claim to their Parliaments Sitting to Redress Grievances, and Provide for the Common Safety; by the Known Laws and Constitutions of the Nation* (London, 1681), is reprinted in Malcolm, *The Struggle for Sovereignty* 2:651–69.
8. "Manus haec inimica tyrannis / Ense petit placidam sub libertate quietam." Like so much else in Sidney's life, even the provenance of this celebrated motto is uncertain. He never acknowledged having written the second line, and the first line may be a quotation from an unknown source. See Chester N. Greenough, "Algernon Sidney and the Motto of the Commonwealth of Massachusetts," *Proceedings of the Massachusetts Historical Society* 51 (1917–18): 262. On Sidney's life, see Alan Craig Houston, *Algernon Sidney and the Republican Heritage in England and America* (Princeton, 1991).*
9. Sidney to Bulstrode Whitelock, November 13, 1659, in *Sydney Papers, consisting of a journal of the Earl of Leicester, and original letters of Algernon Sydney*, ed. Robert Blencowe (London, 1825), 169–73; Sidney to [his father] the Earl of Leicester, July 28, 1660, in *Sydney Papers*, 189–94.

10. Algernon Sidney, *Court Maxims*, ed. Hans W. Blom, Eco Haitsma Mulier, and Ronald Janse (Cambridge, 1996), 188. See also Sidney, "The Character of Sir Henry Vane," reprinted in Violet A. Rowe, *Sir Henry Vane the Younger* (London, 1970), 278–82. For Sidney's inscription, "Sit Sanguinis Ultor Justorum," see Jonathan Scott, *Algernon Sidney and the English Republic, 1623–1677* (Cambridge, 1988), 171.
11. Sir George Downing to Edward Hyde, Earl of Clarendon, June 23, 1665, in T. H. Lister, *Life and Administration of Edward, First Earl of Clarendon . . .*, 3 vols. (London, 1837), 3:388; and William Scot to Lord Arlington, c. August 18–21, 1666, in Houston, *Algernon Sidney and the Republican Heritage in England and America*, 42.
12. Sidney, *Court Maxims*, 44, 197.
13. Sidney, *Court Maxims*, 4, 15.
14. Sidney, *Court Maxims*, 24.
15. The learned, Sidney observed, might invoke Littleton, Coke, and the common law, but he counseled reading only ancient philosophers and the Bible. Sidney, *Court Maxims*, 123, 125.*
16. Sidney, *Court Maxims*, 4, 12.
17. Algernon Sidney, *Discourses concerning Government*, ed. Thomas G. West (Indianapolis, 1990), 192.
18. See Blair Worden, "Republicanism, Regicide and Republic: The English Experience," in *Republicanism: A Shared European Heritage*, ed. Martin van Gelderen and Quentin Skinner, 2 vols. (Cambridge, 2002), 1:307–27, esp. 326n13.
19. On Sidney's exile and return to England, see Houston, *Algernon Sidney and the Republican Heritage in England and America*, 30–45.*
20. Englishmen with resources routinely purchased their neighbors' votes; the word "sham" entered the English language in the 1670s to describe such corrupt practices. See William Penn [using the pseudonym Philanglus], *England's Great Interest in the Choice of this New Parliament, Dedicated to All Her Freeholders and Electors* (London, 1679), 1.*
21. "I must confess," Sidney wrote, "I do not know three men of a mind, and that a spirit of giddiness reigns among us, far beyond any I ever observed in my life." Sidney to George Savile, May 5, 1679, in *Letters of the Honourable Algernon Sidney* (London, 1742), 53–54.
22. Royal spies suspected Sidney of allying with Shaftesbury in the Exclusion Crisis and participating in the Rye House Plot, both of which now seem false; and of helping to write seditious pamphlets challenging the legitimacy of the king's repeated dissolutions of Parliament, which was almost certainly true. Sidney to Benjamin Furly, October 13, 1680, in *Original Letters of John Locke, Algernon Syndey and Lord Shaftesbury*, ed. T. Forster (London, 1847), 98.*
23. On Sidney's role in this crisis, see Jonathan Scott, *Algernon Sidney and the Restoration Crisis, 1677–1683* (Cambridge, 1991).*
24. George Jeffreys, *The Tryal of Algernon Sydney*, in *Sydney on Government*, ed. J. Robertson (London, 1772), quoted in Scott, *England's Troubles*, 362.

25. Sidney and his contemporaries saw the world in terms of neither a market economy nor a classical polis but above all in terms of their understanding of the responsibilities of Protestant Christians. See Houston, *Algernon Sidney and the Republican Heritage in England and America*, 3–11, 122–30; and Scott, *England's Troubles*, 290–97, 352–55.*
26. "Liberty solely consists in an independency upon the will of another, and by the name of slave we understand a man, who can neither dispose of his person nor goods, but enjoyes all at the will of his master." Sidney, *Discourses*, 17.
27. Sidney, *Discourses*, 102–3.
28. Sidney, *Discourses*, 99, 166.
29. Sidney, *Discourses*, 478–79.
30. Sidney, *Discourses*, 13.
31. Sidney, *Discourses*, 396–97, 502–7; and see J. R. Pole, *Political Representation in England and the Origins of the American Republic* (1966; Berkeley, 1971), 13–17.*
32. Sidney considered federal governments such as Switzerland or the United Provinces inferior to England's legislature, because Parliament was premised on the assumption that "every county does not make a distinct body, having in itself a sovereign power, but is a member of that great body which comprehends the whole nation. 'Tis not therefore for *Kent* or *Sussex*, *Lewis* or *Maidstone*, but for the whole nation, that the members chosen in those places are sent to serve in parliament." Sidney, *Discourses*, 451.
33. Sidney, *Discourses*, 443–44.
34. Sidney, *Discourses*, 559.
35. As we shall see, on that point Sidney disagreed with William Penn's less prudent assessment of human potential. Sidney, *Discourses*, 461, 451, 173; and cf. 149–50, 357, and 524–25.*
36. Sidney, *Discourses*, 548.
37. Individuals are merely "rough pieces of timber or stone" to be shaped to fit together. Sidney, *Discourses*, 83–85.*
38. Sidney described the jury that found him guilty as "a rabble of men of the meanest callings," lacking autonomy, experience in public affairs, and the ethic of reciprocity that Sidney prized—those most likely to favor absolute monarchy and least likely to embrace Sidney's republican values. For *The Apology of A. Sydney, in the Day of his Death*, in *Sydney on Government*, see Scott, *England's Troubles*, 448.*
39. Sidney, *The Very Copy of a Paper Delivered to the Sheriffs, upon the Scaffold on Tower-Hill, on Friday Decemb. 7, 1683* (London, 1683), 2.*
40. Free nations "are governed by their own laws and magistrates according to their own mind"; only the enslaved are content with aristocracy or monarchy. Sidney, *Discourses*, 440; see also 502–503.*
41. The most influential of such misreadings were those of Leo Strauss and C. B. Macpherson.*
42. This now-standard way of reading Locke originated with Peter Laslett's introduction to his edition of Locke, *Two Treatises of Government* (1960; Cambridge,

1963), 15–135; and John Dunn, *The Political Thought of John Locke: An Historical Account of the Argument of the "Two Treatises of Government"* (Cambridge, 1969).*

43. In his unpublished *Tracts* and his correspondence, Locke acknowledged his relief, at that stage in his life, that the monarchy had been restored. Locke's letters to his father and to Thomas Westrow are in *The Correspondence of John Locke*, ed. E. S. de Beer, 8 vols. (Oxford, 1976–1989), 1:136–37, 124–25.*
44. Locke's status as a Carolina "landgrave" never yielded him a penny. On the relation between Locke's ownership of stock in the Royal African Company, which profited from the slave trade, and his political writings, cf. Jeremy Waldron, *God, Locke, and Equality: Christian Foundations in Locke's Political Thought* (Cambridge, 2002), 198–206; and David Armitage, "John Locke, Carolina, and the *Two Treatises of Government*," *Political Theory* 32 (2004): 602–27.*
45. Maurice Cranston, *John Locke: A Biography* (1957; Oxford, 1985), 202, 246–57.
46. Locke to the Earl of Pembroke, December 8, 1684, in Locke, *Correspondence* 2:664.*
47. Locke, *Correspondence* 3:634.*
48. Locke to Clarke, April 19/29, 1687, *Correspondence* 3:173. In a letter to William Molyneux written January 19, 1694, Locke wrote, "Every one, according to what way Providence has placed him in, is bound to labour for the public good, as far as he is able, or else he has no right to eat." *Correspondence* 4:786.*
49. "Every man has an immortal soul," Locke wrote, "capable of eternal happiness or misery," and doing what is "necessary to the obtaining of God's favor" is "the highest obligation that lies upon mankind." Locke, *Letter concerning Toleration*, ed. Mark Goldie (Indianapolis, 2010), 11–15, 44–45.*
50. Locke first expressed this conviction, which he reached in the early 1670s, in *A Letter from a Person of Quality to his Friend in the Country*. Not coincidentally, he left for France immediately after that tract was published anonymously in 1675. The *Letter* is included in the appendix to Locke, *Political Essays*, ed. Mark Goldie (Cambridge, 1997), 360–65, even though its authorship remains contested.*
51. Notwithstanding Locke's eloquent defense of toleration, he considered both Catholics and atheists beyond the pale. Cf. Duncan Ivison, "The Nature of Rights and the History of Empire," in *British Political Thought in History, Literature and Theory*, ed. David Armitage (Cambridge, 2006), 191–211; and Waldron, *God, Locke, and Equality*, 218–23.
52. Locke's case against absolutism depends on arguments developed in *The Second Treatise*, in which he laid out his own principles of government. That makes *The First Treatise* hard to follow for readers not immersed in Filmer, and it corroborates the claim that Locke was working on both books simultaneously in the late 1670s and early 1680s, at just the time when he was deeply engaged with Shaftesbury in the Exclusion Crisis.*
53. Locke, *Second Treatise*, in *Two Treatises of Government*, ed. Peter Laslett (1960; Cambridge, 1988), 268. All citations to the *First Treatise* and the *Second Treatise* are to the 1988 version of Laslett's edition.*

54. Locke, *Second Treatise*, 268–69.
55. In England, the people had established episcopal government in the domain of religion and Parliament in the realm of politics; in both spheres Hooker considered those appointed the legitimate agents of the people. On Hooker's explosive ideas, see Richard Tuck, *Philosophy and Government, 1572–1651* (Cambridge, 1993), 146–53.*
56. To that ethic of reciprocity Hooker and Locke added the "relation of equality between our selves and them, that are as our selves," a relation that "natural reason hath drawn for direction of Life," a principle of which "no Man is ignorant." Locke quoting from Hooker, *Ecclesiastical Polity*, the edition of 1676, in *Second Treatise*, 310–11.*
57. Locke, *Second Treatise*, 271.
58. On Grotius in historical context, see Tuck, *Philosophy and Government, 1572–1651*, 154–201.
59. See Grotius, *The Free Sea*, ed. David Armitage (Indianapolis, 2004); and Martine van Ittersum, "Profit and Principle: Hugo Grotius, Natural Rights Theories and the Rise of Dutch Power in the East Indies, 1595–1615" (unpub. Ph.D. diss., Harvard University, 2002).
60. Oldenbarnevelt was a prominent public official—for a time the chief minister of Holland, the most powerful among the United Provinces—and the decision of the States-General to arrest him and Grotius indicated that religious unrest in the United Provinces had escalated to a point near civil war. Oldenbarnevelt was convicted, in part on the basis of testimony given by his associate Grotius, and was martyred, just as Sidney was, for the cause of religious toleration. After his escape from prison, Grotius remained in France for the rest of his life, first on a royal pension for his services to the French government, then as an envoy from Sweden to France—except for a brief sojourn in 1631 back in the United Provinces, from which he was again expelled.
61. Pufendorf, *De jure naturae et gentium libri octo*, trans. C. H. Oldfather and W. A. Oldfather, 2 vols. (Oxford, 1934), 2:1010–11, 1064, 1077.
62. Pufendorf, *De jure naturae et gentium libri octo* 2:205.*
63. On natural law theory, see Leonard Krieger, *The Politics of Discretion: Pufendorf and the Acceptance of Natural Law* (Chicago, 1965); and Richard Tuck, *Natural Rights Theories: Their Origin and Development* (Cambridge, 1979).*
64. Locke, *Second Treatise*, 331–33.
65. Locke, *Second Treatise*, 329–32.*
66. As the suspicions aroused by Locke's unpublished arguments suggest, his arguments for equality and popular sovereignty, although less radical than those of some Levellers and clearly far short of our standard of universal suffrage, placed him among the more democratically inclined of English political writers.*
67. The problem was hard to fix because current arrangements suited those in Parliament, but those arrangements reflected custom, not "true reason." Locke, *Second Treatise*, 372–74.*

68. Locke, *First Treatise*, 211–16; *Second Treatise*, 363, 353. On Locke's ideas concerning property, see James Tully, *A Discourse on Property: John Locke and His Adversaries* (Cambridge, 1980); Richard Ashcraft, *Revolutionary Politics and Locke's "Two Treatises of Government"* (Princeton, 1986), 120–23; and Waldron, *God, Locke, and Equality.* A recent addition to these arguments for seeing "divine command," not individual property rights, as the "bedrock" of Locke's philosophy is Steven Forde, *Locke, Science and Politics* (Cambridge, 2014), 1–10, 175–81.*
69. Were the government to dissolve for any reason, Locke argued, power would logically revert to the people, who would then "constitute a new Form of Government." The body exercising this ultimate power was not necessarily "a Democracy" or any other particular form of government, but merely the "independent community" that maintains "the supreme power" in any political system. Locke, *Second Treatise*, 354.*
70. Locke was familiar with the writings of Henry Parker and John Wildman and with the monarchomach tradition, which held that power reverts to the legislature in cases of usurpation. Locke also knew the now-obscure writings of George Lawson, who criticized the Commonwealth for constituting its authority on the basis of the already discredited Parliament rather than appealing directly to the English people. On the influence of Lawson on Locke, see Julian Franklin, *John Locke and the Theory of Sovereignty: Mixed Monarchy and the Right of Resistance in the Political Thought of the English Revolution* (Cambridge, 1978).*
71. Locke refused assignment as ambassador to the court of Frederick III, Elector of Brandenburg, on the grounds that he could not hold his beer. Either his constitution had changed since he had claimed in 1684 that he had gone to Holland for the beer, or the explanation of 1689 was as specious as that he offered five years earlier. See Cranston, *Locke*, 312.
72. Locke's letter to William Clarke, written in late 1689 or early 1690, is reprinted in James Farr and Clayton Roberts, "John Locke on the Glorious Revolution: A Rediscovered Document," *Historical Journal* 28 (1985): 385–98.*
73. Farr and Roberts, "John Locke on the Glorious Revolution."
74. John Locke, *An Essay concerning Human Understanding*, ed. Peter H. Nidditch (Oxford, 1979), bk. 1, chap. 4, par. 17, 95.
75. For contrasting judgments concerning the implications of Locke's religious convictions for our "post-Christian" age, cf. Dunn, *The Political Thought of John Locke*, 262–67; and Waldron, *God, Locke, and Equality*, 240–43.*
76. Locke, *Essay*, bk. 3, chap. 11, par. 16, 517; bk. 2, chap. 11, par. 10, 159. See also Waldron, *God, Locke, and Equality*, 50–81; and Ivison, "The Nature of Rights and the History of Empire," 194.*
77. Locke, *Essay*, bk. 4, chap. 10, par. 6, 621.
78. "Such a submission as this of our *reason* to *faith*, takes not away the landmarks of knowledge; this shakes not the foundations of reason, but leaves us that use of our faculties, for which they were given us." Locke, *Essay*, bk. 4, chap. 18, par. 10, 696.

79. See Locke, *Essay*, bk. 4, chap. 19, par. 12, 703; and Dunn, *The Political Thought of John Locke*, 249–50.
80. Locke and many of his interpreters write "Christianity" when they mean "Protestant Christianity."*
81. Locke's egalitarianism and his ethics flowed from his conviction that rational capacity exists in every person. Locke, *Essay*, bk. 4, chap. 20, par. 3, 708.*
82. Locke, *Essay*, bk. 4, chap. 20, par. 16, 717.
83. Locke's journal quoted in Cranston, *John Locke*, 265n1.
84. Locke, *Essay*, bk. 2, chap. 21, par. 52, 267; and cf. Locke's letter to Edward Clarke, April 19/29, 1687, discussed on pp. 155–56 above.
85. Locke, *Some Thoughts concerning Education*, ed. John W. Yolton and Jean S. Yolton (Oxford, 1989), 103. Cf. the following passage from 170: "Covetousness, and the Desire of having in our Possession, and under our Dominion, more than we have need of, being the Root of all Evil, should be early and carefully weeded out, and the contrary Quality of a Readiness to impart to others, implanted."
86. Locke, *Some Thoughts concerning Education*, 111, the same wording as that in the letter to Edward Clarke discussed on pp. 155–56 above.
87. John Locke, *The Reasonableness of Christianity: As Delivered in the Scriptures*, ed. John C. Higgins-Biddle (Oxford, 1999), 89, 150.*
88. Locke, *The Reasonableness of Christianity*, 149.
89. Locke, *Second Treatise*, 358.
90. See Locke's letter to William Molyneux, January 19, 1694, on the universal obligation "to labour for the public good." On Locke's conception of what follows from the duty to develop one's God-given capacities through labor, see Duncan Kelly, *The Propriety of Liberty: Persons, Passions, and Judgment in Modern Political Thought* (Princeton, 2011), 20–58.*
91. These passages come from two of the tracts printed in the spring of 1689, *A Brief Collection of Some Memorandums* and *A Letter to a Friend, Advising him, in this extraordinary Juncture, how to free the Nation from Slavery for ever*, both quoted in Lois G. Schwoerer, "The Bill of Rights: Epitome of the Revolution of 1688–89," in *Three British Revolutions, 1641, 1688, 1776*, ed. J. G. A. Pocock (Princeton, 1980), 230–31. For others of these tracts, see Malcolm, *The Struggle for Sovereignty* 2:847–1064.*
92. "A Paper which was delivered to the house of Commons on Monday 28th January 1688 [i.e., 1689]...said to be written by the Marquis of Halifax" (Rawlinson Ms. D 1079, 8, Bodleian Library); and "Proposals to this present Convention," in *The Eighth Collection of Papers Relating to the Present Juncture of Affairs* (London, 1689), 33.*
93. These judgments, of course, remain contested. These years also saw the first appearance of what might be called a women's-rights sensibility, notably in the work of Lady Mary Chudleigh and Mary Astell. See Mary Astell, *Political Writings*, ed. Patricia Springborn (Cambridge, 1996); and Patricia Springborn, *Mary Astell: Theorist of Freedom from Domination* (Cambridge, 2005).*

94. See Linda Colley, *Britons; Forging the Nation, 1707–1837* (New Haven, 1992); and David Armitage, *The Ideological Origins of the British Empire* (Cambridge, 2000).
95. Cf. Derek Hirst, *The Representative of the People? Voters and Voting in England under the Early Stuarts* (Cambridge, 1975); Mark Kishlansky, *Parliamentary Selection: Social and Political Choice in Early Modern England* (Cambridge, 1986); and John A. Cannon, *Parliamentary Reform, 1640–1832* (Cambridge, 1973).*
96. On politics after 1689, see Tim Harris, *Politics under the Later Stuarts: Party Conflict in a Divided Society, 1660–1715* (London, 1993); John Brewer, *Party Ideology and Popular Politics at the Accession of George III* (Cambridge, 1976); and J. H. Plumb, *The Growth of Political Stability in England, 1675–1725* (London, 1967).
97. *The Manuscripts of His Grace the Duke of Portland*, quoted in Hoppit, *A Land of Liberty?*, 271.
98. James quoted in Edmund S. Morgan, *Inventing the People: The Rise of Popular Sovereignty in England and America* (New York, 1988), 125. James understood that the capacity of representative assemblies to make trouble was more than a fiction.*
99. For the 1678 Petition from the Massachusetts General Court, see *Records of the Governor and Company of the Massachusetts Bay in New England, 1628–1686*, ed. Nathaniel Bradstreet Shurtleff, 5 vols. (Boston, 1853–54), 5:200.
100. The petitions from 1683 and 1685 are in Shurtleff, *Records of the Governor and Company of the Massachusetts Bay* 5:201, 495.
101. Wise and Dudley quoted in Perry Miller, *The New England Mind*, vol. 2, *From Colony to Province* (1953; Boston, 1961), 156. The record of the court case against the Ipswich men, August 23, 1687, is in Gay Transcripts 3:59, 62–68, Massachusetts Historical Society.*
102. On Bulkeley, see Timothy Breen, *The Character of the Good Ruler: A Study of Puritan Political Ideas in New England, 1630–1730* (New Haven, 1970), 176–79; and Brendan McConville, *The King's Three Faces: The Rise and Fall of Royal America* (Chapel Hill, 2006), 94–95.*
103. Cotton Mather's *Declaration, of the Gentlemen, Merchants, and Inhabitants of Boston, and the Country adjacent* quoted in Samuel Eliot Morison, *The Intellectual Life of Colonial New England* (1936; New York, 1956), 199. For a more comprehensive view of New Englanders' complaints against Andros, see *The Andros Tracts*, ed. William Whitmore, 3 vols. (Boston, 1868–74).*
104. Increase Mather quoted in Miller, *From Colony to Province*, 169. On the persistence and transformation of piety as New England was drawn into transatlantic economic and religious networks, cf. Breen, *The Character of the Good Ruler*, 134–79; and Mark Peterson, "*Theopolis Americana*: The City-State of Boston, the Republic of Letters, and the Protestant International, 1689–1739," in *Soundings in Atlantic History: Latent Structures and Intellectual Currents, 1500–1830*, ed. Bernard Bailyn and Patricia L. Denault (Cambridge, MA, 2009), 329–70.*

105. On voter eligibility and turnout in Massachusetts, see Richard Beeman, *The Varieties of Political Experience in Eighteenth-Century America* (Philadelphia, 2004), 69–79.*

106. For an excellent analysis of the relation between the Puritan tradition of covenant and the Charter of 1691, see John Brooke, *The Heart of the Commonwealth: Society and Political Culture in Worcester County, Massachusetts, 1713–1861* (Cambridge, 1989), 19–25.

107. Writing in support of Sidney's candidacy for Parliament, Penn defended the "Right and Title to your own Lives, Liberties and Estates," recommended "governing on a ballance, as near as possible, of the severall Religious interests," and urged voters to choose "the most Wise, Sober and Valiant of the People, not Men of mean Spirits or sordid *Passions* that would sell the *Interest* of the People that chuse them to advance their own, or be at the Beck of some great Man, in the hopes of a *Lift* to a good Employ; pray beware of these." The early history of Pennsylvania would test Penn's convictions. Penn, *One Project for the Good of England* (1679), in Penn, *Works*, 2 vols. (London, 1726), 1:482; and Penn [Philanglus], *Englands Great Interest in the Choice of this New Parliament* (London, 1679), 3.

108. [William Penn and Thomas Rudyard], *The Peoples Antient and Just Liberties*, quoted in Gary De Krey, "The First Restoration Crisis: Conscience and Coercion in London, 1667–1673," *Albion* 25 (1993): 573. See Richard S. Dunn and Mary Maples Dunn, eds., *The World of William Penn* (Philadelphia, 1986).*

109. William Penn, *England's Present Interest Considered* (1675), in *Works* 1:674.

110. See John E. Pomfret, *Colonial New Jersey: A History* (New York, 1973).*

111. Penn sought to create a refuge for Quakers and others seeking freedom of conscience, establish a form of government free of corruption, and improve his own economic prospects. Penn's letter to Sidney, October 13, 1681, shows that Sidney helped Penn frame the government of Pennsylvania. See Houston, *Algernon Sidney and the Republican Heritage in England and America*, 232–34.*

112. "All differences between the planters and the natives" were to be resolved by a body of twelve mediators, "six planters and six natives," so that "we may live friendly together" and prevent "all occasions of heart-burnings and mischief." Penn sought to secure for Native Americans the same rights and legal protections that settlers would enjoy. Penn's "Concessions to the Province of Pennsylvania" (1681) is reprinted in *Colonial Origins of the American Constitution: A Documentary History*, ed. Donald Lutz (Indianapolis, 1998), 266–70.

113. Penn, "Charter of Liberties and Frame of Government of the Province of Pennsylvania in America," from *Votings and Proceedings* 1:xxvii–xxviii; reprinted in Lutz, *Colonial Origins*, 272–86.

114. Penn, "Charter of Liberties and Frame of Government."

115. William Penn, *The Great Question to be Considered by the King, and this approaching Parliament...* (London, 1680), 4.

116. William Penn, "Some Account of the Province of Pennsylvania" (1681), in *Narratives of Early Pennsylvania, West New Jersey and Delaware, 1630–1707*, ed. Albert Cook Myers (1912; New York, 1956), 203–207.
117. Penn, "A Further Account of the Province of Pennsylvania" (1685), in Myers, *Narratives of Early Pennsylvania, West New Jersey and Delaware, 1630–1707*, 255–78.*
118. William Penn to Thomas Lloyd, in Penn, *Letters* 3: 50.
119. Locke's journal, with his critical commentary on Penn's Frame of Government, is quoted in Cranston, *Locke*, 261–62.*
120. Cranston, *Locke*, 298.
121. Penn retained executive authority and vast land holdings in Pennsylvania, which sparked the earliest political battles in the colony. William Penn, *Papers* 4:283; and Alan Tully, *Forming American Politics: Ideals, Interests, and Institutions in Colonial New York and Pennsylvania* (Baltimore, 1994), 408–21.*
122. Of course many fewer than were eligible actually voted, and rates of participation, as well as the meaning of voting, varied as widely as eligibility did. See Beeman, *Varieties of Political Experience in Eighteenth-Century America,* 22, 52, 75, 103–6, 211; and David Hackett Fischer, *Albion's Seed: Four British Folkways in America* (New York, 1989), 815.*
123. See chapters 2 and 3 above.
124. John Davenport quoted in Miller, *The New England Mind: The Seventeenth Century* (1939; Boston, 1961), 421.*
125. On Gershom Bulkeley, see pp. 175–76 above.
126. The relation between colonial legislation and English law was contested from the start and never clarified.*

Chapter 5

1. Scholarship on the Enlightenment is immense: a list of judiciously selected titles, limited to works on political theory alone, runs to seventy densely packed pages: *The Cambridge History of Eighteenth-Century Political Thought* (hereafter *CHECPT*), ed. Mark Goldie and Robert Wokler (Cambridge, 2006), 830–900. Two classics are Ernst Cassirer, *The Philosophy of Enlightenment*, trans. Fritz C. A. Koellen and James P. Pettegrove (1936; Princeton, 1951); and Peter Gay, *The Enlightenment: An Interpretation*, 2 vols. (New York, 1966–69). Recent studies include Anthony Pagden, *The Enlightenment and Why It Still Matters* (New York, 2013); Michael L. Frazier, *The Enlightenment of Sympathy: Justice and the Moral Sentiments in the Eighteenth Century and Today* (Oxford, 2010); and three volumes by Jonathan Israel, *Radical Enlightenment: Philosophy and the Making of Modernity, 1650–1750* (Oxford, 2001); *Enlightenment Contested: Philosophy, Modernity, and the Emancipation of Man, 1670–1752* (Oxford, 2006); and *Democratic Enlightenment: Philosophy, Revolution, and Human Rights, 1750–1790* (New York, 2011). Notable essays include Jonathan Israel, "Enlightenment! Which Enlightenment?" *Journal of the History of Ideas* 67

(2006): 523–45, on *Encyclopedia of the Enlightenment*, ed. Alan Charles Kors et al., 4 vols. (New York, 2003); Anthony LaVopa, "A New Intellectual History? Jonathan Israel's Enlightenment," *Historical Journal* 52 (2009): 717–38; and Darrin M. McMahon, "What Are Enlightenments?" *Modern Intellectual History* 4 (2007): 601–16.*

2. Scholars have long recognized the limited penetration of enlightened ideas: Robert Darnton, "In Search of Enlightenment: Recent Attempts to Create a Social History of Ideas," *Journal of Modern History* 43 (1971): 113–32; J. H. Plumb, "Reason and Unreason in the Eighteenth Century: The English Experience," in *Some Aspects of Eighteenth-Century England*, ed. J. H. Plumb and Venton Dearing (Los Angeles, 1971), 3–26; Henry May, *The Enlightenment in America* (New York, 1976); Robert A. Ferguson, *The American Enlightenment, 1750–1820* (Cambridge, MA, 1997). On the persistence of religious practices and popular resistance to Enlightenment, see James E. Bradley and Dale Van Kley, eds., *Religion and Politics in Enlightenment Europe* (Notre Dame, 2001).*
3. These two French terms express the conviction of many champions of Enlightenment that they were engaged in a project that was both an exercise in philosophical inquiry and something broader than that, a project that would bring to European cultures the illumination of reason through the efforts of writers who were hardly technical or professional philosophers but rather men and (at least toward the end of the eighteenth century) women of letters. Both terms have become so firmly entrenched in English discourse that they do not require translation.*
4. Baruch Spinoza, one of the Enlightenment's most radical figures, thought the risks of democracy in practice outweighed its attractiveness in theory. See Israel, *The Radical Enlightenment*, 14–22, 72–77, 258–62, 270–74; and Richard H. Popkin and Mark Goldie, "Scepticism, Priestcraft, and Toleration," in *CHECPT*, 70–109.*
5. Voltaire, *Letters concerning the English Nation* (London, 1778), 46, in *The Enlightenment: A Comprehensive Anthology*, ed. Peter Gay (New York, 1973), 147–74. For Voltaire's assessment of Newton, see his letter to the abbé d'Olivet, October 18, 1736, in *Correspondence*, ed. Theodore Besterman, 13 vols. (Paris, 1977–), 1:281.*
6. Joseph Addison, *Spectator* 1, no. 44 (March 12, 1711).
7. Anthony Ashley Cooper, 3rd Earl of Shaftesbury, to Jean Le Clerc, *The Life, Unpublished Letters and Philosophical Regimen of Anthony, Earl of Shaftesbury* (1900), quoted in Roy Porter, *The Creation of the Modern World* (New York, 2000), 3; and see 487–88n9.*
8. Anthony Ashley Cooper, 3rd Earl of Shaftesbury, *An Inquiry concerning Virtue or Merit*, vol. 1 of *Characteristics of Men, Manners, Opinions, Times, etc.*, ed. John M. Robertson (1900), excerpted in *British Moralists, 1650–1800*, ed. D. D. Raphael 2 vols. (1969; Indianapolis, 1991), 1:167–88; the passages quoted are from bk. 2, pts. 1 and 2, on pp. 175, 188.*

9. Voltaire, *Political Writings*, ed. and trans. David Williams (Cambridge, 1994), 59–60.
10. That such offices, primarily judicial but to a degree legislative, could be bought and sold occasioned understandable criticism. Montesquieu defended the practice because he deemed it preferable to enhancing even further the power of the monarchy—and the possibility of corruption—by making such offices appointive. By custom, royal decrees became law only when registered by the provincial parlements. A parlement could—and sometimes did—simply ignore such decrees, thereby providing a check against royal absolutism prized by many aristocrats in a nation still rooted in its diverse local traditions.
11. See Mark Hulliung, *Montesquieu and the Old Regime* (Berkeley, 1976); and Judith Shklar, *Montesquieu* (Oxford, 1987).*
12. Or did it? Montesquieu also wrote a supplement to the fable that he never published, in which the tale ended with a new king taking advice from a wise subject who urges him to avoid extravagance and exemplify virtue both through his own moderation and by eradicating extreme poverty and great wealth. Montesquieu, *Persian Letters*, ed. and trans. Christopher J. Betts (New York, 1973), 53–61, 166, 219, 286–87. See Michael Sonenscher, *Before the Deluge: Public Debt, Inequality, and the Intellectual Origins of the French Revolution* (Princeton, 2007), 95–172, on Montesquieu's ideas concerning the implications of luxury for government.*
13. On Fénelon, see Nannerl Keohane, *Philosophy and the State in France: The Renaissance to the Enlightenment* (Princeton, 1980), 332–46; Michael Sonenscher, *Sans-Culottes: An Eighteenth-Century Emblem in the French Revolution* (Princeton, 2008), 202–59; and Patrick Riley's introduction to his edition of Fénelon, *Telemachus* (Cambridge, 1994).
14. On Mandeville, see E. J. Hundert, *The Enlightenment's Fable: Bernard Mandeville and the Discovery of Society* (Cambridge, 1994); and Donald Winch, *Riches and Poverty: An Intellectual History of Political Economy in Britain, 1750–1834* (Cambridge, 1996), 57–89.
15. Montesquieu, *Considerations on the Causes of the Romans' Greatness and Decline*, in Melvin Richter, *The Political Theory of Montesquieu* (Cambridge, 1977), 53.
16. On the wide range of responses to *The Spirit of the Laws*, see Sonenscher, *Before the Deluge*, 173–74; Duncan Kelly, *The Propriety of Liberty: Persons, Passions and Judgement in Modern Political Thought* (Princeton, 2011), 59–116; and Aurelian Craiutu, *A Virtue for Courageous Minds: Moderation in French Political Thought, 1740–1830* (Princeton, 2012).*
17. See Shklar, *Montesquieu*, 97–98.*
18. Only those voters willing to state their preference in public, as citizens did in Athens, possessed sufficient virtue to participate in electoral politics. Montesquieu, *The Spirit of the Laws*, ed. Franz Neumann, trans. Thomas Nugent (New York, 1949), 12.*
19. Montesquieu, *The Spirit of the Laws*, 13, 15.*

20. The French term *moeurs*, central to Montesquieu and later to Rousseau and Tocqueville, presents a challenge to all translators. Sometimes it is best rendered by the English word "customs," at other times by "manners," at other times by "morals." It refers to the bundle of practices that constitute a culture and give it a distinctive quality related to, but not reducible to, its laws, religion, and ethical convictions.
21. Montesquieu, *The Spirit of the Laws*, 40–45, 120–21. On Montesquieu's debts to earlier thinkers, see Eric Nelson, *The Greek Tradition in Republican Thought* (Cambridge, 2007), 159–76.*
22. Montesquieu, *The Spirit of the Laws*, 109–11, 149–51.
23. Montesquieu, *The Spirit of the Laws*, 151–62.
24. Such a representative government Montesquieu judged superior to ancient democracies because the people as a whole were incapable of executing the laws: "They ought to have no share in the government but for the choosing of representatives, which is within their reach." Montesquieu, *The Spirit of the Laws*, 307–11, 154–55.*
25. Duty as Montesquieu conceived of it took diverse forms, including religious and ethical virtue as well as political virtue, as he was at pains to indicate to critics who accused him of atheism.*
26. On Montesquieu's ambivalence, see Hulliung, *Montesquieu and the Old Regime*; and Kelly, *The Propriety of Liberty*.
27. Montesquieu's reply to his critics, first printed as the preface to the posthumous edition of *The Spirit of the Laws* (1757), in *The Spirit of the Laws*, pp. lxvii–lxix in the Neumann edition.*
28. Jean le Rond d'Alembert, *Preliminary Discourse to the Encyclopedia of Diderot* (1751), ed. and trans. Richard N. Schwab and Walter E. Rex (Indianapolis, 1963), 99–100.
29. According to d'Alembert, once Rome's citizens became accustomed to imperial luxury, they subjected themselves to masters—precisely the logic of the fable of the Troglodytes. D'Alembert's eulogy is reprinted in vol. 1 of André Masson's *Oeuvres complètes de Montesquieu*, 3 vols. (Paris, 1950–55).*
30. Catholics in France as well as Christians elsewhere in Europe adapted to the scientific revolution and the Enlightenment without adopting a secular or skeptical orientation. See Bradley and Van Kley, *Religion and Politics in Enlightenment Europe*; and Jonathan Sheehan, *The Enlightenment Bible: Translation, Scholarship, Culture* (Princeton, 2005).*
31. D'Alembert, *Preliminary Discourse*, 6–7, 36, 74–84.
32. D'Alembert, *Preliminary Discourse*, 22; Denis Diderot, "Encyclopedia," from *The Encyclopedia*, in *Rameau's Nephew and Other Works*, trans. Jacques Barzun and Ralph H. Bowen (Indianapolis, 1956), 294.*
33. Voltaire, *Essay on Manners and Spirits of Nations*, excerpted in *The Portable Enlightenment Reader*, ed. Isaac Kramnick (New York, 1995), p. 375. On aspirations to uniformity, see David W. Bates, *Enlightenment Aberrations: Error and*

Revolution in France (Ithaca, 2002); and Henry Vyverberg, *Human Nature, Cultural Diversity, and the French Enlightenment* (Oxford, 1989).*

34. Voltaire, *Histoire du parlement de Paris*, ed. J. Renwick (Oxford, 2005), 467.*
35. In his *Preliminary Discourse*, D'Alembert offered a miniature version of social contract theory, locating humans' understanding of natural law not in God's will, as Locke believed, but in conscience. D'Alembert, *Preliminary Discourse*, 36, 12–13, 44–45, 26.*
36. Although the phrase "*laissez-faire, laissez-passer*" did not originate with the physiocrats, it became the slogan associated with their campaign to reorganize the French economy and French politics by circumventing traditional constraints.*
37. In Turgot's words, "Manners are gradually softened, the human mind takes enlightenment, separate nations draw nearer to each other, commerce and policy connect at last all parts of the globe"—in sum, humanity "marches always, although slowly, toward still higher perfection." Anne-Robert-Jacques Turgot, "A Philosophical Review of the Successive Advances of the Human Mind," in *Turgot on Progress, Sociology and Economics*, ed. and trans. Ronald L. Meek (Cambridge, 1973).*
38. Because the mature economic conditions necessary for free trade were not yet in place, Turgot considered it necessary at times to provide public employment, support food imports, revise taxes temporarily, and prevent landowners from removing tenants.*
39. In a treatise intended to explain his rationale, Turgot adopted, in the words of his contemporary François Métra, "the tone of a father who explains to his children the measures he has taken for their welfare and who desires that their submission be as enlightened as it is willing." See Emma Rothschild, *Economic Sentiments: Adam Smith, Condorcet, and the Enlightenment* (Cambridge, 2001), 17–39; and Keith Michael Baker, *Condorcet: From Natural Philosophy to Social Mathematics* (Chicago, 1975), 55–64.
40. On Turgot's and Condorcet's plans for a system of assemblies ranging from the local to the national, see Baker, *Condorcet*, 56–57, 193, 208–14.*
41. Denis Diderot, "Political Authority," in *The Encyclopedia*, ed. and trans. Stephen J. Gendzier (New York, 1967), 185–88.
42. Denis Diderot, "Citoyen," in *Encyclopédie*, ed. Denis Diderot and Jean le Rond D'Alembert, 17 vols. (Paris, 1751), 3:489.
43. Diderot spelled out the implications of the general will for ethics with little more precision: "The general will in each individual is a pure act of understanding that reasons in the silence of the passions about what man can demand of his fellow man and about what his fellow man can rightfully demand of him." Diderot, "Natural Rights," in *The Encyclopedia*, 170–75.*
44. See Robert Darnton, *The Business of Enlightenment: A Publishing History of the Encyclopédie* (Cambridge, 1979).*
45. On the 1770 decree against d'Holbach, see Jerome Schneewind, *The Invention of Autonomy: A History of Modern Moral Philosophy* (Cambridge, 1998), 413.

46. In *De l'esprit* (1758), Helvétius vociferously denied the existence of God and left no room for an eternal reward to prod individuals toward virtue. That was the job of the legislator. Helvétius, *De l'Esprit* (Paris, 1973), 2:xv, 139. In his posthumously published *De l'homme* (1772), Helvétius declared that sociability springs not from any "innate quality" such as the moral sense or a divine spark but from "the necessity of mutual assistance." Helvétius, "Sociability," in *A Treatise on Man: His Intellectual Faculties and His Education*, ed. and trans. W. Hooper, 2 vols. (London, 1810), 1:134, 140.*
47. Paul Henri Thiry Baron d'Holbach, *Système social: ou principes naturels de la morale et de la politique... (1781)*, 2 vols. (Hildesheim, 1969), 1:7–8.
48. Holbach argued that distinct social orders, including the clergy, the nobility, the magistrates, the merchants, and the farmers, required their own representatives because members of these orders, self-interested as humans always are, can never know the interests of the others, and only a king can transcend particular interests and represent the interests of the nation as a whole. Holbach, "Representatives," in *The Encyclopedia*, 214–22.*
49. See Robert Darnton, *The Forbidden Best-Sellers of Pre-Revolutionary France* (New York, 1995); and Derek Beales, *Enlightenment and Reform in Eighteenth-Century Europe* (London, 2005), 28–35.
50. Voltaire's amusing articles on law and the state in his *Philosophical Dictionary* offer only equal-opportunity indictments of existing legal codes. Voltaire, *Philosophical Dictionary*, ed. Peter Gay (New York, 1962), 42, 58, 190–94, 272–73, 281–88, 322, 386–94, 398–400. On the controversies generated by Voltaire's religious ideas, see René Pomeau, *La religion de Voltaire*, 2nd ed. (Paris, 1969).
51. See Beales, *Enlightenment and Reform in Eighteenth-Century Europe.*
52. Voltaire, *Idées républicaines*, in *Oeuvres de Voltaire* (Paris, 1869), 5:396–403.
53. Voltaire to d'Alembert, October 16, 1765, in *Oeuvres complètes de Voltaire*, vol. 43, *Correspondance avec M. d'Alembert* (Paris, 1821), 331–33.
54. On Rousseau's life, the best sources are his *Confessions* (1781), ed. and trans. J. M. Cohen (London, 1953), quotations from 34, 40; Maurice Cranston's two-volume biography, *Jean-Jacques: The Early Life and Work of Jean-Jacques Rousseau, 1712–1754* (New York, 1983) and *The Noble Savage: Rousseau, 1754–1762* (Oxford, 1991); and Jean Starobinski, *Jean-Jacques Rousseau: Tranparency and Obstruction*, trans. Arthur Goldhammer, 2nd ed. (1957, 1971; Chicago, 1988).
55. Rousseau, *Confessions*, 106, 205.
56. Rousseau, *Confessions*, 225–26.
57. Rousseau, *Confessions*, 252–57. Initiated into the wonders of music along with other mysteries by Mme. de Warens, Rousseau wrote an opera entitled *La découverte du nouveau monde*, inspired perhaps by the departure of his uncle Bernard for South Carolina. While a member of the Mably household, Rousseau produced his first treatise on education.*
58. Rousseau, *Confessions*, 306.

59. During this period Rousseau also provided the research notes necessary for M. and Mme. Dupin to compose their three-volume critique of Montesquieu's *Spirit of the Laws*.*
60. This question, stated in these words by the Academy of Dijon, is often rendered as Rousseau himself did: "Has the restoration of the sciences and arts tended to purify or corrupt morals?" By introducing "or corrupt," Rousseau signaled his dramatic departure. See the editor's notes to Rousseau, *The First and Second Discourses*, ed. Roger D. Masters, trans. Roger D. Masters and Judith R. Masters (New York, 1964), 66–67n7.
61. Rousseau's account of this life-changing incident shows the distance he had traveled from his early affinity with ancient stoicism and the reasons why variants of the adjective "Rousseau-esque" soon entered most European languages to convey the onset of irresistibly powerful emotions almost beyond expression: "All at once I felt my mind dazzled by a thousand lights, a crowd of splendid ideas presented themselves to me with such force and in such confusion, that I was thrown into a state of indescribable bewilderment." Rousseau to Malesherbes, January 12, 1762, *Correspondance complète de J.-J. Rousseau*, ed. R. A. Leigh, 14 vols. (Geneva, 1965–95), 10:24–29.*
62. Rousseau, *Confessions*, 327; and cf. Cranston, *Jean-Jacques*, 226–29.
63. Rousseau referred to Voltaire as "famed Arouet" to avoid using Voltaire's pen name, a symbol of lost authenticity in the quest for mere celebrity. See Rousseau, *First Discourse*, 53, 72–73n41.*
64. Rousseau, *First Discourse*, 36, 51; and cf. 46–47.
65. Rousseau's self-conscious adoption of a simple life of virtue has struck many commentators as an attempt to justify abandoning to a state orphanage the five children he and Thérèse had together.*
66. On the contrast between Rousseau's two ideals, the rustic simplicity of family life in a Swiss mountain village and the austere, disciplined civic republicanism of Sparta, see Judith Shklar, *Men and Citizens* (Cambridge, 1969).*
67. Rousseau, *Oeuvres complètes*, ed. B. Gagnebin, M. Raymond, et al., 5 vols. (Paris, 1959–95), 4: 245.
68. Rousseau, *Second Discourse*, 92–93; and cf. 108–41, 180–81.*
69. Voltaire to Rousseau, August 30, 1755, in *Correspondance complète de J.-J. Rousseau*.*
70. Rousseau rejected Hobbes's bleak portrait of the state of nature, but he conceded that the pity operating among savages evaporated through an inevitable and irreversible process set in motion by instinct and reason, the engine of human perfectibility.*
71. Rousseau, *Second Discourse*, 133.
72. Rousseau, *Second Discourse*, 150–60.
73. Rousseau, *Second Discourse*, 163–70.
74. Rousseau, *Second Discourse*, 167–68.
75. Rousseau, *Second Discourse*, 168–72.

76. Rousseau, *Second Discourse*, 202.
77. To understand Rousseu's writings historically, we must bracket those who later invoked his ideas. See Starobinski, *Jean-Jacques Rousseau*, 29–30, 382 n. 20.*
78. Rousseau, *Emile; or, On Education*, ed. and trans. Allan Bloom (New York, 1979), 444–46, 473, 325.*
79. Rousseau, *Emile*, 235, 289–90; see also 233–36 for the relation between the experience of friendship and the development of an ethical sensibility, and the relation between morality and justice.*
80. *Emile* is the story of an isolated child growing up in a world largely without politics. His development mirrors the transformation of society from the state of nature to the degraded state of civilization. His education counteracts that tendency and teaches Emile how to transmute the primitive impulse of pity into a mature ethic of reciprocity, thereby keeping at bay the fatal danger of self-love. Rousseau's paeans to the innocence of childhood and his celebrations of play and reverie reversed traditional views of children as miniature adults. His portraits of women, by contrast, merely reinforced male dominance and helped usher in a new, romantic ideal of swooning women dependent on their fathers, lovers, and husbands. Transferring to a civic setting the tutor's maxim to place duty before inclination is the challenge Rousseau would tackle in the *Social Contract*. Rousseau, *Emile*, 211–36.*
81. Rousseau, "Political Economy," in Rousseau, *On the Social Contract, with "Geneva Manuscript" and "Political Economy,"* ed. Roger D. Masters, trans. Judith R. Masters (New York, 1978), 209–11, 229–36.
82. Rousseau, "Political Economy," 211–15.
83. Rousseau, "Political Economy," 214–16.
84. Rousseau, "Political Economy," 216–18.
85. Rousseau, "Political Economy," 220.
86. Rousseau, "Political Economy," 223–24.
87. Rousseau, "Political Economy," 224–31.
88. Rousseau was restating one of the crucial arguments of the *First Discourse* that Diderot resisted, which explains why Diderot printed an article by Nicolas-Antoine Boulanger under the heading "Political Oeconomy" in volume 10 of the *Encyclopedia*. See Robert Derathé, *Jean-Jacque Rousseau et la science politique de son temps* (Paris, 1979), 248–94.
89. Rousseau, *Geneva Manuscript*, 157–63.*
90. See Robert R. Palmer, *The Age of Democratic Revolutions*, vol. 1, *The Challenge* (1959; Princeton, 1969), 119.
91. See C. Girard, "Jean-Jacques Rousseau et la démocratie deliberative: bien commun, droits individuels et unanimité," *Lumières* 15 (2010): 199–221; and Nadia Urbinati, *Representative Democracy: Principles and Genealogy* (Chicago, 2006), 6–16, 60–100.*
92. As astute translators have pointed out, Rousseau not only had an available alternative that lacked the ambiguity of his chosen formulation (viz., the French

verb *naisser*, to be born); he employed that alternative when he wanted to avoid the ambiguity he preferred for the opening of the book.*

93. Rousseau, *On the Social Contract*, 53–55; Rousseau's emphasis.
94. Rousseau, *On the Social Contract*, 55. Though not universally accepted, this interpretation of the general will has had distinguished champions ever since Kant.*
95. Rousseau, *On the Social Contract*, 55–56.
96. Madison identified a similar problem; for his solution, see chapters 8 and 9 below.
97. Rousseau, *On the Social Contract*, 61–67.
98. To explain Rousseau's emphasis on the generality of the general will and his anxiety about the negative consequences of individualism and partial associations, different interpreters have emphasized the psychodynamics of Rousseau, the Catholic tradition, scientific accounts of Nature, philosophical paeans to Reason, and the French veneration of the semidivine figure of the king.*
99. Rousseau's letter to Mirabeau is quoted in Keohane, *Philosophy and the State in France*, 443.*
100. Rousseau, *Geneva Manuscript*, 168.*
101. Rousseau, *On the Social Contract*, 67–71.
102. Rousseau, *On the Social Contract*, 67, 71–75.
103. Only the island nation of Corsica, Rousseau concluded, met the criteria for establishing a democracy.*
104. Rousseau, *On the Social Contract*, 84–85; and cf. *Emile*, 465–66.
105. René-Louis de Voyer de Paulmy, marquis d'Argenson, *Considérations sur le gouvernement ancien et présent de la France* (Amsterdam, 1764), 8, 27–28.*
106. Rousseau, *On the Social Contract*, 111–12.*
107. Rousseau claimed that his plan for Poland was "deduced" from the "principle" of the *Social Contract*. Rousseau, *Considerations on the Government of Poland*, in *Rousseau: Political Writings*, ed. and trans. Frederick Watkins (London, 1953), 193–95.*
108. Rousseau, *Constitutional Project for Corsica*, an incomplete and unpublished manuscript, in *Rousseau: Political Writings*, 277–330.*
109. Rousseau, *Second Discourse*, 79.*
110. Rousseau, *Second Discourse*, 80.*
111. Rousseau, *Second Discourse*, 82–83.
112. Rousseau, *Second Discourse*, 79, 81–82, 85. Rousseau believed the abstract ideal of the general will was likelier to be achieved in practice not through "pure" democracy—suitable only to gods—but through the institutions of representative democracy, the means best suited to lubricating the inevitable frictions of politics.*
113. On the 1766 quarrel between Hume and Rousseau, see E. C. Mossner, *The Life of David Hume*, 2nd ed. (Oxford, 1980); and Donald Winch, *Riches and Poverty*, 52–56, which includes a reprint of the 1766 illustration *The Savage Man* poking fun at Rousseau's squabbles with Hume and Voltaire.

114. David Hume, *Enquiry concerning the Principles of Morals*, in Hume, *Enquiries concerning Human Understanding and concerning the Principles of Morals*, ed. L. A. Selby-Bigge, 3rd ed. rev, ed. P. H. Niddich (Oxford, 1978), 2:270. Rousseau and Hume did have one thing in common: they were the least characteristic figures of the French and Scottish Enlightenments.*
115. On Hume's politics, see Duncan Forbes, *Hume's Philosophical Politics* (Cambridge, 1975); and David Miller, *Philosophy and Ideology in Hume's Political Thought* (Oxford, 1981).*
116. David Hume, "Idea of a Perfect Commonwealth" (1752), in Hume, *Political Essays*, ed. Knud Haakonssen (Cambridge, 1994), 221–33.*
117. David Hume, *The History of England from the Invasion of Julius Caesar to the Abdication of James the Second* (1688), 6 vols. (Indianapolis, 1983), 5:569.
118. David Hume, "Of the Rise and Progress of the Arts and Sciences" (1742), in *Political Essays*, 70–72.
119. David Hume, "Of Refinement in the Arts" (1752), in *Political Essays*, 102.
120. David Hume, "Of the First Principles of Government" (1741), in *Political Essays*, 16.
121. David Hume, "Of the Independency of Parliament" (1741), in *Political Essays*, 24.
122. David Hume, "Of the Rise and Progress of the Arts and Sciences" (1742), in *Political Essays*, 59.
123. David Hume, "That Politics May Be Reduced to a Science" (1741), in *Political Essays*, 5.
124. David Hume, "Whether the British Government Inclines More to Absolute Monarchy, or to a Republic" (1741), in *Political Essays*, 28.
125. David Hume, "Of Parties in General" (1741), in *Political Essays*, 34–36.
126. David Hume, "Of the Independency of Parliament" (1741), in *Political Essays*, 24.
127. Hume, "Of the First Principles of Government," 17–19; "Of the Independency of Parliament," 26; "Whether the British Government Inclines More to Absolute Monarchy, or to a Republic," 31–32.
128. David Hume, "Of the Original Contract" (1748), in *Political Essays*, 186–201.
129. Douglass Adair, "'That Politics May Be Reduced to a Science': David Hume, James Madison, and the Tenth *Federalist*," *Huntington Library Quarterly* 20, no. 2 (June 1957): 343–60, is among the most widely cited pieces of scholarship on the Constitution and the process of ratification. Cf. my discussion of Madison in chapters 8 and 9 below.
130. David Hume, "Idea of a Perfect Commonwealth," in *Political Essays*, 221–33.*
131. David Hume, "Idea of a Perfect Commonwealth."*
132. David Hume, "Of the Coalition of Parties" (1758), in *Political Essays*, 206–12.
133. David Hume, "Of the Origin of Government" (1777), in *Political Essays*, 20–23.
134. See Richard Teichgraeber III, *"Free Trade" and Moral Philosophy: Rethinking the Sources of Adam Smith's "Wealth of Nations"* (Durham, NC, 1986), p. 84.

135. Fletcher quoted in Nicholas Phillipson, "The Scottish Enlightenment," in *The Enlightenment in National Context*, ed. Roy Porter and M. Teich (Cambridge, 1981), 23.*
136. Francis Hutcheson, *An Inquiry into the Original of Our Ideas of Beauty and Virtue* (1725), in Raphael, *British Moralists, 1650–1800* 1:265, 272.
137. Hutcheson, *An Inquiry*, 274, 284.*
138. Francis Hutcheson, *An Inquiry into the Original of Our Ideas of Beauty and Virtue*, ed. Wolfgang Leidhold, 2 vols. in 1 (Indianapolis, 2004), 134–35.
139. Francis Hutcheson, *System of Moral Philosophy*, 3 vols. (London, 1755), 1:77.*
140. Adam Smith, *The Theory of Moral Sentiments*, ed. Dugald Stewart (London, 1853), 3; or in the more recent and accessible Glasgow edition, ed. D. D. Raphael and J. I. Macfie (Oxford, 1976), 1.
141. Smith, *The Theory of Moral Sentiments*, 137.
142. Smith never moved as boldly toward atheism as Hume did; whether his caution reflected his own deep uncertainty—or merely prudence induced by the abuse Hume endured—cannot be known conclusively.*
143. Smith, *The Theory of Moral Sentiments*, 152.
144. Smith, *The Theory of Moral Sentiments*, 233–34.
145. Smith's review of Rousseau's *Second Discourse* appeared in the *Edinburgh Review* in 1756; see Robert Wokler, "Rousseau's Reading of the Book of Genesis and the Theology of Commercial Society," *Modern Intellectual History*, 3 (2006): 85–94; and Istvan Hont, *Politics in Commercial Society: Jean-Jacques Rousseau and Adam Smith* (Cambridge, MA, 2015).*
146. Smith, *Lectures on Jurisprudence*, ed. R. L. Meek, D. D. Raphael, and P. G. Stein (Oxford, 1978), 435.
147. Smith, *The Theory of Moral Sentiments*, 25–28; and see Donald Winch, *Adam Smith's Politics: An Essay in Historiographic Revision* (Cambridge, 1978), 158.
148. Smith, *The Wealth of Nations*, bk. 4, chap. 7, pt. 3.*
149. Smith, *The Theory of Moral Sentiments*, 25–28.*
150. On this decades-long process of resolving the so-called Adam Smith problem, related in some respects to the transformation of our understanding of the relation between Locke's philosophy and his politics, see Hont, *Politics in Commercial Society*; Charles Griswold, *Adam Smith and the Virtues of Enlightenment* (Cambridge, 1999); and Winch, *Adam Smith's Politics*.*
151. On the legacy of Adam Smith, see Winch, *Adam Smith's Politics*; and Rothschild, *Economic Sentiments*.
152. For a recent overview, see James Moore, "Natural Rights and the Scottish Enlightenment," in *CHECPT*, 291–317.
153. Hume, *The History of England* 5:146–47.
154. Hume quoted in Ernest C. Mossner, "Hume's Early Memoranda, 1729–1740: The Complete Text," *Journal of the History of Ideas* 9 (1948): 504.
155. Grieg, J. Y. T., *The Letters of David Hume*, 2 vols. (Oxford, 1932), 2:237.*

156. Grieg, *The Letters of David Hume* 2:300–301.
157. Grieg, *The Letters of David Hume* 2:302–3.
158. Grieg, *The Letters of David Hume* 2:308.
159. Grieg, *The Letters of David Hume* 2:286.
160. Denis Diderot, *Oeuvres politiques*, ed. P. Vernière (Paris, 1963), 491.*

Chapter 6

1. A wide-ranging collection of documents is *The Enlightenment in America, 1720–1825*, ed. Jose R. Torre, 4 vols. (London, 2008). See also Caroline Winterer, "What Was the American Enlightenment?" in *The Worlds of American Intellectual History*, ed. Joel Isaac, James T. Kloppenberg, Michael O'Brien, and Jennifer Ratner-Rosenhagen (New York, 2016); and Nathalie Caron and Naomi Wulf, "American Enlightenments: Continuity and Renewal," *Journal of American History* 99 (2013): 1072–91.*
2. The decades-old notion of a quarrel between champions of the "social" and "ideological" interpretations of the Revolution now impedes historical understanding.*
3. The two leading historians often characterized by their critics as offering an "ideological" or idea-centered explanation of the American Revolution have insisted on the necessity of a multidimensional account that attends to social, economic, and political as well as intellectual history. See Bernard Bailyn, *Faces of Revolution: Personalities and Themes in the Struggle for American Independence* (New York, 1990), ix–xiii; and Gordon Wood, preface to the 1998 edition of *The Creation of the American Republic, 1776–1787* (1969; Chapel Hill, 1998), v–xiii.*
4. On the dying gasps of royalism, see Brendan McConville, *The King's Three Faces: The Rise and Fall of Royal America, 1688–1776* (Chapel Hill, 2006); and Eric Nelson, *The Royalist Revolution: Monarchy and the American Founding* (Cambridge, 2014).
5. Recent years have seen an upsurge of scholarly interest in Franklin. The most detailed biography is J. A. Leo Lemay, *The Life of Benjamin Franklin*; of the projected seven volumes, the first two, covering the years 1706–47, have been published (Philadelphia, 2006).
6. Franklin's article in the *Gazette*, October 9, 1729, in *The Papers of Benjamin Franklin*, ed. Leonard Labaree et al., 41 vols. to date (New Haven, 1959–), is quoted in Alan Houston's edition of Franklin, *Autobiography and Other Writings on Politics, Economics, and Virtue* (Cambridge, 2004), 51. A comprehensive and up-to-date critical edition of Franklin's classic is *Benjamin Franklin's Autobiography*, ed. Joyce E. Chaplin (New York, 2012).
7. Franklin's debts to Milton as well as Shaftesbury and Hutcheson, and his aversion to the moral egoism of Hobbes and Mandeville, manifest themselves in *A Dissertation on Liberty and Necessity, Pleasure and Pain* (1725) and "Articles of Belief and Acts of Religion" (1728). See Douglas Anderson, *The Radical*

Enlightenments of Benjamin Franklin (Baltimore, 1997), 33–89; and on Franklin's lifelong reverence for God and adherence to Christian beliefs, see Joyce E. Chaplin, *The First Scientific American: Benjamin Franklin and the Pursuit of Genius* (New York, 2006), 29, 59–62, 337, 362.

8. For the controversy surrounding the Reverend Hemphill and Franklin's defense of his preaching, see Franklin, *Papers* 2:37–125.*
9. As imperfect creatures, Franklin believed, we should concede the limits of our knowledge: "Surrounded as we are on all sides with Ignorance and Error, it little becomes poor fallible Man to be Positive and dogmatical in his Opinions." Only forbearance could prevent conflict in a culture awash with conflicting forms of religious enthusiasm. Franklin, "Dialogue between Two Presbyterians," printed in the *Gazette*, April 10, 1735, in *Papers* 2:27–33.*
10. Franklin, *Autobiography*, ed. Houston, 79.
11. Voltaire, "Virtue," *Philosophical Dictionary*, ed. Peter Gay (New York, 1962), 398–400.
12. Women as well as men were avid readers of Addison and Steele's *Spectator* in the 1740s. A family portrait by John Greenwood, *The Greenwood-Lee Family*, painted in 1747 and held by Boston's Museum of Fine Arts, shows a woman reading the *Spectator*. As Dana Comi notes in "'In the Shade of Solitude': The Mind of New England Women, 1630–1805" (Ph.D. dissertation, Brandeis University, 2003), in the seventeenth century the woman would have been shown reading the Bible (117–18).*
13. Not that there was any necessary contradiction: by the age of forty-two, Franklin had become one of the richest men in Pennsylvania.*
14. From Homer and Virgil to *Athenian Sports*, Cicero, and Tacitus; from Montaigne, More, and Bacon to Milton, Harrington, Sidney, and Locke; from Montesquieu and Voltaire to Defoe and Hume; and from Increase and Cotton Mather to a wide range of Christian devotional literature, extant catalogs from 1641 and 1647 show the interests of a readership with strikingly wide-ranging and eclectic tastes. See Edwin Wolfe, "Franklin and His Friends Choose Their Books," *Pennsylvania Magazine of History and Biography* 80 (1956): 11–36.*
15. On the American Philosophical Society, see James E. McClellan III, *Science Reorganized: Scientific Societies in the Eighteenth Century* (New York, 1985).*
16. "The *Principal End* of Education is," according to Hutcheson, "to *form us wise and good Creatures, useful to others and happy ourselves*." In Locke's words, "'Tis VIRTUE, then, direct VIRTUE, which is to be *aim'd at* in Education." Franklin, *Proposals Relating to the Education of Youth in Pennsylvania*, in *Papers* 3: 419–20.*
17. Franklin, *Autobiography*, ed. Houston, 78–79.
18. Franklin, *Autobiography*, ed. Houston, 76–77.
19. Franklin admitted that politics usually devolves into the pursuit of self-interest, but he thought moving toward the common good would be possible if Christian benevolence replaced sectarian dogma, and the humility of Jesus and Socrates replaced arrogance. Franklin, *Autobiography*, ed. Houston, 96–97.*

20. "Manus haec inimica tryannis / Ense petit placidam sub libertatae quietem," *Pennsylvania Gazette*, November 20, 1755; the quoted passages are drawn from Sidney's *Discourses concerning Government*, ed. Thomas G. West (Indianapolis, 1990), 209, 205. See Alan Craig Houston, *Algernon Sidney and the Republican Heritage in England and America* (Princeton, 1991), 231–36.
21. Franklin, *Plain Truth*, and *Form of the Association and Remarks into which Numbers are daily entering, for the Defence of this City and Province—With Remarks on each Paragraph*, in *Papers* 3:180–204, 205–11, reprinted in *Autobiography*, ed. Houston, 180–92, 193–99. See also Franklin's own account of the process of forming the militia, and his role in it, in *Autobiography*, ed. Houston, 91–96.*
22. Franklin, "Appeal for the Hospital" (August 8, 1751), in *Papers* 4:150.
23. William Penn, "Some Account of the Province of Pennsylvania" (1681), in *Narratives of Early Pennsylvania, West New Jersey and Delaware, 1630–1707*, ed. Albert Cook Myers (1912; New York, 1956), 208. Thomas Penn quoted in Bernard Bailyn, *The Origin of American Politics* (New York, 1967), 158; Anon. [Joseph Galloway], *A True and Impartial State of the Province of Pennsylvania* (Philadelphia, 1759), 38.
24. See, for example, Richard R. Beeman, *The Varieties of Political Experience in Eighteenth-Century America* (Philadelphia, 2006); and Alan Tully, *Forming American Politics: Ideals, Interests, and Institutions in Colonial New York and Pennsylvania* (Baltimore, 1994).
25. See A. G. Roeber, "Constitutions, Charity, and Liberalism by Default: Germany and the Anglo-American Tradition," in *Republicanism and Liberalism in America and the German States, 1750–1850*, ed. Jürgen Heideking and James Henretta (Cambridge, 2002), 73–90.*
26. Franklin, *Observations concerning the Increase of Mankind, People of Countries, &c.*, in *Papers* 4:234, and *Autobiography*, ed. Houston, 221.*
27. Franklin, *Observations*, in *Autobiography*, ed. Houston, 217–21. In the first version of the essay, Franklin wrote that "every Slave" is "*by Nature* a Thief." In the revised version of 1769, in which he omitted the slur against Germans, he altered *"by Nature"* to read "from the nature of slavery." Franklin eventually admitted that slavery is morally wrong, yet he never emancipated his own slaves. See Edmund S. Morgan, *Benjamin Franklin* (New Haven, 2002), 38–39, 304–14. Like the rejection of women's equality, the acceptance of race-based slavery showed the limits of eighteenth-century conceptions of reason and the boundaries of the principles of autonomy and equality, not their hollowness. Women and nonwhites eventually won—to a still-limited degree—equal protection under the law not by repudiating those principles but by demanding that they be extended to all people. On the widespread racism of many eighteenth-century European and American thinkers, see Emmanuel Chukwudi Eze, ed., *Race and the Enlightenment* (Oxford, 1997).*
28. John Woolman, *Some Considerations on the Keeping of Negroes* (1754; New York, 1976); Anthony Benezet, *Epistle of Caution and Advice concerning the Buying and Keeping of Slaves* (Philadelphia, 1754).*

29. Franklin, *Autobiography*, ed. Houston, 109. The Plan of Union, in Franklin, *Papers* 5:374–91, is reprinted in *Autobiography*, ed. Houston, 238–55. On the origins of the idea of a federal union in the writings of Grotius, Pufendorf, and Vattel, three thinkers familiar to Franklin, see Alison LaCroix, *The Ideological Origins of Federalism* (Cambridge, 2010).*
30. On Franklin in the international network of scientists, see Chaplin, *The First Scientific American*.
31. Franklin's letter to Benjamin Rush and Jonathan Potts, December 20, 1766, in *Papers* 13:530. The passage from *The Autobiography of Benjamin Rush* is quoted in Andrew Hook, "Scottish Thought and Culture in Early Philadelphia," in *Scotland and America in the Age of Enlightenment*, ed. Richard B. Sher and Jeffrey R. Smitten (Princeton, 1990), 236–37.
32. Franklin, *Autobiography*, ed. Houston, 139–42. On the depth of Franklin's loyalism and the path he took from being "the king's man" to becoming a partisan of American independence, see Gordon Wood, *The Americanization of Benjamin Franklin* (New York, 2004).
33. Franklin to Robert Livingston, July 22, 1783, in *The Writings of Benjamin Franklin*, ed. A. Henry Smyth, vol. 9 (London, 1906), 59–73; the quotation is on 61. In a letter to Richard Morris, March 7, 1783, Franklin characterized Adams as "a certain mischievous madman" (*Writings* 9:17).
34. Wise has been a lightning rod for many historians. Cf. Timothy Breen, *The Character of the Good Ruler: A Study in Puritan Political Ideas in New England, 1630–1730* (New Haven, 1970), 251–61; and Seth Cotlar, "Languages of Democracy in America from the Revolution to the Election of 1800," in *Re-imagining Democracy in the Age of Revolutions: America, France, Britain, Ireland, 1750–1850*, ed. Joanna Innes and Mark Philp (Oxford, 2013), 15.
35. John Wise, *A Vindication of the Government of New England Churches* (Boston, 1717), 33.
36. Wise, *A Vindication*, 33–35.
37. Wise, *A Vindication*, 36–39.
38. Wise, *A Vindication*, 46–51.
39. On Walpole and his critics, see Paul Langford, *A Polite and Commercial People: England, 1727–1783* (Oxford, 1989), 9–57. On *Cato's Letters* and *The Craftsman*, see Caroline Robbins, *The Eighteenth-Century Commonwealthman* (Cambridge, 1959).*
40. Many Americans resisted the appeal of Trenchard and Gordon not because of their politics but because of their lack of piety. See Mark A. Noll, *America's God: From Jonathan Edwards to Abraham Lincoln* (Oxford, 2002), 61–63.
41. On the international dimension of the Great Awakening, see Susan O'Brien, "A Transatlantic Community of Saints: The Great Awakening and the First Evangelical Network, 1735-1755," *American Historical Review* 91 (1986): 811–32.*
42. Elisha Williams, *The Essential Rights and Liberties of Protestants. A Seasonable Plea for the Liberty of Conscience and the Right of Private Judgment, in Matters of*

Religion, Without any Controul from human Authority (Boston, 1744), reprinted in *Political Sermons of the American Founding Era, 1730–1805*, ed. Ellis Sandoz (Indianapolis, 1991), pp. 55, 62.

43. Williams, *The Essential Rights and Liberties of Protestants,* 56–60.

44. Williams, *The Essential Rights and Liberties of Protestants*, 57–58, 40, 93. The legitimacy of the people's chosen representatives—and the implicit illegitimacy of lawmakers not chosen by the people, such as Parliament in relation to the American colonists, was a standard theme of New Yorker William Livingston's *Independent Reflector* (1752–53), republished and edited by Milton M. Klein (Cambridge, 1963).

45. *Independent Advertiser*, January 11 and February 8, 1748, quoted in Peter Linebaugh and Marcus Rediker, *The Many-Headed Hydra: Sailors, Slaves, Commoners, and the Hidden History of the Revolutionary Atlantic* (Boston, 2000), 88.*

46. William Shirley to Lords of Trade, December 1, 1747, in *Correspondence of William Shirley, Governor of Massachusetts and Military Commander in America, 1731–1760*, ed. Charles H. Lincoln, 2 vols. (New York, 1912), 1:418.

47. See Robert Middlekauff, "Democracy in America before Tocqueville," Harmsworth Lecture, Oxford University, 1997.*

48. George Whitefield, *Britain's Mercies, and Britain's Duties* (Boston, 1746), 10–11, 21.*

49. Charles Chauncy, *Civil Magistrates must be just, ruling in the Fear of God* (Boston, 1747), 53, 55, 33–34.

50. Jonathan Mayhew, *A Discourse concerning Unlimited Submission and Non-Resistance to the Higher Powers: With some Reflections on the Resistance made to King Charles I* (Boston, 1750), 29–30, 32, 39.*

51. As Henry May pointed out in *The Enlightenment in America* (New York, 1976), the "skeptical Enlightenment" of Spinoza and Hume exerted almost no influence in America, whereas the "moderate Enlightenment" of Locke, Newton, Montesquieu, and the Scottish philosophers of common sense was of crucial importance.*

52. See Knud Haakonssen, "Scottish Common Sense Realism," in *A Companion to American Thought*, ed. Richard W. Fox and James T. Kloppenberg (Oxford, 1995), 618–20; and Mark Noll, "The Rise and Long Life of the Protestant Enlightenment in America," in *Knowledge and Belief in America: Enlightenment Traditions and Modern Religious Thought*, ed. William M. Shea and Peter A. Huff (Cambridge, 1995), 88–124.*

53. See Noll, *America's God*, 31–157; Jerome Huyler, *Locke in America: The Moral Philosophy of the Founding Era* (Lawrence, 1995); and Joshua Foa Dienstag, "Serving God and Mammon: The Lockean Sympathy in Early American Thought," *American Political Science Review* 90 (1996): 497–511.*

54. When Adams entered Harvard, the class was ranked according to the eminence of each student's family. Because Adams's mother was a member of the Boylston family, he ranked near the middle of the class. His father's lineage and the economic standing of his family would have placed him near the bottom. Even

though his father sold ten acres of land to finance John's education, without a partial scholarship he would have been unable to attend Harvard.

55. Even as an adolescent, Adams was appalled by "Frigid" Calvinist theology. Briant at times exchanged pulpits with Jonathan Mayhew, and Adams was powerfully drawn to their unorthodox version of Protestantism. John Adams to Nathan Webb, September 1, 1755, in *Papers of John Adams*, ed. Robert J. Taylor et al., 17 vols. to date (Cambridge, MA, 1977–), 1:1. Adams wrote that one of the ministers he met in Worcester told Adams "very civilly" that he "supposed that I took my faith on Trust from Dr. Mayhew." See *Diary and Autobiography of John Adams*, ed. L. H. Butterfield, 4 vols. (Cambridge, MA, 1962), 1:14–15.*
56. Adams, *Diary and Autobiography* 1:42–43; Adams to Samuel Quincy, April 22, 1761, in *Papers* 1:49.
57. See C. Bradley Thompson, *John Adams and the Spirit of Liberty* (Lawrence, 1998), 7–8, on the Worcester reading club; and David McCullough, *John Adams* (New York, 2001), 38, on teaching.
58. Adams to Jonathan Sewall, February 1760, in *Papers* 1:42.*
59. Draft of a letter from Adams to Jonathan Sewall, in *Diary and Autobiography* 1:123.
60. Adams, *Diary and Autobiography* 1:43.
61. Adams, *Diary and Autobiography* 1:117; John Adams, *The Earliest Diary of John Adams*, ed. L. H. Butterfield et al. (Cambridge, 1966), 66.
62. Adams, *Diary and Autobiography*1:43.
63. Adams to Charles Cushing, April 1, 1756, in *Papers* 1:12.
64. Adams, *Diary and Autobiography* 1:25.
65. Adams, *Earliest Diary*, 71.
66. Adams, *Diary and Autobiography* 1:31.
67. Adams, *Diary and Autobiography* 1:222.
68. Adams was aware of his own vanity—and equally aware of others' failures to achieve the humility that eluded him. See Adams, *Diary and Autobiography* 1:22–24, 33–34, 37, 221–22.
69. Jefferson's letter appears in *The Papers of Thomas Jefferson*, ed. Julian Boyd, 41 vols. to date (Princeton, 1950–), 11:94.
70. In his diary entry dated "January 1759," Adams resolved to allow "no Girl, no Gun, no Cards, no flutes, no Violins, no Dress, no Tobacco, no Laziness, decoy you from your Books." He vowed to study "Roman, grecian, french, English Treatises of natural, civil, common, Statute Law" and achieve "an exact Knowledge of the Nature, End, and Means of Government" by studying "Seneca, Cicero, and all other good moral Writers," including "Montesque, Bolinbroke, [illegible], &c. and all other good, civil Writers, &c." and internalize the choice of Hercules, a life of "Industry, temperance, and Honour." See John Adams, *Revolutionary Writings, 1755–1775*, ed. Gordon S. Wood (New York, 2011), pp. 36–37.
71. John Adams to Nathan Webb, October 12, 1755, in *Revolutionary Writings, 1755–1775*, 3–4.

72. See Edith Gelles, *Portia: The World of Abigail Adams* (Bloomington, 1992).*
73. See Jill Lepore, *The Book of Ages: The Life and Opinions of Jane Franklin* (New York, 2013).
74. Rev. Mather Byles quoted in Comi, "'In the Shade of Solitude,'" 143, 19–58, 69–116.*
75. John Adams to Abigail Adams, October 29, 1775, in *Adams Family Correspondence*, ed. L. H. Butterfield, 10 vols. (Cambridge, 1963), 1:316–17.*
76. Abigail Adams to Mercy Otis Warren, December 11, 1773, in *Adams Family Correspondence* 1:89.*
77. Abigail Adams to John Adams, November 27, 1775, in *Adams Family Correspondence* 1:329.
78. On these tenants' revolts and the struggles between backcountry farmers and coastal or English landlords, see Gary B. Nash, *The Unknown American Revolution: The Unruly Birth of Democracy and the Struggle to Create America* (New York, 2005), 3–8, 88–114.
79. *Boston Gazette*, May 5, 1760.
80. Adams to William Tudor, March 29, 1817, in *Works* 10:247–48; and Adams's account of the writs of assistance case in *Diary and Autobiography* 3:276.
81. Samuel Sewall, *The Selling of Joseph* (Boston, 1700).
82. Sven Beckert, Katherine Stevens, et al., *Harvard and Slavery* (Cambridge, MA, 2011).
83. The corrupt practices of British elections and patronage politics—and those of many southern colonies, where an elite of white male slaveholders persuaded less affluent white males to perpetuate their power—differed from the norms and practices of public life in the middle and New England colonies and the backcountry.*
84. James Otis, *The Rights of the British Colonies Asserted and Proved* (Boston, 1764).*
85. On the relation between English law and colonial law, see Mary Sarah Bilder, *The Transatlantic Constitution: Colonial Legal Culture and the Empire* (Cambridge, MA, 2004); and Daniel J. Hulsebosch, *Constituting Empire: New York and the Transformation of Constitutionalism in the Atlantic World, 1664–1830* (Chapel Hill, 2005). On the relation between Otis's arguments and changing conceptions of law, see *Pamphlets of the American Revolution, 1750–1776*, vol. 1, *1750–1765*, ed. Bernard Bailyn (Cambridge, MA, 1965), 446–466.*
86. See Morgan, *Benjamin Franklin*, 128–44.
87. Adams in *Boston Gazette*, August 29, 1763.
88. See J. L. Bullion, *A Great and Necessary Measure: George Grenville and the Genesis of the Stamp Act, 1763–1765* (Princeton, 1982); and Edmund S. Morgan and Helen M. Morgan, *The Stamp Act Crisis: Prologue to Revolution*, 2nd ed. (1953; New York, 1963).
89. Otis, *Vindication of the British Colonies*, in Bailyn, *Pamphlets*. Cf. Bailyn, *Ideological Origins*, 78–79, 85, 186; and Wood, *The Creation of the American Republic*, 292–95.*

90. "If those now so considerable places are not represented," Otis observed, "they ought to be." See the discussion of this point in Bailyn, *Ideological Origins*, 168–69.
91. Daniel Dulany, *Considerations on the Propriety of Imposing Taxes in the British Colonies* (Boston, 1765), 7.
92. See Jack P. Greene, *The Constitutional Origins of the American Revolution* (Cambridge, 2011); and John Phillip Reid, *Constitutional History of the American Revolution: The Authority of Law* (Madison, 1993).*
93. Mayhew played a leading role in the controversy that raged from 1762 through 1764 concerning the Anglican Society for the Propagation of the Gospel in America, which New England Puritans interpreted as a sign that the Church of England was planning to bring episcopacy to Massachusetts.*
94. Mayhew confessed that he had been goaded into the sermon by his critics and wished he had never delivered it. Mayhew's letters to Hutchinson and Samuel Clarke are quoted in Bailyn, *Faces of Revolution*, 128–32.*
95. Mayhew, *The Snare Broken: A Thanksgiving Discourse...* (Boston, 1766), reprinted in Sandoz, *Political Sermons of the American Founding Era, 1730–1805*,. 233–66; the quotations are from 247–49.
96. Mayhew's sermon mirrored the conflicts felt by countless New Englanders who cherished both liberty and law. Mayhew, *The Snare Broken*, 258–59, 262–63.*
97. On forms of popular unrest exemplified by the Stamp Act protests, see Edward Countryman, "Social Protest and the Revolutionary Movement, 1765–1776," in *The Blackwell Encyclopedia of the American Revolution*, ed. Jack P. Greene and J. R. Pole (Oxford, 1991), pp. 184–97.*
98. John Adams, *A Dissertation on the Canon and Feudal Law*, in *Papers* 1:111.
99. Adams defended the erudite, liberty-loving founders of New England, who established self-government in church and state alike. Adams, *A Dissertation*, in *Papers* 1:113–16.*
100. Adams, *A Dissertation*, 116.
101. Adams, *A Dissertation*, 120–21.
102. Adams, *A Dissertation*, 121.
103. Adams, *A Dissertation*, 123–24, 126.*
104. Adams, *A Dissertation*, 122, 126–27.
105. Adams, *A Dissertation*, 128.
106. Adams, *A Dissertation*, 128.*
107. John Adams to Thomas Jefferson, August 24, 1815, in *The Adams-Jefferson Letters: The Complete Correspondence between Thomas Jefferson and Abigail and John Adams*, ed. Lester J. Cappon (Chapel Hill, 1959), 455; John Adams to Hezekiah Niles, February 13, 1818, in *Works* 10:282–83.
108. On the colonists' blending of different traditions, see James T. Kloppenberg, "The Virtues of Liberalism: Christianity, Republicanism, and Ethics in Early American Political Discourse," *The Journal of American History* 74, no. 1 (June 1987): 9–33, reprinted in Kloppenberg, *The Virtues of Liberalism* (New York, 1998), 21–37, 183–92.*

109. Adams, *Diary and Autobiography* 1:263.

110. "Instructions of the Town of Braintree to Their Representative" (1765), in Adams, *Papers* 1:137–39.

111. "Instructions of the Town of Braintree," 138, 139–40.

112. On these issues cf. Greene, *The Constitutional Origins of the American Revolution*, 139–86; J. R. Pole, *Political Representation in England and the Origins of the American Republic* (London, 1966), 9–75, 277–78; and Nash, *The Unknown American Revolution*, 98.*

113. John Adams, "The Earl of Clarendon to William Pym," no. 2, January 20, 1766, in *Papers* 1:164. Adams used much the same language writing in his diary on December 18, 1765; see *Diary* 1:263.

114. Adams, "The Earl of Clarendon to William Pym," no. 2, 167–69, 163, 170, and no. 3, January 27, 1766, in *Papers* 1:170.

115. Adams, *Diary and Autobiography* 3:287.

116. The final sentence of Adams's final essay as the Earl of Clarendon, January 27, 1766, rebukes his antagonist for "exploding the whole system of popular power with regard to the Americans." Adams, *Papers*, 1:170).*

117. Benjamin Franklin, Examination before the Committee of the Whole of the House of Commons, (1766), in *Papers* 13:124–58; the quotation is from 153.

118. Franklin to Lord Kames, February 25, 1767, in *Papers* 14:62–70, and in *Autobiography*, ed. Houston, 281–85.*

119. Thomas Hutchinson to Richard Jackson, November 19, 1767, Thomas Hutchinson Letterbooks 26:215–19, Massachusetts Historical Society.

120. Thomas Gage to the Earl of Hillsborough, October 31, 1768, published in the *Providence Gazette and Country Journal*, April 29, 1769; *Georgia Gazette*, June 14, 1769; *Boston Gazette and Country Journal*, July 31, 1769.

121. Bernard Bailyn, in *The Origins of American Politics* (New York, 1968), notes that English officials identified the colonists' excessive "democracy" as the source of their unruliness, yet he denies the colonists themselves wanted democracy.*

122. "Populus" [Samuel Adams], *Boston Gazette*, March 14, 1768.

123. Johnson's report also suggests the racism and xenophobia that, like most colonists' equally rabid anti-Catholicism, crossed boundaries of class and region. William Johnston to the Earl of Dartmouth, November 4, 1772, in *Documents Relative to the Colonial History of the State of New York*, ed. E. B. O'Callaghan (Albany, 1853), 8:314–17.*

124. As Adams put it, in a "*free* Country" counsel "ought to be the very last thing that an accused Person should want." Adams, *Diary and Autobiography* 3:293.*

125. Adams, *Legal Papers of John Adams*, ed. L. K. Wroth and H. B. Zobel, 3 vols. (Cambridge, 1965), 3:266, 270.*

126. Joseph Warren, *An Oration Delivered March 5th, 1772, At the Request of the Inhabitants of the Town of Boston; To commemorate the Bloody Tragedy of the Fifth of March, 1770*, reprinted in the *Newsletter* of the Roxbury Latin School, October 2001, 14–18.

127. John Adams, "Notes for an Oration at Braintree," in *Papers* 2:58. It is unknown whether Adams ever delivered the speech.*
128. Adams, "Notes for an Oration at Braintree," 59, 57.
129. From the time that Queen Elizabeth granted Walter Raleigh the charter of Virginia, Adams argued, no English monarch had made a declaration concerning the extent of Parliament's authority as audacious as Hutchinson's. With characteristic exhaustiveness, Adams compiled multiple examples from English law, founding charters, and colonial practice to demonstrate "that the Colonies were not intended or considered to be within the Realm of England, though within the Allegiance of the English Crown." Adams, "Answer to His Excellency's Speech at the Opening of the Session," in *Papers* 1:324–25.*
130. Adams, entry of April 30, 1771, in *Diary and Autobiography* 2:7.
131. Hutchinson had quoted Edward Randolph, no friend of colonial presumptions, who admitted in 1676 that "no Law is in Force or Esteem" in New England "but such as are made by the General Court." John Adams, "Answer to His Excellency's Speech at the Opening of the Session," 324–25.*
132. Adams, "Answer to His Excellency's Speech at the Opening of the Session," 329.
133. Adams concluded by quoting Richard Hooker and Locke, who agreed that feudal claims to absolute authority are contrary to God's will; legitimate authority comes only from popular consent. Adams, "Answer to His Excellency's Speech at the Opening of the Session," 332, 334–35.*
134. See Conrad E. Wright, *Revolutionary Generation: Harvard Men and the Consequences of Independence* (Amherst, 2005).
135. Franklin, "The Colonist's Advocate: VI, 29," January 29, 1770, in *Papers* 17:47–48. The passage quoted is from Sidney, *Discourses*, chap. 3, sec. 8, p. 288.
136. Franklin quickly produced two deft rapier thrusts in place of Adams's lawyer-like bludgeoning. "Rules by Which a Great Empire May Be Reduced to a Small One" explained that if the colonists' grievances were not addressed, Britain would find itself with no colonies left to govern. "An Edict by the King of Prussia" contended that the Prussian monarch had at least as good a case against England as England had against the colonies. Franklin, "An Edict by the King of Prussia," September 22, 1773, in *Papers* 20:413–18.*
137. See Wood, *The Americanization of Benjamin Franklin*, 139–51. This cathartic experience transformed Franklin's attitude toward England; when he returned to Philadelphia in the spring of 1775, he was committed to American independence.*
138. Gouverneur Morris to John Penn, May 20, 1774, in *American Colonial Documents to 1776*, ed. Merrill Jensen, vol. 10 of *English Historical Documents* (London, 1955), 861–63. Economic, social, political, religious, and ideological factors were all at work in the process of altering American sensibilities, and they all worked against British authority.*
139. The Quebec Act preserved the privileges of the Catholic Church, which inflamed the anti-Catholic sensibilities of Puritans, Quakers, Lutherans, and many other Protestants, especially those whose faith had been reinvigorated by

the egalitarian thrust of the Great Awakening. John Adams later wrote that "the apprehension of Episcopacy" contributed "as much as any other cause, to arouse the attention, not only of the inquiring mind, but of the common people" in the 1760s and 1770s. Religious fervor "was a fact as certain as any in the history of North America." John Adams to Jedediah Morse, December 2, 1815, in *Works* 10:185. The Bible remained the single most widely cited book in the revolutionary era.*

140. *The American Journal of Ambrose Serle, Secretary to Lord Howe, 1776–1778*, ed. Edward H. Tatum Jr. (San Marino, 1940), 149–50.
141. Patrick Henry quoted in Nash, *The Unknown Revolution*, 90–91.*
142. Adams's "Novanglus" letters are in *Papers* 2:380.
143. Adams, *Papers* 2:328, 300.
144. Adams, *Papers* 2:313, 319.
145. Adams, *Papers* 2:327, 323–24. According to Leonard and other Tories on both sides of the Atlantic, "There is no medium between absolute independence and subjection to the authority of parliament." If so, Adams replied, then the colonies would indeed be "as fully convinced of their independence, their absolute independence, as they are of their own existence." Adams rejected Leonard's premise, though, and claimed the colonies wanted only to continue making their own laws governing their internal affairs. Adams, *Papers* 2:335.*
146. Adams quoted Locke: when men have entered into "society and civil government" and established laws "among themselves"—as the colonists had done for over a century—"those who set up force again, in opposition to the laws, do *rebellare*, that is, do bring back again the state of war, and are properly, rebels." Adams, *Papers* 2:292–93.
147. Adams, *Papers* 2:230–31; John Adams to Abigail Adams, in *Adams Family Correspondence* 1:131.*
148. The argument of "Massachusettensis" concerning the all-but-certain anarchical consequences of the ideas of equality and popular sovereignty serves as the conclusion to Bailyn, *Ideological Origins of the American Revolution*, 318–19.*
149. Adams, *Papers* 2:287.
150. In his "Novanglus" letters, Adams explicitly denied Leonard's claim that the effect of the controversy was to strengthen the appeal of absolute monarchy in the colonies.*
151. Alexander Hamilton, "A Full Vindication of the Measures of the Congress, from the Calumnies of Their Enemies," December 15, 1774, in *The Papers of Alexander Hamilton*, 27 vols., ed. Harold C. Syrett (New York, 1961–87) 1:47; Hamilton, "The Farmer Refuted," February 23, 1775, in *Papers* 1:105.*
152. James Iredell, *Address to the Inhabitants of Great Britain* (n. p., 1774).
153. James Wilson, *Considerations on the Nature and the Extent of the Legislative Authority of the British Parliament* (1774), in *Collected Works of James Wilson*, ed. Kermit L. Hall and Mark David Hall, 2 vols. (Indianapolis, 2007), 1:3–31. Wilson drafted *Considerations* in 1768, but he chose to publish it in 1774, at

the moment when his argument would resonate with those flowing from the pens of other colonial writers.*

154. Benjamin Franklin to William Franklin, March 13, 1768, in *Papers* 15:74–78.

155. On Jefferson's life and thought, see Noble Cunningham, *In Pursuit of Reason: The Life of Thomas Jefferson* (Baton Rouge, 1987). On Sally Hemings, a slave who was the daughter of Jefferson's deceased wife's father and the mother of several of his children, and who was finally freed only after Jefferson's death by his daughter Martha (Sally's niece), see Annette Gordon-Reed, *The Hemingses of Monticello: An American Family* (New York, 2008).*

156. The phrases quoted come from the best source on Jefferson's early life, his own "Autobiography, 1743–1790," completed in January of 1821, in Jefferson, *Writings*, ed. Merrill D. Peterson (New York, 1984), 3–18.

157. Jefferson, *A Summary View*, in *Writings*, 105–10. In his "Autobiography," Jefferson offered a slightly different version of his rationale, which resembled even more closely Adams's reasoning in his "Novanglus" essays: because the right to expatriation is grounded in natural law, "our emigration from England to this country gave her no more rights over us" than the emigrations of Danes and Saxons gave those nations sovereignty over England (9).

158. Jefferson, "Autobiography," 10.

159. Jefferson, "Autobiography," 118.

160. Jefferson proclaimed that "all the lands within the limits which any particular society has circumscribed around itself are assumed by that society," subject only to their decisions. Jefferson, "Autobiography," 118–20.*

161. In this case Jefferson's public actions proved as good as his private words. After he returned from the Congress in Philadelphia that declared the colonies independent in the summer of 1776, his first priority was to undertake the revision of Virginia's laws, and his first target was the law of primogeniture. Although it took a decade to complete, he judged this reform among his most significant achievements.*

162. Jefferson, "Autobiography," 32.*

163. See Jefferson, "Autobiography," 5.*

164. Jefferson, *A Summary View*, 115–16; Abigail Adams to John Adams, September 22, 1774, in *Adams Family Correspondence* 1:161–62.*

165. On the role white Virginia Protestants played in justifying slavery by creating the category of "hereditary heathenism" to exclude Indians and blacks, see Rebecca Anne Goetz, *The Baptism of Early Virginia: How Christianity Created Race* (Baltimore, 2012).

166. *The Carolina Backcountry on the Eve of the Revolution: The Journal and Other Writings of Charles Woodmason*, ed. Richard J. Hooker (Chapel Hill, 1969), 240–41.

167. Jefferson, *A Summary View*, 122.

168. Jefferson to Robert Skipwith, August 3, 1771, in *Writings*, 740–45.*

169. On this point see note 108 above.

170. For evidence of Jefferson's deep albeit unconventional Christianity, see his letter to Benjamin Rush, April 21, 1803, in *Writings*, 1122–26; and his letter to John Adams after the death of Abigail Adams, November 13, 1818, in Cappon, *The Adams-Jefferson Letters*, 529.*
171. *Pietas et gratulatio* (Boston, 1761).
172. On literacy in the colonies and the central role of the Bible, the book most often quoted during these years, see May, *The Enlightenment in America*, 35.

Chapter 7

1. The oft-cited reply of ninety-one-year-old Levi Preston to the questions posed by historian Mellen Chamberlain in 1842 is quoted in Samuel Eliot Morison, *The Oxford History of the American People* (New York, 1965), 212–13.*
2. "The Interest of America," *Freeman's Journal, or New-Hampshire Gazette* (Portsmouth, NH); "Spartanus," *New York Journal*, June 20, 1776, in *American Archives*, 4th ser., 6:994; *Maryland Gazette*, August 15, 1776; instructions to the delegates of Mecklenburg County to the North Carolina Constitutional Convention, November 1, 1776, in *The Colonial Records of North Carolina...* (Raleigh, 1886–90), 10:870a; *Providence Gazette*, August 9, 1777.
3. For a convincing argument establishing that "democracy" and "republic" were used interchangeably in the debates over state constitutions during the early stages of the war for independence, see Willi Paul Adams, *The First American Constitutions: Republican Ideology and the Making of the State Constitutions in the Revolutionary Era*, trans. Rita Kimber and Robert Kimber, 2nd ed. (1973; Lanham, MD, 2001). The online directory of newspapers in the Library of Congress lists only 29 newspapers with "Democrat" in the title and 342 with the variations on the name "Republican" for the 1790–1820 period. During the 1830–1860 period, 1,465 publications used some version of "Democrat" in their titles and 1,039 "Republican." Though usage clearly changed over time, variants of both "democracy" and "republic" were in use when Americans debated and established new forms of popular government, nonmonarchical and nonaristocratic, in the 1770s and 1780s.*
4. Earl of Clarendon to William Pym, January 27, 1766; "Humphrey Ploughjogger" to Philanthrop, ante January 5, 1767; "U" to the *Boston Gazette*, July 18, 1763, in *The Papers of John Adams*, ed. Robert Taylor, 17 vols. to date (Cambridge, MA, 1977–), 1:167–68, 179, 71.*
5. Andrew Burnaby, *Travels through the Middle Settlements in North America...*, 2nd ed. (London, 1775), 86, 118, 122; John Adams, *Diary and Autobiography of John Adams*, ed. Lyman H. Butterfield et al., 4 vols. (Cambridge, MA, 1961), 2:107.*
6. Benjamin Franklin to William Franklin, Journal of Negotiations in London, March 22, 1775, in *The Papers of Benjamin Franklin*, ed. Leonard Labaree et al., 41 vols. to date (New Haven, 1959–), 21:582–83. On July 5, 1775, in a draft of a letter addressed to his lifelong friend William Strahan, Franklin cleverly registered his disillusionment: "You are a Member of Parliament, and one of

that Majority which has doomed my Country to Destruction. . . . You are now my Enemy, and I am, Yours, B. Franklin." See Franklin, *Papers* 22:85. Franklin never mailed this celebrated letter, which he displayed to some of his Philadelphia friends only to convince them he had decisively renounced mother England.*

7. John Adams to Isaac Smith, June 1, 1776, in *The Works of John Adams*, ed. Charles Francis Adams, 10 vols. (Boston, 1850–56), 9:584.
8. Adams to James Warren, June 1, 1776, in *Works* 9:339.
9. Adams, *Autobiography*, in *Works* 3:16.
10. Adams, *Autobiography*, in *Works* 3:45; Adams to Abigail Adams, May 17, 1776, in *Adams Family Correspondence*, ed. L. H. Butterfield et al., 12 vols. to date (Cambridge, MA, 1963–), 1:110.
11. Gordon Wood, in *The Creation of the American Republic, 1776–1787* (1969; Chapel Hill, 1998), contends that Adams's *Thoughts on Government* was "the most influential pamphlet in the early constitution-writing period" (203). Although an aged and disgruntled Adams later made even more exaggerated claims for its significance, it did play a decisive role in shaping American constitutionalism. See *Diary and Autobiography*, 3:358; and for the context of its writing, 331–32.
12. John Adams, "Thoughts on Government," in Adams, *The Revolutionary Writings of John Adams*, ed. C. Bradley Thompson (Indianapolis, 2000), 293. Adams wrote, "In New England the Thoughts on Government will be disdained because they are not popular enough; in the Southern colonies they will be despised and dissected because too popular."
13. Thomas Paine, *Common Sense* (1776), in Paine, *Collected Writings*, ed. Eric Foner (New York, 1995), 52–53.
14. Paine, *Common Sense*, 12–15.*
15. Paine, *Common Sense*, 17, 9.
16. Paine, *Common Sense*, 23.*
17. Paine, *Common Sense*, 35–36, 43.
18. Paine, *Common Sense*, 8–9.
19. Paine, *Common Sense*, 8–9.*
20. Paine, *Common Sense*, 33.
21. Paine, *Common Sense*, 33–34.
22. Paine knew that some critics of British colonial policy, such as Edmund Burke, had no interest in popular sovereignty but nevertheless thought the colonies were heading toward independence. Paine had certainly read the *Political Disquisitions* (1774–75) of the Scottish writer James Burgh, whom he cited in *Common Sense*. He was familiar with both the Court and Country wings of Whig radicalism. He had experienced firsthand the mobs that gathered in support of John Wilkes. The principal focus of English dissidents, however, was either corruption—if their emphasis was political, like Bolingbroke's and Trenchard and Gordon's—or the need to extend religious toleration to dissenting sects of Christians.*
23. James Chalmers, *Plain Truth*, in *Pamphlets of the American Revolution, 1750–1776*, ed. Bernard Bailyn (Cambridge, MA, 1965), 2:64.*

24. "To the People of Pennsylvania—Letter VI," signed "Cato," *Pennsylvania Packet*, April 15, 1776, in *American Archives*, 4th ser., 5:545; Charles Inglis, *The True Interest of America impartially stated in certain strictures on a pamphlet intitled Common Sense* (Philadelphia, 1776), 53, vii.
25. Inglis, *The True Interest*, 34; Gouverneur Morris quoted in Eric Foner, *Tom Paine and Revolutionary America* (New York, 1976), 85.*
26. For a survey of responses to Paine's *Common Sense*, see Foner, *Tom Paine*, 71–106.
27. John Witherspoon, "The Dominion of Providence over the Passions of Men," a sermon preached at Princeton, New Jersey, on May 17, 1776, and reprinted in Ellis Sandoz, ed., *Political Sermons of the American Founding Era, 1730–1805* (Indianapolis, 1991), 533–58; see 538–39 on Paine.
28. Adams, *Diary and Autobiography* 3:333.
29. On Paine's *Age of Reason* and its hostile reception in the United States, see Foner, *Tom Paine*, 246–49; and see chapter 12 below.
30. Adams, *Diary and Autobiography* 3:333; Adams to Abigail Adams, March 19, 1776, in *Adams Family Correspondence* 1:362–64.
31. Paine, *Common Sense*, 6–7.
32. John Adams, "Notes for an Oration at Braintree," Spring 1772, in *Diary and Autobiography* 2:56–57.
33. Adams to Horatio Gates, March 23, 1776, in *Papers* 4:59; Adams to Patrick Henry, June 3, 1776, in *Papers* 4:234–35.*
34. See John Adams's entries for September 5–6, 1774, in *Diary and Autobiography* 2:122–26.*
35. Critics from James Madison and James Wilson to writers in our own day have judged the equal representation of all states in the United States Senate antithetical to democracy. Such criticism takes for granted the individualism that Ward and many of his contemporaries challenged.*
36. Adams, "Thoughts on Government," 288–89.
37. Adams to James Warren, May 12, 1776, in *Papers* 4:26.
38. Adams, "Thoughts on Government," 289–90.
39. Adams to Abigail Adams, June 4, 1777, in *Adams Family Correspondence* 2:255.
40. For example, Gary Nash, a harsh critic of Adams, describes Henry as "a man with deeply democratic sensibilities." See Nash, *The Unknown American Revolution: The Unruly Birth of Democracy and the Struggle to Create America* (New York, 2005), 202.
41. Patrick Henry to Richard Henry Lee, May 20, 1776, in *Patrick Henry: Life, Correspondence and Speeches*, ed. William Wirt Henry, 3 vols. (New York, 1891), 1:411; Richard Henry Lee to Charles Lee, June 29, 1776, in *The Letters of Richard Henry Lee*, ed. James Curtis Ballagh, 2 vols. (1911–14; New York, 1970), 1:2–3.
42. Carter Braxton, "An Address to the Convention of the Colony of the Ancient Dominion of Virginia on the subject of government in general, and recommending a particular form to their consideration. By a native of that colony"

(Philadelphia, 1776), 6, 15; Carter Braxton to Landon Carter, April 14, 1776, in *Letters of Delegates to Congress, 1774–1789*, ed. Paul H. Smith et al., 26 vols. (Washington, 1976–2000), 3:520–23.

43. The argument that a democracy was distinguished from a republic during these years has a long lineage and remains widely accepted among historians. In 1776, however, Paine, Adams, and most of their contemporaries agreed that representative democracy was the only appropriate and workable form of government for a republic grounded on the principle of popular sovereignty. Why do so many Americans accept the argument that there was a distinction from the beginning between a republic and a democracy? To those on the political right, that distinction discredits those who claim the United States should be more egalitarian: the founders wanted a (hierarchical) republic, not a (radical) democracy. To those on the left, it explains why the United States is not more egalitarian: the "founders" did not trust the people. Both judgments project into the 1760s and 1770s a distinction that developed only during the late 1780s and hardened into dogma as a result of the divisions generated by the French Revolution. European commentators from the 1770s until the present, by contrast, have taken for granted that the American Revolution was a democratic revolution.*
44. On the origins of democracy in Rhode Island and Connecticut, see chapter 2 above.
45. *Providence Gazette*, August 9, 1777.*
46. Jonathan Sewall to General Frederick Haldimand, May 30, 1775, in *Colonies to Nation, 1763–1789: A Documentary History of the American Revolution*, ed. Jack P. Greene (New York, 1975), 266; Ambrose Serle to the Earl of Dartmouth, November 8, 1776, quoted in Jonathan C. D. Clark, *The Language of Liberty, 1660–1832: Political Discourse and Social Dynamics in the Anglo-American World* (Cambridge, 1994), 204.*
47. Adams to Elbridge Gerry, June 18, 1775, in *Works* 9:358.
48. The fullest account of colonial political practice is Richard R. Beeman, *The Varieties of Political Experience in Eighteenth-Century America* (Philadelphia, 2004). The appendices contain evidence on voter qualifications; days in session of, and laws enacted and petitions received by, colonial assemblies; the number of assembly elections; and the average turnover of legislators.*
49. James Wilson, "Speech Delivered in the Convention for the Province of Pennsylvania, in January, 1775," in *Collected Works of James Wilson*, ed. Kermit L. Hall and Mark David Hall, 2 vols. (Indianapolis, 2007), 1:37; and Thomas Jefferson, "A Summary View of the Rights of British America," in Jefferson, *Writings*, ed. Merrill D. Peterson (New York, 1984), 118.*
50. Although Vermont, which patterned its constitution on Pennsylvania's, and Georgia both adopted unicameral systems, both of them preserved much of the spirit and the function of an upper house through the institution of executive councils.*
51. [Democritus], "Loose Thoughts on Government," Purdie's *Virginia Gazette*, June 7, 1776, in *American Archives*, 4th ser., 6:731; Novanglus [John Adams],

Boston Gazette, January 30, 1775, in Adams, *Revolutionary Writings, 1775–1783*, ed. Gordon S. Wood (New York, 2011), 406.*

52. Jefferson, "Draft Constitution of Virginia," in *Writings*, 343, 338; Jefferson, *Autobiography*, *The Life and Selected Writings of Thomas Jefferson*, ed. Adrienne Koch and William Peden (New York, 1944), in *The Papers of Thomas Jefferson*, ed. Julian Boyd, 41 vols. to date (Princeton, 1950–), 1:363, 560.*
53. Jefferson to Edmund Pendleton, August 26, 1776, in *Writings*, 755–58.*
54. Adams, "Thoughts on Government," 290.*
55. Jefferson to Pendleton, August 26, 1776, in *Writings*, 755–58.*
56. Many historians have hailed the Pennsylvania Constitution of 1776 as a product of popular agitation and lamented its replacement in 1790 as a repudiation of the people's will. Adams opposed unicameralism as unworkable and unwise. Writing to James Warren, May 12, 1776, he criticized "crude, ignorant Notions of a Government by one Assembly." Adams, *Papers* 4:181–83.*
57. Thomas Smith to Arthur St. Clair, August 22, 1776, in Arthur St. Clair, *The St. Clair Papers*, ed. William Henry Smith, 2 vols. (Cincinnati, 1882), 1:374.
58. Demophilus [George Bryan?], *The Genuine Principles of the Ancient Saxon, or English Constitution* (Philadelphia, 1776), 17.
59. Alexander Hamilton to Gouverneur Morris, May 19, 1777, in *The Papers of Alexander Hamilton*, ed. Harold C. Syrett, 27 vols. (New York, 1961–87), 1:255.
60. Salus Populi, "Salus Populi to the People of North-America: On the Different Kinds of Government," in *American Archives*, ser. 4, 5:180; *Pennsylvania Journal*, March 13, 1776.
61. [James Cannon], *To the Several Battalions of Military Associators in the Province of Pennsylvania*, Philadelphia, June 26, 1776.*
62. Pennsylvania Constitution of 1776, in *Federal and State Constitutions…*, ed. Francis Newton Thorpe, 7 vols. (Washington, 1909), 5:3083.*
63. Pennsylvania Constitution of 1776, 3086.
64. *Journals of the Continental Congress*, ed. Worthington Chauncey Ford et al., 34 vols. (Washington, 1904–37), 4:358.
65. In his *Autobiography*, Adams gave several reasons for declining to draft the Declaration. See Adams, *Revolutionary Writings, 1775–1783*, 613–14. For Jefferson's own bare-bones account of the events of June 1776, which resulted in his authorship of the first draft of the Declaration of Independence, see his *Autobiography*, in *Writings*, 13–18.*
66. Jefferson, *Writings*, 1501.
67. Samuel West, "A Sermon Preached before the Honorable Council, and the Honorable House of Representatives of the Colony of Massachusetts-Bay, in New-England," May 29, 1776 (Boston, 1776), in John Wingate Thornton, ed., *The Pulpit of the American Revolution* (Boston, 1860), 279, 281.
68. *Act of the Assembly of Rhode-Island repealing an act entitled "an Act for the more effectual securing to his Majesty the allegiance of his Majesty's subjects in this his Colony and Dominion of Rhode-Island and Providence Plantations,"* in *American Archives*, ser. 4, 5:1215.

69. "Declaration by the Delegates of Maryland," in *American Archives*, ser. 4, 6:1506.
70. "Declaration on the subject of the independence of Pennsylvania on the Crown of Great Britain," in *American Archives*, ser. 4, 6:1506.
71. William Henry Drayton, "Judge Drayton's Address to the Grand Jury at Charleston, South Carolina," in *American Archives*, ser. 4, 5:1025.
72. Drayton, "Judge Drayton's Address," 1033; Cheraws District Grand Jury, in *American Archives*, ser. 4, 6:514–15.*
73. For the resolutions from the Massachusetts towns of Topsfield, Palmer, and Wrentham, see *American Archives*, ser. 4, 6:704, 702, 700.
74. George Mason, "Committee Draft of the Virginia Declaration of Rights, May 27, 1776," in *The Papers of George Mason*, ed. Robert A. Rutland, 3 vols. (Chapel Hill, 1970), 1:283. See also the final draft of the Virginia Declaration of Rights, in Thorpe, *Federal and State Constitutions* 7:4077; and James Wilson, *Considerations on the Nature and Extent of the Legislative Authority of the British Parliament* (1774), in *Works* 1:4.
75. See Jon Butler, *Becoming America: The Revolution before 1776* (Cambridge, MA, 2000), 243–44; and for the opposite case, Clark, *The Language of Liberty*, 110–12.*
76. Only much later did some Americans begin protesting government taxing "their" property, a preposterous idea unknown in the eighteenth century, when the necessity of government to secure property rights seemed too obvious to be controversial.*
77. When the issue of slavery was raised in the debate over the Declaration of Independence, most northern delegates agreed not to antagonize southerners committed to its perpetuation. Jefferson's rhetorical strategy in his draft pivoted on his condemnation of George III for waging "cruel war against human nature itself" by authorizing that "assemblage of horrors," the slave trade. Later explaining why Congress deleted his comments on this "execrable commerce," Jefferson pointed to Georgia and South Carolina and the "tender" feelings of "our northern brethren" who profited from shipping slaves, even though fewer owned slaves themselves. He failed to note that his fellow Virginia slave owners were equally averse to critiques of slavery. See Jefferson, *Writings*, 19–24, 16–18.*
78. Historians disagree about whether Jefferson was more indebted to the ideas of Thomas Reid, who considered the moral sense a rational faculty, or Thomas Hutcheson. The evidence is inconclusive.*
79. The chaplain of the Massachusetts legislature, William Gordon, had admonished New Englanders at the dawn of the Revolution that a republican society of "comprehensive benevolence" could be constructed only by following God's will. Jacob Duchë assured a Philadelphia congregation that only a God-fearing republic would serve as "the eminent example of every divine and social virtue." William Gordon, *A Sermon Preached before the Honorable House of Representatives* (Watertown, 1765), 22; Jacob Duchë, *The American Vine, a Sermon Preached in Christ-Church, Philadelphia, before the Honorable Continental Congress, July 20, 1775* (Philadelphia, 1775), 29.

80. Adams, "Thoughts on Government," 288, 292–93.
81. John Adams to Abigail Adams, July 3, 1776, in *Adams Family Correspondence* 2:28.
82. Benjamin Rush to John Adams, August 8, 1777, in *Letters of Benjamin Rush*, ed. L. H. Butterfield, 2 vols. (Princeton, 1951), 1:152.
83. Samuel Adams to John Scollay, December 30, 1780, in *The Writings of Samuel Adams*, ed. Harry Alonzo Cushing, 4 vols. (1904–8; New York, 1968), 4:238; Samuel Adams to John Langdon, August 7, 1777, in *Writings* 3:403.*
84. Nine of the fifty-five delegates to the Constitutional Convention, including most notably James Madison, had degrees from the College of New Jersey.*
85. John Witherspoon, *The Dominion of Providence over the Passions of Man*, 1776, in Sandoz, *Political Sermons of the American Founding Era, 1730–1805*, 544. Witherspoon acknowledged that such praise of New England might strike readers as a convenient compliment in light of the war being fought, but noted that his praise of their "invincible fortitude" dated from "a sermon on Psal. lxxiv, 22, prepared and preached in Scotland, in the month of August, 1758."*
86. Witherspoon contended that virtue also paid rewards of another kind. "Habits of industry prevailing in a society, not only increase its wealth, as their immediate effect, but they prevent the introduction of many vices, and are intimately connected with sobriety and good morals." Witherspoon's sermon offered a classic formulation of the Protestant ethic and the spirit of productivity, if not capitalism, and the contributions of both to the patriots' cause. Witherspoon, *The Dominion of Providence*, 545–58.*
87. Witherspoon's counsel was multiplied countless times throughout the colonies.*
88. Abigail Adams to John Quincy Adams, January 19, 1780; and March 20, 1780, in *Adams Family Correspondence* 3:268, 310.
89. Benjamin Rush, "Of the Mode of Education," in Rush, *Essays, Literary, Moral, and Philosophical* (Philadelphia, 1798), 8.
90. Wood, *Creation of the American Republic*, 72n58, details the educational provisions of many of the new constitutions.
91. Adams, "Thoughts on Government," 292.
92. John Adams to James Sullivan, May 26, 1776, in *Revolutionary Writings, 1775–1783*, 73.*
93. John Adams to Abigail Adams, April 14, 1776, in *Adams Family Correspondence*, 1: 381; John Adams to Patrick Henry, June 3, 1776, in *Papers* 4:235.
94. Abigail Adams to John Adams, March 31, 1776, in *Adams Family Correspondence* 1:370.
95. Judith Apter Klinghoffer and Lois Elkis, "'The Petticoat Electors': Women's Suffrage in New Jersey, 1776-1807," *Journal of the Early Republic* 12 (1992): 159–93.*
96. John Adams to Abigail Adams, April 14, 1776, in *Adams Family Correspondence* 1:397–98.
97. Abigail Adams to Mercy Otis Warren, April 27, 1776, in *Adams Family Correspondence* 1:397–98.

98. James Otis, *The Rights of the British Colonies Asserted and Proved*, 2nd ed. (London, 1765), 5, 7.

99. Abigail Adams to John Adams, May 7, 1776, in *Adams Family Correspondence* 1:402.

100. Although John agreed, at Abigail's insistence, to allow their daughter Nabby to study Latin, he cautioned that she should keep it quiet, "for it is scarcely reputable for young ladies to understand Latin and Greek." John Adams to Abigail Adams 2nd (i.e., Nabby), April 18, 1776, in *Adams Family Correspondence* 1:388. Adams also encouraged, and took pride in, Abigail's own wide reading. He wrote to her from Passy, France, on December 2, 1778, "Have you ever read J. J. Rousseau? If not, read him—your Cousin smith has him. What a Difference between him and Chesterfield, and even Voltaire? But he was too virtuous for the Age, and for Europe. I wish I could not say for another Country." Adams, *Revolutionary Writings, 1775–1783*, 172–74.*

101. Abigail Adams to John Adams, March 31, 1776, in *Adams Family Correspondence* 1:367; John Adams to Colonel Ward, January 8, 1810, Adams Papers, reel 118, Massachusetts Historical Society.

102. See Linda K. Kerber, *Women of the Republic: Intellect and Ideology in Revolutionary America* (Chapel Hill, 1980); Mary Beth Norton, *Liberty's Daughters: The Revolutionary Experience of American Women, 1750–1800* (Boston, 1980); and Rosemarie Zagarri, *Revolutionary Backlash: Women and Politics in the Early American Republic* (Philadelphia, 2007).

103. Wayne E. Carp, *To Starve the Army at Pleasure: Continental Army Administration and American Political Culture, 1775–1783* (Chapel Hill, 1984); Charles Royster, *A Revolutionary People at War: The Continental Army and American Character, 1775–1783* (Chapel Hill, 1979).

104. An up-to-date guide to the social and economic history of the American Revolution is *The Oxford Handbook of the American Revolution*, ed. Edward G. Gray and Jane Kamensky (New York, 2013).*

105. Louis Duportail's letter, Papers of Sir Henry Clinton, William L. Clements Library, University of Michigan, Ann Arbor, is quoted in John Shy, *A People Numerous and Armed* (Ann Arbor, 2004), 20, 301n17.

106. Theophilus Parsons, *Result of the convention of delegates holden at Ipswich* (Newburyport, MA, 1778), 20, 11, 33.*

107. Diary entry, April 6, 1778, in Adams, *Diary and Autobiography* 2:296; John Adams to Abigail Adams, April 12 and December 2, 1778, in *Adams Family Correspondence* 3:9, 125.

108. Instructions of the people of Stoughton to their delegate to the state constitutional convention, in Oscar Handlin and Mary Handlin, eds., *The Popular Sources of Political Authority: Documents of the Massachusetts Convention of 1780* (Cambridge, 1966), 424–26.

109. Adams, *The Report of a Constitution, or Form of Government, for the Commonwealth of Massachusetts*, in *Revolutionary Writings*, 297–322.

110. Adams, *Works* 4:216.

111. Adams's draft began by paraphrasing the preamble to Jefferson's Declaration: "All men are born equally free and independent, and have certain natural, essential, and unalienable rights, among which may be reckoned the right of enjoying and defending their lives and liberties; that of acquiring, possessing, and protecting their property; in fine, that of seeking and obtaining their safety and happiness." Like all rights as understood by Adams and all good republicans, the right to property was circumscribed by duties: Adams stressed the necessity of collecting taxes to pay for the services government must provide. Adams also declared religious observance a civic obligation: "It is the duty of all men in society, publicly, and at stated seasons, to worship the SUPREME BEING, the great Creator and Preserver of the universe." Yet no one should be penalized "for worshipping GOD in the manner most agreeable to the dictates of his own conscience" so long as he does "not disturb the public peace, or obstruct others in their religious worship." Adams's commitment to religion as the glue holding society together never wavered, but his willingness to entertain religious diversity showed how far he had traveled from the strict Calvinism that had troubled him in his youth. Most members of the convention were not persuaded by Adams's latitudinarianism; they provided for state support of Congregationalism, which was not disestablished until 1833. Adams's draft was fully consistent with Jefferson's submission, on returning to Virginia after the Continental Congress, of a Bill to Establish Religious Freedom. Adams, *The Report of a Constitution*; and see Jefferson, "A Bill to Establish Religious Freedom," in *Writings*, 346–48.

112. *Independent Chronicle* (Boston), June 11, 1778; Ezra Stiles, *The United States Elevated to Glory and Honor* (New Haven, 1783), 21; William Hornby, *Gazette of the State of South Carolina* (Charleston), July 17, 1784; Christopher Gadsden, *The Writings of Christopher Gadsden, 1746–1805*, ed. Richard Walsh (Columbia, SC, 1966), 200–38.*

113. *Address of the Inhabitants of Grafton County*, in *Documents and Records relating to the State of New Hampshire*, ed. Nathaniel Bouton (Concord 1874); 10:233.

114. [William Whiting], *An Address to the Inhabitants of the County of Berkshire*... (Hartford, 1778), 24–27.

115. That understanding also lay behind the arguments of influential proponents of the United States Constitution, such as James Wilson and James Madison, at the Constitutional Convention and during the debates over ratification. See chapters 8 and 9 below.

116. See Beeman, *Varieties of Political Experience in Eighteenth-Century America*, 54 and appendices; and David Hackett Fischer, *Albion's Seed: Four British Folkways in America* (New York, 1989), 815.*

117. See J. R. Pole, *Political Representation in England and the Origins of the American Republic* (London, 1966), 277–79; and Wood, *Creation of the American Republic*, 184–85n42.

118. Adams proposed that in order "to provide for a representation of the citizens of this commonwealth, founded upon the principle of equality, every corporate town, containing one hundred and fifty ratable polls, may elect one representative." Smaller towns would "associate" with larger towns so that their citizens' views might be heard. Forty senators would be elected by different districts, to be determined by legislation and population, consistent with the conviction that Adams shared with many of his contemporaries: members of the upper house should provide a broader view than those chosen for the lower house.*

119. Thus not the wealth of individuals but of communities was to determine the allocation of Senate seats. The convention stated the principle clearly enough: "The House of Representatives is intended as the Representatives of the Persons, and the Senate of the property of the Common Wealth." Massachusetts Constitution, part 2, section 2, article 1, in *Popular Sources*, ed. Handlin and Handlin, 437.*

120. Jefferson, *Notes on the State of Virginia*, in *Writings*, 245–46.*

121. James Madison to Caleb Wallace, August 23, 1785, in Madison, *Writings*, ed. Jack Rakove (New York, 1999), 39–47.

122. Samuel Chase, *Maryland Journal*, February 9, February 13, 1787.

123. Arthur St. Clair, *Pennsylvania Journal*, February 14, 1784.*

124. "Resolutions Passed at a Meeting in the State House, Philadelphia, Pa., *Journal*, Oct. 22, Nov. 13, 1776," *Pennsylvania Gazette*, October 23, 1776, in *American Archives*, ser. 4, 2:1149–50.

125. See Joyce Appleby, "America as a Model for the Radical French Reformers of 1789," *William and Mary Quarterly*, 3rd ser., 28 (1971): 267–86; and chapters 10 and 11 below.*

126. Benjamin Rush, *Observations upon the Present Government of Pennsylvania* (Philadelphia, 1777), 9.

127. William Gordon proposed a change in nomenclature to signal the shift. Since "the Senate will be as much a representative body" as the lower house, that chamber should no longer be designated "the House of *Representatives*" but instead the "House of Assembly." William Gordon, *Continental Journal* (Boston), April 9, 1778.

128. Samuel Cooper, *A Sermon on the Day of the Commencement of the Constitution*, in Sandoz, *Political Sermons*, 631–35.*

129. Cooper, *A Sermon on the Day of the Commencement of the Constitution*, 637, 639; and cf. the discussion of Sidney in chapter 4 above.*

130. The grandeur of the Constitution of the Commonwealth of Massachusetts, now often proclaimed the longest-lived constitution still in effect anywhere, would be enhanced if its origins were less murky.*

131. Cooper drew on Montesquieu as well as Locke, Sidney, and Milton: "Virtue is the spirit of a republic; for where all power is derived from the people, all depends on their good disposition." As Adams observed, most people in his-

tory had found themselves bound by their circumstances, but Americans, Cooper wrote, "though surrounded by the flames of war," nevertheless enjoyed the precious opportunity of "deliberating and deciding upon this most interesting of all human affairs with calmness and freedom." Having now "framed the constitution under which you choose to live," his contemporaries in Massachusetts would henceforth be "subject to no laws, by which you do not consent to bind yourselves." Cooper, *A Sermon on the Day of the Commencement of the Constitution*, 642–45, 647–48, 655.*

132. On these changes, see Wood, *The Creation of the American Republic*, 197–391; and Wood, *The Radicalism of the American Revolution*, pt. 3.
133. Henry Cumings, "A Sermon Preached at Lexington on the 19th of April" (1781), in Sandoz, *Political Sermons*, 681.
134. See Seymour Drescher, *Abolition: A History of Slavery and Antislavery* (Cambridge, 2009).*
135. See Ruth Bogin, "'Liberty Further Extended': A 1776 Antislavery Manuscript by Lemuel Haynes," *William and Mary Quarterly*, 3rd ser., 40 (1983): 85–105.*
136. [Benjamin Lincoln], "The Free Republican," *Independent Chronicle*, November 24, 1785, to February 9, 1786.*
137. Benjamin Franklin, *A Comparison of the Conduct of the Ancient Jews and of the Anti-Federalists in the United States of America*, in *The Works of Benjamin Franklin*, ed. Jared Sparks, 10 vols. (London, 1882), 5:168.*
138. When General Cornwallis surrendered to Washington's army at Yorktown, one of the tunes said to be played was "The World Turned Upside Down," which dated from the Levellers' agitation in 1646.*
139. See Craig Calhoun, ed., *Habermas and the Public Sphere* (Cambridge, MA, 1992), which includes Habermas's response to critics who accused him of ignoring the dynamics of power and exclusion; and John L. Brooke, "Consent, Civil Society, and the Public Sphere in the Age of Revolution and the Early American Republic," in *Beyond the Founders: New Approaches to the Political History of the Early American Republic*, ed. Jeffrey L. Pasley, Andrew W. Robertson, and David Waldstreicher (Chapel Hill, 2004), 207–50.
140. See the discussion of Franklin's 1785 warning in Edmund S. Morgan, *Benjamin Franklin* (New Haven, 2002), 307–8.*
141. [John Adams], "Letters from a Distinguished American," no. 9, July 1780, in *Revolutionary Writings, 1775–1783*, 372.
142. Condorcet, *Oeuvres du Marquis de Condorcet*, ed. A. Condorcet O'Connor and M. F. Arago, 2nd ed., 12 vols. (Paris, 1847–49), 3:420.

Chapter 8

1. *Pennsylvania Packet*, October 14, 1786.
2. See Barbara Clark Smith, "Food Rioters and the American Revolution," *William and Mary Quarterly*, 3rd ser., 51 (January 1994): 3–38; Terry Bouton, *Taming Democracy: "The People," the Founders, and the Troubled Ending of the*

American Revolution (New York, 2007); and Woody Holton, *Unruly Americans and the Origins of the Constitution* (New York, 2007).*

3. William Findley in *Debates and Proceedings of the General Assembly, on the Memorial Praying a Repeal or Suspension of the Law Annulling the Charter of the Bank*, ed. Matthew Carey (Philadelphia, 1786), 129, 123.*
4. A population under fifty thousand generated two thousand cases at the same time in the Worcester County Court of Common Pleas; more people in the town of Springfield were in debt than were solvent.*
5. Holton, *Unruly Americans and the Origins of the Constitution*, 3–176.
6. *Pennsylvania Packet*, October 14, 1786.
7. See Jürgen Heideking, *The Constitution before the Judgment Seat: The Prehistory and Ratification of the American Constitution, 1787–1791*, ed. John P. Kaminski and Richard Leffler (Charlottesville, 2012), 7–52.*
8. See Maya Jasanoff, *Liberty's Exiles: American Loyalists in the Revolutionary World* (New York, 2011); and Philip Gould, *Writing the Rebellion: Loyalists and the Literature of Politics in British America* (New York, 2013).
9. See Max M. Edling, *A Revolution in Favor of Government: Origins of the U.S. Constitution and the Making of the American State* (New York, 2003); and Peter S. Onuf, "Federalism, Democracy, and Liberty in the New American Nation," in *Exclusionary Empire: English Liberty Overseas, 1600–1900*, ed. Jack P. Greene (Cambridge, 2009), 132–59.
10. Alexander Hamilton to John Laurens, September 11, 1779, in *The Papers of Alexander Hamilton*, ed. Harold C. Syrett, 27 vols. (New York, 1961–87), 2:166–67; and Hamilton, *The Continentalist* 6 (July 4, 1782), in *Papers* 3:103.
11. Thomas FitzSimons quoted in Bouton, *Taming Democracy*, 166, and see also 145–67; Benjamin Hawkins to Richard Caswell, September 26, 2785, in *The State Records of North Carolina*, ed. Walter Clark, 30 vols. (Goldsboro, 1886–1914), 17:525; David Daggett, *An Oration Pronounced in the Brick Meeting-House, in the City of New-Haven, on the Fourth of July, A.D. 1787* (New Haven, 1787), 14.
12. David P. Szatmary, *Shays' Rebellion: The Making of an Agrarian Insurrection* (Amherst, 1980); Leonard L. Richards, *Shays' Rebellion: The American Revolution's Final Battle* (Philadelphia, 2002).*
13. George Richards Minot, *History of the Insurrections in Massachusetts*, 2nd ed. (Boston, 1810), 10, 21.*
14. Thomas Dawes Jr., *An Oration Delivered July 4, 1787, at the request of the inhabitants of the town of Boston, in celebration of the anniversary of American independence* (Boston, 1787).*
15. James Wilson, *Commentaries on the Constitution of the United States of America, with that Constitution prefixed, in which are unfolded, the principles of free government, and the superior advantages of republicanism demonstrated* (London, 1792), 68.
16. Henry Lee to Madison, October 19, 1786, in *Papers of James Madison*, 17 vols. (hereafter *PJM*), ed. William T. Hutchinson et al. (Chicago and Charlottesville, 1962–91), 9:144; Washington to Madison, November 5, 1786, *PJM* 9:174;

William Grayson to Madison, November 22, 1786, *PJM* 9:231. Madison communicated his heightened anxiety in an extraordinary letter to Jefferson, a letter in which he uncharacteristically signaled his alarm by encoding many of his words in cipher. Madison to Jefferson, March 19, 1787, in James Madison, *Writings*, ed. Jack Rakove (New York, 1999), 66.*

17. As Madison, Wilson, and many other Americans knew, Montesquieu had warned that all democracies disappear when the desire for wealth replaces virtue, and they worried that the United States would be only the latest in an endless series of popular governments to fail. For a pointed statement of these anxieties, see Madison's letter to Jefferson, August 12, 1786, in *Writings*, 52–59.*
18. See the discussion of Wilson's *Considerations* in chapter 6 above.
19. See *Collected Works of James Wilson*, ed. Kermit L. Hall and Mark David Hall, 2 vols. (Indianapolis, 2007); and Mark David Hall, *The Political and Legal Philosophy of James Wilson, 1742–1798* (Columbia, MO, 1997).*
20. Wilson's home was located on the southwest corner of Third and Walnut. See John K. Alexander, "The Fort Wilson Incident of 1779," *William and Mary Quarterly*, 3rd ser., 31 (October 1974): 589–612.
21. On criticism of Wilson as a greedy speculator only posing as a democrat, which began during Wilson's life and has continued until the present, see Hall, *The Political and Legal Philosophy of James Wilson*, 34n70.*
22. Aristotle, *Politics* 1296a7.
23. On Madison's years in Princeton, see Irving Brandt, *James Madison*, 6 vols. (Indianapolis, 1941–61). For Witherspoon's syllabus, see Dennis Thompson, "Bibliography: The Education of a Founding Father. The Reading List for John Witherspoon's Course in Political Theory, as Taken by James Madison," *Political Theory* 4 (November 1976): 523–29.*
24. Madison to William Bradford, January 24, 1774, in *Writings*, 5–6, 7; Madison to William Bradford, September 25, 1773, in *PJM* 1:96; Madison to William Bradford, April 1, 1774, in *Writings*, 8, 9.*
25. Madison to Bradford, July 28, 1775, in *PJM* 1:161.*
26. See the discussion of the Virginia Constitution in chapter 7 above.
27. When Jefferson returned from the Continental Congress to participate in the Virginia debates, he joined with Madison and Henry to remove the remaining powers of the state to license preachers and the continuing reliance on parishes to perform some civil functions. Jefferson took great pride in the bill he introduced in 1779, the Statute for Establishing Religious Freedom, but not until the next decade did he and Madison succeed in achieving their goal of securing religious freedom by separating church and state. The point of their campaign was not to remove religion from secular politics but to prevent politics from interfering with—whether by authorizing and thereby contaminating the purity of, or by prohibiting and thereby inciting hatred of—the free exercise of religious belief. Madison's amendment is in *Writings*, 10.*

28. Madison to Randolph, January 22, 1783, in *PJM* 6:55.
29. On January 28, 1783, the physically unimposing Madison delivered a bold address contrary to Virginia's instructions and most delegates' positions. If the individual states continued to make their own decisions about funding the national government, the United States would establish "our national independence on the ruins of public faith." The nation could no longer depend on the whim of state legislatures to pay its debts, particularly its debts to its soldiers. The severity of the crisis was forcing Madison to reconsider the relation between a representative and those who sent him. Though "the declared sense of constituents" should be taken as "a law in general to these representatives, still there were occasions on which the latter ought to hazard personal consequences from a respect to what his clear conviction determines to be the true interest of the former." Only six months later, the ominous threat of unrest among unpaid members of the Continental Army forced Congress to move from Philadelphia to Princeton. Indispensable French funds and personnel had enabled the United States to defeat Britain militarily, but now the new nation's soldiers seemed ready to turn against their own government. Madison, "Notes on Debates," January 28, 1783, in *PJM* 6:143–44, 146, 147.*
30. Lance Banning, *The Sacred Fire of Liberty: James Madison and the Founding of the Federal Republic* (Ithaca, 1995), 88–91.*
31. Madison's "Memorial and Remonstrance" is in *Writings*, 29–36.*
32. Madison, "Memorial and Remonstrance," 30, 34.
33. Madison, "Memorial and Remonstrance," 30–36.*
34. Madison to James Monroe, October 5, 1786, in *PJM* 9:141.*
35. So enamored of this image was Jefferson that he offered several alternate versions of it in several letters written within the following year. Jefferson to Madison, January 30, 1787, in *Writings*, 881–87.*
36. Jefferson to Abigail Adams, February 22, 1787, in *Writings*, 190; Jefferson to William Smith, November 13, 1787, in *Writings*, 911; Jefferson to Madison, December 20, 1787, in *Writings*, 917; Adams to Jefferson, November 30, 1786, in *The Papers of Thomas Jefferson*, ed. Julian Boyd, 41 vols. to date (Princeton, 1950–), 10:557.
37. Jefferson to Charles Bellini, September 30, 1785, in *Writings*, 833.
38. Jefferson to John Bannister Jr., October 15, 1785, in *Writings*, 838–39.
39. Jefferson to Madison, October 28, 1785, in *Writings*, 840–43.
40. On the contexts within which Adams wrote, see C. Bradley Thompson, *John Adams and the Spirit of Liberty* (Lawrence, KS, 1998), 91–106.
41. Adams, fragment entitled "Literary Drafts and Notes," Adams Papers, reel 188, Massachusetts Historical Society.*
42. Adams to Francis Adrian Vanderkemp, April 20, 1812, Adams Papers, reel 118, Massachusetts Historical Society.
43. Adams, preface to *Defence of the Constitutions of Government of the United States of America*, in *Works* 4:290.

44. Adams, *Defence*, in *Works* 6:142, 95. Jefferson wrote in February of 1787 to congratulate Adams and express the "infinite satisfaction and improvement" the book brought him and his belief that it would do "great good." "It's [*sic*] learning and it's [*sic*] good sense will I hope make it an institute for our politicians, old as well as young." More than mere politeness, Jefferson's letter reflected his agreement with the central argument of the *Defence*. Many of Adams's specific critiques of the American constitutions, particularly the lack of a strong executive and the lack of a clear distinction between the Assembly and the Senate, paralleled the reservations about Virginia's constitution expressed in Jefferson's *Notes on the State of Virginia*. Jefferson to Adams, February 23, 1787, in *Papers* 11:177.*
45. That feature of New England culture remained visible in the later Federalist, Whig, and mid-nineteenth-century Republican parties. Adams, *Defence*, in *Works* 4:382, 6:66, 4:395.
46. Adams, *Defence*, in *Works* 6:115.
47. Madison's prediction concerning the hostile reception of Adams's *Defence* proved accurate, not only at the time but ever since. Madison to Jefferson, June 6, 1787, in *Writings*, 95–97. This letter is dated the same day as Madison's opening speech at the Constitutional Convention, in which, as I will make clear in chapter 9, he emphasized the democratic quality of the Virginia Plan for the federal constitution.*
48. Madison, "Notes on Ancient and Modern Confederacies," in *PJM* 9:3–22.*
49. It is important to keep in mind how contingent the Constitutional Convention was. Those who planned and executed it had no warrant for it, and there was considerable ambivalence throughout the United States about the entire project.*
50. On the process whereby Madison came to see the desirability of a Constitutional Convention, see Banning, *Sacred Fire of Liberty*, 43–75.
51. Madison, "Vices of the Political System of the United States," in *Writings*, 69–71.*
52. See Edmund S. Morgan, *American Slavery, American Freedom* (New York, 1975); and the concise account in David Brion Davis, *Inhuman Bondage: The Rise and Fall of Slavery in the New World* (New York, 2006), 141–56.
53. Madison, "Vices of the Political System of the United States," 71–76.*
54. Madison writing as Publius, *Federalist* 51, February 6, 1788, in *Writings*, 298.
55. Not content with the notion of politics as a slugfest in which individuals compete by advancing their own narrow self-interest, the image Rousseau deprecated as "the will of all" rather than the "general will," Madison was struggling to find the words to express his alternative. Madison, "Vices of the Political System of the United States, " 78–80; Madison writing as Publius, *Federalist* 51, February 6, 1788, in *Writings*, 298.*
56. Findley admitted that he pursued wealth himself; he owned "more land than I can make a proper use of." Unlike those backing the bank, however, he enjoyed only enough wealth "to give a spring to industry" and "procure the necessaries and a competence of the comforts of life." He had been lucky; many of his constituents had lost everything in the postwar downturn.* For the Findley-Morris

debate, see Carey, *Debates and Proceedings of the General Assembly of Pennsylvania*, 64–73, 128–30.*

57. Madison to Caleb Wallace, August 23, 1785, in *Writings*, 39–47.
58. Benjamin Franklin, James Wilson, Robert Morris, and Gouverneur Morris would be able to live in their comfortable homes during the summer of 1787, while the other delegates (except the venerable Washington, who accepted his friend Robert Morris's invitation to be his houseguest) stayed in boardinghouses. Washington to Madison, March 31, 1787, in *The Papers of George Washington*, Confederation Series, 6 vols. (Charlottesville, 1992–), 5:115; Madison to Washington, April 16, 1787, in *Writings*, 80–85.*
59. Madison's comment on Richard Morris quoted in Richard Beeman, *Plain, Honest Men: The Making of the American Constitution* (New York, 2009), 48; see also 44–57.*
60. The first scholar to characterize the Constitution as a repudiation of the democratic thrust of the Revolution was Charles Beard, *An Economic Interpretation of the Constitution of the United States* (1913; New York, 1961). That tradition has continued until the present.*
61. Jared Sparks, journal entry, April 19, 1830, in Max Farrand, ed., *The Records of the Federal Convention of 1787*, 3 vols. (New Haven, 1911), 3:479; the passage is usually attributed to Madison himself.*
62. Jefferson to Adams, August 30, 1787, in *Writings*, 906–9; George Mason to George Mason Jr., June 1, 1787, in Farrand, *Records* 3:33; Madison in Farrand, *Records* 1:13.*
63. See Jack N. Rakove, *Original Meanings: Politics and Ideas in the Making of the Constitution* (New York, 1996); and Beeman, *Plain, Honest Men*.
64. For Randolph's speech, see Madison, *Notes of Debates in the Federal Convention of 1787 Reported by James Madison*, ed. Adrienne Koch (Athens, OH, 1966), 28–33.
65. For Sherman's, Gerry's, and Randolph's remarks, see Madison, *Notes of Debates*, 39–42.
66. Mason, Wilson, and Madison in Madison, *Notes of Debates*, 39–50.*
67. For Pierce's portrait of Wilson, see Farrand, *Records* 3:91–92.
68. See Bruce H. Mann, *Republic of Debtors: Bankruptcy in the Age of American Independence* (Cambridge, MA, 2002), on the tangled webs of borrowing that ensnared even small farmers and artisans operating in a world of people with big ambitions and little money.
69. As he did in "Vices," Madison outlined the multiple rifts in every society, adding classical allusions and contemporary illustrations. In his own day some debtors "have defrauded their creditors," in others "the landed interest has borne hard on the mercantile interest," and in still others "holders of one species of property" have taxed disproportionately "holders of another species." Madison's diagnosis was accurate: from the humblest farmers to the richest financiers, many, perhaps even most, Americans in the mid-1780s both owed and lent money. There was plenty of ambition, and plenty of injustice, to go around. Madison's speech of June 6, 1787, is in *Notes of Debates*, 75–77, and in *Writings*, 92–93.*

70. Forrest McDonald, in *Novus Ordo Seclorum: The Intellectual Origins of the Constitution* (Lawrence, KS, 1985), 205–9, argues that only thirty-one of Madison's seventy-one specific proposals made it into the Constitution. It can be argued that the Supreme Court ended up playing a role similar to that Madison envisioned for the national government vis-à-vis the state legislatures, but the delegates to the convention had no idea how crucial these justices, appointed for life, would prove to be.*
71. Mason in Farrand, *Records* 2:94; Gerry in Farrand, *Records* 2:114; Wilson in Farrand, *Records* 2:103. The ultimate resolution of this conundrum, the electoral college, was almost an afterthought, and it did not take long—the contested election of 1800—for evidence to emerge showing just how poorly thought-out was the convention's scheme.*
72. Hamilton in Farrand, *Records* 1:146. For Butler's remarks, see *Notes of Debates*, 63. Hamilton's speech of June 18, 1787, in *Notes of Debates*, 129–139, shows the chasm dividing his approach to government from Madison's and Wilson's, and indeed from those of almost all the other delegates at the convention. Madison and Hamilton forged a strategic alliance to collaborate on the *Federalist* solely to achieve the ratification of the Constitution.*
73. Although George Read of Delaware wanted to replace the Articles of Confederation, he announced that the Delaware delegation was under strict instructions to oppose any plan that deviated from equal representation of each state. Delaware's John Dickinson, who had trained Wilson in the law and was among the architects of the Articles of Confederation, and Roger Sherman from Connecticut argued that the convention needed to recognize the importance of the states as states, an argument with the force of tradition on its side. Farrand, *Records* 3:574–75.*
74. Madison's July 9 speech is in *Writings*, 101–8. The record does not show how many delegates were still awake when Madison finished his exhaustive and exhausting history of the world's experiments in confederation.*
75. The notorious three-fifths clause has often been taken to indicate the triumph of the South over the North, but it might just as easily be seen, as indeed it was seen by Frederick Douglass and others, as a defeat for the South. Don Fehrenbacher, *The Slaveholding Republic: An Account of the United States Government's Relations to Slavery* (New York, 2001), points out that the alternative to the three-fifths compromise under discussion in 1787 was to count slaves as full persons for the purposes of apportioning representatives, just as women and children were counted, an outcome that would have increased substantially the number of congressional representatives from southern states.
76. Wilson compared the proposed Senate to the most rotten of England's notorious rotten boroughs; both he and Madison railed against its injustice and tried to show how unlikely was the feared alliance among large states. Wilson's speech of June 30, 1787, is in *Notes of Debates*, 220–22.
77. Farrand, *Records* 1:197–98.

78. Madison viewed this result as a far more bitter defeat than his loss of the national veto over state legislation, and his later alignment with Jefferson and other southerners on the issue of states' rights can be traced to his disillusionment with small-state delegations from the North who opposed him in Philadelphia. For Wilson's major speeches relating to these issues, see Madison, *Notes of Debates*, 208, 220–22, 226, 295; and for Madison's, 204–8, 213–15, 223–25, 228, 239–40, 263, 292–95, and Madison, *Writings*, 108–27.*
79. Some delegates thought the decision should be left to the states, since their practices were hardly uniform. In ten states, to cite just one example of such diversity, free blacks enjoyed the right to vote. In New Jersey, women had been voting for over a decade.*
80. Only Delaware voted in favor of Gouverneur Morris's proposal to limit the franchise; the Maryland delegation was divided. All the other states, including Virginia and Pennsylvania, voted no. See *Notes of Debates*, 401–5. For Madison's reflections on the learning that occurred during the debates, see Farrand, *Records* 3:455.*
81. Madison, *Writings*, 93.
82. Jefferson, *Notes on the State of Virginia*, in *Writings*, 263–64.
83. Jefferson, *Notes on the State of Virginia*, 288–89.
84. Adams to Jefferson, May 22, 1785, in *Papers of Thomas Jefferson* 8:160.
85. See Davis, *Inhuman Bondage*, 144. In 1791 Madison made preliminary notes for an essay demonstrating the incompatibility of slavery and democracy. He never published it. His notes for that proposed *National Gazette* essay are in *PJM* 14: 163–64.
86. The bizarre idea of the three-fifths ratio, proposed by the slave-owning delegates from South Carolina, appeared originally in 1783, when delegates to the Confederation Congress were wrangling over whether each state's payments to the central government should be proportional to that state's wealth. Because it was estimated that a slave produced roughly 60 percent of the economic value of a free laborer, it was proposed that each slave should be counted as three-fifths of a person when calculating that state's contribution. Although the scheme was never enacted, the ratio stuck in the minds of those who convened in Philadelphia four years later.*
87. Madison, *Writings*, 93.
88. Dickinson's entry in his notebook is in James H. Hutson, *Supplement to Max Farrand's "The Records of the Federal Convention of 1787"* (New Haven, 1987), 158.*
89. In Gouverneur Morris's words, "The rights of human nature and the principles of our holy religion loudly call on us to dispense the blessing of freedom to all mankind." Gouverneur Morris in Farrand, *Records* 2:221–23.*
90. At the convention, Mason echoed Jefferson's lament: slavery had "the most pernicious effect" on "the manners" of every white southerner, who "is born a petty tyrant" and learns to "despise labor." Mason in Farrand, *Records* 2:370.*

91. Hendrik Hartog, "The Constitution of Aspiration and 'The Rights That Belong to Us All,'" *Journal of American History* 74, no. 3 (December 1987): 1013–34, remains a valuable meditation on the double-sided character of the Constitution. Hartog exposes its limitations and also its role establishing rights not only as trumps but also as "a duty on public authority to undo—to destroy—the structures that maintain hierarchy and oppression."*

Chapter 9

1. Also laboring on the final draft was Gouverneur Morris, Madison's and James Wilson's closest associate at the convention and the likeliest author of the ringing preamble that located the power of the Constitution in the people themselves rather than the states.*
2. Much of the controversy surrounding Madison's position has come from critics who disagree with his analysis of politics. Those who believe politics is about nothing but self-interest, whether from the right or the left, either distort Madison's position in order to enlist him into their ranks or dismiss him as an apologist for antidemocratic conspiracies he never joined.*
3. Madison to Jefferson, October 24, 1787, in Madison, *Writings*, ed. Jack Rakove (New York, 1999), 142–58.
4. [Alexander Hamilton], *The Farmer Refuted* (1775), 6.*
5. Jefferson to Madison, December 30, 1787, in Jefferson, *Writings*, ed. Merrill D. Peterson (New York, 1984), 914–18. In an earlier letter to Adams, Jefferson complained primarily about the office of the presidency, which he described as a "bad edition of a Polish king." The fact that the president could be reelected to successive four-year terms meant, Jefferson feared, that he would be "an officer for life." Jefferson to Adams, November 13, 1787, in *Writings*, 912–14.
6. See Bernard Bailyn, ed., *Debates on the Constitution: Federalist and Antifederalist Speeches, Articles, and Letters during the Struggle over Ratification*, 2 vols. (New York, 1993) (hereafter *DOTC*): vol. 1, *Debates in the Press and in Private Correspondence, September 17, 1787–January 12, 1788; and Debates in the State Ratifying Conventions, Pennsylvania, November 20–December 15, 1787; Connecticut, January 3–9, 1788; Massachusetts, January 9–February 7, 1788*; and vol. 2, *Debates in the Press and in Private Correspondence, January 14–August 9, 1788; and Debates in the State Ratifying Conventions, South Carolina, May 12–24, 1788; Virginia, June 2–27, 1788; New York, June 17–July 26, 1788; North Carolina, July 21–August 4, 1788.**
7. Less than six weeks after the convention closed, the Constitution had been reprinted in every newspaper in the United States. Robert A. Rutland, "The Great Newspaper Debate: The Constitutional Crisis of 1787–1788," *Proceedings of the American Antiquarian Society* 97 (1987): 47.
8. Despite the shortcomings of the Constitution from our vantage point, when it is considered historically it is clear that it advanced the cause of popular government and provided the framework for further democratization.*

9. Several dichotomies have been used to characterize the differences between those in favor and those opposed to ratification—including liberal vs. republican, Court vs. Country, cosmopolitan vs. local, conservative vs. radical, forward-thinking vs. tradition-bound, and, perhaps most common of all, elites vs. the common people—but none of those binaries captures the range of individuals involved or opinions expressed between the fall of 1787 and the summer of 1788.*
10. George Turner to Winthrop Sargent, November 6, 1787, and John Breckinridge to James Breckinridge, January 25, 1788, in Merrill Jensen, John P. Kaminski, and Gaspare J. Sardino et al., eds., *The Documentary History of the Ratification of the Constitution*, 30 vols. (Madison, 1976–) (hereafter *DHRC*), 13:565–66, 8:320–21.
11. "William Penn," *Independent Gazetteer* (Philadelphia), January 2 and 3, 1788, in *The Complete Anti-Federalist*, ed. Herbert Storing, 7 vols. (Chicago, 1963–81), 3:168–73.*
12. For the range of Antifederalist essays, see *Debates on the Constitution*, which depends, as does all scholarship on the ratification process, on *The Documentary History of the Ratification of the Constitution*.*
13. Rawlins Lowndes, *Debates Which Arose in the House of Representatives of South Carolina on the Constitution Framed for the United States by a Convention of Delegates Assembled at Philadelphia*, in *DOTC* 2:19–25.
14. Patrick Henry's speech in the Virginia Convention, June 11, 1787, in *DHRC* 9:1161.
15. George Mason's speech in the Virginia Convention, June 17, 1788, in *DHRC* 10:1342.
16. Brutus III [Robert Yates?], November 15, 1787, in *DOTC* 1:317–23.
17. Benjamin Gale's speech in the Killingworth town meeting, November 12, 1787, in *DHRC* 3:421; *Carlisle Gazette*, March 5, 1788. The *Massachusetts Centinel* observed that northerners thought "that in the new Constitution, the southern states have preeminence," whereas southerners thought "in all things the eastern states out-wit and unhinge us." Because the complaints balanced out, the Constitution was deemed fair by many commentators. *DHRC* 4:419.
18. Saul Cornell, *The Other Founders: Anti-Federalism and the Dissenting Tradition in America, 1788–1828* (Chapel Hill, 1999), which demonstrates the diversity of the Antifederalists and their arguments, shows why it is no longer plausible to treat the Antifederalists as if they expressed a unified sensibility.*
19. Centinel complained that the Constitution provided no bill of rights, unlimited power to tax, the possibility of a standing army, a Supreme Court accountable to no one, and, worst of all, a bicameral legislature that departed from the wise precedent of Pennsylvania's unicameral popular assembly. Centinel railed against a Senate that would shelter "the *better sort*, the *well born*" and nurture "a *permanent* ARISTOCRACY." Centinel 1 appeared in Philadelphia's *Independent Gazetteer* on October 5, 1787; it is reprinted in *DOTC* 1:52–62.*

20. Melancton Smith in the New York Ratifying Convention, June 21, 1788, in *DOTC* 2:761; Rusticus, *New York Journal*, September 13, 1787.
21. Cato Uticensis [George Mason?], "To the Freemen of Virginia," *Virginia Independent Chronicle* (Richmond), October 17, 1787, in *DHRC* 8:70–72.
22. One of the most comprehensive, and widely reprinted, Antifederalist tracts, probably written by Samuel Bryan, provides an excellent summation of their objections. See "The Address and Reasons of Dissent of the Minority of the Convention of the State of Pennsylvania to Their Constituents," in *DOTC* 1:526–52.*
23. [James Winthrop], "Agrippa Letters," in *Essays on the Constitution of the United States*, ed. Paul L. Ford et al. (1892; New York, 1970), 73.
24. "William Penn," *Independent Gazetteer* (Philadelphia), January 2 and 3, 1788, in Storing, *The Complete Anti-Federalist* 3:168–73.
25. An Old Whig [James Hutchinson], *Independent Gazetteer* (Philadelphia): no. 4, October 27, 1787; no. 5, November 1, 1787,; and no. 8, February 6, 1788, in Storing, *The Complete Anti-Federalist* 3:32–34, 35, 49.
26. The rifts among the Antifederalists showed the accuracy of Madison's analysis concerning crosscutting cleavages on the basis of religion, economics, geography, and cultural tradition. Mercy Otis Warren was among the many Americans anxious about excessive democracy and excessive aristocracy. On the one hand, she fumed about those who would reject all authority; on the other, she denounced the new constitution as the work of those who "secretly wish for aristocracy." A Columbian Patriot, [Mercy Otis Warren], *Observations on the new Constitution, and on the foederal and state conventions* (New York, 1788), 20–21.*
27. Brutus I in *DOTC* 1:172.
28. Federal Farmer I in *DOTC* 1:253; Melancton Smith in *DOTC* 2:759.
29. Cincinnatus in *DOTC* 1:119.
30. Federal Farmer flatly rejected the idea that the people would remain sovereign in the Constitution. Since power "must be lodged somewhere in every society," it would gravitate toward the executive and his "aristocratical" associates in the Senate. The authorship of this widely read pamphlet, published with the title *Observations Leading to a Fair Examination of the System of Government Proposed by the Late Convention: and to Several Essential and Necessary Alterations in It. In a Number of Letters from the Federal Farmer to the Republican*, remains unknown. Contemporaries thought it was the work of Virginia's Richard Henry Lee; more recent scholars have proposed New Yorker Melancton Smith. It is published in *DOTC* 1:245–88.*.
31. Federal Farmer, *Observations*, 249–69, 277–83.*
32. Smith's reasoning echoed Madison's as well as Federal Farmer's: "The interest of both the rich and the poor are involved in that of the middling class. No burden can be laid on the poor, but what will sensibly affect the middling class." Melancton Smith in the New York Ratifying Convention, June 21, 1788, in *DOTC* 2:757–65, 773–75.
33. On middling Antifederalists such as Federal Farmer, Philadelphiensis, Smith, Findley, Bryan, and John Nicholson, see Cornell, *The Other Founders*, 97–99,

148–50, 180–87, and 191–94; on the differences between them and plebeian Antifederalists such as William Petriken and William Manning, see 46–47, 84, 107–109, and 187.

34. Even the Federalists with the least sympathy for "the people" conceded that the decision was theirs. Fisher Ames of Massachusetts, who notoriously declared that "a democracy is a volcano" that "conceals the fiery materials of its own destruction," acknowledged that "the people always mean right," and "if time is allowed for reflection and information, they will do right." In any case, "all power resides" in their judgment because by choosing delegates to the state ratifying conventions, the American people would decide whether the Constitution best secured the foundations of their democracy. Fisher Ames, speech in the Massachusetts Ratifying Convention, January 15, 1788, in *DOTC* 2:891–95.*

35. James Wilson, *Lectures on Law, Delivered in the College of Philadelphia, in 1790 and 1791*, in *Collected Works of James Wilson*, ed. Kermit L. Hall and Mark David Hall, 2 vols. (Indianapolis, 2007), 1:432.

36. For that reason, Wilson claimed, the absence of a bill of rights made no difference: "It would have been superfluous and absurd to have stipulated with a foederal body of our own creation, that we should enjoy those privileges, of which we are not divested either by the intention or the act, that has brought that body into existence." "Wilson's Speech at a Public Meeting," October 6, 1787, in *DOTC* 1:63–69.

37. "Wilson's Speech." On 1142, Bailyn describes this now little-known speech as "the single most influential and most frequently cited document in the entire ratification debate." By the end of 1787, it had been printed in thirty-four newspapers, in twenty-seven towns, scattered across twelve states.*

38. Wilson's preferred term for citizens' freedom to follow the general will harkened back to a word familiar to seventeenth-century Puritans, "Foederal liberty." Sovereign power "remains and flourishes with the people," and it is "under the influence of that truth," Wilson declared, that "we, at this moment, sit, deliberate, and speak." America's democracy would reach decisions not by armed conflict, as other nations had done, but through the deliberative "means of obtaining a superior knowledge of the nature of government, and of accomplishing its end." Wilson's "great panacea of human politics" was Rousseau's: "The supreme power, therefore, should be vested in the people," who retain the power to alter their government as they see fit, not only by choosing their representatives but also because they preserve the power of amendment. "Wilson's Opening Address," November 24, 1787, is in *DOTC* 1:791–803.*

39. William Findley challenged Wilson's logic at the Pennsylvania Ratifying Convention, reasoning that officers in the federal government would maximize their power at the expense of the states and the people. Wilson replied that if they exceeded their authority, they would be checked not by state or local institutions but by the irresistible force of the people themselves. Wilson emphasized how direct the popular control over the new government would

be: "I have no idea that a safe system of power, in the government, sufficient to manage the general interest of the United States, could be drawn from any other source, or rested in any other authority than that of the people at large," which he called "the rock on which this structure will stand." "Wilson's Replies to Findley," December 1, 1787, and December 3, 1787, are in *DOTC* 1:820–28, 829–30.*

40. Distinctive as Wilson's rhetoric was, he and Madison were hardly alone in emphasizing the democratic dimensions of the Constitution. Writing as "Americanus" in the *New York Daily Advertiser*, Federalist John Stevens Jr. distinguished the new nation from earlier republics. Whereas Spartan civic virtue turned rival states into "nests of hornets," in the United States "the gusts of passion, which faction is ever blowing up in '*a small territory*,'" will "lose their force before they reach the seat of *Federal* Government." By forming "mutual checks on each other," the layers and branches of government will foster a spirit of moderation. "Representation is the grand secret in the formation of republican government," Stevens later wrote, because it transforms self-interest into a vision of the public good. November 2 and December 5–6, 1787, in *DOTC* 1:227–30, 457–64.*
41. The town of Norwich instructed those it sent to the ratifying convention only to act "as their wisdom shall direct." Norfolk empowered its delegates to "act as they think best." In the town of Wingham, "after a very able and lengthy discussion of the subject" and two decisions to adjourn, a substantial majority of voters decided they should not make a decision: "As the proposed Constitution was to be determined on by a state Convention, it was not proper for this town to pass any vote on the subject." See *DHRC* 3:405–51.*
42. Roger Sherman, August 15, 1789, in *Annals of Congress* 1789, 763.
43. Anyone familiar with debate, Fisher Ames and Noah Webster argued, understands how ideas can change in that crucible. Had the delegates to the Constitutional Convention been under binding instructions, Ames pointed out, the document would never have been written. Fisher Ames, speech at the Massachusetts Ratifying Convention, January 15, 1787, in *DOTC* 1:891–95; Giles Hickory [Noah Webster], *American Magazine*, February 1788, in *DOTC* 2:304–15.*
44. James Innes, speech in the Virginia Ratifying Convention, in *DHRC* 10:1520; Edmund Randolph in *DHRC* 10:1366; John Jay, speech in the New York Ratifying Convention, in *DOTC* 2:784–88.
45. For Archibald Maclaine's challenge to instructing delegates, see Publicola, "An Address to the Freemen of North Carolina," in *DHRC* 16:438–39; James Iredell, speech in the North Carolina Ratifying Convention, in Jonathan Elliot, ed., *The Debates in the Several State Conventions, on the Adoption of the Federal Constitution*, 5 vols. (Philadelphia, 1907), 4:4–13.*
46. John Adams, when looking for an exemplary ancient lawgiver as he wrote his draft of the Massachusetts Constitution, chose the Athenian Solon, who also served as the model for Adam Smith. Hamilton, Jay, and Madison made good

their intentions to remain engaged in public affairs for the remainder of their lives.

47. Even though later commentators inflated the significance of the *Federalist* beyond its influence at the time, understanding its historical significance remains indispensable. Unlike most careful works of political philosophy, these essays present debaters' points intended to respond to specific claims by their opponents. Only by ripping the *Federalist* from its historical context can it be seen, as commentators seem increasingly inclined to do—and as the Supreme Court has tended more and more to do in recent years—as an authoritative statement of the meaning of the United States Constitution.*

48. The authorship of individual essays has remained a vexed question since the essays' original publication. Even though recent scholarship has resolved most of these disputes, the persistence of disagreements about who wrote which essays suggests how conscious the authors were of making a consistent argument that masked their deep differences. See the Introduction to the most comprehensive edition of the *Federalist*, ed. Jacob Cooke (Middletown, CT, 1961), xi–xxx.*

49. Hamilton writing as Publius, *Federalist* 1, October 27, 1787, ed. Cooke, 3–7. This essay first appeared in the *Independent Journal* and was reprinted, as were most of the essays, in the *New-York Packet* and the *Daily Advertiser*.*

50. On the theme of union in the new nation, see Daniel Wewers, "The Specter of Disunion in the Early American Republic, 1783–1815" (unpub. Ph.D. diss., Harvard University, 2008).

51. Hamilton writing as Publius, *Federalist* 9, November 21, 1787, ed. Cooke, 50–56.

52. Primarily because of the layers of polemic that now surround it, the task of understanding *Federalist* 10 historically becomes ever more challenging. If, as one of the characters in David Lodge's novel *Small World* observes, we cannot avoid the influence of T. S. Eliot on Shakespeare, we likewise cannot avoid the influence of two centuries of commentary on Madison.

53. The most detailed and persuasive accounts of the reasons for Madison's judgment on this complex question, which critics think shows his fear of popular sentiment, are Rakove, *Original Meanings*, and Banning, *The Sacred Fire of Liberty*.

54. More than a century of sophisticated analysis of class formation challenging Marx's framework, from Jean Jaurès to Dipesh Chakrabarty, has failed to shake the certainty of some historians still committed to the idea that "the people," conceived as a unitary force with shared interests and aspirations, lost their battle against "the elite" during the 1780s.*

55. See the discussion of Adams and Paine on pp. 383–85 above. Writing about the *Federalist* late in his life, Adams discerned the peculiar nature of the attempt to differentiate between a "democracy" and a "republic" in *Federalist* 10: The "distinction between a republic and a democracy cannot be justified. A democracy is as really a republic as an oak is a tree, or a temple a building. There are, in strictness of speech and in the soundest technical language, democratical and aristocratical republics, as well as an infinite variety of mixtures of

both." Adams understood that the two terms were employed more or less interchangeably throughout the 1770s and 1780s to designate forms of popular government in contradistinction to monarchy, with different shadings depending on the circumstances in which, and the purposes for which, the terms were used. Adams contended, sensibly enough, that the apparently hard and fast distinction in *Federalist* 10 was inconsistent with common practice in 1787. John Adams to J. H. Tiffany, March 31, 1819, in *The Works of John Adams*, ed. Charles Francis Adams, 10 vols. (Boston, 1850–56), 10: 377–78.

56. Whatever the source of faction, a charismatic demagogue, devotion to a religious sect, or an economic campaign such as "a rage for paper money, for an abolition of debts," or "for an equal division of property, or for any other improper or wicked project," its effects could best be checked through the institutions of representative government and the extended sphere of the great republic. Madison surely did oppose both the radical transformation of the money supply and the equalization of wealth, as did almost all eighteenth-century Americans. The ban on states issuing paper money and canceling contracts was adopted by the delegates in Philadelphia with little debate. Madison's repeated references to religious zealots and scheming party leaders, however, were not smokescreens; they expressed genuine concerns with the obstacles posed by enthusiasm to deliberation.*

57. Madison writing as Publius, *Federalist* 10, November 22, 1787, ed. Cook, 56–65. The commentary on this essay is enormous and continues to grow.*

58. Readers did not know *Federalist* 10 was Madison's first as Publius, nor did they seem to find its arguments any more compelling than those of numbers 1 through 8. Those essays focused on the importance of unity in face of the multiple threats facing the new nation, threats from European powers, threats from the wilderness and the Indians it contained, and threats from each other if they were to split apart. Madison's penetrating analysis of faction and his sophisticated case for deliberative democracy seem to have left his contemporaries underwhelmed.*

59. See Akhil Amar, *America's Constitution: A Biography* (New York, 2010).

60. As the first essays of the *Federalist* were appearing in print, Madison emphasized that he was not engaged in writing political philosophy. As in Philadelphia, the Federalists had to keep their eyes on the target. "If any Constitution is to be established by deliberation and choice," Madison wrote to Archibald Stuart on October 30, 1787, "it must be examined with many allowances and must be compared, not with the theory which each individual may frame in his own mind, but with the system which it is meant to take the place of and with any other which there might be a probability of obtaining." Wilson delivered his great Rousseauvian oration at the Pennsylvania Ratifying Convention just two days after Madison's *Federalist* 10 was published. Given Wilson's explicit endorsement of Rousseau and the already noted parallels between Wilson's arguments and Madison's, only the stubborn insistence that Madison must have meant something different from Rousseau has blinded commentators to the

similarities between his idea of a public good emerging from the deliberation of representatives and Rousseau's conception of the general will. Given the distinction that Madison and Hamilton had sketched in *Federalist* 9 and 10, Madison now had to establish the point that Wilson had made so powerfully in Pennsylvania. Replying to Antifederalists who worried that those elected to the United States Congress would be too remote from the people, Madison insisted in *Federalist* 14, his first contribution after Wilson's intervention in Pennsylvania, that their foes' objections foundered on two crucial considerations, the principle of popular sovereignty and the practice of representation. Wilson had described "a chain of connection with the people"; Madison in *Federalist* 14 claimed for "America the merit of making the discovery" of representation as "the basis of unmixed"—i.e., nonmonarchical and nonaristocratic—"and extensive republics." Their terminologies now differed. Their arguments did not. Madison writing as Publius, *Federalist* 14, November 30, 1787, ed. Cooke, 83–89.*

61. Madison's summary expressed his awareness of the problems faced in Philadelphia by those who produced the Constitution: "Here then are three sources of vague and incorrect definitions; indistinctness of the object, imperfection of the organ of conception, inadequateness of the vehicle of ideas." Although Madison offered no examples, his own creative substitution of "republic" for "democracy" would have provided an excellent illustration of his point. Given all these obstacles, he concluded, the "real wonder" was not the flaws that remained in the Constitution but that "so many difficulties should have been surmounted, and surmounted with a unanimity almost unprecedented." Madison writing as Publius, *Federalist* 37, January 11, 1788, ed. Cooke, 231–39.*

62. Franklin in Max Farrand, ed., *The Records of the Federal Convention of 1787*, 3 vols. (New Haven, 1911), 2:641–43. In several later essays, Madison emphasized the principle of popular sovereignty: all government officials "are in fact but different agents and trustees of the people." Madison writing as Publius, *Federalist* 39, January 16, 1788, ed. Cooke, 250–57; *Federalist* 45, January 26, 1788, ed. Cooke, 308–14; *Federalist* 46, January 29, 1788, ed. Cooke, 315–23. The quotation comes from 315. Rather than being constituted by members of a separate social order, the United States Senate would provide only another deliberative forum that would balance the House, represent each state equally, and provide greater stability because of the longer terms of office. The Constitution explicitly prohibited the creation of an aristocracy. Madison writing as Publius, *Federalist* 48, February 1, 1788, ed. Cooke, 332–38.*

63. John Stevens Jr. writing as Americanus, *New York Daily Advertiser*, November 30, 1787, in *DOTC* 1:437–42.

64. A Columbian Patriot [Mercy Otis Warren], *Observations on the Constitution*, February 1788, in *DOTC* 2:284–303. At the end of 1788, reflecting on Jefferson's suggestion that members of the upper house of the Virginia Assembly serve only two-year terms, Madison defended the longer terms of United States senators by decrying the "spirit of *locality*" that was developing in the state legislature as

representatives focused too narrowly on the particular interests of their constituencies. That obsession with their own neighbors caused them to "lose sight of the aggregate interests of the community, and even to sacrifice them to the interests or prejudices of their respective constituents." Whereas most Antifederalists believed that such close attention to local interests was the point of popular government, and agreed with Columbian Patriot that annual elections were the best guarantee of responsibility so conceived, Madison disagreed. Madison writing as Publius, *Federalist* 62, February 27, 1788, ed. Cooke, 415–22; and *Federalist* 63, March 1, 1788, ed. Cooke, 422–31. Madison's "Observations on the 'Draft for the Constitution for Virginia,'" his reply to the sketch in Jefferson's *Notes on the State of Virginia,* in Madison, *Writings*, 409–18.*

65. Madison writing as Publius, *Federalist* 55, February 13, 1788, ed. Cooke, 372–78.
66. Madison writing as Publius, *Federalist* 51, February 6, 1788, ed. Cooke, 347–53.
67. From the most generous benevolence to the narrowest self-interest, Madison found multiple reasons why representatives would pursue the general interest. Madison writing as Publius, *Federalist* 57, February 19, 1788, ed. Cooke, 384–90.*
68. Federal Farmer concluded that delegates to the state ratifying conventions would represent "the solid sense and the real political character of the country." Federal Farmer in *DOTC* 1: 287, 285.*
69. In New York, the state to which the essays in the *Federalist* were devoted, so much was printed in so many publications that a truly comprehensive analysis of all the primary sources may never be possible.*
70. Wilson's speech of December 11, 1787, in *DOTC* 1:832–68.*
71. Smilie contended that because fewer than one-sixth of Pennsylvania's electorate had voted in the selection of delegates, the unrepresented majority might take matters into its own hands if the convention endorsed a Constitution "the people" deemed despotic. Federalists, who held a two-to-one majority at the convention, howled at the charge and insisted that Pennsylvanians would not be swayed by the ranting of disgruntled losers. William Shippen to Thomas Lee Shippen, December 12, 1788, in *DHRC* 2: 601.*
72. *DHRC* 5: 995–1001.*
73. As Federalists had argued elsewhere, two-year terms made sense because it would take time to learn how to cope with the more complicated problems facing the entire nation. The South, they insisted, would simply never have accepted a Constitution that abolished slavery, and slavery would die when the supply of slaves was shut off. Finally the Senate, instead of serving as a breeding ground for aristocrats, simply registered the integrity of the state governments and guarded against excesses of popular passion.
74. See Pauline Maier, *Ratification: The People Debate the Constitution, 1787–1988* (New York, 2010), 138–213.*
75. Massachusetts Federalists earnestly engaged their opponents, in part because they knew that the arrogance of Wilson and the Morrises had antagonized

many delegates. See Smith in *DHRC* 6:1510, 1514; and Backus in *DHRC* 6:1215, 1224–26.*

76. Jefferson to Madison, December 20, 1787, in *Writings*, 914–18.
77. Madison's initial objections to a declaration of rights stemmed from his judgment that rights were hopelessly vague, were impossible to enforce, and had proved ineffective in the states.*
78. Madison, "Speech in the Virginia Ratifying Convention on the Judicial Power," June 20, 1788, in *Writings*, 393–400.*
79. See, for example, "Melancton Smith Speaks in Support of Ratification without Condition," July 23, 1787, *DOTC* 2:852–53.
80. Madison to Jefferson, October 17, 1788, in *Writings*, 418–23. After his election, Madison wrote, "Circumstances are now changed: The Constitution is established," and now "amendments, if pursued with a proper moderation and in a proper mode, will be not only safe, but may serve the double purpose of satisfying the minds of well meaning opponents, and of providing additional guards in favour of liberty." Madison to George Eve, January 2, 1789, in *Writings*, 427–28.*
81. Madison, "Speech in Congress Proposing Constitutional Amendments," June 8, 1789, in *Writings*, 437–52.
82. Madison, "Speech in Congress Proposing Constitutional Amendments," 441–42.
83. Madison, "Remarks in Congress on the 'Most Valuable Amendment,'" in *Writings*, 470.*
84. Widgery and Taylor in *DHRC* 6:1487–89.*
85. The festivities were described in the *Massachusetts Centinel*, February 13, 1788, in *DHRC* 7:1623–27. Baltimore followed with a celebration "allamode de Boston" designed to outdo the New Englanders. According to Baltimore's *Maryland Journal*, the procession attracted more than three thousand participants, again including "Farmers, Mechanics and Merchants, to form the most interesting Scene ever exhibited in this Part of the World." The comprehensive array of workers, representing every occupation practiced in the state, was designed to demonstrate that "the people" were delighted with the new Constitution. After-dinner toasts at the post-parade feast began with a rousing one to "The Majesty of the People." *Maryland Journal*, May 6, 1788, *DOTC* 2: 430–38.*
86. The "Account of the Grand Federal Procession" appeared in three Philadelphia newspapers on July 9, 1788, and was later published as a pamphlet and in German translation. See *DHRC*,18:246–49. Excerpts from Wilson's notes for his address are in *DHRC* 18:242–46.*
87. The toast by the Boston artisans' committee was published in the *Independent Chronicle* (Boston), February 14, 1788, in *DHRC* 7:1630–31.The temptation to issue a final rebuke was too strong for one Massachusetts partisan to resist: now that the Constitution had been ratified, the word "federal" expresses "national honour, dignity, freedom, happiness, and every republican privilege," whereas "anti-federalism" means only "anarchy, confusion, rebellion, treason, sacrilege, and rapine." *Massachusetts Gazette*, January 18, 1788, in *DHRC* 5:744. New

York's procession, which included professors in academic regalia along with the usual farmers and artisans, attracted twenty thousand spectators; even in the smaller city of Charleston, more than three thousand participated.*

88. Benjamin Rush in *DHRC* 18:265.*

89. [John Stevens], *Observations on Government* (New York, 1787), 50; James Iredell's speech at the North Carolina Ratifying Convention, July 28, 1788, *DOTC* 2:882–87; David Ramsay, *The History of the American Revolution* (Trenton, 1811), 452; Thomas Pownall, *A Memorial Addressed to the Sovereigns of America* (London, 1783), 53; Nathaniel Chipman, *Sketches of the Principles of Government* (Rutland, VT, 1793), 289–90.

90. Thomas Paine, *The Rights of Man*, in Paine, *Writings*, ed. Eric Foner (New York, 1984), 594; Paine to George Washington, July 30, 1796, in *The Life and Works of Thomas Paine*, ed. William M. Van der Weyde (New Rochelle, 1925), quoted in Alfred F. Young, "The Framers of the Constitution and the 'Genius' of the People," *Radical History Review* 42 (1988): 8–18.*

91. Adams to John Jay, December 16, 1787, in *Works* 8:467.

92. Wilson, "Lectures on Law, Introductory Lecture: Of the study of law in the United States," *The Works of James Wilson*, ed. Robert Green McCloskey, 2 vols. (Cambridge, MA, 1967), 1: 79.*

93. Alexander Graydon, who did not share Wilson's enthusiasm for popular government, wrote in his memoir that "Wilson was truly great, but enthusiastically democratic." Graydon wrote that Wilson's conception of popular sovereignty reminded him of Rousseau: "*Ces Pauvres Savoyards sont si bonnes gens!* As Jean-Jacques says. And who could say less of the good souls of Pennsylvania?" See Alexander Graydon, *Memoirs of a Life, Chiefly Passed in Pennsylvania, Within the Last Sixty Years* (Edinburgh and London, 1822), 371–72.

94. Wilson, "Lectures on Law, Lecture 10: Of Government," in *Works* 1:305.

95. Max Edling, *A Revolution in Favor of Government: Origins of the U.S. Constitution and the Making of the American State* (Oxford, 2003), 222–29.

96. John Stevens dissented from Madison's and Wilson's talk of justice and argued that representative democracy could function very well without "heroic virtues which we admire" in the ancient world. "The sacrifice of our dearest interests, self-denial and austerity of manners, are by no means necessary." If instead American citizens "pursue merely their own true interest and happiness," the republic will "flourish for ages." The reasons, Stevens insisted, could be traced to the enlarged sphere of the republic, the responsibility forced on representatives by regular elections, and the difference between "self denial" on the one hand and citizens' "true interest and happiness" on the other. Americanus [John Stevens Jr.], "On Representation and the Modern State," *New York Daily Advertiser*, November 30, 1787, in *DOTC* 1:437–42.

97. Benjamin Rush, "A Plan for the Establishment of Public Schools," in *Essays on Education in the Early Republic*, ed. Frederick Rudolph (Cambridge, MA, 1965), 19. The scholarly literature on the *doux commerce* thesis is extensive.*

98. Hamilton echoed the argument he had made in the Constitutional Convention, departing from Madison and Wilson by applauding the prospect of a growing difference between rich and poor. Hamilton at the New York Ratifying Convention, June 21, 1788, in *DOTC* 2: 771.*

99. Jefferson also recommended, as guides to ethics, the works of Plato, Cicero, Locke, Hutcheson, Kames, Ferguson, Adam Smith, and the novelist Laurence Sterne. He urged Carr above all to "lose no occasion of exercising your dispositions to be grateful, to be generous, to be charitable, to be human, to be true, just, firm, orderly, courageous &c. Consider every act of this kind as an exercise which will strengthen your moral faculties, & increase your worth." Jefferson to Peter Carr, August 10, 1787, in *Writings*, 900–906. Twenty-six years later, Jefferson wrote, "Self-love, therefore, is no part of morality. . . . It is the sole antagonist of virtue, leading us constantly by our propensities to self-gratification in violation of our moral duties to others." Jefferson to Thomas Law, June 13, 1814, in *Writings*, 1335–39; see also Jefferson to John Minor, August 30, 1814, in *Writings*, 1557–61.*

100. Adams, *Discourses on Davila*, in *Works* 6:114–15, 232–49.*

101. Mercy Otis Warren, "Alphabet for Marcia," (n.d.), Mercy Warren Papers, box 1, Massachusetts Historical Society.*

102. Ezra Stiles, *The United States Elevated to Glory and Honor* (New Haven, 1783), 7–8.

103. Charles Chauncy, *The Benevolence of the Deity* (Boston, 1784), 186.

104. Asa Burton, *A Sermon Preached at Windsor . . . on the Day of the Anniversary Election, October, 1785* (Windsor, VT, 1786), 22.

105. Charles Backus, *A Sermon Preached in Long-Meadow at the Publick Feast, April 17, 1788* (Springfield, MA, 1788), 13, 21.

106. Aaron Bancroft, "An Account of His Ministry in the Second Parish" (1785), 7–8, Aaron Bancroft Papers, 1789–1839, American Antiquarian Society; and David Barnes, "Sermon on Timothy 6:9," November 13, 1785, David Barnes Sermons, 2 manuscript vols., 1:1091, American Antiquarian Society.*

107. Enos Hitchcock, *An oration: delivered July 4, 1788, at the request of the inhabitants of the town of Providence, in celebration of the anniversary of American independence, and of the accession of nine states to the Federal Constitution* (Providence, 1788), 21–22.*

108. Benjamin Rush to John Adams, July 21, 1789, in *Letters of Benjamin Rush*, ed. L. H. Butterfield, 2 vols. (Princeton, 1951), 1:523; Rush to Elhanan Winchester, November 12, 1791, in *Letters* 1:611; Rush to Jefferson, August 22, 1800, in *Letters* 2:820–21.

109. Adams to Charles Francis Adams, January 9, 1794, in *Adams Family Correspondence*, ed. L. H. Butterfield et al., 12 vols. to date (Cambridge, MA, 1963–), 10:20.

110. Jefferson to Rush, September 23, 1800, in *Writings*, 1080–82.

111. Jefferson to Moses Robinson, March 23, 1801, in *Writings*, 1087–88. See also the book of selections from the New Testament that Jefferson pieced together

to form the ethical code he considered the heart of Christianity: *Jefferson's Extracts from the Gospels*, ed. Dickenson W. Adams (Princeton, 1983).

112. See Stephen A. Marini, "Religion, Politics, and Ratification," in *Religion in a Revolutionary Age*, ed. Ronald Hoffman and Peter J. Albert (Charlottesville, 1994), 184–217.*

113. Many historians have shown the wide variety of forms this new democratic sensibility took in the early national period. See, for example, Sean Wilentz, *The Rise of American Democracy: Jefferson to Lincoln* (New York, 2005); Robert Shalhope, *A Tale of New England: The Diaries of Hiram Harwood, Vermont Farmer, 1810–1837* (Baltimore, 2003); Joyce Appleby, *Inheriting the Revolution: The First Generation of Americans* (Cambridge, MA, 2000); and Andrew Robertson, *The Language of Democracy: Political Rhetoric in the United States and Britain, 1790–1900* (Ithaca, 1995).*

114. Montesquieu, *The Spirit of the Laws*, ed. Franz Neumann, trans. Thomas Nugent (New York, 1949), 96.

115. François-Alexandre Frédérique, duc de la Rochefoucauld, *Constitutions des treize Etats-Unis de l'Amérique* (Paris, 1783); François-Alexandre Frédérique, duc de la Rochefoucauld, *Travels through the United States of North America, the Country of the Iroquois, and Upper Canada in the Years 1795, 1796, and 1797*, 2 vols. (London, 1799), 1:64–66.*

Chapter 10

1. Guillaume-Thomas Raynal, *Histoire philosophique et politique des établissemens et du commerce des européens dans les Deux Indes* (1772; Geneva, 1781), 6:427–28; Raynal, *A Philosophical and Political History of the Settlements and Trade of the Europeans in the East and the West Indies*, trans. J. O Justamond, 6 vols. (1776; New York, 1969).*
2. Robert R. Palmer, *The Age of the Democratic Revolution*, vol. 1, *The Challenge* (Princeton, 1959), 244, lists both the dates of the appearance of the major assessments of the new nation and the dates of the books' translations into the major European languages.*
3. Louis Genty, *L'influence de la découverte de l'Amérique sur le bonheur du genre humain* (Paris, 1787), cited in Bernard Faÿ, *L'Esprit révolutionnaire en France et aux Etats-Unis à la fin du XVIIIe siècle* (Paris, 1925), 133.
4. Guillaume-Thomas Raynal, *Révolution de l'Amérique* (London, 1781), 85.
5. Lafayette's letter quoted in Patrice Higonnet, *Sister Republics: The Origins of French and American Republicanism* (Cambridge, MA, 1988), 166.
6. Jacques-Pierre Brissot de Warville quoted in Durand Echeverria, *Mirage in the West: A History the French Image of American Society to 1815* (Princeton, 1957).*
7. Jacques-Pierre Brissot de Warville and Etienne Clavière, *Le Philadelphien à Genève, ou lettres d'un Américain sur la dernière révolution de Genève, sa constitution nouvelle, l'émigration en Irlande, etc., pouvant servir de tableau politique de Genève jusqu'en 1784* (Dublin, 1783). See also James Livesey, *Making Democracy in the French Revolution* (Cambridge, MA, 2001).

8. Louis André Vigneras, "La Société gallo-américaine de 1787," in *Bulletin de l'Institut français de Washington*, December 1952.*
9. Brissot, *Plan de conduite pour les députés du peuple aux Etats-Généraux de 1789* (Paris, 1789), 240–42.
10. See William Doyle, *The Oxford History of the French Revolution* (Oxford, 1990); and Colin Jones, *The Great Nation: France from Louis XIV to Napoleon* (London, 2002).*
11. Dale Van Kley, *The Religious Origins of the French Revolution: From Calvin to the Civil Constitution, 1560–1791* (New Haven, 1996); William Doyle, *Jansenism* (London, 2000).*
12. Jacques Bénigne Bossuet, *Politique tirée des propres paroles de l'Ecriture sainte*, ed. J. Le Brun (Geneva, 1967), 185; Bossuet, *Politics Drawn from the Very Words of Holy Scripture*, ed. and trans. Patrick Riley (Cambridge, 1990).
13. Antoine-Louis Séguier quoted in Keith Michael Baker, *Inventing the French Revolution* (Cambridge, 1990), 116.*
14. Alexis de Tocqueville, *The Old Regime and the French Revolution*, trans. Alan Kahan, ed. François Furet and Françoise Mélonio (Chicago, 1998), 142.
15. The king's declaration, "C'est légal parce que je le veux," quoted in Jones, *Great Nation*, 387. See also Durand Echeverria, *The Maupeou Revolution: A Study in the History of Libertarianism, France, 1770–1774* (Baton Rouge, 1985); and Nannerl Keohane, *Philosophy and the State in France* (Princeton, 1980), 458.*
16. Thomas Jefferson to James Madison, October 28, 1785, in Jefferson, *Writings*, ed. Merrill D. Peterson (New York, 1984), 840–43.*
17. Jefferson to George Wythe, August 13, 1786, and to Edward Carrington, January 16, 1787, in *Writings*, 857–60, 879–81.
18. Jefferson to J. Hector St. John de Crèvecoeur, August 9, 1788, and to the Rev. James Madison, July 19, 1788, in *Writings*, 927–29, 923–27.*
19. Comparisons of the French and American Revolutions include Palmer, *The Age of the Democratic Revolution*; Higonnet, *Sister Republics*; Anne Sa'adah, *The Shaping of Liberal Politics in Revolutionary France: A Comparative Perspective* (Princeton, 1990); and Mark Hulliung, *Citizens and Citoyens: Republicans and Liberals in America and France* (Cambridge, MA, 2002).*
20. See Higonnet, *Sister Republics*, 121–70.
21. Jean-Antoine-Nicolas de Caritat, Marquis de Condorcet, *Vie de Turgot*, in Condorcet, *Oeuvres complètes de Condorcet*, 12 vols. (Paris, 1847–49), 5:209–10, 211.*
22. On Turgot's *Mémoire sur les municipalités*, written between 1774 and 1776, see Baker, *Inventing the French Revolution*, 120–22.
23. Turgot quoted in Jones, *Great Nation*, 295.*
24. Turgot's letter to Price, in Richard Price, *Observations on the Importance of the American Revolution and the Means of Making It a Benefit to the World* (London, 1784), 95–114.*
25. John Adams claimed that the Massachusetts Constitution he wrote in 1780 was "Locke, Sidney, and Rousseau and de Mably reduced to practice." Adams, *The Works of John Adams*, ed. Charles Francis Adams, 10 vols. (Boston, 1850–56), 4:216.*

26. Gabriel Bonnot de Mably, *Des droits et des devoirs du citoyen* (Paris, 1789), 126–27, 99.*
27. Mably, along with almost every other writer in France, considered a king indispensable.*
28. Adams did not read *De la législation* until 1791; he reread it in 1806. His marginal notations, in his copy of *De la législation* in the Adams Papers at the Boston Public Library, reflect his increasing ire concerning the course of the French Revolution as well as his changing attitudes toward Mably's political ideas.*
29. Johnson Kent Wright, *A Classical Republican in Eighteenth-Century France: The Political Thought of Mably* (Stanford, 1997).*
30. Although Jefferson possessed shrewder political instincts than Condorcet, he aligned himself with Condorcet's belief that, as Jefferson put it, "the mind is perfectible to a degree of which we cannot as yet form any conception." See Jefferson to William Green Mumford, June 18, 1799, in *Writings,* 1065. On Condorcet, see Keith Michael Baker, *Condorcet: From Natural Philosophy to Social Mathematics* (Chicago, 1975); and *Condorcet: homme des Lumières et la Révolution*, ed. Anne-Marie Chouillet and Pierre Crépel (Fontenay-aux-Roses, 1997).*
31. Julie de Lespinasse left a charming portrait of the young Condorcet in *Lettres inédites de Mlle de Lespinasse*, ed. Charles Henry (Paris, 1887), 232–42.*
32. Condorcet's notes for the speech accepting admission to the French Academy in 1782, Bibliothèque de l'Institut de France, MS 855, f. 7.*
33. Condorcet, *Discours prononcé dans l'Académie française, le jeudi 21 février 1782, à la réception de M. Le marquis de Condorcet*, in *Oeuvres de Condorcet*, ed. A. Condorcet-O'Connor and F. Arago (Paris, 1887), 1:392.
34. Condorcet, *Essai sur l'application de l'analyse à la probabilité des décisions rendues à la pluralité des voix* (Paris, 1785), cvi.*
35. Condorcet, *De l'influence de la Révolution d'Amérique*, in *Oeuvres de Condorcet*, 8:13.*
36. Condorcet quoted in Baker, *Condorcet*, 223; and Condorcet, *De l'influence de la Révolution d'Amérique*, 7.
37. Filippo Mazzei, *Recherches historiques et politiques sur les Etats-Unis*, 4 vols. (Paris, 1788).*
38. Only at the municipal level would citizens vote directly for electors, who would then choose those who would participate in assemblies, and so on all the way to the national assembly. All but the local selections would be indirect, yet Condorcet contended that those chosen for the unicameral national assembly would discern the wishes of the nation because they would be "representatives of the citizens chosen by themselves." Condorcet, *Oeuvres complètes* 8:234.*
39. Condorcet, *Oeuvres complètes* 8:601.
40. Deliberation incites "momentary passions," so it causes "error" and "incoherence" in legislative assemblies. Condorcet, *Oeuvres complètes* 8:208, 211.*
41. Because Condorcet's early scheme was soon mooted by events, its details matter less to historians than to mathematically inclined social scientists. Condorcet, *Oeuvres complètes* 9:97–135, 8:117–659.*

42. Emmanuel-Joseph Sieyès, *Political Writings*, ed. Michael Sonenscher (Indianapolis, 2003), contains the most important of Sieyès's early writings.*
43. Sieyès, undated fragment in Archives Nationales, 284 AP 4, dossier 5. More extensive collections of Sieyès's writings are Roberto Zapperi, *Emmanuel-Joseph Sieyès: Ecrits politiques* (Montreux, 1998); and *Des Manuscrits de Sieyès*, 2 vols., vol. 1: *1773–1779*, vol. 2: *1770–1815*, ed. Christine Fauré, Jacques Guilhaumou, and Jacques Valier (Paris, 2000, 2007). English translations of some of his manuscripts in the French National Archives are available in Murray Forsyth, *Reason and Revolution: The Political Thought of the Abbé Sieyès* (Leicester, 1987); and in Sonenscher's incisive Introduction to Sieyès, *Political Writings* (hereafter *PW*).*
44. Sieyès, *Views of the Executive Means*, in *PW*, 48.
45. Sieyès, *Views of the Executive Means*, in *PW*, 48; and Sieyès, "Représentation du tout n'a rien au-dessus," Archives Nationales, 284 AP 5, 1:2.*
46. Sieyès, *What Is the Third Estate?* in *PW*, 134–35.
47. Sieyès, *Views of the Executive Means*, in *PW*, 15–16.
48. See two undated fragments: Sieyès, "Représentation du tout n'a rien audessus," Archives Nationales, 284 AP 5, 1:2; and "Ordre politique, base démographiqe, édifice représentation," Archives Nationales, 284 AP 5, 1:3.*
49. Sieyès, *Views of the Executive Means*, in *PW*, 9–11.
50. In sum, "the legislative power is always the product of the generality of individual wills." Only in that way can the "general will" or the "general view," the view that best incorporates the different perspectives of different individuals, emerge through the process of deliberation. Sieyès, "Views of the Executive Means," in *PW*, 12–13, 36–37.
51. Sieyès addressed these issues directly in *What Is the Third Estate?* in *PW*, 140–44.
52. Sieyès, *What Is the Third Estate?* in *PW*, 127–30.
53. Sieyès, *Views of the Executive Means*, in *PW*, 50–51.
54. Sieyès, *Views of the Executive Means,* in *PW*, 54–55; and *What Is the Third Estate?* in *PW*, 142–43.
55. Sieyès, *Views of the Executive Means*, in *PW*, 56–60.
56. Sieyès, *Essay on Privileges*, in *PW*, 69–88.
57. Sieyès, *What Is the Third Estate?* in *PW*, 147–50.
58. Sieyès, *What Is the Third Estate?* in *PW*, 110.
59. Sieyès, "Représentation du tout n'a rien au-dessus," Archives Nationales, 284 AP 5, 1:2.*
60. There is no evidence that Sieyès had read either Madison or John Adams, whose ideas concerning those "natural aristocrats" to be elected by the people also bore some resemblance to the argument Sieyès advanced in 1788–89.
61. Sieyès, *What Is the Third Estate?* in *PW*, 154–55.
62. Sieyès, *What Is the Third Estate?* in *PW*, 96.
63. Marie-Vic Ozouf-Marignier, *La formation des départements: la représentation du territoire français à la fin du XVIII*[e] *siècle* (Paris, 1989).
64. Sieyès, *What Is the Third Estate?* in *PW*, 157–58.*

65. Robespierre's pamphlet is quoted in Ruth Scurr, *Fatal Purity: Robespierre and the French Revolution* (New York, 2006), 75.*
66. François Furet wrote, "There are two ways of totally misunderstanding Robespierre as a historical figure: one is to detest the man, the other is to make too much of him." Furet, *Interpreting the French Revolution*, trans. Elborg Forster (Cambridge, 1981), 61. The temptation to revere or revile Robespierre persists.*
67. Mirabeau wrote to Sieyès that if reform were to come, it would be led by renegades from the first and second estates. Mirabeau to Sieyès, February 23, 1789, quoted in Michael Sonenscher, *Before the Deluge: Public Debt, Inequality, and the Intellectual Origins of the French Revolution* (Princeton, 2007).*
68. Timothy Tackett, *Becoming a Revolutionary: The Deputies of the French National Assembly and the Emergence of a Revolutionary Culture, 1789–1790* (Princeton, 1996). *
69. Timothy Tackett, "Conspiracy Obsession in a Time of Revolution: French Elites and the Origins of the Terror, 1789–1792," *American Historical Review* 105 (June 2000): 691–713.
70. See Peter M. Jones, *Reform and Revolution in France: The Politics of Transition, 1774–1791* (Cambridge, 1995).
71. See Patrice Gueniffey, *Le nombre et la raison: la Révolution française et les élections* (Paris, 1993), and Malcolm Crook, *Elections in the French Revolution* (Cambridge, 1996).*
72. Sieyès, "Motion sur la vérification des pouvoirs," June 10, 1789, in *Orateurs de la Révolution française*, ed. Ran Halévi and François Furet, vol. 1, *Les Constituants* (Paris, 1989), 1001.
73. Sieyès, "Motion sur la constitution des communes en Assemblée des représentants connus et vérifiés de la nation française," June 15, 1789, in *Orateurs de la Révolution française* 1:1002.
74. Sieyès's notes from July 20–21, 1789, Archives Nationales, 284 AP 5.*
75. Detailed accounts include Jacques Godechot, *The Taking of the Bastille: July 14, 1789*, trans. Jean Stewart (London, 1970); Simon Schama, *Citizens: A Chronicle of the French Revolution* (New York, 1989), 369–425; and William H. Sewell Jr., "Historical Events as Transformations of Structures: Inventing Revolution at the Bastille," in Sewell, *Logics of History: Social Theory and Social Transformation* (Chicago, 2005), 225–70.
76. Robespierre to Antoine Buissart, July 23, 1789, in Maximilien Robespierre, *Oeuvres complètes*, ed. E. Hamel et al., 10 vols. (Paris, 1910–67), 3a:42–50.*
77. Morris embarked on an affair with a French noblewoman, and through her he became acquainted with philosophes such as Condorcet and Buffon, Lafayette, and various ministers, diplomats, and members of the fashionable salons such as Necker's daughter Madame de Staël.*
78. Both the passage from Gouverneur Morris, *A Diary of the French Revolution*, 2 vols., ed. Beatrix Davenport (Boston, 1939), 1:159, and Morris's letter to Mrs. Robert Morris, July 22, 1789, are quoted in Philipp Ziesche, *Cosmopolitan Patriots: Americans in Paris in the Age of Revolution* (Charlottesville, 2010), 29.

79. Jefferson to Lafayette, February 28, 1787, in *The Papers of Thomas Jefferson*, ed. Julian Boyd et al., 41 vols. to date (Princeton: Princeton University Press, 1950–), 11:186; and Jefferson to David Humphreys, March 18, 1789, in *Papers* 14: 676–79; Jefferson to John Jay, May 9, 1789, in *Writings*, 949–54.*
80. Jefferson to "Rabaut St. Etienne," June 3, 1789, in *Writings*, 954–56.
81. Jefferson to Diodati, August 3, 1789, in *Writings*, 956–59.
82. See Georges Lefebvre, *The Great Fear: Rural Panic in Revolutionary France*, trans. Joan White (1932; New York, 1973); and Clay Ramsay, *The Ideology of the Great Fear: The Soissonnais in 1789* (Baltimore, 1992).*
83. Accounts of August 4, 1789, include Jean-Pierre Hirsch, *La nuit du 4 août* (Paris, 1978); and Michael P. Fitzsimmons, *The Night the Old Regime Ended: August 4, 1789, and the French Revolution* (University Park, PA, 2003).*
84. Etienne Dumont, *Souvenirs sur Mirabeau et sur les deux premières assemblées législatives* (Paris, 1832), 146, 147.
85. This early draft of a constitution provided for amendments, a feature notably lacking in all the constitutions adopted and discarded in France during these years except for the Constitution of 1795, which was superseded in 1799. See articles 336–350 of the 1795 Constitution. Jefferson described his dinner with those debating a new constitution in his autobiography, *Writings*, 96.*
86. All quotations from the Declaration come from the translation by Keith Michael Baker, "Declaration of the Rights of Man and of the Citizen," in *Readings in Western Civilization*, vol. 7, *The Old Regime and the French Revolution*, ed. Keith Baker (Chicago, 1987), 237–39.
87. Sieyès's speech in *Archives parlementaires* 8:259, quoted by Marcel Gauchet, "Rights of Man," in *A Critical Dictionary of the French Revolution*, ed. François Furet and Mona Ozouf, trans. Arthur Goldhammer (Cambridge, MA, 1989), 825.
88. Sieyès, *Ecrits politiques*, ed. Roberto Zapperi (Paris, 1985), 238.
89. "Declaration of the Rights of Man and of the Citizen," in Baker, *The Old Regime and the French Revolution*, 237–39.*
90. Jacques-Pierre Brissot de Warville, *Plan de conduite pour les députés du peuple aux états-généraux de 1789* (Paris, 1789), 21.
91. Sieyès, *Quelques idées de constitution applicables à la ville de Paris en juillet 1789* (Versailles, 1789), 3. See also Pierre Rosanvallon, "The History of the Word 'Democracy' in France," trans. Philip J. Costopoulos, *Journal of Democracy* 6 (1995): 140–54; Raymonde Monnier, "Démocratie et révolution française," *Mots* 59 (1999): 50–56; Ruth Scurr, "Varieties of Democracy in the French Revolution," in *Re-imagining Democracy in the Age of Revolutions: America, France, Britain, Ireland, 1750–1850*, ed. Joanna Innes and Mark Philp (Oxford, 2013), 57–68; and Pierre Rosanvallon, *Le Sacre du citoyen: histoire du suffrage universel en France* (Paris, 1992), 45–180.*
92. Sieyès, "Sur l'organisation du pouvoir législatif et la sanction royale," in *Orateurs de la Révolution française*, 1: 1031.
93. Robespierre, *Oeuvres complètes* 6:86–95, 364–65.

94. On Sieyès's attempt to combine the ideas of representation and the general will, see Baker, *Inventing the French Revolution*, 251.
95. Among the problems was a drought that had prevented the water mills from grinding flour; identifying the culprits conspiring against rain would have been challenging.
96. Louis Gottschalk and Margaret Maddox, *Lafayette in the French Revolution through the October Days* (Chicago, 1969).
97. Robespierre, *Oeuvres complètes* 6:115.
98. Condorcet, *Oeuvres complètes* 9:445–46.*
99. Condorcet's *Prospectus* for the journal envisioned by the Society of 1789 is quoted in Baker, *Condorcet*, 274.*
100. Condorcet, *Oeuvres complètes* 10:71.*
101. *Chronique de Paris*, June 15, 1790.*
102. See Patrice Higonnet, *Goodness beyond Virtue: Jacobins during the French Revolution* (Cambridge, MA, 1998).*
103. See Dale Van Kley, "Christianity as Casualty and Chrysalis of Modernity: The Problem of Dechristianization in the French Revolution," *American Historical Review* 108 (2003): 1081–103. Maultrot and Mey quoted in Dale Van Kley, "Piety and Politics in the Century of Lights," in *The Cambridge History of Eighteenth-Century Political Thought*, ed. Mark Goldie and Robert Wokler (Cambridge, 2006), 110–43.*
104. Bertrand Capmartin de Chaupy, *Réflexions d'un avocat sur les remontrances du parlement du 27 novembre 1755*... (London, 1756), 54.
105. Jean-Georges Lefranc de Pompignan, *Défense des actes du clergé de France, concernant la religion, publiée en l'assemblée de 1765*, in *Oeuvres complètes de Jean-Georges Lefranc de Pompignan*, ed. M. Emery, 2 vols. (Paris, 1855), 1:574.
106. See James E. Bradley and Dale Van Kley, eds., *Religion and Politics in Enlightenment Europe* (Notre Dame, 2001); and Suzanne Desan, *Reclaiming the Sacred: Lay Religion and Popular Politics in Revolutionary France* (Ithaca, 1990).*
107. Recent scholarship challenging the argument that eighteenth-century France underwent a process of "dechristianization" includes John McManners, *Church and Society in Eighteenth-Century France*, 2 vols. (Oxford, 1998); Nigel Aston, *Christianity and Revolutionary Europe, 1750–1830* (Cambridge, 2002); Stewart J. Brown and Timothy Tackett, eds., *Enlightenment, Reawakening, and Revolution, 1680–1815* (Cambridge, 2006); and Jonathan Sheehan, "Enlightenment, Religion, and the Enigma of Secularization," *American Historical Review* 108 (2003): 1061–80.*
108. See Ruth Necheles, "The Curés in the Estates-General of 1789," *Journal of Modern History* 46 (1974): 125–44.
109. On the persistence of religious belief and the emergence of opposition to the Revolution, see Eric F. Johnson, "The Sacred, Secular Regime: Catholic Ritual and Revolutionary Politics in Avignon, 1789–1791," *French Historical Studies* 30, no. 1 (2007): 49–76.*

110. Proclamation quoted in Pierre de la Gorce, *Histoire religieuse de la Révolution française*, 5 vols. (Paris, 1902–1923), 1:303; trans. in Doyle, *French Revolution*, 144. On the transformative effect of the Civil Constitution of the Clergy, see Timothy Tackett, *Religion, Revolution, and Regional Cultures in Eighteenth-Century France: The Ecclesiastical Oath of 1791* (Princeton, 1986). A map in Furet and Ozouf, *Critical Dictionary of the French Revolution*, 332, shows that opposition to the Civil Constitution of the Clergy was strongest—and emigration from France highest—in the peripheral regions of the northeast, the Massif Central, and the west; support was strongest in Paris, in the center of France, and in the southeast, the regions where Jansenism exerted the strongest appeal. In rural areas the clergy and the laity tended either to accept or reject the Civil Constitution together. In cities, though, they diverged, except in Paris, where the juring clergy constituted an overwhelming majority. These religious divisions, Tackett shows, followed their own logic and cannot be reduced to socioeconomic or other characteristics. The significance of these divisions persists into the twenty-first century: the regions in which opposition to the Civil Constitution was most pronounced remain the most staunchly Catholic regions in France.*
111. Johnson, "The Sacred, Secular Regime," 70–76.
112. For Robespierre's speech of June 9, 1790, see *Archives parlementaires* 16:154–56.
113. For this speech, the first of Robespierre's speeches to attract widespread attention, see Dumont, *Souvenirs sur Mirabeau*, 60–61.
114. Madame de Houdetot to Jefferson, in *Papers of Thomas Jefferson* 17:485.

Chapter 11

1. On British responses, see Pamela Clemit, ed., *The Cambridge Companion to British Literature of the French Revolution in the 1790s* (Cambridge, 2011); and Gareth Stedman Jones, *An End to Poverty? A Historical Debate* (New York, 2004).*
2. "*Lord*," Price concluded, "*now lettest thy servant depart in peace, for mine eyes have seen thy salvation*," first in England's Revolution of 1688 and now in the American and French Revolutions. "Behold, the light you have struck out, after setting America free, reflected to France and there kindled into a blaze that lays despotism in ashes and warms and illuminates Europe!" Richard Price, "A Discourse on the Love of Our Country," 4th ed., in Richard Price, *Political Writings*, ed. D. O. Thomas (Cambridge, 1991), 176–96; the quotations are from 191–96.*
3. Thomas Paine to Edmund Burke, January 17, 1790, in which Paine predicted "the Revolution in France is certainly a forerunner to other Revolutions in Europe," in *The Correspondence of Edmund Burke*, ed. Thomas W. Copeland (Cambridge, 1958–78), 6:69.
4. Edmund Burke, "Speech on Conciliation," March 22, 1775, in Burke, *Works*, 6 vols. (London, 1854), 1:490–91.
5. See Joseph Priestley, *Political Writings*, ed. Peter Miller (Cambridge, 1993); and the essays collected in *Science, Medicine, and Dissent: Joseph Priestley (1733–1804)*, ed. R. G. W. Anderson and Christopher Lawrence (London, 1987).*

6. See Nigel Aston, "Horne and Heterodoxy: The Defence of Anglican Beliefs in the Late Enlightenment," *English Historical Review* 108 (1993): 895–919; and Boyd Hilton, *A Mad, Bad, and Dangerous People? England, 1783–1846* (Oxford, 2006), 57–64.
7. Edmund Burke, *Reflections on the Revolution in France*, ed. Thomas H. D. Mahoney (Indianapolis, 1955), 103, 8.*
8. "If in the moment of riot and in a drunken delirium from the hot spirit drawn out of the alembic of hell," the usually sensible people of Britain too were tempted to "uncover [their] nakedness by throwing off that Christian religion" that had warmed, comforted, and civilized them, they would follow France into chaos. Burke, *Reflections*, 97, 99, 103.
9. All these abominations came to a head for Burke in the revolutionaries' shameful treatment of the royal family. Burke, *Reflections*, 87, 82.*
10. Joseph Priestley, *Letters to the Right Honourable Edmund Burke, occasioned by his reflections on the revolution in France, &c.*, 3rd ed. (New York, 1791), 67. Friedrich von Gentz quoted in Robert R. Palmer, *The Age of the Democratic Revolution*, vol. 1, *The Challenge* (Princeton, 1959), 456.*
11. In contrast to Burke's "wilderness of rhapsodies," fictional chapters "in which he asserts whatever he pleases," Paine invoked the authority of a trustworthy eyewitness, his friend Lafayette. Thomas Paine, *The Rights of Man*, in Paine, *Collected Writings*, ed. Eric Foner (New York, 1995) (hereafter *CW*), 456–62.*
12. Paine to Benjamin Rush, March 16, 1790, in *CW*, 371–73. The key to the Bastille still hangs in Washington's Mount Vernon.*
13. See Patrice Gueniffey, "Terminer la Révolution: Barnave et la révision de la Constitution (Août 1791)," in *Terminer la Révolution: Mounier et Barnave dans la Révolution française*, ed. François Furet and Mona Ozouf (Grenoble, 1991); and Barry M. Shapiro, "Self-Sacrifice, Self-Interest, or Self-Defense? The Constituent Assembly and the 'Self-Denying Ordinance' of May 1791," *French Historical Studies* 25 (2002): 625–56.
14. Maximilien Robespierre, *Oeuvres complètes*, ed. E. Hamel et al., 10 vols. (Paris, 1910–1967) 7: 268.*
15. Patrice Higonnet, *Goodness beyond Virtue: Jacobins during the French Revolution* (Cambridge, MA, 1998), 31.*
16. The exchange appeared first in Paris—Paine's letter in *Le Républicain* and Sieyès's reply in the *Moniteur*—and then in London, where the *European Magazine and London Review* published translations of both in August 1791.*
17. Paine, "To the Authors of the Republican," in *CW*, 276–379.
18. Condorcet, *Mémoires sur l'instruction publique*, in *Oeuvres complètes de Condorcet*, 12 vols. (Paris, 1847–49), 7:226–27.* For a discussion of these issues and Condorcet's decisions in the summer of 1791, see Keith Michael Baker, *Condorcet: From Natural Philosophy to Social Mathematics* (Chicago, 1975), 304–42.
19. Robespierre, *Oeuvres complètes* 8:151.

20. Robespierre, *Oeuvres complètes* 4:34; 8:315. On Jefferson's letter to Charles Jarvis, September 28, 1820, see p. 6 above.
21. This observation, first made by Jean Jaurès, *Histoire socialiste de la Révolution française*, ed. Albert Mathiez (Paris, 1922), has been restated by Jean-Daniel Piquet, *L'émancipation des noirs dans la Révolution française* (Paris, 2002).
22. On slavery in the Enlightenment and revolution, see Louis Sala-Molins, *Le Code Noir; ou, le calvaire de Canaan* (Paris, 1987); Louis Sala-Molins, *Les Misères des Lumières: sous la raison, l'outrage* (Paris, 1992); Laurent Dubois, *A Colony of Citizens: Revolution and Slave Emancipation in the French Caribbean, 1787–1804* (Chapel Hill, 2004); and Laurent Dubois, "An Enslaved Enlightenment: Rethinking the Intellectual History of the French Atlantic," *Social History* 31, no. 1 (February 2006): 1–14.*
23. John D. Garrigus, *Before Haiti: Race and Citizenship in French Saint-Domingue* (New York, 2006).*
24. Sue Peabody, *"There Are No Slaves in France": The Political Culture of Race and Slavery in the Ancien Régime* (New York, 1996).
25. Paine to Benjamin Rush, March 16, 1790, in *CW*, 372.
26. *Philadelphia General Advertiser*, October 11, 1791, and J. Félix Carteau, *Soirées Bermudiennes, ou entretiens sur les événemens qui ont opéré la ruine de la partie française de l'île Saint-Domingue* (Bordeaux, 1802), quoted in Dubois, "An Enslaved Enlightenment," 9–10.*
27. See Malick Ghachem, *The Old Regime and the Haitian Revolution* (Cambridge, 2012); and John Thornton, "'I Am the Subject of the King of Congo': African Political Ideology and the Haitian Revolution," *Journal of World History* 4 (1993): 181–214.*
28. On Brissot's speech, see Wim Klooster, *Revolutions in the Atlantic World: A Comparative History* (New York, 2009), 96–97.*
29. See Pierre Pluchon, *Toussaint Louverture: un révolutionnaire noir d'Ancien Régime* (Paris, 1989); and Carolyn Fick, *The Making of Haiti: The Saint Domingue Revolution from Below* (Knoxville, 1990).*
30. Louis Boisrond-Tonnerre quoted in Thomas Madiou, *Histoire d'Haïti*, 8 vols. (1847–48; Port-au-Prince, 1989–91), 3:145. On the 1804 Haitian Declaration of Independence, see David Armitage, *The Declaration of Independence: A Global History* (Cambridge, MA, 2007), 114–17, 193–98.
31. Dessalines quoted in Hubert Cole, *Christophe, King of Haiti* (New York, 1967), 144.*
32. See David Geggus, "The Caribbean in the Age of Revolution," in *The Age of Revolutions in Global Context, c. 1760–1840*, ed. David Armitage and Sanjay Subrahmanyam (New York, 2010), 83–100.*
33. See David Brion Davis, *Inhuman Bondage: The Rise and Fall of Slavery in the New World* (New York, 2006), 157–74; and Ashli White, *Encountering Revolution: Haiti and the Making of the Early Republic* (Baltimore, 2010).*
34. *Doléances des Femmes françaises*, March 5, 1789, in the National Archives, Paris, quoted in Carol Blum, *Rousseau and the Republic of Virtue: The Language of Politics in the French Revolution* (Ithaca, 1986), 205. Madame B. B., *Cahier des*

doléances et réclamations des femmes, quoted in Jane Abray, "Women in the French Revolution," in *Becoming Visible: Women in European History*, ed. Renata Bridenthal and Claudia Koonz (Boston, 1977), 239.

35. Exceptions include Christine de Pisan; Marie de Jars de Gournay, author of *Egalité des hommes et des femmes* (1622), whom Montaigne described as his "*fille d'alliance*"; and Mary Astell. Even those who called for women's education, as Astell did, tended to assume that women should be educated for different purposes, for lives as wives and mothers.*
36. Sophie de Grouchy's commentaries on Adam Smith's *Theory of Moral Sentiments*, which she appended to her translation, have been published as Sophie de Grouchy, *Letters on Sympathy: A Critical Edition*, ed. Karin Brown, trans. James E. McClellan III, *Transactions of the American Philosophical Society* 98, no. 4 (Philadelphia, 2008).
37. Catherine Larrère, "Women, Republicanism and the Growth of Commerce," in *Republicanism*, vol. 2: *The Values of Republicanism in Early Modern Europe*, ed. Martin van Gelderen and Quentin Skinner (Cambridge, 2002), 139–56.*
38. See Olympe de Gouges, *Ecrits politiques, 1788–1791*, ed. Olivier Blanc, 2 vols. (Paris, 1993); Sophie Mousset, *Women's Rights and the French Revolution: A Biography of Olympe de Gouges* (New Brunswick, 2007); and Olivier Blanc, *Olympe de Gouges*, 2nd ed. (Paris, 1989).*
39. Olympe de Gouges, "Declaration of the Rights of Woman," in *Women in Revolutionary Paris, 1789–1795*, ed. Darline Gay Levy, Harriet Branson Applewhite, and Mary Durham Johnson (Urbana, 1979), 89–96.
40. Janet Todd, *Mary Wollstonecraft: A Revolutionary Life* (London, 2000); Barbara Taylor, *Wollstonecraft and the Feminist Imagination* (Cambridge, 2003); Claudia Johnson, ed., *The Cambridge Companion to Mary Wollstonecraft* (Cambridge, 2002).*
41. Mary Wollstonecraft, *A Vindication of the Rights of Men*, in *A Vindication of the Rights of Woman and A Vindication of the Rights of Men*, ed. Janet Todd (Oxford, 1993), 45, 47.
42. Wollstonecraft, *Vindication of the Rights of Men*, 33.
43. Wollstonecraft, *Vindication of the Rights of Men*, 22, 65–66.
44. Wollstonecraft elaborated her critique of the duplicity and deception of refined culture, where women were merely "insignificant objects of desire" fit "only for a seraglio." *Vindication of the Rights of Men*, 75, 72, 102, 74.*
45. Wollstonecraft, *Vindication of the Rights of Men*, 86–95, 128–29, 131, 150–66.
46. Wollstonecraft, *Vindication of the Rights of Men*, 131–49.*
47. Wollstonecraft, *Vindication of the Rights of Woman*, 103, 113, 122, 197.*
48. Wollstonecraft, *Vindication of the Rights of Woman*, 138, 215, 219–20.
49. Wollstonecraft, *Vindication of the Rights of Woman*, 221.
50. László Kontler, "Beauty or Beast, or Monstrous Regiments? Robertson and Burke on Women and the Public Scene," *Modern Intellectual History* 1, no. 3 (2004): 305–30.
51. Wollstonecraft, *Vindication of the Rights of Woman*, 222–31.*
52. J. G. A. Pocock, *Virtue, Commerce, and History*, 5th ed. (Cambridge, 1995), 103.

53. Wollstonecraft, *Vindication of the Rights of Men*, 57–59.*
54. As already noted, Franklin, Adams, and Jefferson agreed with Madison that "without violating the rights of property," graduated taxation was the best means to "reduce extreme wealth to a state of mediocrity, and raise extreme indigence toward a state of comfort." Madison, *The Papers of James Madison*, ed. William T. Hutchinson et al., 17 vols. (Chicago and Charlottesville, 1962–91), 14:197–98.*
55. See Paine to Jefferson, February 1788, in *CW*, 368–69; and Paine, *Rights of Man*, in *CW*, 552–56.
56. Paine, *Rights of Man*, in *CW*, 596–657.*
57. Burke, *Reflections*, 193.
58. Paine conjured up a striking image: "A nation is not a body, the figure of which is to be represented by the human body," the image familiar to all readers of Hobbes's *Leviathan*. The nation is instead "like a body contained within a circle, having a common center, in which every radius meets, and that center is formed by representation." Those representatives, through their discussions of their constituents' interests, come to understand—more clearly than would be possible for any single individual—where the different interests intersect, or, to return to Paine's image, where "every radius meets." Paine, *Rights of Man*, in *CW*, 564–78.*
59. See Michael Sonenscher, *Sans-Culottes: An Eighteenth-Century Emblem of the French Revolution* (Princeton, 2009).*
60. Gouverneur Morris, diary entry for June 20, 1790, in *The Diary and Letters of Gouverneur Morris*, ed. Anne Cary Morris, 2 vols. (New York, 1888), 1:546.
61. Robespierre, *Oeuvres complètes* 8:408–19.
62. Robespierre, *Oeuvres complètes* 4:351–52, 358.
63. For a vivid account of the events of August 10, 1792, see Simon Schama, *Citizens: A Chronicle of the French Revolution* (New York, 1989), 597–618.
64. *Collection complète des lois*, ed. J.-B. Duvergier (Paris, 1825–28), 4:297.
65. See Malcolm Crook, "Elections and Democracy in France, 1789–1848," in *Re-imagining Democracy in the Age of Revolutions: America, France, Britain, Ireland, 1750–1850*, ed. Joanna Innes and Mark Philp (Oxford, 2013), 83–97.*
66. Condorcet, *Adresse de l'Assemblée nationale aux français*, September 19, 1792, in Condorcet, *Oeuvres complètes* 7: 226.
67. Robespierre, *Oeuvres complètes* 5:17.
68. Marat in *L'ami du peuple*, September 21, 1792, 8.
69. Robespierre, *Oeuvres complètes* 9:93.*
70. Robespierre, *Oeuvres complètes* 9:122.
71. Robespierre, *Oeuvres complètes* 9:198; 9:228.
72. Paine's speeches against executing the king, January 15, 1793, and January 19, 1793, are in *CW*, 382–91.
73. Perhaps Robespierre was right. To have tried the king and pardoned him would have prevented France from extinguishing the flame of monarchy.*
74. Brissot quoted in Mona Ozouf, "The King's Trial," in *Critical Dictionary of the French Revolution*, ed. François Furet and Mona Ozouf, trans. Arthur Goldhammer

(Cambridge, MA, 1989), 96. On the trial and death of Louis XVI, see Jules Michelet, *Histoire de la Révolution française*, 2 vols. (Paris, 1952); and Jean Jaurès, *Histoire socialiste de la Révolution française*, vol. 4, *La Conventioned*, ed. Albert Soboul (Paris, 1969).*

75. See Stedman Jones, *An End to Poverty*, 18–63.*
76. Condorcet, *Oeuvres complètes* 10:612, 12:340–441.*
77. Condorcet's defenders have emphasized his awareness of the tension between his confidence in reason and his desire to enable informed popular choices, but there is a difference between Condorcet's having acknowledged that tension and his having resolved it.*
78. See Michael Sonenscher, *Before the Deluge: Public Debt, Inequality, and the Intellectual Origins of the French Revolution* (Princeton, 2007); and Emma Rothschild, *Economic Sentiments: Adam Smith, Condorcet, and the Enlightenment* (Cambridge, MA, 2001).*
79. On educational reform, see Baker, *Condorcet*, 316–20; and James Livesey, *Making Democracy in the French Revolution* (Cambridge, MA, 2001), 169–77.
80. Robespierre, "On the Principles of Revolutionary Government," December 25, 1793, in Robespierre, *Virtue and Terror*, ed. Slavoj Žižek, trans. John Howe (London, 2007), 98–107; *Oeuvres complètes* 10:273–92, and see also 9:399 and 9:569.*
81. See Malcolm Crook, *Elections in the French Revolution* (Cambridge, 1996), 105–11, on the vote for ratification, and 115–16 on resistance.
82. Paine to Danton, May 6, 1793, in *CW*, 392–95.
83. For de Gouges's final political writings, see "Défenseur officieux de Louis Capet," "Mon dernier mot," "Testament politique," "Les trois urnes ou le salut de la patrie," and "Olympe de Gouges au Tribunal révolutionnaire," in de Gouges, *Ecrits politiques*; and the English translations of her writings by Clarissa Palmer at www.olympedegouges.eu.
84. Colin Lucas, *The Structure of the Terror: The Example of Javogues and the Loire* (Oxford, 1973).*
85. Condorcet, *Esquisse d'un tableau historique des progrès de l'esprit humain*, ed. O. H. Prior (Paris, 1933), 238–39.*
86. Robespierre, "On the Principles of Political Morality," February 5, 1784, in Robespierre, *Virtue and Terror*, 108–25.*
87. Although disagreements persist, this interpretation of Robespierre and those engaged in the Terror, which sees their fatal flaw as their unwillingness to accept the inevitability of disagreement, has become more widely accepted in recent years. For an incisive discussion of the historiography, which shows how central participants in the Revolution anticipated explanations advanced by nineteenth- and twentieth-century historians and how Marx's account of the conflict between bourgeois individualism and egalitarian universalism illuminates the Jacobins' dilemma, see Patrice Higonnet, "Terror, Trauma, and the 'Young Marx' Explanation of the Terror," *Past and Present* 191 (May 2006): 121–64. *
88. Camille Desmoulins, *Oeuvres de Camille Desmoulins*, ed. Jules Claretie, 2 vols. (Paris, 1874), 1:218–19; Danton's comment to Paine quoted in Hilaire Belloc, *Danton: A Study* (London, 1910), 301.

89. Robespierre, "On the Principles of Political Morality," February 5, 1784, in Robespierre, *Virtue and Terror*, 112.*
90. Robespierre's speech of July 26, 1794, is in Robespierre, *Virtue and Terror*, 126–41.*
91. David A. Bell, *The First Total War: Napoleon's Europe and the Birth of Warfare as We Know It* (New York, 2007).

Chapter 12

1. In addition to the classic study by Robert R. Palmer, *The Age of the Democratic Revolution: A Political History of Europe and America, 1760–1800*, rev. ed. with a new foreword by David Armitage (1959, 1964; Princeton, 2014), see Janet Polasky, *Revolutions without Borders: The Call to Liberty in the Atlantic World* (New Haven, 2015), which expands the canvas to include the Caribbean world and the circulation of information concerning democratic revolutions; *The Age of Revolutions in Global Context, 1760–1840*, ed. David Armitage and Sanjay Subrahmanyam (London, 2010); and Wim Klooster, *Revolutions in the Atlantic World: A Comparative History* (New York, 2009).*
2. See Matthew Rainbow Hale, *The French Revolution and the Transformation of American Democracy* (Charlottesville, forthcoming); and Rachel Hope Cleves, *The Reign of Terror in America: Visions of Violence from Anti-Jacobinism to Antislavery* (Cambridge, 2009).
3. Maya Jasanoff, *Liberty's Exiles: American Loyalists in the Revolutionary World* (New York, 2011); Brendan McConville, *The King's Three Faces: The Rise and Fall of Royal America, 1688–1776* (Chapel Hill, 2007).
4. On Elijah Parish, "Psalm 136.2, Thanksgiving 1789," the reprinting of Robespierre's article in the American press, and the article "Club des Jacobins. Paris, August 18," *Gazette of the United States*, November 6, 1789, see Cleves, *The Reign of Terror in America*, 61–62.
5. See the discussion of Jefferson's response to Adams's *Defence* in n. 44, p. 777 above. Adams to Elbridge Gerry, April 25, 1785, in Adams Papers, reel 107, Massachusetts Historical Society, and in James T. Austin, *Life of Elbridge Gerry*, 2 vols. (Boston, 1828), 1:427–31.
6. "Mirabeau" quoted in Marcus Daniel, *Scandal and Civility: Journalism and the Birth of American Democracy* (New York, 2009), 122, 138–39; *Independent Gazetteer*, cited in *Aurora General Advertiser*, September 21, 1795.
7. Adams to Adrian Van der Kemp, March 27, 1790, Van der Kemp Papers, quoted in John Howe Jr., *The Changing Political Thought of John Adams* (Princeton, 1966), 184.
8. Adams to Benjamin Rush, October 25, 1809, in *Old Family Letters: Copied from the Originals for Alexander Biddle*, series A (Philadelphia, 1892), 245.
9. Adams, "Reply to the Massachusetts Militia," October 11, 1789, Adams Papers, reel 119, Massachusetts Historical Society. On de la Rochefoucauld-Liancourt, see pp. 452–53 above.

10. "Too many Frenchmen, like too many Americans, pant for equality of persons and property. The impracticality of this God Almighty has decreed" by giving men unequal abilities, "and the advocates of liberty who attempt it will surely suffer for it." John Adams to Richard Price, April 19, 1790, in *The Works of John Adams*, ed. Charles Francis Adams, 10 vols. (Boston, 1850–56), 9:564.*
11. Adams selected the title *Discourses on Davila* in deliberate homage to Machiavelli's *Discourses on Livy*.*
12. See David McCullough, *John Adams* (New York, 2001), 374–79; for responses to the book, see "On the New Constitution," *State Gazette of South Carolina*, January 28, 1788, in *Debate on the Constitution*, ed. Bernard Bailyn (New York, 1993), 2:107–108.
13. John Adams, *Defence*, in *Works* 6:116, 4:308–9, 6:116, 4:359.
14. Adams, *Defence*, in *Works* 6:116, 118, 171–72, 130–31, 116–17.
15. See Joyce Appleby, "The Jefferson-Adams Rupture and the First French Translation of John Adams's *Defence*," *American Historical Review* 73 (1968): 1084–91.
16. Jefferson's note in Dumas Malone, *Jefferson and His Time*, vol. 2, *Jefferson and the Rights of Man* (Boston, 1951), 357.
17. Jefferson to Adams, November 13, 1787, in Jefferson, *Writings*, ed. Merrill D. Peterson (New York, 1984), 912–14; and *The Adams-Jefferson Letters*, ed. Lester J. Cappon (Chapel Hill, 1959), 213. On this exchange of letters, see McCullough, *Adams*, 380.
18. Adams to Jefferson, December 10, 1787, in *Works* 4:587.
19. John Quincy Adams's "Publicola" essays are reprinted in *The Writings of John Quincy Adams*, ed. Worthington Chauncey Ford, 7 vols. (New York, 1913–17), 1:65–110. See also Paul Nagel, *John Quincy Adams: A Public Life, a Private Life* (Cambridge, MA, 1997), 73–74.
20. Adams never repudiated representative democracy. He feared, with good reason, that the campaign of Jefferson and Madison to brand him a monarchist had done permanent (and unjustifiable) damage to his reputation.*
21. Writing to Jefferson in the spring of 1791, Madison sided with his fellow Virginian and expressed his own righteous fury about Adams, whose *Defence* and *Davila* Madison inaccurately characterized as "antirepublican discourses." Madison to Jefferson, May 12, 1791, in James Madison, *Writings*, ed. Jack Rakove (New York, 1999), 490–91.*
22. Madison, *Writings*, 472–73, 480–90.
23. Madison's essays, which appeared in the *National Gazette* from November 21, 1791, through December 22, 1792, show his continuing commitment to representative democracy as the best means to attain the common good. See Madison, *Writings*, 490–534.*
24. The passages from the *National Gazette*, *Providence Gazette*, and *Newport Mercury* are quoted in Hale, *The French Revolution and the Transformation of American Democracy*.
25. *National Gazette*, May 29, 1793.*

26. Civis Mundi's article from the *New York Diary* appeared in the *Gazette of the United States*, January 30, 1795.*
27. *Gazette of the United States*, January 31, 1795.*
28. "An American," writing in *Independent Chronicle*, cited in *Eastern Herald*, October 26, 1793.*
29. Barlow's lyrics were printed in the *North-Carolina Gazette*, November 29, 1794.*
30. On these developments see Hale, *The French Revolution and the Transformation of American Democracy*; and Cleves, *The Reign of Terror in America*.*
31. The French word *chute*, which conveys not only fall, downfall, and collapse but also overthrow, seems singularly appropriate for the events of late July. The *chute de Robespierre* is typically designated in studies of the French Revolution as 9 Thermidor, the date according to the revolutionary calendar that was put in place on October 5, 1793, and abandoned on January 1, 1806.*
32. See Pierre Rosanvallon, *La démocratie inachevée* (Paris, 2000), 90–100.*
33. For the passages from Anton François Boissy-Anglas, Jean-Denis Lanjuinais, and Merlin de Douai, see Malcolm Crook, *Elections in the French Revolution* (Cambridge, 1996), 115–30.*
34. On Sieyès and the 1795 Constitution, see Michael Sonenscher, *Before the Deluge: Public Debt, Inequality, and the Intellectual Origins of the French Revolution* (Princeton, 2007), 350–51; and James Sheehan, "The Problem of Sovereignty in European History," *American Historical Review* 111 (2006): 1–15.
35. On Sieyès's final scheme, see Sonenscher's introduction to Sieyès, *Political Writings*, ed. Michael Sonenscher (Indianapolis, 2003), xxxi–xxxiii.*
36. Jacques Necker, *Dernières vues de politique et de finance* (1802), in Necker, *Oeuvres*, 12 vols. (Paris, 1821), 11:15–16, 21.*
37. Mona Ozouf, *L'école de la France: essais sur la Révolution, l'utopie, et l'enseignement* (Paris, 1984).
38. Roger Martin, *Rapport fait par Roger Martin, au nom de la commission d'instruction publique, sur l'organisation des écoles primaires* (Paris, Year V).*
39. François de Neufchâteau quoted in James Livesey, *Making Democracy in the French Revolution* (Cambridge, MA, 2001), 116.*
40. See Mona Ozouf, "Revolutionary Calendar," in *Critical Dictionary of the French Revolution*, ed. François Furet and Mona Ozouf, trans. Arthur Goldhammer (Cambridge, MA, 1989), 538–59.*
41. See Dale Van Kley, *The Religious Origins of the French Revolution: From Calvin to the Civil Constitution, 1560–1791* (New Haven, 1996), 374–75.
42. Jacques Necker, *Dernières vues*, in *Oeuvres* 11:94.
43. Jefferson to Gouverneur Morris, December 30, 1792, in *Writings*, 1001–2.
44. Jefferson to William Short, January 3, 1793, in *Writings*, 1003–6; and cf. Jefferson to Francis Hopkinson, March 13, 1789, in *Writings*, 940–42.
45. James Sullivan, *The Altar of Baal Thrown Down; or, The French Nation Defended, against the Pulpit Slander of David Osgood, A. M. Pastor of the Church in Medford: A Sermon* (Stockbridge, MA, 1795), 23; and Joseph Eckley, *A Sermon, Preached*

at the Request of the Ancient and Honourable Artillery Company, June 4, 1792 Being the Anniversary of Their Election of Officers (Boston, 1792), 16–20.*

46. See *A Specimen of Unrelenting Cruelty of Papists in France, and the Unshaken Faith & Patience of the Protestants of That Kingdom: Now Entering upon the Seventieth Year of Their Persecutions* (London, 1756).*
47. Noah Webster, *An Oration Pronounced before the Citizens of New Haven on the Anniversary of the Declaration of Independence, July 1802*, in *American Political Writing during the Founding Era, 1760–1805*, ed. Charles S. Hyneman and Donald S. Lutz, 2 vols. (Indianapolis, 1983), 2:1220–40.*
48. Robespierre, *Report upon the Principles of Political Morality: Which Are to Form the Basis of the Administration of the Interior Concerns of the Republic. Made in the Name of the Committee of Public Safety, the 18th Pluviôse, Second Year of the Republic (February 6, 1794)*, trans. Benjamin Franklin Bache (Philadelphia, 1794).
49. "New Jersey. Schallenburg, July 6," *Aurora General Advertiser*, July 20, 1795.
50. Elijah Parish, "Ezra 8.23, Fast (April) 1794," quoted in Cleves, *The Reign of Terror in America*, 68–69.
51. *Gazette of the United States*, May 17, 1798.
52. Massachusetts *Minerva* quoted in *Gazette of the United States*, July 14, 1798.
53. Monongahela County writer quoted in *Aurora*, April 15, 1799.*
54. On Madison's use of Adams's *Defence* in Philadelphia, see Darren Staloff, *Hamilton, Adams, Jefferson: The Politics of Enlightenment and the American Founding* (New York, 2005), 195–96.
55. Since 1793, when France went to war against Britain, France had captured American ships because the British navy had put the French fleet out of commission. The XYZ Affair heightened tensions between the United States and France, and the Quasi-War consisted of a few naval engagements rather than full-scale hostilities. Republican Francophiles accused the Federalists of capitulating to Britain and needlessly antagonizing France, but Adams peacefully resolved the dispute in the Treaty of Mortefontaine.*
56. Madison, "Political Reflections," *Aurora General Advertiser*, February 23, 1799, in *Writings*, 599–607.
57. On the political history of the 1790s, see Andrew W. Robertson, "Afterword: Reconceptualizing Jeffersonian Democracy," *Journal of the Early Republic* 33 (2013): 317–34; Rosemarie Zagarri, "The Family Factor: Congressmen, Turnover, and the Burden of Public Service in the Early American Republic," *Journal of the Early Republic* 33 (2013): 283–316; and Jeffrey L. Pasley, Andrew W. Robertson, and David Waldstreicher, eds., *Beyond the Founders: New Approaches to the Political History of the Early American Republic* (Chapel Hill, 2004).
58. Candor in *Independent Chronicle*, June 26, 1800.*
59. Moderate, writing in *Centinel of Freedom*, September 17, 1799.
60. John Adams, diary entry on March 9, 1783, in Adams, *Revolutionary Writings, 1775–1783*, ed. Gordon S. Wood (New York, 2011), 549.

61. Adams, *Diary and Autobiography of John Adams*, ed. L. H. Butterfield, 4 vols. (Cambridge, MA, 1962), 3:240–41. *
62. Adams to John Taylor in *Works*, 6:461; Adams to Jefferson, July 9, 1819, in *The Adams-Jefferson Letters*, 350–52.
63. Noah Webster, *The Revolution in France, Considered in Respect to Its Prospects and Effects* (New York, 1794), 59–60.*
64. Adams, *Discourses on Davila* (Boston, 1805), 74, 83, 92.
65. See Laura Edwards, "The Contradictions of Democracy in American Institutions and Practices," in *Re-imagining Democracy in the Age of Revolutions: America, France, Britain, Ireland, 1750–1850*, ed. Joanna Innes and Mark Philp (Oxford, 2013), 40–54; and Andrew Robertson, "Democracy: America's Other 'Peculiar Institution,'" ms. in author's possession.*
66. Adams to Benjamin Rush, September 9, 1806, in *The Spur of Fame: Dialogues of John Adams and Benjamin Rush, 1805–1813*, ed. Douglass Adair and John A. Schutz (San Marino, CA, 1966), 66–67.*
67. Friedrich von Gentz, *The Origin and Principles of the American Revolution, Compared with the Origin and Principles of the French Revolution*, trans. "an American gentleman" [John Quincy Adams] (Philadelphia, 1800).
68. See Alison LaCroix, *The Intellectual Origins of American Federalism* (Cambridge, 2010).
69. Samuel Hopkins to Levi Hart, January 29, 1788, in Samuel Hopkins Papers, New York Historical Society.*
70. See Susan Branson, *Those Fiery Frenchified Dames: Women and Political Culture in Early National Philadelphia* (Philadelphia, 2001); and Rosemarie Zagarri, *Revolutionary Backlash: Women and Politics in the Early American Republic* (Philadelphia, 2007).*
71. Murray produced prodigious amounts of mediocre poetry, mostly in rhyming couplets. Although she claimed to share the anxiety of many other New Englanders concerning the effect of fiction and drama on public morals, she wrote novellas and plays that were published and performed.
72. See Sheila L. Skemp, *Judith Sargent Murray: A Brief Biography with Documents* (Boston, 1998); Sheila L. Skemp, *First Lady of Letters: Judith Sargent Murray and the Struggle for Female Independence* (Philadelphia, 2009); and the introduction by Nina Baym to *The Gleaner* (Schenectady, 1992), originally published by Murray in 1798 under the pseudonym "Constantia."*
73. Murray, "On the Equality of the Sexes," in Skemp, *Judith Sargent Murray*, 176–82.
74. Multiple editions of Wollstonecraft's *Vindication of the Rights of Woman* appeared in the United States. In 1792 it was published in Boston by Peter Edes, for Thomas and Andrews, and in Philadelphia by William Gibbons; two years later another edition was published in Philadelphia by Matthew Carey.*
75. For Murray's letter to Mrs. K——, April 21, 1802, see Skemp, *Judith Sargent Murray*, 113.
76. Murray, *Gleaner* 89, ed. Baym, 709–16; Murray to Mrs. Barrell of York, November 25, 1800, quoted in Skemp, *Judith Sargent Murray*, 114.
77. Murray, *Gleaner* 91, ed. Baym, 727–28.

78. Murray *Gleaner* 26, ed. Baym, 206–13.
79. Murray, *Gleaner* 27, ed. Baym, 214–22.
80. Murray, "Dedication to John Adams, L. L. D., President of the United States," in *Gleaner*, ed. Baym, 11.
81. On Abigail's admonition to John Adams, see pp. 342–46 above. On female academies, see Mary Kelley, *Learning to Stand and Speak: Women, Education, and Public Life in America's Republic* (Chapel Hill, 2006).*
82. See Gareth Stedman Jones, *An End to Poverty? A Historical Debate* (New York, 2004), 64–132; and Patrice Higonnet, *Goodness beyond Virtue: Jacobins during the French Revolution* (Cambridge, MA, 1998), 240–58.*
83. See the discussion of the "Fort Wilson Riot" in pp. 372–373 above. Cf. Paine to Danton, May 6, 1793, in Paine, *CW*, 392–95; and Paine's "Response to the Riot Outside James Wilson's House," October 16, 1779, in Paine, *Collected Writings*, ed. Eric Foner (New York, 1995), 218–21.
84. On the responses to Paine's *Age of Reason*, see Harvey J. Kaye, *Thomas Paine and the Promise of America* (New York, 2005), 82–155.*
85. Thomas Paine, "Dissertation on First Principles of Government," in *The Works of Thomas Paine* (Boston, 1796), 423.*
86. On this dynamic, see Seth Cotlar, *Tom Paine's America: The Rise and Fall of Transatlantic Radicalism in the Early* Republic (Charlottesville, 2011), 161–214.*
87. Paine to Samuel Adams, January 1, 1803, in *Collected Writings*, 416–21.
88. Jefferson, First Inaugural Address, in *Writings*, 492–96. Jefferson's insistence on unity was hardly exceptional. On Americans' pervasive fear of disunion, and the equally pervasive calls to unite, see Daniel Wewers, "The Specter of Disunion in the Early American Republic, 1783–1815" (unpub. Ph.D. diss., Harvard University, 2008).*

Chapter 13

1. Gareth Stedman Jones, *An End to Poverty? A Historical Debate* (New York, 2004); Pierre Rosanvallon, *La démocratié inachevée: histoire de la souveraineté du peuple en France* (Paris, 2000), 101–238; Sean Wilentz, *The Rise of American Democracy: Jefferson to Lincoln* (New York, 2005); and Daniel Walker Howe, *What Hath God Wrought: The Transformation of America, 1815–1848* (New York, 2007).*
2. Fisher Ames and George Cabot quoted in Gordon Wood, *The Radicalism of the American Revolution* (New York, 1991), 229–43. On the mock epic poem by "Aquiline Nimble Chops, Democrat," see Wilentz, *The Rise of American Democracy*, 61.
3. Elias Smith, *The Loving Kindness of God Displayed in the Triumph of Republicanism in America; Being a Discourse Delivered at Taunton, (Mass.), July Fourth, 1809* (Taunton, MA, 1809), 13–14.
4. [Edward Tyrrel Channing], "The Abuses of Political Discussion," *North American Review* 4 (1817): 197–201.*
5. See Alexander Keyssar, *The Right to Vote: The Contested History of Democracy in the United States* (New York, 2000), 26–52, 42–43 quoted; and Wilentz, *The Rise of American Democracy*, 116–25.

6. The fullest account of the disfranchisement of women is Rosemarie Zagarri, *Revolutionary Backlash: Women and Politics in the Early American Republic* (Philadelphia, 2007).*
7. *Washington Globe*, July 26, 1832.*
8. See Daniel T. Rodgers, *Contested Truths: Keywords in American Politics since Independence* (New York, 1987); and Andrew Robertson, *The Language of Democracy: Political Rhetoric in the United States and Britain, 1790–1900* (Ithaca, 1995).*
9. See Malcolm Crook, "Elections and Democracy in France, 1789–1848,"; Joanna Innes, Mark Philp, and Robert Saunders, "The Rise of Democratic Discourse in the Reform Era: Britain in the 1830s and 1840s"; and Joanna Innes, "People and Power in British Politics to 1850," all in *Re-imagining Democracy in the Age of Revolutions: America, France, Britain, Ireland 1750–1850*, ed. Joanna Innes and Mark Philp (Oxford, 2013), 93–97, 114–28, 129–46.*
10. Matthew Arnold, "Democracy," originally written in 1859 as the introduction to his official *Report on the Systems of Popular Education in France, Holland, and the French Cantons of Switzerland*, published in 1861, and later republished separately in 1871 with Arnold's *Mixed Essays*, in Arnold, *"Culture and Anarchy" and Other Writings*, ed. Stefan Collini (Cambridge, 1993), 1–25; the quoted passage appears on 8.
11. See John Belcham, *"Orator" Hunt: Henry Hunt and English Working-Class Radicalism* (Oxford, 1985), 137–61.
12. Recent overviews include Boyd Hilton, *A Mad, Bad, and Dangerous People: England, 1783–1846* (Oxford, 2006); K. Theodore Hoppen, *The Mid-Victorian Generation, 1846–1886* (Oxford, 1998); Pierre Rosanvallon, *Le sacre du citoyen: histoire du suffrage universel en France* (Paris, 1992); and Alan S. Kahan, *Liberalism in Nineteenth-Century Europe* (New York, 2003).*
13. European champions of postreligious rationality, including the new ruling elites that assumed power after the Napoleonic wars, were quick to declare religion dead, yet piety made a comeback, often explicitly in opposition to the anti-Catholicism of the most radical French revolutionaries.*
14. "A Christian," in the words of Benjamin Rush, "cannot fail of being a republican, for every precept of the Gospel inculcates those degrees of humility, self-denial, and brotherly kindness, which are directly opposed to the pride of monarchy and the pageantry of the court." Benjamin Rush, *A Plan for the Establishment of Public Schools and the Diffusion of Knowledge in Pennsylvania; To Which Are Added Thoughts upon the Mode of Education Proper in a Republic. Addressed to the Legislature and Citizens of the State* (Philadelphia, 1786), 16.*
15. Tocqueville's liminal status has been a central theme of most biographical studies written in recent decades, from Andre Jardin, *Tocqueville: A Biography*, trans. Lydia Davis and Robert Hemenway (1984; New York, 1988) to Jean-Louis Benoit, *Tocqueville: un destin paradoxal* (Paris: Bayard, 2005). *
16. Despite Hervé's gruesome and grueling experience during his months in prison, the family remained resilient. After 1815 Hervé served as mayor of the town of Verneuil and as prefect in multiple postings from Metz to Versailles,

exhibiting a relatively progressive public spiritedness rare among Restoration ministers. On the Tocqueville family history, see Jardin, *Tocqueville*, 3–55.*

17. See Rémy Hebding, *Benjamin Constant: le libéralisme tourmenté* (Paris, 2009); Steven K. Vincent, *Benjamin Constant and the Birth of French Liberalism* (New York, 2011); Helena Rosenblatt, ed., *The Cambridge Companion to Constant* (Cambridge, 2009); and Helena Rosenblatt, "Why Constant? A Critical Overview of the Constant Revival," *Modern Intellectual History* 1 (2004): 439–53.*
18. Constant's early writings contrasted the *hauteur* of Bourbon rule with Britain's milder monarchy. Benjamin Constant, *The Spirit of Conquest and Usurpation and Their Relation to European Civilization* (1814), in Constant, *Political Writings*, ed. Biancamaria Fontana (Cambridge, 1988), 86–87.
19. Constant, *The Spirit of Conquest and Usurpation*, 122–29.
20. Constant, *The Spirit of Conquest and Usurpation*, 113.
21. Constant, *The Spirit of Conquest and Usurpation*, 77.
22. "The citizens possess individual rights independently of all social and political authority, and any authority which violates these rights becomes illegitimate." Constant, *Principles of Politics Applicable to all Representative Government* (1815), in *Political Writings*, 175–289; the quoted passage appears on 180.
23. See Constant, *Principles of Politics*; and his 1806 manuscript, only recently published, *Principes de politique applicable à tous les gouvernements*, ed. Etienne Hoffmann, 2 vols. (Geneva, 1980), now translated as *Principles of Politics Applicable to All Governments*, trans. Dennis O'Keefe (Indianapolis, 2003).*
24. On the *idéologues*, see Cheryl Welch, *Liberty and Utility: The French Idéologues and the Transformation of Liberalism* (New York, 1984); on the doctrinaires, cf. Pierre Rosanvallon, *Le moment Guizot* (Paris, 1985), and Aurelian Craiutu, *Liberalism under Siege: The Political Thought of the French Doctrinaires* (Lanham, MD, 2003).*
25. François Guizot, "Elections," *Encyclopédie progressive* (1821), in *Discours académiques, suivis des discours prononcés pour la distribution des prix au concours général de l'Université et devant diverses sociétés religieuses et de trois essais de philosophie littéraire et politique* (Paris, 1861), 395.*
26. Guizot, "Elections," 406.*
27. François Guizot, *Histoire parlementaire de France* (Paris, 1864), 2:223.
28. Guizot was among many French liberals who adopted a version of Constant's distinction between the liberty of the ancients and that of the moderns.*
29. See Guizot, "Discours du 18 Août, 1842," in *Histoire parlementaire de France* 3:685.*
30. In the history of democratic thought, Guizot's contributions were crucial because his historical scholarship established the existence of earlier experiments with representative government; his conception of the "sovereignty of reason" legitimated excluding most citizens from active participation in politics and relying on educated elites; and his emphasis on public debate inadvertently helped erode the public's trust in those experts.*

31. On Pierre Rosanvallon, who has probed the shortcomings of French liberals' solutions to the problems of postrevolutionary France, see Samuel Moyn and Andrew Jainchill, "French Democracy between Totalitarianism and Solidarity: Pierre Rosanvallon and Revisionist Historiography," *Journal of Modern History* 76 (2004): 107–54. Rosanvallon has recently begun more explicitly to compare French and American thought and experience; see Pierre Rosanvallon, *Democratic Legitimacy: Impartiality, Reflexivity, Proximity*, trans. Arthur Goldhammer (Princeton, 2011).
32. Tocqueville described this crisis in a letter dated February 26, 1857, in Tocqueville, *Oeuvres complètes*, ed. J. P. Mayer (Paris, 1951–), 15:315.
33. Louis-Philippe, Tocqueville wrote, "was an unbeliever in religion like the eighteenth century, and skeptical in politics like the nineteenth; having no belief in himself, he had none in the belief of others." Tocqueville, *Recollections*, trans. George Lawrence, ed. J. P. Mayer and A. P. Kerr (Garden City, NY, 1970), 6–7.
34. Tocqueville's 1835 letter to an unnamed correspondent, probably either Eugene Stoffels or Louis de Kergolay, is in *Oeuvres complètes* 1:373–75.
35. Sailing across the Atlantic in 1831, Beaumont wrote to his father that he and Tocqueville would study America's "inhabitants, its cities, its institutions, its mores. We will learn how the republican government works." Gustave de Beaumont, *Lettres d'Amérique, 1831–1832*, ed. André Jardin and George W. Pierson (Paris, 1973), 28.
36. See, for example, René Rémond, *Les Etats-Unis devant l'opinion françaises, 1815–1852* (Paris, 1962); Kathleen Burk, *Old World, New World: Great Britain and America from the Beginning* (New York, 2007); and Aurelian Craiutu and Jeffrey C. Isaac, eds., *America through European Eyes: English and French Reflections on the New World from the Eighteenth Century to the Present* (University Park, PA, 2009).*
37. Alexis de Tocqueville to Louis de Kergolay, December 15, 1850, in Tocqueville, *Selected Letters on Politics and Society*, ed. Roger Boesche, trans. J. Toupin and Roger Boesche (Berkeley, 1985), 252–58, reprinted in *The Tocqueville Reader: A Life in Letters and Politics*, ed. Olivier Zunz and Alan S. Kahan (Oxford, 2002), 255–59. Tocqueville's writings on the 1848 revolution, whether intended for publication or not, appeared in an incomplete version, entitled *Souvenirs*, in 1893. The entire text, published only in 1942, is available in English as *Recollections*, trans. George Lawrence, ed. J. P. Mayer (Garden City, NY, 1970).*
38. On Tocqueville and Beaumont's trip and the writing of *Democracy in America*, cf. George Wilson Pierson, *Tocqueville in America* (1938; Baltimore, 1996); James T. Schleifer, *The Making of Tocqueville's "Democracy in America,"* 2nd ed. (1980; Indianapolis, 2000); and the critical edition of *Democracy in America*, ed. Eduardo Nolla, trans. James T. Schleifer (Indianapolis, 2006).*
39. Robert T. Gannett Jr., *Tocqueville Unveiled: The Historian and His Sources for "The Old Regime and the Revolution"* (Chicago, 2003).*
40. Distinct from Guizot, but equally convinced that centralization breeds atomistic individualism, were early nineteenth-century legitimists such as Joseph Fiévée, Joseph de Villèle, Ferdinand Béchard, and the writers clustering around

Tocqueville's friend Louis de Kergolay's *La Revue provinciale* and the Catholic journal *L'Avenir*. See Annelien de Dijn, "Aristocratic Liberalism in Post-revolutionary France," *Historical Journal* 48 (2005): 661–81; and Annelien de Dijn, "The Intellectual Origins of Tocqueville's *L'Ancien Régime et la Révolution*," *Modern Intellectual History* 5 (2008): 1–25.

41. See Pierson, *Tocqueville in America*; and cf. Schleifer, *The Making of Tocqueville's "Democracy in America,"* 325–39.*
42. Thomas Jefferson to Dupont de Nemours, April 24, 1816, in Jefferson, *Writings*, ed. Merrill D. Peterson (New York, 1984), 1387.
43. Jefferson to John Taylor, May 28, 1816, in *Writings*, 1392–93.
44. Jefferson to Samuel Kercheval, July 12, 1816, in *Writings*, 1399.
45. See Keyssar, *The Right to Vote*, 36–42; and Wilentz, *The Rise of American Democracy*, 196–202.
46. Cf. Wilentz, *The Rise of American Democracy*, 222–31; and Daniel Walker Howe, *What Hath God Wrought*, 147–60.
47. John Quincy Adams, First Annual Message, December 6, 1825, printed in *Journal of the House of Representatives*, 19th Congress, 1st Session, December 6, 1825 (Washington, 1825).
48. On John Quincy Adams, see Fred Kaplan, *John Quincy Adams, American Visionary* (New York, 2014); and Cory M. Pfarr, "John Quincy Adams's Republicanism: 'A Thousand Obstacles Apparently Stand before Us,'" *Massachusetts Historical Review* 16 (2014): 73–121.*
49. Daniel Webster, *A Discourse, Delivered at Plymouth, December 22, 1820* (Boston, 1821).*
50. On Webster's two replies to South Carolina senator Robert Y. Hayne, see Harlow Sheidley, "The Webster-Hayne Debate," *New England Quarterly* 67 (1994): 5–29; and Sandra M. Gustafson, *Imagining Deliberative Democracy in the Early American Republic* (Chicago, 2011), 52–57, 102–12.*
51. Cf. Andrew W. Robertson, "'Look on this Picture . . . And on This!' Nationalism, Localism, and Partisan Images of Otherness in the United States, 1787–1820," *American Historical Review* 106 (2001): 1263–80; and Mary Babson Fuhrer, *A Crisis in Community: The Trials and Transformation of a New England Town, 1815–1848* (Chapel Hill, 2014).*
52. See Yonatan Eyal, *The Young America Movement and the Transformation of the Democratic Party, 1828–1861* (Cambridge, 2007).*
53. Only on the issue of slavery did Leggett distance himself from the Democratic Party mainstream. See William Leggett, *Democratick Editorials: Essays in Jacksonian Political Economy*, ed. Lawrence H. White (Indianapolis, 1984), 58, 178–80, 254–62; and on slavery and antislavery, 192–98.*
54. These passages from Calvin Colton, *A Voice from America to England* (London, 1839), were quoted in the book responsible for identifying the Whigs with elitism and the Jacksonians with democracy, Arthur M. Schlesinger Jr., *The Age of Jackson* (New York, 1945), 279–82.

55. James Madison to W. T. Barry, August 4, 1822, in Madison, *Writings*, ed. Jack Rakove (New York, 1999), 790–94.
56. See Gordon S. Wood, "The Trials and Tribulations of Thomas Jefferson," in *Jeffersonian Legacies*, ed. Peter S. Onuf (Charlottesville, 1993), 395–417; and Drew McCoy, *The Last of the Fathers: James Madison and the Republican Legacy* (Cambridge, 1989).*
57. See William Novak, *The People's Welfare: Law and Regulation in Nineteenth-Century America* (Chapel Hill, 1996); and Howe, *What Hath God Wrought*.
58. Jefferson to Kercheval, July 12, 1816, in *Writings*, 1403.*
59. See Leonard P. Curry, *The Free Black in Urban America, 1800–1850: The Shadow of the Dream* (Chicago, 1981).*
60. Members of one of those cultures would have been charmed by Jefferson's discussing with John Quincy Adams, in a quiet corner of Madison's inaugural party in 1809, the merits of Homer, Virgil, and the "minor poets" of the ancient world; the other would have recoiled from such unmanly snobbery. John Quincy Adams to Louisa Catherine Adams, March 5, 1809, in *The Writings of John Quincy Adams*, ed. Worthington Chauncey Ford, 7 vols. (New York, 1913–17), 3:288–90.*
61. As the Jackson Party took shape between 1824 and 1828, John Quincy Adams and his supporters tried to place themselves "above party" because they considered partisanship inimical to what they called "the public good." Thomas Coens, "The Formation of the Jackson Party, 1822–1825" (unpub. Ph.D. diss., Harvard University, 2004).*
62. See Wilentz, *The Rise of American Democracy*, 327, 370–74.*
63. Tocqueville, *Democracy in America*, ed. J. P. Mayer, trans. George Lawrence (Garden City, NY, 1969), 35–36; John Quincy Adams, *An Oration at Plymouth, December 22, 1802, at the Anniversary Commemoration of the First Landing of Our Ancestors at That Place* (Boston, 1802).
64. Tocqueville, *Democracy in America*, 46–47.
65. Tocqueville, *Democracy in America*, 58–60.
66. Tocqueville, *Democracy in America*, 344, and more generally, 316–95.
67. Tocqueville, *Democracy in America*, 339.
68. Tocqueville, *Democracy in America*, 250, and more generally, 248–61.*
69. Adam I. P. Smith, "The 'Fortunate Banner': Languages of Democracy in the United States, c. 1848," in Innes and Philp, *Re-imagining Democracy in the Age of Revolutions*, 29n4.*
70. On Franklin's civic activities and his conviction that the associations he founded might contribute to fostering benevolence and preventing factionalism, see pp. 255–259 above.
71. Tocqueville, *Democracy in America*, 274, and more generally, 270–76, 295–300.
72. Tocqueville, *Democracy in America*, 315.
73. Tocqueville, *Democracy in America*, 94, and more generally 190–95.
74. Tocqueville's unpublished letter to his father, dated May 7, 1835, is in the Tocqueville archives; see Jardin, *Tocqueville*, 235.

75. On the consequences of the Reform Act, cf. E. P. Thompson, *The Making of the English Working Class* (1963; New York, 1966), 816–32; John A. Phillips and Charles Wetherell, "The Great Reform Act of 1832 and the Political Modernization of England," *American Historical Review* 100, no. 2 (1995): 411–36; and Philip Salmon, *Electoral Reform at Work: Local Politics and National Parties, 1832–1841* (London, 2002).*
76. John Russell, *Hansard*, December 12, 1831, 166.
77. Earl Grey, *Hansard*, October 3, 1831, 934.
78. John Russell, *Hansard*, December 17, 1831, 497; John Campbell, *Hansard*, July 6, 1831, 822.
79. Henry Bunbury, *Hansard*, September 19, 1831, 227.*
80. See Sir Charles Wetherell, Commons, August 3, 1831, in *Hansard*, 2nd ser., 5:689; and Lord Wharncliffe, Lords, May 24, 1832, in *Hansard*, 2nd ser., 13:20.*
81. John A. Roebuck, *Pamphlets for the People* (London, 1835), 6–8.*
82. On the rise of the language of democracy in Chartist organizations and publications, see Joanna Innes, Mark Philp, and Robert Saunders, "The Rise of Democratic Discourse in the Reform Era," 121–28.
83. William Lovett and John Collins, *Chartism: A New Organisation of the People*, in *The Chartist Movement in Britain, 1838–1850*, ed. Gregory Claeys (London, 2001), 214.
84. Cf. Gareth Stedman Jones, "Rethinking Chartism," in *Languages of Class: Studies in English Working Class History, 1832–1982* (Cambridge, 1983), 90–178; and William H. Sewell Jr., *The Logics of History: Social Theory and Social Transformation* (Chicago, 2005), 62–67.*
85. Malcolm Chase, *Chartism: A New History* (Manchester, 2007).*
86. Tocqueville's letter to Mill, dated June 13, 1835, in *Oeuvres completes* 6:293–95; Tocqueville, "Etat social et politique de la France avant et depuis 1789," originally published in Mill's *London and Westminster Review*, April 1836, in Tocqueville, *Oeuvres*, ed. François Furet and Françoise Mélonio (Paris, 2004), 3:33–66.*
87. Tocqueville to Mill, dated June 13, 1835, *Oeuvres complètes*, 6: 293–95.*
88. James Mill, "Education," Supplement to *Encyclopedia Britannica* (London, 1825), reprinted in *James Mill on Education* (Cambridge, 1969).
89. In the *Autobiography* that Mill wrote near the end of his life, he contended modestly that "any boy or girl of average capacity and healthy physical constitution" could do what he had done if given similar opportunities. Yet in Mill's own estimation, his extraordinary training had given him "an advantage of a quarter of a century over my contemporaries." *Autobiography of John Stuart Mill*, ed. John Jacob Coss (New York, 1924), 21; in John Stuart Mill, *Collected Works*, ed. John M. Robson et al., 33 vols. (Toronto, 1963–91), 1:33.
90. Mill, *Autobiography*, 118–21.*
91. On Mill's falling-out with Roebuck, precipitated by their formal debate concerning the relative merits of Wordsworth, whom Mill preferred, and Byron, see Mill, *Autobiography*, 102–10.

92. Mill, *Autobiography*, 94–136; Mill to John Sterling, July 10, 1833, in *Collected Works* 12:164–67.*
93. In a letter to Mill, the only reviewer whom Tocqueville credited with seeing his aim in both volumes, he admitted that volume 2 lost "the ordinary reader" by trying to "depict the general features of democratic societies" rather than adding new details to his earlier portrait of American democracy. Tocqueville's letter to Mill, December 30, 1840, is in Zunz and Kahan, *The Tocqueville Reader*, 213–14.*
94. The perennial appeal of *Democracy in America* in the United States stems partly from the *lack* of congruence between Tocqueville's ideas and those prevailing in American politics at any time, which makes possible his adoption by disparate guardians eager to embrace or excoriate him for their own purposes. Because he was, by his own admission, neither simply a democrat nor simply an aristocrat, Tocqueville fits awkwardly into standard American categories.*
95. Mill's review of Tocqueville's second volume appeared in *Edinburgh Review*, 1840; Mill, *Collected Works* 18:156.
96. Tocqueville, *Democracy in America*, 506–8.
97. Tocqueville, *Democracy in America*, 524–26.
98. Tocqueville, *Democracy in America*, 572.
99. Tocqueville, *Democracy in America*, 509.
100. Tocqueville, *Democracy in America*, 515. The lessons Tocqueville drew from Madison were quite different from the lessons drawn by post–World War II American political scientists.*
101. Mill's review of Tocqueville's vol. 2, *Collected Works* 18:169.
102. On Tocqueville's loss of conventional religious faith, see his letter to Mme. Swetchine, February 26, 1857, in Zunz and Kahan, *The Tocqueville Reader*, 334–36; and Agnès Antoine, *L'impensé de la démocratie: Tocqueville, la citoyenneté, et la religion* (Paris, 2003).*
103. Tocqueville, *The European Revolution and Correspondences with Gobineau*, trans. John Lukacs (Gloucester, MA, 1968), 190–91; Tocqueville, *Selected Letters on Politics and Society*, ed. Roger Boesche, trans. James Toupin and Roger Boesche (Berkeley, 1985), 342–44.*
104. Tocqueville, *Democracy in America*, 289, 294, 445.
105. See Sean Wilentz, "Many Democracies: On Tocqueville and Jacksonian America," in *Reconsidering Tocqueville's "Democracy in America,"* ed. Abraham E. Eisenstadt (New Brunswick, 1988), 207–28.
106. Mill, who had little interest in or patience with religious faith, mentioned religion in his review of Tocqueville only in connection with the danger of mob violence. See Mill's review of Tocqueville, *Collected Works* 18:176–78.*
107. Tocqueville, *Democracy in America*, 689.
108. See Robert Gannett Jr., "Bowling Ninepins in Tocqueville's Township," *American Political Science Review* 97, no. 1 (2003): 1–16.*

109. In the city of Worcester, an hour west of Boston, stands a nineteenth-century neoclassical courthouse with the following words carved in stone: "Obedience to law is liberty." It would be hard to find a clearer statement of the sensibility of the proto-Whigs who served as some of the most influential of Tocqueville's informants.*

110. Herbert Baxter Adams, "Jared Sparks and Alexis de Tocqueville," *Johns Hopkins Studies in Historical and Political Science* 16 (1898): 7–49.*

111. For a compilation of these documents see Donald Lutz, ed., *Colonial Origins of the American Constitution: A Documentary History* (Indianapolis, 1998).*

112. See Holly Brewer, "Entailing Aristocracy in Colonial Virginia: 'Ancient Feudal Restraints' and Revolutionary Reform," *William and Mary Quarterly*, 3d ser., 54, no. 2 (April 1997): 307; and Holly Brewer, "Tocqueville as Historian of the Struggle between Democracy and Aristocracy in America," *Tocqueville Review/La Revue Tocqueville* 27 (2006): 381–402.

113. Tocqueville learned the same lesson from another northerner, Benjamin Richards, who was soon to begin a second term as mayor of Philadelphia when he met with Tocqueville. "Our republic is the triumph and the government of the middle classes," Richards reported. Tocqueville's notes on his conversation with John Quincy Adams and Benjamin Richards quoted in Pierson, *Tocqueville in America*, 419, 483.

114. Mill, *Autobiography,* 134, and *Collected Works*, 1:199.

115. The central themes of Mill's reviews of Tocqueville echo almost perfectly the central themes of Sparks's outline of American democracy: 1) citizens' participation in New England towns; 2) the political and moral education that citizens derive from participating in civic life; 3) the unlikelihood that anything other than the common good will emerge from decisions made by majority vote after citizens deliberate; 4) the distinction between individual self-interest in the economic sphere and the broadening of citizens' sensibilities through political engagement; and 5) the connection between economic equality and citizens' willingness to engage in democratic debate. Mill's reviews of Tocqueville's *Democracy in America* appeared in the *London Review* in 1835 and in the *Edinburgh Review* in 1840; they are reprinted in Mill, *Dissertations and Discussions: Political, Philosophical, Historical* (London, 1859); and in Mill, *Collected Works* 18:47–90, 153–204.*

116. In his review of volume 2 of *Democracy in America*, Mill highlighted the importance of "public spirit" and the danger to liberty deriving from the conformity that would result if citizens abandoned civic engagement to concentrate on material gain. Mill, *Collected Works* 18: 153, 204.*

117. Mill, *Autobiography*, 162–63.*

118. Lincoln, "Address to the Young Men's Lyceum of Springfield, Illinois, January 27, 1838," in Lincoln, *Speeches and Writings, 1832–1858*, ed. Don E. Fehrenbacher (New York, 1989), 28–36.

119. Lincoln, "Address to the People of Sangamo County, New Salem, Illinois, March 9, 1832," in *Speeches and Writings, 1832–1858*, 1–5.

120. Lincoln's 1844 lines of poetry, from a letter to Andrew Johnston dated April 18, 1846, are in *Speeches and Writings, 1832–1858*, 138–39.*
121. "Representative Government," *American Review: A Whig Journal Devoted to Politics and Literature* 1, no. 3 (March, 1848): 280–81.
122. *National Intelligencer* (Washington), April 29, 1834.*
123. John Quincy Adams, *The Social Compact Exemplified in the Constitution of the Commonwealth of Massachusetts, with Remarks on the Theories of Divine Right of Hobbes and Filmer, and the Counter Theories of Sidney, Locke, Montesquieu, and Rousseau* (Providence, 1842), 1–31.*
124. Adams, *The Social Compact Exemplified*, 31–32.
125. Cf. George M. Dennison, *The Dorr War: Republicanism on Trial, 1831–1861* (Lexington, KY, 1976); and Marvin Gettleman, *The Dorr Rebellion: A Study in American Radicalism, 1833–1849* (New York, 1973).*
126. Junius [Calvin Colton], *Democracy* (New York, 1844), 2–5, 11.
127. Orestes Brownson, "The Laboring Classes," *Boston Quarterly Review* 3 (1840): 358–95.
128. Orestes Brownson, "Democracy," *Boston Review* 1 (January 1838): 33–74, in Orestes Brownson, *Works*, ed. Henry F. Brownson, 20 vols. (Detroit, 1882–87), 15:1–34.*
129. Brownson, *Works* 16:88–90.*
130. See James H. Read, *Majority Rule versus Consensus: The Political Thought of John C. Calhoun* (Lawrence, KS, 2009); Michael O'Brien, *Conjectures of Order: Intellectual Life and the American South*, 2 vols. (Chapel Hill, 2004), 2:817–36, 849–62; and Manisha Sinha, *The Counterrevolution of Slavery: Politics and Ideology in Antebellum South Carolina* (Chapel Hill, 2000).*
131. See James G. Basker et al., eds., *American Abolitionists: A Collection of Anti-Slavery Writings, 1760–1820* (New York, 2005).*
132. Lovejoy's article in the *Alton Observer*, July 20, 1837, is reprinted in Joseph C. Lovejoy and Owen Lovejoy, *Memoir of the Rev. Elijah P. Lovejoy: Who Was Murdered in Defence of the Liberty of the Press at Alton, Illinois*, with an introduction by John Quincy Adams (New York, 1838), 236.
133. See Thomas Bender, ed., *The Antislavery Debate: Capitalism and Abolitionism as a Problem in Historical Interpretation* (Berkeley, 1992); Elizabeth B. Clark, "The Sacred Rights of the Weak," *Journal of American History* 82 (1995): 463–93; Lacy Ford, *Deliver Us from Evil: The Slavery Question in the Old South* (New York, 2009); and Margaret Abruzzo, *Polemical Pain: Slavery, Cruelty, and the Rise of Humanitarianism* (Baltimore, 2011).*
134. See Jefferson's chilling letter to Jared Sparks, February 4, 1824, in which he explained his rationale for favoring the compulsory relocation of all black children to Saint-Domingue. Jefferson, *Writings*, 1484–87. Although some African Americans likewise favored colonization, usually because they thought white Americans' racism would deny them equality in the United States, the vast majority opposed the idea.*

135. William Lloyd Garrison to the *Patriot* (London), August 6, 1833; Garrison, "To the Public," the lead editorial in the first issue of the *Liberator*, January 1, 1831. Caleb McDaniel, *The Problem of Democracy in the Age of Slavery: Garrisonian Abolitionists and Transatlantic Reform* (Baton Rouge, 2013), locates Garrison within the transatlantic community of antislavery discourse.*
136. Wendell Phillips, "Speech of Wendell Phillips," *Liberator*, August 14, 1857; Phillips, "Public Opinion," in Phillips, *Speeches, Lectures, and Letters* (Boston, 1870), 40.*
137. Wendell Phillips, "Public Opinion," "Women's Rights," and "Sims Anniversary," in *Speeches, Lectures, and Letters*; the quotations are on 45, 18, and 82.
138. For the Ashman amendment, see *Congressional Globe*, 30th Congress, 1st Session, 95. Henry David Thoreau, "Resistance to Civil Government," in Thoreau, *Collected Essays and Poems*, ed. Elizabeth Hall Witherell (New York, 2001), 208.
139. According to John L. O'Sullivan, the Democratic Party journalist who coined the term "manifest destiny," it was God's will that the United States spread across the continent. Without the war, Europeans might obstruct the nation's divinely ordained expansion.*
140. On the American ideology of endless expansion as an alternative to class conflict, see Aziz Rana, *The Two Faces of American Freedom* (Cambridge, MA, 2010).*
141. M. Ducos's speech, in the *Moniteur Universel*, February 15, 1842.*
142. Guizot's speech, in the *Moniteur Universel*, March 26, 1847.
143. Tocqueville, *Recollections*, 27–28.
144. Tocqueville, *Recollections*, 38, 41.
145. Tocqueville to Pierre Royer-Collard, September 27, 1841, in Zunz and Kahan, *The Tocqueville Reader*, 155–57.
146. Tocqueville, *Recollections*, 86–95.
147. Tocqueville, *Recollections*, 136–54.*
148. Tocqueville, *Recollections*, 105–6.
149. Tocqueville, *Recollections*, 132.
150. Tocqueville, *Recollections*, 14, 191–92, 177.
151. Tocqueville, *Recollections*, 181.
152. Tocqueville, *Recollections*, 105.*
153. John Stuart Mill to John Pringle Nichol, September 30, 1848, in Mill, *Collected Writings* 13:738–39; Harney quoted in Innes, Philp, and Saunders, "The Rise of Democratic Discourse in the Reform Era," 125.

Chapter 14

1. Leopold von Ranke, *Über die Epochen der neueren Geschichte: Historisch-kritische Ausgabe*, ed. Theodor Schieder and Helmut Berding (Munich, 1971), 415–17.*

2. See James T. Kloppenberg, *Uncertain Victory: Social Democracy and Progressivism in European and American Thought, 1870–1920* (New York, 1986).*
3. *Washington Daily Union*, March 2, 1850; *Philadelphia Public Ledger*, February 20 and 25, 1850, quoted in Elizabeth Varon, *Disunion! The Coming of the American Civil War, 1789–1859* (Chapel Hill, 2008), 214–15. See also Timothy Mason Roberts, *Distant Revolutions: 1848 and the Challenge to American Exceptionalism* (Charlottesville, 2009).*
4. *Christian Inquirer* (New York), April 7, 1849; *New York Tribune*, March 29, 1848; *New York Tribune*, April 20, 1849.*
5. *Times* (London), July 17, 1847.*
6. Derek Fraser, *The Evolution of the British Welfare State: A History of Social Policy since the Industrial Revolution* (New York, 2003).*
7. Eric Foner, *Free Soil, Free Labor, Free Men: The Ideology of the Republican Party before the Civil War* (New York, 1970); Michael F. Holt, *The Fate of Their Country: Politicians, Slavery Extension, and the Coming of the Civil War* (New York, 2004); Varon, *Disunion!**
8. Speech on the Kansas-Nebraska Act, Peoria, Illinois, October 16, 1854, in Abraham Lincoln, *Speeches and Writings, 1832–1858*, ed. Don Fehrenbacher (New York, 1989), 315.
9. On Lincoln's voracious reading in philosophy and political theory, see Ronald C. White Jr., *A. Lincoln: A Biography* (New York, 2009); for an unmatched analysis of the Peoria address, see John Burt, *Lincoln's Tragic Pragmatism: Lincoln, Douglas, and Moral Conflict* (Cambridge, MA, 2013), 27–93.*
10. Lincoln, *Speeches and Writings, 1832–1858*, 334.
11. Lincoln, *Speeches and Writings, 1832–1858*, 316; see also 329.
12. On Lincoln's evolving ideas about slavery and race, see Eric Foner, *The Fiery Trial: Abraham Lincoln and American Slavery* (New York, 2010).*
13. Lincoln, *Speeches and Writings, 1832–1858*, 326–27. On the sources of Lincoln's moral philosophy, the most thorough study is William Miller, *Lincoln's Virtues: An Ethical Biography* (New York, 2002).*
14. Lincoln, *Speeches and Writings, 1832–1858*, 81.
15. George Fredrickson, *Big Enough to Be Inconsistent: Abraham Lincoln Confronts Slavery and Race* (Cambridge, 2006).*
16. Lincoln, *Speeches and Writings, 1832–1858*, 328.
17. Lincoln's fragment on slavery is in *Speeches and Writings, 1832–1858*, 303.
18. Sumner's speech is in *The Works of Charles Sumner* (Boston, 1873), 4:125–48.*
19. Chief Justice Roger Taney held that the Constitution should not be interpreted as applying to blacks, whether slave or free. Because slaves were not citizens, Dred Scott lacked the standing necessary to file suit as a citizen in a federal court. Don E. Fehrenbacher, *The Dred Scott Case: Its Significance in American Law and Politics* (New York, 1978).*
20. On Lincoln's romantic nationalism, see Stewart Winger, *Lincoln, Religion, and Romantic Cultural Politics* (DeKalb, 2003).

21. Speech of Abraham Lincoln, Springfield, June 16, 1858, in *The Lincoln-Douglas Debates of 1858*, ed. Robert W. Johannsen (New York, 1965), 14–15.
22. Speech of Stephen A. Douglas, Chicago, July 9, 1858, in Johannsen, *The Lincoln-Douglas Debates of 1858*, 22–36; the quotations are from 23, 27, 30, and 35.
23. On Lincoln's physical appearance and its enduring significance, see Richard Wightman Fox, *Lincoln's Body: A Cultural History* (New York, 2015). On the Lincoln-Douglas debates, see Burt, *Lincoln's Tragic Pragmatism*; Alan Guelzo, *Lincoln and Douglas: The Debates That Defined America* (New York, 2008); and David Zarefsky, *Lincoln, Douglas and Slavery: In the Crucible of Public Debate* (Chicago, 1993).*
24. Johannsen, *The Lincoln-Douglas Debates*, 37–114.
25. Douglass, "What to the Slave Is the Fourth of July?," first delivered in Rochester, New York, July 5, 1852, is in *The Frederick Douglass Papers, Series One: Speeches, Debates, and Interviews*, ed. John W. Blassingame et al., 2 vols. (New Haven, 1982), 2:359–88.
26. *Life and Times of Frederick Douglass Written by Himself*, first published in 1881 and reissued in 1892, is in Frederick Douglass, *Autobiographies*, ed. Henry Louis Gates Jr. (New York, 1994); the quotation is from 921.*
27. On Lincoln's reverence for Clay and the reasons why he invoked this phrase, see Richard Carwardine, *Lincoln* (London, 2003), 11–28; William E. Gienapp, *Abraham Lincoln and Civil War America* (New York, 2002), 40–45; and Burt, *Lincoln's Tragic Pragmatism*, 356–59, 596–97.*
28. Johannsen, *The Lincoln-Douglas Debates*, 219–20.
29. Johannsen, *The Lincoln-Douglas Debates*, 316, 226.
30. See Edouard Laboulaye, *Le parti libéral, son programme et son avenir*, 3rd ed. (Paris, 1863), 149–50.*
31. Macaulay's letter to Henry S. Randall, May 23, 1857, was reprinted from the *Southern Literary Messenger* in *New York Times*, March 24, 1860.
32. For Gladstone's speech, see *Hansard*, May 11, 1864, 324–25.
33. Arnold, "Democracy," in *"Culture and Anarchy" and Other Writings*, ed. Stefan Collini (Cambridge, 1993), 5–13.*
34. F. B. Smith, *The Making of the Second Reform Bill* (Cambridge, 1966), 160.
35. See K. Theodore Hoppen, *The Mid-Victorian Generation, 1846–1886* (Oxford, 1998), 263–71.*
36. See Hannah Mather Crocker, *Observations on the Real Rights of Women, with Their Appropriate Duties, Agreeable to Scripture, Reason, and Common Sense*, ed. Constance J. Post (1818; Lincoln, NE, 2011).*
37. Tocqueville, *Democracy in America*, ed. Olivier Zunz, trans. Arthur Goldhammer (New York, 2004), 695–97.*
38. See Cheryl Welch, *De Tocqueville* (New York, 2001), 190–207.*
39. Frances Wright, *Views of Society and Manners in America*, ed. Paul R. Baker (1821; Cambridge, MA, 1963), 167.*

40. Sarah Grimké, *Letters on the Equality of the Sexes and the Condition of Women, Addressed to Mary S. Parker, President of the Boston Female Anti-Slavery Society* (Boston, 1838), 4, 7, 46, 17, 122–23, 127, 128, 10.*

41. Margaret Fuller, *Woman in the Nineteenth Century* (New York, 1845), 154, 158, 161.

42. Margaret Abruzzo, *Polemical Pain: Slavery, Cruelty, and the Rise of Humanitarianism* (Baltimore, 2011).*

43. "When in the course of Human Events," the Litchfield Declaration began, "it becomes necessary for the Ladies to dissolve those bonds by which they have been subjected to others, and to assume among the self styled Lords of Creation that separate and equal station to which the laws of nature and their *own talents* entitle them," they must explain "the causes which impel them to the separation." "The Ladies Declaration of Independence," from Miss Pierce's School Papers, 1839, Litchfield Historical Society, Litchfield, CT, in Linda Kerber, *Women of the Republic: Intellect and Ideology in Revolutionary America* (Chapel Hill, 1980), 278–79.*

44. The 1837 Proceedings, reprinted in *Turning the World Upside Down: The Anti-Slavery Convention of American Women*, ed. Dorothy Sterling (New York, 1987), 19.

45. See Margaret Hope Bacon, *Valiant Friend: The Life of Lucretia Mott* (New York, 1980), 125.

46. Stanton's speech, delivered often in the 1840s, is in *The Selected Papers of Elizabeth Cady Stanton and Susan B. Anthony*, ed. Ann D. Gordon (New Brunswick, 1997), 94–123.

47. See Lori D. Ginzberg, *Untidy Origins: A Story of Woman's Rights in Antebellum New York* (Chapel Hill, 2005); and Linda Kerber, *No Constitutional Right to Be Ladies: Women and the Obligations of Citizenship* (New York, 1998).*

48. *North American Review* 109, no. 225 (October 1869): 556–65.

49. Harriet Taylor Mill, "Enfranchisement of Women," originally published in *Westminster Review*, July 1851, and republished as a pamphlet in 1868, is Appendix C in John Stuart Mill, *Collected Works*, ed. John M. Robson et al., 33 vols. (Toronto, 1963–91), 21:405, and is also reprinted in *Sexual Equality: Writings by John Stuart Mill, Harriet Taylor Mill, and Helen Taylor*, ed. Ann P. Robson and John M. Robson (Toronto, 1994).

50. The reviewer noted that the most notable progress along the path toward equality had been made with the end of slavery and the ratification of the Fourteenth and Fifteenth Amendments to the United States Constitution. Now it was women's turn. *North American Review* 109, no. 225 (October 1869): 565.

51. Mill quoted in William Thompson, *Appeal of One Half the Human Race, Women, against the Pretensions of the Other Half, Men, to Retain Them in Political, and Thence in Civil and Domestic Slavery* (1825; London, 1983), 9.

52. Harriet Taylor to J. W. Fox, May 10, 1848, in *John Stuart Mill and Harriet Taylor: Their Correspondence and Subsequent Marriage*, ed. F. A. Hayek (London, 1951), 123. On the Chartists' lack of interest in woman suffrage, see Anna

Clark, *The Struggle for the Breeches: Gender and the Making of the British Working Class* (Berkeley, 1995), 220–47.

53. See Bonnie S. Anderson, *Joyous Greetings: The First International Women's Movement, 1830–1860* (New York, 2000), for the struggles between women's rights groups and the broader reform movements of which they were a part.
54. Mill to Harriet Taylor [1850?], in the Mill-Taylor Papers, London School of Economics, in Hayek, *John Stuart Mill and Harriet Taylor*, 166–67.*
55. Reprinted in Elizabeth Cady Stanton, Susan B. Anthony, and Matilda Joslyn Gage, *History of Woman Suffrage*, 6 vols. (Rochester, 1881), 1:853.*
56. Deroin's response was published in *L'Opinion des Femmes* 4 (May 1849), 4.*
57. On the relation between the 1848 revolutions and the struggle for women's rights, see Roberts, *Distant Revolutions*, 90–104; and Anderson, *Joyous Greetings*, 15–18, 164–78.
58. Harriet Taylor Mill, "The Enfranchisement of Women," in Mill, *Collected Works*, Appendix C, 21:415, and in Robson and Robson, *Sexual Equality*, 203.*
59. John Stuart Mill, *The Subjection of Women*, in *"On Liberty" and Other Writings* ed. Stefan Collini (Cambridge, 1989), 120–21.*
60. Mill, *Subjection of Women*, 123–30.*
61. Mill, *Subjection of Women*, 131, 135–36, 138, 143–45.*
62. Mill, *Subjection of Women*, 148, 153, 158–59.*
63. "We are entering into an order of things in which justice will again be the primary virtue; grounded as before on equal, but now also on sympathetic association; having its root no longer in the instinct of equals for self-protection, but in a cultivated sympathy between them; and no one being now left out, but an equal measure being extended to all." Mill, *Subjection of Women*, 159–60.*
64. "The moral regeneration of mankind" could not begin, Talor and Mill concluded, until marriage "is placed under the rule of equal justice, and when human beings learn to cultivate their strongest sympathy with an equal in rights and in cultivation." Mill, *Subjection of Women*, 195, 207–208, 211.*
65. Mill, *Subjection of Women*, 213.*
66. Mill, *Autobiography*, 186.*
67. Mill, *Considerations on Representative Government* (1861), in *Collected Works* 19:380–94.*
68. Mill, *Considerations on Representative Government*, in *Collected Works* 19: 410–12, 436.
69. Mill, *Autobiography*, 162–63.*
70. Mill, *Utilitarianism*, 3rd ed. (London, 1867), 40–45; see also 27–28, 36, 46–47, 53, 95–96; and Mill, "Speech to the London National Society for Women's Suffrage, March 26, 1870," in *Collected Works* 29:387.
71. Mill, "The Utility of Religion," in *Three Essays on Religion* (London, 1874), 108–9.*
72. Having condemned slavery in *Democracy in America*, Tocqueville joined the French Society for the Abolition of Slavery as early as 1835. Tocqueville's 1843 report to the Chamber of Deputies, "The Emancipation of Slaves," in Tocqueville, *Writings on Empire and Slavery*, ed. Jennifer Pitts (Baltimore, 2001), 199–226.*

73. See John M. Robson, *The Improvement of Mankind: The Social and Political Thought of John Stuart Mill* (Toronto, 1968), 224–25; and James T. Kloppenberg, "The Canvas and the Color: Tocqueville's 'Philosophical History' and Why It Matters Now," *Modern Intellectual History* 3 (2006): 495–521.*
74. Mill, *Autobiography*, 187–90; and Mill, "The Contest in America," in *Collected Works* 21:136–41. "The South are in rebellion," Mill wrote, "not for simple slavery; they are in rebellion for the right of burning human creatures alive." Mill was much more ambivalent about the British role in India than he was about the need to abolish slavery in the United States.*
75. Cooper Union Address, in Abraham Lincoln, *Speeches and Writings, 1859–1865*, ed. Don Fehrenbacher (New York, 1989), 129–30.
76. A compilation of speeches and writings on John Brown is *The Tribunal: Responses to John Brown and the Harpers Ferry Raid*, ed. John Stauffer and Zoe Trodd (Cambridge, 2012).*
77. For Lincoln's defense of free labor and his ideal of America as a land of independent yeomen, see his address to the Wisconsin State Agricultural Society, September 30, 1859, in Lincoln, *Speeches and Writings, 1859–1865*, 90–101.
78. Lincoln, First Inaugural Address, March 4, 1861, in *Speeches and Writings, 1859–1865*, 215–24.
79. Lincoln, Speech on Discoveries and Inventions, Jacksonville, Illinois, February 11, 1859, in *Speeches and Writings, 1859–1865*, 3–12; the quoted passages are on 6.
80. For the roots of Lincoln's preference for moderate change, see his address to the Washington Temperance Society of Springfield, Illinois, February 22, 1842, in *Speeches and Writings, 1859–1865*, 81–90.*
81. On Lincoln's gradual development from skepticism to the embrace of religious faith in the last decade of his life, see Michael Burkhimer, *Lincoln's Christianity* (Yardley, 2007). Although Lincoln himself disliked evangelicals' fervor, their increasingly enthusiastic support of his presidency ended up sustaining him into his second term.*
82. Lincoln, First Inaugural Address.
83. On this theme see William Novak, "The Myth of the 'Weak' American State," *American Historical Review* 113 (2008): 752–72; and Steven Conn, ed., *To Promote the General Welfare: The Case for Big Government* (New York, 2012), a collection that establishes the presence of the federal government throughout American history despite its usual "invisibility," a paradox first noted by Tocqueville: in the United States "government authority seems anxiously bent on keeping out of sight." Tocqueville, *Democracy in America*, 77.*
84. Lincoln, Message to Congress, July 4, 1861, in *Speeches and Writings, 1859–1865*, 246–61.*
85. See Lincoln, Address on Colonization to a Committee of Colored Men, Washington, DC, August 14, 1862, in *Speeches and Writings, 1859–1865*, 353–57; and Annual Message to Congress, December 1, 1862, in *Speeches and Writings, 1859–1865*, 493–15.*

86. Lincoln to Horace Greeley, August 22, 1862, in *Speeches and Writings, 1859–1865*, 357–58.
87. See Carwardine, *Lincoln*, on the paradoxical consequences of the Emancipation Proclamation, which rallied to the Union cause—and bolstered Lincoln's own standing among—those radicals whose fervor he had distrusted and whose strategies he had rejected.
88. Paradoxically, as James M. McPherson argued in *Battle Cry of Freedom: The Civil War Era* (Oxford, 1988), had the Union succeeded in suppressing the Confederate rebellion in 1861 or 1862, it is unlikely that slavery would have ended in the 1860s.
89. See Garry Wills, *Lincoln at Gettysburg: The Words That Remade America* (New York, 1992); and Dean Grodzins, *American Heretic: Theodore Parker and Transcendentalism* (Chapel Hill, 2002).*
90. Lincoln, Address at the Sanitary Fair in Baltimore, Maryland, April 18, 1864, in *Speeches and Writings, 1859–1865*, 589–91.
91. See, for example, Lincoln's letter to Albert G. Hodges, April 4, 1864, in *Speeches and Writings, 1859–1865*, 585–86.
92. Today that percentage would total nearly six million persons. Although twenty-first-century Americans lament the casualties from the wars and disasters of our own day, and although the scale of the slaughter was similar for mid-twentieth-century Europeans, most Americans find it hard even to imagine carnage on the scale of the United States Civil War.
93. Lincoln, Second Inaugural Address, in *Speeches and Writings, 1859–1865*, 686–87.
94. Lincoln to Thurlow Weed, March 15, 1865, in *Speeches and Writings, 1859–1865*, 689.*
95. The best study of the consequences of the North's retreat from Reconstruction is Eric Foner, *Reconstruction: America's Unfinished Revolution, 1863–1877* (New York, 1988).*
96. On this process and its consequences, see David Blight, *Race and Reunion: The Civil War in American Memory* (Cambridge, 2002).
97. Mill, "The Contest in America" (February 1862), in *Collected Works* 21:136–41.
98. Mill also wrote that Lincoln provided "an example of how far singleminded honesty will often go, in doing the work and supplying the place of talent." Mill to John Elliot Cairnes, December 26, 1863, in *Collected Works* 15:911–13.*
99. On Tocqueville and Mill, see the splendid introduction by Françoise Mélonio and François Furet to their edition of Alexis de Tocqueville, *The Old Regime and the French Revolution*, trans. Alan S. Kahan, 2 vols. (Chicago, 1998), 1:1–73*.
100. Tocqueviile, *The Old Regime* 1:87.
101. On the *Manifeste des soixante*, see Pierre Rosanvallon, *La question syndicale* (Paris, 1988), 204.*
102. Edouard Laboulaye, *Histoire des Etats-Unis*, 5th ed., 3 vols. (Paris, 1870), 3:v–xii.*
103. Francis Lieber, *On Civil Liberty and Self-Government*, 3rd ed. (1853; Philadelphia, 1888), 159–70, argued that representative government should not be considered

second best, compared with the direct democracies of Greece and Rome, but should be seen as the ideal form of democratic government.*

104. Edouard Laboulaye, *La république constitutionelle* (Paris, 1871).*
105. Charles Eliot Norton, "American Political Ideas," *North American Review*, October 1865, 550–56. Norton's arguments could be multiplied many times.*
106. Daniel W. Hamilton, *The Limits of Sovereignty: Property Confiscation in the Union and the Confederacy during the Civil War* (Chicago, 2007).
107. Mill to Norton, November 24, 1865, Norton Papers, Houghton Library, Harvard University.*
108. Walt Whitman, "Democratic Vistas," in Whitman, *Complete Poetry and Collected Prose* (New York, 1982).*
109. On the relation between Mill's and Tocqueville's writings and Kant's ideas of reason and right, see Jürgen Habermas, *The Structural Transformation of the Public Sphere: An Inquiry into a Category of Bourgeois Society*, trans. Thomas Burger with the assistance of Frederick Lawrence (1962; Cambridge, MA, 1989), 89–140.*
110. See Foner, *Reconstruction*, 604, 610; and Carl N. Degler, *Place over Time: The Continuity of Southern Distinctiveness* (Baton Rouge, 1977).*
111. Matthew 22: 37–40.*
112. St. Paul to the Philippians 2:2–4.*
113. Tocqueville, *Democracy in America*, 689.*

INDEX